The Interpretation of Contracts

THE INTERPRETATION OF CONTRACTS

7TH EDITION

SIR KIM LEWISON
A Lord Justice of Appeal

SWEET & MAXWELL

THOMSON REUTERS

First Edition 1989
Second Edition 1997
Third Edition 2004
Fourth Edition 2007
Fifth Edition 2011
Sixth Edition 2015
Seventh Edition 2020

Published in 2021 by Thomson Reuters,
trading as Sweet & Maxwell.
Thomason Reuters is registered in England & Wales, Company
No.1679046.
Registered Office and address for service:
5 Canada Square, Canary Wharf, London, E14 5AQ.

For further information on our products and services, visit
http://www.sweetandmaxwell.co.uk

Printed and bound by CPI Group (UK) Ltd, Croydon, CR0 4YY.
A CIP catalogue record of this book is available from the British Library.

ISBN (print): 978-0-414-07041-7

ISBN (e-book): 978-0-414-07083-7

ISBN (print and e-book): 978-0-414-07084-4

FSC
www.fsc.org
MIX
Paper from
responsible sources
FSC® C013604

PREFACE

Who would not say that commentaries increase doubt and ignorance, since there is no book to be found, human or divine, with which the world has any business, in which the difficulties are cleared up by the interpretation?

Montaigne: *On Experience*

It is now over 30 years since I first embarked upon attempting to provide a modern account of the interpretation of contracts. I have been gratified by the warm reception that successive editions have received among practitioners; and its occasional approval in court. It has been a very educational journey for me.

The aim of this book remains constant. I do not advance a grand theory of interpretation. I seek to gather together the principles of interpretation that the courts have laid down, in the hope of providing the practical lawyer with a source book of arguments that will advance the client's cause. I hope that this commentary will not increase doubt and ignorance, as Montaigne feared.

In the preface to the last edition of this book I commented that there was a tension between a decision of the Supreme Court which had emphasised the primacy of the contractual language over background facts on the one hand, and the repeated statements that contractual interpretation is an iterative exercise which requires consideration of the commercial consequences of rival interpretations. To the surprise of many, the Supreme Court subsequently confidently denied that there was any tension between these two approaches.[1]

It is notable that in *Wood v Capita* the recent history of contractual interpretation was traced from *Rainy Sky*[2] rather than from Lord Hoffmann's restatement in *Investors Compensation Scheme*. And in *Marks & Spencer v BNP Paribas*,[3] the Supreme Court pulled back from Lord Hoffmann's elegant analysis of the implication of terms. The processes of interpretation and implication are now seen by the Supreme Court as connected but sequential processes. To the outsider it appeared that much of Lord Hoffmann's outstanding contributions to contractual interpretation was being sidelined. Partly for that reason this edition contains an entirely new Ch.1, which can no longer rest solely on the foundations that Lord Hoffmann laid in *Investors Compensation Scheme*.

Yet, at the same time, the Supreme Court has in other cases amalgamated the two processes of interpretation and implication, in claiming to interpret a contract by relying on words that were never expressed, and even bringing body language into the process of interpretation.[4]

So despite the confident denial, it is the view of this commentator at least, that the tension still remains.

In addition to these cases, the Supreme Court has also considered the scope of the principle that a contract should be validated if possible[5]; the scope of the prevention principle[6]; and, somewhat unusually, a boundary dispute made its way right up to the Privy Council.[7] There has, of course, been a steady stream of cases

---

[1] *Wood v Capita Insurance Services Ltd* [2017] UKSC 24; [2017] A.C. 1173.
[2] *Rainy Sky SA v Kookmin Bank* [2011] UKSC 50; [2011] 1 W.L.R. 2900.
[3] [2015] UKSC 72; [2016] A.C. 742.
[4] *Wells v Devani* [2019] UKSC 4; [2020] A.C. 129.
[5] *Tillman v Egon Zehnder Ltd* [2019] UKSC 32; [2020] A.C. 154.
[6] *Duval v 11-13 Randolph Crescent Ltd* [2020] UKSC 18; [2020] 2 W.L.R. 1167.
[7] *Lovering v Atkinson* [2020] UKPC 14.

decided by the Court of Appeal and the High Court. As in previous editions, I have tried to incorporate those which are of interest to practitioners engaged both in interpreting and in drafting contracts.

I have not been shy about changing my mind on some of the knottier points where keen minds have exposed flaws in the text. As Alan Coren wrote[8]:

> "If a man spends 30 years banging a key for money, it must follow that not everything he writes will come up to impeccable snuff."

On the other hand, where I disagree with the current direction of travel I have said so.

In this edition, as well as updating and revising the text, I have also broken it down into smaller numbered paragraphs. I hope that this will make the text more user-friendly, particularly for those who use an online edition. The text is based on materials available to me on 31 July 2020.

May I conclude, as I have done in previous editions, with the wise words of Megarry J in *Cordell v Second Clanfield Properties Ltd*[9]:

> "It seems to me that words in a book written or subscribed to by an author who is or becomes a judge have the same value as words written by any other reputable author, neither more nor less."

Kim Lewison
Royal Courts of Justice
London WC2A 2LL

---

[8] *Nothing But the Truth.*
[9] [1969] 2 Ch 9.

TABLE OF CONTENTS

TABLE OF CASES

TABLE OF STATUTES

TABLE OF STATUTORY INSTRUMENTS

CHAPTER 1

AN OVERVIEW

A certain heathen came to Hillel and said to him, "Make me a proselyte, on condition that you teach me the whole Torah in the time I can stand on one foot." Hillel said to him, "What is hateful to you, do not do to your neighbour: that is the whole Torah; all the rest is commentary."

The Talmud

1.   THE BASIC PRINCIPLES

Interpretation is the ascertainment of the objective meaning of the language in which the parties have chosen to express their agreement, in its documentary, factual and commercial context. That meaning is what a reasonable person having all the background knowledge which would have been available to the parties would have understood them to be using the language in the contract to mean. Both the text and the context are tools in the process of interpretation.

The text must be assessed in the light of (i) the natural and ordinary meaning of the words, (ii) any other relevant provisions of the contract, and (iii) the overall purpose of the clause and the contract. The factual context includes facts and circumstances known or assumed by the parties at the time that the document was executed. It also includes background knowledge which would reasonably have been available to the parties in the situation in which they were at the time of the contract.

The process is a unitary and iterative one by which each suggested interpretation is checked against the provisions of the contract and its commercial consequences are investigated. The weight to be given to each will depend on a number of factors, including the formality of the agreement and the quality of the drafting.

If the language of the contract is unambiguous the court must apply it. But if there are two possible interpretations, the court is entitled to prefer the interpretation which is consistent with business common sense as at the date of the contract and to reject the other. Nevertheless, the commercial consequences of one interpretation as against another do not detract from the importance of the words.

In exceptional circumstances the court may conclude that the parties have used the wrong words. If it is clear what the error is, and the nature of the correction required, the court may correct it.

In carrying out its task, the court must disregard the parties' subjective intentions, and (except for limited purposes) the negotiations that preceded the making of the contract.

Shortly after the second edition of this book was published, Lord Hoffmann gave   **1.01** his speech in *Investors Compensation Scheme v West Bromwich Building Society*.[1] He said:

"I do not think that the fundamental change which has overtaken this branch of the law, particularly as a result of the speeches of Lord Wilberforce in *Prenn v Simmonds*[2] and *Reardon Smith Line Ltd v Hansen-Tangen, Hansen-Tangen v Sanko Steamship Co*,[3] is always sufficiently appreciated. The result has been, subject to one important exception, to assimilate the way in which such documents are interpreted by judges to the common-sense principles by which any serious utterance would be interpreted in ordinary life. Almost all the old intellectual baggage of 'legal' interpretation has been discarded. The principles may be summarised as follows.

(1) Interpretation is the ascertainment of the meaning which the document would convey to a reasonable person having all the background knowledge which would reasonably have been available to the parties in the situation in which they were at the time of the contract.

(2) The background was famously referred to by Lord Wilberforce as the 'matrix of fact', but this phrase is, if anything, an understated description of what the background may include. Subject to the requirement that it should have been reasonably available to the parties and to the exception to be mentioned next, it includes absolutely anything.[4]

(3) The law excludes from the admissible background the previous negotiations of the parties and their declarations of subjective intent. They are admissible only in an action for rectification. The law makes this distinction for reasons of practical policy and, in this respect only, legal interpretation differs from the way we would interpret utterances in ordinary life. The boundaries of this exception are in some respects unclear. But this is not the occasion on which to explore them.[5]

(4) The meaning which a document (or any other utterance) would convey to a reasonable man is not the same thing as the meaning of its words. The meaning of words is a matter of dictionaries and grammars; the meaning of the document is what the parties using those words against the relevant background would reasonably have been understood to mean. The background may not merely enable the reasonable man to choose between the possible meanings of words which are ambiguous but even (as occasionally happens in ordinary life) to conclude that the parties must, for whatever reason, have used the wrong words or syntax (see *Mannai Investment Co Ltd v Eagle Star Life Assurance Co Ltd*).[6]

(5) The 'rule' that words should be given their 'natural and ordinary meaning' reflects the commonsense proposition that we do not easily accept that people have made linguistic mistakes, particularly in formal documents. On the other hand, if one would nevertheless conclude from the background that something must have gone wrong with the language,

---

[1] [1998] 1 W.L.R. 896.
[2] [1971] 1 W.L.R. 1381 at 1384–1386.
[3] [1976] 1 W.L.R. 989.
[4] In *BCCI v Ali* [2002] 1 A.C. 251 at 269 Lord Hoffmann qualified this. See para.1.22.
[5] In *Chartbrook Ltd v Persimmon Homes Ltd* [2009] A.C. 1101 the House of Lords reaffirmed this exclusionary rule.
[6] [1997] A.C. 749.

the law does not require judges to attribute to the parties an intention which they plainly could not have had. Lord Diplock made this point more vigorously when he said in *Antaios Cia Naviera SA v Salen Rederierna AB, The Antaios*[7]:

'... if detailed semantic and syntactical analysis of words in a commercial contract is going to lead to a conclusion that flouts business common sense, it must be made to yield to business common sense.[8]'

For many years that was the starting point for the interpretation of contracts. But in the years that followed, successive decisions of the Supreme Court have refined and developed those principles. Nevertheless, in its most recent decision[9] the Supreme Court has emphasised that: **1.02**

"The recent history of the common law of contractual interpretation is one of continuity rather than change. One of the attractions of English law as a legal system of choice in commercial matters is its stability and continuity, particularly in contractual interpretation."

The principles were restated by the Supreme Court in *Rainy Sky SA v Kookmin Bank*[10]—Lord Clarke said: **1.03**

"For the most part, the correct approach to construction of the bonds, as in the case of any contract, was not in dispute. The principles have been discussed in many cases, notably of course, as Lord Neuberger of Abbotsbury MR said in *Pink Floyd Music Ltd v EMI Records Ltd*, by Lord Hoffmann in *Mannai Investment Co Ltd v Eagle Star Life Assurance Co Ltd* in *Investors Compensation Scheme Ltd v West Bromwich Building Society* and in *Chartbrook Ltd v Persimmon Homes Ltd (Chartbrook Ltd Part 20 defendants)*. I agree with Lord Neuberger ... that those cases show that the ultimate aim of interpreting a provision in a contract, especially a commercial contract, is to determine what the parties meant by the language used, which involves ascertaining what a reasonable person would have understood the parties to have meant. As Lord Hoffmann made clear in the first of the principles he summarised in the *Investors Compensation Scheme* case ... the relevant reasonable person is one who has all the background knowledge which would reasonably have been available to the parties in the situation in which they were at the time of the contract."

Later in his judgment he said:

---

[7]   [1985] A.C. 191 at 201.
[8]   Professor J.W. Carter subjects Lord Hoffman's five principles to sustained criticism in *The Construction of Commercial Contracts* [5–05] to [5–17]. The author also drew attention to certain respects in which a contract is not like an utterance in ordinary life in *The Interpretation of Contracts*, 6th edn, para.1.03. That discussion is not repeated here.
[9]   *Wood v Capita Insurance Services Ltd* [2017] A.C. 1173.
[10] [2011] UKSC 50; [2011] 1 W.L.R. 2900, reversing the Court of Appeal. See O'Sullivan, "Absurdity and ambiguity—making sense of contractual construction" (2012) C.L.J. 34. Lord Clarke repeated this description in *Aberdeen City Council v Stewart Milne Group Ltd* [2011] UKSC 56; [2012] S.L.T. 205.

"The language used by the parties will often have more than one potential meaning. I would accept the submission made on behalf of the appellants that the exercise of construction is essentially one unitary exercise in which the court must consider the language used and ascertain what a reasonable person, that is a person who has all the background knowledge which would reasonably have been available to the parties in the situation in which they were at the time of the contract, would have understood the parties to have meant. In doing so, the court must have regard to all the relevant surrounding circumstances. If there are two possible constructions, the court is entitled to prefer the construction which is consistent with business common sense and to reject the other."

But he also added:

"Where the parties have used unambiguous language, the court must apply it."

1.04   In *Arnold v Britton*[11] Lord Neuberger said:

"When interpreting a written contract, the court is concerned to identify the intention of the parties by reference to 'what a reasonable person having all the background knowledge which would have been available to the parties would have understood them to be using the language in the contract to mean', to quote Lord Hoffmann in *Chartbrook Ltd v Persimmon Homes Ltd* [2009] AC 1101 para 14. And it does so by focussing on the meaning of the relevant words, in this case clause 3(2) of each of the 25 leases, in their documentary, factual and commercial context. That meaning has to be assessed in the light of (i) the natural and ordinary meaning of the clause, (ii) any other relevant provisions of the lease, (iii) the overall purpose of the clause and the lease, (iv) the facts and circumstances known or assumed by the parties at the time that the document was executed, and (v) commercial common sense, but (vi) disregarding subjective evidence of any party's intentions."[12]

In the following passages of his judgment Lord Neuberger stressed the importance of the words of the contract, and what appeared to be their primacy over surrounding circumstances or business common sense. This led to the widespread perception in lower courts that *Arnold v Britton* heralded a return to more conventional principles of interpretation.

1.05   However, despite the widespread perception of the effect of *Arnold v Britton*, in *Wood v Capita Insurance Services Ltd*[13] the Supreme Court did not accept that *Arnold v Britton* represented any departure from the approach to interpretation described in *Rainy Sky SA v Kookmin Bank*. Lord Hodge explained:

"The court's task is to ascertain the objective meaning of the language which the parties have chosen to express their agreement. It has long been accepted that this

---

[11] [2015] A.C. 1619. He had already expressed this view in *Marley v Rawlings* [2015] A.C. 157 (a case about the interpretation of a will).

[12] This has been described as "essentially a 'check-list' of the factors that have been treated as relevant in the decided cases; it is not a statement of the intellectual process that is involved in interpreting a contract", *HOE International Ltd v Andersen* [2017] CSIH 9; 2017 SC 313. Scottish courts are thus more wary of taking Lord Neuberger's summary at face value. See *Scanmudring AS v James Fisher MFE Ltd* [2019] CSIH 10; 2019 S.L.T. 295.

[13] [2017] A.C. 1173.

is not a literalist exercise focused solely on a parsing of the wording of the particular clause but that the court must consider the contract as a whole and, depending on the nature, formality and quality of drafting of the contract, give more or less weight to elements of the wider context in reaching its view as to that objective meaning. In *Prenn v Simmonds* and in *Reardon Smith Line Ltd v Yngvar Hansen-Tangen*, Lord Wilberforce affirmed the potential relevance to the task of interpreting the parties' contract of the factual background known to the parties at or before the date of the contract, excluding evidence of the prior negotiations. When in his celebrated judgment in *Investors Compensation Scheme Ltd v West Bromwich Building Society* Lord Hoffmann reformulated the principles of contractual interpretation, some saw his second principle, which allowed consideration of the whole relevant factual background available to the parties at the time of the contract, as signalling a break with the past. But Lord Bingham in an extra-judicial writing, 'A New Thing Under the Sun? The Interpretation of Contracts and the ICS Decision', persuasively demonstrated that the idea of the court putting itself in the shoes of the contracting parties had a long pedigree."

In *Wood v Capita Insurance Services Ltd*[14] Lord Hodge described the correct approach as follows: **1.06**

"Interpretation is ... a unitary exercise; where there are rival meanings, the court can give weight to the implications of rival constructions by reaching a view as to which construction is more consistent with business common sense. But, in striking a balance between the indications given by the language and the implications of the competing constructions the court must consider the quality of drafting of the clause...; and it must also be alive to the possibility that one side may have agreed to something which with hindsight did not serve his interest.... Similarly, the court must not lose sight of the possibility that a provision may be a negotiated compromise or that the negotiators were not able to agree more precise terms."

He continued:

"12. ...This unitary exercise involves an iterative process by which each suggested interpretation is checked against the provisions of the contract and its commercial consequences are investigated ... To my mind once one has read the language in dispute and the relevant parts of the contract that provide its context, it does not matter whether the more detailed analysis commences with the factual background and the implications of rival constructions or a close examination of the relevant language in the contract, so long as the court balances the indications given by each.

13. Textualism and contextualism are not conflicting paradigms in a battle for exclusive occupation of the field of contractual interpretation. Rather, the lawyer and the judge, when interpreting any contract, can use them as tools to ascertain the objective meaning of the language which the parties have chosen to express their agreement. The extent to which each tool will assist the court in its task will vary according to the circumstances of the particular agreement or agreements.

---

[14]   [2017] A.C. 1173.

Some agreements may be successfully interpreted principally by textual analysis, for example because of their sophistication and complexity and because they have been negotiated and prepared with the assistance of skilled professionals. The correct interpretation of other contracts may be achieved by a greater emphasis on the factual matrix, for example because of their informality, brevity or the absence of skilled professional assistance. But negotiators of complex formal contracts may often not achieve a logical and coherent text because of, for example, the conflicting aims of the parties, failures of communication, differing drafting practices, or deadlines which require the parties to compromise in order to reach agreement. There may often therefore be provisions in a detailed professionally drawn contract which lack clarity and the lawyer or judge in interpreting such provisions may be particularly helped by considering the factual matrix and the purpose of similar provisions in contracts of the same type. The iterative process, … assists the lawyer or judge to ascertain the objective meaning of disputed provisions."

1.07   In Singapore the Court of Appeal has stressed the importance of both text and context, while adding that the text must be "the first port of call".[15] On the other hand, the Supreme Court of Ireland continues to apply the principles in *Investors Compensation Scheme* as originally formulated by Lord Hoffmann.[16] Lord Hoffmann's five principles have been adopted by the courts in Scotland,[17] Ireland (with some qualification),[18] Hong Kong,[19] New Zealand[20] and Singapore,[21] although the High Court of Australia has taken a more cautious view.[22]

In *ICDL GCC Foundation FZ LLC v European Computer Driving Licence*

---

[15]   *YESF & B Group Pte Ltd v Soup Restaurant Singapore Pte Ltd* [2015] SGCA 55; [2016] 1 LRC 318; *Lucky Realty Co Pte Ltd v HSBC Trustee (Singapore) Ltd* [2015] SGCA 68. These cases are discussed in Daniel Y.M. Tan, "Divergent Interpretations? Leases and Contractual Interpretation in Singapore and the UK" [2016] J.B.L. 409.

[16]   See *Law Society of Ireland v The Motor Insurers' Bureau of Ireland* [2017] IESC 31.

[17]   *City Wall Properties (Scotland) Ltd v Pearl Assurance Plc* [2007] CSIH 79; *Inveresk Plc v Papermakers Ltd* [2010] UKSC 19. The Inner House has since applied the approach found in *Rainy Sky SA v Kookmin Bank and Wood v Capita Insurance Services Ltd*: see *Ashtead Plant Hire Co Ltd v Granton Central Developments Ltd* [2020] CSIH 2.

[18]   *Analog Devices BV v Zurich Insurance Company* [2005] IESC 12.

[19]   *Jumbo King Ltd v Faithful Properties Ltd* (1999) H.K.C.F.A.R. 279.

[20]   *Boat Park Ltd v Hutchinson* [1999] 2 N.Z.L.R. 74; *Yoshimoto v Canterbury Golf International Ltd* [2001] 1 N.Z.L.R. 523, reversed by the Privy Council [2004] 1 N.Z.L.R. 1 (but not on these principles); *Firm PI 1 Ltd v Zurich Australian Insurance and Body Corporate 398983* [2014] NZSC 147.

[21]   *Sandar Aung v Parkway Hospitals Singapore Pte Ltd* [2007] 2 S.L.R. 891; *China Insurance Co (Singapore) Pte Ltd v Liberty Insurance Pte Ltd* [2005] 2 S.L.R. 509; *Seiko Epson Corp v Sepoms Technology Pte Ltd* [2008] F.S.R. 14.

[22]   *Royal Botanic Gardens and Domain Trust v South Sydney City Council* (2001) 76 A.J.L.R. 436. The debate in Australia has still not been settled. The High Court considered principles of interpretation in *Mount Bruce Mining Pty Ltd v Wright Prospecting Pty Ltd* [2015] HCA 37 but declined to rule one way or the other. In the joint judgment of French CJ and Nettle and Gordon JJ at [52] the principles were said not to mark any departure from *Codelfa Construction Pty Ltd v State Rail Authority of New South Wales* (1982) 149 C.L.R. 337 or *Electricity Generation Corp v Woodside Energy Ltd* (2014) 251 C.L.R. 640. The court also pointed out that *Western Export Services Inc v Jireh International Pty Ltd* (2011) 86 A.L.J.R. 1 was a decision on an application for leave to appeal and had no precedential value. For an excellent overview of multiple jurisdictions see Winkelmann CJ, Glazebrook and Ellen France JJ, *Contractual Interpretation* a paper presented to Asia Pacific Judicial Colloquium on 28 May 2019 (available on the Courts of New Zealand website).

Foundation Ltd, the Supreme Court of Ireland, while approving Lord Hoffmann's five principles, has stressed that although evidence of surrounding circumstances is admissible it "will not normally be allowed to alter the plain meaning of words".[23] In addition, the court said that the fourth principle:

> "should not be misunderstood as advocating a loose and unpredictable path to interpretation. A court will always commence with an examination of the words used in the contract."[24]

In *Marlan Holmes Ltd v Walsh*,[25] the Supreme Court of Ireland also adopted this theme. It said: **1.08**

> "It is important however to note that where the parties have committed their responsibilities to written form, in a particular manner, it must be assumed that they have intended to give effect to their obligations in that way. Such must be recognised as their right, both commercially and under contract law. Accordingly it is important that, when faced with a construction issue, a court should focus its mind on the language adopted by the parties being that which they have chosen to best reflect their intentions. It is not for the court, either by means of giving business or commercial efficacy or otherwise, to import into such arrangement a meaning, that might also be available from an understanding of the more general context in which the document came to exist, but is one not deducible by the use of the interpretive rules as mentioned."

The High Court of Australia has accepted Lord Hoffmann's description of the nature of interpretation (i.e. the first principle).[26] In *Toll (FGCT) Pty Ltd v Alphapharm Pty Ltd*,[27] their Honours said: **1.09**

> "References to the common intention of the parties to a contract are to be understood as referring to what a reasonable person would understand by the language in which the parties have expressed their agreement. The meaning of the terms of a contractual document is to be determined by what a reasonable person would have understood them to mean. That, normally, requires consideration not only of the text, but also of the surrounding circumstances known to the parties, and the purpose and object of the transaction."

In *Synergy Protection Agency Pty Ltd v North Sydney Leagues' Club Ltd*,[28] the New South Wales Court of Appeal held that there was no need to find an ambiguity in a contract before resorting to background. This is the predominant view of intermediate appellate courts in Australia although the position of the High Court remains uncertain.[29]

It is also not clear whether the High Court of Australia has also accepted Lord   **1.10**

---

23 [2012] IESC 55. This appears to be a less than whole-hearted acceptance of Lord Hoffmann's fifth principle.

24 More recent cases in England and Wales favour an iterative approach.

25 [2012] IESC 23.

26 *Maggbury Pty Ltd v Hafele Australasia Pty Ltd* (2000) 216 C.L.R. 451.

27 (2004) 219 C.L.R. 165.

28 [2009] NSWCA 140.

29 The authorities are surveyed in *Franklins Pty Ltd v Metcash Trading Ltd* [2009] NSWCA 407 and *Masterton Homes Pty Ltd v Palm Assets Pty Ltd* [2009] NSWCA 234.

Hoffmann's more controversial description of the admissible background (i.e. the second principle).[30] In *Western Export Services Inc v Jireh International Pty Ltd*,[31] the High Court of Australia held that the law in Australia is still represented by *Codelfa*.[32] It seems, therefore, that Lord Hoffmann's second principle is not yet accepted in Australia.[33] The decision of the High Court of Australia in *Electricity Generation Corp v Woodside Energy Ltd*[34] does not expressly refer to this principle, although it did say that interpretation "will require" consideration of surrounding circumstances.[35] In *Rinehart v Hancock Prospecting Pty Ltd*[36] the High Court of Australia placed heavy reliance on purpose and background in interpreting the scope of an arbitration clause. It did not, at least expressly, find that the words of the clause were ambiguous.

1.11   Although Lord Hodge said in *Wood v Capita Insurance Services Ltd* that the legal profession has had enough syntheses of the principles of contractual interpretation, some judges nevertheless attempt to reconcile the various cases. In *Lukoil Asia Pacific Pte Ltd v Ocean Tankers (Pte) Ltd (Ocean Neptune)*[37] Popplewell J said:

> "The court's task is to ascertain the objective meaning of the language which the parties have chosen in which to express their agreement. The court must consider the language used and ascertain what a reasonable person, that is a person who has all the background knowledge which would reasonably have been available

---

[30] In *Pacific Carriers Ltd v BNP Paribas* (2004) C.L.R. 451, the court referred in a footnote to the *Investors Compensation Scheme* case, but the text of the judgment refers only to "surrounding circumstances". See J.J. Spigelman, *"From Text to Context"* (Address to the Risky Business Conference 21 March 2007); Peden and Carter, "Taking Stock: The High Court and Contract Construction" (2005) 21 J.C.L. 172; *International Air Transport Association v Ansett Australia Holdings Ltd* [2008] HCA 3.

[31] [2011] HCA 45. See also *Velvet Glove Holdings Pty Ltd v Mount Isa Mines Ltd* [2011] QCA 312; *McCourt v Cranston* [2012] WASCA 60; *Pepe v Platypus Asset Management Pty Ltd* [2013] VSCA 38; *Canberra Hire Pty Ltd v Koppers Wood Products Pty Ltd* [2013] ACTSC 162; *W & K Holdings (NSW) Pty Ltd v Mayo* [2013] NSWSC 1063; McLauchlan and Lees, More Construction Controversy (2012) J.C.L. 97.

[32] *Codelfa Construction Pty Ltd v State Rail Authority of New South Wales* (1982) 149 C.L.R. 337. On the difference between the approach in England and Wales and the approach in Australia, see also Spigelman, "Extrinsic material and the interpretation of insurance contracts" (2011) 22 *Insurance Law Journal* 143; *W & K Holdings (NSW) Pty Ltd v Mayo* [2013] NSWSC 1063. The differences are also highlighted in Lewison and Hughes, *The Interpretation of Contracts in Australia* (Lawbook Co, 2012).

[33] Whether ambiguity is a necessary pre-condition to recourse to extrinsic evidence is still a matter of controversy in Australia: see *Cordon Investments Pty Ltd v Lesdor Properties Pty Ltd* [2012] NSWCA 184; *W & K Holdings (NSW) Pty Ltd v Mayo* [2013] NSWSC 1063; *Canberra Hire Pty Ltd v Koppers Wood Products Pty Ltd* [2013] ACTSC 162. However, Australian judges are, perhaps, more ready to find ambiguities sufficient to let in extrinsic evidence than their English counterparts.

[34] [2014] HCA 7.

[35] Subsequent cases tend to hold that context must be examined in every case, whether or not there is an ambiguity: *Mainteck Services Pty Ltd v Stein Heurtey SA* [2014] NSWCA 184; *Stratton Finance Pty Ltd v Webb* [2014] FCAFC 110; *Newey v Westpac Banking Corp* [2014] NSWCA 319.

[36] [2019] HCA 13; 366 A.L.R. 635.

[37] [2018] EWHC 163 (Comm); [2018] 1 C.L.C. 94; *Edgeworth Capital (Luxembourg) SARL v Aabar Investments PJS* [2018] EWHC 1627 (Comm); [2018] EWHC 1627, approved by the Court of Appeal in *Ark Shipping Co LLC v Silverburn Shipping (IOM) Ltd* [2019] EWCA Civ 1161; [2019] 7 WLUK 122; *Cape Distribution Ltd v Cape Intermediate Holdings Plc* [2016] EWHC 1119 (QB); *Deutsche Trustee Co Ltd v Duchess VI Clo BV* [2019] EWHC 778 (Ch) at [29]–[30], approved on appeal at [2020] EWCA Civ 521 sub nom *Barings (UK) Ltd v Deutsche Trustee Co Ltd* [2020] EWCA Civ 521.

to the parties in the situation in which they were at the time of the contract, would have understood the parties to have meant. The court must consider the contract as a whole and, depending on the nature, formality and quality of drafting of the contract, give more or less weight to elements of the wider context in reaching its view as to the objective meaning of the language used. If there are two possible constructions, the court is entitled to prefer the construction which is consistent with business common sense and to reject the other. Interpretation is a unitary exercise; in striking a balance between the indications given by the language and the implications of the competing constructions, the court must consider the quality of drafting of the clause and it must also be alive to the possibility that one side may have agreed to something which with hindsight did not serve his interest; similarly, the court must not lose sight of the possibility that a provision may be a negotiated compromise or that the negotiators were not able to agree more precise terms. This unitary exercise involves an iterative process by which each suggested interpretation is checked against the provisions of the contract and its commercial consequences are investigated. It does not matter whether the more detailed analysis commences with the factual background and the implications of rival constructions or a close examination of the relevant language in the contract, so long as the court balances the indications given by each."

In *Minera Las Bambas SA v Glencore Queensland Ltd*[38] Leggatt LJ said: **1.12**

"In short, the court's task is to ascertain the objective meaning of the relevant contractual language. This requires the court to consider the ordinary meaning of the words used, in the context of the contract as a whole and any relevant factual background. Where there are rival interpretations, the court should also consider their commercial consequences and which interpretation is more consistent with business common sense. The relative weight to be given to these various factors depends on the circumstances. As a general rule, it may be appropriate to place more emphasis on textual analysis when interpreting a detailed and professionally drafted contract such as we are concerned with in this case, and to pay more regard to context where the contract is brief, informal and drafted without skilled professional assistance. But even in the case of a detailed and professionally drafted contract, the parties may not for a variety of reasons achieve a clear and coherent text and considerations of context and commercial common sense may assume more importance."

2. CONTINUITY AND CHANGE

The recent history of the principles of the interpretation of contracts is one of continuity rather than change.

As long ago as 1905, Wigmore[39] described the history of the law of interpretation as "a progress from a stiff and superstitious formalism to a flexible rationalism". **1.13**

---

38 [2019] EWCA Civ 972.
39 *Wigmore on Evidence*, Vol.4, para.2462.

Lord Hoffmann's summary of principle in *Investors Compensation Scheme*[40] was seen by some judges, including himself, as no more than a step along the same road.

Lord Bingham, speaking extra-judicially, has commented that Lord Hoffmann's five principles are more a change of emphasis than a fundamental change.[41]

In *Chartbrook Ltd v Persimmon Homes Ltd*[42] Lord Hoffmann himself said:

> "As Lord Bingham pointed out, there was little in that statement of principle which could not be found in earlier authorities. The only points it decided that might have been thought in the least controversial were, first, that it was not necessary to find an 'ambiguity' before one could have any regard to background and, secondly, that the meaning which the parties would reasonably be taken to have intended could be given effect despite the fact that it was not, according to conventional usage, an 'available' meaning of the words or syntax which they had actually used."

Many other cases took the same view.[43]

1.14   It had been thought that *Arnold v Britton*[44] changed the relationship between the words of a contract and its factual background. Judges expressed this change in different ways. In *Process Components Ltd v Kason Kek-Gardner Ltd*[45] Proudman J commented that *Arnold v Britton* "has put the language of the contract firmly back into the spotlight". Likewise, in *Globe Motors Inc v TRW Lucas Varity Electric Steering Ltd*[46] Beatson LJ said that *Arnold v Britton* had made a "change of emphasis ... to give greater weight to the words used in the document"; and in *Evangelou v McNicol*[47] he said that *Arnold v Britton* "adjusted the balance between the words of the contract and its context and background by giving greater weight to the words used". In *Fluor Ltd v Shanghai Zhenhua Heavy Industries Ltd*[48] Edwards-Stuart J said that the Supreme Court has "taken a rather harder approach". In *Nobahar-Cookson v Hut Group Ltd*[49] Briggs LJ said that Arnold v Britton encouraged him "to treat the natural meaning of language as the best guide to interpretation". Commentators were divided over whether there had been a retreat from Lord Hoffmann's principles. Sir Geoffrey Vos considers that there had been.[50]

---

[40] [1998] 1 W.L.R. 896.
[41] "A New Thing under the Sun?" (2008) Edin L.R. 374. *Wood v Capital Insurance Services Ltd* [2017] A.C. 1173 made the same point by reference to this article. Paul S. Davis discusses the impact of Lord Hoffmann's five principles in "The Meaning of Commercial Contracts" in *The Jurisprudence of Lord Hoffmann* (Hart Publishing, 2015).
[42] [2009] A.C. 1101.
[43] See, e.g. *Bromarin v IMD Investments Ltd* [1998] S.T.C. 244; *WRM Group v Woods* [1998] C.L.C. 189; *Mora Shipping Inc of Monrovia, Liberia v Axa Corporate Solutions Assurance SA* [2005] 2 Lloyd's Rep. 769 CA. Other cases are collected in the 6th edition of this book: para.1.02. They are principally of historical interest only.
[44] [2015] UKSC 36; [2015] A.C. 1619.
[45] [2016] EWHC 2198 (Ch).
[46] [2016] EWCA Civ 396.
[47] [2016] EWCA Civ 817.
[48] [2016] EWHC 2062 (TCC).
[49] [2016] EWCA Civ 128.
[50] "Contractual Interpretation: Do judges sometimes say one thing and do another?" [2017] 23 Canterbury L. Rev. 1. See also Daniel Y.M. Tan, "Divergent Interpretations? Leases and Contractual Interpretation in Singapore and the UK" [2016] J.B.L. 409. Professor Gerard McMeel criticises *Arnold v Britton* in "Foucault's Pendulum: Text, Context and Good Faith in Contract Law" [2017] C.L.P. 365.

Professor McLauchlan, on the other hand, does not.[51] Lord Sumption has discussed the shifts in emphasis in "A Question of Taste: The Supreme Court and the Interpretation of Contracts".[52] Lord Hoffmann has defended his original approach in "Language and Lawyers".[53]

In *Wood v Capita Insurance Services Ltd*[54] the Supreme Court emphasised the continuity between Lord Hoffmann's restatement and previous authority. Lord Hodge said: **1.15**

> "14. On the approach to contractual interpretation, the *Rainy Sky* and *Arnold* cases were saying the same thing.
>
> 15. The recent history of the common law of contractual interpretation is one of continuity rather than change. One of the attractions of English law as a legal system of choice in commercial matters is its stability and continuity, particularly in contractual interpretation."

Thus, in *Dynniq UK Ltd v Lancashire County Council*[55] Coulson J said:

> "The rules of construction are now well-known: there has been a plethora of cases in the House of Lords and the Supreme Court in recent years in which the relevant rules have been repeatedly set out, including *Chartbrook Ltd v Persimmon Homes Ltd*; *Rainy Sky SA v Kookmin Bank*; *Arnold v Britton* and *Woods v Capita Insurance Service Ltd*. As I have pointed out elsewhere, some practitioners and legal commentators, with nothing better to do, have sought to exploit certain fine linguistic differences between the various judgments in those cases but, in my view, they all point in the same general direction."

In *Actavis UK Ltd v Eli Lilly and Co*[56] Lord Neuberger observed that:

> "the applicable principles [of interpreting documents] are tolerably clear, and were recently affirmed by Lord Hodge JSC in *Wood v Capita Insurance Services Ltd*,[57] paras 8–15."

In *Law Society of Ireland v Motor Insurers Bureau of Ireland*,[58] applying Lord Hoffmann's five principles as originally formulated, O'Donnell J said: **1.16**

> "The common law is treated as a coherent and consistent body of law developing incrementally by subtle changes, and only on occasion by sharp and dramatic turns. It is sometimes only after a period of time that the significance of a development is understood and it becomes apparent that the direction of the law has altered considerably. The modern approach to the interpretation of contracts is one which would probably be unrecognisable to, and might be regarded as

---

[51] "Continuity, not change, in contract interpretation?" (2017) L.Q.R. 546.
[52] J. Sumption, "A Question of Taste: The Supreme Court and the Interpretation of Contracts", The Supreme Court, *https://www.supremecourt.uk/docs/speech-170508.pdf* [Accessed 10 October 2020].
[53] (2018) L.Q.R. 553.
[54] [2017] A.C. 1173.
[55] [2017] EWHC 3173 (TCC); [2018] B.L.R. 81; *Zayo Group International Ltd v Ainger* [2017] EWHC 2542 (Comm); [2017] 10 WLUK 335; *Fishbourne Developments Ltd v Stephens* [2020] EWHC 932 (Ch).
[56] [2017] Bus. L.R. 1731.
[57] [2017] A.C. 1173.
[58] [2017] IESC 31.

heresy, by the Victorian judges who expounded so confidently on commercial matters."

3.   The Meaning Which the Document Would Convey

Interpretation is the ascertainment of the meaning which the document would convey to a reasonable person having all the background knowledge which would reasonably have been available to the parties in the situation in which they were at the time of the contract.

1.17   This principle is taken from the first of Lord Hoffman's five principles in *Investors Compensation Scheme v West Bromwich Building Society*.[59] It remains valid today. Therefore, in *Arnold v Britton*[60] Lord Neuberger said:

> "When interpreting a written contract, the court is concerned to identify the intention of the parties by reference to 'what a reasonable person having all the background knowledge which would have been available to the parties would have understood them to be using the language in the contract to mean', to quote Lord Hoffmann in *Chartbrook Ltd v Persimmon Homes Ltd*."

In the same case, Lord Hodge said that:

> "The role of the construct, the reasonable person, is to ascertain objectively, and with the benefit of the relevant background knowledge, the meaning of the words which the parties used."

In *Wood v Capita Insurance Services Ltd*[61] he said:

> "The court's task is to ascertain the objective meaning of the language which the parties have chosen to express their agreement."

1.18   Beguilingly simple though the formulation of Lord Hoffmann's first principle is, it contains the fundamental philosophy underlying the English approach to the interpretation of contracts. That is that interpretation does not involve the search for the actual intentions of the parties, but for an objective meaning. The purpose of interpretation is not to find out what the parties intended, but what the language of the contract would signify to a properly informed ordinary speaker of English.[62] The

---

[59]   [1998] 1 W.L.R. 896, repeated in *Chartbrook Ltd v Persimmon Homes Ltd* [2009] A.C. 1101.
[60]   [2015] UKSC 36; [2015] A.C. 1619.
[61]   [2017] A.C. 1173.
[62]   See Steyn, "Written Contracts: To What Extent May Evidence Control Language" [1998] C.P.L. 23; Steyn, "The Intractable Problem of the Interpretation of Legal Texts" (2003) Syd L. Rev. 1; Hoffmann, "The Intolerable Wrestle with Words and Meanings" (1997) 114 S.A.L.J. 656; Stevens, *Contract Interpretation: What it says on the tin* (Inner Temple Reading, 2014). The interpretation of utterances is that branch of linguistics called "pragmatics". For an introduction see P. Grundy, *Doing Pragmatics*, 2nd edn. Many of the classic papers are also reprinted in A.P. Martinich (ed.), *The Philosophy of Language*, 3rd edn (New York: Oxford University Press, 1996). Studies of legal interpretation from an American perspective may be found in L. Solan, *The Language of Judges* and S. Levinson and S. Mailloux (eds), *Interpreting Law and Literature* (Evanston: Northwestern University Press, 1988). Professor McMeel introduces the subject in *The Construction of Contracts*, 3rd edn (Oxford University Press, 2017), Ch.2. For discussions of the theory of language in articles accessible for lawyers, see also Gerard McMeel, "Language and the Law Revisited: an Intellectual

refocusing of attention on the impression made by the words on the reader, rather than on the intended message of the writer, is a departure from the traditional formulation of the aim of interpretation, namely to ascertain the presumed intention of the parties.[63] Although some judges continue to describe the object of interpretation as the ascertainment of the intention of the parties,[64] this is a distraction from the real question, which is: what does the contract mean?[65] It is this philosophy that explains the rationale for such of the exclusionary rules of evidence as remain in English law. In this respect, as Lord Hoffmann acknowledged, the five principles do not follow the way in which serious utterances are interpreted in ordinary life.[66]

The author prefers concentrating attention on the meaning of the contract rather than a fictional intention of the parties. **1.19**

4. TEXT AND CONTEXT

Both the text and the context are tools in the process of interpretation. The text must be assessed in the light of (i) the natural and ordinary meaning of the words, (ii) any other relevant provisions of the contract, and (iii) the overall purpose of the clause and the contract.

In *Arnold v Britton*[67] Lord Neuberger said that the meaning of a clause (in that case a clause in a lease) must be: **1.20**

"… assessed in the light of (i) the natural and ordinary meaning of the clause, (ii) any other relevant provisions of the lease, (iii) the overall purpose of the clause and the lease, (iv) the facts and circumstances known or assumed by the parties at the time that the document was executed, and (v) commercial common sense, but (vi) disregarding subjective evidence of any party's intentions."

He went on to say:

History of Contractual Interpretation" (2005) C.L.W.R. 343 and Adam Kramer, "Common Sense Principles of Contract Interpretation" (2003) O.J.L.S. 23. Ryan Catterwell, *A Unified Approach to Contract Interpretation* (Hart, 2020) presents a structured theory of contract interpretation.

[63] See Collins, *Objectivity and Committed Contextualism in Interpretation* (reprinted in Worthington, *Commercial Law and Commercial Practice*).

[64] See, e.g. *Marley v Rawlings* [2014] UKSC 2; [2014] 2 W.L.R. 213; *Arnold v Britton* [2015] UKSC 36; [2015] A.C. 1619 at [15].

[65] Sir George Leggatt has argued that even this formulation is unsatisfactory, and that contract interpretation does not depend on what the parties to the contract actually meant or would have been understood by a reasonable person to have meant when the contract was made: "Making sense of contracts: the rational choice theory" (2015) L.Q.R. 454. See also Stevens, *Contract Interpretation: What it says on the tin* (Inner Temple Reading, 2014).

[66] In "The Intolerable Wrestle with Words and Meanings", Lord Hoffmann argues that any interpretation, even in everyday life, is necessarily objective since the interpreter does not have a window into the speaker's mind, and hence cannot know his subjective intention. However, in everyday life a listener may ask for clarification in cases of ambiguity; whereas it is precisely in those cases that the court is called upon to interpret a contract, with no possibility of seeking clarification. In addition, in everyday life a speaker whose words are interpreted in a way he did not intend may legitimately say that he has been misunderstood. It would be a churlish response to say that he has not, simply because his words conveyed a different meaning to a reasonable listener.

[67] [2015] A.C. 1619.

"The exercise of interpreting a provision involves identifying what the parties meant through the eyes of a reasonable reader, and, save perhaps in a very unusual case, that meaning is most obviously to be gleaned from the language of the provision."

1.21   In *Wood v Capita Insurance Services Ltd*[68] Lord Hodge said:

"The court's task is to ascertain the objective meaning of the language which the parties have chosen to express their agreement. It has long been accepted that this is not a literalist exercise focused solely on a parsing of the wording of the particular clause but that the court must consider the contract as a whole and, depending on the nature, formality and quality of drafting of the contract, give more or less weight to elements of the wider context in reaching its view as to that objective meaning."

He added:

"Textualism and contextualism are not conflicting paradigms in a battle for exclusive occupation of the field of contractual interpretation. Rather, the lawyer and the judge, when interpreting any contract, can use them as tools to ascertain the objective meaning of the language which the parties have chosen to express their agreement. The extent to which each tool will assist the court in its task will vary according to the circumstances of the particular agreement or agreements."

5.   THE ADMISSIBLE EVIDENCE

The admissible background includes anything which a reasonable person would have regarded as relevant and which would have affected the way in which they would have understood the language of the document, and which would reasonably have been available to the parties.[69]

1.22   This principle is taken from Lord Hoffmann's second principle in *Investors Compensation Scheme v West Bromwich Building Society*.[70] As originally formulated, Lord Hoffmann's second principle was:

"The background was famously referred to by Lord Wilberforce as the 'matrix of fact', but this phrase is, if anything, an understated description of what the background may include. Subject to the requirement that it should have been reasonably available to the parties and to the exception to be mentioned next, it includes absolutely anything which would have affected the way in which the language of the document would have been understood by a reasonable man."[71]

---

[68]   [2017] A.C. 1173.

[69]   This paragraph was approved in *Northrop Grumman Mission Systems Europe Ltd v BAE Systems (Al Diriyah C4I) Ltd* [2014] EWHC 2955 (TCC).

[70]   [1998] 1 W.L.R. 896.

[71]   Steven Pinker explains that:

"language itself could not function if it did not sit atop a vast infrastructure of tacit knowledge about the world and about the intentions of other people. When we understand language, we have to listen between the lines to winnow out the unintended readings of an ambiguous sentence, piece together fractured utterances, glide over slips of the tongue, and fill in the countless unsaid steps in a complete train of thought. When the shampoo bottle says 'Lather, rinse, repeat', we don't

Soon after Lord Hoffmann's speech, some disquiet was expressed about the width of this principle.[72] That disquiet was shared not only by commentators but also by judges.[73] Lord Hoffmann qualified the original formulation in *BCCI v Ali*.[74] He said:

"I should in passing say that when, in *Investors Compensation Scheme Ltd v West Bromwich Building Society, Investors Compensation Scheme Ltd v Hopkin & Sons (a firm), Alford v West Bromwich Building Society, Armitage v West Bromwich Building Society*,[75] I said that the admissible background included 'absolutely anything which would have affected the way in which the language of the document would have been understood by a reasonable man', I did not think it necessary to emphasise that I meant anything which a reasonable man would have regarded as relevant. I was merely saying that there is no conceptual limit to what can be regarded as background. It is not, for example, confined to the factual background but can include the state of the law (as in cases in which one takes into account that the parties are unlikely to have intended to agree to something unlawful or legally ineffective) or proved common assumptions which were in fact quite mistaken. But the primary source for understanding what the parties meant is their language interpreted in accordance with conventional usage: '… we do not easily accept that people have made linguistic mistakes, particularly in formal documents.' I was certainly not encouraging a trawl through 'background' which could not have made a reasonable person think that the parties must have departed from conventional usage."

Even that more restricted formulation was not universally welcomed.[76] But in *Wood v Capita Insurance Services Ltd*[77] Lord Hodge referred to Lord Hoffmann's second principle without any sign of disapproval or qualification.

In *Arnold v Britton*[78] Lord Neuberger preferred the expression "factual context". **1.23** He described that as:

---

spend the rest of our lives in the shower; we infer that it means 'repeat once'. And we know how to interpret ambiguous headlines such as 'Kids Make Nutritious Snacks', 'Prostitutes Appeal to Pope', and 'British Left Waffles on Falkland Islands', because we effortlessly apply our background knowledge about the kind of things that people are likely to convey in newspapers", *The Blank Slate* (Penguin, 2002), pp.210–211. See also S. Pinker, *The Language Instinct* (William Morrow and Company, 1994), pp.225–230.

72 See Sir Christopher Staughton, "How do the Courts Interpret Commercial Contracts?" [1999] C.L.J. 303; J.J. Spigelman in "*Contractual Interpretation: A Comparative Perspective*", a paper presented to the Third Judicial Seminar on Commercial Litigation, 23 March 2011.

73 For example, *National Bank of Sharjah v Dellborg* Unreported 9 July 1997, part cited with approval in *NLA Group v Bowers* [1999] 1 Lloyd's Rep. 109. See also *Beazer Homes Ltd v Stroude* [2006] 2 P. & C.R. 6. In these cases, the perceived problem was the position of third parties or assignees who might be unaware of the background facts at the date of the contract. Other judges expressed disquiet at the volume of evidence that might potentially be adduced in what was essentially a dispute about interpretation: *Wire TV Ltd v CableTel (UK) Ltd* [1998] C.L.C. 244 at 257; *Persimmon Homes (South Coast) Ltd v Hall Aggregates (South Coast) Ltd* [2008] EWHC 2379 (TCC); *Standard Life Assurance Ltd v Oak Dedicated Ltd* [2008] 2 All E.R. (Comm) 916.

74 [2002] 1 A.C. 251.

75 [1998] 1 W.L.R. 896 at 913.

76 *MSC Mediterranean Shipping Co SA v Owners of the ship "Tychy"* [2001] 2 Lloyd's Rep. 403.

77 [2017] A.C. 1173.

78 [2015] A.C. 1619.

"the facts and circumstances known or assumed by the parties at the time that the document was executed ..."

He went on to say:

"When interpreting a contractual provision, one can only take into account facts or circumstances which existed at the time that the contract was made, and which were known or reasonably available to both parties."

In *Impact Funding Solutions Ltd v Barrington Support Services Ltd*[79] Lord Hodge repeated this terminology. He said:

"The court looks to the meaning of the relevant words in their documentary, factual and commercial context."

1.24   Recourse to the background should not deflect the court from the task of interpreting the words that the parties have actually used. As Lord Steyn put it in *Society of Lloyd's v Robinson*[80]:

"Loyalty to the text of a commercial contract, instrument, or document read in its contextual setting is the paramount principle of interpretation. But in the process of interpreting the meaning of the language of a commercial document the court ought generally to favour a commercially sensible construction. The reason for this approach is that a commercial construction is likely to give effect to the intention of the parties. Words ought therefore to be interpreted in the way in which a reasonable commercial person would construe them. And the reasonable commercial person can safely be assumed to be unimpressed with technical interpretations and undue emphasis on niceties of language."

It thus remains the case that:

"The court does not, through the guise of interpretation, make for the parties a bargain which they did not themselves choose to make. It is not for the court, through the guise of interpretation to substitute for the bargain which the parties did make a different bargain which in its view they would have made if they had been better advised or had had better regard for their own interests."[81]

1.25   But the debate about admissibility is in some ways a sterile debate. As Lord Steyn pointed out in *Mannai Investments Co Ltd v Eagle Star Life Assurance Co Ltd*[82]:

"what is *admissible* as a matter of the rules of evidence under this heading is what is arguably relevant. But admissibility is not the decisive matter. The real question is what evidence of surrounding circumstances may ultimately be allowed to influence the question of interpretation. That depends on what meanings the language read against the objective contextual scene will let in."

---

[79]   [2017] A.C. 73.
[80]   [1999] 1 W.L.R. 756. In *Phillips v Rafiq* [2007] 1 W.L.R. 1351 the Court of Appeal held that nothing in the background would drive a reasonable man to conclude that the words meant something quite different from what they "so plainly and obviously literally mean".
[81]   *Megaro v Di Popolo Hotels Ltd* [2007] EWCA Civ 309.
[82]   [1997] A.C. 749 at 778. Lord Steyn has elaborated on this extra-judicially: "Written Contracts: To What Extent May Evidence Control Language" [1998] C.P.L. 23.

Lord Steyn's observations in *Mannai* about weight rather than admissibility were followed by the majority of the Court of Appeal in *Cherry Tree Investments Ltd v Landmain Ltd*.[83]

In addition, more recent statements at the highest level have reaffirmed the importance of the contractual language. Thus in *Arnold v Britton*,[84] Lord Neuberger warned that:

> "the reliance placed in some cases on commercial common sense and surrounding circumstances ... should not be invoked to undervalue the importance of the language of the provision which is to be construed. The exercise of interpreting a provision involves identifying what the parties meant through the eyes of a reasonable reader, and, save perhaps in a very unusual case, that meaning is most obviously to be gleaned from the language of the provision. Unlike commercial common sense and the surrounding circumstances, the parties have control over the language they use in a contract. And, again save perhaps in a very unusual case, the parties must have been specifically focussing on the issue covered by the provision when agreeing the wording of that provision."

J.J. Spigelman has pointed out[85] that:

> "... it remains pertinent, not least as a precedent, to approach the task of interpretation on the basis that a significant commercial purpose of the written agreement was to state the obligations of the parties with sufficient certainty to avoid the very dispute that has eventuated. The further one travels beyond the text, the less likely it is that that commercial purpose will be served."

In Australia the High Court has taken a more restrictive view of what is admissible in order to interpret a contract. It has said that if there is any conflict between Lord Hoffmann's second principle and *Codelfa*,[86] Australian courts should continue to follow *Codelfa*.[87] Whether there is any inconsistency has not been authoritatively settled. In *Ray Brooks Pty Ltd v NSW Grains Board*,[88] Palmer J held that there was no inconsistency between *Codelfa* and Lord Hoffmann's second principle. But in *LMI Australasia Pty Ltd v Baulderstone Hornibrook Pty Ltd*,[89] the New South Wales Court of Appeal accepted that Australia had kept while England had discarded the concept that ambiguity is necessary to be shown before one looks at the surrounding circumstances. In *BP Australia Pty Ltd v Nyran Pty Ltd*,[90] RD Richardson J refused to follow Palmer J and held that *Codelfa* and Lord Hofmann's second

1.26

1.27

---

83 [2012] EWCA Civ 736; [2013] Ch 305.
84 [2015] UKSC 36; [2015] 2 W.L.R. 1593.
85 "Extrinsic material and the interpretation of insurance contracts" (2011) 22 *Insurance Law Journal* 143.
86 See *Codelfa Construction Pty Ltd v State Rail Authority of New South Wales* (1982) 149 C.L.R. 337.
87 *Royal Botanic Gardens and Domain Trust v South Sydney City Council* (2001) 76 A.J.L.R. 436. However, in *Pacific Carriers Ltd v BNP Paribas* (2004) C.L.R. 451, the court referred in a footnote to the *Investors Compensation Scheme* case, but the text of the judgment refers only to "surrounding circumstances". See D.W. McLauchlan, "Objectivity in Contract" [2005] U.Q.L.J. 28; J.J. Spigelman, "*From Text to Context*" (Address to the Risky Business Conference 21 March 2007). The position in Australia remains, to some extent, unclear.
88 [2002] NSWSC 1049.
89 [2003] NSWCA 74.
90 [2003] FCA 520.

principle were not consistent. More recently, however, in *Lion Nathan Australia Pty Ltd v Coopers Brewery Ltd*,[91] Finn J held that *BP Australia Pty Ltd v Nyran Pty Ltd* could not be considered to be correct.

In *Western Export Services Inc v Jireh International Pty Ltd*,[92] the High Court of Australia held that the law in Australia is still represented by *Codelfa*.[93] The most recent decision of the High Court of Australia in *Electricity Generation Corp v Woodside Energy Ltd*[94] does not refer to this principle; so the position remains uncertain.[95] In other respects, however, the statement of principle by the High Court appears to coincide with the approach in England and Wales.

6. A Unitary and Iterative Process

The process of interpretation is a unitary and iterative one by which each suggested interpretation is checked against the provisions of the contract and its commercial consequences are investigated. The weight to be given to each will depend on a number of factors, including the formality of the agreement and the quality of the drafting.

1.28   In *Rainy Sky SA v Kookmin Bank*[96] Lord Clarke said:

"the exercise of construction is essentially one unitary exercise in which the court must consider the language used and ascertain what a reasonable person, that is a person who has all the background knowledge which would reasonably have been available to the parties in the situation in which they were at the time of the contract, would have understood the parties to have meant. In doing so, the court must have regard to all the relevant surrounding circumstances."

In *Re Sigma Finance Corp*,[97] Lord Mance, approving Lord Neuberger's dissenting judgment in the Court of Appeal, said:

"Lord Neuberger was right to observe that the resolution of an issue of interpretation in a case like the present is an iterative process, involving 'checking each

---

[91] [2005] FCA 1812.

[92] [2011] HCA 45. See also *Velvet Glove Holdings Pty Ltd v Mount Isa Mines Ltd* [2011] QCA 312; *McCourt v Cranston* [2012] WASCA 60; *Pepe v Platypus Asset Management Pty Ltd* [2013] VSCA 38; *Canberra Hire Pty Ltd v Koppers Wood Products Pty Ltd* [2013] ACTSC 162; *W & K Holdings (NSW) Pty Ltd v Mayo* [2013] NSWSC 1063; McLauchlan and Lees, "More Construction Controversy" (2012) J.C.L. 97.

[93] On the difference between the approach in England and Wales and the approach in Australia see also Spigelman, "Extrinsic material and the interpretation of insurance contracts" (2011) 22 *Insurance Law Journal* 143; *W & K Holdings (NSW) Pty Ltd v Mayo* [2013] NSWSC 1063. The differences are also highlighted in Lewison and Hughes, *The Interpretation of Contracts in Australia* (Lawbook Co, 2012).

[94] [2014] HCA 7.

[95] Whether ambiguity is a necessary pre-condition to recourse to extrinsic evidence is still a matter of controversy in Australia: see *Cordon Investments Pty Ltd v Lesdor Properties Pty Ltd* [2012] NSWCA 184; *W & K Holdings (NSW) Pty Ltd v Mayo* [2013] NSWSC 1063; *Canberra Hire Pty Ltd v Koppers Wood Products Pty Ltd* [2013] ACTSC 162. However, Australian judges are, perhaps, more ready to find ambiguities sufficient to let in extrinsic evidence than their English counterparts.

[96] [2011] 1 W.L.R. 2900.

[97] [2009] UKSC 2; [2010] 1 All E.R. 571; *MT Hojgaard A/S v E.On Climate and Renewables UK Robin Rigg East Ltd* [2015] EWCA Civ 407.

of the rival meanings against other provisions of the document and investigating its commercial consequences'."

In *Arnold v Britton*[98] Lord Hodge drew these threads together. As he put it:

"This unitary exercise involves an iterative process by which each of the rival meanings is checked against the provisions of the contract and its commercial consequences are investigated."

He repeated this description in *Wood v Capita Insurance Services Ltd*[99] and added:

"To my mind once one has read the language in dispute and the relevant parts of the contract that provide its context, it does not matter whether the more detailed analysis commences with the factual background and the implications of rival constructions or a close examination of the relevant language in the contract, so long as the court balances the indications given by each."

The relative weight to be given to text and context depends on a number of factors. One of those factors is the quality of the drafting. In *Arnold v Britton*[100] Lord Neuberger said:

1.29

"when it comes to considering the centrally relevant words to be interpreted, I accept that the less clear they are, or, to put it another way, the worse their drafting, the more ready the court can properly be to depart from their natural meaning. That is simply the obverse of the sensible proposition that the clearer the natural meaning the more difficult it is to justify departing from it. However, that does not justify the court embarking on an exercise of searching for, let alone constructing, drafting infelicities in order to facilitate a departure from the natural meaning. If there is a specific error in the drafting, it may often have no relevance to the issue of interpretation which the court has to resolve."

Lord Hodge elaborated on this theme in *Wood v Capita Insurance Services Ltd*.[101] He said:

"The extent to which each tool will assist the court in its task will vary according to the circumstances of the particular agreement or agreements. Some agreements may be successfully interpreted principally by textual analysis, for example because of their sophistication and complexity and because they have been negotiated and prepared with the assistance of skilled professionals. The correct interpretation of other contracts may be achieved by a greater emphasis on the factual matrix, for example because of their informality, brevity or the absence of skilled professional assistance."

In *Fishbourne Developments Ltd v Stephens*[102] it was held that the general poor quality of the drafting of an option agreement and muddled sequence of contractual obligations entitled the court to place rather greater weight on the surrounding facts

---

[98] [2015] A.C. 1619.
[99] [2017] A.C. 1173.
[100] [2015] A.C. 1619.
[101] [2017] A.C. 1173.
[102] [2020] EWHC 932 (Ch).

known to the parties than might otherwise be the case; reinforced by the commercial purpose of the agreement.

1.30   Likewise, in *Buckinghamshire v Barnardo's*[103] Lord Hodge said:

> "In deciding which interpretative tools will best assist in ascertaining the meaning of an instrument, and the weight to be given to each of the relevant interpretative tools, the court must have regard to the nature and circumstances of the particular instrument."

Among the factors that he regarded as justifying concentration on the text rather than the context were the facts that the instrument (in that case a pension scheme) had been drafted by skilled specialists; that it was intended to operate over the long term; that it was not the product of negotiations; and that it conferred rights on persons who were not party to it. But he added:

> "The emphasis on textual analysis as an interpretative tool does not derogate from the need both to avoid undue technicality and to have regard to the practical consequences of any construction."

7.   BUSINESS COMMON SENSE

If the language of the contract is unambiguous the court must apply it. But if there are two possible interpretations, the court is entitled to prefer the interpretation which is consistent with business common sense as at the date of the contract and to reject the other. Nevertheless, the commercial consequences of one interpretation as against another do not detract from the importance of the words.

1.31   In *Rainy Sky SA v Kookmin Bank*[104] Lord Clarke said:

> "Where the parties have used unambiguous language, the court must apply it."[105]

He added:

> "where a term of a contract is open to more than one interpretation, it is generally appropriate to adopt the interpretation which is most consistent with business common sense."

In *Wood v Capita Insurance Services Ltd*[106] Lord Hodge said:

> "where there are rival meanings, the court can give weight to the implications of rival constructions by reaching a view as to which construction is more consistent with business common sense."

1.32   In *Arnold v Britton*[107] Lord Neuberger made two cautionary points about reli-

---

[103] [2019] I.C.R. 495.
[104] [2011] 1 W.L.R. 2900.
[105] *Sun Alliance (Bahamas) Ltd v Scandi Enterprises Ltd* [2017] UKPC 10; [2017] 2 All E.R. (Comm) 1019.
[106] [2017] A.C. 1173.
[107] [2015] A.C. 1619.

ance on business common sense. First, he said:

"... the reliance placed in some cases on commercial common sense and surrounding circumstances should not be invoked to undervalue the importance of
the language of the provision which is to be construed. The exercise of interpreting a provision involves identifying what the parties meant through the eyes of
a reasonable reader, and, save perhaps in a very unusual case, that meaning is
most obviously to be gleaned from the language of the provision. Unlike commercial common sense and the surrounding circumstances, the parties have
control over the language they use in a contract. And, again save perhaps in a
very unusual case, the parties must have been specifically focussing on the issue covered by the provision when agreeing the wording of that provision."

Second, he said:

"... commercial common sense is not to be invoked retrospectively. The mere
fact that a contractual arrangement, if interpreted according to its natural
language, has worked out badly, or even disastrously, for one of the parties is not
a reason for departing from the natural language. Commercial common sense is
only relevant to the extent of how matters would or could have been perceived
by the parties, or by reasonable people in the position of the parties, as at the date
that the contract was made."

8.   CORRECTION OF ERRORS

**In exceptional circumstances the court may conclude that the parties have used
the wrong words. If it is clear what the error is, and the nature of the correction required, the court may correct it.**

Lord Hoffmann's fifth principle in *Investors Compensation Scheme v West
Bromwich Building Society*[108] was: **1.33**

"The 'rule' that words should be given their 'natural and ordinary meaning'
reflects the commonsense proposition that we do not easily accept that people
have made linguistic mistakes, particularly in formal documents. On the other
hand, if one would nevertheless conclude from the background that something
must have gone wrong with the language, the law does not require judges to attribute to the parties an intention which they plainly could not have had."

In *Chartbrook Ltd v Persimmon Homes Ltd*[109] he made two further points. First:

"in deciding whether there is a clear mistake, the court is not confined to reading the document without regard to its background or context. As the exercise is
part of the single task of interpretation, the background and context must always
be taken into consideration."

Second:

---

[108]   [1998] 1 W.L.R. 896. He repeated this in *Chartbrook Ltd v Persimmon Homes Ltd* [2009] A.C. 1101.
[109]   [2009] A.C. 1101.

"there is not, so to speak, a limit to the amount of red ink or verbal rearrangement or correction which the court is allowed. All that is required is that it should be clear that something has gone wrong with the language and that it should be clear what a reasonable person would have understood the parties to have meant."[110]

1.34   Both these requirements must be satisfied. In *Arnold v Britton*[111] Lord Hodge said:

"Nor is this a case in which the courts can identify and remedy a mistake by construction. Even if, contrary to my view, one concluded that there was a clear mistake in the parties' use of language, it is not clear what correction ought to be made. The court must be satisfied as to both the mistake and the nature of the correction."

1.35   Even in a case where the court ascribes primacy to the text of the instrument, this principle may still apply. In *Buckinghamshire v Barnardo's*[112] Lord Hodge said:

"a focus on textual analysis in the context of the deed containing the scheme must not prevent the court from being alive to the possibility that the draftsman has made a mistake in the use of language or grammar which can be corrected by construction, as occurred in *Chartbrook Ltd v Persimmon Homes Ltd*, where the court can clearly identify both the mistake and the nature of the correction."

9.   Exclusionary Rules

In carrying out its task, the court must disregard the parties' subjective intentions, and (except for limited purposes) the negotiations that preceded the making of the contract.

1.36   Lord Hoffmann's third principle in *Investors Compensation Scheme v West Bromwich Building Society*[113] was:

"The law excludes from the admissible background the previous negotiations of the parties and their declarations of subjective intent. They are admissible only in an action for rectification. The law makes this distinction for reasons of practical policy and, in this respect only, legal interpretation differs from the way we would interpret utterances in ordinary life. The boundaries of this exception are in some respects unclear. But this is not the occasion on which to explore them."

1.37   The exclusion of the parties' subjective declarations of intent from the admissible material is a reflection of the principle that a contract must be interpreted objectively.[114] Where the contract is a written one, this principle has never been

---

[110] However, in *Chipsaway International Ltd v Kerr* [2009] EWCA Civ 320, the CA held that where it is clear that something has gone wrong with the language, such that the clause must be rewritten, the rewriting that is required is that which involves the minimum changes necessary to achieve a sensible meaning and which gives effect to the commercial purpose of the clause.

[111] [2015] A.C. 1619.

[112] [2019] I.C.R. 495.

[113] [1998] 1 W.L.R. 896. He repeated this in *Chartbrook Ltd v Persimmon Homes Ltd* [2009] A.C. 1101.

[114] See Steyn, "Written Contracts: To What Extent May Evidence Control Language" [1998] C.P.L. 23;

doubted.[115] In *Arnold v Britton*[116] Lord Neuberger made it clear that subjective evidence of any party's intentions was to be disregarded.[117]

After intense debate the rule has been settled in England and Wales by the decision of the House of Lords in *Chartbrook Ltd v Persimmon Homes Ltd*[118] confirming the rule that excludes evidence of negotiations. The scope of the exclusion is considered in para.3.41.

1.38

Hoffmann, "The Intolerable Wrestle with Words and Meanings" (1997) 114 S.A.L.J. 656. See also *SDI Retail Services Ltd v The Rangers Football Club Ltd* [2019] EWHC 1929 (Comm).

[115] In the case of a contract which is either wholly oral, or partly oral and partly in writing, it has been held that evidence of a party's subjective intention is admissible: *Blyth v Nelsons Solicitors* [2019] EWHC 2063 (QB); [2019] Costs L.R. 1409.

[116] [2015] A.C. 1619.

[117] The position differs in a claim for the equitable remedy of rectification.

[118] [2009] 1 A.C. 1101.

CHAPTER 2

THE PURPOSE OF INTERPRETATION

Whatever reader desires to have a thorough comprehension of an author's thoughts cannot take a better method than by putting himself into the circumstances and postures of life that the author was in, upon every important passage as it flowed from his pen; for this will introduce a parity and strict correspondence of ideas between the reader and the author.

Swift: *A Tale of a Tub*

1. The Process of Interpretation

The interpretation of a written contract involves the ascertainment of the words used by the parties and the determination, subject to any rule of law, of the legal effect of those words.

This book is concerned with the interpretation of written contracts. In the last resort, when parties have differing views about what their contract means, or what its effect on their legal rights and obligations is, their difference must be settled by the court.[1] In *Wasa International Insurance Co Ltd v Lexington Insurance Co*,[2] Sedley LJ said:

> "It is the rule of law and the principle of finality which forms part of it which make the meaning and effect of a contract whatever a court of competent jurisdiction holds them to be."

The settlement of differences is to a large extent governed by the proper interpretation (or construction) of the contract.[3] In arriving at its conclusion the court

2.01

---

[1] Or by arbitration. Some contracts, however, are framed in such a way that makes the content of the parties' obligations dependent on what a third party thinks they are. See para.14.12.

[2] [2008] Bus. L.R. 1029. The decision of the Court of Appeal was reversed, sub nom *Lexington Insurance Co v AGF Insurance Ltd* [2010] 1 A.C. 180 but without affecting this point.

[3] A distinction is sometimes drawn between "construction" and "interpretation". Thus in *Life Insurance Co of Australia v Phillips* (1925) 36 C.L.R. 60, Isaacs J said at 78:

> "But the term 'ambiguity' is itself not inflexible. It may arise from doubt as to the construction in their totality of the ordinary and in themselves well-understood English words the parties have employed. That is true construction. Or it may arise from the diversity of subjects to which those words may in the circumstances be applied. That is rather interpretation of terms. Or again it may arise from obscurity as to the full expression in ordinary language of some abbreviated term or arbitrary form that has been adopted. That again is interpretation of terms."

It is doubtful whether this distinction serves any useful purpose, particularly since in practice "construction" and "interpretation" are used interchangeably. In *Cream Holdings Ltd v Davenport* [2009] B.C.C. 183 Sedley LJ said:

applies relatively well-established principles of interpretation. The purpose of this book is to gather together those principles.

2.02   However, at the outset the scope of the inquiry must be ascertained. In *Chatenay v The Brazilian Submarine Telegraph Co Ltd*,[4] Lindley LJ said:

> "The expression 'construction', as applied to a document, at all events as used by English lawyers, includes two things: first the meaning of the words; and secondly their legal effect, or the effect which is to be given to them."

As a working definition, however, this is incomplete. First, the determination of the legal effect of a contract may involve the application of external rules of law (for example the intervention of a statute, or some rule of public policy) which has nothing to do with the intention of the parties as expressed in their contract. Secondly, the determination of the legal effect to be given to the contract may turn in part on words which the parties have not actually used, but which are properly to be implied. Although the interpretation of express words in a contract, and the implication of terms are part of the process of determining the scope and meaning of the contract, they are different processes and governed by different rules.[5] It has also been suggested that determining the scope of a claim for damages for breach of contract is also a question of interpretation of the contract in question, rather than the application of an external rule of foreseeability.[6]

2.03   It is also difficult, in any practical sense, to draw a realistic boundary between examining documents (and sometimes conduct) in order to determine whether a contract has been formed at all, and examining the same material in order to ascertain what the terms of a concluded agreement are.

2.04   Finally it must be said that the boundary between the interpretation of a document, the emergence of a canon or principle of interpretation and its eventual ossification into a rule of law is a difficult one to discern. Over time a particular interpretation may develop into a principle, as a judicial consensus grows.[7] The

---

"Many law students are initially puzzled by the expression 'construction of contracts'. They think it must mean the process of assembling the elements of a contract; it takes them some time to realise that it means interpreting them. The realisation, moreover, may not come rapidly because the law reports which they study are often as consistent with the first as with the second meaning of 'construction', because the courts, although mandated only to make sense of what the parties have agreed to, repeatedly find themselves repairing or rebuilding contracts which simply do not cater for the problem which has arisen."

It is partly for this reason that the author prefers to speak of the interpretation of contracts. However, in *Sembcorp Marine Ltd v PPL Holdings Pte Ltd* [2013] SGCA 43; (2013) 151 Con. L.R. 170 the Singapore Court of Appeal drew a sharp distinction between "interpretation" on the one hand and "construction" on the other. Interpretation is concerned only with the meaning of the express words contained in the contract, whereas construction embraces wider considerations, such as the implication of terms to fill gaps in the contract for which the express terms make no provision. This is not a view to which the author subscribes. In general, it is little more than an arid semantic debate. However, the distinction may be valid where the question is whether a contractual provision is a penalty. See para.17.06.

4   [1891] 1 Q.B. 79 at 85.

5   *Marks and Spencer Plc v BNP Paribas Securities Services Trust Co (Jersey) Ltd* [2016] A.C. 742. For implied terms, see Ch.6.

6   *Transfield Shipping Inc v Mercator Shipping Inc* [2009] 1 A.C. 61. For comment see (2009) 125 L.Q.R. 408 (Adam Kramer).

7   *The Mercini Lady* [2010] EWCA Civ 1145.

boundary may have been crossed at times, but there is no general intention to deal with matters of substantive rules of law.

2. ASCERTAINMENT OF MEANING TO A REASONABLE READER

Interpretation is the ascertainment of the meaning which the document would convey to a reasonable person having all the background knowledge which would reasonably have been available to the parties in the situation in which they were at the time of the contract.

The modern starting point is Lord Hoffmann's statement that[8]:　　　　　　　**2.05**

"Interpretation is the ascertainment of the meaning which the document would convey to a reasonable person having all the background knowledge which would reasonably have been available to the parties in the situation in which they were at the time of the contract."[9]

As he explained in *Kirin Amgen Inc v Hoechst Marion Roussel Ltd*[10]:

"Construction, whether of a patent or any other document, is of course not directly concerned with what the author meant to say. There is no window into the mind of the patentee or the author of any other document. Construction is objective in the sense that it is concerned with what a reasonable person to whom the utterance was addressed would have understood the author to be using the words to mean. Notice, however, that it is not, as is sometimes said, 'the meaning of the words the author used', but rather what the notional addressee would have understood the author to mean by using those words. The meaning of words is a matter of convention, governed by rules, which can be found in dictionaries and grammars. What the author would have been understood to mean by using those words is not simply a matter of rules. It is highly sensitive to the context of and background to the particular utterance. It depends not only upon the words the author has chosen but also upon the identity of the audience he is taken to have been addressing and the knowledge and assumptions which one attributes to that audience."

In *Attorney General of Belize v Belize Telecom Ltd*,[11] Lord Hoffmann reiterated that the meaning of a contract is not necessarily the same as the intention of the parties. He said:

8　In *Investors Compensation Scheme v West Bromwich Building Society* [1998] 1 W.L.R. 896.

9　Sir George Leggatt has argued that even this formulation is unsatisfactory, and that contract interpretation does not depend on what the parties to the contract actually meant or would have been understood by a reasonable person to have meant when the contract was made: "Making sense of contracts: the rational choice theory" (2015) L.Q.R. 454. Lord Hoffmann's statement in *Attorney General of Belize v Belize Telecom Ltd* that the court is only concerned "to discover what the instrument means" goes a long way to meet Sir George's objection. Professor David McLauchlan has written a riposte to Sir George Leggatt's article: "A better way of making sense of contracts?" (2016) 132 L.Q.R. 577. See also Stevens, *Contract Interpretation: What it says on the tin* (Inner Temple Reading, 2014)

10　[2004] UKHL 46; [2005] R.P.C. 9.

11　[2009] 1 W.L.R. 1988; *Anthracite Rated Investments (Jersey) Ltd v Lehman Brothers Finance SA* [2011] EWHC 1822 (Ch).

"The court has no power to improve upon the instrument which it is called upon to construe, whether it be a contract, a statute or articles of association. It cannot introduce terms to make it fairer or more reasonable.[12] It is concerned only to discover what the instrument means. However, that meaning is not necessarily or always what the authors or parties to the document would have intended. It is the meaning which the instrument would convey to a reasonable person having all the background knowledge which would reasonably be available to the audience to whom the instrument is addressed."

Similarly, Lord Steyn said in *Equitable Life Assurance Society v Hyman*[13]:

"The purpose of interpretation is to assign to the language of the text the most appropriate meaning which the words can legitimately bear."[14]

2.06   The more traditional formulation of the goal of interpretation was that it was designed to ascertain the intention of the contracting parties. Thus in *Pioneer Shipping Ltd v BTP Tioxide Ltd*,[15] Lord Diplock said:

"The object sought to be achieved in construing any contract is to ascertain what the mutual intentions of the parties were as to the legal obligations each assumed by the contractual words in which they sought to express them."

The framing of the goal by reference to the intention of the parties was liable to give rise to the common but erroneous thought that the task of the court was to ascertain the real intention of the actual parties to the contract. As will be seen this was never the approach taken by English law.

2.07   Despite references to the intention of the parties, the English approach to the interpretation of contracts has always been an objective one. This is one of the principal features of the English approach that distinguishes it from many European jurisdictions.[16] Lord Hoffmann explained in *Chartbrook Ltd v Persimmon Homes Ltd*[17]:

"Both the *Unidroit Principles of International Commercial Contracts* (1994 and 2004 revision) and the *Principles of European Contract Law* (1999) provide that in ascertaining the 'common intention of the parties', regard shall be had to prior negotiations: articles 4.3 and 5.102 respectively. The same is true of the United Nations Convention on Contracts for the International Sale of Goods (1980). But these instruments reflect the French philosophy of contractual interpretation, which is altogether different from that of English law. As Professor Catherine

---

[12]   *Ilott v Williams* [2013] EWCA Civ 645.

[13]   [2000] 3 All E.R. 961 at 969.

[14]   See also *Commerzbank AG v Jones* [2003] EWCA Civ 1663:

"The aim of construction is to determine from the documents, read, of course, in their factual setting, what the parties agreed. It is not the function of the court to substitute for the agreement of the parties what it thinks would have been the sensible commercial agreement for the parties to have made", per Mummery LJ.

[15]   [1982] A.C. 724.

[16]   Comparative surveys may be found in Kötz and Flessner, *European Contract Law* (Clarendon Press), Ch.7, and Vogenauer, "Interpretation of Contracts: Concluding Comparative Observations" in Burrows and Pee (eds), *Contract Terms* (Oxford University Press).

[17]   [2009] A.C. 1101.

Valcke explains in an illuminating article ('On Comparing French and English Contract Law: Insights from Social Contract Theory') (16 January 2009), French law regards the intentions of the parties as a pure question of subjective fact, their *volonté psychologique*, uninfluenced by any rules of law. It follows that any evidence of what they said or did, whether to each other or to third parties, may be relevant to establishing what their intentions actually were. There is in French law a sharp distinction between the ascertainment of their intentions and the application of legal rules which may, in the interests of fairness to other parties or otherwise, limit the extent to which those intentions are given effect. English law, on the other hand, mixes up the ascertainment of intention with the rules of law by depersonalising the contracting parties and asking, not what their intentions actually were, but what a reasonable outside observer would have taken them to be."

Lord Hoffmann's reformulation by reference to the reasonable outsider, rather than by reference to the parties themselves, emphasises the objective nature of the task. Indeed, the phrase "the intention of the parties" does not appear at all in the five principles he laid down. This is a reflection of the philosophical basis of interpretation in English law; namely that it is an objective exercise.[18] It would be conducive to greater clarity if references to the intention of the parties (whether actual or presumed) were abandoned.

In *Arnold v Britton*[19] Lord Neuberger defined the court's task as "to identify the intention of the parties". Lord Hodge, on the other hand, described it as to ascertain "the meaning of the words which the parties used". In *Wood v Capita Insurance Services Ltd*[20] Lord Hodge again referred to the "objective meaning of the words the parties have chosen".[21] The author prefers the latter formulation, which concentrates attention on the meaning of the contract rather than a fictional intention of the parties. **2.08**

Nevertheless the mixing up of the meaning of the contract and the intention of the parties continues in pronouncements at the highest level. Thus in *Aberdeen City Council v Stewart Milne Group Ltd*,[22] Lord Clarke said: **2.09**

> "the ultimate aim in construing a contract is to determine what the parties meant by the language used, which involves ascertaining what a reasonable person would have understood the parties to have meant; the relevant reasonable person being one who has all the background knowledge which would reasonably have been available to the parties in the situation in which they were at the time of the contract."

This is not a new approach. Even in the more traditional formulations of the purpose of interpretation judges have been careful to stress that when they speak of the intention of the parties, they are ascertaining their presumed intention objectively.

---

[18] See Stevens, *"Contract Interpretation: What it says on the tin"* (Inner Temple Reading, 2014); Leggatt, "Making sense of contracts: the rational choice theory" (2015) L.Q.R. 454.
[19] [2015] UKSC 36; [2015] A.C. 1619.
[20] [2017] UKSC 24, [2017] A.C. 1173.
[21] Lord Hoffmann emphasises this point in his article "Language and Lawyers" (1018) L.Q.R. 553.
[22] [2011] UKSC 56; [2012] S.L.T. 205.

Thus in *Reardon-Smith Line Ltd v Hansen-Tangen*,[23] Lord Wilberforce said:

"When one speaks of the intention of the parties to the contract one speaks objectively—the parties cannot themselves give direct evidence of what their intention was—and what must be ascertained is what is to be taken as the intention which reasonable people would have had if placed in the situation of the parties."

A similar point was made by Lord Reid in *McCutcheon v David MacBrayne Ltd*,[24] approving the following quotation from *Gloag on Contracts*[25]:

"The judicial task is not to discover the actual intentions of each party it is to decide what each was reasonably entitled to conclude from the attitude of the other."

In *Codelfa Construction Pty Ltd v State Rail Authority of New South Wales*,[26] Mason J said:

"… when the issue is which of two or more possible meanings is to be given to a contractual provision we look not to the actual intentions, aspirations or expectations of the parties before or at the time of the contract, except in so far as they are expressed in the contract, but to the objective framework of facts within which the contract came into existence, and to the parties' presumed intention in this setting. We do not take into account the actual intentions of the parties and for the very good reason that an investigation of those matters would not only be time consuming but would also be unrewarding as it would tend to give too much weight to these factors at the expense of the actual language of the contract."

2.10   Sir John Donaldson MR gave a rather more cynical explanation of the unimportance of the actual intentions of the parties in *Summit Investment Inc v British Steel Corp*[27]:

"their actual intentions are happily irrelevant, since, were it otherwise, many, and perhaps most, disputes upon points of construction would be resolved by holding that the parties were not *ad idem*."

Nevertheless, this is an important point for it emphasises the objectivity of the court's task of interpretation. In many cases the contract is one which will be relied upon by third parties (for example a bill of lading or a conveyance) and it is important for such persons to have a reasonable degree of certainty as to the meaning of the contract. Both these reasons were confirmed by the Ontario Court of Appeal in *Dumbrell v The Regional Group of Companies Inc*,[28] Doherty JA said:

---

[23]   [1976] 1 W.L.R. 989.
[24]   [1964] 1 W.L.R. 125.
[25]   2nd edn (1985), p.7.
[26]   (1982) 149 C.L.R. 337.
[27]   [1987] 1 Lloyd's Rep. 230 at 233.
[28]   (2007) 279 D.L.R. (4th) 201.

"In my view, when interpreting written contracts, at least in the context of commercial relationships, it is not helpful to frame the analysis in terms of the subjective intention of the parties at the time the contract was drawn. This is so for at least two reasons. First, emphasis on subjective intention denudes the contractual arrangement of the certainty that reducing an arrangement to writing was intended to achieve. This is particularly important where, as is often the case, strangers to the contract must rely on its terms. They have no way of discerning the actual intention of the parties, but must rely on the intent expressed in the written words. Second, many contractual disputes involve issues on which there is no common subjective intention between the parties. Quite simply, the answer to what the parties intended at the time they entered into the contract will often be that they never gave it a moment's thought until it became a problem."

More modern descriptions of the process of interpretation also stress the objectivity of the exercise. In *Deutsche Genossenschaftsbank v Burnhope*,[29] Lord Steyn[30] said: **2.11**

"It is true the objective of the construction of a contract is to give effect to the intention of the parties. But our law of construction is based on an objective theory. The methodology is not to probe the real intentions of the parties but to ascertain the contextual meaning of the relevant contractual language. Intention is determined by reference to expressed rather than actual intention. The question therefore resolves itself in a search for the meaning of language in its contractual setting. That does not mean that the purpose of a contractual provision is not important. The commercial or business object of a provision, *objectively ascertained*, may be highly relevant: ... But the court must not try to divine the purpose of the contract by speculating about the real intention of the parties. It may only be inferred from the language used by the parties, judged against the objective contextual background. It is therefore wrong to speculate about the actual intention of the parties in this case, as Staughton LJ apparently did in the first sentence in the passage quoted and as counsel for the insurers undoubtedly did throughout his argument."

In *Cream Holdings Ltd v Davenport*,[31] Mummery LJ said:

"The language chosen to express the parties' intentions, the intended purpose of the provision and its overall context are all relevant to construction. The object of the exercise is to end up, if possible, with a reasonable result within the ambit of the parties' probable intentions."

Similarly, in *Bekker NO v Total South Africa (Pty) Ltd*,[32] Kriegler J said:

"The interpretation of a written document is not an exercise in the arcane. It is a logical process in which the interpreter seeks to ascertain the intention of the draftsman as embodied in the instrument. The mutual intention of the parties to a bilateral contract is, of course, an abstraction. The primary method to find out

---

[29]   [1995] 4 All E.R. 717.
[30]   A dissenting speech.
[31]   [2009] B.C.C. 183.
[32]   [1990] 3 S.A. 159.

what that abstraction was is to ask: what did the parties say? This does not mean picking away at words like a guinea fowl down a row of maize seed. One looks at the words used with common sense and perspective."

2.12 However, the logical aspects of the process of construction must not be exaggerated. As Robert Walker LJ explained in *John v Price Waterhouse*[33]:

"The process of construction often (and certainly in this case) involves the assessment of disparate (and therefore incommensurable) factors to reach what is ultimately an intuitive (but not irrational) conclusion. If a judge makes a point-by-point evaluation of the opposing arguments addressed to him he is performing his duty to give reasons for his decision. But point-by-point analysis of that sort cannot fully reflect the nature of the judicial process of construing a complex and difficult commercial agreement."

2.13 The reasonable reader, who is the medium through whom the contract is interpreted is, of course, a legal construct. The reasonable reader's characteristics may vary depending on the nature of the contract under consideration. *Spire Healthcare Ltd v Royal & Sun Alliance Insurance Plc*[34] concerned the interpretation of a liability insurance policy where there was a potential conflict between different parts of the policy. Simon LJ said:

"In approaching the issue of construction, the Court assumes that the reasonable reader of this policy has the characteristic of a sophisticated assured who is assisted by professional advice; and does not confine his or her reading of the policy to the Limits of Indemnity contained in the schedule."

In other cases, the court has said that the reasonable reader does not read the whole of the document. Thus the reasonable reader of a bill of lading may not read the small print on the back.[35] In other cases, the reasonable reader may have to be equipped with knowledge of the legal background against which the contract was made.[36] In *Munich Re Capital Ltd v Ascot Corporate Name Ltd*[37] the dispute concerned insurance cover for an offshore drilling rig. Carr J said that the reasonable reader "is someone with substantial expertise and experience of the offshore construction all-risks market, familiar with the ordinary workings of that market and of the ordinary expectations of parties to an offshore CAR[38] policy."

---

[33] [2002] EWCA Civ 899 at [94]. See also *Morrells of Oxford Ltd v Oxford United Football Club* [2001] Ch. 459.

[34] [2018] EWCA Civ 317; [2018] 1 C.L.C. 327; *Warborough Investments Ltd v Lunar Office SARL* [2018] EWCA Civ 427; [2018] L. & T.R. 24.

[35] *Homburg Houtimport BV v Agrosin Private Ltd* [2004] 1 A.C. 715.

[36] See para.4.32.

[37] [2019] EWHC 2768 (Comm).

[38] Construction all risks.

3. INTERPRETATION IS OBJECTIVE

The interpretation of a contract is an objective exercise.[39]

The words of Lord Steyn in *Deutsche Genossenschaftsbank v Burnhope*[40] have already been cited.[41] Lord Steyn has repeatedly stressed the objective nature of interpretation. In *Sirius International Insurance Co v FAI General Insurance Ltd*,[42] his Lordship said: **2.14**

> "The aim of the inquiry is not to probe the real intentions of the parties but to ascertain the contextual meaning of the relevant contractual language. The inquiry is objective: the question is what a reasonable person, circumstanced as the actual parties were, would have understood the parties to have meant by the use of specific language. The answer to that question is to be gathered from the text under consideration and its relevant contextual scene."

Likewise, in *Wood v Capita Insurance Services Ltd*[43] Lord Hodge said:

> "The court's task is to ascertain the objective meaning of the language which the parties have chosen to express their agreement."

In *First National Trustco (UK) Ltd v McQuitty*[44] Peter Jackson LJ said:

> "When construing a document the court must determine objectively what the parties to the document meant at the time they made it. What they meant will generally appear from what they said, particularly if they said it after a careful process. The court will not look for reasons to depart from the apparently clear meaning of the words they used, but elements of the wider documentary, factual and commercial context will be taken into account to the extent that they assist in the search for meaning. That wider survey may lead to a construction that departs from even the clearest wording if the wording does not reflect the objectively ascertained intention of the parties."

The stress on the objectivity of the English approach[45] is not new. In *IRC v Raphael*,[46] Lord Wright spoke to similar effect. He said: **2.15**

> "The words actually used must no doubt be construed with reference to the facts known to the parties and in contemplation of which the parties must be deemed to have used them; such facts may be proved by extrinsic evidence or appear in

---

[39] The equivalent paragraph in a previous edition was cited with approval by Young CJ in Eq in *Greenwood v Kingston Properties Pty Ltd* [2007] NSWSC 1108.

[40] [1995] 4 All E.R. 717. See also *Credit Lyonnais Bank Nederland NV v Export Credit Guarantee Department* [1998] 1 Lloyd's Rep. 19 at 38, per Hobhouse LJ ("The purpose [of interpretation] is to enable the Court to attribute the appropriate *objective* meaning to the words used by the parties in the document"); *Brogden v Investec Bank Plc* [2014] EWHC 2785 (Comm).

[41] See para.2.11.

[42] [2004] 1 W.L.R. 3251; *Weston v Dayman* [2006] B.P.I.R. 1549.

[43] [2017] A.C. 1173.

[44] [2020] EWCA Civ 107; *Gilbert v Duchess Wellesley* [2020] EWHC 777 (Ch).

[45] The Scottish courts take the same approach: *Soccer Savings (Scotland) Ltd v Scottish Building Society* [2012] CSOH 104.

[46] [1935] A.C. 96.

recitals; again the meaning of the words used must be ascertained by considering the whole context of the document and so as to harmonize as far as possible all the parts; particular words may appear to have been used in a technical or trade sense, or in a special meaning adopted by the parties as shown by the whole document. Terms may be implied by custom and on similar grounds. But allowing for these and other rules of the same kind, the principle of the common law has been to adopt an objective standard of construction and to exclude general evidence of the intention of the parties; the reason for this has been that otherwise all certainty would be taken from the words in which the parties have recorded their agreement or their dispositions of property. If in some cases hardship or injustice may be effected by this rule of law, such hardship or injustice can generally be obviated by the power in equity to reform the contract, in proper cases and on proper evidence that there has been a real intention and a real mistake in expressing that intention; these matters may be established, as they generally are, by extrinsic evidence. The Court will thus reform or rewrite the clauses to give effect to the real intention. But that is not construction, but rectification."

2.16   In *Kirin Amgen Inc v Hoechst Marion Roussel Ltd*,[47] Lord Hoffmann also emphasised that construction is an objective exercise:

"Construction is objective in the sense that it is concerned with what a reasonable person to whom the utterance was addressed would have understood the author to be using the words to mean."

As he explained in *Chartbrook Ltd v Persimmon Homes Ltd*[48]:

"English law ... mixes up the ascertainment of intention with the rules of law by depersonalising the contracting parties and asking, not what their intentions actually were, but what a reasonable outside observer would have taken them to be."

2.17   Accordingly, the subjective intention of one party to a contract, even if communicated to the other party before the contract is made, will not usually be a relevant consideration.[49]

It is for this reason that evidence of the parties' subjective intention is inadmissible. Given the objective nature of the exercise, it is, quite simply, irrelevant. In *Young v Brooks*,[50] Rimer LJ said:

"One thing, however, which is clear is this. Although the task of the court is to ascertain the intentions of the parties as expressed in the language in which they have chosen to frame the grant, the one area of evidence that is wholly inadmissible for that purpose is the direct evidence of what the parties, or either of them, actually intended by it. That is not part of the admissible background evidence

---

[47] [2005] R.P.C. 169.
[48] [2009] A.C. 1101.
[49] *Windwood v Bifa Waste Services Ltd* [2011] EWCA Civ 108. However, Professor McLauchlan has argued that the law does not preclude the court from giving effect to a clearly proved actual mutual intention, even where that intention is to be found in the parties' pre-contractual negotiations: "Common intention and contract interpretation" [2011] L.M.C.L.Q. 30. In the author's opinion that is the proper subject for rectification rather than contract interpretation.
[50] [2008] 3 E.G.L.R. 27.

and such evidence is admissible only in a claim for rectification, which the present claim was not."

The objective approach is also applied in Australia and New Zealand. Thus in **2.18** *Pacific Carriers Ltd v BNP Paribas*,[51] the High Court of Australia said:

"What is important is not Ms Dhiri's subjective intention, or even what she might have conveyed, or attempted to convey, to NEAT about her understanding of what she was doing. The letters of indemnity were, and were intended by NEAT and BNP to be, furnished to Pacific. Pacific did not know what was going on in Ms Dhiri's mind, or what she might have communicated to NEAT as to her understanding or intention. The case provides a good example of the reason why the meaning of commercial documents is determined objectively: it was only the documents that spoke to Pacific."

Similarly in *Toll (FGCT) Pty Ltd v Alphapharm Pty Ltd*,[52] their Honours said:

"This Court, in *Pacific Carriers Ltd v BNP Paribas*, has recently reaffirmed the principle of objectivity by which the rights and liabilities of the parties to a contract are determined. It is not the subjective beliefs or understandings of the parties about their rights and liabilities that govern their contractual relations. What matters is what each party by words and conduct would have led a reasonable person in the position of the other party to believe. References to the common intention of the parties to a contract are to be understood as referring to what a reasonable person would understand by the language in which the parties have expressed their agreement. The meaning of the terms of a contractual document is to be determined by what a reasonable person would have understood them to mean. That, normally, requires consideration not only of the text, but also of the surrounding circumstances known to the parties, and the purpose and object of the transaction."

In *Ryledar Pty Ltd v Euphoric Pty Ltd*,[53] Campbell JA said:

"For the purpose of deciding whether a contract has been entered, or what construction it bears, the common intention that the court seeks to ascertain is what is sometimes called the 'objective intention' of the parties. That is the intention that a reasonable person, with the knowledge of the words and actions of the parties communicated to each other, and the knowledge that the parties had of the surrounding circumstances, would conclude that the parties had, concerning the subject matter of the alleged contract."

Similar statements are made in cases from New Zealand. In *Benjamin Developments Ltd v Robt Jones (Pacific) Ltd*,[54] Gallen J said:

---

51 (2004) 218 C.L.R. 451.
52 (2004) 219 C.L.R. 165. See also *Equuscorp Pty Ltd v Glengallen Investments Pty Ltd* (2004) 218 C.L.R. 471 (HCA). For criticism of the stress on objectivity see D.W. McLauchlan, "Objectivity in Contract" [2005] U.Q.L.J. 28.
53 (2007) 69 NSWLR 603 at [262].
54 [1994] 3 N.Z.L.R. 189 CA.

"It should not be forgotten that other persons not parties to the contract are also entitled and may need to order their affairs in line with what they understand the agreement to be."

2.19 The courts in Scotland also take an objective approach to interpretation. In *Soccer Savings (Scotland) Ltd v Scottish Building Society*,[55] Lord Hodge said:

"This objective approach to interpretation focuses on the language which the parties have used. Three points may be made to expand that summary as some contracts are easier to construe than others. First, where the words which the parties have used are unambiguous and there is no absurdity or unreasonableness in the result when viewed against the admissible background, the court will have particular regard to the reality that the terms are those which the parties were able to agree. A concluded deal may favour one party more than the other. But the court will enforce an improbable commercial result if the contractual provision is unambiguous ... Secondly, it is in the nature of language that the words which parties use in a contract may have more than one potential meaning. Where the words of a provision in a commercial agreement are open to different constructions, the court prefers a commercially sensible construction which produces a reasonable result as that is likely to be what reasonable business people would intend ... Thirdly, where the court identifies poor drafting and where it is driven by syntactical analysis towards a conclusion which flouts business common sense, it will give great weight to achieving a commercially sensible construction undeterred by niceties of language ...".

2.20 In Canada, a distinction has been drawn between an intentionalist approach and a textualist approach to interpretation. The prevailing authority seems to favour the latter.[56]

2.21 The principle that a contract must be construed objectively does not confine the court to looking only at the contract itself. As Hardie Boys J pointed out in *Quainoo v NZ Breweries Ltd*[57]:

"Often the words the parties use have only one meaning, and then there is unlikely to be occasion to look outside the contract itself. But where the words are susceptible of more than one meaning, even if one of them be an unusual meaning the Court is entitled to look, indeed it must look, at the surrounding circumstances in order to ascertain from them, if it can, what the intention was. This is quite different from listening to the parties' version of what they each meant. A contract must be construed objectively, but not in disregard of its factual context and purpose."

In *Vitol BV v Compagnie Europeene des Petroles*,[58] Saville J said:

"The approach of the English law to questions of the true construction of contracts of this kind is to seek objectively to ascertain the intentions of the par-

[55] [2012] CSOH 104.
[56] See *Dumbrell v The Regional Group of Companies Inc* (2007) 279 D.L.R. (4th) 201, quoted in para.2.10.
[57] [1991] 1 N.Z.L.R. 165 CA.
[58] [1988] 1 Lloyd's Rep. 574 at 576.

ties from the words which they have chosen to use. If those words are clear and admit of only one sensible meaning, then that is the meaning to be ascribed to them and that meaning is taken to represent what the parties intended. If the words are not so clear and admit of more than one sensible meaning, then the ambiguity may be resolved by looking at the aim and genesis of the agreement, choosing the meaning which seems to make the most sense in the context of the contract and its surrounding circumstances as a whole.[59] In some cases, of course, having attempted this exercise, it may simply remain impossible to give the words any sensible meaning at all in which case they (or some of them) are either ignored, that is to say, treated as not forming part of the contract at all, or (if of apparent central importance) treated as demonstrating that the parties never made an agreement at all, that is to say, had never truly agreed upon the vital terms of their bargain."

This approach means, of course, that the parties do run the risk that they have inaccurately conveyed their real intentions by the words they have used. Thus in *Ireland v Livingston*,[60] a question arose about the interpretation of a written order from principal to agent. Lord Chelmsford said: **2.22**

"Now it appears to me that if a principal gives an order to an agent in such uncertain terms as to be susceptible of two different meanings, and the agent bona fide adopts one of them and acts upon it, it is not competent to the principal to repudiate the act as unauthorised because he meant the order to be read in the other sense of which it is equally capable. It is a fair answer to such an attempt to disown the agent's authority to tell the principal that the departure from his intention was occasioned by his own fault, and that he should have given his order in clear and unambiguous terms."

Clearly, the agent is allowed to set up his real (subjective) understanding of the order communicated to him by his principal; and presumably he is, in addition, allowed to prove his good faith in acting in the way that he did on the strength of that understanding. If so, the question of construction will be answered, if at all, on the strength of evidence of subjective intention. It is interesting to note that in *Ireland v Livingston*, the court's approach to the duty of the principal to express himself unambiguously was held by the court to relieve it from the necessity of construing the contract at all. It was enough that the order could have had the meaning ascribed to it by the agent; it was not necessary to determine whether that meaning was in fact correct.

In the paragraphs that follow it will be seen that from time to time judges speak of the intention of the parties. But it must not be forgotten that when they do so they use the expression in an objective sense. Since a reference to the parties themselves is apt to suggest that the real intention of the actual parties to the contract is relevant, it is better to stay with the modern formulation of the meaning that the contract would convey to a reasonable reader. Although it has consistently been held that the interpretation of a contract is objective, in *Huntington v Imagine Group Hold-* **2.23**

---

[59] It is no longer the case that it is necessary to find an ambiguity before looking at the background to the contract, or to choose the meaning that makes most sense.
[60] (1871) L.R. 5 App. Cas. 395.

ings Ltd,[61] Dyson LJ said:

> "I have described the sixth sentence as difficult to construe. It can, with some force, be said that, for the reasons I have given, it is ambiguous. In these circumstances it seems to me that one is entitled to have regard to what the parties to the negotiations said about what they intended, in order to resolve the ambiguity of the sixth sentence."

It seems that Dyson LJ was prepared to look at the parties' subjective declarations of intent in the course of negotiations. If so, this represents a major departure from established principles, recently reaffirmed by the House of Lords in *Chartbrook Ltd v Persimmon Homes Ltd*,[62] and it is submitted that in this respect the reasoning is erroneous.

2.24   There are also practical reasons for the objective approach to interpretation. The primary reason for adopting an objective approach to the interpretation of contracts is the promotion of certainty. As Lord Goff of Chieveley explained in *President of India v Jebsens (UK) Ltd*[63]:

> "I must confess I am reluctant to speculate on the motives of a party for adopting a clause in any particular form. For once a clause is embodied in a commercial contract, it has simply to be construed in its context, from the objective point of view of reasonable persons in the shoes of the contracting parties. Of course it has to be construed sensibly, and regard has to be had to its practical effect. But the objective interpretation is of paramount importance in commercial affairs; commercial men have frequently to take important decisions with some speed, and it is of great importance that they all know that they can rely on Courts and arbitrators, if any dispute should later arise, to adopt the same objective approach as they themselves have to adopt in the daily administration of their contracts."

Similarly, in *AIB Group (UK) Plc v Martin*,[64] Lord Hutton said:

> "It is a general rule in the construction of deeds that the intention of the parties is to be ascertained from the words used in the deed and that, with certain limited exceptions, extrinsic evidence cannot be given to show the real intention of the parties. On occasions this rule may lead to the actual intention of the parties being defeated but the rule is applied to ensure certainty in legal affairs."

2.25   There are other reasons as well.[65] In *Tartsinis v Navona Management Co*,[66] Leggatt J said:

> "These rules have many advantages. Such advantages include: (i) enabling a party to predict with a reasonable degree of certainty when entering into a contract how its provisions will be interpreted, without having to probe or be

---

61   [2008] EWCA Civ 159.
62   [2009] A.C. 1101.
63   [1991] 1 Lloyd's Rep. 1 at 9, HL.
64   [2002] 1 W.L.R. 94.
65   The Court of Appeal discussed the reasons in *FSHC Group Ltd v GLAS Trust Corp Ltd* [2019] EWCA Civ 1361; [2020] 2 W.L.R. 429 [148]–[153].
66   [2015] EWHC 57 (Comm).

concerned about whether the other party shares this understanding or with trying to lay a favourable paper trail in pre-contractual correspondence; (ii) enabling
a lawyer advising a party, or a judge or arbitrator required to interpret the
contract, to do so on the basis of relatively little information and without the need
for an extensive and expensive factual inquiry; and (iii) respecting the autonomy
of the contracting parties by treating them as rational agents who have chosen
the words of their document to give appropriate expression to their bargain."

Leggatt LJ repeated these advantages in *FSHC Group Holdings Ltd v GLAS Trust
Corpn Ltd*,[67] adding that:

"… this approach facilitates contractual ventures by giving content to contractual
obligations even in circumstances which the parties did not specifically
envisage."

Moreover, as Vos J pointed out in *Spencer v Secretary of State for Defence*[68]:

"I would venture to suggest that the subjective element of the normal usage of
the word 'intention' may in the past have caused much confusion. But it is now
clear that the process of interpretation is an objective one. One might ask
rhetorically: how could it be otherwise? It would be impossible for the court to
construe contracts by reference to the subjective intentions of the parties, when
by the time every case came to be decided, the competing parties would be swearing blind that they had subjectively 'intended' the meaning for which they were
now contending."

In *Franklins Pty Ltd v Metcash Trading Ltd*,[69] Allsop P gave a further reason to
justify the objective approach:

"In many cases, the reality of commercial life and bargaining can be seen to
underpin and explain the objective theory. Sometimes, beyond platitudes and
obvious commercial aims, negotiating parties may well be at pains not to expose
what they want from the terms and operation of an agreement. To do so may
damage their bargaining position. In such cases, as in many cases, the bargaining that takes place is over what *words* are acceptable and the commercial aims
and objects of negotiation give a framework and context to understanding what
the bargained-for words mean."

The promotion of certainty is a theme that has run through English commercial **2.26**
law for centuries. The rationale behind this approach was amplified by Lord Devlin
in his lecture "Morals and the Law of Contract"[70] as follows:

"If a man minded only about keeping faith, the spirit of the contract would be
more important than the letter. But in the service of commerce the letter is in
many ways the more significant. This is because in most commercial contracts
many more than the original parties are concerned. The contract is embodied in

---

[67] [2019] EWCA Civ 1361; [2020] 2 W.L.R. 429.
[68] [2012] EWHC 120 (Ch); [2012] L. & T.R. 318. An appeal from Vos J was dismissed, but this point
      was not discussed: [2012] EWCA Civ 1368; [2013] All E.R. (Comm) 287.
[69] [2009] NSWCA 407 at [21] (emphasis in original).
[70] Reprinted in *The Enforcement of Morals* (1965).

a document which may pass from hand to hand when the goods it represents are sold over and over again to a string of buyers, or when money is borrowed on it, or insurances arranged. The spirit of the contract gets lost on these travels and the outward form is all that matters. For the common law the sanctity of the contract means the sanctity of the written word in the form in which it is ultimately enshrined. Normally, evidence is not admissible of conversations or correspondence leading up to the contract; they cannot be used to amplify or modify the final document. That document must speak for itself. For the common law has its eye fixed as closely on the third man as on the original parties; and the final document is the only thing that can speak to the third man."[71]

2.27   The stress that English law places on objectivity is probably the principal difference between English law and other legal systems, particularly civilian ones. Both the Unidroit principles[72] and the Principles of European Contract Law[73] require the contract to be interpreted according to the common intention of the parties; and only where that cannot be ascertained should it be interpreted according to the meaning that reasonable persons in the circumstances of the parties would have given it. Lord Hoffmann explained in *Chartbrook Ltd v Persimmon Homes Ltd*[74]:

> "Both the *Unidroit Principles of International Commercial Contracts* (1994 and 2004 revision) and the *Principles of European Contract Law* (1999) provide that in ascertaining the 'common intention of the parties', regard shall be had to prior negotiations: articles 4.3 and 5.102 respectively. The same is true of the United Nations Convention on Contracts for the International Sale of Goods (1980). But these instruments reflect the French philosophy of contractual interpretation, which is altogether different from that of English law. As Professor Catherine Valcke explains in an illuminating article ('On Comparing French and English Contract Law: Insights from Social Contract Theory') (16 January 2009), French law regards the intentions of the parties as a pure question of subjective fact, their *volonté psychologique*, uninfluenced by any rules of law. It follows that any evidence of what they said or did, whether to each other or to third parties, may be relevant to establishing what their intentions actually were. There is in French law a sharp distinction between the ascertainment of their intentions and the application of legal rules which may, in the interests of fairness to other parties or otherwise, limit the extent to which those intentions are given effect. English law, on the other hand, mixes up the ascertainment of intention with the rules of law by depersonalising the contracting parties and asking, not what their intentions actually were, but what a reasonable outside observer would have taken them to be."

4.   A CONTRACT HAS ONLY ONE MEANING

Although a contract may potentially have more than one possible meaning, the court can select only one meaning. In making its selection the court applies the

---

[71]   Considerations of this kind led the Court of Appeal to hold that since negotiability is of the essence of a bill of exchange "a strict approach to construction should be adopted": *Hong Kong & Shanghai Banking Corp v GD Trade Co Ltd* [1998] C.L.C. 238.

[72]   Principle 4.1.

[73]   Principle 5.101.

[74]   [2009] A.C. 1101.

same principles, whatever the subject matter of the contract. The meaning of the contract, once interpreted, does not change.[75]

As Diplock LJ explained in *Slim v Daily Telegraph Ltd*[76]:　　　　　　　　**2.28**

"Everyone outside a court of law recognises that words are imprecise instruments for communicating the thoughts of one man to another. The same words may be understood by one man in a different meaning from that in which they are understood by another and both meanings may be different from that which the author of the words intended to convey; but the notion that the same words should bear different meanings to different men, and that more than one meaning should be 'right' conflicts with the whole training of a lawyer. Words are the tools of his trade. He uses them to define legal rights and duties. They do not achieve that purpose unless there can be attributed to them a single meaning as a 'right' meaning. And so the argument between lawyers starts with the unexpressed major premise that any particular combination of words has one meaning, which is not necessarily the same as that intended by him who published them or understood by any of those who read them, but is capable of ascertainment as being the 'right' meaning by the adjudicator to whom the law confides the responsibility of determining it."

Briggs LJ pointed out in his dissenting judgment in *Credit Suisse Asset Management LLC v Titan Europe 2006-1 Plc*[77]:

"English law assumes that every question of construction has a right and a wrong answer. In reality there can often be as much scope for reasonable differences of view as there is in many questions about the exercise of a discretion."

In *Egan v Static Control Components (Europe) Ltd*,[78] Arden LJ referred to the　　**2.29**
first of Lord Hoffmann's five principles and added:

"Lord Hoffmann's principle (1) ... makes it clear that there are not two possible constructions in any given situation, namely a purely linguistic one and one in the light of the factual background, but only one, the true interpretation. This is because the object of interpretation is to discover the meaning of the provision in question in its context."

The same conclusion follows from the principle that the interpretation of a contract is an iterative process, testing competing interpretations against their commercial consequences.

The theory that a contract has only one meaning is pervasive. Thus there is only　　**2.30**
one system of interpretation. There is no such thing as an equitable interpretation as opposed to a common law interpretation. As Lord Chelmsford LC said in *Scott v Liverpool Corp*[79]:

---

[75]　This paragraph was referred to with apparent approval in *Trust Risk Group Spa v Amtrust Europe Ltd* [2015] EWCA Civ 437.

[76]　[1968] 2 Q.B. 157 CA (a libel case).

[77]　[2016] EWCA Civ 1293.

[78]　[2004] 2 Lloyd's Rep. 429.

[79]　(1858) 3 De G. & J. 334.

"There is no equitable construction of an agreement distinct from its legal construction. To construe is nothing more than to arrive at the meaning of the parties to an agreement, and this must be the aim and end of all Courts which are called upon to enforce any rights created by and growing out of contract."

Similarly, in *BCCI v Ali*,[80] Lord Nicholls of Birkenhead said:

"Today there is no question of a document having a legal interpretation as distinct from an equitable interpretation."[81]

2.31   The same principles apply irrespective of the type of contract under consideration, although there are specific rules that apply, for example, to consumer contracts. Thus it has been said that there are no special principles that apply to the interpretation of badly drafted contracts,[82] charterparties,[83] consent orders,[84] covenants in restraint of trade,[85] CVAs,[86] deeds in general,[87] guarantees,[88] insurance policies,[89] leases,[90] partnership agreements,[91] pension schemes,[92] planning and highway agreements,[93] settlement agreements,[94] trust deeds[95] and releases.[96] The same principles also apply to the interpretation of unilateral notices,[97] wills,[98] a unilateral undertak-

---

[80]   [2002] 1 A.C. 251.
[81]   Lord Mansfield expressed the same thought in *Hotham v East India Co* (1779) 1 Doug 272, as did Lord Romilly MR in *Parkin v Thorold* (1852) 16 Beav. 69 and Rolt LJ in *Tilley v Thomas* (1867) L.R. 3 Ch. App. 61. So this is hardly revolutionary.
[82]   *Mitsui Construction Co Ltd v Att.-Gen. of Hong Kong* (1986) 33 Build. L.R. 1.
[83]   *Total Transport Corp v Arcadia Petroleum Ltd (The Eurus)* [1998] 1 Lloyd's Rep. 351.
[84]   *Sirius International Insurance Co v FAI General Insurance Ltd* [2004] 1 W.L.R. 3251; *Weston v Dayman* [2006] EWCA Civ 1165; *Alexiou v Campbell* [2007] UKPC 11. None of these authorities were referred to in *Secretary of State for Business, Innovation and Skills v Feld* [2014] EWHC 1383 (Ch); [2014] 1 W.L.R. 3396, which concerned an order that (although not a consent order) was one that the parties had drafted.
[85]   *Arbuthnot Fund Managers v Rawlings* [2003] All E.R. (D) 181; *Beckett Investment Management Group Ltd v Hall* [2007] EWCA Civ 613.
[86]   *Appleyard v Ritecrown Ltd* [2009] B.P.I.R. 1.
[87]   *Weardale Coal and Iron Co v Hodson* [1894] 1 Q.B. 598.
[88]   *Egan v Static Control Components (Europe) Ltd* [2004] 2 Lloyd's Rep. 429; *Mora Shipping Inc v Axa Corporate Solutions Assurance SA* [2005] 2 Lloyd's Rep. 769; *National Merchant Buying Society Ltd v Bellamy* [2013] EWCA Civ 452.
[89]   *Hayward v Norwich Union Insurance Ltd* [2001] Lloyd's Rep. IR 410.
[90]   *Co-Operative Wholesale Society v National Westminster Bank* [1995] 1 E.G.L.R. 97.
[91]   In *Re White (Dennis), dec'd White v Minnis* [2001] Ch. 393.
[92]   *The Law Debenture Trust Plc v Lonrho Africa Trade & Finance Ltd* [2003] O.P.L.R. 167. The principles applicable to the interpretation of pension trust deeds have been elaborated in *British Airways Pension Trustees Ltd v British Airways Plc* [2002] EWCA Civ 672; [2002] P.L.R. 247; *Alitalia-Linee Aeree Italiane SPA v Rotunno* [2008] EWHC 185 (Ch); [2008] Pens L.R. 175; and *Foster Wheeler Ltd v Hanley* [2009] Pens L.R. 39. The summary of principle in the last-mentioned case was not in issue on the appeal: *Foster Wheeler Ltd v Hanley* [2009] Pens L.R. 229. See also Independent *Trustee Services Ltd v Knell* [2010] EWHC 650; [2010] Pens L.R. 195; *Stena Line Ltd v Merchant Navy Ratings Pension Fund Trustees Ltd* [2011] EWCA Civ 543.
[93]   *Stroude v Beazer Homes Ltd* [2006] 2 P. & C.R. 6.
[94]   *Point West London Ltd v Mivan Ltd* [2012] EWHC 1223 (TCC); *Stretchline Intellectual Properties Ltd v H&M Hennes & Mauritz UK Ltd* [2015] EWCA Civ 516.
[95]   *First National Trustco (UK) Ltd v McQuitty* [2020] EWCA Civ 107.
[96]   *BCCI v Ali* [2002] 1 A.C. 251.
[97]   *Mannai Investment Co Ltd v Eagle Star Life Assurance Co Ltd* [1997] A.C. 749.
[98]   *Charles v Barzey* [2003] 1 W.L.R. 437; *Baynes v Hedger* [2008] 2 F.L.R. 1805; *Royal Society for the Prevention of Cruelty to Animals v Sharp* [2010] EWCA Civ 1474, per Lord Neuberger of Ab-

ing given under the Town and Country Planning Act 1990[99] and at least in general terms, to patent claims and specifications.[100]

The principles that apply to the interpretation of contracts also apply to the interpretation of wills[101] and mortgages; although mortgages "come to us laden with old equitable doctrines which mean that the legal effect of the document sometimes has to be qualified".[102]

Similar principles apply to the interpretation of collective agreements made in the context of employment, although in interpreting such an agreement which is the product of a compromise between conflicting interests, the court will bear in mind that a collective agreement may be deliberately silent on contentious issues.[103]

However, they do not apply where the question is whether one party has made an offer capable of acceptance, rather than what a concluded contract means.[104]

Whether they apply to "smart contracts" (i.e. contracts expressed wholly or partly in computer code) has yet to be decided.[105] It can generally be expected that computer code is unambiguous; but there are likely to be sources of the agreement external to the computer code, expressed in natural language.[106]

2.32

Although there are no special principles applicable to the interpretation of particular categories of contract, the nature of the contract may influence the relative weight to be given to the text of the contract, and the overall context (including the factual background, and the commercial common sense) on the other. The relevant factors include whether the contract has been professionally drawn, whether it is a standard form contract; whether it is a publicly registrable contract; whether it is designed to operate over the long term; and whether it affects the interests of person who are not parties to it.[107] In addition, in the case of a long-term contract, the court may be more willing to adopt a flexible interpretation, even though the basic principles of interpretation remain the same.[108] Where a contract has been professionally drafted, there is less room for departure from a textual analysis. As Hamblen LJ explained in *National Bank of Kazakhstan v The Bank of*

2.33

---

botsbury MR.

[99] *R. (Robert Hitchins Ltd) v Worcestershire County Council* [2015] EWCA Civ 1060.

[100] *Kirin Amgen Inc v Hoechst Marion Roussel Ltd* [2005] R.P.C. 169.

[101] *Thomas v Kent* [2007] W.T.L.R. 177; *Scarfe v Matthews* [2012] EWHC 3071 (Ch); *Marley v Rawlings* [2014] UKSC 2; [2014] 2 W.L.R. 213.

[102] *West Bromwich Building Society v Wilkinson* [2005] UKHL 44; [2005] 1 W.L.R. 2303.

[103] *East Midlands Trains Ltd v National Union of Rail, Maritime and Transport Workers* [2013] EWCA Civ 1072.

[104] *Crest Nicholson (Londinium) Ltd v Akaria Investments Ltd* [2010] EWCA Civ 1331; *Credit Suisse International v Stichting Vestia Groep* [2014] EWHC 3103 (Comm); although in *Bexbes LLP v Beer* [2008] EWHC 2559 (Ch) and *London & Medway Ltd v Sunley Holdings Plc* [2013] EWHC 1420 (Ch) it was held that they did apply to an offer letter.

[105] See Green, "Smart contracts, interpretation and rectification" [2018] L.M.C.L.Q. 234.

[106] The interpretation of smart contracts is discussed in The LawTech Delivery Panel: Legal Statement on Cryptoassets and Smart Contracts available at *https://35z8e83m1ih83drye28oo9d1-wpengine.netdna-ssl.com/wp-content/uploads/2019/11/6.6056_JO_Cryptocurrencies_Statement_FINAL_WEB_111119-1.pdf* [Accessed 7 September 2020].

[107] See *Wood v Capita Insurance Services Ltd* [2017] A.C. 1173; *Barnardo's v Buckinghamshire* [2019] 1 I.C.R. 495; *Thales UK Ltd v Thales Pension Trustees Ltd* [2017] EWHC 666 (Ch); [2017] Pen LR 15; *British Telecommunications Plc v BT Pension Scheme Trustees Ltd* [2018] EWHC 69 (Ch); [2018] Pens. L.R. 7.

[108] *Globe Motors Inc v TRW Lucas Varity Electric Steering Ltd* [2016] EWCA Civ 396; [2016] 1 C.L.C. 712.

New York Mellon SA/NV, London Branch[109]:

> "In the present case, the [contract] is a carefully drafted and formal contract, drawn up with the assistance of lawyers and concluded between sophisticated parties. There is no suggestion that anything has gone wrong in the drafting process. Nor is there any patent ambiguity in the terms used in clause 16(i). In accordance with the guidance provided in *Wood*, it is the type of agreement in relation to which textual analysis will be of particular importance."

2.34   Nevertheless, as Lord Hodge explained in *Barnardo's v Buckinghamshire*[110]:

> "The emphasis on textual analysis as an interpretative tool does not derogate from the need both to avoid undue technicality and to have regard to the practical consequences of any construction. Such an analysis does not involve literalism but includes a purposive construction when that is appropriate."

2.35   The theory that a contract has only one meaning is also part of the justification for the refusal by the courts to admit evidence of subsequent conduct. In *James Miller & Partners Ltd v Whitworth Street Estates (Manchester) Ltd*,[111] Lord Reid said:

> "I must say that I had thought that it is now well settled that it is not legitimate to use as an aid in the construction of the contract anything which the parties said or did after it was made. Otherwise one might have the result that a contract meant one thing the day it was signed, but by reason of subsequent events meant something different a month or a year later."

5.   WHAT IS INTENTION?

For the purpose of the interpretation of contracts, the intention of the parties is the meaning of the contract. There is no intention independent of that meaning.

2.36   Part of the confusion into which the process of interpretation has fallen stems from the differing meanings given to the word "intention" both by advocates and, on occasion, judges.[112] In *Great Western Railway v Bristol Corp*,[113] Lord Shaw said:

> "… one hears much use made of the word 'intention,' but courts of law when on the work of interpretation are not engaged upon the task or study of what parties intended to do, but of what the language which they employed showed that

---

[109]   [2018] EWCA Civ 1390.

[110]   [2019] 1 I.C.R. 495.

[111]   [1970] A.C. 583.

[112]   Vos J noted the confusion in *Spencer v Secretary of State for Defence* [2012] EWHC 120 (Ch); [2012] L. & T.R. 318. An appeal from Vos J was dismissed, but this point was not discussed: [2012] EWCA Civ 1368; [2013] All E.R. (Comm) 287. See also *Byrnes v Kendle* [2011] HCA 26 in which the Australian High Court pointed out that "intention" could be used in two different senses, viz (1) of that which the parties intended to do, or (2) of the meaning of the words that they have employed; and that in the case of interpretation it is the second sense which is the relevant one. See also Stevens, *Contract Interpretation: What it says on the tin* (Inner Temple Reading, 2014); Leggatt, "Making sense of contracts: the rational choice theory" (2015) L.Q.R. 454.

[113]   (1918) 87 L.J.Ch. 414. See also *Igote v Badsey* [2001] 4 I.R. 511, Irish Supreme Court.

they did; in other words, they are not constructing a contract on the lines of what may be thought to have been what the parties intended, but they are construing the words and expressions used by the parties themselves. What do these mean? That when ascertained is the meaning to be given effect to, the meaning of the contract by which the parties are bound. The suggestion of an intention of parties different from the meaning conveyed by the words employed is no part of interpretation, but is mere confusion."

Later in his speech he said:

"… experience has shown that the attempt seems to be inevitable in the pleader's mind … to confuse evidence of the writer's intention as such, with the intention conveyed by the words which he employed. The latter alone is legitimate."

Nowadays the "intention of the parties" is equated with the objective meaning of the contract.[114] As the High Court of Australia said in *Toll (FGCR) Pty Ltd v Alphapharm Pty Ltd*[115]:   **2.37**

"References to the common intention of the parties to a contract are to be understood as referring to what a reasonable person would understand by the language in which the parties have expressed their agreement. The meaning of the terms of a contractual document is to be determined by what a reasonable person would have understood them to mean."

In *Board of Trustees of the National Provident Fund v Shortland Securities Ltd*,[116] the New Zealand Court of Appeal said:

"The parties, particularly knowledgeable and experienced parties, legally advised, are to be taken as having intended what they have said."

So also in *IRC v Raphael*,[117] Lord Wright said: **2.38**

"It must be remembered at the outset that the court, while it seeks to give effect to the intention of the parties, must give effect to that intention as expressed, that is, it must ascertain the meaning of the words actually used. There is often an ambiguity in the use of the word 'intention' in cases of this character. The word is constantly used as meaning motive, purpose, desire, as a state of mind, and not as meaning intention as expressed."

In the same case Lord Warrington of Clyffe said:

"The fact is that the narrative and operative parts of a deed perform quite different functions, and 'intention' in reference to the narrative and the same word in reference to the operative parts respectively bear quite different significations. As appearing in the narrative part it means 'purpose'. In considering the intention of the operative part the word means significance or import—'the way in which

---

[114] *Gladman Commercial Properties v Fisher Hargreaves Proctor* [2013] EWCA Civ 1466.
[115] (2004) 219 C.L.R. 165.
[116] [1996] 1 N.Z.L.R. 45 CA.
[117] [1935] A.C. 96.

anything is to be understood' (*Oxford English Dictionary*) supported by the illustration: 'The intention of the passage was sufficiently clear.'"[118]

The distinction between the two was also pointed out by Lord Simon of Glaisdale in *Schuler (L.) AG v Wickman Machine Tool Sales Ltd*,[119] approving the following passage in *Norton on Deeds*[120]:

"... the question to be answered always is, 'What is the meaning of what the parties have said?' not 'What did the parties mean to say?' ... it being a presumption *juris et de jure* ... that the parties intended to say that which they have said."

As Jackson LJ put it in *Daejan Properties Ltd v Campbell*[121]:

"In construing a written contract, the governing principle is that the parties mean what they say."

2.39   In other words "intention" is equivalent to "meaning". In *Gladman Commercial Properties v Fisher Hargreaves Proctor*,[122] Briggs LJ confirmed that the "intention of the parties":

"means no more than the meaning of the agreement which they have made, objectively ascertained, read against the relevant background."

In *Attorney General of Belize v Belize Telecom Ltd*,[123] Lord Hoffmann reiterated that the meaning of a contract is not necessarily the same as the intention of the parties. He said:

"The court has no power to improve upon the instrument which it is called upon to construe, whether it be a contract, a statute or articles of association. It cannot introduce terms to make it fairer or more reasonable. It is concerned only to discover what the instrument means. However, that meaning is not necessarily or always what the authors or parties to the document would have intended. It is the meaning which the instrument would convey to a reasonable person having all the background knowledge which would reasonably be available to the audience to whom the instrument is addressed."

As Lord Hodge put it in *Arnold v Britton*[124]:

"The role of the construct, the reasonable person, is to ascertain objectively, and with the benefit of the relevant background knowledge, the meaning of the words which the parties used."

---

[118] See also *Byrnes v Kendle* [2011] HCA 26 in which the Australian High Court pointed out that "intention" could be used in two different senses, viz (1) of that which the parties intended to do, or (2) of the meaning of the words that they have employed; and that in the case of interpretation it is the second sense which is the relevant one.
[119] [1974] A.C. 235.
[120] 2nd edn (1928), p.50.
[121] [2012] EWCA Civ 1503; [2013] 1 E.G.L.R. 34.
[122] [2013] EWCA Civ 1466.
[123] [2009] 1 W.L.R. 1988.
[124] [2015] UKSC 36; [2015] 2 W.L.R. 1593.

However, Lord Hoffmann has also pointed out an important qualification to this **2.40** principle. In *Mannai Investment Co Ltd v Eagle Star Life Assurance Society Ltd*,[125] he said:

"It is of course true that the law is not concerned with the speaker's subjective intentions. But the notion that the law's concern is therefore with the 'meaning of his words' conceals an important ambiguity. The ambiguity lies in a failure to distinguish between the meanings of words and the question of what would be understood as the meaning of a person who uses words. The meaning of words, as they would appear in a dictionary, and the effect of their syntactical arrangement, as it would appear in a grammar, is part of the material which we use to understand a speaker's utterance. But it is only a part; another part is our knowledge of the background against which the utterance was made. It is that background which enables us, not only to choose the intended meaning when a word has more than one dictionary meaning but also, in the ways I have explained, to understand a speaker's meaning, often without ambiguity, when he has used the wrong words.

When, therefore, lawyers say that they are concerned, not with subjective meaning but with the meaning of the language which the speaker has used, what they mean is that they are concerned with what he would objectively have been understood to mean.[126] This involves examining not only the words and the grammar but the background as well."[127]

Likewise, in *Kirin Amgen Inc v Hoechst Marion Roussel Ltd*,[128] he said:

"Construction is objective in the sense that it is concerned with what a reasonable person to whom the utterance was addressed would have understood the author to be using the words to mean. Notice, however, that it is not, as is sometimes said, 'the meaning of the words the author used', but rather what the notional addressee would have understood the author to mean by using those words. The meaning of words is a matter of convention, governed by rules, which can be found in dictionaries and grammars. What the author would have been understood to mean by using those words is not simply a matter of rules. It is highly sensitive to the context of and background to the particular utterance. It depends not only upon the words the author has chosen but also upon the identity of the audience he is taken to have been addressing and the knowledge and assumptions which one attributes to that audience."

The equation of "intention" and "meaning" may give rise to apparently hard **2.41** cases. Thus in *Smith v Lucas*,[129] Jessel MR said:

---

[125] [1997] A.C. 749 at 775.

[126] In his article "Language and lawyers" (2018) L.Q.R. 553 Lord Hoffmann emphasises the importance of "speaker meaning" as opposed to "word meaning".

[127] In his subsequent formulation of the principles in *Investors Compensation Scheme v West Bromwich Building Society* ([1998] 1 W.L.R. 896) Lord Hoffmann laid emphasis on the reader rather than the speaker. The role of the reader in interpreting a bilateral written contract is less of a fiction than what a listener understands a single speaker to mean.

[128] [2005] R.P.C. 169 (a case of patent construction).

[129] (1881) 18 Ch. D. 531.

"The settlement is one which I cannot help thinking was never intended by the framer of it to have the effect I am going to attribute to it; but of course, as I very often say, one must consider the meaning of the words used, not what one may guess to be the intention of the parties."

So also in *Philpots (Woking) Ltd v Surrey Conveyancers Ltd*,[130] Nourse LJ, reversing the trial judge on a question of construction of a rent review clause in a lease, said:

"I think it very probable that, in accepting the landlord's construction, the learned judge has correctly assessed what the parties did indeed believe and desire to be the effect of [the clause]. But a court of construction can only hold that they intended it to have that effect if the intention appears from a fair interpretation of the words which they have used against the factual background known to them at or before the date of the lease, including its genesis and objective aim."

2.42   Moreover, it must not be forgotten that many contracts have effect upon persons other than the original contracting parties. In the example of the settlement given by Jessel MR, it is entirely possible that the settlor may have taken one view of the meaning of the settlement, while the trustees of the settlement accepted office on the basis of a quite different understanding of their powers and duties. And in the case of a lease there are potential successors in title of each party. Hence the court is right to insist that the intention must be made clear by the words of the contract read in the light of the admissible background.

6.   HOW THE MEANING OF THE CONTRACT IS TO BE ASCERTAINED

The meaning of the contract must be ascertained from the language the parties have used, considered in the light of the surrounding circumstances and the overall purpose of the contract, in so far as that has been agreed or proved.

2.43   In *Marley v Rawlings*,[131] Lord Neuberger said:

"When interpreting a contract, the court is concerned to find the intention of the party or parties, and it does this by identifying the meaning of the relevant words, (a) in the light of (i) the natural and ordinary meaning of those words, (ii) the overall purpose of the document, (iii) any other provisions of the document, (iv) the facts known or assumed by the parties at the time that the document was executed, and (v) common sense, but (b) ignoring subjective evidence of any party's intentions."

He repeated this in slightly different terms in *Arnold v Britton*.[132]

2.44   In recent years the court has paid increasing attention to what it has determined to be the commercial purpose of the contract, or even a particular clause in it. In many cases the commercial purpose has not been proved by evidence or even formally agreed, but has been determined by the judge. Such determination is likely

---

[130] [1986] 1 E.G.L.R. 97.
[131] [2014] UKSC 2; [2015] A.C. 129.
[132] [2015] A.C. 1619.

to be based on the judge's general experience of contracts of a similar type to that under scrutiny. However, there is high authority deploring that approach. In *Leader v Duffey*,[133] Lord Halsbury LC said:

"… I agree that you must look at the whole instrument, and inasmuch as there may be inaccuracy and inconsistency, you must, if you can, ascertain what is the meaning of the instrument taken as a whole in order to give effect, if it be possible to do so, to the intention of the framer of it. But it appears to me to be arguing in a vicious circle to begin by assuming an intention apart from the language of the instrument itself, and having made that fallacious assumption to bend the language in favour of the assumption so made."

So too in *Smith v Cooke*,[134] he said:

"I must say I for one have always protested against endeavouring to construe an instrument contrary to what the words of the instrument itself convey, by some sort of preconceived idea of what the parties would or might or perhaps ought to have intended when they began to frame their instrument."

From time to time the same view is heard in modern cases. Thus in *Pagnan SpA v Tradax Ocean Transportation*,[135] Steyn J said: **2.45**

"The task of the court is to construe the meaning of the special condition without any pre-conception as to what the parties intended. In other words, it is wrong to introduce uncertainty by starting from the viewpoint of a general rule governing such clauses, and then to resolve the question of construction by reference to it. The court's task is simply to determine the meaning of the provision, against its contractual and contextual scene."

This approach was reaffirmed by the Court of Appeal in *Equity & Law Life Assurance Society Plc v Bodfield Ltd*,[136] in which Dillon LJ (who gave the only judgment) said that guidelines as to construction of a particular type of clause (a rent review clause):

"cannot entitle the court to construe and apply not the clause into which the parties have entered but the different clause which they might have, or probably would have, entered into if their lawyers had thought rather more deeply about how the intricate scheme they were setting up would work in practice."

Similarly, in *Bank St Petersburg v Savelyev*,[137] Hildyard J said:

"To favour a construction which fits the likely purpose, influenced by knowledge of what has happened after the event, and forgetting other factors that may have influenced the parties at the time, would, I have concluded, be to seek to mend

---

[133] (1888) 13 App. Cas. 294.
[134] [1891] A.C. 297.
[135] [1987] 1 All E.R. 81; affirmed [1987] 3 All E.R. 565.
[136] [1987] 1 E.G.L.R. 124. See also *Ashville Investments Ltd v Elmer Contractors Ltd* [1989] 1 Q.B. 488, per May LJ. ("In seeking to construe a clause in a contract, there is no scope for adopting either a liberal or a narrow approach, whatever that may mean. The exercise which has to be undertaken is to determine what the words mean.")
[137] [2013] EWHC 3529 (Ch).

or improve the bargain actually made. The agreement must be construed as it was, and not as subsequent events might suggest would have been wise to have made it."

So also in construing a charter party:

"The starting point must be the words and phrases the parties have chosen to use. It is not a permissible method of construction to propound a general or generally accepted principle for sharing the risk of delay between owners and charterers or seeking in the abstract to determine a reasonable allocation of risk of delay and then ... to seek to force the provisions of the charter into the straitjacket of that principle or into that concept of reasonableness."[138]

2.46   In *Mitsubishi Heavy Industries Ltd v Gulf Banfi*,[139] Potter LJ said:

"It is of course both useful and frequently necessary when construing a clause in a contract to have regard to the overall commercial purpose of the contract in the broad sense of the type and general content, the relationship of the parties and such *common* commercial purpose as may clearly emerge from such an exercise. However, it does not seem to me to be a proper approach to the construction of a default clause in a commercial contract to seek or purport to elicit some self-contained 'commercial purpose' underlying the clause which is or may be wider than the ordinary or usual construction of the words of each sub-clause will yield."[140]

In *Temple Legal Protection Ltd v QBE Insurance (Europe) Ltd*,[141] Beatson J confirmed that the task of the court is to interpret a contract in its objective commercial context without any preconception as to what the parties intended. The court's task is simply to determine the meaning of the provision, against its contractual and contextual scene, also referred to as the matrix of fact.

2.47   In *Re Golden Key Ltd*,[142] Henderson J said that:

"... it is dangerous to start with assumptions about what the parties must or are likely to have intended, and there is in my judgment no substitute for a close examination of the language of the contractual terms in order to ascertain what their rights may be."

Although his decision was reversed on appeal[143] it is not thought that this statement is invalidated.

2.48   In *Cargill International SA v Bangladesh Sugar & Food Industries Corp*,[144] Potter LJ balanced the two approaches. He said:

---

[138] *Palm Shipping Inc v Kuwait Petroleum Corp (The Sea Queen)* [1988] 1 Lloyd's Rep. 500 at 502, per Saville J; *Suek AG v Glencore International AG* [2011] EWHC 1361 (Comm). Cf. *SA Marocaine de L'Industrie du Raffinage v Notos Maritime Corp (The Notos)* [1987] 1 Lloyd's Rep. 503 at 506, per Lord Goff of Chieveley.
[139] [1997] 1 Lloyd's Rep. 343.
[140] Sic.
[141] [2008] Lloyd's Rep. IR 643.
[142] [2009] EWHC 148 (Ch).
[143] [2009] EWCA Civ 636.
[144] [1998] 1 W.L.R. 461 CA.

"In this connection [counsel] has rightly made the point that, when construing the effect of particular words in a commercial contract, it is wrong to put a label on the contract in advance and thus to approach the question of construction on the basis of a pre-conception as to the contract's intended effect, with the result that a strained construction is placed on words, clear in themselves, in order to fit them within such pre-conception …

On the other hand, modern principles of construction require the court to have regard to the commercial background, the context of the contract and the circumstances of the parties, and to consider whether, against that background and in that context, to give the words a particular or restricted meaning would lead to an apparently unreasonable and unfair result."

In addition to the words of the instrument itself the court may also receive evidence in aid of interpretation. The circumstances in which and the extent to which evidence may be admitted are discussed in Ch.3.   **2.49**

7. Business Common Sense

In addition to the words of the instrument, and the particular facts proved by evidence admitted in aid of interpretation, the court may also be assisted by a consideration of the commercial purpose of the contract, and in considering that purpose may rely upon its own experience of contracts of a similar character to that under examination. However, a court must be cautious before concluding that a particular interpretation does not accord with commercial common sense. In addition commercial common sense should not be invoked retrospectively.

(a) Business common sense

In the course of the last five decades the court has increasingly sought to elucidate the commercial purpose of the contract under consideration, and as between competing interpretations to select that meaning which best serves the commercial purpose of the contract, as perceived by the court.[145] Although tradition-ally judges have been wary of passing commercial judgment on a contract,[146] this   **2.50**

---

[145] This observation was approved by the majority of the *New Zealand Supreme Court in Firm PI 1 Ltd v Zurich Australian Insurance and Body Corporate 398983* [2014] NZSC 147. Derrington J offers a thoughtful discussion of the role of business common sense and its limits in *Pipe Networks Pty Ltd v 148 Brunswick Street Pty Ltd (Trustee)* [2019] FCA 598.

[146] Cf. *Manchester Sheffield & Lincolnshire Railway Co v Brown* (1883) 8 App. Cas. 703 at 716 per Lord Bramwell ("For here is a contract made by a fishmonger and a carrier of fish who know their business, and whether it is just and reasonable is to be settled by me who am neither fishmonger nor carrier, nor with any knowledge of their business"). J.J. Spigelman has pointed out that

"… it remains pertinent, not least as a precedent, to approach the task of interpretation on the basis that a significant commercial purpose of the written agreement was to state the obligations of the parties with sufficient certainty to avoid the very dispute that has eventuated. The further one travels beyond the text, the less likely it is that that commercial purpose will be served."

"Extrinsic material and the interpretation of insurance contracts" (2011) 22 Insurance Law Journal 143. Likewise in *Firm PI 1 Ltd v Zurich Australian Insurance and Body Corporate 398983* [2014] NZSC 147 the majority judgment stated:

"It should not be over-looked, however, that the language of many commercial contracts will have features that ordinary language (even a "serious utterance") is unlikely to have, namely that it

[51]

approach is not new. In *Glynn v Margetson & Co*,[147] the House of Lords construed a bill of lading in a printed form under which oranges were shipped from Malaga to Liverpool, Lord Herschell LC said:

"Where general words are used in a printed form which are obviously intended to apply, so far as they are applicable, to the circumstances of a particular contract to be embodied or introduced into that printed form, I think you are justified in looking at the main object and intent of the contract and in limiting the general words used, having in view that object and intent."

Lord Halsbury LC added:

"Looking at the whole of the instrument, and seeing what one must regard ... as its main purpose, one must reject words, indeed whole provisions, if they are inconsistent with what one assumes to be the main purpose of the contract."

In that case, the main object of the contract was clear from the terms of the contract itself.[148] Moreover, the contract was a standard printed form, rather than a contract which had been negotiated in detail by the parties themselves (or their solicitors). These points, however, do not seem to matter.

2.51 The court will adopt the same approach to the interpretation of a "one off" contract negotiated in detail. As Lord Steyn said in *Mannai Investment Co Ltd v Eagle Star Life Assurance Co Ltd*[149]:

"In determining the meaning of the language of a commercial contract, and unilateral contractual notices, the law therefore generally favours a commercially sensible construction. The reason for this approach is that a commercial construction is more likely to give effect to the intention of the parties. Words are therefore interpreted in the way in which a reasonable commercial person would construe them. And the standard of the reasonable commercial person is hostile to technical interpretations and undue emphasis on niceties of language."

2.52 The same approach will also extend to the interpretation of a deed, which was formerly interpreted in a more traditional manner. In *Weardale Coal and Iron Co v Hodson*,[150] Lord Esher MR said:

"We must give to the language used the ordinary sense that business men would give to it. The ordinary view of a business man would be that the payment of interest on money borrowed is to be made in respect of that money so long as it is unpaid, and no longer. In this view the covenant to pay interest on a sum of money which is repayable by instalments would be to pay interest on the amount remaining unpaid at any given time. The strict grammatical construction may be

---

will result from a process of negotiation, will attempt to record in a formal way the consensus reached and will have the important purpose of creating certainty, both for the parties and for third parties (such as financiers)."

[147] [1893] A.C. 351.
[148] i.e. the carriage of oranges from Malaga to Liverpool.
[149] [1997] A.C. 749 at 771.
[150] [1894] 1 Q.B. 598. See, however, the division of opinion on a similar question of construction in *Britoil Plc v Hunt Overseas Oil Inc* [1994] C.L.C. 561 CA.

that for which Mr Jelf contends; but the business meaning is that which I have stated, and that is the meaning that must be given to the covenant."

Similarly, in *Bailey (CH) Ltd v Memorial Enterprises Ltd*,[151] Sir Eric Sachs said:

"The objective of the courts in a case relating to office leases is naturally to determine the intended commercial effect of the particular agreement reached between the parties. In this respect a lease is no less a contract relating to the use of premises than an agreement in relation to the supply of furniture for those premises is also a contract. It follows, to my mind that the courts should in this class of case avoid resort, so far as practicable, to any of the highly technical points that stem from the intricacies of the ancient law of landlord and tenant."

This approach was carried further in *Law Land Company Ltd v Consumers' Association Ltd*.[152] In that case the court was guided by the commercial purpose of the clause considered rather than by the words of the clause itself. Brightman LJ said:

"Some modification has to be made to the strict wording of the rent review clause if it is to work. I fully recognise the attractiveness of the arguments advanced by [counsel], but they lead to a solution which, to my mind, is not practical and cannot possibly have been contemplated by the parties. The lease is a commercial document and we have to find a commercial solution to the problem posed."

(b)   Is absurdity a pre-condition?

In *Antaios Cia Naviera SA v Salen Rederierna AB*,[153] Lord Diplock said: **2.53**

"While deprecating the extension of the use of the expression 'purposive construction' from the interpretation of statutes to the interpretation of private contracts,[154] I agree with the passage I have cited from the arbitrators' award and I take this opportunity of restating that, if a detailed semantic and syntactical analysis of words in a commercial contract is going to lead to a conclusion that flouts business common sense, it must be made to yield to business common sense."

This dictum was applied to the construction of a rent review clause in *MFI*   **2.54**
Properties Ltd v BICC Group Pension Trust Ltd.[155] In *Secretary of State for Defence v Turner Estate Solutions Ltd*,[156] Coulson J held that one party's suggested interpretation of a construction contract was such as to "flout common sense". However, in *The Sounion*,[157] Gatehouse J suggested that this dictum was only applicable when the literal construction of a document leads to absurdity. Such a view

---

[151] [1974] 1 W.L.R. 728.
[152] [1980] 2 E.G.L.R. 109.
[153] [1985] A.C. 191. In *Mannai Investment Co Ltd v Eagle Star Life Assurance Co Ltd* [1997] A.C. 749, Lord Steyn drew attention to the change in attitude of the court over the last 50 years and said that it was better to speak of "a shift towards commercial interpretation".
[154] The adjective "teleological" is sometimes substituted for "purposive" without any discernible change in meaning: *Phillips v Rafiq* [2007] 1 W.L.R. 1351 at 1363.
[155] [1986] 1 All E.R. 974.
[156] [2015] EWHC 1150 (TCC).
[157] *Summit Invest Inc v British Steel Corp (The Sounion)* [1986] 2 Lloyd's Rep. 593.

would be consistent with the "golden rule" of construction enunciated in *Grey v Pearson*.[158] However, it no longer represents the law. The decision of Gatehouse J was reversed by the Court of Appeal[159] in which Lloyd LJ described the problem of construction as being:

"designed to separate the purposive sheep from the literalist goats."

The sheep won.[160]

2.55   The testing of rival interpretations against their commercial consequences is part of the iterative process of interpretation. In *Re Sigma Finance Corp*,[161] Lord Mance said:

"Lord Neuberger was right to observe that the resolution of an issue of interpretation in a case like the present is an iterative process, involving 'checking each of the rival meanings against other provisions of the document and investigating its commercial consequences'."

In *Napier Park European Credit Opportunities Fund Ltd v Harbourmaster Pro-Rata CLO 2 BV*,[162] Lewison LJ emphasised that the iterative process thus described is not confined to textual analysis and comparison. It extends also to placing the rival interpretations within their commercial setting and investigating (or at any rate evaluating) their commercial *consequences*. The court looks to see where different constructions lead, how they fit with other provisions in the contract (or other phrases in the same clause), what obstacles to a particular interpretation are met upon the way, and what results are reached.[163] So in *Barnardo's v Buckinghamshire*[164] Lord Hodge explained:

"The emphasis on textual analysis as an interpretative tool does not derogate from the need both to avoid undue technicality and to have regard to the practical consequences of any construction. Such an analysis does not involve literalism but includes a purposive construction when that is appropriate."

Likewise, in *Ravennavi SpA v New Century Shipbuilding Co Ltd*,[2007] 2 Lloyd's Rep. 24. Moore-Bick LJ said:

"Unless the dispute concerns a detailed document of a complex nature that can properly be assumed to have been carefully drafted to ensure that its provisions dovetail neatly, detailed linguistic analysis is unlikely to yield a reliable answer. It is far preferable, in my view, to read the words in question fairly as a whole in the context of the document as a whole and in the light of the commercial and factual background known to both parties in order to ascertain what they were intending to achieve."

---

[158] (1857) 6 H.L. Cas. 61 (see para.5.06).

[159] [1987] 1 Lloyd's Rep. 230.

[160] The "merits" are not always against the literalists as Portia demonstrated in the literal construction she placed upon the bond given by Antonio to Shylock in *The Merchant of Venice*.

[161] [2009] UKSC 2; [2010] 1 All E.R. 571. See also *Classic Maritime Inc v Limbungan Makmur Sdn Bhd* [2019] 4 All E.R. 1145.

[162] [2014] EWCA Civ 984.

[163] *Wood v Sureterm Direct Ltd & Capita Insurance Services Ltd* [2015] EWCA Civ 839.

[164] [2019] 1 I.C.R. 495.

In *Re Golden Key Ltd*,[165] Arden LJ said that the court must have regard to the par-   **2.56**
ties' aim, objectively ascertained, even if there is little extrinsic evidence about the
surrounding circumstances apart from the document itself. She added:

> "… unless the contrary appears, the court must assume that the parties to a com-
> mercial document intended to produce a commercial result, and the court must
> thus take into account the commerciality of the rival constructions, if that com-
> merciality can be identified. The commerciality of a particular construction may
> be a crystallising factor in its favour where it is implausible that parties would
> have intended any other result."

In *Barclays Bank Plc v HHY Luxembourg SARL*,[166] Longmore LJ said:

> "The Judge said that it did not flout common sense to say that the clause provided
> for a very limited level of release, but that, with respect, is not quite the way to
> look at the matter. If a clause is capable of two meanings, as on any view this
> clause is, it is quite possible that neither meaning will flout common sense. In
> such circumstances, it is much more appropriate to adopt the more, rather than
> the less, commercial construction."

These observations were specifically approved by the Supreme Court in *Rainy
Sky SA v Kookmin Bank*[167]; and have been widely applied.[168]

Likewise in *Norwich Union Life and Pensions v Linpac Mouldings Ltd*,[169]   **2.57**
Lewison J said:

> "The language of the licence must also be interpreted in a way that makes com-
> mercial sense. Commercial commonsense is not merely a cross-check; it is an es-
> sential part of the process of interpretation. Commercial commonsense must also
> be considered from the perspective of both parties."

In *Napier Park European Credit Opportunities Fund Ltd v Harbourmaster Pro-
Rata CLO 2 BV*,[170] Lewison LJ said:

> "Thus we must seek to discern the commercial intention, and the commercial
> consequences from the terms of the contract itself; and that feeds in to the process
> of deciding whether a particular word or phrase is in reality clear and
> unambiguous. It follows in my judgment that, where possible, the court should

---

[165] [2009] EWCA Civ 636 at [28].
[166] [2010] EWCA Civ 1248; *Wollenberg v Casinos Austria International Holding GmbH* [2011] EWHC
103 (Ch).
[167] [2011] UKSC 50; [2011] 1 W.L.R. 2900, reversing the Court of Appeal.
[168] See, e.g. *Teal Assurance Co Ltd v WR Berkley Insurance (Europe) Ltd* [2011] EWCA Civ 1570;
[2012] 1 All E.R. (Comm) 969; *RGI International Ltd v Synergy Classic Ltd* [2011] EWHC 3417
(Comm); *Chalabi v Agha-Jaffar* [2011] EWCA Civ 1535; *Durham v BAI (Run Off) Ltd* [2012]
UKSC 14; [2012] 1 W.L.R. 867; *Danks v Qinetiq Holdings Ltd* [2012] EWHC 570 (Ch); *Re Employers' Liability Policy "Trigger" Litigation* [2012] UKSC 14; *Barbudev v Eurocom Cable Management Bulgaria EOOD* [2012] EWCA Civ 548; [2012] All E.R. (Comm) 963; *BP Oil International
Ltd v Target Shipping Ltd* [2012] EWHC 1590 (Comm); [2012] 2 Lloyd's Rep. 245; *Aston Hill
Financial Inc v African Minerals Finance Ltd* [2012] EWHC 2173 (Comm); *Royal Mail Group Ltd
v Evans* [2013] EWHC 1572 (Ch). See also *Axa S.A. v Genworth Financial International Holdings, Llc* [2020] EWHC 2024 (Comm) where commercial common sense was influential in the result.
[169] [2010] 1 P. & C.R. 218; affirmed [2010] EWCA Civ 395; [2010] L. & T.R. 10.
[170] [2014] EWCA Civ 984.

test any interpretation against the commercial consequences. That is part of the iterative exercise of interpretation. It is not merely a safety valve in cases of absurdity."

2.58   As Leeming JA pointed out in *Mainteck Services Pty Ltd v Stein Heurtey SA*[171]:

"... to say that a legal text is 'clear' reflects the *outcome* of that process of interpretation. It means that there is nothing in the context which detracts from the ordinary literal meaning. It cannot mean that context can be put to one side."

Thus in *LB Re Financing No.3 Ltd v Excalibur Funding No.1 Plc*,[172] Briggs J pointed out that:

"Questions of commercial common sense falling short of absurdity may however enable the court to choose between genuinely alternative meanings of an ambiguous provision. The greater the ambiguity, the more persuasive may be an argument based upon the apparently greater degree of common sense of one version over the other."

Similarly, in *Royal Mail Group Ltd v Evans*,[173] Asplin J said:

"Where there are two possible interpretations, the weight to be given to the commercial consequences must depend on the degree of ambiguity of the language concerned."

But as Briggs J also said in *Sugarman v CJS Investments LLP*[174]:

"There can unfortunately be a fine dividing line between that which appears commercially unattractive and even unreasonable and that which appears nonsensical or absurd. It causes continuing difficulty in the application of English law to problems of construction, not least because it is not unusual for apparently reasonable judicial minds to disagree on the question whether a particular contractual or other documentary provision has crossed it ... ."

Similarly, in *African Minerals Ltd v Renaissance Capital Ltd*,[175] Sir Stanley Burnton said:

"The less the commercial sense of a construction of an agreement, the greater the need to scrutinise its literal wording and if possible to depart from it to give a commercially sensible interpretation."

2.59   However, a rather harder line is taken in Australia, where the courts place greater emphasis on the natural meaning of the words of the contract.[176]

---

[171] [2014] NSWCA 184.
[172] [2011] EWHC 2111 (Ch).
[173] [2013] EWHC 1572 (Ch).
[174] [2014] EWCA Civ 1239. Despite his use of the adjectives "nonsensical" and "absurd" it is not thought that his Lordship meant to elevate this into a pre-condition before the commercial consequences of rival interpretations could be considered as part of the iterative process. It is clear that absurdity is not a pre-condition: see *Rainy Sky SA v Kookmin Bank* [2011] 1 W.L.R. 2900.
[175] [2015] EWCA Civ 448.
[176] See *Demlakian Engineers Pty Ltd v The Owners of Strata Plan* 80453 [2014] NSWSC 401.

In considering rival interpretations the court must also consider whether the rival interpretations are workable. As Christopher Clarke LJ put it in *Unite the Union v Liverpool Victoria Banking Services Ltd*[177]:

"It is, of course, possible for the parties to reach an agreement that is unworkable. But a construction which has that result is unlikely to be what the parties meant their words to mean."

(c) Approach to business common sense

In considering the choice between rival meanings, the court must consider all the factual circumstances in which the construction selected might apply. Thus in *Miramar Maritime Corp v Holborn Oil Trading Ltd*,[178] Lord Diplock said: **2.60**

"The words in the Exxonvoy bill of lading on which this appeal turns are the same irrespective of whether it is issued in respect of a complete or a part of the cargo received on board at the first or a subsequent loading port for carriage to and discharge at the last or any previous discharging port, there must be ascribed to the words a meaning that would make good commercial sense in any of these situations, and not some meaning that imposed on a transferee to whom the bill of lading for goods afloat was negotiated a financial liability of unknown extent that no businessman in his senses would be willing to incur."

In addition, as the Court of Appeal said in *Bank of Nova Scotia v Hellenic Mutual War Risks Association (Bermuda) Ltd*[179]:   **2.61**

"It is nonetheless important, in attributing a purpose to a commercial transaction, to be sure that it is the purpose of both parties and not just one. If the purpose of the transaction is seen through the eyes of one party only an unbalanced view of the transaction may result. Many contracts represent a compromise between what one party wishes to obtain and the other is willing to give."

In *Wood v Sureterm Direct Ltd & Capita Insurance Services Ltd*,[180] Christopher Clarke LJ observed: **2.62**

"What is business common sense may depend on the standpoint from which you ask the question. Further the court will not be aware of the negotiations between the parties. What may appear, at least from one side's point of view, as lacking in business common sense, may be the product of a compromise which was the only means of reaching agreement."

Similarly, in *Royal Society for the Prevention of Cruelty to Animals v Sharp*,[181] Lord Neuberger of Abbotsbury pointed out that:

"One obvious difference between a bilateral document such as a contract and a unilateral document such as a will, is that parties negotiating a contract may well

---

[177] [2015] EWCA Civ 285.
[178] [1984] A.C. 676.
[179] [1990] Q.B. 818 at 870 CA; *Churchill v Temple* [2011] 17 E.G. 72.
[180] [2015] EWCA Civ 839, affirmed [2017] A.C. 1173.
[181] [2010] EWCA Civ 1474.

be consciously content to include an obscurely drafted provision, on the basis that it represents an acceptable compromise, which enables overall agreement to be reached, whereas, save in a most exceptional case, which it is hard to conceive, a person making a will has no interest in obscurity."

(d)   Nature of business common sense

2.63   In *Ashtead Plant Hire Co Ltd v Granton Central Developments Ltd*[182] the Inner House discussed the nature of business common sense in detail. Lord Drummond Young said:

"The concept has been the subject of criticism in commentaries on the case law, largely on the ground that it is too uncertain or nebulous to be of practical use. We are nevertheless of opinion that commercial common sense is an important aid to the construction of contracts, and indeed commercial dealings of every sort. Common sense at a general level is frequently used in practical reasoning. In general, it involves a double process: is a conclusion (a deduction or inference) one that is widely held by those with a knowledge of the particular field under consideration ('common')? And does the converse of the conclusion make sense? If it does not, it is likely that the conclusion is correct (or makes 'sense'). The notion of common sense has been the subject of a considerable amount of philosophical commentary. For present purposes, it is sufficient to note the writings of Thomas Reid, notably his Essays on the Intellectual Powers of Man, Essay 1, chapters 2, 7 and 8 (1785). Reid placed particular emphasis on the manner in which conclusions may be derived from the use of language, properly analyzed. "Commercial" common sense involves applying these concepts to business transactions or business relationships, but with the addition of elementary microeconomics; 'microeconomics' is merely the branch of economics that covers the behaviour of individual firms (or individuals or families) in their commercial dealings with other persons. We would emphasize the word 'elementary'. The court should not embark on anything approaching a full professional economic analysis."

The factors which bear on business common sense include the practice that is followed in a particular trade; the principle that equivalence of obligation is a feature of most contracts; the avoidance of disproportionate burdens and (conversely) of windfalls; the approach which judges have taken in previous cases; and the general type of contract which can be seen as "a norm against which the particular features of the parties' contract can be judged".[183]

---

[182]   [2020] CSIH 2; *Ardmair Bay Holdings Ltd v Craig* [2020] CSIH 21.
[183]   *Ashtead Plant Hire Co Ltd v Granton Central Developments Ltd* [2020] CSIH 2.

(e) Cautionary words

Nevertheless, there are limits on the application of Lord Diplock's dictum.[184] In **2.64** *Co-Operative Wholesale Society Ltd v National Westminster Bank Plc*,[185] Hoffmann LJ said:

> "This robust declaration does not, however, mean that one can rewrite the language which the parties have used in order to make the contract conform to business common sense. But language is a very flexible instrument and, if it is capable of more than one construction, one chooses that which seems most likely to give effect to the commercial purpose of the agreement."

In *Arnold v Britton*,[186] Lord Neuberger said:

> "... while commercial common sense is a very important factor to take into account when interpreting a contract, a court should be very slow to reject the natural meaning of a provision as correct simply because it appears to be a very imprudent term for one of the parties to have agreed, even ignoring the benefit of wisdom of hindsight. The purpose of interpretation is to identify what the parties have agreed, not what the court thinks that they should have agreed. Experience shows that it is by no means unknown for people to enter into arrangements which are ill-advised, even ignoring the benefit of wisdom of hindsight, and it is not the function of a court when interpreting an agreement to relieve a party from the consequences of his imprudence or poor advice. Accordingly, when interpreting a contract a judge should avoid re-writing it in an attempt to assist an unwise party or to penalise an astute party."

As Briggs J observed in *Jackson v Dear*[187]:

> "The dictates of common sense may enable the court to choose between alternative interpretations (with or without implied terms), not merely where one would 'flout' it, but where one makes more common sense than the other. But this does not elevate commercial common sense into an overriding criterion, still less does it subject the parties to the individual judge's own notions of what might have been the most sensible solution to the parties' conundrum."

This observation was approved by the Court of Appeal in *BMA Special Opportunity Hub Fund Ltd v African Minerals Finance Ltd*[188] in which Aikens LJ added that:

---

[184] Professor McLauchlan has suggested that more recent decisions of the courts have departed from the principles in ICS and now propound a return to the pre-ICS days of the "plain meaning rule": "The Lingering Uncertainty in the Law of Contract Interpretation" [2015] L.M.C.L.Q. 406.

[185] [1995] 1 E.G.L.R. 97 CA.

[186] [2015] UKSC 36; [2015] A.C. 1619; *Wood v Sureterm Direct Ltd & Capita Insurance Services Ltd* [2015] EWCA Civ 839.

[187] [2012] EWHC 2060 (Ch). See also Grabiner, "The Iterative Process of Contractual Interpretation" (2012) 128 L.Q.R. 41.

[188] [2013] EWCA Civ 416; *Alegro Capital Llp v Allproperty Media PTE Ltd* [2013] EWHC 3376 (QB); *Cottonex Anstalt v Patriot Spinning Mills Ltd* [2013] EWHC 236 (Comm); [2014] 1 Lloyd's Rep. 615; *Tartsinis v Navona Management Co* [2015] EWHC 57 (Comm); *Edgeworth Capital (Luxembourg) SARL v Ramblas Investments BV* [2015] EWHC 150 (Comm); *Trust Risk Group Spa v Amtrust Europe Ltd* [2015] EWCA Civ 437.

"... the parties should not be subjected to '... the individual judge's own notions of what might have been the sensible solution to the parties' conundrum'. I would add, still less should the issue of construction be determined by what seems like 'commercial common sense' from the point of view of one of the parties to the contract."

Likewise, in *Procter & Gamble Co v Svenska Cellulosa Aktiebolaget SCA*,[189] Moore-Bick LJ said:

"I entirely agree that if a clause is reasonably capable of bearing two possible meanings (and is therefore ambiguous), the court should prefer that which better accords with the overall objective of the contract or with good commercial sense, but the starting point must be the words the parties have used to express their intention and in the case of a carefully drafted agreement of the present kind the court must take care not to fall into the trap of re-writing the contract in order to produce what it considers to be a more reasonable meaning."

2.65   The invocation of business common sense may not help in the detailed interpretation of the disputed words.[190] As Lord Hodge observed in *Wood v Capita Insurance Services Ltd*[191]:

"Business common sense is useful to ascertain the purpose of a provision and how it might operate in practice. But in the tug o' war of commercial negotiation, business common sense can rarely assist the court in ascertaining on which side of the line the centre line marking on the tug o' war rope lay, when the negotiations ended."

2.66   However, if there is no doubt about what the words mean commercial common sense has little (if any) part to play.[192] In *BNY Corporate Trustee Services Ltd v Eurosail UK 2007 3BL Plc*,[193] Lord Hope said that the role of business common sense is:

"... to find out what the parties meant when they entered into the arrangement, not to replace it with something which is not to be found in the documents at all."

Likewise, in *RWE Npower Renewables Ltd v JN Bentley Ltd*,[194] Akenhead J said:

"It is however fair to assume that these two commercial parties must be taken to have read and understood what they were signing up to. There is no suggestion that this is a case for rectification. Contractual interpretation should not be swayed in the case of a commercial contract between two commercial parties by

---

[189] [2012] EWCA Civ 1413; *Greatship (India) Ltd v Oceanografia SA de CV* [2012] EWHC 3468 (Comm); [2013] 2 Lloyd's Rep. 359.
[190] Professor Neil Andrews considers the use of commercial common sense in "Interpretation of Contracts and 'Commercial Common Sense': Do Not Overplay This Useful Criterion" (2017) 76 C.L.J. 36.
[191] [2017] A.C. 1173.
[192] *Flanagan v Liontrust Investment Partners LLP* [2015] EWHC 2171 (Ch) at [137], per Henderson J.
[193] [2013] UKSC 28; [2013] 1 W.L.R. 1408.
[194] [2013] EWHC 978 (TCC).

sympathy for one side or the other which may have inadvertently signed up to something which it later regrets."

From time to time judges have been cautious about adopting too robust a view **2.67** of what constitutes commercial sense. In *Merthyr (South Wales) Ltd v Merthyr Tydfil County Borough Council*[195] Leggatt LJ said:

"It is salutary to recall that the persons best placed to judge what is a commercially sensible agreement to make are the parties who have chosen to make it, and courts should be correspondingly wary of rejecting a natural interpretation of contractual language because it appears to produce a commercially unreasonable result. But just as there are degrees of naturalness of linguistic usage, so too there are degrees of unreasonableness of result, ranging from the merely imprudent or surprising to the obviously irrational or absurd."

In *Torvald Klaveness A/S v Arni Maritime Corp*,[196] Lord Mustill said:

"Naturally no judge will favour an interpretation which produces an obviously absurd result unless the words drive him to it, since it is unlikely that this is what the parties intended. But where there is no obvious absurdity, and simply assertions by either side that its own interpretation yields the more sensible result, there is room for error."

As Lord Donaldson MR pointed out in *The World Symphony*[197]:

"... arguments based upon apparent commercial absurdity need to be regarded with caution not least because, whilst judges of commercial experience are in a position to make some evaluation of the benefits and burdens of liberties and limitations contained in a charter-party, they are unlikely to be able to evaluate the countervailing burden or benefit of a particular rate of hire or length of charter, which depends upon current market conditions and because the alleged absurdity of a particular provision has to be judged in the context of the whole package."

So also in *Skanska Rashleigh Weatherfoil Ltd v Somerfield Stores Ltd*,[198] **2.68** Neuberger LJ said:

"[I]t seems to me that the court must be careful before departing from the natural meaning of the provision in the contract merely because it may conflict with its notions of commercial common sense of what the parties may, must or should have thought or intended. Judges are not always the most commercially-minded, let alone the most commercially experienced, of people, and should, I

[195] [2019] EWCA Civ 526.
[196] [1994] 1 W.L.R. 1465 HL.
[197] *Chiswell Shipping and Liberian Jaguar Transports Inc v National Iranian Tankers Co (The World Symphony and The World Renown)* [1992] 2 Lloyd's Rep. 115. Lord Donaldson considered that the position was different in the case of maritime arbitrators who were in day-to-day contact with the market.
[198] [2006] EWCA Civ 1732; [2007] C.I.L.L. 2449. See also *Forrest v Glasser* [2006] 2 Lloyd's Rep. 392; *K/S Victoria Street v House of Fraser (Stores Management) Ltd* [2010] EWHC 3344 (Ch); *Napier Park European Credit Opportunities Fund Ltd v Harbourmaster Pro-Rata CLO 2 BV* [2014] EWCA Civ 984; *Tartsinis v Navona Management Co* [2015] EWHC 57 (Comm).

think, avoid arrogating to themselves overconfidently the role of arbiter of commercial reasonableness or likelihood."

Similarly, in *Royal and Sun Alliance Insurance Plc v Dornoch Ltd*,[199] Longmore LJ said:

"[T]here are dangers in judges deciding what the parties must have meant when they have not said what they meant for themselves. This is particularly dangerous when the parties have selected from the shelf or the precedent book a clause which turns out to be unsuitable for its purpose. The danger is then intensified if it is only one part of such a clause which is to be construed in accordance with 'business common sense'. If the parties had addressed their mind to the question which clause out of a number of standard terms they would have used for the particular requirement which they had in mind, it is by no means obvious that they would have selected a form which was as draconian as the one unwisely but in fact chosen."

In *AMEC Foster Wheeler Group Ltd v Morgan Sindall Professional Services Ltd*[200] Edwards-Stuart J observed:

"... judges—even specialist commercial judges—are not, perhaps, always best placed to reach conclusions in any particular situation as to what constitutes commercial common sense."

2.69   In *North Sydney Leagues Club Ltd v Synergy Protection Agency Pty Ltd*,[201] Einstein J said that:

"it is extraordinary difficult to be certain of what is or is not *commonsense* in any particular business dealing which has been reduced to writing in the form of a contract. The court requires to be *very* wary before applying the so-called 'business commonsense' test" (emphasis in original).

Likewise in *Kahn v Dunlop Haywards (DHL) Ltd*,[202] Foskett J said:

"It seems to me that a case can be made by each party that the other's interpretation has economic consequences that were not what that party would have intended from a subjective point of view. However, this does not really help with determining what the agreement meant, objectively speaking. If, of course, one objective interpretation of an agreement leads to an absurd result or, to borrow Lord Diplock's expression, it 'flouts business common sense', then one needs to look for another meaning that cannot be so characterised. But where there are reasonable arguments both ways this principle of construction does not help greatly."

In *Cottonex Anstalt v Patriot Spinning Mills Ltd*,[203] Hamblen J said:

---

[199] [2005] 1 All E.R. (Comm) 590.
[200] [2016] EWHC 902 (TCC); 166 Con. L.R. 130.
[201] [2008] NSWSC 413.
[202] [2007] EWHC 2659 (QB).
[203] [2014] EWHC 236 (Comm); [2014] 1 Lloyd's Rep. 615; *Edgeworth Capital (Luxembourg) SARL v Ramblas Investments BV* [2015] EWHC 150 (Comm).

"... it will only be appropriate to give effect to the interpretation which is most consistent with business common sense where that can be ascertained by the court. In many cases that is only likely to be so where it is clear to the court that one interpretation makes more business common sense. If, as frequently happens, there are arguments either way the court is unlikely to be able to conclude with confidence that there is an interpretation which makes more business common sense. It is often difficult for a court of law to make nice judgments as to where business common sense lies."

Since the decision of the Supreme Court in *Arnold v Britton*,[204] the courts have become much more cautious in giving weight to alleged considerations of commercial common sense. In *Teva Pharma-Produtos Farmaceuticos Lda v Astrazeneca-Produtos Farmaceuticos Lad*,[205] the Court of Appeal held that the clear and natural meaning of a contractual definition should not be subverted by considerations of the court's perception of business common sense. In *Carillion Construction Ltd v Emcor Engineering Services Ltd*,[206] Jackson LJ explained:

2.70

"Recent case law establishes that only in exceptional circumstances can considerations of commercial common sense drive the court to depart from the natural meaning of contractual provisions."

Even though in that case the natural meaning of the words produced anomalies likely to give one party or the other a windfall benefit, the court declined to depart from the natural meaning of the contractual words. Nevertheless, in deciding whether there is any ambiguity in the contractual language, the court must have regard to the commercial consequences of rival interpretations. As Patten LJ put it in *Liontrust Investment Partners LLP v Flanagan*[207]:

"Although Lord Neuberger recognised in *Arnold v Britton*[208] at [17] that the importance of the language used by the parties to the contract should not be undervalued, what is usually referred to as commercial common sense is relevant to the ascertainment of how matters would have been perceived at the time when the contract was made. In *Wood v Capita Insurance Services Ltd*[209] the Supreme Court re-affirmed that the construction of a contract is a unitary exercise in which each suggested interpretation is checked against the provisions of the contract and its commercial consequences: see Lord Hodge JSC at [12]."

However, in *Grove Investments Ltd v Cape Building Products Ltd*,[210] the Inner House took a more sanguine view. Lord Drummond Young said:

2.71

"In a number of cases warnings have been given against 'excess of confidence that the judge's view as to what might be commercially sensible coincides with

204 [2015] UKSC 36; [2015] A.C. 1619.
205 [2017] EWCA Civ 2135.
206 [2017] EWCA Civ 65; [2017] B.L.R. 203.
207 [2017] EWCA Civ 985.
208 [2015] UKSC 36; [2015] A.C. 1619.
209 [2017] UKSC 24; [2017] A.C. 1173.
210 [2014] CSIH 43. He expressed the same view in *Ashtead Plant Hire Co Ltd v Granton Central Developments Ltd* [2020] CSIH 2. Commercial common sense played an influential role in *Guest Services Worldwide Ltd v Shelmerdine* [2020] EWCA Civ 85.

the views of those actually involved in commercial contracts'.[211] That is clearly correct. In particular, in construing contracts it is important to recognize that an unfortunate result for one party may simply be the result of a bad bargain, and apparent anomalies may be the result of trade-offs made during the negotiation of the contract. The court cannot correct a bad bargain, and it must respect the substance of the transaction that the parties have actually entered into. Nevertheless, many judges tend to develop considerable experience of commercial contracts over the years, both in practice in the legal profession (where they may have advised on the terms of contracts as they were being concluded) and on the bench. For that reason, although they must be sensitive to the possibility of trade-offs and bad bargains, they will usually be in a good position to decide what is commercially sensible."

In the event they decided that each of the argued interpretations was a possible meaning of the clause, and decided that one made better commercial sense than the other. One of the main reasons for that conclusion was that their preferred interpretation was more congruent with the common law.

2.72   Often, each party asserts that its preferred interpretation makes better commercial sense. As Eder J said in *Aston Hill Financial Inc v African Minerals Finance Ltd*[212]:

"... although there is no doubt that when construing a commercial contract the court should strive to attribute to it a meaning which accords with business common sense, it is not always easy for the court to identify which of two possible constructions is more consistent with business common sense particularly where, as in the present case, each side trumpets that its own construction is plainly the more consistent."

Having considered the rival arguments he concluded:

"For all these reasons, I have found the plea by both sides that I should construe the Facility in accordance with business common sense difficult to apply in the particular circumstances of the present case. The arguments fly in different directions or at least are not clear-cut. In such circumstances, I think there is considerable difficulty—and potential danger—in the court relying upon such arguments in reaching its conclusion."

Likewise, in *ENER-G Holdings Plc v Hormell*,[213] Gross LJ said that:

"... one of the difficulties in the present case is that considerations of business common sense can properly be relied upon for each of the rival constructions."

Similarly, in *Enterprise Inns Plc v Palmerston Associates Ltd*,[214] Morgan J said:

---

[211] *Credential Bath Street Ltd v Venture Investment Placement Ltd* [2008] Housing L.R. 2 at [24], per Lord Reed.

[212] [2012] EWHC 2173 (Comm) (affirmed on appeal [2013] EWCA Civ 416); *Ted Baker Plc v Axa Insurance UK Plc* [2012] EWHC 1406 (Comm); *Cottonex Anstalt v Patriot Spinning Mills Ltd* [2013] EWHC 236 (Comm); [2014] 1 Lloyd's Rep. 615; *Soufflet Negoce SA v Fedcominvest Europe Sarl* [2014] EWHC 2405 (Comm).

[213] [2012] EWCA Civ 1059.

[214] [2011] EWHC 3165 (Ch).

"Applying the approach identified in *The Rainy Sky*, I do not think that either of the rival constructions is inconsistent with business common sense nor do I think that either of the rival constructions is more consistent with business common sense than the other. I think that this is a case where an appeal to commercial purpose or business common sense does not advance the arguments as to what the parties are to be taken to have meant by the words which they have used."

Conversely, in *BP Oil International Ltd v Target Shipping Ltd*,[215] Andrew Smith J said of the two rival interpretations of a charterparty that each would be a perfectly workable arrangement; but that both interpretations produced a result:

"that businessmen would consider unusual and would be commercially surprising."

In *MT Hojgaard A/S v E.On Climate & Renewables UK Robin Rigg East Ltd* MT Højgaard A/S v E.On Climate & Renewables UK Robin Rigg East Ltd,[216] Stuart-Smith J drew the threads together. He said: **2.73**

"What is also clear is that the weight to be given to the implications or consequences of an interpretation will depend upon the clarity of the contractual language and the confidence with which the Court can form a view about whether the consequences of a given interpretation are genuinely uncommercial or otherwise tend to suggest that the parties to the contract did not intend them. In my judgment the Court should always be cautious when invited to take a view about whether consequences of an interpretation are commercially unacceptable or otherwise militate against a particular interpretation. This is for two main reasons. First, the Court will seldom, if ever, know what motivated the parties to agree either the particular terms in issue or the terms of a contract as a whole in the terms that they did—and, even if it did, pre-contract negotiations and aspirations are generally inadmissible as an aid to construction. Second, as Lord Hoffmann said in *ICS*, the Courts should adopt the common sense proposition that we do not easily accept that people have made linguistic mistakes, particularly in formal documents."

(f) No retrospective application

In *Arnold v Britton*,[217] Lord Neuberger said: **2.74**

"… commercial common sense is not to be invoked retrospectively. The mere fact that a contractual arrangement, if interpreted according to its natural language, has worked out badly, or even disastrously, for one of the parties is not a reason for departing from the natural language. Commercial common sense is only relevant to the extent of how matters would or could have been perceived by the parties, or by reasonable people in the position of the parties, as at the date that the contract was made."

---

[215] [2012] EWHC 1590 (Comm); [2012] 2 Lloyd's Rep. 245.
[216] [2013] EWHC 967 (TCC). His decision and his reasoning were approved on appeal: [2014] EWCA Civ 710.
[217] [2015] UKSC 36; [2015] 2 W.L.R. 1593; *Wood v Sureterm Direct Ltd & Capita Insurance Services Ltd* [2015] EWCA Civ 839.

(g) Boilerplate clauses

2.75   There may be more scope for the application of business common sense in the interpretation of boilerplate clauses. In *HOE International Ltd v Andersen*[218] Lord Drummond Young said:

> "... when a contract is drafted, it is in practice extremely difficult — indeed impossible — to foresee every contingency that might result. This means that the central terms of the contract (eg the property sold, the price, the basis on which the price will be adjusted to deal with contingencies and the key warranties) will usually be considered and drafted with scrupulous care. On the other hand, terms dealing with less central features are likely to receive much less attention by those drafting the contract. For this reason we think that there must be limits to how far it is legitimate to state that the parties must have specifically focused on an issue when agreeing the wording of a particular provision; in practice, for obvious reasons, parties and their advisers tend to concentrate on the key terms of the contract and draft the others on the basis of standard forms or past precedents, which may not be perfectly adapted to their particular circumstances."

He went on to point out:

> "... if all possible contingencies have to be catered for and contracts become longer in consequence, that will impose greater transaction costs on the parties when a contract is drafted. That can be avoided if the courts adopt a purposive and contextual approach to contractual construction and have due regard to commercial common sense. It can be said that in cases where a dispute arises such an approach may lead to more protracted and more expensive litigation, which in itself increases transaction costs. Nevertheless, it is important to bear in mind that such cases are the exception, not the rule, and consequently the overall increase in cost is likely to be reduced and for the most part confined to difficult cases. If, by contrast, the parties are compelled to draft every contract with the most meticulous foresight, that will impose substantial transaction costs in every case other than the simplest; in addition, the longer contracts that result will not necessarily lend themselves to easy interpretation. That itself produces uncertainty and unpredictability, which is clearly undesirable. Overall, relying on the courts to adopt a sensible commercial interpretation is in our opinion likely to produce a reduction in transaction costs. It is also likely to produce greater predictability, as contracts will be construed according to the standards of a reasonable commercial person."

(h) Forensic difficulties

2.76   The tension between the literal meaning of a contract and its commercial purpose is not without its difficulties for the advocate, as Megaw LJ pointed out in *Bailey (CH) Ltd v Memorial Enterprises Ltd*.[219] He said:

> "As I understood it counsel for both the landlords and the tenants in this court accepted that this is a commercial document between commercial parties which

---

[218] [2017] CSIH 9; 2017 SC 313.
[219] [1974] 1 W.L.R. 728.

ought to be construed as far as possible to give effect to commercial good sense. That approach is one which inevitably tends to give rise to difficulties in submission, because the forensic tendency necessarily is that when the actual literal interpretation of the wording is in favour of the submission that counsel wishes to make, he is disposed to rely on the literal and the grammatical construction; but when the literal and grammatical construction tends perhaps to be adverse to his submission he seeks to rely on broad commercial good sense."

Given the techniques by which advocates attempt to persuade the court that the construction favourable to their client is correct, this is inevitable.[220] Moreover, the court itself selects between the two approaches in different ways for different cases. The likely explanation is that the court sees its prime function as doing justice in the particular dispute before it, rather than in the consistent development of principles of construction and will employ the interpretative tools at its disposal in whatever manner it thinks right in order to achieve a decision in conformity with the "merits" as perceived by the court. The fetters which are from time to time placed on the court by binding authority are less important in the construction of contracts, for as will be seen, the role of precedent is extremely limited.[221] The court is, therefore, freer than in many cases to decide cases purely on the "merits".

Illustrations

1.   A charter party entitled the owner to withdraw the vessel for non-payment of hire or "on any breach of this charter party". It was held that "any breach" meant "any repudiatory breach".
    The Antaios[222]

2.   A contract for the sale of a lease of a club provided for the buyer to go into occupation pending the obtaining of the landlord's consent to the sale. The contract provided that in the event of consent not being obtained within three months "the Purchaser shall vacate the premises". It was held that "shall vacate" meant "shall be entitled to vacate", and that the buyer did not become a trespasser by remaining in occupation after the three months had expired.
    Balabel v Mehmet[223]

3.   A loan agreement by which an American bank lent a sum in US dollars to a Greek shipping company contained a clause by which the borrowers submitted to the jurisdiction of the English courts. It was held that the clause covered all disputes under the agreement, including disputes which could have been litigated in Greece. The answer was to be found not in the niceties of the clause but in commercial common sense.
    Continental Bank NA v Aeakos Compania SA[224]

---

[220]   The same forensic tendency is apparent in *Durham v BAI (Run Off) Ltd* [2011] 1 All E.R. 605 at [209] and [211].
[221]   See Ch.4.
[222]   [1985] A.C. 191 HL.
[223]   [1990] 1 E.G.L.R. 220 CA.
[224]   [1994] 1 Lloyd's Rep. 505 CA.

4.   A building contract contained provision for the adjudication of disputes. The contract gave the adjudicator power to order costs to be paid "as part of his decision". It was held that he was empowered to award costs even where one party had discontinued the adjudication before the adjudicator had made a substantive decision. The alternative interpretation would have produced an odd and uncommercial result.

John Roberts Architects Ltd v Parkcare Homes (No.2) Ltd[225]

5.   A clause in a contract for the maintenance of a council's leisure facilities stated that the council was entitled to terminate the contract if the contractor committed any breach of its obligations under the contract. It was held that the clause could not be literally applied because the notion that this term would entitle the council to terminate a contract such as this at any time for any breach of any term flew in the face of commercial common sense.

Rice (t/a Garden Guardian) v Great Yarmouth Borough Council[226]

6.   A clause in a tenancy agreement provided that either party might serve any notice (including any notice in proceedings) on the other at the address given in the particulars [(at the beginning of the tenancy agreement]) or such other address as had previously been notified in writing. It was held that, as a matter of commercial common sense, the parties must have intended that the new address, once duly notified, should supersede the original one shown in the particulars.

Grimes v Trustees of the Essex Farmers and Union Hunt[227]

7.   A contract for the sale of land and the transfer of the land contained a provision that, if a barn on the land transferred were to be demolished at any time thereafter, the transferees would retransfer a strip of land to the transferors. The sellers also entered into restrictive covenants so as to bind part of the land which they retained for the benefit of the land being sold by prohibiting the carrying on of activities which would be normal in an agricultural or rural setting, but which would be a nuisance to residential estate neighbours. It was held that the strip of land, once retransferred, was subject to the same restrictive covenants as the originally retained land. Although that was not the literal meaning of the words, no other interpretation made sense.

Jones v Oven[228]

8.   THE LIMITS OF BUSINESS COMMON SENSE

Where the words of a contract are clear, the court must give effect to them even if they have no discernible commercial purpose.[229]

2.77   It goes without saying that in the absence of a claim for rectification, the court must give effect to the words chosen by the parties to express their bargain. Accordingly the commercial purpose of the contract, as perceived by the court, can-

---

[225] (2006) 105 Con. L.R. 36.

[226] (2001) 3 L.G.L.R. 4.

[227] [2017] EWCA Civ 361; [2017] L. & T.R. 28.

[228] [2017] EWHC 1647 (Ch).

[229] This paragraph was referred to with apparent approval in *Dorchester Property Management Ltd v BNP Paribas Real Estate Advisory & Property Management UK Ltd* [2012] EWHC 1323 (Ch).

not override the words of a contract where they are clear. Business common sense is not an overriding criterion: it merely assists the choice between possible interpretations of the contract.[230]

Thus in *Rainy Sky SA v Kookmin Bank*,[231] the Supreme Court reaffirmed that:

"Where the parties have used unambiguous language, the court must apply it."

Likewise, in *Townsend v Persistence Holdings Ltd*,[232] the Privy Council applied the "plain and obvious meaning" of a contract, despite the harsh consequences of doing so.

As Jackson LJ put it in *Daejan Properties Ltd v Campbell*[233]:

"In construing a written contract, the governing principle is that the parties mean what they say."

However, as Leeming JA pointed out in *Mainteck Services Pty Ltd v Stein Heurtey SA*[234]:

2.78

"... to say that a legal text is 'clear' reflects the *outcome* of that process of interpretation. It means that there is nothing in the context which detracts from the ordinary literal meaning. It cannot mean that context can be put to one side."

As Christopher Clarke LJ put it in *Wood v Sureterm Direct Ltd & Capita Insurance Services Ltd*[235]:

"... a balance has to be struck between the indications given by the language and the implications of rival constructions. The clearer the language the less appropriate it may be to construe or confine it so as to avoid a result which could be characterised as unbusinesslike. The more unbusinesslike or unreasonable the result of any given interpretation the more the court may favour a possible interpretation which does not produce such a result and the clearer the words must be to lead to that result. Thus if what is prima facie the natural reading produces a wholly unbusinesslike result, the court may favour another, even if less obvious, reading. But, as Lord Neuberger observed in *Arnold v Britton* at [17] 'commercial common sense and surrounding circumstances ... should not be invoked to under value the importance of the language of the provision which is to be construed'."

Thus contractual language that may appear to be unambiguous divorced from the admissible background and the commercial consequences of rival interpretations may nevertheless give rise to difficulties of interpretation when read in context. It

2.79

---

230 *Jackson v Dear* [2012] EWHC 2060 (Ch), unaffected by the appeal at [2013] EWCA Civ 89; [2014] 1 B.C.L.C. 186; *BMA Special Opportunity Hub Fund Ltd v African Minerals Finance Ltd* [2013] EWCA Civ 416; *Procter & Gamble Co v Svenska Cellulosa Aktiebolaget SCA* [2012] EWCA Civ 1413.

231 [2011] UKSC 50; [2011] 1 W.L.R. 2900, reversing the Court of Appeal. See also *Ardagh Group SA v Pillar Property Group Ltd* [2013] EWCA Civ 900; *Joseph v Deloitte NSE LLP* [2019] EWHC 3354 (QB).

232 [2013] UKPC 12.

233 [2012] EWCA Civ 1503; [2013] 1 E.G.L.R. 34.

234 [2014] NSWCA 184.

235 [2015] EWCA Civ 839.

is not considered that *Rainy Sky* is intended to sanction an acontextual interpretation of contracts even if, at first sight, the language seems plain. On the contrary, as Lord Clarke emphasised, the interpretation of a contract is a "unitary process" in which the contractual language must be considered in the light of the background facts and the commercial consequences of the rival interpretations.

2.80   In *Thompson v Goblin Hill Hotels Ltd*,[236] Lord Dyson, giving the advice of the Privy Council, said of articles of association and a clause in a lease:

"In the opinion of the Board, the plain and ordinary meaning of the words used in article 91(1) and clause 5(b) can only be displaced if it produces a commercial absurdity."[237]

In *City Alliance Ltd v Oxford Forecasting Services Ltd*,[238] Chadwick LJ said:

"It is not for a party who relies upon the words actually used to establish that those words effect a sensible commercial purpose. It should be assumed, as a starting point, that the parties understood the purpose which was effected by the words they used; and that they used those words because, to them, that was a sensible commercial purpose. Before the Court can introduce words which the parties have not used, it is necessary to be satisfied (i) that the words actually used produce a result which is so commercially nonsensical that the parties could not have intended it, and (ii) that they did intend some other commercial purpose which can be identified with confidence. If, and only if, those two conditions are satisfied, is it open to the court to introduce words which the parties have not used in order to construe the agreement. It is then permissible to do so because, if those conditions are satisfied, the additional words give to the agreement or clause the meaning which the parties must have intended."

The same principle applies to an interpretation that involves the deletion of words.[239]

2.81   As Jackson LJ put it in *Balfour Beatty Regional Construction Ltd v Grove Developments Ltd*[240]:

"The court will not, indeed cannot, use the canons of construction to rescue one party from the consequences of what that party has clearly agreed. There is no ambiguity in the present case which enables the court to reinterpret the parties' contract in accordance with 'commercial common sense' ... ."

He added:

---

[236] [2011] UKPC 8.

[237] While background facts play a very limited role in relation to articles of association, they may play a greater role in relation to a lease. To hold that in the latter case the plain and ordinary meaning of words can only be displaced in the event of absurdity sets the bar too high.

[238] [2001] 1 All E.R. (Comm) 233 CA; *Lediaev v Vallen* [2009] EWCA Civ 156; *Pink Floyd Music Ltd v EMI Records Ltd* [2010] EWCA Civ 1429; [2011] 1 W.L.R. 770. In *Seakom Ltd v Knowledgepool Group Ltd* [2013] EWHC 4007 (Ch) Carr J said that *City Alliance Ltd v Oxford Forecasting Services Ltd* was "either inconsistent with or has at least been overtaken by the approach of the Supreme Court in *Rainy Sky*". The author is doubtful whether this is correct; and in *Amlin Corporate Member Ltd v Oriental Assurance Corp* [2014] EWCA Civ 1135 the Court of Appeal cited *City Alliance* with evident approval.

[239] *Powell v General Electric Co* [2005] EWHC 644 (Ch).

[240] [2016] EWCA Civ 990; [2017] 1 W.L.R. 1893.

"Commercial common sense can only come to the rescue of a contracting party if it is clear in all the circumstances what the parties intended, or would have intended, to happen in the circumstances which subsequently arose."

So too in *Safeway Food Stores Ltd v Banderway Ltd*,[241] Goulding J rejected an invitation to depart from the literal meaning of the words. He said:

"It may not be what one would think most probable, but there is nothing absurd about it, nothing insensible about it. For all that I am entitled to know in a construction case, the matter may have been so arranged as the result of bargaining on various points between the original landlord and the original tenant. If I assume that they had a common intention different from what the words express, I think I am merely guessing, and accordingly on this point the defendant succeeds."

And in *Charter Reinsurance Co Ltd v Fagan*,[242] Lord Mustill said:

"There comes a point at which the court should remind itself that the task is to discover what the parties meant from what they have said, and that to force upon the words a meaning which they cannot fairly bear is to substitute for the bargain actually made one which the court believes could better have been made. This is an illegitimate role for the court. Particularly in the field of commerce, where the parties need to know what they must do and what they can insist on not doing, it is essential for them to be confident that they can rely on the court to enforce their contract according to its terms."

As David Steel J put it in *BP Exploration Operating Co Ltd v Dolphin Drilling Ltd*[243]:

"... if on the one hand the words used by the parties are straightforward (albeit giving rise to a harsh outcome in the circumstances that have arisen) and on the other hand it is difficult to reformulate the relevant provision in a manner which avoids that harsh result, the Court will be the more ready to accept that commercial parties, with their competing interests feeding the negotiations, meant exactly what they said."

Nevertheless as part of the iterative process of interpretation, in deciding whether **2.82** the language of the contract is clear and unambiguous the court must test the rival interpretations against their commercial consequences. Thus in *Napier Park European Credit Opportunities Fund Ltd v Harbourmaster Pro-Rata CLO 2 BV*,[244] Lewison LJ said:

"Thus we must seek to discern the commercial intention, and the commercial consequences from the terms of the contract itself; and that feeds in to the process

---

[241] [1983] 2 E.G.L.R. 116.
[242] [1997] A.C. 313 HL. In the result, the House of Lords relied heavily on the context of the contract to attribute to the words "actually paid" a meaning which was not obvious at first sight. See also the powerful dissenting judgment of Staughton LJ.
[243] [2010] 2 Lloyd's Rep. 192.
[244] [2014] EWCA Civ 984. See also *Kudos Catering (UK) Ltd v Manchester Central Convention Complex Ltd* [2013] EWCA Civ 38; [2013] 2 Lloyd's Rep 270.

of deciding whether a particular word or phrase is in reality clear and unambiguous. It follows in my judgment that, where possible, the court should test any interpretation against the commercial consequences. That is part of the iterative exercise of interpretation. It is not merely a safety valve in cases of absurdity."

Thus, in *Canary Wharf Finance II Plc v Deutsche Trustee Co Ltd*[245] Phillips J, having decided that the words of the contract were clear and unambiguous, nevertheless considered business common sense by way of cross-check.

2.83   Deciding whether a contract is or is not ambiguous is not always easy. As Briggs LJ observed in *Sugarman v CJS Investments LLP*[246]:

"There can unfortunately be a fine dividing line between that which appears commercially unattractive and even unreasonable and that which appears nonsensical or absurd. It causes continuing difficulty in the application of English law to problems of construction, not least because it is not unusual for apparently reasonable judicial minds to disagree on the question whether a particular contractual or other documentary provision has crossed it ... ."

2.84   The realities of commercial life will often result in the parties agreeing a form of words that represents a compromise between their respective positions. In such a case the parties may well accept a form of words that are deliberately obscure in the hope that no problem will arise. In his dissenting judgment in *Re Sigma Finance Corp*[247] Lord Neuberger of Abbotsbury said:

"Documents such as the [contract in question] are prepared in many different ways. They often have provisions lifted (sometimes with bespoke amendments) from other documents; they often have different provisions drafted inserted or added to by different lawyers at different times; they often include last-minute amendments agreed in a hurry, frequently in the small hours of the morning after intensive negotiations, with a view to achieving finality rather than clarity; indeed, often the skill of the drafting lawyer is in producing obscurity, rather than clarity, so that two inconsistent interests can feel satisfied with the result. If there is subsequent disagreement as to the effect of the document, then other lawyers then have to do their best to determine what, in all the circumstances, the document means."

Similarly, in *Bishops Wholesale Newsagency Ltd v Surridge Dawson Ltd*,[248] Judge Mackie QC said:

"The factual matrix is commonplace with a background of parties entering a merger for a variety of reasons and with a range of bargaining strengths and weaknesses. The merger is recorded in a pair of relatively complex agreements containing terms which were no doubt heavily negotiated. It is clear and understandable that those drafting the Agreement did not subject the potential meaning of the clauses to the same full and exceptionally able analysis they have

---

[245] [2016] EWHC 100 (Comm).
[246] [2014] EWCA Civ 1239.
[247] [2009] B.C.C. 393. The majority decision of the CA was reversed on appeal.
[248] [2009] EWHC 2578 (Ch).

received from Counsel in this case. There are what appear to be anomalies which result, no doubt, not only from what with the wisdom of hindsight are seen to be shortcomings in drafting but also from bargaining and compromise. That is often the case with commercial contracts and the parties often then shape what they do and when they do it to navigate around or exploit difficulties created by the drafting. In this case the subjective intentions of the parties are of course inadmissible but one sees from the evidence and infers from the absence of a claim for rectification that there is disagreement between them about what they had in mind when agreeing the clause in dispute. But of course for the purpose of construction one assumes that they agreed and derives that agreement from the words used in the contract set against the background and in the context of the deal as a whole."

In such a case there is more scope for emphasis to be placed on context rather than text. Lord Hodge explained in *Wood v Capita Insurance Services Ltd*[249]:

"But negotiators of complex formal contracts may often not achieve a logical and coherent text because of, for example, the conflicting aims of the parties, failures of communication, differing drafting practices, or deadlines which require the parties to compromise in order to reach agreement. There may often therefore be provisions in a detailed professionally drawn contract which lack clarity and the lawyer or judge in interpreting such provisions may be particularly helped by considering the factual matrix and the purpose of similar provisions in contracts of the same type."

A well-drafted contract is more likely than a badly drafted contract to make itself plain. Accordingly, there is probably less scope for the use of the apparent commercial purpose as an aid to construction in the case of a well-drawn contract than in the case of a badly drawn one.[250] The quality of the drafting was specifically mentioned by Lord Bridge of Harwich in *Mitsui Construction Co Ltd v Att-Gen of Hong Kong*,[251] in which he said:

2.85

"It is obvious that this is a badly drafted contract. This, of course, affords no reason to depart from the fundamental rule of construction of contractual documents that the intention of the parties must be ascertained from the language they have used, interpreted in the light of the relevant factual situation in which the contract was made. But the poorer the quality of the drafting, the less willing any court should be to be driven by semantic niceties to attribute to the parties an improbable and unbusinesslike intention if the language used, whatever it may lack in precision, is reasonably capable of an interpretation which attributes to the parties an intention to make provision for contingencies inherent in the work contracted for on a sensible and businesslike basis."

---

[249] [2017] A.C. 1173.
[250] *Minera Las Bambas v Glencore Queensland Ltd* [2019] EWCA Civ 972; *Malone v Birmingham Community NHS Trust* [2018] EWCA Civ 1376; [2018] 3 Costs L.R. 627.
[251] (1986) 33 Build. L.R. 1 (a building contract case). See also *Sinochem International Oil (London) v Mobil Sales and Supply Corp* [2000] C.L.C. 878 CA; *Oxonica Energy Ltd v Neuftec Ltd* [2008] EWHC 2127 (Pat) and on appeal [2009] EWCA Civ 668.

2.86   In *Arnold v Britton*,[252] Lord Neuberger said:

"... when it comes to considering the centrally relevant words to be interpreted, I accept that the less clear they are, or, to put it another way, the worse their drafting, the more ready the court can properly be to depart from their natural meaning. That is simply the obverse of the sensible proposition that the clearer the natural meaning the more difficult it is to justify departing from it. However, that does not justify the court embarking on an exercise of searching for, let alone constructing, drafting infelicities in order to facilitate a departure from the natural meaning. If there is a specific error in the drafting, it may often have no relevance to the issue of interpretation which the court has to resolve."

Similarly, in *The Seaflower*,[253] Jonathan Parker LJ said:

"On any reading of cl. 46 of the charter, the conclusion is inescapable (to my mind at least) that the draftsman of the clause gave insufficient consideration to the precise meaning and effect of the terms in which it is framed. That being so, it seems to me that, as a matter of general interpretation of the clause, the court should focus rather more closely than might otherwise have been appropriate on what may be taken to be the parties' underlying commercial aims and objectives in entering into the charter ... and rather less closely on the precise words in which the parties have chosen to use to express their contractual intention."

2.87   In *Sinochem International Oil (London) Co Ltd v Mobil Sales & Supply Corporation*,[254] Mance LJ said:

"The strength of Mr. Milligan's interpretation is that it creates greater (though as will appear by no means complete) grammatical consistency. Its weakness to my mind is that it is very difficult to believe that commercial parties could have selected such a scheme. The clause bears the appearances of drafting expanded during its course to introduce or emphasize additional points, in a way which may explain an element of incoherence."

So also in *MFI Properties Ltd v BICC Group Pension Trust Ltd*,[255] Hoffmann J construed a rent review clause in order to determine the terms to be assumed in the hypothetical letting. He said:

"The terms on which such hypothetical letting must be assumed to take place will naturally depend on the particular language of the rent review clause. In general the purpose of such clauses would point to a prima facie assumption that the parties intended the hypothetical letting to be for the residue of the actual lease held by the tenant on the same terms and in the circumstances which actually exist at the relevant date. Thereby, the tenant would be required to pay on the assumption that he was being granted the interest which he actually held on the rent review date. But the language of the clause may show clearly that a departure from reality was intended. In some cases it will be easy for an outsider who was

---

[252] [2015] UKSC 36; [2015] A.C. 1619.
[253] *BS&N Ltd (BVI) v Micado Shipping Ltd (Malta) (The Seaflower) (No.1)* [2001] C.L.C. 421 at 437.
[254] [2000] 1 Lloyd's Rep. 339.
[255] [1986] 1 All E.R. 974.

not privy to the negotiations between the parties, to see why such an assumption should have been made. For example fairness to the landlord might explain an assumption that the tenant has complied with his repairing covenants even if he had in fact not done so. Similarly, fairness to the tenant will explain an assumption which excludes from consideration any improvements which the tenant has made at his own expense or his acquisition of goodwill which he would pay a higher rent to protect. But there will also be cases in which the language used by the parties shows beyond doubt that they intended an assumption for which, to a third party who knows nothing of the negotiations, no commercial purpose can be discerned. In such circumstances the court has no option but to assume that it was a *quid pro quo* for some other concession in the course of negotiations, the court cannot reject it as absurd merely because it is counterfactual and has no outward commercial justification. On the other hand, if the language is capable of more than one meaning, I think the court is entitled to select the meaning which accords with the apparent commercial purpose of the clause rather than one which appears commercially irrational."

The difficulty inherent in the attempt to construe contracts in accordance with **2.88** their apparent commercial purpose is twofold. In the first place, the parties may not give evidence of their intention in entering into the contract in the form they did. Nor, generally, may the court receive evidence of the negotiations between the parties[256]; so that it is impossible for a judge to discover whether the matter had been the result of bargaining between the parties. Moreover, even if the parties do indicate in the document itself what their purpose was, their statement may itself be overridden by a consideration of the contract as a whole.[257] Secondly, neither the advocates who argue points of construction nor the judges who determine them are commercial men. In deciding without evidence what the commercial purpose of a contract is, there is a danger that the real intention of the parties will be frustrated. This may manifest itself in the application of a preconceived idea of what contracts of that description generally seek to achieve, and a resulting tendency to force the words of the particular contract to fit that preconception. But provided that a consideration of the commercial purpose of the contract is tempered by loyalty to the text, it is a useful tool of interpretation.

9. PRIMA FACIE PRESUMPTIONS

Although the court may not dictate to the parties what their bargain should be, in many areas of the law prima facie presumptions have evolved about the meaning or effect of particular provisions. The usefulness of these presumptions is the promotion of commercial certainty, and thus contracts will usually be interpreted in the light of these presumptions. However, a prima facie presumption may be rebutted on a consideration of the contract as a whole and the circumstances in which it was made.

---

[256] See para.3.43.
[257] See para.9.56.

2.89   The value of presumptions of interpretation is that they give more certainty to commercial transactions. In *Wuhan Guoyu Logistics Group Co Ltd v Emporiki Bank of Greece SA*,[258] Longmore LJ pointed out that:

> "It is a problem of our system of precedent, that as more and more cases get decided, it seems to be necessary for judges at first instance to consider each case and determine how near or how far the document in question differs from the document construed in each past case.[259] The commercial community deserves better than this, if better can be done."

The solution to the problem was a presumption of interpretation. As he went on to say:

> "In deciding whether the document is a traditional 'see to it' guarantee or an 'on demand' guarantee, it would be obviously absurd to say that there are 6 pointers in favour of the former and only 4 pointers in favour of the latter and it must therefore be the former. But if the law does not permit boxes to be ticked in this way, commercial men will need some assistance from the courts in determining their obligations. The only assistance which the courts can give in practice is to say that, while everything must in the end depend on the words actually used by the parties, there is nevertheless a presumption that, if certain elements are present in the document, the document will be construed in one way or the other."

In *The Peonia*,[260] Saville J said:

> "Over the course of the years the English courts have dealt in this way with many disputes over the meaning and effect of commercial bargains. As a result there exists a large body of case law which not only authoritatively reaffirms and from time to time refines the applicable principles ... but also provides authoritative guidance on the meaning and effect of common types of commercial bargain, both generally and with regard to the words and phrases commonly used in such bargains. It follows that if in one case a Court concludes that a particular type of commercial bargain gives rise, or indeed does not give rise, to particular express or implied rights or obligations, another Court or tribunal is likely (or, if required by the laws of precedent, bound[261]) to take the same view of another like bargain, unless there are significant differences in the words or phrases used, or in the context in which they are used. The approach, however, always remains the same. The starting point must be to examine in context the words and phrases

---

[258] [2012] EWCA Civ 1629; [2013] All E.R. (Comm) 1191. *Wuhan Guoyo Logistics Group Co Ltd v Emporiki Bank of Greece* was followed and applied in *Spliethoff's Bevrachtingskantoor BV v Bank of China Ltd* [2015] EWHC 999 (Comm); [2015] 2 Lloyd's Rep. 123; *Bitumen Invest AS v Richmond Mercantile Ltd FZC* [2016] EWHC 2957 (Comm); [2017] 1 Lloyd's Rep. 219; *Shanghai Shipyard Co Ltd v Reignwood International Investment (Group) Co Ltd* [2020] EWHC 803 (Comm).

[259] This practice was roundly condemned by Jessel MR in *Aspden v Seddon* (1874) L.R. 10 Ch. App. 394 at 396n (see para.4.80).

[260] *Hyundai Merchant Marine Co v Gesuri Chartering Co (The Peonia)* [1991] 1 Lloyd's Rep. 100, affirmed [1991] 1 Lloyd's Rep. 100 CA, and approved by Lord Mustill in *Torvald Klaveness A/S v Ami Maritime Corp* [1994] 1 W.L.R. 1465 HL.

[261] See Ch.4.

used in the case under consideration. If this is not done, then there exists the risk that the law will start dictating to the parties what their bargain should be, the antithesis of the philosophy and principles of English common law on this subject."

Saville J speaks of "significant" differences before a new interpretation will be adopted. This is reflected in the judgment of Hoffmann J in *Laura Investment Co Ltd v Havering LBC*[262]:

"The courts have, over the years, formulated various prima facie assumptions as guides to the construction of rent review clauses. Although, of course, the construction of a particular document depends upon its own language, the prima facie assumptions laid down in the authorities are very important. They bring some consistency to the interpretation of leases and they enable parties buying and selling leases and reversions to obtain more realistic advice on what their rights and obligations are likely to be."

Having considered minor differences in wording between the clause he was considering and those considered in the authorities, he concluded:

"It seems to me that it would detract from the value of a prima facie rule of construction if it were to be frittered away on such small distinctions."

Although Lord Hoffmann has subsequently expressed the view[263] that presumptions about what people mean are of limited value, they continue to be applied in practice. In *Fiona Trust v Privalov*,[264] Lord Hoffmann himself said of an arbitration clause:

2.90

"In my opinion the construction of an arbitration clause should start from the assumption that the parties, as rational businessmen, are likely to have intended any dispute arising out the relationship into which they have entered or purported to enter to be decided by the same tribunal. The clause should be construed in accordance with this presumption unless the language makes it clear that certain questions were intended to be excluded from the arbitrators' jurisdiction."

Similarly, in the same case Lord Hope commended:

"a rule of construction ... which presumes, in cases of doubt, that reasonable parties will wish to have the claims arising from their contract decided by the same tribunal irrespective of whether their contract is effective or not."

The value of presumptions of interpretation is that they give greater certainty to commercial transactions. In *British Gas Corp v Universities Superannuation Scheme Ltd*,[265] Browne-Wilkinson VC said:

2.91

---

[262] [1992] 1 E.G.L.R. 155.
[263] *Kirin-Amgen Inc v Hoechst Marion Roussel Ltd* [2005] R.P.C. 169 at [35]. See also *Re White* [2001] Ch. 393 in which Chadwick LJ doubted whether it was correct to approach the construction of a contract on the basis that the court leans towards one conclusion rather than another.
[264] [2008] 1 Lloyd's Rep. 254.
[265] [1986] 1 W.L.R. 398.

"I am conscious that such an approach is perilously close to seeking to lay down mechanistic rules of construction as opposed to principles of construction. But there is an urgent need to produce certainty in this field. Every year thousands of rents are coming up for review on the basis of clauses such as the one before me: witness the growing tide of litigation raising the point. Landlords, tenants and their valuers need to know what is the right basis of valuation without recourse to lawyers, let alone to the courts. The question cannot be left to turn on the terms of each lease without the basic approach being certain."

2.92   In *Phoenix Commercial Enterprises Pty Ltd v City of Canada Bay Council*,[266] Campbell JA offered another justification for the use of presumptions of interpretation:

"If the document in question is drawn by a lawyer, is manifestly intended to effect a legal transaction, and uses an expression that is not an expression in common use but that has a meaning in an area of legal discourse that is relevant to the document in question, that in itself provides a basis for the reasonable reader concluding that that expression is used in its special legal sense, unless there are other factors present that show it is not used in that special legal sense. So understood, the presumption is consistent with the current approach to construction."

2.93   However, these presumptions are only prima facie presumptions, and may be displaced by the words of the contract. In *United Scientific Holdings Ltd v Burnley Borough Council*,[267] the issue was whether a timetable in a rent review clause required strict compliance. Lord Diplock said:

"So upon the question of principle which these two appeals were brought to settle, I would hold that in the absence of any contra-indications in the express words of the lease or in the interrelation of the rent review clause itself and other clauses or in the surrounding circumstances the presumption is that the timetable specified in a rent review clause for completion of the various steps for determining the rent payable in respect of the period following the review date is not of the essence of the contract."

Much of the subsequent litigation about rent review clauses concerned the question whether the presumption had been rebutted.[268]

2.94   In *IIG Capital LLC v van de Merwe*,[269] Waller LJ referred to the presumption that outside a banking context a document called a "guarantee" was not a performance bond, and continued:

"I accept there is a presumption against these being demand bonds or guarantees; I also accept that the documents must be looked at as a whole. I accept that clause 3, which would only be necessary if the deeds were or might be undertaking a secondary liability, points in favour of the presumption and that there are other terms which appear in what I would call normal guarantees given to banks in

---

[266] [2010] NSWCA 64 at [174].

[267] [1978] A.C. 904.

[268] See para.15.65.

[269] [2008] 2 Lloyd's Rep. 187.

relation to a customer's indebtedness. It will thus only be if clear language has been used in the operative clauses that the presumption will be rebutted."

Similarly, in *Wasa International Insurance Co Ltd v Lexington Insurance Co*,[270] Lord Collins of Mapesbury said:

"The presumption that the liability under a proportional facultative reinsurance is co-extensive with the insurance should be a strong one because (as I have said) the essence of the bargain is that the reinsurer takes a proportion of the premium in return for a share of the risk. But this is an unusual case in which the express (and entirely usual) terms of the reinsurance are clear. This is not a case where the reinsurers are relying on a technicality to avoid payment. At the beginning and end of these appeals remains the question whether the provision for the policy period in the reinsurance is to be given the effect it has under English law, or whether the parties must be taken to have meant that the reinsurance was to respond to all claims irrespective of when the damage occurred and irrespective of the period to which the losses related. There is, in my judgment, no principled basis for a conclusion in the latter sense."

As Rix LJ explained in *Durham v BAI (Run Off) Ltd*[271]:

"That was therefore a case in which the language of the contract prevailed over the presumption, created by the commercial purpose of the transactions, that insurance and reinsurance should provide the same cover."

A commercial contract will often specify a measure of damages for breach of its terms. In such a case there is no presumption that the measure of damages will coincide with the measure of damages at common law. As Lord Sumption explained in *Bunge SA v Nidera BV*[272]: **2.95**

"... damages clauses are commonly intended to avoid disputes about damages, ei-ther by prescribing a fixed measure of loss (as in the case of a liquidated damages clause) or by providing a mechanical formula in place of the more nuanced and fact-sensitive approach of the common law (as in cl.20 of GAFTA 49). In either case, it is inherent in the clause that it may produce a different result from the common law. For that reason there can be no scope for a presumption that the parties intended the clause to produce the same measure of damages as the compensatory principle would produce at common law. The mere fact that in some cases its application will over- or under-estimate the injured party's loss is nothing to the point. Such clauses necessarily assume that the parties are willing to take the rough with the smooth. However, I would accept a more moderate version of [the] presumption. A damages clause may be assumed, in the absence of clear words, not to have been intended to operate arbitrarily, for example by producing a result unrelated to anything which the parties can reasonably have expected to approximate to the true loss."

A presumption of this kind is sometimes referred to as "a default rule"; but the **2.96**

270 [2010] 1 A.C. 180 at [116].
271 [2011] 1 All E.R. 605 at 668.
272 [2015] UKSC 43; [2015] Bus. L.R. 987.

court must be wary of holding that a default rule exists. In many cases the supposed default rule will be no more than a conclusion reached on the particular wording of the contract in question.[273]

Illustrations

1.   Where a contract contains an arbitration clause, there is a presumption, called "the presumption in favour of one-stop adjudication", that the parties intended that all disputes should be determined by the same tribunal.
Harbour Assurance Co (UK) Ltd v Kansa General International Assurance Co Ltd[274]

2.   Where a rent review clause contains a procedural timetable, there is a presumption that time is not of the essence of the timetable.
United Scientific Holdings Ltd v Burnley Borough Council[275]

3.   There is a presumption that the scope and nature of the cover afforded by a reinsurance contract is the same as the cover afforded by the insurance.
Groupama Navigation et Transports v Catatumbo CC Seguros[276]

4.   Outside a banking context there is a strong presumption against interpreting the words "on demand" in a guarantee as creating a primary obligation to pay rather than a secondary obligation to stand surety.
Marubeni Hong Kong Ltd v Mongolian Government[277]

5.   A contract provided for payment in a currency which differed from the currency of account. The existence of a default rule about exchange rates proved decisive in interpreting the contract.
Procter & Gamble Co v Svenska Cellulosa Aktiebolaget SCA[278]

6.   A contract for the sale of goods contained an agreed damages clause. There was no presumption that the measure of damages prescribed by the clause corresponded to the common law measure of damages for breach of contract.
Bunge SA v Nidera BV[279]

7.   There is a presumption that an all-risks marine cargo policy is construed as covering only losses flowing from physical loss or damage to goods; and there must

---

[273]   *Drake v Harvey* [2011] EWCA Civ 838.
[274]   [1993] 1 Lloyd's Rep. 455 CA; followed in *Continental Bank NA v Aeakos Compania Naviera SA* [1994] 1 Lloyd's Rep. 505 CA. See also *Ashville Investments Ltd v Elmer Contractors Ltd* [1989] 1 Q.B. 488.
[275]   [1978] A.C. 904 HL.
[276]   [2000] 2 Lloyd's Rep. 350. But see *Wasa International Insurance Co Ltd v Lexington Insurance Co* [2010] 1 A.C. 180 where the wording displaced the presumption.
[277]   [2005] 1 W.L.R. 2497. However, the presumption may be rebutted by other contra-indications in the instrument, read as a whole: *Van Der Merwe v IIG Capital LLC* [2008] 2 Lloyd's Rep. 187.
[278]   [2012] EWCA Civ 1413.
[279]   [2015] UKSC 43.

be clear words indicating a broader intention.

Engelhart CTP (US) LLC v Lloyd's Syndicate 1221 for the 2014 Year of Account[280]

10. Strict Construction

The court will sometimes construe a contract strictly in order to achieve a fair result on the facts of the particular case.

In *Mannai Investment Co Ltd v Eagle Star Life Assurance Co Ltd*,[281] Lord **2.97**
Hoffmann said of a notice exercising a break clause in a lease:

> "But what does it mean to say that a document must be 'strictly' construed, as opposed to the normal process of ascertaining the intentions of the author?[282] The expression does not explain itself. If it operates merely by way of intensification, so that the intention must be clear, unambiguous, incapable of misleading, then I think that the notice in this case satisfied the test at that level."

In many cases, however, the court says that it will not adopt a suggested construc- **2.98**
tion in the absence of clear words. As Lord Hoffmann pointed out in *BCCI v Ali*[283]:

> "When judges say that 'in the absence of clear words' they would be unwilling to construe a document to mean something, they generally mean (as they did in the case of exemption clauses) that the effect of the document is unfair."

In *Liberty Mutual Insurance Co (UK) Ltd v HSBC Bank Plc*,[284] Rix LJ said:

> "It is true that modern authority ... has moved away from technical or hostile attitudes to exclusion clauses. Even so, situations where 'clear words' are required remain."

Among the examples he gave were whether an exclusion clause excludes liability for negligence; whether a contract excludes a remedy for breach; and whether a release surrenders rights of which the parties were unaware. A conclusive evidence clause is also one to be strictly construed.[285]

It is traditionally the case that covenants in leases prohibiting alienation are strictly construed, because a breach may result in a forfeiture[286]; but it is doubtful whether this represents the modern law.[287]

Where it is alleged that a right or remedy available under the general law has **2.99**
been contractually removed, the court will often require clear words to achieve that effect.[288]

---

[280] [2018] EWHC 900 (Comm); [2018] 2 Lloyd's Rep. 24.
[281] [1997] A.C. 749 at 776.
[282] One possibility is that the court will give less weight to background at the expense of the text. In the case of a contract that is negotiable, the court often adopts this approach: *Hong Kong & Shanghai Banking Corp v GD Trade Co Ltd* [1998] C.L.C. 238.
[283] [2002] 1 A.C. 251, in a dissenting speech. See further para.7.169.
[284] [2002] EWCA Civ 691.
[285] *Northshore Ventures Ltd v Anstead Holdings Inc* [2011] EWCA Civ 230; *Carey Value Added SL v Grupo Urvasco SA* [2010] 132 Con. L.R. 15.
[286] *Lam Kee Ying Sdn Bhd v Lam Shes Tong* [1975] A.C. 247.
[287] *Akici v LR Butlin Ltd* [2006] 2 All E.R. 872.
[288] See para.12.144.

2.100   A strict construction, in the sense of one that pays closer attention to the words of the contract than to its background, may also be warranted where the contract is transmissible to third parties.[289] Likewise, in *Opua Ferries Ltd v Fullers Bay of Islands Ltd*,[290] the Privy Council held that extrinsic evidence should not be permitted to qualify the meaning borne by a public document contained in a register because members of the public should be entitled to take the registered document at face value. As has been seen, greater emphasis on the text is also justified where the contract has been professionally drawn, where it is a standard form contract; where it is designed to operate over the long term; and where it affects the interests of person who are not parties to it.[291]

Illustration

An agreement provided that any notice "may be served by delivering it personally or by sending it by pre-paid recorded delivery post". The intended recipient received a notice, but it was not served in either of the ways specified in the contract. The Court of Appeal held by a majority that clear words would be necessary before concluding that the contract meant that someone who had actually received a notice was entitled to say that he had not. Consequently the specified methods of service were not exclusive.
ENER-G Holdings Plc v Hormell[292]

11.   MANIPULATIVE INTERPRETATION

The court will sometimes manipulate the construction of the contract in order to achieve a fair result on the facts of the particular case. This approach is rarely overtly recognised, and has been disapproved in the case of exemption clauses.

2.101   All those who have experience of the decisions of the courts on points of construction will be aware that the court will frequently arrive at a construction which accords with the "merits" of the case. The process was graphically described by Lord Denning M.R. in *Mitchell (George) (Chesterhall) Ltd v Finney Lock Seeds Ltd*.[293] In discussing the approach of the court to exemption clauses he said:

"Faced with this abuse of power, by the strong against the weak, by the use of the small print of the conditions, the judges did what they could to put a curb on it. They still had before them the idol, 'freedom of contract.' They still knelt down and worshipped it, but they concealed under their cloaks a secret weapon. They used it to stab the idol in the back. This weapon was called 'the true construc-

---

[289] *Hong Kong & Shanghai Banking Corp v GD Trade Co Ltd* [1998] C.L.C. 238.

[290] [2003] 3 N.Z.L.R. 740; [2003] UKPC 19.

[291] See *Wood v Capita Insurance Services Ltd* [2017] A.C. 1173; *Barnardo's v Buckinghamshire* [2019] 1 I.C.R. 495; *Thales UK Ltd v Thales Pension Trustees Ltd* [2017] EWHC 666 (Ch); [2017] Pen. L.R. 15; *British Telecommunications Plc v BT Pension Scheme Trustees Ltd* [2018] EWHC 69 (Ch); [2018] Pens. L.R. 7.

[292] [2012] EWCA Civ 1059. Note that in *The Port Russel* [2013] EWHC 490 (Comm); [2013] 2 Lloyd's Rep. 57, Popplewell J preferred the reasoning in the dissenting judgment of Longmore LJ.

[293] [1983] Q.B. 284. See also Atiyah, "Judicial Techniques and the Law of Contract" (reprinted in *Essays on Contract* (1986)).

tion of the contract.' They used it with great skill and ingenuity. They used it to depart from the natural meaning of the words of the exemption clause and to put on them a strained and unnatural construction. In case after case, they said that the words were not strong enough to give the big concern exemption from liability, or that in the circumstances the big concern was not entitled to rely on the exemption clause. If a ship deviated from the contractual voyage, the owner could not rely on the exemption clause. If a warehouseman stored goods in the wrong warehouse, he could not pray in aid the limitation clause. If the seller supplied goods different in kind from those contracted for, he could not rely on any exemption from liability. If a shipowner delivered goods to a person without production of the bill of lading, he could not escape liability by reference to an exemption clause. In short, whenever the wide words, in their natural meaning, would give rise to an unreasonable result, the judges either rejected them as repugnant to the main purpose of the contract or else cut them down to size in order to produce a reasonable result. ... But when the clause was itself reasonable and gave rise to a reasonable result, the judges upheld it, at any rate when the clause did not exclude liability entirely but only limited it to a reasonable amount. So, where goods were deposited in a cloakroom or sent to a laundry for cleaning, it was quite reasonable for the company to limit their liability to a reasonable amount, having regard to the small charge made for the service."

This historical description was referred to in the House of Lords without disapproval.[294] The judicial approach towards exemption clauses described by Lord Denning MR was deprecated by the House of Lords in *Photo Production Ltd v Securicor Transport Ltd*,[295] in which it was said that strained interpretations should not be put upon exemption clauses. Indeed Lord Denning himself abjured it (with the approval of the House) in the *Finney Lock Seeds* case itself.

Nevertheless, some judges do recognise that the court has a creative role in interpreting a contract. As Sedley LJ put it in *Casson v PJ Ostley Ltd*[296]:   **2.102**

"'Construction' has two meanings, one derived from the verb to construe, the other from the verb to construct. It may be as well to admit that under the guise of the first, the courts in cases like this are doing the second. We mitigate the uncovenanted effects of literalism not by nakedly writing a new contract for the parties but by construing the words according to principles which enable the contract, in effect, to be reconstructed. It is a very reasonable stopping place on the road that runs between second guessing parties who have simply contracted incautiously and leaving a party at the mercy of unconsidered words."

Similarly, in *Durham v BAI (Run Off) Ltd*,[297] Rix LJ referred to a number of cases in which "the courts have manipulated language in order to make sense of a contract or unilateral notice, on the basis that such manipulated language would reflect the reasonable understanding of the parties, readers or addressees."

---

[294] [1983] 2 A.C. 803.
[295] [1980] A.C. 827.
[296] [2003] B.L.R. 147.
[297] [2011] 1 All E.R. 605 at [209] et seq.

12.   MATTERS OF IMPRESSION[298]

Much of interpretation is intuitive. A question of interpretation may be said to be a matter of impression when it is too difficult to explain why words convey a particular meaning in context.

2.103   In many cases the court decides a question of interpretation intuitively. As Robert Walker LJ acknowledged in *Welsh v Greenwich LBC*[299]:

"questions of construction are frequently a matter of impression and are not readily susceptible of precise explanation."

In *Designers Guild Ltd v Russell Williams (Textiles) Ltd*,[300] Lord Hoffmann said:

"When judges say that a question is one of impression, they generally mean that it involves taking into account a number of factors of varying degrees of importance and deciding whether they are sufficient to bring the whole within some legal description. It is often difficult to give precise reasons for arriving at a conclusion one way or the other (apart from an enumeration of the relevant factors) and there are borderline cases over which reasonable minds may differ."

In *Ashville Investments Ltd v Elmer Contractors Ltd*,[301] Balcombe LJ said:

"As on any question of construction the issue is incapable of much elaboration: it is a matter of how the words strike the reader."

2.104   Similarly, in *Skanska Rashleigh Weatherfoil Ltd v Somerfield Stores Ltd*,[302] Neuberger LJ, having described the question of construction as a "matter of impression", added:

"Notwithstanding the benefit of all the guidance from the House of Lords and all the arguments of counsel, the natural meaning which the words in question convey to a particular reader, whether or not a judge, must inevitably play a very significant part in his or her decision as to that effect."

In *Norwich Union Life Insurance Society v British Railways Board*,[303] Hoffmann J said:

"The use of ordinary language to convey meaning often involves subtle discriminations which for most people are intuitive rather than capable of lucid explanation. An explanation of why ordinary English words in a particular context convey a given meaning is frequently more likely to confuse than to

---

[298] This paragraph was referred to with apparent approval in *Bywater Properties Investments LLP v Oswestry Town Council* [2014] EWHC 310 (Ch); [2014] 2 P. & C.R. 1.
[299] (2001) 81 P. & C.R. 12.
[300] [2000] 1 W.L.R. 2416 (a case of copyright infringement rather than contractual interpretation).
[301] [1989] Q.B. 488.
[302] [2006] EWCA Civ 1732; [2007] C.I.L.L. 2449.
[303] [1987] 2 E.G.L.R. 137; *Northrop Grumman Sperry Marine BV v Thales Electronics Ltd* [2015] EWHC 1255 (Ch).

enlighten. Perhaps this is what judges mean when they say that questions of construction are often matters of impression."[304]

Similarly, where the question is whether a contractual term is ambiguous, it is sometimes difficult to explain why one has reached a particular conclusion.[305] In *Ambatielos v Anton Jurgen Margarine Works*,[306] Lord Sterndale MR said: **2.105**

"... it is very difficult indeed to say what is ambiguous and what is not, and I do not think any test can be applied except that of the person who is dealing with it. If it does not seem ambiguous to him I am afraid he can only say 'It may seem ambiguous to others, but it does not to me.'"

But it remains the case that "where a collection of words, whose interpretation is in dispute, convey a particular meaning to a judge, the parties are entitled to the best explanation the judge can give as to why the words convey that particular meaning to him, even though, as Hoffmann J said, carrying out that exercise may confuse rather than enlighten."[307] In *Cameron v Boggiano*,[308] Mummery LJ said: **2.106**

"Even after the necessary process of analysing the purpose, structure and language of a document is over, the meaning conveyed may still remain a matter of overall impression of the document in its unique setting. It is not particularly surprising to find that different readers of a document sometimes have different impressions of its meaning."

Likewise, in *Kazeminy v Siddiqi*,[309] Moore-Bick LJ said of a settlement agreement:

"In the end, however much one subjects wording of this kind to textual analysis, the question whether the clause was intended to have the effect of extinguishing in Mr Kazeminy's hands rights obtained from third parties inevitably elicits a response that is largely intuitive, but which is for that reason no less sound, being based on the nature of the agreement and the context in which it was made."

In *Geofizika DD v MMB International Ltd*,[310] Lord Neuberger of Abbotsbury MR warned: **2.107**

"First impression can be a dangerous guide to meaning: it is liable to be subjective, it is normally impossible to explain, and it not infrequently turns out to be wrong. However, as the purpose of interpretation is to work out what meaning the words in question convey, the initial impression they make on the tribunal charged with interpretation is often of relevance—not least in a case such as this,

---

[304] See, e.g. *Taupo Totara Timber Co Ltd v Rowe* [1978] A.C. 537; *Wasa International Insurance Co Ltd v Lexington Insurance Co* [2007] All E.R. (D) 206 (Apr).

[305] In *Boots UK Ltd v Trafford Centre Ltd* [2008] EWHC 3372 (Ch) Morgan J described this as "the elephant test".

[306] [1922] 2 K.B. 185.

[307] *C & J Clark International Ltd v Regina Estates Ltd* [2003] EWHC 1622 (Ch) (per Neuberger J).

[308] [2012] EWCA Civ 157.

[309] [2012] EWCA Civ 416. See also *Bywater Properties Investments LLP v Oswestry Town Council* [2014] EWHC 310 (Ch); [2014] 2 P. & C.R. 1.

[310] [2010] 2 Lloyd's Rep. 1.

where the recipient of the document concerned will, in practice, read its provisions pretty quickly (if at all)."

Similarly, in *Charter Reinsurance Co Ltd v Fagan*,[311] Lord Mustill said:

"This is ... an occasion when a first impression and simple answer no longer seem the best, for I recognise that the focus of the argument is too narrow. The words must be set in the landscape of the instrument as a whole. Once this is done the shape of the policy and the purpose of the terms become quite clear."

2.108   Even where a judge can explain why language conveys a particular meaning, much of the mental processing of the language is intuitive. As Robert Walker LJ explained in *John v Price Waterhouse*[312]:

"The process of construction often (and certainly in this case) involves the assessment of disparate (and therefore incommensurable) factors to reach what is ultimately an intuitive (but not irrational) conclusion. If a judge makes a point-by-point evaluation of the opposing arguments addressed to him he is performing his duty to give reasons for his decision. But point-by-point analysis of that sort cannot fully reflect the nature of the judicial process of construing a complex and difficult commercial agreement."

Similarly, in *Morrells of Oxford Ltd v Oxford United Football Club Ltd*,[313] he said:

"The judicial mind does not in practice proceed in an orderly series of immutable choices in order to reach a conclusion on a question of construction. In practice it scans repeatedly from one point or proposition to another, often forming and rejecting provisional views in the search for the most satisfactory (or least unsatisfactory) resolution."

2.109   In his dissenting judgment in *Re Sigma Finance Corp*,[314] Lord Neuberger of Abbotsbury described a similar process:

"However, while one is seeking to interpret the document as a whole, the ultimate issue between the parties turns on the meaning of the provision, and, in order to resolve the issue, the reasoning and analysis have to start somewhere. The natural, indeed, I would have thought, the inevitable, point of departure is the language of the provision itself. However, where the interpretation of a word or phrase is in dispute, the resolution of that dispute will normally involve something of an iterative process, namely checking each of the rival meanings against the other provisions of the document and investigating its commercial consequences."

---

[311] [1997] A.C. 313, cited with approval in *Re Sigma Finance Corp* [2010] 1 All E.R. 571.
[312] [2002] EWCA Civ 899; *Northrop Grumman Sperry Marine BV v Thales Electronics Ltd* [2015] EWHC 1255 (Ch).
[313] [2001] Ch. 459; *Altera Voyageur Production Ltd v Premier Oil E&P UK Ltd* [2020] EWHC 1891 (Comm).
[314] [2009] B.C.C. 393.

On appeal to the Supreme Court[315] Lord Mance said that:

"Lord Neuberger was right to observe that the resolution of an issue of interpretation in a case like the present is an iterative process, involving 'checking each of the rival meanings against other provisions of the document and investigating its commercial consequences'. ... Like him, I also think that caution is appropriate about the weight capable of being placed on the consideration that this was a long and carefully drafted document, containing sentences or phrases which it can, with hindsight, be seen could have been made clearer, had the meaning now sought to be attached to them been specifically in mind. ... Even the most skilled drafters sometimes fail to see the wood for the trees, and the present document on any view contains certain infelicities, as those in the majority below acknowledged."

The description of the process of interpreting a contract as an "iterative process" was subsequently endorsed by the Supreme Court in *Rainy Sky SA v Kookmin Bank*.[316] The "iterative process" can be seen at work in *Al-Sanea v Saad Investments Co Ltd*.[317] The approach in *Re Sigma Finance Corp* was also followed in *McKillen v Maybourne Finance Ltd*.[318]

Lord Neuberger returned to the theme in *Fabio Perini Spa v LPC Group Plc*[319] in which he said: **2.110**

"The process of construction has to start somewhere, and when the ultimate issue is the interpretation of a common English word, it is often helpful to begin with its ordinary meaning before one turns to its documentary context and other relevant factors. After all, issues of interpretation (whether arising in connection with patents or any other commercial documents) often require an intracranial iterative process, involving multiple factors, including natural meaning, documentary context, technical considerations, commercial context, and business common sense."

In *Multi-Link Leisure Developments Ltd v Lanarkshire Council*,[320] Lord Rodger suggested:

"When translating a document written in a foreign language, it often makes sense to start with the parts whose meaning is clear and then to use those parts to unravel the meaning of the parts which are more difficult to understand. The same applies to interpreting contracts or statutes."

Lady Hale agreed, saying:

"construe the words you can understand and see where that takes you."

---

[315] [2010] 1 All E.R. 571; *Anthracite Rated Investments (Jersey) Ltd v Lehman Brothers Finance SA* [2011] EWHC 1822 (Ch).
[316] [2011] UKSC 50; [2011] 1 W.L.R. 2900, reversing the Court of Appeal. See also Grabiner, "The Iterative Process of Contractual Interpretation" (2012) 128 L.Q.R. 41.
[317] [2012] EWCA Civ 313.
[318] [2012] EWCA Civ 864.
[319] [2010] EWCA Civ 525 (a case of patent construction).
[320] [2010] UKSC 47; [2011] 1 All E.R. 175.

2.111   In *OneSteel Manufacturing Pty Ltd v BlueScope Steel (AIS) Pty Ltd*,[321] Allsop P said:

> "That there is one true meaning does not detract from the pervasive reality that a contract will often have potentially more than one meaning, that words are inherently contextual in their meaning and that reasonable minds often differ about what is the true meaning. That is partly because, as Holmes J said in *Towne v Eisner*,[322] a 'word is not a crystal, transparent and unchanged, it is the skin of a living thought and may vary greatly in color and content according to the circumstances and the time in which it is used.' Further, structure of the text and the relative weight and influence of context and purpose can strike people differently. That is why the process of construction is not a process necessarily concluded by logical reasoning or a priori analysis. It involves the weighing of different considerations partly logical and partly intuitive (though rational) leading to a choice. Analysis of competing arguments assists in that process, but the 'correct' answer is not arrived at merely by seeing which side has the greater number of 'good' points."

2.112   The retreat into the safety of describing a question as "a matter of impression", particularly if otherwise unexplained, can make litigation very unpredictable. As Professor McLauchlan lamented[323]:

> "The outcome of interpretation litigation is notoriously difficult to predict. This is partly because questions of interpretation are often seen as 'matters of impression' or intuition, and inevitably the way in which judges mentally process language and apply it to the facts will vary according to their background and experience. Even so, the division of opinion that one finds in the cases is remarkable. Time and again judges will disagree on such elementary questions as whether particular words have a plain meaning and what is the 'commonsense' or 'commercially realistic' interpretation."

But as Lord Hoffmann observed in *Chartbrook Ltd v Persimmon Homes Ltd*[324]:

> "It is, I am afraid, not unusual that an interpretation which does not strike one person as sufficiently irrational to justify a conclusion that there has been a linguistic mistake will seem commercially absurd to another. ... The subtleties of language are such that no judicial guidelines or statements of principle can prevent it from sometimes happening. It is fortunately rare because most draftsmen of formal documents think about what they are saying and use language with care."

---

[321] [2013] NSWCA 27.

[322] [1918] U.S.S.C. 6; 245 U.S. 418 (1918) at 425.

[323] "Contract Interpretation: What Is It About?" (2009) 31 *Sydney Law Review* 5. Professor McLauchlan has repeated his criticism of *Multi-Link Leisure Developments Ltd v North Lanarkshire Council* in "A construction conundrum?" [2011] L.M.C.L.Q. 428. However, it was referred to with apparent approval by the Supreme Court in *L Batley Pet Products Ltd v North Lanarkshire Council* [2014] UKSC 27; [2014] Bus. L.R. 615.

[324] [2009] 1 A.C. 1101.

13. WHY NOT SAY IT?

Since almost any dispute about the interpretation of a contract involves rival meanings, it is seldom helpful to ask why the parties did not adopt one of those rival meanings in their contract.[325]

One question which is frequently posed for forensic effect is to ask: "if the parties meant that, why did they not say it?" It is, however, inherent in most disputes about the interpretation of a contract that the words in question are susceptible of more than one meaning. As Mance LJ put it in *Dodson v Peter H Dodson Insurance Services*[326]:

2.113

> "It is almost always possible to say after the event that the point could have been put beyond doubt, either way, by express words."

If the words were clear, there would be no room for dispute.[327]
In *Charrington & Co v Wooder*,[328] Lord Dunedin said:

> "I do not think it rests with either party to say to the other 'If the meaning is as you contend, why did you not express it otherwise?' Both contentions as to the true meaning can be expressed by a gloss. ... If either of these glosses had been expressed there would be no possibility of dispute. It therefore comes back to the question, What is the true interpretation of the expression in the contract?"

In *Conister Trust Ltd v John Hardman & Co*,[329] Lawrence Collins LJ said:

> "To some extent the present exercise is one of impression. No assistance can be derived from dictionary definitions, and I have already concluded that no assistance can be derived from the cases on consumer credit law. Nor do I derive any assistance from the point made by Hardmans that Conister could have made the point clear beyond doubt by appropriate wording. That can always be said when parties differ on the meaning of a contract."

Likewise, in *Transfield Shipping Inc v Mercator Shipping Inc*,[330] Lord Hoffmann said:

> "I suppose it can be said of many disputes over interpretation, especially over implied terms, that the parties could have used express words or at any rate expressed themselves more clearly than they have done. But, as I have indicated, the implication of a term as a matter of construction of the contract as a whole in its commercial context and the implication of the limits of damages liability

---

[325] This paragraph was cited with approval in *Fitzpatrick Contractors Ltd v Tyco Fire and Integrated Solutions (UK) Ltd* (2008) 119 Con. L.R. 155 and *Trust Risk Group Spa v Amtrust Europe Ltd* [2015] EWCA Civ 437. See also *Bovis Lend Lease Ltd v Cofely Engineering Services* [2009] EWHC 1120 (TCC) and *Barbudev v Eurocom Cable Management Bulgaria EOOD* [2011] EWHC 1560 (Comm); [2011] 2 All E.R. (Comm) 951.
[326] [2001] 1 W.L.R. 1012 at 1029.
[327] Cf. *The Rio Assu* [1999] 1 Lloyd's Rep. 115 at 126 CA; *Crest Nicholson Residential (South) Ltd v MacAllister* [2003] 1 All E.R. 46.
[328] [1914] A.C. 71 at 82 HL.
[329] [2008] EWCA Civ 841 at [85].
[330] [2009] 1 A.C. 61.

seem to me to involve the application of essentially the same techniques of interpretation. In both cases, the court is engaged in construing the agreement to reflect the liabilities which the parties may reasonably be expected to have assumed and paid for. It cannot decline this task on the ground that the parties could have spared it the trouble by using clearer language."

In *Spire Healthcare Ltd v Royal & Sun Alliance Insurance Plc*[331] Simon LJ said:

"In construing a contract of insurance, the Court seeks to give effect to all the words of the policy that bear on the issue. Doubtless clearer words in proviso 5A would have put the question of whether it was an aggregation clause beyond doubt; but the Court construes the contract as it is and not as it might have been drafted. In almost any dispute over contractual terms a party can argue that a contentious term could have been better expressed to achieve the effect that the other party avows."

Similarly, in his dissenting judgment in *Re Sigma Finance Corp*,[332] Lord Neuberger of Abbotsbury said:

"I do not think it is normally convincing to argue that, if the parties had meant a phrase to have a particular effect, they would have made the point in different or clearer terms. That is a game which all parties can normally play on issues of interpretation. Save in relatively rare circumstances (e.g. where the document concerned contains a provision elsewhere in different words which has the effect contended for by one of the parties), it does not take matters further."

2.114 However, the argument that "if the draftsman had meant that he could have easily said so" does sometimes find favour.[333]

2.115 In many, if not most, cases, the problem occurs because the parties did not foresee the factual situation which has arisen, and to which the contract applies.

2.116 Where the question is whether a prima facie presumption has been displaced, or whether the contract expresses a result in clear words, the fact that the contract could have been differently drafted so as to produce the result for which one party contends is often of considerable importance. Thus where the question is whether an exclusion clause covers liability for negligence, clarity of expression is important. In *EE Caledonia Ltd v Orbit Valve Co Europe*,[334] Hobhouse J said:

"The parties are always able, by the choice of appropriate language, to draft their contract so as to produce a different legal effect. The choice is theirs. In the present case there would have been no problem in drafting the contract so as to produce the result for which the plaintiffs have contended; however, the contract was not so drafted and contains only general wording and is seriously lacking in clarity."

---

[331] [2018] EWCA Civ 317; [2018] 1 C.L.C. 327; *Warborough Investments Ltd v Lunar Office SARL* [2018] EWCA Civ 427; [2018] L. & T.R. 24.

[332] [2009] B.C.C. 393.

[333] See *Fomento de Construcciones y Contratas SA v Black Diamond Offshore Ltd* [2016] EWCA Civ 1141; *Singularis Holdings Ltd v Chapelgate Credit Opportunity Master Fund Ltd* [2020] EWHC 1616 (Ch).

[334] [1994] 1 W.L.R. 221 at 228 (affirmed [1994] 1 W.L.R. 1515 CA).

14.   Unforeseen Changes in Circumstances

Where the circumstances in which the contract is to be applied have unexpectedly changed, the court's task is to decide, in the light of the agreement that the parties made, what they must have been taken to have intended in relation to the events which have arisen which they did not contemplate.

Chadwick LJ explained in *Bromarin v IMD Investments Ltd*[335]:   **2.117**

"that it is commonplace that problems of construction, in relation to commercial contracts, do arise where the circumstances which actually arise are not circumstances which the parties foresaw at the time when they made the agreement. If the parties have foreseen the circumstances which actually arise, they will normally, if properly advised, have included some provision which caters for them. What that provision may be will be a matter of negotiation in the light of an appreciation of the circumstances for which provision has to be made.

It is not, to my mind, an appropriate approach to construction to hold that, where the parties contemplated event A, and they did not contemplate event B, their agreement must be taken as applying only in event A and cannot apply in event B. The task of the court is to decide, in the light of the agreement that the parties made, what they must have been taken to have intended in relation to the event, event B, which they did not contemplate. That is, of course, an artificial exercise, because it requires there to be attributed to the parties an intention which they did not have (as a matter of fact) because they did not appreciate the problem which needed to be addressed. But it is an exercise which the courts have been willing to undertake for as long as commercial contracts have come before them for construction. It is an exercise which requires the court to look at the whole agreement which the parties made, the words which they used and the circumstances in which they used them; and to ask what should reasonable parties be taken to have intended by the use of those words in that agreement, made in those circumstances, in relation to this event which they did not in fact foresee."

Similarly, in *Casson v PJ Ostley Ltd*,[336] Sedley LJ said: **2.118**

"One of the dubious wares in which lawyers deal is the plain meaning of words. Words often have a meaning which linguistically is perfectly straightforward but which makes no sense, or unacceptable sense, when it is applied to particular facts. Interpretation, moreover, only happens when words are applied to facts. The example beloved of law teachers is the proposal to put a World War II tank on a plinth in a park regulated by a by-law which bans motor vehicles. Contracts, a form of law made for themselves by private parties, are no more immune to this fate than are statutes, of which Stair remarked more than three centuries ago:

'... the lawgiver must at once balance the conveniences and inconveniences; wherein he may and often doth fall short ... .'

---

[335] [1998] S.T.C. 244. In *W. Nagel v Pluczenik Diamond Co NV* [2018] EWCA Civ 2640; [2019] 1 All E.R. 194 the court discussed the approach to applying contractual wording to unforeseen circumstances.
[336] [2003] B.L.R. 147.

In the present case, as in most cases on the interpretation of contracts which reach this court, the words fall short of the facts. It may be axiomatic that we are to deduce the parties' intention from the words they have used, but the intention itself is in most such cases a fiction. Occasionally, it is true, something which has been agreed on has just been poorly expressed and can be elucidated; but far more often the parties have simply and understandably not even thought about the event which has now caused a problem. No more than a legislature can they be expected to anticipate every eventuality; but when the unexpected happens, as it regularly does, they and the courts have only the now insufficient words on the page to fall back on.

What is the court then to do? It may not simply make the contract which it believes the parties would have made if they had thought about the issue. It must keep in focus those agreed purposes which are evident. It must give what effect it can to the words on the page. But since, ex hypothesi, the words on the page do not fit the facts, the court has to work creatively; and consistency requires it to do so by adopting and observing principles—in lawyers' language, rules of construction."

2.119   In *W. Nagel v Pluczenik Diamond Co NV*[337] Leggatt LJ said:

"It is, however, commonplace for circumstances to arise which the parties to a contract did not foresee when the contract was made. When this happens, it does not follow that the contract ceases to be binding or ceases to apply. On the contrary, unless the change of circumstances is so radical or fundamental as to frustrate the contract by making it impossible to perform, the parties are held to their bargain. What the contract requires in the changed circumstances depends on its proper construction."

Likewise, in *Munich Re Capital Ltd v Ascot Corporate Name Ltd*[338] the issue was the relation between an insurance policy and a reinsurance policy relating to a substantial construction project which unexpectedly overran. Carr J said:

"It is a question of contractual interpretation in changed factual circumstances. The task of the court is to decide, in the light of the agreement that the parties made, what they must have been taken to have intended in relation to the events which have arisen which they did not contemplate, namely an extension to the Project Period in the Insurance Policy but no corresponding extension to the Project Period in the Reinsurance Policy."

2.120   The unforeseen changes may be changes in the factual situation, changes in practice, or changes in the law.

2.121   In *Debenhams Retail Plc v Sun Alliance and London Assurance Co Ltd*,[339] a lease provided for a turnover rent as a percentage of the tenant's "gross amount of total sales". When the lease was granted in 1965, purchase tax was levied on certain goods. Purchase tax was replaced by VAT in 1973. The issue was whether VAT was to be included in the "gross amount of sales". The Court of Appeal held that it was. Mance LJ said:

---

[337] [2018] EWCA Civ 2640; [2019] Bus. L.R. 692.
[338] [2019] EWHC 2768 (Comm).
[339] [2005] 3 E.G.L.R. 34.

"To speak even of objective intention in such circumstances involves some artificiality. Even if we were judicial archaeologists, we would find in the wording of the lease negotiated in 1965 no actual or buried intention regarding VAT, since it was introduced in April 1973, and the regime in force in 1965 was the different purchase tax regime. But no-one suggests that the lease cannot or should not apply in the changed circumstances. We have to promote the purposes and values which are expressed or implicit in its wording, and to reach an interpretation which applies the lease wording to the changed circumstances in the manner most consistent with them."

In the result the court held that the "gross amount" included that part of the purchase price of goods that was attributable to output tax for VAT. In *Lloyds TSB Foundation for Scotland v Lloyds Banking Group Plc*,[340] the Supreme Court applied the approach in *Debenhams Retail Plc v Sun Alliance and London Assurance Co Ltd*. Lord Mance said:

"No-one suggests or could suggest that the change meant that the 1997 Deed was frustrated, so the question is how its language best operates in the fundamentally changed and entirely unforeseen circumstances in the light of the parties' original intentions and purposes."

Illustration

A section 106 agreement required a developer to pay the city council a sum equal to the amount of Social Housing Grant necessary to secure affordable rented homes of an equivalent type and size on another site. The Social Housing Grant was unexpectedly abolished. It was held that the obligation was not discharged, but that the developer had to pay an amount equivalent to what the Social Housing Grant would have been if it had continued to exist.
Council of the City of York v Trinity One (Leeds) Ltd[341]

---

[340] [2013] UKSC 3; [2013] 1 W.L.R. 366.
[341] [2018] EWCA Civ 1883.

CHAPTER 3

THE MATERIALS AVAILABLE

Words, words. They're all we have to go on.

Tom Stoppard: *Rosencrantz and Guildenstern Are Dead*

1. THE DOCUMENT TO BE INTERPRETED

The primary material available is the document to be interpreted. In the absence of fraud or mistake the parties are bound by the terms of a written document which they have signed or which has been signed on their behalf.

In the absence of fraud or misrepresentation a party signing a contract is bound by its terms, and it is wholly immaterial whether he has read the document or not.[1] One possible reason is that by signing the document the signatory represents to the other party that he has made himself acquainted with its contents and assented to them.[2] Thus formulated, the rule may be seen as a branch of the law of estoppel. However, it may be doubted whether this is the true foundation of the rule. In *McCutcheon v Macbrayne (David) Ltd*,[3] Lord Devlin said:

> "It seems to me that when a party assents to a document forming the whole or part of his contract, he is bound by the terms of the document, read or unread, signed or unsigned, simply because they are in the contract; and it is unnecessary and possibly misleading to say that he is bound by them because he represents to the other party that he has made himself acquainted with them."

As Moore-Bick LJ pointed out in *Peekay Intermark Ltd v Australia and New Zealand Banking Group Ltd*[4]:

> "It is an important principle of English law which underpins the whole of commercial life; any erosion of it would have serious repercussions far beyond the business community. Nonetheless, it is a rule which is concerned with the content of the agreement rather than its validity."

In *Internaut Shipping GmbH v Fercometal SARL*,[5] Rix LJ said:

> "The signature is, as it were, the party's seal upon the contract; and that remains the case even where, as here, the contract has already been made … Prima facie

3.01

---

[1] *L'Estrange v Graucob* [1934] 2 K.B. 395.
[2] *Harris v Great Western Railway Co* (1896) 1 Q.B.D. 515 at 530, per Blackburn J.
[3] [1964] 1 W.L.R. 125 at 134.
[4] [2006] 2 Lloyd's Rep. 511. See also the comprehensive discussion by the High Court of Australia in *Toll (FGCT) Pty Ltd v Alphapharm Pty Ltd* [2004] HCA 52.
[5] [2003] 2 All E.R. (Comm) 760.

a person does not sign a document without intending to be bound under it, or, to put that thought in the objective rather than subjective form, without properly being regarded as intending to be bound under it. If therefore he wishes to be regarded as not binding himself under it, then he should qualify his signature or otherwise make it plain that the contract does not bind him personally."

3.02   Accordingly, in the absence of a claim for fraud, rectification or misrepresentation it is clear that the process of interpretation must start by a consideration of the language used by the parties to the document itself. Thus in *Re Jodrell*,[6] Lord Halsbury said:

"I do not know what the testator meant except by the words he has used. ... For myself, I am prepared to look at the instrument such as it is; to see the language that is used in it; to look at the whole of the document and not to part of it; and having looked at the whole of the document to see, if I can, through the document what was in the mind of the testator. Those are general principles for the construction of all instruments, and to that extent it may be said that they are canons of construction."

3.03   In most cases, the identification of the relevant document will not be in doubt. There will be a self-contained document which purports to be, and is, the parties' contract. But there are also cases in which it is not clear which documents constitute the contract, with the result that the instrument must first be identified before it can be interpreted.

3.04   Usually the court will be entitled to look at the whole of the document, but there may be cases in which the court must disregard words which appear in the identified instrument. In addition, the court is not nowadays confined to the four corners of the document in order to reach a conclusion about what the contract means. This chapter will explore the extent to which other materials are available to assist in the process of interpretation.

2.   SUPPLEMENTAL DOCUMENTS

A document to which the primary document is expressed to be supplemental may itself be looked at in its entirety for the purpose of construing the primary document.

3.05   Section 58 of the Law of Property Act 1925 provides:

"Any instrument (whether executed before or after the commencement of this Act) expressed to be supplemental to a previous instrument, shall as far as may be, be read and have effect as if the supplemental instrument contained a full recital of the previous instrument."

The effect of this section is that the previous instrument is treated as having been incorporated verbatim into the supplemental instrument as a recital. Since any instrument must be construed as a whole, it follows that the recital may be looked at for the purpose of interpreting the instrument. Thus the whole of the previous

---

[6] (1890) 44 Ch. D. 590 (a will case). Lord Halsbury also reiterated the same thought process in *Leader v Duffey* (1888) 13 App. Cas. 294 (see para.2.44).

instrument is available to assist the process of construction.[7] As Knox J noted in *Historic Houses Ltd v Cadogan Estates*[8]: "[t]he statutory shorthand ... only creates a recital and not an operative provision". It is a word saving provision.[9] Thus in *Scottish Widows Fund and Life Assurance Society v BGC International*,[10] the Court of Appeal interpreted a lease by reference to a supplemental agreement executed contemporaneously with the lease.

3. DOCUMENTS FORMING PART OF THE SAME TRANSACTION

A document executed contemporaneously with, or shortly after, the primary document to be construed may be relied upon as an aid to construction, if it forms part of the same transaction as the primary document.[11]

Many transactions take place by the entry into a series of contracts, for example **3.06** a sale of land involving an exchange of identical contracts; a sale and lease-back of property; an agreement of sale and a bill of sale and so on. In such cases, where the transaction is in truth one transaction,[12] all the contracts may be read together for the purpose of determining their legal effect. This principle is a more specific example of the general principle that background is admissible in interpreting a written contract. It applies to other documents executed as part of the same transaction, whether they happen to be executed before, at the same time as, or after the document requiring to be interpreted.[13]

In *Smith v Chadwick*,[14] Jessel MR said:

"... when documents are actually contemporaneous, that is two deeds executed at the same moment, ... or within so short an interval that having regard to the nature of the transaction the Court comes to the conclusion that the series of deeds represents a single transaction between the same parties, it is then that they are treated as one deed; and of course one deed between the same parties may be read to show the meaning of a sentence and may be equally read, although not contained in one deed but in several parchments, if all the parchments together in the view of the Court make up one document for this purpose."

The rationale behind this principle was explained by Fletcher Moulton LJ in **3.07**

---

7   *Plumrose Ltd v Real and Leasehold Estate Investment Society Ltd* [1970] 1 W.L.R. 52. See also para.10.32.
8   [1993] 2 E.G.L.R. 151 at 152.
9   *Barclays Bank Plc v Prudential Assurance Co Ltd* [1998] B.C.C. 928 at 930; *Fattal v Walbrook Trustees (Jersey) Ltd* [2010] EWHC 2767 (Ch).
10   [2012] EWCA Civ 607.
11   This section was cited with approval in *ING Lease (UK) Ltd v Harwood* [2008] Bus. L.R. 762 (affirmed but without reference to this point: [2009] Bus. L.R. 972); by the Court of Appeal of Western Australia in *Secure Parking (WA) Pty Ltd v Wilson* [2008] WASCA 268 and *Sunny Metal & Engineering Pte Ltd v Ng* [2007] SGCA 36 (Singapore Court of Appeal). See also *Encia Remediation Ltd v Canopius Managing Agents Ltd* [2007] 2 All E.R. (Comm) 947.
12   Or, as it is called in modern jargon, a "composite transaction". For the converse case of one document containing several transactions see *Wilkinson v Clements* (1872) L.R. 8 Ch. App. 96 (cited in para.16.121). See also para.3.66 (expressly incorporated terms). The question whether terms have been incorporated into a contract is a somewhat different question to that whether another document may be looked at in order to construe a contract; it has therefore been treated separately.
13   *Cherry Tree Investments Ltd v Landmain Ltd* [2012] EWCA Civ 736; [2013] Ch. 305.
14   (1882) 20 Ch. D. 27 at 62 (on appeal (1884) 9 App. Cas. 187).

Manks v Whiteley[15] as follows:

> "… where several deeds form part of one transaction and are contemporaneously executed they have the same effect for all purposes such as are relevant to this case as if they were one deed. Each is executed on the faith of all the others being executed also and is intended to speak only as part of the one transaction, and if one is seeking to make equities apply to the parties they must be equities arising out of the transaction as a whole. It is not open to third parties to treat each one of them as a deed representing a separate and independent transaction for the purpose of claiming rights which would only accrue to them if the transaction represented by the selected deed was operative separately. In other words, the principles of equity deal with the substance of things, which in such a case is the whole transaction, and not with unrealities such as the hypothetical operation of one of the deeds by itself without the others."

Applying this principle, a will was read together with two assents giving effect to the gifts in the will.[16]

3.08   Where a contract is one of a series of linked contracts (e.g. a contract of insurance and a contract of reinsurance) the relevant terms in a proportional facultative reinsurance and in particular those relating to the risk should in principle be construed so as to be consistent with the terms of the insurance contract on the basis that the normal commercial intention is that they should be back-to-back.[17] As Lord Mance put it in *Durham v BAI (Run Off) Ltd*[18]:

> "Where two contracts are linked, the law will try to read them consistently with each other."

However, in such a case although the provisions of the other contracts are important and must be considered together with the commercial context, the starting point of the analysis must be the provisions of the contract under consideration itself.[19]

3.09   On the other hand, it is not permissible to read together agreements made between different parties where those agreements are separated by a significant period.[20]

3.10   As is clear, whether or not documents are to be read together may have important legal consequences. In *Samuel v Jarrah Timber and Wood Paving Corp Ltd*,[21] first mortgage debenture stock was mortgaged to secure an advance. The mortgagee was also given an option to buy the stock within 12 months of the arrangement. The House of Lords held that the option was void as being a clog on the equity. Lord Halsbury LC said:

---

[15] [1912] 1 Ch. 735 at 754. This was a dissenting judgment but the decision of the majority was reversed by the House of Lords sub nom. *Whiteley v Delaney* [1914] A.C. 132.

[16] *Bee v Thompson* [2010] Ch. 412.

[17] *Lexington Insurance Co v AGF Insurance Ltd* [2009] UKHL 40.

[18] [2012] UKSC 14; [2012] 1 W.L.R. 867 at [69].

[19] *Temple Legal Protection Ltd v QBE Insurance (Europe) Ltd* [2008] EWHC 843 (Comm).

[20] *Kason Kek-Gardner Ltd v Process Components Ltd* [2017] EWCA Civ 2132; [2018] 2 All E.R. (Comm) 381.

[21] [1904] A.C. 323.

"A perfectly fair bargain made between two parties to it, each of whom was quite sensible of what they were doing, is not to be performed because at the same time a mortgage arrangement was made between them. If a day had intervened between the two parts of the arrangement, the part of the bargain which the appellant claims to be performed would have been perfectly good and capable of being enforced ...".[22]

Contracts of long duration are often varied from time to time. It is undoubtedly   **3.11**
the case that the variations must be read together with the original contract. It is not, however, clear whether in reading the original terms together with the variations the latter may be held to alter the meaning of an original unaltered clause. It seems unlikely that the parties would have wished to alter the meaning of a clause without actually altering its words, although an amendment may show what the parties thought their original contract meant.[23] On the other hand, it may be forcefully argued that having taken the opportunity to review their contract, the parties must be taken to have entered into a new contract on the date of the (last) variation of it.[24] If the latter view is correct, it may also alter the nature of the background that may be considered in construing the contract.[25] Where a clause has itself been amended, the amended clause should be construed in the light of the background knowledge available to the parties at the date of the amendment.[26] Thus where, for instance, a pension scheme is altered by the introduction of a new clause, that clause must be interpreted by reference to the circumstances prevailing at the date of its introduction. In *Stena Line Ltd v Merchant Navy Ratings Pension Fund Trustees Ltd*,[27] Arden LJ said:

"The point under discussion here is the question whether, given that a clause in a trust deed (and, it would follow, a provision in the rules) should be interpreted against the relevant factual background, a clause should be interpreted in the light of the circumstances prevailing at the time of the execution of the trust deed notwithstanding that the clause in question was added later. My answer in the passage just quoted is in the negative. Rather, the circumstances should be those prevailing at the (later) date of the first introduction of the relevant clause. I go on to add that, similarly, the clause must be interpreted in the context of the rest of the deed as it stood at that time."

The principle just described is only a principle of interpretation. It does not mean   **3.12**
that linked documents are to be treated as a single document for the purposes of a substantive rule of law, where that rule requires a single document.[28]

---

[22] It is, however, over-simplified to say that the mere intervention of a day would have validated the option. The real question is whether the two arrangements were part of the same transaction. In *Ford v Stuart* (1852) 15 Beav. 493, four deeds bearing four consecutive dates were held to be sufficiently connected to be read together.

[23] *National Grid Co Plc v Mayes* [2001] 1 W.L.R. 864 at 881A.

[24] In *Groveholt Ltd v Hughes* [2010] EWCA Civ 538 this proposition was said to be "reasonably arguable". See also *St Martin's Property Investments Ltd v Cable & Wireless Plc* [2007] EWHC 582 (Ch).

[25] See *Rembrandt Group Ltd v Philip Morris International Inc* [1999] All E.R. (D) 196.

[26] *Portsmouth City Football Club Ltd v Sellar Properties (Portsmouth) Ltd* [2004] EWCA Civ 760 CA.

[27] [2011] EWCA Civ 543.

[28] *Cherry Tree Investments Ltd v Landmain Ltd* [2012] EWCA Civ 736; [2013] Ch. 305.

Illustrations

1.   A lease contained a discrepancy between the habendum and the reddendum. The court looked at the counterpart to resolve it. Amphlett JA said:

"... the lease and counterpart are really but one document. Formerly they used to be written on one piece of paper or parchment. They are still but one deed and we have a right to look at both to ascertain the construction."

Burchell v Clark[29]

2.   A husband and wife assigned chattels by bill of sale to secure the payment of a debt. By a contemporaneous deed the wife mortgaged a reversionary interest under a will to secure payment of a like sum. The bill of sale was duly registered but the mortgage was not. It was held that the bill of sale and the mortgage had to be read together as part of the same transaction, and the bill of sale was void.
Edwards v Marcus[30]

3.   A man applied for and was allotted profit sharing deposit notes in a company. He applied for them on the strength of a written prospectus. It was held that the notes and the prospectus could be read together as together constituting the contract between the subscribers and the company.
Jacobs v Batavia and General Plantations Trust Ltd[31]

4.   A mortgaged property to B to secure a loan. After B's death his personal representatives called in the loan. A arranged for them to be paid by C who took a transfer of the mortgage. On the same day, A and C entered into an agreement under which C agreed not to call in the loan for two years, and A granted C an option to buy part of the mortgaged property. It was held that the loan and the option were "part and parcel of one transaction" and accordingly the option was void.
Lewis v Love (Frank) Ltd[32]

5.   A landlord granted to a tenant a lease for a term of 16 years, and a reversionary lease for a term of 34 years immediately following. The lease contained a rent review clause. It was held that for the purpose of interpreting the rent review clause, regard could be had to the fact that the two leases were executed as part of a single transaction.
Toyota (GB) Ltd v Legal & General Assurance (Pensions Management) Ltd[33]

6.   Under the terms of the sale of a business, a series of seven leases was granted. One of the leases contained a self-contradictory repairing obligation. By

---

[29]   (1876) 2 C.P.D. 88. See also *Matthews v Smallwood* [1910] 1 Ch. 777.
[30]   [1894] 1 Q.B. 587.
[31]   [1924] 1 Ch. 287 (affirmed [1924] 2 Ch. 329). And in *Re Capital Fire Insurance Association* (1882) 21 Ch. D. 209, a company's memorandum and articles of association were read together, the latter being used to explain the former.
[32]   [1961] 1 W.L.R. 261.
[33]   [1989] 2 E.G.L.R. 123.

comparison between that lease and the other six, the court held that the seventh lease contained an obvious error, which could be corrected as a matter of construction.

Holding & Barnes Plc v Hill House Hammond Ltd (No.1)[34]

4. DELETED WORDS[35]

Despite older authority to the contrary, the court will nowadays often look at words which the parties have deleted from their contract in order to construe the words which remain, although they are an unsafe guide to meaning.

The function of the court is to construe that which has been agreed between the parties; not that which has not been agreed. For this reason the court is not usually prepared to look at negotiations preceding the making of a written contract or a draft of the contract. Sometimes, however, parties do not go to the trouble of re-engrossing a contract after its final draft or the parties may have contracted on the basis of a standard printed form and have simply deleted those clauses which were not to apply. As a matter of principle, it is difficult to see how the court is able to differentiate between a case where the parties have re-engrossed the final version of the contract, and a case where the deletions remain visible on the face of the contract. At one time, this appeared to be the law.

3.13

In *Inglis v Buttery*,[36] the House of Lords held that a deleted sentence in a contract for the overhaul and repair of a ship could not be looked at in construing the agreement. Lord Hatherley said[37]:

3.14

"When I turn to the deleted words and find that in spite of a line being drawn through them I can read the words ... it appears to me that, those words being deleted, and a marginal note affixed shewing that they were deleted before the contract was finally concluded, it is not in the power of any Court to look at words, which have been so dealt with and absolutely taken out of the contract, for any purpose whatever connected with the construction of that contract of which they form no part whatsoever. ... It is to my mind perfectly immaterial whether the instrument was torn up and rewritten, written out again with those words no longer contained in it, or whether the course was taken of running through those words as they stood in writing."

Lord O'Hagan said[38]:

"When those words were removed from the paper which had presented the full contract between the parties, they ceased to exist to all intents and purposes; and whether it was possible, as in point of fact it was, still to read them, in consequence of their simply having a line drawn through them, or whether they had been absolutely obliterated appears to me not to make the smallest difference."

---

[34] [2002] L. & T.R. 7 CA.
[35] This paragraph was referred to with approval in *Gard Marine & Energy Ltd v China National Chartering Co Ltd* [2013] EWHC 2199 (Comm); [2014] 1 Lloyd's Rep. 59.
[36] (1878) 3 App. Cas. 552.
[37] (1878) 3 App. Cas. 552 at 569.
[38] (1878) 3 App. Cas. 552 at 571.

Lord Blackburn agreed, but Lord Gordon did not express an opinion directly on the point. Nevertheless, it is submitted that the proposition that the court is not entitled to have recourse to deleted words as an aid to construction is part of the ratio decidendi of that case.

A similar view was taken by Viscount Sumner, delivering the advice of the Privy Council in *Sassoon (MA) & Sons Ltd v International Banking Corp.*[39] He said:

> "There is a good deal of authority, now old, about the effect of deleting words in a printed form of mercantile contract, which it is not now necessary to cite; but they [i.e. their Lordships] take it to be settled in such a case as this, that the effect is the same as if the deleted words had never formed part of the print at all."

In *Wates Construction (London) v Frantham Property*,[40] Beldam LJ said:

> "It may well be that exceptionally, in the case of a standard form of contract contained in a printed document, the fact that a particular deleted provision may assist in the resolution of an ambiguity in another part of the agreement justifies looking at the deleted part. But I have no doubt that the general rule is that stated by Viscount Sumner, Lord Hatherley and Lord O'Hagan. In any event, even if there may be exceptional cases, in my view, they are of no assistance in construing the agreement in this case."

3.15   Despite the high authority of *Inglis v Buttery* and *Sassoon (MA) & Sons Ltd v International Banking Corp*, the court has on occasion paid attention to deleted portions of drafts in construing concluded contracts.

In *Baumvoll Manufactur von Scheibler v Gilchrest & Co*,[41] Lord Esher MR asserted:

> "We have a right to look at what is written in to the printed form and at what is struck out."

Neither of the other members of the court[42] based themselves on that proposition. However, in *Caffin v Aldridge*,[43] a charterparty was in a printed form, according to which the ship was to load "a full and complete cargo" but the words "full and complete" were struck out. The charterers argued that the natural construction of the remaining word "cargo" was that it meant the full carrying capacity of the ship. An identically constituted Court of Appeal rejected that argument. Lord Esher MR said[44]:

> "In order to see what it meant one must look at the rest of the document. We find that the words 'full and complete' which were in the printed form, had been struck out. The plaintiff's counsel contends that, these words having been deliberately struck out, by necessary implication the Court must put them in again. I cannot agree with him."

---

[39]   [1927] A.C. 711 at 721.
[40]   (1991) 53 B.L.R. 23.
[41]   [1892] 1 Q.B. 253.
[42]   Lopes and Kay LJJ.
[43]   [1895] 2 Q.B. 648.
[44]   [1895] 2 Q.B. 648 at 650.

Lopes LJ agreed, and relied on the deleted words as showing what the parties had not agreed. Kay LJ did not rely on the deleted words. *Inglis v Buttery* was not cited in either case, and accordingly it may be that they were both decided *per incuriam*.

The legitimacy of the approach of the Court of Appeal was doubted by Harman J in *City and Westminster Properties* (1934) Ltd v Mudd,[45] and confined (if legitimate) to commercial cases where the words struck out appear on the face of the signed document.[46] However, in *Louis Dreyfus & Cie v Parnaso Cia Naviera SA*,[47] Diplock J took a different view. He said:

3.16

"Where there is a standard form of words familiar to commercial men and contained in a printed form in general use ... it seems unreal to suppose that when the contracting parties strike out a provision dealing with a specific matter, but retain other provisions, they intend to effect any alteration other than the exclusion of the words struck out. I cannot prima facie, at any rate, ascribe to them any intention of altering the meaning of the words in the provisions which they have chosen to retain. I say 'prima facie' because there may be added or substituted words which drive one to the conclusion that they did intend to ascribe to the words retained a meaning modified by the added or substituted provisions; but while I think that I must first look at the clause in its actual form, without the deleted words, if I find the clause ambiguous, I think that I am entitled to look at the deleted words to see if any assistance can be derived from them in solving the ambiguity, bearing in mind the prima facie rule I have indicated."

A similar approach was adopted by Lord Cross of Chelsea delivering the judgment of the majority of the House of Lords in *Mottram Consultants Ltd v Sunley (Bernard) & Sons Ltd*.[48] He said:

"When the parties use a printed form and delete parts of it one can, in my opinion pay regard to what has been deleted as part of the surrounding circumstances in the light of which one must construe what they have chosen to leave in."

So too in *Timber Shipping Co SA v London & Overseas Freighters Ltd*,[49] Lord Reid said (obiter):

"There is a controversy as to whether one can ever look at deleted words in an agreement. If the words were first inserted by the draftsman of the agreement and then deleted before signature then I have no doubt that they must not be considered in construing the agreement. They are in the same position as any other preliminary suggestion put forward and rejected before the final agreement was made. But it appears to me that striking out words in a printed form is

---

[45] [1959] Ch. 129.
[46] It is difficult to see why "commercial" contracts should be singled out for special treatment. A contract made on a printed form might be treated differently for pragmatic reasons, but such contracts are only a sub-species of the genus "commercial" contract. This observation was approved in *Mopani Copper Mines Plc v Millennium Underwriting Ltd* [2008] EWHC 1331 (Comm); [2008] Bus. L.R. D121.
[47] [1959] 1 Q.B. 498 at 513.
[48] [1975] 2 Lloyd's Rep. 197 at 209.
[49] [1972] A.C. 1 at 15; observations described as "highly persuasive" by Bingham J in *Ben Shipping Co (Pte) Ltd v An Bord Bainne (The C Joyce)* [1986] 2 Lloyd's Rep. 285 at 291.

quite a different matter. The process of adapting a printed form to make it express the parties' intentions requires two things to be done. Those parts which are not to be part of the agreement are struck out and the words are inserted to complete the rest of the form so as to express the agreement. There is no inference that in striking out words the parties had second thoughts; the words struck out were never put there by the parties or any of them or by their draftsman."

Inglis v Buttery was apparently not cited in either case.

3.17   Lord Reid was using the fact of deletion as an aid to construction. In *Punjab National Bank v de Boinville*,[50] Staughton LJ said:

"It is a different process to that of Diplock J who used the deleted words as a guide to the meaning of similar words elsewhere. ... The fact of deletion shows what the parties did not want in their agreement. No doubt one may on occasion still find the same term elsewhere, as a matter of construction or implication. But there is at least a prima facie indication that it was not required."

The formulation expressed by Diplock J[51] is, however, restrictive in its scope. Firstly, it applies only to a contract in a standard form in general use. It would not, therefore, apply to a one-off contract (such as that considered in *Inglis v Buttery*). However, it appears that the bill of exchange considered by the Privy Council in *Sassoon & Sons Ltd v International Banking Corp* was in a standard printed form. Secondly, the deleted words may only be looked at if the remaining words of the contract produce an ambiguity. The second limb is not supported by the speeches in *Inglis v Buttery* or *Sassoon and Sons Ltd v International Banking Corp*. It is submitted that despite the narrow formulation of the judge's approach it is irreconcilable with the two cases last mentioned. The authorities were cited to Bingham J in *The C Joyce*.[52] He concluded that he was not entitled to look at the deleted terms of a bill of lading, although it was on a standard printed form.

3.18   More recently, the courts have adopted a more liberal approach. In *Team Services Plc v Kier Management and Design Ltd*,[53] Lloyd LJ said:

"One-off contracts are often composed of ready-made clauses taken from one or more sources, together with ad hoc clauses drafted afresh for the purpose of the particular contract. I can see no difference in principle between looking at a deletion in a printed form of contract, and looking at a deletion in a printed form of clause included in a one-off contract."

That case concerned an omission from the printed form rather than a visible deletion. Lloyd LJ said:

"Then comes the question whether there is a difference between a deletion and an omission. I can see no sense in such a distinction. What difference can it make whether the parties incorporated clause 11(b) in their contract by means of scissors and paste and then deleted [the words], or whether they omitted the words

---

[50] [1992] 1 W.L.R. 1138.
[51] Which seems to represent the current practice of one "school of thought" in the Commercial Court: see *The Golden Leader* [1980] 2 Lloyd's Rep. 573 at 575, per Lloyd J.
[52] [1986] 2 Lloyd's Rep. 285.
[53] (1993) 63 B.L.R. 76 CA, Hoffmann LJ dissenting.

when retyping the clause without physical incorporation? Of course, it would be necessary to show that the omission was deliberate. But if the court is satisfied as to that, then the omission is as much a surrounding circumstance as a deletion."[54]

In *Jefco Mechanical Services Ltd v Lambeth LBC*,[55] Slade LJ accepted that it was, in principle, open to the court in an appropriate case to deduce parties' intentions from deletions in a standard form of contract but derived no assistance from the adoption of one formula in a standard form rather than another one. In *Bovis Lend Lease Ltd v Cofely Engineering Services*,[56] Coulson J held that when construing construction contracts, deletions and amendments to standard form terms are a legitimate tool to aid interpretation.

In *Mopani Copper Mines Plc v Millennium Underwriting Ltd*,[57] which contains a full review of the authorities, Christopher Clarke J concluded: **3.19**

"The diversity of authority, of which Diplock J spoke, renders it difficult for a judge of first instance to recognise when recourse to deleted words may properly be made. The tenor of the authorities appears to be that in general such recourse is illegitimate, save that (a) deleted words in a printed form may resolve the ambiguity of a neighbouring paragraph that remains; and (b) the deletion of words in a contractual document may be taken into account, for what (if anything) it is worth, if the fact of deletion shows what it is the parties agreed that they did not agree and there is ambiguity in the words that remain. This is classically the case in relation to printed forms ... or clauses derived from printed forms ..., but can also apply where no printed form is involved."

In *Narandas-Girdhar v Bradstock*[58] the Court of Appeal approved the decision in *Mopani Copper Mines Plc v Millennium Underwriting Ltd*. Briggs LJ said:

"For present purposes, the relevant principle is that if the fact of deletion shows what it is the parties agreed that they did not agree and there is ambiguity in the words that remain, then the deleted provision may be an aid to construction, albeit one that must be used with care."

Where a contract has been varied by agreement, the court is able to look at the contract both before and after the variation.[59] In *Punjab National Bank v de Boinville*,[60] Staughton LJ said: **3.20**

---

[54] However, in the first place this approach appears to let in evidence of the negotiations in order to interpret the contract, which is generally impermissible. Second, as Lloyd J himself pointed out in *The Golden Leader* [1980] 2 Lloyd's Rep. 573 parties may have all sorts of reasons for omitting a clause.
[55] (1983) 24 B.L.R. 1 at 8.
[56] [2009] EWHC 1120 (TCC).
[57] [2008] EWHC 1331 (Comm); [2008] Bus. L.R. D121. In *Ted Baker Plc v Axa Insurance UK Plc* [2012] EWHC 1406 (Comm), Eder J agreed with the analysis in *Mopani Copper Mines*.
[58] [2016] EWCA Civ 88; [2016] 1 W.L.R. 2366. See also *J. Murphy & Sons Ltd v Beckton Energy Ltd* [2016] EWHC 607 (TCC); [2016] B.L.R. 448; *Commercial Management (Investments) Ltd v Mitchell Design & Construct Ltd* [2016] EWHC 76 (TCC); 164 Con. L.R. 139.
[59] *Trasimex Holding SA v Addax BV (The Red Sea)* [1997] 1 Lloyd's Rep. 610. See also *HIH Casualty and General Insurance Ltd v New Hampshire Insurance Co* [2001] 2 Lloyd's Rep. 161 and para.3.23.
[60] [1992] 1 W.L.R. 1138 at 1148, CA.

"… if the parties to a concluded contract subsequently agree in express terms that some words in it are to be replaced by others, one can have regard to all aspects of the subsequent agreement, in construing the contract, including the deletions, even in a case which is not, or not wholly, concerned with a printed form."

But where the parties have made a contract and then enter into a subsequent contract with the deletion of part of the antecedent contract, the court must be even more cautious about drawing any inference from the fact of the deletion.[61]

3.21   The assistance to be gained from deleted words must necessarily be limited. In *The Golden Leader*,[62] Lloyd J said:

"… the use of a word or phrase in the deleted part of the clause may throw light on the meaning of the same word or phrase in what remains of the clause. … But it seems to me quite another thing to say that the deletion itself has any contractual significance; or that by deleting a provision in a contract the parties must be deemed to have agreed the converse. The parties may have had all sorts of reasons for deleting the provision; they may have thought it unnecessary; they may have thought it inconsistent with some other provision in the contract; it may even have been deleted by mistake."

At best, the consideration of deleted words may negative the implication of a term in form of the deleted words.[63] Even in the cases where the fact of deletion is admissible as an aid to interpretation, there is a great difference between a case where a self-contained provision is simply deleted and another case where a draft is amended and effectively re-cast. It is one thing to say that the deletion of a term which provides for "X" is suggestive that the parties were agreeing on "not X"; it is altogether a different thing where the structure of the draft is changed so that one provision is replaced by another provision. Further, where the first provision contains a number of ingredients, some assisting one party and some assisting the other, and that provision is removed, it by no means follows that the parties intended to agree the converse of each of the ingredients in the earlier provision.[64]

In *Bou-Simon v BGC Brokers LP*,[65] Asplin and Singh LJJ discussed (obiter) the admissibility of deleted words for the purpose of negativing a suggested implied term. Asplin LJ was rather more sceptical than Singh LJ about the admissibility of such material. Not surprisingly, the author agrees with Singh LJ that there is:

"force in the suggestion made in Lewison, *The Interpretation of Contracts* (6th ed.,) at p.96, that 'the consideration of deleted words may negative the implication of a term in the form of deleted words'. This is because what would be admitted in that scenario is the fact that the same words which it is now argued should be implied into a contract had been deleted by the parties. It seems to me that fact could well have a bearing on the question whether the test for implica-

---

[61] *Bou-Simon v BGC Brokers LP* [2018] EWCA Civ 1525; 179 Con. L.R. 32; *Health & Case Management Ltd v The Physiotherapy Network Ltd* [2018] EWHC 869 (QB).
[62] [1980] 2 Lloyd's Rep. 573 at 575.
[63] See *Codelfa Construction Pty Ltd v State Rail Authority of New South Wales* (1982) 149 C.L.R. 337 at 352, per Mason J. This was in fact the result in *Caffin v Aldridge* [1895] 2 Q.B. 648 (above).
[64] *Berkeley Community Villages Ltd v Pullen* [2007] EWHC 1330 (Ch), per Morgan J, approved on this point in *Narandas-Girdhar v Bradstock* [2016] EWCA Civ 88; [2016] 1 W.L.R. 2366.
[65] [2018] EWCA Civ 1525; 179 Con. L.R. 32.

tion of a term into a contract has been met. That fact would not be admitted in order to construe the express terms which eventually found their way into the final version of the contract."

Even where there is a simple deletion of a clause it is considered that the explanation given by Lloyd J points powerfully to the conclusion that a consideration of deleted words is an unsafe guide to the meaning of a contract.[66]   **3.22**

In *Mopani Copper Mines Plc v Millennium Underwriting Ltd*,[67] Christopher Clarke J added:

"Even if recourse is had to the deleted words, care must be taken as to what inferences, if any, can properly be drawn from them. The parties may have deleted the words because they thought they added nothing to, or were inconsistent with, what was already contained in the document; or because the words that were left were the only common denominator of agreement, or for unfathomable reasons or by mistake. They may have had different ideas as to what the words meant and whether or not the words that remained achieved their respective purposes."

Illustrations

1.   A deed of partnership provided that on dissolution of the partnership the sum to be paid for an outgoing partner's share was to be a sum of money equal to the share of the outgoing partner "in the net profits arising from the said business" during a certain period. The word "net" was deleted. In an arbitration the arbitrator ruled that he was entitled to take into account in construing the deed the alteration which appeared on its face. The Divisional Court held that he was wrong.
   Re Duncan and Pryce[68]

2.   A charterparty was made, based on a printed form, part of which had been deleted. Collins MR said:

"I find in the printed form upon which these persons are working, a provision which would have carried out that which is the now contention of the shipowners, namely a contract for a lump freight. I find these words 'for the full reaches and burden of the steamer's hold and every available space the lump sum of' so much. All that is scratched out and what is left in is the alternative form, which indicates freight in the ordinary way. So it was not a mere case ... of a contract written out on a blank sheet of paper; but it was a deliberate deletion of that part of the printed contract which would have formed the obligation which the shipowners now set up."

London Transport Co Ltd v Trechmann Brothers[69]

---

[66]   This passage in the previous edition of this book was approved by the CA in *Rhodia Chirex Ltd v Laker Vent Engineering Ltd* [2004] B.L.R. 75, where Auld LJ doubted whether deleted words should be looked at to interpret a contract, except to the limited extent mentioned. On the facts, recourse to the deleted words did not help.

[67]   [2008] Bus. L.R. D121.

[68]   [1913] W.N. 117.

[69]   [1904] 1 K.B. 635.

5.   ANTECEDENT AGREEMENTS

A concluded antecedent agreement may be relied upon in interpreting a later instrument made pursuant to the agreement.[70]

3.23   Where a transaction is effected by deed, it is traditionally said that a contract which preceded the deed cannot be relied on as an aid to interpreting the deed. In *Leggott v Barrett*,[71] Brett LJ said:

> "... where there is a preliminary contract in words which is afterwards reduced into writing, or where there is a preliminary contract in writing which is afterwards reduced into a deed, the rights of the parties are governed in the first case entirely by the writing, and in the second case entirely by the deed; and if there be any difference between the words and the written document in the first case, or between the written agreement and the deed in the other case, the rights of the parties are entirely governed by the superior document and by the governing part of that document."

This is a branch of the parol evidence rule,[72] and is also related to the principle of construction that a contract merges in a conveyance on completion. But the latter is not a rule of law but a principle of interpretation, and will therefore yield to any contrary intention of the parties. In order to ascertain that intention, the court examines the antecedent agreement. Accordingly, the antecedent agreement is admitted in evidence. Even if, logically, it is not permitted to take account of it in interpreting the later instrument, it is unlikely that the court will remain wholly uninfluenced by it.

Moreover, where the contract is recited in the deed (as many are) then it is permissible to look at the contract for the purpose of interpreting the deed, although not for the purpose of enlarging, diminishing or modifying its terms.[73]

3.24   The traditional approach is no longer the law. Nowadays the court does not adopt a narrowly restrictive approach to a preliminary agreement in the light of the decisions of the House of Lords in *Prenn v Simmonds*[74] and *Reardon Smith Line Ltd v Hansen-Tangen*.[75] In the former case, the rationale of excluding negotiations was that no consensus had then been reached. This objection is not open in the case of reference to an antecedent agreement. In the latter case it was said that the court should be placed in thought in the same factual matrix as that in which the parties were when they made their agreement. If they had already reached an agreement, that would have been one objective fact which would have been known to both of them, and ought therefore to be admissible in evidence.[76] This principle also ap-

---

[70]   This section was approved in *Enterprise Inns Plc v Palmerston Associates Ltd* [2011] EWHC 3165 (Ch); *Grainmarket Asset Management LLP v PGF II SA* [2013] EWHC 1879 (Ch); *Cape Distribution Ltd v Cape Intermediate Holdings Plc* [2016] EWHC 1119 (QB); [2016] Lloyd's Rep. I.R. 499.

[71]   (1880) 15 Ch. D. 306.

[72]   See para.3.87.

[73]   *Leggott v Barrett* (1880) 15 Ch. D. 306, per James LJ. A contrary view was expressed by Cozens Hardy MR in *Millbourn v Lyons* [1914] 2 Ch. 231, but it is thought that the court would be readier to allow a prior agreement to be admitted in evidence nowadays. See further paras 10.26–10.53.

[74]   [1971] 1 W.L.R. 1381.

[75]   *Reardon Smith Line Ltd v Hansen-Tangen (The Diana Prosperity)* [1976] 1 W.L.R. 989. *Mawdsley's WI Inc v Mawdsley's GNS Ltd* [2007] EWHC 501 (Ch).

[76]   *Multiplex Constructions (UK) Ltd v Cleveland Bridge UK Ltd* [2007] 111 Con. L.R. 48.

plies to an agreed draft. So in *Ladbroke Group Plc v Bristol City Council*,[77] a lease was granted pursuant to an agreement for lease which annexed the agreed form of draft. The lease as executed gave rise to a difficulty of construction, and in order to resolve it the court looked at the draft lease annexed to the agreement. So also in *Squarey v Harris-Smith*,[78] where it was alleged that a conveyance carried with it an implied right of way, the court looked at the contract pursuant to which the conveyance was executed in order to rebut the implication. In *Crown Estates Commissioners v Roberts*,[79] an auction memorandum was used as an aid to interpreting a conveyance giving effect to the auction contract recorded in the memorandum.[80] And in *Peacock v Custins*,[81] the Court of Appeal looked at the contract which a conveyance was intended to implement (but not a statement made by the auctioneer) in order to determine the extent of a right of way.

In *Re BCA Pension Plan*[82] Snowden J said: **3.25**

"It is also clear that earlier contractual documents (but not drafts produced in negotiation) can be used as part of the background to the construction of later documents."[83]

In *KPMG LLP v Network Rail Infrastructure Ltd*,[84] the Court of Appeal looked at an agreed draft lease annexed to an agreement for lease in interpreting the completed document. Carnwath LJ said:

"In my view, the 1974 agreement, including the form and content of the draft lease attached to it, was an important part of the background and is a permissible aid in the construction of the lease in its final form."

Where the relevant terms of the two agreements are the same the background to the earlier agreement may be influential.[85]

In *St Ivel Ltd v Wincanton Group Ltd*,[86] the Court of Appeal reaffirmed that an antecedent agreement may be relied on in interpreting a later agreement. In *Electrosteel Castings Ltd v Scan-Trans Shipping & Chartering Sdn Bhd*,[87] Gross J held that the court could consider both a booking note and a recap telex, both of which had contractual force, in determining the meaning of the ultimate formal contract contained in a charterparty. In the realm of maritime disputes there are no technical evidential rules which preclude reference to fixture recaps when seeking to resolve ambiguities in the later, formal charterparties. However, the judge said that this applied only to antecedent agreements, and did not apply to pre-contractual negotiations.

But, although antecedent agreements are admissible, judges often say that they   **3.26**

---

[77] [1988] 1 E.G.L.R. 126.
[78] (1981) 42 P. & C.R. 118, CA.
[79] [2008] 2 E.G.L.R. 165.
[80] See also *Westvilla Properties Ltd v Dow Properties Ltd* [2010] EWHC 30 (Ch).
[81] [2001] 1 E.G.L.R. 87.
[82] [2015] EWHC 3492 (Ch); [2016] 4 W.L.R. 5.
[83] *Health & Case Management Ltd v The Physiotherapy Network Ltd* [2018] EWHC 869 (QB).
[84] [2007] EWCA Civ 363.
[85] *Grainmarket Asset Management LLP v PGF II SA* [2013] EWHC 1879 (Ch).
[86] [2008] EWCA Civ 1286.
[87] [2003] 1 Lloyd's Rep. 190.

are of little practical help.[88] In *Enterprise Inns Plc v Palmerston Associates Ltd*,[89] Morgan J said:

> "To say that the earlier terms are admissible as a potential aid to construction of the 2001 Deed is not to say that a consideration of the earlier terms will be helpful, much less decisive. In fact, in this case, I do not find that a consideration of the earlier terms, which were later superseded, provides any real help. The principal reason for this is that the same, or similar, arguments would have arisen in relation to the earlier terms as now need to be considered in relation to the current terms."

3.27 However, in *Glenmere Plc v F Stokes & Sons Ltd*,[90] the court ruled that heads of terms were inadmissible as being part of the parties' negotiations. It is not entirely clear from the judgment, but it may be that they were inadmissible because they had not been agreed by both parties, but merely prepared by one side. If they were agreed heads of terms, it is thought that they ought in principle to have been admissible as recording the genesis of the transaction. In *Matchbet Ltd v Openbet Retail Ltd*,[91] Henderson J held that non-contractual heads of terms were not admissible in interpreting a subsequent agreement; and to the extent that the heads of terms were contractually binding, they were also irrelevant to interpretation of the subsequent agreement because the subsequent agreement contained an entire agreement clause.

3.28 Where a contract expressly purports to vary another contract, there can be no reason for excluding the varied contract from consideration. In such a case the parties can be taken to have had the common intention that the contract as varied should not mean the same as the contract before the variation. Consequently, the case is far stronger than that of looking at words deleted from printed forms, for in the case of a variation there are two expressions of common intention to which to appeal. Since it may be assumed that each expression bears a different meaning, valuable light and shade may throw a problem of construction into sharper relief. Thus in *Punjab National Bank v de Boinville*,[92] Staughton LJ said:

> "… if the parties to a concluded contract subsequently agree in express terms that some words in it are to be replaced by others, one can have regard to all aspects of the subsequent agreement in construing the contract, including the deletions, even in a case which is not, or is not wholly, concerned with a printed form."

3.29 In *HIH Casualty and General Insurance Ltd v New Hampshire Insurance Co*,[93] Rix LJ said:

> "In principle it would seem to me that it is always admissible to look at prior *contracts* as part of the matrix or surrounding circumstances of a later contract.

---

[88] *Barnardo's v Buckinghamshire* [2016] EWCA Civ 1064; *National Bank of Abu Dhabi PJSC v BP Oil International Ltd* [2016] EWHC 2892 (Comm); *British Telecommunications Plc v BT Pension Scheme Trustees Ltd* [2018] EWHC 69 (Ch); [2018] Pens. L.R. 7.

[89] [2011] EWHC 3165 (Ch); *Grainmarket Asset Management LLP v PGF II SA* [2013] EWHC 1879 (Ch).

[90] [2008] All E.R. (D) 92 (Jan).

[91] [2013] EWHC 3067.

[92] [1992] 1 W.L.R. 1138 at 1149, CA.

[93] [2001] 2 Lloyd's Rep. 161, followed in *Standard Life Assurance Ltd v Oak Dedicated Ltd* [2008] 1 C.L.C. 59; *Hageman v Holmes* [2009] EWHC 50 (Ch).

I do not see how the parol evidence rule can exclude prior contracts, as distinct from mere negotiations. The difficulty of course is that, where the later contract is intended to *supersede* the prior contract, it may in the generality of cases simply be useless to try to construe the later contract by reference to the earlier one. ...

Where, however, it is not even common ground that the later contract is intended to supersede the earlier contract, I do not see how it can ever be permissible to exclude reference to the earlier contract."

But as Stadlen J pointed out in *Giedo Van Der Garde BV v Force India Formula One Team Ltd*[94]:

"I would however observe that Rix LJ was at pains to emphasise that even if a prior written agreement is, as he held to be the case, admissible for the purpose of construing a later one its usefulness as an aid to construction is likely to be limited in most cases. Where the language in the two documents is identical, the former is unlikely to add anything to the exercise of construing the latter. If the wording in the later contract is different the prima facie influence is that the difference is a deliberate decision to depart from the earlier wording which thus provides no assistance. Hence his emphasis for the need for a cautious and sceptical approach to finding any assistance in the earlier contract."

Sometimes a change in language as between an earlier contract and a later one **3.30** will be significant. In *Thorney Park Golf Ltd v Myers Catering Ltd*,[95] a contract for the provision of catering services was terminable on notice. It was replaced by a contract which stated that "an initial three-year term" must be agreed. A later clause in the agreement provided for termination by notice. The Court of Appeal held that notice could not be given during the initial three-year term. McCombe LJ said:

"The argument is also inconsistent with the significant point that the parties clearly intended a change from the previous agreement operated at the Club. It is clear to me that the terms in which that change is expressed shows that it was to go beyond the mere change of the notice period from three months to four months. They expressly stated that they wanted (what amounted to a change from past) a fixed initial term in order to make the new contract 'reasonable' and to enable them to develop and invest in a viable business plan. In such circumstances, in my view, to focus upon the syntax of cl 6 gives too much force to one clause at the expense of the commercial sense of the Agreement as a whole."

6.   PUBLISHED PRECEDENTS

Where a clause in a contract is taken from a published precedent known to both parties the precedent may be relied on as an aid to interpretation.[96]

In *Bogg v Raper*,[97] Millett LJ said: **3.31**

---

[94]   [2010] EWHC 2373 (QB) at [161].
[95]   [2015] EWCA Civ 19.
[96]   This section was referred to with apparent approval in *The Bank of New York Mellon (London Branch) v Truvo NV* [2013] EWHC 136 (Comm).
[97]   [1998] 1 I.T.E.L.R. 267.

"I reached this conclusion before I discovered the source of the clause and without the assistance of the precedents to which I have referred. My conclusion is, however, fortified by the evidence of those precedents, which provide material on which the Court can take notice when construing a legal document: see *Re Follett dec.*[98] It is gratifying that what appears to have been merely a clerical error in transcription has not affected the meaning to be ascribed to the clause."

Accordingly, if a draft agreement is a standard printed form, then the court may look at the standard form draft as part of the surrounding circumstances, although the weight to be given to the draft may differ according to the nature of the contract.[99] Thus in *The Starsin*,[100] words in a bill of lading were supplied by reference to the Conline bill of lading on which the clause in the contract was "closely modelled" and which had been omitted by a copyist's error.

3.32   This approach cannot be carried too far. The court should not, for instance, enter into detailed comparisons between earlier and later versions of a standard form. As Moore-Bick LJ explained in *Seadrill Management Services Ltd v OAO Gazprom*[101]:

"In cases where it is possible to identify with a degree of confidence the reason for a particular amendment to a standard form, for example, where a change has been made to respond to the effect of a particular decision of the courts, a change in legislation or a widely publicised event, that may be appropriate. Such cases are usually well-known within the industry and are often documented in the trade press. Both parties are therefore likely to be aware of them. I am doubtful, however, whether it is legitimate simply to compare the earlier and later versions of the contract form on the assumption that the parties consciously intended to achieve a particular result by adopting the later version. Such an exercise is not wholly removed from that of referring to drafts produced during the course of negotiations, which are not a proper aid to construction. The earlier version does, of course, serve as an example of how the contract could have been worded differently, but in that respect it has no greater persuasive force than a text created for the purposes of the trial. The fact is that in the present case we have no evidence of why specific changes were made, nor any evidence that the parties turned their minds to the differences between the two forms and there must be a real likelihood that they simply reached for the current form without any consideration of the earlier version. In any event, times have moved on and one cannot assume that the commercial background has not moved with them. In my view the right course when seeking to ascertain the intention of the parties is to consider this contract on its own terms against the commercial background as it existed at the time it was made."

Although there may be occasions when previous versions of a standard form may be looked at in order to resolve ambiguities, in general the archaeology of forms is

---

[98]   [1954] 1 W.L.R. 1430 (reversed on the evidential value of the material which was available at [1955] 1 W.L.R. 429).

[99]   See *Fraser v Canterbury Diocesan Board of Finance (No.2)* [2003] W.T.L.R. 1125.

[100]   [2004] 1 A.C. 715.

[101]   [2010] EWCA Civ 691.

discouraged because it makes the task of interpretation over-elaborate and adds to the time and expense of litigation.[102]

In addition it has been said that the court will only have regard to a published precedent where the published precedent is known to both parties. In *Company Developments (Finance) Ltd v Coffee Club Restaurants Ltd*,[103] Lloyd LJ said: **3.33**

> "We know in fact that Butterworths precedent provided, directly or indirectly, the basis for the drafting of the lease, so it may be possible to infer that the landlord's solicitors, who will have prepared the first draft, are likely to have used either the draft precedent itself or their own office adaptation of it or a previous lease derived directly or indirectly from it as the basis for working out and formulating the draft lease to be put to the tenant in this case. Which of those possibilities applied we do not know. Equally we do not know whether the tenant's solicitor was equally familiar with this precedent. It is possible that both solicitors knew that this was the source. It is equally possible that neither of them did or that only one of them did. It does not seem to me that we can properly assume, without evidence on the point—and there was none—that the provenance of the draft from this precedent and therefore the provenance of the actual lease from this precedent was a fact known to both parties. Accordingly, despite the judge's understandable reference to it in the absence of any objection before him and despite the known direct or indirect derivation from the precedent, for my part I would disregard it in construing the lease."[104]

On the other hand, in *TRW Steering Systems Ltd v North Cape Properties Ltd*,[105] a conveyance contained a covenant by the purchaser to observe and perform encumbrances "so far as the same affect the Property". Precedent books showed that these words were used by conveyancers in a context which included positive as well as restrictive covenants. It was held that the words should be given that meaning in the conveyance. Whether the parties to the conveyance knew of the existence of those precedents was not explored. Equally the courts have corrected mistakes in written instruments where the actual instrument imperfectly followed a well-known form, even though the parties' knowledge of the form in question had not been established.[106] **3.34**

7. DRAFT AGREEMENTS

A draft agreement which does not represent the final consensus between the parties is not generally taken into account in interpreting the concluded agreement.[107]

---

[102] *Polestar Maritime Ltd v YHM Shipping Co Ltd* [2012] EWCA Civ 153; [2012] 1 Lloyd's Rep. 510.

[103] [2011] EWCA Civ 766.

[104] It might, however, be argued that even if not a fact known to both parties, a published precedent may have been "reasonably available" to the parties. See also para.4.78.

[105] (1993) 69 P. & C.R. 265 CA.

[106] See *Re Hargraves' Trusts* [1937] 2 All E.R. 545, referred to in para.9.21.

[107] This section was referred to with approval in *Bank St Petersburg v Savelyev* [2013] EWHC 3529 (Ch).

3.35   In the case of drafts, which do not represent a final consensus, the common law is clear. Evidence of drafts is inadmissible.[108] In *National Bank of Australasia v Falkingham & Sons*,[109] Lord Lindley, delivering the advice of the Privy Council, said:

> "Drafts of this deed were prepared, and objections were made to them as prepared; but ultimately the deed as printed in the record was executed. ... No claim is made to rectify this deed. The drafts cannot therefore properly be received in evidence to alter its language; still less to explain or assist in the interpretation of the deed as finally executed."

3.36   The same principle applies to contracts which are not under seal, and also to voluntary settlements. For the same reason that a draft is not admissible in interpreting a contract, so the opinion of counsel who settled the draft is inadmissible.[110]

However, if the draft is a standard printed form, then the court may look at the standard form draft as part of the surrounding circumstances, although the weight to be given to the draft may differ according to the nature of the contract.[111] This seems consistent with the willingness of the court to look at deletions from standard form contracts.

3.37   Similarly, if the draft represents the final consensus (as in the case of an agreed draft lease annexed to an agreement for lease) the court may look at the agreed draft.[112]

In *Tucker v Gold Fields Mining LLC*,[113] the Court of Appeal held that formal proposals for a creditors' voluntary arrangement could be taken into account in interpreting the final form of CVA as approved by the creditors of an insolvent company.

8.   EXPLANATORY NOTES

The court may take into account published explanatory notes in interpreting the contract that they are intended to explain.

3.38   In *Investors Compensation Scheme v West Bromwich Building Society*,[114] deficiencies in the drafting of the contract were solved partly by reference to the explanatory notes that accompanied the contract. Lord Hoffmann said:

> "First, the claim form was obviously intended to be read by lawyers and the explanatory note by laymen. It is the terms of the claim form which govern the legal relationship between the parties. But in construing the form, I think that one

---

[108] *Lola Cars International Ltd v Dunn* [2004] EWHC 2616 (Ch).

[109] [1902] A.C. 585.

[110] *Rabin v Gerson Berger Association Ltd* [1986] 1 W.L.R. 526. However, since the court will look at explanatory notes which accompany a contract, this may require reconsideration.

[111] See *Fraser v Canterbury Diocesan Board of Finance (No.2)* [2003] W.T.L.R. 1125; and para.3.23.

[112] *KPMG LLP v Network Rail Infrastructure Ltd* [2007] EWCA Civ 363.

[113] [2009] 1 B.C.L.C. 567.

[114] [1998] 1 W.L.R. 896.

should start with the assumption that a layman who read the explanatory note and did not venture into the claim form itself was being given an accurate account of the effect of the transaction."

This is not new. Thus where investors applied to subscribe to an investment scheme described in a brochure, the brochure was admissible to construe the contract.[115] Similarly, a standard form of engineering contract was construed in the light of Guidance Notes supplied in order to assist in its drafting,[116] and explanatory notes were considered in interpreting an agreement between the Motor Insurers' Bureau and the Secretary of State.[117] However, the Court of Appeal has also held that it was uncertain whether a practice note issued by the JCT to explain amendments to the JCT form of Agreement for Minor Works was admissible to interpret its operative provisions; but that even if it was it was not helpful.[118]

3.39

In *Global Maritime Investments Ltd v STX Pan Ocean Co Ltd*,[119] Christopher Clarke J in interpreting a clause in a charterparty drafted by the Documentary Committee of The Baltic and International Maritime Council took into account a circular issued by the Committee explaining the thinking behind the clause. In *Pacific Basin IHX Ltd v Bulkhandling Handymax A/S*,[120] Teare J took a similar approach.

3.40

In *Lehman Brothers International (Europe) v Lehman Brothers Finance SA*,[121] the court took into account a published User Guide in interpreting the Master Agreement issued by the International Swap Dealers Association which explained the reason for changes in a revised version of the agreement. In *Lomas v Burlington Loan Management Ltd*,[122] the court took into account a "Readers' Guide" supplied by Lehman Brothers' administrators to potential creditors who entered into a claims resolution agreement, although David Richards J stressed the fact that administrators' statutory duties as regards all creditors differentiated the agreement from an ordinary commercial agreement. In *AIG Europe Ltd v OC320301 LLP*[123] the Court of Appeal considered the terms of a professional indemnity insurance policy applicable to all solicitors. In so doing they took into account a publication in the Law Society Gazette in which the Law Society explained the rationale for changes being made to the standard form of policy.

In *MPloy Group Ltd v Denso Manufacturing UK Ltd*,[124] it was held that DTI guidance on the operation of certain regulations formed part of the admissible background.

In *Starbev GP Ltd v Interbrew Central European Holdings BV*,[125] Blair J held that

---

[115] *R. v Clowes (No.2)* [1994] 2 All E.R. 316 CA.
[116] *Matthew Hall Ortech Ltd v Tarmac Roadstone Ltd* (1997) 87 B.L.R. 96.
[117] *Phillips v Rafiq* [2007] 1 W.L.R. 1351.
[118] *TFW Printers Ltd v Interserve Project Services Ltd* (2006) 109 Con. L.R. 1. It is thought that in principle explanatory notes ought to be admissible.
[119] [2012] EWHC 2339 (Comm); [2012] 2 Lloyd's Rep. 354.
[120] [2011] EWHC 2862 (Comm); [2012] 1 Lloyd's Rep. 151.
[121] [2013] EWCA Civ 188. It was followed by Andrews J in *Greenclose Ltd v National Westminster Bank Plc* [2014] EWHC 1156 (Ch); and by Knowles J in *Lehman Brothers Special Financing Inc v National Power Corporation* [2018] EWHC 487 (Comm); [2019] 3 All E.R. 53.
[122] [2015] EWHC 2270.
[123] [2016] EWCA Civ 367, reversed on a different point sub nom *AIG Europe Ltd v Woodman* [2017] UKSC 18; [2017] 1 W.L.R. 1168.
[124] [2014] EWHC 2992 (Comm).
[125] [2014] EWHC 1311 (Comm).

a worked example in a contract should be treated in the same way as explanatory notes.

In *The State of the Netherlands v Deutsche Bank AG*[126] the Court of Appeal considered that the available background included not only the ISDA User Guide at the date of the contract, but also one that post-dated it.[127]

But in *The Arundel Castle*[128] Knowles J declined to take into account a definition of "port" contained in Laytime Definitions for Charterparties which the parties had not incorporated into their charterparty. In *Yuanda (UK) Co Ltd v Multiplex Construction Europe Ltd*[129] Fraser J declined to take into account guidance notes published by the Association of British Insurers about the interpretation of a model form of guarantee bond. First, he held that to do so would "come perilously close to construing the words in the Guarantee by using the subjective intentions of one of the parties". Secondly, he said that the form of the clause in question was not the same as that in the model form. It is thought that the second reason is stronger than the first.

3.41   Explanatory notes will not usually override the plain meaning of the contract[130]; in many cases, especially those concerning pension schemes, an explanatory booklet will often contain a statement that in case of conflict the terms of the formal documents prevail. In such a case reliance on the explanatory booklet is unlikely to give rise to an estoppel.[131]

In *CA Blackwell (Contractors) Ltd v Gerling Allegemeine Verischerungs-AG*,[132] the court considered the scope of an exclusion clause in an insurance policy. One party referred to a report by the Advanced Study Group of the Institute of Insurance which gave the history of such clauses. Tuckey LJ said:

> "This report is instructive about the purpose of defect exclusion clauses and how they have evolved. But it cannot be used as an aid to construction of the clause in question which must be construed according to its terms. The intention of those who drafted it and other similar clauses is not relevant or admissible."

3.42   Explanatory notes must also be distinguished from the parties' subjective declarations of intent, which are inadmissible.[133] As Rimer LJ put it in *Young v Brooks*[134]:

> "Although the task of the court is to ascertain the intentions of the parties as expressed in the language in which they have chosen to frame the grant, the one area of evidence that is wholly inadmissible for that purpose is the direct evidence of what the parties, or either of them, actually intended by it. That is not part of the admissible background evidence and such evidence is admissible only in a

---

[126] [2019] EWCA Civ 771.
[127] [2019] EWCA Civ 771.
[128] [2017] EWHC 116 (Comm); [2017] 1 Lloyd's Rep 370.
[129] [2020] EWHC 468 (TCC).
[130] *Phillips v Rafiq* [2007] 1 W.L.R. 1351.
[131] *Steria Ltd v Hutchison* [2007] I.C.R. 445.
[132] [2008] 1 All E.R. (Comm) 885.
[133] In the case of a contract which is either wholly oral, or partly oral and partly in writing, it has been held that evidence of a party's subjective intention is admissible at least where those subjective intentions have been contemporaneously communicated: *Blyth v Nelsons Solicitors* [2019] EWHC 2063 (QB); [2019] Costs L.R. 1409; *Moorgate Capital (Corporate Finance) Ltd v Sun European Partners LLP* [2020] EWHC 593 (Comm).
[134] [2008] 3 E.G.L.R. 27.

claim for rectification, which the present claim was not. The principles applicable to the interpretation of contracts explained by Lord Hoffmann in his speech in *Investors Compensation Scheme Ltd v West Bromwich Building Society*,[135] make this clear, and they apply as much to the interpretation of an express grant of an easement as they do to a contract: see *Mobil Oil Co Ltd v Birmingham City Council*[136]; and *Partridge v Lawrence*.[137] In my judgment, if and so far as the judge placed reliance on the two documents or either of them as reflecting Pendle Borough Council's intentions as to the nature of the grant, he was wrong to do so. They were inadmissible. Alternatively, if the documents amounted to no more than Pendle Borough Council's opinion as to the true interpretation of the grant, they were similarly inadmissible. The interpretation of the grant raised a pure question of English law upon which opinion evidence is inadmissible."

However, in *Huntington v Imagine Group Holdings Ltd*,[138] Dyson LJ said:

"I have described the sixth sentence as difficult to construe. It can, with some force, be said that, for the reasons I have given, it is ambiguous. In these circumstances it seems to me that one is entitled to have regard to what the parties to the negotiations said about what they intended, in order to resolve the ambiguity of the sixth sentence."

It seems that Dyson LJ was prepared to look at the parties' subjective declarations of intent in the course of negotiations. If so, this represents a major departure from established principles, recently reaffirmed by the House of Lords in *Chartbrook Ltd v Persimmon Homes Ltd*,[139] and it is submitted that in this respect the reasoning is erroneous.

9. PRE-CONTRACTUAL NEGOTIATIONS

Evidence of pre-contractual negotiations is not generally admissible to interpret the concluded written agreement. But evidence of pre-contractual negotiations is admissible to establish that a fact was known to both parties; to decide (in a consumer contract) whether a term has been individually negotiated; to determine which party put forward a particular term; and to elucidate the general object of the contract. Evidence that parties negotiated on the basis of an agreed meaning is only admissible in support of a claim of estoppel or rectification.[140]

(a) The general rule

The third of Lord Hoffmann's five principles[141] was: 3.43

---

[135] [1998] 1 W.L.R. 896.
[136] [2002] 2 P. & C.R. 186 at [24].
[137] [2004] 1 P. & C.R. 176 at [28].
[138] [2008] EWCA Civ 159.
[139] [2009] UKHL 38; [2009] 1 A.C. 1101.
[140] This section was approved in *Northrop Grumman Mission Systems Europe Ltd v BAE Systems (Al Diriyah C4I) Ltd* [2014] EWHC 2955 (TCC).
[141] *Investors Compensation Scheme v West Bromwich Building Society* [1998] 1 W.L.R. 896.

"The law excludes from the admissible background the previous negotiations of the parties and their declarations of subjective intent. They are admissible only in an action for rectification. The law makes this distinction for reasons of practical policy and, in this respect only, legal interpretation differs from the way we would interpret utterances in ordinary life. The boundaries of this exception are in some respects unclear."

One reason for the exclusion was explained by Lord Wilberforce in *Prenn v Simmonds*[142] as follows:

"The reason for not admitting evidence of these exchanges is not a technical one or even mainly of convenience ... It is simply that such evidence is unhelpful. By the nature of things, where negotiations are difficult, the parties' positions, with each passing letter are changing and until the final agreement, though converging, still different. It is only the final document which records a consensus. If the previous documents use different expressions, how does construction of those expressions, itself a doubtful process, help on the construction of the contractual words? If the same expressions are used, nothing is gained by looking back; indeed something may be lost since the relevant surrounding circumstances may be different. And at this stage there is no consensus of the parties to appeal to."

3.44   Other reasons that have been advanced to justify the rule are: that it reduces uncertainty and unpredictability in the resolution of disputes; that it prevents unfairness to third parties who may be unaware of the course of negotiations; and that the admission of evidence about the course of negotiations would subvert the objective approach to the interpretation of contracts that is the bedrock of the English approach.[143]

In *The Rio Assu (No.2)*,[144] Waller LJ said:

"[T]he negotiations of a contract can often be a compromise. It is dangerous to make the assumption that one party intended to have something supplied or provided for by the contract, or that the other party intended to have something else supplied or provided by the contract. Contracts are negotiated and ultimately each may think that he has what he wishes, but it is for the Court to interpret the language of the contract. There is no doubt about the correctness of the principle."

3.45   Despite this ringing endorsement the principle has not won universal acceptance; and it is not a principle that is recognised by some other jurisdictions.[145] In *Investors Compensation Scheme v West Bromwich Building Society*, Lord Hoffmann said that the boundaries of this principle are unclear[146]; and in *BCCI v Ali*,[147] Lord

---

[142] [1971] 1 W.L.R. 1381.

[143] See Lord Nicholls of Birkenhead, "My Kingdom for a Horse" (2005) 121 L.Q.R. 577; *Chartbrook Homes Ltd v Persimmon Homes Ltd* [2009] 1 A.C. 1101.

[144] [1999] 1 Lloyd's Rep. 115 at 124 CA.

[145] Both the Unidroit Principles for International Contracts (para.4.3(1)(a)) and the European Principles of Contract Law (para.5.102(a)) permit the parties' negotiations to be taken into account in interpreting their contract. However, civilian systems do not adopt the objective approach to interpretation that is the foundation of the English approach.

[146] Professor D.W. McLauchlan suggests that Lord Hoffmann's subsequent reasoning, and in particular

Nicholls questioned whether the policy underlying the principle still holds good today. The most sustained attack on the principle in a common law jurisdiction is that of Thomas J in *Yoshimoto v Canterbury Golf International Ltd*.[148] On appeal to the Privy Council[149] their Lordships said that this was not the occasion to re-examine the scope of the principle, as the evidence of earlier drafts of the contract was, as Lord Wilberforce had predicted, unhelpful.

A subsequent lecture by Lord Nicholls,[150] and somewhat inconclusive discus-sion in the Court of Appeal,[151] suggested that English law might take the step

3.46

---

his treatment of the example of the conversation between Alice and Humpty Dumpty, is not consist-ent with the general proposition that direct evidence of intention is inadmissible: see "Objectivity in Contract" [2005] U.Q.L.J. 28.

[147] [2002] A.C. 251.

[148] [2001] 1 N.Z.L.R. 523, to which Lord Nicholls referred in *BCCI v Ali*. His Honour said:

> "I would also reiterate that, for the purposes of this case, I am not seeking to entirely abrogate the rule that evidence of prior contractual negotiations is not receivable to ascertain the mean-ing of a contract. What I am suggesting is that the rule should not be treated as an absolute and rigid rule to the point where the court is called upon to impose an interpretation which does not accord with the parties' actual intention. The objective basis would remain. But that basis would be enhanced by approaching the task of determining what the contract would convey to a reason-able person without artificially restricting the background knowledge available to the parties at the time they completed the contract. Subject to the caution which I will shortly stress, that background knowledge should be able to include reference to matters that might otherwise come under the general heading of negotiations where such a reference would undoubtedly assist to ascertain the true meaning of the parties' contract. Thus, in this case, the clause in the draft agree-ment and the deleted recital E would assist the reasonable person reading the words of the contract to determine what the parties intended cl 6.3 to mean, as distinct from their subjective inten-tions divorced from the wording used.
>
> > [77] Nor is it remotely suggested that such evidence be received without caution. Obviously, the evidence must be reliable. No doubt documentary evidence will tend to be more reli-able than oral evidence. The reason usually given to justify the exclusion of prior negotia-tions is that the parties' position will change with each passing communication until the final agreement which records a consensus. That reason is essentially a generality. Whether or not this is so and, if so, the extent to which it is so, will depend on the particular circumstances of each case. Those particular circumstances can be taken into account in determining the weight, if any, to be given to the evidence of the prior negotiations.
> > [78] In so far as what I have urged is not a total rejection of the rule excluding evidence of prior negotiations, it is unnecessary to address the perceived policy reasons for that rule. Relaxing the absolute and rigid nature of the rule can be done without corroding the underlying policy."

The NZCA was subsequently reversed by the Privy Council, but their Lordships said that this was not the occasion to re-examine the rule: [2004] N.Z.L.R. 1.

[149] [2004] N.Z.L.R. 1.

> "It seems to them pointless to try to speculate upon why the change was made. No doubt each party had their reasons for proposing it on the one hand and accepting it on the other. All a court can do is to decide what the final contract means", per Lord Hoffmann at [28].

[150] See Lord Nicholls of Birkenhead, "My Kingdom for a Horse" (2005) 121 L.Q.R. 577. The case for admitting evidence of negotiations is also argued by Professor McLauchlan, "A Contract Contradic-tion" [1999] VU L. Rev. 33 and "Objectivity in Contract" [2005] U.Q.L.J. 28. Arguments for and against relaxing the rule are marshalled in McMeel, "Prior Negotiations and Subsequent Conduct" (2002) 119 L.Q.R. 272. See also McMeel, *The Construction of Contracts*, 3rd edn (Oxford University Press, 2017), paras 5.74 and 5.87. Lord Bingham, speaking extra-judicially, had aligned himself with the "judicial dinosaurs" in supporting the general rule that evidence of pre-contractual negotiations should be excluded: "A New Thing under the Sun?" (2008) Edin. L.R. 374. So, for what it is worth, did the author: "*If It Ain't Broke Don't Fix It: Rectification and the Boundaries of Interpretation*", The Jonathan Brock Memorial Lecture, 21 May 2008 (reprinted as

towards admitting evidence of pre-contractual negotiations as part of the relevant background to the interpretation of a concluded written agreement.[152] The question arose directly for decision in *Chartbrook Homes Ltd v Persimmon Homes Ltd*,[153] where developers sought to rely on pre-contractual negotiations to interpret a development agreement. The decision of the House of Lords in that case has settled the debate in England and Wales.[154] Although, strictly speaking, the Lords' discussion of this question was obiter, it is thought that it will be treated as authoritative. Their Lordships reaffirmed the exclusionary rule prohibiting the admission of pre-contractual negotiations for the purpose of interpreting a contract.[155] Lord Hoffmann said:

(1) the exclusionary rule applied not only in a case where the pre-contractual negotiations were irrelevant[156];

(2) it would not be inconsistent with the English objective theory of contractual interpretation to admit evidence of previous communications as part of the background[157];

(3) thus, while it is true that normally evidence of negotiations is excluded because it is irrelevant, there are cases in which its exclusion can only be justified on pragmatic grounds.[158]

3.47 The first ground is that exclusion of this kind of evidence creates greater uncertainty of outcome and adds to the costs of advice, arbitration and litigation. This ground is based on:

"a sound practical intuition that the law of contract is an institution designed to enforce promises with a high degree of predictability and that the more one allows conventional meanings or syntax to be displaced by inferences drawn from background, the less predictable the outcome is likely to be."

Pre-contractual negotiations differ from other kinds of background material:

"Whereas the surrounding circumstances are, by definition, objective facts, which

---

an Appendix to the Supplement to the 4th edition of this book). Professor McLauchlan cogently argued the opposite point of view in "Contract Interpretation: What is it all About?" (2009) *Sydney Law Review* 5.

[151] *Proforce Recruit Ltd v The Rugby Group Ltd* [2006] EWCA Civ 69. This case was an application for summary judgment, so the question was whether evidence of the negotiations was arguably admissible. In addition, the allegation was that the parties had negotiated on the basis of an agreed meaning, which has been said to be an exception to the general principle. Nevertheless many cases adhered to the traditional view: *Full Metal Jacket Ltd v Gowlain Building Group Ltd* [2005] EWCA Civ 1809; *Beazer Homes Ltd v Stroude* [2005] EWCA Civ 265; *IN Newman Ltd v Ric Adlem* [2006] F.S.R. 16; *Square Mile Partnership Ltd v Fitzmaurice McCall Ltd* [2007] 2 B.C.L.C. 23; *Berkeley Community Villages Ltd v Pullen* [2007] EWHC 1330 (Ch); *Great Hill Equity Partners II LLP v Novator One LLP* [2007] EWHC 1210 (Comm); *Alexiou v Campbell* [2007] UKPC 11; [2007] 1 All E.R. (Comm) 1083.

[152] Spigelman CJ of the New South Wales CA has given a spirited defence of the traditional exclusionary rule: "From Text to Context: Contemporary Contractual Interpretation", Address to the Risky Business Conference, 21 March 2007. The author finds it convincing.

[153] [2009] 1 A.C. 1101.

[154] See *Bright Asset Ltd v Lewis* [2011] EWCA Civ 122. Professor McLauchlan remains unconvinced: (2010) L.Q.R. 8.

[155] [2009] 1 A.C. 1101.

[156] [2009] 1 A.C. 1101 at [32].

[157] [2009] 1 A.C. 1101 at [33].

[158] [2009] 1 A.C. 1101 at [32].

will usually be uncontroversial, statements in the course of pre-contractual negotiations will be drenched in subjectivity and may, if oral, be very much in dispute. It is often not easy to distinguish between those statements which (if they were made at all) merely reflect the aspirations of one or other of the parties and those which embody at least a provisional consensus which may throw light on the meaning of the contract which was eventually concluded. But the imprecision of the line between negotiation and provisional agreement is the very reason why in every case of dispute over interpretation, one or other of the parties is likely to require a court or arbitrator to take the course of negotiations into account."

Support for the admissibility of evidence of pre-contractual negotiations could not be obtained from the Unidroit Principles of International Commercial Contracts or the Principles of European Contract Law, because their underlying philosophy was the French legal philosophy of subjective intent; and it is not possible to transpose rules based on one philosophy of contractual interpretation to another.[159] It might be thought, however, that this particular point does not sit easily with Lord Hoffmann's earlier acceptance that admitting evidence of pre-contractual negotiations is not incompatible with the English theory of objectivity. There was strength in the argument that the admission of such evidence would prejudice third parties,[160] but:

"The law sometimes deals with the problem by restricting the admissible background to that which would be available not merely to the contracting parties but also to others to whom the document is treated as having been addressed."

Ordinarily, however, a contract is addressed to the parties alone and:

"an assignee must either inquire as to any relevant background or take his chance on how that might affect the meaning a court will give to the document."[161]

The exclusionary rule had not been shown to be unjustified and should therefore be retained. Lord Hoffmann added[162]:

"The rule may well mean, as Lord Nicholls has argued,[163] that parties are sometimes held bound by a contract in terms which, upon a full investigation of the course of negotiations, a reasonable observer would not have taken them to have intended. But a system which sometimes allows this to happen may be justified in the more general interest of economy and predictability in obtaining advice and adjudicating disputes. It is, after all, usually possible to avoid surprises by carefully reading the documents before signing them and there are the safety nets of rectification and estoppel by convention."

The debate may, in time, shift to the question of whether the evidence sought to   **3.48**

---

[159] [2009] 1 A.C. 1101 at [39].
[160] [2009] 1 A.C. 1101 at [40].
[161] In the author's view this does not adequately address the difficulty of inquiring in cases of very long-term contracts, e.g. a long lease. However, the solution may lie in the conclusion that in such a case the reasonable reader of the contract would not be affected by background in his understanding of what the words of the contract mean. See paras 3.143–3.182.
[162] [2009] 1 A.C. 1101 at [41].
[163] In "My Kingdom for a Horse" (2005) 121 L.Q.R. 577.

be introduced is directed towards establishing some objective fact or is merely evidence of subjective intent. In *Oceanbulk Shipping and Trading SA v TMT Asia Ltd*,[164] Lord Clarke said:

> "Trial judges frequently have to distinguish between material which forms part of the pre-contractual negotiations which is part of the factual matrix and therefore admissible as an aid to interpretation and material which forms part of the pre-contractual negotiations but which is not part of the factual matrix and is not therefore admissible. This is often a straightforward task but sometimes it is not."

3.49 From time to time the attempt is made to introduce evidence of negotiations on the ground that it is part of the "matrix of fact". In *Secured Income Real Estate (Australia) Ltd v St Martins Investments Pty Ltd*,[165] the purchasers of an office block were liable to make certain payments if the income from leases of parts of the block produced a certain amount. The vendors offered to take leases in order to make up the shortfall in income. The purchasers sought to adduce evidence that in the course of negotiations both parties had "commercial" leases in mind. Mason J said:

> "This was said to be evidence of surrounding circumstances to which recourse could be had in interpreting the contract. In truth the evidence is not evidence of surrounding circumstances; it is evidence of antecedent oral negotiations and expectations of the parties and as such it cannot be used for the purpose of construing the words of a written contract intended by the parties to comprehensively record the terms of the agreement which they have made."

The increasing trend of attempts to introduce evidence of what parties say or do in the course of negotiations for the purpose of drawing inferences about what the contract means has been strongly deprecated.[166]

3.50 The exclusionary rule precludes recourse to evidence of a provisional consensus or to evidence of the parties' mistaken understandings about objective background facts.[167] Even if evidence of negotiations is admitted because the action raises a question of rectification, or misrepresentation, the court should not allow itself to be influenced by that evidence when it comes to construe the agreement.[168] Naturally, this is difficult to achieve in practice.[169]

(b) Evidence of negotiations to establish knowledge of a fact

3.51 There are, however, some cases in which the court will admit evidence of pre-contractual negotiations. First, the court will admit evidence to establish the parties' state of knowledge of facts. In *Governor and Company of The Bank of Scotland v Dunedin Property Investment Co Ltd*,[170] Lord Rodger, having considered the English authorities, said:

---

[164] [2010] UKSC 44; [2011] 1 A.C. 662.

[165] (1979) 144 C.L.R. 596.

[166] *Falkonera Shipping Co v Arcadia Energy Pte Ltd* [2012] EWHC 3678 (Comm); [2013] 1 Lloyd's Rep. 582, per Eder J.

[167] *Stena Line Ltd v Merchant Navy Ratings Pension Fund Trustees Ltd* [2010] EWHC 1805 (Ch).

[168] *Arrale v Costain Civil Engineering Ltd* [1976] 1 Lloyd's Rep. 98.

[169] See Denning, *The Discipline of the Law* (Butterworths, 1979), p.55 and *Attorney-General v Dreux Holdings* (1996) 7 T.C.L.R. 617 NZCA.

[170] 1998 S.C. 657. This case has since been followed in England: *Seagate Shipping Ltd v Glencore*

"As these authorities demonstrate, the rule which excludes evidence of prior communings as an aid to interpretation of a concluded contract is well-established and salutary. The rationale of the rule shows, however, that it has no application when the evidence of the parties' discussions is being considered, not in order to provide a gloss on the terms of the contract, but rather to establish the parties' knowledge of the circumstances with reference to which they used the words in the contract."

Likewise, in *Codelfa Construction Pty Ltd v State Rail Authority of New South Wales*,[171] Mason CJ said:

"Obviously the prior negotiations will tend to establish objective background facts which were known to both parties and the subject matter of the contract. To the extent to which they have this tendency they are admissible."

This was confirmed by the House of Lords in *Chartbrook Homes Ltd v Persimmon Homes Ltd*.[172] Lord Hoffmann said:

"The rule excludes evidence of what was said or done during the course of negotiating the agreement for the purpose of drawing inferences about what the contract meant. It does not exclude the use of such evidence for other purposes: for example, to establish that a fact which may be relevant as background was known to the parties, or to support a claim for rectification or estoppel. These are not exceptions to the rule. They operate outside it."

In *Globe Motors Inc v TRW Lucas Varity Electric Steering Ltd*[173] Beatson LJ reaffirmed the principle that:

"the pre-contractual negotiations of the parties cannot be taken into account in interpreting its terms and determining what they mean. The exceptions are where a party seeks to establish that a fact which may be relevant as background was known to the parties or to support a claim for rectification or estoppel."

In *Q-Park v HX Investments Ltd*,[174] Kitchin LJ confirmed that:

"the background knowledge may well include objective facts communicated by one party to the other in the course of the negotiations."

Thus evidence may be admitted in order to prove additional consideration to that stated in the written contract.[175] It does not matter that the communication of the fact relied on was made in a "without prejudice" communication.[176]

Professor McLauchlan has argued that this exception to the exclusionary rule has deprived it of almost all content.[177]

International AG [2008] 2 Lloyd's Rep. 440; *Bernard Schulte Shipmanagement (Bermuda) Ltd Partnership v BP Shipping Ltd* [2009] 1 All E.R. (Comm) 601.

[171] (1982) 149 C.L.R 337 at 352.
[172] [2009] 1 A.C. 1101.
[173] [2016] EWCA Civ 396; [2016] 1 C.L.C. 712.
[174] [2012] EWCA Civ 708.
[175] *Latimer Management Consultants v Ellingham Investments Ltd* [2005] EWHC 1732 (Ch).
[176] *Oceanbulk Shipping and Trading SA v TMT Asia Ltd* [2010] UKSC 44; [2011] 1 A.C. 662.
[177] "Common intention and contract interpretation" [2011] L.M.C.L.Q. 30.

3.52   This exception to the exclusionary rule does not enable the court to receive evidence of the parties' mistaken understandings about objective background facts.[178] Nor does it enable the court to take into account what amounts to no more than the parties' negotiating positions.[179]

(c)   Consumer contracts

3.53   Evidence of negotiations may be admissible in determining the effect of a consumer contract governed by the Unfair Terms in Consumer Contracts Regulations 1999. Regulation 5 stated:

> "A contractual term which has not been individually negotiated shall be regarded as unfair if, contrary to the requirement of good faith, it causes a significant imbalance in the parties' rights and obligations arising under the contract, to the detriment of the consumer."

In many cases the visual appearance of the contract will show that the term in question has not been individually negotiated. But in other cases, this may not be visually apparent. In such a case it seems that evidence about the negotiations would be admissible. Strictly however, evidence of this kind is adduced, not for the purpose of interpreting the contract, but for the purpose of determining which of its terms are enforceable. In *African Export-Import Bank v Shebah Exploration & Production Co Ltd*,[180] the question was whether a contract had been made on one party's "standard terms of business". The Court of Appeal held that in order to determine that question it was legitimate to look at the course of negotiations. The fact that there had been extensive negotiations and revisions to the original draft was one of the reasons why the contract could not be said to have been made on standard terms of business.

3.54   Section 62(4) of the Consumer Rights Act 2015 does not repeat the reference to the course of the negotiations. It says simply that:

> "A term is unfair if, contrary to the requirement of good faith, it causes a significant imbalance in the parties' rights and obligations under the contract to the detriment of the consumer."

It appears, therefore, that recourse to negotiations is irrelevant, with the consequence that such evidence ought not to be admitted.

3.55   In addition, an inquiry into the drafting process may be undertaken for the purpose of identifying an objective fact known to both parties, namely who drafted a clause where the *contra proferentem* principle is in play. Such an inquiry does not therefore infringe the rule that evidence of negotiations is inadmissible for the purpose of identifying the subjective intentions of the parties.[181]

---

[178] *Stena Line Ltd v Merchant Navy Ratings Pension Fund Trustees Ltd* [2010] EWHC 1805 (Ch).
[179] *Northrop Grumman Missions Systems Europe Ltd v BAE Systems (Al Diriyah C4I) Ltd* [2015] EWCA Civ 844.
[180] [2017] EWCA Civ 845; [2018] 1 W.L.R. 487.
[181] See para.7.78.

(d) General object of the contract

In *Investec Bank (Channel Islands) Ltd v The Retail Group Plc*,[182] Sales J said: **3.56**

"… in interpreting a contract, regard may be had to the content of the parties' negotiations to establish 'the genesis and object' of a provision. This seems to me to be a relevant part of the factual matrix, since if the parties in the course of their negotiations are agreed on a general objective which is to be achieved by inclusion of a provision in their contract, that objective would naturally inform the way in which a reasonable person in the position of the parties would approach the task of interpreting the provision in question."

However, in *Excelsior Group Productions Ltd v Yorkshire Television Ltd*,[183] Flaux J said:

"It seems to me that there is a very fine line between looking at the negotiations to see if the parties have agreed on the general objective of a provision as part of the task of interpreting the provision and looking at the negotiations to draw an inference about what the contract meant (which is not permissible), a line so fine it almost vanishes."

In *Elmfield Road Ltd v Trillium (Prime) Property GP Ltd*,[184] the deputy judge   **3.57** declined to follow *Investec Bank (Channel Islands) Ltd v Retail Group Plc*[185] on the question of the admissibility of pre-contractual negotiations and preferred the approach in *Excelsior Group Productions Ltd v Yorkshire Television Ltd*.[186] He said:

"The genesis and aim of a particular provision may be sufficiently important to qualify as part of the genesis and aim of the whole transaction. If so, it will be admissible pursuant to *Prenn v Simmonds*; if not, it is contrary to *Prenn v Simmonds* to allow it to be admitted."

In *Merthyr (South Wales) Ltd v Merthyr Tydfil County Borough Council*[187] the Court of Appeal agreed with the author's view that that was correct. Leggatt LJ said:

"Sir Kim Lewison considers this approach to be correct (see *The Interpretation of Contracts*, 2017 supplement, at 3.09), and so do I."

He added that to the extent that such material is admissible, it is restricted to identifying the general aim of the transaction, rather than to draw inferences about what the contract means.[188] But the court recognised that there may be borderline cases in which the line between referring to previous communications to identify the "genesis and aim of the transaction" and relying on such evidence to show what the parties intended a particular provision in a contract to mean may be hard to draw.

Evidence of pre-contractual negotiations should not be used to elucidate detailed   **3.58**

---

[182] [2009] EWHC 476 (Ch), followed in *Barclays Bank Plc v Landgraf* [2014] EWHC 503 (Comm); a case which should now be treated with caution.

[183] [2009] EWHC 1751 (Comm).

[184] [2016] EWHC 3122 (Ch) (affirmed [2018] EWCA Civ 1556 but without reference to this point).

[185] [2009] EWHC 476 (Ch).

[186] [2009] EWHC 1751 (Comm).

[187] [2019] EWCA Civ 526; [2019] J.P.L. 989.

[188] *Gwynt Y Mor Ofto Plc v Gwynt Y Mor Offshore Wind Farm Ltd* [2020] EWHC 850 (Comm).

points of interpretation. In *Scottish Widows Fund and Life Assurance Society v BGC International*,[189] Arden LJ said:

> "Pre-contractual negotiations rarely descend into detail on every point; the negotiations are unlikely to throw any light on the detailed points of interpretation that generally arise after execution.
>
> However this does not necessarily mean that the pre-contractual negotiations should be accepted as evidence even as to the general object of the transaction. Statements made in the course of negotiations are often no more than statements of a negotiating stance at that point in time, thus shedding more heat than light on issues as to interpretation of the final deal."

She concluded that "judges should exercise considerable caution before treating as admissible communications in the course of pre-contractual negotiations relied on as evidencing the parties' objective aim in completing the transaction."

In *Barclays Bank Plc v Landgraf*,[190] Popplewell J held that regard could be had to the parties' negotiations for the purpose of determining the genesis and object of a contractual provision.[191] In the light of *Scottish Widows Fund and Life Assurance Society v BGC International* it is questionable whether this is correct.

3.59   But evidence of negotiations may be admitted in order to decide whether a provision alleged to be a penalty had a commercial justification.[192]

(e)   The private dictionary principle

3.60   In *Arrale v Costain Civil Engineering Ltd*,[193] Stephenson LJ suggested that evidence of negotiations could be admitted in order to clarify ambiguities. This suggestion was followed by Kerr J in *The Karen Oltmann*.[194] He said:

> "If a contract contains words which, in their context, are fairly capable of bearing more than one meaning, and if it is being alleged that the parties have in effect negotiated on an agreed basis that the words bore only one of the two possible meanings, then it is permissible for the Court to examine the extrinsic evidence relied upon to see whether the parties have in fact used the words in question in one sense only, so that they have in effect given their own dictionary meaning to the word as the result of their common intention."

In *Proforce Recruit Ltd v The Rugby Group Ltd*,[195] on an application for summary judgment, the Court of Appeal endorsed this approach. The principle as formulated is contrary to *The Nita*[196] in which evidence of exchanges between the parties prior to execution of a charterparty was rejected, even though it was tendered to explain an ambiguity. When *Proforce Recruit Ltd v The Rugby Group Ltd* reached

---

[189] [2012] EWCA Civ 607; (2012) 142 Con. L.R. 27, reversing [2011] EWHC 729 (Ch).
[190] [2014] EWHC 503 (Comm).
[191] Following Sales J in *Investing Bank Channel Islands Ltd v The Retail Group Plc* [2009] EWHC 476 (Ch). The author has already expressed his doubts about the correctness of that decision.
[192] *Azimut-Benetti SpA v Healey* [2011] 1 Lloyd's Rep. 473.
[193] [1976] 1 Lloyd's Rep. 98.
[194] [1976] 2 Lloyd's Rep. 708. See also *Nicholson v Markham* (1997) 75 P. & C.R. 428 at 435–436, per Staughton LJ.
[195] [2006] EWCA Civ 69.
[196] [1892] P. 411.

trial,[197] the trial judge, Cresswell J, said:

"The present case serves to illustrate some of the difficulties with this (the agreed dictionary) exception to the rule that the law excludes from the admissible background the previous negotiations of the parties and their declarations of subjective intent. It is in my opinion important that it should be recognised that this is an exception which will seldom arise in the interpretation of commercial contracts. If commercial parties wish to contract on the basis of their own diction-ary meaning, they might be expected to include that dictionary meaning in the contract itself. ... Where the parties have included their own dictionary mean-ing in the contract itself, the exception will not apply. Where the agreement is silent as to the meaning of the words in question, and those words have been used in a particular sense in correspondence preceding the agreement (which forms part of the factual matrix), it would be surprising if commercial parties intended to contract on the basis of some other meaning, without saying so in the contract. The exception under consideration should not be allowed to become a means, regularly adopted by litigants, of attempting to circumvent the fundamental principle that generally the law excludes from the admissible background the previous negotiations of the parties and their declarations of subjective intent."

The judge found on the facts that there was no agreed meaning.[198]

The House of Lords examined this principle in *Chartbrook Homes Ltd v Persim-* **3.61** *mon Homes Ltd*.[199] Lord Hoffmann pointed out that *The Karen Oltmann* was not a case of specialised usage of words.[200] The choice was between two conventional meanings. He also said that Kerr J was wrong to have held that rectification was not an available remedy.[201] He continued:

"On its facts, *The Karen Oltmann* was in my opinion an illegitimate extension of the 'private dictionary' principle which, taken to its logical conclusion, would destroy the exclusionary rule and any practical advantages which it may have. There are two legitimate safety devices which will in most cases prevent the exclusionary rule from causing injustice. But they have to be specifically pleaded and clearly established. One is rectification. The other is estoppel by conven-tion, which has been developed since the decision in *The Karen Oltmann*.[202] If the parties have negotiated an agreement upon some common assumption, which may include an assumption that certain words will bear a certain meaning, they may be estopped from contending that the words should be given a different

---

[197] [2007] EWHC 1621 (QB).
[198] An attempt to prove an agreed meaning failed on the facts in *Cavell USA Inc v Seaton Insurance Co* [2008] 2 C.L.C. 898.
[199] [2009] 1 A.C. 1101.
[200] At first instance Briggs J held that the private dictionary principle could not apply to terms which the contract expressly defined. In *Harper v Interchange Group Ltd* [2007] EWHC 1834 (Comm), Aikens J agreed with him. But in the light of the decision of the House of Lords this limitation seems too narrow.
[201] This is the analysis that the author advocated in *"If It Ain't Broke Don't Fix It: Rectification and the Boundaries of Interpretation"*, The Jonathan Brock Memorial Lecture, 21 May 2008 (reprinted as an Appendix to the Supplement to the 4th edition of this book).
[202] See *Amalgamated Investment & Property Co Ltd v Texas Commerce International Bank Ltd* [1982] Q.B. 84. In *Air New Zealand Ltd v Nippon Credit Bank Ltd* [1997] N.Z.L.R. 218, Gault J analysed the principle expressed in *The Karen Oltmann* as based on estoppel by convention. In *Chartbrook Homes Ltd v Persimmon Homes Ltd* [2007] 1 All E.R. (Comm) 1083, Briggs J would have analysed it in the same way.

meaning. Both of these remedies lie outside the exclusionary rule, since they start from the premise that, as a matter of construction, the agreement does not have the meaning for which the party seeking rectification or raising an estoppel contends."

3.62   This explanation of the principle was adopted by the Supreme Court of New Zealand. In *Vector Gas Ltd v Bay of Plenty Energy Ltd*,[203] Tipping J said:

"Although an estoppel will usually arise from the adoption of a special meaning, it is in cases where words are capable of bearing more than one meaning that estoppel is likely to have its primary application. A party may be estopped from denying that one of two possible meanings was the meaning the parties intended their words to bear. This, or an agreement as to meaning, is the best analysis of the controversial decision of Kerr J in *The Karen Oltmann*. ... *The Karen Oltmann* is sometimes referred to as a special (private dictionary) meaning case because of Kerr J's reference to the parties' 'own dictionary meaning'. But I agree with the House of Lords in *Chartbrook* that this is not its true basis. The case was one where the word 'after' was, on its face, capable of two meanings. If the parties agreed or represented to each other in the telexes that the word 'after' meant 'on the expiry of' and the agreement or representation was relied on when they entered into the time charter, the parties were each estopped by that agreement or representation from contending that the word 'after' bore the alternative meaning. Indeed, on the basis discussed earlier, they were bound by any such definitional agreement. Of course, the court must be satisfied that an agreement or representation as to meaning, reached or made during negotiations, was still operating at the time the contract was formed and represented a linguistic premise on which it had been formed. *The Karen Oltmann* was correctly decided; but on the basis of agreement or estoppel as to meaning, not on the basis of special meaning. There was nothing special about the meaning of the word 'after'. It was, however, capable of two meanings. The parties had consensually resolved which meaning was to apply, or an estoppel had been created, and evidence to that effect was admissible."

In *London Weekend Television Ltd v Paris & Griffith*,[204] Megaw J considered this situation in a more traditional way. He is reported as having said:

"Where two persons agreed expressly with one another what was the meaning of a particular phrase but did not record their definition in the contract itself, if one of the parties sought to enforce the agreement on the basis of some other definition, he could be prevented by an action for rectification."

(f)   When the question should be decided

3.63   Where one party wishes to rely on pre-contractual communications, the question arises whether his ability to do so should be decided at an early stage. In *Standard Life Assurance Ltd v Oak Dedicated Ltd*,[205] Tomlinson J said that it is very difficult for a judge at the interlocutory stage to rule that evidence is inadmissible,

---

[203] [2010] NZSC 5.
[204] (1969) 113 S.J. 222.
[205] [2008] 1 C.L.C. 59.

and that the trial judge is usually better placed to do so. Likewise, in *Beazer Homes Ltd v Stroude*,[206] Mummery LJ said:

"In general, disputes about the admissibility of evidence in civil proceedings are best left to be resolved by the judge at the substantive hearing of the application or at the trial of the action, rather than at a separate preliminary hearing. The judge at a preliminary hearing on admissibility will usually be less well informed about the case. Preliminary hearings can also cause unnecessary costs and delays."

However, in *Anglo Continental Educational Group (GB) Ltd v Capital Homes (Southern) Ltd*,[207] Arden LJ said:

"Time and costs should not be unnecessarily spent on evidence about communications before an agreement is made. If a party is served with a witness statement which it considers may contain material which is inadmissible on a question of interpretation, it should seek to establish from the other party the basis on which the evidence is said to be admissible. If he is dissatisfied with the answer, he may in appropriate circumstances make an application to exclude the evidence before replying to it. Another course would be to issue an application to be heard at trial, but this may lead to increased costs and a diversion of the time available for trial to this subsidiary issue. Yet another course would be for the court at the case management conference to direct the parties to identify in writing the precise point which they say the evidence establishes and why they say that that evidence is admissible. This may shorten the time spent at trial on any application to exclude it. At all events, the court should not allow the focus of a case about interpretation to be distorted by a detailed enquiry about material that plays a minor role, if any, in resolving the case."

These varying alternatives demonstrate that the reception of evidence of pre-contractual material tends to distract from the court's main task of deciding what a contract means.

(g) Other jurisdictions

The traditional approach was robustly defended by the Court of Appeal of Alberta in *Gainers Inc v Pocklington Financial Corp*[208]: **3.64**

"If hindsight, implication, unspoken thoughts, and unwritten statements could have so pivotal a role as they appear to have had here, then written contracts would become a mere trap for the credulous. Almost all commercial certainty would evaporate, and commercial litigation become a swearing contest. A suit on a commercial contract, no matter how carefully drafted, would become a long historical investigation of an insoluble mystery. Often who said what to whom by telephone 15 years ago is impossible to unravel. A formal written contract should not rise or fall with such mysteries."

In other jurisdictions Lord Hoffmann's support for the exclusionary rule has not **3.65**

[206] [2005] EWCA Civ 265.
[207] [2009] EWCA Civ 218.
[208] 2000 ABCA 151.

won universal acceptance. In *Vector Gas Ltd v Bay of Plenty Energy Ltd*,[209] the New Zealand Supreme Court considered the admissibility of pre-contractual negotiations. Tipping J said:

> "[27]   Against that background I come to the subject of the admissibility of prior negotiations. Some of the difficulties in this area may derive from the concept of 'prior negotiations' being employed in a more or less expansive way. Sometimes the concept seems to be used as if it encompassed all conduct and circumstances associated with negotiations towards the formation of a contract. It is necessary, however, to distinguish between the subjective content of negotiations; that is, how the parties were thinking, their individual intentions and the stance they were taking at different stages of the negotiating process on the one hand, and, on the other, evidence derived from the negotiations which shows objectively the meaning the parties intended their words to convey. Such evidence includes the circumstances in which the contract was entered into, and any objectively apparent consensus as to meaning operating between the parties.
>
> [28]   The vice in admitting subjective evidence of negotiations, is that doing so would be inconsistent with the objective basis on which interpretation issues are resolved. As already seen, evidence of a party's subjective intention is not relevant to an objective resolution of interpretation issues. Although the common law takes the view that it is only the final written contract which records the ultimate consensus of the parties, the way that consensus is expressed may be based on an agreement as to meaning reached during negotiations.
>
> [29]   There is no problem with objective evidence directed to the context, factual or linguistic, in which the negotiations were taking place. That kind of evidence can properly inform an objective approach to meaning. Whereas evidence of the subjective content of negotiations is inadmissible on account of its irrelevance, evidence of facts, circumstances and conduct attending the negotiations is admissible if it is capable of shedding objective light on meaning. It is often said in contract interpretation cases that evidence of surrounding circumstances is admissible. Circumstances which surround the making of the contract can operate both before and after its formation. In either case irrelevance should be the touchstone for the exclusion of evidence. I do not consider there are any sufficiently persuasive pragmatic grounds on which to exclude evidence that is relevant."[210]

Illustrations

1.   A hotel owner agreed to sell the hotel. The contract provided that the conveyance should contain a restrictive covenant for the benefit of certain houses. After

---

[209]   [2010] NZSC 5.

[210]   The other members of the court differed in their approach. Blanchard J (with whom Gault J agreed) referred to the established exceptions to the inadmissibility of pre-contractual negotiations, and said that whether the courts of New Zealand should go further should wait for another day. McGrath J said that *Chartbrook* had set sound limits to the admission of pre-contractual negotiations. Wilson J took the view that recourse to extrinsic evidence was permissible only in cases of ambiguity. But if ambiguity is established then all evidence is admissible (except evidence of undeclared intention).

the contract, but before the completion, the vendor sold the houses. The terms of sale did not mention the proposed restrictive covenant. The conveyance was duly completed containing the covenant. It was held that since the vendor had no land capable of being benefited by the covenant at the date of the conveyance, the covenant did not bind a successor in title of the purchaser, and the antecedent contract did not affect the position.
Millbourn v Lyons[211]

2.   A lightening contract recited that a stricken vessel had requested assistance and provided that the lightening ship would render assistance. It was held that the master's request for assistance could be examined for the purpose of construing the word "assistance".
The Pacific Colocrotronis[212]

3.   A reinsurance slip is inadmissible in construing a reinsurance policy.
Youell v Bland Welch[213]

4.   A written agreement to end an employee's employment after a certain date which would benefit his pension entitlement said that it was made in confirmation of "the substance of our discussion" at an earlier meeting. Evidence of the meeting prior was admissible in order to resolve any doubts about what was intended by the reference to a pension.
Engineering Training Authority v The Pensions Ombudsman[214]

10.   EXPRESSLY INCORPORATED TERMS

Where parties expressly incorporate terms into a contract, the incorporated terms must be interpreted as if they had been written out in full in the contract, and, accordingly, must be interpreted in the context of the contract into which they have been incorporated.

---

[211] [1914] 2 Ch. 231. Cozens Hardy MR said:

"speaking generally, it is perfectly clear that when you have a conveyance which expresses the final concluded deliberate terms of the contract between the parties you cannot alter or affect that by reference to the antecedent contract".

He continued: "It makes no difference that the prior agreement is itself recited in the conveyance". Swinfen Eady LJ held the vendor's argument to be wrong because:

"it would be a departure from the well established principle that when you have negotiations leading to a contract you do not look at the negotiations to construe the contract in writing, you only look to the written contract, and so where there is a contract followed by a conveyance you look at the terms of the conveyance".

[212] [1981] 2 Lloyd's Rep. 40. Eveleigh LJ said:

"One is not going outside the contract in a real sense to determine its meaning; one is following the instructions of the contract to discover its meaning. It is in effect defining its terms by reference to what has already been requested. But if I am wrong in that approach, I nonetheless take the view that the negotiations and what occurred during them are 'permissible' factors to take into account in order to construe the words of this contract".

[213] [1990] 2 Lloyd's Rep. 422.
[214] [1996] Pens. L.R. 409. See also *Lewis v Pensions Ombudsman* [2005] Pens. L.R. 195.

(a) Incorporation of other contractual terms

3.66   The first question to be determined is what terms the parties have incorporated into their contract. A term may be incorporated in a contract where an electronic order form refers to a website; and a hyperlink links to terms and conditions on the website.[215] The second question is what the incorporated terms mean in the context of the contract into which they have been incorporated. These two questions are to some extent interlinked.

In *Tradigrain SA v King Diamond Shipping SA*,[216] Rix LJ said:

"The first rule relating to the incorporation of one document's terms into another is to construe the incorporating clause in order to decide on the width of the incorporation ... A second rule, however, is to read the incorporated wording into the host document *in extenso* in order to see if, in that setting, some parts of the wording nevertheless have to be rejected as inconsistent or insensible when read in their new context."[217]

In *TJH and Sons Consultancy Ltd v CPP Group Plc*,[218] the Court of Appeal applied this two-step approach.

In *Skips A/S Nordheim v Syrian Petroleum Co Ltd*,[219] the Court of Appeal considered the effect of a bill of lading which incorporated by reference the "conditions" of the charterparty under which the shippers held the vessel carrying the cargo. Oliver LJ said:

"The purpose of referential incorporation is not, or at least is not generally, to incorporate the intention of the parties to the contract whose clauses are incorporated but to incorporate the clauses themselves in order to avoid the necessity of writing them out verbatim. The meaning and effect of the incorporated clause is to be determined as a matter of construction of the contract into which it is incorporated having regard to the terms of that contract."[220]

In *Northrop Grumman Missions Systems Europe Ltd v BAE Systems (Al Diriyah C4I) Ltd*,[221] a licence agreement stated that it was to "be governed by" the terms of an enabling agreement. Briggs LJ said:

"Literally construed, the phrase 'the terms contained within the Enabling Agree-

---

[215] *Cockett Marine Oil DMCC v Ing Bank NV* [2019] EWHC 1533 (Comm). There is a wide-ranging discussion of the incorporation of terms electronically in F. Wang, "The incorporation of terms into commercial contracts: a reassessment in the digital age" [2015] J.B.L. 87.

[216] [2000] 2 Lloyd's Rep. 319; *Cottonex Anstalt v Patriot Spinning Mills Ltd* [2014] EWHC 236 (Comm); [2014] 1 Lloyd's Rep. 615; *TJH and Sons Consultancy Ltd v CPP Group Plc* [2017] EWCA Civ 46.

[217] See *Porteous v Watney* (1878) 3 Q.B.D. 534 at 542. Where a bill of lading had an oblique cross-reference to an earlier version of conditions of carriage, but the reverse of the bill set them out clearly, the latter took preference over the former: *Golden Endurance Shipping SA v RMA Watanya SA* [2014] EWHC 3917 (Comm).

[218] [2017] EWCA Civ 46.

[219] [1984] Q.B. 599; *Northrop Grumman Missions Systems Europe Ltd v BAE Systems (Al Diriyah C4I) Ltd* [2015] EWCA Civ 844.

[220] Compare the statement of Lord Esher MR in *Hamilton & Co v Mackie & Sons* (1889) 5 T.L.R. 677 that: "the conditions of the charterparty must be read verbatim into the bill of lading as though they were there printed in extenso".

[221] [2015] EWCA Civ 844.

ment ...' prima facie mean all of them. Clause 5.1 does not itself provide any guidelines for the application of only some of them. But unlike the bill of lading in the *Skips* case, clause 5.1 does not use words of incorporation (at least in the sense explained by Oliver LJ). Rather it uses the phrase 'governed by'. Considerable effort was devoted by counsel in an attempt, by reference to synonyms, such as ruled or regulated. I did not find those efforts to be helpful. The parties have chosen 'governed', and it is a word with a sufficiently clear meaning. Although it points slightly away from Oliver LJ's concept of notionally writing the incorporated clauses into the agreement being construed, it is a no less forceful word than incorporated. But even the concept of being governed would give way where, for example, a clause in the Enabling Agreement was flatly inconsistent with a clause in the Licence Agreement dealing with the same subject matter. In such a case, the general would give way to the particular."

The problem identified by the first rule in *Tradigrain SA v King Diamond Shipping SA* has arisen frequently where parties to a bill of lading incorporate some or all of the terms of the charterparty binding the shipper of the cargo. Frequently the dispute is whether the arbitration clause in the charterparty is incorporated into the bill of lading. The authorities recognise a distinction in approach between cases in which the parties incorporate the terms of a contract between two other parties or between one of them and a third party and those in which they incorporate standard terms.[222]   **3.67**

The general approach to the problem was described by Brandon J as follows:

"First, in order to decide whether a clause under a bill of lading incorporates an arbitration clause in the charterparty it is necessary to look at both the precise words in the bill of lading alleged to do the incorporating, and also the precise terms of the arbitration clause in the charterparty alleged to be incorporated. Secondly, it is not necessary, in order to effect incorporation that the incorporating clause should refer expressly to the arbitration clause. General words may suffice, depending on the words of the latter clause. Thirdly, when the arbitration clause is, by its terms, applicable only to disputes under the charterparty, general words will not incorporate it into the bill of lading so as to make it applicable to disputes under the contract contained in or evidenced by that document. Fourthly, where the arbitration clause by its terms applies both to disputes under the charterparty and to disputes under the bill of lading, general words of incorporation will bring the clause into the bill of lading so as to make it applicable to disputes under that document."[223]

In the case of a bill of lading which incorporates the terms of a charterparty (a two-contract case) a distinction is drawn between provisions germane to the bill of lading (for example the shipment, carriage and delivery of goods) and other provisions. The former may be incorporated by a general reference to the terms and conditions of the charterparty. The latter (e.g. an arbitration clause) must be   **3.68**

---

[222] *Habas Sinai Ve Tibbi Gazlar Istihsal Endustrisi AS v Sometal Sal* [2010] EWHC 29 (Comm); [2010] 1 Lloyd's Rep. 661 containing a full review of the authorities, on which the text of this section is largely based.
[223] *The Annefield* [1971] P. 169 at 173; affirmed by the Court of Appeal.

expressly incorporated.[224] This approach has been applied to a contract of holiday insurance,[225] but it has been held subsequently that the distinction between clauses which are germane and clauses which are not is a special rule applicable to charterparties or perhaps arbitration clauses. In other cases the question is simply one of construction.[226]

In *The Federal Bulker*,[227] the issue was whether a clause in a charterparty requiring bills of lading to provide for arbitration of "all disputes arising out of this contract" was incorporated in bills which provided "all terms ... as per charterparty ... to be considered as fully incorporated as if fully written". The Court of Appeal held that the arbitration clause was not incorporated. Bingham LJ said:

> "64   Generally speaking, the English law of contract has taken a benevolent view of the use of general words to incorporate by reference standard terms to be found elsewhere. But in the present field a different, and stricter, rule has developed, especially where the incorporation of arbitration clauses is concerned. The reason no doubt is that a bill of lading is a negotiable commercial instrument and may come into the hands of a foreign party with no knowledge and no ready means of knowledge of the terms of the charterparty. The cases show that a strict test of incorporation having, for better or worse, been laid down, the Courts have in general defended this rule with some tenacity in the interests of commercial certainty. If commercial parties do not like the English rule, they can meet the difficulty by spelling out the arbitration provision in the bill of lading and not relying on general words to achieve incorporation.
>
> 65   The importance of certainty in this field was emphasised by Lord Denning, M.R. in *The Annefield* ... by Sir John Donaldson, M.R. in *The Varenna* ... and by Lord Justice Oliver in the same case ... This is indeed a field in which it is perhaps preferable that the law should be clear, certain and well understood than that it should be perfect. Like others, I doubt whether the line drawn by the authorities is drawn where a modern commercial lawyer would be inclined to draw it. But it would, I think, be a source of mischief if we were to do anything other than try to give effect to settled authority as best we can."

In *Caresse Navigation Ltd v Zurich Assurances Maroc*,[228] the Court of Appeal had difficulty with the principle underlying this approach, and preferred to apply the general approach to the interpretation of contracts to the question whether a jurisdiction clause had been incorporated. The rule developed in *The Federal Bulker* and other cases was acknowledged to be a pragmatic one only.

3.69   In *The Athena (No.2)*,[229] Langley J described the cases in which the strict test of incorporation of an arbitration agreement was applied as being "two-contract" cases, whereas in "single contract" cases, general words of incorporation sufficed.

---

[224] *The Federal Bulker* [1989] 1 Lloyd's Rep. 103 CA.

[225] *Pine Top Insurance Co Ltd v Unione Italiana Anglo-Saxon Reinsurance Co Ltd* [1987] 1 Lloyd's Rep. 476.

[226] *Hong Kong Borneo Services Co Ltd v Pilcher* [1992] 2 Lloyd's Rep. 593; *OK Petroleum v Vitol Energy* [1995] 2 Lloyd's Rep. 160; *Excess Insurance Co Ltd v Mander* [1997] 2 Lloyd's Rep. 119; *Navigas Ltd of Gibraltar v Enron Liquid Fuels Ltd* [1997] 2 Lloyd's Rep. 759.

[227] [1981] 1 Lloyd's Rep. 103.

[228] [2014] EWCA Civ 1366; [2015] 2 W.L.R. 43.

[229] [2007] 1 Lloyd's Rep. 280.

He said:

"In principle, English law accepts incorporation of standard terms by the use of general words and, I would add, particularly so when the terms are readily available and the question arises in the context of dealings between established players in a well-known market. The principle ... does not distinguish between a term which is an arbitration clause and one which addresses other issues. In contrast, and for the very reason that it concerns other parties, a "stricter rule" is applied in charterparty/bills of lading cases. The reason given is that the other party may have no knowledge nor ready means of knowledge of the relevant terms. Further, as the authorities illustrate, the terms of an arbitration clause may require adjustment if they are to be made to apply to the parties to a different contract."

He said, however, that an extension of the stricter rule should not be encouraged. He concluded:

"General words of incorporation may serve to incorporate an arbitration clause save in the exceptional two-contract cases ... in which some express reference to arbitration or perhaps provision of the relevant clause is also required."

In *Habas Sinai Ve Tibbi Gazlar Istihsal Endustrisi AS v Sometal Sal*,[230]   **3.70**
Christopher Clarke J said:

"48.   I accept that, if the terms of an earlier contract or contracts between the parties are said to have been incorporated it is necessary for it to be clear which terms those were. But, like Langley J, I do not regard this to be the position only if the terms said to be incorporated include an arbitration or jurisdiction clause. Whenever some terms other than those set out in the incorporating document are said to be incorporated it is necessary to be clear what those terms are. Since arbitration clauses are not terms which regulate the parties' substantive rights and obligations under the contract but are terms dealing with the resolution of disputes relating to those rights and obligations it is also necessary to be clear that the parties did intend to incorporate such a clause. But, if a contract between A and B incorporates all the terms of a previous contract between them other than the terms newly agreed in the later contract, there should be no lack of clarity in respect of what is to be incorporated.

49.   There is a particular need to be clear that the parties intended to incorporate the arbitration clause when the incorporation relied on is the incorporation of the terms of a contract made between different parties, even if one of them is a party to the contract in suit. In such a case it may not be evident that the parties intended not only to incorporate the substantive provisions of the other contract but also provisions as to the resolution of disputes between different parties, particularly if a degree of verbal manipulation is needed for the incorporated arbitration clause to work. These considerations do not, however, apply to a single contract case."

The more restrictive approach requires express reference to the arbitration or   **3.71**
jurisdiction clause before it will be taken to be incorporated into the contract. This more restrictive approach will apply to cases in which:

---

[230] [2010] EWHC 29 (Comm); [2010] 1 Lloyd's Rep 661.

(1) A and B make a contract incorporating terms agreed between A (or B) and C.

Common examples are a bill of lading incorporating the terms of a charter to which A is a party[231]; reinsurance contracts incorporating the terms of an underlying insurance; excess insurance contracts incorporating the terms of the primary layer of insurance; and building or engineering sub-contracts incorporating the terms of a main contract or sub-sub-contracts incorporating the terms of a sub-contract.

(2) A and B make a contract incorporating terms agreed between C and D.

Bills of lading, reinsurance[232] and insurance contracts and building contracts may fall into this category.

However, it will not apply where:

(3) A and B make a contract in which they incorporate standard terms.

These may be the standard terms of one party set out on the back of an offer letter or an order, or contained in another document to which reference is made; or terms embodied in the rules of an organisation of which A or B or both are members; or they may be terms standard in a particular trade or industry.

(4) A and B make a contract incorporating terms previously agreed between A and B in another contract or contracts to which they were both parties.[233]

3.72 Where terms of one agreement are said to "govern" another agreement, those terms rule or regulate that other agreement. Not only would those terms be incorporated but they would generally, depending on the particular context, prevail over the other terms of the other agreement.[234] In *Edgeworth Capital (Luxembourg) SARL v Aabar Investments PJS*[235] Popplewell J reaffirmed the principle that where there is a conflict between the express terms contained in a contract and those which are incorporated by reference from another document, the terms of the contract will ordinarily prevail over those from the incorporated document. This reflects the fact that the parties are more likely to have had in mind and given attention to the express terms of the contract itself when negotiating and signing it than to the terms of a different document which is merely referred to.

---

[231] See e.g. *OK Petroleum AB v Vitol Energy SA* [1995] 2 Lloyd's Rep. 160, per Colman J:

"In particular, in approaching the question whether a charterparty arbitration clause is incorporated by general words of incorporation into a bill of lading contract, the courts have repeatedly held that great weight is to be attached to the consideration that an arbitration clause between shipowner and charterer is not 'germane' or relevant to those contractual rights and obligations which arise under the bill of lading contract. There is in the authorities a well-developed approach to construction of general words of incorporation that only such provisions will be incorporated as are in substance relevant or germane to, and, if incorporated, capable of being operated in conjunction with the subject-matter of the bill of lading."

[232] See e.g. *Assicurazioni Generali SPA v Ege Sigorta AS* [2002] Lloyd's Rep. I.R. 480, per Colman J:

"... general words of incorporation in a reinsurance contract will not generally incorporate jurisdiction clauses from the primary policy. The reason for this is that such clauses are not germane to the primary risk reinsured, but are merely ancillary provisions which the parties to the reinsurance would not normally intend to incorporate".

[233] *Habas Sinai Ve Tibbi Gazlar Istihsal Endustrisi AS v Sometal Sal* [2010] EWHC 29 (Comm); [2010] 1 Lloyd's Rep. 661.

[234] *Northrop Grumman Mission Systems Europe Ltd v BAE Systems (Al Diriyah C4I) Ltd* [2014] EWHC 2955 (TCC).

[235] [2018] EWHC 1627 (Comm); [2018] 2 P. & C.R. DG21.

The general principle that where a contract incorporates the terms of another document, and the terms of that other document conflict with the terms of the host contract, the terms of the host contract will prevail is not determinative in a case in which the terms of a contract of employment have to be gathered from a patchwork of sources. In such a case the court must resolve the inconsistency in the way which it believes best reflects the intentions of the parties, and for that purpose may have regard to the way in which the contract had been operated in practice and the realities of the situation.[236]

In some cases the parties intend to incorporate standard terms which are subject to alteration from time to time (e.g. the Standard Conditions of Sale or a standard freight scale). If the contract is silent as to the possibility of amendment the question may arise as to which version of the terms should be taken to have been incorporated. Prima facie a reference to standard terms or conditions is a reference to the terms or conditions current at the date of the contract,[237] although this may be rebutted by other indications in the documents comprising the contract.[238] In *Ford Motor Company of Australia Ltd v Arrowcrest Group Pty Ltd*,[239] Finkelstein J said: **3.73**

> "... prima facie a reference to standard terms and conditions is a reference to the terms and conditions current at the date of the contract. ... There will be occasions when the incorporation includes amendments made from time to time ... [u]sually this will only occur when the amendments are of a procedural, and not a substantive, type."

It was held in *MPloy Group Ltd v Denso Manufacturing UK Ltd*[240] that clear words are necessary before words of incorporation are effective to incorporate amendments made to standard terms from time to time.

But where the parties provided for arbitrations arising out of the contract to be governed by the rules of the International Chamber of Commerce, it was held that they had incorporated those rules as amended from time to time.[241] Similarly, where the parties incorporate a standard scale of charges which is designed to be brought up to date from time to time, a reference to the scale in a continuing contract should be read as a reference to that scale as amended from time to time.[242] However, there may be a distinction between the incorporation of procedural provisions and substantive provisions. It may be that while a reference to the former will be taken to mean the provisions as amended from time to time, a reference to the latter will   **3.74**

---

[236] *Pimlico Plumbers Ltd v Smith* [2017] EWCA Civ 51; [2017] I.C.R. 657. It is not considered that this statement of principle was affected by the subsequent appeal to the Supreme Court: [2018] UKSC 29; [2018] I.R.L.R. 872.

[237] *Smith v South Wales Switchgear Ltd* [1978] 1 W.L.R. 165 (standard terms of sale). Where parties incorporate the terms of a statute which has been amended, it appears that there is no presumption that they intend to incorporate the statute as amended by the date of the contract: *Brett v Brett Essex Golf Club Ltd* [1986] 1 E.G.L.R. 154 CA (Landlord and Tenant Act 1954 and amendments made in 1969). However, the court did not refer to the Interpretation Act 1978 s.23(3), which suggests the contrary in the case of legislation passed after 1 January 1979.

[238] *Aqua Design & Play International Ltd v Kier Regional Ltd* [2002] EWCA Civ 797 (corrections made to superseded form).

[239] [2002] FCA 156 at [6].

[240] [2014] EWHC 2992 (Comm).

[241] *Offshore International SA v Banco Central SA* [1976] 2 Lloyd's Rep. 402 (not reported on this point at [1976] 3 All E.R. 749).

[242] *The Bungamawar* [1978] 1 Lloyd's Rep. 263.

be taken to mean a reference to the provisions as they exist at the date of the contract.[243] A reference to a non-existent version of a standard form may be corrected by the court.[244]

3.75   In considering whether an arbitration clause has been validly incorporated the court is entitled, in an appropriate case to conclude that something has gone wrong with the language. Thus in *Caresse Navigation Ltd v Office National De L'electricite*,[245] a charterparty contained a clause that stated that it was to be governed by English law and that disputes should be resolved by the English courts. A bill of lading stated that all the terms of the charterparty "including the Law and Arbitration clause" were incorporated. The court held that since the charterparty contained no arbitration clause, but did contain a law and jurisdiction clause, the words of incorporation were sufficient to incorporate that clause. It was a case in which the reasonable reader would have understood that something had gone wrong with the language.

(b)   Incorporation of statutory provisions

3.76   The starting point is to decide whether the terms of a statute (or part of it) are incorporated at all. In *NRAM Plc v McAdam*,[246] a contract stated that: "This is a Credit Agreement regulated by the Consumer Credit Act 1974". In fact it was not, and it was held that the parties had not incorporated any part of the Act. Nor did the statement amount to a promise to treat the borrowers as if the agreement had been regulated or estop the lender from contending that it was not.

3.77   If the terms of a statute are incorporated into a contract by reference, the contract has to be read as if the words of the statute are written out in the contract and construed, as a matter of contract, in their contractual context[247]; but where a contract incorporates a statutory definition, the meaning of the word in the contract will usually be given the same meaning as it bears in the statute. In *Enviroco Ltd v Farstad Supply A/S*,[248] a contract defined an "affiliate" as including a "Subsidiary", and provided that "Subsidiary" shall have the meaning assigned to it in s.736 of the Companies Act 1985. Patten LJ said:

> "In the present case, clause 1(a) of Part B of the charterparty defines 'Affiliate' as including a subsidiary of the charterer or a company of which the charterer is also a subsidiary. It then goes on to state that 'for the purposes of this definition 'Subsidiary' shall have the meaning assigned to it in Section 736 of the Companies Act 1985'. That seems to me to be an unequivocal direction to the parties and to the court that the statutory definition is to be applied. Not some alternative meaning of the same words. If Enviroco's case depends upon giving to the words of s.736 a meaning which they would not have in their statutory context then ... the effect is either to require one to read the last sentence of clause 1(a) as a direction to give the word 'subsidiary' a meaning which is not assigned to it by s.736 or simply to delete that last sentence altogether from the contract."

---

[243] *Bunge SA v Kruse* [1979] 1 Lloyd's Rep. 279.

[244] *Modern Building Wales Ltd v Limmer and Trinidad Ltd* [1975] 1 W.L.R. 1281.

[245] [2014] EWCA Civ 1366, affirming [2013] EWHC 3081 (Comm); [2014] 1 Lloyd's Rep. 337.

[246] [2015] EWCA Civ 751, reversing [2014] EWHC 4174 (Comm).

[247] *Adamastos Shipping Co Ltd v Anglo-Saxon Petroleum Co Ltd* [1959] A.C. 133; *Farstad Supply A/S v Enviroco Ltd* [2011] UKSC 11.

[248] [2009] EWCA Civ 1399; [2010] Bus. L.R. 1008 (affirmed [2011] UKSC 16; [2011] 1 W.L.R. 921).

Longmore LJ said:

"Words in a statute necessarily have to have a certain meaning and, if the parties incorporate the words of the statute into their contract, the words must have the same meaning as they had when the statute was enacted and the charterparty was agreed. It is only if the words of the contract are actually inconsistent with the meaning of the (incorporated) statutory words (as they were in *Adamastos Shipping v Anglo-Saxon Petroleum Ltd* [1958] A.C. 133) that an ambiguity can be said to arise which requires the court to choose between alternative meanings."

This has been said to be "the normal approach to the incorporation of statutory provisions in contracts".[249] In some cases, however, the incorporated parts of a statute may need to be interpreted in a different sense in order to make the contract work.[250] Where the parties incorporate the words of a statute verbatim, those words must be construed in the context of the contract, and their meaning in the context of the contract is not necessarily the same as their meaning in the context of the statute.[251]   **3.78**

In *William Hare Ltd v Shepherd Construction Ltd*,[252] Coulson J said:

"Where a contract or deed incorporates the provisions of a statute or subordinate legislation there is no presumption either way as to whether the reference is to the law for the time being in force."[253]

The question depends on the proper interpretation of the words of incorporation in the context in which they are used.[254] In *Brewers' Company v Viewplan Plc*,[255] a lease contained a covenant which defined the permitted use by reference to Class III of the Town and Country Planning (Use Classes) Order 1972. Class III consisted of light industrial use. The Order was revoked by the Town and Country Planning (Use Classes) Order 1987, which introduced new use classes, including Class B1, which included both office use and light industrial use. It was held that the terms of the covenant had incorporated the 1972 definition and was not modified by the subsequent revocation of the 1972 Order.

It seems, however, that in the case of an Act passed on or after 1 January 1979 a different rule applies. Section 17(2) of the Interpretation Act 1978 provides: **3.79**

"Where an Act repeals and re-enacts, with or without modification, a previous enactment then, unless the contrary intention appears,—

(a)   any reference in any other enactment to the enactment so repealed shall be construed as a reference to the provision re-enacted."

---

[249] *BNY Corporate Trustee Services Ltd v Eurosail—UK 2007—3bl Plc* [2011] EWCA Civ 227.
[250] *Brett v The Brett Essex Golf Club* (1986) 52 P. & C.R. 330.
[251] *GREA Real Property Investments Ltd v Williams* [1979] 1 E.G.L.R. 121.
[252] [2009] EWHC 1603 (TCC).
[253] This was the view that the author stated in previous editions of this book.
[254] *Brett v Brett Essex Golf Club* [1986] 1 E.G.L.R. 154 CA. However, s.19 of the Interpretation Act 1978 provides that where an Act cites another Act by year, statute, session or chapter, or a section or other portion of another Act by number or letter, the reference, unless the contrary intention appears, is a reference to the Act included in any revised edition of the statutes printed by authority. This section is applied to deeds and other instruments and documents by s.23(3) of the Act. The revised edition of the statutes printed by authority is Statutes in Force. These provisions do not appear to have been cited to the court, although since the legislation in question predated 1979 the sections would not have been relevant on the facts.
[255] [1989] 2 E.G.L.R. 133.

Section 23(3) of the Act provides that in the application of s.17(2)(a) to Acts passed or subordinate legislation made after 1 January 1979:

"… the reference to any other enactment includes any deed or other instrument or document."

In addition legislation may itself expressly provide for the updating of prior contracts.[256]

In *William Hare Ltd v Shepherd Construction Ltd*,[257] Coulson J added that where the provisions of the legislation are not referred to for their normative content but simply used as a convenient shorthand to describe a factual situation, it must be rare that the parties will have intended that situation to vary unpredictably with the vagaries of future legislation. In that case a "pay when paid clause" defined insolvency by reference to certain events, including the making of an administration order under Pt II of the Insolvency Act 1986. The contract was entered into after the changes to the insolvency legislation made by the Enterprise Act 2002, which allowed companies to enter administration without a court order. The Court of Appeal,[258] affirming Coulson J, held that the reference to the making of an administration order could not be read as encompassing entry into administration without a court order.

3.80   Apart from a choice of law clause by which the contract is governed by a foreign legal system, the contract may incorporate specific rules of foreign law. In such a case, as Potter LJ explained in *Shamil Bank of Bahrain v Beximco Pharmaceuticals Ltd*[259]:

"The doctrine of incorporation can only sensibly operate where the parties have by the terms of their contract sufficiently identified specific 'black letter' provisions of a foreign law or an international code or set of rules apt to be incorporated as terms of the relevant contract such as a particular article or articles of the French Civil Code or the Hague Rules. By that method, English law is applied as the governing law to a contract into which the foreign rules have been incorporated. In such a case, in construing and applying those rules, where there is ambiguity or doubt as to their ambit or effect, it may be appropriate for the Court to have regard to evidence from experts in foreign law as to the way in which the provisions identified have been interpreted and applied in their 'home' jurisdiction. However, that is still only as an end to interpretation by the English Court in the course of applying English law and rules of construction to the contract with which it is concerned."

(c)   Incorporation of other documentary material

3.81   It is not necessary for the incorporated document itself to have any contractual force or indeed any legal effect; it may be merely a printed form.[260] The terms of

---

[256] See, e.g. Enterprise Act 2002 Sch.17 para.1.

[257] [2009] EWHC 1603 (TCC).

[258] [2010] EWCA Civ 283. Had the contract been made before the amendments came into force it would have been rescued by Enterprise Act 2002 Sch.17 para.1.

[259] [2004] 2 Lloyd's Rep. 1.

[260] *Aktieselkabet Ocean v B Harding and Sons Ltd* [1928] 2 K.B. 371 at 393, per Russell J.

the incorporated document must, however, be capable of having contractual force. In *Keeley v Fosroc International Ltd*,[261] Auld LJ said:

"On the question of construction ... where a contract of employment expressly incorporates an instrument such as a collective agreement or staff handbook, it does not necessarily follow that all the provisions in that instrument or document are apt to be terms of the contract. For example, some provisions, read in their context, may be declarations of an aspiration or policy falling short of a contractual undertaking; see e.g. *Alexander and others v Standard Telephones and Cables Ltd. (No.2)* [1991] I.R.L.R. 286, per Hobhouse J, as he then was, at paragraph 31; and *Kaur v MG Rover Group Ltd* [2005] I.R.L.R. 40, CA, per Keene LJ, with whom Brooke and Jonathan Parker LJJ agreed, at paragraphs 9, 31 and 32. It is necessary to consider in their respective contexts the incorporating words and the provision in question incorporated by them."

Likewise, in *Martland v Co-operative Insurance Society Ltd*,[262] Elias P said:

"Not all terms typically found in a collective agreement will be incorporated. That is so, even where the contract of employment ostensibly incorporates all relevant terms from the collective agreement. In order to be apt for incorporation the terms must, by their nature and character, be suitable to take effect as contractual terms. Some collective terms will not do so because, for example, they are too vague or aspirational, or because their purpose is solely to regulate the relationship between the collective parties."

In *Harlow v Artemis International Corp Ltd*,[263] an employee's letter of engagement stated that: "All other terms and conditions are as detailed in the Staff Handbook as issued to you, and subject to its most recent update". It was held that certain paragraphs of the employer's redundancy policy described in the Staff Handbook had been incorporated into the contract.

In *Hyundai Merchant Marine Co Ltd v Americas Bulk Transport Ltd (The Pacific Champ)*,[264] the effect of the parties' dealings was to incorporate a pro forma charterparty which had no independent contractual effect, although it was held on the facts that no contract came into existence.

(d) Incorporation of regulatory code

Many contracts are carried out against a regulatory background. Regulatory **3.82** obligations are not necessarily contractual obligations; so the question can arise whether all or any of the regulatory obligations have been incorporated into the contract. In *Larussa-Chigi v CS First Boston Ltd*,[265] Thomas J held that a document which stated that transactions would be "governed by" a Code of Conduct established by the Bank of England achieved the incorporation of that Code. And in *Brandeis (Brokers) Ltd v Black*[266] an agreement which was said to be "subject

---

[261] [2006] I.R.L.R. 961.
[262] *UKEAT/0220/07/RN.*
[263] [2008] I.R.L.R. 629.
[264] [2013] EWHC 470 (Comm); [2013] 2 Lloyd's Rep. 320.
[265] [1998] C.L.C. 277.
[266] [2001] 2 Lloyd's Rep. 359.

to" regulatory rules was held by Toulson J to have the same effect. But the mere fact that a contract recognises the existence of regulatory obligations will not be enough. In *Target Rich International Ltd v Forex Capital Markets Ltd*[267] Mr Adrian Beltrami QC said:

> "In broad terms, claimants have sought to fuse the existence of regulatory obligations with contractual rights agreed between the parties by drawing attention to instances where regulatory rules were mentioned or even described within a set of contractual terms. Such attempts have been uniformly unsuccessful. Whilst the court will give effect to clear expressions of incorporation, the cases demonstrate a consistent recognition that regulatory obligations are distinct from contractual rights, that they may operate in parallel without fusion and, in particular, that mere references in contractual terms to the existence and content of regulatory obligations will not, or at least will not lightly, be treated as an incorporation of any specific obligations mentioned, let alone of the rules as a whole."

(e) Inappropriate incorporation

3.83 The terms of the clauses which are incorporated into the parties' contract may not always be entirely appropriate to the contract into which they are incorporated. The proper approach to interpreting an incorporated document was laid down by the House of Lords in *Thomas (TW) & Co Ltd v Portsea Steamship Co Ltd*,[268] and by the Court of Appeal in *Hamilton & Co v Mackie & Sons*.[269] In the latter case, Lord Esher MR took the approach of reading in the whole terms of the incorporated document, and then treating any term which was inconsistent with the incorporating document as insensible and to be disregarded.[270] In the former case, Lord Gorell and Lord Robson approached the matter from the standpoint of reading in so much of the incorporated document as is not inconsistent with the subject-matter of the incorporating document. The two approaches may differ slightly but they usually achieve the same result.[271] The process was described by Buckley LJ in *Modern Buildings Wales Ltd v Limmer and Trinidad Ltd*[272] as follows:

> "Where parties by an agreement import the terms of some other document as part of their agreement those terms must be imported in their entirety, in my judgment, but subject to this: that if any of the imported terms in any way conflicts with the expressly agreed terms, the latter must prevail over what would otherwise be imported."

3.84 The court may read the incorporated clauses with such modifications as are necessary to make them apply to the contract into which they are incorporated.

---

[267] [2020] EWHC 1544 (Comm).

[268] [1912] A.C. 1.

[269] (1889) 5 T.L.R. 677 (approved in the former case). See also *Skanska Rashleigh Weatherfoil Ltd v Somerfield Stores Ltd* [2007] C.I.L.L. 2449; [2006] EWCA Civ 1732, referring to this passage with approval.

[270] In *Tradigrain SA v King Diamond Shipping SA* [2000] 2 Lloyd's Rep. 319, Rix LJ took the same approach.

[271] See *Adamastos Shipping Co Ltd v Anglo-Saxon Petroleum Co Ltd* [1959] A.C. 133 at 179, per Lord Keith of Avonholm. However, in *Cegelec Projects Ltd v Pirelli Construction Co Ltd* unreported 21 May 1998, they did not.

[272] [1975] 1 W.L.R. 1281.

Thus, in *Adamastos Shipping v Anglo-Saxon Petroleum Ltd*,[273] a charterparty included a clause which stated: "This bill of lading shall have effect subject to the Carriage of Goods by Sea Act of the United States ... 1936". The United States Act provided that it did not apply to charterparties. The House of Lords held that the words "this bill of lading" should be read as "this charterparty" and that the section of the incorporated Act which provided that it did not apply to charterparties should be rejected as meaningless. Lord Somervell of Harrow said:

"The first point taken by the charterers is based on the opening words of the paramount clause 'This bill of lading' ... I agree with the learned judge that the answer to this point is an application of the principle *falsa demonstratio non nocet*. I have nothing I wish to add to his conclusion on this point. The opening words of the paramount clause are to be read as if they were: 'This charterparty.' I also agree with the learned judge on the second point based on the provision of section 5 of the Act that the Act shall not be applicable to charterparties. He said: 'Since the clause paramount says that this charterparty shall be subject to the Act, it is insensible to incorporate into the clause paramount a condition which says that the Act shall not apply to charterparties.' The provisions of the Act are, therefore, to be incorporated as terms of the contract as far as applicable."[274]

However, the court should not indulge in verbal manipulation so as to remake **3.85** the parties' bargain by rewriting clauses in the contract whose terms have been incorporated. In *The Merak*[275] and *The Annefield*,[276] it was suggested in the Court of Appeal that where a bill of lading incorporates the terms of a charterparty, clauses in the charterparty which are directly germane to the shipment carriage and delivery of goods are to be treated as incorporated into the bill of lading even if it may involve manipulation of the words used. This suggestion has now been rejected by the House of Lords in *Miramar Maritime Corp v Holborn Oil Trading Ltd*,[277] in which Lord Diplock emphasised the importance of the overall commercial purpose of a contract and business common sense. He said:

"... no businessman who had not taken leave of his senses would enter into a contract which exposed him to a potential liability of this kind; and this in itself I find to be an overwhelming reason for not indulging in verbal manipulation of the actual contractual words used in the charterparty so as to give them this effect when they are treated as incorporated in the bill of lading."

He concluded:

"... where in a bill of lading there is included a clause which purports to incorporate the terms of a specified charterparty, there is not any rule of construction that clauses in that charterparty which are germane to the shipment carriage or delivery of goods and impose obligations on the 'charterer' under that designation are presumed to be incorporated in the bill of lading with the substitu-

---

[273] [1958] A.C. 133.
[274] This is to apply the principle in *Golodetz v Kersten, Hunik & Co* (1926) 24 Lloyd's Rep. 374.
[275] [1965] P. 223. It was suggested in *Caresse Navigation Ltd v Office National De L'electricite* [2014] EWCA Civ 1366 that *The Merak* might be decided differently today.
[276] [1971] P. 168.
[277] [1984] A.C. 676.

tion of (where there is a cesser clause), or inclusion in (where there is no cesser clause) the designation 'charterer,' the designation 'consignee of the cargo' or 'bill of lading holder'."

This marks a change in the approach to the construction of terms incorporated into other contracts, a change which Lord Diplock himself recognised in his disapproval of older cases which adopted a "literalist" construction without regard to the commercial purpose of the contract under consideration.

3.86   Where the contract purports to incorporate a more nebulous concept such as "market practice" there is no scope for reading down apparent inconsistencies.[278]

Illustrations

1.   The defendant was a building contractor employed under the terms of a written contract. He subcontracted some work to the plaintiff. The subcontract recited that the subcontractor had agreed to carry out the work in accordance with the terms of the main contract. It was held that a mere recital was insufficient to incorporate the terms of the main contract into the subcontract.
Chandler Bros Ltd v Boswell[279]

2.   Contractors tendered for a contract under cover of a letter stating that the tender was subject to adequate supplies of material and labour being available. The tender was successful. The parties entered into a contract which provided that "the said tender" should be construed as part of the agreement. It was held that "the said tender" did not include the covering letter which was not incorporated into the contract.
Davis Contractors Ltd v Fareham Urban District Council[280]

3.   Shipowners chartered a vessel to charterers for the shipment of a cargo on behalf of shippers for delivery to consignees under a bill of lading which stated that "all conditions and exceptions" of the charterparty were deemed to be incorporated into the bill of lading. It was held that, by reason of long-established authority, the words of incorporation did not incorporate into the bill of lading the arbitration clause in the charterparty.
The Varenna[281]

4.   A lease of part of a building contained a rent review clause. Subsequently part of the premises were surrendered and at the same time the tenant was granted an option to renew. Simultaneously the landlord granted the tenant a lease of adjoining premises. That lease stated that, "subject as to the premises demised the terms of years granted the rent reserved and the matters specifically referred to" it was granted upon the same covenants by landlord and tenant "and to the same stipula-

---

[278] *CFH Clearing Ltd v Merrill Lynch International* [2019] EWHC 963 (Comm).
[279] [1936] 3 All E.R. 179. Even a provision requiring the subcontractor to observe and perform the conditions of the main contract does not incorporate the terms of the main contract as to payment: *Dunlop & Ranken Ltd v Hendall* [1957] 1 W.L.R. 1102.
[280] [1956] A.C. 696.
[281] [1984] Q.B. 599.

tions and conditions" as were contained in the first lease. It was held that the second lease did not incorporate the rent review clause in the first lease.
Telegraph Properties (Securities) Ltd v Courtaulds Ltd[282]

11. THE PAROL EVIDENCE RULE

Where a contract is made wholly in writing, evidence is not admissible to add to, vary or contradict the written terms.

The parol evidence rule[283] was stated by P.O. Lawrence J in *Jacobs v Batavia and General Plantations Ltd*[284] as follows: **3.87**

"It is firmly established as a rule of law that parol evidence cannot be admitted to add to, vary or contradict a deed or other written instrument. Accordingly, it has been held that (except in cases of fraud or rectification, and except, in certain circumstances, as a defence to an action for specific performance) parol evidence will not be admitted to prove that some particular term, which had been verbally agreed upon, had been omitted (by design or otherwise) from a written instrument constituting a valid and operative contract between the parties."

Lord Morris expressed the rule in similar terms in *Bank of Australasia v Palmer*.[285]

One justification of the rule is the promotion of certainty. In *Shore v Wilson*,[286] **3.88**
Tindal CJ said:

"If it were otherwise, no lawyer would be safe in advising upon the construction of a written instrument, nor any party in taking under it; for the ablest advice might be controlled, and the clearest title undermined, if, at some future period, parol evidence of the particular meaning which the party affixed to his words, or of his secret intention in making the instrument, or of the objects he meant to take benefit under it, might be set up to contradict or vary the plain language of the instrument itself."

In *AIB Group (UK) Ltd v Martin*,[287] Lord Hutton said:

"It is a general rule in the construction of deeds that the intention of the parties is to be ascertained from the words used in the deed and that, with certain limited exceptions, extrinsic evidence cannot be given to show the real intention of the parties. On occasions this rule may lead to the actual intention of the parties being defeated but the rule is applied to ensure certainty in legal affairs."

---

[282] [1981] 1 E.G.L.R. 104.
[283] The rule is examined in depth in "The Parol Evidence Rule: A Comparative Analysis and Proposal" [2003] U.N.S.W.L.J. 44. Professor David McLauchlan subjects the parol evidence rule to forceful criticism in "The Entire Agreement Clause" (2012) 128 L.Q.R. 521.
[284] [1924] 1 Ch. 287. See also *Goss v Lord Nugent* (1833) 5 B. & Ad. 58 at 64, per Lord Denman CJ.
[285] [1897] A.C. 540 at 545.
[286] (1842) 9 Cl. & F. 355; followed in *Rabin v Gerson Berger Association Ltd* [1986] 1 W.L.R. 526. In *Hope v RCA Photophone of Australia Pty Ltd* (1937) 59 C.L.R. 348 at 357, Latham CJ gave a similar justification for the rule. The Law Commission, however, concluded in 1976 that it "is a technical rule of uncertain ambit which, at best, adds to the complications of litigation without affecting the outcome, and, at worst, prevents the courts getting at the truth" (Working Paper No.70, para.43).
[287] [2002] 1 W.L.R. 94.

More recently in *Shogun Finance Ltd v Hudson*,[288] Lord Hobhouse of Woodborough said:

> "The rule that other evidence may not be adduced to contradict the provisions of a contract contained in a written document is fundamental to the mercantile law of this country; the bargain is the document; the certainty of the contract depends on it. ... This rule is one of the great strengths of English commercial law and is one of the main reasons for the international success of English law in preference to laxer systems which do not provide the same certainty."

3.89   At about the same time the High Court of Australia also asserted the value of the rule. In *Equuscorp Pty Ltd v Glengallen Investments Pty Ltd*,[289] their Honours said:

> "Where parties enter into a written agreement, the Court will generally hold them to the obligations which they have assumed by that agreement. At least, it will do so unless relief is afforded by the operation of statute or some other legal or equitable principle applicable to the case. Different questions may arise where the execution of the written agreement is contested; but that is not the case here. In a time of growing international trade with parties in legal systems having the same or even stronger deference to the obligations of written agreements (and frequently communicating in different languages and from the standpoint of different cultures) this is not a time to ignore the rules of the common law upholding obligations undertaken in written agreements. It is a time to maintain those rules. They are not unbending. They allow for exceptions. But the exceptions must be proved according to established categories. The obligations of written agreements between parties cannot simply be ignored or brushed aside."

In *BMIC Ltd v Chinnakannan Sivasankaran Siva Ltd*,[290] Popplewell J confirmed that:

> "The purpose of a written and formally executed agreement is to avoid the disputes which commonly arise when the parties' bargain is not completely recorded in writing. In a case like this, in which the parties contemplate that their agreement will be reduced to lengthy written agreements, drafted and advised on by lawyers, and formally executed, there is a strong presumption (quite apart from any entire agreement clause) that the parties do not intend to be bound by anything not recorded in their written agreement."

3.90   A more theoretical justification for the parol evidence rule is that it follows logically from a conclusion that the parties agreed to be bound by the written contract objectively interpreted. Seen in this way its justification is that it gives effect to the parties' agreement as objectively manifested.[291] The use of background in interpreting contracts does not contravene the parol evidence rule. Such evidence is consistent with the objectives of finality and certainty because it is used as an interpretive

---

[288] [2004] 1 A.C. 919. Lord Walker of Gestingthorpe agreed with Lord Hobhouse. The value of the rule in promoting certainty is robustly defended by J.J. Spigelman in *"Contractual Interpretation: A Comparative Perspective"*, a paper presented to the Third Judicial Seminar on Commercial Litigation, 23 March 2011.

[289] (2004) 218 C.L.R. 471.

[290] [2014] EWHC 1880 (Comm).

[291] Robert Stevens, *Contract Interpretation: What it says on the tin* (Inner Temple Reading, 2014).

aid for determining the meaning of the written words chosen by the parties, not to change or overrule the meaning of those words. The surrounding circumstances are facts known or facts that reasonably ought to have been known to both parties at or before the date of contracting; therefore, the concern of unreliability does not arise.[292]

Although the rule is known as the parol evidence rule, it in fact applies to all forms of evidence outside the contract itself; not merely to oral evidence. Thus, the principle that drafts of the contract are inadmissible[293] may be seen as a branch of the parol evidence rule.[294]   **3.91**

Although the rule may be clearly stated, there are numerous exceptions to it. Indeed, there are so many exceptions that some scholars assert that there is no such rule at all.[295] In their final report on the topic the Law Commission stated[296]:

> "We have now concluded that although a proposition of law can be stated which can be described as the 'parol evidence rule' it is not a rule of law which, correctly applied, could lead to evidence being unjustly excluded. Rather, it is a proposition of law which is no more than a circular statement: when it is proved or admitted that the parties to a contract intended that all the express terms of their agreement should be as recorded in a particular document or documents, evidence will be inadmissible (because irrelevant) if it is tendered only for the purpose of adding to, varying, subtracting from or contradicting the express terms of that contract."

In *Bolkiah v Brunei Darussalam*,[297] Lord Mance said:

> "For the respondents, Mr Pascoe QC rightly conceded in the Court of Appeal that 'the trouble with the parol evidence rule and the statutory enactments, is one is liable to go round in a circle with the parol evidence rule. If the court finds that all the terms of a written document—all the terms of an agreement have not been reduced to the written document, of course the court is going to let evidence in of other terms'."[298]

In *Masterton Homes Pty Ltd v Palm Assets Pty Ltd*,[299] Campbell JA summarised the principles as follows[300]:   **3.92**

> "(1)   When there is a document that on its face appears to be a complete contract, that provides an evidentiary basis for inferring that the docu-

---

[292] *Sattva Capital Corp v Creston Moly Corp* 2014 SCC 53 (Supreme Court of Canada).
[293] See para.3.31.
[294] *Youell v Bland Welch & Co Ltd* [1990] 2 Lloyd's Rep. 423.
[295] See Professor McMeel, *The Construction of Contracts*, 3rd edn (Oxford University Press, 2017), para.15.08. In *Ezekiel v Kohali* [2009] EWCA Civ 35 the Court of Appeal assumed that the parol evidence rule was still good law, although the point does not appear to have been argued. In *Rafferty v Philip* [2011] EWHC 709 (Ch) Norris J applied the rule.
[296] Law Com (No.154) para.2.7. See *National Westminster Bank v Binney* [2011] EWHC 694 (QB).
[297] [2007] UKPC 63.
[298] Lord Mance's suggestion that even where the contract contains an entire agreement clause the court will allow parol evidence of terms is now shown to be wrong by *Rock Advertising Ltd v MWB Business Exchange Centres Ltd* [2018] UKSC 24; [2019] A.C. 119.
[299] [2009] NSWCA 234.
[300] With very full citation of authority, which is omitted here.

ment contains the whole of the express contractual terms that bind the parties.

(2)   It is open to a party to prove that, even though there is a document that on its face appears to be a complete contract, the parties have agreed orally on terms additional to those contained in the writing ... Conversely, it is open to a party to prove that the parties have orally agreed that a document should contain the whole of the terms agreed between them.

(3)   The parol evidence rule applies only to contracts that are wholly in writing, and thus has no scope to operate until it has first been ascertained that the contract is wholly in writing.

(4)   Where a contract is partly written and partly oral, the terms of the contract are to be ascertained from the whole of the circumstances as a matter of fact ... Similarly, finding the terms of a wholly oral contract is a question of fact.

(5)   In determining what are the terms of a contract that is partly written and partly oral, surrounding circumstances may be used as an aid to finding what the terms of the contract are ... If it is possible to make a finding about what were the words the parties said to each other, the meaning of those words is ascertained in the light of the surrounding circumstances ... If it is not possible to make a finding about the particular words that were used (as sometimes happens when a contract is partly written, partly oral and partly inferred from conduct) the surrounding circumstances can be looked at to find what in substance the parties agreed.

(6)   A quite separate type of contractual arrangement to a contract that is partly written and partly oral is where there is a contract wholly in writing and an oral collateral contract."

3.93   The recognised exceptions to the parol evidence rule are as follows:

3.94   First, evidence is admissible to show that the contract is not yet in force by reason of an unfulfilled condition precedent. So in *Pym v Campbell*,[301] the parties entered into a written agreement for the sale of a share in an invention. The purchaser was allowed to give oral evidence that it had been agreed that the agreement was not to come into operation until the invention had been approved by an engineer appointed by the purchaser. All members of the court distinguished the parol evidence rule. As Erle J said:

"in the present case the defence begins one step earlier."

The reasoning of the court also suggests that evidence would have been admissible to show that the parties had no intention to contract.[302] So also parties are entitled to lead evidence to show that a written document has been executed in escrow only.[303] Thus in *Guardhouse v Blackburn*,[304] Sir J P Wilde said:

"... if the written document is alleged to have been signed under condition that it should not operate except in certain events parol evidence has been admitted at law to prove such condition and the breach of it."

---

[301] (1866) 6 E. & B. 370.
[302] See also *Meyer v Barnett* (1863) 3 F. & F. 696; *Air Great Lakes Pty Ltd v KS Easter (Holdings) Ltd* (1985) 2 N.S.W.L.R. 309 at 337.
[303] *Furness v Meek* (1857) 27 L.J. Ex. 34.
[304] (1866) L.R. 1 P. & D. 109.

These cases were not cited in *Chudley v Clydesdale Bank plc*[305] in which Flaux LJ said:

"Where that condition precedent is not contained in the written document, the party who alleges that there was a condition precedent would have to establish by evidence both that the written document did not contain the entire agreement between the parties and that it had been agreed between the parties that there would be a condition precedent that had to be fulfilled before the contract came into effect."[306]

This statement of principle suggests that where a contract contains an "entire agreement" clause, it is not open to a party to that contract to prove the existence of a condition precedent. At first sight that is not easy to reconcile with the proposition that the defence begins "one step earlier". But it may be justified on the basis that an agreement that a written contract is subject to a condition precedent is itself one of the terms of the overall agreement. That would seem to accord with the emphasis that the court now gives to "entire agreement" clauses.

Secondly, unless the contract contains an "entire agreement" clause,[307] evidence is admissible to show that the writing was not intended to be the entire contract between the parties. On the face of it, this exception to the rule seems to be almost destructive of the rule itself.[308] In *HSBC Bank Plc v 5th Avenue Partners Ltd*,[309] Walker J noted that "the parol evidence rule does not prevent evidence that the parties' agreement was not contained in the written document." In *Harlow v Artemis International Corporation Ltd*,[310] McCombe J held that extrinsic evidence was admissible to identify the documents to which the parties are referring to in a contract if that is not clear from the documents themselves. That is not the admission of evidence for the purpose of interpretation of the written agreement; it is merely identifying what the written agreement is.

However, the party alleging that the written document does not represent the full contract has to counter a presumption that it does. In *Gillespie v Cheney Egar & Co*,[311] Lord Russell of Killowen CJ said:

"When parties have arrived at a definite written contract, the presumption is that the writing was intended to contain all the terms of the contract; but it is a presumption only, and either party may allege an antecedent express stipulation intended to continue in force with the written contract, and may contend that the written contract was not intended to include all the terms."

Sometimes a contract will contain an express term which declares that the writ-

3.95

---

[305] [2019] EWCA Civ 344; [2020] Q.B. 284.
[306] The statement was obiter, as the allegation of condition precedent was neither pleaded nor supported by evidence.
[307] See para.3.132.
[308] This led the Law Commission to conclude that the rule was circular (*Law Commission Final Report (No.154)*, para.2.7). In some cases, however (e.g. contracts for the sale of land), all the terms that the parties have expressly agreed must be in writing and signed by both parties, otherwise there will be no contract.
[309] [2008] 2 C.L.C. 770.
[310] [2008] EWHC 1126 (QB).
[311] [1896] 2 Q.B. 59. Professor Wedderburn puts it thus: "a document which looks like a contract is to be treated as the whole contract". See [1959] C.L.J. 58. The presumption is often reinforced by an entire agreement clause: see para.3.132.

ten terms are the only terms of the contract. In *McGrath v Shah*,[312] such a term was said to be "an insuperable hurdle" to an allegation that the contract was partly contained in statements which were not recorded in the contract. However, it was also held that such a term would not prevent the statements from amounting to a collateral contract. In *Brikom Investments Ltd v Carr*,[313] however, Lord Denning MR held that such a clause was ineffective to negative the effect of an express promise or representation relied on by one of the contracting parties. Although he said that the cases were "legion" to that effect, the only one cited[314] does not support the proposition. But in *Rock Advertising Ltd v MWB Business Exchange Centres Ltd*[315] Lord Sumption said:

> "In *Brikom Investments Ltd v Carr* [1979] QB 467, 480, Lord Denning MR brushed aside an entire agreement clause, observing that 'the cases are legion in which such a clause is of no effect in the face of an express promise or representation on which the other side has relied.' In fact there were at that time no cases in which the courts had declined to give effect to such clauses, and the one case which Lord Denning cited (*J Evans & Son (Portsmouth) Ltd v Andrea Merzario Ltd* [1976] 1 W.L.R. 1078) was really a case of estoppel and concerned a different sort of clause altogether."

However, even where the contract is contained in a deed preceded by a written agreement the court must still ascertain whether the antecedent contract was intended to be entirely superseded by the deed. So in *Palmer v Johnson*,[316] Bowen LJ said:

> "One must construe the preliminary contract by itself, and see whether it was intended to go on to any, and what, extent after the formal deed had been executed."

3.96 Thirdly, unless the contract contains an "entire agreement" clause,[317] evidence is admissible to prove a collateral agreement.[318] This exception to the rule is similar to the second, and the dividing line between a collateral agreement and a contradiction of the written agreement is sometimes hard to draw. A distinction has been drawn in the cases between a collateral agreement which adds to the written agreement, and a collateral agreement which contradicts it. Thus in *Lysnar v National Bank of New Zealand*,[319] Lord Wright, delivering the advice of the Privy Council said:

> "though the collateral contract must, inevitably, it seems, add to the written contract, it must not vary it in the sense of being inconsistent with, or contradic-

---

[312] (1987) 53 P. & C.R. 452.

[313] [1979] Q.B. 467 at 480, CA. The reasoning was criticised in *Business Environment Bow Lane Ltd v Deanwater Estates Ltd* [2007] 32 E.G. 90.

[314] *J Evans & Son (Portsmouth) Ltd v Andrea Merzario Ltd* [1976] 1 W.L.R. 1078 CA.

[315] [2018] UKSC 24; [2019] A.C. 119. The decision of Gray J in *Ryanair Ltd v DR Technics Ireland Ltd* [2007] EWHC 3089 (QB); criticised in the text of the 6th edition of this book was disapproved.

[316] (1884) 13 Q.B.D. 351.

[317] See para.3.132.

[318] In cases concerning contracts for the sale of land, the notion of a collateral contract is problematic as a matter of substantive law: see *Grossman v Hooper* [2001] 2 E.G.L.R. 82. The cases referred to below might not be decided in the same way now.

[319] [1935] N.Z.L.R. 129.

tory of, the written contract to which it is collateral. ... The line between what is contradictory of, and what is merely supplemental to, the written contract may not be easy in all cases to draw."

So in *De Lassalle v Guildford*,[320] parties negotiated for the grant of a lease of a house. Terms were agreed, but the tenant refused to exchange leases unless the landlord warranted that the drains were in order. The landlord gave the warranty. Although the lease contained repairing obligations, it was silent as to the drains. The tenant was held to be entitled to prove the warranty as an agreement collateral to the lease. By contrast, in *Angell v Duke*,[321] a lease of a furnished house specified the furniture which the landlord was to provide. The tenant was not allowed to prove an oral agreement that the landlord would supply more furniture, because it would have contradicted the specification. The distinction, as a matter of the general law of contract, does not appear to survive *City and Westminster Properties* (1934) Ltd v Mudd.[322] In that case a lease contained a covenant by the tenant not to permit any part of the premises to be used as a place of lodging, dwelling or sleeping. The tenant was allowed to prove an antecedent oral agreement with the landlord that if the tenant executed the lease in that form the landlord would not enforce the covenant against him. Similarly, in *Brikom Investments Ltd v Carr*,[323] a prospective tenant was offered a lease of a flat which contained a service charge which would have obliged him to contribute to the cost of repairing the roof. The landlord assured the tenant that the cost of repairing the roof would be borne by the landlord and not passed on to the tenants. It was held by Roskill LJ (with whom Cumming Bruce LJ agreed) that the assurance amounted to a collateral contract.

Fourthly, evidence is admissible to identify the parties to the contract[324] or the subject matter of the contract,[325] or additional consideration.[326] Although evidence is admissible to identify parties to a contract, where the parties are specifically named in a written contract evidence is not admissible for the purpose of showing that others (who were not named) were also parties to the contract.[327] It is thought that this is an orthodox application of the parol evidence rule. In addition, extrinsic evidence is admissible to prove the actual role carried out by a party, even if it is misdescribed in the contract.[328]   **3.97**

Fifthly, evidence is admissible to prove custom.[329]   **3.98**

Sixthly, evidence is admissible to prove the true nature of the transaction. So for example, evidence has been admitted to show that what appeared to be a convey-   **3.99**

---

[320] [1901] 2 K.B. 215.

[321] (1875) 32 L.T. 320.

[322] [1959] Ch. 129. The impact of s.2 of the Law of Property (Miscellaneous Provisions) Act 1989 would now have to be considered. See *Business Environment Bow Lane Ltd v Deanwater Estates Ltd* [2007] 32 E.G. 90.

[323] [1979] Q.B. 467. The question whether evidence of the oral assurance was admissible does not appear to have been argued; and the impact of s.2 of the Law of Property (Miscellaneous Provisions) Act 1989 would now have to be considered. See *Business Environment Bow Lane Ltd v Deanwater Estates Ltd* [2007] 32 E.G. 90, where the reasoning was criticised.

[324] See para.10.15.

[325] See para.11.06.

[326] See para.10.72.

[327] *Barbudev v Eurocom Cable Management Bulgaria EOOD* [2011] EWHC 1560 (Comm); [2011] 2 All E.R. (Comm) 951.

[328] *Mileform Ltd v Interserve Security Ltd* [2013] EWHC 3386 (QB).

[329] See para.6.115.

ance for valuable consideration was really a conveyance on trust[330]; that a written contract for sale was a loan on security[331]; or that what appeared to be an outright conveyance was a conveyance for a limited purpose only.[332]

3.100   Finally, evidence is admissible where it is sought to challenge the validity of the contract (e.g. by claiming rectification or rescission for mistake or misrepresentation).

Illustrations

1.   A lease provided for the payment of the rent quarterly in advance. The tenant was not allowed to attempt to prove an oral agreement that payment of the rent was to be by way of a bill payable at three months, because that would have contradicted the express terms of the lease.
Henderson v Arthur[333]

2.   Parties entered into a written agreement for the assignment of a lease of a farm. The purchaser was permitted to prove an oral agreement that the written agreement should be void if the landlord refused consent to the assignment.
Wallis v Littell[334]

3.   In the course of negotiations for a lease of a flat it was orally agreed that if the prospective tenant took the flat, he should have the use of two rooms for storage, and the garden. The lease referred to neither the rooms nor the garden. It was held that the oral agreement formed part of the overall bargain, and consequently evidence of it was admissible.
Walker Property Investments (Brighton) Ltd v Walker[335]

4.   A tenant agreed to take a lease but refused to sign it until the landlord had promised to destroy rabbits on the land. The landlord gave the promise. The lease contained an obligation by the tenant not to shoot, hunt or sport on the land and to use his best endeavours to preserve game. The tenant was allowed to prove the antecedent oral agreement.
Morgan v Griffith[336]

5.   A shipping contract was made on standard terms, which allowed the forwarding agents complete freedom in the manner of transport of the goods. However, they had told the owners of the goods to be shipped that the goods would not be shipped on deck. The owners were allowed to prove the assurance. The majority of the Court

---

[330] *Haigh v Kaye* (1872) L.R. 7 Ch. 469.
[331] *Maas v Pepper* [1905] A.C. 102.
[332] *Ali v Khan* (2002) 5 I.T.E.L.R. 232.
[333] [1907] 1 K.B. 10.
[334] (1861) 11 C.B.N.S. 369. The impact of s.2 of the Law of Property (Miscellaneous Provisions) Act 1989 would now have to be considered.
[335] (1947) 177 L.T. 204. The impact of s.2 of the Law of Property (Miscellaneous Provisions) Act 1989 would now have to be considered.
[336] (1871) L.R. 6 Exch. 70; and see *Erskine v Adeane* (1873) 8 Ch. App. 756. The impact of s.2 of the Law of Property (Miscellaneous Provisions) Act 1989 would now have to be considered.

of Appeal held that the contract was partly oral, partly written, and partly created by conduct.

Evans (J) and Son (Portsmouth) Ltd v Merzario (Andrea) Ltd[337]

6.   A developer entered into an agreement for lease under which it undertook to build a building in a good substantial and workmanlike manner, and on completion of the building to grant a lease of it to the tenant. The form of the lease contained a tenant's repairing covenant. After the lease had been completed, defects appeared in the building and the tenant sued the developer on the covenant in the agreement for lease. It was held that the covenant did not merge in the lease, for it must have been the intention of the parties that it would survive the grant of the lease, otherwise it would have been of little value to the tenant.

International Press Centre Ltd v Norwich Union[338]

7.   Underwriters subscribed to a contract of reinsurance. In accordance with normal practice the reinsurance cover was initially agreed in the form of a slip. Subsequently a formal policy was issued. It was held that the slip was inadmissible in construing the policy.

Youell v Bland Welch & Co Ltd[339]

12.   TERMS INCORPORATED BY NOTICE

In addition to express verbal incorporation, terms may be incorporated by the conduct of the parties. Such conduct may consist in one party drawing to the attention of the other the terms on which he is willing to contract before the contract is concluded. The more onerous or unusual the terms, the greater the degree of notice required to incorporate them.

In many cases the contract does not consist of a document signed by both parties. In such a case the question often arises whether the standard terms of business of one of the parties to the contract have been incorporated into it.[340] It is often the case that the particular term in dispute is an exemption clause. The early cases were concerned with contracts of carriage, many arising out of the purchase of a railway ticket. In the leading case of *Parker v South Eastern Railway,*[341] it was held that if the person receiving the ticket did not see or know that there was any writing on the ticket, he is not bound by the conditions; if he knew there was writing and knew or believed that the writing contained conditions, then he is bound by the conditions; and if he knew that there was writing on the ticket, but did not know that the writing contained conditions, he is bound if the delivering of the ticket to him in such a manner that he could see that there was writing upon it was, as a matter of

3.101

---

[337] [1976] 1 W.L.R. 1078.

[338] (1986) 36 Build. L.R. 130.

[339] [1990] 2 Lloyd's Rep. 423.

[340] The Principles of European Contract Law (2:104) summarise the principle as follows: (1) Contract terms which have not been individually negotiated may be invoked against a party who did not know of them only if the party invoking them took reasonable steps to bring them to other party's attention before or when the contract was concluded. (2) Terms are not brought appropriately to a party's attention by mere reference to them in a signed contract document. There are additional requirements in the case of consumer contracts imposed by the Consumer Rights Act 2015. The Act is outside the scope of this book.

[341] (1877) 2 C.P.D. 416.

fact, reasonable notice that the writing contained conditions. Thus the three questions of fact to be answered are:

(a) Did the passenger know there was printing on the railway ticket?
(b) Did he know that the ticket contained or referred to conditions?
(c) Did the carrier do what was reasonable in the way of notifying prospective passengers of the existence of conditions and where their terms might be considered?[342]

3.102   The same principles apply to other types of contract where one party seeks to rely upon his standard terms of business which are not contained in a contract signed by both parties.[343] The first and second of these questions are really asking whether a reasonable person would have understood that the ticket or document in question was a contractual document. As Auld LJ put it in *Grogan v Robin Meredith Plant Hire*[344]:

"The central question is ... whether [the document] comes within the class of a document which the party receiving it knew contained, or which a reasonable man would expect to contain, relevant contractual conditions."

If a reasonable person would have thought that the document was no more than a receipt, then a reference in the document to contract terms will not bind him.[345] On the other hand, where a reasonable person would understand that the contract would contain conditions (e.g. a contract of insurance) the ticket cases must be applied with caution.[346]

3.103   What degree of notice is adequate is a question of fact, to be determined according to accepted social standards.[347] If the party putting forward the terms specifically advises the other party to read them, notice is likely to be adequate.[348] Notice must be given before the contract is concluded, otherwise the contract will already be complete. Thus many of the cases turn on the question when the contract was formed.[349]

The degree of notice will vary according to the nature of the term sought to be incorporated.[350] In *Thornton v Shoe Lane Parking Ltd*,[351] Megaw LJ said:

"When the conditions sought to be attached all constitute, ... 'the sort of restric-

---

[342] See also *Richardson Spence & Co v Rowntree* [1894] A.C. 217; *Hood v Anchor Line (Henderson Brothers) Ltd* [1918] A.C. 837; *McCutcheon v Macbrayne (David) Ltd* [1964] 1 W.L.R. 125.

[343] At one level the cases are concerned with a question of pure contractual analysis, whether one party has done enough to give the other notice of the incorporation of a term in the contract. At another level they are concerned with a somewhat different question, whether it would in all the circumstances be fair (or reasonable) to hold a party bound by any conditions or by a particular condition of an unusual and stringent nature. See Interfoto *Picture Library Ltd v Stiletto Visual Programmes Ltd* [1989] 1 Q.B. 433, per Bingham LJ.

[344] [1996] C.L.C. 1127. A time sheet, an invoice and a statement of account will not usually have contractual effect.

[345] *Chapelton v Barry Urban District Council* [1940] 1 K.B. 532.

[346] *William McIlroy Swindon Ltd v Quinn Insurance Ltd* [2010] EWHC 2448 (TCC).

[347] *Hood v Anchor Line (Henderson Brothers) Ltd* [1918] A.C. 837.

[348] *William McIlroy Swindon Ltd v Quinn Insurance Ltd* [2010] EWHC 2448 (TCC).

[349] For example, *Chapelton v Barry Urban District Council* [1940] 1 K.B. 532; *Thornton v Shoe Lane Parking Ltd* [1972] 2 Q.B. 163.

[350] This proposition was approved by the Supreme Court of Ireland in *James Elliott Construction Ltd v Irish Asphalt Ltd* [2014] IESC 74.

[351] [1972] 2 Q.B. 163.

tion ... that is usual', it may not be necessary for a defendant to prove more than that the intention to attach some conditions has been fairly brought to the notice of the other party. But at least where the particular condition relied on involves a sort of restriction that is not shown to be usual in that class of contract, a defendant must show that his intention to attach an unusual condition of that particular nature was fairly brought to the notice of the other party. How much is required as being, ... 'reasonably sufficient to give the plaintiff notice of the condition', depends upon the nature of the restrictive condition."

In *Spurling (J) Ltd v Bradshaw*,[352] Denning LJ put it more graphically:

"I quite agree that the more unreasonable a clause is, the greater the notice which must be given of it. Some clauses which I have seen would need to be printed in red ink on the face of the document with a red hand pointing to it before the notice could be held to be sufficient."

In *Kaye v Nu Skin Ltd*,[353] Kitchin J referred to:

"the requirement that particularly onerous or unusual conditions are brought fairly and reasonably to the attention of the other party, failing which they may be found never to have formed part of the contract; alternatively, the other party may be relieved from liability under them."

But in *Woodeson v Credit Suisse (UK) Ltd*,[354] Longmore LJ said:

"The first step that has to be taken is to consider each term which is said to be onerous or unusual, and decide if it is correctly so characterised. Only if any of them do, does one need to move to the second step of the process, and consider adequacy of notice."

In *Goodlife Foods Ltd v Hall Fire Protection Ltd*[355] a manufacturer of food **3.104** products acquired a sprinkler system for its factory. Clause 11 of the standard terms excluded liability, but offered to arrange insurance for excluded losses. The manufacturer's argument that cl.11 was onerous and not incorporated into the contract was rejected. Coulson LJ set out the general principle:

"It is a well-established principle of common law that, even if A knows that there are standard conditions provided as part of B's tender, a condition which is 'particularly onerous or unusual' will not be incorporated into the contract, unless it has been fairly and reasonably brought to A's attention."

He then went on to consider two questions: (a) was the clause particularly onerous, and (b) if so, was it fairly brought to A's attention? As to the first he said:

"The question of whether or not clause 11 was particularly onerous or unusual has to be considered in the context of the contract as a whole. This was a one-off supply contract carried out, for a modest sum, in 2002. Other than the limited warranty noted by the judge, Hall Fire had no maintenance obligations or any

---

[352] [1956] 1 W.L.R. 461.
[353] [2011] 1 Lloyd's Rep. 40.
[354] [2018] EWCA Civ 1103.
[355] [2018] EWCA Civ 1371; [2018] C.T.L.C. 265.

other connection with the premises at Warrington after they had installed the system. In those circumstances, I consider that it was neither particularly unusual nor onerous for Hall Fire fully to protect themselves against the possibility of unlimited liability arising from future events."

As to the second, he said:

"Clause 11 was not buried away in the middle of a raft of small print, such as occurs in some of the older cases. Instead it was one of the standard conditions which were expressly referred to on the front of the quotation and which were printed in clear type. Moreover, its potentially wide-reaching effect was expressly identified at the very start of those same conditions. In my view, the fact that the warning (paragraph 11 above) was cast in almost apocalyptic terms is a point against (rather than in favour of) Goodlife: if that did not alert them to the effect of clause 11, then nothing would have done. A buyer who started reading these conditions would have seen by the very first words used that, at the very least, the conditions contained terms which were emphatically not in the buyer's interests. Obviously, the buyer should then have read on."

Gross LJ said:

"With regard to the question as to the adequacy of notice, the common law in effect operated a sliding scale."

In *Bates v Post Office (No.3)*[356] Fraser J said:

"The degree of notice depends upon the nature of the clause; the more severe its effect, the greater the notice required. Such a clause must have the potential to act very severely to the detriment of the party in question. It is a principle available to contracting parties who are not consumers, but context and the respective bargaining positions of the parties are relevant. So too is a recommendation that legal advice be sought before the contract is entered into. I also consider that it is a high hurdle that must be passed for a term to be held to be onerous and unusual."

3.105 It is not necessary to the incorporation of trading terms into a contract that they should be specifically set out provided that they are conditions in common form or usual terms in the relevant business. It is sufficient if adequate notice is given identifying and relying upon the conditions and they are available on request. A statement that the terms and conditions are available on a website may be sufficient in the case of a contract made between commercial parties.[357] Clear words of reference suffice to incorporate the terms referred to. Other considerations apply if the conditions or any of them are particularly onerous or unusual.[358] An anti-

---

[356] [2019] EWHC 606 (QB).

[357] *Impala Warehousing and Logistics (Shanghai) Co Ltd v Wanxiang Resources (Singapore) PTE Ltd* [2015] EWHC 25 (Comm).

[358] *Circle Freight International Ltd v Medeast Gulf Exports Ltd* [1988] 2 Lloyd's Rep. 427. This section was approved by the Supreme Court of Ireland in *Noreside Construction Ltd v Irish Asphalt Ltd* [2014] IESC 68.

set-off clause in a commercial contract for the sale of goods is not so unusual or onerous that it must be specifically and separately drawn to the buyer's attention.[359]

In *Interfoto Picture Library Ltd v Stiletto Visual Programmes Ltd*,[360] Interfoto ran a photographic transparency lending library. Following a telephone inquiry by Stiletto, Interfoto delivered to them 47 transparencies together with a delivery note containing nine printed conditions. Condition 2 said that all the transparencies had to be returned within 14 days of delivery otherwise a holding fee of £5 per day and value added tax would be charged for each transparency retained thereafter. Stiletto, who had not used Interfoto's services before, did not read the conditions. Dillon LJ said:

"It is, in my judgment, a logical development of the common law into modern conditions that it should be held ... that, if one condition in a set of printed conditions is particularly onerous or unusual, the party seeking to enforce it must show that that particular condition was fairly brought to the attention of the other party.

In the present case, nothing whatever was done by the plaintiffs to draw the defendants' attention particularly to condition 2; it was merely one of four columns' width of conditions printed across the foot of the delivery note. Consequently condition 2 never, in my judgment, became part of the contract between the parties."

If the test laid down in *Interfoto* is satisfied in relation to an arbitration clause, it will amount to a voluntary renunciation of the right to a fair trial for the purposes of art.6 of the European Convention on Human Rights.[361] **3.106**

Where the question is whether a jurisdiction clause has been incorporated for the purpose of the Recast Regulation[362] or similar international conventions, the test is not governed by domestic law. The question in such cases is whether there has been "real consent" to, or "actual acceptance" of, the clause which must be "clearly and precisely demonstrated".[363] **3.107**

Illustrations

1.   The claimant hired two deck chairs. As he paid, he was handed a receipt on the reverse of which was printed a clause exempting the hirer from liability. It was held that the clause was ineffective because the contract of hire was complete before the clause was drawn to the claimant's attention.
Chapelton v Barry Urban District Council[364]

2.   A man and his wife arrived at a hotel and paid for one week's board and residence in advance. They then went up to their room in which was displayed a notice purporting to exempt the hotelier from liability for lost and stolen articles.

[359] *F.G. Wilson (Engineering) Ltd v John Holt & Co (Liverpool) Ltd* [2012] EWHC 2477 (Comm); [2012] 2 Lloyd's Rep. 479.
[360] [1989] Q.B. 433; *AEG (UK) Ltd v Logic Resource Ltd* [1996] C.L.C. 265.
[361] *Stretford v Football Association Ltd* [2007] 2 Lloyd's Rep. 31 (subject to questions of duress, undue influence or misrepresentation).
[362] Regulation 1215/2012.
[363] *Salotti v RÜWA Polstereimaschinen GmbH* [1977] 1 C.M.L.R. 345; *Mains Schiffahrts-Genossenschaft v Les Gravieres Rhenones (C-106/95)* Mains Schiffahrts-Genossenschaft v Les Gravières Rhénones (C-106/95) [1997] Q.B. 731; *Coreck Maritime GmbH v Handelsveen BV* (C-387/98) [2001] C.L.C 550. See further para.18.83.
[364] [1940] 1 K.B. 532.

It was held that the notice was not incorporated into the contract between the guests and the hotelier because the contract was concluded before the guest had seen it.
Olley v Marlborough Court Ltd[365]

3.   The plaintiff agreed to go on holiday with a friend. The friend received the defendant's brochure, which drew attention to the conditions of carriage. The friend read the brochure. He obtained two tickets on board the defendant's ship and later read the conditions which contained a wide exemption clause. It was held that although the friend was acting as the plaintiff's agent, his contract was complete before the ticket containing the exemption clause was delivered, and the brochure was not sufficient notice.
Hollingworth v Southern Ferries Ltd[366]

4.   An advertising agency inquired of a photographic library whether it had any material suitable for a presentation. The library dispatched 47 transparencies in a bag. Also inside the bag was a delivery note which contained "conditions" including a condition requiring payment of a daily "holding charge" of an exorbitant amount if the transparencies were not returned within 14 days. It was held that since the condition had not been specifically drawn to the attention of the agency, it was not bound by it.
Interfoto Picture Library Ltd v Stiletto Visual Programmes Ltd[367]

5.   A football agent obtained an annual licence from FIFA. The licence stated that "the holder of this licence agrees to abide by the rules and regulations of FIFA, The FA Premier League and the Football League". Those rules and regulations included an annual handbook which had been issued since the 1989/90 season. The handbook had for many years contained an arbitration clause. It was held that the agent was bound by the latest revision to the clause.
Stretford v Football Association Ltd[368]

6.   A work order for aircraft maintenance identified the name of the customer, the aircraft, the place where the work was to be carried out and the items of work to be done. In place of a priced quotation were the letters T&M, standing for "time and materials". It was a short document. At its foot were words in large capital letters stating that no work would commence until the order was signed and returned, below which appeared in smaller but legible capital letters "terms and conditions available upon request". It was held that the more likely interpretation was that the "terms and conditions" were incorporated into the contract.
Rooney v CSE Bournemouth Ltd[369]

13.   TERMS INCORPORATED BY COURSE OF DEALING

Terms may be incorporated by a previous consistent course of dealing between the parties, or by their common understanding.

3.108   In some cases although the standard terms have not been drawn to the attention

---

[365] [1949] 1 K.B. 533.
[366] [1977] 2 Lloyd's Rep. 70, followed in *Daly v General Steam Navigation Co Ltd* [1979] 2 Lloyd's Rep. 257.
[367] [1989] Q.B. 433.
[368] [2007] 2 Lloyd's Rep. 31.
[369] [2011] EWCA Civ 1364.

of the contracting party before the conclusion of the contract in question, nevertheless he is bound by them because of a pre-existing course of conduct, or a common understanding between the parties. The question whether terms have been incorporated by reference to a previous course of dealing is essentially a question of the implication of terms. Thus the usual tests for the implication of terms will need to be satisfied.[370]

Incorporation of terms by prior course of dealing is a question of fact and degree. **3.109** It depends on the number of previous contracts, how recent they are, and their similarity in terms of subject matter and the manner in which they were concluded.[371] As Lord Pearce said in *McCutcheon v Macbrayne (David) Ltd*[372]:

> "It is the consistency of a course of conduct which gives rise to the implication that in similar circumstances a similar contractual result will follow. Where the conduct is not consistent, there is no reason why it should still produce an invariable contractual result."

Accordingly, where a previous course of dealing does not exhibit consistency, it will not have the effect of incorporating terms. Likewise, as Donaldson J said in *Salsi v Jetspeed Air Services Ltd*[373]:

> "Usage apart, no-one can contend that he has usual trading conditions if he has never used them or brought them to the attention of anyone."

In general, a large number of transactions will require to be proved before the **3.110** court will permit one party to a contract to rely on a course of dealing in order to rely upon standard terms of business.[374] In cases of contracts made between commercial organisations of equal bargaining power, it seems that less stringent standards are applied as compared with consumer contracts. In view of the Unfair Contract Terms Act 1977 and the Consumer Rights Act 2015, which give wide protection to consumers against exemption clauses, it is questionable whether this approach is justified any longer.

However, in cases where the number of transactions proved is insufficient to **3.111** amount to a course of conduct, it is still possible that standard terms will be held to have been incorporated into a contract. In *British Crane Hire Corp Ltd v Ipswich Plant Hire Ltd*,[375] it was proved that the hirer of a crane expected that the hire would be subject to conditions imposed by the supplier. However, there was no course of dealing between the parties, and the actual terms of business of the supplier had not been drawn to the attention of the hirer before the contract was concluded. Nevertheless the supplier's terms were held to have been incorporated into the contract of hire. Lord Denning MR (with whom Megaw LJ agreed) said:

---

[370] *Lisnave Estaleiros Navais SA v Chemikalien Seetransport GmbH* [2013] EWHC 338 (Comm); [2013] 2 Lloyd's Rep. 203.

[371] *Capes (Hatherden) Ltd v Western Arable Services Ltd* [2010] 1 Lloyd's Rep. 477.

[372] [1964] 1 W.L.R. 125 at 138.

[373] [1977] 2 Lloyd's Rep. 57.

[374] For example, three or four transactions per month for three years (*Hardwick Game Farm v Suffolk Agricultural Producers* [1969] 2 A.C. 31); 81 contracts over 5 1/2 years (*SLA T di del Ferro v Tradax Overseas SA* [1980] 1 Lloyd's Rep. 53); but not three or four contracts in five years (*Hollier v Rambler Motors (AMC) Ltd* [1972] 2 Q.B. 71).

[375] [1975] Q.B. 303. A similar conclusion was reached in *The Havprins* [1983] 2 Lloyd's Rep. 356, where terms were held to have been incorporated because one party "knew and intended" that the other party's standard terms were to apply.

"I would not put it so much on the course of dealing, but rather on the common understanding which is to be derived from the conduct of the parties, namely that the hiring was to be on the terms of the plaintiff's usual conditions."

Sir Eric Sachs gave a slightly different reason. He said that the terms were incorporated because on the facts the supplier was entitled to conclude that the hirer accepted its conditions.[376]

3.112   Where the question is whether a jurisdiction clause has been incorporated for the purpose of the Judgment Regulation[377] or similar international conventions, the test is not governed by domestic law. The question in such cases is whether there has been "real consent" to, or "actual acceptance" of, the clause which must be "clearly and precisely demonstrated".[378]

3.113   A previous course of dealing may also be relied on in interpreting the terms of a contract that the parties have made.[379]

3.114   In *Transformers & Rectifiers Ltd v Needs Ltd*,[380] Edwards-Stuart J summarised the principles:

"i)   Where A makes an offer on its conditions and B accepts that offer on its conditions and, without more, performance follows, the correct analysis, assuming that each party's conditions have been reasonably drawn to the attention of the other, is that there is a contract on B's conditions;

ii)   Where there is reliance on a previous course of dealing it does not have to be extensive. Three or four occasions over a relatively short period may suffice;

iii)   The course of dealing by the party contending that its terms and conditions are incorporated has to be consistent and unequivocal;

iv)   Where trade or industry standard terms exist for the type of transaction in question, it will usually be easier for a party contending for those conditions to persuade the court that they should be incorporated, provided that reasonable notice of the application of the terms has been given;

v)   A party's standard terms and conditions will not be incorporated unless that party has given the other party reasonable notice of those terms and conditions;

vi)   It is not always necessary for a party's terms and conditions to be included or referred to in the documents forming the contract; it may be sufficient if they are clearly contained in or referred to in invoices sent subsequently;

vii)   By contrast, an invoice following a concluded contract effected by a clear offer on standard terms which are accepted, even if only by delivery, will or may be too late."

---

[376] An approach similar to that of Diplock LJ in *Hardwick Game Farm v Suffolk Agricultural Producers* [1966] 1 W.L.R. 287 at 339.

[377] Regulation 1215/2012.

[378] *Salotti v RÜWA Polstereimaschinen GmbH* [1977] 1 C.M.L.R. 345; *Mains Schiffahrts-Genossenschaft v Les Gravieres Rhenones (C-106/95)* Mains Schiffahrts-Genossenschaft v Les Gravières Rhénones (C-106/95) [1997] Q.B. 731; *Coreck Maritime GmbH v Handelsveen BV* (C-387/98) [2001] C.L.C. 550. See further para.18.83.

[379] *The BBC Greenland* [2012] 1 Lloyd's Rep. 230.

[380] [2015] EWHC 269 (TCC) (omitting references to authority); *Hamad M. Aldrees & Partners v Rotex Europe Ltd* [2019] EWHC 574 (TCC); 184 Con. L.R. 145.

Illustrations

1.   The defendant had dealt with the plaintiff warehousemen for many years. When he delivered goods to them he would receive within a few days a document acknowledging receipt of the goods and containing a printed exemption clause. He was held to be bound by the exemption clause.
Spurling (J) Ltd v Bradshaw[381]

2.   Three or four times a month for three years the sellers sold feedstuff to the buyers. The buyers would order the goods orally, and the order would be accepted orally. A day or two later the sellers would send the buyers a sold note, containing various conditions. It was held that those conditions governed the sales.
Hardwick Game Farm v Suffolk Producers Association[382]

3.   The plaintiff had had his car repaired by the defendant three or four times during a five-year period. On at least two occasions he signed a document which contained a wide exemption clause. It was held that no sufficient course of dealing had been proved.
Hollier v Rambler Motors (AMC) Ltd[383]

4.   An advertising agency inquired of a photographic library whether it had any material suitable for a presentation. The library dispatched 47 transparencies in a bag. Also inside the bag was a delivery note which contained "conditions" including a condition requiring payment of a daily "holding charge" of an exorbitant amount if the transparencies were not returned within 14 days. It was held that since the condition had not been specifically drawn to the attention of the agency, it was not bound by it.
Interfoto Picture Library Ltd v Stiletto Visual Programmes Ltd[384]

5.   Over a number of years, photographers and their representatives supplied transparencies to magazine publishers. The transparencies were accompanied by a delivery note containing terms of business. The delivery of the transparencies was held to be an offer on the terms of the delivery note, with the result that those terms were incorporated into the contract upon acceptance.
Photolibrary Group Ltd v Burda Senator Verlag GmbH[385]

6.   A manufacturer purported to attach terms and conditions (including an exclusion clause) to a quotation given to a customer; but in fact failed to do so. It was unable to rely on a previous course of dealing because its approach to incorporation had been inconsistent and the reasonable businessperson would conclude that the terms were only possibly incorporated, which did not suffice.
Hamad M Aldrees & Partners v Rotex Europe Ltd[386]

14.   BATTLE OF THE FORMS

Where there is an exchange of offer and counter-offer, each referring to different standard terms, whether there is a contract and if so, on whose terms,

---

[381]   [1956] 1 W.L.R. 461.
[382]   [1969] 2 A.C. 31.
[383]   [1972] 2 Q.B. 71.
[384]   [1989] Q.B. 433.
[385]   [2008] 2 All E.R. (Comm) 881.
[386]   [2019] EWHC 574 (TCC); 184 Con. L.R. 145.

must be objectively assessed. But the assessment will usually be conducted on the basis of a traditional analysis of offer and counter offer, with the result that the "last shot" will usually prevail.

3.115 In *RTS Flexible Ltd v Molkerei Alois Muller Gmbh & Co KG*,[387] Lord Clarke said:

"Whether there is a binding contract between the parties and, if so, upon what terms depends upon what they have agreed. It depends not upon their subjective state of mind, but upon a consideration of what was communicated between them by words or conduct, and whether that leads objectively to a conclusion that they intended to create legal relations and had agreed upon all the terms which they regarded or the law requires as essential for the formation of legally binding relations. Even if certain terms of economic or other significance to the parties have not been finalised, an objective appraisal of their words and conduct may lead to the conclusion that they did not intend agreement of such terms to be a pre-condition to a concluded and legally binding agreement."

In *Butler Machine Tool Co Ltd v Ex-Cell-O Corp (England) Ltd*,[388] Lawton LJ said:

"The modern commercial practice of making quotations and placing orders with conditions attached, usually in small print, is indeed likely, as in this case, to produce a battle of forms. The problem is how should that battle be conducted? The view taken by the judge was that the battle should extend over a wide area and the court should do its best to look into the minds of the parties and make certain assumptions. In my judgment, the battle has to be conducted in accordance with set rules. It is a battle more on classical 18th century lines when convention decided who had the right to open fire first rather than in accordance with the modern concept of attrition."

3.116 The set rules are those of offer and acceptance. Although Lord Denning MR appeared to favour a wider test, he nevertheless said that:

"... it will be found that in most cases when there is a 'battle of forms' there is a contract as soon as the last of the forms is sent and received without objection being taken to it."

On the facts the contract was on the buyer's terms and conditions, because the seller had completed and returned the acknowledgment of order which was stated to be on the buyer's terms and conditions. The seller's later letter, which referred to its own terms and conditions, was found to be irrelevant because it simply referred to the price and identity of the machine in question, and did not operate, as a matter of construction, to incorporate the seller's terms back into the contract.

3.117 In *Tekdata Interconnections Ltd v Amphenol Ltd*,[389] Longmore LJ said:

"The way in which I would put it is to say that the traditional offer and acceptance analysis must be adopted unless the documents passing between the par-

---

[387] [2010] 1 W.L.R. 753.
[388] [1979] 1 W.L.R. 401.
[389] [2010] 1 Lloyd's Rep. 357; *Claxton Engineering Services Ltd v TXM Olaj-Es Gazkutato KFT* [2010] EWHC 2567 (Comm).

ties and their conduct show that their common intention was that some other terms were intended to prevail."

In the same case Dyson LJ said:

"[24] The paradigm battle of the forms occurs where A offers to buy goods from B on its (A's) conditions and B accepts the offer but only on its own conditions. As is pointed out in *Cheshire, Fifoot and Furmston's Law of Contract* (15th edn, 2006) p 210, it may be possible to analyse the legal situation that results as being that there is: (i) a contract on A's conditions; (ii) a contract on B's conditions; (iii) a contract on the terms that would be implied by law, but incorporating neither A's nor B's conditions; (iv) a contract incorporating some blend of both parties' conditions; or (v) no contract at all.

[25] In my judgment, it is not possible to lay down a general rule that will apply in all cases where there is a battle of the forms. It always depends on an assessment of what the parties must objectively be taken to have intended. But where the facts are no more complicated than that A makes an offer on its conditions and B accepts that offer on its conditions and, without more, performance follows, it seems to me that the correct analysis is what Longmore LJ has described as the 'traditional offer and acceptance analysis', ie that there is a contract on B's conditions. I accept that this analysis is not without its difficulties in circumstances of the kind to which Professor Treitel refers in the passage quoted at [20], above. But in the next sentence of that passage, Professor Treitel adds: 'For this reason the cases described above are best regarded as exceptions to a general requirement of offer and acceptance.' I also accept the force of the criticisms made in Anson. But the rules which govern the formation of contracts have been long established and they are grounded in the concepts of offer and acceptance. So long as that continues to be the case, it seems to me that the general rule should be that the traditional offer and acceptance analysis is to be applied in battle of the forms cases. That has the great merit of providing a degree of certainty which is both desirable and necessary in order to promote effective commercial relationships."

However, there are cases in which an objective assessment will result in neither set of terms being incorporated into the contract. In *Lidl (UK) GmbH v Hertford Foods Ltd*,[390] Chadwick LJ said: **3.118**

"23. … In my view it is impossible to hold that they were agreed that either set of standard conditions was applicable. As the judge found, they said nothing to each other which indicated agreement on that point; and … there is no basis upon which agreement on that point can be inferred.

24. … On that basis, knowing that they had not—and, in the circumstances, probably could not—reach agreement as to the applicability as to either set of standard terms, the only inference that can be drawn is that their agreement was made on the basis that neither set of standard terms would be applicable. That conclusion seems to me at least as likely to accord with reality as a conclusion either that they reached no binding agreement at all or that either agreed to contract on the standard terms of the other."

---

[390] [2001] EWCA Civ 938.

3.119   In *Transformers & Rectifiers Ltd v Needs Ltd*,[391] Edwards-Stuart J summarised the principles:

> "i)   Where A makes an offer on its conditions and B accepts that offer on its conditions and, without more, performance follows, the correct analysis, assuming that each party's conditions have been reasonably drawn to the attention of the other, is that there is a contract on B's conditions;
>
> ii)   Where there is reliance on a previous course of dealing it does not have to be extensive. Three or four occasions over a relatively short period may suffice;
>
> iii)   The course of dealing by the party contending that its terms and conditions are incorporated has to be consistent and unequivocal;
>
> iv)   Where trade or industry standard terms exist for the type of transaction in question, it will usually be easier for a party contending for those conditions to persuade the court that they should be incorporated, provided that reasonable notice of the application of the terms has been given;
>
> v)   A party's standard terms and conditions will not be incorporated unless that party has given the other party reasonable notice of those terms and conditions;
>
> vi)   It is not always necessary for a party's terms and conditions to be included or referred to in the documents forming the contract; it may be sufficient if they are clearly contained in or referred to in invoices sent subsequently;
>
> vii)   By contrast, an invoice following a concluded contract effected by a clear offer on standard terms which are accepted, even if only by delivery, will or may be too late."

Illustrations

1.   A main contractor engaged a roofing subcontractor. The subcontractor quoted on his own standard terms. At a later meeting, discussion took place on the basis of the main contractor's standard terms. The subcontractor agreed to waive his terms in favour of DOM/1. This was followed by an order placed by the main contractor. Although the order stated that its own standard terms were attached, in fact they were not. The order, interpreted objectively, referred to the terms of DOM/1. Moreover, the main contractor's standard terms stated that if there was conflict between their terms and the terms of the order, the order would prevail. It was held that the contract incorporated the terms of DOM/1.
Cubitt Building and Interiors Ltd v Richardson Roofing (Industrial) Ltd[392]

2.   A manufacturer placed a purchase order for goods expressed to be subject to its own terms and conditions. The seller accepted the purchase order; but on its own terms and conditions. The goods were supplied. It was held that although a contract had been concluded, it was not concluded on either set of terms.

---

[391] [2015] EWHC 269 (TCC) (omitting references to authority).
[392] (2008) 119 Con. L.R. 137.

Consequently it was governed by the implied terms contained in the Sale of Goods Act 1979.
GHSP Inc v AB Electronic Ltd[393]

3. A buyer placed a purchase order for goods on is own terms. The seller acknowledged the order but on its own terms. The goods were supplied. It was held that the terms of the contract were those in the seller's acknowledgement, rather than those in the buyer's purchase order.
Tekdata Interconnections Ltd v Amphenol Ltd[394]

15. WHEN A REPRESENTATION BECOMES A TERM OF THE CONTRACT

Where, in the course of the negotiations for a contract, one of the prospective parties states a fact or expresses an opinion, it will be held to be a term of the contract (or a collateral contract) if the totality of the evidence shows that such was the intention of the parties.[395]

The origins of the law on this topic are to be traced to the famous dictum of Holt CJ[396]:

    3.120

"An affirmation at the time of the sale is a warranty, provided it appear on the evidence to be so intended."

There is no decisive test for determining what was the intention of the parties; it must be deduced from the totality of the evidence.[397] The question whether a warranty was intended depends on the conduct of the parties, on their words and behaviour, rather than on their thoughts. If an intelligent bystander would reasonably infer that a warranty was intended, that will suffice. And this, when the facts are not in dispute, is a matter of law.[398] However, later cases have identified a number of features which assist in reaching a conclusion.

    3.121

First, if an oral representation is put into writing, it is good evidence that it was intended as a warranty.[399] However, there is no reason in principle which would prevent the court from finding an oral warranty collateral to a written contract.[400]

    3.122

Secondly, if the representation is the statement of a fact which is or should be within the knowledge of one party but not of the other, that is evidence of a warranty.[401]

    3.123

---

[393] [2011] 1 Lloyd's Rep. 432.
[394] [2010] 1 Lloyd's Rep. 357; *Claxton Engineering Services Ltd v TXM Olaj-Es Gazkutato KFT* [2010] EWHC 2567 (Comm).
[395] The equivalent paragraph in the Australian edition of this book was approved in *Raphael Shin Enterprises Pty Ltd v Waterpoint Shepherds Bay Pty Ltd* [2014] NSWSC 743.
[396] *Crosse v Gardner* (1699) Sail. 210 (cited with approval by Viscount Haldane LC and Lord Moulton in *Heilbut Symons & Co v Buckleton* [1913] A.C. 30).
[397] *Heilbut Symons & Co v Buckleton* [1913] A.C. 30 at 50–51, per Lord Moulton.
[398] *Oscar Chess Ltd v Williams* [1957] 1 W.L.R. 370.
[399] *Oscar Chess Ltd v Williams* [1957] 1 W.L.R. 370.
[400] *Birch v Paramount Estates Ltd* (1956) 16 E.G. 396. The impact of s.2 of the Law of Property (Miscellaneous Provisions) Act 1989 would now have to be considered. See *Business Environment Bow Lane Ltd v Deanwater Estates Ltd* [2007] 32 E.G. 90.
[401] *Couchman v Hill* [1947] K.B. 554; *Harling v Eddy* [1951] 2 K.B. 739.

3.124   Thirdly, if the representor has no special knowledge it is less likely that the representation will be taken to be a warranty.[402]

3.125   Fourthly, if the representation is made for the very purpose of inducing the representee to enter into the contract, it is prima facie a warranty.[403]

3.126   Fifthly, if the representation is a representation of fact, it is more likely to be intended to have contractual effect than a statement of opinion; so it is much easier to infer that in the former case it was so intended, and more difficult in the latter. Similarly, where statements of future fact or forecasts are under consideration, it will require more cogent evidence to justify the conclusion that such statements were intended to be contractual in character.[404]

3.127   In *Inntrepreneur Pub Co Ltd v East Crown Ltd*,[405] Lightman J summarised the principles as follows:

> "The relevant legal principles regarding the recognition of pre-contractual promises or assurances as collateral warranties may be stated as follows:
>
> 1.   A pre-contractual statement will only be treated as having contractual effect if the evidence shows that the parties intended this to be the case. Intention is a question of fact to be decided by looking at the totality of the evidence.[406]
> 2.   The test is the ordinary objective test for the formation of a contract: what is relevant is not the subjective thought of one party, but what a reasonable outside observer would infer from all the circumstances.
> 3.   In deciding the question of intention, one important consideration will be whether the statement is followed by further negotiations and a written contract not containing any term corresponding to the statement. In such a case, it will be harder to infer that the statement was intended to have contractual effect, because the prima facie assumption will be that the written contract includes all the terms the parties wanted to be binding between them.[407]
> 4.   A further important factor will be the lapse of time between the statement and the making of the formal contract. The longer the interval, the greater the presumption must be that the parties did not intend the statement to have contractual effect in relation to a subsequent deal.
> 5.   A representation of fact is much more likely to have intended to have contractual effect than a statement of future fact or a future forecast."

3.128   Where a representation has become a term of the contract it may override other express terms of the contract even where the overridden terms are reduced to writ-

---

[402] *De Lassalle v Guildford* [1901] 2 K.B. 215 as explained in *Heilbut Symons & Co v Buckleton* [1913] A.C. 30 at 50, per Lord Moulton; *Routledge v McKay* [1954] 1 W.L.R. 615.

[403] *Bentley (Dick) Productions Ltd v Smith (Harold) (Motors) Ltd* [1965] 1 W.L.R. 623.

[404] *Esso Petroleum Co Ltd v Mardon* [1976] Q.B. 801.

[405] [2000] 2 Lloyd's Rep. 611. This summary was referred to with approval in *Business Environment Bow Lane Ltd v Deanwater Estates Ltd* [2007] EWCA Civ 622; [2007] 2 E.G.L.R. 51. It was also referred to with approval in *Hanoman v Mayor and Burgesses of the London Borough of Southwark* [2009] 1 W.L.R. 374. This point did not arise on appeal to the House of Lords: [2009] 1 W.L.R. 1367.

[406] The mere fact that a representation is made "subject to contract" does not of itself prevent it from becoming a term of the contract if and when a contract is made: see *Business Environment Bow Lane Ltd v Deanwater Estates Ltd* [2007] EWCA Civ 622; [2007] 2 E.G.L.R. 51.

[407] See *Business Environment Bow Lane Ltd v Deanwater Estates Ltd* [2007] EWCA Civ 622; [2007] 2 E.G.L.R. 51.

ing[408] and in an extreme case may flatly contradict them.[409] The ability of one party to a written contract to rely upon an oral warranty having become a term of that contract is a major breach of the parol evidence rule which, in theory, precludes the admission of evidence for the purpose or adding to, varying or contradicting a written contract.[410] It is for this reason that it has been said that collateral contracts are viewed with suspicion by the law and must be proved strictly.[411] In *Thinc Group Ltd v Armstrong*,[412] the Court of Appeal confirmed that a collateral contract may contradict the terms of the written contract to which it is collateral. Rix LJ said:

"[Counsel] accepted that the doctrine of collateral warranty could give effect to such a warranty so as to enable it to take precedence over the inconsistent wording of even a signed contract. He was right to do so, see, for instance *Curtis v. The Chemical Cleaning & Dyeing Co Ltd*,[413] as explained in *Peekay Intermark Limited v. ANZ Banking Group* at [43]–[44] or *AXA Sun Life Services plc v. Campbell Martin Ltd*,[414] on the basis that the effect of the collateral warranty is to misrepresent the primary contract."

In practical terms, there will often be no difference between a conclusion that the **3.129** parties have made a collateral contract, and a conclusion that a contract is partly written and partly oral. It may, however, be of significance where a contract is required to be made in writing (by reason of, for example, s.2 of the Law of Property (Miscellaneous Provisions) Act 1989) in which case only a finding of a collateral contract will be effective.[415] In a normal conveyancing transaction in a commercial context with both parties represented by experienced solicitors, the usual course of dealing is to ensure that all agreed terms are put into the contract and conveyance, transfer or lease. Accordingly, it has been held that those who assert a collateral contract in relation to a term not so contained must show that it was intended to have contractual effect separate from the normal conveyancing documents. Otherwise it will be invalidated by s.2 of the Law of Property (Miscellaneous Provisions) Act 1989 even if evidence as to its existence is admitted.[416] On the other hand, it has also been held that the court need not interpret a collateral contract so far as possible to bring it within s.2; and that, on the contrary, on general

---

[408] *Couchman v Hill* [1947] K.B. 554; *Harling v Eddy* [1951] 2 K.B. 739.
[409] *City and Westminster Properties Ltd v Mudd* [1959] Ch. 129; *Evans (J) & Son (Portsmouth) Ltd v Merzario (Andrea) Ltd* [1976] 1 W.L.R. 1078.
[410] See para.3.87.
[411] *Heilbut Symons & Co v Buckleton* [1913] A.C. 30, per Lord Moulton; but see also *Esso Petroleum Co Ltd v Mardon* [1975] Q.B. 801, per Lord Denning MR for a very different approach.
[412] [2012] EWCA Civ 1227.
[413] [1951] 1 K.B. 805.
[414] [2012] Bus. L.R. 203 at 227–228.
[415] *Angell v Duke* (1875) L.R. 10 Q.B. 174; *Record v Bell* [1991] 1 W.L.R. 853; *Tootal Clothing Ltd v Guinea Properties Ltd* (1992) 64 P. & C.R. 452 CA. However, the extent to which s.2 permits proof of a collateral contract is unclear: see *Record v Bell* [1991] 1 W.L.R. 833; *Grossman v Hooper* [2001] 2 E.G.L.R. 82 CA. It is thought that the better view is that it does not unless the collateral contract is truly intended to be distinct from the land contract: see *Business Environment Bow Lane Ltd v Deanwater Estates Ltd* [2007] EWCA Civ 622; [2007] 2 E.G.L.R. 51. At all events the court should be wary of dividing what is in truth a composite bargain part of which involves the creation or disposition of an interest in land and artificially dividing it: see *Kilcarne Holdings Ltd v Targetfollow (Birmingham) Ltd* [2005] 2 P. & C.R. 8.
[416] *Business Environment Bow Lane Ltd v Deanwater Estates Ltd* [2007] EWCA Civ 622; [2007] 2 E.G.L.R. 51.

principle the court should so far as possible interpret it so that it can be enforced and party autonomy respected.[417]

3.130   In the past the distinction between a representation and a warranty was often of crucial significance because, before the passing of the Misrepresentation Act 1967, no action lay for damages for misrepresentation (unless the misrepresentation was fraudulent) and once the contract had been completed it was often too late to rescind. The distinction is nowadays of less importance because of the effect of the Misrepresentation Act 1967.[418]

3.131   In the case of consumer contracts, ss.12 and 38 of the Consumer Rights Act 2015 provide for a wide variety of pre-contractual information to become terms of the contract.

Illustrations

1.   A reply to preliminary enquiries in a conveyancing transaction was made before the purchasers showed any real intention to contract, and was made by a solicitor who had no actual or ostensible authority to contract. It was held that the replies did not amount to warranties.
Gilchester Properties Ltd v Gomm[419]

2.   A car dealer stated to a prospective buyer "It's a good little bus, I would stake my life on it, you will have no trouble with it". The words amounted to a warranty that the car was in good condition and reasonably safe and fit for use on a highway.
Andrews v Hopkinson[420]

3.   The owner of a motor car, a dealer, told a prospective purchaser that the car had done 20,000 miles since having been fitted with a new gearbox. It was held that the statement was a warranty.
Bentley (Dick) Productions Ltd v Smith (Harold) (Motors) Ltd[421]

4.   A water authority invited tenders for a dredging contract. A potential tenderer, with no experience of dredging, wished to tender but before doing so needed to establish the cost of hiring barges. The tenderer invited five firms who hired barges to quote prices. The defendant quoted a price "subject to availability and charterparty". In the course of further negotiations, the defendant made various statements about the carrying capacity of the barge. It was held that those statements were not warranties because the offer to hire was made "subject to contract"; in those circumstances it was unlikely that an oral statement was intended to be

---

[417] *Hanoman v Mayor and Burgesses of the London Borough of Southwark* [2009] 1 W.L.R. 374. Of these two approaches, the author prefers the former, which is more consistent with the policy underlying s.2. *Business Environment Bow Lane Ltd v Deanwater Estates Ltd* appears to have been approved by the CA in *North Eastern Properties Ltd v Coleman* [2010] 1 W.L.R. 2715.

[418] See *Esso Petroleum Co Ltd v Mardon* [1976] Q.B. 801, per Lord Denning MR.

[419] [1948] 1 All E.R. 493. It makes no difference where the answers are confirmed by way of requisitions on title: *Mahon v Ainscough* [1952] 1 All E.R. 337.

[420] [1957] 1 Q.B. 229.

[421] [1965] 1 W.L.R. 623.

contractually binding. The barges were to be the subject of a survey by the hirer, and there was to be a formal charterparty.

Howard Marine and Dredging Co Ltd v Ogden (A) & Sons (Excavations) Ltd[422]

16.   ENTIRE AGREEMENT CLAUSES

Where a contract contains a clause stating that the written contract contains the parties' entire agreement, that will usually prevent a finding that a collateral contract was made. If, in addition, the contract contains an acknowledgment that neither party has relied on pre-contractual representations, then depending on the terms of the contract that may give rise to an estoppel.[423]

Sometimes a contract will contain an express term which declares that the written terms are the only terms of the contract.[424] In *McGrath v Shah*,[425] such a term was said to be "an insuperable hurdle" to an allegation that the contract was partly contained in statements which were not recorded in the contract. But it was also held that such a term would not prevent the statements from amounting to a collateral contract.[426]

3.132

Subsequently, however, in *Deepak Fertilisers and Petrochemical Corp v Davy McKee*,[427] the Court of Appeal[428] held that an entire agreement clause did preclude reliance on a collateral contract.

3.133

This was followed in *Inntrepreneur Pub Co v East Crown*[429] in which Lightman J said:

"The purpose of an entire agreement clause is to preclude a party to a written agreement from thrashing[430] through the undergrowth and finding, in the course of negotiations, some (chance) remark or statement (often long-forgotten or difficult to recall or explain) upon which to found a claim, such as the present, to the existence of a collateral warranty. The entire agreement clause obviates the occasion for any such search, and the peril to the contracting parties posed by the need that may arise in its absence to conduct such a search. For such a clause constitutes a binding agreement between the parties that the full contractual terms are to be found in the document containing the clause and not elsewhere, and that, accordingly, any promises or assurances made in the course of the negotiations (which, in the absence of such a clause, might have effect as a collateral war-

---

[422] [1978] Q.B. 574.
[423] This section was referred to with approval in *Papanicola v Sandhu* [2011] EWHC 1431 (QB); [2011] 2 B.C.L.C. 811; and *Mileform Ltd v Interserve Security Ltd* [2013] EWHC 3386 (QB).
[424] Professor David McLauchlan discusses entire agreement clauses in "The Entire Agreement Clause" (2012) 128 L.Q.R. 521.
[425] (1987) 57 P. & C.R. 452.
[426] This appears to be supported by the judgments of Roskill and Cumming-Bruce LJJ in *Brikom Investments v Carr* [1979] Q.B. 467. However, although the contract in that case contained an entire agreement clause, neither of the Lords Justices referred to it. *Brikom Investments v Carr* was distinguished by Park J in *Inntrepreneur Pub Co (CPC) v Sweeney* [2002] 2 E.G.L.R. 132 at 140, but without reference to these two judgments.
[427] [1999] 1 Lloyd's Rep. 387.
[428] Upholding Rix J [1998] 2 Lloyd's Rep. 139.
[429] [2000] 2 Lloyd's Rep. 611 at 614 and in *Inntrepreneur Pub Co (CPC) v Sweeney* [2002] 2 E.G.L.R. 132.
[430] The report reads "threshing", but this is a transcription error: see *Inntrepreneur Pub Co (CPC) v Sweeney* [2002] 2 E.G.L.R. 132 at 139.

ranty) shall have no contractual force, save in so far as they are reflected and given effect in that document. The operation of the clause is not to render evidence of the collateral warranty inadmissible in evidence, as is suggested in *Chitty on Contracts* (28th ed.) vol 1 para. 12–102; it is to denude what would otherwise constitute a collateral warranty of legal effect."

It has subsequently been said that this purpose of an entire agreement clause is "obvious".[431] In *Rock Advertising Ltd v MWB Business Exchange Centres Ltd*,[432] Lightman J's description of the purpose of an entire agreement clause was affirmed. In the same case Lord Briggs said:

"[An entire agreement clause] may well serve the same objective of promoting legal certainty as to what the agreement is but, as Lord Sumption explains, these clauses do not purport to bind the parties as to their future conduct. They leave the scope and the procedure for subsequent variation entirely unaffected."

3.134   But despite this general description of the purpose of an entire agreement clause the court should not approach such a clause with the pre-conceived idea that its sole intention is to ensure that the parties cannot subsequently contradict the wording of the agreement by reference to agreements or understandings supposedly arrived at in the course of negotiations (which is undoubtedly normally the main object of such clauses).[433] Such a clause may also "serve the valuable purpose, (in a composite transaction which includes, but does not entirely consist of, a land contract), of ensuring that the land contract will not accidentally be construed as conditional upon the other expressly agreed terms, so as to render the land contract void" under s.2 of the Law of Property (Miscellaneous Provisions) Act 1989.[434] That said, an entire agreement clause in a signed agreement will take effect according to its terms.[435] As Longmore LJ put it in *North Eastern Properties v Coleman*[436]:

"If the parties agree that the written contract is to be the entire contract, it is no business of the courts to tell them that they do not mean what they have said."

3.135   Thus, as Moore-Bick LJ pointed out in *Ravennavi SpA v New Century Shipbuilding Co Ltd*[437]:

"The effect of an entire agreement clause ... must depend primarily on its terms, since it is the language chosen by the parties to express their agreement (wherever it appears) which, construed in its proper context, provides the primary source of their intentions. It is for that reason that I am unable to accept the suggestion in the Buyer's skeleton argument that clauses of this kind can be construed by reference to their supposed purpose or that their significance is diminished if they are found among what are sometimes called the 'boilerplate' provisions of a formal contract of this kind. There may be circumstances, of course, in which the

---

[431] *Axa Sun Life Services Plc v Campbell Martin Ltd* [2011] EWCA Civ 133.
[432] [2018] UKSC 24; [2019] A.C. 119.
[433] *Satyam Computer Services Ltd v Upaid Systems Ltd* [2008] 2 All E.R. (Comm) 465.
[434] *North Eastern Properties v Coleman* [2010] 1 W.L.R. 2715.
[435] *Springwell Navigation Corp v JP Morgan Chase Bank* [2010] EWCA Civ 1221; *Axa Sun Life Services Plc v Campbell Martin Ltd* [2011] EWCA Civ 133.
[436] [2010] 3 All E.R. 528.
[437] [2007] 2 Lloyd's Rep. 24.

court can be satisfied that a clause of that kind, although apparently couched in language wide enough to encompass the particular matter on which one or other party seeks to rely, was not intended by the parties to operate in the way in which its terms would suggest, but any such conclusion must be borne out by the particular circumstances of the case."

In *The Federal Republic of Nigeria v JP Morgan Chase Bank NA*,[438] Mr Andrew Burrows QC said:

"It is unnecessary to regard there as being a separate rule for the interpretation of an entire agreement clause. However, where the entire agreement clause will have the effect of excluding an implied term that would otherwise arise, one should recognise that a party is unlikely to have agreed to give up a valuable right that it would otherwise have had without clear words. The more valuable the right, the clearer the words will need to be. It follows that an entire agreement clause may or may not exclude an implied term. This will primarily depend on the words used, in their context, but it will also be relevant to consider, for example, the nature of the implied term. So it may be that a term implied by law, at common law or by statute, as opposed to some terms implied by fact or by custom, confers a particularly valuable right so that it is unlikely that a party has agreed to give up that right other than by clear wording."

In general, an entire agreement clause gives rise to a contractual estoppel, **3.136** precluding a party from asserting that something outside the four corners of the contract was a term of the contract or a contract collateral to it.[439] For this reason an entire agreement clause is a powerful pointer (although not conclusive) that an undisclosed principal may not sue or be sued on the contract.[440]

Here English law is not on its own. The Unidroit Principles for International **3.137** Commercial Contracts state:

"A contract in writing which contains a clause indicating that the writing completely embodies the terms on which the parties have agreed cannot be contradicted or supplemented by evidence of prior statements or agreements. However, such statements or agreements may be used to interpret the writing."[441]

Where a contract contains an entire agreement clause it is obviously important **3.138** to decide what document (or documents) constitute the entire agreement. In *Ryanair Ltd v SR Technics Ireland Ltd*,[442] Gray J gave effect to a collateral contract, despite the existence of an entire agreement clause. He did so on the basis that both parties proceeded on the common assumption that the collateral contract would be

---

[438] [2019] EWHC 347 (Comm) (affirmed [2019] EWCA Civ 1641).

[439] *Matchbet Ltd v Openbet Retail Ltd* [2013] EWHC 3067 (Ch); *Dubai Islamic Bank PJSC v PSI Energy Holding Co BSC* [2013] EWHC 3781 (Comm).

[440] *Kaefer Aislamientos SA de CV v AMS Drilling Mexico SA de CV* [2019] EWCA Civ 10; [2019] 1 W.L.R. 3514; *Ivy Technology Ltd v Martin* [2020] EWHC 94 (Comm); *Filatona Trading Ltd v Navigator Equities Ltd* [2020] EWCA Civ 109.

[441] Para.2.17.

[442] [2007] EWHC 3089 (QB). This decision undermines the general purpose of an entire agreement clause. In *Mileform Ltd v Interserve Security Ltd* [2013] EWHC 3386 (QB) Gloster LJ agreed with this criticism. Ryanair was disapproved in *Rock Advertising Ltd v MWB Business Exchange Centres Ltd* [2018] UKSC 24; [2019] A.C. 119.

honoured despite the existence of the entire agreement clause. The entire agreement clause did not prevent the contention that the entire agreement was found partly in the formal contract and partly in the collateral contract.

In *Cheverny Consulting Ltd v Whitehead Mann Ltd*,[443] an entire agreement clause stated that:

> "This agreement constitutes the entire agreement between the parties to it with respect to its subject matter and shall have effect to the exclusion of any other memorandum, agreement or understanding of any kind between the parties hereto preceding the date of this agreement and touching or concerning its subject matter."

Sir Donald Rattee held that the words "any other agreement *preceding* the date of this agreement" were to be read as not excluding agreements which were part of a package of agreements entered into as a composite transaction. Accordingly, the entire agreement clause did not preclude the enforcement of a collateral agreement contained in a side letter. Similarly, in *Satyam Computer Services Ltd v Upaid Systems Ltd*,[444] the Court of Appeal held that:

> "reliance on the Entire Agreement clause is circular since it applies to supersede prior agreements 'concerning this subject matter herein and the terms and conditions applicable hereto', and 'all other documents' inconsistent with 'the documents constituting the Entire Agreement' (namely the Services Agreement and its Annexures). The question still remains whether the subject matter of the Assignment Agreement is included within the Services Agreement or whether it is inconsistent with the Services Agreement in any material respect."

Likewise, in *Easyair Ltd v Opal Telecom Ltd*,[445] an entire agreement clause stated that the entire agreement was contained in the contract and the documents referred to in it. The contract was construed together with another contemporaneous contract between the same parties, forming part of the overall package. The same approach has been applied in Scotland.[446]

3.139   A term which would otherwise be implied as a result of custom or usage may be excluded by an "entire agreement" clause.[447] But a conventional "entire contract" clause does not affect the question whether some matter of fact (whether or not in documentary form) is admissible as an aid to the process of construing a contractual document.[448] On that basis it is considered that an entire agreement clause would not usually preclude the implication of a term because the implication of a term is elucidating what the written contract means.[449] In *Axa Sun Life Services Plc v*

---

[443] [2007] EWHC 3130 (Ch).

[444] [2008] 2 All E.R. (Comm) 465.

[445] [2009] EWHC 339 (Ch); *Nas Air Co v Genesis Aviation Trading 3 Ltd* [2020] EWHC 507 (Comm) (entire agreement contained in "Operative Documents" as defined).

[446] *Macdonald Estates Plc v Regenesis (2005) Dunfermline Ltd* 2007 S.L.T. 791.

[447] *Exxonmobile Sales and Supply Corp v Texaco Ltd* [2004] 1 All E.R. (Comm) 435.

[448] *John v Price Waterhouse* [2002] EWCA Civ 899. It may, however, entitle the court to treat such matters with caution: *Giedo Van Der Garde BV v Force India Formula One Team Ltd* [2010] EWHC 2373 (QB) at [167].

[449] See *Harrison v Shepherd Homes Ltd* [2011] EWHC 1811 (TCC). This proposition was approved in *Novoship (UK) Ltd v Mikhaylyuk* [2015] EWHC 992 (Comm) and *Essex County Council v UBB Waste (Essex) Ltd* [2020] EWHC 1581 (TCC).

Campbell Martin Ltd,[450] the Court of Appeal held that an entire agreement clause did not preclude the implication of terms, because they were "intrinsic" to the agreement. In *Kason Kek-Gardner Ltd v Process Components Ltd*[451] the Court of Appeal confirmed that an entire agreement clause does not preclude the implication of a term. In *The Federal Republic of Nigeria v JP Morgan Chase Bank, NA*[452] an entire agreement clause did not exclude a bank's implied duty of skill and care towards its customer; and in particular its duty to refrain from making a payment (despite an instruction on behalf of its customer to do so) where it has reasonable grounds for believing that that payment is part of a scheme to defraud the customer. However, terms that would be implied as a result of matters "extrinsic" to the agreement would be excluded by the entire agreement clause.[453] In *Great Elephant Corp v Trafigura Beheer BV*,[454] Teare J held that an entire agreement clause did not have the effect of excluding terms implied by the Sale of Goods Act 1979 because implied terms spell out the terms which the parties have agreed. They were not part of any collateral contract or warranty with which "express terms of the contract" were compared in the clause.[455] Likewise, in *Barden v Commodities Research Unit*,[456] Vos J held that an entire agreement clause did not preclude the implication of a term necessary to make the contract work and to prevent commercial absurdity. On the other hand, the existence of an entire agreement clause may preclude the parties from asserting that undisclosed principals are entitled to the benefit of the contract or liable under it; although it is not decisive.[457]

In *NHS Commissioning Board v Vasant*[458] the Court of Appeal held that neither an entire agreement clause, nor a no oral modification clause, precluded the admission of extrinsic evidence to explain the meaning of the written terms that the parties had agreed. Nor will an entire agreement clause in conventional terms preclude a claim for rectification[459] or an estoppel which arises after the making of the agreement.[460] However, a suitably worded clause could prevent such an estoppel **3.140**

---

[450] [2011] EWCA Civ 133; [2012] Bus. L.R. 203; *Compass Group UK and Ireland Ltd v Mid Essex Hospital Services NHS Trust* [2012] EWHC 781 (QB); [2012] 2 All E.R. (Comm) 300.

[451] [2017] EWCA Civ 2132; [2018] 2 All E.R. (Comm) 381.

[452] [2019] EWCA Civ 1641.

[453] It is unclear what the distinction is. In general, an entire agreement clause in conventional form does not restrict the nature of evidence admissible to interpret the contract. In so far as there are matters extrinsic to a contract which would support the implication of a term, they would appear to fall within the scope of evidence admissible to interpret the contract. However, in *Matchbet Ltd v Openbet Retail Ltd* [2013] EWHC 3067 (Ch), Henderson J held that an entire agreement clause precluded reliance on preceding heads of terms as an admissible aid to the interpretation of the contract containing the entire agreement clause. In *Bhasin v Hrynew* [2014] 3 S.C.R. 495 the Supreme Court of Canada held that the common law of Canada recognised an overarching duty of good faith in the performance of contracts. Since this was an overarching duty rather than an implied term, it was not excluded by an entire agreement clause.

[454] [2012] EWHC 1745 (Comm); [2012] 2 Lloyd's Rep. 503.

[455] Older authority, however, suggests that an entire agreement clause may be effective to exclude implications of this kind: *L'Estrange v F Graucob Ltd* [1934] 2 K.B. 394; *Eccles v Mills* [1898] A.C. 360.

[456] [2013] EWHC 1633 (Ch).

[457] *Kaefer Aislamientos SA De CV v AMS Drilling Mexico SA De CV* [2019] EWCA Civ 10; [2019] 1 W.L.R. 3514.

[458] [2019] EWCA Civ 1245.

[459] *JJ Huber Ltd v The Private DIY Co Ltd* (1995) 70 P. & C.R. 33; *Surgicraft Ltd v Paradigm Biodevices Inc* [2010] EWHC 1291 (Ch).

[460] *Lloyd v MGL (Rugby) Ltd* [2007] EWCA Civ 153 (sub nom. *Sutcliffe v Lloyd* [2007] 2 E.G.L.R. 19).

arising.[461] In *Barclays Bank Plc v Unicredit Bank AG*,[462] Popplewell J held that the entire agreement clause in that case did not preclude reliance on an estoppel, where the estoppel involved an assumption as to future conduct which was not akin to an additional contractual promise; but related to the manner in which one party would exercise a contractual discretion. In the result the argument failed on the facts. However, on appeal[463] it is doubtful whether the Court of Appeal agreed with him. Commenting on the entire agreement clause in that case Longmore LJ said:

> "[27] The entire agreement clause is concerned with identifying the terms of the contract. The use of the phrase 'constitute the entire agreement and understanding' is intended to exclude any evidence or argument to the effect that the terms of the contract are to include any mutual understanding that is not recorded in the contract. It is not intended to exclude admissible evidence or argument about the way in which parties exercise rights given to them by the terms of the contract.
>
> [28] Courts have tended to construe entire agreement clauses strictly. A clause framed in the way in which it is framed in the contract with which this case is concerned would not, for example, preclude a claim for misrepresentation because that is not a claim which depends on a term of the contract which is not expressed in the contract. ... Consistently with this approach, the clause has, in my view, no relevance to the way in which parties may exercise rights given to them by the contract."

3.141   An entire agreement clause, as opposed to a non-reliance clause, will not usually exclude liability for a pre-contractual misrepresentation.[464] The distinction between the two types of clause was pointed out in *Inntrepreneur Pub Co v East Crown Ltd*[465] in which Lightman J said:

> "An entire agreement provision does not preclude a claim in misrepresentation, for the denial of contractual force to a statement cannot affect the status of the statement as a misrepresentation. The same clause in an agreement may contain both an entire agreement provision and a further provision designed to exclude liability for misrepresentation and breach of duty."

In *BSkyB Ltd v HP Enterprise Services UK Ltd*,[466] an entire agreement clause said that the agreement and its schedules "constitute the whole agreement between the parties in relation to the subject matter and supersede any previous discussions, correspondence, representations and agreement between the parties with respect thereto ...". Ramsey J held that the clause did not exclude liability for non-fraudulent misrepresentation. He said:

> "[382] Those words do not, in my judgment, amount to an agreement that

---

[461] *Jet2.com Ltd v Blackpool Airport Ltd* [2010] EWHC 3166 (Comm).

[462] [2012] EWHC 3655 (Comm); [2013] 2 Lloyd's Rep. 1.

[463] [2014] EWCA Civ 302 at [29].

[464] *Deepak Fertilisers v ICI Chemicals* [1999] 1 Lloyd's Rep. 387; *BSkyB Ltd v HP Enterprises Ltd* [2010] EWHC 86 (TCC). However, a contract may also contain an acknowledgement that neither party has relied on pre-contractual representations, in which case an evidential or contractual estoppel may arise.

[465] [2000] 2 Lloyd's Rep. 611; *Trident Turboprop (Dublin) Ltd v First Flight Couriers Ltd* [2008] 2 Lloyd's Rep. 581.

[466] [2010] EWHC 86 (TCC).

representations are withdrawn, overridden or of no legal effect so far as any liability for misrepresentation may be concerned. It provides that the Agreement represents the entire understanding and constitutes the whole agreement. It is in that context that the Agreement supersedes any previous representations. That is, representations are superseded and do not become terms of the Agreement unless they are included in the Agreement. If it had intended to withdraw representations for all purposes then the language would, in my judgment, have had to go further. ...

[385]   In this case the statement that the Agreement superseded any previous discussions, correspondence, representations or agreement between the parties with respect to the subject matter of the agreement prevented other terms of the agreement or collateral agreement from having contractual effect. It did not supersede those matters so far as there might be any liability for misrepresentation based on them. ...

[387]   Secondly, while there is a reference to representations, there is nothing in the clause that indicates that it is intended to take away a right to rely on misrepresentations. ... I consider that clear words are needed to exclude a liability for negligent misrepresentation and that this clause does not include any such wording."

In *Axa Sun Life Services Plc v Campbell Martin Ltd*,[467] cl.24 of an agreement provided:

"This Agreement and the Schedules and documents referred to herein constitute the entire agreement and understanding between you and us in relation to the subject matter thereof. Without prejudice to any variation as provided in clause 1.1, this Agreement shall supersede any prior promises, agreements, representations, undertakings or implications whether made orally or in writing between you and us relating to the subject matter of this Agreement but this will not affect any obligations in any such prior agreement which are expressed to continue after termination."

Rix LJ said:

"In context the language of 'representations' and 'supersede' is the language of defining contractual obligations rather than the language of excluding liability in misrepresentation. There was there, as here, no language to the effect that the parties were agreed that no representations had been made or relied upon."

He added:

"No doubt all such cases are only authority for each clause's particular wording: nevertheless it seems to me that there are certain themes which deserve recognition. Among them is that the exclusion of liability for misrepresentation has to be clearly stated. It can be done by clauses which state the parties' agreement that there have been no representations made; or that there has been no reliance on any representations; or by an express exclusion of liability for misrepresentation. However, save in such contexts, and particularly where the

---

[467] [2011] EWCA Civ 133.

word 'representations' takes its place alongside other words expressive of contractual obligation, talk of the parties' contract superseding such prior agreement will not by itself absolve a party of misrepresentation where its ingredients can be proved."

3.142   Since non-reliance clauses have the effect of excluding remedies, they are considered further in Ch.12.

17.   BACKGROUND

In construing any written agreement the court is entitled to look at evidence of the objective factual background known to the parties or reasonably available to them[468] at or before the date of the contract. This principle applies even if the contract appears to be unambiguous. There is no conceptual limit to background. It can include anything relevant which would have affected the way in which the document would have been understood by a reasonable person. However, this does not entitle the court to look at evidence of the parties' subjective intentions; nor to ascribe to the words of the contract a meaning that they cannot legitimately bear.

(a)   The general principle

3.143   In *Investors Compensation Scheme v West Bromwich Building Society*,[469] Lord Hoffmann said:

"The background was famously referred to by Lord Wilberforce as the 'matrix of fact', but this phrase is, if anything, an understated description of what the background may include. Subject to the requirement that it should have been reasonably available to the parties and to the exception to be mentioned next,[470] it includes absolutely anything[471] which would have affected the way in which the language of the document would have been understood by a reasonable man."[472]

---

[468] See *Norcross v Georgallides (Estate of)* [2015] EWHC 2405 (Comm). The extent to which objective factual background unknown to the parties but reasonably available to them is relevant to interpretation remains uncertain.
[469] [1998] 1 W.L.R. 896.
[470] i.e. that evidence of negotiations and declarations of subjective intention are not admissible.
[471] In *BCCI v Ali* [2002] 1 A.C. 251 Lord Hoffmann qualified this, saying:

"When ... I said that the admissible background included 'absolutely anything which would have affected the way in which the language of the document would have been understood by a reasonable man', I did not think it necessary to emphasise that I meant anything which a reasonable man would have regarded as relevant. I was merely saying that there is no conceptual limit to what can be regarded as background. It is not, for example, confined to the factual background but can include the state of the law (as in cases in which one takes into account that the parties are unlikely to have intended to agree to something unlawful or legally ineffective) or proved common assumptions which were in fact quite mistaken. But the primary source for understanding what the parties meant is their language interpreted in accordance with conventional usage: '... we do not easily accept that people have made linguistic mistakes, particularly in formal documents.' I was certainly not encouraging a trawl through 'background' which could not have made a reasonable person think that the parties must have departed from conventional usage."

[472] Lord Hoffmann expanded on this theme extra-judicially in "The Intolerable Wrestle with Words and Meanings" (1997) 114 S.A.L.J. 656; and "Language and Lawyers" (2019) L.Q.R. 553.

It has, however, always been the case that the court must construe a written agree-   **3.144**
ment (even under seal) in the light of the circumstances (or background) surrounding its making. Although recent decisions have emphasised the importance of the
background to a contract, the principle has long been part of English law. Over 150
years ago in *Shore v Wilson*,[473] Erskine J said:

"in all cases, even where the words are in themselves plain and intelligible, and
even where they have a strict legal meaning, it is always allowable, in order to
enable the Court to apply the instrument to its proper object, to receive evidence
of the circumstances by which the testator or founder was surrounded at the date
of the execution of the instrument in question, not for the purpose of giving effect to any intention of the writer not expressed in the deed, but for the purpose
of ascertaining what was the intention evidenced by the expressions used; to
ascertain what the party has said; not to give effect to any intention he has failed
to express."

In the same case Parke B said[474]:

"For the purpose of applying the instrument to the facts, and determining what
passes by it, and who takes an interest under it, a second description of evidence
is admissible, viz., every material fact that will enable the Court to identify the
person or thing mentioned in the instrument, and to place the Court, whose
province it is to declare the meaning of the words of the instrument as near as
may be in the situation of the parties to it."

The principle expressed by Erskine J is formulated in wider terms than those used   **3.145**
by Parke B. and it is the former which has gained widespread acceptance in the
modern law. It will be noted that the principle thus formulated applies even where
the words of the contract are plain and intelligible. Thus in *River Wear Commissioners v Adamson*,[475] Lord Blackburn said:

"In all cases the object is to see what is the intention expressed by the words used.
But, from the imperfection of language, it is impossible to know what that intention was without enquiring farther, and seeing what the circumstances were with
reference to which the words were used, and what was the object, appearing from
those circumstances, which the person using them had in view, for the meaning
of words varies according to the circumstances with respect to which they were
used."

So also in *Hvalfangerselkapet Polaris A/S v Unilever Ltd*,[476] Lord Russell of Killowen said:

"Before a Court begins to construe a written contract, it must know all the
relevant circumstances which exist and are within the knowledge of the contracting parties at the time when they make their contract."

A similar approach was adopted by Lord Wilberforce in his two speeches in   **3.146**

---

[473] (1842) 9 Cl. & Fin. 355 at 512.
[474] (1842) 9 Cl. & Fin. 355 at 556.
[475] (1877) 2 App. Cas. 743 (a case of statutory construction).
[476] (1933) 46 Lloyd's Rep. 29.

Prenn v Simmonds[477] and *Reardon Smith Line Ltd v Yngvar HansenTangen*,[478] which are the foundation stones of the modern approach. In the former case Lord Wilberforce said:

"The time has long since passed when agreements, even those under seal, were isolated from the matrix of facts in which they were set and interpreted purely on internal linguistic considerations. ... We must ... inquire beyond the language and see what the circumstances were with reference to which the words were used, and the object appearing from those circumstances, which the person using them had in view."

He continued:

"... evidence should be restricted to evidence of the factual background known to the parties at or before the date of the contract, including evidence of the 'genesis' and objectively the 'aim' of the transaction."

In the latter case Lord Wilberforce said:

"No contracts are made in a vacuum: there is always a setting in which they have to be placed. The nature of what is legitimate to have regard to is usually described as 'the surrounding circumstances' but this phrase is imprecise; it can be illustrated but hardly defined. In a commercial contract it is certainly right that the court should know the commercial purpose of the contract and this in turn presupposes knowledge of the genesis of the transaction, the background, the context, the market in which the parties are operating."

He continued:

"... what the court must do must be to place itself in thought in the same factual matrix as that in which the parties were."

In *Arbuthnott v Fagan*,[479] Sir Thomas Bingham MR said:

"Courts will never construe words in a vacuum. To a greater or lesser extent, depending on the subject matter, they will wish to be informed of what may variously be described as the context, the background, the factual matrix or the mischief. To seek to construe any instrument in ignorance or disregard of the circumstances which gave rise to it or the situation in which it is expected to take effect is in my view pedantic, sterile and productive of error. But that is not to say that an initial judgment of what an instrument was or should reasonably have been intended to achieve should be permitted to override the clear language of the instrument, since what an author says is usually the surest guide to what he meant. To my mind construction is a composite exercise, neither uncompromisingly literal nor unswervingly purposive: the instrument must speak for itself, but it must do so in situ and not be transported to the laboratory for microscopic analysis."

3.147 Thus it came about that the practice of the late twentieth century was to refer to

---

[477] [1971] 1 W.L.R. 1381.
[478] [1976] 1 W.L.R. 989.
[479] [1995] C.L.C. 1396, cited in *The Fina Samco* [1995] 2 Lloyd's Rep. 344 at 350, CA.

the "matrix of fact" or the "factual matrix" in which a contract was made.[480] The practice was approved by the House of Lords in *Forsikringsaktieselskapet Vesta v Butcher*.[481] Now, however, the more fashionable phrase is "background", or "factual context".

However, although background is an important aid to the interpretation of a contract, the important question remains: what does the contract mean? The use of background does not absolve the court from paying close attention to the contractual text.[482] Background "cannot obscure the court's task, which is to construe the terms that the parties in the event agreed".[483] Nor should background be invoked to undervalue the importance of the language of the provision to be interpreted.[484] Where the words of a contract are clear, the court must give effect to them.[485]

(b)   Ambiguity unnecessary

In *Charrington & Co v Wooder*,[486] Viscount Haldane LC said: **3.148**

"If the language of a written contract has a definite and unambiguous meaning, parol evidence is not admissible to shew that the parties meant something different from what they have said. But if the description of the subject-matter is susceptible of more than one interpretation, evidence is admissible to shew what were the facts to which the contract relates. If there are circumstances which the parties must be taken to have had in view when entering into the contract, it is necessary that the Court which construes the contract should have these circumstances before it."

It was at one time thought that ambiguity was necessary before recourse could   **3.149**
be had to extrinsic evidence of background. It is now clear, however, that this is not
the law.[487] The more modern formulations of the principle make no reference to the
need to find ambiguity.[488]

In *Kingscroft Insurance Co Ltd v Nissan Fire and Marine Insurance Co Ltd*,[489]
Moore-Bick J said he was:

"unable to accept, therefore, that the court can only take account of the background in cases where the contract itself gives rise to doubts about its meaning."

Similarly, in *Persimmon Homes (South Coast) Ltd v Hall Aggregates (South*

---

[480] Sir Bernard Eder criticises the use of background in "The construction of shipping and marine insurance contracts" [2016] L.M.C.L.Q. 220.
[481] [1989] A.C. 852 at 909, per Lord Lowry.
[482] *TJH and Sons Consultancy Ltd v CPP Group Plc* [2017] EWCA Civ 46.
[483] *Starbev GP Ltd v Interbrew Central European Holdings BV* [2014] EWHC 1311 (Comm), per Blair J approving Grabiner, "The iterative process of contractual interpretation" (2012) 128 L.Q.R. 41.
[484] *Arnold v Britton* [2015] UKSC 36; [2015] 2 W.L.R. 1593.
[485] *Sun Alliance (Bahamas) Ltd v Scandi Enterprises Ltd* [2017] UKPC 10; [2017] 2 All E.R. (Comm) 1019.
[486] [1914] A.C. 71. A similar view was expressed by Tindal CJ in *Shore v Wilson* (1842) 9 Cl. & Fin. 355 at 565.
[487] It may still be the law in Australia where the position remains unclear.
[488] In *Chartbrook Ltd v Persimmons Homes Ltd* [2009] A.C. 1101 Lord Hoffmann said of *Investors Compensation Scheme v West Bromwich Building Society* that it decided "that it was not necessary to find an 'ambiguity' before one could have any regard to background".
[489] [1999] C.L.C. 1875.

Coast) Ltd,[490] Coulson J pointed out that:

"it is always necessary for the court to consider the factual background to a commercial contract even if the wording of that contract might be regarded as unambiguous or sensible."

In *YES F & B Group Pte Ltd v Soup Restaurant Singapore Pte Ltd*[491] the Singapore Court of Appeal discussed the role of background in the light of the decision of the Supreme Court in *Arnold v Britton*.[492] They pointed out that the Supreme Court had said that evidence of background was very limited, and referred to Lord Hodge's description of the process of interpretation as iterative. The Singapore Court of Appeal continued:

"Given that the context in *Arnold* was of limited assistance, it is not surprising, in our view, that the majority of the court gave full effect to what it felt was the clear and unambiguous language in the clauses concerned. In this regard, the absurd result in that decision ... aptly justified as being in accord with the intention of the parties at the time that they entered into the contract concerned. We would venture to suggest that the situation might have been quite different had the relevant context been clearer and therefore more helpful. Indeed, even though Lord Carnwath was of the view that the context was of limited assistance, he nevertheless proceeded to consider much more general and broader facts (including the historic inflation figures), thereby expanding, so to speak, the scope of the factual matrix which (in turn) assisted him in arriving at a different decision from that of the majority. Thus, it is not that the context was not referred to; it is that, pursuant to the unitary approach, the context was looked at but it did not change anything with regard to the text."

3.150   Accordingly, evidence of the surrounding circumstances is admissible in all cases to place the contract in its correct setting, even where there is no ambiguity apparent on the face of the document. Thus in *St Edmundsbury & Ipswich Diocesan Board of Finance v Clark (No.2)*,[493] Sir John Pennycuick, delivering the judgment of the Court of Appeal said it was contended:

"that the proper method of construction is first to construe the words of the instrument in isolation and then look at the surrounding circumstances in order to see whether they cut down the prima facie meaning of the words. It seems to us that this approach is contrary to well-established principle. It is no doubt true that in order to construe an instrument one looks first at the instrument and no doubt one may form a preliminary impression on such inspection. But it is not until one has considered the instrument and the surrounding circumstances in conjunction that one concludes the process of construction."

Similarly, in *Bright Asset Ltd v Lewis*,[494] Arden LJ said:

"The agreement cannot be abstracted from the admissible factual matrix. The

---

[490] [2008] EWHC 2379 (TCC).
[491] [2015] SGCA 55; [2016] 1 L.R.C. 318. See Daniel Y.M. Tan, "Divergent interpretations? Leases and contractual interpretation in Singapore and the UK" [2016] J.B.L. 409.
[492] [2015] UKSC 36; [2015] A.C. 1619.
[493] [1975] 1 W.L.R. 468.
[494] [2011] EWCA Civ 122.

interpretative exercise is the single exercise taking into account the factual matrix."

(c) No conceptual limit

In *BCCI v Ali*,[495] Lord Hoffmann said: **3.151**

"… there is no conceptual limit to what can be regarded as background. It is not, for example, confined to the factual background but can include the state of the law (as in cases in which one takes into account that the parties are unlikely to have intended to agree to something unlawful or legally ineffective) or proved common assumptions which were in fact quite mistaken."[496]

It is not thought that this statement has been invalidated by subsequent cases, although the weight to be given to background may have been.

British Overseas Bank Nominees Ltd v Stewart Milne Group Ltd[497] concerned the   **3.152**
interpretation of a collateral warranty given by a design and build contractor. The Inner House dealt with "context" rather than "background", but that is no more than a choice of words. Lord Drummond Young said:

"Contextual construction means that the wording used in the contract must be construed against the background known to the parties at the time. Context can take many forms. First, with building projects, the roles of the various persons involved, in the totality of the contracts governing the project, including subcontractors, are an important component. Secondly, the collateral warranty itself, like any other contract, must be construed as a whole. Thirdly, the general legal context will usually be relevant. In the present case that includes the rules of prescription,[498] and also the rules of law relating to contractual defences and limitations. It also includes the primary legal reasons that collateral warranties are used: the principle of privity of contract, the impact of the decision in *Murphy v Brentwood District Council*, and the consequent need to prevent loss caused by the failure of a contractor or a member of the design team to use proper care and skill from falling into a so-called 'black hole', so that the person suffering the loss is unable to obtain compensation."

Thus in interpreting a contract the court is entitled to have regard to expert   **3.153**
evidence about market practice, even if that practice falls short of a trade custom, at least where knowledge of that practice was known to the parties or reasonably available to them at the time of the contract.[499] Expert evidence may also be admissible to show what the parties would have known or believed, although in most

---

[495] [2002] 1 A.C. 251.

[496] Where the parties to a contract for the sale of land were mistaken about the true extent of the property, but the contract stated that the buyer was deemed to have inspected before contract, and the mistake would have been evident on inspection, the contract was interpreted by reference to the true facts, rather than the parties' mistaken understanding of them: *Bashir v Ali* [2010] EWHC 2320 (Ch). This point was not dealt with on the subsequent appeal: [2011] EWCA Civ 707.

[497] [2019] CSIH 47; [2020] P.N.L.R. 2.

[498] The Scots equivalent of limitation.

[499] *Crema v Cenkos Securities Plc* [2010] EWCA Civ 1444; [2011] Bus. L.R. 943. In *Pink Floyd Music Ltd v EMI Records Ltd* [2010] EWCA Civ 1429; [2011] 1 W.L.R. 770 the CA held that expert evidence about the practices of the music industry was admissible to interpret a licence agreement. Note, however, that in *Reardon Smith Line Ltd v Yngvar HansenTangen* [1976] 1 W.L.R. 989,

cases it is unlikely to take the case much further.[500] The background may include the state of medical knowledge at the time of the contract even if medical knowledge has subsequently moved on.[501] In the case of an agreement recorded in a recital to a court order, the court looked at transcripts of the proceedings in order to see the context in which the recital was made.[502] If the parties share cultural traditions, they too may be part of the relevant background.[503] The background may also include the setting of social practices and institutions (including the law) within which the contract will operate.[504] In *Yam Seng PTE Ltd v International Trade Corp Ltd*,[505] Leggatt J said that:

"... the relevant background against which contracts are made includes not only matters of fact known to the parties but also shared values and norms of behaviour. Some of these are norms that command general social acceptance; others may be specific to a particular trade or commercial activity; others may be more specific still, arising from features of the particular contractual relationship. Many such norms are naturally taken for granted by the parties when making any contract without being spelt out in the document recording their agreement."

3.154   Accordingly, if a reasonable person with the relevant background knowledge would read some particular contractual provision in light of the provisions of a statutory context within which the contract is to operate, then that statutory context can be a legitimate aid to construction.[506] The use of legal background is discussed later.[507]

3.155   The court must also have regard to the purpose of the contract. In *Batey v Jewson Ltd*,[508] an assignment by a company called Starlcroft Ltd read: "The company as beneficial owner Assigns to Barry Batey any sums of money recoverable from the dispute with Jewsons in lieu of wages owing". The issue was whether the assignment was an assignment of a right of action or only an assignment of the fruits of any action. Mummery LJ said:

---

evidence of Japanese shipbuilding practices was rejected as inadmissible to interpret a contract between two foreign companies, even if those practices had been known to them. In *Barlee Marine Corp v Mountain* [1987] 1 Lloyd's Rep. 471, a policy of marine insurance provided that any amendment addition or deletion of the policy agreed by the leading underwriter was to be binding on all other underwriters. One of the following underwriters sought to adduce evidence of market practice, and the understanding in the market of such a clause. Hirst J rejected the evidence as inadmissible. He said it was "essentially an attempt to influence the construction of the agreement subjectively, by reference to the opinions of market practitioners as to the normal and proper scope of a clause of this character, albeit on a very vague basis". But in *Phillips and Stratton v Dorintal Insurance Ltd* [1987] 1 Lloyd's Rep. 482 Steyn J admitted and relied on evidence of their understanding of a contractual provision given by "market men" in the reinsurance market. In the light of *Crema v Cenkos Securities Plc* and *Pink Floyd Music Ltd v EMI Records Ltd* it is considered that this debate has now been settled up to the level of the Court of Appeal. However, it remains the case that such evidence does not extend to the subjective understanding of the meaning of the contract.

[500]   *Pink Floyd Music Ltd v EMI Records Ltd* [2010] EWCA Civ 1429; [2011] 1 W.L.R. 770.
[501]   *Durham v BAI (Run Off) Ltd* [2011] 1 All E.R. 605, per Smith LJ.
[502]   *Warren v Calzaghe* [2010] EWCA Civ 1447.
[503]   *Khan v Khan* [2008] Bus. L.R. D73.
[504]   *Phoenix Commercial Enterprises Pty Ltd v City of Canada Bay Council* [2010] NSWCA 64 at [172].
[505]   [2013] EWHC 111 (QB); [2013] 1 Lloyd's Rep. 526.
[506]   *Phoenix Commercial Enterprises Pty Ltd v City of Canada Bay Council* [2010] NSWCA 64 at [176].
[507]   See para.4.32.
[508]   [2008] EWCA Civ 18.

"In my judgment, the Recorder was wrong in construing this assignment so as to confine it to the fruits of an action by Starlcroft. I agree that it could be read in that way by simply looking at the wording of it. The Recorder reached the wrong decision because he construed the language of the assignment without sufficient regard to the evidence before him on the practical purpose for making it and on its relevant background."

But where the contract in question is the memorandum or articles of association of a company, extrinsic circumstances cannot be relied on to justify the implication of a term, although they may be relied on for the limited purpose of identifying persons, places or other subject matter referred to in them.[509]   **3.156**

(d) Known or reasonably available?

Lord Hoffmann's proposition was that background included what "should have been reasonably available to the parties". That formulation does not restrict background to what the parties actually knew; and raises questions about how to judge what would have been "reasonably available". To take the second point first, it has been pointed out in Australia that in the age of the internet the range of material "reasonably available" is almost limitless; and that a fact that is reasonably available to the parties should only be used as an aid to interpretation if it can be inferred that the parties actually knew it.[510] This limitation has been held to be equally applicable in English law.[511] In *SAS Institute Inc v World Programming Ltd*,[512] Lewison LJ said: **3.157**

"Almost anything is available on the internet these days, and simply because something is available on the internet does not mean that it is relevant background."

As Hildyard J noted in *Challinor v Juliet Bellis & Co*,[513] "the test of reasonable availability is not always easy to apply, and requires restraint in its application." The need for restraint in the use of background was emphasised by Briggs LJ in *Gladman Commercial Properties v Fisher Hargreaves Proctor*.[514] He said: **3.158**

"I recognise that, in the words of Lord Hoffmann in *ICS Limited v West Bromwich Building Society*.[515] The background matrix of fact may include 'absolutely anything which would have affected the way in which the language of the document would have been understood by a reasonable man'. Nonetheless it seems to me that this broad invitation has tended to lead to levels of minute examination of the contextual background extending way beyond the sensible boundaries of any legitimate aid to interpretation. This is a case in point. The Settlement Agreement is a short, simple, one page document negotiated between sophisticated lawyers. Lord Hoffmann's reasonable man might be forgiven for

---

[509] *Bratton Seymour Service Co Ltd v Oxborough* [1992] B.C.L.C. 693; *HSBC Bank Middle East v Clarke* [2007] UKPC 31; [2007] L.R.C. 544.
[510] *The Movie Network Channels Pty Ltd v Optus Vision Pty Ltd* [2010] NSWCA 111 at [97]–[106].
[511] *Toth v Emirates* [2012] EWHC 517 (Ch); [2012] F.S.R. 26; *SAS Institute Inc v World Programming Ltd* [2013] EWCA Civ 1482; [2014] R.P.C. 8.
[512] [2013] EWCA Civ 1482; [2014] R.P.C. 8.
[513] [2013] EWHC 347 (Ch) at [277].
[514] [2013] EWCA Civ 1466.
[515] [1998] 1 W.L.R. 896 at 912–913.

thinking that its meaning was easily to be ascertained from its straightforward language, without the need for a painstaking recollection or analysis of events which had taken place between the parties to it during the previous six months, a process which it took counsel most of a day to develop before this court."

3.159 Where the contract is one of a contemporaneous series of contracts between the same parties, the other contracts in the series may be looked at as part of the background.[516]

3.160 In *Hamid (t/a Hamid Properties) v Francis Bradshaw Partnership*,[517] Jackson LJ said that the statement of principle in *Investors Compensation Scheme*:

"does not require the court, when construing a document, to take into account matters which the parties might have discovered but did not in fact discover."[518]

In *Revenue and Customs v Secret Hotels2 Ltd*,[519] Lord Neuberger said that:

"When interpreting an agreement, the court must have regard to the words used, to the provisions of the agreement as whole, to the surrounding circumstances in so far as they were known to both parties, and to commercial common sense."

These formulations appear to restrict background to what was known to the parties rather than also encompassing what was reasonably available to them.

3.161 However, in *Tidal Energy Ltd v Bank of Scotland Plc*,[520] the Court of Appeal were divided on whether the details of the mode of operation of the CHAPS banking transfer system were relevant to the interpretation of an instruction by a customer to a bank, in the absence of evidence showing that the customer knew or could readily have discovered that information. Actual knowledge was not the criterion. Similarly, in *Norcross v Georgallides (Estate of)*,[521] Andrew Smith J rejected the proposition that background was limited to what the parties actually knew, and extended at least to knowledge of the practices of the market in which they were operating, whether they knew those practices or not.[522] But he added that the requirement of reasonable availability to the parties was a flexible requirement, which needed to be glossed over in some cases, especially where a document was addressed to a wide class of readers.

3.162 To confine the use of background to those objective facts which were actually known to the parties is difficult to reconcile with the insistence in English law on the objective approach to the interpretation of contracts, because it would pay too close attention to the subjective state of mind of the actual parties to the contract. It would seem right in principle, therefore, to widen the scope of the relevant background beyond what the parties actually knew. On the other hand, especially in the light of more recent stress on the primacy of the contractual language, the peripheral and the speculative should be excluded.

---

[516] *Holding & Barnes Plc v Hill House Hammond (No.1)* [2002] L. & T.R. 7 CA.

[517] [2013] EWCA Civ 470.

[518] Jackson LJ did not deal with the extent to which knowledge of the law was to be attributed to the parties, if they did not in fact know it.

[519] [2014] UKSC 16; [2014] 2 All E.R. 685.

[520] [2014] EWCA Civ 1107.

[521] [2015] EWHC 2405 (Comm).

[522] As noted evidence of market practices was held to be admissible in *Crema v Cenkos Securities Plc* [2010] EWCA Civ 1444; [2011] Bus. L.R. 943 and *Pink Floyd Music Ltd v EMI Records Ltd* [2010] EWCA Civ 1429; [2011] 1 W.L.R. 770.

In *Challinor v Juliet Bellis & Co*,[523] Hildyard J summarised his view as follows:

"(1)   At least where there is no direct evidence as to what the parties knew and did not know, and as a corollary of the objective approach to the interpretation of contracts, the question is what knowledge a reasonable observer would have expected and believed both contracting parties to have had, and each to have assumed the other to have had, at the time of their contract[524];

(2)   that includes specialist or unusual knowledge which only parties entering into a contractual engagement of the sort in question might reasonably be assumed to have; and it also includes knowledge which it is to be inferred, from the nature of the actions they have in fact undertaken, that they had or must have had;

(3)   however, it does not include information that a reasonable observer would think that the parties merely might have known: that would open the gate too far to subjective or idiosyncratic speculation;

(4)   the fact that material is readily available or notorious may support an inference as to what the parties actually knew;

(5)   but (subject to (6) below) where it is demonstrated that one or more of the parties did not in fact have knowledge of the matter in question such knowledge is not to be imputed[525]; nor is the test what reasonable diligence would or might have revealed: in either case, that would be inappropriately to introduce impermissible concepts of constructive notice or a duty (actionable or otherwise) to make inquiries or investigations[526];

(6)   the exception is that a reasonable person cannot be assumed to be in ignorance of clear and well known legal principles affecting or incidental to the contractual engagement in question.[527]"

(e)   Limitations on use of background[528]

Despite the modern emphasis on the importance of the background, there are limits on its use.[529] In *Durham v BAI (Run Off) Ltd*,[530] Burton J pointed out three important qualifications to the use of background: **3.163**

"The first is relevance. ... The second is knowledge: the facts in question 'should

---

[523] [2013] EWHC 347 (Ch) at [277]. This case also contains a useful summary of the principles about the use of background.

[524] *Spencer v Secretary of State for Defence* [2012] EWHC 120 (Ch); [2012] 2 All E.R. (Comm) 480 at [65]–[74].

[525] It is not entirely clear how this proposition sits with the objective theory of interpretation. Hildyard J remains of the view that the positive fact that when making their contract the parties did not know of as particular fact or circumstance is as much as part of the factual matrix as anything else: *Lehman Brothers International (Europe) v Exotix Partners LLP* [2019] EWHC 2380 (Ch). The case is discussed by Parker and Fu, "Knowledge and ignorance in contractual construction: an analysis of Lehman Brothers v Exotix" (2020) 1 J.I.B.F.L. 28.

[526] *Toth v Emirates* [2012] EWHC 517 (Ch) at [44]; *The Movie Network Channel Pty Ltd v Optus Vision Pty Ltd* [2010] NSWCA 111 at [97].

[527] *Spencer v Secretary of State* [2012] EWHC 120 (Ch); [2012] 2 All E.R. (Comm) 480 at [72].

[528] This section was approved in *Bates v Post Office (No.3)* [2019] EWHC 606 (QB).

[529] The limitations are neatly summarised in *Potter v Potter* [2003] 3 N.Z.L.R. 145 (NZCA), affirmed by PC but without discussion of these principles.

[530] [2009] 2 All E.R. 26 at [202]. The statement of principle was not criticised on appeal: [2011] 1 All E.R. 605.

have been reasonably available to the parties'. ... The third qualification is objectivity, so as not to introduce by a side wind evidence of the subjective intention of the parties, but subject ... to a certain degree of flexibility ...".

3.164   The first limitation, that of relevance, is of particular importance in considering standard form contracts or a contract of a nature such that third parties may acquire rights under it.[531]

3.165   Secondly, the relevant background consists of facts that were known or reasonably available to both (or all) parties to a contract. Facts that were known or reasonably available to only one of them will not be relevant. In *Arnold v Britton*,[532] Lord Neuberger said:

> "When interpreting a contractual provision, one can only take into account facts or circumstances which existed at the time that the contract was made, and which were known or reasonably available to both parties. Given that a contract is a bilateral, or synallagmatic, arrangement involving both parties, it cannot be right, when interpreting a contractual provision, to take into account a fact or circumstance known only to one of the parties."

It is, of course, the case that facts which were not known or reasonably available to either party at the date of the contract are not relevant to the construction of their contract, for if the facts were neither known nor reasonably available they cannot have played any part in forming the presumed intention which is embodied in the contract. However, where a fact is known to one party and not to the other, in theory it may well have played a part in forming the intention of the party who knew that fact. However, unless a fact was known or reasonably available to both parties, it will not be admitted in evidence, because what the court is seeking is not the actual intention of one party to the contract, but the presumed mutual intention of both of them.[533]

3.166   Thirdly, the background cannot be used to introduce by a sidewind evidence of the subjective intention of the parties, since that is contrary to the objective theory of interpretation of contracts.[534] Thus in *Plumb Brothers v Dolmac (Agriculture) Ltd*,[535] May LJ said:

> "There has grown up a tendency to speak about construing documents in or against what is described as the 'factual matrix' in which the contract or documents first saw the light of day. In truth that is only, I think, a modern way of saying what has been the rule for a long time that, in construing a document, one must look at all the circumstances surrounding the making of the contract at the time it was made. There is the danger, if one stresses reference to 'the factual matrix,' that one may be influenced by what is in truth a finding of the subjective intention of the parties at the relevant time, instead of carrying out what I understand to be the correct exercise, namely determining objectively the intent of the parties from the words of the documents themselves in the light of the

---

[531] See para.3.171.
[532] [2015] UKSC 36; [2015] A.C. 1619.
[533] Cf. *K.C. Sethia (1944) Ltd v Partabmull Rameshwar* [1950] 1 All E.R. 51.
[534] In the case of a contract which is either wholly oral, or partly oral and partly in writing, it has been held that evidence of a party's subjective intention is admissible: *Blyth v Nelsons Solicitors* [2019] EWHC 2063 (QB); [2019] Costs L.R. 1409.
[535] [1984] 2 E.G.L.R. 1.

circumstances surrounding the transaction. It is not permissible, I think, to take into account a finding of fact about what the parties intended a document to achieve when one is faced with a problem some five, 10 or many years later of construing it."

In *Rabin v Gerson Berger Association Ltd*,[536] Fox LJ reiterated the need to restrict the admission of evidence of background to evidence of objective facts.[537] He said:

"... It is, I think, necessary to observe that 'surrounding circumstances' cannot be literally interpreted: practically anything can be described as 'surrounding circumstances' or information which places the court in the same position as the settlor. Direct evidence of the settlor's intentions, for example, seems to me to be capable of being so described, but it is plainly not admissible ... Nor, I think, can one say that since the object is to discover the intentions of the parties, the court has a roving commission to search for evidence for that purpose."

Fourthly, reliance on background must be tempered by loyalty to the contractual text. It is not permissible to construct from the background a meaning that the words of the contract will not legitimately bear.[538]   **3.167**

In *Commerzbank AG v Jones*,[539] Mummery LJ said:

"I agree ... that the deputy judge paid insufficient attention to the actual language of the documents. He placed far too much reliance on what, in the surrounding circumstances, would have been the sensible commercial agreement between the parties. In the result he constructed from the context alone a contract that the parties in their respective situations might have made. In doing so he has not construed the language of the two letters in which the terms of the contract were in fact formally expressed. Of course, the context of a contract matters as an aid to construction, but it should not be used to construct a contract which does not properly reflect the language employed in formal contractual documents."

As Lord Steyn has put it[540]:

"It is true, as counsel submitted, that the court ought to approach the construction of commercial contracts in a practical and businesslike manner. On the other hand, the paramount principle to which all other principles of construction are subordinate requires loyalty to the contractual text viewed in its relevant context. Loyalty to the text does not permit the construction counsel put forward."

Fifthly, the background should not be used to create an ambiguity where none   **3.168**

---

[536] [1986] 1 W.L.R. 526.

[537] Although there is no burden of proof on a question of construction, nevertheless a party asserting the relevance of surrounding circumstances must both plead them and prove them: *Hallman Holdings Ltd v Webster* [2016] UKPC 3; *Scott v Martin* [1987] 1 W.L.R. 841.

[538] Although in *Chartbrook Ltd v Persimmons Homes Ltd* [2009] A.C. 1101 Lord Hoffmann said of *Investors Compensation Scheme v West Bromwich Building Society* that it decided that: "the meaning which the parties would reasonably be taken to have intended could be given effect despite the fact that it was not, according to conventional usage, an 'available' meaning of the words or syntax which they had actually used".

[539] [2003] EWCA Civ 1663; *Armitage v Staveley Industries Plc* [2006] Pens. L.R. 191.

[540] *National Commercial Bank Jamaica Ltd v Guyana Refrigerators Ltd* [1998] 4 L.R.C. 36; *Society of Lloyds v Robinson* [1999] 1 All E.R. (Comm) 545; *Total Gas Marketing Ltd v Arco British Ltd* [1998] 2 Lloyd's Rep. 209.

exists. The court must be careful to ensure that the background is used to elucidate the contract, and not to contradict it. In *Benjamin Developments Ltd v Robt Jones (Pacific) Ltd*,[541] Hardie Boys J said:

> "What the judge appears to have done is allow the background to create the uncertainty of meaning and then use it again to resolve that uncertainty in a manner in which, in my view at least, contrary to the plain meaning of the words. Such an approach is not in accordance with the authorities. ... It is not permissible to inquire into preliminary or background matter in order to find a different meaning; for that would amount to the court holding that the parties really meant something different from what they choose to say."

Similarly, in *Roar Marine Ltd v Bimeh Iran Insurance Co*,[542] Mance J said:

> "Even if the most generous examination of surrounding circumstances is permitted, any decision on interpretation must pay due regard to the explicitness of particular wording and the nature and strength of any circumstances suggested as putting a different complexion upon it."

In *Well Energy Group Ltd v ECNZ*,[543] McGechan J said:

> "It may seem old-fashioned, but the first step in interpreting words in a document is to read the words concerned. They are the central focus, and the point of departure. *Boat Park* principles[544] do not require anything different. The question is the meaning of the words used, in light of surrounding circumstances. Reference to surrounding circumstances is particularly appropriate where words used give rise to ambiguity or literal meaning gives rise to unreasonable outcomes. One does not start from surrounding circumstances and on that basis invent wording which might have made more sense but which does not exist. The task is interpretation, not reconstruction."

In *Ryledar Pty Ltd v Euphoric Pty Ltd*,[545] the New South Wales Court of Appeal approved the following statement by the primary judge:

> "31 However, that does not mean that when the Court begins the task of construction it puts the words of the document aside and endeavours first to ascertain the commonly known factual context and purpose of the transaction, often only by resolving a strenuous contest between the parties. The Court does not, once it has found the commonly known factual context and purpose, then look at the words of the contract and, if they do not readily accommodate the context and purpose so found, force them to do so by a process of interpretation.

---

[541] [1994] 3 N.Z.L.R. 189 CA. This approach was adopted by the Privy Council in *The Melanesian Mission Trust Board v Australian Mutual Provident Society* [1997] 2 E.G.L.R. 128, and by the Supreme Court in *Arnold v Britton* [2015] UKSC 36; [2015] 2 W.L.R. 1593.

[542] [1998] 1 Lloyd's Rep. 423 at 429.

[543] [2001] 2 N.Z.L.R. 1; approved by NZCA [2001] 2 N.Z.L.R. 1 at 18 and *Potter v Potter* [2003] 2 N.Z.L.R. 145.

[544] *Boat Park Ltd v Hutchinson* [1999] 2 N.Z.L.R. 74, in which the NZCA held that the principles stated in *Investors Compensation Scheme v West Bromwich Building Society* [1998] 1 W.L.R. 896 applied in New Zealand.

[545] (2007) 69 N.S.W.L.R. 603. This formulation was adopted by the same court in *Moraitis Fresh Packaging (NSW) Pty Ltd v Fresh Express (Australia) Pty Ltd* [2008] NSWCA 327.

32   When the Court is construing a commercial contract, it begins with the words of the document: there it often finds expressed the factual context known to both parties and the common purpose and object of the transaction. But the Court is alive to the possibility that what seems clear by reference only to the words on the printed page may not be so clear when one takes into account as well what was known to both parties but does not appear in the document. When that is taken into account, the words in the contract may legitimately have one or more of a number of possible meanings. It is then the Court's task to identify which of the possible meanings represents the parties' contractual intention.

33   However, when a party to a contract argues that the known context and common purpose of the transaction gives the words of the contract a meaning which, by no stretch of language or syntax they will bear then, in truth, one has a rectification suit, not a construction suit."

A different approach was adopted by McHugh JA in *Manufacturers Mutual Insurance Ltd v Withers*[546] in which he said:

"… few, if any, English words are unambiguous or not susceptible of more than one meaning or have a plain meaning. Until a word, phrase or sentence is understood in the light of the surrounding circumstances, it is rarely possible to know what it means."

It is thought that this is too pessimistic a view.[547]

(f)   Date for ascertainment of background

Since a contract must be interpreted according to its meaning at the date when it was made, it ought to follow that the relevant background is likewise to be ascertained by reference to the date at which the contract became binding on the parties. This is also consistent with the general principle that subsequent conduct of the parties does not affect the interpretation of the contract. The point arose in *BlueCo Ltd v BWAT Retail Nominee (1) Ltd*[548] where a management lease was granted pursuant to an obligation contained in a forward sale agreement. There was some disagreement between Etherton C. and Briggs LJ about whether the relevant background was to be ascertained at the date of execution of the management lease in 1998 or at the earlier date in 1996 of the forward sale agreement pursuant to which the management lease was granted. Briggs LJ took the view that, at least arguably, the earlier date was the relevant date for ascertaining the factual background. He said that there were two reasons for that view. The first was that "the objective analysis of the meaning of an agreement is to be conducted by reference to the background in which the parties were at the time when they made their bargain". The second was that on the facts of the case there had been an agree-

3.169

---

[546] (1988) 5 A.N.Z. Insurances Cases 60–853, followed in *Trawl Industries of Australia Pty Ltd v Effem Foods Pty Ltd* (1992) 27 N.S.W.L.R. 326 CA; *B & B Constructions (Aust.) Pty Ltd v Brian A Cheeseman & Associates Pty Ltd* (1994) 35 N.S.W.L.R. 227 CA.

[547] This approach may be attributable to the traditional rule in Australia that an ambiguity is necessary before the courts will have regard to extrinsic evidence. Intermediate appeal courts have taken the view that no ambiguity is necessary, but the position of the High Court remains unclear: see *Franklins Pty Ltd v Metcash Trading Ltd* [2009] NSWCA 407.

[548] [2014] EWCA Civ 154.

ment that the earlier rights under the forward sale agreement were not to be altered. It is considered that the view expressed by Briggs LJ is right in principle.

3.170   By the same token, where a contract has been amended, the background will include facts available to the parties at the date of the amendment.[549]

Illustrations

1.   In determining the standard of repair required by a covenant to keep property in repair, the court must know the age, character and locality of the demised property at the time of the demise.
Proudfoot v Hart[550]

2.   Prima facie the grant of a right of way is the grant of a right of way having regard to the nature of the road over which it is granted and the purpose for which it is to be used; and both those circumstances may be legitimately called in aid in determining whether it is a general right of way, or a right of way restricted to foot-passengers, or restricted to foot passengers and horsemen or cattle, or a general right of way for carts, horses carriages and everything else.
Cannon v Villars[551]

3.   A rent review clause was construed in the light of valuation methods which the parties must have envisaged would be applied at the review date.
Pivot Properties Ltd v Secretary of State for the Environment[552]

4.   A bill of lading was construed in the light of the practice that consignees of goods do not take delivery of goods at the ship's rail but normally collect them after some period of storage on or near the wharf.
The New York Star[553]

5.   A brewer demised a public house to a publican, who covenanted to take all his beer from the brewer, provided that the brewer was willing to supply him at the fair market price. The evidence showed that there was a two-tier market, and that brewers allowed discounts to tenants of tied houses. The House of Lords held that having regard to the surrounding circumstances, the fair market price meant the fair market price charged to tenants of tied houses.
Charrington & Co Ltd v Wooder[554]

6.   A contract for the supply of whale oil was construed in the light of the manner and methods of producing whale oil during the seasonal period to which it related, and in particular the practice among those in the pelagic whaling industry

---

[549] *Renaissance Capital Ltd v African Minerals Ltd* [2014] EWHC 2004 (Comm), referring to *Portsmouth City FC v Sellar Properties (Portsmouth) Ltd* [2004] EWCA Civ 760.

[550] (1890) 25 Q.B.D. 42. See also *Basildon Development Corp v Mactro Ltd* [1986] 1 E.G.L.R. 137 (use clause in a lease construed by reference to the size of the property).

[551] (1878) 8 Ch. D. 415. See also *Johnstone v Holdway* [1963] 1 Q.B. 601; *Keefe v Amor* [1965] 1 Q.B. 334; *St Edmundsbury & Ipswich Diocesan Board of Finance v Clark (No.2)* [1975] 1 W.L.R. 468.

[552] (1980) 41 P. & C.R. 248. See also *Standard Life Assurance Co v Oxoid Ltd* [1987] 2 E.G.L.R. 140.

[553] [1980] 2 Lloyd's Rep. 317.

[554] [1914] A.C. 71.

to own or charter tank accommodation in addition to the tank capacity of a factory ship.
Hvalfangerselskapet Polaris A/S v Unilever Ltd[555]

7. A contract for the building of a ship identified the ship by naming the contractor who was to build her and the yard number allocated to the hull. She was in fact built by a sub-contractor half of whose shareholding was owned by the contractor. It was held that the name of the contractor and the yard number were not essential parts of the description of the vessel, and that accordingly the ship built by the sub-contractors was the ship contracted for.
Reardon Smith Line Ltd v Hansen-Tangen[556]

8. A planning permission in existence at the date of a conveyance, being a public document which could have been available to a purchaser of land, was admissible as an aid to construing the grant of a right of way contained in the conveyance.
Scott v Martin[557]

9. Investors applied to subscribe to an investment scheme described in a brochure. The brochure was admissible to construe the contract.
R. v Clowes (No.2)[558]

10. An IATA ticketing handbook which was present in the office of one of the parties, but rarely referred to, was not reasonably available to the parties and hence was inadmissible for the purpose of construing an IATA Passenger Sales Agency Agreement. However, a glossary of terms commonly used in the airline industry was admissible.
Association of British Travel Agents Ltd v British Airways Plc[559]

11. A standard form of engineering contract was construed in the light of Guidance Notes supplied in order to assist in its drafting.
Matthew Hall Ortech Ltd v Tarmac Roadstone Ltd[560]

18. BACKGROUND AND STANDARD FORMS NEGOTIABLE CONTRACTS AND PUBLIC DOCUMENTS

In the case of a standard form contract, a negotiable contract or a public document evidence of background to an individual contract has a more limited part to play. The same principle applies to documents where the need for certainty is paramount.[561]

---

[555] (1933) 26 Lloyd's Rep. 29.
[556] [1976] 1 W.L.R. 989.
[557] [1987] 1 W.L.R. 841.
[558] [1994] 2 All E.R. 316 CA.
[559] [2000] 1 Lloyd's Rep. 169; on appeal [2000] 2 Lloyd's Rep. 209 CA.
[560] (1997) 87 B.L.R. 96. Contrast *TFW Printers Ltd v Interserve Project Services Ltd* (2006) 109 Con. L.R. 1.
[561] This section was approved by Longmore LJ in *Cherry Tree Investments Ltd v Landmain Ltd* [2012] EWCA Civ 736; [2013] Ch. 305; and in *77m Ltd v Ordnance Survey Ltd* [2019] EWHC 2322 (Ch).

3.171   In *AIB Group (UK) Plc v Martin*,[562] Lord Millett said[563]:

"A standard form is designed for use in a wide variety of different circumstances. It is not context-specific. Its value would be much diminished if it could not be relied upon as having the same meaning on all occasions. Accordingly the relevance of the factual background of a particular case to its interpretation is necessarily limited. The danger, of course, is that a standard form may be employed in circumstances for which it was not designed. Unless the context in a particular case shows that this has happened, however, the interpretation of the form ought not to be affected by the factual background."

This approach has since been applied to standard form contexts. In *Re Lehman Brothers (No.8)*[564] Hildyard J said:

"… a standard form is not context-specific and evidence of the particular factual background or matrix has a much more limited, if any, part to play."

That observation has since been approved by the Court of Appeal.[565]

In *GSO Credit—A Partners LP v Barclays Bank Plc*[566] Knowles J discussed the principles applicable to the interpretation of standard terms, concluding that:

"Overall, the principles described above provide for an approach that seeks to respect the parties' choice, to understand the commercial context, and to provide certainty and consistency in matters of business."

Likewise, in *LSREF III Wight Ltd v Millvalley Ltd*[567] Cooke J said:

"In the context of standard form contracts, consistency, predictability and certainty are essential and so they are much less susceptible to interpretation by reference to background circumstances or matrix. An ISDA standard form cannot therefore be subjected to any 'manipulation' of the language used, because of the potential im-pact on other transactions governed by it."

3.172   The fact that parties are aware their contract might be relied upon by a third party may justify a more restrictive approach to the use of background in some instances, the parties' awareness being itself part of the relevant background.[568] In *LB Re Financing No.3 Ltd v Excalibur Funding No.1 Plc*,[569] Briggs J correctly said:

---

[562] [2002] 1 W.L.R. 94. See also *Yarm Road Ltd v Hewden Tower Cranes Ltd* (2003) 90 Con. L.R. 1, per Laws LJ.

[563] In a dissenting speech.

[564] [2016] EWHC 2417 (Ch); [2017] 2 All E.R. (Comm) 275.

[565] *State of Netherlands v Deutsche Bank AG* [2019] EWCA Civ 771; *Lamesa Investments Ltd v Cynergy Bank Ltd* [2020] EWCA Civ 821.

[566] [2016] EWHC 146 (Comm); [2017] 1 All E.R. (Comm) 421.

[567] [2016] EWHC 466 (Comm); 165 Con. L.R. 58.

[568] *Firm PI 1 Ltd v Zurich Australian Insurance and Body Corporate 398983* [2014] NZSC 147 (NZSC by majority).

[569] [2011] EWHC 2111 (Ch).

"Identification of the relevant audience is important, because it serves to identify the range of background facts relevant to interpretation."

Similarly, in *Dairy Containers Ltd v Tasman Orient CV*,[570] Lord Bingham of Cornhill said:

"There may reasonably be attributed to the parties to a contract such as this such general commercial knowledge as a party to such a transaction would ordinarily be expected to have, but with a printed form of contract, negotiable by one holder to another, no inference may be drawn as to the knowledge or intention of any particular party. The contract should be given the meaning it would convey to a reasonable person having all the background knowledge which is reasonably available to the person or class of persons to whom the document is addressed."

In the case of a public document, members of the public are entitled to take the **3.173** document at face value. Thus in *Slough Estates Ltd v Slough Borough Council*,[571] which concerned the interpretation of a planning permission, Lord Reid said:

"Of course, extrinsic evidence may be required to identify a thing or place referred to, but that is a very different thing from using evidence of facts which were known to the maker of the document but which are not common knowledge to alter or qualify the apparent meaning of words or phrases used in such a document. Members of the public, entitled to rely on a public document, surely ought not to be subject to the risk of its apparent meaning being altered by the introduction of such evidence."

Likewise, in *Secretary of State for Communities & Local Government v Bleaklow Industries Ltd*,[572] Keene LJ said:

"A planning permission runs with the land and should be capable of being relied on by later landowners and others who may well not have access to officers' reports and other extrinsic material."

This approach was applied by the Privy Council in *Opua Ferries Ltd v Fullers* **3.174** *Bay of Islands Ltd*.[573]
Lord Hodge discussed the difference between public documents and private

---

[570] [2005] 1 W.L.R. 215.

[571] [1971] A.C. 958.

[572] [2009] EWCA Civ 206. The same approach applies to the interpretation of a local development plan: *R. (on the application of TW Logistics Ltd) v Tendring District Council* [2013] EWCA Civ 9; *Phides Estates (Overseas) Ltd v Secretary of State for Communities and Local Government* [2015] EWHC 827 (Admin).

[573] [2003] 3 N.Z.L.R. 740; [2003] UKPC 19. In the case of an injunction which may affect third parties, it has been held that the order must "speak for itself" and reference to extrinsic material is inadmissible: *Masri v Consolidated Contractors (Oil and Gas) Co Sal* [2009] EWCA Civ 36. However, in *Sans Souci Ltd v VRL Services Ltd* [2012] UKPC 6 (an appeal from Jamaica) Lord Sumption discussed the interpretation of a court order remitting an arbitration award and held that:

"The reasons for making the order which are given by the court in its judgment are an overt and authoritative statement of the circumstances which it regarded as relevant. They are therefore always admissible to construe the order."

Although he said that these principles applied to orders generally, he did not expressly deal with the case of injunctions (which might be seen as a special case, especially where they are capable of contracts in *Trump International Golf Club Scotland Ltd v Scottish Ministers*[574] (which concerned a licence granted under s.36 of the Electricity Act 1989). He said:

"Differences in the nature of documents will influence the extent to which the court may look at the factual background to assist interpretation. Thus third parties may have an interest in a public document, such as a planning permission or a consent under s.36 of the 1989 Act, in contrast with many contracts. As a result, the shared knowledge of the applicant for permission and the drafter of the condition does not have the relevance to the process of interpretation that the shared knowledge of parties to a contract, in which there may be no third party interest, has. There is only limited scope for the use of extrinsic material in the interpretation of a public document, such as a planning permission or a s.36 consent. ...

When the court is concerned with the interpretation of words in a condition in a public document such as a s.36 consent, it asks itself what a reasonable reader would understand the words to mean when reading the condition in the context of the other conditions and of the consent as a whole. This is an objective exercise in which the court will have regard to the natural and ordinary meaning of the relevant words, the overall purpose of the consent, any other conditions which cast light on the purpose of the relevant words, and common sense. Whether the court may also look at other documents that are connected with the application for the consent or are referred to in the consent will depend on the circumstances of the case, in particular the wording of the document that it is interpreting. Other documents may be relevant if they are incorporated into the consent by reference ... or there is an ambiguity in the consent, which can be resolved, for example, by considering the application for consent."

In the same case Lord Carnwath said:

"I do not think it is right to regard the process of interpreting a planning permission as differing materially from that appropriate to other legal documents. As has been seen, that was not how it was regarded by Lord Denning in Fawcett. Any such document of course must be interpreted in its particular legal and factual context. One aspect of that context is that a planning permission is a public document which may be relied on by parties unrelated to those originally involved. (Similar considerations may apply to other forms of legal document, for example leases which may need to be interpreted many years, or decades, after the original parties have disappeared or ceased to have any interest.)"

---

affecting third parties). In *Group Seven Ltd v Allied Investment Corp Ltd* [2013] EWHC 1509 (Ch), Hildyard J took the view that a freezing order had to be interpreted without reference to evidence that is only available to the original parties. *JSC BTA Bank v Ablyazov* [2013] EWCA Civ 928; [2014] 1 W.L.R. 1414 adopted a similar approach. For the further appeal, see [2015] UKSC 64; [2015] 1 W.L.R. 4752. None of these authorities were referred to in *Secretary of State for Business, Innovation and Skills v Feld* [2014] EWHC 1383; [2014] 1 W.L.R. 3396. In general, however, the court's reasons are admissible in interpreting a court order: *Sarkar v Secretary of State for the Home Department* [2014] EWCA Civ 195; *Re A (a child)* [2014] EWCA Civ 871; *Davison v Davison* [2015] EWCA Civ 587, all following *Sans Souci Ltd v VRL Services Ltd* [2012] UKPC 6.

[574] [2015] UKSC 74; [2016] 1 W.L.R. 85; *Lambeth LBC v Secretary of State for Communities and Local Government* [2019] UKSC 33; [2019] 1 W.L.R. 4317. Publicly available documents may, however, be admissible: *R. (Skelmersdale Ltd) v West Lancashire Borough Council* [2016] EWCA Civ 1260. See also *UBB Waste Essex Ltd v Essex County Council* [2019] EWHC 1924 (Admin).

In *Cherry Tree Investments Ltd v Landmain Ltd*,[575] the question was whether an erroneous omission from a registered charge could be corrected by interpretation having regard to a facility letter that preceded it. The Court of Appeal held that the facility letter was admissible in evidence; but the majority[576] held that since the registered charge was a public document open to inspection by third parties the omission would have to be corrected (if at all) by rectification rather than by interpretation. Lewison LJ said:

> "The reasonable reader's background knowledge would, of course, include the knowledge that the charge would be registered in a publicly accessible register upon which third parties might be expected to rely. In other words a publicly registered document is addressed to anyone who wishes to inspect it. His knowledge would include the knowledge that in so far as documents or copy documents were retained by the registrar they were to be taken as containing all material terms, and that a person inspecting the register could not call for originals. The reasonable reader would also understand that the parties had a choice about what they put into the public domain and what they kept private. He would conclude that matters which the parties chose to keep private should not influence the parts of the bargain that they chose to make public. There is, in my judgment, a real difference between allowing the physical features of the land in question to influence the interpretation of a transfer or conveyance (which we do)[577] and allowing the terms of collateral documents to do the same (which we should not). Land is (almost) invariably registered with general boundaries only, so the register is not conclusive about the precise boundaries of what is transferred. Moreover, physical features are, after all, capable of being seen by anyone contemplating dealing with the land and who takes the trouble to inspect. But a third party contemplating dealing with the land has no access to collateral documents."

Longmore LJ said:

> "The legal charge in the present case is not just an agreement made by two parties to the transaction who are themselves alone affected. It is a public document on a public register open to inspection and potentially to be relied on by third parties. I do not think that mistakes in such documents can be construed away by a process of construction of the kind envisaged in Lord Hoffmann's principle (5)."

Bryant Homes Southern Ltd v Stein Management Ltd[578] concerned a restrictive covenant, particulars of which were registered at HM Land Registry and a collateral agreement which was not. Norris J held, following *Cherry Tree Invest-*

---

[575] [2012] EWCA Civ 736; [2013] Ch. 305, noted at [2012] Conv. 349 and (2013) L.Q.R. 24. See also *TW Logistics, R. (on the application of) v Tendring District Council* [2013] EWCA Civ 9; [2013] 2 P. & C.R. 190 (local development plan). *Cherry Tree Investments Ltd v Landmain Ltd* was followed and applied in *Network Rail Infrastructure Ltd v Freemont Ltd* [2013] EWHC 1733 (Ch) and *British Malleable Iron Co Ltd v Revelan (IOM) Ltd* [2013] EWHC 1954 (Ch).
[576] Longmore and Lewison LJJ. Arden LJ dissented.
[577] See para.11.14.
[578] [2016] EWHC 2435 (Ch); [2017] 1 P. & C.R. 6.

ments Ltd v Landmain Ltd,[579] that the collateral agreement could not be given weight as an aid to interpretation of the registered covenant. On the other hand, in *Pathway Finance SARL v The Defendants Set Out In Annex 1 To the Claim*[580] extrinsic evidence was admitted to correct (by way of interpretation) an erroneous reference to a facility agreement which was contained in a charge registrable under the Companies Act.

3.176   In *Egyptian Salt and Soda Co Ltd v Port Said Salt Association Ltd*,[581] the documents in question were the memorandum and articles of association of a limited company. The judge reached an interpretation which relied in part on the surrounding circumstances at the time when the company was incorporated. Lord Macmillan, giving the advice of the Privy Council, said:

> "As regards the aid to interpretation to be derived from surrounding circumstances the learned judge has in their Lordships' view taken too wide a scope. It must be borne in mind that the purpose of the memorandum is to enable shareholders, creditors and those who deal with the company to know what is its permitted range of enterprise, and for this information they are entitled to rely on the constituent documents of the company. They have not access to other sources of information such as the antecedent transactions which the learned judge invokes, and have no means of knowing, for example, 'that the intention of the promoters that the company should not export salt was known to the defendant company', a circumstance which the learned judge adduces. The intention of the framers of the memorandum must be gathered from the language in which they have chosen to express it."

In *Cosmetic Warriors Ltd v Gerrie*[582] it was held, in relation to a company's memorandum and articles of association that:

> "... the cases establish that (a) there is no absolute prohibition on considering extrinsic material for the purpose of interpreting the articles of association of a company; (b) however, the admissible background for the purposes of construction is limited to what any reader of the articles would reasonably be supposed to know; and (c) in contrast, an implication based on extrinsic evidence of which only a limited number of people would have known is impermissible."

This approach was accepted on the appeal.[583] These principles also apply to the constitution of a charity, which is required to be registered with the Charity Commission and open to public inspection.[584] They have been held not to apply to a letter of credit.[585]

These cases are consistent with Lord Hoffmann's description of the role of

---

579   [2012] EWCA Civ 736; [2013] Ch. 305. The issue was raised in the Supreme Court of New Zealand in *Lakes International Golf Management Ltd v Vincent* [2017] NZSC 99, but the court did not have to resolve it. There is further discussion by the Supreme Court of New Zealand in *Green Growth No.2 Ltd v Queen Elizabeth National Trust* [2018] NZSC 75.

580   [2020] EWHC 1191 (Ch).

581   [1931] A.C. 677.

582   [2015] EWHC 3718 (Ch).

583   *Cosmetic Warriors Ltd v Gerrie* [2017] EWCA Civ 324; [2017] 2 B.C.L.C. 456.

584   *Celestial Church of Christ, Edward Street Parish (A Charity) v Lawson* [2017] EWHC 97 (Ch); [2017] P.T.S.R. 790.

585   *Yuchai Dongte Special Purpose Automobile Co Ltd v Suisse Credit Capital (2009) Ltd* [2018] EWHC 2580 (Comm).

background. The reason for this is that in these cases the background to an individual contract would not have affected what a reasonable person would have understood the language of the contract to mean. As he himself said of articles of association in *Attorney General of Belize v Belize Telecom Ltd*[586]:

"Because the articles are required to be registered, addressed to anyone who wishes to inspect them, the admissible background for the purposes of construction must be limited to what any reader would reasonably be supposed to know. It cannot include extrinsic facts which were known only to some of the people involved in the formation of the company."

It will be noted also that in *Dairy Containers Ltd v Tasman Orient CV* one of the features of the contract that limited the role of background was that it was negotiable by one holder to another. The circumspection with which a court should approach the question of background in the case of a tradable financial instrument was emphasised by the Supreme Court in *LBG Capital No.1 Plc v BNY Mellon Corporate Trustee Services Ltd*.[587] Likewise, in the case of a negotiable bill of lading the role of background is very restricted.[588] In *Toth v Emirates*,[589] the parties were adherents to an agreement with Nominet which allocated internet domain names and which also made provision for dispute resolution. Mann J said: **3.177**

"... the contracts in this case were in the nature of a contract which would have a number of adherents from time to time and in relation to which the concept of the background matrix of fact is not going to be of much assistance."

It is suggested that in the case of a contract that contemplates its assignment this is also a reason for limiting the role or scope of background. In *Phoenix Commercial Enterprises Pty Ltd v City of Canada Bay Council*,[590] Campbell JA, having referred to the principle that surrounding circumstances must be taken into account, said: **3.178**

"However, the way those principles come to be applied to a particular contract can be affected by aspects of the contract such as whether it is assignable, whether it will endure for a longer time rather than a shorter time, and whether the provision that is in question is one to which indefeasibility attaches by virtue of the contract being embodied in an instrument that is registered on a Torrens title register. All these are matters that would be taken into account by the reasonable person seeking to understand what the words of the document conveyed. That is because the reasonable person seeking to understand what the words convey would understand that the meaning of the words of the document does not change with time or with the identity of the person who happens to be seeking to understand the document. That reasonable person would therefore understand that the sort of background knowledge that is able to be used as an

---

[586] [2009] 1 W.L.R. 1988.
[587] [2016] UKSC 29; [2016] 2 Lloyd's Rep 119; *Hayfin Opal Luxco 3 SARL v Windermere VII Cmbs Plc* [2016] EWHC 782 (Ch); *CBRE Loan Servicing Ltd v Gemini (Eclipse 2006-3) Plc* [2015] EWHC 2769 (Ch); *The State of the Netherlands v Deutsche Bank AG* [2018] EWHC 1935 (Comm). Similar circumspection is necessary where the question is one of implying terms into such an instrument: *Law Debenture Trust Corp Plc v Ukraine* [2017] EWHC 655.
[588] *Glencore International AG v MSC Mediterranean Shipping Co SA* [2015] EWHC 1989 (Comm).
[589] [2012] EWHC 517 (Ch); [2012] F.S.R. 26.
[590] [2010] NSWCA 64 at [151].

aid to construction, has to be background knowledge that is accessible to all the people who it is reasonably foreseeable might, in the future, need to construe the document."[591]

He continued:

"The fact that a lease is to endure for a long time, is assignable, is to be registered as a dealing under the RPA, and may well on occasions need to be understood and acted upon by people other than the original parties to its creation are themselves relevant surrounding circumstances to the entering of the lease. They are the sort of background circumstances that anyone could infer from a perusal of the lease document itself. They are not background circumstances that are the particular, private knowledge of the people who entered the lease, but rather background circumstances of a type ascertainable by anyone who set out to understand the lease, even many years after it was entered. They are the type of background circumstances not dependent upon the chance of the person seeking to understand the document being able to locate and communicate with the people who negotiated it, and the negotiators still having documents or enough reliable memory for the surrounding circumstances to become known. They are surrounding circumstances that should lead a reasonable person seeking to understand the meaning of the document, to leave out of consideration other surrounding circumstances that are not likely to be ascertainable by others who wish to construe the document in the future."[592]

So, in *Public Trustee v Harrison*[593] Marcus Smith J held that an indenture executed by a settlor and approved by the court should be interpreted without reference to external factors. As he put it:

"The trustee and future beneficiaries are, as it seems to me, entitled to rely on the wording of the instrument, unaffected by materials that may (or may not) have weighed upon the mind of the settlor."

3.179   Likewise, in *Re Sigma Finance Corp*,[594] a finance deed secured a variety of creditors holding different instruments issued at different times and in different circumstances. Lord Collins said:

"Consequently this is not the type of case where the background or matrix of fact is or ought to be relevant, except in the most generalised way. I do not consider, therefore, that there is much assistance to be derived from the principles of interpretation re-stated by Lord Hoffmann in the familiar passage in *Investors Compensation Scheme Ltd v West Bromwich Building Society*.[595] Where a security document secures a number of creditors who have advanced funds over a long period it would be quite wrong to take account of circumstances which are not known to all of them. In this type of case it is the wording of the instrument which is paramount. The instrument must be interpreted as a whole in the

---

[591] Lewison LJ endorsed this passage in *Cherry Tree Investments Ltd v Landmain Ltd* [2012] EWCA Civ 736; [2013] Ch. 305.
[592] See also *Burns Phillip Hardware Ltd v Howard China Pty Ltd* (1987) 8 N.S.W.L.R. 642 at 655.
[593] [2018] EWHC 166 (Ch); [2018] W.T.L.R. 299.
[594] [2010] 1 All E.R. 571.
[595] [1998] 1 W.L.R. 896 at 912–913.

light of the commercial intention which may be inferred from the face of the instrument and from the nature of the debtor's business. Detailed semantic analysis must give way to business common sense."

In the author's view this is a sound approach.
However, in *Chartbrook Ltd v Persimmon Homes Ltd*,[596] Lord Hoffmann said: **3.180**

"Ordinarily, however, a contract is treated as addressed to the parties alone and an assignee must either inquire as to any relevant background or take his chance on how that might affect the meaning a court will give to the document. The law has sometimes to compromise between protecting the interests of the contracting parties and those of third parties. But an extension of the admissible background will, at any rate in theory, increase the risk that a third party will find that the contract does not mean what he thought. How often this is likely to be a practical problem is hard to say."

Lord Hoffmann qualified this view in the case of articles of association and negotiable instruments which are addressed to a wider readership, and limited this observation to "ordinary contracts". But as Mr Nicholas Strauss QC (sitting as a judge of the Chancery Division) pointed out in *Churchill v Temple*[597]:

"In many cases, including this one, the issue of construction arises long after the contract was entered into, and as between parties who are not the original parties to the contract. It is then usually impossible to know what were all the facts known, or reasonably available, to the parties, to which *Investors Compensation* requires the court to have regard, because the parties are not there to provide the evidence. Some of the facts may be clear, but there is a real risk that the court is proceeding on the basis of incomplete evidence as to the relevant background, and that it may therefore misunderstand it."

The Supreme Court adopted a similar approach in *Barnado's v Buckingham-*   **3.181**
shire,[598] which concerned the rules of a pension scheme intended to confer rights on persons who were not parties to the instrument; and to operate over a long term. As Lord Hodge explained:

"A pension scheme, such as the one in issue on this appeal, has several distinctive characteristics which are relevant to the court's selection of the appropriate interpretative tools. First, it is a formal legal document which has been prepared by skilled and specialist legal draftsmen. Secondly, unlike many commercial contracts, it is not the product of commercial negotiation between parties who may have conflicting interests and who may conclude their agreement under considerable pressure of time, leaving loose ends to be sorted out in future. Thirdly, it is an instrument which is de-signed to operate in the long term, defining people's rights long after the economic and other circumstances, which existed at the time when it was signed, may have ceased to exist. Fourthly, the scheme confers important rights on parties, the members of the pension scheme, who were not parties to the instrument and who may have joined the scheme many years after it was initiated. Fifthly, members of a pension scheme may not

---

[596] [2009] A.C. 1101.
[597] [2011] 1 E.G.L.R. 73.
[598] [2018] UKSC 55; [2019] I.C.R. 495.

have easy access to expert legal advice or be able readily to ascertain the circumstances which existed when the scheme was established."

These characteristics "make it appropriate for the court to give weight to textual analysis, by concentrating on the words which the draftsman has chosen to use and by attaching less weight to the background factual matrix than might be appropriate in certain commercial contracts".

3.182   Some contracts may expressly contemplate that a third party will have to act on the basis of the contract (e.g. a valuer). The parties' awareness of that fact is itself part of the background.[599] In such circumstances it is unlikely that they would have intended any but the most obvious extrinsic circumstances to be taken into account in interpreting the contract.[600] Likewise, in *Mannai Investment Co Ltd v Eagle Star Life Assurance Co Ltd*,[601] Lord Hoffmann said:

> "There are documents in which the need for certainty is paramount and which admissible background is restricted to avoid the possibility that the same document may have different meanings for different people according to their knowledge of the background. Documents required by bankers' commercial credits fall within this category."

On the same principle the courts of Australia are much more cautious in admitting extrinsic evidence in interpreting conveyancing documents (e.g. grants of easements) because the Torrens system of land registration is dependent on a publicly accessible register.[602] It is not clear whether this approach will be applied in New Zealand.[603] The move in England and Wales to a system of title by registration (rather than registration of title) as a result of the Land Registration Act 2002 is likely to cause a shift in prevailing judicial attitudes to the admission of extrinsic evidence (other than topographical evidence) to interpret conveyancing documents.[604]

19.   SUBSEQUENT CONDUCT OF THE PARTIES

The court may not generally look at the subsequent conduct of the parties to interpret a written agreement. However, where the agreement is partly written and partly oral, subsequent conduct may be examined for the purpose of determining what were the full terms of the contract.[605] In addition the subsequent conduct of the parties may be examined where an estoppel by convention is alleged; where it is alleged that the agreement was a sham; and probably for the purposes of determining the boundaries of an ambiguous grant of land.[606]

[599] *Firm PI 1 Ltd v Zurich Australian Insurance Ltd* [2014] NZSC 147.
[600] See *Burns Phillip Hardware Ltd v Howard China Pty Ltd* (1987) 8 N.S.W.L.R. 642 at 655; *Meritz Fire and Marine Insurance Co Ltd* [2010] EWHC 3362 (Comm).
[601] [1997] A.C. 749.
[602] *Westfield Management Ltd v Perpetual Trustee Co Ltd* (2007) 239 A.L.R. 75.
[603] *Big River Paradise Ltd v Congreve* [2008] NZCA 78; *Thompson v Trounson* [2008] NZCA 84.
[604] See *Cherry Tree Investments Ltd v Landmain Ltd* [2012] EWCA Civ 736; [2013] Ch. 305.
[605] Referred to with approval in *Kellogg Brown & Root Inc v Concordia Maritime AG* [2006] EWHC 3358 (Comm); *Jones v Southwark London Borough Council* [2016] EWHC 457 (Ch); [2016] P.T.S.R. 1011 and *Stobart Ltd v Stobart* [2019] EWCA Civ 1376.
[606] The equivalent section in a previous edition of this book was cited with approval in *Excelsior Group*

(a) The general rule

At one time the courts were prepared to admit evidence of subsequent conduct **3.183** in cases where the contract was ambiguous and subsequent conduct was probative. Thus in *Houlder Bros & Co Ltd v Public Works Commissioner*,[607] Lord Atkinson said:

> "There is no doubt that the construction of a contract cannot be affected by the declarations of the parties made subsequent to its date, as to its nature or effect, or as to their intention in entering into it. But it is equally true that, where the words of the contract are ambiguous, the acts, conduct, and course of dealing of the parties before, and at the time, they entered into it may be looked at to ascertain what was in their contemplation, the sense in which they used the language they employ, and the intention which their words in that sense reveal."

Likewise, in *Watcham v Att.-Gen. of East Africa Protectorate*,[608] it was held by the Privy Council that where an instrument contains an ambiguity, evidence of use under it may be given to show the sense in which the parties used the language employed; and that that principle applied to a modern as well as to an ancient instrument, and to a case of latent as well as patent ambiguity.

However, the general authority of this case in English law as applied to com- **3.184** mercial contracts has since been seriously undermined.[609] In *Union Insurance Society of Canton Ltd v George Wills & Co*,[610] Lord Parmoor said:

> "It is immaterial to the construction of the contract to consider subsequent events. The intention of the parties must be gathered from the language of the contract, the subject-matter, and the circumstances in existence at the time it was made."

In *James Miller and Partners Ltd v Whitworth Street Estates (Manchester) Ltd*,[611] it was held by the House of Lords that subsequent conduct of the parties could not be looked at in order to construe a written contract unless that conduct amounted to a variation of the contract, or gave rise to an estoppel. Lord Reid said:

> "I must say that I had thought it now well settled that it is not legitimate to use as an aid in the construction of the contract anything which the parties said or did after it was made. Otherwise one might have the result that a contract meant one thing the day it was signed, but by reason of subsequent events meant something different a month or a year later."

Watcham's Case was not cited to the House of Lords, and this omission was **3.185** pointed out to their Lordships in *Schuler (L.) AG v Wickman Machine Tool Sales Ltd*.[612] In that case the House of Lords confirmed that the law was as laid down in *Whitworth's Case* and that *Watcham's Case*, if still good law, should be confined to the interpretation of title deeds by reference to acts of possession under them.

Productions Ltd v Yorkshire Television Ltd [2009] EWHC 1751 (Comm); and *Entrust Pension Ltd v Prospect Hospice Ltd* [2012] EWHC 1666 (Ch).

[607] [1908] A.C. 276 (a case of a charterparty).
[608] [1919] A.C. 533. See also para.11.24.
[609] It was described by Lord Wilberforce in *Schuler (L) AG v Wickman Machine Tool Sales Ltd* [1974] A.C. 235 as "nothing but the refuge of the desperate".
[610] [1916] 1 A.C. 281.
[611] [1970] A.C. 583.
[612] [1974] A.C. 235; applied by the Privy Council in *Australian Mutual Provident Society v Chaplin*

A possible fallacy in Lord Reid's statement was exposed by Tipping J in *Wholesale Distributors v Gibbons*[613]:

"Evidence of subsequent conduct does not invite a subsequent meaning. It is directed to the original meaning; that is, the meaning of the contract when it was signed. It is a distraction to suggest that post-contract evidence is capable of changing the contract date meaning, when its sole purpose is to elucidate that meaning."

Nevertheless the rule remains part of current English law.[614] Lord Reid's statement was applied by the Court of Appeal in *Amalgamated Investment & Property Co Ltd v Texas Commerce International Bank Ltd*[615] in which Lord Denning quoted Lord Reid's statement and said:

"I can understand the logic of it when the construction is clear: but not when it is unclear. Still, we must accept it."

3.186   In addition, in *Rembrandt Group Ltd v Philip Morris International Inc*,[616] Morritt LJ (with whom Butler-Sloss and Sedley LJJ agreed) said of certain post-contractual statements:

"Each of the events amounts to the description by one party in the presence or to the knowledge of the other of the legal effect of the contract or contracts already concluded. Such views cannot be relevant to or of assistance in the determination by the court of the point of law on which the party is expressing its opinion. Nor, without more, can it be of any assistance in the determination, for the purposes of the Novation Agreement, what obligations had been previously undertaken by PMI. I can understand that the views and opinions so expressed might give rise to some estoppel by convention for the future or to some further or collateral contract to the effect represented in the statement; cf *Amalgamated Investment & Property Co Ltd v Texas Commerce International Bank Ltd*.[617] But in the absence of such an estoppel or contract, and none was suggested, I do not see how the statements relied on can have any effect on the issues we have to determine."

In *Sattar v Sattar*,[618] Sales J ruled that post-contractual conduct was inadmissible on the ground that:

"Conduct of a party after the making of the contract does not provide relevant factual context to explicate the meaning with which the parties used the words at the time they made the contract."

(1978) 18 A.L.R. 385.
[613] [2007] NZSC 37 at [59].
[614] *Crema v Cenkos Securities Plc* [2011] Bus. L.R. 943.
[615] [1982] Q.B. 84 at 120.
[616] *25 February 1999.*
[617] [1982] 1 Q.B. 84.
[618] [2009] EWHC 289 (Ch). See also *Wollenberg v Casinos Austria International Holding GmbH* [2011] EWHC 103 (Ch).

In *Hyundai Merchant Marine Co Ltd v Daelim Corp The Gaz Energy*,[619] Flaux **3.187**
J, referring to the equivalent paragraph in a previous edition of this book, said:

"reliance on a subsequent contract to construe a written contract is, to say the
least, a heretical approach to construction.[620] Although [counsel] did not press the
point, I consider it should be addressed, if only to dismiss it. The inadmissibility of a subsequent contract as an aid to construction of a written contract is
merely one aspect of the general principle of English contract law that (save in
exceptional circumstances not applicable in the present case) the subsequent
conduct of the parties cannot be looked at to interpret a written contract. ... It
seems to me that the principle that the subsequent contract is inadmissible is
equally applicable whether it is made the following day or long after."

In *Agricultural and Rural Finance Pty Ltd v Gardiner*,[621] a majority of the High
Court of Australia reaffirmed the general principle that "it is not legitimate to use
as an aid in the construction of [a] contract anything which the parties said or did
after it was made". Since the general rule is that the subsequent conduct of the parties is not a permissible aid to interpretation, it follows that the subsequent conduct
of different parties cannot be either.[622]

There are some purposes for which subsequent conduct may be admissible and **3.188**
relevant. In *HMRC v Secret Hotels2 Ltd*[623] Lord Neuberger said:

"The subsequent behaviour or statements of the parties can, however, be relevant,
for a number of other reasons. First, they may be invoked to support the contention that the written agreement was a sham—i.e. that it was not in fact intended
to govern the parties' relationship at all. Secondly, they may be invoked in support of a claim for rectification of the written agreement. Thirdly, they may be
relied on to support a claim that the written agreement was subsequently varied,
or rescinded and replaced by a subsequent contract (agreed by words or conduct).
Fourthly, they may be relied on to establish that the written agreement
represented only part of the totality of the parties' contractual relationship."

Subsequent conduct may also be relied on to prove the true nature of the agreement or the legal relationship of the parties, even though this may vary or add to
the written instrument.[624] In addition, subsequent conduct may give rise to an estoppel; and may also be relied on in the case of a contract partly oral and partly writ-

---

[619] [2011] EWHC 3108 (Comm); [2012] 1 Lloyd's Rep. 211.
[620] In *CLP Holding Co Ltd v Singh* [2014] EWCA Civ 1103 the Court of Appeal appears to have relied
to some extent on conduct subsequent to the conclusion of the contract in deciding a dispute about
its meaning. The principle was not discussed.
[621] [2008] HCA 57. Kirby J dissented. He said: "I do not agree that later communications and conduct
of parties to an agreement are inadmissible when tendered to indicate acceptance by the parties of
a particular meaning of the language used in their agreement. For example, if an agreement included
technical words, the communications and conduct of the parties after the execution of that agreement might be admitted to throw light on a common understanding as to the meaning of such words.
In particular circumstances, the common understanding of the language of a written agreement might
assist in deriving the objective meaning of the text." The Australian authorities are comprehensively
reviewed by Campbell JA in *Franklin Pty Ltd v Metcash Trading Ltd* [2009] NSWCA 407.
[622] *Kason Kek-Gardner Ltd v Process Components Ltd* [2017] EWCA Civ 2132; [2018] 2 All E.R.
(Comm) 381.
[623] [2014] UKSC 16; [2014] 2 All E.R. 685.
[624] *Barclays Bank Plc v Landgraf* [2014] EWHC 503 (Comm).

ten or to identify the boundaries of an ambiguous conveyance.[625] Where a clause is alleged to amount to a penalty, evidence of subsequent events may be valuable evidence of what could reasonably have been expected to be the loss at the time that the contract was made.[626]

(b) Identification of terms[627]

3.189 Evidence of post-contractual conduct is admissible in deciding what terms the parties agreed (as opposed to interpreting the meaning of the terms that they did agree), at all events where the contract is not contained wholly in writing.[628] Thus in *Wilson v Maynard Shipbuilding Consultants AG Ltd*,[629] the Court of Appeal held that where one cannot ascertain from the terms of the contract itself what was agreed about a relevant term (in that case the place where under his contract an employee normally works), one may look at what has happened and what the parties have done under the contract during the whole contemplated period of the contract for the limited purpose of ascertaining what that term is. In *Maggs v Marsh*,[630] Smith LJ, approving the equivalent passage in the previous edition of this book, said:

> "In my judgment it is clear that the principle set out in *Miller*'s case,[631] does not apply to an oral contract. Determining the terms of an oral contract is a question of fact. Establishing the facts will usually, as here, depend upon the recollections of the parties and other witnesses. The accuracy of those recollections may be tested and elucidated by things said and done by the parties or witnesses after the agreement has been concluded. Receiving evidence of such words or actions does not mean that the judge is losing sight of his task of deciding what the parties agreed at the time of the contract. It is simply helping him to decide whose recollection is right. It is not surprising to me that the editor[632] of Lewison should observe that there is nothing in the authorities to prevent the court from looking at post-contract actions of the parties. As a matter of principle, I can see every reason why such evidence should be received."

In *Great North Eastern Rly Ltd v Avon Insurance Plc*,[633] Longmore LJ said:

> "If the question is whether a term was incorporated into a contract, the subsequent conduct of the parties may be very relevant to the inquiry whether

---

[625] See *Bank St Petersburg v Savelyev* [2013] EWHC 3529 (Ch). In *Wood v Waddington* [2014] EWHC 1358 (Ch) Morgan J suggested that this principle may need modification in the light of *Cherry Tree Investments Ltd v Landmain Ltd* (see para.3.175). However, *Cherry Tree Investments Ltd v Landmain Ltd* was not concerned with objective facts verifiable on inspection of the property in question; and the two principles may yet be capable of reconciliation.

[626] *Philips Hong Kong Ltd v The Attorney General of Hong Kong* [1993] 61 B.L.R. 41.

[627] Campbell JA discusses the difference between interpretation of terms and identification of terms in typically compelling and learned fashion in *Lym International Pty Ltd v Marcolongo* [2011] NSWCA 303; *Johnston v Brightstars Holding Co Pty Ltd* [2014] NSWCA 150.

[628] *Wollenberg v Casinos Austria International Holding GmbH* [2011] EWHC 103 (Ch).

[629] [1978] Q.B. 665; followed in *Todd v British Midland Airways Ltd* [1978] I.C.R. 959 and *Mears v Safecar Security Ltd* [1983] Q.B. 54.

[630] [2006] B.L.R. 395; *Crema v Cenkos Securities Plc* [2011] Bus. L.R. 943.

[631] *James Miller and Partners Ltd v Whitworth Street Estates (Manchester) Ltd* [1970] A.C. 583.

[632] In fact the author.

[633] [2001] 2 All E.R. (Comm) 526; *ED&F Man Commodity Advisers Ltd v Fluxo-Cane Overseas Ltd* [2009] EWCA Civ 406.

such a term was or was not agreed. Mr Flaux's submissions to the contrary were, with respect, a misapplication of the principle that the subsequent conduct of the parties cannot be relied on as an aid to the construction of the contract (see *James Miller & Partners Ltd v Whitworth Street Estates (Manchester) Ltd*[634]). No such principle exists in relation to the question whether an alleged term of a contract was, in fact, agreed."

In *Kier Regional Ltd v City & General (Holborn) Ltd*,[635] Coulson J said that:

"where a contract is partly oral and partly in writing, the court may have regard to subsequent conduct to ascertain what the oral agreement might have been."

In *BVM Management Ltd v Yeomans*,[636] Aikens LJ confirmed that:

"... in the case of a contract which is entirely oral or partly oral, evidence of things said and done after the contract was concluded are admissible to help decide what the parties had actually agreed."

In *Sea Containers Services Ltd*,[637] Hildyard J also distinguished between admitting evidence of subsequent conduct for the purpose of identifying terms, and admitting such evidence for the purpose of interpreting terms. Only the former is permissible.

(c) Identification of subject matter

Where the question is not the interpretation of written terms, but the identification of the subject matter of the contract which is not recorded in writing, post-contractual conduct is admissible. In *County Securities Pty Ltd v Challenger Group Holdings Pty Ltd*,[638] Spigelman CJ said[639]:   **3.190**

"Where, as here, the issue is the identification, as a matter of fact, of the subject matter of the contract, as distinct from the interpretation of the contract, subsequent conduct, especially conduct at the time of settlement is, in my opinion, entitled to significant weight ... In my opinion, subsequent conduct, especially how a contract for purchase and sale was settled, is relevant, on an objective basis, to the identification of the subject matter of the contract or the determination of necessary terms, as distinct from deciding the meaning of words."

(d) Estoppel

Nevertheless, the recognition by the House of Lords that, even in the context of a commercial contract, subsequent conduct of the parties may give rise to an estoppel was seized on as "a way of escape" by Lord Denning MR in *Amalgamated*   **3.191**

---

[634] [1970] A.C. 583 at 603, 615, per Lord Reid and Lord Wilberforce respectively.
[635] [2009] B.L.R. 90; *Crema v Cenkos Securities Plc* [2011] Bus. L.R. 943.
[636] [2011] EWCA Civ 1254.
[637] [2012] EWHC 2547 (Ch).
[638] [2008] NSWCA 193.
[639] Referring to the equivalent section in a previous edition of this book.

Investment & Property Co Ltd v Texas Commerce International Bank Ltd.[640] In that case the conduct of the parties was held to give rise to an estoppel by convention which precluded them from relying upon the true construction of the written agreement, as opposed to what they had erroneously supposed it to mean. Lord Denning said:

> "So here we have available to us, in point of practice if not in law, evidence of subsequent conduct to come to our aid. It is available, not so as to construe the contract, but to see how they themselves acted upon it. Under the guise of estoppel we can prevent either party from going back on the interpretation they themselves gave to it."

He added:

> "There is no need to inquire whether their particular interpretation is correct or not, or whether they were mistaken or not, or whether they had in mind the original terms or not. Suffice it that they have by the course of dealing, put their own interpretation on their contract, and cannot be allowed to go back on it."

(e) Sham

3.192   In addition, evidence of the subsequent conduct of the parties is admissible where it is alleged that some or all of the terms of a contract are a sham. In *AG Securities Ltd v Vaughan*,[641] Lord Jauncey said:

> "Accordingly, although the subsequent actings of the parties may not be prayed in aid for the purposes of construing the agreement they may be looked at for the purposes of determining whether or not parts of the agreements are a sham in the sense that they were intended merely as 'dressing up' and not as provisions to which any effect would be given."

(f) Title deeds

3.193   *Watcham's Case* itself was concerned with title deeds; whereas the two cases in the House of Lords were not. This distinction was drawn on by Megarry J in *St. Edmundsbury & Ipswich Diocesan Board of Finance v Clark (No.2).*[642] He said:

> "Parcels clauses and plans in a conveyance not infrequently give rise to disputes on the application of what appears on the piece of paper to what lies physically

---

[640] [1982] Q.B. 84, following prior expressions of regret at the House's decision, e.g. in *Port Sudan Cotton Co v Govindaswamy Chettiar and Sons* [1977] 2 Lloyd's Rep. 5. The doctrine enunciated by Lord Denning MR is that of estoppel by convention. Discussion of the doctrine is outside the scope of this book. The reader is referred to, e.g. Spencer Bower: *Reliance-Based Estoppel*, 5th edn (Bloomsbury Professional, 2017). See also *The Vistafjord* [1988] 2 Lloyd's Rep. 343.

[641] [1990] 1 A.C. 417 HL.

[642] [1973] 1 W.L.R. 1572 (affirmed [1975] 1 W.L.R. 468). In *Neilson v Poole* (1969) 20 P. & C.R. 909 Megarry J had previously drawn attention to possible justifications of *Wateham's Case*. He noted particularly:

    (a) the modern tendency against exclusionary rules of evidence in civil cases; and

    (b) the particular pressure on the court in construing a parcels clause to produce a decisive result.

Evidence of subsequent conduct has been held to be irrelevant to the construction of a reservation of an incorporeal hereditament: *Inglewood Investment Co v Forestry Commission* [1988] 1 W.L.R. 959 (affirmed [1988] 1 W.L.R. 1278).

on the ground. Even if there is no uncertainty as to the meaning of the words used or the ambit of what is coloured on the plan, there may still be serious problems of application. Furthermore, in these problems of application the passage of time often brings its own cure; the passage of 12 years may stifle an incipient boundary dispute, whereas it would do nothing to resolve the extent of a contractual obligation. In such circumstances, it seems to me that the doctrine may still play a useful part."

In *Clarke v O'Keefe*,[643] Peter Gibson LJ said:

"It was said, as long ago as 1969, by no less an authority than Megarry J in *Neilson v Poole*,[644] that the then modern tendency was towards admitting evidence in boundary disputes and assessing the weight of that evidence rather than excluding it. That tendency has, in my experience, not diminished in the intervening years."

However, by 2004 he appears to have changed his mind. In *Beale v Harvey*,[645] he referred to many judicial criticisms of *Watcham's Case* and having said that a decision of the Privy Council was not binding on the Court of Appeal, declined to follow it.

In *Ali v Lane*,[646] Carnwath LJ reviewed the authorities and concluded:

"The conclusion I would be inclined to draw from this review is that *Watcham* remains good law within the narrow limits of what it decided. In the context of a conveyance of land, where the information contained in the conveyance is unclear or ambiguous, it is permissible to have regard to extraneous evidence, including evidence of subsequent conduct, subject always to that evidence being of probative value in determining what the parties intended."

The special rule that probative post-contractual conduct may be taken into account in interpreting a conveyance has since been reaffirmed by the Court of Appeal.[647] *Watcham's Case* appears to be making a come-back, at least in cases involving title deeds. In *Armbrister v Lightbourn*,[648] the Privy Council cited *Watcham v Attorney General of the East African Protectorate*[649] without any disapproval in support of the proposition that: **3.194**

"where there is doubt or inconsistency as to the description of land in a conveyance, extrinsic evidence is admissible to resolve the difficulty."

They added that the case shows that "the admissible extrinsic evidence may include later events".

The courts of Australia are much more cautious in admitting extrinsic evidence in interpreting conveyancing documents (e.g. grants of easements) because the Tor-

---

[643] (1997) 80 P. & C.R. 126 at 133.
[644] (1969) 20 P. & C.R. 909 at 912.
[645] [2004] 2 P. & C.R. 18.
[646] [2007] 1 P. & C.R. 26.
[647] *Bradford v James* [2008] B.L.R. 538; *Piper v Wakeford* [2008] EWCA Civ 1378; *Norman v Sparling* [2014] EWCA Civ 1152; [2015] 1 P. & C.R. 104.
[648] [2012] UKPC 40; [2013] 1 P. & C.R. 17. See also *Wood v Waddington* [2014] EWHC 1358 (Ch), although on the facts subsequent conduct was of no real help.
[649] [1919] A.C. 533.

rens system of land registration is dependent on a publicly accessible register.[650] It is not clear whether this approach will be applied in New Zealand.[651]

(g) Other jurisdictions

3.195   The current English approach is not shared internationally. The Unidroit Principles for International Commercial Contracts state that in interpreting a contract regard shall be had to all the circumstances including "any conduct of the parties subsequent to the conclusion of the contract".[652] Likewise the Principles of European Contract Law state that in interpreting a contract, regard must be had to "the conduct of the parties, even subsequent to the conclusion of the contract".[653]

Even in some other common law jurisdictions evidence of subsequent conduct is admissible.[654] In *Valentine Properties Ltd v Huntco Corp Ltd*,[655] the New Zealand Court of Appeal held that the interpretation of a contract could be illuminated by the subsequent conduct of the parties. Although their decision was reversed on appeal to the Privy Council,[656] the principle was not discussed further.

Subsequently, in *Gibbons Holding Ltd v Wholesale Distributors Ltd*,[657] the New Zealand Supreme Court decided that evidence of subsequent conduct was admissible to interpret a contract. Tipping J said:

> "As a matter of principle, the court should not deprive itself of any material which may be helpful in ascertaining the parties' jointly intended meaning, unless there are sufficiently strong policy reasons for the court to limit itself in that way. I say that on the basis that any form of material extrinsic to the document should be admissible only if capable of shedding light on the meaning intended by both parties. Extrinsic material which bears only on the meaning intended or understood by one party should be excluded. The need for the extrinsic material to shed light on the shared intention of the parties applies to both pre-contract and post-contract evidence. Provided this point is kept firmly in mind, I consider the advantages of admitting evidence of post-contract conduct outweigh the disadvantages."

He returned to the theme in *Vector Gas Ltd v Bay of Plenty Energy Ltd*[658] in which he said:

> "[29] There is no problem with objective evidence directed to the context, factual or linguistic, in which the negotiations were taking place. That kind of evidence can properly inform an objective approach to meaning. Whereas evidence of the subjective content of negotiations is inadmissible on account of its irrelevance, evidence of facts, circumstances and conduct attending the negotiations is admissible if it is capable of shed-

---

[650] *Westfield Management Ltd v Perpetual Trustee Co Ltd* (2007) 239 A.L.R. 75.
[651] *Big River Paradise Ltd v Congreve* [2008] NZCA 78; *Thompson v Trounson* [2008] NZCA 84.
[652] Para.A.3(1)(c).
[653] Para.5.102(b).
[654] Arguments for and against relaxing the rule are marshalled in McMeel, "Prior Negotiations and Subsequent Conduct" (2002) 119 L.Q.R. 272. See also McMeel, *The Construction of Contracts*, 2nd edn (Oxford University Press, 2011), paras 5.161 to 5.163.
[655] [2000] 3 N.Z.L.R. 16.
[656] [2001] 2 N.Z.L.R. 305.
[657] [2007] NZSC 37.
[658] [2010] NZSC 5.

ding objective light on meaning. It is often said in contract interpretation cases that evidence of surrounding circumstances is admissible.
Circumstances which surround the making of the contract can operate
both before and after its formation. In either case irrelevance should be
the touchstone for the exclusion of evidence. I do not consider there are
any sufficiently persuasive pragmatic grounds on which to exclude
evidence that is relevant.

[30]   In *Gibbons Holdings Ltd v Wholesale Distributors Ltd* I expressed the
view that evidence of subsequent conduct should be admissible, if capable
of providing objective guidance as to intended meaning. I suggested that,
in order to be admissible, post-contract conduct should be shared or
mutual. I saw that as a way of emphasising the need to exclude evidence
which demonstrated only a party's subjective intention or understanding
as to meaning. I now consider that the approach I am taking in these
present reasons is a simpler and clearer articulation of the appropriate
principle, but one which still preserves the essential line between
subjectivity and objectivity of approach."

In England, Lord Nicholls of Birkenhead has questioned whether the policy   **3.196**
underlying the principle that the subsequent conduct of the parties is inadmissible
still holds good today.[659]

In *A.-G. v Dreux Holdings*,[660] Blanchard J conducted a tour d'horizon of other
jurisdictions:

"In North America it is, however, a well established practice to consider
subsequent conduct, as illustrated by *Montreal Trust Company of Canada v
Birmingham Lodge Ltd*[661] in Canada and by Article 2–208 of the Uniform Com-
mercial Code and Article 202(4) of the Restatement (2nd) 'Contracts' in the
United States. That conforms with international practice. It should not go un-
noticed that the United Nations Convention on Contracts for the International
Sale of Goods, known as the Vienna Sales Convention, is now, by virtue of the
Sale of Goods (United Nations Convention) Act 1994, part of New Zealand law.
It governs international trading contracts made under New Zealand law or the law
of another State Party unless otherwise stipulated and provides in Article 8(3):

'In determining the intent of a party or the understanding a reasonable person
would have had, due consideration has to be given to all relevant circumstances of the case including the negotiations, any practices which the parties
have established between themselves, usages *and any subsequent conduct of
the parties*. [emphasis added]'

There is something to be said for the idea that New Zealand domestic contract
law should be generally consistent with the best international practice. The
United Kingdom position may need to be re-thought in view of developments
elsewhere. Lord Denning MR has criticised the approach taken by the House of
Lords as being 'contrary to the rule in every other civilised country, including the

---

[659]   *BCCI v Ali* [2002] 1 A.C. 251. In a subsequent lecture Lord Nicholls argued that the rule should be
abandoned: "My Kingdom for a Horse" (2005) 121 L.Q.R. 577.
[660]   (1996) 7 T.C.L.R. 617.
[661]   (1995) 24 O.R. (3d) 97.

other countries of the Common Market': *Port Sudan Cotton Co v Govindaswamy Chettiar & Sons.*[662]

In Australia, our major trading partner, the question appears to remain open: see the review by Priestley JA in *Hide & Skin Trading Pty Ltd v Oceanic Meat Traders Ltd*[663] and the survey by Stephen Charles Q.C. (as he then was) in *Interpretation of Ambiguous Contracts by Reference to Subsequent Conduct.*[664] Australia has also ratified the Vienna Sales Convention, as have several others of New Zealand's major trading partners: see the Law Commission's report *The United Nations Convention on Contracts for the International Sale of Goods: New Zealand's Proposed Acceptance.*[665] On the other hand, in *FAI Traders Insurance Co Ltd v Savoy Plaza Pty Ltd*[666] the Appeal Division of the Supreme Court of Victoria determined that the conduct of a party subsequent to the making of a contract was not relevant to the interpretation of the contract. Whichever view ultimately prevails in Australia, New Zealand Courts will need to consider questions of consistency with Australian domestic law: see generally Professor John Farrar, Closer Economic Relations and Harmonisation of Law Between Australia and New Zealand in *Essays on the Constitution.*"[667]

The Australian courts appear to be moving towards the position that post-contractual conduct, if probative of intention or meaning at the date of the contract, is admissible. In *Sagacious Procurement Pty Ltd v Symbion Health Ltd*,[668] Giles JA (with whom Hodgson and Campbell JA agreed) said:

"I respectfully suggest that subsequent communications are not simply aids to interpretation, or a source of information as to matters with which a concluded contract should deal. Their probative value may be more direct. To repeat, the objective intention of the parties is fact-based, and found in all the circumstances. That in their subsequent communications the parties have continued in negotiations, or have expressed the common understanding that they are not legally bound unless and until a formal contract is executed, is of itself probative as to their contractual intention: see *Howard Smith and Co Ltd v Varawa*, stating simply that any statements or conduct inconsistent with the existence of a concluded contract are relevant."

However, there was a difference of opinion on this question in the Full Court of South Australia in *Symbion Medical Centre Operations Pty Ltd v Thomco (No.2113) Pty Ltd.*[669]

20. ANCIENT DOCUMENTS

Where the meaning of an ancient document is in question, evidence is admissible to show the ordinary meaning of words as used at the date of the document; and if the document is ambiguous, evidence of contemporaneous usage under it may also be admitted as an aid to construction.

---

[662] [1977] 2 Lloyd's Rep. 5 at 11.
[663] (1990) 20 N.S.W.L.R. 310 at 326–328.
[664] (1991) 4 J.C.L. 16.
[665] (1992) N.Z.L.C.R. 23.
[666] [1993] 2 V.R. 337.
[667] P.A. Joseph (ed.), p.158.
[668] [2008] NSWCA 149.
[669] [2009] SASC 65.

In *Shore v Wilson*,[670] Coleridge J said: **3.197**

"… in proportion as we are removed from the period in which an author writes, we become less certain of the meaning of the words he uses; we are not sure that at that period the primary meaning of the words was the same as now, for by the primary is not meant the etymological, but that which the ordinary usage of society affixes to it. We are also equally uncertain whether at that period the words did not bear a technical or conventional sense; and whether they were not so used by the writer."

Accordingly, he concluded the court was not only entitled but bound to inquire into the contemporaneous meaning of the words used. In the same case Tindal CJ held[671] that evidence "dehors the instrument itself" might be admitted:

"where by lapse of time and change of manners, the words have acquired in the present age a different meaning from that which they bore when originally employed."

In *Schuler (L) AG v Wickman Machine Tool Sales Ltd*,[672] Lord Wilberforce said:

"In the case of ancient documents, contemporaneous or subsequent action may be adduced in order to explain words whose contemporary meaning may have become obscure."

In addition to (or in lieu of) evidence, the court may inform itself "from history, **3.198** and other general sources of information, of the meaning of the language used at that particular time".[673] A more modern example of this process may be seen in *Earl of Lonsdale v Att.-Gen.*[674] Chapter 5 will consider further the extent to which evidence is admissible to explain the meaning of words.

If, despite the reception of evidence, an ancient document remains ambiguous the **3.199** court is entitled to look at acts done under the instrument, particularly those done at or shortly after its execution.[675] This is known as *contemporanea expositio*. If the instrument is not ambiguous, evidence of contemporaneous acts is not admissible.[676] As Vaughan Williams LJ said in *Lord Hastings v North Eastern Railway Co*[677]:

"There can be no doubt that contemporaneous usage may be resorted to for the purpose of explaining any uncertainty or ambiguity in an ancient grant; but then there must be uncertainty or ambiguity."

This principle has been of particular value in the case of wills and trust **3.200**

[670] (1842) 9 Cl. & Fin. 355 at 527.
[671] (1842) 9 Cl. & Fin. 355 at 566.
[672] [1974] A.C. 235.
[673] [1974] A.C. 235 at 557, per Parke B.
[674] [1982] 1 W.L.R. 887.
[675] *Attorney General v Corporation of Rochester* (1854) 5 De G.M. & G. 797.
[676] *Earl De La Warr v Miles* (1881) 17 Ch. D. 535.
[677] [1899] 1 Ch. 656.

instruments. In *Attorney General v Sidney Sussex College*[678] a will executed in 1641 left money to two colleges for the education of the testator's descendants. In 1869 the question arose whether the two colleges were entitled to use the funds for more general educational purposes. The Lord Chancellor said:

> "I think the appellants are entitled to apply that principle of the Court which says, that if there be an ambiguity, the course of construction and action upon the bequest may be called in aid, as inferring that the persons who are concerned in the trust have not been committing a breach of trust from the commencement downwards to the present time. The reasons why the Court relies upon that rule with reference to charities, where there is anything doubtful in the construction of the will, is, that there have been persons alive who are competent to controvert any such conclusion, and it is not to be assumed that, where many persons were interested in controverting such conclusion, a course of action has been adopted which has been a plain and clear breach of trust."

3.201   An ancient document for this purpose is one that dates from before living memory.[679] Even so, it must, however, be shown that the lapse of time since the execution of the instrument is such that the words may have changed their meaning in the interval.[680]

Whether the post-contractual acts of the parties under modern instruments may be relied on as an aid to construction has already been discussed in para.3.186.

---

[678] (1869) L.R. 4. Ch. 722, applied in *Fafalios v Apodiacos* [2020] EWHC 1189 (Ch).

[679] *North Eastern Railway Co v Lord Hastings* [1900] A.C. 260 at 269, per Lord Davey. However, it is considered that to the extent that this remains a rule of law, it does not preclude the court from admitting evidence of contemporaneous usage of words (as opposed to contemporaneous acts) even where the contract in question was made within living memory.

[680] *Lord Hastings v North Eastern Ry Co* [1899] 1 Ch. 656, per Lindley MR.

CHAPTER 4

LAW AND PRECEDENT

Judges, too, even though their sentence be erroneous and illegal, must be allowed, for the sake of peace and order, to have decisive authority, and ultimately to determine property.

David Hume: *An Enquiry Concerning the Principles of Morals*

1. LAW AND FACT

The proper construction of a written contract is a question of law. However, the ascertainment of the meaning of a particular word is a question of fact.[1]

The division between what is a question of law and what is a question of fact is extremely difficult to draw.[2] However, it has been said on many occasions that the proper interpretation of a contract is a question of law. Thus it is for the judge to interpret the contract, even when he is assisted by a jury,[3] and the jury is bound to accept the judge's direction upon the construction of the contract. Indeed, it is largely because trials were heard by juries that the construction of a contract is classified as a question of law at all. As Lord Diplock pointed out in *Pioneer Shipping Ltd v BTP Tioxide Ltd*[4]:

4.01

"... in English jurisprudence, as a legacy of the system of trial by juries who might not all be literate, the construction of a written agreement, even between private parties, became classified as a question of law ... A lawyer nurtured in a jurisdiction which did not owe its origin to the common law of England would not regard it as a question of law at all ... Nevertheless, despite the disappearance of juries, literate or illiterate, in civil cases in England, it is far too late to change the technical classification of the ascertainment of the meaning of a written contract between private parties as being 'a question of law' for the purposes of judicial review?...".

---

[1] This section was referred to with approval in *Canada (Attorney General) v Rostrust Investments Inc* [2007] Can. LII 1878.
[2] The problem notably arose in connection with the law of mistake: see *Midland Great Western Railway of Ireland v Johnson* (1858) 6 H.L. Cas. 798; *Cooper v Phibbs* (1867) L.R. 2 H.L. 149; *Solle v Butcher* [1950] 1 K.B. 671. The distinction between law and fact in that context is nowadays of little, if any, importance.
[3] For example, to determine whether a trade custom has been proved, or whether a word bears a secondary trade meaning. In *Turner v Sawdon & Co* [1901] 2 K.B. 653, the trial judge left a question of construction to the jury. The Court of Appeal held that he was wrong to do so, as there was no question proper to be left to the jury. See also *Grenfell v E Meyrowitz Ltd* [1936] 2 All E.R. 1313.
[4] [1982] A.C. 724.

4.02   In *Carmichael v National Power Plc*,[5] Lord Hoffmann, while agreeing with Lord Diplock's account of the original reason for the classification, added a further historical gloss:

> "[T]he rule was adopted in trials by jury for purely pragmatic reasons. In mediaeval times juries were illiterate and most of the documents which came before a jury were deeds drafted by lawyers. In the eighteenth and nineteenth centuries the rule was maintained because it was essential to the development of English commercial law. There could have been no precedent and no certainty in the construction of standard commercial documents if questions of construction had been left in each case to a jury which gave no reasons for its decision."

4.03   The Supreme Court of Canada has now abandoned this historical approach in favour of the view that the interpretation of a contract is generally a mixed question of fact and law.[6] But in *Ledcor Construction Ltd v Northbridge Indemnity Insurance Co*[7] the same court held that the interpretation of a standard form contract was an exception to that principle. As Wagner J put it:

> "In my view, where an appeal involves the interpretation of a standard form contract, the interpretation at issue is of precedential value, and there is no meaningful factual matrix that is specific to the parties to assist the interpretation process, this interpretation is better characterised as a question of law subject to correctness review."

4.04   In *Khan v Khan*,[8] Arden LJ said that there can be no difference in principle between the rules which apply to the interpretation of contractual documents and those which apply to oral contracts.[9] The Court of Appeal appears to have taken a similar view in *Barton v Gwyn-Jones*.[10]

4.05   On the other hand, in *Thorner v Majors*,[11] in the context of a discussion of proprietary estoppel rather than contract, Lord Neuberger of Abbotsbury said:

> "(a) the interpretation of a purely written contract is a matter of law, and depends on a relatively objective contextual assessment, which almost always excludes evidence of the parties' subjective understanding of what they were agreeing, but (b) the interpretation of an oral contract is a matter of fact (I suggest inference from primary fact), rather than one of law, on which the parties' subjective understanding of what they were agreeing is admissible."

Apart from the historical origins of the rule (trial by jury) Lord Neuberger suggested that the dichotomy was underpinned by practical reasons. He said:

---

5   [1999] 1 W.L.R. 2042.
6   *Sattva Capital Corp v Creston Moly Corp* 2014 SCC 53.
7   2016 SCC 37; [2016] 2 SCR 23.
8   [2008] Bus. L.R. D73. *Khan v Khan* was followed in *Kahn v Dunlop Haywards (DHL) Ltd* [2007] EWHC 2659 (QB). This corresponds with the view expressed in a previous edition of this book. That edition referred to *Torbett v Faulkner* [1952] 2 T.L.R. 659, in which Romer LJ said that the ascertainment of the effect of an oral contract was "entirely a question of fact and no question of construction arises". Cf. *Yorkshire Insurance Co Ltd v Campbell* [1917] A.C. 218 at 221, per Lord Sumner. In the author's view this approach conflates the identification of contract terms and their interpretation.
9   See also *Masterton Homes Pty Ltd v Palm Assets Pty Ltd* [2009] NSWCA 234.
10   [2019] EWCA Civ 1999.
11   [2009] 1 W.L.R. 776; *ANZ Bank New Zealand Ltd v Bushline Trustees Ltd* [2020] NZSC 71.

"If the contract is solely in writing, the parties rarely give evidence as to the terms of the contract, so it is cost-effective and practical to exclude evidence of their understanding as to its effect. On the other hand, if the contract was made orally, the parties will inevitably be giving evidence as to what was said and done at the relevant discussions or meetings, and it could be rather artificial to exclude evidence as to their contemporary understanding. Secondly, and perhaps more importantly, memory is often unreliable and self-serving, so it is better to exclude evidence of actual understanding when there is no doubt as to the terms of the contract, as when it is in writing. However, it is very often positively helpful to have such evidence to assist in the interpretation of an oral contract, as the parties will rarely, if ever, be able to recollect all the details and circumstances of the relevant conversations."

The practical considerations to which he referred do not appear to differentiate between identifying the terms of an oral contract (upon which oral evidence is admissible) and interpreting those terms once they have been identified. In the penultimate sentence of the cited passage Lord Neuberger refers to a written contract where "there is no doubt as to the terms". This can only mean that there is no doubt about what terms were agreed, rather than no doubt about what they mean. The final sentence, however, refers to admitting evidence of subjective intention, not for the purpose of identifying the terms of the contract (what terms were agreed?) but for the purpose of interpreting it (what do the agreed terms mean?). It is submitted that this would be a major departure from the objective nature of contractual interpretation, and indeed seems at variance with the actual decision in the case itself, which was that a representation or assurance should be objectively interpreted, albeit in the context of the particular relationship between the representor and the representee.

In *Blyth v Nelsons Solicitors Ltd*[12] Stewart J held that, in the context of an oral agreement, subjective evidence of one of the parties was admissible. It is not entirely clear whether the evidence was admitted for the purpose of identifying what was agreed, as opposed to explaining the meaning of what was agreed.

Since the proper construction of a written contract is a question of law, the court **4.06** is not bound by concessions about its meaning made by counsel in the course of argument; or by the parties' agreement about what it means. In *Bahamas International Trust Co Ltd v Threadgold*,[13] Lord Diplock said:

"In a case which turns, as this one does, on the construction to be given to a written document, a court called on to construe the document in the absence of any claim to rectification, cannot be bound by any concession made by any of the parties as to what its language means. That is so even in the court before which the concession is made; a fortiori in the court to which an appeal from the judgment of the court is brought. The reason is that the construction of a written document is a question of law. It is for the judge to decide for himself what the law is, not to accept it from any or even all of the parties to the suit; having so decided it is his duty to apply it to the facts of the case. He would be acting contrary to his judicial oath if he were to determine the case by applying what the parties conceived to be the law, if in his own opinion it were erroneous."

---

[12] [2019] EWHC 2063 (QB); [2019] Costs L.R. 1409.
[13] [1974] 1 W.L.R. 1514 HL, applied in *Biggin Hill Airport Ltd v Bromley LBC* [2001] EWCA Civ 1089 CA.

Likewise, in *Ross v Bank of Commerce (Saint Kitts Nevis) Trust and Savings Association Ltd*[14] the Privy Council held that "on an issue of construction the Board is not bound by counsel's concession." In *Singapore Airlines Ltd v Buck*,[15] Arden LJ confirmed that a court "cannot be bound by the parties' agreement on the matter of the true interpretation of a document". On the same principle the court is not confined to the way in which the parties plead and argue their respective cases. In *Teesside Gas Transportation Ltd v CATS North Sea Ltd*,[16] Butcher J said:

> "In [the] process of construction [the court] cannot be limited to the positions taken by the parties: it is open to the Court to say that the proper construction of the document is not one for which either party has contended. Furthermore, I consider it problematic to say that the Court charged with a process of construction can only consider some points which go to the proper interpretation of the relevant provisions of the contract and not others."

4.07   However, in *HLB Kidsons v Lloyd's Underwriters*,[17] Rix LJ said that "a judge should be very sure of his ground" before rejecting a concession about a one-off document, affecting only the parties to the contract, where the party making the concession was as experienced in reading and evaluating such documents as anyone.

4.08   For the same reason, the court is not restricted to an interpretation which has been advanced by counsel. Since the question of construction is one of law, it is at large.[18] One further consequence of the principle that the interpretation of a contract is a question of law is that there is no evidential burden on either party to establish its preferred interpretation.[19]

4.09   Although the ascertainment of the meaning of a written contract is a question of law, many steps in the process of ascertaining that meaning are classified as questions of fact.[20] In *Brutus v Cozens*,[21] an appeal concerned the meaning of the word "insulting" as applied to the phrase "insulting behaviour" in the Public Order Act 1936. Lord Reid said:

> "It is not clear to me what precisely is the point of law which we have to decide. The question in the case stated for the opinion of the court is 'Whether, on the above statement of facts, we came to a correct decision in point of law.' This seems to assume that the meaning of the word 'insulting' in s.5 is a matter of law. And the Divisional Court appear to have proceeded on that footing. In my judgment that is not right. The meaning of an ordinary word of the English language is not a question of law. The proper construction of a statute is a question of law. If the context shows that a word is used in an unusual sense the court will

---

[14] [2012] UKPC 3.

[15] [2011] EWCA Civ 1542; [2012] Pens. L.R. 1.

[16] [2019] EWHC 1220 (Comm).

[17] [2009] 1 Lloyd's Rep. 8 at [84].

[18] *Charter Reinsurance Co Ltd v Fagan* [1997] A.C. 313 CA (reversed by HL on different grounds).

[19] *Redrow Regeneration (Barking) Ltd v Edwards* [2012] UKUT 373 (LC); [2013] L. & T.R. 8. By contrast there is an evidential burden to establish facts that are relied upon as relevant background.

[20] In *Torbett v Faulkner* [1952] 2 T.L.R. 659, Romer LJ said that the ascertainment of the effect of an oral contract was "entirely a question of fact and no question of construction arises". Cf. *Yorkshire Insurance Co Ltd v Campbell* [1917] A.C. 218 at 221, per Lord Sumner. These views seem to conflate two stages in the overall question of interpretation.

[21] [1973] A.C. 854.

determine when that unusual sense is. But here there is in my opinion no question of the word 'insulting' being used in any unusual sense."

This distinction applies to written contracts in the same way.[22]

Nor is this approach confined to "ordinary" words. The ascertainment of a technical term is equally a question of fact. So in *Hill v Evans*,[23] Lord Westbury LC said:

4.10

"It is true, as a proposition of law, that the construction of a specification (like the construction of all other written instruments) belongs to the Court; but the specification of an invention contains generally, if not always, some technical terms, some phrases of art, some description of processes which require the light to be derived from what are called the surrounding circumstances. It is therefore an admitted rule of law, that the explanation of the words or technical terms of art, the phrases used in commerce and the proof and results of the processes which are described (and in a chemical patent, the ascertainment of chemical equivalents) that all these are matters of fact upon which evidence may be given, contradictory testimony may be adduced, and upon which it is the province and the right of a jury to decide."

The process of construction or interpretation, therefore, consists of at least two elements, one element of which is factual, and the other legal. The two-stage process was summarised by Lindley LJ in *Chatenay v Brazilian Submarine Telegraph Co Ltd*[24] as follows:

4.11

"The expression 'construction,' as applied to a document, at all events as used by English lawyers, includes two things: first the meaning of the words; and secondly their legal effect, or the effect to be given to them. The meaning of the words I take to be a question of fact in all cases, whether we are dealing with a poem or a legal document. The effect of the words used is a question of law."

Thus in a criminal trial it is the function of the judge to rule on the interpretation of a contract, rather than the function of the jury to decide what it means as a question of fact.[25] However, in a libel action although the question whether words are *capable* of bearing a defamatory meaning is a question of law of the judge, whether they *do* bear such a meaning is a question of fact for the jury.[26]

Most questions of fact cannot be determined by the court without evidence to prove them. Sometimes, however, the court may take judicial notice of facts, in which case they may be regarded as proved without the necessity of evidence. Even in such a case, however, it seems unlikely that a party could be prevented from leading evidence on such a fact. In the case of the determination of the meaning of an ordinary English word, evidence of meaning is positively inadmissible. Thus in

4.12

22 *Commonwealth Smelting Ltd v Guardian Royal Exchange Assurance Ltd* [1986] 1 Lloyd's Rep. 121; *Belgravia Navigation Co SA v Cannor Shipping Inc, The Times* 18 April 1988; *Norwich Union Life Insurance Society v P&O Property Holdings Ltd* [1993] 1 E.G.L.R. 164 CA; *Fitzroy House Epworth Street (No.1) Ltd v Financial Times Ltd* [2006] 2 All E.R. 776; *Giles v Tarry* [2012] EWCA Civ 837; [2012] 2 P. & C.R. 12.
23 (1862) 4 De G.P. & J. 288 (a case of interpretation of patents).
24 [1892] 1 Q.B. 79. See also *Neilson v Harford* (1841) 8 M. & W. 806 at 823, per Parke B.
25 *R. v Spens* [1991] 1 W.L.R. 624 CA.
26 *Slim v Daily Telegraph* [1968] 2 Q.B. 157.

Lovell and Christmas Ltd v Wall,[27] Fletcher Moulton LJ said:

> "I think that it is arguable that evidence may be taken as to the meaning of the word 'provision merchants'. I say that it is arguable because it must not be thought that the court cannot take judicial cognisance of the fact that the words have different meanings in different contexts. For instance I doubt very much whether the court ought to take evidence as to the meaning of the word 'chair'. That word in connection with domestic furniture has one meaning. But 'chair' in connection with a railway has another. I very much doubt whether a court would consider itself perfectly entitled to take cognisance of the fact that 'chair' used in connection with a railway, means a mode of fastening a rail to a sleeper."

It is, therefore, a curiosity that the ascertainment of the meaning of an ordinary English word is a question of fact which cannot be proved by any admissible evidence.[28]

2. FACT

The ascertainment of the terms of a contract which is partly written and partly oral or which is wholly oral is a question of fact.[29]

4.13 Whether the parties intended their contract to be wholly written is a question of fact. If they did not, then the ascertainment of the full terms of the contract is also a question of fact.[30]

In *Moore v Garwood*,[31] Pollock CB directed the jury that:

> "... the nature of the contract into which the parties had entered was rather a question of fact than of law, because it did not consist of one distinct contract between the parties, but of a series of acts and things done, from which the jury were to determine what was the real intention and meaning of the parties when they entered into the mutual relation in which they stood ...".

His direction was upheld on appeal. Similarly, in *Maggs v Marsh*,[32] Smith LJ said:

> "Determining the terms of an oral contract is a question of fact. Establishing the facts will usually, as here, depend upon the recollections of the parties and other witnesses. The accuracy of those recollections may be tested and elucidated by things said and done by the parties or witnesses after the agreement has been concluded."

---

27 (1911) 104 L.T. 85. See also *Marquess Camden v IRC* [1913] 1 K.B. 641. In 1977 the word "supermarket" was sufficiently out of the ordinary for evidence to be admissible to explain it: *Calabar (Woolwich) Ltd v Tesco Stores Ltd* [1978] 1 E.G.L.R. 113.

28 The logic of the rule has been questioned in Australia: *Pepsi Seven-Up Bottlers Perth Pty Ltd v Commissioner of Taxation* (1995) 62 F.C.R. 289; *Dyson v Pharmacy Board* (2000) 50 N.S.W.L.R. 523.

29 This proposition was approved in *Masterton Homes Pty Ltd v Palm Assets Pty Ltd* (2009) 261 A.L.R. 382.

30 *Carmichael v National Power Plc* [1999] 1 W.L.R. 2042.

31 (1849) 4 Exch. 681.

32 [2006] B.L.R. 395.

Similarly, in *BVM Management Ltd v Yeomans*,[33] Aikens LJ said:

"When the terms of a contract have to be ascertained from oral exchanges and conduct that is a question of fact… [m]oreover, in the case of a contract which is entirely oral or partly oral, evidence of things said and done after the contract was concluded are admissible to help decide what the parties had actually agreed."

However, in *Keeley v Fosroc International Ltd*,[34] Auld LJ pointed out that: **4.14**

"[W]here document A, acknowledged to have contractual effect, expressly incorporates by reference document B, and there are no other candidates for contractual contribution to the agreement, the construction of a particular provision in document B does not become a fact-finding exercise on the strength of extraneous evidence as to the true intention of the parties, any more than it would have done if the provision had originally appeared in document A. It simply becomes a matter of construction of the two documents read together."

In *Torbett v Faulkner*,[35] Romer LJ said that the ascertainment of the effect of an **4.15**
oral contract was "entirely a question of fact and no question of construction arises." It is thought, however, that this bald statement goes too far. While the ascertainment of the terms of an oral contract is a question of fact, the determination of the legal effect of those terms is a question of law. In that sense the construction of a contract is always a question of law. As Arden LJ put it in *Khan v Khan*[36]:

"[T]here can be no difference in principle between the rules which apply to the interpretation of contractual documents and those which apply to oral contracts."

3. CATEGORISATION AND CONSTRUCTION

The legal effect of a written contract may involve a two-stage process: first to ascertain what rights and obligations the contract creates; and second to determine what kind of contract has been made.

Many substantive legal rules apply only to contracts of a particular kind. In *A1* **4.16**
Lofts Ltd v HMRC,[37] Lewison J said:

"The court is often called upon to decide whether a written contract falls within a particular legal description. In so doing the court will identify the rights and obligations of the parties as a matter of construction of the written agreement; but it will then go on to consider whether those obligations fall within the relevant legal description."

---

[33] [2011] EWCA Civ 1254.
[34] [2006] I.R.L.R. 961.
[35] [1952] 2 T.L.R. 659.
[36] [2008] Bus. L.R. D73. See also *Masterton Homes Pty Ltd v Palm Assets Pty Ltd* [2009] NSWCA 234.
[37] [2010] S.T.C. 214. This statement was approved by the Supreme Court in *Revenue and Customs v Secret Hotels2 Ltd* [2014] UKSC 16; [2014] 2 All E.R. 685. See also *IIG Capital LLC v Van Der Merwe* [2008] 2 Lloyd's Rep. 187, per Waller LJ: "It was common ground before us that it ultimately depends on the true construction of the agreement whether a particular label is the right one to apply to any instrument".

The latter process is conveniently referred to as categorisation.[38] During the 1970s and 1980s, for example, the courts were frequently required to determine whether a contract created a licence or a tenancy. Whether the occupier of residential property acquired security of tenure depended on the answer to that question. As Lord Templeman put it in *Street v Mountford*[39]:

"Both parties enjoyed freedom to contract or not to contract and both parties exercised that freedom by contracting on the terms set forth in the written agreement and on no other terms. But the consequences in law of the agreement, once concluded, can only be determined by consideration of the effect of the agreement. If the agreement satisfied all the requirements of a tenancy, then the agreement produced a tenancy and the parties cannot alter the effect of the agreement by insisting that they only created a licence. The manufacture of a five-pronged implement for manual digging results in a fork even if the manufacturer, unfamiliar with the English language, insists that he intended to make and has made a spade."

Likewise, in *McEntire v Crossley*,[40] Lord Herschell LC said:

"Coming then to the examination of the agreement, I quite concede that the agreement must be regarded as a whole—its substance must be looked at. The parties cannot, by the insertion of any mere words, defeat the effect of the transaction as appearing from the whole of the agreement into which they have entered. If the words in one part of it point in one direction and the words in another part in another direction, you must look at the agreement as a whole and see what its substantial effect is. But there is no such thing, as seems to have been argued here, as looking at the substance, apart from looking at the language which the parties have used. It is only by a study of the whole of the language that the substance can be ascertained."

4.17   In *Agnew v Commissioner of Inland Revenue*,[41] the Privy Council considered whether an agreement created a fixed charge or a floating charge. Lord Millett explained:

"In deciding whether a charge is a fixed charge or a floating charge, the court is engaged in a two-stage process. At the first stage it must construe the instrument of charge and seek to gather the intentions of the parties from the language they have used. But the object at this stage of the process is not to discover whether the parties intended to create a fixed or a floating charge. It is to ascertain the nature of the rights and obligations which the parties intended to grant each other in respect of the charged assets. Once these have been ascertained, the court can then embark on the second stage of the process, which is one of categorisation. This is a matter of law. It does not depend on the intention of the parties. If their intention, properly gathered from the language of the instrument, is to grant the company rights in respect of the charged assets which are inconsistent with the nature of a fixed charge, then the charge cannot be a fixed

---

[38] *Progress Property Co Ltd v Moorgarth Group Ltd* [2011] 2 All E.R. 432.
[39] [1985] A.C. 809. See also *Progress Property Co Ltd v Moorgarth Group Ltd* [2011] 2 All E.R. 432.
[40] [1895] A.C. 457. See also *Welsh Development Agency v Export Finance Co Ltd* [1992] B.C.L.C. 148.
[41] [2001] 2 A.C. 710.

charge however they may have chosen to describe it. A similar process is involved in construing a document to see whether it creates a licence or tenancy."

Equally, the classification of a contract may bring with it particular non-statutory legal rights and obligations. In *Socimer International Bank Ltd v Standard Bank London Ltd*,[42] Lloyd LJ said: **4.18**

"If parties enter into a transaction which is a mortgage, then the law imposes certain obligations on the mortgagee, and confers certain rights on the mortgagor, which go back to the intervention of equity in the early development of mortgages. Although a mortgage is a contractual transaction, the imposition of such duties has nothing to do with the implication of terms in a contract under the general law of contracts ... Whether these duties are imposed on a given party depends only on whether, on the true analysis of the transaction, it is or is not a mortgage."

Similarly, because of the different legal consequences that may attach to a guarantee on the one hand and an indemnity on the other, it may be important to classify the document as one or the other.[43]

In each case there is a public interest which overrides unrestrained freedom of contract, namely to ensure that the substantive law is properly applied. Lord Walker explained this in *Re Spectrum Plus Ltd*[44]:   **4.19**

"it is the court's duty to characterise the document according to the true legal effect of its terms ... In each case there is a public interest which overrides unrestrained freedom of contract. On the lease/licence issue, the public interest is the protection of vulnerable people seeking living accommodation. On the fixed/floating issue, it is ensuring that preferential creditors obtain the measure of protection which Parliament intended them to have."

In considering how to classify a contract, "the task is to decide the nature of the instrument by looking at it as a whole without any preconceptions as to what it is".[45] So in *AXA SA v Genworth Financial International Holdings, Inc*,[46] Bryan J said: **4.20**

"This approach of assigning the clause to a category of obligation first and then construing the clause amounts, I am satisfied, to the tail wagging the dog."

In the case of a composite transaction, the court will assess the substance of the transaction taken as a whole.[47]   **4.21**

The question of false labels is considered further in para.9.56.

4.   PRINCIPLES OF INTERPRETATION ARE NOT RULES OF LAW

A principle of interpretation is a guideline rather than a rule of law; and accordingly will only be applied in the absence of a contrary intention expressed in the contract.

---

[42] [2008] 1 Lloyd's Rep. 558.
[43] *Associated British Ports v Ferryways NV* [2009] 1 Lloyd's Rep. 595.
[44] [2005] 2 A.C. 680.
[45] *Gold Coast Ltd v Caja de Ahorros del Mediterraneo* [2002] 1 Lloyd's Rep. 617.
[46] [2019] EWHC 3376 (Comm).
[47] *Brighton & Hove City Council v Audus* [2009] EWHC 340 (Ch).

4.22   The court often construes contracts with the assistance of principles of interpretation (often called canons of construction). Over time a particular interpretation may
develop into a principle, as a judicial consensus grows.[48] In *Mitchell (George)
(Chesterhall) Ltd v Finney Lock Seeds Ltd*,[49] Kerr LJ pointed out that:

> "Rules of construction are not rules of law; they are merely guidelines to the
> presumed intention of the parties in the light of events which have occurred."

4.23   In some cases these principles of interpretation become rebuttable presumptions of substantive law. But the parties are free to modify or exclude any principle
of interpretation. For example, it is a principle of interpretation that a timetable in
a rent review clause in a lease need not be strictly adhered to.[50] However, the parties may provide expressly, or by implication from contra-indications in the lease,
that such a timetable is of the essence of the contract. Nevertheless, the existence
of a principle of interpretation or guideline does not absolve the court from its duty
of construing the actual agreement which the parties made, and not the agreement
which they would have made if they had been wiser.[51]

4.24   By contrast, a rule of law operates irrespective of the intention of the parties, and
may sometimes controvert it. Thus the grant of exclusive possession of residential
accommodation for a term at a rent, where the landlord does not provide services
or attendance, results in the creation of a tenancy, whatever the actual intention of
the parties was.[52] Whether a substantive legal rule applies is a question of classification of the contract, once the rights and obligations that it creates have been
determined as a question of interpretation.[53]

5.   INTERPRETATION NOT TO BE AFFECTED BY LEGAL RESULT

**The interpretation of a contract should not be influenced by the question of
whether interpretation in one way as opposed to another would produce a different legal result. However, if one interpretation will result in the contract (or
clause) being invalid that may be taken into account.**

4.25   Questions of interpretation often arise against the background of substantive law.
Answering the question of interpretation in one way will produce a different legal
result from answering it in another way. In theory at least, the court should be
uninfluenced in interpreting a contract by what the legal result will be. Thus it has
been said that in interpreting a covenant in restraint of trade, the court should not
approach the task with a prima facie assumption that the covenant is illegal. "You
are to construe the contract, and then see whether it is legal."[54] Similarly, in *Moenich
v Fenestre*,[55] Lindley LJ said:

> "The true principle to be applied in construing agreements in restraint of trade

---

[48]   *The Mercini Lady* [2010] EWCA Civ 1145.
[49]   [1983] Q.B. 284. See also *Sabah Flour and Feedmills v Comfez Ltd* [1988] 2 Lloyd's Rep. 647.
[50]   *United Scientific Holdings v Burnley Borough Council* [1978] A.C. 904.
[51]   *Equity and Law Life Assurance Society Plc v Bodfield Ltd* [1987] 1 E.G.L.R. 124, cited in para.2.45.
[52]   *Street v Mountford* [1985] A.C. 809.
[53]   See para.4.16.
[54]   *Mills v Dunham* [1893] 1 Ch. 577, per Lindley LJ.
[55]   (1892) 67 L.T. 602 CA; *Littlewoods Organisation Ltd v Harris* [1977] 1 W.L.R. 1472 CA; *Clarke*

is … that the agreement must be approached without reference to the question of its legality or illegality."

In the same case Lopes LJ said:

"… you must construe the agreement according to the reasonable meaning of the words used, without regard to what may be the effect of such construction."

Similarly, in considering the effect of a document for the purposes of tax, the court should not approach the problem with any predisposition that the document should, or should not, attract tax. In *IRC v Wesleyan and General Assurance Society*,[56] Lord Greene MR said: **4.26**

"In considering tax matters a document is not to have placed upon it a strained or forced construction in order to attract tax, nor is a strained or forced construction to be placed upon it in order to avoid tax. The document is to be construed in the ordinary way and the provision of the tax legislation then applied to it. If on its true construction, it falls within a certain taxing category, then it is taxed. If, on its true construction, it falls outside the taxing category, then it escapes tax."

The same approach applies when considering whether a document creates a licence or a tenancy. In *Shell-Mex and BP Ltd v Manchester Garages Ltd*,[57] Buckley LJ said:

"One has first to find out the true nature of the transaction and then see how the Act operates on that state of affairs. One should not approach the problem with a tendency to attempt to find a tenancy because unless there is a tenancy the case will escape the effects of the statute."

Similarly, in *Street v Mountford*,[58] Lord Templeman said:

"I accept that the Rent Acts are irrelevant to the problem of determining the legal effect of the rights granted by the agreement. Like the professed intention of the parties the Rent Acts cannot alter the effect of the agreement."

Likewise in deciding whether a clause was a penalty clause, the High Court of Australia said in *Gumland Property Holdings Pty Ltd v Duffy Bros Fruit Market (Campbelltown) Pty Ltd*[59]:   **4.27**

"if the contractual words clearly have one meaning, the consequence that in that meaning they create a penalty cannot cause them to be given another meaning."

These cases concern the effect of statutes or substantive rules of law on the parties' rights and obligations. Public policy is not treated in quite the same way. So   **4.28**

---

v Newland [1991] 1 All E.R. 397 CA; *Arbuthnot Fund Managers v Rawlings* [2003] All E.R. (D) 181 (Mar); *Beckett Investment Management Group Ltd v Hall* [2007] I.C.R. 1539.
[56] [1946] 2 All E.R. 749, affirmed [1948] 1 All E.R. 555; *Reed Employment Plc v HMRC* [2015] EWCA Civ 805.
[57] [1971] 1 W.L.R. 612.
[58] [1985] A.C. 809.
[59] (2008) 234 C.L.R. 237 at [60].

in *Nickerson v Barraclough*,[60] Brightman LJ said:

"... I cannot accept that public policy can play any part at all in the construction of an instrument; in construing a document the court is endeavouring to ascertain the expressed intention of the parties. Public policy may require the court to frustrate that intention where the contract is against public policy, but in my view public policy cannot help the court to ascertain what that intention was."

This is, however, too dogmatic a view. If a contract admits of two interpretations, one of which is legal and the other illegal, the courts prefer that which leads to a legal result.[61] Likewise, if a contract admits of two realistic interpretations, one of which makes the contract valid, and the other makes it invalid, the courts prefer that which makes it valid.[62]

4.29   In relation to wills Lord Hoffmann explained the position as follows in *Charles v Barzey*[63]:

"They are substantive rules of public policy which prohibit certain kinds of dispositions or the imposition of certain kinds of conditions. In principle, the application of these rules of public policy comes after the question of construction. One first ascertains the intention of the testator and then decides whether it can be given effect. But nowadays the existence of the rules of public policy may influence the question of construction. If the testator's words can be construed in two different ways, one of which is valid and the other void, then unless the testator obviously did not intend to make the kind of gift which would be valid, the court will usually be inclined to construe his will in that sense."

In *Lancashire CC v Municipal Mutual Insurance Ltd*,[64] Simon Brown LJ said:

"The only way in which public policy can properly be invoked in the construction of a contract is under the rule *verba ita sunt intelligenda ut res magis vale at quam pereat*[65]: if the words are susceptible of two meanings, one of which would validate the particular clause or contract and the other render it void or ineffective, then the former interpretation should be applied, even though it might otherwise, looking merely at the words and their context, be less appropriate."

Likewise, in *Turner v Commonwealth & British Minerals Ltd*,[66] Waller LJ said:

"There is in my view some interconnection between the question of construction and the doctrine of restraint of trade. That, as it seems to me, must be so for at least one reason. If a particular construction was to lead to the view that the clause was unenforceable, then an alternative view, which did not lead to the same result if legitimate, ought to be preferred."

---

[60]   [1981] Ch. 426.

[61]   See para.7.119.

[62]   See para.7.154.

[63]   [2003] 1 W.L.R. 437.

[64]   [1996] 3 All E.R. 545. See also *Arab African Energy Corp Ltd v Olieprodukten Nederland NV* [1983] 2 Lloyd's Rep. 419 (change in public policy justified change in approach to construction of arbitration agreements excluding rights of appeal).

[65]   See para.7.154.

[66]   [2000] I.R.L.R. 114.

In *PSG Franchising Ltd v Lydia Darby Ltd*,[67] Males J held that in choosing between two possible meanings of a covenant in restraint of trade, and without rewriting the clause, it is legitimate to adopt an interpretation which limits the clause to reasonable protection of a legitimate business interest, with the consequence that the clause will be valid and enforceable, and to reject an interpretation which would render the clause void.

A desire to uphold the validity of a contract cannot, however, be taken too far. Simon Brown LJ said in *JA Mont (UK) Ltd v Mills*[68]: **4.30**

"As a matter of policy, courts should not too urgently strive to find, within restrictive covenants ex facie too wide, implicit limitations such as alone would justify their imposition. Otherwise, employers would have no reason ever to impose restraints in appropriately limited terms. Thus would be perpetuated the long-recognised vice of ex-employees being left subject to apparently excessive restraints and yet quite unable, short of expensive litigation and at peril of substantial damages claims, to determine precisely what their rights may be."

This approach was followed in *Advantage Business Systems Ltd v Hopley*,[69] in which Judge Seymour QC said that although the court should construe a covenant in restraint of trade in a contract of employment against the background that the parties to it presumably intended, or at least accepted, that the covenant was enforceable, it should not strain to achieve a construction that produces the result that the covenant is enforceable.

In addition, the substantive law may form part of the surrounding circumstances which may properly be taken into account in interpreting a contract. Thus a consideration of the legal position may justify attaching a particular meaning or particular weight to a term of the contract whose purpose is not otherwise apparent. In addition, the legal background will supply the meaning of a term of art.[70] **4.31**

6.   THE LEGAL BACKGROUND

The legal background against which the contract was made may influence the interpretation of the contract.[71]

Parties do not make contracts in a legal vacuum. They always negotiate against the background of the law. It is, therefore, reasonable to suppose that they take into account the general law in reaching their ultimate consensus. And, accordingly, the proper interpretation of their agreement is properly influenced by the legal background against which it is made.[72] The legal context includes "both the surrounding contractual and other legal arrangements and the general law".[73] **4.32**

---

67   [2012] EWHC 3707 (QB).
68   [1993] I.R.L.R. 172.
69   [2007] EWHC 1783 (QB).
70   See para.5.63.
71   This section was approved in *Enterprise Inns Plc v Palmerston Associates Ltd* [2011] EWHC 3165 (Ch).
72   *BCCI v Ali* [2002] 1 A.C. 251 at 269, per Lord Hoffmann. Although the principle is well-established, Professor J.W. Carter subjects it to criticism in *The Construction of Commercial Contracts* (Oxford: Hart Publishing Ltd, 2013), para.13-17.
73   *Ardmair Bay Holdings Ltd v Craig* [2020] ScotCS CSIH 21.

(a)   Common law

4.33   In *Winter Garden Theatre (London) Ltd v Millennium Productions Ltd*,[74] the House of Lords considered the question whether a licence to use a theatre was determinable on reasonable notice. Lord Porter said:

> "there are few, if any, contracts which can be construed without taking into consideration a long background of gradual development and the implication of customary provisions, and I do not think that the meaning of a licence can be reached by considering the matter, as it were, in the air; its incidents have a long history behind them."

In *Oxonica Energy Ltd v Neuftec Ltd*,[75] Peter Prescott QC (sitting as a judge of the Chancery Division) said of a patent licence:

> "The background knowledge that the neutral, reasonable person employs when understanding a commercial document can include a knowledge of the relevant law ... Indeed a person could not properly understand the Licence Deed in this case unless he had a good general knowledge of patent law and international practice in that regard. The problem is that the more of that knowledge he had the more he might be baffled by the document."

His decision was upheld on appeal.[76]

4.34   The point was put more forcefully by Lord Cairns LC in *Llanelly Railway and Dock Co v London and North Western Railway*[77]:

> "With regard to contracts of partnership they also are already ruled and settled, by law, to be capable of termination at any moment unless a definite limit is prescribed upon the face of them. And, the law being well settled, when you have a contract of that kind, you apply the understood law, and you hold that the parties, knowing what the law was, must be supposed to have intended entering into a partnership which could at any time be terminated, if they did not provide upon the face of their contract that it should be a continuing partnership."

Similarly, in considering the scope of a force majeure clause the court will take into account the common law doctrine of frustration, which forms part of the legal backdrop against which such clauses are framed.[78] In *Cape Distribution Ltd v Cape Intermediate Holdings Plc*,[79] Picken J held that the legal background included the statutory context, the relevant law and market practice falling short of trade usage.

4.35   Where, however, there is no settled practice (or principle of interpretation), then the court must confine itself to the words of the contract itself. Even then the court

---

[74] [1948] A.C. 173 at 193.
[75] [2008] EWHC 2127 (Pat).
[76] [2009] EWCA Civ 668. See also *Maggbury Pty Ltd v Hafele Australia Pty Ltd* (2001) 210 C.L.R. 181.
[77] (1875) L.R. 1 App. Cas. 550 at 560. See also *Bracknell Development Corp v Greenlees Lennards Ltd* [1981] 2 E.G.L.R. 105.
[78] *Thames Valley Power Ltd v Total Gas & Power Ltd* [2006] 1 Lloyd's Rep. 441.
[79] [2016] EWHC 1119 (QB); [2016] Lloyd's Rep. I.R. 499.

may take into account the relevant legal background. As Lord Donaldson MR said in *The World Symphony*[80]:

"… it is for the parties to give expression to the terms of their bargain and this always has to be done against a background of general law and accepted principles, such as the prima facie risk of loss by delay in performance under a time-charter falls upon the charterer."

Similarly, in *Toomey v Eagle Star Insurance Co Ltd*,[81] Hobhouse LJ said:

"It is also necessary that the Court should have regard to previous decisions of the Courts upon the same or similar wording. Parties to a commercial contract are to be taken to have contracted against a background which includes the previous decisions upon the construction of similar contracts."

In *MDIS Ltd v Swinbank*,[82] Clarke LJ referred to an earlier decision of Devlin J and said that:

4.36

"both the decision and the dicta in that case can in my judgement properly be treated as relevant to the construction of this clause since they have been known amongst insurance lawyers and indeed brokers for many years and would be likely to have been in the back of the minds of those negotiating this contract."

In *Linpac Mouldings Ltd v Aviva Life and Pensions Ltd*,[83] interpreting a break clause in a lease, the Court of Appeal took into account both the common law rules relating to the giving of notice to quit and also "a number of cases since 1994, which would be well known to commercial property lawyers, in which the Court of Appeal has considered the operation of a tenant's right to break the lease". In *Newcastle NHS Trust v Haywood*,[84] the Supreme Court took into account a consistent line of cases in the Employment Appeal Tribunal in deciding what term about the effective date of contractual notices should be implied in a contract of employment.

In *Tesco Stores Ltd v Constable*,[85] a policy of public liability insurance was interpreted as limited to insurance against claims on tort, thus excluding liability for pure economic loss. The fact that it was described as insurance against "public liability" was an important factor in the court's reasoning. Tuckey LJ said:

4.37

"A public liability policy provides cover against liability to the public at large. By contrast private liability arises from contracts entered into between individuals. Public liability in this sense arises in tort; it does not and cannot arise only in contract. As a general rule a claim in tort cannot be founded upon pure economic loss. So the judge was right to say that the fact that this was public liability insurance was important and that such policies do not generally cover liability in contract for pure economic loss. It is a strong pointer to the meaning of the words used. Of course it is not conclusive: the wording may extend cover

---

80 [1992] 2 Lloyd's Rep. 115 CA.
81 [1994] 1 Lloyd's Rep. 516 CA.
82 [1999] 2 All E.R. (Comm) 722. See Clarke LJ's similar remarks in *Eridiana SpA v Oetker* [2000] 2 All E.R. (Comm) 108.
83 [2010] EWCA Civ 395.
84 [2018] UKSC 22; [2018] 1 W.L.R. 2073.
85 [2008] 1 C.L.C. 727.

to third party claims in contract even for pure economic loss although one would expect it to say so clearly and for such insurance to be described as contract liability, financial or consequential loss cover."

4.38   In *Grove Investments Ltd v Cape Building Products Ltd*,[86] the Inner House held that the common law may serve another function, namely to enable the court to select an interpretation that made the best commercial sense. As Lord Drummond Young explained:

> "A further factor that may be important in construing a commercial contract is the rules of the common law. In giving a contract a contextual interpretation it is clear that the legal context must be considered as well as the factual context. The relevance of the common law goes beyond that, however, because in the field of contract its rules represent the considered attempts of judges, over many years, to strike a fair balance between the interests of contractual parties. Usually, therefore, the common law will achieve a result in accordance with commercial common sense. For this reason, when a contract is interpreted, the common law can often serve as a benchmark against which considerations of fairness can be measured. If a particular construction of a contractual term achieves a result that is radically different from the rules of the common law, that is a factor that *may* in some circumstances indicate that that construction is commercially unreasonable. Such a factor is unlikely to be of great importance in construing the main terms of a contract, dealing with the parties' substantive rights and obligations, since these will almost invariably be the subject of specific negotiation. With many of the subsidiary terms, however, such as a term providing for a payment that does not form part of the main consideration, the consequences of the wording used may not have been well thought through and there may be no active intention either to abrogate or to follow the common law rule. In a case of that sort the common law may provide considerable assistance in deciding what is commercially sensible."

4.39   In *@SIPP (Pension Trustees) Ltd v Insight Travel Services Ltd*,[87] the trial judge had held, based on observations in *Grove Investments Ltd v Cape Building Products Ltd*, that:

> "... a contract is a co-operative enterprise entered into by parties for the mutual benefit, that it should normally be construed in such a way as to avoid arbitrary or unpredictable burdens, that the common law often serves as a benchmark against which considerations of fairness can be measured and that radical departure from the common law could indicate that that construction is commercially unreasonable."

The Inner House disagreed. Lady Smith said:

> "... the general observations in Grove ought not, we consider, to be taken as indicating that the considerations of co-operation and mutuality that would be appropriate to, say, partnership or joint venture apply across the board. Com-

---

[86]   [2014] CSIH 43.
[87]   [2015] ScotCS CSIH 91; [2016] 1 P. & C.R. 17.

mercial contracts may, equally, be hard fought with each party intent on securing their own particular objective."

(b) Statute law

The relevant legal background can include statutory regimes as well as the common law.

4.40

In *Doleman v Shaw*,[88] the "legal landscape" against which the Court of Appeal interpreted an authorised guarantee agreement of the liabilities of an assignee of a lease included the statutory provisions about the effect of a disclaimer of the lease, as interpreted by a previous decision of the House of Lords. Elias LJ said that "the words used must be read in the context of the common law and statutory background". In *Standard Life Assurance Ltd v Oak Dedicated Ltd*,[89] the relevant legal background included "a working understanding of the regulatory regime introduced by the Financial Services Act 1986" to which the contract expressly referred. Likewise, in interpreting the terms of a pension scheme the court will always take account of the fiscal background.[90] In *Amcor Ltd v Construction, Forestry, Mining & Energy Union*,[91] Kirby J referred to the legislative background against which an industrial agreement was made and certified. He said:

> "It was a background that would have been in the minds of both parties (Amcor and its agent on the one side and the Union on the other) who negotiated the Agreement and hammered out its terms. The legislative background is therefore part of the common knowledge attributable to the parties to the Agreement. So far as it is relevant, the parties intended the Agreement to take its place within the industrial setting created by the Act."

And in *Phoenix Commercial Enterprises Pty Ltd v City of Canada Bay Council*,[92] Campbell JA said:

> "… if a reasonable person with the relevant background knowledge would read some particular contractual provision in light of the provisions of a statutory context within which the contract is to operate, then that statutory context can be a legitimate aid to construction."

Thus where a contract is intended to give effect to a statutory provision, it should be interpreted in the light of the statutory provision to which it was intended to give effect.[93] Similarly, a contract which was intended to implement a directive of the EU was construed so as to be compatible with the directive.[94] However, although a contract will be construed in the light of the legislative background, ultimately a question of interpretation will be resolved by construing the contract itself. In *Of-*

4.41

---

88   [2009] Bus. L.R. 1175.
89   [2008] 1 C.L.C. 59.
90   *Mettoy Pension Trustees Ltd v Evans* [1990] 1 W.L.R. 1587; *National Grid Plc v Mayes* [2001] 1 W.L.R. 864; *Armitage v Staveley Holdings Ltd* [2006] Pens. L.R. 191.
91   (2005) 222 C.L.R. 241 at [64].
92   [2010] NSWCA 64 at [176].
93   *Reinwood Ltd v L Brown & Sons Ltd* [2008] 2 All E.R. 885; *Allied Domecq (Holdings) Ltd v Allied Domecq First Pension Trust Ltd* [2008] Pens. L.R. 425 at [38]; *Digby v General Accident Fire and Life Assurance Corp Ltd* [1943] A.C. 121. There was a division of opinion on this point in *Great Estates Group Ltd v Digby* [2011] EWCA Civ 1120; [2011] 3 E.G.L.R. 101.
94   *White v White* [2001] 1 W.L.R. 481 HL.

fice of Telecommunications v Floe Telecom Ltd,[95] the Court of Appeal was concerned with the scope of a licence to operate a mobile phone network which had been granted by the Secretary of State. The particular question was whether the licence permitted the connection to the network of GSM gateways, which were permitted by a regulation of the EC. Mummery LJ said:

> "109. Floe's alternative argument on construction relied on the EC directives as aids to construction of the licence. Of course, the language in which the licence is expressed must be construed in context. The context may include EC or domestic legislation. For example, a licence may use technical terms without defining them, but against the background of legislation, including EC legislation, in which they are defined. The terms as defined in the related legislation would be aids to the interpretation of the licence.
>
> 110. In this case, however, the licence defines its own terms. It is they and not the contents of the directives which control the meaning of the licence. The licence authorises the use of Radio Equipment. The definition of Radio Equipment does not include GSM gateways, which fall within the definition of different apparatus, 'User Stations'."

4.42   In *R & S Pilling (t/a Phoenix Engineering) v UK Insurance Ltd*,[96] a motor insurance policy certified that it met the statutory requirements of the Road Traffic Act 1988. On a literal interpretation of the scope of the cover, it did not. The Supreme Court applied a corrective interpretation, inserting words into the description of the cover, so as to make it conform to the statutory requirements.

(c) How much law?

4.43   Although the admissible background may include the law, the knowledge of the law imputed to the parties need not be extensive. In *Enterprise Inns Plc v Palmerston Associates Ltd*,[97] Morgan J said:

> "... there is room for discussion as to how much of the legal background should be regarded as reasonably available to both of the parties; in this respect, the court is concerned with the position of both parties and not just of one of them. There is also room for discussion as to whether the court is confined to considering the law as it was thought to be at the date of the contract or whether the court can take into account the law as it has developed thereafter.[98] There is also room for discussion as to whether the court should presume that the parties know the relevant principles of English law or whether something more by way of evidence as to their actual position is required."

---

[95] [2009] Bus. L.R. 1116.

[96] [2019] UKSC 16; [2019] 2 W.L.R. 1015.

[97] [2011] EWHC 3165 (Ch).

[98] See *Durham v BAI (Run Off) Ltd* [2012] UKSC 14; [2012] 1 W.L.R. 867 at [70] in which changes in the law were taken into account. This and other cases are referred to below.

With reference to the last point, the preponderance of authority is to the effect **4.44** that the parties must be taken to know established principles of English law. In *Spencer v Secretary of State for Defence*,[99] Vos J said:

"There might be considerable argument about whether a particular fact should be regarded as being reasonably available to the reasonable third party observer, but in respect of the law (at least clear law) the position seems to me to be less difficult. A reasonable person cannot be assumed to be in ignorance of clear and well known legal principles."

In *Challinor v Juliet Bellis & Co*,[100] Hildyard J said that:

"a reasonable person cannot be assumed to be in ignorance of clear and well known legal principles affecting or incidental to the contractual engagement in question."

Likewise, in *Procter & Gamble Co v Svenska Cellulosa Aktiebolaget SCA*,[101] the question was whether parties had agreed a fixed rate of exchange for converting euros into sterling. Rix LJ said:

"… that the principle by which, in the normal way, a difference between currency of account and currency of payment leads to an exchange rate as at the time of payment rather than at some other time or rate is a deep-rooted principle of nominalism, and not a mere question of the interpretation or implication of one among other contracts. In this connection I refer to *Dicey, Morris & Collins*, 14th ed, 2006, at rule 236 and paras 36–005–008. In my judgment, therefore, if that principle is to be dislodged by contrary provision, then it must be done clearly."

In *C v D*,[102] the question was whether an offer to settle proceedings amounted to **4.45** a Pt 36 offer. Rix LJ said that:

"Both the writer and the reader of that offer must be taken, objectively, to know the legal context."

In *Lehman Brothers International (Europe) v Lehman Brothers Finance SA*,[103] Arden LJ said that case law on the meaning of a standard form of agreement was part of the relevant background.

In *Gladman Commercial Properties v Fisher Hargreaves Proctor*,[104] the parties were credited with knowledge of the legal consequences of releasing joint tortfeasors; and in *Richards v Wood*,[105] the way in which the general law of trusts had treated a council tenant's entitlement to discount on exercise of the statutory right

---

[99] [2012] EWHC 120 (Ch); [2012] L. & T.R. 318. An appeal from Vos J was dismissed, but this point was not discussed: [2012] EWCA Civ 1368; [2013] 1 All E.R. (Comm) 287. Vos J adhered to this reasoning in *Barden v Commodities Research Unit* [2013] EWHC 1633 (Ch) in which he held that the requirement on an employer to pay wages or salary net of income tax was a matter that the parties must be taken to have known. Knowledge of the law appears to be placed on a footing that may differ from factual knowledge to be attributed to the parties.

[100] [2013] EWHC 347 (Ch) at [277].

[101] [2012] EWCA Civ 1413.

[102] [2011] EWCA Civ 646; [2012] 1 All E.R. 302.

[103] [2013] EWCA Civ 188.

[104] [2013] EWCA Civ 1466.

[105] [2014] EWCA Civ 327.

to buy was treated as part of the legal background for the purpose of interpreting a professionally drafted declaration of trust.

In *First Abu Dhabi Bank PJSC v BP Oil International Ltd*,[106] the Court of Appeal held, approving this section of previous edition, that:

"… it is a recognised principle of construction that a contract should be construed on the basis that the law (at least clear law) is known."

4.46   However, the Court of Appeal has refused to attribute to a hirer of a motor car a detailed knowledge of consumer credit legislation.[107] In *Crosstown Music Company v Rive Droite Music Ltd*,[108] it was argued that a publishing agreement between a writer and a publishing house should be interpreted against the background of foreign copyright law. Mann J rejected that contention. He said:

"It is said that the effect on foreign copyrights is something that should be taken into account in construing the agreement. For that to be the case the foreign copyright position would have to be something that was known to both parties of each agreement, or treated as being known to both parties. In that way it would become part of the relevant factual background. There was no evidence which would justify such a finding. First, there is no evidence that the Writers knew anything about foreign copyright law at all. Second, there is no evidence that RD knew anything about the foreign copyright position either, or at least as to the extent of its knowledge of this technical point. Third, there is no evidence of what any relevant foreign copyright law was anyway. For these reasons the foreign copyright position is not a relevant factor to take into account in construing the agreements."

4.47   It is not considered that proof of actual knowledge of the parties is necessary in all cases. Where the legal background in question is English law, it is considered that the principles of English law, if not actually known to the parties, would at least have been reasonably available to them.

(d)   Changes in the law

4.48   When considering the legal background represented by the common law, the court is not generally restricted to what the law was thought to be at the date of the contract if it has subsequently been developed. In *Henry Smith's Charity v AWADA Trading and Promotion Services Ltd*,[109] the question was whether time was of the essence of machinery for rent review contained in a lease. After the date of the lease, the House of Lords had laid down a general presumption[110] that time was not of the essence. Sir John Donaldson MR said:

"[Counsel] also submitted that, as the terms of the lease were agreed before the decision of the House of Lords in *United Scientific*, the lease had to be construed and the intention of the parties deduced on the basis of the law as it was thought to be at that time. While this argument is not without its attractions, I think that

[106] [2018] EWCA Civ 14; *Bates v Post Office (No .3)* [2019] EWHC 606 (QB).
[107] *Zoan v Rouamba* [2000] 2 All E.R. 620.
[108] [2009] EWHC 600 (Ch); on appeal [2010] EWCA Civ 1222.
[109] (1983) 46 P. & C.R. 74.
[110] *United Scientific Holdings Ltd v Burnley Borough Council* [1978] A.C. 904.

it must be rejected as involving an undesirable extension of the doctrine of *stare decisis*."

In *Lymington Marina Ltd v MacNamara*,[111] Arden LJ said:

"In my judgment there can be no necessary implication that, where parties come to an agreement, that agreement must be interpreted on the basis of the law as it stood when the agreement was made as if it were in some time warp. It is part of the factual matrix known to both parties that both statute law and the common law develop over time. Developments in the common law apply retrospectively unless, exceptionally, the court makes an order for prospective overruling. … If the parties have been content to leave a matter to the general law, they must be taken to have agreed that their agreement should be interpreted in the light of the general law from time to time."

However, in *BCCI v Ali*,[112] an employee signed a release of claims against his former employer. The question was whether the release included claims for so-called "stigma damages". The House of Lords held that it did not, largely because the concept of "stigma damages" was unknown at the date of the contract. Lord Nicholls of Birkenhead said: **4.49**

"I consider these parties are to be taken to have contracted on the basis of the law as it then stood. To my mind there is something inherently unattractive in treating these parties as having intended to include within the release a claim which, *as a matter of law*, did not then exist and whose existence could not then have been foreseen."

It is considered that in general the view expressed by Arden LJ is the better one. It is supported by *Durham v BAI (Run Off) Ltd*[113] in which Lord Mance said in relation to the interpretation of insurance policies: **4.50**

"Furthermore, if the common law during or even after the currency of an insurance develops in a manner which increases employers' liability, compared with previous perceptions as to what the common law was, that is a risk which the insurers must accept, within the limits of the relevant insurance and insurance period. Eady J. correctly identified this in *Phillips v Syndicate 992 Gunner*.[114] The declaratory theory 'does not presume the existence of an ideal system of the common law, which the judges from time to time reveal in their decisions. But it does mean that, when judges state what the law is, their decisions do … have a retrospective effect'—in the sense that the law as stated 'will, generally speaking, be applicable not only to the case coming before [them] but, as part of the common law, to other comparable cases which come before the courts, whenever the events which are the subject of those cases': *Kleinwort Benson Ltd v Lincoln CC*.[115] The declaratory theory is a pragmatic tool, essential when cases can only come before the court 'some time, perhaps some years' after the relevant events occurred, and when 'the law [must] be applied equally to all, and yet be capable

---

[111] [2007] EWCA Civ 151; [2007] Bus. L.R. D29.
[112] [2002] 1 A.C. 251.
[113] [2012] UKSC 14; [2012] 1 W.L.R. 867 at [70].
[114] [2003] EWHC 1084 (QB); [2004] Lloyd's Insurance and Reinsurance Reports 426 at 429 (left).
[115] [1999] 2 A.C. 349 at 378G–H, per Lord Goff.

of organic change'. A similar principle must, generally speaking, apply in relation to a statute such as the Compensation Act 2006, which changes or corrects the common law to what Parliament perceives to be a more appropriate result for the purposes of all future cases coming before the courts, whenever the events giving rise to them."

Nevertheless, if the change in the law (even the common law) is unique and unprecedented, the court may adopt a more creative solution.[116]

4.51 In *Cape Distribution Ltd v Cape Intermediate Holdings Plc*,[117] Picken J, referring to this section, said that he was "wary" of the submission that a contract should be interpreted in accordance with the common law as it stood at the date of the contract. It is thought that he was right not to accept that argument.

4.52 Lord Mance restricted his observations to changes in the common law. Although Arden LJ referred to changes both in the common law and in statute law, whether changes in statute law are treated in the same way as changes in the common law is more controversial.[118]

4.53 Where statute law changes, the court must decide how to apply the words of the contract to the changed circumstances. In *Debenhams Retail Plc v Sun Alliance and London Assurance Co Ltd*,[119] a lease provided for a turnover rent as a percentage of the tenant's "gross amount of total sales". When the lease was granted in 1965, purchase tax was levied on certain goods. Purchase tax was replaced by VAT in 1973. The issue was whether VAT was to be included in the "gross amount of sales". The Court of Appeal held that it was. Mance LJ said:

"To speak even of objective intention in such circumstances involves some artificiality. Even if we were judicial archaeologists, we would find in the wording of the lease negotiated in 1965 no actual or buried intention regarding VAT, since it was introduced in April 1973, and the regime in force in 1965 was the different purchase tax regime. But no-one suggests that the lease cannot or should not apply in the changed circumstances. We have to promote the purposes and values which are expressed or implicit in its wording, and to reach an interpretation which applies the lease wording to the changed circumstances in the manner most consistent with them."

In the result the court held that the "gross amount" included that part of the purchase price of goods that was attributable to output tax for VAT. In *Lloyds TSB Foundation for Scotland v Lloyds Banking Group Plc*,[120] the Supreme Court applied the approach in *Debenhams Retail Plc v Sun Alliance and London Assurance v Co Ltd*.[121] Lord Mance said:

"No-one suggests or could suggest that the change meant that the 1997 Deed was

---

116 *Equitas Insurance Ltd v Municipal Mutual Insurance Ltd* [2019] EWCA Civ 718; [2020] 1 All E.R. 16.
117 [2016] EWHC 1786 (QB); [2017] Lloyd's Rep. I.R. 1.
118 See *Frobisher (Second Investments) Ltd v Kiloran Trust Co Ltd* [1980] 1 W.L.R. 452 (no term implied to take account of change in statute); *Brewers Co v Viewplan Plc* [1989] 2 E.G.L.R. 133 (change in Use Classes Order did not change construction of use covenant in a lease); *Brett v Brett Essex Golf Club Ltd* (1986) 52 P. & C.R. 330 (reference to s.34 of the Landlord and Tenant Act 1954 in a rent review clause was to the Act as unamended). See para.3.66.
119 [2005] 3 E.G.L.R. 34. See also *The Woodland Trust v Loring* [2014] EWCA Civ 1314; [2015] 2 All E.R. 32 where Lewison LJ applied this observation to the interpretation of a will.
120 [2013] UKSC 3; [2013] 1 W.L.R. 366.
121 [2005] 3 E.G.L.R. 34.

frustrated, so the question is how its language best operates in the fundamentally changed and entirely unforeseen circumstances in the light of the parties' original intentions and purposes."

Similarly, in *Shebelle Enterprises Ltd v Hampstead Garden Suburb Trust Ltd*,[122] the Court of Appeal interpreted a covenant for quiet enjoyment in the light of changes in the legal structure following the grant of the lease, and in particular the implementation of a scheme of management under the Leasehold Reform Act 1967.

In some cases a statute itself may make provision for updating references in contracts.[123]   **4.54**

More difficult questions may arise where an existing instrument is alleged to have been affected by the Human Rights Act 1988. In *Re Erskine 1948 Trust*,[124] a settlement made in 1948 provided that the ultimate beneficiaries should be the "statutory next of kin" of the principal beneficiary. Legislation in force at the date of the settlement defined "next of kin" in terms that excluded adopted children. Although subsequent legislation provided that adopted children were in principle to be treated the same as biological children, that legislation was expressed not to affect dispositions made before 1950. The question was whether the reference in the settlement to "statutory next of kin" could be interpreted in conformity with current legislation, bearing in mind that the legislation in force in 1948 would have been incompatible with the European Convention on Human Rights, because it discriminated against adopted children. Mr Mark Herbert QC, sitting as a judge of the Chancery Division, held that the settlement could be interpreted compatibly with the Convention if it could be done without unfairness. On the point of principle he said: **4.55**

"First, I must avoid a decision which is unreasonable, arbitrary or blatantly inconsistent with the prohibition of discrimination established by art 14 (though I do not see that anything is added by the adverb 'blatantly'). ... Second, I must not put words into the settlor's mouth, so to speak, and I should construe the disposition in a way which corresponds to national law and the convention as developed in the ECtHR's case law. ... Third, if the disposition, as worded by the settlor, did make a distinction between biological and adopted children, then I have to give effect to that distinction. ... The priorities between those points are not spelled out."

He added:

"I am prepared to accept in principle that the convention becoming part of English law can have an effect on the construction and effect of an existing trust, if that can be achieved without unfairness. This is not fully retrospective. The new construction derived from the convention would operate only from 2 October 1998. But it would, from that date, alter beneficial interests under the settlement."

On the other hand, in *Hand v George*[125] the testator had made a will dividing his estate between his children for life with remainder to their children. At the time   **4.56**

---

[122] [2014] EWCA Civ 305; [2014] 2 P & CR 114.
[123] See, e.g. Enterprise Act 2002 Sch.17 para.1; Human Fertilisation and Embryology Act 2008 s.48(5).
[124] [2012] EWHC 732 (Ch); [2013] Ch. 135.
[125] [2017] EWHC 533 (Ch); [2017] Ch. 449, followed in Monkcom Re JC Druce Settlement [2019] EWHC 3701 (Ch).

when the will was made (and at the time when the testator died), domestic law provided that adopted children did not count as children for the purposes of inheritance. Domestic law had since changed, and the previous legislation had been repealed. One of the children died after the coming into force of the Human Rights Act 1998, leaving adopted children. Rose J refused to follow *Re Erskine 1948 Trust*. She held that the question was not simply one of interpretation of the will, but whether the repealed domestic legislation could be read down in the light of the jurisprudence of the European Court of Human Rights. She held that it could, and that the adopted children took under the will.

7. THE USE OF PRECEDENT IN THEORY

Since the interpretation of a contract is a question of law, it follows that the decision of the court is, in theory, a binding authority. However, it is an authority which can be easily distinguished.

4.57   Since the decision of the court on the meaning of a contract decides a question of law, the doctrine of stare decisis theoretically means that any inferior court is bound by the point of law decided. However, any contract is a consensual arrangement between particular parties made against the background of particular circumstances. In those circumstances it has proved a relatively simple task for the court to distinguish a decision made in relation to a different contract when it so desires. Indeed some judges have asserted that the decision of a superior court on a question of interpretation of a written contract does not bind even an inferior court. Sir George Jessel MR held particularly strong views in this regard. In *Pedlar v Road Block Gold Mines of India Ltd*,[126] Warrington J said:

> "In a question of construction, no judge is bound by the decision of another judge. He is obliged to express his view of the meaning of the document which he has to construe, and in expressing that view, in my opinion, he is not bound by the view of somebody else. I remember hearing Sir George Jessel say that he should not regard himself as bound by the decision of a previous judge on the construction of the identical document and the identical passage of the document which he had to construe."[127]

In *Westcott v Hahn*[128] Scrutton LJ said:

> "A flood of authorities in and since the seventeenth century were poured out upon the Court, in which somewhat similar words to this covenant had received a construction from the Courts. In my view, however, the first thing to be done is to endeavour to ascertain from the words the parties have used in this case their actual intention. If they have used words which by a settled course of authority have acquired a technical meaning, the Court will give effect to those authori-

---

[126] [1905] 2 Ch. 427.

[127] Sir George expressed similar views in *Re New Callao Ltd* (1882) 22 Ch. D. 484 at 488, and *Hack v London Provident Building Society* (1883) 23 Ch. D. 103 at 111. See also *Re Coleman's Depositories Ltd* [1907] 2 K.B. 798 at 812, per Buckley LJ; and, for a more moderate view, *Ashville Investments Ltd v Elmer Contractors Ltd* [1989] 1 Q.B. 488, per May LJ (quoted in para.4.88).

[128] [1918] 1 K.B. 495 at 511 and, to similar effect, *Welsh v Greenwich LBC* [2000] 3 E.G.L.R. 41, per Robert Walker LJ. However, in *BCCI v Ali* [2002] 1 A.C. 251, the House of Lords was heavily influenced by a long line of authority in interpreting an instrument of release.

ties; but, unless this is so, it appears to me very unprofitable to consider what Courts have thought that other words in other documents meant and to see which reported case has the least differences from the present."

Thus in *Hawley v Luminar Leisure Ltd*,[129] Hallett LJ stressed: **4.58**

"the caution which a court, seeking to identify the meaning of a word in a particular contract, must adopt when considering what assistance can be derived from either the word's acontextual meaning, or judicial decisions as to the meaning of the same word in a different contract. Because the contractual and commercial circumstances of each case are inevitably different, it can be positively dangerous to draw assistance from the acontextual meaning or from decisions of other courts as to the meaning, of a particular word, when context is so important on issues of interpretation. Of course, very different considerations may apply where a particular word or phrase has a specific well established meaning in a certain type of contract."

Similarly, in *Midland Bank Plc v Cox McQueen*,[130] Mummery LJ said:

"As has been repeatedly remarked, every document must be construed according to its particular terms and in its unique setting. Detailed comparisons of one document with another and of one precedent with another do not usually help the court to reach a decision on construction. Indeed, that exercise occupies a disproportionate amount of valuable time which would be better spent on the arguments that really count: those which focus on the precise terms of the relevant documents and the illuminating environment of the transaction."

In *JHP Ltd v BBC Worldwide Ltd*,[131] Norris J said:

"The process of construction is the ascertainment of the meaning which the document would convey to a reasonable person having all background knowledge which would reasonably have been available to the parties in the situation in which they were at the time of the contract. In this process reported decisions on the meaning of the same or similar words in other documents are of very little assistance (unless the words have a technical meaning in formal documents which the draftsman may be taken to have known), save for pointing up occasions on which the point may have arisen before and alerting the court to the arguments then advanced. That is in part because the factual background known to the parties will invariably differ from document to document."

In *Khanty-Mansiysk Recoveries Ltd v Forsters LLP*,[132] Sir Bernard Eder said: **4.59**

"In my view, reference to earlier authorities as to the meaning of a particular word or phrase is often unhelpful and sometimes dangerous particularly where the context in which that word or phrase may have been used is different from the instant case or wording."

---

[129] [2006] I.R.L.R. 817; *Persimmon Homes Ltd v Country Weddings (Cardiff) Ltd* [2020] EWHC 302 (Ch).
[130] [1999] 1 F.L.R. 1002.
[131] [2008] EWHC 757 (Ch).
[132] [2016] EWHC 522 (Comm).

Similarly, in *Lukoil Mid-East v Barclays Bank Plc*,[133] Stuart-Smith J said:

"Because different authorities typically discuss different wordings, they are likely to be of limited assistance as aids to interpretation except to the extent that they state general principles of construction."

4.60   On the other hand, where both the language and the context are similar, precedent may have a greater role to play. In *Enterprise Inns Plc v The Forest Hill Tavern Public House Ltd*,[134] Morritt C said of a previous decision:

"Plainly such a decision cannot be conclusive as to the interpretation of other contracts made at different times, between different parties and in different circumstances even though both are questions of law. But a decision on the interpretation of a contract may be persuasive as to the interpretation of another contract using similar language by parties involved in a similar trade and in similar circumstances, particularly where knowledge of the previous decision may be imputed to the parties."

In *AFFCO New Zealand Ltd v New Zealand Meat Workers and Related Trades Union Inc*,[135] the New Zealand Court of Appeal observed:

"Integration of relevant case law into the contractual context is a logical extension of the current emphasis on business common sense as a guide to interpretation. While decisions on disputes between certain parties cannot determine the interpretation of contracts made between other parties at a later date, the earlier decisions may well be persuasive where the provisions at issue in a later contract use similar language, in a similar trade and in similar circumstances. Earlier judicial authority and practice on the construction of similar contracts is relevant where the words used in a particular contract cannot properly be understood without reference to meanings ascribed to them in previous judgments."

4.61   In addition, where a case construing a "one-off" contract lays down a principle of construction, the principle may amount to a binding precedent for later cases.[136] Over time a particular interpretation may develop into a principle, as a judicial consensus grows. *Bominflot v Petroplus Marketing ("The Mercini Lady")*[137] is an illustration of this principle. In that case Rix LJ said:

"If therefore I were construing this clause untrammelled by past authority, or if such authority was plainly limited, in the way that so many decisions on the construction of individual clauses are limited, by considerations of the precise language and context of those particular clauses, I would feel it open, in the modern world, to give to clause 18 the construction which I believe that it realistically bears: that is to say, that 'guarantees' and 'warranties' are intended to cover all terms, both those which entitle the innocent party in the case of breach to treat

---

[133] [2016] EWHC 166 (TCC); [2016] B.L.R. 162; *Zayo Group International Ltd v Ainger* [2017] EWHC 2542 (Comm).

[134] [2010] EWHC 2368 (Ch).

[135] [2016] NZCA 482, referring to this section.

[136] *Jolley v Carmel Ltd* [2000] 3 E.G.L.R. 68 CA; *Starmark Enterprises v CPL Distribution* [2002] Ch. 306 CA.

[137] [2010] EWCA Civ 1145; [2011] 1 Lloyd's Rep. 442.

the contract as repudiated and those which sound only in damages. As section 11(3) of the 1979 Act itself records, 'a stipulation may be a condition, though called a warranty in the contract': and clause 18 itself demonstrates that buyer's warranties there set out are treated by the contract as conditions. It might be said that what is good enough for Lord Diplock (see at para 55 above) is good enough for commercial traders. However, I am not so free. The jurisprudence extends beyond individual decisions and has become expressive of a principle, and what is more the principle also encompasses clauses very similar to clause 18. I must consider that the parties to this English law contract, foreign as both of them are and quite possibly ignorant of the consequences of their choice of language, intended to contract by reference to what English law had to say about the language which they have adopted."

Moreover, as Waller LJ explained in *British Sugar Plc v NEI Power Projects Ltd*[138]:

"once a phrase has been authoritatively construed by a court in a very similar context to that which exists in the case in point, it seems to me that a reasonable businessman must more naturally be taken to be having the intention that the phrase should bear the same meaning as construed in the case in point. It would again take very clear words to allow a court to construe the phrase differently."

Even if one might consider that the parties to the contract themselves might not have had previous decisions of the Courts in mind when making their contracts, their lawyers will have done so in deciding whether or not to pursue a dispute subsequently.[139]

On the other hand, where an erroneous decision has departed from orthodoxy, **4.62** and a contract is entered into while the erroneous decision was thought to represent the law, that will not provide a reason for applying the erroneous decision to the contract in question.[140]

It is well known that certain types of contract are made on the basis of standard **4.63** terms common throughout one sector of the economy. Examples which figure frequently both in the Law Reports and in practice are: standard forms of charterparty of various kinds; the JCT form of building contract; the Standard Conditions of Sale; and many others. A common feature of such cases is that the standard form is printed, and the parties fill in a printed form, sometimes also deleting parts and adding clauses specially negotiated.[141] The provenance of the resulting contract is usually clear on the face of the completed document. Parties who

---

[138] (1997) 87 B.L.R. 42 at 50. See also *Re National Coffee Palace Co, Ex p. Panmure* (1883) 24 Ch. D. 367 at 370, per Brett MR:

"The reason for doing so, is that when Courts of Law have construed a contract in a particular way, and the interpretation which has been put upon it by the Court of Law comes to be accepted in the trade or business and people afterwards make contracts on that understanding, a Court of Appeal ought to hold itself bound by that decision; because if it altered the principle of interpretation the Court would be construing the contracts contrary to the meaning of those who made them".

[139] *The Radauti* [1987] 2 Lloyd's Rep. 276 CA; *The Kalliopi A* [1988] 2 Lloyd's Rep. 101 CA; *The Solon* [2000] C.L.C. 593.

[140] See *Shell International Petroleum Ltd v Gibbs* [1983] 2 A.C. 375 HL; *Trustees of Henry Smith's Charity v AWADA Trading & Promotion Services* (1983) 47 P. & C.R. 607 CA.

[141] It is frequently the ill-considered adaptation of the standard form which gives rise to the dispute, e.g.

adopt one of these standard forms as the basis of their contract may well do so against the background of previous decisions of the court on the meaning of the words of the standard form. As Lord Hoffmann put it in *Beaufort Developments (NJ) Ltd v Gilbert-Ash (NJ) Ltd*[142]:

> "It is also important to have regard to the course of earlier judicial authority and practice on the construction of similar contracts. The evolution of standard forms is often the result of interaction between the draftsmen and the courts and the efforts of the draftsman cannot be properly understood without reference to the meaning which the judges have given to the language used by his predecessors."

Similarly, in *Sunport Shipping Ltd v Tryg-Baltica International (UK) Ltd*,[143] Clarke LJ said:

> "When a contract has been professionally drawn ... the draftsman is certain to have in mind decisions of the courts on earlier editions of the clauses. Such decisions are part of the context or background circumstances against which the particular contract falls to be construed. If the draftsman chooses to adopt the same words as previously construed by the courts, it seems to me to be likely that, other things being equal, he intends that the words should continue to have the same meaning."

In *Ferryways NV v Associated British Ports*,[144] cl.9(c) of a contract excluded liability for loss "of an indirect or consequential nature". Teare J said:

> "Where a party seeks to protect himself from liability for losses otherwise recoverable by law for breach of contract he must do so by clear and unambiguous language. Clause 9(c) provides that liability for such losses as are 'of an indirect or consequential nature' is excluded. In the light of the well-recognised meaning which has been accorded to such words in a variety of exemption clauses by the courts from 1934 to 1999 it would require very clear words indeed to indicate that the parties' intentions when using such words was to exclude losses which fall outside that well-recognised meaning."

4.64   A different approach is warranted in such cases, for the contractual terms are not wholly private to the parties, but are semi-public in that they are in widespread use in a sector of the economy. An intermediate position arises where the contract has its origins in a published precedent but that fact is not clear on the face of the document, or the precedent has been adapted before the contract is finally concluded. This situation is relatively common in conveyancing, especially leasehold conveyancing. The current practice of the court seems not to treat such cases as

---

in *General Accident Fire and Life Assurance Corp Ltd v Midland Bank Ltd* [1940] 2 K.B. 388, Sir Wilfred Greene MR said:

> "Most of the difficulties in the case have arisen from the circumstance so frequently found, that a printed form has been used for a purpose for which it was not intended, and the alterations which that purpose required in order to avoid ambiguity were not made."

See also *Mottram Consultants Ltd v Sunley (Bernard) & Sons Ltd* [1975] 2 Lloyd's Rep. 197 at 204, per Lord Cross of Chelsea.

[142] [1999] A.C. 266.
[143] [2003] 1 Lloyd's Rep. 138 CA.
[144] [2008] 1 Lloyd's Rep. 639.

standard form cases, but to treat them as one-off cases of construction.[145] It is suggested that this approach has little to commend it, and that parties to conveyancing transactions who base their transaction upon a published precedent are in a similar position to those who contract upon the basis of a published printed form.[146]

8.   STANDARD FORMS OF COMMERCIAL AGREEMENTS

In a case where the contract is based upon a standard form of commercial agreement, the court recognises the desirability of certainty, and is reluctant to disturb an established construction.[147]

In *Dunlop & Sons v Balfour Williamson & Co*,[148] Lord Esher MR said: **4.65**

"It is a wholesome rule that has often been laid down that when a well-known document has been in constant use for a number of years, the Court, in construing it, should not break away from previous decisions, even if in the first instance they would have taken a different view, because all documents made after the meaning of one has been judicially determined are taken to have been made on the faith of the rule so laid down."

Similarly, in *The Annefield*,[149] the Court of Appeal had to construe a charterparty in the Centrocon form. A challenge was made to a decision on a point of construction on the same form in 1936 which had itself paid regard to a practice in existence since 1914. Lord Denning MR said:

"Once a court has put a construction on commercial documents in a standard form, commercial men act upon it. It should be followed in all subsequent cases. If the business community is not satisfied with the decision, they should alter the form."

The same point was made at slightly greater length by Lord Diplock (with whom   **4.66**
the other Lords of Appeal agreed) in *Federal Commerce and Navigation Co Ltd v Tradax Export SA*.[150] He drew attention to the need for standard forms in assisting the making of contracts in a free market, partly to enable ready comparison between offers, but also because:

---

[145] There are remarkable examples of judges coming to different conclusions in relation to very similar words. Compare *Drebbond Ltd v Horsham District Council* (1978) 37 P. & C.R. 237 and *Touche Ross & Co v Secretary of State for the Environment* (1983) 46 P. & C.R. 187.

[146] However, where a contract is taken from a published precedent, the precedent may be used as an aid to interpretation: see para.3.31.

[147] The interpretation of standard form agreements is discussed by Aaron Taylor, "Interpretation of Industry Standard Contracts" [2017] L.M.C.L.Q. 261.

[148] [1892] 1 Q.B. 507.

[149] [1971] P. 168. See also *Atlantic Trading and Shipping Co v Louis Dreyfus & Co* [1922] 2 A.C. 250 at 257, per Lord Dunedin:

"My Lords, in these commercial cases it is, I think, of the highest importance that authority should not be disturbed, and if your Lordships find that a certain doctrine has been laid down in former cases and presumably acted on in the framing of other contracts you will not be disposed to alter that doctrine unless you think it is clearly wrong".

Re an Arbitration between Hooley Hill Rubber and Chemical Co Ltd and Royal Insurance Co Ltd [1920] 1 K.B. 257; *The Radauti* [1987] 2 Lloyd's Rep. 276 at 278; *Excess Insurance Co Ltd v Mander* [1997] 2 Lloyd's Rep. 119 at 124.

[150] [1978] A.C. 1.

"they become the subject of exegesis by the courts so that the way in which they will apply to the adventure contemplated by the charterparty will be understood in the same sense by both the parties when they are negotiating its terms and carrying them out."

He continued:

"It is no part of the function of a court of justice to dictate to charterers and shipowners the terms of the contracts into which they ought to enter on the freight market; but it is an important function of a court, and particularly of your Lordships' House, to provide them with legal certainty at the negotiation stage as to what it is they are agreeing to. And if there is that certainty, then when occasion arises for a court to enforce the contract or award damages for its breach, the fact that the members of the court themselves may think that one of the parties was unwise in agreeing to assume a particular misfortune risk or unlucky in its proving more expensive to him than he expected, has nothing to do with the merits of the case or with enabling justice to be done. The only merits of the case are that parties who bargained on equal terms in a free market should stick to their agreements. Justice is done by seeing that they do so or compensating the party who has kept his promise for any loss he has suffered by the failure of the other party to keep his."

In the result the House of Lords refused to alter the test of what constituted an arrived ship in a port charterparty which had been laid down in *The Johanna Oldendorff*.[151]

4.67   Lord Diplock returned to the theme of certainty in *Pioneer Shipping Ltd v TP Tioxide Ltd; The Nema*,[152] where he said:

"... when contracts are entered into which incorporate standard terms it is the interests alike of justice and of the conduct of commercial transactions that those standard terms should be construed and treated by arbitrators as giving rise to similar legal rights and obligations in all arbitrations in which the events which have given rise to the dispute do not differ from one another in some relevant respect. It is only if parties to commercial contracts can rely on a uniform construction being given to standard terms that they can prudently incorporate them in their contracts without the need for detailed negotiation or discussion. Such uniform construction of standard terms had been progressively established up to 1979, largely through decisions of the courts on special cases stated by arbitrators. In the result English commercial law has achieved a degree of comprehensiveness and certainty that has made it acceptable for adoption as the appropriate proper law to be applied to commercial contracts wherever made by parties of whatever nationality."

Similarly, in *The World Symphony*,[153] Hobhouse J said:

"It is axiomatic in English commercial law that where certain contractual provisions have achieved an established and recognised meaning the Courts should not decline to follow earlier authorities in which that meaning is recognised unless

---

[151] [1974] A.C. 479.
[152] [1982] A.C. 724. See also *The Kalliopi A* [1988] 2 Lloyd's Rep. 101 at 105.
[153] [1991] 2 Lloyd's Rep. 251 at 257 (aff'd [1992] 2 Lloyd's Rep. 115).

those previous authorities are clearly wrong. Without such a principle the certainty and continuity of commercial law is lost and there is a risk of frustrating rather than giving effect to the intentions of the parties. Parties must be able to contract on the basis of established decisions about the words they are choosing to use to express their contractual intention."

And in *The Chikuma*,[154] Lord Bridge said:

"The ideal at which the courts should aim, in construing such clauses, is to produce a result such that in any given case both parties seeking legal advice as to their rights and obligations can expect the same clear and confident answer from their advisers and neither will be tempted to embark on long and expensive litigation in the belief that victory depends on winning the sympathy of the court. This ideal may never be fully attainable, but we shall certainly never even approximate to it unless we strive to follow clear and consistent principles and steadfastly refuse to be blown off course by the supposed merits of individual cases."

In *GSO Credit—A Partners LP v Barclays Bank Plc*,[155] Knowles J discussed the **4.68** principles applicable to the interpretation of standard terms, quoting in particular Lord Diplock in *Pioneer Shipping Ltd v BTP Tioxide Ltd (The Nema)*, and concluding that:

"Overall, the principles described above provide for an approach that seeks to respect the parties' choice, to understand the commercial context, and to provide certainty and consistency in matters of business."

The dividing line between a contract which is a standard form with amend- **4.69** ments and one which is not, may be difficult to define. Indeed in *The Nema* itself, the basis of the charterparty was a standard form, but it had been so heavily amended that it was categorised as a "one off" contract both by Lord Diplock and by Lord Roskill.

The desirability of promoting certainty in relation to commercial contracts goes **4.70** further than the mere application of the principle of stare decisis. The court should strive to achieve a common and stable approach to legal problems.[156] The importance of certainty is all the greater where the contract is made in the context of an international market. In *Walter Rau Neusser Oel und Fett AG v Cross Pacific Trading Ltd*,[157] Allsop J said:

"[S]tandard form contracts, including in particular standard forms [and] international terms and conditions of organisations ... using phrases that have had meanings given to them by commercial courts, should be interpreted, in the interests of international comity and international commercial certainty, in a consistent way, giving weight to those previous decisions. Of course, if the particular circumstances of the case or the other provisions of the contract point in a different direction, a different construction may obtain."

---

[154] [1981] 1 W.L.R. 314 HL.
[155] [2016] EWHC 146 (Comm); [2017] 1 All E.R. (Comm) 421.
[156] *AIG Europe (Ireland) Ltd v Faraday Capital Ltd* [2007] 1 All E.R. (Comm) 527.
[157] [2005] FCA 1102 at [45]. See also *Leonie's Travel Pty Ltd v Qantas Airways Ltd* (2010) 183 F.C.R. 246 at [58].

4.71   Where a decision is of long standing the court is unlikely to depart from it unless it is persuaded that the decision has been demonstrated to work unsatisfactorily in the market place and to produce manifestly unjust results.[158] However, the reluctance of the courts to overrule a long-standing decision is less when the decision in question is only a few years old and itself represents a deviation from orthodoxy,[159] or is one given at first instance only, even where it has stood for 25 years. Thus in *Re Spectrum Plus Ltd*,[160] Lord Hope of Craighead said:

> "It is a tribute to the great respect which Slade LJ's outstandingly careful judgments, both at first instance and the Court of Appeal, have always commanded that his decision in that case has remained unchallenged for so many years. But the fact is that it was a decision that was taken at first instance, and it has now been conclusively demonstrated that the construction which he placed on the debenture was wrong. This is not one of those cases where there are respectable arguments either way. With regret, the conclusion has to be that it is not possible to defend the decision on any rational basis. It is not enough to say that it has stood for more than 25 years. The fact is that, like any other first instance decision, it was always open to correction if the country's highest appellate court was persuaded that there was something wrong with it. Those who relied upon it must be taken to have been aware of this. It provided guidance, and no criticism can reasonably be levelled at those who felt that it was proper to rely on it. But it was no more immune from review by the ultimate appellate court than any other decision which has been taken at first instance."

Moreover, as Lord Scott said in *Golden Strait Corp v Nippon Usen Kubishka Kaisha*[161]:

> "Certainty is a desideratum and a very important one, particularly in commercial contracts. But it is not a principle and must give way to principle. Otherwise incoherence of principle is the likely result. The achievement of certainty in relation to commercial contracts depends, I would suggest, on firm and settled principles of the law of contract rather than on the tailoring of principle in order to frustrate tactics of delay to which many litigants in many areas of litigation are wont to resort."

4.72   A consistent approach to the interpretation of similar forms of contract does, however, have its costs. As Beatson LJ said in *Caresse Navigation Ltd v Zurich Assurances Maroc*[162]:

> "It is, however, not surprising in a commercial context, that where a settled construction has been given to a particular form of words, courts will recognise that other commercial parties are entitled to rely and act on it. If, however, a settled construction involves courts having to make fine distinctions between the particular form of words given the construction and very similar forms of words that cannot be explained by reference to differences in the ordinary meaning of

---

[158] *Jindal Iron and Steel Co Ltd v Islamic Solidarity Shipping Co Jordan Inc* [2005] 1 W.L.R. 1363.

[159] *Shell International Petroleum Co Ltd v Gibbs, The Salem* [1983] 2 A.C. 375.

[160] [2005] 2 A.C. 680, overruling *Siebe Gorman & Co Ltd v Barclays Bank Ltd* [1979] 2 Lloyd's Rep. 142.

[161] [2007] 2 Lloyd's Rep. 164.

[162] [2014] EWCA Civ 1366; [2015] 2 W.L.R. 43.

the two forms of words or the objectively ascertained intention of the parties, the certainty achieved may come at a cost. That cost arises because any deviation from the form that has been sanctified by the construction may lead to a different result which can be explained only in formal terms and not on the basis of any substantial linguistic difference or principle. While the consequent complexity may not, in itself, be objectionable, ultimately such differences may not be healthy for the coherence of the law and perceptions as to its fairness."

9.   STANDARD FORMS OF CONVEYANCING AGREEMENTS

Where the purpose of a particular clause in a conveyancing agreement can be discerned, the court will construe the clause so as to give effect to the underlying purpose and so as to assimilate it with the meaning given to other clauses of the same nature.

Conveyancing agreements are rarely made on standard printed forms.[163] Usually such agreements are the subject of lengthy negotiations between the parties' solicitors. However, particularly in a complicated transaction, the contract will often be based upon a precedent taken from a published work, and there are many such books available. To that extent, therefore, they are contracts in standard terms. Even where the words are not identical, the purpose of the varieties of clause is the same. This is particularly so in the case of rent review clauses.

4.73

For many years landlords granting long terms of years have insisted on the insertion in the lease of a rent review clause whereby the rent is periodically adjusted to reflect changes in the value of money and property. The most common method of revision is by requiring a valuer to assume a hypothetical letting of the premises in the open market on the terms of the actual lease but subject to various artificial assumptions. Many cases turned on the question of whether those assumptions required the valuer to assume a letting of the premises on terms which themselves contained no provision for revising the rent. These cases involved a meticulous analysis of the precise words in the lease.[164] However, in *British Gas Corp v Universities Superannuation Scheme Ltd*,[165] Sir Nicolas Browne-Wilkinson VC laid down the correct approach to such problems of construction. He said:

4.74

"I am conscious that such an approach is perilously close to seeking to lay down mechanistic rules of construction as opposed to principles of construction. But there is an urgent need for certainty in this field. Every year thousands of rents are coming up for review on the basis of clauses such as the one before me: witness the growing tide of litigation raising the point. Landlords, tenants and their valuers need to know what is the right basis of valuation without recourse to lawyers let alone to the courts. The question cannot be left to turn on the terms of each lease without the approach being certain."

---

[163] With the exception of executory contracts for the sale of land which are frequently governed by a set of standard terms (known as general conditions) which are supplemented or modified by the parties (by special conditions).

[164] For example, *Equity and Law Life Assurance Society Plc v Bodfield Ltd* [1985] 2 E.G.L.R. 144; *Datastream Ltd v Oakeep Ltd* [1986] 1 W.L.R. 404.

[165] [1986] 1 W.L.R. 398. These guidelines were "welcomed and approved" (but distinguished) by the Court of Appeal in *Equity and Law Life Assurance Plc v Bodfield Ltd* [1987] 1 E.G.L.R. 124. The same approach is manifested by the decision of the Court of Appeal in *Basingstoke and Deane District Council v The Host Group Ltd* [1988] 1 W.L.R. 348 (presumption of construction that the valuation is to be based on the actual rights and obligations of the parties).

4.75   It may be noted that both the Court of Appeal and the House of Lords in *United Scientific Holdings Ltd v Burnley Borough Council*[166] assimilated different forms of rent review clause in adopting a basic approach to the question whether time is of the essence of a timetable for rent review. However, despite the adoption of a broad approach and despite constant reminders that fine distinctions between clauses should not be drawn,[167] small differences in language produce widely different results.[168]

4.76   As in the case of commercial agreements, where previous cases have given a particular meaning to an expression used in conveyancing documents, the court will give effect to that meaning. As Jessel MR said in *Wallis v Smith*[169]:

"Of course if cases have laid down a rule that in certain events words are to have a particular meaning and that has become a settled rule, it may be assumed that persons in framing their agreements have had regard to settled law, and may have purposely used words which, though on the face of them they may have a different meaning, they know by reason of the decided cases must bear a particular or special meaning; and therefore we must consider whether there are cases which lay down any such rule making settled law in the sense of being binding on this court."

In *Simons v Associated Furnishers Ltd*,[170] Clauson J said:

"Such a form—or one so closely resembling it as to be practically indistinguishable—has been in common use for more than a century past. It has been before the court many times, and it would be dangerous to depart a hair's breadth from decisions upon it in former cases."

In *C&G Homes Ltd v Secretary of State for Health*,[171] Nourse LJ said:

"No less to be taken into account is that parties to a conveyancing transaction, having entered into a covenant in a long established and familiar form, must have intended that it should have the effect which earlier authorities have said that it has."

Similarly, in *Akici v LR Butlin Ltd*,[172] Neuberger LJ said:

"While interpretation of a word or phrase in a document must ultimately depend upon the documentary and factual circumstances in which it was agreed, it is desirable that the courts are as consistent as they properly can be when construing standard phrases in standard contexts."

4.77   In some cases the court will recognise that the drafter has adapted a standard form

---

[166] [1976] Ch. 128; [1978] A.C. 904.
[167] For example, *Trustees of Smith's (Henry) Charity v AWADA Trading and Promotion Services Ltd* (1983) 46 P. & C.R. 74, per Sir John Donaldson MR; *Mecca Leisure Ltd v Renown Investments (Holdings) Ltd* (1984) 49 P. & C.R. 12, per Browne-Wilkinson LJ (dissenting). The dissenting judgment of Browne-Wilkinson LJ was approved in *Starmark Enterprises Ltd v CPL Distribution Ltd* [2002] Ch. 306 CA.
[168] See *Touche Ross & Co v Secretary of State for the Environment* (1983) 46 P. & C.R. 187.
[169] (1882) 21 Ch. D. 243 at 254 CA.
[170] [1931] 1 Ch. 379.
[171] [1991] Ch. 365.
[172] [2006] 1 W.L.R. 201; *Linpac Mouldings Ltd v Aviva Life and Pensions UK Ltd* [2010] L. & T.R. 10.

of contract, and in such a case is prepared to adopt a liberal approach to construction. In *British Railways Board v Mobil Oil Co Ltd*,[173] a lease reserved a series of fixed stepped rents followed by a rent review clause. The rent review clause was to take effect by assessing the rise in rents since the commencement of the term or, "if" the rent had been previously increased, since the date of the last increase. The tenant argued that the last increase in rent was the last of the fixed rises. Hoffmann LJ said:

> "The only argument against [the tenant's] construction is that it gives no effect to the conditional word 'if' which precedes the words 'the rent payable hereunder shall previously have been increased'. This is because, given the stepped rents provided for in the reddendum, it was certain that the rent would have increased before any rent notice could be served. But this is easily accounted for. The rent review was a standard clause whereas the reddendum is custom made for this particular lease. This is the kind of ruck in the texture of a document which frequently happens when the draftsman inserts a one-off clause without checking through the rest of the document to see what effect it is going to have on other standard clauses. It is certainly not enough to justify implying words into the clause which will produce a commercially absurd result."

10. THE PRACTICE OF CONVEYANCERS

In construing a conveyancing document the court is often influenced by the practice of conveyancers. However, the practice of conveyancers cannot alter the meaning of a contract whose terms are clear.

Where conveyancers have consistently interpreted a form of words in a particular sense, or as having a particular legal effect, the court will be slow to depart from that practice. In *Burch v Farrows Bank Ltd*,[174] Neville J said: **4.78**

> "I have been referred to the practice of conveyancers and the meaning they attribute to words such as these, and in both the books of the distinguished authors to which I have been referred it has been laid down as deduced from the cases, and I think rightly deduced, that words such as these do create conditions precedent. That being the practice of conveyancers, it seems to me in the last degree undesirable to make minute distinctions between one form of expression and another when to my mind the intention of the parties is identical."

But where the contract is clear in its meaning, the court will give effect to that meaning, even if conveyancers habitually use a different form of words to achieve the same result. In *Estates Gazette Ltd v Benjamin Restaurants Ltd*,[175] Nourse LJ said: **4.79**

> "[Counsel] submitted that the court should take notice of the invariable practice of conveyancers, when drafting a licence containing a covenant intended to make the assignee liable throughout the term, to include words such as 'during the residue of the term'. He referred us to precedents in that form … While certainly

---

[173] [1994] 1 E.G.L.R. 146 CA.
[174] [1917] 1 Ch. 606, followed in *Trane (UK) Ltd v Provident Mutual Life Insurance* [1995] 1 E.G.L.R. 33.
[175] [1994] 1 W.L.R. 1528 CA.

accepting that it must be best practice to include the words suggested by [counsel], I doubt whether the sources he referred to were enough to establish an invariable practice to that effect. In any event I am unable to see how even an invariable practice to adopt a particular formula for a particular provision can affect the construction of a provision in another form whose effect is neither ambiguous nor doubtful."

Illustration

A conveyance contained a covenant by the purchaser to observe and perform encumbrances "so far as the same affect the Property". Precedent books showed that these words were used by conveyancers in a context which included positive as well as restrictive covenants. It was held that the words should be given that meaning in the conveyance.

TRW Steering Systems Ltd v North Cape Properties Ltd[176]

11. ONE-OFF CONTRACTS

The court discourages the citation of authority on the interpretation of a one-off contract, and will not usually be greatly assisted by it.

4.80　　The use of precedent as an aid to interpreting one-off contracts has been the subject of varying judicial responses. In *Ata Ul Haq v Nairobi City Council*,[177] Lord Morris of Borth-y-Gest delivering the opinion of the Privy Council said:

"Their Lordships consider that the decision in the present case must depend on the construction of its own particular contractual documents and though the opinions of courts on other words, in other contracts, in other cases is of assistance, the adjudication in this case involves thereafter a return to a study of the contract under review."

4.81　　The citation of authority was there considered to be "of assistance" albeit not decisive. This is a favourable response. However, in *Schuler (L) AG v Wickman Machine Tool Sales Ltd*,[178] Lord Morris of Borth-y-Gest adopted a different response. He said:

"If it is correct to say, as I think it is, that where there are problems of the construction of an agreement the intention of the parties to it may be collected from the terms of their agreement and from the subject matter to which it relates, then I doubt whether, save in so far as guidance on principle is found, it is of much value (although of much interest) to consider how courts have interpreted various differing words in various contracts. Nor is it of value to express either agreement or disagreement with the conclusions reached in particular cases."

This is assigning a more restrictive role to precedent. It is no longer said to be "of assistance" but is only of value in so far as guidance on principle may be found.

---

[176] (1993) 69 P. & C.R. 265 CA.
[177] (1962) 28 Build. L.R. 76 applied in *National Coal Board v Neill (William) & Son (St Helens) Ltd* [1985] Q.B. 300.
[178] [1974] A.C. 235.

In *Luxor (Eastbourne) Ltd v Cooper*,[179] Lord Wright expressed a similar view:

> "I deprecate in general the attempt to enunciate decisions on the construction of agreements as if they embodied rules of law. To some extent decisions on one contract may help by way of analogy and illustration in the decision of another contract. But however similar the contracts may appear, the decision as to each must depend on the consideration of the language of the particular contract, read in the light of the material circumstances of the parties in view of which the contract is made."

Here too, authority is accorded some value, if only by way of analogy and illustration. But a stronger warning was issued in *Foulger v Arding*,[180] in which the court construed a covenant in a lease to pay "impositions" charged on the premises. Collins MR said: **4.82**

> "It has often been my fortune, or perhaps misfortune, in the course of my professional experience to have to go through the series of cases on this subject up to date, but I do not propose to go through them again on the present occasion. It appears to me that a lamentable waste of judicial time and power is often involved in examining decisions with regard to the meaning of words which with one context are capable of one meaning and with another context of another meaning."

Lord Roskill in *Pioneer Shipping Ltd v BTP Tioxide Ltd*,[181] spoke to similar effect:

> "... on the first issue your Lordships were referred to a number of decisions on consecutive voyage charterparties. I do not propose to refer to them for each was a decision on the particular contract then in issue and decisions on one particular contract are of no assistance whatever in interpreting another and quite different contract and ought not to be cited for this purpose."

Perhaps the strongest deprecation of the citation of authority is to be found in the judgment of Jessel MR in *Aspden v Seddon*,[182] where he said: **4.83**

> "No judge objects more than I do to referring to authorities merely for the purpose of ascertaining the construction of a document; that is to say, I think it is the duty of a Judge to ascertain the construction of the instrument before him, and not to refer to the construction put by another judge upon an instrument, perhaps similar, but not the same. The only result of referring to authorities for that purpose is confusion and error, in this way, that if you look at a similar instrument, and say that a certain construction was put upon it, and that it differs only to such a slight degree from the document before you, that you do not think the difference sufficient to alter the construction, you miss the real point of the case, which is to ascertain the meaning of the instrument before you. It may be quite

---

[179] [1941] A.C. 108.
[180] [1902] 1 K.B. 700.
[181] [1982] A.C. 724.
[182] (1874) L.R. 10 Ch. App. 394 at 396n, approved by the Court of Appeal in *Equity & Law Life Assurance Plc v Bodfield Ltd* [1987] 1 E.G.L.R. 124. See also the opening observations of Dillon LJ in *Pagnan SpA v Tradax Ocean Transportation SA* [1987] 3 All E.R. 565 at 577; *Rees v Peters* [2011] EWCA Civ 836.

true that in your opinion the difference between the two instruments is not sufficient to alter the construction, but at the same time the Judge who decided on that other instrument may have thought that that very difference would be sufficient to alter the interpretation of that instrument. You have in fact no guide whatever; and the result especially in some cases of wills has been remarkable. There is, first document A, and a Judge formed an opinion as to its construction. Then came document B, and some other Judge has said that it differs very little from document A—not sufficiently to alter the construction—therefore he construes it in the same way. Then comes document C, and the Judge there compares it with document B, and says it differs very little, and therefore he shall construe it in the same way. And so the construction has gone on until we find a document which is in totally different terms from the first, and which no human being would think of construing in the same manner, but which has by this process come to be construed in the same manner."

In *Caterpillar (NI) Ltd v John Holt & Co (Liverpool) Ltd*,[183] Longmore LJ said:

"The judge declined to be beguiled into considering the numerous authorities that exist on retention of title clauses, no doubt because they were all considering clauses framed in different terms and the duty of the court is to construe the clause in the contract before it and not get bogged down into comparisons with other clauses construed in other cases ... I would, for my part, applaud such an approach."

Likewise, in *T&L Sugars Ltd v Tate & Lyle Industries Ltd*,[184] Flaux J said that:

"... in any given case, the court has to construe the particular contract before it, applying the principles of construction to that contract, not some other contract considered by another judge in another case."

4.84 In practice, however, most advocates do cite authority even on questions involving the construction of one-off contracts. Why? First, the citation of authority may establish a general principle of interpretation (or guideline) which is relevant to the particular type of contract under discussion.[185] As Lord Neuberger explained in *Cusack v London Borough of Harrow*[186]:

"... particularly in a system which accords as much importance to [precedent][187] as the common law, considerable help can often be gained from considering the approach and techniques devised or adopted by other judges when considering questions of interpretation. Even though such approaches and techniques cannot amount to rules, they not only assist lawyers and judges who are subsequently faced with interpretation issues, but they also ensure a degree of consistency of approach to such issues."

4.85 Secondly, as Lord Wright acknowledged in *Luxor (Eastbourne) Ltd v Cooper*,[188] authority can provide analogies and illustrations of particular arguments on

---

[183] [2013] EWCA Civ 1232; [2014] 1 All E.R. 785.
[184] [2014] EWHC 1066 (Comm).
[185] See *Jolley v Carmel Ltd* [2000] 3 E.G.L.R. 68 CA.
[186] [2013] UKSC 40; [2013] 1 W.L.R. 2022 (a case of statutory interpretation).
[187] The text reads "precedence" but this seems to be a typographical error.
[188] [1941] A.C. 108.

interpretation. Thus in *Enterprise Inns Plc v The Forest Hill Tavern Public House Ltd*,[189] Morritt C said:

"Plainly such a decision cannot be conclusive as to the interpretation of other contracts made at different times, between different parties and in different circumstances even though both are questions of law. But a decision on the interpretation of a contract may be persuasive as to the interpretation of another contract using similar language by parties involved in a similar trade and in similar circumstances, particularly where knowledge of the previous decision may be imputed to the parties."

In *AFFCO New Zealand Ltd v New Zealand Meat Workers and Related Trades Union Inc*,[190] the New Zealand Court of Appeal observed:

"Integration of relevant case law into the contractual context is a logical extension of the current emphasis on business common sense as a guide to interpretation. While decisions on disputes between certain parties cannot determine the interpretation of contracts made between other parties at a later date, the earlier decisions may well be persuasive where the provisions at issue in a later contract use similar language, in a similar trade and in similar circumstances. Earlier judicial authority and practice on the construction of similar contracts is relevant where the words used in a particular contract cannot properly be understood without reference to meanings ascribed to them in previous judgments."

For a judge at first instance, previous decisions may be of considerable value. In **4.86** *CSSA Chartering and Shipping Services SA v Mitsui OSK Lines Ltd*,[191] Popplewell J said:

"That process of interpretation is informed by the established case law, including that at first instance, because the standard charterparty forms and the adaptation of them have been developed in accordance with the well-established principles governing commonly used expressions and devices; and the parties may be taken to have contracted on the basis of those principles when adopting or adapting those forms, and when using those expressions and devices. The desiderata of certainty in commercial contracts and of giving effect to the parties' bargain dictate that when interpreting the particular charter in question the court should apply reported decisions on similar wording, including those at first instance unless there is good reason to depart from them."

This approach is not confined to first instance judges. When the appeal from Popplewell J reached the Court of Appeal,[192] Longmore LJ accepted that every charterparty must be construed on its own terms, but added:

"But in a business world (such as the shipping world) previous decisions on the same or similar clauses must be treated as authoritative in the interests of busi-

---

[189] [2010] EWHC 2368 (Ch).
[190] [2016] NZCA 482, referring to this section.
[191] [2017] EWHC 2579 (Comm); [2017] Bus. L.R. 2125; *Re Olympia Securities Commercial Plc* [2017] EWHC 2807 (Ch).
[192] *CSSA Chartering and Shipping Services SA v Mitsui OSK Lines Ltd* [2018] EWCA Civ 2413; [2020] Bus. L.R. 192.

ness certainty. Although phrases such as 'hallowed doctrine' … should perhaps best be avoided, previous cases on similar wording should be regarded as helpful guides in situations similar to situations that have arisen before."

4.87   So also in *Navigators Insurance Co Ltd v Atlasnavios-Navegacao Lda*,[193] Lord Mance said that certain clauses in a policy of marine insurance "must also be read in the context of established authority, particularly at the time when they were drafted and, on 1 October 1983, issued. … While the clauses were freshly drafted, they did not abandon, but sought to bring fresh order and clarity to, many of the time-honoured concepts used in the market. In the present context, prior authority on the concept of persons acting maliciously is therefore potentially relevant".

4.88   Thirdly, citation of authority can establish a climate of judicial opinion which may be of assistance in persuading the particular tribunal. Fourthly, in a case where the tribunal may not be altogether familiar with the intricacies of the subject matter of the contract, the citation of authority may provide an authoritative conspectus of the way in which such contracts work in practice. Fifthly, there is a trend in current judicial thinking which actively promotes the assimilation of different forms of words, so that legal results flow from the type of contract under discussion, rather than from the particular words.[194] And lastly, it must be recognised that some tribunals are influenced by the thought process which Sir George Jessel derided.[195]

4.89   There is nevertheless a difference of approach in the attitude of the higher courts towards the interpretation of contracts made on standard terms and those which are one-off. In the former case high emphasis is (rightly) placed on the value of certainty, and consequently it follows that authorities on earlier contracts using those standard terms may assist the court in resolving the particular dispute which has arisen. In the latter case, however, a lower value is placed on producing broadly similar results in broadly similar cases; instead emphasis is laid on the particularity of the bargain which the parties have made. In a sense this is an artificial distinction, for even a one-off contract may itself have been influenced by the parties' experience and expectations of contracts made on standard terms. The problem is all the more real where the contract is based upon a precedent in standard form, but then altered by the parties.

4.90   An appeal court is less constrained, at all events where the body of case law

---

[193] [2018] UKSC 26; [2018] 2 W.L.R. 1671.

[194] For example, *Linpac Mouldings Ltd v Aviva Life and Pensions UK Ltd* [2010] L. & T.R. 10.

[195] A much more receptive approach to the citation of authority was displayed by May LJ in *Ashville Investments Ltd v Elmer Contractors Ltd* [1989] 1 Q.B. 488, in which the Court of Appeal considered an arbitration clause in the JCT form. Authority was cited involving arbitration clauses in different forms. May LJ said:

"However, I do not think that there is any principle of law to the effect that the meaning of certain specific words in one arbitration clause is immutable and that the same specific words in another arbitration clause in other circumstances in another contract must be construed in the same way. This is not to say that the earlier decision on a given form of words will not be persuasive to a degree dependent on the extent of the similarity between the contracts and the surrounding circumstances in the two cases. In the interests of certainty and clarity a court may well think it right to construe words in an arbitration agreement, or indeed in a particular type of contract, in the same way as those words have been construed in another case involving an arbitration clause by another court. But in my opinion the subsequent court is not bound by the doctrine of stare decisis to do so."

In addition, in *BCCI v Ali* [2002] 1 A.C. 251, the House of Lords was heavily influenced (some might say too much influenced) by authority in interpreting the scope of a release from liability.

consists of first instance decisions. In *Allianz Insurance Plc v Tonicstar Ltd*,[196] Leggatt LJ said:

"… where the meaning of a clause in a standard form of agreement has been interpreted by a court, later courts may think it right to adhere to the interpretation previously adopted even if, had they been deciding the question for the first time, they would have taken a different view. There are two reasons for this. One is that the earlier decision may form part of the relevant background against which the parties have contracted. … A second, related reason for adhering to an established interpretation is the value of certainty in commercial law."

He added:

"In any case, while certainty is an important value in commerce, so too is the ability of the legal system to correct error, and contracting parties may be taken to know that a decision of a court of first instance is not immutable and is capable of being overruled. The value of certainty is greatest where the members of a trade can be expected to rely on the determination of a point which is otherwise unclear. Such cases epitomise Lord Mansfield's famous dictum that 'it is of more consequence that a rule should be certain than whether the rule be established one way or the other; because speculators in trade then know which ground to go upon': *Vallejo v Wheeler*.[197] But if a decision is not one on which significant reliance is likely to be placed or if the consequences of such reliance are unlikely to be significant, the importance of certainty is diminished. And if a decision is untenable, it should not in any case be allowed to stand."

---

[196] [2018] EWCA Civ 434; [2018] 1 Lloyd's Rep. 389.
[197] 98 E.R. 1012; (1774) 1 Cowp. 143, 153.

CHAPTER 5

THE MEANING OF WORDS

*The tacit conventions on which the understanding of everyday language depends
are enormously complicated.*

Ludwig Wittgenstein: *Tractatus Logico-Philosophicus*

1. THE STARTING POINT

**The words of a contract should be interpreted in their natural and ordinary
sense in context, unless there is good reason to adopt a different meaning.**

In *Tophams Ltd v Earl of Sefton*,[1] Lord Upjohn said: **5.01**

"The words which the parties have used in the conveyance, being ordinary words
of the English language, must be construed in their ordinary and natural meaning unless the context otherwise requires."

Even after *Investors Compensation Scheme v West Bromwich Building Society*,[2]   **5.02**
it remains the case that "the primary source for understanding what the parties
meant is their language interpreted in accordance with conventional usage".[3] The
court "reads the terms of the contract as a whole, giving the words used their natural
and ordinary meaning in the context of the agreement, the parties' relationship and
all the relevant facts surrounding the transaction so far as known to the parties".[4]
In *Arnold v Britton*,[5] Lord Neuberger referred to "the natural and ordinary meaning of the clause"; and considered that there had to be good reason (such as lack
of clarity or poor drafting) to depart from that meaning. In *Bardardo's v Buckinghamshire*,[6] considerable importance was given to "the word order and grammatical construction" of the disputed phrase. In *Lambeth LBC v Secretary of State for*

---

[1]   [1967] A.C. 50 at 73; *The Olympic Brilliance* [1982] 2 Lloyd's Rep. 205 CA; *African Minerals Ltd
v Renaissance Capital Ltd* [2015] EWCA Civ 448.
[2]   [1998] 1 W.L.R. 896. The expression "conventional usage" is preferred by linguists to the more
traditional expressions "ordinary meaning" or "natural meaning". For practical purposes, there is little difference between them.
[3]   *BCCI v Ali* [2002] 1 A.C. 251, per Lord Hoffmann. See also *GE Frankona Reinsurance Ltd v CMM
Trust No.1400* [2006] 1 All E.R. (Comm) 665; *Golden Fleece Maritime Inc v St Shipping and
Transport Inc* [2007] EWHC 1890 (Comm):

"The primary source for understanding what the parties meant by the language which they
employed is that language, interpreted in accordance with conventional usage, but without excessive literalism" per Cooke J.

[4]   *BCCI v Ali* [2002] 1 A.C. 251, per Lord Bingham of Cornhill.
[5]   [2015] UKSC 36; [2015] A.C. 1619.
[6]   [2018] UKSC 55; [2019] I.C.R. 495.

Communities and Local Government,[7] Lord Carnwath said:

"In summary, whatever the legal character of the document in question, the starting point—and usually the end point—is to find 'the natural and ordinary meaning' of the words there used, viewed in their particular context (statutory or otherwise) and in the light of common sense."

5.03   In *Jumbo King Ltd v Faithful Properties Ltd*,[8] Lord Hoffmann said:

"If the ordinary meaning of the words makes sense in relation to the rest of the document and the factual background, then the court will give effect to that language, even though the consequences may appear hard for one side or the other. The court is not privy to the negotiation of the agreement—evidence of such negotiations is inadmissible—and has no way of knowing whether a clause which appears to have an onerous effect was a quid pro quo for some other concession. Or one of the parties may simply have made a bad bargain."

5.04   In *Warborough Investments Ltd v Lunar Office SARL*,[9] Patten LJ said:

"… it is normally safe to assume that the parties intended to give the words they chose their natural meaning. In particular, there is a danger in approaching the construction of the document with pre-conceived ideas about what the parties, acting commercially, are likely to have intended and to allow those ideas to subvert the clear language of the document."

In *Pratt v Aigaion Insurance Co SA*,[10] Sir Anthony Clarke MR said:

"As Lord Hoffmann expressly noted in *BCCI v Ali*, none of this is to say that the language is not important. As Lord Mustill put it in *Charter Reinsurance v Fagan*[11]:

'Subject to [the use of a specialist vocabulary] the inquiry will start, and usually finish, by asking what is the ordinary meaning of the words used.'"

Similarly, in *Martin v David Wilson Homes Ltd*,[12] Buxton LJ said:

"One has to remember, when looking at issues about the factual matrix, that although reference to that matrix is not limited to cases where the words are clearly ambiguous, the first place where one expects to find the meaning of the words and the intention of the draftsmen is in the words themselves. If they yield a fairly clear conclusion, and in my judgment these words do, then one has to pause long before concluding that at that point the draftsmen has used words with a meaning that do not fit in with the objective that he was seeking to attain".

---

[7]   [2019] UKSC 33; [2019] 1 W.L.R. 4317; *Atos IT Services UK Ltd v Atos Pension Schemes Ltd* [2020] EWHC 145 (Ch).

[8]   (1999) H.K.C.F.A.R. 279, cited with approval by the CA in *Holding & Barnes Plc v Hill House Hammond Ltd* [2002] L. & T.R. 7.

[9]   [2018] EWCA Civ 427; [2018] 2 P. & C.R. 5.

[10] [2009] 1 Lloyd's Rep. 225.

[11] [1997] A.C. 313 at 384C–D.

[12] [2004] 3 E.G.L.R. 77.

As Patten J put it in *Ellse v Hill-Pickford*[13]:

"[T]he starting point is necessarily the words which they actually used and the natural and ordinary meaning of those words. It remains a reasonable (but not a necessary) assumption that the parties did adopt the usual rules of grammar and dictionary meanings. As Lord Hoffmann said in the *ICS* case, one does not easily assume that the lawyers or others who drafted the document made a linguistic mistake. The document (looked at in its proper factual context) may however indicate that a mistake was made or that a departure from the dictionary or grammar book was intended and that the parties did in fact intend the words to bear a special or unusual meaning."

Similarly, in *Franklins Pty Ltd v Metcash Trading Ltd*,[14] Giles JA said:　**5.05**

"Words are ordinarily used in a conventional and grammatical way, and a formal written contract prepared over a period, with drafts exchanged, referred for instructions and varied as in the present case, has considerable claim to adherence to the ordinary grammatical meaning. It comes down to a determination in each case whether the words are to be understood otherwise in the light of the context and purpose revealed by the admissible evidence, including whether they are intractable and do not admit of departure from the conventional and grammatical use."

Likewise, in *Chartbrook Ltd v Persimmon Homes Ltd*,[15] Lord Hoffman said:

"It is of course true that the fact that a contract may appear to be unduly favourable to one of the parties is not a sufficient reason for supposing that it does not mean what it says. The reasonable addressee of the instrument has not been privy to the negotiations and cannot tell whether a provision favourable to one side was not in exchange for some concession elsewhere or simply a bad bargain."

Accordingly, the court should be very slow to reject the natural meaning of a　**5.06** provision simply because it appears to have been a very imprudent term for one of the parties to have agreed.[16] In *First National Trustco (UK) Ltd v McQuitty*,[17] Peter Jackson LJ said:

"When construing a document the court must determine objectively what the parties to the document meant at the time they made it. What they meant will generally appear from what they said, particularly if they said it after a careful process. The court will not look for reasons to depart from the apparently clear meaning of the words they used, but elements of the wider documentary, factual and com-

---

[13] [2006] EWHC 2093 (Ch); *Best Beat Ltd v Mourant & Co Trustees Ltd* [2008] EWHC 3156 (Ch).
[14] [2009] NSWCA 407.
[15] [2009] 1 A.C. 1101; *Anthracite Rated Investments (Jersey) Ltd v Lehman Brothers Finance SA* [2011] EWHC 1822 (Ch). In his article "Language and Lawyers" (2018) L.Q.R. 553, Lord Hoffmann wrote that "we should not depart from the conventional meaning of the language of a contract merely because, either at the time or in the light of the events which have happened, that would have been more fair or reasonable. No one has ever supported such a rule. We must give effect to what they appear to have used the language to mean, whether that would have been fair and reasonable or not. We must take into account that legal documents are drawn up by people who can be expected to have chosen their words with care and not to have left things out."
[16] *Arnold v Britton* [2015] UKSC 36; [2015] 2 W.L.R. 1593.
[17] [2020] EWCA Civ 107.

mercial context will be taken into account to the extent that they assist in the search for meaning. That wider survey may lead to a construction that departs from even the clearest wording if the wording does not reflect the objectively ascertained intention of the parties."

This has been the approach of English law for over 150 years. In *Grey v Pearson*,[18] Lord Wensleydale said:

"In construing all written instruments, the grammatical and ordinary sense of the words is to be adhered to, unless that would lead to some absurdity, or some repugnance or inconsistence with the rest of the instrument, in which case the grammatical and ordinary sense of the words may be modified, so as to avoid that absurdity and inconsistency, but no further."

This is what he used to call "the golden rule".[19] It deals with two different aspects of language used in written documents, namely the words themselves, and the grammatical sense in which those words are used. In the context of modern contract interpretation, this overstates the principle, because it is not necessary to go as far as to find "absurdity, inconsistency or repugnancy" before adopting some other interpretation.[20]

5.07   Thus in *L Batley Pet Products Ltd v North Lanarkshire Council*,[21] Lord Hodge said that:

"The starting point is the words the parties have chosen to use."

As Cooke J put it in *The Captain Stefanos*[22]:

"The initial search must be for the ordinary and natural, or conventional, meaning of the language used, in the context of the agreement, the parties' relationship, and all the relevant facts surrounding the transaction, so far as known to the parties. The primary source for understanding what the parties meant is the language used by them in the Charterparty, interpreted in accordance with conventional usage. Regard must be had to the particular words used and the grammatical structure and syntax of the clause in question."

In *Lehman Brothers International (Europe) v Lehman Brothers Finance SA*,[23] Arden LJ said:

"In my judgment, it is well established that, until the contrary is shown, the court should proceed on the basis that ordinary English words are used in their ordinary

18 (1857) 6 H.L. Cas. 61 at 106; *Watson v Phipps* (1985) 60 A.J.L.R. 1.
19 *Caledonian Railway Co v North British Railway Co* (1881) 6 App. Cas. 114 at 131, per Lord Blackburn.
20 In *Entrust Pension Ltd v Prospect Hospice Ltd* [2012] EWHC 1666 (Ch), Henderson J questioned whether the principle stated in this section has any continued application in the light of the decision of the Supreme Court in *Rainy Sky SA v Kookmin Bank* [2011] UKSC 50; [2011] 1 W.L.R. 2900 that the interpretation of a contract is a single unitary exercise.
21 [2014] UKSC 27; [2014] Bus. L.R. 615.
22 [2012] EWHC 571 (Comm); [2012] 2 Lloyd's Rep. 46.
23 [2013] EWCA Civ 188. See also *British Telecommunications Ltd v Rail Safety and Standards Board Ltd* [2012] EWCA Civ 553; [2012] L. & T.R. 35; *Anthracite Rated Investments (Jersey) Ltd v Lehman Brothers Finance SA* [2011] EWHC 1822 (Ch); [2011] 2 Lloyd's Rep. 538.

meaning. I will call this the 'ordinary meaning' principle. If the term is a technical one, then this precept does not of course apply."

Likewise, in *West v Ian Finlay & Associates (a firm)*,[24] Vos LJ said:

"The first consideration in any construction exercise is to consider the normal meaning of the words."

So too in *Amlin Corporate Member Ltd v Oriental Assurance Corp*,[25] Gloster LJ said:

"In accordance with well-established principles of construction, the typhoon warranty should be construed having regard to the language actually chosen by the parties and giving those words their ordinary natural meaning, unless the background indicates that such meaning was not the intended meaning."

Deficiencies in drafting should not lead the court to depart from the natural meaning of the words used.[26] If one has to choose between giving a phrase little meaning or an un-natural meaning, then, in the absence of a good reason to the contrary, the former option is preferable.[27]   **5.08**

Where a contract has been professionally drafted, there is less room for departure from a textual analysis. As Hamblen LJ explained in *National Bank of Kazakhstan v The Bank of New York Mellon SA/NV, London Branch*[28]:   **5.09**

"In the present case, the [contract] is a carefully drafted and formal contract, drawn up with the assistance of lawyers and concluded between sophisticated parties. There is no suggestion that anything has gone wrong in the drafting process. Nor is there any patent ambiguity in the terms used in clause 16(i). In accordance with the guidance provided in *Wood*, it is the type of agreement in relation to which textual analysis will be of particular importance."

This principle is all the more important where the contract in question is one which is not tailored to a particular factual situation. In *Napier Park European Credit Opportunities Fund Ltd v Harbourmaster Pro-Rata Clo 2 BV*,[29] Etherton C distinguished two types of instrument. He said:

"The principles for the interpretation of a contract are the same whether the document relates to a single commercial venture, in which the contracting parties will remain the same throughout, or the document is intended to confer rights and obligations which it is contemplated may pass to persons other than the original contracting parties, such as title documents to property or, as in the present case, tradable financial instruments. In the case of the second category, however, it is reasonable to assume that the parties will have been particularly conscious of the

---

[24] [2014] EWCA Civ 316.

[25] [2014] EWCA Civ 1135.

[26] *@SIPP (Pension Trustees) Ltd v Insight Travel Services Ltd* [2015] Scot CS CSIH 91; [2016] 1 P. & C.R. 17; *Barnardo's v Buckinghamshire* [2016] EWCA Civ 1064.

[27] *Re Lehman Bros International (Europe) (in administration) (No .4)* [2017] UKSC 38; [2018] A.C. 465 at [67].

[28] [2018] EWCA Civ 1390.

[29] [2014] EWHC 1083 (Ch). This statement of principle is unaffected by the reversal of the decision itself: [2014] EWCA Civ 984.

need for clarity and certainty in the language they have used. It is for that reason that the court should be particularly cautious about departing from the ordinary and natural meaning of the words in documents of that kind."

5.10   This chapter is concerned with the meaning of words. Easy as it is to state, the golden rule may not be of very much assistance in practice. As Lord Blackburn pointed out[30]:

"Unfortunately in the cases in which there is real difficulty it does not help us much, because the cases in which there is real difficulty are those in which there is a controversy as to what the grammatical and ordinary sense of the words, used with reference to the subject matter, is."

5.11   The first question which must be addressed is, therefore: for the purpose of interpreting a contract, what is the ordinary meaning of a word?[31]

The question itself is not without artificiality, because it assumes that there is only one correct meaning to be attributed to the words in question. As Diplock LJ explained in *Slim v Daily Telegraph Ltd*[32]:

"Everyone outside a court of law recognises that words are imprecise instruments for communicating the thoughts of one man to another. The same words may be understood by one man in a different meaning from that in which they are understood by another and both meanings may be different from that which the author of the words intended to convey; but the notion that the same words should bear different meanings to different men, and that more than one meaning should be 'right' conflicts with the whole training of a lawyer. Words are the tools of his trade. He uses them to define legal rights and duties. They do not achieve that purpose unless there can be attributed to them a single meaning as a 'right' meaning. And so the argument between lawyers starts with the unexpressed major premise that any particular combination of words has one meaning, which is not necessarily the same as that intended by him who published them or understood by any of those who read them, but is capable of ascertainment as being the 'right' meaning by the adjudicator to whom the law confides the responsibility of determining it."

5.12   This principle is of great importance in achieving certainty. As Kirby J put it in *Agricultural and Rural Finance Pty Ltd v Gardiner*[33]:

"Courts, however, do no service to such parties by adopting atextual meanings of words of strictness such as 'punctually'. Such interpretations simply encourage the kind of litigation that has occurred in the present case.

Increasing numbers of contractual agreements today involve international parties that use the English language to express their bargains. They often provide for the resolution of their disputes in courts or by arbitration which will apply the

---

[30] See *Caledonian Railway Co v Northern British Railway Co* (1881) 6 App. Cas. 114 at 131.

[31] Many linguists would also dispute the idea that there is an "ordinary" or "natural" meaning of a word, or even of a sentence. The essence of the argument is that words on their own do not refer to anything. It is people who use words to refer to things. There is thus a distinction between "word meaning" and "speaker meaning".

[32] [1968] 2 Q.B. 157 CA (a libel case).

[33] [2008] HCA 57. See also Kirby J's observations in *B & B Constructions (Australia) Pty Ltd v Brian A Cheeseman & Associates Pty Ltd* (1994) 35 N.S.W.L.R. 227.

foregoing principles. Adopting atypical meanings of words such as 'punctually' tends to defeat the expectation of such parties. It diminishes their capacity to agree in advance on their respective legal obligations and entitlements. It erodes confidence in the capacity of the law to uphold the bargains, upon which the parties have agreed, according to their terms."

In *BP Exploration Operating Co Ltd v Kvaerner Oilfield Products Ltd*,[34] Colman J's summary of principle included the following:

"The whole basis of contractual certainty is the words actually used in their ordinary meaning. It is thus ordinarily to be inferred that the parties mutually intended the contract to have that ordinary meaning ... English commercial law does not permit any other inference to be drawn unless on the evidence before it there are cogent grounds for concluding that although the ordinary meaning can be identified as X, the parties could only have mutually intended Y. ... Departure from the ordinary meaning cannot normally be justified merely because another construction would have produced a result more reasonable in commercial terms for both parties ... The exercise in construction which is called for is to identify the meaning which it is inferred that the parties mutually intended. In a case where, to use Lord Diplock's words,[35] the ordinary meaning of the words used 'flouts business common sense' the inference that such meaning was mutually intended is displaced because experienced commercial contractors do not intentionally make such bargains. But, flouting business common sense is not a comprehensive test to justify departure from the inference. Lord Hoffman's approach by reference to the conclusion that 'something must have gone wrong with the language' presents itself to me as a somewhat more useful approach."

In *Thompson v Goblin Hill Hotels Ltd*,[36] Lord Dyson, giving the advice of the Privy Council, said of articles of association and a clause in a lease:

"In the opinion of the Board, the plain and ordinary meaning of the words used in article 91(1) and clause 5(b) can only be displaced if it produces a commercial absurdity."[37]

However, as Leggatt J pointed out in *Zhoushan Jinhaiwan Shipyard Co Ltd v Golden Exquisite Inc*[38]:　　　　　　　　　　　　　　　　　　　　　　　　**5.13**

"In order to ascertain the meaning of the words used by the parties to record their bargain, a judge or arbitrator must bring to bear both their understanding of how words are commonly used and their understanding of the purposes which someone using the words in the relevant context could be expected to have. Where the document to be interpreted is a contract, the assumption made is that the parties to the contract chose its language to express an intention which they shared. The assumption is also made that the parties were reasonable people with

---

[34] [2005] 1 Lloyd's Rep. 307 at 321.
[35] In *Antaios Cia Naviera SA v Salen Rederierna AB* [1985] A.C. 191.
[36] [2011] UKPC 8.
[37] In New Zealand, the Court of Appeal has held that there is no presumption in favour of the ordinary meaning of words: *Trustees Executors Ltd v QBE Insurance (International) Ltd* [2010] NZCA 608; *Technix Group Ltd v Fitzroy Engineering Group Ltd* [2011] NZCA 17.
[38] [2014] EWHC 4050 (Comm); [2015] 1 Lloyd's Rep. 283.

the purposes and values which reasonable parties in their situation who had a shared intention may fairly be supposed to have had ...

Identifying the meaning of the words used, however, and the shared purposes and values which the parties may be taken to have had are not two separate inquiries. The meaning of all language depends on its context. To paraphrase a philosopher of language,[39] a sentence is never not in a context. Contracting parties are never not in a situation. A contract is never not read in the light of some purpose. Interpretive assumptions are always in force. A sentence that seems to need no interpretation is already the product of one. At the same time the main source from which the shared purposes and values of the parties can be ascertained is the contract they have made. It is for these reasons that it is a fundamental principle of the interpretation of contracts that the contractual document must be read as a whole."

Illustrations

1. Clause 7.6.3 of a contract provided that for the avoidance of doubt compensation would not be payable where "the death, accidental injury or illness resulted from amongst other things, the Officer's wilful act, default or misconduct". Teare J held that this included suicide. He said:

"In my judgment it is difficult to envisage a clearer example of a wilful act than suicide. The act is deliberate and the consequences are intended. Although suicide could have been made an express exception the fact that the draftsman did not do so does not, in my judgment, require clause 7.6.3 to be given anything other than its natural meaning."

Braganza v BP Shipping Ltd[40]

2. An engineering contract provided for payment by reference to costs. The costs excluded those due to default by the contractor in carrying out its obligations. It was held that "default" bore its ordinary meaning of any failure by the contractor to comply with its obligations under the contract.

Network Rail Infrastructure Ltd v ABC Electrification Ltd[41]

3. A trust deed relating to a time share complex provided for an indemnity to be given to the trustee for liabilities incurred in performance of its duties. The indemnity did not extend to a tax liability imposed on its subsidiary which was the operator of the complex.

First National Trustco (UK) Ltd v McQuitty[42]

2. THE ORDINARY MEANING OF WORDS

The ordinary meaning of a word is its meaning in its plain, ordinary and popular sense, although that sense may be a sense among a particular group of persons.

---

[39] Stanley Fish, *Is there a Text in this Class?*
[40] [2012] EWHC 1423 (Comm); [2013] 2 Lloyd's Rep. 351. This question of interpretation did not arise on appeal: [2013] EWCA Civ 230; [2013] I.C.R. D18; [2015] UKSC 17; [2015] I.C.R. 449.
[41] [2019] EWHC 1769 (TCC); [2019] B.L.R. 522.
[42] [2020] EWCA Civ 107.

As Lord Hoffmann said in *Investors Compensation Scheme v West Bromwich*   **5.14**
Building Society[43]:

> "The 'rule' that words should be given their 'natural and ordinary meaning' reflects the commonsense proposition that we do not easily accept that people have made linguistic mistakes, particularly in formal documents."

In *Chartbrook Ltd v Persimmon Homes Ltd*,[44] Lord Hoffmann re-emphasised that:

> "we do not easily accept that people have made linguistic mistakes, particularly in formal documents."

In *Cosmos Holidays Plc v Dhanjal Investments Ltd*,[45] Sir Anthony Clarke MR said:

> "As Lord Hoffman noted ... the primary source for understanding what the parties meant is their language interpreted in accordance with conventional usage. Of course, the particular provision must be construed in the context of the clause as a whole, and the clause itself must be construed in the context of the contract as a whole, which must in turn be considered in its factual matrix or against the circumstances surrounding it."

Nearly 200 years earlier Lord Ellenborough CJ had expressed the principle thus[46]:   **5.15**

> "It [namely, a written instrument] is to be construed according to its sense and meaning as collected in the first place from the terms used in it, which terms are themselves to be understood in their plain ordinary and popular sense, unless they have generally in respect to the subject matter, as by the known usage of a trade, or the like, acquired a peculiar sense of the same words; or unless the context evidently points out that they must in the particular instance, and in order to effectuate the intention of the parties to that contract, be understood in some other special and peculiar sense."

The application of this principle often means that the popular sense of a word   **5.16**
prevails over the scientific sense of the same word, unless the court is persuaded
by evidence that the parties intended the latter meaning. Thus in *Stanley v Western
Insurance Co*,[47] Kelly CB said of an insurance policy:

> "The words of the policy are to be construed not according to their strictly philosophical or scientific meaning, but in their ordinary and popular sense."

---

43 [1998] 1 W.L.R. 896.
44 [2009] A.C. 1109.
45 [2009] EWCA Civ 316.
46 *Robertson v French* (1803) 4 East. 130 at 135.
47 (1868) L.R. 3 Exch. 71 (construing the word "gas" in an insurance policy); *Hart v Standard Marine Insurance Co Ltd* (1889) 22 Q.B.D. 499 (construing the word "iron" in a marine insurance policy); *Clark v Adie (No.2)* (1877) 2 App. Cas. 423 (construing the word "parallel" in a patent specification); *Yorke v Yorkshire Insurance Co Ltd* [1918] 1 K.B. 662 (in an insurance policy "the words 'sober and temperate' must receive such an interpretation as would be placed upon them by ordinary men of normal intelligence and average knowledge of the world").

5.17   In *Reilly v National Insurance & Guarantee Corporation Ltd*,[48] Moore-Bick LJ referred to "a presumption that the words in question should be construed in their ordinary and popular sense". Likewise, in *Harlow v Artemis International Corp Ltd*,[49] McCombe J said that employment contracts "are designed to be read in an informal and common sense manner in the context of a relationship affecting ordinary people in their everyday lives".

In *Dino Services Ltd v Prudential Assurance Co Ltd*,[50] Kerr LJ said of the word "violent" in an insurance policy:

> "The word 'violent' is an ordinary English word, which here appears in a common commercial document. It seems to me that there is no reason why its meaning should be in any way different from what any ordinary person would understand. At first sight I therefore conclude that there should be no need to resort either to a dictionary, or to authorities, to interpret this word; nor to the rule that, this being an insurers' document, it must be construed against them."

Similarly, in *Yorke v Yorkshire Insurance Co Ltd*,[51] speaking of a phrase in an insurance policy, McCardie J said:

> "I think that the words 'sober and temperate' must receive such an interpretation as would be placed upon them by ordinary men of normal intelligence and average knowledge of the world."

5.18   Thus judges frequently express themselves as having decided the meaning of a word using their knowledge as an "ordinary speaker of English".[52] In *Tophams Ltd v Earl of Sefton*,[53] however, Lord Upjohn referred to the meaning of a word:

> "used between laymen bent on serious business or other affairs intended to have legal consequences."

It is doubtful whether this formulation was intended to be more restrictive than the meaning of a word as used by an ordinary speaker of English.

5.19   In *Brisbane City Council v Attorney-General for Queensland*,[54] Lord Wilberforce said:

> "Showground is a word of normal parlance; not a term of art requiring interpreta-

---

[48] [2009] 1 All E.R. (Comm) 1166.

[49] [2008] I.R.L.R. 629.

[50] [1989] 1 Lloyd's Rep. 379 CA.

[51] [1918] 1 K.B. 662.

[52] For example, *Barnett v National Parcels Insurance Co Ltd* [1942] 1 All E.R. 221, per Atkinson J: "As there is no evidence as to how the general public understand the word 'garage', I suppose one is entitled to use one's own knowledge."; *Young v Sun Alliance and London Assurance Ltd* [1976] 1 W.L.R. 104, per Cairns LJ: "giving oneself for the moment the credit of assuming that one is an ordinary Englishman"; *Post Office v Aquarius Properties Ltd* [1985] 2 E.G.L.R. 105, per Hoffmann J: cases on the meaning of "repair" illustrate contexts in which "judges, as ordinary speakers of English" have decided that work was or was not within a covenant to repair; *Commonwealth Smelting Ltd v Guardian Royal Exchange Ltd* [1986] 1 Lloyd's Rep. 121. It may, perhaps, be thought to be unduly modest for such highly trained and experienced lawyers and former advocates to describe themselves as "ordinary" speakers of English, especially when it has been judicially observed that "judges are philologists of the highest order": *Ex p. Davis* (1857) 5 W.R. 522 at 523, per Pollock CB.

[53] [1967] A.C. 50 at 75.

[54] [1979] A.C. 411 at 423 PC.

tion with expert assistance. It is a word to be interpreted by the judge, using his knowledge of the language, and his acquaintance with accepted applications of the word to situations arising in the normal life of the community in which he lives. Judicial knowledge is the knowledge of the ordinary wide-awake man, used by one who is trained to express it in terms of precision."

However, the popular sense of a word is not necessarily the meaning it has among the public at large. Its meaning may be restricted to its popular sense among persons of a particular class or occupation, even without going so far as to prove a trade custom. In *SS Garston Co v Hickie*,[55] the Court of Appeal considered the meaning of the word "port" in a charterparty. Brett MR said:

    5.20

"My Brother Wills has taken exception to the language used by other judges. He does not like their use of the words 'popular' and 'commercial' when they say that the word 'port' is to be understood in its 'popular' sense, or its 'commercial' sense. I dare say those words are not the best possible words. ... But they are not the only words which have been used for the purpose. Some judges have said 'in the business sense of the word,' 'in the ordinary sense,' 'in the common and ordinary sense.' All these phrases mean the same thing. ... [W]hen you are trying to define the port with regards to which persons who enter into a charterparty are contracting, you endeavour to find words which will shut out those things which you know they did not intend. What do they intend? They intend the port as commonly understood by all persons who are using it as a port, i.e. for sailing to or from it with goods and merchandise. What persons are they? Shippers of goods, charterers of vessels, and shipowners. What do all those persons in their ordinary language mean by a 'port'? What they understand by the word is the port in its ordinary sense, in its business sense, in its popular sense—i.e. the popular sense of such persons. It is also the port in its commercial sense, for, with them, business means commercial business."

In *Crema v Cenkos Securities Plc*,[56] the Court of Appeal held that expert evidence was admissible to explain the "shorthand" of a particular market even though it fell short of a trade custom. Expert evidence is also admissible to explain market practice "if that is relevant background knowledge for the purposes of interpreting the terms of the contract, both explicit and implicit". In *Ted Baker Plc v Axa Insurance UK Plc*,[57] Eder J accepted the submission that:

    5.21

"the courts have moved away from the strict principles previously adhered to in respect of the relevance of custom and practice[58]; that the court is entitled to hear evidence of market practice falling short of trade usage or custom in order to as-

---

[55] (1885) 15 Q.B.D. 580. See also *Hart v Standard Marine Insurance Co Ltd* (1889) 22 Q.B.D. 499: "words are not to be construed in the sense in which they would be used amongst men of science, but as they would be used in mercantile transactions": at 500, per Lord Esher MR construing the word "iron" in a marine insurance policy. Fry LJ reached the same conclusion by asking what the words meant "as they are used in the English language by ordinary persons".

[56] [2011] Bus. L.R. 943.

[57] [2012] EWHC 1406 (Comm). In *Eitzen Bulk A/S v TTMI Sarl* [2012] EWHC 202 (Comm); [2012] 2 All E.R. (Comm) 100, Eder J had earlier said that that evidence of "market understanding" falling short of custom was inadmissible. There was no reference in the judgment to *Crema v Cenkos Securities Plc*. It is thought that Eder J's second thoughts accurately reflect the current state of the law.

[58] *Crema v Cenkos Securities Plc* [2010] EWCA Civ 1444; [2011] 1 W.L.R. 2066 CA.

sist it in a full understanding of the factual background ... and that this can include the evidence of persons other than expert witnesses, such as brokers and insurers experienced in the relevant market.[59] Further, [counsel] relied upon the decision in *Lancashire County Council v Municipal Mutual Ins*[60] in support of the proposition that, unlike a traditional plea of custom and practice, it is sufficient if most reasonable persons in the position of the contracting parties would have understood the words used to have a particular effect. In particular [counsel] submitted that that case provides an example of how this approach to construction defeats literalism. The issue was whether exemplary damages were 'compensation' for the purpose of a liability insurance policy covering, inter alia, liabilities for assault and wrongful arrest. The Court of Appeal held that exemplary damages fell outside what lawyers would understand to be the natural meaning of the term 'compensation': see per Simon Brown LJ at p903H–904B, Thorpe LJ agreeing (911B). Thus, [counsel] submitted that the case is also a good example of the courts resisting literalism in the interpretative process, an approach reaffirmed by Lord Steyn in *Sirius International Insurance Co (Publ) v FAI General Insurance Ltd*[61]; that it is consistent with the approach endorsed in *Reardon Smith Line v Yngvar Hansen-Tangen*[62]; that in this case the dealings between the brokers and the Defendants [sic] insurers were conducted by experienced insurance professionals who are to be taken to be familiar with market practices and understanding against the background of which the words used must be construed; and that the insurance market, its practices and the understanding of individuals operating therein are an important part of the relevant background."

In *Hobartville Stud Pty Ltd v Union Insurance Co Ltd*,[63] a question arose whether a colt had been destroyed for "humane reasons". Giles J said:

"A cloistered speculation upon humanity would hardly be satisfactory. ... It was not a case of a meaning acquired by custom and usage ... but a case of arriving at the application of the words in the policy having considered their usage amongst those in the veterinary profession and the insurance industry in relation to the destruction of a horse."

5.22 Thus the correct meaning of words is to be found—not by their derivation or by literal analysis—but by the meaning commonly attached to them by the users of them.[64] A business sense will be given to business documents. The business sense is that which businessmen, in the course of their ordinary dealings, would give the document.[65] So in construing an exception of mines and minerals the meaning of that phrase is to be determined in accordance with the vernacular of the mining world and commercial world and landowners at the date of the instrument, rather

---

[59] *Gard Marine & Energy Ltd v Lloyd Tunnicliffe* [2011] EWHC 1658 at [38]–[39] and [44]; [2011] N.L.J.R. 954.
[60] [1997] Q.B. 897.
[61] [2004] UKHL 54; [2005] 1 All E.R. 191.
[62] [1976] 1 W.L.R. 989.
[63] (1990) 6 ANZ Ins. Cas. 61-032.
[64] *The Tropwind* [1982] 1 Lloyd's Rep. 232 at 236, per Lord Denning MR.
[65] *Homburg Houtimport BV v Agrosin Private Ltd* [2004] 1 A.C. 715 at 737, per Lord Bingham of Cornhill.

than by reference to a true scientific meaning.[66] Similarly, in construing the rules of a trade union, the court must bear in mind that they are addressed to a readership consisting of members of that trade rather than judges or lawyers versed in the semantic technicalities of statutory draftsmanship.[67] This does not of course mean that the court cannot adopt a precise or technical meaning of a word if that is its ordinary meaning.[68]

There is of course a premise underlying the concept of the ordinary meaning of words, namely that words do have an ordinary meaning.[69] In *Shogun Finance Ltd v Hudson*,[70] Lord Phillips of Worth Matravers said:

5.23

"Words in a language have one or more ordinary meaning, which will be known to anyone who speaks that language."

On the other hand, some judges have not always found this a helpful concept. In *Charter Reinsurance Co Ltd v Fagan*,[71] Lord Hoffmann said:

"I think that in some cases[72] the notion of words having a natural meaning is not a very helpful one. Because the meaning of words is so sensitive to syntax and context, the natural meaning of words in one sentence may be quite unnatural in another. Thus a statement that words have a particular natural meaning may mean no more than that in many contexts they will have that meaning. In other contexts their meaning will be different but no less natural."[73]

In *Ryledar Pty Ltd v Euphoric Pty Ltd*,[74] Campbell JA said:

5.24

"… a subjective intention to use words with some meaning other than the meaning that an ordinary hearer of the words would put on them, if the hearer were not in the specific context in which the words were spoken, comes to be taken into account, in deciding what are the terms of the contract, only because there is some form of communication between the parties, or context, such that a reasonable person would realise that the more usual meaning of the words was

---

66 *Hext v Gill* (1872) L.R. 7 Ch. App. 699, per James LJ; *North British Railway Co v Budhill Coal and Sandstone Co* [1910] A.C. 116. However, this is not a rigid rule: see *Borys v Canadian Pacific Railway Co* [1953] A.C. 217.

67 *Porter v National Union of Journalists* [1980] I.R.L.R. 404; *Jacques v AUEW* [1987] I.C.R. 683.

68 *Commonwealth Smelting Ltd v Guardian Royal Exchange Assurance Ltd* [1986] 1 Lloyd's Rep. 121.

69 Many linguists would also dispute the idea that there is an "ordinary" or "natural" meaning of a word, or even of a sentence. The essence of the argument is that words on their own do not refer to anything. It is people who use words to refer to things. There is thus a distinction between "word meaning" and "speaker meaning".

70 [2004] 1 A.C. 919.

71 [1997] A.C. 313 HL.

72 But not in all. See the quotation from Lord Hoffmann's speech in *Investors Compensation Scheme v West Bromwich Building Society* at the beginning of this section and the quotation from his judgment in *Jumbo King Ltd v Faithful Properties Ltd* in para.5.03.

73 Although language is undoubtedly sensitive to context, this may be too dismissive of the concept of the natural or conventional meaning of words. As Professor Steven Pinker explains in *The Language Instinct* (New York, NY: William Morrow and Co, 1994), p.151)):

"A word is the quintessential symbol. Its power comes from the fact that every member of a linguistic community uses it interchangeably in speaking and understanding. If you use a word, then as long as it is not too obscure I can take it for granted that if I later utter it to a third party, he will understand my use of it the same way I understood yours".

74 (2007) 69 N.S.W.L.R. 603 at [266].

not intended. But a subjective intention to use words with some meaning other than their usual meaning, not communicated in any way to the person with whom one is dealing, and not ascertainable from the context within which one is speaking or acting, is not sufficient to stop a contract being entered in which the terms are accorded the meaning that a reasonable observer would take them to have."

5.25   It is plainly right that an uncommunicated subjective intention to use words otherwise than according to their conventional meaning and not ascertainable from context cannot prevent words from being interpreted according to their conventional meaning. However, it is the author's view that where the sole reason for according to words an unconventional meaning is a prior communication between the parties, the case ought more properly to be treated as one for rectification rather than interpretation. It is thought that the discussion by Lord Hoffmann of the "private dictionary" principle in *Chartbrook Ltd v Persimmon Homes Ltd*[75] supports that view.

Illustrations

1.   A testator devised property on trust for his grandson Robert but in case he should die under the age of 21 years and without issue then upon different trusts. Robert attained the age of 21 but died without issue. It was held that the word "and" must be read in its ordinary sense as a copulative, and that accordingly the property did not pass on the alternative trusts declared by the will.
Grey v Pearson[76]

2.   A reinsurance policy on a steamer contained a warranty not to carry cargo other than kerosene oil, and was warranted "no contraband of war." During the Russo-Japanese war the ship sailed from Shanghai to Vladivostock but was captured by a Japanese cruiser. It was then discovered that on board the ship were two Russian naval officers travelling under assumed German names. Their presence was not known to the captain or owners of the vessel, but nevertheless the Japanese confiscated it. It was held that the word "contraband" was to be given its ordinary meaning of prohibited goods, and did not extend to persons. Accordingly, the reinsurers were liable on the policy.
Yangtsze Insurance Association v Indemnity Mutual Marine Assurance Co[77]

3.   An aviator bought a pair of goggles described as "safety-glass". Evidence was admitted to show that at the time of the contract "safety-glass" denoted glass made by a particular method of manufacture, and was understood by the parties as such; and did not amount to a warranty of safety.
Grenfell v E Meyrowitz Ltd[78]

4.   A contract provided that deferred consideration was payable if "drilling" of an offshore oil well no longer formed part of an approved programme or had not been commenced within a certain time. It was held that the natural meaning of

[75] [2009] A.C. 1109.
[76] (1857) 6 H.L. Cas. 61.
[77] [1908] 2 K.B. 504.
[78] [1936] 2 All E.R. 1313.

"drilling" was the physical penetration of the sea bed rather than the broader concept of the drilling process as a whole, beginning with mobilisation of the rig.
Vitol E & P Ltd v Africa Oil and Gas Corp[79]

3. THE USE OF DICTIONARIES AND OTHER MATERIALS

Where the court does not understand the language of a written instrument it may look at dictionaries and other materials in order to elucidate the meaning of the words.

A dictionary is at least a guide to the conventional meaning of words, and dictionary definitions of words are frequently referred to.[80] Lord Hoffmann recognised this in *Mannai Investment Co Ltd v Eagle Star Life Assurance Co Ltd*,[81] in which he said: **5.26**

"The meaning of words, as they would appear in a dictionary, and the effect of their syntactical arrangement, as it would appear in a grammar, is part of the material which we use to understand a speaker's utterance. But it is only a part; another part is our knowledge of the background against which the utterance was made. It is that background which enables us, not only to choose the intended meaning when a word has more than one dictionary meaning but also, in the ways I have explained, to understand a speaker's meaning, often without ambiguity, when he has used the wrong words."

But although it is not sufficient to have regard to dictionary definitions of particular words or expressions, that is not to say that it is not permissible to have regard to them.[82] In *Heronslea (Mill Hill) Ltd v Kwik-Fit Properties Ltd*,[83] Sharp J said that: **5.27**

"It [is] clear ... that the Court is entitled to have regard to dictionary definitions as an aid to construction to ascertain the natural and ordinary meaning of the words in their relevant context."

She added:

"When construing the natural meaning of the language in its context I see no reason why the court should not derive assistance from various dictionary definitions, in particular where the ambit of the activities covered by a particular word is in doubt or dispute, as it is here. Indeed it is clear from the judgment of Sir

---

[79] [2016] EWHC 1677 (Comm); 167 Con. L.R. 268.
[80] This section was referred to with apparent approval in *Rocker v Full Circle Asset Management* [2017] EWHC 2999 (QB). For recent examples see *Biggin Hill Airport Ltd v Bromley LBC* [2001] EWCA Civ 1089; *Crystal Palace FC (2000) Ltd v Paterson* [2005] EWCA Civ 180; *Lloyd v MGL (Rugby) Ltd* [2007] EWCA Civ 153; *Absalom v TRCU Ltd* [2006] 2 Lloyd's Rep. 129 CA; *Durham Tees Valley Airport Ltd v BMI Baby Ltd* [2009] EWHC 852 (Ch); *CPC Group Ltd v Qatari Diar Real Estate* [2010] EWHC 1535 (Ch); *AET Inc Ltd v Arcadia Petroleum Ltd* [2011] 1 All E.R. (Comm) 153; *Farstad Supply AS v Enviroco Ltd* [2010] 2 Lloyd's Rep. 387; *Wollenberg v Casinos Austria International Holding Gmbh* [2011] EWHC 103 (Ch); *Durham v BAI (Run Off) Ltd* [2011] 1 All E.R. 605.
[81] [1997] A.C. 749.
[82] *Crystal Palace FC (2000) Ltd v Paterson* [2005] EWCA Civ 180; *King v Brandywine Reinsurance Co (UK) Ltd* [2004] 2 Lloyd's Rep. 670 at 686.
[83] [2009] EWHC 295 (QB).

Anthony Clarke MR in the *Crystal Palace* case, that such an approach (while not sufficient in itself) is permissible."

In *Shore v Wilson*,[84] Parke B said that there was no doubt:

"that not only where the language of the instrument is such as the Court does not understand, it is competent to receive evidence of the proper meaning of that language, as when it is written in a foreign tongue; but it is also competent, where technical words or peculiar terms, or indeed any expressions are used which at the time the instrument was written had acquired an appropriate meaning, either generally or by local usage, or amongst particular classes."

In *S&T (UK) Ltd v Grove Developments Ltd*[85] the court applied the dictionary definition of "specify" to determine the validity of a notice. In *Acon Equity Management, LLC v Apple Bidco Ltd*,[86] Cockerill J referred to dictionary definitions which, she said, was "of some significance where a document has been drafted by professionals, who may be assumed to have a propensity to use words precisely". However, since dictionaries are only part of the relevant aids to interpretation, it follows that a court may ascribe to words a meaning not found in the dictionary.

5.28   It is not entirely clear whether the use of a dictionary is to be regarded as evidence given to the court as to the meaning of a word which it does not fully understand or whether it is no more than refreshing the memory of the court as to matters to which it is presumed to have knowledge.[87] In *R. v Peters*,[88] Lord Coleridge CJ said:

"I am quite aware that dictionaries are not to be taken as authoritative exponents of the meanings of words used in Acts of Parliament, but it is a well-known rule of courts of law that words are to be taken to be used in their ordinary sense, and we are sent for instruction to these books."

The word "instruction" suggests that the court is finding out something it did not know before.

5.29   On the other hand, in *Marquis Camden v IRC*,[89] the Court of Appeal decisively rejected the suggestion that evidence be received to prove the meaning of ordinary English words. Nevertheless, Cozens-Hardy MR said:

"It is for the Court to interpret the statute as best they can. In so doing the Court may no doubt assist themselves in the discharge of their duty by any literary help which they can find, including of course the consultation of standard authors and reference to well-known and authoritative dictionaries, which refer to the sources in which the interpretation which they give to the words of the English language is to be found."

This approach clearly differentiates between the ascertaining of meaning through the use of a dictionary, and the ascertaining of meaning by evidence. To the same

---

[84] (1842) 9 Cl. & Fin. 355 at 555.
[85] [2018] EWCA Civ 2448.
[86] [2019] EWHC 2750 (Comm).
[87] In *Hills v London Gaslight Co* (1857) 27 L.J. Ex. 60 at 63, Martin B asked: "Is not the Judge bound to know the meaning of all words in the English language?"
[88] (1886) 16 Q.B.D. 636.
[89] [1914] 1 K.B. 641.

effect is the judgment of Fry J in *Holt & Co v Collyer*[90] where, having refused to admit evidence of the meaning of "beerhouse", he proceeded to consider the word according to:

"its ordinary signification, not neglecting the use of dictionaries or any other means of information which may assist me in coming to a conclusion as to what is the ordinary meaning of the word."

The dividing line between the receiving of evidence and the use of "other means of information" is a difficult one to draw. Moreover, the fact that a word is defined in a widely used dictionary does not of itself mean that that word is an ordinary English word. Thus in *Calabar (Woolwich) Ltd v Tesco Stores Ltd*,[91] the Court of Appeal in 1977 upheld the judge's ruling that evidence was admissible to explain the meaning of the word "supermarket" notwithstanding that it was defined in a number of dictionaries. It seems, therefore, as if the court must first decide whether the word it is asked to construe is an ordinary English word before deciding whether to rely solely on dictionaries and other printed matter, or whether to allow evidence to be led. In reaching such a decision, the court has only its own linguistic capabilities and experience to rely on. In the end, therefore, the question whether a word is an ordinary English word may come to no more than the question whether the particular judge is sufficiently confident of his own familiarity with it, so as not to need the assistance of a third party.[92] Thus in *Sussex Investments Ltd v Secretary of State for the Environment*,[93] Robert Walker LJ said:

"In principle, the court is presumed to know the English language and the meaning of ordinary English words. In principle, therefore, the court does not admit evidence as to the meaning of ordinary words (as opposed to non-legal technical terms, in relation to which evidence is admissible). But there are obvious difficulties in making any sharp distinction between ordinary and technical terms. A judge who read Greats and whose pastime is riding will have a different perception of what is technical and what is ordinary from that of a judge who read chemistry and whose pastime is sailing. In practice, the courts do look at English dictionaries, and sometimes at other literary materials, although it has often been said that dictionaries are generally of limited usefulness."

On the same principle it is legitimate to refer to a glossary of terms commonly used in a particular industry where the contract is made between parties operating in that industry.[94]

Where, however, the contract uses a word which is neither an ordinary word nor

5.30

5.31

---

[90] (1881) 16 Ch. D. 718. See also *Biggin Hill Airport Ltd v Bromley LBC* [2001] EWCA Civ 1089 ("business aviation"); *AET Inc Ltd v Arcadia Petroleum Ltd* [2011] 1 All E.R. (Comm) 153 ("free pratique").

[91] [1978] 1 E.G.L.R. 113. It seems improbable, though, that in 1977 any of their Lordships asked "What is a supermarket?"

[92] For example, *Cooper (Max) and Sons Pty Ltd v Sydney City Council* (1980) 54 A.L.J. 234 at 239 where Lord Diplock said of the expression "pay loadings":

"it is not an expression that is used in ordinary speech; without extrinsic evidence from a witness experienced in the building industry and familiar with the technical terms used in it, a judge could only speculate as to the meaning".

[93] [1998] P.L.C.R. 172.

[94] For example, *Association of British Travel Agents Ltd v British Airways Plc* [2000] 2 Lloyd's Rep. 209 (glossary of terms used in the airline industry).

a term of art, but merely a coined word, the court cannot give it a plain meaning, for the obvious reason that it has none.[95]

5.32   Reference to a dictionary is permissible to show not only the meaning of a word but also its application. Thus in *Pepsi-Cola Co of Canada v Coca-Cola Co of Canada Ltd*,[96] Lord Russell of Killowen, delivering the advice of the Privy Council, said:

> "there can ... be no doubt that dictionaries may properly be referred to in order to ascertain not only the meaning of a word, but also the use to which the thing (if it be a thing) denoted by the word is commonly put."

5.33   Of course, the fact that a word is defined in a dictionary does not mean that the court will necessarily apply the dictionary definition to the contract. As Lord Herschell said in *Southland Frozen Meat and Produce Export Co Ltd v Nelson Brothers Ltd*[97]:

> "... the words must not be applied to everything that might be said to come within a possible dictionary use of them, but must be interpreted in the way in which business men would interpret them, when used in relation to a business matter of this description."

5.34   Moreover a dictionary will list all possible conventional meanings of a word; and the bigger dictionaries will give contextual examples of contextual usage. But a court can select only one meaning, because a contract can only have one meaning. Thus as P.O. Lawrence J said in *Mills v Cannon Brewery Co*[98]:

> "One of the main objects of every dictionary of the English language is to give an adequate and comprehensive definition of every word contained in it, which involves setting forth all the different meanings which can properly be given to the particular word. The Court, on the other hand, in determining what is the true meaning of a particular word used in an instrument which it has to construe, has to ascertain in what sense the parties to that instrument have used the word: all the help the Court can derive from dictionaries in such a case is, in case of doubt, to ascertain that the meaning which it comes to the conclusion ought to be attributed to the words is one which may properly be given to it."

So also in *Arbuthnott v Fagan*,[99] Steyn LJ said:

> "Dictionaries never solve concrete problems of construction. The meaning of words cannot be ascertained divorced from their context. And part of the contextual scene is the purpose of the provision."

As Zacaroli J pointed out in *British Telecommunications Plc v BT Pension*

---

[95] See *London & North Western Railway Co v Neilson* [1922] 2 A.C. 263 ("misconveyance" described as "a coined word of no recognised significance").
[96] (1942) 49 R.P.C. 127 (concerning the meaning of the particle "Cola" in Pepsi-Cola and Coca-Cola respectively).
[97] [1898] A.C. 442.
[98] [1920] 2 Ch. 38 at 44.
[99] [1995] C.L.C. 1396 cited in *The Fina Samco* [1995] 2 Lloyd's Rep. 344 at 350, CA.

Scheme Trustees Ltd[100]:

> "When faced with a word in common usage such as 'inappropriate', there is in my judgment little to be gained from, and potential for confusion in, replacing it with another word of similar, but not necessarily identical, meaning found in a dictionary definition."

Although the court may look at a dictionary to see whether a particular meaning of a word is one of the conventional meanings that the dictionary ascribes to the word in question, the court may also ascribe to it a meaning that is not in the dictionary. As Lord Hoffmann explained in *Investors Compensation Scheme v West Bromwich Building Society*[101]:

5.35

> "The meaning of words is a matter of dictionaries and grammars; the meaning of the document is what the parties using those words against the relevant background would reasonably have been understood to mean. The background may not merely enable the reasonable man to choose between the possible meanings of words which are ambiguous but even (as occasionally happens in ordinary life) to conclude that the parties must, for whatever reason, have used the wrong words or syntax."

As Lord Hoffmann also pointed out in *R. v Brown*[102]:

> "The fallacy in the Crown's argument is, I think, one common among lawyers, namely to treat the words of an English sentence as building blocks whose meaning cannot be affected by the rest of the sentence. ... This is not the way language works. The unit of communication by means of language is the sentence and not the parts of which it is composed. The significance of individual words is affected by other words and the syntax of the whole."

Some judges have found resort to dictionaries positively unhelpful. In the US Supreme Court, Jackson J has observed that "dictionaries are the last resort of the baffled judge",[103] and Lord Wilberforce is reported to have said that he never used dictionaries and shut his ears if they were referred to in court.[104]

5.36

4.   MULTIPLE MEANINGS

Where a word has both an ordinary meaning and a specialised meaning, evidence will not be admitted of the specialised meaning the court is satisfied,

---

[100]   [2018] EWHC 69 (Ch); [2018] Pens. L.R. 7.

[101]   [1998] 1 W.L.R. 896 HL.

[102]   [1996] A.C. 543 (a case of statutory construction).

[103]   *Jordan v De George* 341 US 223 at 234 (1951) dissenting.

[104]   Francis Bennion, *Statutory Interpretation*, 5th edn (LexisNexis, 2008), p.1222 (this anecdote is not repeated in the current edition). In his dissenting judgment in *Re Rowland* [1963] Ch.1 Lord Denning MR said:

> "True it is that you must discover his intention from the words he used: but you must put upon his words the meaning which they bore to him. If his words are capable of more than one meaning, or of a wide meaning and a narrow meaning, as they often are, then you must put upon them the meaning which he intended them to convey, and not the meaning which a philologist would put upon them. And in order to discover the meaning which he intended, you will not get much help by going to a dictionary. It is very unlikely that he used a dictionary, and even less likely that he used the same one as you".

either from the contract itself or from the context that the word ought to be interpreted in the latter sense.

5.37   Many words have more than one meaning. Only the context can reveal in which sense it is used. Often the choice is between a popular or ordinary meaning and a technical or scientific meaning. But before the court will admit evidence about the latter meaning it must be satisfied, either from the context and circumstances of the agreement or by other evidence, that the parties intended to displace the primary meaning of the word.

5.38   Thus in *Holt & Co v Collyer*,[105] a landlord sought to adduce evidence that the word "beerhouse" had a special meaning in the brewing trade, and to argue that it ought to be given that meaning in a covenant in a lease of a shop. Fry J refused to admit the evidence. He said:

> "Now is there anything here from which I can infer that the word 'beerhouse' was not used in its primary and popular sense? The covenant which the Plaintiff desires to have enforced against the Defendant is contained in an indenture of lease, which is not a trade instrument in any sense of the term. It is an ordinary lease by a landlord, who is not shown to be a brewer or connected with the brewing trade, to a person who was not ... connected with the business of selling beer at that time, and in respect of whom there is no evidence to shew that he was in any way engaged in the business."

Holt & Co v Collyer was a case where neither party to the lease had a connection with the brewing trade, and consequently could not be supposed to have intended a technical meaning current only in that trade to be given to their contract. It may, however, happen that one party is conversant with the trade in question but the other is not. In such a case, unless the transaction takes place in a recognised market, and possibly through the intervention of a broker in that market, the primary popular meaning of the word will prevail.[106]

5.39   But where both parties are aware of the secondary meaning and that fact is proved by evidence, the secondary meaning will be given effect, even though it may not amount to a technical term or trade custom. Thus in *Scragg v United Kingdom Temperance & General Provident Institution*,[107] the question arose whether a sprint event was within the words "motor racing" in an insurance policy. Mocatta J held that as a matter of ordinary English it was, but that both the insured and the insurers had been aware that the words were used in a special sense by those interested in motor sports, and admitted evidence as to that special meaning.

So also in *Lovell and Christmas Ltd v Wall*,[108] the Court of Appeal construed a covenant in an agreement for the sale of the business of a provision merchant. It was held that the trial judge had rightly admitted evidence of a secondary meaning of the word "provision" in the phrase "provision merchant".

5.40   Many words, however, do not have a recognised "ordinary" or "primary" meaning. In such a case the court selects the meaning to be given to the word from

---

[105] (1881) 16 Ch. D. 719. See also *Biggin Hill Airport Ltd v Bromley LBC* [2001] EWCA Civ 1089 ("business aviation": special meaning not proved on the evidence).
[106] *Lord Forres v Scottish Flax Co Ltd* [1943] 2 All E.R. 366.
[107] [1976] 2 Lloyd's Rep. 227.
[108] (1911) 104 L.T. 85.

an examination of the context in which it is used and of the facts to which the word is to be applied.[109]

Illustrations

1.   A contract to insure was made by persons not in the insurance world. It was held that it could not be construed in the way in which it might have been by persons whose business was that of insurers.
Yuill & Co v Robson[110]

2.   A lease contained a covenant to insure against loss or damage by fire. Sargant J said that it would be wrong to construe a document made between an ordinary lessor and ordinary lessees, having no special knowledge of insurance practice, in the way in which it might be perfectly well understood by persons conversant with insurance practice and dealing on that market. He expressed the principle thus:

> "The plaintiffs rely ... upon the plain rule of construction applicable to all contracts, that where there is nothing to show that the parties have used language in any other than its strict and ordinary sense, and where the words interpreted in that sense are sensible in reference to extrinsic circumstances, it is an inflexible rule of construction that the words shall be interpreted in that strict and primary sense and no other, and although the most conclusive evidence of intention to use them in such popular sense be tendered."

Enlayde Ltd v Roberts[111]

3.   A reinsurance policy warranted "no contraband of war". It was argued that contraband extended to the transport of military personnel of a belligerent. It was held that the dictionary definition of contraband which restricted contraband of goods should apply. Farwell LJ said:

> "The general rule of construction is that words used in documents must receive their primary signification, unless the context of the instrument read as a whole, or surrounding contemporaneous circumstances, shew that the secondary meaning expresses the real intention of the parties, or unless the words are used in connection with some place, trade or the like in which they have acquired the secondary meaning as their customary meaning quoad hoc."

Yangtze Insurance Association v Indemnity Mutual Marine Assurance Co[112]

5.   WORDS OF IMPRECISE MEANING

Where words are of imprecise meaning or describe a quality of continuous variation, the court must decide as a question of fact whether a given set of circumstances is within or outside the contractual stipulation. Such cases are often decided as a matter of impression.

---

[109] See para.5.102. We distinguish between a "Pork Butcher" and a "Family Butcher" because of our background knowledge of what butchers do.
[110] [1908] 1 K.B. 270.
[111] [1917] Ch. 109.
[112] [1908] 2 K.B. 504.

5.41   In *Tophams Ltd v Earl of Sefton*,[113] Lord Wilberforce said:

> "There are some words or expressions used in legal contexts which can be called definitive, or normative: words of which it can be said in advance, or *in abstracto*, with fair precision, what factual situations they comprehend or exclude. The reason is that the situations are typical and involve one or more of a limited range of identifiable facts. Other words or expressions are more of a factual character: they are often plain English words devised to deal with more varied and coarser-grained segments of experience; which can be applied with common sense to most situations without difficulty as to their application or the reverse; these the ordinary man would think to be clear enough even though it is possible to think of cases near the border, or even to find a band of difficulty as to their inclusion or exclusion."

5.42   Whether any given state of affairs falls within the language of the stipulation is in a sense a question of fact. It is true that the answer depends on the true interpretation of the written instrument, but as has been seen the meaning of an ordinary English word is classified as a question of fact.[114]

5.43   In addition to the problems posed by determining the factual limits of the embrace of ordinary English words, many words have different shades of meaning according to the context in which they are used. In *Earl of Lonsdale v Att.-Gen.*,[115] Slade J said:

> "Of many, perhaps the majority, of the words used by English speaking people there can be little doubt as to the ordinary meaning, or 'literal' or 'primary' meaning, as it is often called. To take an example at random, the court would not, I conceive find much difficulty in attaching a literal or primary meaning to the word 'elephant,' if it found it in a written instrument.[116] In contrast, however, some English words and phrases fall into a second, quite different category. There are words and phrases which are readily capable of bearing two or more alternative meanings and to which the court is not willing to ascribe a prima facie meaning, so as to impose upon any party the onus of displacing it. In any such case the court finds itself obliged to construe the word in its particular context, having regard to the admissible evidence, without any predisposition to give it one meaning in preference to another."

5.44   Furthermore, many words describe what on the face of it appear to be opposites, but which in truth are separated by a middle ground of continuous variation. Thus although "day" and "night" are clearly antonyms, there is a whole range of gradations in between, and it is difficult to say where one stops and the other

---

[113] [1967] A.C. 50 at 83 (a dissenting judgment). See also Glanville Williams, "Language and the Law II" (1945) 61 L.Q.R. 179, 181–192 ("The upshot is that the words we use, though they have a central core of meaning that is relatively fixed, are of doubtful application to a considerable number of marginal cases").

[114] para.4.01.

[115] [1982] 1 W.L.R. 887.

[116] Even "elephant" might have a different primary meaning in a contract about sizes of paper.

begins.[117] In *Durham Tees Valley Airport Ltd v BMI Baby Ltd*,[118] Davis J considered the meaning of the word "summer" in the context of an agreement regulating flights from a regional airport. He said:

"The word 'summer' can have varying meanings depending on context, as I see it. Sometimes it can be used to connote a 3 month season (June, July, August) to be contrasted with the other 3 month seasons of autumn, winter and spring. According to the Shorter Oxford English Dictionary, sometimes in popular usage it connotes the period from mid-May to mid-August. Sometimes again it may be used in contrast simply to winter, in denoting one half of the year. I was told, in evidence, that for the scheduling purposes of the International Air Transport Association, 'summer' is defined as meaning from the last Sunday in March (corresponding presumably to the start of British Summer Time) until the last Saturday in October, with 'winter' being for the remainder of the year: although there was no evidence that this particular definition was widely accepted for airport/airline contracts (which, as I have said, are individually negotiated). All the same, I think, on the whole, that it is this last sense it has here."

The court is not allowed the luxury of indecisions. If parties enter into a contract **5.45** containing an obligation framed by reference to such a word or concept, the court must decide, in relation to a given set of circumstances, whether the contract bites or not. In *Gregg v Fraser*,[119] FitzGibbon LJ said:

"This is in each case a pure question on the construction of a written document, whether the case lies on the one side or on the other of a definite line in the mathematical sense—a line without breadth—every case must lie on one side of that line or on the other and 'line balls' are barred."

It is difficult to lay down any principle to assist in resolving the question whether **5.46** a particular decision will go one way or the other. So much depends upon the individuality of the particular tribunal hearing the case, and its particular experience that one is bound to retreat into some such phrase as "the point is one of impression". As has been seen, all that this phrase describes is the common phenomenon of reaching a very clear conclusion as to the meaning of a particular word or stipulation, without being able to attribute the forming of that conclusion to any process of reasoning.[120] As Hoffmann J said in *Norwich Union Life Insurance Society v British Railways Board*[121]:

"The use of ordinary language to convey meaning often involves subtle discriminations which for most people are intuitive rather than capable of lucid explanation. An explanation of why ordinary English words in a particular context convey a given meaning is frequently more likely to confuse than to enlighten. Perhaps this is what judges mean when they say that questions of construction are often matters of impression."

A similar experience is often encountered in construing stipulations which refer **5.47**

---

[117] See *Hobbs v London & South Western Railway* (1875) L.R. 10 Q.B. 111 at 121, per Blackburn J; and Glanville Williams, "Language and the Law II" (1945) 61 L.Q.R. 179, 181–189.
[118] [2009] EWHC 852 (Ch).
[119] [1906] 1 I.L.R. 545 at 578.
[120] See also para.2.103.
[121] [1987] 2 E.G.L.R. 137.

to classes of things. In *Att.-Gen. v Brighton & Hove Co-operative Supply Association*,[122] Lindley MR said:

"Nothing is more common in life than to be unable to draw the line between two things. Who can draw the line between plants and animals? And yet, who has any difficulty in saying that an oak tree is a plant and not an animal?"

Similarly, in *Stevens v Gourley*,[123] Byles J said:

"The imperfection of human language renders it not only difficult, but absolutely impossible, to define the word 'building' with any approach to accuracy. One may say of this or that structure, this or that is not a building; but no general definition can be given and our lexicographers do not attempt it."

Illustrations

1.   A conveyance contained a covenant not to permit the Aintree racecourse to be used otherwise than for the purpose of horse racing and agriculture. The owner, who was bound by the covenant, proposed to sell it to a developer knowing that the developer intended to build houses on the land. It was held that the word permit denoted a measure of control, and accordingly once the land had been sold to the developer the former owner could not be said to have permitted any breach of the covenant.
Tophams Ltd v Earl of Sefton[124]

2.   A conveyance made in 1880 conveyed the mineral substances and all other mines and minerals under a portion of the sea bed. The question arose whether the conveyance operated to pass title to oil and natural gas under the sea. It was held that the meaning of mines and minerals was to be ascertained according to the vernacular usage among mining men at the date of the grant. At that date there was no definite meaning that could be attached to the phrase, but other indications in the conveyance, read as a whole, showed that the parties did not intend the oil or natural gas to pass.
Earl of Lonsdale v Att.-Gen.[125]

6.   FOREIGN WORDS

The court may receive evidence as to the meaning of foreign words and documents, but having received that evidence, the construction of the foreign document remains a matter of law for the court. Where the court has knowledge of the language concerned, it may construe the words or documents without such evidence.

5.48   In *Di Sora v Phillips*,[126] Lord Chelmsford said:

"The office of construction of a written instrument, whether foreign or domestic,

---

[122] [1900] 1 Ch. 276.
[123] (1859) 7 C.B.N.S. 99.
[124] [1967] A.C. 50.
[125] [1982] 1 W.L.R. 887.
[126] (1863) 10 H.L. Cas. 624. Latin does not appear to be treated as a foreign language for this purpose.

brought into controversy before our tribunals, properly belongs to the judge. In the case of a foreign instrument, he necessarily requires some person's assistance. In the first place he must have a translation of the instrument, a translator being a witness to the meaning and also the grammatical construction of the words. He must then have the way cleared for him by explanatory evidence, of any words which are of a technical description, or which have a peculiar meaning, different from that which, literally translated into our language, they would bear; and if there is any established principle of construction by the foreign tribunal, proof of it must be given. But the witnesses having supplied the judge with all these facts, they must retire and leave his sufficiently informed mind to his proper office—that of ascertaining for himself the intention of the parties; or, in other words, of construing the language of the instrument in question."

A somewhat more restrictive approach was taken by Lord Greene MR in *Rouyer Guillet et Cie v Rouyer Guillet & Co Ltd*,[127] where he said: **5.49**

"... evidence on the construction of a private document, such as articles of association, is admissible so far as it deals with [foreign] rules of construction or [foreign] rules of law or the explanation of [foreign] technical terms, but evidence as to its meaning after those aids have been taken into account is not admissible. It is for the court to construe the document, having fortified itself with the permissible evidence."

This approach deals with the question as one of admissibility of evidence, whereas Lord Chelmsford's approach dealt with the matter as one of necessity. Thus, while Lord Chelmsford suggests that evidence is obligatory, according to Lord Greene's approach, evidence is permissible but not obligatory. It seems, therefore, that according to Lord Greene's formulation it would be open to a judge conversant with the foreign language in question to construe the document without the aid of any evidence at all.   **5.50**

Until recently this might have appeared contrary to principle. All judges take judicial notice of the English language, and accordingly evidence as to the meaning of ordinary words is unnecessary and inadmissible. However: **5.51**

"the court cannot take judicial notice of [a foreign] language and it must have recourse to the assistance of those who understand it."[128]

In other words, the need for evidence as to the meaning of a foreign document is based not so much on the court's ignorance of the foreign language but upon the court's inability to take judicial notice of it, just as the court may require proof of facts which the judge might privately already know. However, there are clear signs that the approach of the court has changed, particularly since the entry of the UK into the EU.[129] Thus in *Buchanan (James) & Co Ltd v Babco Forwarding and Shipping (UK) Ltd*,[130] Lord Wilberforce said that there was nothing illegitimate in the court looking at the foreign text of a convention to which the UK was a party without the aid of evidence as to its meaning. However, Viscount Dilhorne, Lord Edmund-Davies and Lord Fraser of Tullybelton seem to have had misgivings at that course of action.

---

[127] [1949] 1 All E.R. 244n.
[128] *Chatenay v Brazilian Submarine Telegraph Co Ltd* [1891] 1 Q.B. 79, per Lindley LJ.
[129] It is not thought that this will change after Brexit.
[130] [1978] A.C. 141.

5.52   Lord Wilberforce returned to the same theme in *Fothergill v Monarch Airlines Ltd*,[131] in which the court was required to construe the Warsaw Convention. He said:

> "The process of ascertaining the meaning must vary according to the subject matter. If a judge has some knowledge of the relevant language, there is no reason why he should not use it; this is particularly true of the French or Latin language, so long languages of our courts. There is no reason why he should not consult a dictionary, if the word is such that a dictionary can reveal its significance; often of course it may substitute one doubt for another. In all cases he will have in mind that ours is an adversary system; it is for the parties to make good their contentions. So he will inform them of the process he is using, and if they think fit, they can supplement his resources with other material, other dictionaries, other books of reference and other decided cases. They may call evidence of an interpreter, if the language is unknown to the court, or of an expert if the word or expression is such as to require expert interpretation. Between a technical expression in Japanese and a plain word in French there must be a whole spectrum which calls for suitable and individual treatment."

The other Law Lords (including Lord Fraser of Tullybelton) agreed. Lord Scarman seems to have followed a narrower line than the majority, for he seems to have held that since the French text of the Convention was scheduled to the Carriage by Air Act 1961, it was part of English law and hence the court was required to take judicial notice of it. In theory it is possible that different rules would apply to the method by which the court interprets an Act of Parliament as opposed to a private contract, but none of their Lordships, with the possible exception of Lord Scarman, expressly confined their discussion of judicial linguistic ability to cases concerning statutory construction. It is submitted, therefore, that the modern law is that the court is entitled, without the assistance of oral evidence, to construe a document in a foreign language, but that at the same time, evidence is admissible to explain its meaning, though not its legal effect.[132] It is considered, however, that where one or both parties adduce evidence of a translation (and a fortiori if the translation is agreed) the court would in practice be bound to work from that translation.

5.53   In principle, where a document has been translated, its proper interpretation is a matter for the court, and not a proper subject of expert evidence.[133] An expert (as well as translating the document itself) is entitled to give evidence of any special canons of construction applicable to the document if it is governed by foreign law; but the construction of the document itself remains the province of the court.[134] However, where a document is translated for the benefit of the court, there is a

---

[131] [1981] A.C. 251.

[132] In Australia the courts have taken a different approach. The rule there is that for a tribunal to act upon a document, applying its own understanding of the foreign language uncommunicated to the parties would involve an abuse of natural justice. Accordingly, if a document is sought to be tendered in a foreign language, and the document is objected to, evidence of the meaning of the document must be given: *Zoeller v Federal Republic of Germany* (1989) 23 F.C.R. 282. However, Lord Wilberforce said in terms that the judge should inform the parties of his proposed course of action; and allow them to adduce their own translation. Thus, it is thought, the rules of natural justice would be followed.

[133] *Gemstar-TV Guide International Inc v Virgin Media Ltd* [2011] EWCA Civ 302 (a patent specification rather than a contract).

[134] *Rouyer Guillet et Cie v Rouyer Guillet & Co Ltd* [1949] 1 All E.R. 244n; *King v Brandywine Reinsurance Co (UK) Ltd* [2004] 2 Lloyd's Rep. 670; *Rendall v Combined Insurance Co of America* [2005]

danger that the process of translation will itself filter the meaning of the document. This danger was pointed out by Stable J in *Dies v British and International Mining and Finance Corp Ltd*[135]:

"The precise mental process of translating a word or sentence spoken or written in one language into another language is or may be somewhat complex. In fact, to say that you translate one word by another seems to me to be a summary method of stating a process the exact nature of which is a little obscure. A substantive word is merely a symbol which, unless it be part of a tale told by an idiot, signifies something. If that something is a concrete object such as an apple or a particular picture, the process of translation from one language to another is easy enough for anyone well acquainted with both languages. Where the words used signify not a concrete object but a conception of the mind, the process of the translator seems to be to ascertain the conception or thought which the words used in the language to be translated conjure up in his own mind, and then, having got that conception or thought clear, to re-symbolize it in words selected from the language into which it is to be translated. A possible danger, when the document to be translated is one on which legal rights depend, is apparent, inasmuch as the witness who is in theory a mere translator in practice may construe the document in the original language and then impose on the Court the construction at which he has arrived by the medium of the translation which he has selected."

The *Principles of European Contract Law* state[136]:   **5.54**

"Where a contract is drawn up in two or more language versions none of which is stated to be authoritative, there is, in case of discrepancy between the versions, a preference for the interpretation according to the version in which the contract was originally drawn up."

There is no English authority on this point.

7.   SCIENTIFIC AND TECHNICAL TERMS

Where a document contains technical terms which the court does not understand, the court may discover the meaning of such terms through the use of an appropriate dictionary, unless the meaning of the term is in dispute, in which case it seems that the court can only proceed upon evidence.[137]

This section was referred to with apparent approval in *Rocker v Full Circle As-*   **5.55**
set Management[138] where it was pointed out that the distinction between ordinary and technical terms is not always clear. In this context, the court may consider extrinsic evidence from a witness experienced in the field. Such evidence is admis-

---

1 C.L.C. 565; *Svenska Petroleum Exploration AB v Government of the Republic of Lithuania (No.2)* [2007] 1 Lloyd's Rep. 193.
[135] [1939] 1 K.B. 724 at 733.
[136] (The Hague: Kluwer Law International, 2000), para.5:107.
[137] This proposition was approved in *Kellogg Brown & Root Inc v Concordia Maritime AG* [2006] EWHC 3358 (Comm) and *Encia Remediation Ltd v Canopius Managing Agents Ltd* [2007] 1 C.L.C. 818.
[138] [2017] EWHC 2999 (QB) concerning the meaning of "stop loss" in an investment agreement.

sible as part of the relevant background, and it is admissible even if the meaning falls short of a trade custom.

5.56   In *Shore v Wilson*,[139] it was agreed by all the judges consulted by the House of Lords that evidence was admissible for the purpose of explaining scientific or technical terms. In *Baldwin & Francis Ltd v Patents Appeal Tribunal*,[140] the Court of Appeal was asked to construe a specification full of technical terms. Counsel began to explain the technicalities to the court, but the court held that it could not construe the specification in the absence of evidence as to the meaning of the technical terms. In the House of Lords,[141] a different approach prevailed. Lord Reid said:

> "A judge is supposed to know the law, the English language and such facts as are common knowledge. If he refers to authorities or dictionaries or other works dealing with these matters he can safely do so because his general knowledge enables him to check and appreciate them. But if without assistance he attempts to handle highly technical matters he may easily go astray. Some fairly simple technical matters can nowadays be considered to be common knowledge, and I would not attempt to draw the line—it may alter from time to time. In this case some of the terms are simple enough but some are certainly not. So what is a court to do if on the face of a record there are technical terms which cannot be understood without expert assistance? There may be cases where a very little assistance is all that is necessary, and I think it would be unfortunate if such a strict rule were laid down that the mere presence of some technicality is enough to prevent a court from proceeding further in the absence of evidence to explain it.
>
> Technicalities crop up in a great variety of cases and, when the parties are not in dispute about them they are often explained without evidence. Counsel give explanations and by doing so they are not giving anything away; if they were not in agreement evidence would be led. But in a case where it is not competent to lead evidence counsel could not, in my view, properly be asked to help in this way unless there is some other way for the court to get the necessary information. If the court finds that there is a genuine dispute and real doubt about any technical matter, then I do not think that it can proceed further without evidence."

5.57   Lord Denning put the matter somewhat differently, and with echoes of Lindley LJ in *Chatenay v Brazilian Submarine Telegraph Co Ltd*.[142] He said:

> "The one thing that the court ought not to do is to refuse jurisdiction in a case because it does not understand the technical terms employed in it. Scientists and engineers are entitled to have their rights enforced and their wrongs redressed as well as anyone else; and the court must possess itself of whatever information is necessary for the purpose. Some judges may have it already because of their previous experience. Others may have to acquire it for the first time. But in either case the information they glean is not evidence strictly so called.
>
> When an assessor explains the technicalities, he does not do so on oath, nor can he be cross-examined. And no one ever calls the author of a dictionary to give evidence. All that happens is that the court is equipping itself for its task by tak-

---

[139] (1839) 9 Cl. & F. 355.
[140] [1959] 1 Q.B. 105.
[141] [1959] A.C. 663.
[142] [1891] 1 Q.B. 79.

ing judicial notice of such things as it ought to know in order to do its work properly."[143]

If this approach is correct, it is submitted that it considerably extends the scope of taking judicial notice, to which it becomes difficult to see any limit. Logically, where the court hears evidence of the background against which a contract is made, it would, on this approach, be merely taking judicial notice of such things as it needs to know in order to do its work properly. Yet in such cases it cannot be doubted that the court is hearing evidence properly so called. Moreover as Lord Reid pointed out the problem only arises where there is dispute about the meaning of a technical term. If there is no dispute there can be no objection to counsel explaining technical terms to the judge.[144] It is submitted that the approach of Lord Reid is to be preferred. Lord Reid's approach seems to have found favour with the Privy Council in *Cooper (Max) and Sons Pty Ltd v Sydney City Council*,[145] in which Lord Diplock said of the expression "pay loadings" in a building contract: **5.58**

"it is not an expression that is used in ordinary speech; without extrinsic evidence from a witness experienced in the building industry and familiar with the technical terms used in it, a judge could only speculate as to the meaning".

Similarly, in *Lloyds TSB Bank Plc v Clarke*,[146] two banks entered into a "sub-participation agreement." Lord Hoffmann said: **5.59**

"The term 'sub-participation agreement' is not a legal term of art like 'assignment' or 'trust'. It is however a term commonly used in the market and there was before the courts in The Bahamas a good deal of evidence about what it meant. Such evidence, showing what certain words would have been understood to mean in the relevant trade at the time of the agreement, is in their Lordships' opinion admissible as part of the background against which the agreement should be construed".

In *Crema v Cenkos Securities Plc*,[147] the Court of Appeal held that expert evidence was admissible to explain the "shorthand" of a particular market even though it fell short of a trade custom. Expert evidence is also admissible to explain market practice "if that is relevant background knowledge for the purposes of interpreting the terms of the contract, both explicit and implicit". **5.60**

But as Robert Walker LJ observed in *Sussex Investments Ltd v Secretary of State for the Environment*[148]:

"[T]here are obvious difficulties in making any sharp distinction between ordinary and technical terms. A judge who read Greats and whose pastime is riding will have a different perception of what is technical and what is ordinary from that of a judge who read chemistry and whose pastime is sailing. In practice, the

---

[143] An assessor may be appointed under s.70 of the Senior Courts Act 1981. An appointed assessor may give the court private instruction in the scientific discipline under consideration. This power is used from time to time in cases concerning the interpretation of "high tech" patents.
[144] In patent cases where the meaning of the claims or specification is in dispute the parties are encouraged to prepare an agreed primer of the technicalities for the assistance of the court.
[145] (1980) 54 A.L.J. 234 at 239.
[146] [2002] UKPC 27; [2002] 2 All E.R. (Comm) 992.
[147] [2011] Bus. L.R. 943.
[148] [1998] P.L.C.R. 172.

courts do look at English dictionaries, and sometimes at other literary materials, although it has often been said that dictionaries are generally of limited usefulness."

5.61   Although expert evidence may be necessary to explain technical terms to the court, it is not the function of an expert to interpret the contract.[149] That remains the function of the judge.[150]

8.   LEGAL TERMS OF ART

Where a document contains a legal term of art the court should give it its technical meaning in law, unless there is something in the context to displace the presumption that it was intended to carry its technical meaning.[151]

5.62   The proposition at the head of this section was approved in *ICICI Bank UK Plc v Assam Oil Co Ltd.*[152]

5.63   Draftsmen of contracts frequently use legal terms of art (or technical terms). Sometimes this comes from tradition or laziness, but there are more powerful reasons for their use. They were pointed out by Lord Simon of Glaisdale in *Falkiner v Commissioner of Stamp Duties (NSW)*[153] as follows:

> "Certain words have been legally construed as having a prima facie meaning (not generally differing from their most ordinary meaning) when contained in documents intended to have legal effect—particularly, wills and settlements. In the absence of a contrary intention appearing, the court will assume that it is this prima facie meaning which was intended. In the first place the existence of the rule will enable legal advisers to predict how a court will construe the words in various circumstances within the contemplation of the client and advisers; and, if the prima facie legal meaning does not represent the clients' intention, to make that intention plain. Secondly, the rule leads to economy: the meaning need not be spelled out at length, but words can rather be used in the knowledge that they will prima facie carry the meaning put on them by the law. Thirdly, if as often happens, the actual forensic situation was probably not foreseen by settlor or testator, the court is relieved from a purely impressionistic interpretation, which might well vary from judge to judge; and the unsuccessful litigant will at least have the consolation of knowing that his case has been adjudged by an objective standard, which has been applied in the past to others in a similar situation to his, and which will be so applicable to others in the future."

A similar explanation was given by Diplock LJ in *Sydall v Castings Ltd,*[154] as follows:

---

[149] Or, in patent cases, the claims and specification.
[150] *Kingscroft Insurance Co Ltd v Nissan Fire and Marine Insurance Co Ltd* [2000] 1 All E.R. (Comm) 272; *JP Morgan Chase Bank v Springwell Navigation Corp* [2007] 1 All E.R. (Comm) 549.
[151] This proposition was approved in *Programme Holdings Pty Ltd v Van Gogh Holdings Pty Ltd* [2009] WASC 79. However, Prof. J.W. Carter criticises the principle in *The Construction of Commercial Contracts* (Hart Publishing, 2013), paras [13.19]–[13.21].
[152] [2019] EWHC 750 (Comm) ("set-off" and "counterclaim"); Jeffreys v Scruton [2020] EWHC 536 (Ch).
[153] [1973] A.C. 565 ("next of kin" construed in technical sense, i.e. the next of kin at the date of the death of the person whose death is spoken of).
[154] [1967] 1 Q.B. 302 at 313.

"Documents which are intended to give rise to legally enforceable rights and duties contemplate enforcement by due process of law which involves their being interpreted by courts composed of judges, each one of whom has his personal idiosyncrasies of sentiment and upbringing, not to speak of age. Such documents would fail in their object if the rights and duties which could be enforced depended on the personal idiosyncrasies of the individual judge or judges upon whom the task of construing them chanced to fall. It is to avoid this that lawyers, whose profession is to draft and to construe such documents, have been compelled to evolve an English language of which the constituent words and phrases are more precise in their meaning than they are in the language of Shakespeare or of any of the passengers on the Clapham omnibus this morning. These words and phrases to which a more precise meaning is so ascribed are called by lawyers 'terms of art' but are in popular parlance known as 'legal jargon'. We lawyers must not allow this denigratory description to obscure the social justification for the use of 'terms of art' in legal documents. It is essential to the effective operation of the rule of law."

Thus in *IDC Group Ltd v Clark*,[155] Nourse LJ said: **5.64**

"In deciding what this professional draftsman intended in 1969 by the use of the expression 'grant licence', we must start from the position that for over 300 years it had been well known to lawyers in general, and to conveyancers in particular, that a licence properly so called is a permission to do something on or over land which creates no interest in it. ... We must start with the proper legal meaning of 'licence' which, even if it is no longer a term of art, is certainly the next best thing. That is something which [counsel's] submissions have at every point failed to recognise. He says that words must be construed according to their ordinary meaning, but where a word has a proper legal meaning it is that meaning which must ordinarily be given to it in a legal document."

The first question for the court is to decide whether the term in dispute is indeed   **5.65**
a term of art. It is not difficult to see that differences of opinion can arise. In *Ageas (UK) Ltd v Kwik-Fit (GB) Ltd*,[156] a sale and purchase agreement provided that any claim for breach of warranty would not be valid unless it was commenced by validly "issuing and serving legal process" within six months of the making of the claim. Green J held that the word "serving" was not a legal term of art sufficient to incorporate the provisions in the CPR about deemed dates of service. He said:

"The expression is one which can bear a number of different and conflicting meanings covering points in time before, on, and after receipt. For instance it can mean dispatch in the sense that a document is 'served' from the point in time of its dispatch or sending and therefore prior to its receipt. In such cases the modes of dispatch are frequently spelled out (fax, DX, first class recorded post, etc). The parties by this method in effect agree a risk transfer away from the sender and on to the other party ... Alternatively, the phrase 'service' (and its cognates) might be read simply to mean delivery in a form which brings the contents of the document being served to the actual attention of the intended recipient. In such circumstances a document or other instrument will be served only when it is

---

[155] [1992] 2 E.G.L.R. 184 CA.
[156] [2013] EWHC 3261 (QB).

proven that the intended recipient was in actual possession of the document or instrument in issue. This is in my view the normal meaning of the concept of 'service'. And yet further it is possible that 'service' (and cognates) may be treated as having occurred at a point of time after actual receipt by the inclusion in the contract of provisions which define service as having occurred, for example, 'x' days or hours following proof of actual receipt. This analysis shows that the phrase 'service' is not a term which necessarily imports a fixed or technical meaning. Its ordinary meaning is delivery upon and receipt by the intended recipient, but that can be modified by contractual provisions. This is not, in my view, one of those cases where the parties have carefully and deliberately chosen a very precise legal term of art which, according to consistent case law, should be accorded its technical meaning and which the parties would accordingly understand as having a precise legal meaning".

However, in *T&L Sugars Ltd v Tate & Lyle Industries Ltd*,[157] Flaux J declined to follow that decision. The contract in that case also required claims to have been "both issued and served" by a contractual time limit. Flaux J said:

"[15]   In my judgment, the word 'served' in clause 11.3 means 'served' in accordance with the CPR for the following reasons. First, the word is used in the phrase 'has issued and served proceedings'. Clearly the word 'issued' in that phrase must mean issued in accordance with English procedural rules (since the only proceedings permitted by virtue of the exclusive jurisdiction clause were before the English courts) in other words issued and sealed by the court in accordance with CPR 7.2. 'Issued' in that context cannot have some ordinary, non-legal meaning, for example the sending of a draft claim form and Particulars of Claim, as sometimes occurs to facilitate settlement before proceedings are formally issued. That would not amount to proceedings being 'issued'. On the basis that 'issued' in this context means issued in accordance with the CPR, it would be very odd if 'served' in the same phrase did not also connote served in accordance with the CPR, but had some ordinary non-legal meaning, whatever that entails. So far as I can tell, the significance of the word 'issuing' in the provision Green J was considering does not seem to have been discussed in that case.

[16]   Second, following on from that, in its context it seems to me that, when clause 11.3 talks about proceedings (which by necessity means proceedings before the English courts) being 'issued and served', the natural meaning of the word 'served' in that context is 'served in accordance with the procedural rules in force in England at the relevant time'. I am afraid that I do not find the contrary reasoning of Green J in *Ageas* that the parties as reasonable businessmen would have intended 'served' to have some ordinary meaning of delivered and received at all compelling. It seems to me that, if the parties had intended to convey that it should be sufficient that the defendant had notice of the proceedings within the twelve month period by receipt of the claim form even though actual service under the CPR had not occurred, they would more naturally have used words such as 'the buyer has delivered the claim form' or 'the seller has received notice of proceedings' within 12 months in clause 11.3."

---

157   [2014] EWHC 1066 (Comm).

In addition, the contract in that case contained a different regime for the service of contractual notices.

In *Phoenix Commercial Enterprises Pty Ltd v City of Canada Bay Council*,[158] **5.66** Campbell JA considered the interrelation between a presumption that legal terms of art were used in their technical sense and the modern approach to interpretation which, by and large, eschews presumptions. He said:

"If the document in question is drawn by a lawyer, is manifestly intended to effect a legal transaction, and uses an expression that is not an expression in common use but that has a meaning in an area of legal discourse that is relevant to the document in question, that in itself provides a basis for the reasonable reader concluding that that expression is used in its special legal sense, unless there are other factors present that show it is not used in that special legal sense. So understood, the presumption is consistent with the current approach to construction."

Accordingly where an instrument uses a legal term of art, it is to be presumed **5.67** in the absence of clear indications to the contrary, that the term of art is being used in its correct legal sense. Thus in *Infiniteland Ltd v Artisan Contracting Ltd*,[159] a share sale agreement qualified warranties by reference to the purchaser's "actual knowledge". It was argued that constructive knowledge was also included. Carnwath LJ said:

"In my view, it is important in the interests of legal certainty that such established distinctions should be respected, both by those drafting contracts, and by the courts in their interpretation. In the context of a professionally drawn legal document such as this, the court should start from a strong presumption that such expressions are used in their ordinary legal meanings."

In *Bedfordshire Police Authority v Constable*,[160] an insurance policy covered **5.68** sums that the insured might become "legally liable to pay as damages". It was argued that the words "liable as damages" had a settled meaning and that reasonable persons, having the background knowledge reasonably available at the time of the contract, would not have had a detailed knowledge of the law. Longmore LJ said:

"This submission confuses two separate concepts. It may well be correct that 'liable as damages' has the comparatively technical meaning that an English lawyer would give to the concept of 'damages'. But if that is right it is then wrong to say that it must be construed against 'reasonably available background knowledge' so as to limit the technical sense of the phrase under the consideration. We are already outside the principle that an ordinary term in a contract is to be construed against the commercial background or the 'aim and genesis' of the transaction. A technical phrase has been used and it must be interpreted in its technical sense without regard to reasonably available background knowledge. If, therefore, the phrase 'legally liable to pay as damages' has connotations which a reasonably experienced layman might not appreciate or if the phrase leads to an inquiry which only a lawyer or a historian

---

158 [2010] NSWCA 64 at [174].
159 [2006] 1 B.C.L.C. 632.
160 [2009] 2 All E.R. (Comm) 200.

would be qualified to conduct, the concept of limiting this inquiry to background knowledge reasonably available to an insurance broker or an insurer must necessarily fade into the background."

Likewise, in *Lowe v National Insurance Bank of Jamaica*,[161] reference to background (including allegations of agreements made in the course of negotiations) were held by the Privy Council to be insufficient to displace the conventional legal meaning of "hypothecation" used in a loan agreement.

5.69   *Durham v BAI (Run Off) Ltd*[162] concerned the interpretation of a number of different insurance policies. One of the issues was the meaning of the word "injury". Rix LJ said[163]:

"In legal discourse, the word or concept 'injury' is not an everyday matter like a garden or a house. Of course, there may be legal disputes of line drawing as to whether even such things as houses and gardens are houses rather than mansions, or gardens rather than patios. In the law, however, it seems that 'injury' is very much a term of art. A trivial injury is not an injury for the purpose of the law of tort. *De minimis non curat lex*. The law does not care about trivial things. However, if a trivial injury, such as a scratch or an insect bite leads on to more serious consequences, then the law does care about it. What is trivial? Not something which has material consequences."

5.70   The same presumption applies even if there are indications that the drafter misunderstood the law.[164] Thus in *Akici v LR Butlin Ltd*,[165] where a covenant in a lease prohibited both parting with and sharing possession, it was held that even though possession is indivisible:

"the covenant against parting with possession of the whole or part of the premises in the present case should be given its normal, and technically legally correct, meaning, unless there is any good reason to construe it in some other way."

The same meaning was given to the word "possession" in the covenant against sharing possession, even though sharing possession might be thought a legal solecism. Similarly, in *William Hare Ltd v Shepherd Construction Ltd*,[166] the draftsman had probably overlooked changes to the insolvency legislation; and had defined "insolvency" by reference to the previous law. The contractual definition of "insolvency" by reference to the making of an administration order was held not to extend to entry into administration without a court order.

5.71   Sometimes it is clear that the drafter has misunderstood the law. In such a case the court will put less weight on a detailed linguistic analysis than might otherwise be the case. In *Oxonica Energy Ltd v Neuftec Ltd*,[167] the deputy judge said:

"we quite often come across agreements that concern specialised legal subjects— and intellectual property licences fall into that category—which have been

[161] [2008] UKPC 26.
[162] [2011] 1 All E.R. 605.
[163] [2011] 1 All E.R. 605 at [278].
[164] *IRC v Williams* [1969] 1 W.L.R. 1197 ("the rule against perpetuities" construed in its correct sense even though the draftsman may have misunderstood the complicated rules about lives in being).
[165] [2006] 2 All E.R. 872.
[166] [2010] EWCA Civ 283.
[167] [2008] EWHC 2127 (Pat).

drafted by non-specialists. We can tell this from the way that technical expressions have been employed in the document. Sometimes those documents contain crucial ambiguities, not so much because of the misuse of the technical expressions, but because the draftsman had not enough understanding of the subject-matter to beware of the ambiguities that ought to be avoided. Such draftsmen, inspired by their word processors, are sometimes apt to cut and paste choice phrases and expressions where it was not necessary to do so."

On appeal[168] Jacob LJ said that:

"Initially I felt uncomfortable with ignoring the closing words 'or Licensed Patent' in the definition of Licensed Products for the purposes of deciding what was royalty bearing. But in the end, I think that has to be done to make rational sense of this appallingly drafted document."

The mere fact that a contract uses a word that is defined by statute does not make that word a legal term of art. Thus where the holder of an option agreed to apply for planning permission for "development" of property it was held that the word "development" was to be construed in a non-technical sense rather than in accordance with its statutory definition in town and country planning legislation.[169] So in *Risegold Ltd v Escala Ltd*,[170] Mummery LJ said: **5.72**

"It does not follow that because 'rebuilding' has a restricted meaning in planning legislation, in a planning permission or in a leasehold covenant that it should bear a similarly restricted meaning in a right of entry provision. This really is a case in which, in a well-worn phrase, 'context is everything'."

However, where an agreement has been drawn with the provisions of statutorily defined words in mind, some particular context is required before the court can attribute to the parties an intention to use such a term in a different sense to that which it has in the legislative context.[171] But where words are defined by statutory instrument (e.g. the Town and Country Planning (Use Classes) Order 1987) and the contract uses different words, the statutory definition affords little, if any, help in interpreting the contract.[172]   **5.73**

Moreover, although the court approaches legal terms of art on the footing that they are to be given their technical meaning, there is no inflexible rule to that effect. As in all cases of interpretation of contracts, the question is one of reading words in their proper context.[173] In *Marquis Cholmondeley v Lord Clinton*,[174] Plumer MR said: **5.74**

"When technical words or phrases are made use of, the strong presumption is that the party intended to use them according to their correct technical meaning, but this is not conclusive evidence that this was his real meaning. If the technical meaning is found, in the particular case, to be an erroneous guide to the real one,

---

[168] [2009] EWCA Civ 668.
[169] *Hallam Land Management Ltd v UK Coal Mining Ltd* [2002] 2 E.G.L.R. 80.
[170] [2009] 2 P. & C.R. 1.
[171] *Castlebay Ltd v Asquith Properties Ltd* [2006] 2 P. & C.R. 22.
[172] *Walker v Kenley* [2008] EWHC 370 (Ch); [2008] 1 P. & C.R. DG21.
[173] *Sunport Shipping Ltd v Tryg-Baltica International (UK) Ltd* [2003] 1 Lloyd's Rep. 138 CA.
[174] (1820) 2 Jac. & W. 1 at 92. See also *Roddy v Fitzgerald* (1858) 6 H.L. Cas. 823 (a will case).

leading to a meaning contrary to what the party intended to convey by it, it ceases to answer its purpose."

In such a case the presumption is displaced and the technical expression construed according to the real meaning the parties intended to place on it. Thus in *Re Kaupthing Singer & Friedlander*,[175] Blair J interpreted the phrase "winding up" in a trust deed for a subordinated bond issue as including entry into administration. Although he recognised the principle that "where a legal term of art is used in a document, the court will normally give the term its technical meaning in law", he nevertheless held that there were sufficient contra-indications to displace the presumption.[176] In *Gaia Ventures Ltd v Abbeygate Helical (Leisure Plaza) Ltd*,[177] a development agreement was made subject to a number of conditions, one of which was that "the registered leases are merged in the Superior Lease and the Superior Lease is merged in the freehold". The court held that "merged" was not to be interpreted in its strict technical sense, but could include surrender.

5.75 The presumption may also be displaced in a contract intended to have extra-territorial effect. In *Wooldridge v Canelhas Comercio Importacao E Exportacao Ltd*,[178] an English insurance policy covered a Brazilian insured against robbery in Brazil. It was held that concepts employed in it such as "robbery" had to be understood, not in any technical English legal sense, but in the sense in which "ordinary commercial men" would understand them. Mance LJ said:

> "It is of course true that one would expect any ordinary reasonable commercial person obtaining or issuing a policy such as the present to have a general conception of 'robbery' which one might also expect to correspond broadly with that used by legislators here and elsewhere. But a proper understanding of the Holdup or Robbery Limit clause requires consideration of how such a person would understand the whole clause in its context."

5.76 The presumption may be more easily displaced in a case where it is clear that the document in question was not drafted by a lawyer, for:

> "where a word or phrase which is a 'term of art' is used by an author who is not a lawyer, particularly in a document which he does not anticipate may have to be construed by a lawyer, he may have meant by it something different from its meaning when used by a lawyer as a term of art."[179]

This robust approach pays proper attention to the reality that many contracts are not the work of the parties at all, but of lawyers acting on their behalf, and that a different attitude may be appropriate where the contract in question is "home-made".

5.77 The presumption may also be more easily displaced where a contract has been written in "plain English" intended to be understandable to non-lawyers. Thus, in

---

[175] [2010] EWHC 316 (Ch).

[176] Contrast the very different approach of the Court of Appeal in *William Hare Ltd v Shepherd Construction Ltd* [2010] EWCA Civ 283.

[177] [2019] EWCA Civ 823; [2019] E.G.L.R. 25.

[178] [2004] Lloyd's Rep. I.R. 915.

[179] See *Sydall v Castings Ltd* [1967] 1 Q.B. 302, per Diplock LJ.

Homeowners Insurance Pty Ltd v Job,[180] Hutley JA said:

> "There is a current demand by law reformers for policies of insurance expressed in ordinary language and this policy suggests that this is one of its objectives. ... [T]here is no ... justification for retaining the impediments of the past in interpreting household insurance policies. To seek enlightenment as to the meaning of this policy in the ancient criminal law is, in my opinion, to frustrate modern needs ...".

Where, however, the expression has no meaning other than as a technical term **5.78** of art, the court has little choice but to construe it as meaning that. In *Leach v Jay*,[181] Jessel MR said:

> "In this particular will the testatrix, for what reason I know not, has used a technical word—a word not only technical, but a word that has no signification in ordinary language at all. It is a purely technical word; and it appears to me that the whole of my duty consists in ascertaining whether she was at the time of her death 'seised'—according to the technical meaning of that technical term—of this real estate."

Some terms of art do not, however, have immutable meanings. For example the **5.79** concept of "negligence" may have been enlarged or diminished by judicial policy from time to time in defining the limits of a duty of care or of remoteness of damage. In theory the court in such cases is merely declaring what the common law has always been. In those circumstances, it seems likely that the court would interpret such a term of art in the sense in which it was understood at the date of the hearing.[182]

Illustrations

1. A group life assurance scheme was set up by a company for its employees. Payments were made to certain classes of people including "descendants" of the employee in question. It was held that "descendant" was a legal term of art meaning legitimate descendant, and consequently no payment could be made to an illegitimate child of the employee.
   Sydall v Castings Ltd[183]

2. A policy of insurance insured stock in trade against loss or damage by "burglary and housebreaking as hereinafter defined". The risk insured against was expressed to be "by theft following upon actual and violent entry upon the premises". It was held that the words "as hereinafter defined" negatived any intention to use the words "burglary" and "housebreaking" as legal terms of art.

---

[180] (1993) 2 ANZ Ins. Cas. 60-53560-535 at 78,102 (dissenting). Cf. per Priestly JA at 78,133.
[181] (1877) 6 Ch. D. 496.
[182] *Lymington Marina Ltd v MacNamara* [2007] EWCA Civ 15; [2007] Bus. L.R. D 291. See also para.4.32.
[183] [1967] 1 Q.B. 302.

Consequently, the policy did not cover loss arising out of theft following an entry without violence.

Re George and the Goldsmiths and General Burglary Insurance Assn Ltd[184]

3.   A settlement settled funds on such trusts as "shall not infringe the rule against perpetuities" as the trustees should think fit. It was held that the reference to the rule against perpetuities was a reference to the true rule and that the "dictionary principle" could not justify construing the reference according to the draftsman's possibly erroneous appreciation of the law.

IRC v Williams[185]

4.   A building contract contained a clause which set out the rights of the parties as regards "set-off". It was held that "set-off" meant set-off as defined by decisions of the court, and did not extend to other types of defence to liability.

Acsim (Southern) Ltd v Danish Contracting and Development Ltd[186]

5.   A policy of insurance excluded loss caused directly or indirectly or in consequence of riot. It was held that the word "riot" bore its legal meaning in the criminal law, and that loss caused by a robbery by four armed men was not covered by the policy.

London and Lancashire Fire Insurance Co Ltd v Bolands Ltd[187]

6.   A policy of motor insurance excluded loss due to theft while the insured's keys were left unattended in the car. It was held that "theft" was to be given the definition in the Theft Act 1968 and included robbery, which was a form of theft.

Hayward v Norwich Union Insurance Ltd[188]

9.   CUSTOMARY MEANINGS

Where a word has a customary meaning in a particular locality or trade, or among a particular class of persons, evidence is admissible to show that the parties intended to give the word that meaning, and upon proof of such intention, the word should be construed accordingly.[189]

---

[184] [1899] 1 Q.B. 595.

[185] [1969] 1 W.L.R. 1197 at 1203, per Megarry J:

> "If an instrument refers to 'the rule against perpetuities' or any other rule, then in my judgment the reference is to the true rule unless the instrument makes it sufficiently plain that something else is meant, and what that something else is. I do not consider that a mere appearance in the instrument of a lack of comprehension of the true rule, or some error in its application, is sufficient to prevent the reference bearing its primary meaning".

[186] (1989) 47 B.L.R. 55 CA.

[187] [1924] A.C. 836 HL, per Lord Sumner:

> "There is, however, no warrant here for saying that, when the proviso uses a word which is emphatically a term of legal art, it is to be confined, in the interpretation of the policy, to circumstances which are only within popular notions on the subject, but are not within the technical meaning of the word. It clearly must be so with regard to martial law; it clearly, I think, must be so with regards to acts of foreign enemies; and I see no reason why the word 'riot' should not include its technical meaning here as clearly as 'burglary' and 'house-breaking' do."

[188] [2001] 1 All E.R. (Comm) 545 CA.

[189] This section was referred to with approval in *Legal Services Commission v Loomba* [2012] EWHC 29 (QB) at [74]; [2012] 1 W.L.R. 2461 at [74].

In *Shore v Wilson*,[190] Parke B. said that evidence was admissible to enable the court to construe a word where:

> "any expressions are used, which at the time the instrument was written had acquired an appropriate meaning, either generally or by local usage, or among particular classes."

In the same case, Tindal CJ said that evidence was admissible to explain words which:

> "have acquired, by custom or otherwise, a well-known peculiar idiomatic meaning in the particular country in which the party using them was dwelling, or in the particular society of which he formed a member and in which he passed his life."

5.80

Thus in *Smith v Wilson*,[191] a lease of a warren in Suffolk required the tenant to leave 10,000 rabbits in the warren at the end of the term. Evidence was admitted to show that according to the custom of the country, a thousand meant 1,200. Lord Tenterden CJ said:

> "we must suppose the term thousand to have been used by the parties in the sense in which it is usually understood in the place where the contract was made, when applied to the subject of rabbits, and parol evidence was admissible to shew what that sense was."

5.81

Similarly, in *Produce Brokers Co Ltd v Olympia Oil and Cake Co Ltd*,[192] Scrutton LJ said:

> "But it is quite clear that, though the meaning of a contract is varied, you may use a custom first of all in the case where you are using the custom as a dictionary to explain what words in the contract mean; where the contract says 'twelve' you may show that by custom 'twelve' means 'thirteen' (a baker's dozen), and where the contract says 'one hundred' you may prove by custom that 'one hundred' means the long hundred (one hundred and twenty) and where the contract says 'payment at thirty days' as in the case of an ordinary bill of exchange or promissory note, you may prove that thirty days means thirty-three days, or that three months means three months and three days. You may use the custom to define places. 'Alongside' without a custom may mean a certain area, and 'alongside' with a custom may mean a much larger area."

This principle complements, and to some extent overlaps with, the principle that the court will interpret non-legal technical terms in their technical sense, if it appears from the circumstances that the parties intended the words to be so construed. It is difficult to distinguish (if distinction is needed) between cases in which the court is construing a technical term, and cases where the court is recognising a trade

5.82

---

[190] (1842) 9 Cl. & Fin. 355.
[191] (1832) 3 B. & Ad. 732.
[192] [1917] 1 K.B. 320 at 330.

usage. In *Myers v Sarl*,[193] a building contract required the builder to deliver a "weekly account" of work done. It was found by the arbitrator, upon oral evidence, that the expression "weekly account" had a special meaning in the building trade. On a case stated, Cockburn CJ said:

> "Now, although parol evidence is not admissible to contradict a contract the terms of which have but one ordinary meaning and acceptation, yet if the parties have used terms which bear not only an ordinary meaning, but one also peculiar to the department of trade or business to which the contract relates, it is obvious that due effect would not be given to the intention, if the terms were interpreted according to their ordinary and not according to their peculiar signification. Therefore it has always been held that where the terms of a contract have, besides their ordinary and popular sense, also a peculiar and scientific meaning, the parties who have drawn up the contract with reference to some particular department of trade or business, must have intended to use the words in the peculiar sense."

5.83   Whether this is described as a case involving a technical term or a trade usage does not seem to matter. The court's approach is the same. However, where a word or phrase does not have a customary meaning in a particular trade or industry, no assistance is gained by admitting evidence from those practising in the industry of what they think particular words or phrases mean.[194]

5.84   Further, in the same way as the court may sometimes inform itself as to the meaning of a technical term by consulting an appropriate dictionary, so also the court may sometimes inform itself of a particularly notorious trade usage by consulting reported cases recognising such usages, or even by taking judicial notice of them.[195]

Illustration

A contract under which an actress was engaged for three years at a weekly salary was held to entitle her to be paid only during the theatrical season, for the word year had that special meaning in theatrical circles.
Grant v Maddox[196]

10.   PARTIES' OWN DICTIONARY

Examination of the context in which words are used may reveal that the parties have attributed their own peculiar meaning to words, in which case it is the duty of the court to give effect to that meaning.[197]

5.85   It is well-established that, in construing a contract, evidence is admissible to show that the parties have used terms bearing a special or technical meaning. However in a case in which the only issue is the interpretation of a contract the parties may

---

[193]   (1860) 3 E. & E. 306.
[194]   *Sunrock Aircraft Corp Ltd v Scandinavian Airlines System* [2007] 2 Lloyd's Rep. 612.
[195]   See 32 *Halsbury's Laws of England*, 4th edn (Butterworths), para.86 where examples are given.
[196]   (1846) 15 M. & W. 737.
[197]   This section was referred to with approval in *Legal Services Commission v Loomba* [2012] EWHC 29 (QB) at [74]; [2012] 1 W.L.R. 2461 at [74].

not adduce evidence that they negotiated on the basis of an idiosyncratic meaning.[198] However, the contract in the light of the admissible background may reveal that the parties have used language in an unconventional way. This principle is often described as a case in which the parties have made their own dictionary, for they are using words neither in the sense to be found in a published dictionary, nor yet in some recognised technical sense. It is the principle that is at the heart of the contextual interpretation of contracts, and it has been part of English law for many years. The best-known formulation of this principle is that of Lord Cottenham LC in *Lloyd v Lloyd*[199]:

"If the provisions are clearly expressed and there is nothing to enable the court to put upon them a construction different from that which the words impart, no doubt the words must prevail; but if the provisions and expressions be contradictory, and if there be grounds, appearing from the face of the instrument, affording proof of the real intention of the parties, then that real intention will prevail against the obvious and ordinary meaning of the words. If the parties have themselves furnished a key to the meaning of the words used, it is not material by what expressions they convey their intention."

In *Re Sassoon*,[200] Romer LJ said:

"Except in actions for rectification the Court has no power whatsoever of adding to or subtracting from the words of a written instrument. A testator or settlor may, however, in the instrument itself indicate sufficiently plainly that he is using certain words or phrases in other than their literal and ordinary meaning. In such cases he is said to have provided his own dictionary, and the Court will construe such words and phrases in the light of that dictionary."

In *Electric & Musical Industries Ltd v Lissen*,[201] Lord Russell of Killowen said: **5.86**

"I would point out that there is no question here of words in the first claim bearing any special or unusual meaning by reason either of a dictionary found elsewhere in the specification or of technical knowledge possessed by persons skilled in the art. The prima facie meaning of words used in a claim may not be their true meaning when read in the light of such a dictionary, or of such technical knowledge, and in those circumstances, a claim, when so construed, may bear a meaning different from that which it would have borne had no such assisting light been available."

In *NHS Commissioning Board v Vasant*,[202] the court admitted evidence to explain the meaning of "an intermediate minor oral surgery service" in a contract made between the NHS Commissioning Board and three dentists. Lewison LJ said:

"Although each word, considered separately, is an ordinary English word, I do not consider that it is possible to give meaning to the phrase as a whole without extrinsic evidence."

[198] *Alexiou v Campbell* [2007] UKPC 11; *Chartbrook Ltd v Persimmon Homes Ltd* [2009] A.C. 1101 (where a more expansive application of the "private dictionary" principle was disapproved).
[199] (1837) 2 My. & Cr. 192.
[200] [1933] 1 Ch. 858. See also *Re Birks* [1900] 1 Ch. 417 at 419, per Sir F. H. Jeune.
[201] [1938] 4 All E.R. 221 HL.
[202] [2019] EWCA Civ 1245.

Neither the existence of an "entire agreement" clause nor a "no oral modification" clause precluded the admission of such evidence to explain the meaning of the words actually used.

5.87 Although Lord Cottenham said that the proof must appear "from the face of the deed", the modern approach is not to confine the search for meaning so narrowly. A modern court of construction may conclude, by reference to the admissible background to the contract, that parties used words in a special sense, or even that they used the wrong words.

5.88 In *Chartbrook Ltd v Persimmon Homes Ltd*,[203] Lord Hoffmann said:

> "It is true that evidence may always be adduced that the parties habitually used words in an unconventional sense in order to support an argument that words in a contract should bear a similar unconventional meaning. This is the 'private dictionary' principle, which is akin to the principle by which a linguistic usage in a trade or among a religious sect may be proved."

It is to be noted that Lord Hoffmann is here considering a case in which the parties "habitually" use words in an unconventional sense.

5.89 Where, however, it is alleged that the parties agreed a particular meaning of words in the course of pre-contractual negotiations of a one-off contract, the case will normally be one for estoppel or rectification, which must be pleaded and proved. In *Vector Gas Ltd v Bay of Plenty Energy Co Ltd*,[204] Tipping J said:

> "A private dictionary meaning is a meaning the words linguistically cannot reasonably bear. It is, nevertheless, open to a party to show that, despite that fact, the parties intended their words to have that special meaning for the purposes of their contract. This represents a consensual parallel with cases in which words have a special meaning by trade custom. It can also be regarded as a linguistic example of estoppel by convention. The estoppel prevents the accepted special meaning from later being disavowed. Estoppels can also arise in interpretation cases not involving a special meaning. They are then normally based on a common assumption or representation as to meaning … If parties wish, they may contract on the basis that black means white; albeit the unlikelihood of their doing so, without expressly saying so, will no doubt be a powerful factor when it comes to questions of proof. Whether the parties have adopted a private dictionary meaning must be determined objectively in the same way as other disputes as to meaning are determined."

5.90 A will written in cipher would be explicable by evidence.[205] However, where parties use their own private code, they must ensure that it is intelligible to each other.

---

[203] [2009] A.C. 1101.

[204] [2010] NZSC 5. His Honour's view may go further than the current state of English law. His Honour acknowledged the influence of Professor McLauchlan's powerful article "Contract Interpretation: What is it all About" (2009) *Sydney Law Review* 5. But Professor McLauchlan's view on the general admissibility of pre-contractual negotiations was rejected by the HL in *Chartbrook Ltd v Persimmon Homes Ltd*.

[205] *Clayton v Lord Nugent* (1844) 13 M. & W. 200 at 206, per Alderson B. In that case the testator made bequests to persons identified only by a single capital letter. The will stated that a key to the letters could be found in the testator's desk. However, the only key found was one which post-dated the will by many years. It was held that the key was inadmissible.

So where two persons interpreted a coded telegram differently it was held that no contract resulted.[206]

Illustrations

1.   A post-nuptial settlement settled funds to be held on trust for E described as the wife of JK, and after her death for her children. Although E went through a ceremony of marriage with JK the marriage was invalid. The question was whether the word "children" bore its usual legal meaning of "legitimate children". The court held that it did not. Buckley LJ said:

"... I am entitled to say that the settlor in this instrument was using such a dictionary as that 'child' means the offspring of this union."

Ebbern v Fowler[207]

2.   A shipbroker and a chartering agent communicated in code. The agent sent the shipbroker a coded message by which he intended to instruct the shipbroker to load a ship with copra in Fiji for delivery in the UK. The shipbroker interpreted it as instructing him to charter the ship to carry shale from Sydney to Barcelona. It was held that no contract resulted.
Falck v Williams[208]

3.   A testator bequeathed to one of his sons the sum of "i.x.x." and to another the sum of "o.x.x.". In his lifetime the deceased had been a jeweller, and had used those private symbols to denote specific sums of money. The court admitted evidence to explain them.
Kell v Charmer[209]

11.   DEFINITION CLAUSES

Where a word or expression is expressly defined by the contract the court will give effect to the agreed definition in preference to the conventional meaning of the word or expression.

Parties are, of course, free to provide express definitions of terms which they employ in their contract. If they do so the court will uphold the definitions so agreed, even where the meaning attributed to the defined term by the definition is not its ordinary meaning.[210] If a contract defines a term, there is no permissible basis for ignoring it save in exceptional circumstances. In *T&N Ltd (in administration) v Royal & Sun Alliance Plc*,[211] an insurance policy excluded liability for pneumoconiosis. The policy contained a definition of "pneumoconiosis". Lawrence Collins J said:

5.91

"I do not consider that there is any legitimate process of interpretation which can

---

[206] *Falck v Williams* [1900] A.C. 176.
[207] [1909] 1 Ch. 578. This is a case in which the context alone showed that the word was being used in a special sense.
[208] [1900] A.C. 176.
[209] (1856) 23 Beav. 195.
[210] *Re George and the Goldsmiths and General Burglary Insurance Association Ltd* [1899] 1 Q.B. 595.
[211] [2003] 2 All E.R. (Comm) 939.

yield the meaning for which the Royal contends, either on the basis of an appeal to the idea of something having gone wrong with the words, or on the basis of an appeal to the factual matrix. The exclusion contains its own specific definition of 'pneumoconiosis' and there is no permissible basis for ignoring that express definition. I accept T&N's case that any attempt by the Royal to widen the factual matrix for the purpose of putting a different, wider meaning on the word 'pneumoconiosis' will plainly be not for the purpose of explaining the words used, but rather for the purpose of contradicting them, i.e. that 'white is black and that a dollar is fifty cents'."

5.92   So also in *JIS (1974) Ltd v MCE Investment Nominees I Ltd*,[212] a lease contained a definition of the "demised premises" and it was argued the expression should be given a more limited meaning in the context of a tenant's break clause and that part of the demise should be excluded. Carnwath LJ said:

"'Demised premises', for the purposes of the break clause, are defined as including the shop units. To put it beyond doubt, the schedule says that they are excluded only for the purpose of the rent review. That is what the language says, and no amount of background evidence will change that stark fact."

In *Pierse Developments Ltd v Liberty Property Investment Ltd*,[213] cl.15(g) of a contract defined "Completion Date". Etherton LJ said:

"It would be a highly unusual approach to interpretation to give the expression in cl 15(g) a meaning other than that expressly ascribed to it by the parties, especially since the parties did not state that the definition was subject to any contrary intention apparent from the Agreement."

5.93   A definition clause contained in a contract will take priority over a recital to the contract.[214]

5.94   If a contract contains an express definition, then in the absence of a claim for rectification or a plea of estoppel, evidence of the negotiations is not admissible for the purpose of contradicting the definition, even where it is alleged that the parties negotiated on the basis of an agreed meaning.[215]

5.95   In deciding what a defined term means, the court may have regard to the contractual label chosen by the parties as the defined term. In *Chartbrook Ltd v Persimmon Homes Ltd*,[216] Lord Hoffmann said:

"But the contract does not use algebraic symbols. It uses labels. The words used as labels are seldom arbitrary. They are usually chosen as a distillation of the meaning or purpose of a concept intended to be more precisely stated in the definition. In such cases the language of the defined expression may help to elucidate ambiguities in the definition or other parts of the agreement."

In *Cattles Plc v Welcome Financial Services Ltd*,[217] Lloyd LJ said that the label:

---

[212] [2003] EWCA Civ 721.
[213] [2009] EWCA Civ 1423.
[214] *Brookfield Construction (UK) Ltd v Foster & Partners Ltd* [2009] EWHC 307 (TCC).
[215] *Chartbrook Homes Ltd v Persimmon Homes Ltd* [2009] A.C. 1101.
[216] [2009] A.C. 1101.
[217] [2010] EWCA Civ 599.

"is not something to which reference should only be made if the matter is otherwise in doubt. The word used by way of a label may well not be arbitrary or neutral, and here I have no doubt that the labels used were not arbitrary or neutral."

There are, of course, different forms of definition clause. In *Singapore Airlines Ltd v Buck*,[218] Arden LJ said:

    5.96

"Definitions in statutes and deeds can be exhaustive or non-exhaustive. Non-exhaustive definitions are usually prefaced by the word 'include'. More often, however, a definition is intended to be exhaustive and it will then generally begin with the word 'mean' or 'means'. It is difficult to read a definition which begins with the word 'means' as other than exhaustive."

Thus where a term is defined as "including" certain things, the definition is not exhaustive, and anything which falls within the natural meaning of the term in the context of the particular contract will also be held to fall within the defined term.[219] Sometimes a definition is qualified by the phrase "where the context so admits". These two forms of definition clause have been said to be "weaker" than a clause which simply states what a defined word "means".[220]

In *Johnsey Estates Ltd v Webb*,[221] a lease defined "tenant" as including the tenant's successors in title where the context so admits. A surety covenanted to guarantee the tenant's obligations "so long as the term hereby granted is vested in the tenant". The landlord argued that the definition of "tenant" meant that the surety remained liable after the lease ceased to be vested in the original tenant. Millett J rejected the argument. He said:

"In my judgment that is not the effect of the words 'where the context so admits'. They are not the same as 'save where the context otherwise requires'. Unless the court is of the opinion not only that the extended definition is capable of being given effect but also that the context admits of that extended definition, then the court must construe the words 'the tenant' as meaning only the original tenant. In my judgment, it would be wrong, by reliance on the words 'where the context so admits' to place on words which in themselves are plain and unambiguous and have an easily understood and commercially acceptable sense, a highly technical and artificial meaning which only a very experienced conveyancer and, I might add, insolvency practitioner at that would think of."

However, in *Parkside Clubs (Nottingham) Ltd v Armgrade Ltd*,[222] the Court of Appeal took a rather different approach. A lease of a casino defined "the Tenant" as including the tenant's successors in title where the context so admits. The rent review clause required the assumption that all necessary licences had been granted to the "Tenant". The Court held that the "Tenant" meant the actual tenant and not the hypothetical tenant to be assumed for the purposes of the review. Leggatt LJ said:

"The lease stipulates at the outset that the appellants are to be called the 'Ten-

---

[218] [2011] EWCA Civ 1542; [2012] Pens. L.R. 1.
[219] *Adelphi (Estates) Ltd v Christie* [1984] 1 E.G.L.R. 19.
[220] *Franklins Pty Ltd v Metcash Trading Ltd* [2009] NSWCA 407 at [343] and [344].
[221] [1990] 1 E.G.L.R. 80.
[222] [1995] 2 E.G.L.R. 96 CA.

ant' and that the expression shall, where appropriate, include successors in title and assigns. For my part, I cannot see how, in default of rectification, the term can then be construed as meaning something else, at any rate unless in context it would be absurd to treat it as referring to the actual tenant."

In *Yafai v Muthana*,[223] Sir Andrew Morritt C said:

"It is trite law that the Partnership Deed must be construed as a whole. Thus the definitions contained in cl 2.1 must be applied throughout the document unless a particular context otherwise requires."

5.97   The use of the phrase "unless the context otherwise requires" may itself be ambiguous. The context may mean the context in which the contract is made, in other words, the whole background or the matrix of fact. It may, however, be that the relevant context is the context in the contract itself, in other words the context in which the word is used from time to time and place to place in the contract. In most cases this will not matter,[224] but context will not usually be allowed to contradict an express definition. In *Hammonds v Jones*,[225] Lloyd LJ said:

"The definitions in the Partnership Deed apply 'unless the context otherwise requires'. This does enable the definition to give way to the context if necessary. I accept Mr Croxford's point that it must be necessary, rather than merely sensible or reasonable."

In that case, having regard to the agreement as a whole the definition was disapplied to one provision of the agreement because the context required that.

In *Horsell International Pty Ltd v Divetwo Pty Ltd*,[226] the New South Wales Court of Appeal held that a definition clause preceded by the words "means and includes" indicated "an exhaustive explanation of the content of the term which is the subject of the definition, and conveys the idea both of enlargement and exclusion". But a sentence beginning with the words "includes" and "relating to" had an enlarging effect.[227]

5.98   In *AIB Group (UK) Ltd v Martin*,[228] a mortgage entered into by two people named as 'the mortgagor' contained a clause which said:

"If the expression "the mortgagor" includes more than one person it shall be construed as referring to all and/or any one of those persons and the obligations of such persons hereunder shall be joint and several."

The question was whether each of the named persons was liable not only for his own debts but also those of the other named borrower. A majority of the House of Lords held that he was. Lord Millett[229] said:

"The fact that the question concerns the application of an interpretation clause is also significant. The purpose of such a clause is twofold. It shortens the draft-

[223] [2012] EWCA Civ 289.
[224] *Phillips v Rafiq* [2007] 1 W.L.R. 1351.
[225] [2009] EWCA Civ 1400.
[226] [2013] NSWCA 368 at [161].
[227] [2013] NSWCA 368 at [165].
[228] [2002] 1 W.L.R. 94.
[229] In a dissenting speech.

ing and avoids unnecessary repetition; and it enables the form to be used in a variety of different situations. It is not the purpose of such a clause to enlarge the parties' rights and obligations beyond those provided by the operative provisions by imposing, for example, a secondary liability as surety in addition to a primary liability as principal debtor. The application of such a clause is not merely a question of construction. If it is capable of being applied to the operative provisions in more than one way, it should be applied in a way which serves its purpose rather than in a way which extends the parties' obligations beyond those contemplated by the operative provisions. Of course, an interpretation clause may have this effect; but if so it should do so plainly and unambiguously."

However, Lord Scott of Foscote considered that the clause in that case was plain and unambiguous; and Lord Rodger of Earlsferry regarded it as not merely a definition clause. He considered that it was concerned not with the question who is to be taken to be the borrower—that is to say, with the person or persons to whom that expression extends—but with the measure of the obligations undertaken by those persons in that capacity. Accordingly, a provision found in the definition clause was capable of extending the substantive obligations of the parties.

Where the background or usage elsewhere in the contract plainly shows that something has gone wrong with the definition, the court should not adopt an excessively literal interpretation.[230] In some cases this may lead the court to disapply the definition. In *City Inn (Jersey) Ltd v Ten Trinity Square Ltd*,[231] Jacob LJ said: **5.99**

"It is obviously a strong thing to say that where a draftsman has actually defined a term for the purposes of his document that in some places (but not others) where he uses his chosen term he must have intended some other meaning. It is not impossible, however. If, approaching the document through the eyes of the intended sort of reader (here a conveyancer), the court concludes that notwithstanding his chosen definition the draftsman just must have meant something else by the use of the term, it will so construe the document. Such a conclusion will only be reached where, if the term is given its defined meaning the result would be absurd, given the factual background, known to both parties, in which the document was prepared. Nothing less than absurdity will do—it is not enough that one conclusion makes better commercial sense than another."

However, in *Margerison v Bates*,[232] Edward Bartley-Jones QC, sitting as a judge of the Chancery Division, said of *City Inn*:

"I note, in particular, that Jacob L.J. went on to construe the relevant Transfer. He did not confine himself, solely, to issues of commercial absurdity. Ultimately (paragraph 31) Jacob L.J. addressed the rival contentions as to 'commercial sense'. Indeed, he pointed out that the submissions (on commercial sense) as to why the definition should not be applied according to its express terms had caused him to 'pause long and hard'. Taking the judgment as a whole, I see Jacob L.J. doing nothing more than construing the relevant Transfer in accordance with the principles I have identified above, albeit against the background that strong

---

[230] *Ellis v Coleman* [2004] EWHC 3407 (Ch). In *Hopkinson v Towergate Financial (Group) Ltd [2019] EWCA Civ* [2018] EWCA Civ 2744 the CA had real difficulty where the contract was not consistent in its use of defined terms and capitalised words.
[231] [2008] EWCA Civ 156.
[232] [2008] 3 E.G.L.R. 165; *Churchill v Temple* [2010] EWHC 3369 (Ch); [2011] 1 E.G.L.R. 73.

and cogent reasons must be advanced as to why a definition in a professionally prepared document should be departed from or given in different places alternative meanings. I do not see Jacob L.J. establishing any point of law to the effect that only commercial absurdity would suffice for departure, as a question of construction, from a specific definition. I am fortified in reaching this conclusion not merely by the terms of Jacob L.J.'s judgment as a whole but, also, from the whole basis of the approach to issues of construction as identified by Lord Hoffmann in *West Bromwich* (at 912G) where he indicated that, under the modern approach, 'Almost all the old intellectual baggage of "legal" interpretation has been discarded'. The modern approach to construction involves an interpretation of meaning applying the principles I have identified above, not an approach which is governed in respect of specific issues or instances by fixed rules of law."

In the result he held that a covenant in a conveyance not to erect buildings except with the consent of "the Vendor" meant the original vendor alone and did not extend to her successors in title. Similarly, in *Starlight Shipping Co v Allianz Marine And Aviation Versicherungs AG*,[233] Flaux J was doubtful whether the approach of Jacob LJ was consistent with the decision of the Supreme Court in *Rainy Sky v Kookmin Bank*.[234]

5.100   In *Europa Plus SCA SIF v Anthracite Investments (Ireland) Plc*[235] Popplewell J said:

"Where the Court is interpreting a contractual provision which uses a defined term, the starting point for a textual analysis will often be the defined meaning, because the fact that the parties have chosen to use it in the provision being interpreted is often an indication that they intended it to bear its defined meaning when so used. Often, but not always. It is a common experience that defined terms are not always used consistently by contractual draftsmen throughout a commercial contract. Where a de-fined term is used inconsistently within a contract, so as sometimes to bear the de-fined meaning and sometimes a different meaning, the potency of the inference that the parties intended it to bear its defined meaning in a particular provision is much diminished. The question becomes whether they intended to use it in its defined meaning, as in some other clauses, or as meaning something other than its defined meaning, as in different other clauses. Even where there is no inconsistency of use within the contract outside the provision being interpreted, it does not follow that effect must always be given to the defined meaning. If, as is well known, parties some-times use defined terms inappropriately, it follows that they may have done so only once, in the provision which is being interpreted. The process of interpretation remains the iterative process in which the language used must be tested against the commercial consequences and the background facts reasonably available to the parties at the time of contracting. Such an exercise may lead to the conclusion that the parties did not intend the defined term to bear the defined meaning in the provision in question. That is no different from the Court concluding that the parties intended a word or phrase to have a different meaning from what would at first sight seem to be its ordinary or natural meaning."

---

[233] [2014] EWHC 3068 (Comm).
[234] [2011] UKSC 50; [2011] 1 W.L.R. 2900.
[235] [2016] EWHC 437 (Comm).

He held further that:

"... the dictum of Jacob LJ in *City Inn Jersey Ltd v 10 Trinity Square Ltd*, to the effect that the court will only fail to give effect to the use of a defined term if absurdity is established, is not consistent with the reasoning of the Supreme Court in Rainy Sky (or indeed subsequent authority) and is not the law."

On the other hand, in *Anglo Continental Educational Group (GB) Ltd v Capital Homes (Southern) Ltd*,[236] a clause in a contract stated that "the following words and expressions shall have the following meanings for all purposes". Arden LJ said: **5.101**

"Accordingly the possibility of defined terms being excluded by the context is ruled out."

In the author's opinion this uncompromising statement may go too far. Even where the contract contains an apparently comprehensive definition, it is thought that the court could depart from it if the application of the definition produced an absurd result; or if other features in the contract so required. The fact that a term in a contract is a defined term is a factor to be considered in construing the contract, but not a decisive factor.[237] In *Chipsaway International Ltd v Kerr*,[238] the court departed from a defined term, because application of the definition would have produced a nonsense. This point is not affected by the subsequent reversal of that decision by the Court of Appeal[239] which departed even further from the defined term.

Illustrations

1. A lease of a flat required the tenant to pay a service charge equal to 2.9 per cent of the expenditure on services incurred by the lessors. The lease contained a clause defining "the lessors" as including the person for the time being entitled to the immediate reversion to the lease. The original lessor granted an overriding lease of the flat in consequence of which the tenant's immediate landlord paid by way of service charge a sum of money to the superior landlord who in fact performed the services. It was held that the expression "lessors" was apt to include the "superior lessors" having regard to the scheme of management of the building.
   Adelphi (Estates) Ltd v Christie[240]

2. An insurance policy covered loss or damage by "burglary or housebreaking as hereinafter defined". The Divisional Court considered whether the particular loss was occasioned by burglary in the sense in which the law was understood as a matter of criminal law. The Court of Appeal held that that approach was wrong. Collins LJ said:

"They have chosen to frame for themselves a definition of burglary and housebreaking for the purposes of their contract, and by that definition their rights

---

[236] [2009] EWCA Civ 218.
[237] *Starlight Shipping Co v Allianz Marine and Aviation Versicherungs AG* [2014] EWHC 3068 (Comm).
[238] [2008] EWHC 1887 (Ch).
[239] [2009] EWCA Civ 320.
[240] [1984] 1 E.G.L.R. 19.

in this case must be determined."

Re George and The Goldsmiths and General Burglary Insurance Association Ltd[241]

3.   A partnership agreement defined "Partners" in terms that excluded "Partners who shall ... have ceased to be Partners under the provisions hereof or otherwise." A dispute arose between an outgoing partner and the remaining partners who had exercised an option to buy his partnership share. The option was exercised after his retirement from the partnership. An arbitration clause provided for arbitration of disputes "between the Partners touching the Partnership". It was held that the definition of "Partner" should not be strictly applied to the arbitration clause; and that the dispute fell within the jurisdiction of the arbitrator.
Ellis v Coleman[242]

4.   A licence described "the Licensor" as A, B and C and "the Licensee" as B and D. The licence was liable to be terminated upon the failure of B and D to remedy any remediable breaches within the time specified by a notice given by "the Licensor" to "the Licensee". Although B was both licensor and licensee, it was held that despite practical difficulties the notice had to be given by all those making up "the Licensor" as defined.
Fitzhugh v Fitzhugh[243]

5.   A deed of covenant described the covenantee as the "Adjoining Owner". In deciding whether the benefit of the covenant was annexed to land, the court considered that the defined term itself indicated that the covenantee had the benefit of the covenant in his capacity as landowner.
89 Holland Park Management Ltd v Hicks[244]

12.   CONTEXT

Even where a word has a single primary meaning, the choice between meanings is determined by the context in which the word is used.

5.102   It is difficult to over-state the importance that the modern court attaches to the context in which words are used.[245] As Lord Hoffmann said in *Kirin Amgen Inc v Hoechst Marion Rousel Ltd*[246]:

"No one has ever made an acontextual statement. There is always some context to any utterance, however meagre."

In *Zhoushan Jinhaiwan Shipyard Co Ltd v Golden Exquisite Inc*,[247] Leggatt J said:

---

[241] [1899] 1 Q.B. 595.

[242] [2004] EWHC 3407 (Ch).

[243] [2012] EWCA Civ 694; [2012] 2 P. & C.R. 14. This is a particularly stark example, and the author is not convinced that it is correct.

[244] [2013] EWHC 391 (Ch).

[245] In *R. v Secretary of State for the Home Department Ex p. Daly* [2001] 2 A.C. 532 at 548 (statutory construction) Lord Steyn said: "In law, context is everything". Jacob LJ repeated this in a contractual context: *Debenhams Retail Plc v Sun Alliance and London Assurance Co Ltd* [2005] 3 E.G.L.R. 34. The phrase has since been repeated many times.

[246] [2005] R.P.C. 169 at [64].

[247] [2014] EWHC 4050 (Comm); [2015] 1 Lloyd's Rep. 283.

"Identifying the meaning of the words used, however, and the shared purposes and values which the parties may be taken to have had are not two separate inquiries. The meaning of all language depends on its context. To paraphrase a philosopher of language,[248] sentence in never not in a context. Contracting parties are never not in a situation. A contract is never not read in the light of some purpose. Interpretive assumptions are always in force. A sentence that seems to need no interpretation is already the product of one. At the same time the main source from which the shared purposes and values of the parties can be ascertained is the contract they have made. It is for these reasons that it is a fundamental principle of the interpretation of contracts that the contractual document must be read as a whole."

Similar statements were made at the beginning of the 20th century, and earlier. **5.103** Traditionally the principle was summarised in the Latin maxim *noscitur a sociis*.[249] In *Cave v Horsell*,[250] Buckley LJ said:

"There are few words, if indeed there be any, which bear a meaning so exact as that the reader can disregard the surrounding circumstances and the context in which the word is employed. Not even words expressive of number escape the ordeal. There are trades in which a dozen does not mean twelve nor a hundred five score. There are words upon whose primary meaning there is no room for doubt. I may instance again the word 'dozen'. But this is not true of all words. Many are not of fixed, but of flexible meaning. Such a word may have many primary meanings. It is for the reader, looking at the context, to say in which of those meanings it is employed."

In *Tektrol Ltd v International Insurance Co of Hanover Ltd*,[251] an insurance **5.104** policy excluded liability for "erasure loss distortion or corruption of information on computer systems". One question was whether theft of a computer which stored information fell within the clause. Sir Martin Nourse said:

"If, however, 'loss' is read in its context, its meaning becomes plain. The expression 'other erasure loss distortion or corruption of information' demonstrates that the loss contemplated is loss by means of electronic interference; *noscitur a sociis*. It is not just the effect of the other three words, but the order in which the four appear. 'Loss' follows 'erasure'. While erasure can be expected to result in loss, a careful draftsman would not necessarily assume that it was the only way in which information might be lost. Then follow 'distortion or corruption', which seem to refer to interference causing something less than erasure or loss and between which, as Buxton LJ has observed, it is difficult to suggest a clear distinction."

In *Phillips and Strattan v Dorintal Insurance Ltd*,[252] Steyn J said: **5.105**

"Words and phrases in contractual documents do not usually have one im-

---

[248] Stanley Fish, *Is there a Text in this Class?*
[249] See para.7.150.
[250] [1912] 3 K.B. 533. A similar point was made by Slade J in *Earl of Lonsdale v Att.-Gen.* [1981] 1 W.L.R. 887.
[251] [2005] 2 Lloyd's Rep. 701.
[252] [1987] 1 Lloyd's Rep. 482.

mutable meaning. Often there is more than one meaning available for selection. One cannot then simply turn to a dictionary for an answer, in choosing the appropriate meaning, the contextual scene is usually of paramount importance."

Similarly, in *Arbuthnott v Fagan*,[253] he said:

"Dictionaries never solve concrete problems of construction. The meaning of words cannot be ascertained divorced from their context."

In *Hawley v Luminar Leisure Ltd*,[254] Hallett LJ warned:

"Because the contractual and commercial circumstances of each case are inevitably different, it can be positively dangerous to draw assistance from the acontextual meaning or from decisions of other courts as to the meaning, of a particular word, when context is so important on issues of interpretation. Of course, very different considerations may apply where a particular word or phrase has a specific well-established meaning in a certain type of contract."

5.106   In an appropriate case, the context may be strong enough to indicate that a word which has a primary sense should be construed in a sense which is not its primary sense. Thus in *The Niobe*,[255] Lord Watson said:

"I admit the force of the appellant's argument that contracts ought to be construed according to the primary and natural meaning of the language in which the contracting parties have chosen to express the terms of their mutual agreement. But there are exceptions to the rule. One of these is to be found in the case where the context affords an interpretation different from the ordinary meaning of the words; and another in the case where their conventional meaning is not the same as their legal meaning."

5.107   Some judges, indeed, go as far as to say that the idea that words have a primary meaning is unhelpful. In *Charter Reinsurance Co Ltd v Fagan*,[256] Lord Hoffmann said:

"I think that in some cases the notion of words having a natural meaning is not a very helpful one. Because the meaning of words is so sensitive to syntax and context, the natural meaning of words in one sentence may be quite unnatural in another. Thus a statement that words have a particular natural meaning may mean no more than that in many contexts they will have that meaning. In other contexts their meaning will be different but no less natural."

Illustrations

1.   A distributorship agreement provided that it was a condition of the agreement that the distributor should visit six named firms at least once a week for the purpose of soliciting orders. The question arose whether the word "condition" meant that any breach of the term could be treated as a repudiation of the agreement. The House of Lords held that in the context of the agreement as a whole it did not.

---

[253] [1995] C.L.C. 1396, cited in *The Fina Samco* [1995] 2 Lloyd's Rep. 344 at 350, CA.
[254] [2006] I.R.L.R. 817.
[255] [1891] A.C. 401 at 408.
[256] [1997] A.C. 313. See para.5.23.

Lord Morris of Borth-y-Gest said:

"If a word employed by the parties in a contract has only one possible meaning then, unless any question of rectification arises, there will be no problem. If a word either by reason of general acceptance or by reason of judicial construction has come to have a particular meaning then, if used in a business or technical document, it will often be reasonable to suppose that the parties intended to use the word in its accepted sense. But if a word in a contract may have more than one meaning then, in interpreting the contract, a court will have to decide what was the intention of the parties as revealed by or deduced from the terms and subject-matter of their contract."

Schuler (L) AG v Wickman Machine Tool Sales Ltd[257]

2.   A lease of an office building imposed on the tenant a liability to repair. It was held that the liability did not extend to making the basement of the building waterproof. Hoffmann J said:

"All words take meaning from context and it is, of course, necessary to have regard to the language of the particular covenant and the lease as a whole, the commercial relationship between the parties, the state of the premises at the time of the demise and any surrounding circumstances which may colour the way the word is used. In the end, however, the question is whether the ordinary speaker of English would consider that the word 'repair' as used in the covenant was appropriate to describe the work which has to be done. The cases do no more than illustrate specific context in which judges, as ordinary speakers of English, have thought that it was or was not appropriate to do so."

Post Office v Aquarius Properties Ltd[258]

3.   A reinsurance contract provided for reinsurers to be liable to indemnify insurers for their net loss. That was defined as meaning the sum "actually paid" by insurers in settlement of claims. It was held that the context of the contract as a whole was such that there did not have to be an actual disbursement of money before the liability of reinsurers arose.
Charter Reinsurance Co Ltd v Fagan[259]

4.   A cleaning contract for a term of two years said that the cleaning company would have "preferred supplier status" during that period. It was held that the quoted phrase did not have an obvious natural and ordinary meaning, and that its meaning in the contract could only be determined by an examination of the context in which the contract was made.
Proforce Recruit Ltd v The Rugby Group Ltd[260]

13. HEADINGS

A heading to a clause may be taken into account in construing the clause, but it cannot override clear words in a clause or create an ambiguity where, but

---

[257] [1974] A.C. 235.
[258] [1985] 2 E.G.L.R. 105 (affirmed on different grounds: (1987) 54 P. & C.R. 61).
[259] [1997] A.C. 313.
[260] [2006] EWCA Civ 69.

for the heading, none would otherwise exist. Where the contract so provides, headings should not be taken into account.

5.108   Traditionally, the courts have not been influenced by marginal notes or headings in contracts. In *National Farmers' Union Mutual Insurance Society Ltd v Dawson*,[261] an insurance policy contained a marginal note. Viscount Caldecote CJ rejected an argument based on the marginal note, holding that it was "an unsafe guide" to construction. In *Navrom v Callitsis Ship Management SA*,[262] a charterparty contained a clause headed "Force Majeure" which provided that delays caused by "hindrances" were not to count as laytime. At first instance Staughton J said:

> "In my view it is clearly legitimate to look at the title. The draftsman put it there as an indication to the reader of the topic he was going to deal with next. But it is no more than that, and cannot alter the meaning conveyed by the clause if it is plain."

On appeal Lloyd LJ said:

> "Finally, Mr. Young relied on the fact that cl. 33 is headed 'Force Majeure'. This means, he says, that 'hindrances happening without the fault of the charterers' should be limited to hindrances which were unpredictable as well as unavoidable. It is sufficient to say that I can see no justification for so limiting the ordinary meaning of the words by reference to the heading. 'Force Majeure' is clearly used as an omnibus description for a variety of different causes. The rubric does not affect the meaning of each individual cause."

Croom-Johnson LJ said:

> "Much has been said about force majeure. Those words are there as a heading to cl. 33. But I do not regard them as more than a label or signpost, and not as contributing to the interpretation of the clause."

Headings were also taken into account in interpreting a charterparty in *The Vale di Cordoba*.[263]

5.109   However, in *Cott UK Ltd v FE Barber Ltd*,[264] Judge Hegarty QC said:

> "[Counsel's] analysis commenced, and indeed concluded, by emphasising the word 'arbitration', which appears at the head of the clause. He pointed out, correctly, that there is not in this particular contract any provision such as is commonly found, whereby it is expressly stated that the headings of any clauses shall have no constructional consequences in the interpretation of the clause.
> Accordingly, he says that the word 'arbitration' appearing at the heading, must be taken into account fully in construing the clause, and that in those circumstances one cannot determine, as I have said, whether it is truly a clause requiring arbitration, or a clause requiring expert determination. It does seem to me that the word 'arbitration' at the outset, in the absence of any such common form provisions as I have referred to, must be given due weight. What is due weight,

[261] [1941] 2 K.B. 424. See also *Garrard v Lewis* (1882) 10 Q.B.D. 30.
[262] [1987] 2 Lloyd's Rep. 276; [1988] 2 Lloyd's Rep. 416.
[263] [2014] EWHC 129 (Comm); [2014] 1 Lloyd's Rep. 550.
[264] [1997] 3 All E.R. 540.

however, must not disregard the fact that it is a catchword, or form of identification, inserted for convenience of reference.

In my judgment, such a catchword or form of identification cannot prevail over the express wording of the clause, or create ambiguity where no ambiguity is present in construing the words of the clause."

Likewise, in *Farstad Supply AS v Enviroco Ltd*,[265] the Supreme Court took into account the heading of a clause in a charterparty entitled "Exceptions/Indemnities" in interpreting its scope. In *Classic Maritime Inc v Limbungan Makmur SDN BHD*[266] the Court of Appeal took into account the heading of the clause, pointing out that the contract did not contain a prohibition on doing so.

Similarly, in *George v Cluning*,[267] a written agreement granted an option to **5.110** purchase a property. A question arose as to the notice required to exercise the option. Barwick CJ found the clauses of the contract to contain a number of inconsistencies, and that it was difficult to favour one interpretation over the other. He said:

"of greater weight, in my opinion, is cl 6 which commences with the heading 'Exercise of Option', thereby indicating that all that follows goes to the mode of exercise of the option. This is one clear characteristic in a document which is otherwise remarkable for its ambiguities and contradictions. It is not a characteristic which should be obscured by dubious implications to be gathered from less certain provisions.

I do not accept the submission that the first sentence only of cl 6 is directed to the exercise of the option. That is to treat the heading as having no application to the second sentence."

Where the contract states expressly that the headings are not to affect its **5.111** interpretation the cases are divided. In *SBJ Stephenson Ltd v Mandy*,[268] Bell J said:

"Although interpretation clause 21(B) of the agreement provides that clause headings are inserted for convenience only and shall not affect the construction of the agreement, it seems to me that the convenience which they provide is to tell the reader at a glance what the clause is about."

In *Doughty Hanson & Co Ltd v Roe*,[269] Mann J took the same view as Bell J in *SBJ Stephenson Ltd v Mandy*, namely, that the "convenience" of headings was to tell the reader what the clause in question was all about. In *Ace Capital Ltd v CMS Energy Corp*,[270] Christopher Clarke J used the heading of a clause to reach the conclusion that words had been left out by mistake and thus enabled him to read in the missing words.

On the other hand, in *Orleans Investments Pty Ltd v MindShare Communica-* **5.112** *tions Ltd*,[271] the New South Wales Court of Appeal held that headings were not to be taken into account in interpreting a contract, where a clause in the contract said that headings were "for convenience only and do not affect interpretation". In

---

[265] [2011] 1 W.L.R. 921.
[266] [2019] EWCA Civ 1102.
[267] (1979) 28 A.L.R. 57 at 61–62 (HC).
[268] [2000] F.S.R. 286.
[269] [2009] B.C.C. 126.
[270] [2008] 2 C.L.C. 318.
[271] [2009] NSWCA 40.

Gregory Projects (Halifax) Ltd v Tenpin (Halifax) Ltd,[272] Lewison J said:

"Where, as here, the contract says in terms that headings 'shall not affect the interpretation' it seems to me that respect for party autonomy means that the headings cannot be allowed to alter what would otherwise have been the interpretation of the clause in question."

Burton J took the same view in *Rathbone Brothers Plc v Novae Corporate Underwriting*.[273] But in *Citicorp International Ltd v Castex Technologies Ltd*,[274] a trust deed provided that "headings shall be ignored in construing this Trust Deed". The question arose whether the heading should be ignored in interpreting bond conditions. In an obiter part of his judgment, Burton J held that it should not for two reasons. The first was that the bond conditions were not part of the trust deed or its schedule. The second reason is of more general application. He said that he would follow the decisions in *SBJ Stephenson Ltd v Mandy*[275] and *Doughty Hanson & Co Ltd v Roe*[276] in preference to that in *Gregory Products (Halifax) Ltd v Tenpin (Halifax) Ltd* at all events where the heading was consistent with the body of the clause to which it applied. Thus, despite the express statement that headings should be ignored, Burton J was prepared to take them into account. This does not appear to be consistent with his earlier decision in *Rathbone Brothers Plc v Novae Corporate Underwriting* which was upheld on appeal to the Court of Appeal. In that appeal,[277] Elias LJ said that "the heading cannot be used to cut back on the clear language used in the clause".

In *Philp v Cook*,[278] where the agreement stated that "headings do not affect the interpretation of this agreement", May J refused to take them into account. Fraser J also took no account of headings in *Multiplex Construction Europe Ltd v Dunne*.[279] In *Universities Superannuation Scheme Ltd v Scragg*,[280] Rose J held that the Pension Ombudsman had been wrong to take into account the headings to the rules of a pension scheme, which were no more than an inexact paraphrase of the rules in question. It is thought that this is the better view. Ms Joanna Smith QC took this view in *Network Rail Infrastructure Ltd v ABC Electrification Ltd*,[281] in which she said:

"... I can see no sensible basis for the proposition that a heading to one clause in a contract may be used, however obliquely, as a guide to the construction of an entirely different clause, where the parties have agreed (as they have in this Contract) that headings are not to be taken into account in the interpretation or construction of the Contract."

---

[272] [2010] 2 All E.R. (Comm) 646. Not surprisingly, the author considers that this is the better view. See also *Bank of New York Mellon v GV Films (No.2)* [2010] 1 Lloyd's Rep. 425.
[273] [2013] EWHC 3457 (Comm).
[274] [2016] EWHC 349 (Comm).
[275] [2000] FSR 286.
[276] [2007] EWHC 2212 (Ch).
[277] [2014] EWCA Civ 1464; [2014] 2 CLC 818.
[278] [2017] EWHC 3023 (QB).
[279] [2017] EWHC 3073 (TCC); [2018] B.L.R. 36.
[280] [2019] EWHC 51.
[281] [2019] EWHC 1769 (TCC); [2019] B.L.R. 522.

14.   LAYOUT AND PUNCTUATION

The court will take account of punctuation and will probably take account of layout in construing a contract, but font size on its own is of little importance.

In order to enhance the clarity of a document many, if not all, draftsmen pay close attention to layout and punctuation. More often than not, however, judges criticise the standard of punctuation used by draftsmen, and find it of little assistance.[282]   **5.113**

In the case of punctuation, opinions as to its utility in principle differed in the nineteenth century,[283] but in *Houston v Burns*,[284] the House of Lords held that in construing a will punctuation should be considered. Lord Shaw of Dunfermline observed: **5.114**

> "Punctuation is a rational part of English composition, and is sometimes quite significantly employed. I see no reason for depriving legal documents of such significance as attaches to punctuation in other writings."

However, in *Sammut v Manzi Jr*,[285] interpreting a will, the Privy Council placed no weight on punctuation and layout. They distinguished *Houston v Burns*, saying: **5.115**

> "That case concerned a will that was written in 1894, no doubt in manuscript. Their Lordships would not consider it safe in this case to attach significance to the formatting achieved by a word processor that may well have been operated by a secretary."

The modern practice is to take account of punctuation both in construing wills[286] and statutes.[287] In the author's opinion, there is no reason in principle why the court's approach to the construction of contracts should be any different.[288] However, a prerequisite to relying on punctuation is being satisfied that it has been used consciously and not haphazardly.[289] In *Legg v Sterte Garage Ltd*,[290] David Richards LJ said:

> "In an agreement where care appears to have been taken with the lay-out of the terms, it will be taken into account by the court in construing the contract: see Lewison: *The Interpretation of Contracts* (6th ed. 2015) at page 282. But it is only a factor to be taken into account and its effect may well be displaced by the context or sense of the clause in question."

---

[282] See, e.g. *Mapeley Acquisition Co (3) Ltd v City of Edinburgh Council* [2015] CSOH 29.

[283] Contrast *Sanford v Raikes* (1816) 1 Mer. 646 and *Gauntlet v Carter* (1853) 17 Beav. 586.

[284] [1916] A.C. 337.

[285] [2009] 2 All E.R. 234.

[286] *Re Stell* [1979] Ch. 218.

[287] *Hanlon v Law Society* [1981] A.C. 124.

[288] See R.E. Megarry, "Copulatives and Punctuation in Statutes" (1959) 75 L.Q.R. 29, 31. But in *Chalmers Leask Underwriting Agencies v Mayne Nickless Ltd* (1983) 155 C.L.R. the High Court of Australia held that "the mere absence of a comma is of dubious worth as an aid to construction of a clause in which punctuation has plainly been a haphazard matter". Perhaps the position would have been different if the court had concluded that punctuation had been careful.

[289] *Mainteck Services Pty Ltd v Stein Heurtey SA* [2014] NSWCA 184.

[290] [2016] EWCA Civ 97.

5.116 In *AMCI Investments Pty Ltd v Rio Doce Australia Pty Ltd*,[291] the Queensland Court of Appeal paid close attention to the punctuation of a clause in a share sale agreement. Similarly, in *Possfund Custodial Trustee Ltd v Kwik-Fit Properties Ltd*,[292] the Inner House of the Court of Session relied on, among other things, the absence of a comma in an otherwise punctuated lease. If there is no punctuation in the contract its complete absence is difficult to rely on.[293]

In *The Captain Stefanos*,[294] Cooke J paid close attention to the punctuation of a clause in a charterparty. Conversely, in *Soufflet Negoce SA v Fedcominvest Europe Sarl*,[295] although punctuation was heavily relied on other considerations carried the day.

5.117 In *Burchell v Raj Properties Ltd*,[296] one of the issues was whether a defined term spelled with an upper case letter bore the same meaning when spelled with a lower case letter. The Upper Tribunal held that it did, observing:

> "While it is permissible to rely on punctuation and the layout of documents as an aid to their interpretation, such features can only be of limited significance and are unlikely to override what is otherwise the clear and obvious meaning of the contractual language. It will be a very rare case where a defined expression used consistently and unambiguously throughout the remainder of the document can acquire a different meaning by de-capitalisation. To reach that conclusion it would be necessary to be satisfied that the change from upper case to lower case was a deliberate act intended to change the meaning of the word."

Likewise, in *Vitol E&P Ltd v New Age (African Global Energy) Ltd*,[297] Moulder J held that it was necessary to construe the clause in issue as a whole, including the words, syntax and punctuation, to determine the objective meaning.

5.118 However, where a comma was omitted in error when reproducing a standard form, the clause in question was construed as if the comma was there.[298] Punctuation, while relevant, cannot override the obvious meaning of a contract.[299] Likewise, where the drafter's use of commas was "erratic", no weight could be placed on punctuation.[300]

The court's approach to layout has traditionally been less accommodating. The layout of an insurance proposal had a cold reception by the Privy Council in *Yorkshire Insurance Co Ltd v Campbell*,[301] in which Lord Sumner said:

---

[291] [2008] QCA 387.
[292] [2009] 1 E.G.L.R. 39.
[293] *Reilly v National Insurance & Guarantee Corporation Ltd* [2009] 1 All E.R. (Comm) 1166.
[294] [2012] EWHC 571 (Comm); [2012] 2 Lloyd's Rep. 46.
[295] [2014] EWHC 2405 (Comm).
[296] [2014] L. & T.R. 4. In *Hopkinson v Towergate Financial (Group) Ltd* [2019] EWCA Civ; [2018] EWCA Civ 2744 the CA had real difficulty where the contract was not consistent in its use of defined terms and capitalised words.
[297] [2018] EWHC 1580 (Comm).
[298] *Dorset CC v Southern Felt Roofing Co Ltd* (1989) 48 B.L.R. 96 CA.
[299] *Scheldebouw BV v St James Homes (Grosvenor Dock) Ltd* (2006) 105 Con. L.R. 90 (TCC).
[300] *Wood v Capita Insurance Services Ltd* [2017] UKSC 24; [2017] A.C. 1173.
[301] [1917] A.C. 218.

"The appellants use a proposal form which is printed in at least ten different founts of type. This no doubt diversifies its appearance, but for purposes of construction founts of type have no legal meaning."[302]

However, in *Sudbrook Trading Estate Ltd v Eggleton*,[303] the House of Lords attached significance to the fact that a word in a contract began with a capital letter. Lord Diplock said:

5.119

"The term 'valuer' (with a capital 'V' at any rate) is used nowadays to denote a member of a recognised profession comprised of persons possessed of skill and experience in assessing the market price of property, particularly real property."

In *BMBF (No.12) Ltd v Harland and Wolff Shipbuilding and Heavy Industries Ltd*,[304] Sir Martin Nourse was influenced by the fact that some parts of the contract were in upper case type and by the layout of the clause in question.

It seems likely that a modern court will give due weight to the layout of a clause. In *BP Exploration Operating Co Ltd v Kvaerner Oilfield Products Ltd*,[305] Colman J considered both the punctuation and the layout of the disputed clause in an insurance policy, but came to the conclusion that these pointers were outweighed by other parts of the contract. He therefore concluded that something had gone wrong with the punctuation and layout. In *Aquila WSA Aviation Opportunities II Ltd v Onur Air Tasimacilik AS*,[306] Cockerill J took into account that fact that the clause under consideration was in upper case, bold face font and in part underlined. In *Emeraldian Ltd Partnership v Wellmix Shipping Ltd*,[307] cl.5 of a charterparty provided that time lost as a result of a number of causes listed in separate subparagraphs would not count as laytime. Clause 5 (ix) specified "any cause of whatsoever kind or nature beyond the control of seller, preventing cargo preparation, loading or berthing of the vessel". Teare J held that the reference to causes "beyond the control of seller" could not be read back into the other causes listed in the preceding sub-paragraphs.

5.120

15. DATE FOR APPLICATION OF MEANING

There is a presumption that a contract must be interpreted as at the date when it was made; that words must be given the meaning which they bore at that date, and where the meaning has changed, evidence is admissible to prove the original meaning. However, in the case of a contract intended to endure for a long time, the presumption may be rebutted.[308]

---

[302] See *Hamburg Houtimport BV v Agrosin Private Ltd* [2004] A.C. 715 HL. Where, however, the question is whether a term forms part of a contract (e.g. an exemption clause) the size of the type and the clarity of the term may well have a part to play. See *Spurling (J) Ltd v Bradshaw* [1956] 1 W.L.R. 461 at 468, per Denning LJ: "Some clauses which I have seen would need to be printed in red ink on the face of the document with a red hand pointing to it before the notice could be held to be sufficient".

[303] [1983] A.C. 444.

[304] [2001] EWCA Civ 862; [2001] 2 All E.R. (Comm) 385.

[305] [2004] 2 All E.R. (Comm) 266.

[306] [2018] EWHC 519 (Comm).

[307] [2011] 1 Lloyd's Rep. 301.

[308] This section was cited with approval in *Excelsior Group Productions Ltd v Yorkshire Television Ltd* [2009] EWHC 1751 (Comm).

5.121   In *Shore v Wilson*,[309] Coleridge J said:

> "But in proportion as we are removed from the period of which an author writes, we are not sure of the meaning of the words he has used; we are not sure that at that period the primary meaning of the words was the same as now, for by the primary is not meant the etymological, but that which the ordinary usage of society affixes to it. We are also equally uncertain whether at that period the words did not bear a technical or conventional sense; and whether they were not so used by the writer. When, therefore, we are called on to construe deeds of the years 1704 and 1707, it seems to me that we are not only at liberty, but are bound, to inquire what at that time was the meaning of the phrases used in them; not taking for granted, because they bear a certain clear meaning now, that they did so then."

In the same case, Tindal CJ said that extrinsic evidence was admissible:

> "where by the lapse of time and change of manners, the words have acquired in the present age a different meaning from which they bore when originally employed."

5.122   Thus in construing a grant of mines or minerals, the correct approach is to determine what the words meant in the vernacular of the mining world, the commercial world and landowners at the time when the words were used in the instrument.[310] In *Coleman v Ibstock Brick Ltd*,[311] the Court of Appeal gave detailed consideration to the interpretation of an exception and reservation of rights to minerals in a 1921 conveyance. The first important consideration was:

> "that unless the meaning is clear on the face of the legislation or the instrument, the first duty of the court in construing a grant of mines and minerals is to try to ascertain what the phrase meant in the vernacular of the mining world, the commercial world and landowners at the time of the grant."

5.123   However, in *Caledonian Railway Co v Glenboig Union Fireclay Co*,[312] Lord Loreburn said:

> "the evidence given as to common meaning is evidence given of the common meaning at the present day; I should assume that it was the same at the time of the sale, unless sufficient ground was given for coming to a contrary conclusion."

This dictum suggests that there is some burden of proof placed upon a party who asserts that a word has changed its meaning since the contract was made.[313]

5.124   Some contracts, notably contracts of insurance are expressed in archaic language

---

[309] (1842) 9 Cl. & Fin. 355.
[310] *Glasgow Corp v Fairie* (1888) 13 App. Cas. 657; *Borys v Canadian Pacific Railway Co* [1953] A.C. 217.
[311] [2008] EWCA Civ 73.
[312] [1911] A.C. 290 (a case of statutory construction).
[313] Since the meaning of a word is a question of fact, this is compatible with principle. Cf. *Scott v Martin*

which has grown up over many centuries. Such contracts are to be treated as composed of terms of art. In *Shell International Petroleum Co Ltd v Gibbs*,[314] Mustill J said of the Lloyd's S.G. policy:

"The old words in the policy must still be given their former meaning. This does not however provide a complete solution to the problem, for the established interpretation tells one only that barratry may be committed against one owner pro hac vice. It is still necessary to consider whether, in a given case, the charterer is such an owner. This requires the charter to be construed, and construed, like any other contract, in the light of its commercial context. This is the context of today, not of 150 years ago."

In *Joint London Holdings Ltd v Mount Cook Land Ltd*,[315] a lease granted in 1950 prohibited use of the property for carrying on the trade of a victualler. The restriction had appeared in the standard form of lease on the estate in question since the 1790s. In the Court of Appeal Etherton J said:

"Notwithstanding that the presence of the word in that clause can be traced back to restrictions in the standard Estate lease from the 1790s, the question is what meaning the parties to the Lease intended it to bear in 1950."

However, in *Shell International Petroleum Co Ltd v Gibbs*, in the Court of Appeal,[316] Kerr LJ said:

"As it has been said many times in many authorities, in construing the various archaic expressions which are still to be found in this form of policy, one cannot go by their ordinary meaning in our language today, but one must treat them as terms of art and interpret them in accordance with their original meaning."

The principle that a contract is to be interpreted as of the date when it was made **5.125** does not necessarily freeze the meaning of its words. The court may choose between a "static" meaning and a "mobile" meaning. Thus a right of way for carriages granted in the nineteenth century may encompass motor vehicles, even though they were unknown at the date of grant. Thus where parties entered into a restrictive covenant, intended to last in perpetuity, restricting the use of land to housing "the working classes", it was held that they must have intended the meaning of that phrase to change with social and economic changes.[317]

Likewise, in *Excelsior Group Productions Ltd v Yorkshire Television Ltd*,[318] Flaux J said:

"Of course, it may be that, even if a particular concept or entity did not exist at the time the contract was made, the contract, properly construed by reference to what words or phrases used meant at the time, may have used words of sufficient width to encompass that concept or entity when it comes into existence.

[1987] 1 W.L.R. 841.
[314] [1982] Q.B. 946.
[315] [2006] 2 P. & C.R. 306.
[316] [1982] Q.B. 946. See also *Sea and Land Securities Ltd v William Dickinson and Co Ltd* [1942] 2 K.B. 65 at 69, per MacKinnon LJ.
[317] *Dano v Cadogan* [2003] 2 P. & C.R. 10; *Lloyds TSB Foundation for Scotland v Lloyds Banking Group Plc* [2013] UKSC 3; [2013] 1 W.L.R. 366.
[318] [2009] EWHC 1751 (Comm).

An example of that principle in the context of the present case is the use of the words in clause 4(2) of the Frost Agreement 'any and all media now known or hereafter devised'. Equally, the parties may have used a word or phrase in their contract which properly construed is intended to change its meaning as the ordinary meaning of the word or phrase changes."

In *Durham v BAI (Run Off) Ltd*,[319] Lord Mance said in relation to the interpretation of insurance policies:

"Furthermore, if the common law during or even after the currency of an insurance develops in a manner which increases employers' liability, compared with previous perceptions as to what the common law was, that is a risk which the insurers must accept, within the limits of the relevant insurance and insurance period. Eady J correctly identified this in *Phillips v Syndicate 992 Gunner*.[320] The declaratory theory 'does not presume the existence of an ideal system of the common law, which the judges from time to time reveal in their decisions ... But it does mean that, when judges state what the law is, their decisions do ... have a retrospective effect'—in the sense that the law as stated 'will, generally speaking, be applicable not only to the case coming before [them] but, as part of the common law, to other comparable cases which come before the courts, whenever the events which are the subject of those cases': *Kleinwort Benson Ltd v Lincoln CC*.[321] The declaratory theory is a pragmatic tool, essential when cases can only come before the court 'some time, perhaps some years' after the relevant events occurred, and when 'the law [must] be applied equally to all, and yet be capable of organic change'. A similar principle must, generally speaking, apply in relation to a statute such as the Compensation Act 2006, which changes or corrects the common law to what Parliament perceives to be a more appropriate result for the purposes of all future cases coming before the courts, whenever the events giving rise to them."

Similarly, in *Shebelle Enterprises Ltd v Hampstead Garden Suburb Trust Ltd*,[322] the Court of Appeal interpreted a covenant for quiet enjoyment in the light of changes in the legal structure following the grant of the lease, and in particular the implementation of a scheme of management under the Leasehold Reform Act 1967. In the case of a long-term contract, parties often express themselves in broad, flexible terms in order to enable them to adjust to changes in circumstances. The courts will recognise this kind of contract and adopt a flexible approach to interpretation, although loyalty to the text of the contract remains the first principle. This was recognised by the Court of Appeal in *Globe Motors Inc v TRW Lucas Varity Electric Steering Ltd*.[323]

5.126 Where a contract is in the nature of a constitutional instrument (e.g. articles of association) there is more justification for adopting a dynamic approach to interpretation, rather than ascertaining the meaning that the contract bore at the date of its creation.[324]

But where a court has a choice between a static or a mobile interpretation, the

---

[319] [2012] UKSC 14; [2012] 1 W.L.R. 867 at [70].
[320] [2003] EWHC 1084 (Comm); [2004] Lloyd's Insurance and Reinsurance Reports 426 at 429 (left).
[321] [1999] 2 A.C. 349 at 378G–H, per Lord Goff.
[322] [2014] EWCA Civ 305; [2014] 2 P. & C.R. 114.
[323] [2016] EWCA Civ 396.
[324] *Re GIGA Investments Pty Ltd* [1995] FCA 1348; *Lian v Maxz Universal Development Group Pte*

result of adopting a mobile interpretation is not to change the scope of the underlying contract.[325] As it was put in *Debenhams Retail Plc v Sun Alliance and London Assurance Co Ltd*,[326] the court must "promote the purposes and values which are expressed or implicit in the wording, and to reach an interpretation which applies the … wording to the changed circumstances in a manner consistent with them". This flexibility has its limits. In *St Marylebone Property Co Ltd v Tesco Stores Ltd*,[327] a lease granted in 1950 limited use to the trade of grocers provisions wine spirit and beer merchants. A sub-tenant began to sell newspapers, light bulbs and to hire videos. It was argued that the limitation on use should be interpreted by asking what kind of products one would now expect to find in a shop which was the successor to the early 1950s grocer. Hoffmann J rejected that argument. He said:

> "I do not think that the covenant can be construed as flexibly as that. If that were so a lease containing a covenant only to carry on the trade of blacksmith granted in the 1870s would have entitled the tenant to take on a substantial trade in bicycle repairs in the 1890s and to become a garage by 1920. Though the commercial progress is perfectly reasonable, that does not in my view entitle one to say that the garage is carrying on the trade of a blacksmith. It does not seem to me that the meaning of the term 'grocer and provision merchant' has changed since the 1950s. What has happened is that there are now very few establishments to which that expression could strictly be applied."

Similarly, in *Atos IT Services UK Ltd v Atos Pension Schemes Ltd*,[328] a pension scheme contained a definition of "Retail Price Index", referring to RPI. A different index could be substituted if RPI ceased to be published. The fact that RPI was widely regarded as an unreliable measure of inflation did not permit the substitution of a different index, in circumstances in which RPI continued to be published.

Illustrations

1. A building scheme created in 1925 prohibited the erection of a public garage. The Privy Council considered the meaning which that phrase bore in 1925 rather than at the date of the hearing. However, it was common ground that the former was the relevant date.
Texaco Antilles Ltd v Kernochan[329]

2. A lease contained a covenant by the tenant to use the property for the carrying on of the trade or business of a supermarket. Whitford J held that the tenant was entitled to sell items sold in supermarkets at the date of the lease. However, in the Court of Appeal Balcombe LJ declined to express a view whether "the date of the lease is, in the construction of a covenant of this nature the relevant date".
Basildon Development Corporation v Mactro Ltd[330]

3. A conveyance made in 1880 contained a grant of mines and minerals under

---

Ltd [2009] SGCA 4 (Court of Appeal of Singapore).
[325] *Big River Paradise Ltd v Congreve* [2008] NZCA 78.
[326] [2005] 3 E.G.L.R. 34.
[327] [1988] 2 E.G.L.R. 40.
[328] [2020] EWHC 145 (Ch).
[329] [1973] A.C. 609.
[330] [1986] 1 E.G.L.R. 137.

the sea bed. The question arose whether the conveyance included oil and natural gas. It was held that there was no clear evidence that that expression in 1880 would have included oil and natural gas, and that they did not pass.
Earl of Lonsdale v Att.-Gen.[331]

4.   A lease of a pub contained a reservation entitling the landlord to install flow regulating or monitoring equipment. The landlord wished to install a device for measuring the flow of liquid through pipes or lines and for measuring the quantity passing known as idraught. The tenant argued that that system was unknown at the date of the lease and thus did not fall within the reservation. It was held that the system was no more than a development of known systems, and therefore fell within the reservation.
Unique Pub Properties Ltd v Broad Green Tavern Ltd[332]

16.   STATUTORY MEANINGS

Many words are defined by statute. Where words (particularly words defining weights and measures) are defined by statute, it may be that evidence is inadmissible to contradict the statutory definition. If a contract expressly incorporates a statutory definition the contractual meaning will usually correspond with the statutory meaning.

5.127   Section 61 of the Law of Property Act 1925 provides:

"In all deeds, contracts, wills, orders and other instruments executed, made or coming into operation after the commencement of this Act, unless the context otherwise requires[333]:

(a)   Month means calendar month;
(b)   Person includes a corporation;
(c)   The singular includes the plural and vice versa;
(d)   The masculine includes the feminine and vice versa."

Many documents (especially conveyancing documents) contain definition and interpretation clauses which, in effect, reproduce s.61. Such clauses are quite unnecessary. However, s.61 is designed to save verbosity, and should not be used to change fundamentally the meaning that a clause in a contract would have borne in its absence.[334] Neither s.61, nor a clause in the contract to the same effect, justifies a notional rewriting of every singular reference in a contract as if it were a plural reference.[335] Even without reference to s.61, the use of the indefinite article "a" in a contract does not of itself denote singularity.[336] In *Danks v Qinetiq Holdings Ltd*,[337] Vos J applied s.61(c) of the Law of Property Act 1925 to the interpretation of a pension scheme.

---

[331]   [1981] 1 W.L.R. 887.
[332]   [2012] EWHC 2154 (Ch); [2012] 2 P. & C.R. 344.
[333]   For cases in which the statutory presumption was displaced, see *Re a Solicitors' Arbitration* [1962] 1 W.L.R. 353; *Crest Nicholson Residential (South) Ltd v MacAllister* [2003] 1 All E.R. 46 and *Deutsche Genossenschaftsbank v Burnhope* [1995] 1 W.L.R. 1580 HL.
[334]   *Re a Solicitors' Arbitration* [1962] 1 W.L.R. 353.
[335]   *Windwood v Bifa Waste Services Ltd* [2011] EWCA Civ 108.
[336]   *Martin v David Wilson Homes Ltd* [2004] 3 E.G.L.R. 77.
[337]   [2012] EWHC 570 (Ch).

Section 1(1) of the Family Law Reform Act 1969 reduced the age of majority from 21 to 18. Section 1(2) of that Act provides: **5.128**

"The foregoing subsection applies ... in the absence of a definition or of an indication of a contrary intention, for the construction of 'full age,' 'infant,' 'infancy,' 'minor,' 'minority' and similar expressions in—

   (b)   any deed will or other instrument of whatever nature (not being a statutory provision) made on or after [1 January 1970]."

Section 15(1) of the same Act provides:

"in any disposition made after [1 January 1970]—

   (a)   any reference (whether express or implied) to the child or children of any person shall, unless the contrary intention appears, be construed as, or as including, a reference to any illegitimate child of that person; and

   (b)   any reference (whether express or implied) to a person or persons related in some other manner to any person shall, unless the contrary intention appears, be construed as, or as including, a reference to anyone who would be so related if he, or some other person through whom the relationship is deduced, had been born legitimate." [338]

A disposition means a disposition, including an oral disposition, of real or personal property whether inter vivos or by will or codicil.[339] In some circumstances, however, this does not apply.[340] In *Howard v Howard-Lawson*,[341] Norris J confirmed that the reduction in the age of majority effected by the Family Law Reform Act 1969 did not affect the interpretation of a settlement made before the Act came into force.

Section 39 of the Adoption Act 1976 provides: **5.129**

"(1) An adopted child shall be treated in law—
   (a) where the adopters are a married couple, as if he had been born as a child of the marriage (whether or not he was in fact born after the marriage was solemnized);
   (b) in any other case, as if he had been born to the adopter in wedlock (but not as a child of any actual marriage of the adopter)."

This applies for the construction of enactments or instruments passed or made before the adoption or later, and so applies subject to any contrary intention. But it does not apply to an existing instrument or enactment in so far as it contains a disposition of property, and it does not apply to any public general Act in its application to any disposition of property in an existing instrument or enactment.[342] In *Hand v George*[343] the testator had made a will dividing his estate between his children for life with remainder to their children. At the time when the will was

---

[338]   See also Family Law Reform Act 1987 s.1(1).
[339]   Family Law Reform Act 1969 s.15(8).
[340]   See Family Law Reform Act 1969 s.15(5), and the limitations in s.15(2).
[341]   [2012] EWHC 3258 (Ch).
[342]   Adoption Act 1976 Sch.2 para.6(1).
[343]   [2017] EWHC 533 (Ch); [2017] Ch. 449.

made (and at the time when the testator died) domestic law provided that adopted children did not count as children for the purposes of inheritance. Domestic law had since changed, and the previous legislation had been repealed. One of the children died after the coming into force of the Human Rights Act 1998, leaving adopted children. Rose J held that the question was not simply one of interpretation of the will, but whether the repealed domestic legislation could be read down in the light of the jurisprudence of the European Court of Human Rights. She held that it could, and that the adopted children took under the will.

5.130   Section 1(1) of the Family Law Reform Act 1987 provides that in instruments coming into force after 4 April 1988:

> "references (however expressed) to any relationship between two persons shall, unless the contrary intention appears, be construed without regard to whether or not the father and mother of either of them, or the father and mother of any person through whom the relationship is deduced, have or had been married to each other at any time."

This includes dispositions inter vivos made after that date. In *Monkcom Re JC Druce Settlement*[344] HHJ Keyser QC, following *Hand v George*,[345] held that that section could also be read down under the Human Rights Act 1998 with the consequence that a class of beneficiaries limited to "male descendants" could include illegitimate children, even though the settlement pre-dated 4 April 1988.

5.131   Section 9 of the Gender Recognition Act 2004 states that where a gender recognition certificate is issued to a person, that person's gender becomes the acquired gender for all purposes, including the interpretation of instruments made both before and after the issue of the certificate.

Sections 33 to 47 of the Human Fertilisation and Embryology Act 2008[346] contain detailed provisions about when a person is (or is not) to be treated as the mother, father or parent of a child. Where these provisions apply, s.48(5) provides that:

> "… references to any relationship between two people in any enactment, deed or other instrument or document (whenever passed or made) are to be read accordingly."

However, this rule does not affect the succession to any title of honour or dignity nor the devolution of property limited to devolve along with any title of honour or dignity.[347]

These sections were brought into force on 6 April 2009.[348]

5.132   In the law of England and Wales, with effect from 13 March 2014, marriage has the same effect in relation to same sex couples as it has in relation to opposite sex couples.[349] However, this does not affect the effect of any private legal instrument made before that date.[350] Private legal instruments include a will; an instrument

---

[344] [2019] EWHC 3701 (Ch).

[345] [2017] EWHC 533 (Ch); [2017] Ch. 449.

[346] Amended by Civil Partnership Opposite Sex Couples Regulations 2019 (SI 2019/1458).

[347] Section 48(7).

[348] Human Fertilisation and Embryology Act 2008 (Commencement No.1 and Transitional Provisions) Order 2009 (SI 2009/479).

[349] Marriage (Same Sex Couples) Act 2013 s.11(1).

[350] Marriage (Same Sex Couples) Act 2013 Sch.4 para.1(1).

which settles property; an instrument which provides for the use, disposal or devolution of property; and an instrument which establishes a body or regulates the purposes and administration of a body.[351] Although contracts are not specifically referred to, since the definition is inclusive rather than exhaustive it is thought that contracts would be treated in the same way.

Other statutes also contain definitions which are said to apply to contracts.[352] In **5.133** *De Beeche v South American Stores Ltd*,[353] the question was whether evidence was admissible to explain the phrase "first class bills on London". Viscount Sankey said:

"Without endeavouring to give an exhaustive definition of what evidence may be admitted, there are in cases like the present three conditions precedent to its being accepted:—(1.) the evidence must not conflict with a statutory definition; (2.) the evidence must be of a usage common to the place in question; and (3.) the evidence must expound and not contradict the terms of the contract."

In *Smith v Wilson*,[354] Lord Tenterden CJ said:

"where there is used in any written instrument a word denoting quantity, to which an act of parliament has given a definite meaning, I agree it must be considered to have been used in that sense."

Parke J said:

"I agree that where a word is defined by act of parliament to mean a precise quantity, the parties using that word in a contract, must be presumed to use it in the sense given to it by the legislature, unless it appears from other parts of the contract that they used it differently."

Both judges, therefore, would have ruled inadmissible extrinsic evidence tending to controvert the statutory meaning.[355]

The mere fact that a contract uses a word that is defined by statute does not make **5.134** that word a legal term of art. Thus where the holder of an option agreed to apply for planning permission for "development" of property it was held that the word "development" was to be construed in a non-technical sense rather than in accordance with its statutory definition in town and country planning legislation.[356] However, where an agreement has been drawn with the provisions of statutorily defined words in mind, some particular context is required before the court can attribute to the parties an intention to use such a term in a different sense to that which it has in the legislative context.[357]

The starting point is that if the terms of a statute are incorporated into a contract **5.135** by reference, the contract has to be read as if the words of the statute are written out in the contract and construed, as a matter of contract, in their contractual

---

[351] Marriage (Same Sex Couples) Act 2013 Sch.4 para.1(2).
[352] See, e.g. Recorded Delivery Service Act 1962; Decimal Coinage Act 1971; Interpretation Act 1978.
[353] [1935] A.C. 148.
[354] (1842) 9 Cl. & Fin. 355.
[355] It is not thought that this principle applies to statutory definitions other than definitions of weights and measures.
[356] *Hallam Land Management Ltd v UK Coal Mining Ltd* [2002] 2 E.G.L.R. 80.
[357] *Castlebay Ltd v Asquith Properties Ltd* [2006] 2 P. & C.R. 22.

context.[358] But where a contract incorporates a statutory definition, the meaning of the word in the contract will usually be given the same meaning as it bears in the statute. In *Envoroco Ltd v Farstad Supply A/S*,[359] a contract defined an "affiliate" as including a "Subsidiary"; and provided that "'Subsidiary' shall have the meaning assigned to it in Section 736 of the Companies Act 1985". Patten LJ said:

> "In the present case, clause 1(a) of Part B of the charterparty defines 'Affiliate' as including a subsidiary of the charterer or a company of which the charterer is also a subsidiary. It then goes on to state that 'for the purposes of this definition "Subsidiary" shall have the meaning assigned to it in Section 736 of the Companies Act 1985'. That seems to me to be an unequivocal direction to the parties and to the court that the statutory definition is to be applied. Not some alternative meaning of the same words. If Enviroco's case depends upon giving to the words of s.736 a meaning which they would not have in their statutory context then, as Mummery LJ put to Miss Melwani in argument, the effect is either to require one to read the last sentence of clause 1(a) as a direction to give the word 'subsidiary' a meaning which is not assigned to it by s.736 or simply to delete that last sentence altogether from the contract."

Longmore LJ said:

> "Words in a statute necessarily have to have a certain meaning and, if the parties incorporate the words of the statute into their contract, the words must have the same meaning as they had when the statute was enacted and the charterparty was agreed. It is only if the words of the contract are actually inconsistent with the meaning of the (incorporated) statutory words (as they were in *Adamastos Shipping v Anglo-Saxon Petroleum Ltd* [1958] AC 133) that an ambiguity can be said to arise which requires the court to choose between alternative meanings."

5.136   This has been said to be "the normal approach to the incorporation of statutory provisions in contracts".[360] In some cases, however, the incorporated parts of a statute may need to be interpreted in a different sense in order to make the contract work.[361] Where the parties incorporate the words of a statute verbatim, those words must be construed in the context of the contract, and their meaning in the context of the contract is not necessarily the same as their meaning in the context of the statute.[362]

In *William Hare Ltd v Shepherd Construction Ltd*,[363] Coulson J said:

> "Where a contract or deed incorporates the provisions of a statute or subordinate legislation there is no presumption either way as to whether the reference is to the law for the time being in force."[364]

---

[358] *Adamastos Shipping Co Ltd v Anglo-Saxon Petroleum Co Ltd* [1959] A.C. 133; *Farstad Supply A/S v Enviroco Ltd* [2011] I W.L.R. 921.

[359] [2010] Bus. L.R. 1008 (affirmed [2011] 1 W.L.R. 921).

[360] *BNY Corporate Trustee Services Ltd v Eurosail-UK 2007-3bl Plc* BNY Corporate Trustee Services Ltd v Eurosail—UK 2007—3bl Plc [2011] EWCA Civ 227.

[361] *Brett v The Brett Essex Golf Club* (1986) 52 P. & C.R. 330.

[362] *GREA Real Property Investments Ltd v Williams* [1979] 1 E.G.L.R. 121.

[363] [2009] EWHC 1603 (TCC).

[364] This was the view that the author stated in previous editions of this book.

The question depends on the proper construction of the words of incorporation in the context in which they are used.[365] In *Brewers' Company v Viewplan Plc*,[366] a lease contained a covenant which defined the permitted use by reference to Class III of the Town and Country Planning (Use Classes) Order 1972. Class III consisted of light industrial use. The Order was revoked by the Town and Country Planning (Use Classes) Order 1987, which introduced new use classes, including Class B1, which included both office use and light industrial use. It was held that the terms of the covenant had incorporated the 1972 definition and was not modified by the subsequent revocation of the 1972 Order.

It seems, however, that in the case of an Act passed on or after 1 January 1979, a different rule applies. Section 17(2) of the Interpretation Act 1978 provides: **5.137**

"Where an Act repeals and re-enacts, with or without modification, a previous enactment then, unless the contrary intention appears,—

(a) any reference in any other enactment to the enactment so repealed shall be construed as a reference to the provision re-enacted."

Section 23(3) of the Act provides that in the application of s.17(2)(a) to Acts passed or subordinate legislation made after 1 January 1979:

"... the reference to any other enactment includes any deed or other instrument or document."

In addition, legislation may itself expressly provide for the updating of prior contracts.[367]

Nevertheless, in *William Hare Ltd v Shepherd Construction Ltd*,[368] Coulson J added that where the provisions of the legislation are not referred to for their norma- **5.138** tive content but simply used as a convenient shorthand to describe a factual situation, it must be rare that the parties will have intended that situation to vary unpredictably with the vagaries of future legislation.[369] In that case a "pay when paid clause" defined insolvency by reference to certain events, including the making of an administration order under Pt II of the Insolvency Act 1986. The contract was entered into after the changes to the insolvency legislation made by the Enterprise Act 2002, which allowed companies to enter administration without a court order. The Court of Appeal,[370] affirming Coulson J, held that the reference to the making

---

[365] *Brett v Brett Essex Golf Club* [1986] 1 E.G.L.R. 154 CA. However, s.19 of the Interpretation Act 1978 provides that where an Act cites another Act by year, statute, session or chapter, or a section or other portion of another Act by number or letter, the reference, unless the contrary intention appears, is a reference to the Act included in any revised edition of the statutes printed by authority. This section is applied to deeds and other instruments and documents by s.23(3) of the Act. The revised edition of the statutes printed by authority is *Statutes in Force*. These provisions do not appear to have been cited to the court, although since the legislation in question pre-dated 1979 the sections would not have been relevant on the facts.

[366] [1989] 2 E.G.L.R. 133.

[367] See, e.g. Enterprise Act 2002 Sch.17 para.1.

[368] [2009] EWHC 1603 (TCC).

[369] But the contract may make it clear that a meaning defined by reference to statute is to change if the legislation changes: *BNY Corporate Trustee Services Ltd v Eurosail-UK 2007-3bl Plc BNY Corporate Trustee Services Ltd v Eurosail—UK 2007—3bl Plc* [2011] EWCA Civ 227.

[370] [2010] EWCA Civ 283. Had the contract been made before the amendments came into force, it would have been rescued by the Enterprise Act 2002 Sch.17 para.1.

of an administration order could not be read as encompassing entry into administration without a court order.

Illustrations

1.   An insurance policy covered loss caused by "theft ... committed by persons present on the premises". It was held that notwithstanding s.61 of the Law of Property Act 1925 the word "person" meant a natural person and not an artificial person such as a limited company.
   Deutsche Genossenschaftsbank v Burnhope[371]

2.   A partnership deed provided that if "any partner" committed certain breaches of the agreement then "the other partners" could expel him from the partnership. It was held that notwithstanding s.61 of the Law of Property Act 1925 "the other partners" meant all the other partners, and that one partner could not act alone.
   Re a Solicitors' Arbitration[372]

3.   A restrictive covenant prohibited use of the burdened land except for the purposes of "a private dwellinghouse". It was held that notwithstanding s.61 of the Law of Property Act 1925 this prevented the use of the land for two or more dwellinghouses.
   Crest Nicholson Residential (South) Ltd v MacAllister[373]

4.   An article in a company's articles of association contained provision for the transfer of shares to "any person". A different article referred to "a person or company". The argument that "any person" should be confined to a natural person was rejected. The Court of Appeal held that s.61 of the Law of Property Act 1925 applied; and that much clearer language would have been needed to restrict the normal legal meaning of "any person".
   Cosmetic Warriors Ltd v Gerrie[374]

---

[371]   [1995] 1 W.L.R. 1580 HL.
[372]   [1962] 1 W.L.R. 353.
[373]   [2003] 1 All E.R. 46, criticised in *Martin v David Wilson Homes Ltd* [2004] 3 E.G.L.R. 77.
[374]   [2017] EWCA Civ 324.

CHAPTER 6

IMPLIED TERMS

The gaps in a document, what it does not mention, are often as interesting as what it contains.

Richard J. Evans: *In Defence of History*

1. THE NATURE OF IMPLIED TERMS

Implied terms fall broadly into two classes. The first class consists of default rules brought into operation where the parties enter into a particular kind of contractual relationship. The second class consists of elucidating what a particular contract must mean when read in the light of its purpose and the admissible background.

The expression "implied term" is used by lawyers in a wide variety of senses, and a wider variety of circumstances. In *Luxor (Eastbourne) Ltd v Cooper*,[1] Lord Wright said:

> "The expression 'implied term' is used in different senses. Sometimes it denotes some term which does not depend on the actual intention of the parties but on a rule of law, such as the terms, warranties or conditions which, if not expressly excluded, the law imports, as for instance under the Sale of Goods Act and the Marine Insurance Act. But a case like the present is different because what it is sought to imply is based on an intention imputed to the parties from their actual circumstances."

In this passage Lord Wright distinguishes between two types of implied term; those which are rules of law, and those which are based on an intention imputed to the parties from their actual circumstances. The rules of law arise because of the nature of the contract into which the parties have entered. In other words, the parties have manifested an intention to enter into a relationship of employer and employee, or buyer and seller, or landlord and tenant, and in consequence the law imputes to them a certain intention by virtue of their express intention to enter into that relationship.

Similarly, in *Société Genérale, London Branch v Geys*,[2] Lady Hale said that it was:

> "... important to distinguish between two different kinds of implied terms. First, there are those terms which are implied into a particular contract because, on its

6.01

6.02

---

[1] [1941] A.C. 108 at 137.
[2] [2012] UKSC 63; [2013] 1 A.C. 523; *Myers v Kestrel Acquisitions Ltd* [2015] EWHC 916 (Ch).

[325]

proper construction, the parties must have intended to include them.[3] Such terms are only implied where it is necessary to give business efficacy to the particular contract in question. Second, there are those terms which are implied into a class of contractual relationship, such as that between landlord and tenant or between employer and employee, where the parties may have left a good deal unsaid, but the courts have implied the term as a necessary incident of the relationship concerned, unless the parties have expressly excluded it."[4]

The Supreme Court confirmed the existence of two types of implied term in *Marks & Spencer Plc v BNP Paribas Securities Services Trust Co (Jersey) Ltd*[5] as did the Privy Council in *Vizcaya Partners Ltd v Picard*.[6] In the former case Lord Neuberger said:

"... there are two types of contractual implied term. The first, with which this case is concerned, is a term which is implied into a particular contract, in the light of the express terms, commercial common sense, and the facts known to both parties at the time the contract was made. The second type of implied terms arises because, unless such a term is expressly excluded, the law (sometimes by statute, sometimes through the common law) effectively imposes certain terms into certain classes of relationship."

6.03   Implied terms of the first kind operate as "default rules"[7] as opposed to "ad hoc gap fillers".[8] Where the default rules are those imposed by the common law, it is thought that the parties can in general exclude them by express words.[9] But where they are imposed by statute, it is a question of interpretation of the statute whether they can be excluded. The distinction between standardised implied terms and individual implied terms arising out of a particular contract has become more pronounced over the years. The distinction was drawn by Viscount Simonds and Lord Tucker in *Lister v Romford Ice and Cold Storage Co Ltd*.[10] However, it was not clearly developed until the decision of the House of Lords in *Liverpool City Council v Irwin*.[11] In that case, the House of Lords held that there was to be implied into a contract of tenancy of a flat in a high rise block an obligation on the part of the landlord to take reasonable care to keep in repair and lit essential means of access and rubbish chutes. The clearest expression of the distinction between the two types of implied term is to be found in the speech of Lord Cross of Chelsea who said:

"When it implies a term in a contract the court is sometimes laying down a general rule that in all contracts of a certain type—sale of goods, master and servant, landlord and tenant, and so on—some provision is to be implied unless the

---

[3]   *Attorney General of Belize v Belize Telecom Ltd* [2009] UKPC 10; [2009] 1 W.L.R. 1988.
[4]   *Lister v Romford Ice and Cold Storage Co Ltd* [1957] A.C. 555; *Liverpool City Council v Irwin* [1977] A.C. 239.
[5]   [2015] UKSC 72; [2016] A.C. 742.
[6]   [2016] UKPC 5; [2016] Bus. L.R. 413, where Lord Collins described them as terms implied in law and terms implied in fact.
[7]   *Mahmud & Malik v BCCI* [2000] A.C. 20 at 45, per Lord Steyn.
[8]   *Equitable Life Assurance Society v Hyman* [2002] 1 A.C. 408 at 459, per Lord Steyn.
[9]   *Photo Productions Ltd v Securicor Transport Ltd* [1980] A.C. 827 at 848, per Lord Diplock.
[10]   [1957] A.C. 555.
[11]   [1977] A.C. 239. See also *Duke of Westminster v Guild* [1985] Q.B. 688.

parties have expressly excluded it. In deciding whether or not to lay down such a prima facie rule the court will naturally ask itself whether in the general run of such cases the term in question would be one which it would be reasonable to insert. Sometimes, however, there is no question of laying down any prima facie rule applicable to all cases of a defined type but what the court is being in effect asked to do is to rectify a particular—often a very detailed—contract by inserting in it a term which the parties have not expressed. Here it is not enough for the court to say that the suggested term is one the presence of which would make the contract a better or fairer one; it must be able to say that the insertion of the term is necessary to give—as it is put—business efficacy to the contract and that if its absence had been pointed out at the time both parties assuming them to have been reasonable men—would have agreed without hesitation to its insertion."

A similar distinction was also drawn by Lords Wilberforce, Edmund-Davies and Fraser of Tullybelton.[12]

This approach was repeated by Lord Denning MR in *Shell UK Ltd v Lostock Garage Ltd*,[13] in which he distinguished between: **6.04**

"all those relationships which are of common occurrence, such as the relationship of seller and buyer, owner and hirer, master and servant, landlord and tenant, carrier by land and by sea, contractor for building works, and so forth."[14]

and:

"cases, not of common occurrence in which from the particular circumstances a term is to be implied."

Where the court is concerned with a tailor-made implied term, the general test **6.05** is that of necessity, in the sense that it is what the contract must mean.[15] Where, however, the term in question is said to be a standard term in a contract of a particular nature, wider questions arise. In *Crossley v Faithful & Gould Holdings Ltd*,[16] Dyson LJ said:

"It seems to me that, rather than focus on the elusive concept of necessity, it is better to recognise that, to some extent at least, the existence and scope of standardised implied terms raise questions of reasonableness, fairness and the balancing of competing policy considerations."[17]

In *Makers UK Ltd v Camden London Borough Council*,[18] Akenhead J considered

---

[12] Lord Wilberforce described the term as arising as a matter of necessity from the relationship which the parties had agreed upon. The latter two described the term as a "legal incident" of the kind of contract.

[13] [1976] 1 W.L.R. 1187.

[14] He declined to hold, although tempted, that a "solus" agreement, under which a petrol filling station operator agreed to buy all petrol from a single supplier, was of sufficiently common occurrence to fall within the first category.

[15] For different formulations of the test see para.6.54.

[16] [2004] 4 All E.R. 447. The High Court of Australia has retained the concept of "necessity" even in this class of case: *Commonwealth Bank of Australia v Barker* [2014] HCA 32.

[17] See E. Peden, "Policy concerns behind implication of terms in law" (2001) 117 L.Q.R. 459.

[18] (2008) 120 Con. L.R. 161.

the judgment of Dyson LJ in *Crossley v Faithful & Gould Holdings Ltd*,[19] where a term was implied as an incident of a legal relationship. He said:

"I do not consider that Dyson LJ was rejecting the 'necessity' element of the implication of terms; that is too well established in English law. He found it simpler to concentrate in that case on the other elements."[20]

6.06   It may well be that all circumstances in which the court implies terms (and hence the nature of the terms implied) are but "shades on a continuous spectrum".[21] Professor Glanville Williams observes[22] that there are at least three kinds of implied terms:

(i)   terms that the parties probably had in mind but did not trouble to express;
(ii)   terms that the parties, whether or not they actually had them in mind, would probably have expressed if the question had been brought to their attention; and
(iii)   terms that, whether or not the parties had them in mind or would have expressed them if they had foreseen the difficulty, are implied by the court because of the court's view of fairness or policy or in consequence of rules of law.

He points out that of these three kinds of implied term: (i) is an effort to arrive at actual intention; (ii) is an effort to arrive at hypothetical or conditional intention—the intention that the parties would have had if they had foreseen the difficulty; and (iii) is not concerned with the intention of the parties except to the extent that the term implied by the court may be excluded by an expression of positive intention to the contrary. However, as has been seen in Ch.2, the actual intention of the parties is not what the court is trying to ascertain. What the court seeks to ascertain is the meaning that the contract would convey to a reasonable reader. It is, therefore, more accurate to describe case (i) as an effort to arrive at what the reasonable reader would understand the contract to mean.[23] Both case (i) and case (ii) involve a search for meaning, although case (ii) requires the further assumption that the subsequent difficulty was foreseen at the date of the contract.

6.07   The contrast between actual and presumed intention in this context was explained by Mason J in *Codelfa Construction Pty Ltd v State Rail Authority of New South Wales*[24] as follows:

"The implication of a term is to be compared, and at the same time contrasted, with rectification of a contract. In each case the problem is caused by a deficiency in the expression of the consensual agreement. A term which should have been included has been omitted. The difference is that with rectification the term which has been omitted and should have been included was actually agreed upon; with implication the term is one which the parties would have agreed had they turned their minds to it—it is not a term actually agreed upon. Thus, in the case of the

---

[19] [2004] 4 All E.R. 447.
[20] The author is not convinced that this observation is correct.
[21] *Liverpool City Council v Irwin* [1977] A.C 239 at 253, per Lord Wilberforce.
[22] Professor Glanville Williams in his justly celebrated article "Language and the Law" (1945) 61 L.Q.R. 71 at 401.
[23] *Attorney General of Belize v Belize Telecom Ltd* [2009] 1 W.L.R. 1988.
[24] (1982) 149 C.L.R. 337 at 346. See also *Liverpool City Council v Irwin* [1977] A.C. 239 at 266D, per Lord Edmund-Davies.

implied term the deficiency in the expression of the consensual agreement is caused by the failure of the parties to direct their minds to a particular eventuality and to make explicit provision for it. Rectification ensures that the contract gives effect to the parties' actual intention; the implication of a term is designed to give effect to the parties' presumed intention."

Early expressions of the function of the court in implying terms repeatedly stressed the intention of the parties. Thus in *The Moorcock*,[25] Bowen LJ said: **6.08**

"I believe that if one were to take all the instances, which are many, of implied warranties and covenants in law which occur in the earlier cases which deal with real property, passing through the instances which relate to the warranties of title and of quality, and the cases of executory sale and other classes of implied warranties like the implied authority of an agent to make contracts, it will be seen that in all these cases the law is giving to the transaction such efficacy as both parties must have intended it should have."

In these and similar passages, the judges concentrated on the presumed intention of the parties. In later cases, however, the distinction drawn by Lord Wright[26] and Lady Hale[27] has come to the fore.

In practice, however, the court does not always adhere to any rigid division between different kinds of implied term; rather it treats them as shades on a continuous spectrum.[28] In the case of most commercial contracts, the implication of a term may be based either on textual considerations or on a combination of the text of the contract and the background facts. In some cases, however, the court will not imply a term on the basis of background facts. In *Bratton Seymour Service Co Ltd v Oxborough*,[29] Steyn LJ said of a company's articles of association: **6.09**

"I will readily accept that the law should not adopt a black-letter approach. It is possible to imply a term purely from the language of the document itself: a purely constructional implication is not precluded. But it is quite another matter to seek to imply a term into articles of association from extrinsic circumstances. Here, the company puts forward an implication to be derived not from the language of the articles of association but purely from extrinsic circumstances. That, in my judgment, is a type of implication which, as a matter of law, can never succeed in the case of articles of association. After all, if it were permitted, it would involve the position that the different implications would notionally be possible between the company and different subscribers."

This dictum has been approved by the Privy Council.[30]

---

25 (1889) 14 P.D. 64 at 68. See also *Hamlyn & Co v Wood & Co* [1891] 2 Q.B. 488, per Kay LJ ("the court ought not to imply a term in a contract unless there arises such an inference that the parties must have intended the stipulation in question that the court is necessarily driven to the conclusion that it must be implied").

26 *Luxor (Eastbourne) Ltd v Cooper* [1941] A.C. 108.

27 *Société Genérale, London Branch v Geys* [2012] UKSC 63; [2013] 1 A.C. 523.

28 *Liverpool City Council v Irwin* [1977] A.C. 239 at 253, per Lord Wilberforce.

29 [1992] B.C.L.C. 693.

30 *HSBC Bank Middle East v Clarke* [2006] UKPC 31; [2007] L.R.C. 544; *Attorney General of Belize v Belize Telecom Ltd* [2009] 1 W.L.R. 1988.

6.10   In *Mosvolds Rederi A/S v Food Corp of India*,[31] however, Steyn J spoke of three categories of implied term. He said:

> "Sometimes it is said that a term is implied into the contract when in truth a positive rule of law of contract is applied because of the category in which a particular contract falls. Another type of implied term is a term in order to give business efficacy to the contract. The basis of such an implication is that the contract is unworkable without it. There is, however, another form of implication. It is not permissible to imply a term simply because the court considers it to be reasonable. On the other hand, it is possible to imply a term, if the court or arbitrator, as the case may be, is satisfied that reasonable men, faced with the suggested term which *ex hypothesi* was not expressed in the contract, would without hesitation say: 'yes, of course that is so obvious that it goes without saying.'"

6.11   To these may be added certain "implied terms" imposed upon the parties irrespective of the express terms of their contract, and sometimes in contradiction of those terms (e.g. the implied repairing obligations imposed upon a landlord under the Landlord and Tenant Act 1985 or the Consumer Rights Act 2015). These are not really implied terms at all, but are imposed obligations, and stand on a somewhat different footing to terms implied under the Sale of Goods Act 1979 which originate in a statutory codification of the common law. Legislation may also insert implied terms into contracts, but allow the implied term to be excluded in defined circumstances[32]; but an express term does not negative a term implied by the Act unless inconsistent with it.[33]

In *Dalmare SpA v Union Maritime Ltd*,[34] Flaux J held that this test would not be satisfied in a case where one obvious meaning of the term in question would not be inconsistent with the statutorily implied term, even though another obvious meaning was.

6.12   Where legislation covers a particular area the courts must be especially careful about implying a term covering the same general area.[35]

6.13   In addition, the image of "shades on a continuous spectrum" (which comes from the speech of Lord Wilberforce in *Liverpool City Council v Irwin*)[36] itself suggests that at least at some points on the spectrum, the process of implication is a facet of that of interpretation. At one end of the spectrum the court is doing no more than stating the logical corollary of a term expressly agreed.[37] This is clearly part of the process of interpretation. Towards the middle of the spectrum the court is making explicit that which is implicit, not in a logical sense, but in a practical or commercial sense, in the parties' bargain. And at the other end of the spectrum the court is filling gaps in the bargain as expressed.[38]

However, there are unresolved tensions in the notion of the "continuous

---

[31]   [1986] 2 Lloyd's Rep. 68.

[32]   For example, the Late Payment of Commercial Debts (Interest) Act 1998.

[33]   Sale of Goods Act 1979 s.55. This does not apply to a contract to which Ch.2 of Pt I of the Consumer Rights Act 2015 applies: s.55(2), inserted by Consumer Rights Act 2015 Sch.1 para.33.

[34]   [2012] EWHC 3537 (Comm); [2013] 1 Lloyd's Rep. 509.

[35]   *Johnson v Unisys Ltd* [2003] 1 A.C. 518; *Eastwood v Magnox Electric Plc* [2005] 1 A.C. 503.

[36]   [1977] A.C. 239 at 253.

[37]   See *Metropolitan Electric Supply Co Ltd v Ginder* [1901] 2 Ch. 799 (para.6.89, Illustration 2). This is an example of what Steyn LJ described as "a purely constructional implication"; *Bratton Seymour Service Co Ltd v Oxborough* [1992] B.C.L.C. 693.

[38]   Cited with approval in *The Rio Assu* [1989] 1 Lloyd's Rep. 115 at 120 (Clarke J aff'd on appeal).

spectrum". In construing the express terms of a contract the court often stresses the importance of the reasonableness of the construction selected or of the result achieved.[39] By contrast, in discussing the circumstances in which a term is to be implied, the court repeatedly stresses that the touchstone is necessity, not reasonableness. If the implication of terms is part of a continuous spectrum beginning with the construction of express terms, it would seem to follow that at some point in the spectrum there is a radical change in approach. The location of that point is uncertain. Hence some judges do not draw a rigid distinction between the process of interpretation and the process of implication. Thus in *Chaffe v Kingsley*,[40] Sedley LJ said:

> "The distinction between the construction of documents and the implication of terms, which at the start seemed likely to occupy much of the argument, is often a mare's nest. Attempting the latter inevitably provokes the true but unhelpful response that words are being artificially introduced into a document; attempting the former almost as inevitably provokes the response, equally true and equally unhelpful, that the terms relied on are not visible. It has been helpful, therefore, to be conducted directly on the search for meaning."

On the basis that the implication of a term is an exercise in interpreting the contract as a whole the "same background material that is admissible and relevant in aid of construction of the express terms of the charters may also be admitted in aid of the determination of the existence of an implied term."[41]

Illustrations

1. Employees of a health board had the right to buy additional years of pension entitlement on favourable terms provided that they exercised their right within a given time limit. It was held that where there was a relationship of employer and employee and: (1) the terms of the contract of employment were not negotiated with the individual employee but resulted from negotiation with a representative body or were incorporated by reference; (2) a particular term of the contract makes available to the employee a valuable right contingent on action being taken by him to avail himself of its benefit; and (3) the employee cannot reasonably be expected to be aware of the term unless it is drawn to his attention; it is an implied term of the contract that the employer will take reasonable steps to bring the relevant provision to the attention of the employee.
Scally v Southern Health and Social Services Board[42]

2. Where a contract of employment relates to an engagement of a class where it is the normal practice of employers to require a reference from a previous employer before offering employment, and the employee accepts employment on the basis that a full and frank reference will be provided at the request of a prospective employer, it is an implied term of the contract that the employer will, during

---

[39] See paras 2.50 and 7.161.
[40] [2000] 1 E.G.L.R. 104. See also *Legal & General Assurance Co Plc v Expeditors (UK) Ltd* [2007] 2 P. & C.R. 10, where Clarke and Sedley LJJ reached the same answer, the former by a process of implication, the latter by a process of construction.
[41] *Golden Fleece Maritime Inc v St Shipping and Transport Inc* [2007] EWHC 1890 (Comm), per Cooke J.
[42] [1992] 1 A.C. 294 HL.

the continuance of the employment or within a reasonable time thereafter, provide a reference based on facts revealed after making those reasonable inquiries which a reasonable employer would make.
Spring v Guardian Assurance Plc[43]

3. It is an implied term of an arbitration agreement that the arbitration is confidential.
Ali Shipping Corp v Shipyard Trogir[44]

4. A term precluding the arbitrary or irrational exercise of a contractual discretion falls into the first category of implied terms.
Mid Essex Hospital Services NHS Trust v Compass Group UK and Ireland Ltd (t/a Medirest)[45]

5. The principle that a power (e.g. in articles of association) entitling a majority to bind a minority must be exercised for the purpose of benefiting the class as a whole, and not merely individual members only, is a term generally implied by the law as an incident of contracts or arrangements of particular types.
Assenagon Asset Management SA v Irish Bank Resolution Corp Ltd[46]

2. TEST FOR IMPLIED TERMS AS LEGAL INCIDENTS

Where the court is asked to imply a term as a legal incident of a particular legal relationship, the strict test of necessity need not be satisfied. The court is concerned with broader questions of policy.[47]

6.14   As has been seen, the court has recently isolated a special category of implied terms, namely those where the court is asked to imply a term as a legal incident of a particular relationship, as a default rule which will apply unless specifically excluded. These kinds of implied term are not based upon the intention of the parties, actual or presumed, in a given instance, although the provenance of a particular term may well have been the commonplace use of such a term in earlier times in contracts of that type, so establishing what later would become the default rule.[48]

6.15   Where the court decides that a term should be implied as an incident of the legal relationship it is really deciding a question of substantive law. In *Emmott v Michael Wilson & Partners Ltd*,[49] Lawrence Collins LJ, speaking of the implied obligation of confidentiality in an arbitration agreement, said:

"The implied agreement is really a rule of substantive law masquerading as an implied term."

---

[43] [1995] 2 A.C. 296 HL.

[44] [1998] 1 Lloyd's Rep. 643. This implied term has been described as a rule of law masquerading as an implied term: *Emmott v Michael Wilson & Partners Ltd* [2008] Bus. L.R. 1361. Exceptions to the principle of confidentiality were considered in *Ajayi v Ebury Partners Ltd* [2020] EWHC 166 (Comm).

[45] [2013] EWCA Civ 200.

[46] [2012] EWHC 2090 (Ch); [2013] 1 All E.R. 495.

[47] See *Rosserlane Consultants Ltd v Credit Suisse International* [2015] EWHC 384 (Ch). The High Court of Australia has retained the concept of "necessity" even in this class of case: *Commonwealth Bank of Australia v Barker* [2014] HCA 32.

[48] *University of Western Australia v Gray* (2009) 179 F.C.R. 346. This is an example of a growth of judicial consensus giving rise to a presumption of substantive law. See also *Commonwealth Bank of Australia v Barker* [2014] HCA 32.

[49] [2008] Bus. L.R. 1361.

Is this of any legal significance, in terms of the criteria which must be satisfied before such a term will be implied?

In *Lister v Romford Ice and Cold Storage Co Ltd*,[50] the issue was whether there **6.16** was an implied term in a contract of employment entitling an employee to be indemnified by his employer against liability for negligence in the course of his employment. Viscount Simonds said that the court was concerned, not with a particular contract but:

> "with a general question, which if not correctly described as a question of status, yet can only be answered by considering the relation in which the drivers of motor-vehicles and their employers generally stand to each other."

He continued:

> "If I were to try to apply the familiar tests where the question is whether a term should be implied in a particular contract in order to give it what is called business efficacy, I should lose myself in the attempt to formulate it with the necessary precision. But this is not conclusive, for as I have said, the solution of the problem does not rest on the implication of a term in a particular contract but upon more general considerations."

The "more general considerations" are matters of general policy. It seems reason **6.17** ably clear from this passage that different criteria apply to the implication of terms as legal incidents of particular types of contract. However, the water was muddied by the subsequent case of *Liverpool City Council v Irwin*.[51] Lord Wilberforce[52] treated the case as being simply one in which the court was concerned to complete an obviously incomplete contract. He did, however, recognise that whatever term was to be implied would be a legal incident of the relationship between the parties. He described the appropriate test as follows:

> "... such obligation should be read into the contract as the nature of the contract itself implicitly requires, no more, no less; a test in other words of necessity."

Lord Cross of Chelsea took what seems to be a wholly different view. Dealing with the first category of implied term he said:

> "In deciding whether or not to lay down such a prima facie rule the court will naturally ask itself whether in the general run of such cases the term in question would be one which it would be reasonable to insert."[53]

Lord Edmund-Davies said that he would have rejected the alleged implied term on the test of necessity, but upheld it as a "legal incident" of the contract. Clearly,

---

50   [1957] A.C. 555.
51   [1977] A.C. 239.
52   With whom Lord Fraser of Tullybelton agreed. This view was adopted by the Court of Appeal in *Mears v Safecar Security Ltd* [1983] Q.B. 54.
53   Lord Cross contrasted this situation with one where the court is asked to add a term to a particular contract, in which event the appropriate test is necessity. Since Lord Cross gave no other criterion for the implication of terms in cases falling within the first category, it seems that "reasonableness in the general run of cases" is the only one. The distinction drawn by Lord Cross was approved in *JH Ritchie Ltd v Lloyd Ltd* [2007] 1 W.L.R. 670.

therefore, in his Lordship's opinion the criterion to be satisfied before a term can be implied as a legal incident of a legal relationship falls short of necessity.[54]

6.18   In *Shell UK Ltd v Lostock Garages Ltd*,[55] Lord Denning MR said that in such cases the problem:

"… is to be solved by asking: has the law already defined the obligation or the extent of it? If so, let it be followed. If not, look to see what would be reasonable in the general run of cases … and then say what the obligation shall be."

At this stage the position seems reasonably clear. The views of Lord Cross of Chelsea and Lord Edmund-Davies represent the law. However, a different view was taken in *Tai Hing Cotton Mill Ltd v Liu Chong Hing Bank Ltd*.[56] In that case, a bank argued that the contract between it and its customer contained an implied term to the effect that the customer would take reasonable care to ensure that in the operation of the bank account the bank was not injured. The Privy Council held that:

"the relationship between banker and customer is contractual and its incidents, in the absence of express agreement, are such as must be implied into the contract because they can be seen to be obviously necessary."

Accordingly, the alleged term was rejected on the ground that it was not necessary to give business efficacy to the contract. The test adopted by the Privy Council was applied (obiter) by the Court of Appeal in *The Maira*[57] and again in *National Bank of Greece SA v Pinios Shipping Co (No.1)*[58] and *Bank of Nova Scotia v Hellenic Mutual War Risks Association (Bermuda) Ltd*.[59]

6.19   In *Scally v Southern Health Board*,[60] Lord Bridge held that an alleged implied term could not be justified as necessary for the business efficacy of an employment contract, but went on to draw a clear distinction:

"between the search for an implied term necessary to give business efficacy to a particular contract and the search, based on wider considerations, for a term which the law will imply as a necessary incident of a definable category of contractual relationship."

Although the second test involves wider considerations, Lord Bridge's formulation suggests that an implied term must still be a *necessary* incident of the relationship. In *Crossley v Faithful & Gould Holdings Ltd*,[61] Dyson LJ drew the distinction between an implied term as a legal incident of a contractual relationship and a tailor-made implied term. He said:

"This would be a standardised term to be implied by law, that is to say a term

---

54   This was the view of the Court of Appeal in *Duke of Westminster v Guild* [1985] Q.B. 688 (saying that in respect of the category of case now under consideration Lord Cross stated that "a quite different test" is applicable; and referring to the test for other cases as being "less favourable" to the party asserting the existence of the implied term).
55   [1976] 1 W.L.R. 1187.
56   [1986] A.C. 80.
57   [1988] 2 Lloyd's Rep. 126 at 136, per Lloyd LJ and at 146, per Nicholls LJ.
58   [1990] 1 A.C. 637 CA (reversed on other grounds: loc. cit.).
59   [1990] Q.B. 818 CA.
60   [1992] 1 A.C. 294 HL.
61   [2004] 4 All E.R. 447.

which, in the absence of any contrary intention, is an incident of all contracts of employment. It is not a term implied to give business efficacy to the particular contract in question which is dependent on an intention imputed to the parties from the express terms of the contract and the surrounding circumstances."

He rejected the submission that the test was one of necessity and concluded:

"It seems to me that, rather than focus on the elusive concept of necessity, it is better to recognise that, to some extent at least, the existence and scope of standardised implied terms raise questions of reasonableness, fairness and the balancing of competing policy considerations."[62]

In *Société Générale, London Branch v Geys*,[63] Lady Hale approved the approach of Dyson LJ.

In *Makers UK Ltd v Camden London Borough Council*,[64] Akenhead J considered **6.20** the judgment of Dyson LJ in *Crossley v Faithful & Gould Holdings Ltd*,[65] where a term was implied as an incident of a legal relationship. He said:

"I do not consider that Dyson LJ was rejecting the 'necessity' element of the implication of terms; that is too well established in English law. He found it simpler to concentrate in that case on the other elements."[66]

A more relaxed approach to the implication of terms as legal incidents of a **6.21** particular relationship was taken in *William Morton & Co v Muir Brothers & Co*[67] in which Lord McLaren said:

"The conception of an implied condition is one with which we are familiar in relation to contracts of every description, and if we seek to trace any such implied conditions to their source, it will be found that in almost every instance they are founded either on universal custom or in the nature of the contract itself. If the condition is such that every reasonable man on the one part would desire for his own protection to stipulate for the condition, and that no reasonable man on the other part would refuse to accede to it, then it is not unnatural that the condition should be taken for granted in all contracts of the class without the necessity of giving it formal expression."

This approach was approved by the House of Lords in *J&H Ritchie Ltd v Lloyd Ltd*.[68]

To the extent that necessity is the appropriate test in this class of case, a series **6.22** of Australian decisions suggest that necessity is understood in a different sense. In

---

[62] In an article by Elizabeth Peden, "Policy concerns behind implication of terms in law" (2001) 119 L.Q.R. 459, the policy considerations are grouped under three broad categories: (i) how the implied term will sit with existing law; (ii) how the implied term will affect parties to the relationship; and (iii) wider issues of fairness and society. Dyson LJ referred to this article with apparent approval in *Crossley v Faithful & Gould Holdings Ltd* [2004] 4 All E.R. 447.

[63] [2012] UKSC 63; [2013] 1 A.C. 523.

[64] (2008) 120 Con. L.R. 161.

[65] [2004] 4 All E.R. 447.

[66] The author is not convinced that this observation is correct.

[67] [1907] S.C. 1211, 1224.

[68] [2007] 1 W.L.R. 670.

Renard Constructions (ME) Pty Ltd v Minister for Public Works,[69] Priestly JA said:

"It seems to me that the word necessity, when used in the cases analysed by Hope JA,[70] was not being used in the absolute sense. In regard to classes of contract to which particular implications have been recognised as attaching, it is not possible to say that the implication was always necessary, in the sense that the contracts could not have worked without the implied term. Contracts of sale, contracts of employment, and leases are three classes of contract to which such terms have been attached. In all cases it would have been possible for the main purposes of the contracts to have been attained without the implications the judges have held they include. The rules in regard to each of them have come into existence not because in the particular cases giving rise to recognition of the implication it has been thought that it would be impossible for such contracts to be made and carried out without the implications, but because the Court decided it would be better or more appropriate or more reasonable in accordance with the contemporary thinking of the judges and parties concerned with such contracts that the term should be implied than that it should not. The idea is conveyed I think by Holmes's phrase 'The felt necessities of the time' where necessity has the sense of something required in accordance with current standards of what ought to be the case, rather than anything more absolute.

This seems to me to be the approach that should be adopted when considering implication by law ...".

And in *University of Western Australia v Gray,*[71] Lindgren, Finn and Bennett JJ said:

"What is clear is that necessity in this context has a different shade of meaning from that which it has in formulations of the business efficacy test ... The principal reason for this is ... that implication in law rests 'upon more general considerations' ... Those more general considerations require that regard be had 'to the inherent nature of the contract and of the relationship thereby established' ... But those very considerations themselves can raise issues of 'justice and policy' ... as well as consideration, not only of consequences within the employment relationship, but also of social consequences ...".

6.23 It must be recognised, however, that the relationship giving rise to the implication of a term as an incident of that relationship must be defined with care.[72] Sometimes the description is a general one. Thus the relation of employer and employee gives rise to an implied obligation not to destroy the trust and confidence that must subsist between the two parties to the employment contract if it is to work effectively.[73] On the other hand, sometimes the relationship is more narrowly

---

[69] (1992) 26 N.S.W.L.R. 234 at 261. This passage was approved in *Devefi Pty Ltd v Mateffy Pearl Nagy Pty Ltd* (1993) 113 A.L.R. 225 at 240.

[70] In *Castlemaine Tooheys v Carlton & United Breweries Ltd* (1987) 10 N.S.W.L.R. 468 at 489.

[71] [2009] FCAFC 116 at [142]. See also *Hughes Aircraft Systems International v Airservices Australia* (1997) 76 F.C.R 151 at 195.

[72] See E. Peden, "Policy concerns behind implication of terms in law" (2001) 117 L.Q.R. 459.

[73] The implied term of trust and confidence does not apply to a highway maintenance agreement (*Bedfordshire County Council v Fitzpatrick Contractors Ltd* [1998] 62 Con. L.R. 64) or to a franchise agreement (*Jani-King (GB) Ltd v Pula Enterprises Ltd* [2007] EWHC 2433 (QBD)).

defined. In *Scally v Southern Health and Social Services Board*,[74] the implied term required an employer to take reasonable steps to bring to the attention of the employee his entitlement to buy additional years of pension entitlement on favourable terms provided that they exercised their right within a given time limit. However, such a term is not implied into every relationship of employer and employee. It is only implied where the relation of employer and employee is one where: (1) the terms of the contract of employment were not negotiated with the individual employee but resulted from negotiation with a representative body or were incorporated by reference; (2) a particular term of the contract makes available to the employee a valuable right contingent on action being taken by him to avail himself of its benefit; and (3) the employee cannot reasonably be expected to be aware of the term unless it is drawn to his attention. Likewise, in the case of the relation of landlord and tenant it is an implied term that the tenant will have quiet enjoyment of the demised property. In *Liverpool City Council v Irwin*,[75] the implied term required the landlord to take reasonable care to keep in repair and lit essential means of access and rubbish chutes. But this obligation is not implied into every relation of landlord and tenant. It applies only to a contract of tenancy of a flat in a high rise block. A planning agreement made under s.106 of the Town and Country Planning Act 1971 is not of such a character as to attract standardised implied terms.[76]

There has been some debate whether the approach to standardised implied terms **6.24** enables the court to conclude that contracts generally contain an implied term of good faith. In *Yam Seng PTE Ltd v International Trade Corp Ltd*,[77] Leggatt J said:

> "A paradigm example of a general norm which underlies almost all contractual relationships is an expectation of honesty. That expectation is essential to commerce, which depends critically on trust. Yet it is seldom, if ever, made the subject of an express contractual obligation. Indeed if a party in negotiating the terms of a contract were to seek to include a provision which expressly required the other party to act honestly, the very fact of doing so might well damage the parties' relationship by the lack of trust which this would signify....
>
> As a matter of construction, it is hard to envisage any contract which would not reasonably be understood as requiring honesty in its performance. The same conclusion is reached if the traditional tests for the implication of a term are used. In particular the requirement that parties will behave honestly is so obvious that it goes without saying. Such a requirement is also necessary to give business efficacy to commercial transactions."

The judge discussed extensively the question whether English law recognised a general duty of good faith or fair dealing, and came to the conclusion that it did. As he put it:

> "In addition to honesty, there are other standards of commercial dealing which are so generally accepted that the contracting parties would reasonably be understood to take them as read without explicitly stating them in their

---

[74] [1992] 1 A.C. 294 HL.

[75] [1977] A.C. 239.

[76] *Hampshire County Council v Beazer Homes Ltd* [2010] EWHC 3095 (QB).

[77] [2013] EWHC 111 (QB); [2013] 1 Lloyd's Rep. 526, applied in *D&G Cars Ltd v Essex Police Authority* [2015] EWHC 226 (QB).

contractual document. A key aspect of good faith, as I see it, is the observance of such standards. Put the other way round, not all bad faith conduct would necessarily be described as dishonest. Other epithets which might be used to describe such conduct include 'improper', 'commercially unacceptable' or 'unconscionable'."

There would be a breach of that duty if "in the particular context the conduct would be regarded as commercially unacceptable by reasonable and honest people."

6.25 However, in *TSG Building Services Plc v South Anglia Housing Ltd*,[78] Akenhead J said that he "would not draw any principle from this extremely illuminating and interesting judgment which is of general application to all commercial contracts".[79] He went on to hold that even if there was an implied term of good faith it would not override a clear power to terminate the contract "for no, good or bad reason … at any time". It is not considered that at least at present English law recognises a general implication of a term of good faith.[80]

On the other hand, in *Emirates Trading Agency LLC v Prime Mineral Exports Private Ltd*,[81] Teare J held that a term was to be implied into an alternative dispute resolution clause requiring the parties to act in good faith in resolving their disputes. In addition, a term of good faith may be more readily implied in a contract described as a "relational contract".[82]

6.26 The courts in Canada have taken a very different approach. In *Bhasin v Hrynew*,[83] the Supreme Court of Canada described good faith as a general organising principle of the law of contract rather than a term of a particular contract or type of contract. Second, they decided that it applied to all contracts. Cromwell J, giving the unanimous judgment of the Court, said:

"In my view, it is time to take two incremental steps in order to make the common law less unsettled and piecemeal, more coherent and more just. The first step is to acknowledge that good faith contractual performance is a general organising principle of the common law of contract which underpins and informs the various rules in which the common law, in various situations and types of relationships, recognises obligations of good faith contractual performance. The

---

[78] [2013] EWHC 1151 (TCC); followed by Andrews J in *Greenclose Ltd v National Westminster Bank Plc* [2014] EWHC 1156 (Ch). See also *Myers v Kestrel Acquisitions Ltd* [2015] EWHC 916 (Ch).

[79] The author agrees. Leggatt J's general analysis has not been enthusiastically received: *Compass Group UK and Ireland Ltd v Mid Essex Hospital Services NHS Trust* [2013] EWCA Civ 200; *Hamsard 3147 Ltd v Boots UK Ltd* [2013] EWHC 3251 (Pat); *Carewatch Care Services Ltd v Focus Caring Services Ltd* [2014] EWHC 2313 (Ch); *Myers v Kestrel Acquisitions Ltd* [2015] EWHC 916 (Ch). See also S. Whittaker, "Good faith, implied terms and commercial contracts" (2013) L.Q.R. 463. A term of good faith is more readily implied in Australia: see Lewison and Hughes, *The Interpretation of Contracts in Australia*, 1st Australian edn (Australia: Thomson Reuters, 2012), para.6.14; and a term to this effect was found to exist in *D&G Cars Ltd v Essex Police Authority* [2015] EWHC 226 (QB).

[80] *Greenclose Ltd v National Westminster Bank Plc* [2014] EWHC 1156 (Ch). See also *Myers v Kestrel Acquisitions Ltd* [2015] EWHC 916 (Ch).

[81] [2014] EWHC 2104 (Comm).

[82] See para.6.143; *Wales v CBRE Managed Services Ltd* [2020] EWHC 16 (Comm).

[83] [2014] 3 S.C.R. 494. The case and the decision of Leggatt J in *Yam Seng Pte Ltd v International Trade Corp Ltd* [2013] EWHC 111 (QB); [2013] 1 C.L.C. 662 are discussed by Prof. Carter and Prof. Courtney in "Good faith in contracts: is there an implied promise to act honestly?" [2016] C.L.J. 608 and by Zhong Xing Tan in "Keeping faith with good faith? The evolving trajectory post—Yam Seng and Bhasin" [2016] J.B.L. 620. Some Australian courts take the same view: *Renard Constructions (ME) Pty v Minister for Public Works* (1992) 26 NSWLR 234.

second is to recognise, as a further manifestation of this organising principle of good faith, that there is a common law duty which applies to all contracts to act honestly in the performance of contractual obligations."

The Court rejected the proposition that the duty of good faith was an implied term of the contract. If it had been, the parties would have been able to exclude it. Rather, the Court held:

"Because the duty of honesty in contractual performance is a general doctrine of contract law that applies to all contracts, like unconscionability, the parties are not free to exclude it."

It is not considered that this represents English law. In *Versloot Dredging BV v HDI Gerling Industrie Versicherung AG*,[84] Lord Sumption said of the duty of good faith applicable to insurance contracts:

6.27

"the content of the duty of good faith and the consequences of its breach must be accommodated within the general principles of the law of contract. On that view of the matter, the fraudulent claims rule must be regarded as a term implied or inferred by law, or at any rate an incident of the contract."

The Court of Appeal took a similar approach in *MSC Mediterranean Shipping Co SA v Cottonex Anstalt*[85] in which Moore-Bick LJ said:

"There is in my view a real danger that if a general principle of good faith were established it would be invoked as often to undermine as to support the terms in which the parties have reached agreement."

Illustrations

1.   It is no part of the relationship between a building contractor and a sub-contractor that the former will make sufficient work available to the latter to enable him to maintain reasonable progress or to execute his work in an efficient and economic manner. However, it is part of their relationship that they should cooperate, the degree of cooperation depending on the express terms of the contract.
    Grant (Martin) & Co Ltd v Sir Lindsay Parkinson & Co Ltd[86]

2.   It is a necessary incident of an arbitration agreement that it is confidential to the parties.
    Ali Shipping Corp v Shipyard Trogir[87]

3.   A contract provided that if one party failed to perform his obligations the other could enforce his rights by filing a claim in the London Court of International Arbitration. It was held that where one party agrees that another could file an

---

[84]   [2016] UKSC 45; [2017] A.C. 1.
[85]   [2016] EWCA Civ 789; [2016] 2 Lloyd's Rep. 494.
[86]   (1984) 29 Build. L.R. 31.
[87]   [1998] 1 Lloyd's Rep. 643 CA.

arbitration claim against him, it is implied that he will submit to the jurisdiction of the agreed tribunal.

Yegiazaryan v Smagin[88]

4.   It is an implied term of a contract of employment that a written notice given by an employer to an employee does not take effect until it had come to the notice of the employee and he or she has had a reasonable opportunity to read it.

Newcastle upon Tyne Hospitals NHS Foundation Trust v Haywood[89]

5.   It was an implied term of a building contract that the employer would use due diligence to obtain necessary planning permissions and conservation area consents. The content of the obligation required the employer to make a timely application for any such permission or other approval or ensure a timely application was made on his behalf, to ensure sufficient information was provided to the local planning authority in support of the application, and to cooperate with the authority in the statutory process.

Clin v Walter Lilly & Co Ltd[90]

6.   There is no general implication as a matter of law that exclusive distributors must not compete with their suppliers.

Demand Media Ltd v Koch Media Ltd[91]

3.   IMPLICATION OF TERMS DIFFERS FROM INTERPRETATION

Although (i) interpreting the words which the parties have used in their contract and (ii) implying terms into the contract, involve determining the scope and meaning of the contract, interpreting the words used and implying additional words are different processes governed by different rules.[92]

6.28   There had been debate in the past on the question whether the implication of a term is truly a question of interpreting the contract. In *Trollope & Colls Ltd v North West Metropolitan Regional Hospital Board*,[93] Lord Pearson said that it had been convenient to contrast a "construction point" with an argument on the implication of a term:

"without prejudice to the question whether as a matter of strict theory the implication of a term may properly be considered as an aspect of the construction of the contract."

Lord Steyn gave a negative answer to the question. In *National Commercial Bank*

---

88   [2016] EWCA Civ 1290; [2017] 1 Lloyd's Rep. 102.
89   [2018] UKSC 22; [2018] 1 W.L.R. 2073. However, in *S&T (UK) Ltd v Grove Developments Ltd* [2018] EWCA Civ 2448; 181 Con. L.R. 66 (a case concerning a building contract) the Court of Appeal upheld the validity of two notices sent by email within seven or eight seconds of each other. The court explicitly rejected the implication of a term to the effect that a reasonable time must elapse between receipt of the first notice and receipt of the second, on the ground that such a term would be unworkable and create huge uncertainty.
90   [2018] EWCA Civ 490; [2018] B.L.R. 321.
91   [2020] EWHC 32 (QB).
92   This section in a previous edition was referred to with approval in *Eric Wright Group Ltd v Council of the City of Manchester* [2020] EWHC 2089 (Ch).
93   [1973] 1 W.L.R. 601.

Jamaica Ltd v Guyana Refrigerators Ltd,[94] he said:

"The processes of construction and implication of terms are closely linked, but as a matter of legal analysis they need to be kept separate."

In *Gordon & Gotch Australia Pty Ltd v Horwitz Publications Pty Ltd,*[95] Allsop P and Sackville AJA said:

"That interpretation can shade into implication and, indeed, that both may perhaps be seen as part of the one process of the construction of words in a document to identify linguistic and legal meaning can be accepted. However, the distinction between interpretation and implication of terms is recognised (even if the limits of each are not capable of clear definition)."

However, an affirmative answer of a kind to the question was given by Mason J in *Codelfa Construction Pty Ltd v State Rail Authority of New South Wales*[96]:   **6.29**

"When we say that the implication of a term raises an issue as to the meaning and effect of the contract we do not intend by that statement to convey that the court is embarking upon an orthodox exercise in the interpretation of the language of the contract, that is, assigning a meaning to a particular provision. Nonetheless, the implication of a term is an exercise in interpretation, though not an orthodox instance."

Other judges have been more positive. In *South Australia Asset Management Corp v York Montagu Ltd,*[97] Lord Hoffmann said: **6.30**

"As in the case of any implied term, the process is one of construction of the agreement as a whole in its commercial setting."

Writing extra-judicially,[98] Lord Hoffmann developed this thought. He said:

"In fact, of course, the implication of a term into a contract is an exercise in interpretation like any other. It may seem odd to speak of interpretation when, by definition, the term has not been expressed in words, but the only difference is that when we imply a term, we are engaged in interpreting the meaning of the contract as a whole. For this purpose, we apply the ordinary rule of contractual interpretation by which the parties are depersonalised and assumed to be reasonable."

---

[94] (1998) 53 W.I.R. 229. In *Sembcorp Marine Ltd v PPL Holdings Pte Ltd* [2013] SGCA 43; (2013) 151 Con. L.R. 170 the Singapore Court of Appeal drew a sharp distinction between "interpretation" on the one hand and "construction" on the other. Interpretation is concerned only with the meaning of the express words contained in the contract, whereas construction embraces wider considerations, such as the implication of terms to fill gaps in the contract for which the express terms make no provision. This is not a view to which the author subscribes. It is little more than an arid semantic debate.

[95] [2008] NSWCA 257.

[96] (1982) 149 C.L.R. 337. See also *Winter Garden Theatre (London) Ltd v Millennium Productions Ltd* [1948] A.C. 173 at 198, per Lord Uthwatt ("The question whether any such term can be properly implied is purely a question of the construction of the contract.").

[97] [1996] 3 W.L.R. 87 at 93 HL. See also *Equitable Life Assurance Society v Hyman* [2002] 1 A.C. 408 at 459, per Lord Steyn. His Lordship did, however, say that it was necessary to distinguish between interpretation and implication.

[98] Lord Hoffmann, "The Intolerable Wrestle with Words and Meanings" (1997) 114 S.A.L.J. 656.

In *Meridian International Services Ltd v Richardson*,[99] the Court of Appeal approved the statement of the trial judge that:

"The implication of terms is part of the process of interpretation of contracts, and even when dealing with an oral as opposed to a written contract, it is necessary to consider the matter in the light of the background."

Similarly, in *Transfield Shipping Inc v Mercator Shipping Inc*,[100] Lord Hoffmann said that the implication of a term was "a matter of construction of the contract as a whole in its commercial context".

6.31   In *Attorney General of Belize v Belize Telecom Ltd*,[101] giving the advice of the Privy Council, Lord Hoffmann said:

"[16]   Before discussing in greater detail the reasoning of the Court of Appeal, the Board will make some general observations about the process of implication. The court has no power to improve upon the instrument which it is called upon to construe, whether it be a contract, a statute or articles of association. It cannot introduce terms to make it fairer or more reasonable. It is concerned only to discover what the instrument means. However, that meaning is not necessarily or always what the authors or parties to the document would have intended. It is the meaning which the instrument would convey to a reasonable person having all the background knowledge which would reasonably be available to the audience to whom the instrument is addressed: see *Investors Compensation Scheme Ltd v West Bromwich Building Society* [1998] 1 WLR 896, 912–913. It is this objective meaning which is conventionally called the intention of the parties, or the intention of Parliament, or the intention of whatever person or body was or is deemed to have been the author of the instrument.

[17]   The question of implication arises when the instrument does not expressly provide for what is to happen when some event occurs. The most usual inference in such a case is that nothing is to happen. If the parties had intended something to happen, the instrument would have said so. Otherwise, the express provisions of the instrument are to continue to operate undisturbed. If the event has caused loss to one or other of the parties, the loss lies where it falls.

[18]   In some cases, however, the reasonable addressee would understand the instrument to mean something else. He would consider that the only meaning consistent with the other provisions of the instrument, read against the relevant background, is that something is to happen. The event in question is to affect the rights of the parties. The instrument may not have expressly said so, but this is what it must mean. In such a case, it is said that the court implies a term as to what will happen if the event in

---

[99]   [2008] EWCA Civ 609.
[100] [2009] A.C. 61.
[101] [2009] 2 All E.R. 1127.

question occurs. But the implication of the term is not an addition to the instrument. It only spells out what the instrument means."

That was a view with which the author agreed, and which was widely applied.[102] **6.32**

In *Stena Line Ltd v Merchant Navy Ratings Pension Fund Trustees Ltd*,[103] Arden **6.33**
LJ said:

"The *Belize* case constitutes an important and recent development in the principles of interpretation, which the courts are probably still absorbing and ingesting. In *Belize*, the Privy Council analysed the case law on the implication of terms and decided that the implication of terms is, in essence, an exercise in interpretation. This development promotes the internal coherence of the law by emphasising the role played by the principles of interpretation not only in the context of the interpretation of documents simpliciter but also in the field of the implication of terms. Those principles are the unifying factor. The internal coherence of the law is important because it enables the courts to identify the aims and values that underpin the law and to pursue those values and aims so as to achieve consistency in the structure of the law."

In *Mirador International LLC v MF Global UK Ltd*,[104] Lewison LJ said: **6.34**

"Whether this is described as choosing the more commercially sensible of rival

---

[102] See, e.g. *INTA Navigation Ltd v Ranch Investments Ltd* [2010] 1 Lloyd's Rep. 74; *Mediterranean Salvage & Towage Ltd v Seamar Trading & Commerce Inc* [2010] 1 All E.R. (Comm) 1; *Benedetti v Sawiris* [2009] EWHC 1330 (Ch); *ENE Kos 1 Ltd v Petroleo Brasileiro SA (No.2)* [2010] 1 All E.R. (Comm) 669; *AET Inc Ltd v Arcadia Petroleum Ltd* [2010] 1 All E.R. (Comm) 23; *Town Quay Developments Ltd v Eastleigh Borough Council* [2010] 2 P. & C.R. 19; *Gregory Projects (Halifax) Ltd v Tenpin (Halifax) Ltd* [2010] 2 All E.R. (Comm) 646; *CDV Software Entertainment AG v Gamecock Media Europe Ltd* [2009] EWHC 2965 (Ch); *Rutherford v Seymour Pierce Ltd* [2010] I.R.L.R. 606; *Chantry Estates (Southeast) Ltd v Anderson* (2010) 130 Con. L.R. 11; *North Shore Ventures Ltd v Anstead Holdings Inc* [2011] 1 All E.R. (Comm) 81; *PNPF Trust Co Ltd v Taylor* [2010] EWHC 1573 (Ch); *Re Agrimarche Ltd* [2010] EWHC 1655 (Ch); *Enterprise Inns Plc v The Forest Hill Tavern Public House Ltd* [2010] EWHC 2368 (Ch); *Crema v Centros Securities Plc* [2010] EWCA Civ 1444; [2011] Bus. L.R. 943; *KG Bominflot Bunkergesellschaft fur Mineraloele mbH & Co v Petroplus Marketing AG* [2010] All E.R. (D) 174 (Oct); *Société Générale, London Branch v Geys* [2011] EWCA Civ 307; *Garratt v Mirror Group Newspapers Ltd* [2011] EWCA Civ 425; *Miscela v Coffee Republic Retail Ltd* [2011] EWHC 1637 (QB); *Ross River Ltd v Waveley Commercial Ltd* [2012] EWHC 81 (Ch); *Spencer v Secretary of State for Defence* [2012] EWHC 120 (Ch); [2012] 2 All E.R. (Comm) 480 (on appeal [2012] EWCA Civ 1368; [2013] 1 All E.R. (Comm) 287 where the point did not arise); *McKillen v Misland (Cyprus) Investments Ltd* [2012] EWCA Civ 179; *Procter & Gamble Co v Svenska Cellulosa Aktiebolaget SCA* [2012] EWHC 498 (Ch); *Lomas v JFB Firth Rixson Inc* [2012] EWCA Civ 419; *Shah v HSBC Private Bank (UK) Ltd* [2012] EWHC 1283 (QB); *Fitzhugh v Fitzhugh* [2012] EWCA Civ 694; [2012] 2 P. & C.R. 14; *Consolidated Finance Ltd v McCluskey* [2012] EWCA Civ 1325; *Wuhan Ocean Economic & Technical Cooperation Co Ltd v Schiffarts-Gesellschaft "Hansa Murcia" MBH* [2012] EWHC 3104 (Comm); [2013] 1 Lloyd's Rep. 273; *TSG Building Services Plc v South Anglia Housing Ltd* [2013] EWHC 1151 (TCC); *Marex Financial Ltd v Creative Finance Ltd* [2013] EWHC 2155 (Comm); [2014] 1 All E.R. (Comm) 122; *Aspect Contracts (Asbestos) Ltd v Higgins Construction Plc* [2013] EWCA Civ 1541; [2014] 1 W.L.R. 1220; *McKillen v Misland (Cyprus) Investments Ltd* [2013] EWCA Civ 781; *Greenclose Ltd v National Westminster Bank Plc* [2014] EWHC 1156 (Ch); *Carewatch Care Services Ltd v Focus Caring Services Ltd* [2014] EWHC 2313 (Ch); *Myers v Kestrel Acquisitions Ltd* [2015] EWHC 916 (Ch); *University of Wales v London College of Business Ltd* [2015] EWHC 1280 (QB).
[103] [2011] EWCA Civ 543; *Miscela Ltd v Coffee Republic Retail Ltd* [2011] EWHC 1637 (QB).
[104] [2012] EWCA Civ 1662; *Torre Asset Funding Ltd v Royal Bank of Scotland Plc* [2013] EWHC 2670 (Ch).

interpretations of express terms (*Rainy Sky SA v Kookmin Bank*)[105] or implying a term (*Attorney General of Belize v Belize Telecom Ltd*)[106] does not seem to me to matter; since the objective of both is to determine what the reasonable person with the background knowledge of the parties would have understood the contract to mean (*Rainy Sky* §14; *Belize Telecom* §18)."

Likewise, in *Aspect Contracts (Asbestos) Ltd v Higgins Construction Plc*,[107] Longmore LJ said:

"It does not matter much whether one calls this a process of construction or a process of implication because one is only trying to decide what the words mean."

As the Court of Appeal put it in *NRAM Plc v McAdam*[108]:

"Following the judgment of the Privy Council in *Attorney General of Belize v Belize Telecom Ltd*,[109] the test for the implication of a term into a contract has been largely assimilated with the process of construing the contract."

6.35   Similarly, in *McKillen v Misland (Cyprus) Investments Ltd*,[110] Arden LJ said that on the basis of Lord Hoffmann's approach:

"… the underlying basis for the implication of a term is the interpretation of the document. Thus, the exercise becomes one of ascertaining the reasonable understandings and expectations of the parties. In other words, the meaning and effect of the process of testing necessity for the purposes of an implied term is not an exercise to be carried out in a manner detached from the reasonable expectations of the parties to the particular agreement being interpreted. In that way, the common law continues to insist in this field on party autonomy as a key principle of contract law."

Thus in *Gateway Plaza Ltd v White*,[111] the Court of Appeal did not distinguish between interpretation of the agreement and the implication of terms.

6.36   However, in *Foo Jong Peng v Phua Kiah Mai*,[112] the Court of Appeal of Singapore was critical of the assimilation of the principles of interpretation and implication. They considered that Lord Hoffmann's approach offered too little concrete guidance and stressed the necessity for specific rules and principles. The decision contains a valuable review of current case law and academic commentary.[113] The Court of Appeal of Singapore reaffirmed its position in *Sembcorp Marine Ltd v PPL Holdings Pte Ltd*[114] although it attempted to bridge the gap between its position and that of Lord Hoffmann by adopting a distinction between the interpretation of a contract and the construction of a contract.

---

[105] [2011] UKSC 50; [2011] 1 W.L.R. 2900.
[106] [2009] UKPC 10; [2009] 1 W.L.R. 1988.
[107] [2013] EWCA Civ 1541; [2014] 1 W.L.R. 1220.
[108] [2015] EWCA Civ 751.
[109] [2009] 1 W.L.R. 1988.
[110] [2013] EWCA Civ 781.
[111] [2014] EWCA Civ 555.
[112] [2012] SGCA 55. The case is discussed at [2013] J.B.L. 237.
[113] As well as some critical observations on this book.
[114] [2013] SGCA 43; (2013) 151 Con. L.R. 170.

The Supreme Court has now disavowed Lord Hoffmann's view, and relegated his analysis to "characteristically inspired discussion".[115] In *Marks & Spencer Plc v BNP Paribas Securities Services Trust Co (Jersey) Ltd*,[116] Lord Neuberger said:

6.37

"I accept that both (i) construing the words which the parties have used in their contract and (ii) implying terms into the contract, involve determining the scope and meaning of the contract. However, Lord Hoffmann's analysis in the *Belize Telecom* case could obscure the fact that construing the words used and implying additional words are different processes governed by different rules."

Since the court was unanimous in holding that Lord Hoffmann's restatement had not watered down the test applicable to the implication of terms, it is difficult to see why the majority departed from his formulation of principle.[117] Lord Hoffmann has subsequently robustly defended his approach[118]; and in the author's view it remains a valuable approach to what a contract "must mean".

Although there is an overlap in the material relevant to interpretation on the one hand and implication on the other, Lord Neuberger said:

6.38

"In most, possibly all, disputes about whether a term should be implied into a contract, it is only after the process of construing the express words is complete that the issue of an implied term falls to be considered. Until one has decided what the parties have expressly agreed, it is difficult to see how one can set about deciding whether a term should be implied and if so what term."[119]

As it has subsequently been put[120]:

"The former is concerned with what is there; the latter is concerned with inserting what is not there."

In *Byron v Eastern Caribbean Amalgamated Bank*[121] Lady Hale summarised the difference as follows:

6.39

"As I would put it, construing the words of the contract involves deciding what the parties meant by what they did say. Implying terms into the contract involves deciding whether they would have said something that they did not in fact say had the matter occurred to them. And until one has decided what the parties

---

[115] In New Zealand the Supreme Court approved Lord Hoffmann's approach: *Nielsen v Dysart Timbers Ltd* [2009] NZSC 43; [2009] 3 NZLR 160. However, since *Marks & Spencer* there is scope for argument about whether Lord Hoffmann's "undiluted approach" should continue to be followed in New Zealand: *Mobil Oil New Zealand Ltd v Development Auckland Ltd* [2016] NZSC 89. In the meantime it appears that some lower courts in New Zealand continue to apply *Belize* (*BDM Grange Ltd v Trimex Pty Ltd* [2017] NZCA 12; *Harris v GTV Holdings Ltd* [2016] NZHC 3123); while others adopt a stricter test (*Rintoul Group Ltd v Far North District Council* [2017] NZHC 1132).
[116] [2015] UKSC 72; [2016] A.C. 742.
[117] A view expressed by Lord Carnwath in his dissenting judgment. For differing academic perspectives see Edwin Peel, "Terms implied in fact" (2016) 132 L.Q.R. 531; Janet O'Sullivan, "Silence is golden: implied terms in the Supreme Court" (2016) 75 C.L.J. 199; Yihan Goh, "Lost but found again: the traditional tests for implied terms in fact" (2016) 3 J.B.L. 231; Joanna McCunn, "Belize It or Not: Implied Contract Terms in *Marks and Spencer v BNP Paribas*" (2016) 79 M.L.R. 1090.
[118] Hoffmann "Language and Lawyers" (2018) L.Q.R. 553.
[119] The Court of Appeal applied this two-stage approach in *Bou-Simon v BGC Brokers LP* [2018] EWCA Civ 1525; [2019] 1 All E.R. (Comm) 955.
[120] *Greenhouse v Paysafe Financial Services Ltd* [2018] EWHC 3296 (Comm).
[121] [2019] UKPC 16.

meant by what they did say, it will be difficult to set about deciding what they would have said."[122]

6.40 In *Aberdeen City Council v Stewart Milne Group Ltd*,[123] Lord Clarke[124] distinguished between interpretation and implication. He also purported to apply the traditional tests of business efficacy and the officious bystander. He said:

"If the officious bystander had been asked whether such a term should be implied, he or she would have said 'of course'. Put another way, such a term is necessary to make the contract work or to give it business efficacy. I would prefer to resolve this appeal by holding that such a term should be implied rather than by a process of interpretation."[125]

6.41 In the subsequent case of *Trump International Golf Club Scotland Ltd v Scottish Ministers*,[126] Lord Hodge said:

"Interpretation is not the same as the implication of terms. Interpretation of the words of a document is the precursor of implication. It forms the context in which the law may have to imply terms into a document, where the court concludes from its interpretation of the words used in the document that it must have been intended that the document would have a certain effect, although the words to give it that effect are absent."

In the same case Lord Mance sounded an appropriate warning:

"But I would not encourage advocates or courts to adopt too rigid or sequential an approach to the processes of consideration of the express terms and of consideration of the possibility of an implication. Without derogating from the requirement to construe any contract as a whole, particular provisions of a contract may I think give rise to a necessary implication, which, once recognised, will itself throw light on the scope and meaning of other express provisions of the contract ... [I]t appears to me helpful to recognise that, in a broad sense ... the processes of consideration of express terms and of the possibility that an implication exists are all part of an overall, and potentially iterative, process of objective construction of the contract as a whole."

6.42 In *Globe Motors Inc v TRW Lucas Varity Electric Steering Ltd*,[127] Beatson LJ said:

"In the light of what the Supreme Court has stated about the difference between the process of implication and the process of interpretation, care must be taken

---

Lord Kitchin made the same point in *Duval v 11-13 Randolph Crescent Ltd* [2020] UKSC 18; [2020] 2 W.L.R. 1167.
[123] [2011] UKSC 56; [2012] S.L.T. 205.
[124] With whom Lord Hope, Lady Hale and Lords Mance and Kerr agreed. However, in *Mediterranean Salvage & Towage Ltd v Seamar Trading & Commerce Inc* [2010] 1 All E.R. (Comm) 1 Sir Anthony Clarke MR (as he then was) had said that the implication of a term is an exercise in the construction of a contract as a whole. It seems unlikely that elevation to the Supreme Court changed his mind.
[125] This is, with respect, a mis-statement of the "officious bystander" test. The officious bystander poses the question to the parties. He does not provide the answer himself.
[126] [2015] UKSC 74; [2016] 1 W.L.R. 85.
[127] [2016] EWCA Civ 396; [2016] 1 C.L.C. 712.

not to seek to achieve that which might be achieved by implication by an inappropriate approach to interpretation."

In *Holland and Barrett International Ltd v General Nutrition Investment Co*[128] the Court of Appeal emphasised the difference between the explicit meaning of the words of the contract, and their implicit meaning. So in *The Law Debenture Trust Corpn Plc v Ukraine*[129] the Court of Appeal held that in *Marks & Spencer* the Supreme Court had "conclusively determined" that:

"the exercise of implication of terms is not to be classified as part of the exercise of interpretation, or construction, of the terms of a contract; it is a separate exercise."

Where, however, a contract is alleged to be incomplete there may be close relationship between interpretation and implication. In *Hayfin Opal Luxco 3 SARL v Windermere VII Cmbs Plc*,[130] Snowden J said: **6.43**

"In my judgment, what these authorities show is that there may be cases in which an analysis of the express terms of a contract leads to a clear conclusion that something is missing, and in such a case the court may be able to supply the missing words or terms. Whether that result is characterised as the process of correction of mistakes by construction referred to in *Chartbrook*, or as the process of implication of terms addressed in *M&S v BNP* may be open to debate, but there are certain features common to both lines of authority. On either view, the test that must be satisfied to justify such a result is a strict one. The court will not supply additional words or terms simply because it is reasonable to do so in the circumstances which have arisen. The court will only add words to the express terms of an agreement if it is necessary to do so because the agreement is incomplete or commercially incoherent without them. Even then, the court must be certain both that the absence of the missing words was inadvertent, and that if the omission had been drawn to the attention of the parties at the time of contracting they would have agreed what additional provision should be made."

In *Wells v Devani*[131] the Supreme Court did not adopt the rigid division between interpretation on the one hand and implication on the other. The case concerned an oral rather than a written contract; but it is not thought that the principles differ. In the course of a telephone conversation an estate agent said that his terms "would be 2 per cent plus VAT". The Supreme Court held that, as a matter of interpretation rather than implication, this statement meant that if the agent introduced a purchaser who subsequently completed a purchase, he would be entitled to be paid 2 per cent of the purchase price, plus VAT, payable out of the proceeds of sale. In the course of his judgment Lord Briggs gave the following example: **6.44**

"Take for example, the simple case of the door to door seller of (say) brooms. He rings the doorbell, proffers one of his brooms to the householder, and says

---

128 [2018] EWCA Civ 1586; [2019] F.S.R. 1.
129 [2018] EWCA Civ 2026; [2019] Q.B. 1121 (permission to appeal to the Supreme Court has been given).
130 [2016] EWHC 782 (Ch); [2018] 1 B.C.L.C. 118.
131 [2019] UKSC 4; [2020] A.C. 129. One difficulty with the decision of the Supreme Court is that they "interpreted" words that were never spoken: See Paul S. Davies, *Interpretation and Implication in the Supreme Court* [2019] C.L.J. 267.

'one pound 50'. The householder takes the broom, nods and reaches for his wallet. Plainly the parties have concluded a contract for the sale of the proffered broom, at a price of £1·50, immediately payable. But the subject matter of the sale, and the date of time at which payment is to be made, are not subject to terms expressed in words. All the essential terms other than price have been agreed by conduct, in the context of the encounter between the parties at the householder's front door."[132]

This example is strikingly similar to one that Lord Hoffmann gave in his article.[133]

"The background enables us to convey meaning with considerable economy of words. The person at the supermarket checkout can say 'That will be eight forty-six' and know you will understand 'That will be' as meaning 'The total price for the groceries you wish to buy is', 'eight' as referring to pounds, 'forty-six' as referring to pence and implying that if you produce and hand over the appropriate notes and coin of the realm, you may lawfully take the groceries and go home."

The decision in *Wells v Devani* might have been thought to herald a return to a more unified approach to interpretation and implication. But in *Duval v 11-13 Randolph Crescent Ltd*[134] the Supreme Court reaffirmed that the question of implying terms follows the process of interpreting the contract, because:

"until one has worked out what the parties have expressly agreed, it is difficult to see how one can decide whether a term should be implied into a contract and, if so, what it is."

4. THE DEFAULT POSITION

The default position is that nothing is to be implied into the contract. The more detailed and apparently complete the contract, the stronger this presumption is.

6.45   In *Attorney General of Belize v Belize Telecom Ltd*,[135] Lord Hoffmann said:

"The question of implication arises when the instrument does not expressly provide for what is to happen when some event occurs. The most usual inference in such a case is that nothing is to happen. If the parties had intended something to happen, the instrument would have said so. Otherwise, the express

---

[132] The example attributes to the householder knowledge that the person at the door is a seller of brooms, rather than, say, a person who offers his services of sweeping paths and drives. The postulated price seems more consistent with the latter rather than the former. The person at the door also proffers the broom, so body language is part of the communication, in contrast to communication which takes place solely on the telephone. In addition, the example is one of an immediate exchange of goods for money, rather than an executory contract.

[133] Hoffmann, "Language and Lawyers" (2018) L.Q.R. 553. See also Paul S. Davies, "Interpretation and Implication in the Supreme Court" [2019] C.L.J. 267.

[134] [2020] UKSC 18; [2020] 2 W.L.R. 1167. Lord Kitchin gave the leading judgment in both this case and *Wells v Devani*. The two cases might be thought to reveal a difference in approach.

[135] [2009] 2 All E.R. 1127.

provisions of the instrument are to continue to operate undisturbed. If the event has caused loss to one or other of the parties, the loss lies where it falls."

As Aikens LJ put it in *Crema v Cenkos Securities Plc*[136]:

"The default position is that nothing is to be implied in the instrument. In that case, if that particular event has caused loss, then the loss lies where it falls."

Likewise, in *Philips Electronique Grand Public SA v British Sky Broadcasting Ltd*,[137] Sir Thomas Bingham MR said: **6.46**

"The courts' usual role in contractual interpretation is, by resolving ambiguities or reconciling apparent inconsistencies, to attribute the true meaning to the language in which the parties have themselves expressed their contract. The implication of contract terms involves a different and altogether more ambitious undertaking: the interpolation of terms to deal with matters which, *ex hypothesi*, the parties themselves have made no provision. It is because the implication of terms is so potentially intrusive that the law imposes strict constraints on the exercise of this extraordinary power ...
    The question of whether a term should be implied, and if so what, almost inevitably arises after a crisis has been reached in the performance of the contract. So the court comes to the task of implication with the benefit of hindsight, and it is tempting for the court then to fashion a term which can reflect the merits of the situation as they then appear. Tempting, but wrong ...
    And it is not enough to show that had the parties foreseen the eventuality which in fact occurred they would have wished to make provision for it, unless it can also be shown either that there was only one contractual solution or that one of several possible solutions would without doubt have been preferred."

The Supreme Court approved Sir Thomas Bingham's statement of principle in   **6.47**
Marks & Spencer Plc v BNP Paribas Securities Services Trust Co (Jersey) Ltd.[138]
It is considered, therefore, that the principle at the head of this section remains correct.

This approach has a long history. In *Aspdin v Austin*,[139] Lord Denman CJ said: **6.48**

"Where parties have entered into written engagements with express stipulations, it is manifestly not desirable to extend them by any implication; the presumption is that having expressed some, they have expressed all the conditions by which they intend to be bound under that instrument."

In *Churchward v R.*,[140] Cockburn CJ said:

"... where a contract is silent, the court or jury who are called upon to imply an obligation on the other side which does not appear in the terms of the contract, must take great care that they do not make the contract speak where it was

---

[136] [2010] EWCA Civ 1444; [2011] Bus. L.R. 943.
[137] [1995] E.M.L.R. 472 at 481; *Ultraframe (UK) Ltd v Tailored Roofing Systems Ltd* [2004] 2 All E.R. (Comm) 692; *Port of Tilbury (London) Ltd v Stora Enso Transport & Distribution Ltd* [2009] 1 Lloyd's Rep. 391.
[138] [2015] UKSC 72; [2016] A.C. 742.
[139] (1844) 5 Q.B. 671.
[140] (1865) L.R. 1 Q.B. 173 at 195.

intentionally silent; and above all that they do not make it speak entirely contrary to what, as may be gathered from the whole terms and tenor of the contract was the intention of the parties."

In more modern times, Lord Wright has said[141]:

"It is agreed on all sides that the presumption is against the adding to contracts of terms which the parties have not expressed. The general presumption is that the parties have expressed every material term which they intended should govern their agreement, whether oral or in writing."

6.49   The presumption against adding terms is stronger where the contract is a written contract which represents an apparently complete bargain between the parties.[142] In *Greatship (India) Ltd v Oceanografia SA de CV*,[143] Gloster J said:

"Moreover, there is real difficulty in seeking to imply a term into a detailed standard form contract ... where the strong presumption is likely to be that the detailed terms of the contract are complete."

In *Marks & Spencer Plc v BNP Paribas Securities Services Trust Co (Jersey) Ltd*,[144] the Supreme Court emphasised the difficulty in implying terms into a detailed contract.[145] Where the contract in question is a tradeable financial instrument the court must display the same circumspection in implying terms as it displays in the use of background to interpret such instruments.[146]

6.50   Likewise, in *BP Oil International Ltd v Target Shipping Ltd*,[147] Longmore LJ said that where parties had taken elaborate trouble to set out their agreement over several pages, the idea that there was a lacuna which the court had to fill was inherently unlikely. In *Liberty Investing Ltd v Sydow*,[148] Leggatt J said:

"If the parties had intended to impose an obligation on one or other of them, the ordinary expectation is that they would have said so. That expectation is all the stronger in a case where, as here, the parties have expressed their bargain in a detailed written contract which has been prepared with the assistance of high-powered City solicitors."

The Court of Appeal made a similar point in *Dear v Jackson*[149] where it was also suggested that it was more difficult to imply terms into a contract made by the parties in one capacity which would affect their rights and obligations in another capacity.[150]

6.51   Likewise in the case of a collective agreement made in the context of employ-

---

[141] *Luxor (Eastbourne) Ltd v Cooper* [1941] A.C. 108 at 137.
[142] *Duke of Westminster v Guild* [1985] Q.B. 688 at 698; *Broome v Pardess Co-operative Society of Orange Growers (Est. 1900) Ltd* [1940] 1 All E.R. 603; *Phillips Electronique Grand Public SA v British Sky Broadcasting Ltd* [1995] E.M.L.R. 472 CA.
[143] [2012] EWHC 3468 (Comm); [2013] 2 Lloyd's Rep. 359.
[144] [2015] UKSC 72; [2016] A.C. 742.
[145] See also *Fraser Turner Ltd v Pricewaterhousecoopers LLP* [2019] EWCA Civ 1290.
[146] *Law Debenture Trust Corp Plc v Ukraine* [2017] EWHC 655; [2017] Q.B. 1249.
[147] [2013] EWCA Civ 196; [2013] 1 Lloyd's Rep. 561.
[148] [2015] EWHC 608 (Comm).
[149] [2013] EWCA Civ 89; [2014] 1 B.C.L.C. 186.
[150] In that case a contract made in the capacity of shareholders was alleged to restrict the powers of directors.

ment relations, the agreement may be deliberately silent on contentious issues.[151]
The same approach applied to the case of a contract that incorporates standard forms
or wordings contained in provisions which are the result of careful consideration
over a number of years by experienced industry professionals.[152]

Where, however, the bargain is obviously not complete, the court is less reluctant
to supply the missing terms.[153] Mason J put it thus in *Codelfa Construction Pty Ltd
v State Rail Authority of New South Wales*[154]:   **6.52**

> "For obvious reasons the courts are slow to imply a term. In many cases, what
> the parties have actually agreed upon represents the totality of their willingness
> to agree; each may be prepared to take his chance in relation to an eventuality
> for which no provision is made. The more detailed and comprehensive the
> contract the less ground there is for supposing that the parties have failed to ad-
> dress their minds to the question at issue."

Moreover, in such a case there is more of an overlap between interpretation and
implication.[155]   **6.53**

Illustration

A lease of a flat obliged the tenant to pay a maintenance charge to a maintenance
trustee. The maintenance trustee was obliged to expend the contributions from the
tenant, and from other tenants in the block who held on similar leases, in performing a variety of functions including the repair, maintenance and insurance of the
block, the employment of surveyors, the upkeep of common parts and so on. The
landlord gave no express covenant relating to the physical condition of the building and no obligation to repair. It was held that the presence of an elaborate scheme
for dealing with the repair and maintenance of the block precluded the implication
of a term which would have the effect of imposing on the landlord any liability in
respect of the repair or maintenance of the block.
Gordon v Selico Co Ltd[156]

5. WHEN A TERM WILL BE IMPLIED

**A term will be implied where it is necessary to give business efficacy to the
contract, or where it is so obvious that it goes without saying.**

In *Attorney General of Belize v Belize Telecom Ltd*,[157] Lord Hoffmann said: **6.54**

> "[I]n every case in which it is said that some provision ought to be implied in an
> instrument, the question for the court is whether such a provision would spell out

---

[151] *East Midlands Trains Ltd v National Union of Rail, Maritime and Transport Workers* [2013] EWCA Civ 1072.
[152] *Priminds Shipping (HK) Co Ltd v Noble Chartering Inc* [2020] EWHC 127 (Comm).
[153] *Liverpool City Council v Irwin* [1977] A.C. 239 at 253.
[154] (1982) 149 C.L.R. 337 at 346.
[155] *Wells v Devani* [2019] UKSC 4; [2020] A.C. 129.
[156] [1986] 1 E.G.L.R. 71.
[157] [2009] 1 W.L.R. 1988; *Looney v Trafigura Beheer BV* [2011] EWHC 125 (Ch).

in express words what the instrument, read against the relevant background, would reasonably be understood to mean."[158]

He continued:

"But the implication of the term is not an addition to the instrument. It only spells out what the instrument means."

6.55 Cases which applied this approach emphasised that the test was a stringent one. In *Chantry Estates v Anderson*,[159] Jacob LJ said:

"It follows that what one is looking for as the reasonable addressee is whatever the agreement means in context. That may be something else from what at a first look it apparently means. But that will be so when the *only meaning* consistent with the other provisions of the instrument read against the relevant background is that something else" (emphasis in original).

Thus in *Crema v Cenkos Securities Plc* itself the suggested term was not implied because "it is impossible to say that is the only thing that the contract must mean". In *Marks & Spencer Plc v BNP Paribas Securities Services Trust Co (Jersey) Ltd*,[160] Lord Neuberger made it clear that "there has been no dilution of the requirements which have to be satisfied before a term will be implied"; and that commentary which suggested the contrary were mistaken.[161] Cases in England took the same view.[162]

6.56 In *McKillen v Misland (Cyprus) Investments Ltd*,[163] Rimer LJ said:

"I do not question that as part of the interpretation exercise a court can read words into a document which are not already there. It can and will, however, only do so in a case in which it is satisfied that it is necessary to do so in order to reflect what it is satisfied was its true meaning."

So also in *Fitzhugh v Fitzhugh*,[164] Rimer LJ said:

"Moreover, as clause 4(b) remains workable even if its working out may ... prove cumbersome or expensive, there is no necessity to imply the sort of term that the judge was prepared to imply. There was therefore no justification for implying it."

---

[158] Applied in *Thompson v Goblin Hill Hotels Ltd* [2011] UKPC 8.
[159] [2010] EWCA Civ 316.
[160] [2015] UKSC 72; [2016] A.C. 742.
[161] See Chris Peters, "The Implication of Terms in Fact" [2009] C.L.J. 513; P.S. Davies, "Recent developments in the law of implied terms" [2010] L.M.C.L.Q. 140; J. McCaughran, "Implied terms: the journey of the man on the Clapham omnibus" [2011] C.L.J. 607; J.W. Carter, *The Construction of Commercial Contracts*, 1st edn (Oxford: Hart Publishing, 2013) at [3]–[27]; A. Phang, "The challenge of principled gap-filling" [2014] J.B.L. 263; Carter and Courtney, "Belize Telecom: a reply to Professor McLauchlan" [2015] L.M.C.L.Q. 245. Lord Hoffmann's approach was defended in McLauchlan, "Construction and Implication: in defence of Belize Telecom" [2014] L.M.C.L.Q. 203 and Hooley, "Implied terms after Belize Telecom" [2014] C.L.J. 315.
[162] *SNCB Holding v UBS AG* [2012] EWHC 2044 (Comm); *Jackson v Dear* [2012] EWHC 2060 (Ch); *Grainmarket Asset Management LLP v PGF II SA* [2013] EWHC 1879 (Ch); *Torre Asset Funding Ltd v Royal Bank of Scotland Plc* [2013] EWHC 2670 (Ch); *Consolidated Finance Ltd v McCluskey* [2012] EWCA Civ 1325.
[163] [2012] EWCA Civ 179; [2012] B.C.C. 575.
[164] [2012] EWCA Civ 694; [2012] 2 P. & C.R. 14.

But in *Sembcorp Marine Ltd v PPL Holdings Pte Ltd*,[165] the Court of Appeal of **6.57** Singapore took the view that Lord Hoffmann had substituted a test of reasonableness for that of necessity.[166] Their ultimate conclusion was:

"It follows from these points that the implication of terms is to be considered using a three-step process:

(a) The first step is to ascertain how the gap in the contract arises. Implication will be considered only if the court discerns that the gap arose because the parties did not contemplate the gap.

(b) At the second step, the court considers whether it is necessary in the business or commercial sense to imply a term in order to give the contract efficacy.

(c) Finally, the court considers the specific term to be implied. This must be one which the parties, having regard to the need for business efficacy, would have responded 'Oh, of course!' had the proposed term been put to them at time of the contract. If it is not possible to find such a clear response, then, the gap persists and the consequences of that gap ensue."

In *Marks & Spencer Plc v BNP Paribas Securities Services Trust Co (Jersey)* **6.58** *Ltd*,[167] the Supreme Court reverted to a more traditional approach. Nevertheless, the rejection of Lord Hoffmann's approach is somewhat obscured by Lord Neuberger's statement that:

"... the notion that a term will be implied if a reasonable reader of the contract, knowing all its provisions and the surrounding circumstances, would understand it to be implied is quite acceptable, provided that (i) the reasonable reader is treated as reading the contract at the time it was made and (ii) he would consider the term to be so obvious as to go without saying or to be necessary for business efficacy."

Lord Neuberger made it clear however, that these two tests are alternative tests, in the sense that only one of them needs to be satisfied, although he thought that in practice it would be a rare case where only one of those two requirements would be satisfied.

That these two tests are the applicable tests was confirmed by the Supreme Court **6.59** in *Airtours Holiday Transport Ltd v HMRC*[168] and *Impact Funding Solutions Ltd v AIG Europe Insurance Ltd*.[169] In the latter case Lord Hodge said:

---

[165] [2013] SGCA 43; (2013) 151 Con. L.R. 170.
[166] This is not the author's reading of *Belize*. Although the overall exercise is to determine what the agreement would reasonably be understood to mean, if the agreement makes no provision for a particular case the question is what it *must* mean. Thus the author considers that the criticisms of *Belize* are misplaced.
[167] [2015] UKSC 72; [2016] A.C. 742.
[168] [2016] UKSC 21; [2016] 4 W.L.R. 87.
[169] [2016] UKSC 57; [2017] A.C. 73; *Balfour Beatty Regional Construction Ltd v Grove Developments Ltd* [2016] EWCA Civ 990; [2017] 1 W.L.R. 1893.

"... that a term would be implied into a detailed contract only if, on an objective assessment of the terms of the contract, the term to be implied was necessary to give the contract business efficacy or was so obvious that it went without saying."

In *Ali v Petroleum Co of Trinidad and Tobago*[170] Lord Hughes formulated the principle as follows:

"It is enough to reiterate that the process of implying a term into the contract must not become the re-writing of the contract in a way which the court believes to be reasonable, or which the court prefers to the agreement which the parties have negotiated. A term is to be implied only if it is necessary to make the contract work, and this it may be if (i) it is so obvious that it goes without saying (and the parties, although they did not, ex hypothesi, apply their minds to the point, would have rounded on the notional officious bystander to say, and with one voice, 'Oh, of course') and/or (ii) it is necessary to give the contract business efficacy. Usually the outcome of either approach will be the same. The concept of necessity must not be watered down. Necessity is not established by showing that the contract would be improved by the addition. The fairness or equity of a suggested implied term is an essential but not a sufficient pre-condition for inclusion. And if there is an express term in the contract which is inconsistent with the proposed implied term, the latter cannot, by definition, meet these tests, since the parties have demonstrated that it is not their agreement."

6.60 Whether a term is necessary for business efficacy requires a value judgment: it is not a test of absolute necessity, not least because necessity is judged by reference to business efficacy.[171] The implication of a term will satisfy the "business efficacy" test:

"... if, without the term, the contract would lack commercial or practical coherence."[172]

6.61 The decision of the Supreme Court in *Marks & Spencer Plc v BNP Paribas Securities Services Trust Co (Jersey) Ltd* is now the starting point for a consideration of the question whether terms are to be implied into a contract.[173] As Edwards-Stuart J said in *Manor Asset Ltd v Demolition Services Ltd*[174]:

---

[170] [2017] UKPC 2; [2017] I.C.R. 531.

[171] *Europa Plus SCA SIF v Anthracite Investments (Ireland) Plc* [2016] EWHC 437 (Comm).

[172] In *Marks & Spencer Plc v BNP Paribas Securities Services Trust Co (Jersey) Ltd* at [21].

[173] See, e.g. *Marussia Communications Ireland Ltd v Manor Grand Prix Racing Ltd* [2016] EWHC 809 (Ch); [2016] R.P.C. 698; *Hockin v Royal Bank of Scotland* [2016] EWHC 925 (Ch); *Iceland Foods Ltd v Aldi Stores Ltd* [2016] EWHC 1134 (Ch); *Balfour Beatty Regional Construction Ltd v Grove Developments Ltd* [2016] EWCA Civ 990; [2017] 1 W.L.R. 1893; *Perenco UK Ltd v Bond* [2016] EWHC 1498 (TCC); *Europa Plus SCA SIF v Anthracite Investments (Ireland) Plc* [2016] EWHC 437 (Comm); *Walter Lilly & Co Ltd v Clin* [2016] EWHC 357 (TCC); [2016] B.L.R. 247; *Rosenblatt v Man Oil Group SA* [2016] EWHC 1382 (QB); [2016] 4 Costs L.O. 539; *118 Data Resource v IDS Data Services* [2016] F.S.R. 221; *R. (Skelmersdale Ltd Partnership) v West Lancashire Borough Council* [2016] EWHC 109 (Admin); *Gard Shipping AS v Clearlake Shipping PTE Ltd* [2017] EWHC 1091 (Comm); [2017] 2 Lloyd's Rep 38; *Co-operative Bank Plc v Hayes Freehold Ltd* [2017] EWHC 1820 (Ch); *Al Jaber v Al Ibrahim* [2018] EWCA Civ 1690; [2019] 1 W.L.R. 885; *Wells v Devani* [2019] UKSC 4; [2020] A.C. 129.

[174] [2016] EWHC 222 (TCC).

"... the overriding point to be borne in mind is that before implying any term the court must conclude that the implication of that term is necessary in order to give business efficacy to the contract or, to put it another way, it is necessary to imply the term in order to make the contract work as the parties must have intended."

6.62 Males J pointed out in *Marussia Communications Ireland Ltd v Manor Grand Prix Racing Ltd*[175] that:

"... the implication of a contractual term under English law does not necessarily depend upon an actual (albeit unstated) agreement or consent by the parties. On the contrary, sometimes a term will be implied which is effectively imposed upon the parties, or to which they are deemed to have consented, merely because notional reasonable people in their position would have consented and there is nothing to show that they did not. This will be so if the term is necessary to give commercial or practical coherence to the contract even if the parties themselves did not think about it or if they are in fact unreasonable people who would not have consented. Their subjective thoughts and intentions are irrelevant."

6.63 When the court is considering the implication of a term it must not allow itself to be influenced by hindsight.[176]

Illustrations

1.   A transfer of land contained a right to enter with workmen tools and materials on adjoining land for the purpose of effecting such maintenance repair and decoration of the property transferred as might with more convenience be dealt with by access from the adjoining land. It was held that a right to inspect with a view to seeing whether any such works were required was an implied term of the grant.
Dickinson v Cassillas[177]

2.   It was not an implied term of a contract for the loan of money that interest would be paid on the capital advanced. The alleged term was neither necessary to give business efficacy to the contract, nor so obvious that it went without saying.
Al Jaber v Al Ibrahim[178]

6.   APPLICABLE CRITERIA

For a term to be implied, the following conditions (which may overlap) must be satisfied: (1) it must be reasonable and equitable; (2) it must be necessary to give business efficacy to the contract, so that no term will be implied if the contract is effective without it; (3) it must be so obvious that "it goes without saying"; (4) it must be capable of clear expression; (5) it must not contradict any express term of the contract.

---

[175] [2016] EWHC 809 (Ch); [2016] R.P.C. 698. See also *Hockin v Royal Bank of Scotland Plc* [2016] EWHC 925 (Ch).
[176] *Bou-Simon v BGC Brokers LP* [2018] EWCA Civ 1525; 179 Con. L.R. 32; *Bates v Post Office (No.3)* [2019] EWHC 606 (QB).
[177] [2017] EWCA Civ 1254; [2017] H.L.R. 43.
[178] [2018] EWCA Civ 1690; [2019] 1 W.L.R. 885.

6.64   The clearest statement of the above criteria is to be found in the judgment of the majority of the Privy Council in *BP Refinery (Westernport) Pty Ltd v Shire of Hastings*,[179] in which Lord Simon of Glaisdale said:

> "In their [sc their Lordships'] view, for a term to be implied, the following conditions (which may overlap) must be satisfied: (1) it must be reasonable and equitable; (2) it must be necessary to give business efficacy to the contract, so that no term will be implied if the contract is effective without it; (3) it must be so obvious that 'it goes without saying'; (4) it must be capable of clear expression; (5) it must not contradict any express term of the contract."

These criteria may overlap.[180] This now "effectively the test".[181]

6.65   In *Attorney General of Belize v Belize Telecom Ltd*,[182] Lord Hoffmann suggested that these criteria were best regarded as a collection of different ways in which judges have tried to express the central idea that the proposed implied term must spell out what the contract actually means, or in which they have explained why they did not think that it did so. Nevertheless, they were still regarded in English cases as useful guidelines.[183]

As Arden LJ pointed out in *Consolidated Finance Ltd v McCluskey*,[184] the danger in treating these criteria as conditions is that they may divert attention from the real task of interpretation of the actual agreement.

6.66   In *Foo Jong Peng v Phua Kiah Mai*,[185] the Court of Appeal of Singapore favoured retention of the traditional tests as concrete rules or principles that offered more concrete guidance than Lord Hoffmann's more generalised approach. They also continue to be applied in Australia.[186]

6.67   In *Marks & Spencer Plc v BNP Paribas Securities Services Trust Co (Jersey)*

---

[179] (1978) 52 A.L.J.R. 20; *Philips Electronique Grand Public SA v British Sky Broadcasting Ltd* [1995] E.M.L.R. 472.

[180] The equivalent section in a previous edition of this book was described as "in broad terms a proper reflection of the law" in *Makers UK Ltd v Camden London Borough Council* (2008) 120 Con. L.R. 161; and was referred to with apparent approval in *Clyde & Co LLP v New Look Interiors of Marlow Ltd* [2009] EWHC 173 (QB). However, in the light of *Attorney General of Belize v Belize Telecom Ltd* the criteria can no longer be regarded as "conditions" (as they were described in previous editions).

[181] *The Law Debenture Trust Corpn Plc v Ukraine* [2018] EWCA Civ 2026; [2019] Q.B. 1121 (permission to appeal to the Supreme Court has been given); *Zedra Trust Co (Jersey) Ltd v The Hut Group Ltd* [2019] EWHC 2191 (Comm); *Joseph v Deloitte NSE LLP* [2019] EWHC 3354 (QB).

[182] [2009] 2 All E.R. 1127.

[183] *Fortis Bank SA v Indian Overseas Bank* [2010] EWHC 84 (Comm); *Cassa Di Risparmio Della Repubblica Di San Marino Spa v Barclays Bank Ltd* [2011] EWHC 484 (Comm); *Vigeland v Ennismore Fund Management Ltd* [2012] EWHC 3099 (Ch); *Lombard North Central Plc v Nugent* [2013] EWHC 1588 (QB); *Torre Asset Funding Ltd v Royal Bank of Scotland Plc* [2013] EWHC 2670 (Ch); *Stena Line Ltd v Merchant Navy Ratings Pension Fund Trustees Ltd* [2011] EWCA Civ 543; *Rosserlane Consultants Ltd v Credit Suisse International* [2015] EWHC 384 (Ch); *Lancashire Insurance Co Ltd v MS Frontier Reinsurance Ltd* [2012] UKPC 42; *Lifeplan Products Ltd v Carter* [2013] EWCA Civ 453.

[184] [2012] EWCA Civ 1425, repeating her analysis in *Stena Line v Merchant Navy Ratings Pensions Fund* [2011] EWCA Civ 543.

[185] [2012] SGCA 55. The case is discussed at [2013] J.B.L. 237.

[186] See *Brighton v Australia and New Zealand Banking Group Ltd* [2011] NSWCA 152.

Ltd,[187] the Supreme Court approved the criteria in *BP Refinery (Westernport) Pty Ltd v Shire of Hastings*. Lord Neuberger added some comments on that list. He said that:

"… it is questionable whether Lord Simon's first requirement, reasonableness and equitableness, will usually, if ever, add anything: if a term satisfies the other requirements, it is hard to think that it would not be reasonable and equitable."

Thus, in *Hallman Holding Ltd v Webster*[188] Lord Hodge, giving the advice of the Privy Council, said: **6.68**

"It has long been established that, in order to imply a term into an ordinary business contract such as this, the term must be necessary to give business efficacy to the contract; it must be so obvious that it goes without saying; it must be capable of clear expression; and it must not contradict any express term of the contract."

It will be noted that the first of Lord Simon's criteria has been dropped, consistently with Lord Neuberger's view that it rarely adds anything.[189]

In *Marks & Spencer* Lord Neuberger also said that: **6.69**

"… although Lord Simon's requirements are otherwise cumulative, I would accept that business necessity and obviousness, his second and third requirements, can be alternatives in the sense that only one of them needs to be satisfied, although I suspect that in practice it would be a rare case where only one of those two requirements would be satisfied."

This had been the subject of conflicting observations in previous cases. In *Shell*   **6.70**
UK Ltd v Lostock Garage Ltd,[190] Lord Denning MR said that where an implied term is based on the intention to be imputed to the parties from their circumstances:

"Such an imputation is only to be made when it is necessary to imply a term to give efficacy to the contract and make it a workable agreement in such manner as the parties would clearly have done if they had applied their mind to the contingency which has arisen. These are the 'officious bystander' type of case."

Similarly, in *Bank of Nova Scotia v Hellenic Mutual War Risks Association (Bermuda) Ltd*,[191] the Court of Appeal held that the "officious bystander" test is also known as the "business efficacy" test.

These were cases in which the court held that the two principal formulations   **6.71**
meant the same thing. However, in *Mosvolds Rederi A/S v Food Corp of India*,[192]
Steyn J held that a term which failed the test of necessity was nevertheless to be

---

[187] [2015] UKSC 72; [2016] A.C. 742.
[188] [2016] UKPC 3; *Stevensdrake Ltd (t/a Stevensdrake Solicitors) v Hunt* [2017] EWCA Civ 1173; [2017] B.C.C. 611.
[189] Likewise, in *Marussia Communications Ireland Ltd v Manor Grand Prix Racing Ltd* [2016] EWHC 809 (Ch); [2016] RPC 698, Males J omitted this criterion from his summary of principle for the same reason.
[190] [1976] 1 W.L.R. 1187.
[191] [1990] 1 Q.B. 818 CA.
[192] [1986] 2 Lloyd's Rep. 68. See also *Barrett v Lounova* (1982) Ltd [1990] 1 Q.B. 348.

implied into a charterparty because it was so obvious that it went without saying. So also in *Associated Japanese Bank (International) Ltd v Credit du Nord SA*,[193] Steyn J said:

"In the present contract such a condition may only be held to be implied if one of two applicable tests is satisfied. The first is that such an implication is necessary to give business efficacy to the relevant contract ... In other words, the criterion is whether the implication is necessary to render the contract ... workable. That is usually described as the *Moorcock* test ... But there is another type of implication, which seems more appropriate in the present context. It is possible to imply a term if the court is satisfied that reasonable men, faced with the suggested term which was *ex hypothesi* not expressed in the contract, would without hesitation say: yes, of course, that is 'so obvious that it goes without saying' ... Although broader in scope than the *Moorcock* test, it is nevertheless a stringent test, and it will only be permissible to hold that an implication has been established on this basis in comparatively rare cases ...".

In *The Manifest Lipkowy*,[194] Bingham LJ said:

"I take it to be well-established law that a term will be implied only where it is necessary in a business sense to give efficacy to a contract, or where the term is one which the parties must obviously have intended."

He then proceeded to examine the two criteria separately, and concluded that the suggested term failed on both.

In *Ashmore v Corp of Lloyds (No.2)*,[195] Gatehouse J expressly recognised that a term may sometimes be implied on the basis of one test but not another.

6.72 In the light of *Marks & Spencer* it can be said that the two tests are alternatives.

6.73 In *Europa Plus SCA SIF v Anthracite Investments (Ireland) Plc*[196] Popplewell J tabulated the requirements as follows:

"... in order for a term to be implied each of the following four conditions must be satisfied:

   (i)   it must be reasonable and equitable; and
   (ii) it must either:
       a. be necessary to give business efficacy to the contract; or
       b. be so obvious that 'it goes without saying' (although in practice it would be a rare case where only one of those two requirements would be satisfied); and
   (iii) it must be capable of clear expression; and
   (iv) it must not contradict any express term of the contract."

6.74 Where the contract is partly written and partly oral there may be scope for greater flexibility. In those cases, the actual terms of the contract must first be inferred before any question of implication arises. That is to say, it is necessary to arrive at

---

[193] [1989] 1 W.L.R. 255.
[194] [1989] 2 Lloyd's Rep. 138 at 143 CA.
[195] [1992] 2 Lloyd's Rep. 620.
[196] [2016] EWHC 437 (Comm).

some conclusion as to the actual intention of the parties before considering any presumed or imputed intention.[197] In such a case[198]:

"The most that can be said consistently with the need for some degree of flexibility is that, in a case where it is apparent that the parties have not attempted to spell out the full terms of their contract, a court should imply a term by reference to the imputed intention of the parties if, but only if, it can be seen that the implication of the particular term is necessary for the reasonable or effective operation of a contract of that nature in the circumstances of the case."

7. THE TERM MUST BE REASONABLE

No term will be implied in a contract unless the term is reasonable.

Reasonableness has two roles to play in the process of the implication of terms. **6.75**
First, the express terms of the contract must be construed in a reasonable and business-like manner in order to see whether a term needs to be implied.[199]
Secondly, the implied term must itself be a reasonable term. "The implication of an unreasonable term is of course impossible."[200]

Thus in *Young and Marten Ltd v McManus Childs Ltd*,[201] Lord Reid said:

"No warranty ought to be implied in a contract unless it is in all the circumstances reasonable."

Similarly, Lord Salmon said in *Liverpool City Council v Irwin*[202]:

"... unless a warranty or term is in all the circumstances reasonable there can be no question of implying it into a contract, but before it is implied much else besides is necessary ...".

In *BP Refinery (Westernport) Pty Ltd v Shire of Hastings*,[203] Lord Simon of **6.76**
Glaisdale's first criterion was that the term had to be "reasonable and equitable".
The addition of "equitable" emphasises that the term must be judged from the point of view of both parties to the contract.

The reasonableness of the term in question is thus a necessary, but not a suf- **6.77**
ficient, condition. As Lord Hoffmann put it in *Attorney General of Belize v Belize Telecom Ltd*[204]:

"... it is not enough for a court to consider that the implied term expresses what it would have been reasonable for the parties to agree to. It must be satisfied that it is what the contract actually means."

---

[197] *Byrne v Australian Airlines Ltd* (1995) 185 C.L.R. 410.
[198] *Hawkins v Clayton* (1988) 164 C.L.R. 539 per Deane J, approved in *Byrne v Australian Airlines Ltd* (1995) 185 C.L.R. 410.
[199] See *Hamlyn & Co v Wood & Co* [1891] 2 Q.B. 488 at 491, per Lord Esher MR; *Liverpool City Council v Irwin* [1977] A.C. 239, per Lord Edmund-Davies.
[200] *Beazer Homes Ltd v County Council of Durham* [2010] EWCA Civ 1175.
[201] [1969] 1 A.C. 454 at 465.
[202] [1977] A.C. 239 at 262.
[203] (1978) 52 A.J.L.R. 20.
[204] [2009] 2 All E.R. 1127.

6.78   In view of the other tests which must be satisfied before a term will be implied, this test is rarely of decisive significance. Indeed, it has been said that this criterion adds nothing to the remaining ones. In *Marks & Spencer Plc v BNP Paribas Securities Services Trust Co (Jersey) Ltd*,[205] Lord Neuberger said:

> "... it is questionable whether Lord Simon's first requirement, reasonableness and equitableness, will usually, if ever, add anything: if a term satisfies the other requirements, it is hard to think that it would not be reasonable and equitable."

Thus in *Hallman Holding Ltd v Webster*[206] Lord Hodge, giving the advice of the Privy Council, said:

> "It has long been established that, in order to imply a term into an ordinary business contract such as this, the term must be necessary to give business efficacy to the contract; it must be so obvious that it goes without saying; it must be capable of clear expression; and it must not contradict any express term of the contract."

It will be noted that the first of Lord Simon's criteria has been dropped, consistently with Lord Neuberger's view that it rarely adds anything.[207]

Illustration

An oil company (which was one of a large group of companies) entered into an agreement with a rating authority to build an oil refinery. The agreement provided for the amount of rates to be payable by the company. That rate was very favourable to the company. It was argued that there was an implied term in the agreement to the effect that it would come to an end if the oil company ceased to occupy the refinery site. The term was rejected on the ground that it was unreasonable and inequitable.
BP Refinery (Westernport) Pty Ltd v Shire of Hastings[208]

8.   The Term Must be Necessary to Give Business Efficacy to the Contract

A term will not be implied unless it is necessary to give business efficacy to the contract.

6.79   The expression "business efficacy" seems to derive from the well-known judgment of Bowen LJ in *The Moorcock*.[209] He said:

---

[205] [2015] UKSC 72; [2016] A.C. 742.
[206] [2016] UKPC 3; *Stevensdrake Ltd (t/a Stevensdrake Solicitors) v Hunt* [2017] EWCA Civ 1173; [2017] B.C.C. 611.
[207] Likewise, in *Marussia Communications Ireland Ltd v Manor Grand Prix Racing Ltd* [2016] EWHC 809 (Ch); [2016] RPC 698, Males J omitted this criterion from his summary of principle for the same reason.
[208] (1978) 52 A.J.L.R. 20.
[209] (1889) 14 P.D. 64. The history is traced in Andrew Phang, "Implied terms, business efficacy and the officious bystander—a modern history" [1988] J.B.L. 1.

"In business transactions such as this, what the law desires to effect by the implication is to give such business efficacy to the transaction as must have been intended at all events by both parties who are businessmen …".

However, from being the objective, "business efficacy" has been turned into a condition to be satisfied before a term will be implied. In *Marks & Spencer Plc v BNP Paribas Securities Services Trust Co (Jersey) Ltd*,[210] the Supreme Court held that this was one of the two alternative tests for the implication of a term.

6.80

In *Reigate v Union Manufacturing Co*,[211] Scrutton LJ said:

6.81

"A term can only be implied if it is necessary in a business sense to give efficacy to the contract; that is, if it is such a term that it can be confidently said that if at the time the contract was being negotiated someone had said to the parties 'What will happen in such a case?', they would have replied: 'Of course, so and so will happen; we did not trouble to say that; it is too clear.'"

This formulation shows clearly that there is a substantial degree of overlap between the second and third criteria. In *Re Comptoir Commercial Anversois and Power Son & Co*,[212] the same judge said:

"The court … ought not to imply a term merely because it would be a reasonable term to include if the parties had thought about the matter, or because one party, if he had thought about the matter, would not have made the contract unless the term was included; it must be such a term that both parties must have intended that it should be a term of the contract, and have only not expressed it because its necessity was so obvious that it was taken for granted."

It is the requirement of necessity which gives rise to most difficulty, for opinions can readily differ as to whether a term is "necessary" to give "business efficacy" to a contract. Lord Denning MR made an attempt to assimilate a test of reasonableness and a test of necessity.[213] However, that suggestion was decisively rejected by the House of Lords.[214] Lord Wilberforce said:

6.82

"In my opinion such obligation should be read into the contract as the nature of the contract itself implicitly requires, no more or less: a test, in other words of necessity."

Lord Edmund-Davies said:

"The touchstone is always necessity and not merely reasonableness."

Likewise, in *National Commercial Bank Jamaica Ltd v Guyana Refrigerators*

---

[210] [2015] UKSC 72; [2016] A.C. 742.
[211] [1918] 1 K.B. 592 at 605. See also *Lazarus v Cairn Line of Steamships Ltd* (1912) 106 L.T. 378, per Scrutton LJ ("a term they have not expressed is not to be implied because the court thinks it a reasonable term, but only if it is necessarily implied in the nature of the contract the parties have made").
[212] [1920] 1 K.B. 868. See also *Hamlyn & Co v Wood & Co* [1891] 2 Q.B. 488 to the same effect.
[213] Notably in *Liverpool City Council v Irwin* [1976] Q.B. 319.
[214] *Liverpool City Council v Irwin* [1977] A.C. 239. See also *Trollope & Colls Ltd v North West Metropolitan Regional Hospital Board* [1973] 1 W.L.R. 601 at 609, per Lord Pearson (an implied term must be "necessary to give business efficacy to the contract").

Ltd,[215] Lord Steyn said:

> "The implication put forward is not one that can be implied by law; it is not an incident to be annexed by law to a standardised contract. It is a term implied in fact; if it is sustainable, it must be derived from the particular terms of the special instructions. It is not enough that such an implied term would be a reasonable and sensible one. The touchstone requires no citation of authority; it is always strict necessity."

6.83   The test is whether the term in question is necessary to give business efficacy to the contract; not whether it is necessary to some wider business purpose of a contracting party.[216]

If the test is a test of necessity, the question clearly arises: how necessary is necessary? The word itself has a certain degree of imprecision about it. In *Liverpool City Council v Irwin*,[217] Lord Wilberforce recognised that the test for the implication of a term was strict:

> "though the degree of strictness seems to vary with the current legal trend."

6.84   In *Equitable Life Assurance Society v Hyman*,[218] Lord Steyn said of an implied term that:

> "The implication is essential to give effect to the reasonable expectations of the parties."[219]

What his Lordship had in mind is that the question what is necessary is not to be answered simply by asking whether the contract would work at all without the implied term, but whether, without the implied term, it would work in the way the parties might reasonably have expected it to work. The Court of Appeal approved this statement in *Equitas Insurance Ltd v Municipal Mutual Insurance Ltd*.[220]

But in *Marks & Spencer Plc v BNP Paribas Securities Services Trust Co (Jersey) Ltd*,[221] the Supreme Court held that the test would only be satisfied "if, without the term, the contract would lack commercial or practical coherence".[222] This appears to lay down a more stringent test. The question is not whether the implied terms create a commercially coherent result but rather whether the terms are so necessary or

---

[215] (1998) 53 W.I.R. 229.

[216] *Kason Kek-Gardner Ltd v Process Components Ltd* [2017] EWCA Civ 2132; [2018] 2 All E.R. (Comm) 381.

[217] *Liverpool City Council v Irwin* [1977] A.C. 239.

[218] [2002] 1 A.C. 408. Earlier in his speech he reaffirmed the test as one of necessity. In *Attorney General of Belize v Belize Telecom Ltd* [2009] UKPC 10; [2009] 1 W.L.R. 1988 Lord Hoffmann warned against treating the various formulations as if they had "a life of their own"; but his warning has been unfortunately overridden.

[219] In *Attorney General of Belize v Belize Telecom Ltd* [2009] UKPC 10 | [2009] 1 W.L.R. 1988 Lord Hoffmann explained this: "It is frequently the case that a contract may work perfectly well in the sense that both parties can perform their express obligations, but the consequences would contradict what a reasonable person would understand the contract to mean."

[220] [2019] EWCA Civ 718; [2020] 1 All E.R. 16.

[221] [2015] UKSC 72; [2016] A.C. 742.

[222] There is still room for disagreement on whether this test is satisfied. See the divergence of view in *Tai Hing Cotton Mill Ltd v Liu Chong Hing Bank Ltd* [1984] 1 Lloyd's Rep. 555 (Hong Kong Court of Appeal) and [1986] A.C. 80 (Privy Council).

obvious that, without such terms, the contract would lack commercial or practical coherence.[223]

The test of necessity also informs what term (if any) is to be implied. In *Robin Ray v Classic FM*,[224] Lightman J held: **6.85**

"In short a minimalist approach is called for. An implication may only be made if this is necessary, and then only of what is necessary and no more."

The minimalist approach led the House of Lords in *Liverpool City Council v Irwin*[225] to reject an implied term that imposed on a landlord an absolute obligation to keep in repair and lit essential means of access and rubbish chutes in a tenancy of a flat in a high rise block; but to accept an implied term which required the landlord to take reasonable care to do so. Similarly, in *Paymaster (Jamaica) Ltd v Grace Kennedy Remittance Services Ltd*[226] the claimant bought a software package from the defendant. It was a modified version of a program that had been used before. The Privy Council held that there was no implied term to the effect that the claimant had acquired copyright in the software. One of its reasons was that an assignment of copyright was only one possible outcome: an exclusive licence would have been another. Thus the proposed implied term was not necessary to give business efficacy to the contract.

Where the act complained of is a breach of an express term, there is no need to   **6.86** imply any further term which would have the effect of preventing that act.[227] Likewise where a party to a contract is a public authority which has duties in public law, it is unnecessary to imply contractual terms which replicate those duties, still less contractual terms that would go beyond them.[228]

Where it is alleged that it is necessary to imply a term, the question of necessity   **6.87** must be considered from the perspective of both (or all) parties to the contract, and not just from the perspective of one only of them.[229]

The fact that the proposed term is complex is not, in itself, a bar to its   **6.88** implication.[230]

When the court is considering the implication of a term it must not allow itself   **6.89** to be influenced by hindsight.[231]

---

[223] [2018] EWCA Civ 2026; [2019] Q.B. 1121 (permission to appeal to the Supreme Court has been given).
[224] [1998] F.S.R. 622, part of a summary of the principles described by the CA as "masterful": *R Griggs Group Ltd v Evans* [2005] F.S.R. 31.
[225] [1977] A.C. 239.
[226] [2017] UKPC 40; [2018] Bus. L.R. 492.
[227] *The Kallang (No.2)* [2009] 1 Lloyd's Rep. 124; *The Duden* [2009] 1 Lloyd's Rep. 145.
[228] *Hampshire County Council v Beazer Homes Ltd* [2010] EWHC 3095 (QB).
[229] *Meridian International Services Ltd v Richardson* [2008] EWCA Civ 609.
[230] *Perenco UK Ltd v Bond* [2016] EWHC 1498 (TCC).
[231] *Bou-Simon v BGC Brokers LP* [2018] EWCA Civ 1525; 179 Con. L.R. 32; *Bates v Post Office (No.3)* [2019] EWHC 606 (QB).

Illustrations

    1.   A wharfinger hired out the use of his wharf to a shipowner. It was held that the contract contained an implied term that the wharfinger should take reasonable care to ensure that the wharf was safe to use.
    The Moorcock[232]

    2.   A publican contracted to take all his requirements of electric energy from an electricity company. It was held to be a necessary implication that he would not take electricity from anyone else.
    Metropolitan Electric Supply Co Ltd v Ginder[233]

    3.   Three actresses had an idea for a television series in which they wished to appear. A television company acquired an option to exploit the idea. It was held that it was an implied term of the agreement that the television company would not make use of the idea without offering the three actresses parts in the series.
    Fraser v Thames Television Ltd[234]

    4.   A garage proprietor entered into a solus agreement with an oil company. During a price war between rival oil companies, the oil company introduced a support scheme under which it subsidised garages in the proprietor's neighbourhood. The proprietor was excluded from the scheme. He alleged that the solus agreement was subject to an implied term to the effect that the oil company would not abnormally discriminate against him. The term was rejected, because although it was reasonable, it was not necessary.
    Shell UK Ltd v Lostock Garage Ltd[235]

    5.   A colliery owner appointed agents for the sale of his coal for seven years. The agents agreed not to sell any other coal without the colliery owner's consent, and he undertook not to employ any other agent during the continuance of the agreement. Before the term had expired, the colliery owner sold the colliery. It was held that no term could be implied which would have prevented the colliery owner from selling the colliery.
    Rhodes v Forwood[236]

    6.   A contract gave a haulier the exclusive right to provide for all the defined haulage requirements arising in the ordinary course of a shipper's business for a period of three years. It was held that there was no difficulty in implying a term or applying a rule of law that the shipper would do nothing of its own motion to make it impossible for the haulier to supply those requirements.
    CEL Group Ltd v Nedlloyd Lines UK Ltd[237]

---

[232] (1889) 14 P.D. 64. The implication of this kind of term overlaps with the implication of a term as a legal incident of a particular relationship, here wharfinger and shipowner.

[233] [1901] 2 Ch. 799. This form of implication is simply making explicit that which logically follows from the express words of the contract. It is sometimes described as constructional implication.

[234] [1984] Q.B. 44.

[235] [1976] 1 W.L.R. 1187.

[236] (1876) 1 App. Cas. 256.

[237] [2004] 1 Lloyd's Rep. 381.

7. A share option scheme entitled employees of a public company and its subsidiaries to buy shares in the company at favourable prices. The plaintiff was an employee of one of the subsidiaries, but the subsidiary was sold to a third party, which automatically caused the plaintiff's options to lapse. It was held that no term could be implied to prevent the company from dealing with its subsidiaries.
Thompson v ASDA-MFI Plc[238]

8. A share sale agreement provided for a retention of part of the purchase price to meet "Good Claims". The agreement defined "Good Claims" as claims that counsel of at least 10 years call had given a recent opinion to the buyer in writing stating that the Claim in question was bona fide and had a reasonable chance of success and estimating its quantum. It was held that there was no term to be implied to the effect that counsel's opinion was only binding if given on the basis of true facts. No such term was necessary because counsel's opinion was likely to be given at a time when the facts were (or might be) in dispute.
Interleasing (UK) Ltd v Morris[239]

9. A bond issue was governed by a trust deed under which the trustee was entitled to give notice of acceleration making the bonds repayable in full immediately. An implied obligation on the part of the trustee not to give an invalid notice of acceleration was rejected on the ground that it was not necessary to give business efficacy to the trust deed, because an invalid notice of acceleration would have no contractual effect.
Concord Trust v Law Debenture Trust Corp Plc[240]

9. The Term Must be so Obvious it Goes without Saying

A term will not be implied unless it is obvious both that a term ought to be implied and also what term is to be implied.

In *Marks & Spencer Plc v BNP Paribas Securities Services Trust Co (Jersey) Ltd*,[241] the Supreme Court held that this test is one of the two alternative tests for the implication of a term. It is also known as the "officious bystander" test. **6.90**
In *Shirlaw v Southern Foundries (1926) Ltd*,[242] MacKinnon LJ said:

"Prima facie that which in any contract is left to be implied and need not be expressed is something so obvious it goes without saying; so that if, while the parties were making their bargain, an officious bystander were to suggest some express provision for it in their agreement, they would testily suppress him with a common 'Of course.'"

In *Vardinoyannis v Egyptian General Petroleum Corp*,[243] Donaldson J said:

---

[238] [1988] Ch. 241.
[239] [2003] EWCA Civ 40.
[240] [2006] 1 B.C.L.C. 616.
[241] [2015] UKSC 72; [2016] A.C. 742.
[242] [1939] 2 K.B. 206. MacKinnon LJ first proposed this formulation in a lecture delivered to the London School of Economics in 1926: see Andrew Phang, "Implied terms, business efficacy and the officious bystander—a modern history" [1998] J.B.L. 1.
[243] [1971] 2 Lloyd's Rep. 200.

"Any suggested implied term has to be considered against the general business background to the transaction and the express terms of the charter. Furthermore, if a term is to be implied, it must be such that it would surely have been agreed to both by the reasonable shipowner and the reasonable charterer, not to mention that other immortal abstraction and honorary member of the Baltic Exchange, the maritime officious by-stander."

In *Powell v Lowe*,[244] Moore-Bick LJ said:

"A term will be implied into a contract when it would be regarded as obvious by any person acquainted with the transaction that it went without saying. That is sometimes called the 'officious bystander' test."

6.91   The "officious bystander" is one of the great characters of the common law and although Lord Denning MR did make an attempt to "kill him off"[245] he was resurrected on appeal.[246] Nevertheless, as Lord Hoffmann warned in *Attorney General of Belize v Belize Telecom Ltd*[247]:

"[T]he requirement that the implied term must 'go without saying' is no more than another way of saying that, although the instrument does not expressly say so, that is what a reasonable person would understand it to mean. Any attempt to make more of this requirement runs the risk of diverting attention from the objectivity which informs the whole process of construction into speculation about what the actual parties to the contract or authors (or supposed authors) of the instrument would have thought about the proposed implication."[248]

6.92   The approach of postulating the intervention of an officious bystander is not always a helpful approach. One particular problem was identified by Aicken J in *Codelfa Construction Pty Ltd v State Rail Authority of New South Wales*[249]:

"The first problem is that the manner in which the officious bystander formulates his question will often determine the answer which the parties give ... One may formulate another query—must the officious bystander be satisfied with the first response or may he pose a second question, and if not, why not?"

The first problem that Aicken J identified is illustrated by *Spring v National Amalgamated Stevedores and Dockers Society*.[250] In that case a trade union claimed that it was an implied term of membership of the union that the union should have the right to do all things necessary and proper to comply with its lawful and proper agreements; and further, an implied term that members would act in conformity with the lawful and proper agreements of the union. The particular agreement in is-

---

244 [2010] EWCA Civ 1419.

245 *Liverpool City Council v Irwin* [1976] Q.B. 319.

246 [1977] A.C. 239. Lord Hoffmann has criticised this as a "music hall act" which distracts attention from the objective nature of the exercise: "Anthropomorphic Justice: The Reasonable Man and His Friends" (1995) 29 *Law Teacher* 127.

247 [2009] 2 All E.R. 1127.

248 Lord Hoffmann had previously criticised this as a "music hall act" which distracts attention from the objective nature of the exercise: "Anthropomorphic Justice: The Reasonable Man and His Friends" (1995) 29 *Law Teacher* 127.

249 (1982) 149 C.L.R. 337 at 374.

250 [1956] 1 W.L.R. 585.

sue was an agreement known as the Bridlington agreement, which regulated the transfer of members from one union to another. The judge applied the "officious bystander test", and rejected the suggested term, saying:

> "If ... the bystander had asked the plaintiff at the time he paid his five shillings and signed the acceptance form 'Won't you put in some reference to the Bridlington agreement?' I think (indeed I have no doubt) the plaintiff would have answered 'What's that?' In my judgment, that is sufficient to dispose of this case ...."

However, in this example the form of the question put by the court was suggestive of only one answer, and the question might have produced a different answer if put in a more neutral way, or in a way closer to the term for which the union argued. This shows that it is vital to formulate the question to be posed by the "officious bystander" with the utmost care.[251]

6.93 The "officious bystander" must be equipped with such knowledge as is necessary for him to be able to ask the necessary question. It seems probable that he must be equipped with all the background knowledge that would have been available to the parties and which would have been admissible for the purpose of interpreting the contract.[252] Moreover, the fact that the bystander's first response is to ask for an explanation is not an answer. Thus the fact that the proposed term is complex is not, in itself, a bar to its implication.[253] As Lord Hoffmann explained in *Attorney General of Belize v Belize Telecom Ltd*[254]:

> "... it is not necessary that the need for the implied term should be obvious in the sense of being immediately apparent, even upon a superficial consideration of the terms of the contract and the relevant background. The need for an implied term not infrequently arises when the draftsman of a complicated instrument has omitted to make express provision for some event because he has not fully thought through the contingencies which might arise, even though it is obvious after a careful consideration of the express terms and the background that only one answer would be consistent with the rest of the instrument. In such circumstances, the fact that the actual parties might have said to the officious bystander 'Could you please explain that again?' does not matter."[255]

Thus it is considered that *Spring v National Amalgamated Stevedores and Dockers Society* would not be decided in the same way today.

6.94 In *Little v Courage Ltd*,[256] the Court of Appeal gave an answer to Aicken J's second query. They concluded that the first response to the officious bystander's question would have been for the parties to tell him not to be so silly. But, the Court

---

[251] This statement in the text was approved by the Supreme Court in *Marks & Spencer Plc v BNP Paribas Securities Services Trust Co (Jersey) Ltd* [2015] UKSC 72; [2016] A.C. 742.

[252] This proposition was approved in Claimants in the *Royal Mail Group Litigation v Royal Mail Group Ltd* [2020] EWHC 97 (Ch).

[253] *Perenco UK Ltd v Bond* [2016] EWHC 1498 (TCC).

[254] [2009] 2 All E.R. 1127.

[255] In *Ashmore v Corp of Lloyds (No.2)* [1992] 2 Lloyd's Rep. 620, one of the reasons for rejecting an implied term was that the response would have been "Would you mind putting that in writing because I haven't followed it?" It is considered that that case was wrongly decided.

[256] (1994) 70 P. & C.R. 469 CA.

held:

> "The hypothetical bystander must be persistent as well as officious."

Thus the bystander put his question again, and got an answer.

6.95   However, there is a limit to the number of hypothetical questions that the bystander may ask. In *Roxborough v Rothmans of Pall Mall Australia Ltd*,[257] Hill and Lehane JJ said:

> "The hypothetical dialogue between the parties and the officious bystander ... does not proceed by stages, arriving first at a term and then, through a process of further hypothetical discussion, adding qualifications and exceptions. What is to be implied must meet the tests we have already mentioned and must, we think, appear fully fledged."

Thus in *Bank of Nova Scotia v Hellenic Mutual War Risks Association (Bermuda) Ltd*,[258] an implied term was rejected under this head because the response to the bystander's question would have been:

> "it would no doubt be desirable that the law should imply such a term but that, as to his own agreement thereto, he would prefer not to answer without the advice of his solicitor because of the difficulty of knowing in advance what such a term might entail."

6.96   Similarly, in *Potter v Potter*,[259] the parties had entered into a property sharing agreement which provided for each of them to acquire a half share in a property. When the relationship broke down one party argued that a term ought to be implied into the agreement to defeat the other's half share in the event that the purposes of the agreement had not been carried through. Rejecting the argument, the Privy Council held:

> "The test for the implication into the Agreement of the requisite condition for the defeasance of the Respondent's beneficial half-share in Inlet Road must, in their Lordship's view, be that the Respondent, if asked at the time the Agreement was signed whether the implication of the condition would correspond with her intention, would testily answer 'of course'. The test has only to be stated to be seen to fail. The Respondent, or more likely the lawyer advising her, would have asked very many questions and suggested a number of variations to the Agreement before giving an assent to the inclusion of the suggested implied term."

In *Flynn v Breccia*,[260] the Irish Court of Appeal held that it was not sufficient that a "compelling case" could be made for the introduction of an implied term using this test. Finlay Geoghan J accepted the submission that:

> "... the trial judge was in error in his approach to the question. First, they submit that a 'compelling case' is not sufficient to warrant the implication of a term. They submit that obviousness requires the Court to be satisfied that, firstly,

---

[257] *(1999) 95 F.C.R. 185 at* [53] reversed (2001) 208 C.L.R. 516 on other grounds.
[258] [1990] 1 Q.B. 818 CA.
[259] [2004] W.T.L.R. 1331.
[260] [2017] IECA 74.

reasonable people in the position of the parties would all have agreed to make provision for the contingency in question, and second, that they would 'without doubt', or with something approaching certainty, have accepted the term proposed by the officious bystander."

Just as the question of necessity must be considered from the perspective of both **6.97** (or all) parties to the contract, so also must the question whether a term is so obvious that it goes without saying.[261] Thus where the parties would give different answers to the officious bystander's question that is a strong indication that no term should be implied.[262]

It is to be noted that the officious bystander asks questions. He does not provide **6.98** answers. That is done by the parties themselves. In *Aberdeen City Council v Stewart Milne Group Ltd*,[263] Lord Clarke purported to apply the officious bystander test. He said:

"If the officious bystander had been asked whether such a term should be implied, he or she would have said 'of course'. Put another way, such a term is necessary to make the contract work or to give it business efficacy. I would prefer to resolve this appeal by holding that such a term should be implied rather than by a process of interpretation."

This is, with respect, a mis-statement of the "officious bystander" test. The officious bystander poses the question to the parties. He does not provide the answer himself. In *Lancore Services Ltd v Barclays Bank Plc*,[264] Rimer LJ said:

"... it is not in fact a question of what an officious bystander might think, but how the parties would react if such a bystander raised with them the point that the MSA should provide expressly for the making of the payment to the merchant after the expiry of such reasonable time. Bearing in mind the risks to which Barclaycard Business might be subject if it were to become involved in making payments in respect of illegal or aggregated transactions, it by no means follows that it would have responded with a testy 'Oh, of course'. It might well have responded 'Certainly not'. If so, that points away from the implication of any such term."

In asserting the existence of an implied term, it is also important not to argue for **6.99** a wide variety of alternative implications. The more possibilities there are, the less any one of them is obvious.[265]

In *Port of Tilbury (London) Ltd v Stora Enso Transport & Distribution Ltd*,[266] Rix LJ said that the fact that an implied term may take several different formulations is a classic sign that it is neither necessary nor obvious. In *Socimer International*

---

[261] *Meridian International Services Ltd v Richardson* [2008] EWCA Civ 609.
[262] *Mediterranean Salvage & Towing Ltd v Seamar Trading & Commerce Inc* [2008] 2 Lloyd's Rep. 628.
[263] [2011] UKSC 56; [2012] S.L.T. 205; *Spencer v Secretary of State for Defence* [2012] EWHC 120 (Ch); [2012] 2 All E.R. (Comm) 480.
[264] [2010] 1 All E.R. 763.
[265] See *Trollope & Colls Ltd v North Western Metropolitan Regional Hospital Board* [1973] 1 W.L.R. 601.
[266] [2009] 1 Lloyd's Rep. 391.

Bank Ltd v Standard Bank London Ltd,[267] he said:

"At the end of the day, Mr Millett asks us to imply a term in circumstances where his own proposed implication takes two different forms, and where it is at least possible to take different, equally rational views on an implication either restricting an assessment in Standard's discretion to the traditional concepts of good faith, rationality and the like on the one hand, or an implication imposing entirely independent and objective 'true market price' criteria on the other. This alone demonstrates that the parties would not have been likely to rejoin 'of course' to the officious bystander; and that an implication such as that contended for by Socimer is neither necessary nor sufficiently certain."

As Morgan J put it in *Chantry Estates (South East) Ltd v Anderson*[268]:

"The court is not here to re-write the contract and select from an *à la carte* menu of possibilities the one which the court thinks might have been more even-handed for the parties to have agreed."

6.100   In *IMT Shipping and Chartering GmbH v Chansung Shipping Co Ltd*,[269] Tomlinson J said of an argument that a term was obvious:

"This is always a difficult argument where, as here, the contract in question is a carefully drafted 33-page document built on a standard form in wide usage over very many years in respect of which the relevant inference has never before been drawn nor, so far as is known, suggested."

6.101   Furthermore, the "obviousness" must be not merely that the contract is defective; the means of curing the defect must themselves be obvious. In *Trollope & Colls Ltd v North West Metropolitan Regional Hospital Board*,[270] four formulations of the suggested implied term were discussed by Lord Pearson and a fifth by Lord Cross of Chelsea. If there are four or five possibilities, it is difficult to say of any one of them that it is obvious. Lord Cross of Chelsea said:

"... it is not enough for the party seeking to have the words varied to say to the court 'We obviously did not mean what we have said, so please amend the clause so as to make it read in what you think is the most reasonable way.' He must establish not only that the parties obviously did not mean what they said but also that if they had directed their minds to the question, they would obviously have framed the clause in the way in which he contends."

In *Philips Electronique Grand Public SA v British Sky Broadcasting Ltd*,[271] Sir Thomas Bingham MR said:

"And it is not enough to show that had the parties foreseen the eventuality which in fact occurred they would have wished to make provision for it, unless it can

---

[267] [2008] Bus. L.R. 1304.
[268] [2008] EWHC 2457 (Ch), affirmed [2010] EWCA Civ 316.
[269] [2009] 2 All E.R. (Comm) 177.
[270] [1973] 1 W.L.R. 601.
[271] [1995] E.M.L.R. 472 at 481.

also be shown either that there was only one contractual solution or that one of several possible solutions would without doubt have been preferred."

Similarly, in *R. v Paddington and St Marylebone Rent Tribunal, Ex p. Bedrock Investments Ltd*,[272] Lord Goddard CJ said:

"No covenant ought ever to be implied unless there is such a necessary implication that the court can have no doubt what covenant or undertaking they ought to write into the agreement."

When the court is considering the implication of a term it must not allow itself to be influenced by hindsight.[273]   **6.102**

Illustrations

1.   A charterparty contained a clause providing for laytime to count by reference to the time of arrival of a vessel at a particular place some distance from the port. A term was implied to the effect that time should begin to count from notice of completion of loading if transhipment was effected at a place nearer the port.
   Mosvolds Rederi A/S v Food Corp of India[274]

2.   An agreement between a company and two local authorities provided that during a period of 99 years neither of the local authorities should operate public transport services. In return the company was to pay them a percentage of its profits. A successor to the company argued that there was an implied term terminating the agreement if Parliament should make it unlawful for the company to operate public transport services. Walton J held that it was "very, very far from certain" that the parties would have agreed to such a term, and rejected the argument.
   Kirklees Metropolitan Borough Council v Yorkshire Woollen District Transport Co Ltd[275]

3.   Cattle farmers arranged with a vet for their cattle to be inoculated. It was held that the contract contained an implied term that the substance used to inoculate the cows would be safe. This conclusion was reached on the basis that the term "went without saying".
   Dodd v Wilson[276]

4.   Buyers and sellers entered into a contract for the shipment of jute from India to Genoa. The export of jute from India was subject to a quota, which allotted quota in respect of particular countries by reference to the quantities of jute shipped in a basic year selected by the seller. In fact, the sellers had only a very small quota for Italy and were unable to ship the agreed quantity of jute. They argued that there was an implied term that the sale was subject to quota. The court rejected the term, on

---

[272] [1947] K.B. 984.
[273] *Bou-Simon v BGC Brokers LP* [2018] EWCA Civ 1525; 179 Con. L.R. 32; *Bates v Post Office (No.3)* [2019] EWHC 606 (QB).
[274] [1986] 2 Lloyd's Rep. 68. The term was implied even though the judge held that it was not necessary to give business efficacy to the contract (see para.6.01).
[275] (1978) 77 L.G.R. 448.
[276] [1946] 2 All E.R. 691.

the ground that the quota depended on matters which were wholly within the knowledge of the sellers and not of the buyers, so that it was impossible to be sure how the parties would have wished the question of quota to be dealt with.
  Sethia (KC) (1944) Ltd v Partabmull Rameshwar[277]

5.   A lease contained an option to renew if the landlord and the tenant had agreed a business agreement. It was held that although no obligation could be implied which obliged the landlord to take steps to agree the business agreement, a term would be implied to the effect that the parties need only agree a business agreement if the landlord required them to.
  Little v Courage Ltd[278]

6.   An estate agent informed a property owner that his commission terms would be 2% plus VAT. It was so obvious that it went without saying that if he introduced a purchaser who completed a purchase, he would be entitled to commission of 2% of the sale proceeds, payable out of those sale proceeds.
  Wells v Devani[279]

10.   THE TERM MUST BE CAPABLE OF CLEAR EXPRESSION

A term will not be implied unless it can be clearly formulated.

6.103   This criterion overlaps with the criterion of obviousness, for if a term cannot be clearly formulated it is unlikely to be so obvious that it goes without saying. Thus a term will not be implied at common law unless it satisfies the requirement of certainty.[280]

6.104   In *Torre Asset Funding Ltd v The Royal Bank of Scotland Plc*,[281] Sales J emphasised that "clarity, certainty and predictability of interpretation are always important factors when considering whether a term should be implied into an arm's length commercial agreement"; particularly in the case of a negotiable contract. Thus he approved the principles that:

"In order to satisfy the test for implication, the proposed implied term must be reasonably certain. Where there is a variety of proposed terms or where a proposed term could be expressed in different ways, that may be a good indication that it is not sufficiently certain".

And:

"The proposed implied term must be capable of being defined with sufficient precision to give reasonable certainty of operation."

In *Durham Tees Valley Airport Ltd v BMI Baby Ltd*,[282] Davis J said:

---

[277] [1950] 1 All E.R. 51.
[278] (1994) 70 P. & C.R. 469 CA.
[279] [2019] UKSC 4; [2019] 2 W.L.R. 617.
[280] *Lee v Leeds City Council* [2002] 1 W.L.R. 1488, per Chadwick LJ.
[281] [2013] EWHC 2670 (Ch).
[282] [2009] EWHC 852 (Ch). On appeal it was held that the contract was enforceable without the need to imply any term: [2010] EWCA Civ 485.

"An implied term, no less than an express term, must be sufficiently precise as to be enforceable; it is after all, part of the agreement. If matters essential to a bargain are not agreed, whether expressly or impliedly, then the courts may not be able to cure the defect—and certainly no court can remake a bargain for the parties."

In *Law Debenture Trust Corp Plc v Ukraine*,[283] Blair J rejected a proposed **6.105** implied term relating to breaches of principles of international law because those principles were too uncertain to be incorporated by implication, and raised matters which were non-justiciable. The Court of Appeal upheld his decision that the suggested terms were not capable of clear expression and were too vague and uncertain.[284] In *Paymaster (Jamaica) Ltd v Grace Kennedy Remittance Services Ltd*,[285] the claimant bought a software package from the defendant. It was a modified version of a program that had been used before. The Privy Council held that there was no implied term to the effect that the claimant had acquired copyright in the software. One of its reasons was that it was unclear to what material the proposed implied term would apply. In *Marme Inversiones 2007 SL v NatWest Markets Plc*,[286] implied terms were rejected because they were too vague. In *Russell v Cartwright*,[287] one reason that an implied term was rejected was that its content was not satisfactorily explained.

In *Shell UK Ltd v Lostock Garage Ltd*,[288] it was argued that a solus agreement **6.106** for the supply of petrol contained an implied term that the supplier would not discriminate abnormally against the buyer. The term was rejected, for the reason, among others, that it was not capable of sufficiently precise formulation. Ormrod LJ said:

"The second obstacle is the difficulty in formulating the proposed terms, as demonstrated by the vagueness and the ambiguity inherent in such words as 'discriminate' and 'abnormality'.

I do not think that the court will read a term into a contract unless, considering the matter from the point of view of business efficacy, it is clear beyond a peradventure that both parties intended a given term to operate, although they did not include it in so many words."

However, in the same case, Bridge LJ said in a dissenting judgment:

"It is said that lack of precision in the criterion to be embodied in the implied term is fatal to any implication. But it is no novelty in the common law to find that a criterion on which some important question of liability is to depend can only be defined in imprecise terms which leave a difficult question for decision as to how the criterion applied to the facts of a particular case. A clear and distinct line of demarcation may be impossible to draw in abstract terms; yet the court does not

---

[283] [2017] EWHC 655 (Comm); [2017] Q.B. 1249.
[284] [2018] EWCA Civ 2026; [2019] Q.B. 1121 (permission to appeal to the Supreme Court has been granted).
[285] [2017] UKPC 40; [2018] Bus. L.R. 492.
[286] [2019] EWHC 366 (Comm) at [498] and following. See also *Cassa di Risparmio della Repubblica di San Marino SpA v Barclays Bank Ltd* [2011] EWHC 484 (Comm) [2011] 1 C.L.C. 701 at [544].
[287] [2020] EWHC 41 (Ch).
[288] [1976] 1 W.L.R. 1187.

shrink from the task of deciding on the facts of any case before it on which side of the line the case falls."

It is thought that the approach of Bridge LJ is correct in principle,[289] although on the facts of *Shell UK Ltd v Lostock Garage Ltd* itself the majority were correct in holding that the suggested implied term was too imprecise.

11.   THE TERM MUST NOT CONTRADICT ANY EXPRESS TERM OF THE CONTRACT

A term will not be implied if it is inconsistent with the express terms of the contract or its general tenor.[290]

6.107   Since the implication of a term rests upon what the contract must mean, it is unlikely that the reasonable reader would conclude that the contract was self-contradictory. Hence a term will not be implied if it is inconsistent with an express term.[291]

As it was put by Evershed MR in *Lynch v Thorne*[292]:

"... a term prima facie to be implied must, according to well established principle, always yield to the express letter of the bargain."

In that case it was held that where a building contract specified a particular method of building which turned out to be defective, there was no room for a general implied term requiring the building to be constructed so as to be fit for human habitation when completed.

Similarly, in *Interactive Investor Trading Ltd v City Index Ltd*,[293] Tomlinson LJ said:

"It is trite law that a term will not be implied which contradicts the express terms of the contract."

6.108   A more comprehensive version of the principle is to be found in the speech of Lord Parker of Waddington in *Tamplin (FA) Steamship Co Ltd v Anglo-Mexican Petroleum Products Co Ltd*,[294] in which he said:

"It is, of course, impossible to imply in a contract any term or condition inconsistent with its express provisions, or with the intention of the parties as gathered from those provisions. The first thing, therefore, in every case is to compare the

---

[289] See *Esso Petroleum Co Ltd v David* [2003] EWHC 1730 (Comm).

[290] This section was cited with approval in *BP Gas Marketing Ltd v LA Societe Sonatrach* [2016] EWHC 2461 (Comm); 169 Con. L.R. 141 and *Irish Bank Resolution Corp Ltd v Camden Market Holdings Corp* [2017] EWCA Civ 7; [2017] 2 All E.R. (Comm) 781 followed in *Co-operative Bank Plc v Hayes Freehold Ltd* [2017] EWHC 1820 (Ch).

[291] "The suggested implied term would therefore be inconsistent with an express term of the Agreement, which, as the authorities confirm, is a clear indicator against any such implication": *CDV Software Entertainment AG v Gamecock Media Europe Ltd* [2009] EWHC 2965 per Gloster J.

[292] [1956] 1 W.L.R. 303.

[293] [2011] EWCA Civ 837. See also *Bieber v Teathers Ltd* [2012] EWCA Civ 1466; *Torre Asset Funding Ltd v The Royal Bank of Scotland Plc* [2013] EWHC 2670 (Ch); *Ali v Petroleum Company of Trinidad and Tobago* [2017] UKPC 2; [2017] I.C.R. 531; *UTB LLC v Sheffield United Ltd* [2019] 2322 (Ch); *Priminds Shipping (HK) Co Ltd v Noble Chartering Inc* [2020] EWHC 127 (Comm).

[294] [1916] 2 A.C. 397 at 422.

term or condition which it is sought to imply with the express provisions of the contract, and with the intention of the parties as gathered from those provisions, and ascertain whether there is any inconsistency."

In *Equitable Life Assurance Society v Hyman*,[295] Lord Steyn said:

"This principle is sparingly and cautiously used and may never be employed to imply a term in conflict with the express terms of the text."

In *Johnson v Unisys Ltd*,[296] Lord Hoffmann said:

"… any terms which the courts imply into a contract must be consistent with the express terms. Implied terms may supplement the express terms of the contract but cannot contradict them. Only Parliament may actually override what the parties have agreed."

As Toulson LJ put it in *Anders & Kern UK Ltd v CGU Insurance Plc*[297]:

"you cannot imply a term which contradicts an expressed term, because the parties cannot have intended that."

In *Autoclenz Ltd v Belcher*,[298] Aikens LJ said:

"Once it is established that the written terms of the contract were agreed, it is not possible to imply terms into a contract that are inconsistent with its express terms. The only way it can be argued that a contract contains a term which is inconsistent with one of its express terms is to allege that the written terms do not accurately reflect the true agreement of the parties."

This observation was approved by the Supreme Court.[299]

In *Irish Bank Resolution Corp Ltd v Camden Market Holdings Corp*,[300] Beatson LJ said: **6.109**

"There can be two sorts of inconsistency; direct linguistic inconsistency and substantive inconsistency. The second type of inconsistency may be difficult to distinguish from the position where the parties have entered into express obligations with respect to a particular subject-matter, and it is argued that a further term should be implied in relation to the same subject-matter. It is well established that, particularly where the contract is lengthy and carefully drafted, the courts will be very reluctant to imply a further term even if it does not actually conflict with the express terms."

Similarly, in *Glencore International AG v MSC Mediterranean Shipping Co SA*,[301] Andrew Smith J said that:

---

295 [2002] 1 A.C. 408.
296 [2003] 1 A.C. 518.
297 [2008] 2 All E.R. (Comm) 1185.
298 [2009] EWCA Civ 1046.
299 [2011] UKSC 41.
300 [2017] EWCA Civ 7; [2017] 2 All E.R. (Comm) 781.
301 [2015] EWHC 1989 (Comm); [2015] 1 Lloyd's Rep. 508.

"This requirement of consistency does not only preclude an implied term that is starkly inconsistent with what is expressly agreed, but ... the law implies terms that work harmoniously with the scheme of the agreed arrangements, and the less readily harmonious a term would be, the less readily it is implied."

6.110   The relationship between employer and employee contains an implied term that the employer will not without reasonable and proper cause destroy the relationship of trust and confidence which should exist between employer and employee. But the implied term:

"cannot sensibly be used to extend the relationship beyond its agreed duration; and ... it cannot sensibly be used to circumscribe an express power of dismissal without cause. This would run counter to the general principle that an express and unrestricted power cannot in the ordinary way be circumscribed by an implied qualification."[302]

The principle may go somewhat further than the formulation given above.

6.111   In many cases the court has held that where the parties have entered into express obligations with respect to a particular subject-matter, the court will not imply further terms in relation to the same subject-matter, even if the implied term would not actually conflict with the express terms. Thus in *Broome v Pardess Co-operative Society of Orange Growers (Est. 1900) Ltd*,[303] MacKinnon LJ said:

"Where the parties have made an express provision as regards some matter with regard to the contract, it is, and must be, extremely difficult for either of them to say in regard to that subject-matter, as to which there is an express provision, that there is also an implied provision or condition in the contract."

In *Persimmon Homes (South Coast) Ltd v Hall Aggregates (South Coast) Ltd*,[304] Coulson J said that:

"An express term in a contract excludes the possibility of implying any term dealing with the same subject-matter as the express term."

Likewise, in *Waterman v Boyle*,[305] a transfer contained an express right to park. The question was whether further parking rights could be implied. Arden LJ said:

"where there is an express right attaching to the same property of a similar character to the right which is sought to be implied, it is most unlikely that the further right will arise by implication. The circumstances would have to be quite exceptional."

6.112   The wider form of the principle has been explained as a wider form of inconsistency, namely one based on the common sense precept that, if parties explicitly provide for the giving of rights in a stated way, it is unlikely that they have intended

---

[302] *Reda v Flag Ltd* [2002] I.R.L.R. 747 PC.
[303] [1940] 1 All E.R. 603.
[304] [2008] EWHC 2379 (TCC); *Lancore Services Ltd v Barclays Bank Plc* [2010] 1 All E.R. 763.
[305] [2009] 21 E.G. 104.

to subject themselves by implication to some regime of rights and duties of a similar kind which goes beyond the terms upon which they have agreed.[306]

However, in *Fraser Turner Ltd v Pricewaterhousecoopers LLP*,[307] Vos C approved the statement by the trial judge that there was:

    6.113

"no absolute rule that, if there is an express term covering a particular subject, that necessarily excludes the possibility of any implied term where there is no linguistic inconsistency. Rather, the correct approach, reflecting common sense, is that the existence of such an express term makes the co-existence of a further implied term on the same subject unlikely and especially so in a lengthy and carefully drafted document on which legal professionals have been advising."

Thus, in *Ajayi v Ebury Partners Ltd*,[308] a compromise of various employment claims contained a confidentiality clause, subject to certain express exceptions permitting disclosure. Henshaw J held that it was possible to imply further exceptions, although he accepted that the court should proceed with caution before doing so.

Where the contract is a unilateral contract which imposes no obligations on the promisor, it generally impossible to imply into it terms which do impose obligations on him at a stage before the contract has become bilateral.[309]

    6.114

Illustrations

1.   A lease contained an obligation on the tenant to repair drains belonging to the demised property if called upon to do so by the local authority. The tenant sought to imply a term that the landlord was responsible for the repair of a drain which served the demised premises, but possession of which remained with the landlord. The term was rejected on the ground (among others) that the suggested implied term was inconsistent with the express terms of the lease.

Duke of Westminster v Guild[310]

2.   A mortgage contained a stipulation that the mortgagee would not sell the mortgaged property without notice, except in the case of default by the borrower. The borrower argued that there was an implied term in the mortgage to the effect that the mortgagee would not take possession of the mortgaged property except in like circumstances. The Court of Appeal rejected the implication, partly on the ground that the existence of the stipulation as to sale precluded the implication of the term. The maxim "*expressio unius est exclusio alterius*" was applied.

Western Bank Ltd v Schindler[311]

3.   A charter provided for the payment of commission to brokers of 3 per cent of estimated gross hire on signing the charter. It was held that a custom could not

---

[306] *Biki v Chessells* [2004] ANZ Conv. R. 296.
[307] [2019] EWCA Civ 1290.
[308] [2020] EWHC 166 (Comm).
[309] *Little v Courage Ltd* (1994) 70 P. & C.R. 469 CA. See, however, *Wells v Devani* [2019] UKSC 4; [2020] A.C. 129
[310] [1985] Q.B. 687.
[311] [1977] Ch. 1. The maxim is discussed further in para.7.53.

be set up under which commission was only payable on hire earned, for such a custom would have been inconsistent with the express terms of the charter.
Les Affreteurs Reunis SA v Walford (Leopold) (London) Ltd[312]

4   The use of the word "demise" in a lease will give rise to two implied covenants by the landlord; namely that he is entitled to grant some term in the demised property and that the tenant shall have quiet enjoyment of it during the tenancy. But where a lease contained an express covenant dealing with quiet enjoyment, the court refuses to imply the further covenant dealing with title.
Miller v Emcer Products Ltd[313]

5.   A conditional fee agreement between a liquidator and a solicitor provided "you are personally responsible for any payments that you may have to make under this Agreement; those payments are not limited by reference to the funds available in the liquidation". It was held that it was impossible to imply a term that fees would only be payable out of recoveries, because that would have contradicted the express term.
Stevensdrake Ltd (t/a Stevensdrake Solicitors) v Hunt[314]

6.   A term that an agreement is terminable by reasonable notice cannot be implied into a fixed term agreement.
Edge Tools & Equipment Ltd v Greatstar Europe Ltd[315]

7.   A company limited by guarantee was established to promote dance therapy. Dance therapists became members. There was no inconsistency between the fiduciary duties of directors of the company and the implication of a term that in deciding to terminate a therapist's membership the company would act with procedural fairness.
Dymoke v Association for Dance Movement Pyschotherapy UK Ltd[316]

12.   TERMS IMPLIED BY CUSTOM

A term may be implied from a custom of the relevant trade unless it is inconsistent with the express terms of the contract

6.115   In *Hutton v Warren*,[317] Parke B said:

"It has long been settled that in commercial transactions extrinsic evidence of custom and usage is admissible to annex incidents to written contracts, in matters with respect to which they are silent. The same rule has also been applied to contracts in other transactions of life, in which known usages have been established and prevailed; and this has been done upon the principle of presumption that, in such transactions, the parties did not mean to express in writing the

---

[312] [1919] A.C. 801.
[313] [1956] Ch. 304.
[314] [2017] EWCA Civ 1173 (however the same effect was achieved by an estoppel by convention).
[315] [2018] EWHC 170 (QB).
[316] [2019] EWHC 94 (QB); *AB v University of XYZ* [2020] EWHC 206 (QB).
[317] (1836) 1 M. & W. 466.

whole of the contract by which they intended to be bound, but a contract with reference to those known usages."

It is worthy of note that the presumption applied by Parke B is precisely the opposite to that applied by Lord Denman CJ in *Aspdin v Austin*.[318] In *Baker v Black Sea & Baltic General Insurance Co Ltd*,[319] Lord Lloyd of Berwick explained that:

6.116

"it is very common in mercantile contracts, where there is an established market usage, to add a term to an otherwise complete bilateral contract, on the grounds that it is what the parties would have unhesitatingly agreed. This was indeed the fabric out of which much of the modern commercial law was created in the 18th and early 19th centuries."

A trade usage producing a customary meaning is a trade custom which must be proved as clearly and definitely as any other trade custom. In a market where buyers and sellers meet together habitually, they get into the habit of assuming that certain conditions or usages apply to all contracts that they make. A usage grows up because everybody in the market, knowing the usages, tacitly assumes that the contract he is making, whether as buyer or seller, is subject to the usage. The binding character of a usage is born of innumerable individual transactions entered into by the parties to them in the knowledge that certain usages are in practice habitually followed in that market.[320] For a practice to amount to a recognised usage, it must be certain, in the sense that it is so well known in the market in which it is alleged to exist, that those who conduct business in the market contract with the usage as an implied term; and it must be reasonable.[321] The question is whether there is in the trade a uniform practice so well-defined and recognised that the parties must be assumed to have had it in their minds when they contracted.[322]

6.117

In *Durham v BAI (Run Off) Ltd*[323] Burton J said:

6.118

"I must be astute to ensure that such usage as is alleged and relied upon: (i) existed at the date of the relevant contract; (ii) does not contradict the terms of the contract or clause; (iii) is certain, notorious and universal[324]; (iv) is binding, in the sense that it is not simply a usage which parties choose from time to time to follow."

In *Con-Stan Industries of Australia Pty Ltd v Norwich Winterthur Insurance (Australia) Ltd*[325] the High Court of Australia comprehensively reviewed the authorities and concluded:

6.119

(1) The existence of a custom or usage that will justify the implication of a term into a contract is a question of fact;

---

[318] (1844) 5 Q.B. 671 (see para.6.48). The difference depends on the existence of known usages as opposed to a "one off" contract.

[319] [1998] 1 W.L.R. 974 HL.

[320] *Lord Forres v Scottish Flax Co Ltd* [1943] 2 All E.R. 366.

[321] *Cunliffe-Owen v Teather & Greenwood* [1967] 1 W.L.R. 1421.

[322] *Fox-Bourne v Vernon & Co Ltd* (1894) 10 T.L.R. 647 CA; *The Mathraki* [1990] 2 Lloyd's Rep. 84.

[323] [2009] 2 All E.R. 26, 86 (not challenged on appeal on this point).

[324] In *Devonald v Rosser* [1906] 2 K.B. 728 it was said that the alleged custom must be "reasonable, certain, and notorious".

[325] (1986) 160 C.L.R. 226.

(2) There must be evidence that the custom relied on is so well known and acquiesced in that everyone making a contract in that situation can reasonably be presumed to have imported that term into the contract;

(3) A term will not be implied into a contract on the basis of custom where it is contrary to the express terms of the agreement;

(4) A person may be bound by a custom notwithstanding the fact that he personally had no knowledge of it. In elaboration of this last point their Honours said:

> "Historically the courts approached this question in a rather different way. It was said that, as a general rule, a person who was ignorant of the existence of a custom or usage was not bound by it. To this rule there was a qualification that a person would be presumed to know of the usage if it was of such notoriety that all persons dealing in that sphere could easily ascertain the nature and content of the custom. It would then be reasonable to impute that knowledge to a person, notwithstanding his ignorance of it ... In this way, the issue of notoriety discussed in (2) above came to be co-extensive with the question of imputed knowledge. The achievement of sufficient notoriety was both a necessary and sufficient condition for knowledge of a custom to be attributed to a person who was in fact unaware of it. The result is that in modern times nothing turns on the presence or absence of actual knowledge of the custom; that matter will stand or fall with the resolution of the issue of the degree of notoriety which the custom has achieved."

6.120   If established, the custom is part of the contract, and the custom must be interpreted in the same way as the written part of the contract.[326] However:

> "An alleged custom can be incorporated into a contract only if there is nothing in the express or necessarily implied terms of the contract to prevent such inclusion and, further, a custom will only be imported into a contract where it can be so imported consistently with the tenor of the document as a whole."[327]

Thus in *Les Affeteurs Reunis SA v Walford (Leopold) (London) Ltd*,[328] the House of Lords held that an established custom as to the payment of a chartering broker's commission was inconsistent with the express terms of the agreement between the owners and the broker, and consequently did not form part of the contract.

However, in *National Bank of Greece SA v Pinios Shipping Co (No.1)*,[329] the House of Lords held that a bank was entitled to capitalise interest, because that was the established usage of bankers.

6.121   The role of "custom and practice" leading to the implication of terms is greater in the context of employment contracts than in ordinary commercial contracts.[330]

Where the alleged custom relates to a single organisation a multi-factorial approach is more appropriate. Thus as between an employer and an employee a

---

[326] *Produce Brokers Co Ltd v Olympia Oil and Cake Co Ltd* [1916] 1 A.C. 314.

[327] *London Export Corp Ltd v Jubilee Coffee Roasting Co Ltd* [1958] 1 W.L.R. 661 at 675; *Carey Group Plc v AIB Group (UK) Ltd* [2011] EWHC 567 (Ch).

[328] [1919] A.C. 801; *Palgrave Brown & Son Ltd v Owners of S.S. Turid* [1922] 1 A.C 397 HL.

[329] [1990] 1 A.C. 637 HL.

[330] See *Park Cakes Ltd v Shumba* [2013] EWCA Civ 974; [2013] I.R.L.R. 800; *CSC Computer Sciences Ltd v McAlinden* [2013] EWCA Civ 1435; *Thorne v House of Commons Commission* [2014] EWHC 93 (QB).

unilateral management practice may acquire the status of a contractual term. The factors to be considered in deciding that question include: (a) whether the policy was drawn to the attention of employees; (b) whether it was followed without exception for a substantial period; (c) the number of occasions on which it was followed; (d) whether the nature of communication of the policy supported the inference that the employers intended to be contractually bound; (e) whether the policy was adopted by agreement; (f) whether terms were incorporated in a written agreement; and (g) whether the terms were consistently applied.[331]

Terms may also be implied or incorporated by conduct.[332] But a term which would otherwise be implied as a result of custom or usage may be excluded by an "entire agreement" clause.[333]   **6.122**

13. CORRELATIVE OBLIGATIONS

Where a contract imposes an express obligation on one party to the contract, but is silent as to the obligations of the other party, the court may in appropriate circumstances imply an obligation on that other party correlative to the express obligation.

A contract may often impose express obligations on one party with regard to some particular part of the bargain, while remaining silent as to the other party's obligations (if any) with regard to that aspect of the bargain. In such circumstances the court may imply a correlative obligation, but in so doing the test of necessity must still be satisfied. The general principle was described by Cockburn CJ in *Churchward v R.*[334] as follows: **6.123**

"I entirely concur that although a contract may appear on the face of it to bind and be obligatory on one party, yet there are occasions on which you must imply—although the contract may be silent—corresponding and correlative obligations on the part of the other party in whose favour alone the contract may appear to be drawn up. Where the act done by the party binding himself can only be done upon something of a corresponding character being done by the opposite party, you would there imply a corresponding obligation to do the things necessary for the completion of the contract."

He emphasised, however, that the court must take great care not to "make the contract speak where it was intentionally silent".

Where it is sought to imply correlative obligations, the requisite test is one of necessity.[335] A mere expectation that the party on whom no express obligation is imposed will act in a certain way is not enough. Thus in *Sleafer v Lambeth Borough Council*,[336] a tenancy agreement provided that the tenant should not do any decorative or other work to the premises without the landlord's consent. The landlord had an express right to enter and carry out repairs, and in practice the landlord did carry   **6.124**

---

[331] *Albion Automotive Ltd v Walker* [2002] EWCA Civ 946; *Garratt v Mirror Group Newspapers Ltd* [2011] EWCA Civ 425.

[332] See para.3.108.

[333] *Exxonmobile Sales and Supply Corp v Texaco Ltd* [2004] 1 All E.R. (Comm) 435. For entire agreement clauses see para.3.132.

[334] (1865) L.R. 1 Q.B. 173.

[335] *Duke of Westminster v Guild* [1985] Q.B. 688.

[336] [1960] 1 Q.B. 43.

out all repairs. However, there was no express repairing obligation placed upon either party. It was held that none could be implied. The mere fact that the landlord was expected to carry out repairs was not enough.

Illustrations

1. A lease reserved a fixed weekly rent for the cleaning of the demised premises by a housekeeper. It was held that the reservation of the rent gave rise to a correlative obligation on the part of the landlord to provide the housekeeper to clean the property.
    Barnes v City of London Real Property Co Ltd[337]

2. A lease required the tenant to pay the landlord the cost of redecorating the exterior of the demised property in every third year of the term with two coats at least of good oil paint. It was held that there was a correlative implied obligation on the part of the landlord to carry out the triennial redecoration.
    Edmonton Corp v Knowles (WM) & Son Ltd[338]

3. A printer agreed with the Government of Quebec to execute, during a term of eight years, the printing and binding of certain public documents at prices specified in the agreement. It was held that there was no obligation on the part of the Government to supply the printer with work.
    R. v Demer[339]

4. A lease required the tenant to pay the landlord a fair proportion of the cost to the landlord of repairing party structures, drains and similar matters, and in preserving the amenities of the neighbourhood. It was held that no correlative obligation could be implied to oblige the landlord to do any of those things.
    Duke of Westminster v Guild[340]

5. A tenancy of a council dwelling required the tenant to live on the premises and to carry out internal decoration. It was held that no correlative obligation could be implied which required the landlord to make the dwelling fit for human habitation or to remedy design defects causing excessive condensation.
    Ratcliffe v Sandwell MBC[341]

---

[337] [1918] 2 Ch. 18.

[338] (1962) 60 L.G.R. 124.

[339] [1900] A.C. 103.

[340] [1985] Q.B. 688. However, see *Barrett v Lounova* (1982) Ltd [1990] 1 Q.B. 348 CA, where a tenant agreed to keep the interior of a house in repair. There was no express repairing obligation relating to the structure or exterior imposed on either party. It was held that the obligation to repair the structure and exterior was "correlative" to the obligation to repair the interior, and consequently an obligation on the part of the landlord to that effect ought to be implied. The reasoning seems manifestly unsound, particularly when it is compared with the obligation actually implied in *Liverpool City Council v Irwin* [1977] A.C. 239, which was an obligation to take reasonable care, not an absolute obligation. In addition, the conclusion does not follow from the premise either as a matter of logic or, with respect, as a matter of common sense. *Barrett v Lounova* (1982) was distinguished in *Lee v Leeds City Council Ratcliffe v Sandwell MBC* [2002] 1 W.L.R. 1488 CA, and in *Adami v Lincoln Grange Management Ltd* [1998] 1 E.G.L.R. 58 CA it was said to be confined to its own special facts, which is a polite way of saying that it was wrong.

[341] [2002] 1 W.L.R. 1488.

14. The Prevention Principle

In general, a term is necessarily implied in a contract that neither party will prevent the other from performing it.[342]

Both parties to a contract are taken to contract on the footing that they wish the contract to be performed, and accordingly must be taken to have agreed that neither will actively prevent performance. In the recent cases this has been referred to as "the prevention principle". As Lord Kitchin explained in *Duval v 11–13 Randolph Crescent Ltd*[343]:

> "It is well established that a party who undertakes a contingent or conditional obligation may, depending upon the circumstances, be under a further obligation not to prevent the contingency from occurring; or from putting it out of his power to discharge the obligation if and when the contingency arises."

6.125

It has been suggested that the duty does not rest upon the implication of a term, but may be a positive rule of the law of contract that conduct of either the promisor or the promisee, which can be said to amount to himself of his own motion bringing about the impossibility of performance, is itself a breach of the contract.[344] But it has now been held that the "prevention principle" is not an overriding rule of legal or public policy. Whether it applies, and if so the extent to which it applies, is determined by the ordinary principles applicable to the implication of terms.[345] It is more properly regarded as an implied term because, where appropriate, it involves the interpolation of terms to deal with matters for which the parties themselves have made no express provision.[346]

6.126

The essence of the prevention principle is that the promisee cannot insist upon the performance of an obligation which he has prevented the promisor from performing.[347] The classic formulation of the implied term is that of Cockburn CJ in *Stirling v Maitland*[348]:

6.127

> "I look on the law to be that if a party enters into an arrangement which can only take effect by reason of the continuance of a certain state of circumstances, there is an implied engagement on his part that he shall do nothing of his own motion to put an end to that state of circumstances, under which alone that arrangement can be operative."

---

[342] This section was referred to with approval in *Dubai Islamic Bank PJSC v PSI Energy Holding Co BSC* [2013] EWHC 3781 (Comm); *Plantation Holdings (FZ) LLC v Dubai Islamic Bank PJSC* [2017] EWHC 520 (Comm) and *Jiangsu Guoxin Corporation Ltd v Precious Shipping Public Co Ltd* [2020] EWHC 1030 (Comm).

[343] [2020] UKSC 18; [2020] 2 W.L.R. 1167.

[344] Contrast *Southern Foundries (1926) Ltd v Shirlaw* [1940] A.C. 701 at 717, per Lord Atkin and *Thompson v ASDA-MFI Plc* [1988] Ch. 241.

[345] *North Midland Building Ltd v Cyden Homes Ltd* [2018] EWCA Civ 1744; [2018] B.L.R. 565 (noting that the prevention principle was dealt with in this book in the chapter on Implied Terms); *Duval v 11–13 Randolph Crescent Ltd* [2020] UKSC 18; [2020] 2 W.L.R. 1167.

[346] *Duval v 11–13 Randolph Crescent Ltd* [2020] UKSC 18; [2020] 2 W.L.R. 1167.

[347] *Multiplex Constructions (UK) Ltd v Honeywell Control Systems Ltd* (2007) 111 Con. L.R. 78; *Jerram Falkus Construction Ltd v Fenice Developments Ltd* [2011] EWHC 1935 (TCC) 138 Con. L.R. 21. In *TMF Trustee Ltd v Fire Navigation Inc* [2019] EWHC 2918 Phillips J treated the prevention principle as part of the general principle that a party to a contract cannot rely on his own wrong.

[348] (1864) 5 B. & S. 841; *Cory (William) & Sons Ltd v London Corp* [1951] 2 K.B. 476.

This formulation has been applied many times. In *Ogdens Ltd v Nelson*,[349] Lord Alverstone CJ said:

"It is, I think, clearly established as a general proposition that where two persons have entered into a contract, the performance of which on one or both sides is to extend over a period of time, each contracting party is bound to abstain from doing anything which will prevent him from fulfilling the obligations which he has undertaken to discharge."

6.128   In this context "prevention of performance" can also include delay in performance.[350] Thus the principle has been frequently implied in construction and shipbuilding contracts as a means of extending contractual time limits where the action of the employer (e.g. by requiring extra work to be undertaken) has prevented the contractor from completing on time. The principle does not only apply to breaches of contract by the employer but may extend to actions which are perfectly legitimate in contractual terms.[351] But where the parties have expressly provided for extensions of time to be granted in certain circumstances, they may be taken to have excluded the prevention principle by contract.[352]

In *Barque Quilpue Ltd v Brown*,[353] Vaughan Williams LJ said:

"The second point is, that in this contract, as in every other, there is an implied contract by each party that he will not do anything to prevent the other party from performing the contract or to delay him in performing it. I agree that generally such a term is by law imported into every contract, in the same way as you import into every contract a stipulation that the various things which are to be done by the one party or the other are, if no time is specified, to be done within a reasonable time. In each of these cases that may be called an implied contract. It must not, however, be supposed that the law readily implies any special affirmative contracts; I think the law very rarely does or indeed ought to imply such a contract. But the particular stipulation on which the plaintiffs rely is, as far as I know, implied in every contract."

6.129   In *Southern Foundries (1926) Ltd v Shirlaw*,[354] Lord Porter described it as a "well known principle", and in *Schindler v Northern Raincoat Co Ltd*,[355] Diplock J described it as "that respectable principle". Its resilience as a proposition of law and common sense is undoubted; but "like any such proposition in the law of contract, it needs to be read in the context of the particular contract, interpreted against the factual matrix in which it was made."[356] There is, nevertheless, no general principle that this term will be implied. In *Law Debenture Trust Corp Plc v Ukraine*,[357] Blair J held:

---

[349] [1903] 2 K.B. 287; affirmed by HL: [1905] A.C. 109.

[350] *Adyard Abu Dhabi v SD Marine Services* [2011] EWHC 848 (Comm); (2011) 136 Con. L.R. 190.

[351] *Multiplex Constructions (UK) Ltd v Honeywell Control Systems Ltd* (2007) 111 Con. L.R. 78; *Jiangsu Guoxin Corporation Ltd v Precious Shipping Public Co Ltd* [2020] EWHC 1030 (Comm).

[352] *Adyard Abu Dhabi v SD Marine Services* [2011] EWHC 848 (Comm); *North Midland Building Ltd v Cyden Homes Ltd* [2018] EWCA Civ 1744; *Jiangsu Guoxin Corporation Ltd v Precious Shipping Public Co Ltd* [2020] EWHC 1030 (Comm).

[353] [1904] 2 K.B. 264.

[354] [1940] A.C. 701.

[355] [1960] 1 W.L.R. 1038.

[356] *CEL Group Ltd v Nedlloyd Lines UK Ltd* [2004] 1 Lloyd's Rep. 381 CA, per Carnwath LJ.

[357] [2017] EWHC 655 (Comm); [2017] Q.B. 1249.

"... the general principle that a term is necessarily implied in a contract that neither party will prevent the other party from performing it is inapt where the subject matter of the contract is transferable financial instruments such as the notes because transferees or potential transferees have to be able to ascertain the nature of the obligation they are acquiring (or considering acquiring) from within the four corners of the relevant contracts."

The Court of Appeal upheld his decision on this point.[358] In the course of the judgment the Court said:

"Although in various different contexts the courts have been willing to imply into a contract a term prohibiting one party from 'preventing' the performance of another ... we accept [the] submission that there is no general rule that such a term will be implied. Where there is some agreed precondition for performance that a party to a contract needs the other party's assistance to satisfy, an implied duty not to prevent performance of the condition by failing to provide assistance might follow ... But there is no general rule. The implication of such a term, and, perhaps more importantly, its scope, will depend on the contract under consideration, and in particular its express terms."

There are three main circumstances in which an implied term not to prevent performance needs to be considered. The first is where the action of one party to the contract prevents performance of an obligation imposed on the other. A party will often have an interest in performing his own obligation and may wish to complain if the other party's action prevents him from performing his own obligation. The second is where one party to the contract has an obligation which is to be performed in the future or is a contingent obligation. It is then relevant to ask whether a term should be implied that he should not disable himself from performing those obligations if the contingency were to come about. The third is where one party's obligation is subject to a precondition and the suggested implied term is that he should not do anything to prevent the precondition being satisfied.[359] In addition, the principle applies to a contract made between more than two parties. In such a case one party to a contract may not take steps to prevent performance by a second party to the same contract of an obligation owed to a third party to that contract.[360] But this does not mean that a term is to be implied into a contract between A and B that B will not prevent the performance by C of an obligation to be found in a contract between A and C.[361]

6.130

In order for the implied term to bite, there must be prevention of performance. A lease provided that if a management company failed to perform its obligation, the lessor might do so at the company's expense. There was no breach of the implied term where the lessor exercised that power in circumstances in which the management company was preparing to perform its obligations; but had not yet begun to do so.[362] In the case of a guarantee, there was no implied term that the creditor would not prevent recourse by the guarantor to particular assets out of

6.131

[358] [2018] EWCA Civ 2026; [2019] Q.B. 1121 (permission to appeal to the Supreme Court has been given).
[359] *Berkeley Community Villages Ltd v Pullen* [2007] EWHC 1330 (Ch).
[360] *F&C Alternative Investments (Holdings) Ltd v Barthelemy* [2011] EWHC 1731 (Ch) at [267].
[361] *Royal Bank of Scotland Plc v McCarthy* [2015] EWHC 3626 (QB).
[362] *Wild Duck Ltd v Smith* [2018] EWCA Civ 1704; [2018] L. & T.R. 35.

which to repay. The debt could have been repaid out of other resources, and thus performance was not prevented.[363]

6.132 The limits of the implied term must also be recognised. First, the implied term must not be illegal, contrary to public policy, or (in the case of a corporation) ultra vires the contracting party. Thus no term will be implied preventing a public authority from exercising powers vested in it by statute to be exercised for the public good.[364]

Second, the implied term is limited to the active prevention of performance, and probably does not extend to passivity in the face of the action of some third party[365]; nor does it require positive steps to be taken to facilitate performance.[366]

Third, the act complained of must itself be wrongful, either as being a breach of the express or implied terms of the contract, or wrongful independently of the contract (e.g. tortious).[367]

6.133 As with other implied terms, the test of necessity must be satisfied. In *Mona Oil Equipment & Supply Co Ltd v Rhodesia Railways Ltd*,[368] Devlin J said:

"In truth, the proposed term, like all other implied terms must be judged by the test whether or not it is necessary for the business efficacy of the contract. The fact that an act, if not prohibited by the contract, is one which would result in a party being robbed of the benefits which otherwise the contract would give him is certainly an important matter to be considered in relation to the business efficacy of the contract, but it is not necessarily the most important, and it is certainly not the only matter."

The extent of the implied obligation is governed by the express terms of the contract. As Cooke J explained in *James E McCabe Ltd v Scottish Courage Ltd*[369]:

"A duty to co-operate in, or not to prevent, fulfilment of performance of a contract only has content by virtue of the express terms of the contract and the law can only enforce a duty of co-operation to the extent that it is necessary to make the contract workable. The court cannot, by implication of such a duty, exact a higher degree of co-operation than that which could be defined by reference to the necessities of the contract. The duty of co-operation or prevention/inhibition of performance is required to be determined, not by what might appear reasonable, but by the obligations imposed upon each party by the agreement itself."

6.134 Thus there is no duty to cooperate in bringing about something that the contract

---

[363] *General Mediterranean Holding SA v Qucomhaps Holdings Ltd* [2017] EWHC 1409 (QB). On appeal the argument was put on the basis of equitable duties, rather than implied terms; but the appeal was dismissed: [2018] EWCA Civ 2416.

[364] *Cory (William) & Son Ltd v London Corp* [1951] 2 K.B. 476.

[365] Compare A.H. Clough's famous couplet "Thou shalt not kill but needst not strive / Officiously to keep alive", *The Latest Decalogue*.

[366] *Taylor v Rive Droite Music Ltd* [2006] E.M.L.R. 4 at [158], per Neuberger LJ.

[367] *Luxor (Eastbourne) Ltd v Cooper* [1941] A.C. 108 at 147, explaining *Inchbald v Western Neilgherry Coffee Tea and Cinchona Plantation Co Ltd* (1864) 17 C.B.N.S. 733; *Mona Oil Equipment & Supply Co Ltd v Rhodesia Railways Ltd* [1949] 2 All E.R. 1014; *Little v Courage Ltd* (1994) 70 P. & C.R. 469 CA.

[368] [1949] 2 All E.R. 1014.

[369] [2006] EWHC 538 (Comm).

does not require to happen.[370] Similarly, where the contract contains detailed provisions dealing with what will happen in the event that one party is prevented from performing, no term is to be implied.[371]

Illustrations

1.   A broker was retained by the directors of a company to dispose of shares upon terms that he was to receive £100 down, and £400 when all the shares had been allotted. Without any fault on his part, the company was wound up before all the shares had been disposed of. It was held that the company was in breach of an implied term.
   Inchbald v Western Neilgherry Coffee Tea and Cinchona Plantation Co Ltd[372]

2.   An 18-month charter provided for the payment of commission to shipbrokers on hire earned. After four months the owners sold the vessel to the charterers, and the charter was cancelled. It was held that the owners were not in breach of any implied term.
   French (L) and Co Ltd v Leeston Shipping Co Ltd[373]

3.   A contract gave a haulier the exclusive right to provide for all the defined haulage requirements arising in the ordinary course of a shipper's business for a period of three years. It was held that there was no difficulty in implying a term or applying a rule of law that the shipper would do nothing of its own motion to make it impossible for the haulier to supply those requirements.
   CEL Group Ltd v Nedlloyd Lines UK Ltd[374]

4.   Farmers entered into an agreement with a developer by which the developer agreed to use its property development expertise to maximise the potential of a substantial part of the farmers' land for development, in return for which it would receive a fee on the grant of planning permission. The agreement imposed obligations on the developer to work towards that end. It was an implied term of the agreement that the farmers would not sell the farm before the developer had had an opportunity to earn the fee.
   Berkeley Community Villages Ltd v Pullen[375]

5.   A long lease of a flat in a converted house contained an absolute covenant against alterations. The lease also contained a covenant by the landlord that all leases would contain similar covenants; and that upon request the landlord would enforce those covenants. It was held that the landlord would be in breach of covenant if it licensed what would amount to a breach of the absolute covenant.
   Duval v 11–13 Randolph Crescent Ltd[376]

---

[370]   *Australis Media Holdings Pty Ltd v Telstra Corp Ltd* (1998) 43 N.S.W.L.R. 104.
[371]   *Sabic UK Petrochemicals Ltd v Punj Lloyd Ltd* [2013] EWHC 2916 (TCC); [2014] B.L.R. 43.
[372]   (1864) 17 C.B.N.S. 733. This case must be read in the light of the decision of the House of Lords in *Luxor (Eastbourne) Ltd v Cooper* [1941] A.C. 108.
[373]   [1922] 1 A.C. 451.
[374]   [2004] 1 Lloyd's Rep. 381.
[375]   [2007] EWHC 1330 (Ch).
[376]   [2020] UKSC 18; [2020] 2 W.L.R. 1167.

15. TERMS ABOUT COOPERATION

Where performance of the contract cannot take place without the cooperation of both parties, it is implied that cooperation will be forthcoming.

6.135   In *Mackay v Dick*,[377] Lord Blackburn said:

> "... where in a written contract it appears that both parties have agreed that something shall be done, which cannot be effectually done unless both parties concur in doing it, the construction of the contract is that each agrees to do all that is necessary to be done on his part for the carrying out of that thing, though there may be no express words to that effect."

6.136   Thus, if A employs B for reward to do a piece of work which requires A's cooperation (e.g. to paint a portrait) it is implied that the necessary cooperation will be forthcoming (e.g. A will give sittings to the artist).[378] The formulation of the implied term in cases of this class depends (like any other implied term) on necessity. Thus in *Mona Oil Equipment & Supply Co Ltd v Rhodesia Railways Ltd*,[379] Devlin J said:

> "It is, no doubt, true that every business contract depends for its smooth working on co-operation, but in the ordinary business contract, apart, of course, from express terms, the law can enforce co-operation only in a limited degree—to the extent that it is necessary to make the contract workable. For any higher degree of co-operation the parties must rely on the desire that both of them usually have that the business should get done."

6.137   It follows, therefore, that this principle survives reformulation of the appropriate test for the implication of terms in *Marks & Spencer Plc v BNP Paribas Securities Services Trust Co (Jersey) Ltd*.[380]

6.138   In *Elvanite Full Circle Ltd v AMEC Earth & Environmental (UK) Ltd*,[381] Coulson J said that:

> "Whenever a contracting party has to complete a task by a certain date, the other contracting party has a duty to co-operate to take reasonable steps to ensure that such date can be met."

Likewise, where a shipbuilding contract provided for payment in stages on certification that milestones had been reached, there was an implied obligation on the part of the buyer to cooperate in giving the necessary certificates.[382]

6.139   Where a contract is conditional, it is often implied that neither party will do

---

[377] (1881) 6 App. Cas. 251 at 263. Lord Watson approached the matter at 270 by reference to the fictional fulfilment of conditions precedent. This doctrine stems from the civil law and is not part of the law of England: *Thompson v ASDA-MFI Plc* [1988] Ch. 241; *Little v Courage Ltd* (1994) 70 P. & C.R. 469 CA. *Mackay v Dick* is discussed in *St Shipping & Transport Inc v Kriti Filoxenia Shipping Co SA* [2015] EWHC 997 (Comm).

[378] *Luxor (Eastbourne) Ltd v Cooper* [1941] A.C. 108 at 118, per Viscount Simon LC.

[379] [1949] 2 All E.R. 1014.

[380] [2015] UKSC 72; [2016] A.C. 742. See *Sanderson Ltd v Simtom Food Products Ltd* [2019] EWHC 442 (TCC); [2019] B.L.R. 260 approving this section.

[381] [2013] EWHC 1191 (TCC).

[382] *Swallowfalls Ltd v Monaco Yachting & Technologies SAM* [2014] EWCA Civ 186; [2014] 2 Lloyd's

anything to prevent fulfilment of the condition, and is sometimes implied that one of the parties will make reasonable efforts (or do his best) to see that the condition is fulfilled.[383]

In *The Kallang (No.2)*,[384] Mr Jonathan Hirst QC (sitting as a judge of the Commercial Court) pointed out that Lord Blackburn's dictum in *Mackay v Dick* was "put more in terms of construction of the contract than implication of terms." However, if one subscribes to the theory that the implication of terms is part of the interpretation of the contract considered as a whole against the relevant background, there is no inconsistency between the two.

Although the principle is formulated in terms of a contract to which there are two **6.140** parties, the same principle applies in cases where there are more than two parties. In such a case it is an implied term that no party will prevent performance by another party.[385] But this does not mean that a term is to be implied into a contract between A and B that B will not prevent the performance by C of an obligation to be found in a contract between A and C.[386]

The extent of the implied obligation is governed by the express terms of the **6.141** contract. As Cooke J explained in *James E McCabe Ltd v Scottish Courage Ltd*[387]:

"A duty to co-operate in, or not to prevent, fulfilment of performance of a contract only has content by virtue of the express terms of the contract and the law can only enforce a duty of co-operation to the extent that it is necessary to make the contract workable. The court cannot, by implication of such a duty, exact a higher degree of co-operation than that which could be defined by reference to the necessities of the contract. The duty of co-operation or prevention/inhibition of performance is required to be determined, not by what might appear reasonable, but by the obligations imposed upon each party by the agreement itself."

Accordingly, a duty to cooperate cannot be imposed on a party so as to compel **6.142** him to do something which the contract on its true construction relieves him from doing, and cannot be used to compel a party to do something which he cannot in fact do.[388] Similarly, there is no duty to cooperate in bringing about something that the contract does not require to happen.[389]

Illustrations

1. The relationship between a building contractor and a sub-contractor gives rise to an obligation to cooperate with each other. However, the degree of cooperation will depend on the express terms of any contract which the parties may have made.

Grant (Martin) & Co Ltd v Sir Lindsay Parkinson & Co Ltd[390]

2. In an international contract for the sale of goods, there is no duty on the seller

---

Rep. 50.
[383] See Ch.16.
[384] [2009] 1 Lloyd's Rep. 124.
[385] *F&C Alternative Investments (Holdings) Ltd v Barthelemy (Nos 2 and 3)* [2011] EWHC 1731 (Ch); [2012] Bus. L.R. 891 at [268].
[386] *Royal Bank of Scotland Plc v McCarthy* [2015] EWHC 3626 (QB).
[387] [2006] EWHC 538 (Comm); *Imamovic v Cinergy Global Trading Ltd* [2006] EWHC 323 (Comm).
[388] *North Sea Energy Holdings NV v Petroleum Authority of Thailand* [1999] 1 Lloyd's Rep. 483 CA.
[389] *Australis Media Holdings Pty Ltd v Telstra Corp Ltd* (1998) 43 N.S.W.L.R. 104.
[390] (1984) 1 Const. L.J. 220.

to cooperate with the buyer in enabling the latter to negotiate and finalise the terms of a letter of credit, nor any such duty to cooperate with the bank.
Siporex Trade SA v Banque Indosuez[391]

3.   A contract for the sale of maize f.o.b. required the buyers to tender a vessel ready to load between certain dates. The ship nominated by the buyers could not proceed to berth until some documentation required by the sellers was in order. It was an implied term of the contract that the sellers would do all that was necessary to put their documentation in order so as to enable the buyers' ship to berth.
The World Navigator[392]

4.   A land transfer granted the transferee the right to construct a road on the transferor's retained land; and to have the road adopted as a highway maintainable at public expense. It was an implied term of the transfer that the transferor would not object to the adoption.
Beazer Homes Ltd v County Council of Durham[393]

16.   GOOD FAITH IN RELATIONAL CONTRACTS

A term of good faith may be more readily implied in a relational contract. A relational contract is one in which the parties are committed to collaborating with each other, typically on a long-term basis, in ways which respect the spirit and objectives of their venture but which they have not tried to specify, and which it may be impossible to specify, exhaustively in a written contract.

6.143   Although a general duty of good faith as between contracting parties is not part of English law, in recent years such a term has more frequently been implied into a species of contract labelled a "relational contract." In *Al Nehayan v Kent*,[394] Leggatt LJ offered the following description of this species of contract:

> "a category of contract in which the parties are committed to collaborating with each other, typically on a long term basis, in ways which respect the spirit and objectives of their venture but which they have not tried to specify, and which it may be impossible to specify, exhaustively in a written contract."

6.144   In *Bates v Post Office (No.3)*,[395] Fraser J described the nature of a "relational contract":

> "What then, are the specific characteristics that are expected to be present in order to determine whether a contract between commercial parties ought to be considered a relational contract? I consider the following characteristics are relevant as to whether a contract is a relational one or not:
>
> 1.   There must be no specific express terms in the contract that prevents a duty of good faith being implied into the contract.
> 2.   The contract will be a long-term one, with the mutual intention of the parties being that there will be a long-term relationship.

---

[391] [1986] 2 Lloyd's Rep. 146.
[392] [1991] 2 Lloyd's Rep. 23 CA. See also *Odyssey Aviation Ltd v GFG 737 Ltd* [2019] EWHC 1927 (Comm).
[393] [2010] EWCA Civ 1175.
[394] [2018] EWHC 333 (Comm); [2019] 1 C.L.C. 216.
[395] [2019] EWHC 606 (QB) at [725]; *Wales v CBRE Managed Services Ltd* [2020] EWHC 16 (Comm).

3.   The parties must intend that their respective roles be performed with integrity, and with fidelity to their bargain.
4.   The parties will be committed to collaborating with one another in the performance of the contract.
5.   The spirits and objectives of their venture may not be capable of being expressed exhaustively in a written contract.
6.   They will each repose trust and confidence in one another, but of a different kind to that involved in fiduciary relationships.
7.   The contract in question will involve a high degree of communication, cooperation and predictable performance based on mutual trust and confidence, and expectations of loyalty.
8.   There may be a degree of significant investment by one party (or both) in the venture. This significant investment may be, in some cases, more accurately described as substantial financial commitment.
9.   Exclusivity of the relationship may also be present."

None of these characteristics is determinative, apart from the first.[396] As Fancourt J pointed out in *UTB LLC v Sheffield United Ltd*[397]:

"But there is a danger in using the term 'relational contract' that one is not clear about what exactly is meant by it. There is a great range of different types of contract that involve the parties in long-term relationships of varying types, with different terms and varying degrees of detail and use of language, and to characterise them all as 'relational contracts' may be in one sense accurate and yet in other ways liable to mislead. It is self-evidently not all long-term contracts that involve an enduring but undefined, cooperative relationship between the parties that will, as a matter of law, involve an obligation of good faith."

The mere fact that a contract is a long-term contract is not enough. In *Globe Motors Inc v TRW Lucas Varity Electric Steering Ltd*,[398] the Court of Appeal considered whether there was any special rule of interpretation for long-term contracts. Beatson LJ said of a submission that performance of contractual obligations was subject to a duty of good faith:

6.145

"… an implication of a duty of good faith will only be possible where the language of the contract, viewed against its context, permits it. It is thus not a reflection of a special rule of interpretation for this category of contract."

Likewise, in *General Nutrition Investment Co v Holland and Barrett*,[399] Warren J rejected an attempt to imply a term of good faith into a trademark licensing agreement. He said:

---

[396] In *Essex County Council v UBB Waste (Essex) Ltd* [2020] EWHC 1581 (TCC), Pepperall J questioned wither this feature was relevant to the question whether a contract was a relational contract, rather than simply the general principle that an implied term cannot contradict an express term.
[397] [2019] EWHC 2322 (Ch); *Russell v Cartwright* [2020] EWHC 41 (Ch).
[398] [2016] EWCA Civ 396; [2016] 1 C.L.C. 712.
[399] [2017] EWHC 746 (Ch).

"In my judgment, no general obligation of good faith is to be implied into the LA. I do not consider that the LA is a relational contract in the sense in which that term has been used in the cases. Although the LA is a long-term contract, it is one where there ought to be no need for any ongoing communication of the sort envisaged in the cases and required to enable the contract to operate effectively. In any case, even if the LA is relational in the required sense, it is not necessary to imply an obligation of good faith. Such control as GNIC has over the use of the marks is already subject to express provisions making an implied term in relation to those aspects unnecessary."

6.146   In *Amey Birmingham Highways Ltd v Birmingham City Council*,[400] the parties entered into a 25-year PFI contract for the rehabilitation, maintenance, management and operation of a road network. Jackson LJ said that such a contract could be classified as a relational contract. He added:

"Any relational contract of this character is likely to be of massive length, containing many infelicities and oddities. Both parties should adopt a reasonable approach in accordance with what is obviously the long-term purpose of the contract. They should not be latching onto the infelicities and oddities, in order to disrupt the project and maximise their own gain."

6.147   *In National Private Air Transport Services Co (National Air Services) Ltd v Creditrade LLP*,[401] Blair J held that an aircraft lease was not a relational contract, and that no such term was to be implied into an obligation to redeliver the aircraft. He said:

"These are conventional contracts in which the parties' relationship is 'legislated for in the express terms of the contract' ... There may be an expectation of co-operation upon redelivery, but this does not give rise to an implied term redefining the redelivery obligation. The defendants' case rests on an assertion that in the ordinary course, there will be 'give and take' on the redelivery of an aircraft. That is so, but the lessor is entitled to require that the aircraft is redelivered in accordance with the contractual terms, and there is little room for a distinction between 'compliance' and 'literal compliance' in this context."

In *Property Alliance Group Ltd v Royal Bank of Scotland Plc*,[402] Asplin J rejected the submission that a duty of good faith could be implied into standard banking documentation. In *Wales v CBRE Managed Services Ltd*,[403] HHJ Halliwell rejected an implied duty of good faith in a contract for the provision of services to a pension scheme. He did not consider that the contract was a relational contract.

6.148   In *Flynn v Breccia*[404] in the High Court of Ireland the trial judge implied a term to that effect into a shareholders' agreement which was held to be a relational contract. However, his decision was reversed by the Irish Court of Appeal. Finlay Geoghegan J said:

[400] [2018] EWCA Civ 264; [2018] B.L.R. 225.
[401] [2016] EWHC 2144 (Comm).
[402] [2016] EWHC 3342 (Ch); *Morley v Royal Bank of Scotland PLC* [2020] EWHC 88 (Ch) (non-recourse loan agreement).
[403] [2020] EWHC 16 (Comm).
[404] [2017] IECA 74.

"I accept the submission that there is no general principle of good faith and fair dealing in Irish contract law. There are, of course, certain types of agreements and contracts to which a duty of good faith applies, such as in a partnership agreement or the principle of uberrima fides in insurance contracts."

He went on to say that the shareholders' agreement was not a type of contract which fell within these categories and added that the express terms of the contract required the parties to cooperate "as provided in this agreement". The agreement also identified some respects only in which the parties were to act in good faith, and also contained an entire agreement clause.

It has been authoritatively stated that there are no special rules for interpreting a **6.149** long-term relational contract.[405] Although there has been a suggestion that some terms relating to good faith can be legal incidents of this particular type of contract,[406] it is considered that the appropriate test is still:

"whether a reasonable reader of the contract would consider that an obligation of good faith was obviously meant or whether the obligation is necessary to the proper working of the contract."[407]

Thus where a contract contains clauses which contain a specific and narrow obligation of good faith suggests that the parties considered the situations in which a duty of good faith was necessary and provided accordingly. That militates against the implication of an over-arching duty of good faith.[408] Nevertheless, the nature of the contract may mean that the ordinary tests for the implication of a term requiring good faith are more easily satisfied. In *Al Nehayan v Kent*,[409] Leggatt LJ suggested that once a contract has been found to be a relational contract (in the sense described above):

"the nature of the contract as a relational contract implicitly requires (in the absence of a contrary indication) treating it as involving an obligation of good faith."

So in *D&G Cars Ltd v Essex Police Authority*[410] such a term was implied in a contract for the recovery of vehicles on behalf of a police authority.

One of the characteristics identified in *Bates v Post Office* was that the spirit and **6.150** objectives of their venture may not be capable of being expressed exhaustively in a written contract. So where a franchise agreement contained very detailed terms governing all aspects of the parties' relationship, it was not appropriate to imply a general duty of good faith.[411] Similarly, where a contract contained certain express

---

[405] *Total Gas Marketing Ltd v Arco British Ltd* [1998] 2 Lloyd's Rep. 209 (Lord Steyn); *Baird Textile Holdings Ltd v Marks & Spencer Plc* [2001] C.L.C. 999.

[406] *Bates v Post Office (No.3)* [2019] EWHC 606 (QB) at [743]–[746].

[407] *UTB LLC v Sheffield United Ltd* [2019] EWHC 2322 (Ch); *SPI North Ltd v Swiss Post International (UK) Ltd* [2019] EWHC 2004 (Ch); *SDI Retail Services Ltd v The Rangers Football Club Ltd* [2019] EWHC 1929 (Comm); *Russell v Cartwright* [2020] EWHC 41 (Ch); *Cathay Pacific Airways Ltd v Lufthansa Technik AG* [2020] EWHC 1789 (Ch).

[408] *Portsmouth City Council v Ensign Highways Ltd* [2015] EWHC 1969 (TCC); [2015] B.L.R. 675.

[409] [2018] EWHC 333 (Comm); [2019] 1 C.L.C. 216.

[410] [2015] EWHC 226 (QB).

[411] *Carewatch Care Services Ltd v Focus Caring Services Ltd* [2014] EWHC 2313 (Ch).

terms dealing with good faith in relation to particular obligations, it was inappropriate to imply a more general term to that effect.[412]

6.151 Where a duty of good faith is implied, it goes further than simply a duty to act honestly. In *Bates v Post Office (No.3)*,[413] Fraser J said:

> "I consider that there is a specie of contracts, which are most usefully termed 'relational contracts', in which there is implied an obligation of good faith (which is also termed 'fair dealing' in some of the cases). This means that the parties must refrain from conduct which in the relevant context would be regarded as commercially unacceptable by reasonable and honest people. An implied duty of good faith does not mean solely that the parties must be honest."

Leggatt LJ discussed the content of the duty in *Al Nehayan v Kent*.[414] He referred to Australian authority and said:

> "the usual content of the obligation of good faith [is] an obligation to act honestly and with fidelity to the bargain; an obligation not to act dishonestly and not to act to undermine the bargain entered or the substance of the contractual benefit bargained for; and an obligation to act reasonably and with fair dealing having regard to the interests of the parties (which will, inevitably, at times conflict) and to the provisions, aims and purposes of the contract, objectively ascertained. In my view, this summary is also consistent with the English case law as it has so far developed, with the caveat that the obligation of fair dealing is not a demanding one and does no more than require a party to refrain from conduct which in the relevant context would be regarded as commercially unacceptable by reasonable and honest people."

6.152 In *New Balance Athletics, Inc v The Liverpool Football Club and Athletic Grounds Ltd*,[415] the existence of the duty was common ground. As to its content, Teare J said:

> "It is now clear from a number of decisions that the duty of good faith (or fair dealing) can be breached not only by dishonesty but also by conduct which lacks fidelity to the parties' bargain. In judging whether a party has not been faithful to the parties' bargain it is of course necessary to bear in mind the nature of the bargain, the terms of the contract and the context in which the matter arises. Ultimately, the question for the court is whether reasonable and honest people would regard the challenged conduct as commercially unacceptable."

Illustrations

1. A contract provided for the joint creation of training materials for pilots. It was held to be a "relational contract" which was subject to an implied term that contractual obligations would be performed in good faith.
Bristol Groundschool Ltd v Whittingham[416]

---

[412] *Teesside Gas Transportation Ltd v CATS North Sea Ltd* [2019] EWHC 1220 (Comm).
[413] [2019] EWHC 606 (QB) at [711].
[414] [2018] EWHC 333 (Comm); [2019] 1 C.L.C. 216.
[415] [2019] EWHC 2837 (Comm).
[416] [2014] EWHC 2145 (Ch).

2. A duty of good faith was implied into a joint venture agreement which was a "classic instance" of a relational contract. The implication of a duty of good faith in the contract was essential to give effect to the parties' reasonable expectations and satisfied the business necessity test.
Al Nehayan v Kent[417]

3. A 25-year PFI contract for the design, construction, financing, commissioning, operation and maintenance of a mechanical biological waste treatment (MBT) plant in Basildon to process the county's household waste was held to be a relational contract which contained an implied obligation of good faith.
Essex County Council v UBB Waste (Essex) Ltd[418]

4. A long-term maintenance contract for aircraft engines had some but not all of the indicia of a relational contract; and no good faith obligation was implied.
Cathay Pacific Airways Ltd v Lufthansa Technik AG[419]

17. TIME OF PERFORMANCE

Where a contract does not expressly, or by necessary implication, fix any time for the performance of a contractual obligation, the law usually implies that it shall be performed within a reasonable time.[420]

In *Hick v Raymond & Reid*,[421] Lord Watson said: **6.153**

"When the language of a contract does not expressly, or by necessary implication, fix any time for the performance of a contractual obligation, the law implies that it shall be performed within a reasonable time. The rule is general application, and is not confined to contracts for the carriage of goods by sea. In the case of other contracts the condition of reasonable time has been frequently interpreted; and has invariably been held to mean that the party upon whom it is incumbent duly fulfils his obligation, notwithstanding protracted delay, so long as such delay is attributable to causes beyond his control, and he has neither acted negligently nor unreasonably."

Thus where a bill of lading is silent as to the time within which the consignee is **6.154** to discharge the ship's cargo, his obligation is to discharge within a reasonable time.[422] The same principle applies also to the loading of cargo.[423] So also in the case of a contract for the carriage of goods by rail there is an implied obligation to deliver the goods within a reasonable time.[424]

Similarly, where a contract for the sale of land does not specify a completion date, **6.155** it is an implied term that completion will take place within a reasonable time.[425] But

---

[417] [2018] EWHC 333 (Comm); [2018] 1 C.L.C. 216.
[418] [2020] EWHC 1581 (TCC).
[419] [2020] EWHC 1789 (Ch).
[420] This section was cited with approval in *Rennie v Westbury Homes (Holdings) Ltd* [2007] 20 E.G. 296. See also para.6.160.
[421] [1893] A.C. 22 at 32. See also *Barque Quilpue Ltd v Brown* [1904] 2 K.B. 264.
[422] *Hick v Raymond & Reid* [1893] A.C. 22.
[423] *Carlton Steamship Co Ltd v Castle Mail Packets Co Ltd* [1898] A.C. 486.
[424] *Taylor v Great Northern Railway Co* (1866) L.R 1 C.P. 385.
[425] *Johnson v Humphrey* [1946] 1 All E.R. 460.

where a publishing agreement entitled the writers to give notice to the publishers requiring a breach to be remedied, there was no implied term that such a notice should be given within a reasonable time of the writers becoming aware of the breach.[426]

6.156   In *Wuhan Ocean Economic & Technical Cooperation Co Ltd v Schiffarts-Gesellschaft "Hansa Murcia" MBH*,[427] Cooke J said:

> "Where parties impose a unilateral obligation, without specifying the time in which it is to be done, there must be some implication as to the time in which it is to be done, because the parties cannot have intended the obligation to be of perpetual or indefinite duration. There must be a limit to the time in which the obligation is to be fulfilled."

On the facts, the term implied was that the obligation had to be performed within a reasonable time.

6.157   It is an implied term of every contract of insurance that if the insured makes a claim under the contract, the insurer must pay any sums due in respect of the claim within a reasonable time. A reasonable time includes a reasonable time to investigate and assess the claim. What is reasonable will depend on all the relevant circumstances, but the following are examples of things which may need to be taken into account: (a) the type of insurance, (b) the size and complexity of the claim, (c) compliance with any relevant statutory or regulatory rules or guidance, (d) factors outside the insurer's control. If the insurer shows that there were reasonable grounds for disputing the claim (whether as to the amount of any sum payable, or as to whether anything at all is payable), (a) the insurer does not breach the implied term merely by failing to pay the claim (or the affected part of it) while the dispute is continuing, but (b) the conduct of the insurer in handling the claim may be a relevant factor in deciding whether that term was breached and, if so, when.[428]

6.158   The consideration of whether there has been a breach of an obligation to perform within a reasonable time is not limited to what the parties contemplated or ought to have foreseen at the time of the contract.[429] In *Peregrine Systems Ltd v Steria Ltd*,[430] Maurice Kay LJ approved the formulation[431] that the question whether a reasonable time has been exceeded is:

> "a broad consideration, with the benefit of hindsight, and viewed from the time at which one party contends that a reasonable time for performance has been exceeded, of what would, in all the circumstances which are by then known to have happened, have been a reasonable time for performance. That broad consideration is likely to include taking into account any estimate given by the performing party of how long it would take him to perform; whether that estimate has been exceeded and, if so, in what circumstances; whether the party for whose benefit the relevant obligation was to be performed needed to participate in the performance, actively, in the sense of collaborating in what was needed to be done, or passively, in the sense of being in a position to receive performance, or

---

[426] *Crosstown Music Co 1 LLC v Rive Droite Music Ltd* [2010] EWCA Civ 1222.
[427] [2012] EWHC 3104 (Comm); [2013] 1 Lloyd's Rep. 273.
[428] Insurance Act 2015 s.13A (inserted by Enterprise Act 2016) with effect from 4 May 2017.
[429] *Peregrine Systems Ltd v Steria Ltd* [2005] EWCA Civ 239; [2005] Info. T.L.R. 294.
[430] [2005] EWCA Civ 239; [2005] Info. T.L.R. 294.
[431] In *Astea (UK) Ltd v Time Group Ltd* [2003] EWHC 725.

not at all; whether it was necessary for third parties to collaborate with the performing party in order to enable it to perform; and what exactly was the cause, or were the causes of the delay to performance. The list is not intended to be exhaustive."

In *Automotive Latch Systems Ltd v Honeywell International Inc*,[432] Flaux J said that:

"it is clear that the court can and should look at all the material available, including looking at the question with hindsight. On that basis, although none of the cases specifically touches on this, I do not see why in principle, the reasonableness of the party's conduct should not also be assessed, where appropriate, by reference to matters which ante-date the entering of the contract."

In *Parsot v Greig Developments Ltd*,[433] the New Zealand Court of Appeal held that:

"The law is that, in assessing a reasonable period, a court is entitled to take into account post-contract events, in so far as they may explain the cause or causes of the delay in performance."

Thus in deciding what is a reasonable time, account may be taken of events as they unfold.[434] There is no absolute principle which includes or excludes as relevant to the question what is a reasonable time the fact of whether, as things turn out, one party to the contract was prejudiced as a result of the lapse of time.[435] Another factor which may be considered in assessing reasonableness of actions and delay is the extent to which a particular course of action has been dictated or encouraged or agreed or acquiesced to by the other party.[436]   **6.159**

18.   TERMS ABOUT PRICE

Where a concluded contract does not specify the price to be paid for the benefits conferred by the contract, the court will often imply a term that the price is to be a reasonable price.

In the leading case of *Foley v Classique Coaches Ltd*,[437] the parties entered into a contract for the supply of petrol "at a price to be agreed". Petrol was in fact supplied. The court held that it was an implied term of the contract that the price to be paid for the petrol should be a reasonable price. So too where a lease was granted at a fixed rent for the first five years of a 14-year term and thereafter at a rent to be agreed, it was implied that in the absence of agreement the rent would be the fair market rent, excluding the value of tenant's improvements.[438] But before implying such a term the court must be satisfied that the parties intended an objec-   **6.160**

---

[432] [2008] EWHC 2171 (Comm) at [142].
[433] [2009] NZCA 241.
[434] *Jolley v Carmel Ltd* [2000] 3 E.G.L.R. 68, affirming [2000] 2 E.G.L.R. 153.
[435] *Shinedean Ltd v Alldown Demolition (London) Ltd* [2006] 1 W.L.R. 2696.
[436] *Automotive Latch Systems Ltd v Honeywell International Inc* [2008] EWHC 2171 (Comm).
[437] [1934] 2 K.B. 1.
[438] *Beer v Bowden* [1981] 1 W.L.R. 522; *Thomas Bates & Son Ltd v Wyndham's (Lingerie) Ltd* [1981] 1 W.L.R. 505.

tive criterion to be applied. In *BJ Aviation Ltd v Pool Aviation Ltd*,[439] Chadwick LJ explained:

"[W]here the court is satisfied that the parties intended that their bargain should be enforceable, it will strive to give effect to that intention by construing the words which they have used in a way which does not leave the matter to be agreed in the future incapable of being determined in the absence of future agreement. In order to achieve that result the court may feel able to imply a term in the original bargain that the price or rent, or other matter to be agreed, shall be a 'fair' price, or a 'market' price, or a 'reasonable' price; or by quantifying whatever matter it is that has to be agreed by some equivalent epithet. In a contract for sale of goods such a term may be implied by s 8 of the Sale of Goods Act 1979. But the court cannot imply a term which is inconsistent with what the parties have actually agreed. So if, on the true construction of the words which they have used, the court is driven to the conclusion that they must be taken to have intended that the matter should be left to their future agreement on the basis that either is to remain free to agree or disagree about that matter as his own perceived interest dictates there is no place for an implied term that, in the absence of agreement, the matter shall be determined by some objective criteria of fairness or reasonableness."

6.161   In addition, no such implication will be made in order to turn an unconcluded contract into a concluded bargain.[440] This distinction was drawn by the trial judge[441] in *British Bank for Foreign Trade Ltd v Novinex Ltd*[442] as follows:

"The principle to be deduced from the cases is that if there is an essential term which has yet to be agreed and there is no express or implied provision for its solution, the result in point of law is that there is no binding contract. In seeing whether there is an implied provision for its solution, however, there is a difference between an arrangement which is wholly executory on both sides and one which has been executed on one side or the other. In the ordinary way, if there is an arrangement to supply goods at a price 'to be agreed' or to perform services on terms 'to be agreed,' then although, while the matter is still executory, there may be no binding contract, nevertheless, if it is executed on one side, that is, if the one does his part without having come to an agreement as to the price or the terms, then the law will say that there is necessarily implied, from the conduct of the parties, a contract that, in default of agreement, a reasonable sum is to be paid."

This statement of principle was approved by the Court of Appeal.[443]

6.162   Similarly, in *Grow with US Ltd v Green Thumb (UK) Ltd*,[444] a franchise agreement contained a clause providing for renewal of the agreement with "uplifted minimum performance requirements", but did not specify what they were and did not provide for machinery to determine them. The Court of Appeal rejected the

---

[439] [2002] EWCA Civ 163.
[440] *King's Motors (Oxford) Ltd v Lax* [1970] 1 W.L.R. 426.
[441] Denning J.
[442] [1949] 1 K.B. 623.
[443] [1949] 1 K.B. 623.
[444] [2006] EWCA Civ 1201.

argument that the word "reasonable" should be read into the clause. Buxton LJ said:

"This is not a contract that is in the course of performance and which the parties must be taken to have agreed will be performed. This case concerns a contract that has reached the end of its agreed term, and where the issue of whether and on what terms it should be extended, alternatively be replaced by a different contract, is completely open. There is no reason at all to assume that the parties, and certainly not both of them, must have intended that the term be extended, and therefore some grounds must be found for doing that, and no reason to read terms into the contract to achieve that end."

An agreement for the sale of shares at a valuation will usually imply an objec-   **6.163**
tive test of a fair valuation.[445] However, where a share sale agreement provided for the price to be the open market value of the shares "as determined by an independent chartered accountant" it was held that because there are a number of ways of arriving at the open market value of shares, the opinion of the accountant was an essential part of the ascertainment of the price, and it was not possible to say that the shares were to be valued by an objective criterion.[446]

Illustrations

1.   An option in a lease gave the tenant the right to buy the freehold at a price to be agreed by two valuers, one to be nominated by the landlord and the other to be nominated by the tenant. It was held that there was an implied term that the price was to be fair and reasonable.
   Sudbrook Trading Estate Ltd v Eggleton[447]

2.   A daisy chain contract[448] for the sale of crude oil resulted in an agreement to adjust the prices payable by the participants by reference to a base price to be settled after further discussion. It was held that there was an implied term that in default of agreement the base price was to be ascertained by an appropriate independent adjudicator.
   Voest Alpine Intertrading GmbH v Chevron International Oil Co Ltd[449]

3.   A contract for the handling of crude oil stated that it was valid for a period of 10 years. However, it only fixed a fee for the first two years. It was held that a term should be implied to the effect that the fee for the remaining years would be a reasonable fee.
   Mamidoil-Jetoil Greek Petroleum Co SA v Okta Crude Oil Refinery AD[450]

---

[445] *Money v Ven-Lu-Ree Ltd* [1989] 3 N.Z.L.R. 129 PC.
[446] *Gillatt v Sky Television Ltd* [2000] 2 B.C.L.C. 103.
[447] [1983] A.C. 444.
[448] A "daisy chain" contract is equivalent to a "string" contract. However, where the same person appears twice in the "daisy chain", a "circle" results, and to avoid unnecessary payments and deliveries of oil, the circle is by-passed by an agreed "book-out". This involves the fixing of a commonly acceptable base price, and each of the contract prices is thereupon adjusted by reference to the base price, so that only the difference between the two is payable.
[449] [1987] 2 Lloyd's Rep. 547.
[450] [2001] 2 Lloyd's Rep. 76.

19. Terms about Duration

Where a contract does not expressly provide for its expiry or determination, a term may be implied that the contract may be determined after a reasonable time, on giving reasonable notice.[451]

6.164   The traditional view was expressed by Lord Selborne in *Llanelly Railway and Dock Co v London and North Western Railway Co*[452] as follows:

"... an agreement *de futuro*, extending over a tract of time which on the face of the agreement, is indefinite and unlimited, must (in general) throw upon anyone alleging that it is not perpetual, the burden of proving that allegation, either from the nature of the subject, or from some rule of law applicable thereto."

A similar view had been expressed in the Court of Appeal by James LJ.[453]

6.165   However, in *Winter Garden Theatre (London) Ltd v Millennium Productions Ltd*,[454] a licence was granted under which the licensee was entitled to present plays in a theatre. No provision was made for determination by the licensors. The House of Lords held that the licence was determinable upon reasonable notice. Lord MacDermott pointed out that Lord Selborne's dictum was not expressed as "a universal rule of construction" and doubted whether it was intended to apply to the circumstances then under consideration. By 1962 Lord Devlin, delivering the advice of the Privy Council in *Australia Blue Metal Ltd v Hughes*,[455] was able to say:

"It is true that it does not require very much to induce a court to read into as agreement of a commercial character, either by construction or by implication, a provision that the arrangements between the parties, whatever they may be shall be terminable only upon reasonable notice."

This observation was primarily directed to the distinction between arrangements determinable only on notice, and arrangements determinable at will. Nevertheless, it does indicate the court's willingness to hold that some terms as to the duration and termination of agreements are to be supplied. The position was summarised in *Re Spenborough Urban District Council's Agreement*[456] by Buckley J as follows:

"Authority establishes that, where an agreement does not in terms confer on the parties or one of them a power to determine the agreement, whether such a power should be inferred is a question of construction of the agreement to be determined in accordance with the ordinary principles applicable to such a question ... An agreement which is silent about determination will not be determinable unless

---

[451] There is room for debate whether an ability to terminate a contract on reasonable notice is truly an implied term, rather than a question of interpretation of the terms of the contract: *Ward Equipment Ltd v Preston* [2017] NZCA 444. Since in such a case there are no express words relating to termination, the author considers that it is properly a question of implication.

[452] (1875) L.R. 7 App. Cas. 550.

[453] (1873) 8 Ch. App. 942.

[454] [1948] A.C. 173.

[455] [1963] A.C. 74.

[456] [1968] Ch. 139; approved by the CA in *Colchester and East Essex Co-Operative Society Ltd v Kelvedon Labour Club and Institute Ltd* [2003] EWCA Civ 1671.

the facts of the case, such as the subject matter of the agreement, the nature of the contract or the circumstances in which the agreement was made, support a finding that the parties intended it to be determinable, but there is in my judgment, no presumption one way or the other."

This approach neutralises the force of the dictum of Lord Selborne quoted above. **6.166** In *Staffordshire Area Health Authority v South Staffordshire Waterworks Co*,[457] Lord Denning MR attempted to reverse the onus. He suggested that it was "a modern rule of construction" that where a person agrees to supply goods or services continuously over an unlimited time in return for a fixed monthly or yearly payment, the contract can be determined on reasonable notice. However, the other two members of the court[458] did not agree with this proposition. In *Crawford Fitting Co v Sydney Valve & Fittings Pty Ltd*,[459] McHugh JA said:

"In principle, the better view would seem to be that, although there is a presumption against implying a term that an agreement is terminable, ordinarily the nature of a commercial agreement will lead to the conclusion that the parties must have intended it to be terminable on notice."

The fact that a contract is expressed to endure for an unlimited time does not **6.167** necessarily mean that it is terminable on reasonable notice. In *Harbinger UK Ltd v GEI Information Services Ltd*,[460] software suppliers agreed to provide support for the software "in perpetuity". Evans LJ said:

"The words 'in perpetuity' in clause 10 make it clear that the support and maintenance obligation extends beyond termination of the Agreement under clause 3. Equally clearly, they do not impose any time limit on the existence of that obligation. 'In perpetuity' is inconsistent with a time-limit, and the words mean, in my judgment, that the obligation is to continue 'without limit of time'.

This does not mean literally 'for ever' or 'until the crack of doom'. The contract itself—meaning the unilateral contract under which the obligation to provide support and maintenance arises—will not live forever. The time will come when the technology is superseded and the software is outdated. As a result, customers will require a change in the software (and no doubt in the hardware) which they use and they will no longer make the annual payments in return for which the services are provided. No one can predict definitely when this will occur. But until it does, the contract and the obligation both survive.

'In perpetuity' in my judgment emphasises this negative aspect. There is nothing in the clause 10 contract which imposes a time limit, and the obligation continues as long as the contract survives. Perhaps because the appellants have sought to give the words a positive meaning, the judge was able to reject their construction as uncommercial, and both he and the respondents tried to seek out some other positive meaning. Hence the respondents' alternative suggestion of a reasonable time and the judge's contractual timetable which he devised in order to place a time-limit on the operation of the clause; but the words themselves provide expressly that there is no time-limit. Both of these attempts founder, in

---

457 [1978] 1 W.L.R. 1387.
458 Goff and Cumming-Bruce LJJ.
459 (1988) 14 N.S.W.L.R. 438 at 443–444.
460 [2000] 1 All E.R. (Comm) 166.

my judgment, on the plain fact that the express words 'in perpetuity' are inconsistent with any time-limit on the operation of the clause."

The contract was not, therefore, terminable on reasonable notice.

6.168   Where the contract is not for an unlimited time, but is for a fixed term, there is even less likely to be room for implying further terms as to the termination of the agreement. In *Kirklees Metropolitan Borough Council v Yorkshire Woollen District Transport Co Ltd*,[461] an agreement between a company and two local authorities provided that during a period of 99 years neither of the local authorities should operate public transport services. In return the company was to pay the authorities a percentage of its profits. A successor to the company sought to imply a term that the agreement should determine if the company became unable lawfully to operate public transport services. Walton J held that "by no stretch of the imagination" could such a term be implied.

In *Jani-King (GB) Ltd v Pula Enterprises Ltd*,[462] Judge Coulson QC refused to imply a term that a fixed-term contract could be terminated on reasonable notice. As he put it:

"... the whole point of a commercial contract which will last for a particular period (or until a specified event has happened) is that the contracting parties are committed to both the contract and each other for a known period. It seems to me that it would make a nonsense of such an arrangement if either party could give notice of termination at any time during the term, with minimal consequences, because, say, that party has received a more attractive proposal from someone else."

6.169   So, too, where the agreement already contains terms for termination, it will be difficult to imply further such terms.[463] In *Re Berker Sportscraft Ltd's Agreements*,[464] a dress designer and a dress manufacturer entered into an agreement for the manufacture of dresses. The designer was to receive a commission on goods sold, and the agreement was determinable in the event of the commission not reaching a certain figure. Jenkins J held that no further terms for termination could be implied. Similarly, in *Colchester and East Essex Co-Operative Society Ltd v Kelvedon Labour Club and Institute Ltd*,[465] a licence to use a car park was automatically terminable only in certain specified events. It was held that no general power of termination could be implied.

6.170   Where a contract is terminable on reasonable notice, what period of notice would be reasonable will normally be determined as at the date of the giving of notice. Relevant factors will include the degree of formality of the contract, the length of the relationship; the nature of the commercial enterprise; and the importance of the contract to the parties.[466]

---

[461] (1978) 77 L.G.R. 448.

[462] [2008] 1 All E.R. (Comm) 451.

[463] This statement was approved in *Service Power Pacific Pty Ltd v Service Power Business Solutions Ltd* [2009] EWHC 179 (Ch).

[464] (1947) 177 L.T. 420.

[465] [2003] EWCA Civ 1671.

[466] See, e.g. *Martin-Baker Aircraft Co Ltd v Canadian Flight Equipment Ltd* [1955] 2 Q.B. 556 (12 months); *Decro-Wall v Practitioners in Marketing Ltd* [1971] 1 W.L.R. 361 (12 months); *Alpha Lettings Ltd & Neptune Research & Development Inc* [2003] EWCA Civ 704 (four months); *Jackson*

Illustrations

1.   A gas company and a local authority entered into an agreement under which the gas company agreed to light all the public lamps in the district from 1 September, in every year up to the following 1 May, inclusive. It was held that the agreement was terminable on notice.
Crediton Gas Co v Crediton Urban District Council[467]

2.   A company granted another company the right to make ejector seats and sell them in return for a fixed royalty. The contract made no provision for determination. McNair J held that it was determinable on reasonable notice. He said:

"I have little doubt that the law merchant would regard a contract for sale of a hundred tons of coal monthly at a fixed price, no period being specified, as a contract determinable on reasonable notice."

Martin-Baker Aircraft Co Ltd v Canadian Flight Equipment Ltd[468]

3.   Two companies agreed that neither would employ any person who had been an employee of the other during the previous five years. The agreement was silent as to its duration. It was held that it was terminable on 12 months' notice.
Kores Manufacturing Co Ltd v Kolok Manufacturing Co Ltd[469]

4.   A solicitor was retained in connection with the legal work involved in a building development including the grant of leases of the finished building. The retainer was held to be determinable on reasonable notice.
Milner (JH) & Son v Bilton (Percy) Ltd[470]

5.   An agreement was made between a local authority and an industrialist to regulate discharge of trade effluent into the public sewer. It was held to be terminable on reasonable notice.
Re Spenborough Urban District Council's Agreement[471]

6.   An electricity board agreed to supply electricity to a local authority at a fixed price. The agreement stated that its provisions should apply "for all time hereafter". It was held that the agreement could not be terminated by reasonable notice.
Gore District Council v Power Co Ltd[472]

20.   STANDARD OF PERFORMANCE

In a contract to make an article, (including a building) there will be an implied term that the article made will be reasonably fit for its purpose. A similar term will be implied into a licence of land, but not into a lease of unfurnished

---

Distribution Ltd v Tum Yeto Inc [2009] EWHC 982 (QB) (nine months).
[467] [1928] 1 Ch. 17.
[468] [1955] 2 Q.B. 556; *Jackson Distribution Ltd v Tum Yeto Inc* [2009] EWHC 982 (QB).
[469] [1957] 1 W.L.R. 1012.
[470] [1966] 1 W.L.R. 1582.
[471] [1968] Ch. 139.
[472] [1986] 1 N.Z.L.R. 58.

property. In a contract to perform services, there will generally be an implied term that the party performing the services will do so with reasonable care and skill, but in exceptional circumstances there may be an implied warranty that he will achieve the desired result.

6.171   In *Francis v Cockrell*,[473] the defendant had contracted to erect a grandstand for the purpose of viewing races. Kelly CB said:

> "I do not hesitate to say that I am clearly of opinion, as a general proposition of law, that when one man engages with another to supply him with a particular article or thing, to be applied to a certain use or purpose, in consideration of a pecuniary payment, he enters into an implied contract that the article or thing shall be reasonably fit for the purpose for which it is to be used and to which it is to be applied."

6.172   A like term is implied into a contract to supply goods in the course of a contract to do work or labour.[474] It is a matter of legal indifference whether the contract is one for the sale of goods or one of services to do work and supply materials.[475] In a contract of the latter type, there is also to be implied a term that the work must be good workmanship, and the materials of good quality.[476]

6.173   Similar principles apply to contracts for the execution of building works. It is clear from *Lawrence v Cassel*[477] and *Miller v Cannon Hill Estates Ltd*,[478] that when a purchaser buys a house from a builder who contracts to build it, there is a threefold implication: that the builder will do his work in a good and workmanlike manner; that he will supply good and proper materials; and that it will be reasonably fit for human habitation.[479] Similar implied terms are to be found where the purchaser leases, rather than buys outright.[480]

6.174   A term as to fitness for purpose may be implied into a licence (e.g. the right to stay in a hotel room) or even into a licence of commercial property where such an implication is warranted as a matter of business efficacy.[481] A similar implied warranty of fitness for purpose will be implied into a letting of furnished premises.[482] However, no warranty as to fitness for purpose will be implied into a lease of unfurnished property, either as to physical fitness, or as to legal fitness.[483]

6.175   Contracts for the performance of services stand upon a somewhat different footing. The law does not usually imply a warranty that a professional man will achieve the desired result, but only a term that he will use reasonable care and skill. The surgeon does not warrant that he will cure the patient. Nor does the solicitor

---

[473] (1870) L.R. 5 Q.B. 501.
[474] *Myers (GH) & Co v Brent Cross Service Co* [1934] 1 K.B. 46.
[475] *Samuels v Davis* [1943] 1 K.B. 527.
[476] *Stewart v Ravell's Garage* [1952] 2 Q.B. 545.
[477] [1930] 2 K.B. 83.
[478] [1931] 2 K.B.113.
[479] *Hancock v Brazier (BW) (Anerly) Ltd* [1956] 1 W.L.R. 1317 at 1332, per Lord Denning MR.
[480] *Batty v Metropolitan Property Realisations Ltd* [1978] 1 Q.B. 554.
[481] *Maclenan v Segar* [1917] 2 KB. 235; *Western Electric Ltd v Welsh Development Agency* [1980] Q.B. 796. Contrast *Morris-Thomas v Petticoat Lane Rentals Ltd* (1987) 53 P. & C.R. 238.
[482] *Wilson v Finch Hatton* (1877) 2 Ex. D. 336.
[483] *Hart v Windsor* (1844) 12 M. & W. 68; *Sleafer v Lambeth Borough Council* [1960] 1 Q.B. 43; *Duke of Westminster v Guild* [1985] Q.B. 688 (all as to physical fitness); *Edler v Auerbach* [1950] 1 K.B. 359; *Hill v Harris* [1965] 2 Q.B. 601 (as to legal fitness).

warrant that he will win the case. So where a tour operator agreed to provide a package holiday, it was an implied term of the contract that the services included in the package would be supplied with reasonable care and skill, even though they were to be supplied by other people.[484] But in exceptional circumstances a term may be implied that the desired result will be achieved.[485]

21. EXECUTORY AND EXECUTED CONTRACTS

The court is readier to imply terms into executed contracts, particularly where one party has performed his obligations under it, than into executory contracts.

The statement of Denning J in *British Bank for Foreign Trade v Novinex Ltd*[486] **6.176** has already been quoted. The principle which he put forward was that there is a distinction to be drawn between executory and executed contracts. He repeated the principle in wider terms in *Sykes (Wessex) Ltd v Fine Fare Ltd*[487] as follows:

> "In a commercial agreement the further the parties have gone with their contract, the more ready are the Courts to imply any reasonable term so as to give effect to their intentions. When much has been done, the Courts will do their best not to destroy the bargain. When nothing has been done, it is easier to say that there is no agreement between the parties because the essential terms have not been agreed. But when an agreement has been acted upon and the parties, as here, have been put to great expense in implementing it, we ought to imply all reasonable terms so as to avoid any uncertainties."

Similarly, in *Beer v Bowden*,[488] the Court of Appeal stressed the fact that they **6.177** were dealing with the implication of a term into an executed (and continuing) lease, which had created a subsisting estate in land. Goff LJ said that the case of a wholly executory contract posed "an entirely different problem".

But the device of implying terms should not generally be used to turn a non- **6.178** legally binding arrangement into a contract. In *Aotearoa International Ltd v Scancarriers A/S*,[489] Lord Roskill put it thus:

> "... the first question must always be whether any legally binding contract has been made, for until that issue is decided a court cannot properly decide what extra terms, if any, must be implied into what is *ex hypothesi* a legally binding bargain, as being both necessary and reasonable to make that legally binding bargain work. It is not correct in principle, in order to determine whether there is a legally binding bargain, to add to those terms which alone the parties have expressed, further implied terms upon which they have not expressly agreed and

---

[484] *Wong Mee Wan v Kwan Kin Travel Ltd* [1996] 1 W.L.R. 37 PC. A similar result is achieved by the Package Travel, Package Holidays and Package Tours Regulations 1992 (SI 1992/3288).
[485] *Greaves & Co (Contractors) Ltd v Baynham Meikle* [1975] 1 W.L.R. 1095 (architects and engineers); *Eyre v Measday* [1986] 1 All E.R. 488 (surgeon).
[486] [1949] 1 K.B. 623. See para.6.161.
[487] [1967] 1 Lloyd's Rep. 53.
[488] [1981] 1 W.L.R. 522.
[489] [1985] 2 Lloyd's Rep. 419 PC, applied in *Little v Courage Ltd* (1994) 70 P. & C.R. 469 CA.

then by adding the express terms and the implied terms together thereby create what would not otherwise be a legally binding bargain."

Similarly, in *Grow with US Ltd v Green Thumb (UK) Ltd*,[490] a franchise agreement contained a clause providing for renewal of the agreement with "uplifted minimum performance requirements", but did not specify what they were and did not provide for machinery to determine them. The Court of Appeal rejected the argument that the word "reasonable" should be read into the clause. Buxton LJ said:

"This is not a contract that is in the course of performance and which the parties must be taken to have agreed will be performed. This case concerns a contract that has reached the end of its agreed term, and where the issue of whether and on what terms it should be extended, alternatively be replaced by a different contract, is completely open. There is no reason at all to assume that the parties, and certainly not both of them, must have intended that the term be extended, and therefore some grounds must be found for doing that, and no reason to read terms into the contract to achieve that end."

6.179   However, the observations of Lord Roskill in *Scancarriers A/S v Aotearoa International Ltd*[491] do not support the broad proposition that that it is not possible to turn an incomplete bargain into a legally binding contract by adding expressly agreed terms and implied terms together. Lord Kitchin explained in *Wells v Devani*[492] that:

"… there will be cases where an agreement is so vague and uncertain that it cannot be enforced. So too, there will be cases where the parties have not addressed certain matters which are so fundamental that their agreement is incomplete. Further, an agreement may be so deficient in one or other of these respects that nothing can be done to render it enforceable. But I do not accept that there is any general rule that it is not possible to imply a term into an agreement to render it sufficiently certain or complete to constitute a binding contract. Indeed, it seems to me that it is possible to imply something that is so obvious that it goes without saying into anything, including something the law regards as no more than an offer. If the offer is accepted, the contract is made on the terms of the words used and what those words imply. Moreover, where it is apparent the parties intended to be bound and to create legal relations, it may be permissible to imply a term to give the contract such business efficacy as the parties must have intended. For example, an agreement may be enforceable despite calling for some further agreement between the parties, say as to price, for it may be appropriate to imply a term that, in default of agreement, a reasonable price must be paid."

---

[490] [2006] EWCA Civ 1201.
[491] [1985] 2 Lloyd's Rep. 419.
[492] [2019] UKSC4; [2019] 2 W.L.R. 617.

CHAPTER 7

THE CANONS OF CONSTRUCTION

... where every word is at home
  Taking its place to support the others, ...
  The common word exact without vulgarity,
  The formal word precise but not pedantic,
  The complete consort dancing together

TS Eliot: *Little Gidding*

1.   THE FUNCTION OF CANONS OF CONSTRUCTION

The canons of construction are no more than pointers to ascertaining the meaning of a written contract. They are not to be slavishly applied, and where they point in different directions the court must select those which will produce a reasonable and just result.

The canons of construction are not rules of law; they are as much as anything guidelines to the interpretation of the English language.[1] In *Cusack v London Borough of Harrow*,[2] Lord Neuberger said:

> "With few, if any, exceptions, the canons embody logic or common sense, but that is scarcely a reason for discarding them: on the contrary. Of course there will be many cases, where different canons will point to different answers, but that does not call their value into question. Provided that it is remembered that the canons exist to illuminate and help, but not to constrain or inhibit, they remain of real value."

In *Prestcold (Central) Ltd v Minister of Labour*,[3] Lord Diplock said of them that:

> "many of them are general rules of composition which any writer seeking clarity of expression is likely to follow, such as *expressio unius exclusio alterius*, *ejusdem generis* and *noscitur a sociis* though, unlike lawyers, he does not express them in the arcane obscurity of the Latin tongue."

In *Chandris v Isbrandtsen-Moller Co Inc*,[4] Devlin J said:

7.01

7.02

---

[1]   Although they have been dismissed as "intellectual baggage" (*Investors Compensation Scheme v West Bromwich BS* [1998] 1 W.L.R. 896, per Lord Hoffmann), they still have their supporters.
[2]   [2013] UKSC 40; [2013] 1 W.L.R. 2022 (a case of statutory interpretation).
[3]   [1969] 1 W.L.R. 89.
[4]   [1951] 1 K.B. 240. See also *Bader Properties Ltd v Linley Property Investments Ltd* (1967) 19 & C.R. 620 at 636, per Roskill J ("rules of construction are guides to the truth but must not be allowed to compel a construction which would not otherwise be the natural construction of the language used").

"A rule of construction cannot be more than a guide to enable the court to arrive at the true meaning of the parties. The ejusdem generis rule means that there is implied into the language which the parties have used words of restriction which are not there. It cannot be right to approach a document with the presumption that there should be such an implication. To apply the rule automatically in that way would be to make it the master and not the servant of the purpose for which it was designed—namely to ascertain the intention of the parties from the words they have used."

So too, Bowen LJ observed of the *ejusdem generis* principle[5]:

"It is to be observed that the rule admits, as every rule of construction of documents must admit, as it is after all but a working canon to enable us to arrive at the meaning of the particular document—it admits of being modified by the contents of the document itself, and there are many classes of cases in which it is obvious that the rule will have to bend."

7.03   In *BCCI v Ali*,[6] Lord Clyde said:

"Such guides to construction as have been identified in the past should not be allowed to constrain an approach to construction which looks to commercial reality or common sense. If they are elevated to anything approaching the status of rules they would deservedly be regarded as impedimenta in the task of construction. But they may be seen as reflections upon the way in which people may ordinarily be expected to express themselves."

And Lord Hope of Craighead said in *AIB Group (UK) Plc v Martin*[7]:

"Like any other rule of interpretation, it is there to help to ascertain the objective meaning of the document in question. Like all such rules, it must be used with discrimination."

7.04   Similarly, Aikens J said in *HIH Casualty and General Insurance v Chase Manhattan Bank*[8]:

"The court's task is still to discern what the parties intended by the wording that they have agreed in the particular type of contract under consideration. But although 'rules' of construction are a guide to the intention of the parties, they are not the masters of the parties' intention."

Likewise, in *McCann v Switzerland Insurance Australia Ltd*,[9] Kirby J said:

---

5   In *Earl of Jersey v Neath Poor Law Union Guardians* (1889) 22 Q.B.D. 555. See also *The Golden Leader* [1980] 2 Lloyd's Rep. 573, per Lloyd J. ("Like all rules of construction Lord Morton's test is a guide designed to ascertain the true intentions of the parties. It should not be applied rigidly or mechanically so as to defeat their intentions.")
6   [2002] 1 A.C. 251.
7   [2001] UKHL 63; [2002] 1 W.L.R. 94.
8   [2001] C.L.C. 48 at 71, approved in *National Westminster Bank Plc v Utrecht-American Finance Co* [2001] C.L.C. 1372 at 1386 CA.
9   [2000] HCA 65.

"Maxims and rules of construction, developed as tools to aid the task of interpretation, are subordinate to the primary duty, which is to uphold the contract between the parties."

The same point has been made in more acerbic language[10]:

7.05

"The cynical truth about interpretation in England seems to be that the Bench has been provided with some dozens of 'principles' from which a judicious selection can be made to achieve substantial justice in each individual case. From time to time, all the relevant principles point in the same direction and leave the court no choice, but in most of the cases susceptible of any real dispute, the function of counsel is merely to provide sufficient material for the court to perform its task of selection."

Although often described as rules, they are in truth not rules at all. It is more appropriate to describe them as principles of interpretation. Even so, modern courts are far less influenced by these formulated principles than in former times. In *K/S Victoria Street v House of Fraser (Stores Management) Ltd*,[11] Lord Neuberger of Abbotsbury MR, giving the judgment of the court, said:

7.06

"'rules' of interpretation such as *contra proferentem* are rarely decisive as to the meaning of any provisions of a commercial contract. The words used, commercial sense, and the documentary and factual context, are, and should be, normally enough to determine the meaning of a contractual provision."

2. CONSTRUING THE DOCUMENT AS A WHOLE

In order to arrive at the true interpretation of a document, a clause must not be considered in isolation, but must be considered in the context of the whole of the document.[12]

In *Chamber Colliery Ltd v Twyerould*,[13] Lord Watson said:

7.07

"I find nothing in this case to oust the application of the well known rule that a deed ought to be read as a whole, in order to ascertain the true meaning of its several clauses; and that the words of each clause should be so interpreted as to bring them into harmony with the other provisions of the deed, if that interpretation does no violence to the meaning of which they are naturally susceptible."

The bringing of clauses into harmony has been echoed in more recent cases. In

7.08

---

10 Megarry, "Review" (1945) 61 L.Q.R. 102.
11 [2011] EWCA Civ 904.
12 This section was referred to with approval in *AIC Ltd v Marine Pilot Ltd* [2007] 2 Lloyd's Rep. 101 and *Newall v Lewis* [2008] 4 Costs L.R. 626. In *Persimmon Homes (South Coast) Ltd v Hall Aggregates (South Coast) Ltd* [2008] EWHC 2379 (TCC), Coulson J formulated the principle in the same terms as this section, as he also did in *Secretary of State for Defence v Turner Estate Solutions Ltd* [2015] EWHC 1150 (TCC). Compare the *European Principles of Contract Law*, para.5:105: "Terms are interpreted in the light of the whole contract in which they appear".
13 [1915] 1 Ch. 268 (Note). The principle was applied in, among other cases, *Yafai v Muthana* [2012] EWCA Civ 289; *Waite v Paccar Financial Plc* [2012] EWCA Civ 901; and *Kudos Catering (UK) Ltd v Manchester Central Convention Complex Ltd* [2013] EWCA Civ 38; [2013] 2 Lloyd's Rep. 270.

Phoenix Life Assurance Ltd v Financial Services Authority,[14] Andrew Smith J said:

"… each provision should inform the proper interpretation of the other, and the parties' intention is ascertained by seeking from the start a harmonious interpretation of the contract as a whole, rather than managing to reconcile discordant interpretations of different provisions."

In *EE Ltd v Mundio Mobile Ltd*[15] Carr J said:

"Agreements should be read as a whole and construed so far as possible to avoid inconsistencies between different parts on the assumption that the parties had intended to express their intentions in a coherent and consistent way. One expects provisions to complement each other. Only in the case of a clear and irreconcilable discrepancy would it be necessary to resort to the contractual order of precedence to resolve it."

7.09   Sometimes it is put in terms of rationality. Thus in *C v D*,[16] Rix LJ said:

"There is a general principle of construction that a document which falls to be construed should be read as a whole and its separate parts should be so construed, if that is possible, as to bring rational sense and consistency to that whole."

7.10   In the modern jargon this principle is sometimes labelled a "holistic" interpretation.[17] The expression of this principle of construction is no more than an enlargement of the general proposition that an individual word takes its meaning from the context in which it is found, which is now the single most important principle in the modern approach to the interpretation of contracts.

7.11   So too an individual clause takes its meaning from the context of the document in which it is found. Thus in *Barton v FitzGerald*,[18] Lord Ellenborough CJ said:

"It is a true rule of construction that the sense and meaning of the parties in any particular part of an instrument may be collected *ex antecedentibus et consequentibus*; every part of it may be brought into action in order to collect from the whole one uniform and consistent sense, if that may be done."[19]

7.12   Thus it is of the utmost importance to interpret particular clauses "in the landscape of the instrument as a whole".[20] In *Strachey v Ramage*,[21] Rimer LJ said:

"It is a statement of the obvious that the crucial provision in the conveyance was the parcels clause, since it was there that the parties identified the land being conveyed. It is, however, fundamental that the parcels clause in a conveyance

---

14 [2013] EWHC 60 (Comm).
15 *[2016] EWHC 531 (TCC).*
16 [2011] EWCA Civ 646; [2012] 1 All E.R. 302.
17 See *Adam v Shrewsbury* [2006] 1 P. & C.R. 27, per Neuberger LJ; *Taylor v Rive Droite Music Ltd* [2006] E.M.L.R. 4, per Neuberger LJ; *Shaw v Hutton-Shaw* [2007] 1 F.L.R. 1839, per Arden LJ.
18 (1812) 15 East. 530.
19 See also *The Apostolis (No.2)* [2000] 2 Lloyd's Rep. 337 at 348 CA. ("However, it is hornbook law that a contract must be construed as a whole. One cannot first construe cl. 3 and then afterwards alter the meaning of cl. 20 in order to accord with it", per Waller LJ.)
20 *Charter Reinsurance Co Ltd v Fagan* [1997] A.C. 313 at 384.
21 [2008] 2 P. & C.R. 8.

should not be considered in isolation from the remainder of the document. It is a general, and basic, principle of the construction of documents that questions of interpretation should be answered by considering the document as a whole, since only then can the provision giving rise to the question be seen in its proper context. There can be no reason for this principle not to be equally applicable in relation to the interpretation of a conveyance for the purpose of identifying the limits of the land conveyed by it."

In *Re Sigma Finance Corp*,[22] the Supreme Court interpreted provisions in a **7.13** finance deed. Lord Mance said:

"In my opinion, the conclusion reached below attaches too much weight to what the courts perceived as the natural meaning of the words of the third sentence of clause 7.6, and too little weight to the context in which that sentence appears and to the scheme of the Security Trust Deed as a whole. Lord Neuberger was right to observe that the resolution of an issue of interpretation in a case like the present is an iterative process, involving 'checking each of the rival meanings against other provisions of the document and investigating its commercial consequences' ... Like him, I also think that caution is appropriate about the weight capable of being placed on the consideration that this was a long and carefully drafted document, containing sentences or phrases which it can, with hindsight, be seen could have been made clearer, had the meaning now sought to be attached to them been specifically in mind ... Even the most skilled drafters sometimes fail to see the wood for the trees, and the present document on any view contains certain infelicities, as those in the majority below acknowledged. ... Of much greater importance in my view, in the ascertainment of the meaning that the Deed would convey to a reasonable person with the relevant background knowledge, is an understanding of its overall scheme and a reading of its individual sentences and phrases which places them in the context of that overall scheme. Ultimately, that is where I differ from the conclusion reached by the courts below."

In the same case Lord Collins said:

"In complex documents of the kind in issue there are bound to be ambiguities, infelicities and inconsistencies. An over-literal interpretation of one provision without regard to the whole may distort or frustrate the commercial purpose."

The relevant context may extend beyond a single contract. Where a contract is **7.14** one of a series of linked contracts (e.g. a contract of insurance and a contract of reinsurance) the relevant terms in a proportional facultative reinsurance—and in particular those relating to the risk—should in principle be construed so as to be consistent with the terms of the insurance contract on the basis that the normal commercial intention is that they should be back-to-back.[23] Similarly it has been said that "where parties have used language which means one thing in a contract to which they were parties, and they use the same language in another, it is likely that it will have the same meaning".[24] In *RWE Npower Renewables Ltd v JN Bentley*

---

[22] [2010] 1 All E.R. 571; *Sebastian Holdings Inc v Deutsche Bank AG* [2010] EWCA Civ 998.
[23] *Lexington Insurance Co v AGF Insurance Ltd* [2009] UKHL 40. See para.3.08.
[24] *Shell UK Ltd v Total UK Ltd* [2010] 3 All E.R. 793.

Ltd,[25] Moore-Bick LJ said:

> "I start, as did the judge, from the position that the contract documents should as far as possible be read as complementing each other and therefore as expressing the parties' intentions in a consistent and coherent manner."

7.15   The principle of consistency may also inform the meaning of individual words and expressions where they appear more than once in the same contract. In *Interactive Investor Trading Ltd v City Index Ltd*,[26] Tomlinson LJ said that:

> "... it should ordinarily be presumed that language is used consistently within the four corners of an agreement."

In *Barnardo's v Buckinghamshire*,[27] Lord Hodge said:

> "... it is trite both that a provision in a pension scheme or other formal document should be considered in the context of the document as a whole and that one would in principle expect words and phrases to be used consistently in a carefully drafted document, absent a reason for giving them different meanings."

7.16   The principle of consistency is most likely to be useful where the language is ambiguous. In *Re Birks*,[28] Lindley MR said:

> "I do not know whether it is law or a canon of construction but it is good sense to say that whenever in a deed or will or other document you find that a word used in one part of it has some clear and definite meaning, then the presumption is that it is intended to mean the same thing where, when used in another part of the document, its meaning is not clear."

But in *Watson v Haggitt*,[29] Lord Warrington of Clyffe, delivering the advice of the Privy Council, said:

> "The contention of the appellant and the judgments of the two judges who decided in his favour are based upon a supposed rule of construction that the same meaning ought to be given to an expression in every part of the document in which it appears. ... The truth is there is no such rule of general application as is contended for by the appellant. A difficulty or ambiguity may be resolved by resorting to such a device, but it is only in such cases that it is necessary or permissible to do so."

7.17   Sometimes it may be clear from the contract that the same word is used in different senses, even in the same clause.[30] So in *Tea Trade Properties Ltd v CIN Properties Ltd*,[31] Hoffmann J said:

---

[25]   [2014] EWCA Civ 150; [2014] C.I.L.L. 3488.
[26]   [2011] EWCA Civ 837.
[27]   [2018] UKSC 55; [2019] I.C.R. 495.
[28]   [1900] 1 Ch. 417.
[29]   [1928] A.C. 127.
[30]   In *British Energy Power and Trading Ltd v Credit Suisse* [2008] EWCA Civ 53, the same word was given different meanings in different parts of the contract.
[31]   [1990] 1 E.G.L.R. 155.

"The word 'payable' as used in this lease has two distinct meanings and sometimes it is used in one sense and sometimes in the other. It can mean either 'accruing from time to time' or 'falling due for payment'. So, for example, when the reddendum speaks of 'the rent payable immediately prior to the appropriate review date' it means the rent which was accruing due from time to time immediately prior to the appropriate review date. It had fallen due not immediately prior to the rent review date but a quarter earlier. On the other hand, when the same clause goes on to say 'such rent always to be payable by equal quarterly instalments', it is using 'payable' in the sense of falling due for payment."

Where the draftsman uses different words in different parts of the document, a converse principle applies. It was put by Diplock LJ in *Prestcold (Central) Ltd v Minister of Labour*[32] as follows: **7.18**

"the habit of a legal draftsman is to eschew synonyms. He uses the same words throughout the document to express the same thing or concept and consequently if he uses different words the presumption is that he means a different thing or concept ... a legal draftsman aims at uniformity in the structure of his draft."

To the extent that there are such presumptions, they apply with less force to a contract which has been drafted by many hands rather than by one. So in *Lindsay (WN) & Co Ltd v European Grain & Shipping Agency Ltd*,[33] Diplock LJ said: **7.19**

"As is the case with many standard commercial contracts which have evolved piecemeal over the years, the drafting is not self-consistent, and the nomenclature employed is not uniform. The usual presumption that the same word is used throughout the contract in the same meaning is less strong than in the case of a contract drafted at one time by a single draftsman."

Similarly, in *Shop Distributive & Allied Employees' Association v Woolworths Ltd*,[34] in interpreting a collective agreement, Gray ACJ said:

"If the presumption of consistent use of terminology is so weak in legislative drafting, it must be even weaker in the context of a Certified Agreement. Typically, such agreements are the product of hard negotiation, in which wording of particular clauses is often agreed without reference to other provisions of the same document. Provisions are commonly transmitted from one agreement to the next in a series, without regard to whether their terminology sits well with the words used in newly adopted terms. The use of other agreements, and awards, as precedents can often result in the borrowing of provisions, again without regard to whether the words used in them are consistent with the rest of the agreement under consideration. For these and other reasons, consistency will often be absent. It is easy to see that the same word can be used in different provisions with different meanings."

---

[32] [1969] 1 W.L.R. 89 (a case of statutory construction) applied to the JCT form of contract in *Jarvis (John) Ltd v Rockdale Housing Association Ltd* (1986) 3 Const. L.J. 24.
[33] [1963] 1 Lloyd's Rep. 437.
[34] (2006) 151 F.C.R. 513 at [26]. See also *WN Lindsay and Co Ltd v European Grain Shipping Agency Ltd* [1963] 1 Lloyd's Rep. 437 at 443.

7.20   In some cases a reading of the contract as a whole may result in one clause taking effect subject to another apparently inconsistent clause. In *Howe v Botwood*,[35] a lease imposed a covenant on the tenant to pay outgoings and assessments, and a covenant on the landlord to keep the exterior of the property in repair. The sanitary authority served notice requiring a drain to be replaced. Channell J said:

> "The expense of executing the work would under this covenant fall on the [landlord]. If therefore that covenant stood alone without the covenant by the [tenant] that is how I would construe it. That covenant, however, has to be read with the earlier covenant by the tenant to pay and discharge all outgoings. There are thus two covenants, one placing the burden on the tenant and the other placing it on the landlord. We must construe the lease as a whole so as to make it consistent in both its parts. In my opinion the covenant by the tenant must be read as if it contained the words 'except such as are by this lease imposed on the landlord'. By reading that exception into the covenant the two covenants can be read together."

In *Re Media Entertainment & Arts Alliance, Ex p. Hoyts Corp Pty Ltd (No.1)*,[36] the High Court of Australia held that:

> "A conflict ... involving apparently inconsistent provisions in the one instrument, is to be resolved, if at all possible, on the basis that one provision qualifies the other and, hence, that both have meaning and effect. ... That rule is an aspect of the general rule that an instrument must be read as a whole...".

In *Duval v 11–13 Randolph Crescent Ltd*,[37] a lease contained both an absolute covenant and a qualified covenant against alterations. Read literally, there was an overlap between the two. The Supreme Court held that alterations falling within the scope of the qualified covenant must be taken to have been excluded from the scope of the absolute covenant.

7.21   The context of the document as a whole will not usually override the plain meaning of the words used. In *Multi-Link Leisure Developments Ltd v Lanarkshire Council*,[38] Lord Hope said:

> "The court's task is to ascertain the intention of the parties by examining the words they used and giving them their ordinary meaning in their contractual context. It must start with what is given by the parties themselves when it is conducting this exercise. Effect is to be given to every word, so far as possible, in the order in which they appear in the clause in question. Words should not be added which are not there, and words which are there should not be changed, taken out or moved from the place in the clause where they have been put by the

---

[35] [1913] 2 K.B. 387 DC. See also *Arding v Economic Printing Co* (1898) 79 L.T. 622.
[36] (1993) 178 C.L.R. 379 at 386–387. See also *Fitzgerald v Masters* (1956) 95 C.L.R. 420 at 437; *Australian Guarantee Corp Ltd v Balding* (1930) 43 C.L.R. 140 at 152.
[37] [2020] UKSC 18.
[38] [2010] UKSC 47. Lord Hope's summary of principle was endorsed and applied by the Supreme Court in *Barts and the London NHS Trust v Verma* [2013] UKSC 20; [2013] I.C.R. 727. Professor McLauchlan has argued that Lord Hope's statement of principle is inconsistent with Lord Hoffmann's five principles of interpretation: "A construction conundrum?" (2011) L.M.C.L.Q. 428; but more recent cases in the Supreme Court have placed greater weight on the language of a professionally drawn document.

parties. It may be necessary to do some of these things at a later stage to make sense of the language. But this should not be done until it has become clear that the language the parties actually used creates an ambiguity which cannot be solved otherwise."

In *Hume v Rendell*,[39] Leach VC said:

"In the construction of all instruments it is the duty of the court not to confine itself to the force of a particular expression, but to collect the intention from the whole instrument taken together. But a court is not authorized to deviate from the force of a particular expression, unless it finds, in other parts of the instrument, expressions which manifest that the author of the instrument could not have had the intention which the literal force of a particular expression would impute to him. However capricious may be the intention which is clearly expressed, every court is bound by it, unless it be plainly controlled by other parts of the instrument."

In *Homburg Houtimport BV v Agrosin Private Ltd*,[40] Lord Hoffmann propounded **7.22** an unorthodox approach. The issue was whether a description of the parties on the front of a bill of lading overrode the "small print" on the back. The majority of the House of Lords decided that it did, applying the well-known principle that terms selected by the parties themselves override standard printed terms. However, Lord Hoffmann said:

"I respectfully think that where the majority judgments ... in the Court of Appeal went wrong is that they conscientiously set about trying, as lawyers naturally would, to construe the bill of lading as a whole. In fact the reasonable reader of a bill of lading does not construe it as a whole. For some things he goes no further than what it says on the front. If the words there are reasonably sufficient to communicate the information in question, he does not trouble with the back. It is only if the information on the front is insufficient, or the questions which concern the reader relate to matters which do not ordinarily appear on the front, that he turns to the back. And then he calls in his lawyers to construe the document as a whole."

It is not thought that this approach is generally applicable to commercial contracts.

This principle may be difficult to apply where the contract in question has been **7.23** redacted. Henderson LJ said in *Hancock v Promontoria (Chestnut) Ltd*[41]:

"I have much sympathy with the general thrust of the submission, which I take to be that where the court is called upon to resolve a question of construction of a contractual document, the document must in all normal circumstances be placed before the court as a whole, and it is not for the parties or their solicitors to make a pre-emptive judgment about what parts of the document are irrelevant. Sometimes, ... it may be obvious that they can properly be omitted or blanked out; but even then a clear explanation must in my view be provided of the nature

---

[39] (1824) 2 S. & St. 174.
[40] [2004] 1 A.C. 715 HL.
[41] [2020] EWCA Civ 907.

and extent of the omissions, and the reasons for making them. In general, irrelevance alone cannot be a proper ground for redaction of part of a document which the court is asked to construe, and there must be some additional feature (such as protection of privacy or confidentiality, but no doubt there are others too) which can be relied upon to justify the redaction."

Illustrations

1.   A lease contained a covenant restricting the use of the demised property to use as a private dwelling-house. It also contained a covenant prohibiting subletting or parting with possession of the premises without consent. The question was whether the tenant was entitled to sublet part only of the premises without consent. The Court of Appeal said no. Harman J said:

"The covenants in a lease must be construed by reference to the covenants which follow or precede them; thus where a covenant not to use otherwise than as a private dwelling house is followed by a covenant against subletting a part without consent, you must construe the first by reference to the second."

Dobbs v Linford[42]

2.   Shipowners agreed to charter a named ship to charterers for a series of voyages. The charterparty entitled the owners to substitute a ship of similar size at any time before or during the charterparty. The question arose whether the owners were limited to making one substitution. The Court of Appeal held that they were not. Romer LJ said:

"I think that if one took cl. 38 alone, one could legitimately construe it either in the way contended for by the charterers or in the way relied on by the owners without doing undue violence to the language used. But it is not permissible to construe one clause in isolation from the others."

SA Maritime et Commerciale of Geneva v Anglo-Iranian Oil Co Ltd[43]

3.   A bill of lading contained two exception clauses. The first exempted the shipowner from liability for damage to goods whether arising from a defect existing at the time of the shipment or not, or from the neglect of the master or crew, or from any other cause whatsoever. The second clause exempted the owners from liability for similar damage if reasonable means had been taken against such defects. The question arose whether the clauses exempted the owner from liability in respect of a cargo tainted with the disinfectant with which the ship had been disinfected before shipment. The House of Lords held that they did not. Lord Halsbury LC said:

"It seems to me that if what has been called the large print clause had stood alone I should not have had the smallest doubt that it would have carried the shipowner the whole way. I can give no other construction to it than that which the words express; but the difficulty in his way is that he has thought proper to execute an instrument which has two different sets of phrases in it, and one rule of construc-

---

[42]   [1953] 1 Q.B. 48.
[43]   [1954] 1 W.L.R. 492.

tion which must prevail is that you must give effect to every part of a document if you can—you must read it as a whole."

Elderslie Steamship Co Ltd v Borthwick[44]

4.   Clause 6 of a charterparty provided that on arrival at customary anchorage at each port the master was to give notice of readiness to load, berth or no berth, and that laytime should commence six hours after receipt of such notice or the vessel's arrival in berth, whichever occurred first. However, when delay was caused to the vessel getting into berth for any reason over which the charterer had no control that delay was not to count as laytime. Clause 9 provided that the vessel was to load at any safe place reachable on arrival which should be designated and procured by the charterer. The charterer argued that "berth" in cl.6 meant any berth; but the House of Lords held that, reading the contract as a whole, it meant the berth designated and procured under cl.9. Since the charterer had not procured a berth it was not protected by cl.6.

The Laura Prima[45]

5.   A franchise agreement stated that "to be reasonable for both parties to develop and invest in a viable business development plan an initial term of three years (with the fee reviewed annually) must be agreed". It also provided for the contact to be terminable without reasons on four months' notice. It was held that notice could not be given to terminate the contract earlier than the expiry of the three-year period.

Thorney Park Golf Ltd (t/a Laleham Golf Club) v Myers Catering Ltd[46]

3.   Giving Effect to all Parts of a Contract

In interpreting a contract all parts of it must be given effect where possible, and no part of it should be treated as inoperative or surplus.[47]

The interpretation of a document as a whole necessarily involves giving effect to each part of it in relation to all other parts of it. Accordingly, as a corollary of the principle that a document must be interpreted as a whole, effect must be given to each part of the document. This in turn means that in general each part of the document is taken to have been deliberately inserted, having regard to all the other parts of the document, with the result that there is a presumption against redundant

7.24

---

[44]   [1905] A.C. 93.
[45]   [1981] 3 All E.R. 737.
[46]   [2015] EWCA Civ 19.
[47]   This section was referred to with approval in *Newall v Lewis* [2008] 4 Costs L.R. 626; *Programme Holdings Pty Ltd v Van Gogh Holdings Pty Ltd* [2009] WASC 79; *Jerram Falkus Construction Ltd v Fenice Developments Ltd* [2011] EWHC 1935 (TCC); 138 Con. L.R. 21; *Phoenix Life Assurance Ltd v Financial Services Authority* [2013] EWHC 60 (Comm); and *Merthyr (South Wales) Ltd v Merthyr Tydfil County Borough Council* [2019] EWCA Civ 526. See also *Secretary of State for Defence v Turner Estate Solutions Ltd* [2015] EWHC 1150 (TCC). Compare the *European Principles of Contract Law*, para.5:106: "An interpretation which makes the terms of the contract lawful, or effective, is to be preferred to one which would not". The Unidroit Principles of International Commercial Contracts state at para.4.5: "Contract terms shall be interpreted so as to give effect to all the terms rather than to deprive some of them of effect".

words (usually called "surplusage").[48] This principle is sometimes labelled the argument from redundancy. Although this principle was often given weight in earlier cases, its value is much reduced in more modern cases. As Patten LJ put it in *Al-Hasawi v Nottingham Forest Football Club Ltd*,[49] "arguments based on surplusage or redundancy are rarely reliable or sure ground on issues of construction".

7.25   In *Re Strand Music Hall Co Ltd*,[50] Lord Romilly MR said:

"The proper mode of construing any written instrument is, to give effect to every part of it, if this be possible, and not to strike out or nullify one clause in a deed, unless it be impossible to reconcile it with another and more express clause in the same deed."

So also in *SA Maritime et Commerciale of Geneva v Anglo-Iranian Oil Co Ltd*,[51] Somervell LJ said:

"Although one finds surplusage in contracts, deeds and Acts of Parliament, one leans towards treating words as adding something, rather than as mere surplusage."

In *Dwr Cymru Cyfyngedig (Welsh Water) v Corus UK Ltd*,[52] Moore-Bick LJ said:

"In my view what points most strongly to the conclusion that they intended clause 17 to have contractual effect is the very fact that they chose to include it in the Agreement. Surplusage is by no means unknown in commercial contracts, of course, but it is unusual for parties to include in the operative part of a formal agreement of this kind a whole clause which is not intended to have contractual effect of any kind. One starts, therefore, from the presumption that it was intended to have some effect on the parties' rights and obligations."

7.26   In *Bindra v Chopra*,[53] Etherton J said that the approach of the courts is to try to give effect to each and every part of an agreement or instrument freely negotiated and entered into between parties, rather than to reject outright part of it as having no legal effect. Thus cl.1 of a deed of trust was given a meaning consistent with cl.4 of the same deed, rather than a meaning which would have made cl.4 ineffective. His decision was upheld by the Court of Appeal.[54] In *Beckett Investment Management Group Ltd v Hall*,[55] Maurice Kay LJ described a construction which would have deprived a provision of the contract of any practical effect as "futile". Likewise, in *Jani-King (GB) Ltd v Pula Enterprises Ltd*,[56] Judge Coulson QC said that a court should always "think long and hard before arriving at a construction

---

[48] The presumption against surplusage is "not the strongest of weapons": *The Marielle Bolten* [2010] 1 Lloyd's Rep. 648 at 654.
[49] [2019] EWCA Civ 2242.
[50] (1865) 35 Beav. 153, applied in *Singapore Airlines Ltd v Buck Consultants Ltd* [2011] EWHC 59 (Ch). The principle was accepted on appeal: [2011] EWCA Civ 1542; [2012] Pens. L.R. 1. The principle was also applied in *Morris v Blackpool Borough Council* [2014] EWCA Civ 1384; [2015] L. & T.R. 6.
[51] [1954] 1 W.L.R. 492.
[52] [2007] EWCA Civ 285; *PBS Energo AS v Bester Generacion UK Ltd* [2020] EWHC 223 (TCC).
[53] (2008) 11 I.T.E.L.R. 312.
[54] *Chopra v Bindra* [2009] W.T.L.R. 781.
[55] [2007] I.C.R. 1539.
[56] [2008] 1 All E.R. (Comm) 451.

which renders otiose a part of the written agreement"; although he also noted that the presumption against surplusage is relatively weak.[57] In *Costain Ltd v Tarmac Holdings Ltd*,[58] one reason why Coulson J rejected a suggested interpretation was that it would have "put a red line" through another clause in the contract.

However, in *Secretary of State for Defence v Turner Estate Solutions Ltd*,[59] the same judge said that although a presumption against surplusage was of little weight in interpreting a standard form of contract it has a part to play in the case of "a bespoke contract carefully drafted by the parties to meet the exigencies of this particular and significant commercial arrangement".

7.27

Thus, as Gross LJ pointed out in *ENER-G Holdings Plc v Hormell*[60]:

7.28

"... despite the desirability and importance of certainty, a good many commercial contracts are less tidy than might be desirable as a matter of strict theory. In this respect, commercial contracts reflect the realities of commercial life. It is thus no surprise to find in a commercial contract surplus language, for instance that which merely states the obvious."

In *Mutual Energy Ltd v Starr Underwriting Agents Ltd*,[61] Coulson J observed that while the court should strive to give effect to all parts of a contract, the presumption against surplusage was not a "hard edged" rule. He added:

"... the court should guard against giving such a rule too much prominence in circumstances where, as we all know, some tautology, some overlapping terms, some surplusage, will often be found in commercial contracts."

In *Spire Healthcare Ltd v Royal & Sun Alliance Insurance Plc*,[62] HH Judge Waksman QC referred to:

"... the caution that is to be exercised before applying the so-called 'argument from redundancy' in the context of commercial contracts, particularly those containing standard terms."

More generally, in *Total Transport Corp v Arcadia Petroleum Ltd*,[63] Staughton LJ said:

"It is well-established that the presumption against surplusage is of little value in the interpretation of commercial contracts."

Likewise, in *Antigua Power Co Ltd v Attorney General of Antigua and Barbuda*,[64] Lord Neuberger said that:

---

[57] See also *The Marielle Bolten* [2010] 1 Lloyd's Rep. 648 at 654.
[58] [2017] EWHC 319 (TCC); [2017] 1 Lloyd's Rep. 331.
[59] [2015] EWHC 1150 (TCC).
[60] [2012] EWCA Civ 1059.
[61] [2016] EWHC 590 (TCC); 165 Con. L.R. 220.
[62] [2016] EWHC 3278 (Comm); [2016] 2 C.L.C. 1002.
[63] [1998] 1 Lloyd's Rep. 351 at 357; *Masri v Consolidated Contractors International Co SAL* [2007] EWCA Civ 688; *Antiparos ENE v SK Shipping Co Ltd* [2008] 2 Lloyd's Rep. 237.
[64] [2013] UKPC 23. Longmore LJ made the same point in *Swallowfalls Ltd v Monaco Yachting & Technologies SAM* [2014] EWCA Civ 186.

"... on issues of interpretation, arguments based on surplusage are rarely of much force."

7.29   In relation to some kinds of document, such as conveyancing documents, the presumption is particularly weak. Thus it has been observed that a "torrential" style of drafting[65] has been traditional for many years in leases[66] and conveyances[67]; and that "most draftsmen tend to over-egg the pudding."[68] The same style also surfaces in insurance policies.[69] In such cases the court cannot insist on giving each word in a series a distinct meaning because:

"Draftsmen frequently use many words either because it is traditional to do so or out of a sense of caution so that nothing which could conceivably fall within the general concept which they have in mind should be left out."

More graphically, in *Tea Trade Properties Ltd v CIN Properties Ltd*,[70] Hoffmann J said:

"I have never found the presumption against superfluous language particularly useful in the construction of leases. The draftsmen traditionally employ linguistic overkill and try to obliterate the conceptual target by using a number of phrases expressing more or less the same idea."

7.30   So also in *Tektrol Ltd v International Insurance Co of Hanover Ltd*,[71] an insurance policy excluded liability for "erasure loss distortion or corruption of information on computer systems". One question was whether theft of a computer which stored information fell within the clause. Buxton LJ said:

"The judge was attracted to his reading of the exclusion by the consideration that the word 'loss' would be redundant if purely physical loss were not covered by it, since electronic interference, such as by a hacker, was already fully covered by 'erasure distortion or corruption' of information. I consider that that attributes to the draftsman too precise a use of language. There are already redundancies or potential redundancies in the clause: in particular, one would be hard pressed to provide a definition of the two terms that clearly distinguished 'distortion' of computer information from 'corruption' of computer information. The very strong impression is that the draftsman used all of these overlapping phrases to ensure that he had not omitted any case in which the information on the computer systems or on the records programmes or software was interfered with by electronic means."

7.31   Equally, it has been held that the presumption against surplusage is never very strong when construing charterparties.[72] Indeed, it has been said that draftsmen of

65   That is, a style in which a torrent of words are used.
66   *Norwich Union Life Insurance Society v British Railways Board* [1987] 2 E.G.L.R. 137.
67   *GLN (Copenhagen) Southern Ltd v ABC Cinemas Ltd* [2004] EWCA Civ 1279.
68   *British Overseas Bank Nominees Ltd v Analytical Properties Ltd* [2015] EWCA Civ 43.
69   *Tektrol Ltd v International Insurance Co of Hanover Ltd* [2005] 2 Lloyd's Rep. 701.
70   [1990] 1 E.G.L.R. 155.
71   [2005] 2 Lloyd's Rep. 701.
72   *Royal Greek Government v Minister of Transport* (1949) 83 Ll.L. Rep. 228 at 235; *The Pera* [1985] 2 Lloyd's Rep. 103 CA; *Total Transport Corp v Arcadia Petroleum Ltd* [1998] 1 Lloyd's Rep. 351

charterparties use linguistic overkill as much as draftsmen of leases, so that arguments from redundancy carry little weight.[73]

One reason for this is that charterparties are built up of clauses generally agreed in the trade, and when they are added to or varied from time to time, the commercial draftsmen do not pay much attention to overlapping and are not afraid of repetition.[74]

The presumption against surplusage is also unlikely to be useful in interpreting a standard form of contract whose form has evolved over the years. In *Beaufort Developments (NI) Ltd v Gilbert-Ash (NI) Ltd*,[75] Lord Hoffmann said: **7.32**

"This is the argument from redundancy; the parties are presumed not to say anything unnecessarily and unless the decisions of the architect were binding, there would be no need to confer upon the arbitrator an express power to open up, review and revise them.

I think, my Lords, that the argument from redundancy is seldom an entirely secure one. The fact is that even in legal documents (or, some might say, especially in legal documents) people often use superfluous words. Sometimes the draftsmanship is clumsy; more often the cause is a lawyer's desire to be certain that every conceivable point has been covered. One has only to read the covenants in a traditional lease to realise that draftsmen lack inhibition about using too many words. I have no wish to add to the anthology of adverse comments on the drafting of the J.C.T. Standard Form Contract. In the case of a contract which has been periodically renegotiated, amended and added to over many years, it is unreasonable to expect that there will be no redundancies or loose ends."

Similarly, in *Arbuthnott v Fagan*,[76] Hoffmann LJ said in relation to an agreement between Lloyds' names and underwriters:

"In a document like this, however, little weight should be given to an argument based on redundancy. It is a common consequence of a determination to make sure that one has obliterated the conceptual target. The draftsman wanted to leave no loophole for counter-attack by the recipient or intended recipient of a call. It is no justification for construing the language so as to apply to a situation which, on a fair reading of the general purpose of the clause was not within the target area."

In *Macquarie Internationale Investments Ltd v Glencore UK Ltd*,[77] Lord Neuberger of Abbottsbury MR summarised the principle as follows: **7.33**

---

at 357 CA.

[73] *BP Oil International Ltd v Target Shipping Ltd* [2012] EWHC 1590 (Comm); [2012] 2 Lloyd's Rep. 245.

[74] See *Royal Greek Government v Minister of Transport* (1949) 83 Ll.L. Rep. 228 at 235.

[75] [1999] 1 A.C. 266 at 273–274.

[76] [1995] C.L.C. 1396. See also *Tektrol Ltd v International Insurance Co of Hanover Ltd* [2005] 2 Lloyd's Rep. 701 (insurance policy); *Milton Furniture Ltd v Brit Insurance Ltd* [2015] EWCA Civ 671 (insurance policy).

[77] [2010] EWCA Civ 697, applied in *INEOS Manufacturing Scotland Ltd v Grangemouth Chp Ltd* [2011] EWHC 163 (Comm).

"At different stages of his judicial career Lord Hoffmann, whose contributions to the law of interpretation of contracts, as in so many other areas, has been as remarkable for their perception of analysis as for their elegance of expression, has made illuminating observations on the topic of redundancy. At first instance, in *Norwich Union Life Insurance Society v British Railways Board*[78] he referred to the 'torrential drafting' of leasehold repairing covenants. In the Court of Appeal in *Arbuthnott v Fagan*,[79] discussing Lloyds' agency agreements, he stated that 'little weight should be given to an argument based on redundancy', which he said was 'a common consequence of a determination to make sure that one has obliterated the conceptual target'. And, as Lord Hoffmann in *Beaufort Developments (NI) Ltd v Gilbert-Ash (NI) Ltd*,[80] when discussing a JCT Standard Form, he described 'the argument from redundancy' as 'seldom ... entirely secure', because of 'a lawyer's desire to make sure that every conceivable point has been covered'. These remarks apply, in my view, with as much force to contractual warranties in sales of companies and businesses, perhaps particularly when it comes to the reliability of accounts."

7.34   In *Re Lehman Bros International (Europe) (in administration) (No.4)*[81] concerned the meaning of a phrase in a subordinated loan agreement. Lord Neuberger said:

"... the fact that an expression in a sentence, especially in a very full document, does not, on analysis, have much, if any, effect if it is given its natural meaning is not, at least on its own, a very attractive or a very convincing reason for giving it an unnatural meaning. As Lord Hoffmann put it in *Beaufort Developments (NI) Ltd v Gilbert Ash NI Ltd*, 'the argument from redundancy is seldom an entirely secure one. The fact is that even in legal documents (or, some might say, especially in legal documents) people often use superfluous words'.

    And, if one has to choose between giving a phrase little meaning or an unnatural meaning, then, in the absence of a good reason to the contrary, the former option appears to me to be preferable."

7.35   Even where the presumption is of some value, an argument based on surplusage cannot justify the attribution of a meaning that the contract, interpreted as a whole, cannot bear.[82]

7.36   Even if a contractual provision is redundant, it remains part of the contract and may illuminate the meaning to be given to other parts of the contract.[83] It "cannot be airbrushed out of it simply because there has been duplication".[84]

---

[78] [1987] 2 E.G.L.R. 137 at 138D.

[79] [1995] C.L.C. 1396 at 1404D–E.

[80] [1999] A.C. 266, 274B–D.

[81] [2017] UKSC 38; [2018] A.C. 465.

[82] This proposition was approved in *Merthyr (South Wales) Ltd v Merthyr Tydfil County Borough Council* [2019] EWCA Civ 526 and *Minera Las Bambas SA v Glencore Queensland Ltd* [2019] EWCA Civ 972; [2019] S.T.C. 1642. See also *Landesbank Hessen-Thuringen Girozentrale v Bayerische Landesbank* [2014] EWHC 1404 (Comm).

[83] *Barnardo's v Buckinghamshire* [2016] EWCA Civ 1064; [2017] Pen. L.R. 2.

[84] [2018] UKSC 55; [2019] I.C.R. 495.

Illustration

A lease contained provisions for rent review. One clause provided that if the landlord had not applied within a stipulated time limit for the appointment of an expert, then his notice invoking his right to review the rent would become void. The county court judge construed the lease as though that clause had not been there. On appeal, Stephenson LJ said:

"I have not the smallest hesitation in saying that no principle of construction and no authority of any court compels or even justifies a judge in finding one paragraph in a written document (in this case a sealed lease) to have no effect. Effect must be given to the paragraph if it possibly can be."

Lewis v Barnett[85]

4. Standard Printed Terms and Special Terms

Where the contract is a standard form of contract to which the parties have added special conditions, then unless the contract otherwise provides[86] greater weight must be given to the special conditions, and in case of conflict between the general conditions and the special conditions, the latter will prevail.[87] However, in interpreting a standard form there is less room for the influence of the special background applicable to any particular transaction.

In *Homburg Houtimport BV v Agrosin Private Ltd (The Starsin)*,[88] Lord Bingham of Cornhill said that: **7.37**

"it is common sense that greater weight should attach to terms which the particular contracting parties have chosen to include in the contract than to pre-printed terms probably devised to cover very many situations to which the particular contracting parties have never addressed their minds."

Two hundred years earlier, in *Robertson v French*,[89] Lord Ellenborough CJ had said:

"The only difference between policies of assurance and other instruments in this respect is that the greater part of the printed language of them being invariable and uniform has acquired from use and practice a known and definite meaning, and that the word superadded in writing (subject indeed always to be governed in point of construction by the language and terms with which they are accompanied) are entitled nevertheless, if there should be any reasonable doubt

85 (1982) 264 E.G. 1079.
86 This proposition was approved in *Fenice Investments Inc v Jerram Falkus Construction Ltd* (2009) 128 Con. L.R. 124.
87 Compare the *Principles of European Contract Law*, para.5:104: "Terms which have been individually negotiated take preference over those which are not".
88 [2004] 1 A.C. 715; *Bovis Lend Lease Ltd v Cofely Engineering Services* [2009] EWHC 1120 (TCC). The principle was also applied in *Cubitt Building and Interiors Ltd v Richardson Roofing (Industrial) Ltd* (2008) 119 Con. L.R. 137; *Jani-King (GB) Ltd v Pula Enterprises Ltd* [2008] 1 All E.R. (Comm) 451; and *Jacobs UK Ltd v Skidmore Owings & Merrill LLP* [2008] EWHC 2847 (TCC).
89 (1803) 4 East. 130; *The Brabant* [1967] 1 Q.B. 588 at 600.

upon the sense and meaning of the whole, to have a greater effect attributed to them than to the printed words, inasmuch as the written words are the immediate language and terms selected by the parties themselves for the expression of their meaning, and the printed words are a general formality adapted equally to their case and that of all contracting parties upon similar occasions and subjects."

Similarly, in *The Athinoula*,[90] Mocatta J said:

"Clause 18 … is a typed clause, whereas cl. 8 is a printed clause; and where there is a conflict between two such clauses it is well established that the typed clause should prevail."

In *The Starsin*[91] in the Court of Appeal Rix LJ referred to:

"the well known maxim of construction that written, stamped or typed words which are inconsistent with printed terms usually take effect by superseding the latter."

7.38   This principle has often been put on a broader basis, namely that:

"if one party puts forward a printed form of words for signature by the other, and it is afterwards found that those words are inconsistent with the main object and intention of the transaction as disclosed by the terms specially agreed, the court will limit or reject the printed words so as to ensure that the main object of the transaction is achieved."[92]

This basis stems from the decision of the House of Lords in *Glynn v Margetson & Co*,[93] in which Lord Herschell LC said:

"Where general words are used in a printed form which are obviously intended to apply, so far as they are applicable, to the circumstances of a particular contract which particular contract is to be embodied in or introduced into that printed form, I think you are justified in looking at the main object and intent of the contract and in limiting the general words used, having in view that object and intent."

In the same case, Lord Halsbury LC said that:

"one must reject words, indeed whole provisions, if they are inconsistent with what one assumes to be the main purpose of the contract."

7.39   Although these words are on the face of it very wide, it is submitted that they are to be taken as confined to cases involving printed forms or other standard form contracts and do not entitle the court to make assumptions about the main purpose of a contract independently of the words of the contract itself, interpreted in the light

---

90 [1980] 2 Lloyd's Rep. 481.
91 [2001] 1 Lloyd's Rep. 437 (a dissenting judgment), approved by the *HL* [2004] 1 A.C. 715.
92 *Neuchatel Asphalte Co Ltd v Barnett* [1957] 1 W.L.R. 357, per Denning LJ.
93 [1893] A.C. 351.

of the relevant background. This is made clear by the speech of Lord Halsbury himself, five years earlier in *Leader v Duffy*.[94]

However, the parties may agree in the printed terms themselves that written provisions appended to the printed terms are not to modify or override the printed terms.[95] If they do so, the court will give effect to their agreement, even though this is contrary to the normal principle.[96] Where all the terms are standard terms the mere fact that the parties have selected some only of the possible range of standard terms does not bring this principle into play.[97]   **7.40**

The principle only applies where there is a conflict between printed and written terms. As Langley J explained in *Bayoil SA v Seawind Tankers Corp*[98]:   **7.41**

"The Courts will ... seek to construe a contract as a whole and if a reasonable commercial construction of the whole can reconcile two provisions (whether typed or printed) then such a construction can and in my judgment should be adopted."

Thus where parties have contracted on the basis of both standard terms and special terms, the court should try to arrive at an interpretation which is consistent with both. In *Alchemy Estates Ltd v Astor*,[99] Sales J said: **7.42**

"It is true that special terms take precedence over standard conditions if there is a clear conflict between them. ... However, where the parties have adopted both standard conditions and special conditions, and have not indicated that the standard conditions they have adopted are to be displaced in some respect by a special condition and there is no necessary inconsistency between them, then it appears that the parties' intention is that the standard conditions and the special conditions should be interpreted together as parts of one coherent contractual scheme."

Similarly, in *Rivat Pty Ltd v B&N Elomar Engineering Pty Ltd*,[100] Hamilton J said:

"In my view, what flows from these principles is that, whilst clearly inconsistent provisions of the printed form must be treated as excluded by the typed provisions, the operation of the printed clauses should be preserved so far as is possible. The Court should not lightly accede to a submission that the typed provision covers the field and excludes in whole the corresponding printed clause, if parts of that provision can coexist with the typed clause and still be given effect."

In *Ace Capital Ltd v CMS Energy Corp*,[101] Christopher Clarke J summarised the

---

94 (1888) 13 App. Cas. 294 at 301 (see para.2.44).
95 This proposition was approved in *Fenice Investments Inc v Jerram Falkus Construction Ltd* (2009) 128 Con. L.R. 124.
96 *English Industrial Estates Corp v George Wimpey & Co Ltd* [1973] 1 Lloyd's Rep. 118; *Pagnan v Tradax Ocean Transportation SA* [1987] 2 Lloyd's Rep. 342; *The Starsin* [2001] 1 Lloyd's Rep. 437.
97 *Milton Furniture Ltd v Brit Insurance Ltd* [2015] EWCA Civ 671.
98 [2001] 1 Lloyd's Rep. 533; *Milton Furniture Ltd v Brit Insurance Ltd* [2015] EWCA Civ 671.
99 [2009] 1 P. & C.R. 5.
100 [2007] NSWSC 638.
101 [2008] 2 C.L.C. 318; *Tri-MG Intra Asia Airlines BV v Norse Air Charter Ltd* [2009] 1 Lloyd's Rep.

approach as follows:

> "The meaning of one clause may be affected by the content of other clauses in the agreement. A clause should not be rejected unless manifestly inconsistent with or repugnant to the rest of the agreement. It is only if this cannot successfully be done that the court will treat a clause that has been specifically agreed as prevailing over an incorporated standard term."

There are dangers in this approach. Foxton J observed in *Generali Italia SPA v Pelagic Fisheries Corporation*[102]:

> "Elsewhere, I have suggested that what might be described as a 'jigsaw' approach to construction, under which all the pieces are to be used if at all possible, can sometimes risk a false equivalence between bespoke and boilerplate contractual provisions. Whatever the merits of seeking to read provisions together as a general rule of construction, however, it is clear that the enthusiasm with which this approach should be pursued will vary between contractual terms, and contractual contexts."

7.43   Where a contract is wholly printed, there is generally no legal significance in different sizes of type.[103] But the font size may be of significance if the question is whether adequate notice has been given of an onerous term[104]; or where the contract is a consumer contract required to comply with the statutory requirement that a written term must be legible.[105]

7.44   Since a standard form is designed for use in a wide variety of transactions, there is less room for the interpretation of the form to be influenced by the background facts applicable to any particular transaction. As Lord Millett explained in *AIB Group (UK) Plc v Martin*[106]:

> "A standard form is designed for use in a wide variety of different circumstances. It is not context-specific. Its value would be much diminished if it could not be relied upon as having the same meaning on all occasions. Accordingly the relevance of the factual background of a particular case to its interpretation is necessarily limited. The danger, of course, is that a standard form may be employed in circumstances for which it was not designed. Unless the context in a particular case shows that this has happened, however, the interpretation of the form ought not to be affected by the factual background."

Similarly, in *Dairy Containers Ltd v Tasman Orient CV*,[107] Lord Bingham of Cornhill said:

> "There may reasonably be attributed to the parties to a contract such as this such general commercial knowledge as a party to such a transaction would ordinarily be expected to have, but with a printed form of contract, negotiable by one

---

258.

[102]   [2020] EWHC 1228 (Comm).
[103]   *Yorkshire Insurance Co Ltd v Campbell* [1917] A.C. 218 (see para.5.118).
[104]   *Goodlife Foods Ltd v Hall Fire Protection Ltd* [2018] EWCA Civ 1371; [2018] B.L.R. 491.
[105]   Consumer Rights Act 2015 s.68(2).
[106]   [2002] 1 W.L.R. 94 (a dissenting judgment).
[107]   [2005] 1 W.L.R. 215.

holder to another, no inference may be drawn as to the knowledge or intention of any particular party. The contract should be given the meaning it would convey to a reasonable person having all the background knowledge which is reasonably available to the person or class of persons to whom the document is addressed."

The use of background facts in relation to standard forms is discussed in para.3.171.　　**7.45**

5. GENERAL PROVISIONS AND SPECIAL PROVISIONS

Where a contract contains general provisions and specific provisions, the specific provisions will be given greater weight than the general provisions where the facts to which the contract is to be applied fall within the scope of the specific provisions

The above proposition is a loose rendering of the maxim "*Generalia non*　　**7.46** *specialibus derogant*".[108] As it was put in one case, "the ... specific provision effectively overwrites the ... generic provision".[109] It has been described as "a principle of common sense".[110]

The principle has been described in Ireland as follows[111]:

"The relevant rule of interpretation is that encapsulated in the maxim *generalia specialibus non derogant*. In plain English, when you find a particular situation dealt with in special terms, and later in the same document you find general words used which could be said to encompass and deal differently with that particular situation, the general words will not, in the absence of an indication of a definite intention to do so, be held to undermine or abrogate the effect of the special words which were used to deal with the particular situation. This is but a commonsense way of giving effect to the true or primary intention of the draftsman, for the general words will usually have been used in inadvertence of the fact that the particular situation has already been specially dealt with."

The principle does not apply unless one of the rival provisions is a general provision and the other is a special provision. Where both are special provisions there is no room for the principle to apply.[112]　　**7.47**

In *Marc Rich & Co AG v Portman*,[113] a charterparty contained two clauses dealing with laytime and demurrage; cl.6 which was general, and cl.8 which concerned the time taken to get into berth. Longmore J said:　　**7.48**

---

[108] The maxim was applied in *Telewest Communications Plc v Customs and Excise Commissioners* [2005] S.T.C. 481 and *Milton Furniture Ltd v Brit Insurance Ltd* [2014] EWHC 965 (QB) (affirmed [2015] EWCA Civ 671); and the principle was referred to in *The Genius Star* [2011] EWHC 3083 (Comm); [2012] 1 Lloyd's Rep. 222. See also *R. (on the application of TW Logistics) v Tendring District Council* [2013] EWCA Civ 9; *Mid Essex Hospital Services NHS Trust v Compass Group* [2013] B.L.R. 265 at [154]; *Portsmouth City Council v Ensign Highways Ltd* [2015] EWHC 1969 (TCC); *Minister of Energy and Energy Affairs v Maharaj* [2020] UKPC 13.
[109] *Towergate Financial (Group) Ltd v Hopkinson* [2020] EWHC 984 (Comm).
[110] *Woodford Land Ltd v Persimmon Homes Ltd* [2011] EWHC 984 (Ch).
[111] *Welch v Bowmaker (Ir) Ltd* [1980] 1 I.R. 251.
[112] *Ilkerler Otomotiv v Perkins Engines Co Ltd* [2017] EWCA Civ 183; [2017] 4 W.L.R. 144.
[113] [1996] 1 Lloyd's Rep. 430.

"... cl. 8 is a general clause relating to laytime and demurrage to much the same effect as cl. 6. Clause 6 deals with a specific part of the time needed for loading and discharging viz. the operation of 'getting into the berth'. This is, therefore, a specific provision which, in case of inconsistency with cl. 8, must prevail on the principle '*Specialibus generalia non derogant*'."

In *Yarm Road Ltd v Hewden Tower Cranes Ltd*,[114] the terms of hire of a crane contained a general indemnity by which the supplier was to indemnify the hirer against loss. The terms also incorporated another indemnity by which the supplier was responsible for loss due to or arising during the erection of the plant on site, provided that it was under the supplier's control. The crane collapsed during its assembly on site. Laws LJ said:

"[W]hereas the cl 11 indemnity is perfectly general, cl 13 is dealing with the distribution of contractual responsibility in the specific context of the hiring of plant; and the rule, crisply expressed in the Latin maxim *Generalia non specialibus derogant*, is that the general is taken to give way to the specific."

7.49   In *Golden Fleece Maritime Inc v ST Shipping and Transport Inc*,[115] Longmore LJ said that a particular provision of a charterparty should be given precedence over introducing words:

"on the basis that the 'particular should prevail over the general' if that is an acceptable translation of well-known legal principle, '*Generalia non specialibus derogant*'."

Likewise, in *Jani-King (GB) Ltd v Pula Enterprises Ltd*,[116] Judge Coulson QC said:

"Again I acknowledge that this construction means that cl 13.1 is redundant. Again, it seems to me that this is the result of using a standard form of words in cl 13 and a 'case-specific' form of words in Sch 1. The specific should outweigh the general in such circumstances, and therefore the wording in Sch 1 must be interpreted as meaning that there was no obligation on the part of the claimant to provide a (further) initial training programme."

7.50   In *Margetson v Glynn*,[117] Fry LJ said:

"This principle is applicable wherever specific words are used to express the main object and intent of the instrument, and in some other part general words are used which in their utmost generality would be inconsistent with and destructive of the main object of the contract. When the Court in dealing with a contract or document of any kind finds that difficulty, it always, so far as I know, follows this principle, that the general words must be limited so that they shall be consistent with and shall not defeat the main object of the contracting parties."

---

[114]   (2003) 90 Con. L.R. 1.
[115]   [2008] 2 Lloyd's Rep. 119.
[116]   [2008] 1 All E.R. (Comm) 451.
[117]   [1892] 1 Q.B. 337, affirmed on appeal [1893] A.C. 351.

Similarly, in *William Sindall Plc v Cambridgeshire County Council*,[118] Hoffmann LJ said:

"It is, of course, a principle of construction that words capable of bearing a very wide meaning may have to be given a narrower construction to reconcile them with other parts of the document. This rule is particularly apposite if the effect of general words would otherwise be to nullify what the parties appear to have contemplated as an important element in the transaction."

In *The Eternity*,[119] David Steel J observed that:

"Whilst it is correct that in the face of a conflict between provisions the more specific and tailored provision should prevail, such only arises if the conflict is clear and direct."

A particular application of this principle is invoked when, on one reading, a general or subsidiary clause in a contract would significantly detract from a benefit apparently conferred by one of the principal clauses. In this context, it is sometimes said that the secondary clause will be construed by reference to the principle of non-derogation from grant.[120]

However, like all principles of interpretation, it may have to yield to the wording of the specific contract.[121] Moreover, where the two clauses deal with exactly the same subject-matter there may be no room for the application of the principle.[122] **7.51**

In *CLP Holding Co Ltd v Singh*,[123] a contract for the sale of land contained both special conditions and general conditions. Special condition 1 stated that the seller would sell and the buyer would buy at the purchase price. The purchase price was defined as £300,000. Special condition 2 incorporated the general conditions of sale, but also stated that where there was a conflict between the general conditions and the agreement or where the general conditions were not consistent with the agreement, the agreement would prevail. The general conditions said that any sum made payable by the contract was exclusive of VAT; and that any obligation to pay money included an obligation to pay VAT. The Court of Appeal held that the general conditions did not require the buyer to pay VAT which subsequently turned out to be due in respect of the purchase price. Although they attached importance to the statement that in case of conflict the special provisions prevailed over the general conditions, they did not identify what they perceived the conflict to be.[124] **7.52**

6.   EXPRESS MENTION OF PART OF SUBJECT-MATTER

Where the contract expressly mentions some things, it is often to be inferred that other things of the same general category which are not expressly mentioned were deliberately omitted. Similar principles apply to the express inclusion of obligations dealing with a particular area of application.[125]

---

[118] [1994] 3 All E.R. 932.
[119] [2009] 1 Lloyd's Rep. 107.
[120] *Apache North Sea Ltd v Ineos FPS Ltd* [2020] EWHC 2081 (Comm).
[121] For example, *Tradax Export SA v Andre et Cie* [1976] 1 Lloyd's Rep. 416.
[122] *Peabody Trust Governors v Reeve* [2009] L. & T.R. 9.
[123] [2014] EWCA Civ 1103.
[124] They also appear to have relied on the conduct of the parties after the making of the contract in order to interpret it. That is not generally a permissible approach.
[125] Cited with apparent approval in *Gregor Fisken Ltd v Carl* [2020] EWHC 1385 (Comm).

7.53   The above proposition can be summarised by the Latin maxim *expressio unius est exclusio alterius*.[126] Thus in *North Stafford Steel Iron and Coal Co (Burslem) Ltd v Ward*,[127] Willes J said:

> "But the ordinary rule, that if authority is given expressly, though by affirmative words, upon a defined condition, the expression of that condition excludes the doing of the act under other circumstances than those so defined: *expressio unius est exclusio alterius*."

7.54   In *Prestcold (Central) Ltd v Minister of Labour*,[128] Lord Diplock described the maxim as one of the "general rules of composition which any writer seeking clarity of expression is likely to follow".[129] Likewise in *SCN Pty Ltd v Smith*,[130] McPherson JA said:

> "... it is hardly necessary to clothe the thought in authority or Latin garb. If one alternative is expressly and specifically mentioned, it rationally tends to exclude the implication of another or of any other."

7.55   In *Continental Bank NA v Aeakos Compania Naviera NA*,[131] a banking agreement contained a clause by which the borrowers submitted to the jurisdiction of the English courts, but the bank reserved the right to take proceedings in other jurisdictions. Steyn LJ said:

> "The juxtaposition of a submission by the appellants to the jurisdiction of the English Courts and the option reserved in favour of the bank to sue elsewhere brings into play the *expressio unius exclusio alterius* canon of construction. It suggests that a similar option in favour of the appellants was deliberately omitted. In our judgment the language of cl. 21.02 evinces a clear intention that the appellants, but not the bank, would be obliged to submit disputes in connection with the loan facility to the English Courts."

In *Re an Arbitration between Hooley Hill Rubber Co Ltd and Royal Insurance Co*,[132] an insurance policy stated: "This policy does not cover ... loss or damage by explosion, except loss or damage caused by explosion of illuminating gas". Bankes LJ said:

> "The exception of one particular kind of explosion from the general exclusion of explosions shows that the parties intended to exclude from the risks covered by the policy all kinds of explosion other than the one expressly excepted."

---

[126] Specific mention of one thing indicates an intention to rule out others: *Minister of Energy and Energy Affairs v Maharaj* [2020] UKPC 13.

[127] (1868) L.R. 3 Exch. 172.

[128] [1969] 1 W.L.R. 89.

[129] This approach contrasts with Lord Hoffmann's dismissal of the maxims of construction as "intellectual baggage".

[130] [2006] QCA 360 at [7].

[131] [1994] 1 Lloyd's Rep. 545; *Middle Eastern Oil v National Bank of Abu Dhabi* [2009] 1 Lloyd's Rep. 251.

[132] [1920] 1 K.B. 257.

In *George Hunt Cranes Ltd v Scottish Boiler and General Insurance Co Ltd*,[133] **7.56**
the question was whether a term in an insurance policy which required claims to
be made within a certain time limit was a condition precedent to the liability of
insurers. Potter LJ said:

"In this connection it is frequently pointed out that in relation to clauses of this
kind, if the contract states that the condition is a 'condition precedent' or a 'condition of liability', that is influential but not decisive as to its status, especially when
the label condition precedent is attached on an indiscriminate basis for a number
of terms of different nature and varying importance in the policy. One may at
once observe that that is not the case here. It is also the position that where, in a
policy, individual terms are described as conditions precedent, while others are
not, the label is more likely to be respected in relation to a clause expressly so
identified; for instance, *Stoneham v The Ocean Railway and General Accident
Insurance Co*.[134] However, where one clause is labelled 'condition precedent',
and a question arises as to the status of a clause not so labelled, the latter is not,
ipso facto, precluded from being regarded as such. If, as in this case, the wording of the clause is apt to make its intention unambiguously clear, then in my
view the absence of the rubric need not be fatal. As with any other contract, the
task of construction requires one to construe the policy as a whole."

This principle was one strand in the reasoning of the Court of Appeal in *Port of* **7.57**
Tilbury (London) Ltd v Stora Enso Transport & Distribution Ltd,[135] and in *Chin-
nock v Hocaoglu*.[136] In *Shell UK Ltd v Total UK Ltd*,[137] the question was whether
an indemnity clause covered negligence. Waller LJ said:

"We believe that the right approach is to consider the language used in the various agreements. We say straight away, we are not inclined unless driven to it to
contemplate that where detailed agreements are drawn up, one will have been
tacitly extended or by implication extended. We suggest that where parties have
drawn up a series of detailed agreements and the draftsmen have expressly dealt
with negligence, a more significant canon of construction is that which would
suggest that where it has not been expressly referred to that would be likely to
be a deliberate decision by the draftsman to exclude negligence."

The principal is not a rule of law, but merely a principle of interpretation, which **7.58**
like all other such principles, is no more than a guide to the true meaning of the
contract.[138] A principle of this kind cannot "easily subvert the dominant rationality
of the purpose of a general provision".[139] Even at its highest it can be no more than
a presumption. In *Aspdin v Austin*,[140] Lord Denman CJ said:

"Where parties have entered into written engagements, it is manifestly not desirable to extend them by any implications; the presumption is that, having

---

133 [2001] EWCA Civ 1964; [2003] C.L.C. 1.
134 (1887) 19 Q.B.D. 237, per Kay J at 241.
135 [2009] 1 Lloyd's Rep. 391 at [36].
136 [2009] 1 E.G.L.R. 61.
137 [2010] 3 All E.R. 793.
138 *Masri v Consolidated Contractors International Co SAL* [2007] EWCA Civ 688.
139 *Barts and the London NHS Trust v Verma* [2011] EWCA Civ 1129 at [74], per Rix LJ.
140 (1844) 1 Q.B. 671.

expressed some, they have expressed all the conditions by which they intend to be bound under that instrument."

7.59   Accordingly, like other principles of interpretation, this one must not be rigidly applied. As Lopes LJ said in *Colquhoun v Brooks*[141]:

"It is often a valuable servant, but a dangerous master to follow in the construction of statutes or documents. The *exclusio* is often the result of inadvertence or accident, and the maxim ought not to be applied, when its application, having regard to the subject matter to which it is to be applied, leads to inconsistency or injustice."

In *Dean v Wiesengrund*,[142] Jenkins LJ said that the principle carried:

"little, if any, weight where it is possible to account for the *expressio unius* on grounds other than an intention to effect the *exclusio alterius*."

7.60   Thus in *Aspen Insurance UK Ltd v Pectel Ltd*,[143] Teare J, although acknowledging that this sort of linguistic point can be significant, gave little weight to it when set against the commercial purpose of the clause in question. Likewise, in *Griffon Shipping LLC v Firodi Shipping Ltd*,[144] the same judge, having referred to the principle, said:

"the principle of construction relied upon is no more than a presumption and little weight should be given to it 'where it is possible to account for the *expressio unius* on grounds other than an intention to effect the *exclusio alterius*'."

And in *National Grid v Mayes*,[145] Lord Hoffmann said of an amended trust deed embodying a pension scheme:

"This is an argument of the *expressio unius* variety. I think that such arguments are often perilous, especially when applied to a patchwork document like the pension scheme. The fact that a specific provision is made in one place may throw very little light on whether general words in another place include the power to do something similar."

Illustrations

1.   A lease contained a qualified covenant for quiet enjoyment. The tenant sought to argue that there was an implied covenant for title on the part of the landlord. The Court of Appeal rejected the argument. Romer LJ said:

"It was also, however, decided ... that there is no room for the implication of the covenant in a demise if the lessor enters into some covenant for quiet enjoyment. The reason for this is that an express covenant as to one branch of the covenant

---

[141] (1888) 21 Q.B.D. 52.
[142] [1955] 2 Q.B. 120 (a case of statutory construction).
[143] [2008] EWHC 2804 (Comm).
[144] [2013] EWHC 593 (Comm); [2013] 2 Lloyd's Rep. 50.
[145] [2001] 1 W.L.R. 864.

implied by the word 'demise' excludes the other on the principle *expressio unius est exclusio alterius*."

Miller v Emcer Products Ltd[146]

2. A mortgage mortgaged a foundry and two dwelling-houses together with all grates, boilers, bells and other fixtures in and about the two dwelling-houses. The question arose whether fixtures in the foundry were included in the mortgage. It was held that they were not. Taunton J said:

"But as the deed goes on to say 'together with all grates, boilers, bells and other fixtures in and about the said two dwelling houses' I think the mention of these fixtures excludes those in the foundry, on the principle *'expressio unius est exclusio alterius'*."

Hare v Horton[147]

3. A rent review clause provided for the rent to be a sum specified in a notice served by the landlord before a certain date; or a sum agreed by a certain date (of which time was expressed to be of the essence) or determined by a third party to be appointed in default of agreement by a certain date (of which time was expressed to be of the essence) by the President of the RICS. The question arose whether the time for service of the landlord's notice was also of the essence. The Court of Appeal held that it was not. Sir David Cairns said:

"... where you have an agreement which specifies the time for doing three things and two of the three are stated to have a time limit which is of the essence of the contract and the other one is not, then it follows that in all probability, where it is not stated that it is to be of the essence, it is not intended to be of the essence. If the parties, when they wish something to be of the essence, say so in terms, then obviously it is of the essence if they do say so and the probability is that, where they do not say so, it is not intended to be of the essence."

Amherst v Walker (James) Goldsmith & Silversmith Ltd[148]

4. A time charter contained a clause which provided that "failing punctual and regular payment of hire ... or on any breach of this charterparty" the owners were to be at liberty to withdraw the ship. Kerr J held that the owners were not entitled to withdraw the ship for late payment of additional insurance premium. He said:

"It seems to me that the juxtaposition in a forfeiture clause of a reference to 'the punctual and regular payment of hire' and the words 'or on any breach of the charterparty' requires the application of the rule of construction *expressio unius exclusio alterius*. ... The latter words require to be construed restrictively in their context. They should be read so as to exclude breaches which only consist in delaying some payment beyond the time when it would otherwise be due, in

---

[146] [1956] Ch. 304. See also *Line v Stephenson* (1838) 5 Bing. N.C. 183, per Lord Abinger CB *arguendo* at 184.
[147] (1833) 5 B. & Ad. 715.
[148] [1980] 1 E.G.L.R. 86.

particular when the charter prescribes no time for making the payment in question. The obligation to pay punctually, and therefore without any delay, is expressly dealt with in the preceding words and is confined to the payment of hire."

The Tropwind[149]

5. An agricultural tenancy provided for the making of certain payments by an incoming tenant to the outgoing tenant. The custom of the country included an allowance for foldage which was not specifically mentioned in the tenancy agreement. It was held that the outgoing tenant was not entitled to such a payment and that the custom of the country must be taken to have been waived. Bayley J said:

"if a lease speaks distinctly of the allowances to be made on quitting, it seems to me to exclude all others not named."

Webb v Plummer[150]

6. A lease of a hotel required the rent to be reviewed on the assumption that part of the property was available to let for shopping and retail purposes. It was held that, applying the principle *expressio unius exclusio alterius*, use for shopping and retail purposes was to be assumed to be the only permitted use.
Trusthouse Forte Albany Hotels Ltd v Daejan Investments Ltd (No.2)[151]

7. Clause 30 of a building contract dealt with the effect of the final certificate. Clause 30.8.1 said that the certificate should be conclusive evidence that the employer's requirements as to quality of materials and standard workmanship were satisfied. Clause 30.9 said that save as aforesaid no payment by the employer should be conclusive evidence that any design, works, materials or goods were in accordance with the contract. It was held that clause 30.8.1 did not cover design defects. Otton LJ said:

"The fact that within the same clause (clause 30) one sub-clause (30.9) refers to 'design' as a separate and additional category of contractual requirement (distinct from 'works' and 'materials') strongly suggests that the reference in the sub-clause to 30.8 to only the latter two contractual requirements, and the omission of 'design' was deliberate and reflected the intention of the parties."

London Borough of Dagenham & Barking v Terrapin Construction Ltd[152]

8. A loan facility granted by a bank contained a clause which said: "Each of the borrowers ... hereby irrevocably submits to the jurisdiction of the English courts ... but the bank reserves the right to proceed under this agreement in the courts of any other country claiming or having jurisdiction in respect thereof." It was held that the juxtaposition of a submission by the borrowers to the jurisdiction of the

---

[149] [1977] 1 Lloyd's Rep. 397.
[150] (1819) 2 B. & Ad. 746.
[151] [1989] 2 E.G.L.R. 113 CA.
[152] [2000] B.L.R. 479 CA.

English courts and the option reserved in favour of the bank to sue elsewhere brought into play the *expressio unius exclusio alterius* canon of construction. It followed that a similar option in favour of the borrowers was deliberately omitted.
Continental Bank NA v Aeakos Compania Naviera SA[153]

9.   A shipbuilding contract provided for a 10 per cent deposit to be paid to the sellers' "nominated bank in Singapore" and the balance to be paid to the sellers' "nominated bank". It was held that the omission of "in Singapore" as regards the bank where the balance was to be paid must be assumed to have been deliberate.
PT Berlian Laju Tanker TBK v Nuse Shipping Ltd[154]

10.   A contract of retainer for a solicitor provided expressly that the retainer would terminate on the death of the client, but made no similar provision for termination in the case of mental incapacity. That was one reason for concluding that the retainer did not terminate when the client temporarily lost mental capacity.
Blankley v Central Manchester and Manchester Children's University Hospitals NHS Trust[155]

7.   EXPRESS TERMS NEGATIVE IMPLIED TERMS

An express term in a contract is a strong indication against the possibility of implying any term dealing with the same subject-matter as the express term.

The above proposition can be expressed as the Latin maxim *expressum tacit cessare tacitum*.[156] It is a facet of the general principle that a term will not be implied if it is inconsistent with the express terms of the contract[157] and also of the principle of interpretation discussed in the last preceding section. In *Matthew v Blackmore*,[158] Pollock CB said: **7.61**

> "The rule of law as well as of reason and good sense is '*expressum facit cessare tacitum*'."

The principle is "based on the common sense precept that, if parties explicitly   **7.62**
provide for the giving of rights in a stated way, it is unlikely that they have intended to subject themselves by implication to some regime of rights and duties of a similar kind which goes beyond the terms upon which they have agreed".[159] In *Waterman v Boyle*,[160] a transfer of land contained an express right to park. The question was whether further parking rights could be implied. Arden LJ said:

> "where there is an express right attaching to the same property of a similar character to the right which is sought to be implied, it is most unlikely that the

---

[153] [1994] 1 W.L.R. 588; *Credit Suisse First Boston (Europe) Ltd v MLC (Bermuda) Ltd* [1999] C.L.C. 579.
[154] [2008] 2 Lloyd's Rep. 246.
[155] [2014] EWHC 168 (QB); [2014] 2 All E.R. 1104.
[156] The express makes the implied cease.
[157] See para.6.107.
[158] (1857) 1 H. & N. 762.
[159] *Biki v Chessells* [2004] VSCA 70, per Ormiston JA approving this section in a previous edition.
[160] [2009] 21 E.G. 104.

further right will arise by implication. The circumstances would have to be quite exceptional."

In *Aspdin v Austin*,[161] Lord Denman CJ said:

"Where parties have entered into written engagements with expressed stipulations, it is manifestly not desirable to extend them by any implications; the presumption is that having expressed some, they have expressed all the conditions by which they intend to be bound under that instrument."

7.63   Although this passage was quoted in the preceding section, it has equal relevance to this one. Similarly, the case of *Miller v Emcer Products Ltd*[162] can be analysed as applying the principle stated in this section as easily as that discussed in the last preceding one. This serves to emphasise the closeness of the two principles of interpretation.

7.64   The principle, like all other principles of interpretation, is not absolute. In *Fraser Turner Ltd v Pricewaterhousecoopers LLP*,[163] Vos C approved the statement by the trial judge that there was:

"no absolute rule that, if there is an express term covering a particular subject, that necessarily excludes the possibility of any implied term where there is no linguistic inconsistency. Rather, the correct approach, reflecting common sense, is that the existence of such an express term makes the co-existence of a further implied term on the same subject unlikely and especially so in a lengthy and carefully drafted document on which legal professionals have been advising."

7.65   Accordingly, where the contract in question showed "all of the signs of a scissors and paste pastiche that has evolved haphazardly over time", it was so lacking in precision and coherence that the principle could not be applied.[164]

Illustrations

1.   Upon the sale of an equity of redemption the purchaser entered into a limited indemnity, indemnifying the vendors against certain liabilities attaching to the mortgaged property. It was argued that there was also an implied indemnity against the amount secured by the mortgage. It was held by Eve J:

"that the implication of an unqualified personal liability on the part of the purchaser is negatived in this and in all cases where there is an express qualified indemnity, or where the circumstances and nature of the transaction are otherwise of such a nature to rebut such implication."

This passage was approved on appeal.
Mills v United Counties Bank Ltd[165]

---

[161]   (1844) Q.B. 671.
[162]   See para.7.60, Illustration 1.
[163]   [2019] EWCA Civ 1290.
[164]   *Tattersall's Sweeps Pty Ltd v Veetemp Pty Ltd* [2004] ANZ Conv. R. 296.
[165]   [1912] 1 Ch. 231.

2. A lease contained a covenant by the tenant to erect buildings by a specified date, and a covenant to keep such buildings in repair. The tenant did not build by the specified date and the landlord argued that the repairing covenant contained an implied obligation to build. The argument failed. Swinfen-Eady LJ said:

"In my opinion, no such covenant can be implied: *'expressum facit cessare tacitum'*. There is here an express covenant, both as to time and mode of building, and no further covenant to build can be implied from the covenant to repair. The rule is that where a deed contains express covenants, no implication of any other covenants on the same subject-matter can be raised."

Stephens v Junior Army and Navy Stores Ltd[166]

8. CONSTRUCTION CONTRA PROFERENTEM

Where there is a doubt about the meaning of a contract, the words will be construed against the person who put them forward.[167] However, the rule is reversed in the case of a grant by the Crown, but not in the case of a commercial contract to which the Crown is a party.

(a) The maxim and its origins

The Latin maxim *verba cartarum fortius accipiuntur contra proferentem* has been applied in English law ever since Lord Coke's day.[168] The origins of the *contra proferentem* maxim in Roman law and its migration into English law is described by Peter Prescott QC (sitting as a judge of the Chancery Division) in *Oxonica Energy Ltd v Neuftec Ltd*[169]:

7.66

"The maxim *verba fortius accipiuntur contra proferentem* was introduced into English law by writers such as Sir Edward Coke (Co Litt 36a, 183a), Lord Bacon (Maxims of the Law, Regula III), and Sir Henry Blackstone (2 Commentaries 23, 4). But they discussed it, not in relation to what we would now call commercial agreements, but to unilateral documents, such as grants under deed or pleadings. Thus Blackstone denied that it could apply to indentures, 'for the words of an indenture, executed by both parties, are to be considered as the words of them both'. They must have derived the maxim from the civilian writers. There is a useful comparative law paper by Cserne (Péter Cserne, *'Policy Considerations In Contract Interpretation: The Contra Proferentem Rule From a Comparative Law and Economics Perspective'*, Hungarian Association for Law and Economics, 2007), to which I am indebted. In the classical period of Roman law the principle seems to have been applied, if at all, to situations where in practice one

---

166 [1914] 2 Ch. 516.
167 This section was recast in a previous edition of this book in the light of the illuminating discussion of this principle by Campbell J in *North v Marina* [2003] NSWSC 64. The recast section was referred to with apparent approval by the CA in *Lexi Holdings Plc v Stainforth* [2006] EWCA Civ 988 (and appears also to have met with the approval of Campbell JA: *Rava v Logan Wines* [2007] NSWCA 62). It was also referred to with approval in *NRAM Plc v McAdam* [2015] EWCA Civ 751.
168 Co. Litt 36a. In *Co. Litt.* 183a. Lord Coke says "it is a maxime in law, that every man's grant shall be taken by construction of law most forcibly against him". It was applied in *Manchester College v Trafford* (1679) 2 Show 31.
169 [2008] EWHC 2127 (Pat). The point did not arise on appeal: [2009] EWCA Civ 668.

side alone had the opportunity to formulate the wording. (There were two doctrines, *ambiguitas contra stipulatorem and ambiguitas contra venditorem*; but the reasoning was the same. I. The stipulator was one who formulated the precise language of the promise that he invited the other to repeat verbatim, thus creating a unilateral obligation in his favour. Hence the promisor had little or no opportunity to vary the language, which therefore was construed against the stipulator: Cserne, op cit, note 38. Scattered references may be found in the Digest. I have used the SP Scott translation and numbering. They are in D 34, 5, 27 (Celsus: "Where any question arises as to the intention of the parties in a stipulation, the ambiguity should be interpreted against the stipulator"); D 45, 1, 38, 18 (Ulpianus: "When the intention of a stipulation is examined, the language should be interpreted against the stipulator"); D 45, 1, 99 (Celsus:"Whatever is required to render an obligation binding is understood to have been omitted, if it is not plainly expressed in words; and we almost always interpret it in favour of the promisor, because the stipulator was free to give a broader meaning to the terms. ...") II. In later classical Roman law there were two common types of contract (emptio-venditio and locatio-conductio) where, in practice, it was the vendor or lessor who formulated the language. Thus D 2, 14, 39 (Papianus: "It was established by the ancients that where an agreement was obscure or ambiguous, it must be construed against a vendor and a lessor, because it was in their power to have stated the terms of the contract more clearly"); D18, 1, 21 (Paulus: "Labeo says that the ambiguity of an agreement should rather prejudice the vendor who mentioned the terms, than the purchaser; because the former could have stated them more clearly before anything had been done"); D 50, 17, 172 (Paulus: "In a contract of sale, any sentence of doubtful signification is interpreted against the vendor"). It was the commentators and glossators of the late medieval period who generalised the expressions in order to tackle a wider range of contracts, and they arrived at '*ambiguitas contra proferentem*': Cserne, op cit, p 9. In so doing, they introduced the ambiguity.) In English law it seems that the maxim first came to be applied to commercial agreements out of a desire to tame exclusion clauses—an early form of consumer protection."

(b) Does the principle survive?

7.67   As early as 1877 Jessel MR doubted whether the principle continued to exist. In *Taylor v Corporation of St Helens*,[170] he said:

"... I will take the liberty of making an observation as regards a maxim ... which is to be found I believe in a great many text-books, and I am afraid in a great many judgments of ancient date, and that is, that a grant, if there is any difficulty or obscurity as to its meaning, is to be read most strongly against the grantor. I do not see how, according to the now established rules of construction as settled by the House of Lords in *Grey v Pearson*[171] ... that maxim can be considered as having any force at the present day."

---

[170] (1877) 6 Ch. D. 265, an early attempt to jettison "intellectual baggage". Morgan J expressed similar doubts in *Arnold v Britton* [2012] EWHC 3451 (affirmed [2013] EWCA Civ 902; [2013] L. & T.R. 371 and [2015] UKSC 36; [2015] 2 W.L.R. 1593 but without reference to this point).
[171] See para.5.06.

These doubts have been echoed in more recent cases. In *K/S Victoria Street v* **7.68**
House of Fraser (Stores Management) Ltd,[172] Lord Neuberger of Abbotsbury MR
said:

"… such rules are rarely, if ever, of any assistance when it comes to construing
commercial contracts. Quite apart from raising abstruse issues as to who is the
proferens (and, in particular, whether the issue turns on the precise facts of the
case or hypothetical analysis), 'rules' of interpretation such as *contra proferentem*
are rarely decisive as to the meaning of any provisions of a commercial contract.
The words used, commercial sense, and the documentary and factual context, are,
and should be, normally enough to determine the meaning of a contractual
provision."

In *Multiplex Construction Europe Ltd v Dunne*,[173] Fraser J considered the application of the principle to a contract of suretyship. He concluded that there were "only
skeletal, if any, remains of the contra proferentem maxim, or rule of construction,
in commercial cases". He returned to the principle in *Bates v Post Office (No. 3)*.[174]
He said:

"In my judgment, the modern approach to the contra proferentem rule, in commercial contracts at least, is something of a sceptical one. The 'rule' (if rule is
the correct word) requires ambiguity in a provision—for example, in an exemption clause—to be resolved against the party who put the clause forward and
relies upon it. The rule has been subject to criticism, and is something of a historical remnant. The first and most difficult aspect of the rule is determining in a
commercial contract which party is in fact the *proferens*. Here that is not so difficult, because it was only the Post Office who ever drafted any of the terms
(subject to the involvement of the NFSP, which certainly was not occupying the
position of an opposite negotiating party). However, even if it is clear that the
Post Office is the *proferens*, there are in any event better ways of resolving
problems of construction, not least construing the actual words used."

In *The Federal Republic of Nigeria v JP Morgan Chase Bank, NA*,[175] Mr Andrew
Burrows QC regarded it as unnecessary in interpreting exemption and indemnity
clauses to recognise an independent contra proferentem principle, on the basis that:

"the force of what was the contra proferentem rule is embraced by recognising
that a party is unlikely to have agreed to give up a valuable right that it would
otherwise have had without clear words."

---

[172] [2011] EWCA Civ 904; [2012] Ch. 497. See to the same effect *Sideridraulic Systems SpA v BBC
Chartering & Logistic GmbH & Co KG* [2011] EWHC 3106 (Comm); *Intergraph (UK) Ltd v
Wolfson Microelectronics Ltd* [2012] EWHC 528 (Ch). In *WS Tankship II BV v Kwangju Bank Ltd*
[2011] EWHC 3103 (Comm), Blair J said that a commercial instrument should be construed without
reference to principles such as strict construction or *contra proferentem*.
[173] [2017] EWHC 3073 (TCC); [2018] B.L.R. 36; *Haberdashers' Aske's Federation Trust Ltd v
Lakehouse Contracts Ltd* [2018] EWHC 558 (TCC); [2018] B.L.R. 511.
[174] [2019] EWHC 606 (QB) at [635]. At [638] he doubted whether any part of the principle survives.
But in *Goldman Sachs International v Procession House Trustee Ltd* [2018] EWHC 1523 (Ch);
[2018] L. & T.R. 28 Nugee J was prepared to accept that it had survived.
[175] [2019] EWHC 347 (Comm), affirmed on appeal [2019] EWCA Civ 1641.

7.69   Despite these doubts, it is thought that the principle still survives (perhaps with a weaker and more limited role and a different label)[176] and is one to which the court frequently resorts in the interpretation of deeds and contracts.[177] In *Association of British Travel Agents Ltd v British Airways Plc*,[178] Sedley LJ described it as:

"a principle not only of law but of justice."

7.70   The origin and first purpose of the principle is to limit the power of a dominant contractor who is able to deal on his own take-it-or-leave-it terms with others.[179] Thus in *SAS Institute Inc v World Programming Ltd*,[180] the Court of Appeal applied the principle to the interpretation of "take-it-or-leave-it" terms of a licence to use software, which could only be either accepted or rejected.

7.71   In *ICDL GCC Foundation FZ-LLC v European Computer Driving Licence Foundation Ltd*,[181] the Irish Supreme Court found that principle to be of assistance in interpreting a commercial contract. Similarly, in *Bari v Rosen*[182] Spencer J held that it was only possible to reconcile apparently conflicting provisions in a contract of retainer by applying the *contra proferentem* principle.

7.72   In the interpretation of exclusion and exemption clause the principle has a continuing role. In *Nobahar-Cookson v Hut Group Ltd*,[183] Briggs LJ said:

"recent decisions about exclusion clauses have continued to affirm the utility of the principle that, if necessary to resolve ambiguity, they should be narrowly construed, including in relation to commercial contracts."

In *Taberna Europe CDO II Plc v Selskabet af 1 September 2008*,[184] Moore-Bick LJ said:

"In the past judges have tended to invoke the contra proferentem rule as a useful means of controlling unreasonable exclusion clauses. The modern view, however, is to recognise that commercial parties (which these were) are entitled to make their own bargains and that the task of the court is to interpret fairly the words they have used. The contra proferentem rule may still be useful to resolve cases of genuine ambiguity, but ought not to be taken as the starting point."

In *Newman v Framewood Manor Management Co Ltd*,[185] the Court of Appeal were concerned with an exclusion clause in a lease. Arden LJ said:

---

[176] See *Taylor v Rive Droite Music Ltd* [2006] E.M.L.R. 4, per Neuberger LJ; *Goldman Sachs International v Procession House Trustee Ltd* [2018] EWHC 1523 (Ch); [2018] L. & T.R. 28; *Grant v International Insurance Co of Hanover Ltd* [2019] CSIH 9; 2019 S.C. 379.

[177] Retention of the principle is defended in Peel "Whither Contra Proferentem", in Burrows and Peel (eds), *Contract Terms* (Oxford: Oxford University Press, 2007).

[178] [2000] 2 All E.R. (Comm) 204.

[179] *Association of British Travel Agents Ltd v British Airways Plc* [2000] 2 Lloyd's Rep. 209 at 220, per Sedley LJ.

[180] [2013] EWCA Civ 1482; [2014] R.P.C. 8.

[181] [2012] IESC 55 at [80].

[182] [2012] EWHC 1782 (QB). The principle also appears to have been of some assistance in *ED & F Man Sugar Ltd v Unicargo Transportgesellschaft mbH* [2012] EWHC 2879 (Comm).

[183] [2016] EWCA Civ 128; [2016] 1 C.L.C. 573.

[184] [2016] EWCA Civ 1262; [2017] Q.B. 633; *Natixis SA v Marex Financial, Access World Logistics (Singapore) Pte Ltd* [2019] EWHC 2549 (Comm).

[185] [2012] EWCA Civ 159; [2012] 2 E.G.L.R. 45.

"As the exoneration clause has to be interpreted *contra proferentem*, it is only right to give it its narrower meaning."

(c) The meaning of the maxim

A literal translation of the principle is "the words of documents are to be taken strongly against the one who puts forward". However, the phrase "the one who puts forward" is ambiguous. It might mean: **7.73**

(1) the person who prepared the document as a whole;
(2) the person who prepared the particular clause;
(3) the person for whose benefit the clause operates.

This ambiguity has led to the principle having been formulated in many different ways over the years, and as a result the formulations are not always entirely cohesive.[186]

(d) Responsibility for putting forward the document

One line of authority proceeds on the basis that one party has the responsibility for putting forward the whole contract, and hence the contract will be construed against him, even if the other party has had a hand in the drafting process. This approach was pithily summarised by Binnie J in *Co-operators Life Insurance Co v Gibbens*[187]:   **7.74**

"Whoever holds the pen creates the ambiguity and must live with the consequences."

This applies particularly to insurance contracts.[188] Thus in *Houghton v Trafalgar Insurance Co Ltd*,[189] speaking of a policy of insurance, Somervell LJ said:

"If there is any ambiguity, since it is the defendants' clause, the ambiguity will be resolved in favour of the assured."

In *Tam Wing Chuen v Bank of Credit and Commerce Hong Kong Ltd*,[190] Lord Mustill explained that: **7.75**

"… the basis of the *contra proferentem* principle is that a person who puts forward the wording of a proposed agreement may be assumed to have looked

---

[186] This description and the historical summary that precedes it was approved by the Court of Appeal in *Nobahar-Cookson v Hut Group Ltd* [2016] EWCA Civ 128; [2016] 1 C.L.C. 573.
[187] *2009 SCC 59 (Supreme Court of Canada).*
[188] *Yorkshire Water Services Ltd v Sun Alliance and London Insurance Plc (No.1)* [1997] 2 Lloyd's Rep. 21; *Tektrol Ltd v International Insurance Co of Hanover Ltd* [2005] 2 Lloyd's Rep. 701; *Hawley v Luminar Leisure Ltd* [2006] I.R.L.R. 817.
[189] [1955] 1 Q.B. 247.
[190] [1996] 2 B.C.L.C. 69 at 77.

after his own interests, so that if words leave room for doubt about whether he is intended to have a particular benefit there is reason to suppose that he is not."

7.76   In other cases the court has been prepared to look at who it was who introduced particular words into the contract. In *Birrell v Dryer*,[191] Lord Watson said of a policy of insurance:

> "That the underwriters may be rightly held to be the *proferentes* with regard to many conditions in a policy I do not doubt; whether they ought to be so held depends, in each case, upon the character and substance of the condition. In the present case there are many considerations which lead to the inference that the clause in question is not one constructed and inserted by the appellants alone, and for their own protection merely. It was in point of fact, inserted in the contract by the agent of the respondents; and it is in form a warranty by them that their vessel will not be navigated in certain waters, a matter which it was entirely within their power to regulate. These considerations point rather to the respondents themselves being the *proferentes*; but I think the substance of the warranty must be looked to; and that in substance its authorship is attributable to both parties alike."

Thus in *Lexi Holdings Plc v Stainforth*,[192] the parties entered into a supplemental agreement, drafted by one of them without legal advice. In holding for the other of them Carnwath LJ said:

> "The inadequacies of the agreement may reflect a non-lawyer's attempt to reconcile those competing objectives. Whether or not that it is the correct explanation, there is no unfairness in holding that, having presented the agreement in that form, they should bear the risk of any resulting ambiguity, if it cannot be resolved by more conventional interpretative tools."

7.77   Where this formulation is the preferred approach and the *proferens* cannot be identified, or both parties may with equal force be described as the *proferentes*, the maxim cannot be applied. Thus where a contract is made on standard terms drafted not by the parties but by representative bodies, the court has declined to apply the maxim.[193]

In *Levison v Farin*,[194] it was common ground that as the clause in question "emerged as a result of joint efforts" the maxim was of no relevance. A similar approach was taken by Hirst J in *Kleinwort Benson Ltd v Malaysian Mining Corp Berhad*,[195] where he held that the principle would not apply to "a joint drafting effort".

7.78   In a previous edition of this book, it was suggested that this approach was unsound for two reasons.[196] First, it confused identification of the draftsman with identification of the *proferens*. Second, delving into the question who drafted the clause would infringe the principle that evidence of the negotiations was

---

[191] (1884) 9 App. Cas. 345.

[192] [2006] EWCA Civ 988; *YJL London Ltd v Roswin Estates LLP* [2009] EWHC 3174 (TCC).

[193] *Tersons Ltd v Stevenage Development Corp* [1963] 2 Lloyd's Rep. 333 at 368 CA (not reported on this point at [1965] 1 Q.B. 37).

[194] [1978] 2 All E.R. 1149 at 1156.

[195] [1988] 1 W.L.R. 799.

[196] Lewison, *The Interpretation of Contracts*, 2nd edn (London: Sweet & Maxwell, 1997), para.6.07.

inadmissible.[197] The first of these reasons may be countered by cases of high author- ity in which the court has, indeed, identified the draftsman, at least in the sense of identifying the party responsible for procuring the drafting of the clause. The second may be countered by the argument that inquiry into the drafting process is being undertaken merely for the purpose of identifying an objective fact known to both parties, namely who drafted the clause. Such an inquiry does not therefore infringe the rule that evidence of negotiations is inadmissible for the purpose of identify- ing the subjective intentions of the parties.[198]

(e) Person taken to have put forward the document

In yet other cases the inquiry into who put forward the words is not treated as an exercise in fact finding, but is an analysis of the contract in order to decide who ought to be taken as having put forward the words. It is this approach which has resulted in the principle that a deed of grant is construed against the grantor.   **7.79**

In *Johnson v Edgware Railway Co*,[199] Romilly MR said:

"… It is to be observed, that all deeds are to be construed most strongly against the grantor."

So too in *Neill v Duke of Devonshire*,[200] Lord Selbourne LC said:

"It is well settled that the words of a deed, executed for valuable consideration, ought to be construed, as far as they properly may, in favour of the grantee."

So in *Savill Brothers Ltd v Bethell*,[201] Stirling LJ said:

"It is a settled rule of construction that, where there is a grant and an exception out of it, the exception is to be taken as inserted for the benefit of the grantor, and to be construed in favour of the grantee."

(f) Person in whose favour the clause operates

In other cases the court concentrates on deciding in whose favour the clause operates. In *Burton v English*,[202] Brett MR said: **7.80**

"The general rule is that where there is any doubt as to the construction of any stipulation in a contract, one ought to construe it strictly against the party in whose favour it has been made."

A similar approach has been taken by the court towards exemption and exclu- sion clauses.[203]

Another variant of the principle is that the words of a contract are to be construed   **7.81**

---

[197] In *Growth Management Ltd v Mutafchiev* [2007] 1 B.C.L.C. 645, where one party wished to rely on the principle, Cooke J refused to admit evidence of the negotiations.
[198] See *North v Marina* [2003] NSWSC 64, for convincing criticism of the second edition of this book.
[199] (1866) 35 Beav. 480.
[200] (1883) 8 App. Cas. 135. To similar effect are the judgments of Willes J in *Williams v James* (1867) L.R. 2 C.P. 577 at 581, and Jessel MR in *Leech v Schweder* (1874) L.R. 3 Ch. 463n at 465n.
[201] [1902] 2 Ch. 523.
[202] (1883) 12 Q.B.D. 218.
[203] See Ch.12.

against the party who stipulates. Thus in *Webb v Plummer*,[204] Holroyd J said:

> "For although the words of a covenant are to be construed according to the intent of the parties, yet they are to be taken most strongly against the party who stipulates."

The ambiguity was resolved against the grantee (in that case a tenant) who was none the less the covenantor, and, although the report is silent on this point, it is usually the landlord who puts forward (or proffers) the form of lease. This formulation has thus been interpreted as meaning that the words of a contractual obligation will be construed against the promisor. So in *Amax International Ltd v Custodian Holdings Ltd*,[205] Hoffmann J was prepared to treat the tenant as the proferens in construing a rent review clause because the tenant was the covenantor. However, in *North v Marina*[206] Campbell J suggested that this formulation derives from the rules of Roman law under which the promissory was the one who contracted an obligation by replying to a stipulation proposed by the other contracting party[207] (in modern terms the offeree).

7.82 It has also been held that the principle is not engaged where the clause in question is for the benefit of both parties.[208] In *Steria Ltd v Sigma Wireless Communications Ltd*,[209] Judge Davies said of a clause in a contract enabling the contractor to call for an extension of time provided that he had notified the counterparty of the circumstances giving rise to the delay:

> "In my judgment an extension of time provision confers benefits on both parties; in particular it enables a contractor to recover reasonable extensions of time whilst still maintaining the contractually agreed structure of a specified time for completion (together, in the majority of cases, with the contractual certainty of agreed liquidated damages, as opposed to uncertain unliquidated damages). So far as the application of the *contra proferentem* rule is concerned, it seems to me that the correct question to ask is not whether the clause was put forward originally by Steria or by Sigma; the principle which applies here is that if there is genuine ambiguity as to whether or not notification is a condition precedent, then the notification should not be construed as being a condition precedent, since such a provision operates for the benefit of only one party, i.e. the employer, and operates to deprive the other party (the contractor) of rights which he would otherwise enjoy under the contract."

(g) Two main variants

7.83 There are thus two main formulations of the principle. One concentrates on who put the clause forward. The other concentrates on the party who benefits from the clause.[210]

---

[204] (1819) 2 B. & Ald. 746.

[205] [1986] 2 E.G.L.R. 111.

[206] [2003] NSWSC 64.

[207] See Kersley, *Broom's Legal Maxims*, 10th edn (London: Sweet & Maxwell, 1939), p.406.

[208] *Horwood v Land of Leather Ltd* [2010] EWHC 546 (Comm).

[209] [2008] B.L.R. 79.

[210] *Youell v Bland Welch & Co Ltd* [1992] 2 Lloyd's Rep. 127 at 134, per Staughton LJ; *The Zeus V* [2000] 2 Lloyd's Rep. 587 at 597, per Potter LJ.

In *Financial Services Authority v Asset LI Inc*,[211] Andrew Smith J noted the two main variants:

"Secondly, both limbs of the principle of construction *contra proferentem* are to much the same effect: Asset Land presented the form of contract to the investor and is *proferens in contrahendo*, and the Asset Land companies and their directors rely on clauses in the proceedings and are *proferentes coram iudice*."

In *BHP Petroleum Ltd v British Steel Plc*,[212] Evans LJ said:

"It is common ground that the rule of construction known as contra [proferentem] operates against the respondent for two reasons. First, they rely upon the clause to exclude or to limit the liability alleged against them, and, secondly, they were responsible for introducing during the negotiating process the particular parts of the clause on which they now rely."[213]

In *Whitecap Leisure Ltd v John H Rundle Ltd*,[214] Moore-Bick LJ said of a time bar clause: 7.84

"However, in cases where there is uncertainty about the parties' intention, and therefore about the meaning of the clause, such uncertainty will be resolved against the person relying on the clause and the more significant the departure is said to be from what are accepted to be the obligations ordinarily assumed under a contract of the kind in question, the more difficult it will be to persuade the court that the parties intended that result."

The various formulations of the principle may conflict with each other in some   7.85
cases. In *North v Marina*,[215] Campbell J said:

"When there are these different strands of principle recognised in the case law concerning the application of the maxim, those strands could themselves come into conflict. A common example is the one given by Sir Frederick Jordan in *Fenwick*,[216] that a conveyance of land is commonly prepared by the transferee, yet it is a grant made by the transferor."[217]

It was, perhaps, considerations of this kind that led Hoffmann J to say that in most cases the application of the maxim to a lease would be entirely arbitrary.[218] The

---

[211] [2013] EWHC 178 (Ch). See also the same judge's decision in *Sideridraulic Systems SpA v BBC Chartering & Logistic GmbH & Co KG* [2011] EWHC 3106 (Comm).
[212] [2000] 2 Lloyd's Rep. 277 at 281.
[213] The court considered the clause both in its original form and its form as amended during negotiations.
[214] [2008] 2 Lloyd's Rep. 216.
[215] [2003] NSWSC 64.
[216] *Fenwick & Co Pty Ltd v Federal Steam Navigations Co Ltd* (1943) 44 S.R. (NSW) I.
[217] The author is not convinced that this really is a conflict. Although it is true that in traditional conveyancing the transferee drafts the conveyance, the contents of the conveyance will have been prescribed by the contract that precedes it. The contract will have been drafted by the transferor, or will at best have been a joint drafting effort. In *Earl of Plymouth v Rees* [2019] EWHC 1008 (Ch); [2019] 4 W.L.R. 74 Judge Keyser QC discussed the potential conflicts between this principle and the principle that reservations in a conveyance are to be construed against the vendor.
[218] *Amax International Ltd v Custodian Holdings Ltd* [1986] 2 E.G.L.R. 111.

principle was of no assistance in *Bloomberg LP v Sandberg*,[219] partly because of the difficulty in deciding who the proferens was.

(h)   Exclusion clauses

7.86   A different rationale for the application of the principle applies in the case of exclusion clauses. In *Nobahar-Cookson v Hut Group Ltd*,[220] Briggs LJ said:

> "In my judgment the underlying rationale for the principle that, if necessary to resolve ambiguity, exclusion clauses should be narrowly construed has nothing to do with the identification of the proferens, either of the document as a whole or of the clause in question. Nor is it a principle derived from an identification of *579 the person seeking to rely upon it. Ambiguity in an exclusion clause may have to be resolved by a narrow construction because an exclusion clause cuts down or detracts from the ambit of some important obligation in a contract, or a remedy conferred by the general law such as (in the present case) an obligation to give effect to a contractual warranty by paying compensation for breach of it. The parties are not lightly to be taken to have intended to cut down the remedies which the law provides for breach of important contractual obligations without using clear words having that effect."

(i)   When the maxim applies

7.87   Given the differing, and potentially conflicting, formulations of the principle, it is not possible easily to predict the cases in which the court will find the maxim a useful tool. Thus in *CDV Software Entertainment AG v Gamecock Media Europe Ltd*,[221] Gloster J said that the principle was "of uncertain application and little utility in the context of commercially negotiated agreements". Perhaps the most that can be said is that the court will resort to the maxim where the justice of the case demands it. Some reliance was placed on the *contra proferentem* principle "very much as a last resort" in *Landlord Protect Ltd v St Anselm Development Co Ltd*.[222] The principle was also applied by the Court of Appeal in *Pratt v Aigaion Insurance Co*,[223] interpreting a warranty given in an insurance policy. On the other hand, in the case of a pension scheme, which must be interpreted without a predisposition to favour either the sponsoring employer or the members, the principle probably has no part to play.[224] The principle applies only to contracts. It does not apply to documents that are relied on to evidence the making of an oral contract.[225]

---

[219]   [2015] EWHC 2858 (TCC); [2016] B.L.R. 72.
[220]   [2016] EWCA Civ 128; [2016] 1 C.L.C. 573; *Federal Republic of Nigeria v JP Morgan Chase Bank, NA* [2019] EWHC 347 (Comm) (affirmed on appeal: [2019] EWCA Civ 1641).
[221]   [2009] EWHC 2965.
[222]   [2008] EWHC 1582 (Ch).
[223]   [2009] 1 Lloyd's Rep. 225.
[224]   *Carr v Thales Pension Trustees Ltd* [2020] EWHC 949 (Ch).
[225]   *Blyth v Nelsons Solicitors Ltd* [2019] EWHC 2063 (QB); [2019] Costs L.R. 1409.

(i) Principle to be applied only in cases of doubt

However, the principle only applies where there is a "real doubt"[226] or **7.88** ambiguity.[227] It should not be used for the purpose of creating a doubt or magnifying an ambiguity, where the circumstances of the case raise no real difficulty.[228] Before concluding that the contract is ambiguous, thus opening the way for the application of the *contra proferentem* principle, the court should examine the background and commercial purpose of the contract. In *Direct Travel Insurance v McGeown*,[229] Auld LJ said:

"A court should be wary of starting its analysis by finding an ambiguity by reference to the words in question looked at on their own. And it should not, in any event, on such a finding, move straight to the *contra proferentem* rule without first looking at the context and, where appropriate, permissible aids to identifying the purpose of the commercial document of which the words form part. Too early recourse to the *contra proferentem* rule runs the danger of 'creating' an ambiguity where there is none."

As the Upper Tribunal rightly observed in *Burchell v Raj Properties Ltd*[230]:

"It is wrong in principle to seize on the presence of any ambiguity or difficulty of construction as sufficient justification immediately to resort to the *contra proferentem* principle as a trump card."

This section was referred to with approval in *Nobahar-Cookson v Hut Group Ltd*[231] in which Briggs LJ said:

"... the *contra proferentem* rule in its classic form was by no means limited to, or even mainly about, exclusion clauses. It was a rule designed to resolve ambiguities against the party who prepared the document in which the clause appeared, or prepared the particular clause, or against the person for whose benefit the clause operates."

Similarly, in *Transocean Drilling UK Ltd v Providence Resources Plc*,[232] Moore-Bick LJ said that the principle:

"... is an approach to construction to which resort may properly be had when the language chosen by the parties is one-sided and genuinely ambiguous, that is,

---

[226] *Manchikalapati v Zurich Insurance Plc* [2019] EWCA Civ 2163.

[227] *Joint London Holdings Ltd v Mount Cook Land Ltd* [2005] 3 E.G.L.R. 119 CA (referring to the equivalent section in the previous edition of this book); *Static Control Components v Egan* [2004] 2 Lloyd's Rep. 429; *Quest 4 Finance Ltd v Maxfield* [2007] 2 C.L.C. 706; *Manchikalapati v Zurich Insurance Plc* [2019] EWCA Civ 2163; *Natixis SA v Marex Financial, Access World Logistics (Singapore) Pte Ltd* [2019] EWHC 2549 (Comm).

[228] *Cornish v Accident Insurance Co* (1889) 23 Q.B.D. 453 at 456; *Tektrol Ltd v International Insurance Co of Hanover Ltd* [2005] 2 Lloyd's Rep. 701; *Natixis SA v Marex Financial, Access World Logistics (Singapore) Pte Ltd* [2019] EWHC 2549 (Comm).

[229] [2004] 1 All E.R. (Comm) 609, applied in *West v Ian Finlay & Associates (a firm)* [2014] EWCA Civ 316.

[230] [2014] L. & T.R. 4.

[231] [2016] EWCA Civ 128; [2016] 1 C.L.C. 573.

[232] [2016] EWCA Civ 372; [2016] 2 Lloyd's Rep. 51. Professor Edwin Peel has commented in this case in "Contra proferentem revisited" (2017) 133 L.Q.R. 7. See also *Natixis SA v Marex Financial* [2019] EWHC 2549 (Comm).

equally capable of bearing two distinct meanings. In such cases the application of the principle may enable the court to choose the meaning that is less favourable to the party who introduced the clause or in whose favour it operates."

7.89   So the court's first task is to construe the document properly on ordinary principles.[233] As Warren J explained in *PNPF Trust Co Ltd v Taylor*[234]:

"The fact that there are difficulties about a point of construction does not mean that there is a doubt or ambiguity of a type to which the *contra proferentem* rule may be applicable. If conventional canons of construction are capable of resolving the issue, they should be applied."

So also in *Morris v Blackpool Borough Council*,[235] Gloster LJ said:

"... the presumption can only come into play if the court finds itself unable on the material before it to reach a sure conclusion on the construction of a reservation or other contractual term. The presumption itself is not a factor to be taken into account by the court in reaching its conclusion on construction. In my judgment the wording of the lease is not so vague or ambiguous that the court in the present case is unable to reach a sure conclusion on the material before it, applying the established principles of contractual interpretation."

7.90   In *London and Lancashire Fire Insurance Co Ltd v Bolands Ltd*,[236] Lord Sumner said:

"It is suggested further that there is some ambiguity about the proviso, and that, under the various well-known authorities, upon the principle of reading words *contra proferentes*, we ought to construe this proviso, which is in favour of the insurance company, adversely to them. That, however, is a principle which depends upon there being some ambiguity that is to say, some choice of an expression—by those who are responsible for putting forward the clause, which leaves one unable to decide which of two meanings is the right one. In the present case it is a question only of construction. There may be some difficulty, there may be even some difference of opinion, about the construction, but it is a question quite capable of being solved by the ordinary rules of grammar, and it appears to me that there is no ground for saying that there is such an ambiguity as would warrant us in reading the clause otherwise than in accordance with its express terms."

In *Birrell v Dryer*,[237] Earl of Selbourne LC said:

"I do not think that the evidence discloses any ambiguity or uncertainty, suf-

---

[233] *Cattles Plc v Welcome Financial Services Ltd* [2010] EWCA Civ 599 referring to *Static Control Components (Europe) Ltd v Egan* [2004] 2 Lloyd's Rep. 429 CA.

[234] [2010] EWHC 1573 (Ch).

[235] [2014] EWCA Civ 1384; [2015] L. & T.R. 6.

[236] [1924] A.C. 836 at 848 HL. See also *Cornish v Accident Insurance Co* (1889) 23 Q.B.D. 453 at 456 CA, per Lindley LJ ("In a case on the line, in a case of real doubt, the policy ought to be construed most strongly against the insurers; they frame the policy and insert the exceptions. But this principle ought only to be applied for the purpose of removing a doubt, not for the purpose of creating a doubt, or magnifying an ambiguity, when the circumstances of the case raise no real difficulty");
Singh v Rathour [1988] 2 All E.R. 16 CA.

[237] (1884) 9 App. Cas. 345.

ficient to prevent the application of the ordinary rules and principles of construction. ... There does not appear to me to be any necessity for resorting to presumptions in favour of or against either party, whether founded on the rule *fortius contra proferentem*, or on the onus of proving an exception from the general affirmative terms of this contract."

So too in *Patching v Dubbins*,[238] Page Wood VC said: **7.91**

"I had at first an inclination of opinion, that if the words were doubtful, and it could be construed in favour of the defendants, the general rule would be this, that it being equivalent to a grant on the part of the vendor, the construction must be taken most strongly against the grantor. But, on the other hand, there is another rule of construction well established, namely, that it is right to give effect to every word, if it can be reasonable and properly done. I do not feel, therefore, at liberty to say that it is doubtful, if, in putting one construction upon this covenant, I give complete effect to all the words, whereas I should be leaving a portion of the words without effect in giving to the covenant a contrary construction."

So too in *Parkinson v Barclays Bank Ltd*,[239] Cohen LJ said:

"[Counsel] pressed us with the maxim that a deed must be construed *contra proferentem*. But if, applying the ordinary principles of construction, we arrive at a clear conclusion as to what the parties meant by the language which they used, I do not think that the maxim comes into action."

In *Impact Funding Solutions Ltd v AIG Europe Insurance Ltd*,[240] the Supreme Court was concerned with the interpretation of an exclusion in a solicitors' professional indemnity insurance policy. Lord Hodge said:

"As I see no ambiguity in the way that the Policy defined its cover and as the exclusion clause reflected what The Law Society of England and Wales as the regulator of the solicitors' profession had authorised as a limitation of professional indemnity cover, I see no role in this case for the doctrine of interpretation *contra proferentem*."

On the other hand, in *Burnett v International Insurance Company of Hanover Ltd*,[241] Lord Drummond Young in the Inner House appears to have taken the view that the *contra proferentem* principle applies to the interpretation of an insurance policy whether or not there is ambiguity.

Similarly, in *St Edmundsbury and Ipswich Diocesan Board of Finance v Clark*   **7.92**
(No.2),[242] the Court of Appeal held that the presumption can only come into play if the court finds itself unable to reach a sure conclusion on the construction of the provision in question; and that the presumption is not a factor which may be taken into account in reaching that conclusion. So also in *Mira Oil Resources of Tortola v Bocimar*,[243] Colman J said:

"Further, this is not a case where the meaning of the words is so finely balanced

---

238 (1853) 1 Kay 1.
239 [1951] 1 K.B. 368 CA.
240 [2016] UKSC 57; [2017] A.C. 73.
241 [2019] CSIH 9; 2019 SLT 483. It is doubtful whether this is correct.
242 [1975] 1 W.L.R. 468.
243 [1999] 2 Lloyd's Rep. 101.

that the *contra proferentem* rule should be applied in favour of the owners. If in the view of the Court one of the two suggested meanings is significantly preferable to the other, as a matter of construction, it can safely be concluded that the former meaning reflects the mutual intention of the parties."

In *The Olympic Brilliance*,[244] Eveleigh LJ said that the principle was: "usually a rule of, if not last, very late resort".

7.93　　In *Macey v Qazi*,[245] the Court of Appeal went further, and declared that the presumption is to be used only as a last resort. This appears to be the current view. In *Sinochem International Oil (London) Co Ltd v Mobil Sales & Supply Corp*,[246] Mance LJ said:

"I bear in mind that cl. 18 was proffered by Mobil Delaware. But construction against the party putting forward a clause is a rule of last resort."

In *McCann v Switzerland Insurance Australia Ltd*,[247] Kirby J said:

"Courts now generally regard the *contra proferentem* rule (as it is called) as one of last resort because it is widely accepted that it is preferable that judges should struggle with the words actually used as applied to the unique circumstances of the case and reach their own conclusions by reference to the logic of the matter, rather than by using mechanical formulae."

In *BNY Mellon Corporate Trustee Services Ltd v LBG Capital No.1 Plc*,[248]Lord Neuberger said:

"... the contra proferentem rule is very much a last refuge, almost an admission of defeat, when it comes to construing a document."

7.94　　In the case of contracts of guarantee it is often said that they are to be construed *contra proferentem*; that is in favour of the guarantor.[249] However, in the light of the *ICS* case it is doubtful whether the mere fact that a contract is a contract of guarantee is enough to bring the *contra proferentem* principle into play.[250] Even if it does, the principle cannot be pressed too far. In *Coughlan v SH Lock (Australia) Ltd*,[251] Lord Oliver said:

"At the outset [counsel] has reminded their Lordships of certain well-known principles of construction in relation to guarantees. Such a document falls to be construed strictly; it is to be read *contra proferentem*; and, in case of ambiguity, it is to be construed in favour of the surety. But these principles do not, of course, mean that where parties to such a document have deliberately chosen to adopt wording of the widest possible import that wording is to be ignored. Nor do they oust the principle that where wording is susceptible of more than one meaning

---

[244] [1982] 2 Lloyd's Rep. 205 CA.
[245] *The Independent,* 13 January 1987.
[246] [2000] 1 Lloyd's Rep. 339.
[247] [2000] HCA 65.
[248] [2016] UKSC 29; [2016] Bus. L.R. 725.
[249] See, e.g. *Eastern Counties Building Society v Russell* [1947] 1 All E.R. 500.
[250] *Egan v Static Control Components (Europe) Ltd* [2004] 2 Lloyd's Rep. 429 CA; *Meritz Fire & Marine Insurance Co Ltd* [2010] EWHC 3362 (Comm).
[251] (1987) 3 B.C.C. 183 PC. See also *The Kalma* [1999] 2 Lloyd's Rep. 374.

regard may be had to the circumstances surrounding the execution of the document as an aid to construction."

Similarly, in *Johnsey Estates Ltd v Webb*,[252] Millett J said:

"On the other hand the words have to be fairly construed in their context and in accordance with their proper meaning without in any way favouring the guarantor, who is not placed in any more favourable position in this regard than any other contracting party. The so-called rule of construction is very much a matter of last resort."

(k) Effect of the maxim

Where the principle applies, it does not mean that the court should decide the case against the interest of the *proferens* wherever it can. The maxim was applied to a clause in an employment contract which permitted the employer unilaterally to vary the employee's rights.[253] But the narrow interpretation was in fact relied on by the employee. As the court said: **7.95**

"of course the meaning of the clause cannot vary depending upon who is praying it in aid."

Similarly, where a use clause in a lease was ambiguous, the application of the principle led to the adoption of a broader rather than a narrower permitted use, even though for the purposes of rent review it was in the tenant's commercial interest to argue for a narrow use.[254] Likewise, in a dissenting judgment in *Crawford v Morrow*,[255] Côté J said: **7.96**

"If the doctrine does apply, it tells the Court to select one of the two possible interpretations of the contract, the one less favourable to the party who drafted the contract.
    That refers to selecting one interpretation of the contract, not selecting one result of the suit. The proper interpretation of the contract must exist at the time that it is made, and not change. It cannot come and go as the parties' fortunes wax and wane. It cannot be unknowable and shrouded in fog until after the event. For example, one interprets an insurance contract the same way before and after a fire, and it has meaning before any fire."

It is thought that in principle this is the correct approach.[256] Nor does the principle enable the court to adopt a strained meaning of the contract. In *North v Marina*,[257] Campbell J said: **7.97**

"The role of the maxim is to enable the court to choose between alternative meanings of the document or clause in question, being meanings which are fairly open.

---

252 [1990] 1 E.G.L.R. 80.
253 *Dresdner Kleinwort Ltd v Attrill* [2013] EWCA Civ 394.
254 *Skillion Plc v Keltec Industrial Research Ltd* [1992] 1 E.G.L.R. 123.
255 (2004) 244 D.L.R. (4th) 144.
256 This approach appears to have been endorsed by the Court of Appeal in *Hin-Pro International Logistics Ltd v Compania Sud Americana De Vapores SA* [2015] EWCA Civ 401, although the assessment could not be carried out on the facts.
257 (2003) 11 B.P.R. 21, 359 at [75], approved in *Ravi v Logan Wines* [2007] NSWCA 62.

It is not a legitimate use of the maxim to say that two meanings of a particular contractual provision are possible, and that the meaning unfavourable to the *proferens* should be chosen, if one of those alternative meanings is an unrealistic or unlikely construction of the contract."

(l) Crown grants

7.98 The principle is inverted in the case of grants from the Crown.[258] Thus in *Feather v R.*,[259] Cockburn CJ said:

"It is established on the best authority that, in construing grants from the Crown, a different rule of construction prevails from that by which grants from one subject to another are to be construed. In a grant from one subject to another, every intendment is to be made against the grantor, in favour of the grantee, in order to give full effect to the grant; but in grants from the Crown an opposite rule prevails. Nothing passes except that which is expressed, or which is matter of necessity and unavoidable intendment in order to give effect to the plain and undoubted intention of the grant. And in no species of grant does this rule of construction more especially obtain than in grants which emanate from and operate in derogation of, the prerogative of the Crown."

Similarly, Lord Birkenhead LC, speaking in the Committee of Privileges of the House of Lords,[260] said:

"The rule that the words of an instrument shall be taken most strictly against the party employing them—*verba chartarum fortius accipiuntur contra proferentem*—does not apply to the Crown such a grant is construed most strictly against the grantee and most beneficially for the Crown, so that nothing will pass to the grantee but by clear and express words."

In *Lynn Shellfish Ltd v Loose*,[261] Lord Neuberger and Lord Carnwath said:

"It is well established that, unlike other instruments, grants by the Crown are not construed against the grantor (contra proferentem). Crown grants are 'construed most strictly against the grantee and most beneficially for the Crown, so that nothing will pass to the grantee but by clear and express words'."

7.99 The rationale behind the inversion of the normal principle is that:

"the prerogatives and rights and emoluments of the Crown being conferred upon it for great purposes, and for the public use, it shall not be intended that such prerogatives, rights and emoluments are diminished by any grant, beyond what such grant by necessary and unavoidable construction shall take away."[262]

7.100 However:

---

[258] *Att.-Gen. v Ewelme Hospital* (1853) 17 Beav. 366, per Romilly MR. But where the Crown seeks to rely upon an exemption clause inserted into a contract for its benefit, the *contra proferentem* rule will be applied against it: *Canada Steamship Lines v R.* [1952] A.C. 192.

[259] (1865) 6 B. & S. 257.

[260] *Viscountess Rhondda's Claim* [1922] 2 A.C. 339; *Wynne-Finch v Natural Resources Body for Wales* [2020] EWHC 1924 (Ch).

[261] [2016] UKSC 14; [2017] 1 All E.R. 677.

[262] *The Rebeckah* (1799) 1 Ch. Rob. 227, per Lord Stowell.

"the rule that grants by the Crown should be construed in favour of the Crown has no application to ordinary commercial transactions, let alone those where the contract is in a standard form."[263]

But it has been recently applied to a Crown grant of mines and minerals,[264] and to a Latin charter granted by the Crown in 1115.[265]

(m) Injunctions

In the case of an injunction, breach of which may give rise to an application to commit, any ambiguity is to be resolved in favour of the respondent or defendant.[266] However, in *Marketmaker Technology (Beijing) Co Ltd v CMC Group Plc*,[267] Teare J, while accepting the principle, said that: **7.101**

"in order for an undertaking to be ambiguous there must be, at the least, an alternative interpretation which is an available meaning of the words to be found in the undertaking."

Illustrations

1.   A merchant shipped a box of diamonds on a ship under a bill of lading containing an exemption clause, exempting the shipowner from pirates, robbers, thieves and barratry of master and mariners. The diamonds were stolen during the voyage or on the ship's arrival in port. The question arose whether thieves had to be persons external to the ship or whether the word could include passengers. Lush J said:

"The word is ambiguous, and being of doubtful meaning, it must receive such a construction as is most in favour of the shipowner, and for whose benefit the exceptions are framed."

Taylor v The Liverpool and Great Western Steam Co[268]

2.   A lease contained a covenant restricting the use which the tenant could make of the property. A dispute arose between the landlord and the tenant as to its true meaning. Cairns LJ said:

"I think that the clause is ambiguous, and that this is one of those rare cases where resort should be had to the *contra proferentem* rule and, applying that rule, the clause should be construed in the manner contended for by the tenants."

Killick v Second Covent Garden Property Co Ltd[269]

3.   A conveyance contained a reservation of a right of way. It was held that the

---

[263]   *Lonrho Exports Ltd v Export Credits Guarantee Department* [1999] Ch. 158 at 183, per Lightman J.
[264]   *Earl of Lonsdale v Att.-Gen.* [1982] 1 W.L.R. 887.
[265]   *Crown Estates Commissioners v Roberts* [2008] 2 E.G.L.R. 165.
[266]   *Masri v Consolidated Contractors (Oil and Gas) Co Sal* [2009] EWCA Civ 36; *Jobserve Ltd v Skill Site Ltd* [2004] F.S.R. 762; *Lait v Williams* [2006] EWHC 633 (TCC).
[267]   [2009] EWHC 1445 (QB).
[268]   (1874) L.R. 9 Q.B. 546.
[269]   [1973] 1 W.L.R. 658.

reservation operated as a regrant by the purchaser to the vendor, and that accordingly the purchaser, rather than the vendor, was the *proferens* against whom the reservation would be construed.

St Edmundsbury and Ipswich Diocesan Board of Finance v Clark (No.2)[270]

4.   A building contract contained an extension of time clause. It was held that in case of ambiguity it should be interpreted in favour of the contractor.

Multiplex Constructions (UK) Ltd v Honeywell Control Systems Ltd[271]

9.   CONSTRUCTION IN FAVOUR OF CONSUMER

If there is doubt about the meaning of a written term in a consumer contract, the meaning that is most favourable to the consumer prevails.

7.102   Section 69(1) of the Consumer Rights Act 2015 provides that:

> "If a term in a consumer contract, or a consumer notice, could have different meanings, the meaning that is most favourable to the consumer is to prevail."

In substance this re-enacts reg.7(2) of the Unfair Terms in Consumer Contracts Regulations 1999.[272]

7.103   A consumer contract is a contract between a trader and a consumer.[273] A "trader" is a person acting for purposes relating to that person's trade, business, craft or profession, whether acting personally or through another person acting in the trader's name or on the trader's behalf.[274] A "consumer" is an individual acting for purposes that are wholly or mainly outside that individual's trade, business, craft or profession.[275] Since a consumer is defined as an individual, rather than a person, it follows that a limited company cannot be a consumer.

7.104   The interpretative rule does not apply to proceedings by regulators to enforce the Act. Nor does it apply to a term of a contract, or to a notice, to the extent that it reflects—

(a)   mandatory statutory or regulatory provisions, or

(b)   the provisions or principles of an international convention to which the UK or the EU is a party.[276]

Nor does it apply where the court, having recognised a mistake in the language used, is applying a corrective construction by reading into the clause words, which have not been expressed, to correct the mistake.[277]

7.105   This is one of very few occasions on which legislation has instructed the court how to interpret a contract. The principle contained in the regulation is similar to

---

[270]   [1975] 1 W.L.R. 468.

[271]   (2007) 111 Con. L.R. 78.

[272]   SI 1999/2083. ("If there is a doubt about the meaning of a written term, the interpretation which is most favourable to the consumer shall prevail but this rule shall not apply in proceedings brought under regulation 12", i.e. proceedings by regulators for an injunction prohibiting use of a particular term.)

[273]   Consumer Rights Act 2015 s.62(1).

[274]   Consumer Rights Act 2015 s.2(2).

[275]   Consumer Rights Act 2015 s.2(3).

[276]   Consumer Rights Act 2015 s.74(1).

[277]   *R & S Pilling v UK Insurance Ltd* [2019] UKSC 16; [2019] 2 W.L.R. 1015.

the *contra proferentem* principle. In *Peabody Trust Governors v Reeve*,[278] Gabriel Moss QC (sitting as a judge of the Chancery Division) said of reg.7(2):

"This rule in the Regulation appears to be analogous to the domestic English law principle of *contra proferentem* which is normally to the effect that in the case of ambiguity a document is construed against the party putting it forward."

There appears to be no significant difference between the *contra proferentem* principle and this statutory rule of interpretation.[279] First, as in the case of the *contra proferentem* principle, there is no ambiguity the rule cannot apply.[280] Accordingly, if there is "a single and obvious construction", the rule cannot apply.[281] Moreover, a court should be wary of starting its analysis by finding an ambiguity by reference to the words in question looked at on their own. And it should not, in any event, on such a finding, move straight to the *contra proferentem* rule, without first looking at the context.[282] Second, the court is only required to choose between interpretations that the court might otherwise adopt using ordinary techniques of interpretation. In *AJ Building and Plastering Ltd v Turner*,[283] H.H. Judge Keyser QC said:

7.106

"If the normal principles of construction yield a clear preference, even of two competing interpretations over one, the remaining ambiguity applies only to the preferred interpretations; all others have been rejected before invoking any rule or principle of last resort; and they are still rejected, even if they remain possible interpretations in the sense that there is room for other courts or judges to favour them—a common enough state of affairs in appellate courts. Neither at common law nor, in my view, under regulation 7 (2) is the court that invokes what I may call the tie-breaker required or permitted to apply it in favour of an interpretation that has already been rejected by means of the application of the normal canons of construction."

More generally, in *Foxtons Ltd v Pelkey Bicknell*,[284] Lord Neuberger of Abbotsbury said (without reference to the 1999 Regulations):

7.107

"this case is concerned with Foxtons' standard terms. Accordingly, one should lean in favour of a construction which favours their client, particularly in the field of domestic estate agency contracts, where the agent is an expert, often professionally qualified, and normally legally advised, and the client will normally be a lay person who will not seek legal advice on those terms."

---

278 [2008] 43 E.G. 196.
279 *Financial Services Authority v Asset LI Inc* [2013] EWHC 178 (Ch); *AJ Building and Plastering Ltd v Turner* [2013] EWHC 484 (QB).
280 *du Plessis v Fontgary Leisure Parks Ltd* [2012] EWCA Civ 409; *Lebara Mobile Ltd v Lycamobile UK Ltd* [2015] EWHC 3318 (Ch).
281 *Higgins & Co Lawyers Ltd v Evans* [2019] EWHC 2809 (QB).
282 *West v Ian Finlay & Associates (a firm)* [2014] EWCA Civ 316, following *McGeown v Direct Travel Insurance* [2004] 1 All E.R. (Comm) 609.
283 [2013] EWHC 484 (QB), disapproving a previous edition of this book. That decision was followed in *Khurana v Weber Construction Ltd* [2015] EWHC 758 (TCC). See also *Commission v Spain* (C-70/03) [2004] E.C.R. I-7999.
284 [2008] 2 E.G.L.R. 23.

10. PARTY NOT TO TAKE ADVANTAGE OF OWN WRONG

A contract will be interpreted so far as possible in such a manner as not to permit one party to it to take advantage of his own wrong.[285]

7.108   This principle has a long history, and can be traced back to Lord Coke's day.[286] In *Rede v Farr*,[287] a tenant who had failed to pay his rent asserted that by reason of a proviso for re-entry which said that the lease would be void in the event of breach of obligation his lease was at an end. Lord Ellenborough said:

> "In this case, as to this proviso, it would be contrary to an universal principle of law, that a party shall never take advantage of his own wrong, if we were to hold that a lease, which in terms is a lease for twelve years, should be a lease determinable at the will and pleasure of the lessee; and that a lessee by not paying his rent should be at liberty to say that the lease is void."

This formulation suggests that it is a rule of law. However, the decision could be justified on the basis that the court was construing the word "void" in the proviso for re-entry as meaning "voidable".

7.109   In *New Zealand Shipping Co v Societe des Ateliers et Chantiers de France*,[288] Lord Atkinson seems to have treated it as a matter of construction. He said:

> "It is undoubtedly competent for the two parties to a contract to stipulate by a clause that the contract shall be void upon the happening of an event over which neither of the parties shall have any control, cannot bring about, prevent or retard. ... But if the stipulation be that the contract shall be void on the happening of an event which one or other of them can by his own act or omission bring about, then the party, who by his act or omission brings that event about, cannot be permitted either to insist upon the stipulation himself or to compel the other party, who is blameless, to insist upon it, because to permit the blameable party to do either would be to permit him to take advantage of his own wrong, in the one case directly, and in the other case in a roundabout way, but in either way putting an end to the contract."

In the same case, Lord Finlay LC seems to have treated the principle as a rule of law, while Lord Wrenbury treated it as a question of construction.

7.110   In *Cheall v APEX*,[289] in commenting on the *New Zealand* case, Lord Diplock spoke of:

---

[285] This section was referred to with approval in *Extra MSA Services Cobham Ltd v Accor UK Economy Hotels Ltd* [2010] EWHC 775 (Ch) and *Fitzroy Development Ltd v Fitzrovia Properties Ltd* [2011] EWHC 1849 (Ch).

[286] In Co Litt 206b, Lord Coke says: "If a man make a feoffment in fee, upon condition that the feoffee shall re-infeoff him before such a day, and before the day the feoffor disseise the feoffee, and hold him out by force until the day be past, the state of the feoffee is absolute; for the feoffor is the cause wherefore the condition cannot be performed, and therefore shall never take advantage for non-performance thereof. And so it is if A be bound to B that JS shall marry Jane G before such a day, and before the day B marry with Jane, he shall never take advantage of the bond, for that he himself is the mean that the condition could not be performed. And this is regularly true in all cases." Lord Coke also mentions the principle at Co Litt 148b in its Latin form: *"nullus commodum capere potest de injuria sua propria"*.

[287] (1817) 6 M. & S. 121.

[288] [1918] A.C. 1.

[289] [1983] 2 A.C. 181. See also the dissenting judgment of Donaldson LJ at [1983] Q.B. 126 at 144.

"the well known rule of construction that, except in the unlikely case that the contract contains clear express provisions to the contrary, it is to be presumed that it was not the intention of the parties that either party should be entitled to rely upon his own breaches of his primary obligations as bringing the contract to an end."

He described "this rule of construction" as being paralleled by the "rule of law" that a contract cannot be brought to an end by self-induced frustration. The principle may be seen as an aspect of the principle of interpretation that leans against interpretations that produce unreasonable or absurd consequences that could not have been intended.[290]

In *Great Elephant Corp v Trafigura Beheer BV*,[291] Longmore LJ said:　　　　　　**7.111**

"it would be absurd if Vitol could excuse themselves from the consequences of that breach by reference to the Force Majeure clause when it was their own breach of contract that caused the supposed force majeure in the first place. So to allow Vitol would be to allow them to take advantage of their own wrong."

It is considered that the principle as applied in England and Wales and Australia[292]　**7.112** is one of construction rather than of law, and may be ousted by the express terms of the contract.[293] In *Gyllenhammar & Partners International Ltd v Sour Brodogradevna Industrija*,[294] a shipbuilding contract stated that it was subject to the builder declaring that a guarantee had been obtained; and also declaring that all necessary permissions and approvals had been obtained. It went on to say that if these had not been obtained within 30 days of the date of the contract then the contract should become null and void. Hirst J held that this language was sufficiently clear to oust the principle. He said:

"So far as the *New Zealand* and *Cheall* cases are concerned, it seems to me that the express terms of art. 23 exclude the general rule of construction, since sub-cl. (a) and (c) could not operate in the absence of a breach by the party concerned, thus rendering reliance on the general rule impossible for the same reasons as it was impossible for the plaintiff to rely on APEX's r. 14 in the *Cheall* case."

In *Decoma UK Ltd v Haden Drysys International Ltd*,[295] the Court of Appeal held　**7.113** that the words of a "crystal clear" clause in a contract could not be overridden by

---

[290] *Financial Ombudsman Service v Heather Moor & Edgecomb Ltd* [2009] 1 All E.R. 328, per Stanley Burnton LJ.

[291] [2013] EWCA Civ 905.

[292] *Suttor v Gundowa* (1950) 81 C.L.R. 418 at 441; *Gange v Sullivan* (1966) C.L.R. 418 at 442; *Hope Island Resort Holdings Pty Ltd v Jefferson Properties (Qld) Pty Ltd* [2005] QCA 315; *Gold City Developments Pty Ltd v Portpride Pty Ltd* [2010] WASC 148.

[293] *Micklefield v SAC Technology Ltd* [1990] 1 W.L.R. 1002. However, in *Kensland Realty Ltd v Whaleview Investment Ltd* [2001] HKCFA 57, the Court of Final Appeal of Hong Kong doubted the correctness of this case, because relevant Australian authority was not cited. The Australian cases are *Peter Turnbull & Co Pty Ltd v Mondus Trading Co (Australia) Pty Ltd* (1953) 90 C.L.R. 235 and *Mahoney v Lindsay* (1981) 55 A.J.L.R. 118. But *Decoma UK Ltd v Haden Drysys International Ltd* [2006] EWCA Civ 723 reaffirmed the view that the principle is one of construction only, although *Kensland Realty* does not appear to have been cited. The same appears to be true in Australia. In England and Wales the question has now been resolved by *BDW Trading Ltd v JM Rowe (Investments) Ltd* [2011] EWCA Civ 548 reaffirming that the question is one of interpretation.

[294] [1989] 2 Lloyd's Rep. 430.

[295] [2006] EWCA Civ 723.

the principle. In *Petroplus Marketing AG v Shell Trading International Ltd*,[296] Andrew Smith J said:

"It is a general principle of construction that prima facie it will be presumed that the parties intended that neither should be entitled to rely on his own breach of duty to obtain a benefit under a contract, at least where the breach of duty is a breach of an obligation under that contract: see *Chitty on Contracts*, Vol 1 at para 12-082. This is sometimes presented not as a matter of contractual construction but an implied contractual term that a right or benefit conferred upon a party shall not be available to him if he relies upon his own breach of the contract to establish his claim: Chitty on Contracts Vol 1 at para 13-012. However analysed, the principle is not inflexible or absolute: it may be displaced by express contractual provision or by the parties' intention to be understood from the express terms: *Richco International Ltd. v Alfred C Toepfer International GMBH*."[297]

He held on the construction of the particular contract that the principle had been displaced by the terms of the contract. In *The Law Debenture Trust Corp Plc v Elektrim SA*,[298] Sales J also applied the principle as one of construction. Thus English law continues to take the view that the principle is one of interpretation rather than a rule of substantive law. In *BDW Trading Ltd v JM Rowe (Investments) Ltd*,[299] Patten LJ said:

"Although there has been a certain amount of academic discussion as to whether the principle has the status of a rule of law which is imposed upon the parties to a contract almost regardless of what they have agreed, it is now clear as a matter of authority that the application of the principle can be excluded or modified by the terms of the contract and that its scope in any particular case will depend upon the construction of the relevant agreement."

This may be taken to have settled the question up to the level of the Court of Appeal.

7.114   However, the Court of Final Appeal of Hong Kong has held that the principle may be given effect either as a principle of construction or as a rule of law, according to what is appropriate in the circumstances[300]; and this has been followed at first instance in England.[301] If applied as a rule of substantive law, the principle precludes the wrongdoer from taking advantage of his own wrong however clearly the contract may appear to entitle him to do so.[302]

7.115   The cases thus far referred to concern claims that a contract has been terminated entirely. However, the principle has a broader application. Thus in *Harmsworth*

---

[296] [2009] EWHC 1024 (Comm).

[297] [1991] 1 Lloyd's Rep. 136 at 144.

[298] [2009] EWHC 1801.

[299] [2011] EWCA Civ 548; *Office of Fair Trading v Ashbourne Management Services Ltd* [2011] EWHC 1237 (Ch). In *Zhoushan Jinhaiwan Shipyard Co Ltd v Golden Exquisite Inc* [2014] EWHC 4050 (Comm) the principle was held not to apply on the particular interpretation of the contract.

[300] *Kensland Realty Ltd v Whale View Investment Ltd* [2001] HKCFA 57.

[301] *Rother District Investments Ltd v Corke* [2004] 1 E.G.L.R. 47. In the light of *BDW Trading Ltd v JM Rowe (Investments) Ltd* [2011] EWCA Civ 548, this must be taken to have been wrong on this point.

[302] *Kensland Realty Ltd v Whale View Investment Ltd*, above, doubting *Micklefield v SAC Technology Ltd* [1990] 1 W.L.R. 1002.

Pension Funds Trustees Ltd v Charringtons Industrial Holdings Ltd,[303] it was held that for the purpose of assessing rent under a rent review clause, the tenant must be assumed to have complied with its repairing covenant, for otherwise it would be taking advantage of its own breach of covenant in order to depress the rent which would otherwise be payable.

So also in *Alghussein Establishment v Eton College,*[304] an agreement for lease **7.116** contained a covenant by the intending lessee to build. A clause in the agreement provided that if for any reason due to the wilful default of the tenant the development should remain uncompleted by a certain date the lease should forthwith be completed. The House of Lords held that the tenant was not entitled to take advantage of his own wilful default in securing a benefit under a continuing contract, namely the obtaining of the lease. Lord Jauncey of Tullichettle said:

"Although the authorities to which I have already referred involve cases of avoidance the clear theme running through them is that no man can take advantage of his own wrong. There was nothing in any of them to suggest that the foregoing proposition was limited to cases where the parties in breach were seeking to avoid the contract and I can see no reason for so limiting it. A party who seeks to obtain a benefit under a continuing contract is just as much taking advantage of his own wrong as a party who relies on his breach to avoid a contract and thereby escape his obligations."

In order to bring the principle into operation, the relevant breach of duty must **7.117** be a duty owed by one party to the other under the terms of the contract. Thus where the contract imposes no obligations on one party to it (e.g. because it is a unilateral contract, such as an option) there is no room for the principle to operate.[305] In *Eurobank Ergasias SA v Kalliroi Navigation Co Ltd*[306] it was held that the principle is:

"limited to where the party seeking to enforce is relying on his own breach of contractual duty under the agreement in question, as opposed to some wider wrong."

In addition, breach of a duty whether contractual or non-contractual to a stranger to the contract will not suffice.[307]

It is also necessary to show that the contractual rights or benefits which the party in question is seeking to assert or claim arise as a direct result of that party's prior breach of contract.[308]

In order to displace the principle there must be "a clear contractual intention to **7.118** be gathered from the express provisions of the contract".[309] The contractual intention is to be decided by the application of the ordinary principles applicable to the

---

[303] (1985) 49 P. & C.R. 297.
[304] [1988] 1 W.L.R. 587.
[305] *Little v Courage Ltd* (1994) 70 P. & C.R. 469 CA.
[306] [2015] EWHC 2377 (Comm).
[307] *Cheall v APEX* [1983] 2 A.C. 180.
[308] *Kensland Realty Ltd v Whale View Investment Ltd* [2001] HKCFA 57; *Nina's Bar Bistro Pty Ltd v MBE Corp (Sydney) Pty Ltd* [1984] 3 N.S.W.L.R. 613.
[309] *Richco International v Alfred C. Toepfer International* [1991] 1 Lloyd's Rep. 136; *Sainsbury's Supermarkets Ltd v Bristol Rovers (1883) Ltd* [2015] EWHC 2002 (Ch); [2016] 1 P. & C.R. 6 (the point did not arise on the appeal: [2016] EWCA Civ 160).

interpretation of contracts and the implication of terms.[310] Where a contract gave a party the right to terminate "without prejudice to the rights of any one party against the other for any antecedent breach of the terms" of the contract, those words were insufficient to displace the principle.[311] Likewise, the existence of a contractual "no set-off" clause does not prevent the principle from applying.[312]

Illustrations

1.   A lease of a mine contained a forfeiture clause which provided that the lease would be void if the lessee ceased to mine for two years. It was held that the word "void" should be construed as meaning "voidable at the option of the lessor" and did not entitle the tenant to put an end to the lease.
   Quesnel Forks Gold Mining Co Ltd v Ward[313]

2.   A share option scheme provided for employees of subsidiaries of a public company to acquire shares in the company at favourable prices. The scheme was open only to employees. The company sold one of its subsidiaries to a third party, and an employee of the former subsidiary claimed that the company could not take advantage of its own wrong in selling the subsidiary to defeat the exercise of his option. It was held that the company owed no obligation to the employee not to sell the subsidiary, and consequently the sale was not a wrong for that purpose.
   Thompson v ASDA-MFI Group Plc[314]

3.   A lease contained a covenant by the tenant to register assignments within a stipulated time. In a licence to assign, sureties guaranteed performance of the tenant's covenants by the assignee. A proviso to the licence stated that it was to become void if the assignment was not registered in accordance with the covenant. The assignment was not so registered. It was held that the sureties remained liable because they had guaranteed performance by the assignee of the tenant's covenant to register the assignment, and they could not rely on their own breach of covenant caused by the failure to register the assignment in order to avoid liability.
   Cerium Investments Ltd v Evans[315]

4.   An agreement for the sale of shares gave the seller the option to repurchase the shares, completion to take place on the option completion date. The contract provided that all rights attaching to the shares should vest in the seller on the option completion date. The seller exercised the option but was unable to complete on the option completion date. It was held that since the failure to complete was due to the seller's wilful default, the contract should be construed so as not to permit him to take advantage of his own wrong. Accordingly, the buyer continued to be able to vote the shares as he chose.
   JRRT (Investments) Ltd v Haycraft[316]

5.   A contract for the sale of land provided for completion at 13.00 on 2

---

[310] *BDW Trading Ltd v JM Rowe (Investments) Ltd* [2011] EWCA Civ 548.
[311] *Sainsbury's Supermarkets Ltd v Bristol Rovers (1883) Ltd* [2015] EWHC 2002 (Ch).
[312] *TMF Trustee Ltd v Fire Navigation Inc* [2019] EWHC 2918 (Comm).
[313] [1920] A.C. 222. See also *Doe d. Bryan v Bancks* (1821) 4 B. & Ald. 401.
[314] [1988] 2 W.L.R. 1093.
[315] [1991] 1 E.G.L.R. 80 CA.
[316] [1993] B.C.L.C. 401.

September. Time was of the essence. The contract also provided for payment of the completion monies to be by cashiers' orders or cheques in favour of such person as the vendor might direct. One hour and 47 minutes before the time for completion, the vendor issued a direction about how the completion monies were to be apportioned. That was a breach of an implied term to the effect that a direction had to be given at a time which enabled the purchaser to comply with it before completion. Consequently, the vendor was not entitled to insist on strict compliance with the completion deadline, and a tender of the purchase monies six minutes late was a valid tender.

Kensland Realty Ltd v Whale View Investment Ltd[317]

11. CONTRACT TO BE CONSTRUED SO AS TO BE LAWFUL

Where the words of a contract are capable of two meanings, one of which is lawful and the other unlawful, the former interpretation should be preferred.[318]

This principle is based on the proposition that "the parties are unlikely to have intended to agree to something unlawful".[319] It has also been said to be an aspect of the principle of construction "that leans against interpretations that produce unreasonable or absurd consequences that could not have been intended".[320] Equally it has been said to be an aspect of the principle that contracts are to be validated when possible. As Toulson LJ explained in *Great Estates Group Ltd v Digby*[321]:

7.119

"... if the contract is capable of being read in two ways, one of which would involve a contravention of a statute and the other would not, that may be a powerful reason for reading the contract in the sense which is compliant with the statute, even if it is the less natural construction. (This is to put in modern terms the approach expressed in the maxim *ut magis valeat quam pereat*.)"

Sir Edward Coke[322] expressed the principle thus:

"It is a general rule, that whensoever the words of a deed, or of one of the parties without deed, may have a double intendment, and the one standeth with law and right, and the other is wrongful and against law, the intendment that standeth with law shall be taken."

---

[317] [2001] HKCFA 57.
[318] Referred to with approval in *Manor Asset Ltd v Demolition Services Ltd* [2016] EWHC 222 (TCC); *Cape Distribution Ltd v Cape Intermediate Holdings Plc* [2016] EWHC 1119 (QB); [2016] Lloyd's Rep. I.R. 499; *Chaggar v Chaggar* [2018] EWHC 1203 (QB); *Re Criminal Justice Act 1988 Re Khan* [2019] EWHC 2683 (Admin); *Global Network Services Pty Ltd v Legion Telecall Pty Ltd* [2001] NSWCA 279, per Mason P, dissenting; and by the Court of Appeal of Alberta in *Lust v Foundations For the Future Charter Academy* [2007] 409 A.R. 90. It was also referred to with approval in *Landlord Protect Ltd v St Anselm Development Co Ltd* [2008] EWHC 1582 (Ch) where the principle was said to accord with the general principle that a court should seek to uphold, rather than to defeat, the parties' contract. The first instance decision was reversed by the Court of Appeal on other grounds: [2009] 2 P. & C.R. 9. Compare the *European Principles of Contract Law*, para.5:106: "An interpretation which makes the terms of the contract lawful, or effective, is to be preferred to one which would not".
[319] *BCCI v Ali* [2002] 1 A.C. 251 at 269, per Lord Hoffmann.
[320] *Financial Ombudsman Service v Heather Moor & Edgecomb Ltd* [2009] 1 All E.R. 328, per Stanley Burnton LJ.
[321] [2011] EWCA Civ 1120; [2011] 3 E.G.L.R. 101.
[322] Co.Litt. 42a.

7.120   In more modern times that statement was approved by the Privy Council in *Rodger v Comptoir D'Escompte de Paris*,[323] in which Sir Joseph Napier, delivering the advice of the Board said:

> "The rule that words shall be construed most strongly against him who uses them gives place to a higher rule; higher because it has a moral element, that the construction shall not be such as to work a wrong."

Similarly, in *Fausset v Carpenter*,[324] the House of Lords accepted the submission of counsel that the court:

> "... in judging of the design and object of a deed, will not presume that a party executing the deed meant to do and did what he was wrong in doing, when a construction may be put on the instrument perfectly consistent with his doing only what he had a right to do."

7.121   The traditional view is that the question of construction should not be approached with a leaning in one direction or another. Thus although the law frowns upon covenants in restraint of trade, nevertheless such a covenant should not be approached on the basis that it is prima facie illegal. "You are to construe the contract, and then see whether it is legal."[325]

7.122   However, this may be an over-simplification. As Simon Brown LJ[326] explained in *Lancashire County Council v Municipal Mutual Insurance Ltd*[327]:

> "The only way in which public policy can properly be invoked in the construction of a contract is under the rule *ut res magis valeat quam pereat*: if the words are susceptible of two meanings, one of which would validate the particular clause or contract and the other render it void or ineffective, then the former interpretation should be applied even though it might otherwise, looking merely at the words and their context, be less appropriate."

7.123   Thus in choosing between two possible meanings of a covenant in restraint of trade, and without rewriting the clause, it is legitimate to adopt a construction which limits the clause to reasonable protection of a legitimate business interest, with the consequence that the clause will be lawful, and to reject a construction which would render the clause void.[328]

In the *Lancashire County Council* case Staughton LJ took a more cautious view. He said:

> "Next, it was suggested that the contract of insurance should be interpreted so as to accord with public policy. Here there is another Latin maxim—*verba ita*

---

[323] (1869) L.R. 2 P.C. 393.

[324] (1831) 2 Dow. & Cl. 232.

[325] *Mills v Dunham* [1893] 1 Ch. 577, per Lindley LJ. See also *Metropolitan Electric Supply Co Ltd v Ginder* [1901] 2 Ch. 799, per Buckley J ("my first duty is to construe the contract, and for the purpose of arriving at the true construction of the contract, I must disregard what would be the legal consequences of construing it the one way or the other way").

[326] With whom Thorpe LJ agreed.

[327] [1997] Q.B. 897.

[328] *PSG Franchising Ltd v Lydia Darby Ltd* [2012] EWHC 3707 (QB); *Croesus Financial Services Ltd v Bradshaw* [2013] EWHC 3685 (QB); *Tillman v Egon Zehnder Ltd* [2019] UKSC 32; [2019] 3 W.L.R. 245.

sunt intelligenda ut res magis valeat quam pereat: the contract should be interpreted so that it is valid rather than ineffective. If on one view the contract would be illegal, there is a case for adopting another available interpretation."

However, he considered that, except in the case of one construction that would make a contract illegal, whereas another one would not, there is no principle that requires a contract to be construed in accordance with public policy.[329]

Mason P put it in *Global Network Services Pty Ltd v Legion Telecall Pty Ltd*[330]   **7.124**
as follows:

"The absolute construction contended for by Global involves the parties to the Contract promising in effect that one will act in a grossly uncommercial way that would involve unlawful activity on Legion's part and complicity on Global's part. Unless driven to such an outcome by intractable language, such a construction should be rejected having regard to the principle that, where the words of a contract are capable of two meanings, one lawful and the other unlawful, the former construction should be preferred."

In *Coulson v Newsgroup Newspapers Ltd*, Newsgroup's contract with the edi-   **7.125**
tor of one of its newspapers required it to indemnify him against legal costs. The question was whether this extended to costs incurred in defending himself against a criminal charge. The Court of Appeal[331] held that it did. McCombe LJ said:

"There is nothing in the criminal nature of the proceedings to render it objection-able that the indemnity should apply. Once one allows within the indemnity costs of defence of some criminal charges, the scope of the indemnity cannot be defined simply by the criminal nature of the proceedings in question.
    If I am right to think that there is nothing inherently objectionable in a clause such as this covering the defence of criminal proceedings as such, it seems to me that the limit has to be bounded by the question whether the criminal allega-tions arise out of how the employee went about the performance of his job or whether they arise out of some act having nothing whatever to do with perform-ing the job."

Illustrations

1.   A bond was conditioned to assign all offices. It was held that it should be construed as limited to those offices which it was lawful to assign.
Harrington v Kloprogge[332]

2.   A contract for the assignment of a lease provided that if licence to assign was delayed beyond a certain date, the purchaser would pay the purchase price to the vendor and the vendor would "thereupon allow the purchaser to enter into occupa-tion pending completion" and the purchaser would pay the rent and other outgoings.

---

329   Thorpe LJ also agreed with Staughton LJ.
330   [2001] NSWCA 279 (a dissenting judgment).
331   [2012] EWCA Civ 1547, reversing [2011] EWHC 3482 (QB); [2012] I.R.L.R. 385.
332   (1785) 2 B. & B. 678 n(a).

It was held that "allow" meant "lawfully allow", and consequently did not cover entry into occupation in breach of covenant.
Cantor Art Services Ltd v Kenneth Bieber Photography Ltd[333]

12.   EXPRESSION OF TERMS IMPLIED BY LAW

The expression of a term which the law implies as a necessary part of the contract has no greater effect than the implied term would have had.[334]

7.126   This proposition is enshrined in the Latin maxim *expressio eorum* (or *illorum*) *quae tacite insunt nihil operatur.*[335] Thus in *Doe d. Scholefield v Alexander*,[336] a lease contained a proviso for re-entry if the rent was 21 days in arrear "being lawfully demanded". It was held that since statute passed before the date of the lease had removed the need for a formal demand at common law, the landlord could re-enter without such demand. Dampier J said:

> "The right to re-enter grows out of the stipulation of the parties. A demand is necessary as a consequence of law, and there was the same necessity for a demand before the statute whether the lease contained the words 'lawfully demanded' or not. Therefore the maxim applies *expressio eorum quae tacite insunt nihil operatur.*"

7.127   Similarly in *Doe d. Scruton v Snaith*,[337] a mortgage secured payment of a fixed debt with interest, and contained a covenant by the borrower to pay all the lender's expenses. The question arose whether that covenant required the mortgage to be stamped in a greater amount than was appropriate to the security for the fixed debt. Tindal CJ said:

> "We are of opinion that such a stamp is not necessary; for this deed contains no power which the mortgagee might not enforce under an ordinary mortgage."

Alderson J said:

> "The mortgagee here would have been in no worse situation if the deed had contained no stipulation for the expenses; and *expressio illorum quae tacite insunt nihil operatur.*"

7.128   In *Scott v Avery*,[338] the House of Lords considered the validity of a clause that made arbitration a condition precedent to the right to litigate. In the course of his dissenting judgment Martin B said:

> "It was said that the parties, by express agreement between themselves, had made the decision or award of the arbitrators a condition precedent to the right of any member to maintain an action. This is so; but if the matter be examined into, it will be found to be nothing more than what is included in every such contract. If the provision be binding, the consequences would be, in the event of a dispute,

---

[333] [1969] 1 W.L.R. 1226 CA.
[334] Referred to with apparent approval in *Optus Networks Pty Ltd v Telstra Corp Ltd* [2001] FCA 1798.
[335] Applied in *The Royal Exchange Shipping Co Ltd v WJ Dixon & Co* (1886) 12 App. Cas. 11.
[336] (1814) 2 M. & S. 525.
[337] (1832) 8 Bing. 146.
[338] (1856) 5 H.L. Cas. 811.

recourse must be had to an arbitrator, and an award made; but arbitrators have no power to enforce their awards; they cannot issue execution upon them; a court of law or equity must be called in aid to enforce an award adversely. Therefore, in every case, if the agreement to refer be binding, the award must be a condition precedent to maintaining an action, and such condition is tacitly implied. The maxim of law is, '*Expressio eorum quae tacite insunt nihil operatur*'."

In *Forrestt & Son v Aramayo*,[339] the plaintiffs contracted with the defendants to build and deliver f.o.b. at the port in London a steam launch by a fixed date, but were late by three months in effecting delivery. However, the defendants had not prior to the fixed date named the vessel for taking delivery of the launch. To a claim for the balance of the purchase price the defendants sought to deduct an amount representing liquidated damages. Bucknill J held that as the defendants were not ready and willing to take delivery before the plaintiffs were able to deliver the launch, the defendants were not entitled to the agreed damages. His decision was affirmed on appeal. Lord Halsbury LC said:

7.129

"The sole point which I intend to decide upon this appeal is that whenever there are concurrent obligations the party who seeks to recover against the other must show that he has always been ready and willing to perform the obligation upon him. It is immaterial whether the obligation is express or is implied; *expressio eorum quæ tacite nisunt nihil operatur*. In a contract for the sale or manufacture of a chattel, the one party must be ready and willing to deliver, and the other to accept delivery. The difference between the two acts is quite immaterial. The one party in this case is bound to build the launch, and the other to accept it when built; the one is bound to finish the launch, and the other to provide a vessel to receive it. It is common ground that neither party has performed that obligation. The law has been well ascertained and accepted for many years upon this subject."

Illustration

A prospective buyer ordered a quantity of steel reinforcing bars. The prospective seller accepted the order, stating "I assume that we are in agreement that the usual conditions of acceptance apply". Singleton LJ said:

"Those words may be thought by some to refer to the conditions as to the quality of the goods—an implied condition that they shall be reasonably fit for the purpose for which they are required; an implied condition that they shall be of merchantable quality; conditions arising from section 14 of the Sale of Goods Act 1893. For all I know the defendant may have intended that; in which case they were unnecessary. The words 'I assume that we are in agreement that the usual conditions of acceptance apply' are, to my mind, meaningless, and words which are meaningless can be ignored."

Nicolene Ltd v Simmonds[340]

---

[339] (1900) 83 L.T. 335.
[340] [1953] 1 Q.B. 543.

13. THE EJUSDEM GENERIS PRINCIPLE

If it is found that things described by particular words have some common characteristic which constitutes them a genus, the general words which follow them ought to be limited to things of that genus.[341]

7.130 The above formulation of the ejusdem generis principle is taken from the judgment of Vaughan Williams LJ in *Lambourn v McLellan*,[342] and represents its classical formulation. The ejusdem generis principle of construction is one of those described by Lord Diplock as general rules of composition to be followed by any writer seeking clarity of expression.[343] Arden LJ has recently said that the principle is not "intellectual baggage which has to be discarded but rather the wisdom of experience".[344] Likewise in *BOC Group Plc v Centeon LLC*,[345] Evans LJ said:

> "[Counsel's] submission that there is no such thing as an eiusdem generis rule, particularly in the light of the *ICS* judgment, in my view goes too far. Admittedly the Latin ought to be replaced by English words and the interests of clarity may well be served by doing so. Maybe it is wrong to regard it as a rule. Sometimes it has been called a maxim or an aid to construction. What cannot be denied, in my view, is that the considerations which underlie it are ones which a reasonable man would take into account as a matter of commonsense. It is perhaps better now to refer to it as a factor which, when it is relevant, cannot properly be ignored."

In *Scottish Power Plc v Britoil (Exploration) Ltd*,[346] Robert Walker LJ said:

> "Judges are today reluctant, and properly reluctant, to explain decisions on the use of language by reference to maxims expressed in Latin. But this case can be seen as an illustration of the ejusdem generis rule, which in appropriate circumstances remains sound 'both in law and as a matter of literary criticism'."

In *Sun Fire Office v Hart*,[347] Lord Watson said:

> "It is a well known canon of construction, that where a particular enumeration is followed by such words as 'or other', the latter expression ought, if not enlarged by the context, be limited to matters ejusdem generis with those specially enumerated."

7.131 Looking at it from a different perspective, in *BOC Group Plc v Centeon LLC*,[348] Evans LJ said:

> "… with regard to the rule or maxim of eiusdem generis, it seems to me that that

---

[341] This section was referred to with approval in *Burrows Investments Ltd v Ward Homes Ltd* [2017] EWCA Civ 1577; [2018] 1 P. & C.R. 13. The principle was referred to in *Melinda Holdings SA v Hellenic Mutual War Risks Association (Bermuda) Ltd* [2011] EWHC 181 (Comm); [2011] 2 Lloyd's Rep. 141 at [46].

[342] [1903] 2 Ch. 268.

[343] See para.7.01.

[344] *Biggin Hill Airport Ltd v Bromley LBC* [2001] EWCA Civ 1089.

[345] [1999] 1 All E.R. (Comm) 970.

[346] [1997] EWCA Civ 2752.

[347] (1889) 14 App. Cas. 98 at 103 HL.

[348] [1999] 1 All E.R. (Comm) 970.

is a relevant factor in the present case. It might be summarised as follows. The meaning of general words, even 'whatsoever', may be limited by the context in which they appear. They may be used to refer to a class or category, a genus ... of which some but not necessarily all the members are identified in the clause."

In *Burrows Investments Ltd v Ward Homes Ltd*,[349] Henderson LJ said that the **7.132** ejusdem generis principle was "a flexible aid to construction which reflects the twin requirements of commercial common sense and the need to construe contractual provisions as a whole and in their context".

The main argument of construction which justifies the application of the principle **7.133** is the presumption against surplusage; for if the general words have unrestricted meaning, the enumerated items are surplusage.[350] In *Lend Lease Real Estate Investments Ltd v GPT Re Ltd*,[351] Spigelman CJ said:

"The reading down of general words is one of the most common mechanisms applied in the course of legal interpretation. The Court should not give one word in an interrelated, overlapping list of expressions a meaning that is so broad as to be inconsistent with adjoining words or that renders those words irrelevant."

The purpose of inserting general words into contracts has been said: **7.134**

"to prevent disputes founded on nice distinctions. Their office is to cover in terms whatever may be within the spirit of the cases previously enumerated, and so they have a greater or lesser effect as a narrower or broader view is taken of those cases."[352]

The principle is closely linked to the principle that general words in a standard **7.135** form of contract are to be limited to the particular object of the particular contract. Thus in *The Thames and Mersey Marine Insurance Co Ltd v Hamilton Fraser & Co*,[353] Lord Halsbury LC said:

"... Two rules of construction now firmly established as part of our law may be considered as limiting those words. One is that words, however general, may be limited with respect to the subject matter in relation to which they are used. The other is that general words may be restricted to the same genus as the specific words that precede them."

It is misleading to speak of it as a rule, for as has been stressed by many judges **7.136** it is no more than a canon of construction; a guide to the true meaning of the contract.[354]

Many difficulties surround the real meaning and operation of the ejusdem generis **7.137**

---

349 [2017] EWCA Civ 1577; [2018] 1 P. & C.R. 13.
350 *Chandris v Isbrandsten-Moller Co Inc* [1951] 1 K.B. 240; *Decoma UK Ltd v Haden Drysys International Ltd* (2005) 103 Con. L.R. 1, affirmed on appeal [2006] EWCA Civ 723. In *Zhoushan Jinhaiwan Shipyard Co Ltd v Golden Exquisite Inc* [2014] EWHC 4050 (Comm), Leggatt J seems to have accepted this proposition.
351 [2006] NSWCA 207 at [31].
352 *Thames and Mersey Marine Insurance Co Ltd v Hamilton Fraser & Co* (1887) 12 App. Cas. 484, per Lord Macnaghten.
353 (1887) 12 App. Cas. 484.
354 *Earl of Jersey v Neath Poor Law Union* (1889) 22 Q.B.D. 555; *Chandris v Isbrandtsen-Moller Co Inc* [1951] 1 K.B. 240; *BOC Group Plc v Centeon LLC* [1999] 1 All E.R. (Comm) 970.

principle; and it has been said that there is a risk of it developing into a juristic fetish.[355] Nevertheless high authority has declared the principle to be perfectly sound "both in law and as a matter of literary criticism".[356]

In *S.S. Knutsford Ltd v Tillmanns & Co*,[357] Lord Macnaghten said that in construing a bill of lading he preferred to take the rule from:

> "a case which did deal with bills of lading rather than from cases that dealt with real property and settlements."

However, it is likely that the principle applies in much the same way to all classes of instrument, whether mercantile or not.[358]

7.138   The first question which often arises is whether there is any presumption either for or against the application of the principle. In *Anderson v Anderson*,[359] Lord Esher MR said:

> "... prima facie general words are to be taken in their general sense, unless you can find that in the particular case the true construction of the instrument requires you conclude that they are intended to be used in a sense limited to things ejusdem generis with those which have been specifically mentioned before."

Clearly, this suggests a presumption against the application of the principle. However, in *Thorman v Dowgate Steamship Co*,[360] Hamilton J left open the point whether or not there was a presumption either way. And in *S.S. Magnhild v McIntyre Brothers & Co*,[361] McCardie J doubted the existence of any such presumption. He said:

> "If any real presumption exists one way or the other it might substantially affect the interpretation of many documents. Nowhere perhaps has it been definitively and authoritatively laid down that any presumption exists. It is difficult to see how it could satisfactorily exist. For a fundamental rule of construction is that every portion of a document must be fully considered ere any portion of such document be interpreted. If so, it results that general words which are sequent to specific words cannot well be the subject of any presumption at all, inasmuch as they cannot be considered separately from the preceding words without violating the fundamental rule."

The judgment of Vaughan Williams LJ in *Tillmanns & Co v S.S. Knutsford Ltd*[362] suggests that there may be a presumption in favour of the application of the principle. It is submitted, however, that there is probably no presumption either way, for the reasons given by McCardie J.[363] The absence of any presumption is also

---

[355] *S.S. Magnhild v McIntyre Brothers and Co* [1920] 3 K.B. 321, per McCardie J.
[356] *Larsen v Sylvester & Co* [1908] A.C. 295, per Lord Robertson.
[357] [1908] A.C. 406.
[358] See *Chandris v Isbrandtsen-Moller Co Inc* [1951] 1 K.B. 240 at 245.
[359] [1895] 1 Q.B. 749 (a post-nuptial settlement case).
[360] [1910] 1 K.B. 410.
[361] [1920] 3 K.B. 321.
[362] [1908] 2 K.B. 385 (affirmed [1908] A.C. 406).
[363] In *Skillion Plc v Keltec Industrial Research Ltd* [1992] 1 E.G.L.R. 123, Knox J pointed out the difficulty in reconciling the two views.

more consonant with the modern objective approach to the interpretation of contracts.[364]

In some cases the language of the contract itself signals that the principle is not to apply. In *Chandris v Isbrandtsen-Moller Co Inc*,[365] Devlin J said:

7.139

"Legal draftsmen are all familiar with the existence of the rule, and familiar too with the proper signals to hoist if they do not want it to apply. Phrases such as 'whether or not similar to the foregoing' and 'without prejudice to the generality of the foregoing' are often employed in legal draftsmanship; and if the draftsman has read the report of *Larsen v Sylvester & Co*[366] he will know that the addition of 'whatsoever' generally serves the same purpose."[367]

Similarly, in *Earl of Jersey v Neath Union Rural Sanitary Authority*,[368] Fry LJ said:

"... where you find the word 'whatsoever' following, as it does, upon certain substantives, it is often intended to repel, and in this case does effectually repel, the implication of the so-called doctrine of ejusdem generis...".

Likewise, in *The Laconian Confidence*,[369] Rix J said:

"Those comments bring me back to consider the phrase 'any other cause' in the light of the authorities. In my judgment it is well established that those words, in the absence of 'whatsoever', should be construed either ejusdem generis or at any rate in some limited way reflecting the general context of the charter and clause ...".

He added:

"I would suggest that if the clause had been amended to contain the word 'whatsoever', then the position would probably have been otherwise. The vessel would have been prevented from working, albeit in unexpected circumstances. The cause would not have been ejusdem generis, but with the addition of the word 'whatsoever' would not have to be."

But the mere fact that the word "whatsoever" appears in the clause, does not necessarily oust the application of the principle.[370]

In *Transocean Drilling UK Ltd v Providence Resources Plc*,[371] the contract excluded liability for "loss of use (including, without limitation, loss of use or the cost of use of property, equipment, materials and services including without limitation, those provided by contractors or subcontractors of every tier or by third parties), loss of business and business interruption". The trial judge interpreted this by

7.140

---

[364] See, e.g. *The Argo Fund Ltd v Essar Steel Ltd* [2006] 2 Lloyd's Rep. 134.
[365] [1951] 1 K.B. 240.
[366] [1908] A.C. 295.
[367] But if he had also read *BOC Group Plc v Centeon LLC* [1999] 1 All E.R. (Comm) 970 he might have some doubt.
[368] (1889) 22 Q.B.D. 555.
[369] [1977] 1 Lloyd's Rep. 139 at 150; applied in *The Saldanha* [2011] 1 Lloyd's Rep. 187.
[370] *BOC Group Plc v Centeon LLC* [1999] 1 All E.R. (Comm) 970.
[371] [2016] EWCA Civ 372; [2016] 2 Lloyd's Rep. 51. Professor Edwin Peel has commented in this case in "Contra proferentem revisited" (2017) 133 L.Q.R. 7.

reference to the ejusdem generis principle. Reversing that decision, Moore-Bick LJ said:

> "... the judge expressed the view that the expression 'loss of use' was more naturally to be read as connoting the loss of expected profit or benefit to be derived from the use of property or equipment, a conclusion, he said, which gained strength and colour from the application of the *eiusdem generis* principle to the other identified types of loss. However, I think that Mr Rabinowitz was right in saying that this was not a proper case for the application of the *eiusdem generis* principle of construction, by which general words may be given a limited meaning when they follow a list of specific matters (often causes or events) which can be seen to be of a similar kind. The judge was of course right to construe the expression in the context of the sub-paragraph as a whole. I accept that standing alone the expression 'loss of use' might well refer to a loss of expected profit or benefit to be derived from the use of property or equipment, but in this as in other cases its meaning is shaped by its context. I think, with respect, that the judge failed at that point to have sufficient regard to the words in brackets which follow the expression 'loss of use' or to recognise that the purpose of providing specific examples is to flesh out its meaning."

Moore-Bick LJ also stressed the significance of the words "without limitation" immediately following the defined term.

7.141   Even the word order of a particular clause may affect the question whether the principle is applied. In *Ambatielos v Anton Jurgens Margarine Works*,[372] a charterparty contained the following clause:

> "Should the vessel be detained by causes over which the charterers have no control viz. quarantine, ice, hurricanes, blockade, clearing the steamer after the last cargo is taken over etc., no demurrage is to be charged and lay days not to count."

The ejusdem generis principle was held not to apply. In the Court of Appeal[373] Lord Sterndale MR said:

> "The first difficulty that I feel in applying the doctrine of ejusdem generis to this case is that in this case, unlike any other which has been cited to us, ... the specific words follow the general words and do not precede them."

The same point was made by Viscount Cave LC in the House of Lords[374]:

> "... I know of no authority for applying that rule to a case of this kind, where to begin with the whole clause is governed by the initial general words, where, secondly, the expression to be construed is the expression 'etc.,' and where thirdly there is no genus which comprises all the five cases specified other than the genus described in the general words."

---

[372] [1923] A.C. 175.
[373] [1922] 2 K.B. 185.
[374] [1923] A.C. 175.

In *Sun Fire Office v Hart*,[375] Lord Watson summarised the position by saying:

"The canon is attended with no difficulty, except in its application. Whether it applies at all, and if so, what effect should be given to it, must in every case depend upon the precise terms, subject-matter, and context of the clause under construction."

The next question is what is a genus? The word genus is taken from the language of natural history. In natural history a genus is a classificatory group comprehending one or a number of species possessing certain common structural characters distinct from those of any other group. However, as McCardie J said in *S.S. Magnhild v McIntyre Brothers & Co*[376]:   **7.142**

"The phrases of science deal with precise things. The phrases of law deal with matters of ambiguity and cross division."

Thus it is not necessary that a genus should be "of extreme scientific precision".[377] In applying the ejusdem generis principle it is not necessary to ascertain with exactitude what is the scientific definition of the genus to which the general words are supposed to be confined.

It is sufficient if one can reasonably say that the thing or event was of a like kind to some one or more of the specific things or events which precede the general words.[378] The test is: **7.143**

"whether the specified things which precede the general words can be placed under some common category. By this [is meant] that the specified things must possess some common and dominant feature."[379]

Is the existence of a genus a prerequisite of the application of the principle? Many statements of high authority suggest that unless a genus can be found the principle can have no application. Thus in *Tillmanns & Co v S.S. Knutsford Ltd*,[380] Vaughan Williams LJ said: **7.144**

"if a common genus is not to be found the necessary consequence would be that the words 'or any other cause' could not be limited by the doctrine of ejusdem generis."[381]

In the same case Farwell LJ said:

"Unless you can find a category there is no room for the application of the ejusdem generis doctrine."

This formulation would suggest that the principle can never apply if there is only one specific item before the general words. However, this is not so. In *Foscolo*

---

[375] (1889) 14 App. Cas. 98 at 104 HL.
[376] [1920] 3 K.B. 321.
[377] *Thorman v Dowgate Steamship Co* [1910] 1 K.B. 410 per Hamilton J.
[378] See *Foscolo Mango & Co v Stag Line Ltd* [1931] 2 K.B. 48 per Greer LJ.
[379] *S.S. Magnhild v McIntyre Brothers and Co* [1920] 3 K.B. 321 per McCardie J.
[380] [1908] 2 K.B. 385.
[381] Moulder J took this view in *CFH Clearing Ltd v Merrill Lynch International* [2019] EWHC 963 (Comm).

Mango & Co v Stag Line Ltd,[382] Slesser LJ said:

"On a strict application of the ejusdem generis rule it may be argued with some force that to construct a genus out of one species and undefined general words (which together with the species have gone to form the genus) in order to define the denotation of those general words is but a petitio principii, but however that may be, on the wider consideration of the intention and context there is ample authority for the view expressed by Hamilton J."[383]

In *Manchikalapati v Zurich Insurance Plc*,[384] it was held that:

"a single species and general words may constitute a genus."

7.145   Moreover, even if a genus cannot be found, the principle may still apply. As Devlin J said in *Chandris v Isbrandtsen-Moller Co Inc*[385]:

"If the ejusdem generis principle is a rule of automatic application, it becomes of the first importance to determine exactly what the rule is. If it is merely, as I think, an aid to ascertaining the intention of the parties, no point of controversy need arise at all. If there is something to show the literal meaning of the words is too wide, then they will be given such other meaning as seems best to consort with the intention of the parties. In some cases it may be they will seem to indicate a genus; in others that they perform the simpler office of expanding the meaning of each enumerated item. If a genus cannot be found, doubtless that is one factor indicating that the parties did not intend to restrict the meaning of the words. But I do not take it to be universally true that whenever a genus cannot be found the words must have been intended to have their literal meaning, whatever other indications there may be to the contrary."

This passage blurs, if it does not eliminate, the apparent distinction between the two "rules of construction" to which Lord Halsbury LC referred in his speech in the *Thames and Mersey Marine* case.[386] It has, however, the great merit of adopting a flexible approach to the interpretation of contracts, rather than a rigid application of prescriptive rules.[387] Since the modern approach to the interpretation of contracts eschews rigid rules, it is thought that this is the right approach.[388]

7.146   From time to time judges have warned against a too ready application of the principle. In *Anderson v Anderson*,[389] Lord Esher MR said that "the modern tendency of the Courts has been to construe general words in their ordinary sense", and in the same case Rigby LJ said:

"The doctrine known as that of ejusdem generis has, I think, frequently led to wrong conclusions on the construction of instruments."

---

[382] [1931] 2 K.B. 48.
[383] Namely, that a single species and general words may constitute a genus.
[384] [2019] EWCA Civ 2163, referring to this section.
[385] [1951] 1 K.B. 240.
[386] (1887) 12 App. Cas. 484.
[387] In *Skillion Plc v Keltec Industrial Research Ltd* [1992] 1 E.G.L.R. 123, Knox J approved the approach of Devlin J.
[388] *Burrows Investments Ltd v Ward Homes Ltd* [2017] EWCA Civ 1577; [2018] 1 P. & C.R. 13.
[389] [1895] 1 Q.B. 749.

So too in *Earl of Jersey v Neath Union Rural Sanitary Authority*,[390] Fry LJ said that the ejusdem generis principle:

"has often been urged for the sake of giving not the true effect to the contracts of parties, but a narrower effect than they were intended to have."

These warnings, however, do no more than remind the reader that no principle of interpretation is ever more than a guide to the true meaning of the contract.

Illustrations

1.   A lease contained a covenant to yield up certain scheduled articles together with all doors, wainscots, shelves, presses, drawers, locks, keys, bolts, bars, staples, hinges, hearths, chimney pieces, mantelpieces, chimneyjambs, foot-paces, slabs, covings, window-shutters, partitions, sinks, waterclosets, cisterns, pumps, and rails, water tanks and other additions, improvements, fixtures and things. It was held that the general words could not be restricted as the specific words formed no discernible genus.
Wilson v Whateley[391]

2.   A deed of assignment assigned all household goods and furniture and other chattels in a particular house, and all other personal estate whatsoever of the assignor. It was held that the general words did not pass the assignor's leasehold estate in the house (a lease being regarded at that time as a chattel real). Erle CJ said:

"General words following specific words are ordinarily construed ejusdem generis with those before enumerated."

Harrison v Blackburn[392]

3.   A lease contained a proviso for abatement of rent in the event of destruction or damage by fire, flood, storm, tempest or other inevitable accident. It was held that it did not apply when the premises became unfit for use due to a building failure.
Saner v Bilton[393]

4.   A lease contained a covenant to yield up all doors, locks, keys, etc, wainscots, hearths, stoves, marbles, and other chimney pieces, etc, and all other buildings, erections, improvements, fixtures and things on the demised property. It was held that the general words should be limited to things in the nature of landlord's fixtures and consequently did not include machinery affixed by the tenant for the purpose of his trade.
Lambourn v McLellan[394]

5.   A bill of lading contained an exception should a port be inaccessible on account of ice, blockade or interdict, or should entry and discharge at a port be deemed

---

[390]   (1889) 22 Q.B.D. 555.
[391]   (1860) 1 Joh. & H. 436.
[392]   (1864) 17 C.B.N.S. 678.
[393]   (1878) 7 Ch. D. 815; *The Manchester Bonded Warehouse Co Ltd v Carr* (1880) 5 C.P.D. 507.
[394]   [1903] 2 Ch. 268.

by the master unsafe in consequence of war, disturbance or any other cause. It was held that the words "any other cause" must be construed ejusdem generis with war or disturbance and did not include obstruction by ice which the master deemed made the port unsafe (although not in fact inaccessible).
Tillmanns & Co v S.S. Knutsford Ltd[395]

6.   A policy of marine insurance insured against perils of the sea and all other perils, losses, and misfortunes that have or shall come to the hurt detriment or damage of the ship. It was held that the policy did not cover damage caused to the ship by a boiler which fell during loading. Viscount Haldane said:

> "I am of opinion that it is now settled law that the words of the clause describing the adventure and perils insured against indicate that the scope of this clause is confined to the genus of adventures and perils of the seas, and that the reference to other perils losses and misfortunes, with which the clause concludes, is limited to those which are of this genus."

Stott (Baltic) Steamers Ltd v Marten[396]

7.   A contract provided for the sale of two plots of land and buildings material, etc. It was held that the contract did not pass a right of way. Eve J said:

> "I think that the words 'et cetera' are limited to the word 'material' which immediately precedes them and refer to something of the same character as 'material'."

Re Walmsley and Shaw's Contract[397]

8.   A voyage charterparty stipulated that the cargo was to consist of lawful general merchandise excluding acids, explosives, arms, ammunition or other dangerous cargo. It was held that the shipment of turpentine was prohibited.
Chandris v Isbrandtsen-Moller Co Inc[398]

9.   A charterparty provided that hire should cease to be payable in the event of the loss of time from deficiency and/or default of men or stores, fire, breakdown or damages to hull, machinery or equipment, grounding, detention by average accidents to ship or cargo, dry-docking for the purpose of examination or painting bottom, or by any other cause preventing the full working of the vessel. It was held that the phrase "any other cause" should be construed ejusdem generis with the specified causes and did not include interference by regulatory authorities.
Andre & Cie SA v Orient Shipping (Rotterdam) BV (The "Laconian Confidence")[399]

10.   A guarantee provided "that no indulgence granting of time waiver or forbearance to sue by the Lender or any other matter or thing which but for this provision would operate to discharge the liability of a surety shall in any way release

---

[395] [1908] 2 K.B. 385 (affirmed [1908] A.C. 406), sub nom *S.S. Knutsford Ltd v Tillmanns & Co.*
[396] [1916] A.C. 304.
[397] [1917] 1 Ch. 93.
[398] [1951] 1 K.B. 240.
[399] [1997] 1 Lloyd's Rep. 139.

the Guarantor from liability hereunder". The Privy Council held that the phrase "any other matter or thing" was not to be read ejusdem generis with the preceding matters.
Madden v UDC Finance Ltd[400]

11.   An agreement for the remuneration of travel agents provided that commission would be paid on fares applicable, which was defined as "the fares (including fare surcharges) for the transportation in accordance with the Member's tariffs and shall exclude any charges for excess baggage or excess valuation of baggage as well as all taxes and other charges collected by the Agent". Clarke LJ said:

"In this case the words 'and other charges' does seem to me to be naturally affected by the fact that it does not appear by itself but as part of the phrase 'taxes and other charges'. I have reached the conclusion that the taxes and charges were not intended to refer to contractual charges levied on the airlines by owners or operators of airports, but to refer to taxes and charges imposed by the appropriate government authority."

Association of British Travel Agents Ltd v British Airways Plc[401]

12.   An insurance policy excluded liability for claims arising out of the failure of any "fire or intruder alarm switch gear control panel or machinery" to perform its intended function. It was held that the ejusdem generis principle did not apply and that "machinery" was intended to be a discrete category irrespective of whether there was overlap with the preceding parts of the list.
Reilly v National Insurance & Guarantee Corp Ltd[402]

13.   Clause 15 of a charterparty stated that in the event of the loss of time from default and/or deficiency of men including strike of Officers and/or crew or deficiency of ... stores, fire, breakdown or damages to hull, machinery or equipment, grounding, detention by average accidents to ship or cargo, dry-docking for the purpose of examination or painting bottom, *or by any other cause* preventing the full working of the vessel, the payment of hire shall cease for the time thereby lost. The ship was seized by Somali pirates. It was held that the reference to "any other cause" should be read ejusdem generis with the named events and did not include seizure by pirates.
Cosco Bulk Carrier Co Ltd v Team-Up Owning Co Ltd[403]

14.   A licence for a caravan pitch enabled the pitch fee to be reviewed. The licence stated that it would be reviewed having regard to the following criteria: (i) Any charges which are not within the licensor's control such as rates, water charges and other charges paid to third parties; (ii) Any changes in the cost of living as shown by the General Index of Retail Prices or another index having a similar purpose; (iii) Sums spent by the licensor on the Park and/or its facilities; (iv) Changes in the cost of salaries and wages; (v) Changes in the length of the Season; and (vi) Any other relevant factor. The court rejected the argument that "any other

---

[400]   [1997] UKPC 52.
[401]   [2000] 2 All E.R. (Comm) 204.
[402]   [2008] EWHC 722 (Comm), reversed in part on different grounds: [2009] 1 All E.R. (Comm) 1166.
[403]   [2010] 1 C.L.C. 919.

factor" should be read ejusdem generis with the preceding criteria. "Any other relevant factor" meant any other factor relevant to the pitch fee, and was not limited to costs expended by the licensor.

Du Plessis v Fontgary Leisure Parks Ltd[404]

14. MEANING IS KNOWN BY CONTEXT

The meaning of an unclear word is known by its context.

7.147   The Latin maxim *noscitur a sociis* is closely related to the *ejusdem generis* principle. Put shortly, it stresses the importance of context.[405] In *Compania Naviera Aeolus SA v Union of India*,[406] Lord Guest said:

> "The doctrine '*noscitur a sociis*' is exemplified in the dictum of Lord Halsbury L.C. in *Thames and Mersey Marine Insurance Co v Hamilton, Fraser & Co*[407]: 'words, however general, may be limited with respect to the subject-matter in relation to which they are used'."

7.148   In *Watchorn v Langford*,[408] a policy of fire insurance covered "stock in trade, household furniture, linen, wearing apparel and plate". The insured, who was a coach plater and cow-keeper, had bought a large amount of linen on speculation, which was destroyed in a fire. His claim under the policy was rejected. Lord Ellenborough said:

> "I am clearly of the opinion that 'linen' in the policy does not include articles of this description. Here we may apply '*noscitur a sociis*'. The preceding words are 'household furniture', and the succeeding 'wearing apparel'. The linen must be the 'household linen or apparel'."

7.149   In *Tektrol Ltd v International Insurance Co of Hanover Ltd*,[409] an insurance policy excluded liability for "erasure loss distortion or corruption of information on computer systems". One question was whether theft of a computer which stored information fell within the clause. Sir Martin Nourse said:

> "If, however, 'loss' is read in its context, its meaning becomes plain. The expression 'other erasure loss distortion or corruption of information' demonstrates that the loss contemplated is loss by means of electronic interference; *noscitur a sociis*. It is not just the effect of the other three words, but the order in which the four appear. 'Loss' follows 'erasure'. While erasure can be expected to result in loss, a careful draftsman would not necessarily assume that it was the only way in which information might be lost. Then follow 'distortion or corruption', which seem to refer to interference causing something less than erasure or loss and between which, as Buxton LJ has observed, it is difficult to suggest a clear distinction."

---

[404] [2012] EWCA Civ 409.
[405] *New Hampshire Insurance Co v Philips Electronics North America Corp* [1999] Lloyd's Rep. I.R. 58.
[406] [1964] A.C. 868.
[407] (1887) 12 App. Cas. 484.
[408] (1813) 3 Camp 422; 170 E.R. 1432.
[409] [2005] 2 Lloyd's Rep. 701.

In *Inglewood Investment Co Ltd v Forestry Commission*,[410] a lease reserved to **7.150** the landlord "all game woodcocks snipe and other wild fowl hares rabbits and fish". The issue was whether the reservation of "game" extended to deer. Harman J said:

"To my mind, there is a plain implication in the first eight words of *noscitur a sociis*, that the phrase 'other wild fowl,' attached as it is to the end of the phrase 'game woodcocks snipe,' gives one a feeling that in that collocation of words the draftsman was speaking about feathered creatures. The way he goes on by referring next to 'Hares rabbits,' being things which are mammals as apart from 'game woodcocks snipe and other wild fowl,' gives to my mind a flavour that the whole of the first phrase of that reservation has to do with birds. ... The word 'game' has a real and adequate meaning and, knowing it by its neighbours, which is all the Latin words mean, the phrase 'woodcocks snipe and other wild fowl' points to birds which are habitually shot for sport and eaten, and the word 'game' is coloured by that collocation, so that it means, in my view, feathered game, not anything else. In my view, trying as best I can to bear in mind all the multitude of influences that come to one's thought, I have myself really no doubt at all that 'game' in this reservation means only feathered game and not terrestrial game and does not include deer."

It was once thought to be necessary to identify a common characteristic of the **7.151** surrounding words. As Diplock LJ put it in *Letang v Cooper*[411]:

"The maxim *noscitur a sociis* is always a treacherous one unless you know the *societas* to which the *socii* belong."

But the modern approach to contractual interpretation will always interpret a word or phrase in context, whether or not it forms part of a common class. In *Porter Property Ltd v Dugan*[412] an agreement contained a promise not to object to the grant of planning permission with access along a defined route subject to such variation as "may in the reasonable opinion of [an architect] be reasonably necessary to make the Private Access Road suitable to serve the intended development." Discussing the meaning of the word "suitable" Morgan LCJ said:

"We consider that the phrase 'suitable to serve the intended development' sets the context within which the issue of suitability should be assessed. We reject the submission that suitability in this context should be confined to physical issues of practicality. In this context suitability includes physical issues of practicality but also includes visual amenity, environmental impact, cost and economic viability."

In addition, the principle does not permit self-evident facts to be overlooked. In **7.152** *Re Jenkins's Will Trusts*,[413] Buckley J said:

"However, the principle of *noscitur a sociis* does not in my judgment entitle one to overlook self-evident facts. If you meet seven men with black hair and one with red hair you are not entitled to say that here are eight men with black hair.

---

[410] [1988] 1 W.L.R. 959.
[411] [1965] 1 Q.B. 232 at 247.
[412] [2019] NICA 65.
[413] [1966] Ch. 249.

Finding one gift for a non-charitable purpose among a number of gifts for charitable purposes the court cannot infer that the testator or testatrix meant the non-charitable gift to take effect as a charitable gift when in the terms it is not charitable, even though the non-charitable gift may have a close relation to the purposes for which the charitable gifts are made."

15. DISTRIBUTIVE CONSTRUCTION

In an appropriate case where a plural subject is followed by a plural predicate the plurals may be distributively construed, thereby breaking down the plural into its component singulars.

7.153   This principle of construction was explained by Lord Millett in *AIB Group (UK) Plc v Martin*[414] as follows:

"A distributive construction is commonly adopted when a plural subject is followed by a plural predicate and the plurals are broken down into their component singulars. An example from everyday speech would be to say: 'A and B took their children to school'. Prima facie the word "their" means 'belonging to both of them'. But this is not its only possible meaning, and if A and B are not married it is obviously not its meaning.[415] In that case the word 'their' means 'of each of them'. But this means that A and B took *their respective* children to school, not each other's children. The children are distributed to the relevant parent. And it goes further than that. Although the word 'school' is in the singular, it may conceal a plural. If necessary, the sentence means that A and B took the children to their respective schools.

This is a well-established principle of construction. It often, and perhaps usually, gives the words their most natural meaning. It parades under a Latin name *reddendo singula singulis*. This simply means that, when plurals are broken down, each singular component must be attributed to its respective singular and not to every other possible singular. It is a broad and general principle which departs from the literal and grammatical meaning and does not depend upon minutiae of language."

Like any other principle of interpretation it is only a guide; and will yield to the context of the document as a whole.[416]

16. SAVING THE DOCUMENT

Where there are two alternative interpretations of an instrument each of which is realistic, upon one of which the instrument is valid, and upon the other of which it is invalid, the court should lean towards that interpretation which validates the instrument.[417]

7.154   This principle is based on the proposition that "the parties are unlikely to have

---

[414] [2002] 1 W.L.R. 94 (a dissenting judgment). For a selective reading of singular and plural in the interpretation of a statutory instrument, see *Number 20 Cannon Street v Singer & Friedlander Ltd* [1974] Ch. 229.

[415] See also *Bruyn v Perpetual Trustee Co Ltd* (1974) 131 C.L.R. 387.

[416] *Re Knight* [1957] Ch. 441. See also *Batts Combe Quarry Ltd v Ford* [1943] Ch. 51.

[417] In previous editions, this principle was stated as applicable where two interpretations were "equally plausible". The principle in that form was cited with approval in *Multiplex Constructions (UK) Ltd*

intended to agree to something ... legally ineffective".[418] It is expressed in the Latin maxim *verba ita sunt intelligenda ut res magis valeat quam pereat*.[419] One suggested translation is "validate if possible".[420]

In *Langston v Langston*,[421] Lord Brougham LC said:

"If there are two modes of reading an instrument, and one destroys the instrument and the other preserves it, it is the rule of law and of equity following the law in this respect ... that you should lean towards that construction which preserves, rather than towards that which destroys. *Ut res magis valeat quam pereat* is a rule of common law and common sense, and much the same principle ought surely to be adopted where the question is, not between two rival constructions of the same words appearing in the same instrument, but where the question is on so ready an instrument as that you may either take it verbally and literally, as it is, or with a somewhat larger and more liberal construction, and by so supplying words as to read it in a way in which you have every reason to believe that the maker of it intended it should stand. Thus, again, according to the rule *ut res magis valeat quam pereat*, to supply, if you can safely and easily do it, that which he per incuriam omitted, that which instead of destroying preserves the instrument, and, instead of putting an end to the instrument and defeating the intention of the maker of it, tends rather to keep alive and continue and give effect to that intention."

In more modern times, the principle was described by Lord Wright in *Hillas (WN) & Co v Arcos*[422] as follows: **7.155**

"Business men often record the most important agreements in crude and summary fashion; modes of expression sufficient and clear to them in the course of their business may appear to those unfamiliar with the business far from complete or precise. It is accordingly the duty of the court to construe such documents fairly and broadly, without being too astute or subtle in finding defects; but, on the contrary, the court should seek to apply the old maxim of English law, *verba ita sunt intelligenda ut res magis valeat quam pereat*. That maxim, however, does not mean that the court is to make a contract for the parties, or go outside the words they have used, except in so far as there are appropriate implications of law."

In the same case Lord Tomlin said:

"The problem for a court of construction must always be so to balance matters,

---

v Honeywell Control Systems Ltd (2007) 111 Con. L.R. 78; *Steria Ltd v Sigma Wireless Communications Ltd* [2008] B.L.R. 79; *Chopra v Bindra* [2009] W.T.L.R. 781; *Kooee Communications Pty Ltd v Primus Telecommunications Pty Ltd* [2008] NSWCA 5; *Premier Foods Group Services Ltd v RHM Pension Trust Ltd* [2012] EWHC 447 (Ch); *Property Trustees Ltd v Permira Advisers LLP* [2014] EWHC 145 (Ch); [2014] 1 P. & C.R. 345; *Co-operative Group Food Ltd v A & A Shah Properties Ltd* [2019] EWHC 941 (Ch); [2019] L. & T.R. 433. See also *C v D* [2011] EWCA Civ 646.
[418] *BCCI v Ali* [2002] 1 A.C. 251 at 269 (Lord Hoffmann).
[419] Compare the *European Principles of Contract Law*, para.5:106: "An interpretation which makes the terms of the contract lawful, or effective, is to be preferred to one which would not".
[420] *Rayfield v Hands* [1960] Ch. 1 at 4 (Vaisey J). Patten LJ used the same translation in *Tindall Cobham 1 Ltd v Adda Hotels* [2014] EWCA Civ 1215.
[421] (1834) 2 Cl. & Fin. 194; *Shah v Shah* [2010] EWCA Civ 1408.
[422] (1932) 147 L.T. 503. Lord Wright's statement should not be taken to be confined to documents drawn by businessmen without legal advice: *ABC v Australian Performing Right Assn* (1973) 47 A.J.L.R. 526 at 529, per Gibbs J.

that, without the violation of essential principle, the dealings of men may as far as possible be treated as effective, and that the law may not incur the reproach of being the destroyer of bargains."

In *C v D*,[423] Rix LJ said:

"Another principle or maxim of construction which is applicable in the present circumstances is that words should be understood in such a way that the matter is effective rather than ineffective (*verba ita sunt intelligenda ut res magis valeat quam pereat*)."

In *Ross v Bank of Commerce (Saint Kitts Nevis) Trust and Savings Association Ltd*,[424] Lord Walker said:

"The principle '*ut res magis valeat quam pereat*' encourages courts to construe commercial documents so as to give them the fullest possible effect, even if they are defective in part."

7.156 The principle is closely linked to the principle that a contract should be interpreted so as to be lawful, as Toulson LJ explained in *Great Estates Group Ltd v Digby*[425]:

"... if the contract is capable of being read in two ways, one of which would involve a contravention of a statute and the other would not, that may be a powerful reason for reading the contract in the sense which is compliant with the statute, even if it is the less natural construction. (This is to put in modern terms the approach expressed in the maxim *ut magis valeat quam pereat*)."

7.157 The principle is not confined to agreements drawn up without legal draftsmanship. In *IRC v McMullen*,[426] the question was whether a deed of trust establishing the Football Association Youth Trust was charitable. The House of Lords held that it was not. However, Lord Hailsham of St Marylebone LC would have been prepared to apply the maxim, if he had thought that there was any doubt as to the meaning of the deed.

7.158 As indicated, the doctrine may only be called in aid where there is real doubt as to the meaning of the instrument. In previous cases the required degree of doubt has been expressed in various ways. In *Re Baden's Deed Trusts*,[427] Karminski LJ resorted to the doctrine rather than leave the matter "precariously balanced on a knife-edge of indecision". In the same case Harman LJ said:

"... I am of opinion that the court is at liberty, if the considerations on both sides seem evenly balanced, to lean towards that which may effectuate rather than frustrate the settlor's intentions. This is a true application of the doctrine *ut res magis valeat quam pereat*. I by no means hold that the court may take this course by flying in the teeth of the provisions of the deed, so that the weaker view may

---

[423] [2011] EWCA Civ 646; [2012] 1 All E.R. 302.
[424] [2012] UKPC 3.
[425] [2011] EWCA Civ 1120; [2011] 3 E.G.L.R. 101.
[426] [1981] A.C. 1 ("where it can be claimed that there is an ambiguity, a benignant construction should be given if possible. This was the maxim of the civil law: *semper in dubiis benigniora praeferenda sunt*. There is a similar maxim in English law: *ut res magis valeat quam pereat*").
[427] [1969] 2 Ch. 388.

prevail because it is likely to have an effectual result, but where the terms of the deed produce a balance so even as the present I am of opinion that the doctrine may be called in aid."

In *IRC v Williams*,[428] Megarry J said:

"It is possible that the same approach might be adopted where the scales are tilted only slightly to one side or the other; but plainly it cannot apply where ... the court reaches the conclusion that one construction is clearly preferable to the other. At just what point in the scale the doctrine becomes impotent cannot be said with mathematical accuracy; the right view may well be that, before the doctrine can apply, the court must be left in a state of real and persistent uncertainty of mind."

In *Anglo Continental Educational Group (GB) Ltd v Capital Homes (Southern) Ltd*,[429] Arden LJ said of an agreement for the sale of land with development value:

"The relevant provisions of the agreement are undoubtedly difficult to interpret in the events which have happened, but in my judgement neither party's interpretation produces a satisfactory solution. The agreement is not well drafted. In that situation, a principle which has particular potency and resonance is that, if the agreement is susceptible of an interpretation which will make it enforceable and effective, the court will prefer that interpretation to any interpretation which would result in its being void."

These different descriptions of the circumstances in which the principle can apply were all discussed by the Supreme Court in *Tillman v Egon Zehnder Ltd*[430] as a result of which the statement of general principle has been revised. Lord Wilson referred to a number of different ways in which the principle had been expressed. He said at [42]:

7.159

"To require a measure of equal plausibility of the rival meanings is to make unnecessary demands on the court and to set access to the principle too narrowly; but, on the other hand, to apply it whenever an element of ambiguity exists is to countenance too great a departure from the otherwise probable meaning."

He continued:

"In *Great Estates Group Ltd v Digby*,[431] Toulson LJ explained that, if the contract was 'capable' of being read in two ways, the meaning which would result in validity might be upheld 'even if it is the less natural construction'. And in *Tindall Cobham 1 Ltd v Adda Hotels*,[432] Patten LJ, with whom the other members of the court agreed, observed at para 32 that the search was for a 'realistic' alternative construction which might engage the principle. In my view Megarry J, Toulson LJ and Patten LJ were identifying the point at which the principle is engaged in

---

[428] [1969] 1 W.L.R. 1197.
[429] [2009] C.P. Rep. 30; *Strategic Value Master Fund Ltd v Ideal Standard International Acquisition SARL* [2011] EWHC 171 (Ch).
[430] [2019] UKSC 32; [2019] 3 W.L.R. 245.
[431] [2011] EWCA Civ 1120; [2012] 2 All E.R. (Comm) 361.
[432] [2014] EWCA Civ 1215; [2015] 1 P. & C.R. 5; applied in *EMI Group Ltd v Prudential Assurance Co Ltd* [2020] EWHC 2061 (Ch).

much the same place. Let us work with Patten LJ's adjective: let us require the alternative construction to be realistic."

7.160 The principle may be applied so as to enable a contract to be construed so as to accord with public policy,[433] or to allow the court to assume that documents were executed or served in the correct order.[434] The principle may also be invoked in order to justify the implication of terms.[435] It may also be invoked to interpret a contract in a way which means that the contract actually exists at all, rather than effectively being something close to a nullity.[436]

Illustrations

1. A lessee of a house, whose term expired on 13 December, let it orally until that date. The subtenant occupied it until June when he gave notice and refused to pay any more rent. He argued that the transaction must be taken to have been intended to be an assignment, which was void as it was not in writing. The plea failed. Lord Denman CJ said:

"If we were to decide that the transaction was an assignment, we should at the same time decide that it was no assignment, being by parol only; and we should construe that which was expressed and intended to be a lease to be an assignment, merely *ut res pereat*, which is against a known salutary maxim."

Pollock v Stacy[437]

2. An agreement for lease contained a proviso for re-entry exercisable on breach of covenant. The tenant argued that since the agreement was not under seal, there were no covenants, and consequently the proviso was inoperative. The argument failed. Willes J said:

"Therefore to say that the word 'covenants' here cannot apply to the stipulations contained in this agreement, is to say that the word cannot have any sense at all. But we are bound so to construe the instrument as to give it possible effect to every word contained in it."

Hayne v Cummings[438]

3. An agreement for the employment of a traveller contained a covenant in restraint of trade. The question arose whether the covenant was valid. It was held that it was. Kay LJ said:

---

[433] *Lancashire CC v Municipal Mutual Insurance Ltd* [1997] Q.B. 897.
[434] *Eaglehill Ltd v J Needham Builders Ltd* [1973] A.C. 992.
[435] *Cream Holdings Ltd v Davenport* [2010] EWHC 3096 (Ch).
[436] *Tecnicas Reunidas Saudia for Services and Contracting Co Ltd v Korea Development Bank* [2020] EWHC 968 (TCC).
[437] (1847) 9 Q.B. 1033.
[438] (1864) 16 C.B.N.S. 421.

"It is also a settled canon of construction that where a clause is ambiguous a construction which will make it valid is to be preferred to one which will make it void."

Mills v Dunham[439]

4.   It was a condition of a performance bond guaranteeing repayment of advance sums to a sub-contractor that the sums were paid into its account number 042-117994-03 held with HSBC. The sums were paid into that account number held at a different bank (SABB) in which HBSC had a substantial shareholding. There was no bank trading as HSBC in Saudi Arabia. SABB's logo was similar to that of HSBC and was followed by the HSBC logo. It was held that that payment satisfied the condition, otherwise it would have been impossible to comply with.

Tecnicas Reunidas Saudia for Services and Contracting Co Ltd v Korea Development Bank[440]

17.   THE REASONABLENESS OF THE RESULT

The reasonableness of the result of any particular interpretation is a relevant consideration in choosing between rival interpretations.[441]

In *Tillmanns & Co v S.S. Knutsford Ltd*,[442] Farwell LJ said: **7.161**

"In a mercantile document or a statute there is a presumption that businessmen do not intend to do anything absurd, which is some slight guide; but in all cases it is a matter of construction."

Similarly, in *Schuler (L) AG v Wickman Machine Tool Sales Ltd*,[443] Lord Morris of Borth-y-Gest said:

"Subject to any legal requirements, businessmen are free to make what contracts they choose but unless the terms of their agreement are clear a court will not be disposed to accept that they have agreed something utterly fantastic."

However, this approach goes further than might appear from the use of the words   **7.162**
"absurd" and "utterly fantastic". In the latter case Lord Reid put the point more neutrally, saying:

"The fact that a particular construction leads to a very unreasonable result must be a relevant consideration. The more unreasonable the result the more unlikely it is that the parties can have intended it, and if they do intend it the more necessary it is that they shall make that intention abundantly clear."[444]

In *Australian Broadcasting Commission v Australian Performing Right Associa-*

---

[439] [1891] 1 Ch. 576.

[440] [2020] EWHC 968 (TCC).

[441] The equivalent section in a previous edition was approved by the Singapore Court of Appeal in *Yamashita Tetsuo v See Hup Seng Ltd* [2008] SGCA 49. The reasonableness of the result was a highly influential factor in *The Vale di Cordoba* [2014] EWHC 129 (Comm); [2014] 1 Lloyd's Rep. 550.

[442] [1908] 2 K.B. 385.

[443] [1974] A.C. 235.

[444] This formulation was applied by the Court of Appeal in *The Fina Samco* [1995] 2 Lloyd's Rep. 344.

tion Ltd,[445] Gibbs J said:

"It is trite law that the primary duty of a court in construing a written contract is to endeavour to discover the intention of the parties from the words of the instrument in which the contract is embodied. Of course the whole of the instrument has to be considered, since the meaning of any one part of it may be revealed by other parts, and the words of every clause must if possible be construed so as to render them all harmonious one with another. If the words used are unambiguous the court must give effect to them, notwithstanding that the result may appear capricious or unreasonable, and notwithstanding that it may be guessed or suspected that the parties intended something different. The court has no power to remake or amend a contract for the purpose of avoiding a result which is considered to be inconvenient or unjust. On the other hand, if the language is open to two constructions, that will be preferred which will avoid consequences which appear to be capricious, unreasonable, inconvenient or unjust, 'even though the construction adopted is not the most obvious, or the most grammatically accurate', to use the words from earlier authority cited in *Locke v Dunlop*,[446] which, although spoken in relation to a will, are applicable to the construction of written instruments generally; see also *Bottomley's Case*.[447] Further, it will be permissible to depart from the ordinary meaning of the words of one provision so far as is necessary to avoid an inconsistency between that provision and the rest of the instrument. Finally, the statement of Lord Wright in *Hillas & Co Ltd v Arcos Ltd*[448] that the court should construe commercial contracts 'fairly and broadly, without being too astute or subtle in finding defects', should not, in my opinion, be understood as limited to documents drawn by businessmen for themselves and without legal assistance (cf *Upper Hunter County District Council v Australian Chilling and Freezing Co Ltd*[449])."

7.163   Clearly, this is allied to the attitude of the court in discerning (or attempting to discern) the commercial purpose of a particular transaction, and construing the contract in the light of that commercial purpose. This attitude has grown markedly in recent years, and is perhaps the single most important change in the construction of all classes of written instrument in the last 100 years. The epitome of this approach is to be found in the following observation of Lord Diplock in *The Antaios*[450]:

"... if detailed semantic and syntactical analysis of words in a commercial contract is going to lead to a conclusion that flouts business common sense, it must be made to yield to business common sense."

7.164   However, the flouting of business common sense is not a precondition. In *Barclays Bank Plc v HHY Luxembourg SARL*,[451] Longmore LJ said:

"The Judge said that it did not flout common sense to say that the clause provided

---

[445] (1973) 129 C.L.R. 99 at 109–110.
[446] (1888) 39 Ch. D. 387 at 393.
[447] (1880) 16 Ch. D. 681 at 686.
[448] (1932) 147 L.T. 503 at 514.
[449] (1968) 118 C.L.R. 429 at 437.
[450] [1985] A.C. 191.
[451] [2010] EWCA Civ 1248; but see contrary dictum in *Thompson v Goblin Hill Hotels Ltd* [2011] UKPC 8, per Lord Dyson.

for a very limited level of release, but that, with respect, is not quite the way to look at the matter. If a clause is capable of two meanings, as on any view this clause is, it is quite possible that neither meaning will flout common sense. In such circumstances, it is much more appropriate to adopt the more, rather than the less, commercial construction."

These observations were expressly approved by the Supreme Court in *Rainy Sky SA v Kookmin Bank*.[452]

Likewise, in *Hayward v Norwich Union Insurance Ltd*,[453] Peter Gibson LJ said:

"It is always permissible to test whether words have a given meaning by considering whether they produce an unreasonable result if they have that meaning. The more unreasonable the result, the less likely it is that the parties intended the words to have that meaning."

In *Gan Insurance Co Ltd v Tai Ping Insurance Co Ltd*,[454] Mance LJ said:

"Nonetheless, in my judgment the sub-clause has no very natural meaning and is, at the least, open to two possible meanings or interpretations—one the judge's, the other that it addresses two separate subject-matters. In these circumstances, it is especially important to undertake the exercise on which the judge declined to embark, that is to consider the implications of each interpretation. In my opinion, a court when construing any document should always have an eye to the consequences of a particular construction, even if they often only serve as a check on an obvious meaning or a restraint upon adoption of a conceivable but unbusinesslike meaning. In intermediate situations, as Professor Guest wisely observes,[455] a 'balance has to be struck' through the exercise of sound judicial discretion."

Similarly, in *Laura Investment Co Ltd v Havering London Borough Council*,[456] **7.165** Hoffmann J said of a construction of a lease for which the landlord contended:

"This would be an uncommercial thing to do. It might be the consequence of the express language of the lease or the clear presumption of construction ... In a question such as this, however, where one has to deduce the intention of the parties from all the circumstances ... I think one is free to assume that they intended a fair and commercial result rather than an unfair one."

In *Cargill International SA v Bangladesh Sugar and Food Industries Corp*,[457] Potter LJ said:

"On the other hand, modern principles of construction require the court to have regard to the commercial background, the context of the contract and the circumstances of the parties, and to consider whether, against that background and in that context, to give the words a particular or restricted meaning would lead to an apparently unreasonable and unfair result."

---

452 [2011] UKSC 50; [2011] 1 W.L.R. 2900.
453 [2001] 1 All E.R. (Comm) 545.
454 [2001] C.L.C. 637.
455 In *Chitty on Contracts*, 28th edn (London: Sweet & Maxwell, 1999), Vol.1, para.12-049.
456 [1993] 1 E.G.L.R. 124.
457 [1998] 1 W.L.R. 461 CA.

7.166   This principle does not enable the court to disregard clear words. In *Glofield Properties Ltd v Morley (No.2)*,[458] Nourse LJ said:

> "… the question is whether [the judge] was also correct in deciding that the parties have clearly and unequivocally expressed an intention in the sense for which the plaintiff contends. If they have not, it is open to the court to construe their language in such a way as to produce the more sensible and realistic commercial result."

In *Pratt v Aigaion Insurance Co SA*,[459] Sir Anthony Clarke MR said:

> "I should also refer to this further proposition, … which is stated by Lord Mustill … after referring to Lord Reid's well-known statement in *Wickman Machine Tool Sales Ltd v Schuler AG* … that the more unreasonable the result, the more unlikely it is that the parties can have intended it, and if they do intend it the more necessary it is that they should make their meaning clear:
>
> > 'This practical rule of thumb … must however have its limits. There comes a point at which the court should remind itself that the task is to discover what the parties meant from what they have said, and that to force upon the words a meaning which they cannot fairly bear is to substitute for the bargain actually made one which the court believes could better have been made. This is an illegitimate role for the court.'"

7.167   To stronger effect in *Thompson v Goblin Hill Hotels Ltd*,[460] Lord Dyson said that "the plain and ordinary meaning of the words used … can only be displaced if it produces a commercial absurdity".

7.168   Moreover, the court may not, under the guise of interpreting the contract, rewrite it. In *Kazakstan Wood Processors (Europe) Ltd v Nederlandsche Credietverzekering Maatschappij NV*,[461] Peter Gibson LJ said:

> "The court is entitled to look at those consequences because the more extreme they are, the less likely is it that commercial men will have intended an agreement with that result. But the court is not entitled to rewrite the bargain which they have made merely to accord with what the court thinks to be a more reasonable result, and the best guide to the parties' intentions remains the words which they have chosen to use in the contract."

Similarly, in *Best Beat Ltd v Mourant & Co Trustees Ltd*,[462] Patten J said:

> "there is, I think, a danger in attributing too easily to the parties a different intention from the one expressed in the language used in the interests of arriving at what (with the benefit of hindsight) may appear to be a commercially fair solution."

---

[458] [1989] 2 E.G.L.R. 118 CA.

[459] [2009] 1 Lloyd's Rep. 225.

[460] [2011] UKPC 8. In the author's opinion this sets the bar too high. See *Rainy Sky SA v Kookmin Bank* [2011] UKSC 50; [2011] 1 W.L.R. 2900.

[461] [2000] C.L.C. 822 at 831 CA.

[462] [2008] EWHC 3156 (Ch).

The subject of business common sense and the commercial purpose of contracts is dealt with in paras 2.50–2.88.

Illustrations

1.   A lease contained a rent review clause which provided for the assessment of the rent based upon a hypothetical letting on the terms of the actual lease "other than the amount of rent hereby reserved". The landlord argued that the lease required the exclusion of the rent review clause itself from the terms of the hypothetical letting. The argument failed. Warner J said:

> "Faced with that choice as to the meaning of the word, ... I prefer the meaning that does not produce an unreasonable and unfair result, that is to say does not require the lessee to pay over the next five years for a benefit it will not be enjoying, namely the benefit of a lease with no rent review clause in it."

Datastream International Ltd v Oakeep Ltd[463]

2.   A charterparty contained a clause which provided that the owners were to be responsible for the correct stowage of cargo and for delivery of the cargo in good order and condition (including responsibility for the delivery of the same number of parcels as mentioned in bills of lading). The question arose whether the owners had accepted an absolute liability for the delivery of the cargo. It was held that they had not. Lloyd J. followed and applied the dictum of Lord Reid cited above.

The Golden Leader[464]

3.   A rent review clause did not expressly stipulate all the terms to be contained in the hypothetical lease which fell to be valued for the purpose of the rent review. It was held that the valuation should assume a letting on the terms of the actual lease. The argument that the lease stipulated some of the terms to be contained in the hypothetical lease, and consequently that the maxim *expressio unius est exclusio alterius* applied, was rejected as being of little weight when set against the unfair result which the application of the maxim would produce.

Basingstoke and Deane Borough Council v The Host Group Ltd[465]

4.   A mining agreement contained an obligation on the part of the miner to replant the worked-out land "whenever possible". It was held that those words could not be given literal effect. Megarry VC said:

> "I think that such phrases have to be construed in a reasonable sense when they are contained in business transactions intended to have legal effect. Today there are many things which can be achieved, but only with a vast expenditure of time and effort and money. Because they can be achieved in this way they are literally 'possible'; but in a business document intended to have practical effect, the parties are unlikely to have contemplated an obligation to do something which

---

[463] [1986] 1 W.L.R. 404.
[464] [1980] 2 Lloyd's Rep. 573.
[465] [1988] 1 W.L.R. 348.

is altogether outside the range of the practicable and reasonable merely because they use the word 'possible'."

Tito v Waddell (No.2)[466]

18. THE CLEAR WORDS PRINCIPLE

Where a construction would produce an unfair result, the court will often require clear words to support the construction in question.

7.169   In many cases the court says that it will not adopt a suggested construction in the absence of clear words. As Lord Hoffmann pointed out in *BCCI v Ali*[467]:

"When judges say that 'in the absence of clear words' they would be unwilling to construe a document to mean something, they generally mean (as they did in the case of exemption clauses) that the effect of the document is unfair."

7.170   Thus in *Re Kitchin*,[468] Mr Kitchin guaranteed that all wines supplied by a wine supplier to his old firm "shall be duly paid for". Disputes between the old firm and the supplier were referred to arbitration, and, following an award against the firm not being honoured, judgment was entered against it which itself was not satisfied. The firm pursued Mr Kitchin. James LJ said:

"The real question is, what is the true intent and meaning of the guarantee? ... It is contended that he is liable to pay any sum which arbitrators shall say is the amount of the damages. The guarantee must be expressed in very clear words before I could assent to a construction which could lead to the grossest injustice."

In *Liberty Mutual Insurance Co (UK) Ltd v HSBC Bank Plc*,[469] Rix LJ said:

"It is true that modern authority ... has moved away from technical or hostile attitudes to exclusion clauses. Even so, situations where 'clear words' are required remain."

7.171   Among the examples he gave were whether an exclusion clause excludes liability for negligence; whether a contract excludes a remedy for breach[470]; and whether a release surrenders rights of which the parties were unaware. A "clear words" test is also appropriate where the court is considering the proper construction of an entire agreement clause, and an indemnity clause.[471] Thus the court will require clear words before reaching the conclusion that a clause in a contract excludes the right of set-off[472] or excludes other remedies for breach of contract arising by operation of law[473] or excludes rights of appeal under the Arbitration Act

---

[466] [1977] Ch. 314.
[467] [2002] 1 A.C. 251, in a dissenting speech.
[468] (1881) 17 Ch. D. 668.
[469] [2002] EWCA Civ 691.
[470] *Towergate Financial (Group) Ltd v Hopkinson* [2020] EWHC 984 (Comm). See para.12.129.
[471] *JP Morgan Chase Bank, NA v Federal Republic of Nigeria* [2019] EWCA Civ 1641.
[472] *WRM Group Ltd v Wood* [1998] C.L.C. 189 CA.
[473] *Stocznia Gdanska v Latvian Shipping Co* [1998] 1 W.L.R. 574 HL.

1996.[474] So also clear words are required in order to confer on one party a unilateral power to vary a contract to the detriment of the other.[475] Where one party to a contract alleged that an arbitration agreement conferred on the court wider powers to grant an injunction than were contained in s.44 of the Arbitration Act 1996, Laws LJ held that "very clear provision" would have to be made to achieve that result.[476]

Where a clause in an insurance policy requiring notice to be given as soon as possible after an event likely to give rise to a claim would have the effect of precluding an otherwise valid claim under the policy, the insurer must "ensure that clear wording was used to secure that result".[477]

Clear words will be required in order to entitle an employer to vary the terms of a long-term incentive plan to the detriment of an employee.[478] Similarly, where a landlord wishes to impose on a tenant a precondition to the exercise of a break clause, it is incumbent on it to make it clear what the tenant has to do, rather than to leave it to be argued out when it may be too late to do anything about it.[479]

In *Persimmon Homes (South Coast) Ltd v Hall Aggregates (South Coast) Ltd*,[480] Coulson J referred to the principle that:　　　　**7.172**

> "Where a particular construction may produce an unfair result, the court will often require clear words to support the construction in question."

The principle may also be applied where a party to a contract has already　**7.173** acquired rights under it.[481] In *Marine Trade SA v Pioneer Freight Futures Co Ltd BVI*,[482] Flaux J said:

> "Applying recognised principles of contractual construction, where a contractual obligation (and corresponding contractual right in favour of the other party) has accrued, it would require clear words in the contract to remove that obligation and corresponding right at some later stage."

Likewise where a contract contains an agreed damages clause, there is a　**7.174** presumption that in the absence of clear words it cannot have been intended to operate arbitrarily, for example by producing a result unrelated to anything which the parties can reasonably have expected to approximate to the true loss.[483] So also where a loan agreement contains an obligation to repay a loan, it requires clear words to displace that obligation.[484] The same is true of an obligation on the mart of an insurer to pay a claim under a policy of marine insurance.[485]

In some cases, such is the court's perception of the unfairness of the contract that

---

[474] *Essex County Council v Premier Recycling Ltd* [2007] B.L.R. 233; *Shell Egypt West Manzala GmbH v Dana Gas Egypt Ltd* [2010] 1 Lloyd's Rep. 109.

[475] *Amberley (UK) Ltd v West Sussex County Council* [2011] EWCA Civ 11.

[476] *Sabmiller Africa v East African Breweries* [2010] 2 Lloyd's Rep. 242.

[477] *Zurich Insurance Plc v Maccaferri Ltd* [2016] EWCA Civ 1302; [2018] 1 All E.R. (Comm) 112.

[478] *Daniels v Lloyds Bank Plc* [2018] EWHC 660 (Comm); [2018] I.R.L.R. 813.

[479] *Goldman Sachs International v Procession House Trustee Ltd* [2018] EWHC 1523 (Ch); [2018] L. & T.R. 28.

[480] [2008] EWHC 2379 (TCC).

[481] *Culross Global SPC Ltd v Strategic Turnaround Master Partnership Ltd* [2010] UKPC 33.

[482] [2010] 1 Lloyd's Rep. 631; *Strategic Value Master Fund Ltd v Ideal Standard International Acquisition SARL* [2011] EWHC 171 (Ch).

[483] *Bunge SA v Nidera BV* [2015] UKSC 43.

[484] *Lamesa Investments Ltd v Cynergy Bank Ltd* [2020] EWCA Civ 821.

[485] *Mamancochet Mining Ltd v Aegis Managing Agency Ltd* [2018] EWHC 2643 (Comm).

it requires "the most unambiguous" language to support the suggested construction.[486]

19.   PRESUMPTION AGAINST IMPOSSIBILITY

There is a presumption of interpretation that a contract does not require performance of the impossible, but this may be rebutted by clear words.

7.175   Since the court approaches any problem of construction on the assumption that the parties to the contract are reasonable people, and reasonable people do not require each other to do the impossible, it ought to follow that there is a presumption of construction that a contract does not require the impossible to be done. There is surprisingly little authority on this point. In *The Epaphus*,[487] a contract for the sale of goods provided for the goods to be shipped for one main Italian port to be declared on vessel passing through Suez. The buyers declared Ravenna. The vessel was unable to enter Ravenna because her draft exceeded the allowable maximum. The question arose whether the declaration of Ravenna was good, since it was impossible for the vessel to enter that port. The Court of Appeal held by a majority that it was. Sir John Donaldson MR said:

> "My starting point is that parties to a contract are free to agree upon any terms which they consider appropriate, including a term requiring one of the parties to do the impossible, although it would be highly unusual for parties knowingly so to agree. If they do so agree and if, as is inevitable, he fails to perform, he will be liable in damages. That said, any court will hesitate for a long time before holding that, as a matter of construction, the parties have contracted for the impossible, particularly in a commercial contract. Parties to such contracts can be expected to contemplate performance, not breach."

7.176   Thus in *The New Prosper*,[488] Phillips J found a construction of a clause in a contract which did not require him to hold that the parties had contracted for the impossible.
In *Foster v Wheeler*,[489] Bowen LJ said:

> "If a person agrees to do what is impossible in fact you have only to consider whether on the fair construction of the agreement he made himself liable to pay damages if he did not do it; but if a person binds himself to do what depends on the caprice of the third person he must suffer if he cannot get that third person to exercise his caprice in his favour."

---

[486] *Co-Operative Wholesale Society v National Westminster Bank* [1995] 1 E.G.L.R. 97, per Simon Brown LJ.
[487] [1987] 2 Lloyd's Rep. 213.
[488] [1991] 2 Lloyd's Rep. 93.
[489] (1888) 38 Ch. D. 130.

CHAPTER 8

AMBIGUITY AND UNCERTAINTY

Honest, I can't take nothing you say at face value. Every word you speak is open to any number of different interpretations.

Harold Pinter: *The Caretaker*

1.   THE MEANING OF AMBIGUITY

A statement may be said to be ambiguous when it has two (or more) primary meanings, each of which may be adopted without distortion of the language.[1]

The dictionary definition of ambiguity is a double or dubious meaning. However, for the purposes of construing contracts, the mere fact that a meaning is doubtful is not enough to classify it as ambiguous. In *Schuler (L) AG v Wickman Machine Tool Sales Ltd*,[2] Lord Wilberforce said: **8.01**

"... Ambiguity ... is not to be equated with difficulty of construction, even difficulty to a point where judicial opinion as to meaning has differed."

Similarly, in *Scammell v Ouston*,[3] Lord Wright said:

"Difficulty is not synonymous with ambiguity so long as any definite meaning can be extracted."

So in *Upper Hunter District Council v Australian Chilling and Freezing Co Ltd*,[4] Barwick CJ said that as long as a contract is capable of a meaning: **8.02**

"... it will ultimately bear that meaning which the court, or in an appropriate case, an arbitrator decides is its proper meaning; and the court or arbitrator will decide its application."

In *Burns Philp Hardware Ltd v Howard China Pty Ltd*,[5] Priestley JA said that words are ambiguous if they have: **8.03**

---

[1]   This section was referred to with approval in *United Group Rail Services Ltd v Rail Corp NSW* [2008] NSWSC 1364. In *Procter & Gamble Co v Svenska Cellulosa Aktiebolaget SCA* [2012] EWCA Civ 1413, Moore-Bick LJ described a clause that "is reasonably capable of bearing two possible meanings" as ambiguous. See also *Greatship (India) Ltd v Oceanografia SA de CV* [2012] EWHC 3468 (Comm).
[2]   [1974] A.C. 235.
[3]   [1941] A.C. 251.
[4]   (1968) 118 C.L.R. 429 at 436 (H.C. Aust.).
[5]   (1987) 8 N.S.W.L.R. 642.

"… two or more plausible meanings when the context of the document is taken into account in the light of any knowledge any ordinary intelligent reader of the document would bring to the meaning of it."[6]

8.04   Thus ambiguity can only arise where after ascertaining the meaning of the words used, and after applying all the usual canons of construction, the instrument still conveys a double or multiple meaning.

8.05   However, whether a statement is ambiguous is very much a matter of impression. This was recognised by Lord Sterndale MR in *Ambatielos v Anton Jurgen Margarine Works*,[7] in which he said:

"… it is very difficult indeed to say what is ambiguous and what is not, and I do not think any test can be applied except that of the person who is dealing with it. If it does not seem ambiguous to him I am afraid he can only say 'It may seem ambiguous to others, but it does not to me.'"[8]

Conversely:

"The fact that a Court succeeds in construing a contractual provision does not mean that the provision is unambiguous, let alone that it is clear."[9]

8.06   The Court should not be astute to detect ambiguity, still less to manufacture it. In *The Melanesian Mission Trust Board v Australian Mutual Provident Society*,[10] Lord Hope of Craighead said:

"Various rules may be invoked to assist interpretation in the event that there is an ambiguity. But it is not the function of the court, when construing a document, to search for an ambiguity. Nor should the rules which exist to resolve ambiguities be invoked in order to create an ambiguity which, according to the ordinary meaning of the words, is not there. So the starting point is to examine the words used to see whether they are clear and unambiguous."

8.07   However, the court must still interpret the contract in its factual setting. Thus the court should be wary of finding an ambiguity from the words alone. In *McGeown v Direct Travel Insurance*,[11] Auld LJ said:

"A court should be wary of starting its analysis by finding an ambiguity by reference to the words in question looked at on their own. And it should not, in any event, on such a finding, move straight to the *contra proferentem* rule[12] without first looking at the context and, where appropriate, permissible aids to identifying the purpose of the commercial document of which the words form part."

8.08   Although there is a considerable body of learning on the question of ambiguity

---

6   *Jeffreys v Scruton* [2020] EWHC 536 (Ch) ("language is ambiguous if it can reasonably be interpreted in more than one way or the words used can reasonably be given more than one meaning").

7   [1922] 2 K.B. 185.

8   See also *Newey v Westpac Banking Corp* [2014] NSWCA 319.

9   *Youell v Bland Welch & Co Ltd (No.2)* [1990] 2 Lloyd's Rep. 431.

10   [1997] 2 E.G.L.R. 128 PC. See also *Hayward v Norwich Union Insurance Ltd* [2001] All E.R. (Comm) 545 CA.

11   [2004] 1 All E.R. (Comm) 609.

12   See para.7.66.

and how to resolve it, the modern approach to the interpretation of contracts in England and Wales is a more unitary exercise, not dependent on special rules. Thus even if the words of a contract are apparently unambiguous in themselves, they may give rise to difficulties of interpretation when read against the admissible background facts. In *Sans Souci Ltd v VRL Services Ltd*,[13] Lord Sumption said:

> "It is generally unhelpful to look for an 'ambiguity', if by that is meant an expression capable of more than one meaning simply as a matter of language. True linguistic ambiguities are comparatively rare. The real issue is whether the meaning of the language is open to question. There are many reasons why it may be open to question, which are not limited to cases of ambiguity."

2. Two Types of Ambiguity

Traditionally the law has classified ambiguity into two types; patent ambiguity and latent ambiguity. Patent ambiguity is ambiguity which appears from the language of the instrument; whereas latent ambiguity only becomes apparent when the language is applied to the factual situation. The traditional classification does not appear to have continuing significance in the modern law.

A verbal ambiguity which, in a work of literature, might enrich a text is usually eliminated, in a legal document, by a consideration of its context.[14] A syntactical ambiguity is probably the most common form of ambiguity encountered in practice. Such an ambiguity will typically raise the question whether a subordinate clause in a sentence is governed by a particular verb, or whether an adjective applies to a whole list of nouns or only to one or some of them. Such ambiguities are commonly resolved either by a consideration of the commercial purpose of the contract, or by the application of some other principle of interpretation.   **8.09**

The distinction between patent and latent ambiguity goes back at least as far as Bacon,[15] who declared: **8.10**

> "There be two sorts of ambiguities of words; the one is *ambiguitas patens* and the other *latens*. *Patens* is that which appears to be ambiguous upon the deed or instrument; *latens* is that which seemeth certain and without ambiguity, for anything that appeareth upon the deed or instrument; but there is some collateral matter out of the deed that breedeth the ambiguity."

In more modern times the distinction was explained by Lord Wrenbury in *Great*   **8.11**

---

[13] [2012] UKPC 6 (an appeal from Jamaica). In Australia it is still generally necessary to find an ambiguity before extrinsic evidence is admitted.

[14] Lord Simon of Glaisdale pointed out in *Stock v Frank Tipton Ltd* [1967] 1 W.L.R. 231:

> "Words and phrases of the English language have an extraordinary range of meaning. This has been a rich resource in English poetry (which makes fruitful use of the resonances, overtones and ambiguities), but it has a concomitant disadvantage in English law (which seeks unambiguous precision, with the aim that every citizen shall know, as exactly as possible, where he stands under the law)."

[15] Bacon, *Law Tracts* (London: R. Gosling, 1737), p.99. Literary critics have found more than two types: see William Empson, *Seven Types of Ambiguity*, 3rd edn (London: Chatto & Windus, 1953). However, literature is often deliberately ambiguous, whereas a contract usually is not.

Western Railway v Bristol Corp,[16] as follows:

"It there be ambiguity in the language of a contract itself it may be a patent ambiguity; that is, one apparent on the face of the document itself; or a latent ambiguity; that is, one which arises only when you seek to apply the contract."

8.12   The traditional distinction between the two types of ambiguity was criticised by Lord Simon of Glaisdale in *Schuler (L) AG v Wickman Machine Tool Sales Ltd*[17]:

"... the distinctions between patent ambiguities, latent ambiguities and equivocations as regards admissibility of evidence are based on outmoded and highly technical and artificial rules and introduce absurd refinements."

In *Mannai Investment Co Ltd v Eagle Star Life Assurance Co Ltd*,[18] Lord Hoffmann described the rule that evidence is admissible only to resolve a latent ambiguity and not to resolve a patent ambiguity as being "not merely capricious but also ... incoherent". The traditional distinction between these two types of ambiguity does not appear to have survived into the modern law. In *Credential Bath Street Ltd v Venture Investment Placement Ltd*,[19] Lord Reed said that "the classification of mistakes as 'patent' or 'latent' is no longer determinative of the court's power to cure mistakes by construction". However, for the sake of completeness, the traditional view will be described in the sections that follow.

Illustrations

1.   A lease of offices contained a rent review clause which provided for the rent to be increased to the rack-rental value at five-yearly intervals. The clause defined rack-rental value by reference to a hypothetical letting upon a lease "containing the same provisions (other than as to the yearly rent) as are herein contained". It was held that the words "other than as to the yearly rent" were capable of bearing three meanings:

(1)   that the valuer was to ignore all provisions relating to rent in the lease;
(2)   that the valuer was required to ignore the amount of rent payable and the rent review provisions; and
(3)   that the valuer was to ignore the amount of rent only and take into account the existence of the rent review clause.

It was held that a consideration of the commercial purpose of the clause showed that the third meaning was correct.
British Gas Corp v Universities Superannuation Scheme Ltd[20]

2.   A lease contained a restrictive use covenant by which the tenant covenanted that the premises should not be used "for any other purpose than the trade or business of a printer nor have or permit any sale by auction without the lessors' writ-

---

[16]   (1918) 87 L.J. Ch. 414 at 429.
[17]   [1974] A.C. 235.
[18]   [1997] A.C. 749.
[19]   [2007] CSOH 208, 2008 Hous. L.R. 2. In *Wandsworth London Borough Council v Co-Operative Bank Plc* [2003] EWHC 2418 (Comm) Thomas LJ appears to have assumed that the distinction remained valid, but held on the facts that the contract was not ambiguous.
[20]   [1986] 1 W.L.R. 398.

ten consent which shall not be unreasonably withheld". The landlord contended that its consent could be withheld to any change of use, and that the provisions as to unreasonable withholding of consent related only to the holding of auctions. It was held that any ambiguity in the clause was to be resolved by applying the *contra proferentem* principle.

Killick v Second Covent Garden Property Co Ltd[21]

3. PATENT AMBIGUITY

A patent ambiguity may arise because the contract is self-contradictory, or because it expresses alternative intentions without choosing between them, or because it lacks essential definition. In none of these cases is direct evidence of the intention of the parties admissible to resolve the ambiguity, and the court must do the best it can. In reaching a conclusion the court may, however, have regard to such extrinsic evidence as is admissible to construe any contract. In the last resort the clause in question (or the contract as a whole) will be declared void for uncertainty.

Although the law traditionally classified ambiguities into two classes only, difficulties of interpretation may take a number of forms. The instrument may be self-contradictory; it may express clear alternatives but fail to choose between them; it may lack essential definition of terms or concepts it employs; or it may be meaningless. Each of these types of difficulty may bring into play different techniques for reaching a conclusion as to the meaning or effect of the instrument in question.   **8.13**

The traditional significance of the classification of ambiguities into patent and latent ambiguities was that additional extrinsic evidence was admissible to resolve the latter class of ambiguity but not the former. Thus in *Saunderson v Piper*,[22] Tindal CJ said: **8.14**

"This is a case of *ambiguitas patens*, and according to the rules of law, evidence is not admissible. Where there is doubt on the face of the instrument the law admits no extrinsic evidence to explain it."

So too in *Committee of London Clearing Bankers v IRC*,[23] Wright J said:

"If there be, as I think there is here, an ambiguity which is not latent but patent, that is not a matter to be solved by evidence as to the meaning of the parties ... it is to be solved by the Court as a matter of construction."

And in *Great Western Railway v Bristol Corp*,[24] Lord Wrenbury said: **8.15**

"It is a settled rule that parol evidence is inadmissible to explain a patent ambiguity; that is to say, an ambiguity inherent in the words and incapable of being dispelled by any legal rules of construction applied to the instrument itself or by evidence showing that terms in themselves unmeaning or unintelligible are capable of receiving a known conventional meaning. With a latent ambiguity it

---

[21]   [1973] 1 W.L.R. 658 (see para.7.101).
[22]   (1839) 5 Bing. N.C. 425.
[23]   [1896] 1 Q.B. 222.
[24]   (1918) 87 L.J. Ch. 414.

is otherwise ... Extrinsic evidence has created the ambiguity, and extrinsic evidence is admissible to resolve it."

8.16   Taken literally, these statements are misleading in modern times. As has been seen in Ch.3, extrinsic evidence has always been admissible to enable the court to be appraised of the background knowledge available to the parties when they made their contract. It would be surprising if the court was constrained to reject admissible extrinsic evidence merely because the contract was patently ambiguous. What is in truth in issue is the reception of extrinsic evidence in order to resolve the ambiguity over and above that extrinsic evidence which is admissible to construe any contract. The dicta quoted above should therefore be read as indicating that in the case of a patent ambiguity, no extrinsic evidence is admissible to prove the intention of the parties other than such extrinsic evidence as is admissible in any case.

8.17   In *Watcham v Att.-Gen. of the East Africa Protectorate*,[25] the Privy Council held that evidence of subsequent conduct was admissible to show the sense in which the parties used language in a deed which contained a patent ambiguity. The decision was "long under suspicion of the gravest kind from real property lawyers",[26] and was disapproved in so far as it applied in the law of contract generally by the House of Lords in *Schuler (L) AG v Wickman Machine Tool Sales Ltd*,[27] in which Lord Wilberforce described it as "nothing but the refuge of the desperate". Its future citation in English courts in relation to the interpretation of contracts or written documents generally was deprecated. Nevertheless, it is considered that *Watcham's Case* remains authority for admitting evidence of acts of possession under an ambiguous grant of land, even where the ambiguity is patent.[28] Thus in *Armbrister v Lightbourn*,[29] the Privy Council cited *Watcham's Case* in support of the proposition that:

> "where there is doubt or inconsistency as to the description of land in a conveyance, extrinsic evidence is admissible to resolve the difficulty."

They added that the case shows that "the admissible extrinsic evidence may include later events".

8.18   The contrast between the approach of the court in cases of latent ambiguity and of patent ambiguity was considered by the House of Lords in *Mannai Investment Co Ltd v Eagle Star Life Assurance Co Ltd*.[30] Lord Hoffmann described the rule that evidence is admissible only to resolve a latent ambiguity and not to resolve a patent ambiguity as being "not merely capricious but also ... incoherent". He held that evidence of background facts is admissible in either case.[31]

8.19   In solving the ambiguity the court has a number of devices or rules at its disposal.

---

[25] [1919] A.C. 533.

[26] *Sussex Caravan Parks Ltd v Richardson* [1961] 1 W.L.R. 561, per Harman LJ.

[27] [1974] A.C. 235.

[28] Per Lord Simon of Glaisdale and Lord Kilbrandon. It has also been defended by Megarry J in *Neilson v Poole* (1969) 20 P. & C.R. 909, and *St Edmundsbury & Ipswich Diocesan Board of Finance v Clark (No.2)* [1973] 1 W.L.R. 1572, and had new life breathed into it in *Ali v Lane* [2007] 1 P. & C.R. 26 (see paras 3.193 and 11.29).

[29] [2012] UKPC 40; [2013] 1 P. & C.R. 17.

[30] [1997] A.C. 749 HL.

[31] None of the other judges explicitly agreed with Lord Hoffmann on this point, and Lord Goff of Chieveley (who dissented) disagreed. It is also considered that Lord Hoffmann's description of the kind of evidence that was admissible in cases of latent ambiguity was itself too restrictive: see

Many of them have been considered in the preceding chapter. However, in addition to those devices the court has others. For example it may reject untrue descriptions[32]; it may reject clauses as being repugnant to the main object of the contract[33]; it may declare a preference for the earlier of two inconsistent clauses in a deed[34]; it may declare a clause (e.g. an exception clause) to be ineffective,[35] and in the last resort it may declare the clause (or the contract as a whole) void for uncertainty.[36]

Illustrations

1.   Property was conveyed to husband and wife as "beneficial joint tenants in common in equal shares". It was held that they took as joint tenants.
Joyce v Barker Bros (Builders) Ltd[37]

2.   An option contained a clause providing that the term of the option "is to be for 176 days from the date hereof expiring at the hour of 11.59 pm on the 24th day of July 1964". The period of 176 days in fact expired on 18 July. It was held that the provisions fixing the exact time of expiry of the option took precedence over the miscalculation of the period.
Sawley Agency Ltd v Ginter[38]

3.   A bill of exchange contained a discrepancy between the amounts in words and figures. It was held that the amount in words prevailed.
Saunderson v Piper[39]

4.   A testator appointed as one of his executors "Mr. Percival of Brighton Esquire, the Father". Evidence was admitted to show that William Percival Boxall was known to the testator (who addressed him as Percival); that he resided at Brighton; that he had a son; that he had been appointed an executor under an earlier will of the testator, and that the testator knew no one else named Percival.
In b Rosaz[40]

4.   LATENT AMBIGUITY

A latent ambiguity only arises after evidence of the circumstances surrounding the making of the instrument has been tendered; and in such a case further evidence has always been admissible to resolve the ambiguity.

In *Doe d. Hiscocks v Hiscocks*,[41] Lord Abinger CB described a latent ambiguity thus:

    "… where the meaning of the testator's words is neither ambiguous nor obscure,

8.20

---

    para.8.22.
[32]   See para.9.40.
[33]   See para.9.73.
[34]   See para.9.82.
[35]   See Ch.12.
[36]   See para.8.111.
[37]   (1980) 40 P. & C.R. 512.
[38]   (1966) 58 D.L.R. (2d) 757.
[39]   (1839) 5 Bing. N.C. 425.
[40]   (1877) 2 P.D. 66. Cf. *National Society for the Prevention of Cruelty to Children v Scottish National Society for the Prevention of Cruelty to Children* [1915] A.C. 207 (see para.9.49).
[41]   (1839) 5 M. & W. 363.

but, from some of the circumstances admitted in proof an ambiguity arises, as to which of the two or more things, or which of the two or more persons (each answering the words in the will) the testator intended to express."

So too in *Smith v Thompson*,[42] Maule J said:

"I agree that, generally speaking, the construction of a written contract is for the court; but, when it is shewn by extrinsic evidence, that the terms of the contract are ambiguous, evidence is admissible to explain the ambiguity and to shew what the parties really meant. That is one of Lord Bacon's maxims. Where there is an election between two meanings, it is properly a question for the jury. So, if a man devise land to his 'cousin John' and it appears that he has two cousins John, extrinsic evidence is admissible to shew to which of them he meant the land to go."

8.21   The essential feature of a latent ambiguity was that no ambiguity appeared on the face of the document; it was only when the terms of the document came to be applied to the facts that the ambiguity arose. As Lord Wrenbury put it in *GWR v Bristol Corp*[43]:

"The words of the instrument may be perfectly plain and unambiguous for example 'My nephew, Joseph Grant' or 'fair market price,' but if, from the surrounding circumstances, when you come to apply the instrument, you find that there are two persons who will satisfy the words 'my nephew Joseph Grant,' or two markets to which the parties may have been referring, there is a latent ambiguity, and evidence is admissible to resolve it. Extrinsic evidence has created the ambiguity, and extrinsic evidence is admissible to resolve it."

The justification of this principle was the practical one that it saves instruments from being declared void for uncertainty.

Illustrations

1.   A guarantee was expressed to be made "in consideration of your having this day advanced to our client the sum of £750". It was held that evidence was admissible to prove that the advance was made after the guarantee was given. Rolfe B said:

"The question turns upon the meaning of the words 'your having this day advanced' which may mean, either, in consideration that you have this day advanced, or in consideration that you shall have this day advanced. The expression may mean either. How then are we to arrive at the real meaning? The cases

---

[42]   (1849) 8 C.B. 44. See also the footnote to *Hitchin v Groom* (1848) 5 C.B. 515 at 520:

"A latent ambiguity, i.e. an ambiguity in the terms of the instrument, the existence of which is first shewn by extrinsic evidence, whether written or verbal, may be explained by extrinsic evidence, which may be either written or verbal".

[43]   (1918) 87 L.J. Ch. 414 at 429.

... decide that parol evidence is admissible for the purpose of explanation. These cases are in point. The expression here is equivocal."
Goldshede v Swan[44]

2.   Parties entered into an agreement for the purchase of 125 bales of Surat cotton to arrive ex Peerless from Bombay. Two ships named Peerless sailed from Bombay, one in October and one in December. The goods arrived by the December voyage, and the buyer refused to take delivery of the goods on the ground that he intended to refer to the ship which sailed in October. It was held that evidence was admissible to identify the ship to which each party meant to refer.
Raffles v Wichelhaus[45]

3.   Shipowners and charterers disputed the meaning of a clause in a charterparty that lighterage if any necessary to enable steamer to complete loading at North Dock Swansea to be at merchants' risk and expense. It was held that there was sufficient ambiguity in the language of the charterparty to warrant the admission of evidence to explain it.
The Curfew[46]

4.   A lease of a public-house contained a covenant by the tenant to deal exclusively with the landlord for beer provided that the landlord was willing to supply it at a fair market price. It was held that the word "market" was capable of more than one meaning and that evidence was rightly admitted to prove the existence of a two-tier market, one for "tied" houses and one for "free" houses. The tenant was entitled to a supply of beer at the (lower) "tied" rate.
Charrington & Co Ltd v Wooder[47]

5.   THE NATURE OF THE ADMISSIBLE EVIDENCE

In order to resolve a latent ambiguity, any relevant evidence was admissible, including direct evidence of the intention of the parties.

In the normal course of events, the court will receive evidence of the objective facts surrounding the making of the contract, but will not receive direct evidence of the intention of the parties.[48] In addition the court will not receive evidence which would vary or contradict the terms of the written instrument.[49] However, contradicting or varying the instrument is not the problem in the case of a latent ambiguity. In such a case the problem is that there are two or more meanings each of which is entirely consistent with the language of the written instrument and a choice must

8.22

---

44   (1847) 1 Exch. 154. Although extrinsic evidence was admitted, and the case is traditionally classified as one of latent ambiguity, the words of Rolfe B suggest (rightly) that it was really a case of patent ambiguity. In the nineteenth century, the case would have had to have been classified as one of latent ambiguity in order for the evidence to have been admitted (and hence the contract upheld). Nowadays, however, it is likely that the same evidence as was admitted in that case, would be admitted in any event as part of the background: *Static Control Components (Europe) Ltd v Egan* [2004] 2 Lloyd's Rep. 429.

45   (1864) 2 H. & C. 906.

46   [1891] P. 131.

47   [1914] A.C. 71 (see especially Lord Haldane LC at 79 and Lord Atkinson at 93).

48   See para.3.143.

49   See para.3.87.

be made between them. The extrinsic evidence does not, therefore, vary or contradict the written instrument; it supplements or explains it. This was why the court always received evidence of the factual background to the written instrument. In most cases the ambiguity was solved by reference to evidence which nowadays is routinely admitted as part of the background known to the parties. However, it appears that on occasion the court was also prepared to admit evidence of subjective declarations of intent.

8.23   In *Altham's case*,[50] Sir Edward Coke said:

> "Therefore, if A levies a fine to William his son, to have and to hold to him and his heirs, upon this fine the judge cannot make question for any matter of law, but now the party comes and avers matter in fact; and says that A had two sons named William, an elder and a younger, and his intent was to levy the fine to William the younger. This averment out of the fine is good of this matter of fact, which well stands with the words of the fine, and shall be tried by the country, and therewith agrees YB 47 Edw 3, 16 B."

Similarly, in *Lord Cheyney's Case*,[51] it was held:

> "If a man has two sons both baptized by the name of John, and conceiving the elder (who had been long absent) is dead, devises his land by his will in writing to his son John generally, and in truth the elder is living; in this case the younger son may in pleading or evidence allege the devise to him; and if it be denied he may produce witnesses to prove his father's intent, that he thought the other to be dead or that he at the time of the will made, named his son John the younger and the writer left out the addition of the younger."

This passage suggests that direct evidence is admissible of the intention of the father both by proving his inner state of mind and also by proving his spoken intention at the time of the making of the will.

8.24   In *Lord Waterpark v Fennell*,[52] Lord Wesleydale said (obiter):

> "When the evidence of all material facts is exhausted and there is still ambiguity, no parol evidence of the grantor's intentions as distinguished from extrinsic facts can be admissible, except in the single case of there being two subjects or two objects to which the terms of the instruments are equally applicable, a condition of things which does not exist in the present case."[53]

In *Re Jeffery*,[54] Warrington J held that a gift in a will raised a latent ambiguity. He said:

> "The case is one in which evidence of intention as distinct from evidence merely of surrounding circumstances is admissible, and in the present case I have evidence both of intention and of surrounding circumstances."

---

[50]   (1610) 8 Co. Rep. 150b.
[51]   (1591) 5 Co. Rep. 68.
[52]   (1859) 7 H.L. Cas. 650.
[53]   See also *Shore v Wilson* (1842) 9 Cl. & Fin. 355, per Parke B.
[54]   [1914] 1 Ch. 375; *Re Ray* [1916] 1 Ch. 461.

In *Alampi v Swartz*,[55] McGillivray JA explained the extensive nature of the 8.25
evidence that could be admitted in a case of latent ambiguity. Having referred to
the principle that evidence of surrounding circumstances was admissible to interpret
a written instrument, he continued:

"Evidence so admitted does not offend against the general rule. It may not
contradict a term in the contract but, as has been said, is adduced to assign
definite meaning to the terms used or to relate them to the proper subject-
matter. If, however, after such evidence has been led it then appears that the term
under construction is ambiguous and capable of more than one meaning evidence
of a different class may be admitted, namely evidence of intention. Such an
ambiguity, a "latent ambiguity", because not apparent upon the face of the writing, demands evidence of intention to establish whether there was an agreement
at all, or if the parties intended a particular one of alternate meanings to prevail.
Such latent ambiguities have arisen where it was found that two railway sta-
tions bore the name of the one mentioned in the contract[56] ... or where an agreement was made for a lease of premises 'as per plan agreed upon' and it appeared that two plans had been inspected[57] ...".

Wigmore[58] summarised the rule as follows: 8.26

"The foregoing exception[59] has itself an exception, namely, that declarations of
intention, though ordinarily excluded from consideration, are receivable to assist in *interpreting an equivocation*—that is, a term which upon application to
external objects, is found to fit two or more of them equally" (original emphasis).

In *Sembcorp Marine Ltd v PPL Holdings Pte Ltd*,[60] the Singapore Court of Ap- 8.27
peal reviewed the old law about the nature of the evidence that was admissible in
the case of a latent ambiguity. They held that direct evidence of intention was
admissible in cases of latent ambiguity.

The old rule was applicable only where the court was satisfied that the language 8.28
of the instrument equally fitted two or more conclusions. Thus in *National Society
for the Prevention of Cruelty to Children v Scottish National Society for the Prevention of Cruelty to Children*,[61] a Scotsman made a will in the Scottish form leaving
a legacy to "the National Society for the Prevention of Cruelty to Children". That
description fitted exactly a society with its head office in London and without active operations in Scotland. The legacy was also claimed by the Scottish Society,
of which the testator knew before he made his will. The House of Lords held that
the London Society was entitled to the legacy. Lord Dunedin said:

"Here you have an accurate description of the one person and a description which
is admittedly not quite accurate of the other. You must, I think, have positive

---

55 [1964] 43 D.L.R. (2d) 11.
56 *Robinson v Great Western R Co* (1866) 35 L.J.C.P. 123.
57 *Hodges v Horsfall* (1829) 1 Russ. & My. 116.
58 *Evidence*, Vol.4 para.2427.
59 For example, the inadmissibility of subjective declarations of intent.
60 [2013] SGCA 43; (2013) 151 Con. L.R. 170.
61 [1915] A.C. 207.

evidence of some cogent sort to make you prefer the latter to the former. Such evidence unfortunately in this case I do not find."[62]

8.29   In *Mannai Investment Co Ltd v Eagle Star Life Assurance Co Ltd*,[63] Lord Hoffmann said that the old rule was that in cases of latent ambiguity "evidence of background facts which showed what the testator must have meant, notwithstanding that he had used the wrong words, was admitted". It is suggested that this was too limited a summary of the old rule. In the same case (and in *Investors' Compensation Scheme v West Bromwich Building Society*[64]) Lord Hoffmann reiterated that subjective declarations of intent are not admissible for the purpose of interpreting a contract. At the same time, he said that the special rules relating to latent ambiguities were both capricious and incoherent.

8.30   Whether the former exception to the principle, in the case of latent ambiguities, that subjective declarations of intent are inadmissible has survived the restatement remains to be seen. On the one hand, the approach of the courts is to include rather than exclude relevant evidence; and the admission of direct evidence of intent where a contractual description applies equally to two or more persons or places may be the only way of giving effect to the intention of the parties. On the other hand, the courts have assimilated the approach to be taken to all difficulties of construction and the retention of anomalous exceptions may be thought to be undesirable.

Illustrations

1.   A guarantee was expressed to be made "in consideration of your having this day advanced to our client ... the sum of £750". Evidence was admitted to prove that the guarantee was signed and delivered by the defendant to the plaintiff simultaneously with the delivery of a cheque for the money to the named client, and that accordingly there was no reference to a past consideration.
Goldshede v Swan[65]

2.   A charterparty required a vessel to proceed to North Swansea Dock and there load a full and complete cargo "lighterage if any to enable steamer to complete loading at [the dock] to be at merchant's expense". The tides were such that the vessel had to leave the dock before loading was complete. The charterer argued that the clause did not impose the risk of lighterage on them in these circumstances. It was held that the clause was ambiguous. Evidence was admitted of a conversation between the shipbroker acting for the owners and the agent of the charterers, and of an exchange of telegrams between them, which showed that the point argued by the charterers had been raised and rejected before the charterparty was concluded.
The Curfew[66]

3.   An engineer was employed to supervise the construction of a railway. The

---

[62]   In the light of the majority decision of the House of Lords in *Mannai Investment Co Ltd v Eagle Star Life Assurance Co Ltd* [1997] A.C. 749 it is doubtful whether the strictness of this approach can now be maintained. However, in that case Lord Hoffmann referred to the statement of principle in the speech of Lord Loreburn with approval ("the accurate use of a name in a will creates a strong presumption against any rival who is not the possessor of the name"), although he did not comment on the result of the case.

[63]   [1997] A.C. 749.

[64]   [1998] 1 W.L.R. 896.

[65]   (1847) 1 Exch. 154.

[66]   [1891] P. 131.

terms of his engagement entitled him to a fee based on a percentage of the cost of the works. There was a proviso to the effect that he should be paid an extra 1.5 per cent "on the estimate of £35,000" in the event of being able to reduce "the total cost of the works" below £30,000. The question arose whether the "total cost of the works" included the cost of purchasing the land. Evidence was admitted of a conversation between the engineer and the employer's agent and of a circular prepared by the engineer. That evidence showed that the estimate of £35,000 was an estimate of the cost of the finished railway, including the cost of land purchase. Accordingly, the "total cost of the works" included the cost of land purchase.

Bank of New Zealand v Simpson[67]

4. The dimensions and area of a conveyance were ambiguous. Acts of subsequent possession and use were admitted to resolve the ambiguity.

Wateham v Att.-Gen. of the East African Protectorate[68]

6. ELECTION CURING AMBIGUITY

Where the ambiguity in a contract consists of the expression of defined alternatives the law will sometimes permit the ambiguity to be resolved by the election of one of the parties to it.

As has been seen above, ambiguity in a contract may sometimes take the form of the expression of alternatives, without any choice having been made between them.[69] Where the alternatives are themselves sufficiently defined, the law will often permit the choice to be made by one or other of the parties, rather than declare the contract (or the particular provision) void for uncertainty. It must, however, appear from a fair reading of the contract that the parties intended one or other of them to have a choice. Accordingly, whether or not a contractual provision permits questions of uncertainty to be resolved by the unilateral decision of one party to a contract (or by some third party) is ultimately a matter of interpretation.[70]

8.31

Thus it is stated in Sheppard's Touchstone[71]:

8.32

"If one be seised of two acres of land, and he doth lease them for life, and grant the remainder of one of them, and doth not say of which to IS; in this case if IS make his election which acre he will have, the grant of the remainder to him will be good."

So too in *Mervyn v Lyds*,[72] Dyer CJ said:

"If I give you one of my horses, although that be uncertain, yet by your election that may be a good gift."

---

[67] [1900] A.C. 182.
[68] [1919] A.C. 533, as explained in *Schuler (L) AG v Wickman Machine Tool Sales Ltd* [1974] A.C. 235.
[69] For obligations expressed in the alternative, see para.8.104.
[70] *UYCF Ltd (formerly Night Trunkers (London) Ltd) v Forrester* [2000] 12 WLUK 211 | [2001] 3 E.G. 131 (CS).
[71] W. Sheppard, *Sheppard's Touchstone of Common Assurances*, 8th edn (London: Samuel Brooke, 1826), p.251.
[72] (1553) 1 Dyer 90a.

And in *Miller v Green*,[73] Tindal CJ said:

> "It is undoubtedly true that where a deed may enure to diverse purposes, he to whom the deed is made shall have election which way to make it, and may take it in that way as shall most be for his advantage."

8.33   These statements clearly apply where the choice to be made is a choice between alternatives sufficiently defined. The same principle also applies where the choice is to be made, not between different things but between different legal forms. Thus in *Heyward's Case*,[74] the question arose whether a deed took effect as a sale or a demise (in which latter event an attornment was necessary). It was held that the grantees had the right to elect in what manner the deed took effect. The judges resolved:

> "when a man seised of land in fee, for money demises, grants, bargains and sells his land for years, he who is owner of the land by his express grant, gives election to the lessee to take it by the one way or the other, for he has sole power to pass it by demise or bargain; and therefore the law will not make construction against such express grant, and namely in this case where it will trench to the prejudice of the lessee."

And in the following resolution the judges emphasised that:

> "here is not election to claim one of two several things by one and the same title, but to claim one and the same thing by one of the two several titles."

8.34   So in *Edis v Bury*,[75] a document bore the form of a promissory note, but also resembled a bill of exchange. It was held that the holder of the document had the right to treat it either as a promissory note or as a bill of exchange. Bayley J said:

> "... where a party frames his instrument in such a way that it is ambiguous, whether it be a bill of exchange or a promissory note, the party holding it is entitled to treat it either as one or the other ..."

8.35   Election is also available to cure an ambiguity as to the temporal extent of the interest granted by a deed, at all events where there are clear alternative extents. Thus in *Dann v Spurrier*,[76] a lease was granted for a period of seven, 14 or 21 years. It was held to be determinable by the tenant at the seventh or fourteenth year. So too in *Doe d. Webb v Dixon*,[77] it was held that where a lease was granted for a term of 14 or seven years, the landlord had no power to determine the lease at the seventh year, that power being the tenant's alone. And in *Powell v Smith*,[78] Lord Romilly MR said:

> "The construction of the agreement is unquestionable. When it says 'for seven or fourteen years' those words allow the lessee to have an option of saying whether he will give it up at the end of the seven years. Upon that there is no question whatever."

---

[73]   (1831) 8 Bing. 92.
[74]   (1595) 2 Co. Rep. 35a.
[75]   (1827) 6 B. & C. 433.
[76]   (1803) 3 Bos. & P. 399.
[77]   (1807) 9 East. 15.
[78]   (1872) L.R. 14 Eq. 85.

Election may also be available to cure ambiguity as to the physical extent of the   **8.36**
interest granted by an instrument, although the precise circumstances in which the
right to elect will be permitted are far from clear from the cases. In *Jenkins v Green
(No.1)*,[79] the parties entered into an agreement for a lease of a farm of 437 acres
"except thirty seven acres thereof". The 37 acres were not identified in the
agreement. Romilly MR held that the landlord had the right to select the acres to
be excepted, unless the lease had actually been granted in which case the right to
elect would pass to the tenant.

In *Pearce v Watts*,[80] an agreement for the sale of land reserved: **8.37**

"the necessary land for making a railway through the estate to Prince Town."

Jessel MR held that the reservation was void for uncertainty. He said:

"I neither know what is the amount of land necessary for a railway, nor what line
the railway is to take, nor anything about it, and, therefore, I cannot order specific
performance of the contract."

This case is explicable on the ground that the quantity of land was not defined
by the conveyance, nor did the conveyance provide any machinery for determining how much land was necessary. There was therefore no clear choice to be made.

Savill Brothers Ltd v Bethell[81] is closer on the facts to *Jenkins v Green (No.1)*,   **8.38**
yet the court reached a different conclusion. In that case a conveyance purported
to reserve to the vendor a piece of land not less than 40 feet in width commencing
at a point marked on the plan and terminating at the nearest road to be made by the
purchaser. The Court of Appeal held that the exception was void. Although it was
argued that the vendor had a right to select the route of the strip, it was held that
the election could not be made until after the "nearest road" had been constructed,
and that might happen outside the perpetuity period. The exception was, therefore,
void for perpetuity.[82] It is difficult to reconcile the two cases, although *Jenkins v
Green (No.1)* was referred to without any disapproval in the judgment of Stirling
LJ.[83] It is possible that Romilly MR considered the question as one of personal
contract,[84] or that the fact that the conveyance in *Savill Brothers Ltd v Bethell* had
been executed was decisive, since it passed the land before any election could take
place. *Savill Brothers Ltd v Bethell* was concerned with an exception from a
conveyance.

A more liberal approach is taken where the right arises by reservation rather than   **8.39**
by exception. Thus in *South Eastern Railway Co v Associated Portland Cement
Manufacturers (1900) Ltd*,[85] a conveyance of land to a railway company reserved
to the vendor a right to build a tunnel under the railway to connect the parcels of
his land which had been severed by the railway. The conveyance did not define the
route of the tunnel. Swinfen Eady J said:

---

[79] (1858) 27 Beav. 437.
[80] (1875) L.R. 20 Eq. 492.
[81] [1902] 2 Ch. 523.
[82] Since the passing of the Perpetuities and Accumulations Act 1964, the parties would have been
     entitled to "wait and see" whether a road was made, and an election made, within the perpetuity
     period. The same would apply under the Perpetuities and Accumulations Act 2009.
[83] The judgment of the court.
[84] In which case the perpetuity problem would not have arisen.
[85] [1910] 1 Ch. 12.

"It was contended that the provision was too indefinite because the vendor had a considerable strip of land each side of the railway and the precise point at which the tunnel was to be made was not defined. The answer to this objection is that the right to make the tunnel and select the spot within the limits of the strip where it was to be was vested in the vendor, his heirs appointees and assigns. He or they had the right of making the tunnel and therefore of determining the spot."

The judgment of Swinfen Eady J was affirmed by the Court of Appeal. *Savill Brothers Ltd v Bethell* was distinguished on the narrow technical ground that it was dealing with an exception rather than a reservation.

8.40 The question of selection of the extent of land to be conveyed arose in *Bushwall Properties Ltd v Vortex Properties Ltd*.[86] In that case parties entered into an agreement for the purchase of 51 and a half acres of land for £500,000. The purchase price was to be paid in phases. The agreement provided that:

"Upon each completion a proportionate part of the land shall be released forthwith to us."

Oliver J held that the purchaser had the right to select which part of the land was to be conveyed on the occasion of each completion, and that any uncertainty was curable by those means. The Court of Appeal disagreed. Sir John Pennycuick said:

"Leaving aside the implication of a term, I see no ground on which, under the general law as applied to contracts for the sale of land, where an intending vendor and an intending purchaser enter into a binding contract for sale with completion in phases, the power of selection as to what part of the land is to be included in each phase must be regarded as vested in the purchaser."

He held that since the selection of the land was a matter of substance rather than machinery, in the absence of a clear agreement between the parties, the contract was void for uncertainty. Unfortunately, *Jenkins v Green (No.1)* was not cited, either to Oliver J or to the Court of Appeal, nor were any of the other cases discussed in this section. It is submitted that the decision in *Bushwall* is unsatisfactory, first because it did not consider any of the cases dealing with the possibility of curing ambiguity by election, and secondly because it dealt with the question who was to have the right of election without first considering whether any right to elect existed.[87]

8.41 In *Harewood v Retese*,[88] the Privy Council described *Bushwall* as a "difficult case" but did not need to consider it on the facts. The approach of the Court of Appeal in *Bushwall* stands in marked contrast to that of the Court of Appeal of New South Wales in *Malago Pty Ltd v AW Ellis Engineering Pty Ltd*.[89] In that case an agreement for sale of shares in a marina business provided that there was to be transferred to the seller 21.6 per cent of the surface water area of the berths of the marina. Rejecting the argument that this provision was void for uncertainty, the New

---

[86] [1975] 1 W.L.R. 1649; reversed [1976] 1 W.L.R. 591. Oliver J held that the word "proportionate" referred to acreage, and this was common ground in the Court of Appeal.

[87] This decision can be defended on pragmatic grounds. If the Court of Appeal had upheld Oliver J then probably they would have held (as he did) that the purchaser had the right of selection. If the purchaser has the right of selection, the vendor bears the risk of a default, in which event he might be left with a number of unconnected (and perhaps) useless pieces of land.

[88] (1989) 37 W.I.R. 427.

[89] [2012] NSWCA 227.

South Wales Court of Appeal held that any uncertainty was curable by the election of the buyer who was entitled to select which part of the surface area to transfer. Nicholson JA said:

"The general rule is that where a promise permits performance in a number of ways and does not state which party has the right to elect, the promisor has the right to elect which of the methods of performance he will choose ... There are alternative ways in which the relevant obligation may be performed and it is clear, as a matter of construction of the contract, upon which party the right of election falls."[90]

In the author's opinion the approach of the New South Wales Court of Appeal is to be preferred.

8.42 In *Herbert v Doyle*,[91] parties agreed for a transfer of nine parking spaces by Mr Herbert to Mr Doyle. The precise location of the ninth space was not specified, although the agreement was that it had to be "reasonably accessible" in relation to a particular property. Arden LJ said:

"In my judgment, the failure of Mr Herbert to make a selection of the ninth parking space did not in the circumstances of this case mean that there was no valid contract in this sense. The parties agreed by implication that Mr Herbert would choose which parking space would be transferred to the respondents as the ninth parking space, but that was not the limit of the implication to be made. By necessary implication also, the choice had to be made in a reasonable time.

If Mr Herbert failed to make the choice, the question arises whether there is by necessary implication a further term that the ninth parking space is such space as the court shall determine to be that intended by the parties to be selected in order to make their agreement fully effective. (I need not consider whether the respondents were entitled to take any steps themselves in this regard as they have not asserted any such right). In my judgment, that question must be answered affirmatively. There is nothing to suggest that the agreement of April 2003 should only take effect if Mr Herbert took the step of identifying the ninth space. That would have given him a unilateral right of veto. The agreement of April 2003 would have been unworkable in practice if the court could not step in to make the limited choice between the remaining parking spaces so as to identify the ninth space."

8.43 In some circumstances where a contract confers a right of selection on one party, that party has an obligation to make a selection. In *Mansel Oil Ltd v Troon Storage Tankers SA*,[92] a charterparty required the owners to deliver the vessel at a port in the Ghana/Nigeria range. The charterers were to have the option to choose which of the several ports in that range it was to be. Until they did so the owners could not know where that would be, and, therefore, how they were to comply with their contractual obligation to deliver the vessel. Christopher Clarke J said that:

"It seems to me that owners and charterers would ordinarily understand that charterers' option to select the delivery port was an option that they were obliged to exercise. The expectation of the parties is that the charterer will declare where

90 Approving the equivalent paragraphs in the Australian edition of this work.
91 [2010] EWCA Civ 1095.
92 [2008] 2 Lloyd's Rep. 384.

the vessel is to be delivered, not that he may do so. Further, the nomination is necessary in order to complete the definition of the parties' contractual obligations."

This part of the judge's reasoning was not in issue in the Court of Appeal, where the judge's judgment was affirmed.[93]

8.44 Once a selection has been made it cannot be changed (unless the contract provides clearly to the contrary).[94]

Illustrations

1.   A testator owned two closes. By his will he devised one to his son John and one to his son George. He did not specify which son was to have which close. In fact, they tossed for them. It was held that any uncertainty was curable by election and since the brothers had consented to a particular method of selection the devise was good.
Duckmanton v Duckmanton[95]

2.   A testatrix left "one house to each of my nephews and nieces". It was held that the nephews and nieces had the right to select one house each.
Re Knapton[96]

3.   A contract for the sale of goods provided for the goods to be shipped f.o.b. good Danish port. It was held that the contract was not too vague. The buyer was bound to select the port of shipment.
Boyd (David T) & Co v Louis Louca[97]

4.   An agreement made between a developer and a local planning authority entitled the developer to build 343 houses on a site. It also provided that 1.3 hectares of land were to be reserved for school purposes. The precise location of the area was not defined. It was held that it was for the developers to choose the location of the land to be reserved for school purposes.
Abbey Homesteads (Developments) Ltd v Northamptonshire County Council[98]

7.   WHO HAS THE RIGHT TO ELECT

In general, where the right to elect exists, the right to elect belongs to the party who is to take the first step under the contract. However, the right may be that of the person for whose benefit the right exists, or may be determined by the extent to which the contract has been performed.

---

[93]   [2009] EWCA Civ 425.
[94]   *Antiparos ENE v SK Shipping Co Ltd* [2008] 2 Lloyd's Rep. 237; *Mediterranean Salvage & Towing Ltd v Seamar Trading & Commerce Inc* [2008] 2 Lloyd's Rep. 628.
[95]   (1860) 5 H. & N. 219.
[96]   [1941] Ch. 428.
[97]   [1973] 1 Lloyd's Rep. 209.
[98]   [1986] 1 E.G.L.R. 24 CA.

The classic formulation of the principle is that the right to elect belongs to the party who is to take the first step under the contract. It is stated thus in *Heyward's Case*[99]: **8.45**

"In case election be given of two several things, always he who is the first agent, and who ought to do the first act shall have the election. As if a man grants a rent of 20s or a robe to one and his heirs, the grantor shall have the election, for it is the first agent by payment of the one, or delivery of the other. So if a man makes a lease yielding rent or a robe, the lessee shall have the election, *causa qua supra*. And with that agree the books ... but if I give you one of my horses in my stable, there you shall have election, for you must be the first agent by taking or seizure of one of them. And if one grant to another 20 loads of hasel or 20 loads of maple to be taken in his wood of D, there the grantee shall have election, for he ought to do the first act, *scil*, to cut and take it."

In some cases, however, the allocation of the right to elect is based upon consideration of the party for whose benefit the right to elect exists; and that in turn is often determined on the *contra proferentem* principle. **8.46**

Thus in *Dann v Spurrier*,[100] a lease was granted for 7, 14 or 21 years. It was held that the option to determine was vested in the tenant, upon the principle that where a grant is doubtful it is to be construed in favour of the grantee.

In *Reed v Kilburn Co-operative Society*,[101] the plaintiff agreed to lend the defendant a sum of money "for the term of six or nine months". The plaintiff sued for the money after six months. His claim failed. No reasoned judgment is reported, but in the course of argument Blackburn J observed: **8.47**

"Where it is not said at whose option one of two alternatives is to take place the rule of law is that the option is in the party who is to do the first act; here the borrower is to do the first act by paying."

Cockburn CJ said:

"It is clear the alternative is put in for the benefit of the borrower. The lender is master of the situation and could impose any terms in the first instance."

Sometimes the allocation of the right to elect depends upon the stage which the transaction has reached. In *Jenkins v Green (No.1)*,[102] the parties made an agreement for a lease of a farm of 437 acres except 37 acres thereof. The agreement did not specify the 37 acres. Romilly MR said: **8.48**

"The selection must therefore be made by the person granting the lease, before it is executed and excepted out of the demise. But if the lease had been executed in the very terms of the agreement, without specifying the lands excepted, then the right of selecting the excepted lands would rest with the tenant."

---

[99] (1595) 2 Co. Rep. 35a.
[100] (1803) 3 Bos. & Pull. 399. A similar conclusion was reached upon a similar ground by Lord Ellenborough CJ in *Doe d. Webb v Dixon* (1807) 9 East. 15.
[101] (1875) L.R. 10 Q.B. 264.
[102] (1858) 27 Beav. 437.

The first proposition clearly accords with the principle set out in *Heyward's Case* since the landlord is the first agent; his act consisting of the grant of the lease. The second proposition is harder to justify, for once the lease had been granted it is not easy to see what act the tenant was to perform, unless it be to pay the rent.[103]

8.49 Where election is given to several persons, the first election made by any of the parties is effective.[104] However, where a testatrix left a house each to her nephews and nieces, but did not specify which house each was to have or the order in which they should select, it was held that the order of selection should be determined by lot.[105]

Illustration

A landlord agreed with his tenant to supplement the water supply so as to make it adequate, or otherwise to lay a pipe from a well and supply a pump. It was held that the option lay with the landlord, and not the tenant.
    Christie v Wilson[106]

8.   WHEN THE ELECTION IS TO BE MADE

Where no property passes until the election is made, the election must be made within the perpetuity period. Where property passes on the grant and the only doubt is as to the title, the election may be made at any time. Where an election is to be made under a contract, it may be an implied term of the contract that it is to be made within a reasonable time.

8.50 The principle is stated thus in *Heyward's Case*[107]:

"where the things are several, nothing passes before election, and the election ought to be precedent; but when one and the same thing shall pass, there it passes presently, and the election of the title may be subsequent."

And again:

"1.   When nothing passeth to the feoffee or grantee before the election, to have one thing or the other, there the election ought to be made in the life of the parties, and the heir or executor cannot make the election. But when an estate or interest passeth presently to the feoffee donee or grantee, there election may be made by them, or by their heirs or executors.

2.   When a thing passeth to the donee, or grantee, and the donee or grantee hath election in what manner or degree he will take it, there the interest passeth presently, and the party his heirs or executors may make election when they will."

---

[103] It may be based on the abolished doctrine of *interesse termini*, which was a special species of interest taken by a tenant under a lease before he had taken possession. This was an interest in the land but not an estate and consequently it could not, e.g. support the creation of a sublease. In the context of the rules relating to election, presumably the act to be performed by the tenant was the taking of possession.

[104] *Heyward's Case* (1595) 2 Co. Rep. 35a.

[105] *Re Knapton* [1941] Ch. 428.

[106] 1915 S.C. 645.

[107] (1592) 2 Co. Rep. 35a.

Thus in *Savill Brothers Ltd v Bethell*,[108] land was conveyed subject to the exception of a strip of land terminating at the nearest road to be made by the purchaser on the land. Stirling LJ said:

    8.51

> "If, then, by a deed there had been a grant of a plot of land to be ascertained by election, it follows that until the election, nothing passed; and if the deed granted certain specified lands, with the exception of a plot to be ascertained by election, it seems to us that the deed would at once pass the whole, but subject to an exception which could only be ascertained and take effect when the election was made."

Since the effect of the election would be to revest the land in the erstwhile vendor, it follows that the election would have to be made within the perpetuity period. Under the rule against perpetuities then in force, the exception was void, for the road forming the terminus of the excepted strip might not have been built within the perpetuity period.[109]

Again the case of *Jenkins v Green (No.1)*,[110] is difficult to reconcile, for Romilly MR clearly contemplated a shift in the right to elect, depending upon whether the grant had or had not been made, and did not indicate any limitation on the time during which the election could be made by the lessee once the grant had taken place.

    8.52

In *Mansel Oil Ltd v Troon Storage Tankers SA*,[111] a charterparty required the owners to deliver the vessel at a port in the Ghana/Nigeria range. The charterers were to have the option to choose which of the several ports in that range it was to be. The question arose when the nomination of a port was to be made. Christopher Clarke J said:

    8.53

> "In my judgment the correct formulation of the obligation, in respect of this charterparty, is that it was for charterers to make their nomination within a reasonable time which would be such time as was (a) not so late as would mean that, because of the lateness of the nomination, the vessel could not make her cancelling; and (b) early enough to ensure that the vessel suffered no delay resulting from the absence of nomination. Such a conclusion appears to me to be correct in principle, and consistent with the owners' obligation of co-operation. Before the vessel reaches the deviation point the owners can, without a nomination, do all that they need to do to comply with the charterparty, and without loss to themselves."

The judge's formulation was upheld on appeal.[112]

In *Herbert v Doyle*,[113] parties agreed for a transfer of nine parking spaces by Mr Herbert to Mr Doyle. The precise location of the ninth space was not specified, although the agreement was that it had to be "reasonably accessible" in relation to a particular property. Arden LJ said:

    8.54

> "The parties agreed by implication that Mr Herbert would choose which park-

---

[108] [1902] 2 Ch. 538.
[109] The rule against perpetuities is of little importance at the present day. If the rule does apply, the perpetuity period is, in general, 125 years and the "wait and see" rule applies.
[110] (1858) 27 Beav. 437. See para.8.36.
[111] [2008] 2 Lloyd's Rep. 384.
[112] [2009] EWCA Civ 425.
[113] [2010] EWCA Civ 1095.

ing space would be transferred to the respondents as the ninth parking space, but that was not the limit of the implication to be made. By necessary implication also, the choice had to be made in a reasonable time."

8.55 Where the election consists of the right to terminate a lease at stipulated dates before its expiry by effluxion of time, then, in the absence of other indications in the lease, the election may be made at any time before the date arrives.

8.56 Where the right to elect is the right to select the manner of exercising a vested right, the election may be made at any time.[114]

9. OBLIGATIONS THAT CAN BE PERFORMED IN DIFFERENT WAYS

Where an obligation can be performed in different ways, it is generally for the party obliged to perform the obligation to choose the method of performance. This is a question of interpretation of the contract rather than a rule of law. If one method of performance becomes impossible, it is a question of interpretation of the contract whether he is bound to perform by a remaining method or is discharged from the obligation to perform.

8.57 If a contract contains obligations that can be performed in different ways, it is a question of interpretation of the contract whether the promisor or the promisee has the right to choose how to perform. However, the natural meaning of a clause which imposes an obligation on a party to do A or B is likely to be that it is for the promisor to choose whether to do A or B.[115]

8.58 Similarly, where a contractual obligation may be performed in a number of ways, it is a question of construction whether there is a primary method of performance, subject to an option to substitute a different method, or whether there is no primary obligation until a choice between alternatives has been made. The distinction between the two was explained by Lord Devlin in *Reardon Smith Line v Ministry of Agriculture*.[116] He said:

"An obligation in a contract can frequently be performed in a large number of ways and the party under obligation can choose anyone of the ways he likes.[117] A contract may, for example, provide for September/October shipment and the shipper may then select anyone of the 61 days which he likes. I doubt if in such a case the shipper would, in the ordinary use of language, be described as having 61 options. But when a contract itself limits and enumerates the obligations, as when it obliges the shipper to ship wheat or barley or flour, it is quite sensible and natural to talk of his having an option to ship anyone of these three commodities. There is, however, a narrower sense in which the word can be used, and that is to confer a right of choice specially granted to the holder of the option and to be used solely for his own benefit. It is in this sense, I think, that the word is generally used in the business world.

At first sight this appears to be a distinction without a difference. When a party

---

[114] *South Eastern Railway Co v Associated Portland Cement Manufacturers (1900) Ltd* [1910] 1 Ch.12.
[115] *Mora Shipping Inc of Monrovia, Liberia v Axa Corporate Solutions Assurance SA* [2005] 2 Lloyd's Rep. 769.
[116] [1963] A.C. 691 at 717. See also *Ross T Smyth & Co Ltd v WN Lindsay Ltd* [1953] 1 W.L.R. 1280.
[117] Where a person covenants to keep a building in repair, and the repair may be carried out in a number of ways, the choice of methods is his: *Plough Investments Ltd v Manchester City Council* [1989] 1 E.G.L.R. 244.

under obligation selects between various alternatives, is he not considering simply his own benefit and convenience? A shipper who ships on September 4, and not on the 5th has chosen that date because it suits him better than the other. The difference arises when for some reason or another the pursuit of one alternative is temporarily or permanently barred. Where there is no option in the business sense, the consequence of damming one channel is simply that the flow of duty is diverted into the others and the freedom of choice thus restricted. If then a shipper cannot ship wheat, he must ship either barley or flour. The width of the alternatives is in the contract for the benefit of both parties and it can be a liability as well as a benefit for the shipper.

But where there is a 'business option' the legal position is quite different. There is not then one contractual obligation to be performed in alternative ways, but one obligation to be performed in one way, unless the option holder chooses to substitute another way and does so by the effective exercise of his option. In exercising the option, which he has acquired solely for his own advantage, the holder is not bound to consider the convenience or the interest of the other party. If the obligation is to ship a full and complete cargo of wheat with the option to change to barley or flour and the shipment of wheat is impeded, he is not obliged to change to barley or flour simply because that is the only way in which he could ship a full and complete cargo. So the question here is whether the contractual obligation on the charterer is correctly expressed as an obligation to ship a full and complete cargo of wheat, barley or flour in proportions which can, subject to the specified limits, be selected by the charterer; or whether it is an obligation to ship a full and complete cargo of wheat with an option to the charterer to substitute for that cargo a mixed one."

If there is no primary obligation until an election is made, the party entitled to elect is bound by his election and cannot afterwards retract it.[118]   **8.59**

The principle is equally applicable where the obligor is obliged to do X but there are two or more ways (A or B) in which to achieve that result.[119] In such a case it is for the obligor to choose how to perform his obligation. The existence of such a choice is akin to a contractual discretion and, like a contractual discretion, will normally be governed by the concept of rationality. In *Wandsworth LBC v Waaler*,[120] Lewison LJ said: **8.60**

"… where a contract, in this case a lease, empowers one party to it to make discretionary decisions which affect the rights of both parties, the law recognises that the exercise of that discretion gives rise to a potential conflict of interest. That is all the more so where the discretionary decision of one party to the contract imposes a financial liability on the other. The solution which the law has devised in those circumstances is to restrict the exercise of the discretion to what is rational."

Where a contractual obligation is expressed in the alternative, and one of the alternatives becomes impossible of performance, it is a question of construction whether the contracting party is required to perform the other alternative. Thus in   **8.61**

---

[118] *Schneider v Foster* (1857) 2 H. & N. 4; *Browne v Royal Insurance Co* (1859) 1 E. & E. 853.
[119] *Pease v Henderson Administration Ltd* [2019] EWCA Civ 158 (referring to this section with approval).
[120] [2017] EWCA Civ 45; [2017] 1 W.L.R. 2817.

Reardon Smith Line v Ministry of Agriculture,[121] Viscount Radcliffe said:

"If a shipper has undertaken to ship a full and complete cargo made up of alternative commodities, as in the terms 'wheat and/or maize and/or rye', his obligation is to have ready at the port of shipment a complete cargo within the range of those alternatives. Consequently the fact that he is prevented from loading one of the possible types of cargo by a cause within the exceptions clause, even though that is the type that he has himself selected and provided for, is not an answer to a claim for demurrage. To protect him each of the alternatives or all the alternatives would have to be covered by an excepted clause."

In *Anderson v Commercial Union*,[122] a fire insurance policy contained a clause which gave insurers an option to reinstate the property instead of paying the amount of the loss. Reinstatement became impossible and insurers argued that they were thereby discharged from the entire obligation. The Court of Appeal rejected that argument. Bowen LJ said:

"It is clear law that if one of two things which have been contracted for subsequently becomes impossible, it becomes a question of construction whether, according to the true intention of the document, the obligor is bound to perform the alternative or is discharged altogether."

8.62 There are, however, cases in which the contract, properly construed, does not create a single obligation which may be performed in many ways, but rather creates an obligation to be performed in one way, unless the promisor chooses to substitute another way. In such a case, the right to substitute is a true business option, and if the primary method of performance becomes impossible, the promisor is not obliged to substitute a different method of performance.

8.63 If the contracting party has put it out of his power to perform one of the alternatives, he will usually be obliged to perform the other.[123]

10. UNCERTAINTY

A contract, or a provision in a contract, may be uncertain if it is unintelligible; if it is meaningless; if the court is unable to select between a variety of meanings fairly attributable to it, and the circumstances are not such that one or other party to the contract may elect between meanings; where the court is unable to discern the concept which the parties had in mind; or where the terms of the contract require further agreement between the parties in order to implement them.

8.64 Uncertainty may prevent a contract from arising at all (in which context it is often referred to as incomplete agreement) or it may invalidate one particular term in an otherwise valid contract. It may come about in a variety of ways.

8.65 In *Brown v Gould*,[124] Megarry J said that there were "two main ways" in which a provision may be void for uncertainty:

"A provision may be void for uncertainty because it is devoid of any meaning.

---

[121] [1963] A.C. 691 at 717.
[122] (1885) L.J.Q.B. 146.
[123] *The Super Servant Two* [1990] 1 Lloyd's Rep. 1. See also para.13.43.
[124] [1972] 1 Ch. 53.

As some critics of certain modern writings might testify, there may be an unintelligible collocation of ordinary English words, or there may be mere gibberish, such as the phrase 'Fustum funnidos tantaraboo' cited in *Fawcett Properties Ltd v Buckingham County Council*[125] … The other main head is where there is a variety of meanings which can fairly be put on the provision, and it is impossible to say which of them was intended. Mere ambiguities may sometimes be resolved by the application of legal presumptions, and so on; but where the language used is equally consistent with a wide range of different meanings, it may be impossible to discern the concept which the provision was intended to enshrine. If a case is to be brought under this head, the attack will usually start with the demonstration of a diversity of meanings which are consistent with the language used; and if this is not done, the attack will usually fail."

Similarly, in *Star Shipping AG v China National Foreign Trade Transportation Corp*,[126] Steyn LJ said: **8.66**

"The spectre of a catalogue of possible alternative constructions may at first glance seem to confront us with a daunting task. The reality is different. The fact that a multiplicity of possible meanings of a contractual provision are put forward, and that there are difficulties of interpretation, does not justify a conclusion that the clause is meaningless. The court must do its best to select, among the contending interpretations, the one that best matches the intention of the parties as expressed in the language they adopted."

In practice it is relatively rare for a provision in a contract to be held void for   **8.67**
uncertainty because it is unintelligible or gibberish. In *Mellstrom v Garner*,[127]
however, the court declined to construe a partnership agreement between chartered accountants described by Harman LJ as "a farrago of nonsense". In *Mercantile Credits Ltd v Comblas*,[128] cl.9 of a contract relating to a truck which combined the functions of a loan contract and a bill of sale provided in cl.9 that if the mortgagee had taken possession of the truck it would be entitled to recover from the mortgagor the difference between the value of the goods and "the nett balance due within the meaning of section 29 of [the Consumer Transactions Act 1972]". However, cl.12 of the same contract stated that any reference to any of the provisions of the Act were to be disregarded in interpreting the contract. The Privy Council held that the effect of cl.12 was that the reference to the "nett balance due", which was a statutorily defined term, should be treated as struck out of the contract, with the result that cl.9 was meaningless. In *The Pensions Regulator v A Admin Ltd*,[129] a pension scheme prescribed member benefits as "exclusively the benefits of such kinds as are prescribed by Part 4 FA 2004 and shall be computed in accordance with the limits prescribed by Part 4 FA 2004". The Finance Act 2004 did not set out a method

---

[125] [1961] A.C. 636. The gibberish quoted by Megarry J was quoted by him as counsel in argument in *Fawcett Properties Ltd v Buckingham County Council*, and is itself a hypothetical example attributed to Sir Richard Pepper Arden MR (see [1961] A.C. 636 at 647).

[126] [1993] 2 Lloyd's Rep. 445 at 452. See also *Lobb Partnership Ltd v Aintree Racecourse Co Ltd* [2000] C.L.C. 431.

[127] [1970] 1 W.L.R. 603. See also *Nelson Line (Liverpool) Ltd v Nelson (James) & Sons Ltd* [1908] A.C. 16, per Lord Halsbury. In *Confetti Records v Warner Music (UK) Ltd* [2003] E.M.L.R. 35 the author declined to construe the phrase "shizzle my nizzle".

[128] (1982) 56 A.L.J.R. 499; [1982] UKPC 7.

[129] [2014] Pens. L.R. 319.

of computing pension benefits or give any other assistance in working out what the benefits should be. Rose J said that it was impossible to work out what pension the scheme members could expect to receive under the trust. She concluded that:

> "one is at a loss to ascertain what the Prescribed Benefits are under the trust, and hence what the Primary Pension is and hence how A. Admin (or in default of A. Admin, the court) is supposed to carry out its duties of holding the Fund on trust for the payment of the Primary Pension to the Scheme Member. No amount of judicial knowledge or experience or innate common sense—or at any rate not the amount that I am able bring to bear—seems to arrive at a useful answer."

The trust was therefore void for uncertainty.

8.68 It is more common for a phrase or clause to be rejected as meaningless because it has no application to the circumstances in which it was written. Thus in *Nicolene Ltd v Simmonds*,[130] a buyer ordered a quantity of steel reinforcing bars. The seller accepted the order, stating "I assume that we are in agreement that the usual conditions of acceptance apply". Denning LJ said:

> "There are no usual conditions of acceptance at all, so the words are meaningless. There is nothing to which they can apply. On that account it is said that there never was a contract at all between the parties. In my opinion a distinction must be drawn between a clause which is meaningless and a clause which is yet to be agreed. A clause which is meaningless can often be ignored, whilst still leaving the contract good; whereas a clause which has yet to be agreed may mean that there is no contract at all, because the parties have not agreed on all the terms."

So too in *Richards (Michael) Properties Ltd v Corp of Wardens of St Saviour's Parish, Southwark*,[131] the words "subject to contract" were rejected from the acceptance of a tender offer, on the ground that they were meaningless.

8.69 Sometimes the problem encountered is that the words chosen by the parties have no clear objective meaning, but depend on the subjective state of mind of the author. Thus in *Murray v Dunn*,[132] a building restriction prevented a landowner from erecting "any building of an unseemly description". The House of Lords held that the word "unseemly" was too uncertain to be enforceable. The Earl of Halsbury said:

> "What may reasonably be 'seemly' appears to be a question rather of the personal conduct of the individuals engaged than any characteristic of the building which is supposed to be itself an infraction of the covenant which has been entered into."

So too would a trust for "my old friends". In *Re Lloyd's Trust Instruments*,[133] Megarry J said:

> "If there is a trust for 'my old friends' all concerned are faced with uncertainty as to the concept or idea enshrined in these words. It may not be difficult to

---

[130] [1953] 1 Q.B. 543.
[131] [1975] 3 All E.R. 416. This was, however, an exceptional case: *Munton v Greater London Council* [1976] 1 W.L.R. 649.
[132] [1907] A.C. 283.
[133] *Unreported 24 June 1970*. This passage was cited and applied in *Brown v Gould* [1972] Ch. 53; [1971] 3 W.L.R. 334 and *Bushwall Properties Ltd v Vortex Properties Ltd* [1975] 1 W.L.R. 1649 (reversed [1976] 1 W.L.R. 591).

resolve that 'old' means not 'aged' but 'of long standing'; but then there is the question how long is 'long'. Friendship, too, is a concept with almost infinite shades of meaning. Where the concept is uncertain, the gift is void. Where the concept is certain, then mere difficulty in tracing and discovering those who are entitled normally does not invalidate the gift."

These examples show that there are many ordinary English words which have **8.70** an infinite variety of meanings according to the subjective experience and attitudes of the author and reader of them. In such cases the court does not consider it safe to fix upon one only of such meanings. These are not cases in which there are a limited number of certain meanings. On the contrary these are cases in which each meaning shades imperceptibly into the next. Thus where the court is unable to discern objective criteria to assess what would be reasonable, an alleged contract may fail for want of certainty.[134]

Uncertainty may also arise where the court is unable to choose between differ- **8.71** ent meanings to be attributed to the provision in question. Thus in *Scammell and Nephew Ltd v Ouston*,[135] the respondents agreed to buy a van but stated "this order is given on the understanding that the balance of the purchase price can be had on hire purchase terms over a period of two years". The trial judge held that there was a concluded contract, and that the quoted phrase was in the nature of a condition precedent. In the Court of Appeal the three Lords Justices each took a different view as to the nature of the contract (though all held that there was a concluded contract) and in the House of Lords a further version was advanced by the respondent. The House of Lords held that there was no contract by reason of uncertainty. Lord Russell of Killowen said:

"The existence of this fivefold choice is embarrassing but eloquent. An alleged contract which appeals for its meaning to so many skilled minds in so many different ways, is undoubtedly open to suspicion ... But, in view of the numerous forms of hire-purchase transactions, and the multiplicity of terms and details which they involve, the respondents are faced with what appears to me to be a fatal alternative, namely, either (1) this term of the alleged contract is quite uncertain as to its meaning, and prevents the existence of an enforceable contract, or (2) the term leaves essential contractual provisions for further negotiations between the parties with the same result."

In *Vinci Construction UK Ltd v Beumer Group UK Ltd*,[136] O'Farrell J held that:

"... a provision in a contract will be void for uncertainty if the court cannot reach a conclusion as to what was in the parties' minds or where it is not safe for the court to prefer one possible meaning to other equally possible meanings."

Nevertheless, as Barwick CJ said in *Upper Hunter District Council v Austral-* **8.72** *ian Chilling and Freezing Co Ltd*[137]:

"But a contract of which there can be more than one possible meaning or which

---

[134] *Baird Textile Holdings Ltd v Marks & Spencer Plc* [2001] C.L.C. 999 CA; *Wellington City Council v Body Corp 51702 (Wellington)* [2002] 3 N.Z.L.R. 486 NZCA.
[135] [1941] A.C. 251.
[136] [2017] EWHC 2196 (TCC); 174 Con. L.R. 178.
[137] (1968) 118 C.L.R. 429 at 436 (H.C. Aust.).

when construed can produce in its application more than one result is not void for uncertainty. As long as it is capable of a meaning, it will ultimately bear that meaning which the court or, in an appropriate case, an arbitrator, decides is its proper meaning; and the court or arbitrator will decide its application."

8.73   In *Beddow v Cayzer*,[138] Mummery LJ said:

"There can be no contract without some terms, express or implied. If the express terms that are pleaded are significant, but are too uncertain and vague to be legally enforceable, there can be no concluded and binding agreement creating a partnership or joint venture."

In *Wells v Devani*,[139] Lord Kitchin said that:

"... there will be cases where an agreement is so vague and uncertain that it cannot be enforced. So too, there will be cases where the parties have not addressed certain matters which are so fundamental that their agreement is incomplete. Further, an agreement may be so deficient in one or other of these respects that nothing can be done to render it enforceable. But I do not accept that there is any general rule that it is not possible to imply a term into an agreement to render it sufficiently certain or complete to constitute a binding contract. Indeed, it seems to me that it is possible to imply something that is so obvious that it goes without saying into anything, including something the law regards as no more than an offer. If the offer is accepted, the contract is made on the terms of the words used and what those words imply. Moreover, where it is apparent the parties intended to be bound and to create legal relations, it may be permissible to imply a term to give the contract such business efficacy as the parties must have intended. For example, an agreement may be enforceable despite calling for some further agreement between the parties, say as to price, for it may be appropriate to imply a term that, in default of agreement, a reasonable price must be paid."

8.74   An alleged contract to obtain "third party finance" to pay off a bankrupt's debts as a preliminary to obtaining an annulment of the bankruptcy was too uncertain to have legal effect.[140] Likewise an alleged obligation on the part of a seller to cooperate with the buyer to enable appropriate financing arrangements to be put in place is too vague to be enforceable as a legal obligation.[141]

11.   APPROACH TO UNCERTAINTY

The task of the court is to interpret the document according to the ordinary principles of interpretation and then to determine whether the document as so construed is void for uncertainty.[142]

---

[138] [2007] EWCA Civ 644.
[139] [2019] UKSC 4; [2019] 2 W.L.R. 617.
[140] *Schweppe v Harper* [2008] B.P.I.R. 1090.
[141] *Wittmann (UK) Ltd v Willdav Engineering SA* [2007] EWCA Civ 824.
[142] The corresponding statement in a previous edition of this work was approved in *UYCF Ltd (formerly Night Trunkers (London) Ltd) v Forrester* [2000] 12 WLUK 211; [2001] 3 E.G. 131 (CS). In *Organic Group Ltd v Charterhouse Macmillan Group Inc* [2007] EWHC 1275 (QB), Mackay J said that this proposition was "incontrovertible".

In *Whishaw v Stephens (sub nom Re Gulbenkian's Settlement Trusts)*,[143] Lord **8.75**
Upjohn said:

"There is no doubt that the first task is to try to ascertain the settlor's intention,
so to speak, without regard to the consequences, and then, having construed the
document, apply the test. The court, whose task it is to discover that intention,
starts by applying the usual canons of construction; words must be given their
usual meaning, the clause should be read literally and in accordance with the
ordinary rules of grammar. But very frequently, whether it be in wills, settlements or commercial agreements, the application of such fundamental canons
leads nowhere; the draftsman has used words wrongly, his sentences border on
the illiterate and his grammar may be appalling. It is then the duty of the court
by the exercise of its judicial knowledge and experience in the relevant matter,
innate common sense and desire to make sense of the settlor's or parties'
expressed intentions, however obscure and ambiguous the language that may
have been used, to give a reasonable meaning to the language if it can do so
without doing complete violence to it. The fact that the court has to see whether
the clause is 'certain' for a particular purpose does not disentitle the court from
doing otherwise than, in the first place, try to make sense of it."

Although Lord Upjohn was speaking in the context of the requirement of
certainty of objects for the purposes of a power of appointment, his observations
were clearly intended to be of general application.

12.   MAKING CERTAIN

That which can be made certain is itself certain.

It is a long-standing principle that what can be made certain is itself certain. It **8.76**
is enshrined in the Latin maxim *id certum est quod certum reddi potest*.
In *Welsh Development Agency v Export Finance Co Ltd*,[144] Staughton LJ
described it as:

"the rule that something is certain in law if it can be rendered certain without
future agreement of the parties."

So where an agreement provides for terms to be settled by a third party, the agree- **8.77**
ment is sufficiently certain to be enforceable.[145] As Sir John Donaldson said in
*Deutsche Schachtbau- und Tiefbohrgesellschaft mbH v Ras Al Khaimah National
Oil Co*[146]:

"In this context another maxim is relevant, *id certum est quod certum reddi*

---

[143] [1970] A.C. 508.
[144] [1992] B.C.L.C. 148.
[145] *Foster v Wheeler* (1888) 38 Ch. D. 130.
[146] [1987] 2 All E.R. 769.

potest, and there is a vital distinction between an agreement to agree in future and an agreement to accept terms to be determined by a third party. The former cannot and the latter can form the basis for a legally enforceable agreement."

8.78 The principle is most commonly applied in cases relating to the formation of contract; but that is not its only application.

So in *Scammell v Dicker*,[147] where the parties had compromised a boundary dispute by means of a consent order and a plan, the agreement was sufficiently certain despite difficulties in interpretation. Rix LJ said:

"Any of these three solutions would do justice to the parties' agreement, as working out a detail of it. The applicable legal motto is: that is certain which can be rendered certain (*id certum est quod certum reddi potest*). What would to my mind be a complete injustice would be, just because of the difficulty about the precise position of the boundary line in immediate juxtaposition with the telegraph pole, to conclude that the parties had completely failed on the grounds of uncertainty to settle their litigation at all, although that is what they plainly intended to do and what they did in fact do with the aid of a detailed consent order and plan."

8.79 The principle may also be used to identify a party to a contract. In *Reeves v Watts*,[148] Blackburn J said:

"My own opinion certainly was strongly in favour of the proposition that a person may be made a party to a deed inter partes by description as belonging to the defined class; on the principle *that id certum est quod certum reddi potest*."

8.80 The principle has been held to apply to a notice of rejection of goods under a contract for sale or return of computer games[149]; to the question whether an amount that could be worked out arithmetically by the application of a formula was "a stated amount"[150]; to the question whether a proviso to an insurance policy was void for uncertainty[151]; to the question whether a notice to quit was clear and unambiguous.[152] Similarly, where a ship is required to load or unload at a certain rate per day then if the volume of cargo is known that is equivalent to naming a certain number of days.[153] Similarly, "a fluctuating rent is not, as such, necessarily uncertain—certainly not if it is mathematically calculable, so as to attract the operation of the maxim '*certum est quod certum reddi potest*'".[154]

In *P Phipps and Co (Northampton and Towcester Breweries) Ltd v Rogers*,[155] Bankes LJ said:

"It is not necessary that a notice should be clear and unambiguous in its expressed terms provided it can be rendered clear and unambiguous by the application of

---

[147] [2005] 3 All E.R. 838.
[148] (1866) L.R. 1 Q.B. 413.
[149] *Atari Corp (UK) Ltd v Electronics Boutique Stores (UK) Ltd* [1998] Q.B. 539.
[150] *In re Earl Berkeley Decd* [1945] Ch. 107 (statutory construction).
[151] *O'Reilly v Prudential Assurance Co Ltd* [1934] Ch. 519.
[152] *P Phipps and Co (Northampton and Towcester Breweries) Ltd v Rogers* [1925] 1 K.B. 14.
[153] *Postlethwaite v Freeland* (1880) 5 App. Cas. 599.
[154] *Att-Gen of the Province of Alberta v Huggard Assets Ltd* [1953] 2 All E.R. 951 PC, per Lord Asquith of Bishopstone.
[155] [1925] 1 K.B. 14.

the maxim '*Id certum est quod certum reddi potest.*' There are many decided cases in the books where the Courts have imputed to the tenant knowledge which, when applied to the notice to quit served upon him, renders clear what would without that knowledge have been neither clear nor unambiguous."

The principle has particular application in long-term contracts where the parties leave matters to be worked out as the contract progresses. In *Mamidoil-Jetoil Greek Petroleum Co v Okta Crude Oil Refinery*,[156] Rix LJ said:

8.81

"Particularly in the case of contracts for future performance over a period, where the parties may desire or need to leave matters to be adjusted in the working out of their contract, the courts will assist the parties to do so, so as to preserve rather than destroy bargains, on the basis that what can be made certain is itself certain. *Certum est quod certum reddi potest.*"

It is also upon this principle that extrinsic evidence is admissible to prove the subject matter of a contract for the sale of land.[157]

8.82

Illustrations

1.   A prospective tenant entered into an agreement to take a lease on such terms as the landlord should require. It was held that there was a binding agreement. The agreement furnished a standard from which the terms could be ascertained, and the maxim *id certum est quod certum reddi potest* applied.
   Foster v Wheeler[158]

2.   An order was made securing an annual sum for the maintenance of the wife "upon part of the real property [of the husband] to be agreed or to be referred to the district registrar in default of agreement". The husband died before the security had been identified, and the wife sought to enforce the order against his estate. Sachs J held that as the order laid down what was to be done and how it was to be done, the maxim *certum est quod certum reddi potest* applied, thus creating an enforceable claim against the respondent's estate pursuant to s.1(1) of the Law Reform (Miscellaneous Provisions) Act 1934.
   Mosey v Mosey and Barker[159]

13.   UNWILLINGNESS TO HOLD VOID FOR UNCERTAINTY

Where parties have entered into what they believe to be a binding agreement the court is most reluctant to hold that their agreement is void for uncertainty, and will only do so as a last resort.[160]

In *Greater London Council v Connolly*,[161] a tenant's rent card provided that the rent and other sums payable were liable to be "increased or decreased on notice be-

8.83

---

[156] [2001] 2 Lloyd's Rep. 76. A fuller extract from this judgment is quoted in para.8.128.
[157] *Shardlow v Cotterell* (1881) 20 Ch. D. 90; *Plant v Bourne* [1897] 2 Ch. 281; *Harewood v Retese* (1989) 37 W.I.R. 427 PC; *Westvilla Properties Ltd v Dow Properties Ltd* [2010] 2 P. & C.R. 19.
[158] (1888) 38 Ch. D. 130.
[159] [1956] P. 26.
[160] This proposition was referred to with apparent approval in *Willis Management (Isle of Man) Ltd v*

ing given". It was argued that the provision was void for uncertainty. The argument failed. Lord Denning MR said:

"The courts are always loath to hold a condition bad for uncertainty. They will give it a reasonable meaning wherever possible."

Lord Pearson said:

"… the courts are always loath to hold a clause bad for uncertainty if a reasonable meaning can be given to it, and it seems to me easy to give a reasonable meaning to this clause."

8.84   In *Re Lloyd's Trust Instruments*,[162] Megarry J said:

"I think the starting point on any question of uncertainty must be that of the court's reluctance to hold an instrument void for uncertainty. Lord Hardwicke L.C. once said: 'A court never construes a devise void, unless it is so absolutely dark that they cannot find out the testator's meaning': *Minshull v Minshull*.[163] Lord Brougham said: 'The difficulty must be so great that it amounts to an impossibility, the doubt so grave that there is not even an inclination of the scales one way': *Doe d. Winter v Perratt*.[164] In a well-known statement, Sir George Jessel M.R. said that the court would not hold a will void for uncertainty 'unless it is impossible to put a fair meaning on it. The duty of the court is to put a fair meaning on the terms used, and not, as was said in one case, to repose upon the easy pillow of uncertainty': *In re Roberts*.[165] That this is not a doctrine confined to wills but is one which applies to other instruments, such as planning permissions is shown by cases such as *Fawcett Properties Ltd v Buckingham County Council*,[166] where by a majority, the delphic language of a condition in a planning permission escaped from being held void for uncertainty largely because of its resemblance to a section in a modern Act of Parliament."

In *Whitecap Leisure Ltd v John H Rundle Ltd*,[167] Moore-Bick LJ said:

"The conclusion that a contractual provision is so uncertain that it is incapable of being given a meaning of any kind is one which the courts have always been reluctant to accept, since they recognise that the very fact that it was included demonstrates that the parties intended it to have some effect."

In *Openwork Ltd v Forte*[168] Simon LJ said that:

Cable and Wireless Plc [2005] 2 Lloyd's Rep. 597. In *Organic Group Ltd v Charterhouse Macmillan Group Inc* [2007] EWHC 1275 (QB) Mackay J said that this proposition was "incontrovertible". It was also referred to with approval in *Acertec Construction Products Ltd v Thamesteel Ltd* [2008] EWHC 2966 (Comm) and *Westvilla Properties Ltd v Dow Properties Ltd* [2010] 2 P. & C.R. 19. See also *Maple Leaf Macro Volatility Master Fund v Rouvroy* [2009] 1 Lloyd's Rep. 475, 513.

[161] [1970] 2 Q.B. 100.
[162] *Unreported 24 June 1970* (referred to in *Brown v Gould* [1972] Ch. 53 at 56).
[163] (1737) 1 Atk. 411 at 412.
[164] (1843) 9 Cl. & F. 606 at 689.
[165] (1881) 19 Ch. D. 520 at 529.
[166] [1961] A.C. 636.
[167] [2008] 2 Lloyd's Rep. 216.
[168] [2018] EWCA Civ 783. See also *Council of the City of York v Trinity One (Leeds) Ltd* [2018] EWCA

"The Court should strive to give some meaning to contractual clauses agreed by the parties if it is at all possible to do so."

In *Nea Agrex SA v Baltic Shipping Co Ltd*,[169] Lord Denning MR described an argument that a clause was void for uncertainty as "a counsel of despair". **8.85**

In *Dresdner Kleinwort Ltd v Attrill*,[170] the Court of Appeal held that the announcement by a bank of a bonus pool for employees was not void for uncertainty. Elias LJ said: **8.86**

"The submission on uncertainty was based on the assertion that the announcement of the bonus pool left many problems not determined. For example, it is submitted that there is uncertainty as to whether the individual guaranteed fixed bonuses should come out of the fund; whether the bonus should be paid by way of shares or cash; and what proportion of the fund could be held back for contingencies, it being accepted that an element of the fund could be dealt with in that way. In my judgment, these problems are largely dealt with by the finding of the judge that the fund would be dealt with 'in the usual way'. For example, that confirmed that individual fixed bonuses would be paid from the fund as well as the discretionary bonuses. It would admittedly leave some imprecision, for example, on the question of how much could be withheld for contingencies. But I have no doubt that the parties would recognise that it would be a reasonable figure of the kind typically withheld for this purpose in the past. The fundamental principles of the scheme were entirely clear and the fact that there were some loose ends does not in my view begin to constitute a degree of uncertainty necessary to defeat the parties' intention that the agreement should be capable of enforcement. The court will be slow to hold that otherwise contractually enforceable obligations cannot be enforced because they are too uncertain."

The court's reluctance to hold a provision void for uncertainty applies equally to cases where it is alleged that the provision discloses no clear concept; to cases where it is alleged that a provision is meaningless, and to cases where it is alleged that the agreement is no more than an agreement to agree. In *Wells v Devani*,[171] Lord Kitchin said that: **8.87**

"... there will be cases where an agreement is so vague and uncertain that it cannot be enforced. So too, there will be cases where the parties have not addressed certain matters which are so fundamental that their agreement is incomplete. Further, an agreement may be so deficient in one or other of these respects that nothing can be done to render it enforceable. But I do not accept that there is any general rule that it is not possible to imply a term into an agreement to render it sufficiently certain or complete to constitute a binding contract. Indeed, it seems to me that it is possible to imply something that is so obvious that it goes without saying into anything, including something the law regards as no more than an offer. If the offer is accepted, the contract is made on the terms of the words used and what those words imply. Moreover, where it is apparent the parties intended to be bound and to create legal relations, it may be permis-

---

Civ 1883.

[169] [1976] 1 Q.B. 933 CA.
[170] [2013] EWCA Civ 394.
[171] [2019] UKSC 4; [2019] 2 W.L.R. 617.

sible to imply a term to give the contract such business efficacy as the parties must have intended. For example, an agreement may be enforceable despite calling for some further agreement between the parties, say as to price, for it may be appropriate to imply a term that, in default of agreement, a reasonable price must be paid."

8.88 Similarly, in *The Tropwind*,[172] Lord Denning MR said:

"We have on a few occasions rejected a sentence as meaningless, as in *Nicolene v Simmonds*.[173] But this is only when it is impossible to make sense of it. Rather than find it meaningless, we should strive to find out what was really intended—by amending the punctuation, or by supplying words and so forth."

And in *Brown v Gould*,[174] Megarry J said:

"No doubt there may be cases in which the draftsman's ineptitude will succeed in defeating the court's efforts to find a meaning for the provision in question; but only if the court is driven to it will it be held that a provision is void for uncertainty."

Finally, in *Cudgen Ruttle (No.2) Pty Ltd v Chalk*,[175] Lord Wilberforce said:

"In modern times the courts are readier to find an obligation which can be enforced even though some apparent certainty may be lacking as regards some term such as the price, provided that some means or standard by which that term can be fixed can be found."

8.89 In *Wells v Devani*,[176] the Supreme Court upheld the validity of a contract to pay commission to an estate agent, even though the parties had not expressly agreed the triggering event on which the commission would become due. Likewise, in *Vinci Construction UK Ltd v Beumer Group UK Ltd*,[177] O'Farrell J stressed the court's unwillingness to find a contractual provision void for uncertainty; and on the facts she held that the disputed term was sufficiently certain to be enforceable.

8.90 Words which themselves recognise imprecision, such as "approximate" or "approximately", will not vitiate the effectiveness of a contractual stipulation.[178] But if the contract does not enable the court to find an objective standard by which to fix a term, then even if the parties did intend to enter into legal relations, they may nevertheless have failed to do so. As Morritt LJ put it in *Rembrandt Group Ltd v Philip Morris International Inc*[179]:

"... the existence of such an intention does not do away with the need for the

---

[172] [1982] 1 Lloyd's Rep. 232. See also *King v King* (1980) 41 P. & C.R. 311 at 312, per Nourse J (although the actual decision in that case is no longer good law: see *Beer v Bowden* [1981] 1 W.L.R. 522; *Bates (Thomas) & Son Ltd v Wyndham's (Lingerie) Ltd* [1981] 1 W.L.R. 505).

[173] [1953] 1 Q.B. 543.

[174] [1972] Ch. 53.

[175] [1975] A.C. 520.

[176] [2019] UKSC 4; [2019] 2 W.L.R. 617. One difficulty with the reasoning of the Supreme Court is that it interpreted words that were never spoken: see Paul S. Davies, "Interpretation and Implication in the Supreme Court" [2019] C.L.J. 267.

[177] [2017] EWHC 2196 (TCC); 174 Con. L.R. 178.

[178] See, e.g. *Edwards v Skyways Ltd* [1964] 1 W.L.R. 349; *Three Rivers Trading Co Ltd v Gwinear and District Farmers Ltd* (1967) 111 S.J. 831; *Ashburn Anstalt v Arnold* [1989] Ch.1.

[179] [1999] All E.R. (D) 196.

agreement to be sufficiently certain to be enforceable. The intention to create legal relations and be bound by the agreement is not an alternative to the requirement of sufficient certainty."

In *Dwr Cymru Cyfyngedig (Welsh Water) v Corus UK Ltd*,[180] Moore-Bick LJ said:

"Where many important terms have been left undecided and the contractual machinery for resolving disagreements is incapable of being operated, it may be impossible to avoid the conclusion that the agreement as a whole is unenforceable because the parties have failed to establish objective criteria capable of being applied by the court itself."

It has been said that where the document to be construed is not a bilateral **8.91** contract, but a unilateral document (e.g. a notice), a more stringent test applies. In such a case it is not merely a question of what the document means but whether it expresses its meaning clearly.[181] It seems doubtful, however, whether there is still any special rule for construing notices, although the overall effect of a notice once construed must leave the reasonable recipient in no doubt about what right is being exercised.[182]

By contrast, where it is alleged that a document has given rise to an estoppel, the **8.92** words must be clear and unequivocal. In *Woodhouse AC Israel Cocoa Ltd SA v Nigerian Produce Marketing Co Ltd*,[183] Lord Denning MR said:

"The judge must give the written representation the same meaning, no matter whether it is put forward as a variation or as an estoppel. But that is subject to this difference: If the representation is put forward as a variation, and is fairly capable of one or other of two meanings, the judge will decide between those two meanings and say which is right. But, if it is put forward as an estoppel, the judge will not decide between the two meanings. He will reject it as an estoppel because it is not precise and unambiguous. There is good sense in this difference. When a contract is varied by correspondence, it is an agreed variation. It is the duty of the court to give effect to the agreement if it possibly can: and it does so by resolving ambiguities, no matter how difficult it may be. But, when a man is estopped, he has not agreed to anything. Quite the reverse. He is stopped from telling the truth. He should not be stopped on an ambiguity. To work an estoppel, the representation must be clear and unequivocal."

Illustration

1.   An agreement provided that one party should grant to the other a lease of a shop:

"in a prime position at the development with an area available for trading of approximately 100 square feet and with car parking facilities within the development for a term of 21 years and the rent in respect of such lease shall for the first seven years be 25 per cent less than the market rent."

---

[180] [2007] EWCA Civ 285.
[181] *Nunes v Davies Laing & Dick Ltd* (1986) 51 P. & C.R. 310.
[182] See *Mannai Investment Co Ltd v Eagle Star Life Assurance Co Ltd* [1997] A.C. 749 at 767–768, per Lord Steyn.
[183] [1971] 2 Q.B. 23 at 61 CA.

It was held that "prime position" was a term used in the property world and the court could determine on expert evidence whether the offered shop was in such a position. The car parking facilities were to be reasonable facilities, and the use of the word "approximately" did not entitle the court to declare the agreement as void for uncertainty.

Ashburn Anstalt v Arnold[184]

2.   A building contract contained a dispute resolution clause that stated:

"The adjudication procedure will be the TeCSA adjudication rules (amended to require nomination by the RICS and joining of the members of the professional team in a multi-party dispute situation)."

The TeCSA rules allowed for the determination of only one dispute at a time. It was held that the clause should be interpreted as limited to cases in which the disputant required a member of the professional team to be bound by the result of a dispute, rather than allowing more than one dispute to be determined together. On that basis modest amendments to the rules (as contemplated by the contract) would produce a workable result. The clause was not void for uncertainty.

Yuanda (UK) Ltd v WW Gear Construction Ltd[185]

14.   EXECUTORY AND EXECUTED CONTRACTS

The court's reluctance to hold a provision in a contract void for uncertainty is greater in a case where the agreement is no longer executory but has been partly performed.[186]

8.93   In *Gregory v Mighell*,[187] a tenant had been in possession of land for 11 years under an agreement for lease for 21 years at "a fair and just annual rent" to be fixed and ascertained by two valuers to be chosen respectively by the landlord and the tenant or their umpire. The landlord refused to sign arbitration bonds, without which the arbitrators refused to continue. The court ordered the rent to be fixed by the master. Grant MR said:

"After it was known, that the arbitrators had not fixed any rent and that none of the other means, provided by the agreement, were resorted to, the Defendant still acquiesced in the Plaintiff's retaining possession of these lands. That is a case in which the failure of the arbitrators to fix the rent can never affect the agreement. It is in part performed; and the court must find some means of completing its execution."

8.94   In *British Bank for Foreign Trade Ltd v Novinex Ltd*,[188] the Court of Appeal approved the following statement of the trial judge (Denning J):

---

[184] [1989] Ch.1.

[185] [2011] Bus. L.R. 360.

[186] This section was referred to with approval in *Acertec Construction Products Ltd v Thamesteel Ltd* [2008] EWHC 2966 (Comm).

[187] (1811) 18 Yes. 328.

[188] [1949] 1 K.B. 623. This passage was also approved in *Rembrandt Group Ltd v Philip Morris International Inc* [1999] All E.R. (D) 196. See also *RTS Flexible Systems Ltd v Molkerei Alois Müller GmbH & Co KG* [2010] 1 W.L.R. 753.

"The principle to be deduced from the cases is that if there is an essential term which has yet to be agreed and there is no express or implied provision for its solution, the result in point of law is that there is no binding contract. In seeing whether there is an implied provision for its solution, however, there is a difference between an arrangement which is wholly executory on both sides and one which has been executed on one side or the other. In the ordinary way, if there is an agreement to supply goods at a price 'to be agreed' or to perform services on terms 'to be agreed,' then, although while the matter is still executory, there may be no binding contract, nevertheless, if it is executed on one side, that is, if one does his part without having come to an agreement about the price or the terms, then the law will say that there is necessarily implied from the conduct of the parties, a contract that in default of agreement a reasonable sum is to be paid."

Similarly in *Beer v Bowden*,[189] a tenant took a lease at a rent fixed for the first five years of the term and thereafter at such rent as should be agreed between the landlord and the tenant, not being less than the fixed rent, Geoffrey Lane LJ said: **8.95**

"Had this been a contract of sale or an ordinary commercial contract of some sort, there would be a great deal to be said for the view that from the date of the first rent review in March 1973 the contract was void for uncertainty, the parties having failed to agree on a vital term of the contract. But here there is a subsisting estate, and a subsisting estate in land, the lease, which is to continue until 1982, 14 years from the date of the lease itself. It is conceded by the tenant that some rent must be paid in respect of these premises by the tenant, and therefore it follows that the court must imply something, some term which will enable a rent to be fixed."

The distinction between executed and executory contracts was again drawn by Templeman LJ in *Sudbrook Trading Estate Ltd v Eggleton*,[190] a passage approved on appeal[191]:   **8.96**

"Where an agreement which would otherwise be unenforceable for want of certainty or finality in an essential stipulation has been partly performed so that the intervention of the court is necessary in aid of a grant that has already taken effect, the court will strain to the utmost to supply the want of certainty even to the extent of providing a substitute machinery."

In *Mamidoil-Jetoil Greek Petroleum Co v Okta Crude Oil Refinery*,[192] Rix LJ said:

"Where a contract has once come into existence, even the expression 'to be agreed' in relation to future executory obligations is not necessarily fatal to its continued existence.

Particularly in the case of contracts for future performance over a period, where the parties may desire or need to leave matters to be adjusted in the working out of their contract, the Courts will assist the parties to do so, so as to preserve rather than destroy bargains, on the basis that what can be made certain is itself certain. *Certum est quod certum reddi potest.*

---

[189] [1981] 1 W.L.R. 522.
[190] [1983] 1 A.C. 444.
[191] By Lord Fraser of Tullybelton at 484.
[192] [2001] 2 Lloyd's Rep. 76. A fuller extract from this judgment is quoted in para.8.128.

This is particularly the case where one party has either already had the advantage of some performance which reflects the parties' agreement on a long term relationship, or has had to make an investment premised on that agreement.[193]

For these purposes, an express stipulation for a reasonable or fair measure or price will be a sufficient criterion for the courts to act on. But even in the absence of express language, the Courts are prepared to imply an obligation in terms of what is reasonable.

The presence of an arbitration clause may assist the Courts to hold a contract to be sufficiently certain or to be capable of being rendered so, presumably as indicating a commercial and contractual mechanism, which can be operated with the assistance of experts in the field, by which the parties, in the absence of agreement, may resolve their dispute."

In *Associated British Ports v Tata Steel UK Ltd*,[194] Rose J stressed the court's unwillingness to hold void for uncertainty a contract that had been partly performed. Similarly, in *NHS Commissioning Board v Vasant*,[195] Lewison LJ said:

"Ms Demetriou QC, on behalf of the dentists, forcefully submits that the court should be reluctant to hold that an agreement is too uncertain to be enforced. The court's reluctance should be all the greater where what the parties believe to have been a valid contract has been partly performed. That is undoubtedly the case where the question is whether the parties are legally bound at all. The court's extreme reluctance to find that the parties have failed to make any contract because of their omission to specify particular terms in detail is well illustrated by the recent decision of the Supreme Court in *Wells v Devani* ...".

8.97   In the cases which have expressed this principle, the type of uncertainty under consideration has been of the type which has left further terms to be agreed, or where the machinery for which the contract expressly provided has broken down. The solution has been to imply terms or to provide substitute machinery for that which has broken down. However, where the uncertainty is a complete failure on the part of the parties to express an intelligible concept, the court may well be defeated, even in the case of a partly performed bargain.

Illustrations

1.   A lease contained an option to renew for a term of seven years at such a rental as might be agreed upon between the parties. There was no indication of how the rent was to be agreed, nor on what basis, nor what was to happen if the parties should fail to agree. It was held that the option was void for uncertainty.
King's Motors (Oxford) Ltd v Lax[196]

2.   An executory agreement for a lease specified the length of the term to be granted, but did not specify the date from which the term was to begin. The Court of Appeal held that the agreement was void. Davies LJ said:

---

[193] *Maple Leaf Macro Volatility Master Fund v Rouvroy* [2009] 1 Lloyd's Rep. 475, 513.
[194] [2017] EWHC 694 (Ch); [2017] 2 Lloyd's Rep. 11.
[195] [2019] EWCA Civ 1245; *Avonwick Holdings Ltd v Azitio Holdings Ltd*[2020] EWHC 1844 (Comm).
[196] [1970] 1 W.L.R. 426 (doubted in *Corson v Rhuddlan Borough Council* [1990] 1 E.G.L.R. 255 CA).

"In the case of an agreement for lease, unless the length of the term and the commencement of the term are defined, then the subject of the agreement or contract is uncertain."

Harvey v Pratt[197]

3. A dwelling-house was let in war-time upon a weekly tenancy "furnished for duration". It was argued that the tenancy was a tenancy for the duration of the war. The Court of Appeal held that such a letting was void for uncertainty, because it could not be said at the beginning of the tenancy what its duration would be.
Lace v Chantler[198]

4. A contract for the sale of maize provided that the discharging port was to be agreed between sellers and buyers on the ship passing the Straits of Gibraltar. It was held that that provision was void for uncertainty.
Mallozzi v Carapelli SpA[199]

5. An agreement for the supply of coal provided for the ascertainment of the price for the first five years. Thereafter the price was to be agreed in accordance with general criteria set out in the agreement. The agreement also contained an arbitration clause. It was held that the parties had undertaken primary obligations to use reasonable endeavours to agree on the terms of supply beyond the five-year period, and failing agreement, to do everything reasonably necessary to procure the appointment of an arbitrator. The agreement was not void for uncertainty.
The Queensland Electricity Generating Board v New Hope Collieries Ltd[200]

6. A franchise agreement contained a clause providing for renewal of the agreement with "uplifted minimum performance requirements", but did not specify what they were and did not provide for machinery to determine them. It was held that there was no binding agreement for renewal and that the original franchise agreement expired according to its terms.
Grow with US Ltd v Green Thumb (UK) Ltd[201]

15. THE TEST OF UNCERTAINTY

A provision in a contract will only be void for uncertainty if the court cannot reach a conclusion as to what was in the parties' minds or where it is not safe for the court to prefer one possible meaning to other equally possible meanings.[202]

In *Fawcett Properties Ltd v Buckingham County Council*,[203] Lord Keith of Avonholm said:

8.98

---

[197] [1965] 1 W.L.R. 1025; distinguished in *Liverpool City Council v Walton Group Ltd* [2002] 1 E.G.L.R. 149.
[198] [1944] K.B. 368.
[199] [1976] 1 Lloyd's Rep. 407; distinguished in *Voest Alpine Intertrading GmbH v Chevron International Oil Co Ltd* [1987] 2 Lloyd's Rep. 547.
[200] [1989] 1 Lloyd's Rep. 205 PC. The decision that the parties had undertaken primary obligations to use reasonable endeavours to agree the terms of supply is difficult to reconcile with the decision of the House of Lords in *Walford v Miles* [1992] 2 A.C. 128 and of the Court of Appeal in *Little v Cour-*

"As stated the point is one of uncertainty of concept. If it is impossible on construction of the condition, to reach a conclusion as to what was in the draftsman's mind, the condition is meaningless and must be read as *pro non scripto*. It is not a question of ambiguity. If a clause may convey several different meanings it is for the court to say, looking to the general background, surrounding circumstances, subject-matter of discourse and other aids derived from the context of the clause, supplemented not infrequently by certain legal presumptions, what meaning is to be attributed to the clause ... But the question here is different. It is whether one or more intelligible concepts can be extracted from the condition here under challenge."

In *Vinci Construction UK Ltd v Beumer Group UK Ltd*,[204] O'Farrell J held that:

"... a provision in a contract will be void for uncertainty if the court cannot reach a conclusion as to what was in the parties'' minds or where it is not safe for the court to prefer one possible meaning to other equally possible meanings."

8.99 A clear distinction must be drawn between linguistic or semantic uncertainty, which if unresolved by the court renders a provision void for uncertainty, and the difficulty of application of the provision once it has been construed, and its meaning determined.[205] So in *Anangel Atlas Compania Naviera SA v Ishikawajima-Harima Heavy Industries Co Ltd*,[206] Hirst J said:

"An important and well-recognised distinction must be drawn between conceptual uncertainty on the one hand, which invalidates the instrument, and evidential uncertainty, which merely means that a party may on a given set of facts be unable to establish that he comes within a particular aspect of the provision in question."

8.100 However, in seeking the intention of the parties, the court must approach the provision under challenge with reasonable goodwill:

"The question is not ... whether the clause is proof against wilful misinterpretation, but whether someone genuinely seeking to discover its meaning is able to do so."[207]

8.101 In *Jet2.com Ltd v Blackpool Airport Ltd*,[208] the operator of an airport entered into an agreement with an airline. The agreement required the parties to "co-operate together and use their best endeavours to promote Jet2.com's low cost services

---

age Ltd (1994) 70 P. & C.R. 469.
[201] [2006] EWCA Civ 1201.
[202] In *Organic Group Ltd v Charterhouse Macmillan Group Inc* [2007] EWHC 1275 (QB), Mackay J said that this proposition was "incontrovertible". This section was approved in *Openwork Ltd v Forte* [2018] EWCA Civ 783. See also *Council of the City of York v Trinity One (Leeds) Ltd* [2018] EWCA Civ 1883.
[203] [1961] A.C. 636.
[204] [2017] EWHC 2196 (TCC); 174 Con. L.R. 178.
[205] *Whishaw v Stephens (sub nom Re Gulbenkian's Settlement Trusts)* [1970] A.C. 508, per Lord Upjohn; *McPhail v Doulton (sub nom Re Baden's Deed Trusts)* [1971] A.C. 424, per Lord Wilberforce.
[206] [1990] 2 Lloyd's Rep. 526 at 545.
[207] *Brown v Gould* [1972] Ch. 53.
[208] [2012] EWCA Civ 417.

from" the airport. The Court of Appeal held by a majority[209] that the obligation was sufficiently certain to be enforced. Moore-Bick LJ said:

"I think there is an important difference between a clause whose content is so uncertain that it is incapable of creating a binding obligation and a clause which gives rise to a binding obligation, the precise limits of which are difficult to define in advance, but which can nonetheless be given practical content. A famous example of the former is to be found in *Scammell and Nephew Ltd v Ouston*, in which the court held that a contract to purchase a van on terms that part of the price should be paid 'on hire-purchase terms over a period of two years' was too uncertain to be enforceable. An example of the latter is an obligation to promote the sale of the Claimant's product, as in *Terrell v Mabie Todd and Co Ltd*. The content of an obligation to use best endeavours to promote another person's business is not so uncertain as to be incapable of giving rise to a legally binding obligation, although it may be difficult to determine in any given case whether there has been a breach of it. In my view the obligation to use best endeavours to promote Jet2's business is no more uncertain than the obligation to use best endeavours to develop a railway's traffic (*Sheffield District Railway Co v Great Central Railway Co*), or to promote the sales of fountain pens and ink bottles (*Terrell v Mabie Todd and Co Ltd*). There may be argument about what constitutes best endeavours in any particular circumstances (see, for example, *Terrell v Mabie Todd and Co Ltd*), but that is a different matter."

Longmore LJ said:

"The combination of these cases and the twentieth century cases referred to in my Lords' judgments, to my mind, justify the conclusion that an obligation to use best endeavours should usually be held to be an enforceable obligation unless:

i)   the object intended to be procured by the endeavours is too vague or elusive to be itself a matter of legal obligation; or

ii)   the parties have, in the words of Potter LJ in *Phillips Petroleum v Enron Europe Ltd*,[210] provided no criteria on the basis of which it is possible to assess whether best endeavours have been, or can be used."

In his dissenting judgment Lewison LJ said:

"In my judgment the object of the endeavours and the range of possible endeavours must be considered together in order to decide whether there is a justiciable obligation. Moreover it is wrong in principle to focus on the particular factual situation which has given rise to the dispute without considering to what other factual situations the clause might extend if one side or the other is correct."

In *Associated British Ports v Tata Steel UK Ltd*,[211] a licence agreement contained **8.102** a clause which entitled either party to go to arbitration in the event of any major physical or financial change in circumstances affecting the operation of a steelworks or the port serving it. It was argued that the trigger event was too uncertain to be

---

[209] The author dissented. Not surprisingly he considers that the majority decision was wrong.
[210] [1997] C.L.C. 329 at 343.
[211] [2017] EWHC 694 (Ch); [2017] 2 Lloyd's Rep. 11. See also *Kitcatt v MMS UK Holdings Ltd* [2017] EWHC 675 (Comm); [2017] 2 B.C.L.C. 352 ("material adverse impact").

legally binding. Rose J rejected that argument. She followed the approach of Moore-Bick LJ in *Jet2.com Ltd v Blackpool Airport Ltd* and held that:

> "... provided one can posit some changes which would definitely fall within the scope of the phrase 'major physical or financial change in circumstances' and some changes which clearly fall outside it, then the phrase is sufficiently certain to be enforceable even though it may be difficult in the abstract to draw the precise divide between changes falling on either side of the line."

8.103   The potential diversity of meaning, and the consequent danger of holding the parties to any one such meaning, was the principal ground upon which Lord Wright based his speech in *Scammell and Nephew v Ouston*.[212] He said:

> "The object of the court is to do justice between the parties, and the court will do its best, if satisfied that there is an ascertainable and determinate intention to contract, to give effect to that intention, looking at substance and not mere form. It will not be deterred by mere difficulties of interpretation. Difficulty is not synonymous with ambiguity as long as any definite meaning can be extracted. But the test of intention is to be found in the words used. If these words, considered however broadly and untechnically and with due regard to all just implications, fail to evince any definite meaning on which the court can safely act, the court has no choice but to say that there is no contract. Such a position is not often found. But I think that it is found in this case. My reason for so thinking is not only based on the actual vagueness and unintelligibility of the words used, but is confirmed by the startling diversity of explanations, tendered by those who think there was a bargain, of what the bargain was."

He concluded:

> "It is a necessary requirement that an agreement in order to be binding must be sufficiently definite to enable the court to give it a practical meaning. Its terms must be so definite, or capable of being made definite without further agreement of the parties, that the promises and performances to be rendered by each party are reasonably certain."

Illustrations

1.   A lease of a coal mine contained a declaration that nothing was to prevent the landlord from working coal and other minerals not demised provided that in exercising that right the working of the demised coal should not be prevented or unnecessarily interfered with. The Court of Appeal held that the proviso was unintelligible.
Mundy v Duke of Rutland[213]

2.   Suppliers of woollen cardigans purported to accept an order for a number of cardigans subject to "war clause". The Court of Appeal held that there was no contract. Scott LJ said:

---

[212] [1941] A.C. 251.
[213] (1883) 23 Ch. D. 81.

"War clauses take many forms, and the protection afforded to a seller by one may differ from that given by another. Until the parties had met and agreed on a particular form and content of a war clause, there was and could be no consensus *ad idem.*"

Bishop & Baxter Ltd v Anglo Eastern Trading and Industrial Co Ltd[214]

3.   A contract for the sale of a foundry provided for "a large portion" of the purchase money to be left in the business. It was held that since the contract did not specify how much was to be left in the business, nor when it was to be paid, nor how it was to be secured, the whole contract was void for uncertainty.
Cooper v Hood[215]

4.   An agreement upon dissolution of a partnership contained a covenant by the outgoing partner "to retire wholly and absolutely from the partnership and so far as the law allows from the trade or business thereof in all its branches". It was held that since the law might allow a variety of restrictions, many of which might be mutually inconsistent, the second limb of the clause was void for uncertainty.
Davies v Davies[216]

5.   A banking agreement required the customer to pay interest on an overdraft "at the Bank's usual rate of interest". The bank did not publish its rates of interest which depended on a number of factors (including the cost of funds, the personality of the customer, the security offered, and the size of the transaction). Thus the Bank did not have a single rate of interest, with the result that the clause was void for uncertainty.
Financial Institutions Services Ltd v Negril Negril Holdings Ltd[217]

6.   A pension deed said that the benefits were to be as "prescribed by Part 4 FA 2004 and shall be computed in accordance with the limits prescribed by Part 4 FA 2004". In fact, Pt 4 of the Finance Act 2004 provided no means of calculating benefits. The court was thus "at a loss" to understand what the prescribed benefits were intended to be. In consequence the deed was void for uncertainty.
The Pensions Regulator v A Admin Ltd[218]

16.   BLANK SPACES

Where a clause in a contract contains a blank space which was intended to be filled in, the court will ignore the blank space unless it can deduce with reasonable certainty what was intended to have been included in the blank space. Ignoring the blank space may have the effect that the clause in question, or the contract as a whole, is too uncertain to be enforced.

---

[214] [1944] K.B. 12.
[215] (1858) 26 Beav. 293.
[216] (1887) 36 Ch. D. 359.
[217] [2004] UKPC 40.
[218] [2014] EWHC 1378 (Ch).

8.104   In *Caltex Oil (Aust) Pty Ltd v Alderton*,[219] a guarantee left blank the amount that was to be guaranteed. Sugerman P said:

> "A blank left in an instrument generally renders meaningless the portion of the instrument in which it appears. But this may leave the instrument as one which is capable of being carried into effect and enforced, disregarding the meaningless provision, just as may happen where some inessential provision of a contract is so vague and uncertain as to be incapable of any precise meaning."

In *The Goods of De Rosaz*,[220] Sir James Hannen said:

> "A complete blank cannot be filled up by parol testimony, however strong. Thus a legacy to Mr. — cannot have any effect given to it ... nor a legacy to Lady — :... But if there are any words to which a reasonable meaning may be attached, parol evidence may be resorted to shew what that meaning is."

8.105   Thus the two questions are: whether the blank can be filled in by reference to admissible extrinsic evidence; and, if not, what is the effect on the clause or the contract as a whole. It is thought that this applies whatever the extent of the blank.

8.106   In *Liverpool City Council v Walton Group Ltd*,[221] an agreement for lease provided for the grant of a lease:

> "during the term of 999 years from and including the ... day of ... 199 ... (the Term)."

Neuberger J said:

> "The question that therefore falls to be determined is whether, after considering all those matters that can properly be taken into account when construing the agreement and the draft lease, one can, with 'reasonable certainty', be satisfied as to the date upon which the parties intended the lease to start."

After detailed consideration he concluded that the lease was to run from the date of execution of the document.

8.107   In *Westvilla Properties Ltd v Dow Properties Ltd*,[222] the parties entered into a contract for the sale of freehold property subject to a lease back of part. The lease was intended to contain a service charge, but the percentage had been left blank. Vos J held that he could say with reasonable certainty, based on the background facts and the underlying commercial realities, that the blank could be filled in as 36 per cent.

In *Scheldebouw BV v St James Homes (Grosvenor Dock) Ltd*,[223] Jackson J held that a blank space in a contract was "obviously a slip" and that it could be filled in by recourse to other documents.

---

[219] (1964) 81 WN (Pt 1) (NSW) 297.
[220] (1877) 2 P.D. 66.
[221] [2002] 1 E.G.L.R. 149.
[222] [2010] EWHC 30 (Ch).
[223] [2006] EWHC 89 (TCC).

In *Quantum Advisory Ltd v Quantum Actuarial LLP*,[224] an introducer was entitled to a fee for introducing "all those clients whose names are set out on the Q list". The Q List was defined to mean "the existing clients of QFC as listed in Schedule 1 of this Agreement". Schedule 1 was blank. But the court held that the identity of the Q list was proved by extrinsic evidence, with the consequence that the agreement was not void for uncertainty.

In *Davies, Middleton & Davies Ltd v Cardiff Corp*,[225] a contract contained an arbitration clause which said: **8.108**

"such dispute or difference shall be and is hereby referred to the arbitration and final decision of — or, in the event of his death or unwillingness or inability to act, of a person to be appointed on the request of either party by the president or a vice-president for the time being of the Royal Institute of British Architects."

The blank space for the named arbitrator was not filled in. The Court of Appeal held that the arbitration agreement was not void for uncertainty. Sellers LJ said:

"Then, it is said that the words 'or, in the event of his death or unwillingness or inability to act' were left in and that they make this a meaningless and unacceptable contract, but the fact is that in the absence of any insertion of the name those words are of no effect and can be ignored."

Pearson LJ said:

"Be it assumed that the last part of the provision is not operable by reason of the condition precedent not being fulfilled, is the clause then void for uncertainty? In my view, the answer is that this clause is not void for uncertainty and is easily operable."

In *Phoenix General Insurance Co of Greece SA v Administratia Asigurarilor de Stat*,[226] a reinsurance slip provided for a full reinsurance clause. It was agreed that this was a reference to a clause which required blanks to be filled in but that they had not been. Kerr LJ said: **8.109**

"Admittedly, the reinsurance slip must be construed as though the 'full reinsurance clause' had been inserted in it. But it does not follow that it must also be assumed that the parties intended to agree on the completion of the blank in the second part of the clause, let alone by some agreed percentage. For instance, leaving the second blank uncompleted might imply agreement that there should be no retention. Another possibility, in my view more realistic, is that the parties never addressed themselves to the question of any, or any quantum of, retention. They clearly intended, probably as a matter of routine, that the 'full reinsurance clause' should be incorporated, because it usually is, and because its first part is an uncontroversial and virtually universal feature of reinsurance business, viz that the reinsurance is on the basis of the same rate, terms and conditions as the primary insurance, and that the reinsurers are bound to follow the settlements of the reinsured made properly and in good faith. In my judgment this is a suf-

---

[224] [2020] EWHC 1072 (Comm).
[225] (1964) 62 L.G.R. 134.
[226] [1987] 2 All E.R. 152.

ficient explanation of the parties' intention to include this clause, though without any agreement about any retention by Phoenix. It would be pure speculation whether or not any, let alone what, figure was intended to be inserted in the blank space in the second part of the clause. And the court could in any event go no further than to consider the insertion of the minimum figure of 1%. But the evidence was that, in the light of the overrider at 5%, this would not provide any deterrent to Phoenix to control the quality or administration of the primary contracts, so that there would be no basis for the insertion of even this minimum figure."

8.110   Although a blank space may be ignored in a concluded contract, where the question is whether a contract has been concluded at all "it becomes progressively more unreal for the court to adopt that approach when it means, as here, ignoring the majority of a document, in circumstances where the blanks or uncertainties existed because the relevant terms were still being negotiated".[227]

Illustration

Four gifts in a will each devised "All that newly built house, being No ... *Sudeley Place, Cotsfield Road*"; one to each of the testator's four sons. It was held that the blanks could not be filled as a matter of interpretation; and the uncertainty could not be cured by election by the devisees. Accordingly the gifts failed for uncertainty. *Asten v Asten*[228]

17.   Agreements to Agree

Save in exceptional circumstances the court will not recognise a bare agreement to agree as having any legal effect.[229] But where a binding contract contains an obligation to negotiate or provides for a term to be agreed, the court may give effect to it.

8.111   One category of agreement has consistently been treated by the court as being void for uncertainty; namely an agreement to agree.
8.112   The orthodox view was stated by Viscount Dunedin in *May & Butcher Ltd v R.*[230] as follows:

"To be a good contract there must be a concluded bargain, and a concluded contract is one which settles everything that is necessary to be settled and leaves nothing to be settled by agreement between the parties."

So in that case a letter agreeing to purchase goods at a price to be agreed was held not to create a legally binding contract.
8.113   The suggestion was made by Lord Wright[231] that even though there could not be

[227] *Arcadis Consulting (UK) Ltd v AMEC (BSC) Ltd* [2016] EWHC 2509 (TCC) (reversed [2018] EWCA Civ 2222, but without affecting this point).
[228] [1894] 3 Ch. 260.
[229] In *Organic Group Ltd v Charterhouse Macmillan Group Inc* [2007] EWHC 1275 (QB) Mackay J said that this proposition was "incontrovertible".
[230] [1934] 2 K.B. 17n.
[231] In *Hillas & Co Ltd v Arcos Ltd* (1932) 147 L.T. 503.

a binding agreement to agree, it was possible in law to have a binding agreement to negotiate, breach of which could at least give rise to a claim for nominal damages. But that suggestion was unanimously rejected by the Court of Appeal in *Courtney & Fairburn Ltd v Tolaini Bros (Hotels) Ltd*,[232] Lord Denning MR said:

"If the law does not recognise a contract to enter into a contract (when there is a fundamental term yet to be agreed) it seems to me that it cannot recognise a contract to negotiate. The reason is because it is too uncertain to have any binding force. No court could estimate the damages because no one can tell whether the negotiations would be successful or would fall through; or if successful what the result would be. It seems to me that a contract to negotiate, like a contract to enter into a contract, is not a contract known to the law."

This general statement of principle does not, however, prevent the court from upholding a term in a binding oral contract that the parties would negotiate in good faith about further terms to be inserted into a written agreement.[233] The distinction, it seems, is that in the latter case if negotiations fail, there is a pre-existing legally binding agreement to fall back on. But this distinction may not be clear-cut, since the court has held that one clause in an agreement which is otherwise legally binding may be void as being an agreement to agree.[234] However, it has been said that where an obligation to negotiate in good faith is contained in a binding and professionally drafted contract, it would defeat the reasonable expectations of honest men to hold that it had no legal content.[235] "It is only in the absence of agreement as to essential terms that a contract is in danger of failing for uncertainty because further agreement is required. The world is otherwise full of perfectly sound contracts which require further agreement for the purpose of their implementation."[236]

8.114

However, in *Walford v Miles*,[237] the House of Lords held that an agreement to negotiate was unenforceable as lacking in legal content.[238] Although in that case it was suggested that the same defect does not apply to an agreement to use best endeavours, it was subsequently pointed out by Millett LJ in *Little v Courage Ltd*[239] that an agreement to use best endeavours to agree was equally inefficacious. He said:

8.115

"An undertaking to use one's best endeavours to obtain planning permission or an export licence is sufficiently certain and is capable of being enforced: an

---

[232] [1975] 1 W.L.R. 297.

[233] *Donwin Productions Ltd v EMI Films Ltd, The Times,* 9 March 1984.

[234] See *Mallozzi v Carapelli SpA* [1976] 1 Lloyd's Rep. 407.

[235] *Petromec Inc v Petrolio Brasiliero SA* [2006] 1 Lloyd's Rep. 121, 152, per Longmore LJ.

[236] *Scammell v Dicker* [2005] 3 All E.R. 838, per Rix LJ (consent order fixing a boundary was not uncertain despite difficulties of implementation).

[237] [1992] 2 A.C. 128. The New South Wales Court of Appeal has refused to follow *Walford v Miles United Group Rail Services Ltd v Rail Corp New South Wales* [2009] NSWCA 177.

[238] The baldness of this holding has been questioned: *Petromec Inc v Petrolio Brasiliero SA* [2006] 1 Lloyd's Rep. 121, 153, per Longmore LJ. See also *United Group Rail Services Ltd v Rail Corp New South Wales* [2009] NSWCA 177 where Alsopp P analysed the authorities in great detail.

[239] (1994) 70 P. & C.R. 469; *London & Regional Investments Ltd v TBI Plc* [2002] EWCA Civ 355 at [39]. However, in *The Queensland Electricity Generating Board v New Hope Collieries Ltd* [1990] 2 Lloyd's Rep. 526, the Privy Council held that the parties had undertaken primary obligations to endeavour to agree.

undertaking to use one's best endeavours to try to agree, however, is no different from an undertaking to agree, to try to agree, or to negotiate with a view to reaching agreement; all are equally uncertain and incapable of giving rise to an enforceable legal obligation."[240]

8.116   Whether a provision to use best endeavours is or is not sufficiently definite to be enforceable turns, on this approach, on the object of the endeavour. It may, as with the obtaining of a specific planning permission or a particular export licence, involve persuading an authority or other third party to adopt a particular position. The same is true of a provision to use all reasonable endeavours.[241] Whether the objective of a "best endeavours" obligation was sufficiently certain to be enforceable was considered in *Jet2.com Ltd v Blackpool Airport Ltd*.[242] The case is quoted in para.8.101.

8.117   As with other allegations of uncertainty, the court will strain to the utmost to find a construction which will not avoid the contract, particularly where it has been partly performed.[243] Indeed, it may be that the court is readier than before to supply machinery to resolve a dispute between parties to an agreement to agree, so as to turn it into a binding legal obligation. This tendency is particularly manifest when the contract contains an arbitration clause, which may be seized upon by the court as providing the necessary certainty to enable a legally binding agreement to be spelled out.[244] If the contract specifies criteria which may be objectively applied, the court will determine any dispute between the parties according to those criteria.[245] In *Tramtrack Croydon Ltd v London Bus Services Ltd*,[246] the contract provided that the parties should agree financial terms in good faith and acting reasonably. There was also a clause providing for expert determination in the event of failure to agree. Christopher Clarke J said:

> "The parties did not limit their agreement to an obligation to act in good faith. They agreed (a) to act *reasonably* in agreeing and (b) that any failure to agree should be referred to expert determination. In those circumstances the court can, in my judgment, decide, in the case of dispute, at least what they, and the expert, acting reasonably, are bound to take into account or ignore. An agreement such as this should not be construed to mean that the parties (or the expert) may legitimately take into account anything (however unreasonable or irrelevant) they

---

[240] It has been held in Scotland that this statement is too dogmatic: *R&D Construction Group Ltd v Hallam Land Management Ltd* [2010] CSIH 96.

[241] *R&D Construction Group Ltd v Hallam Land Management Ltd* [2010] CSIH 96 (Court of Session Inner House).

[242] [2012] EWCA Civ 417.

[243] *Sudbrook Trading Estate Ltd v Eggleton* [1983] 1 A.C. 444, per Templeman LJ in the Court of Appeal (approved by Lord Fraser of Tullybelton at 484). See also e.g. *Nile Company for the Export of Agricultural Crops v Bennett (H & J M) (Commodities) Ltd* [1986] 1 Lloyd's Rep. 555; *Voest Alpine Intertrading GmbH v Chevron International Oil Co Ltd* [1987] 2 Lloyd's Rep. 547.

[244] *Didymi Corp v Atlantic Lines and Navigation Co Inc* [1988] 2 Lloyd's Rep. 108. That case built upon the willingness of the House of Lords to substitute machinery for the ascertainment of a price when the contractual machinery for that ascertainment broke down: *Sudbrook Trading Estate Ltd v Eggleton* [1983] 1 A.C. 444. It has yet to be determined how far the court will go in substituting machinery of its own to supplement or replace machinery which for one reason or another has not been capable of implementation in the circumstances in which the parties find themselves.

[245] *Scottish Wholefoods Collective Warehouse Ltd v Raye Investments Ltd* [1994] 1 E.G.L.R. 244 (Ct of Sess. I.H.).

[246] [2007] EWHC 107 (Comm).

choose, or that their contractual fate is to be determined by whatever the appointed expert happens (on whatever basis) to decide. Reasonableness is a criterion on which the court (and the expert) can make a judgment; and, if the parties cannot agree whether it would be unreasonable to take into account, or to exclude, a particular consideration, the court may determine the question."

In *FBO 2000 (Antigua) Ltd v Vere Cornwall Bird Jr*,[247] the Privy Council held **8.118** that a binding agreement for lease had been concluded, even though some terms remained to be agreed.

On the other hand, in *Dwr Cymru Cyfyngedig (Welsh Water) v Corus UK Ltd*,[248] **8.119** Moore-Bick LJ said:

"Where many important terms have been left undecided and the contractual machinery for resolving disagreements is incapable of being operated, it may be impossible to avoid the conclusion that the agreement as a whole is unenforceable because the parties have failed to establish objective criteria capable of being applied by the court itself."

Thus in *Dhanani v Crasnianski*,[249] two businessmen signed a term sheet, intended to be legally binding, which committed them to setting up a private equity fund. Although many of the characteristics of the fund were agreed, and a timetable for agreement on the remaining matters was also agreed, the overall agreement was too uncertain to amount to an enforceable contract. Teare J said:

"In my judgment the agreement into which the Claimant and Defendant entered by signing the letter and term sheet was in essence an agreement to agree upon the exact structure of the fund and the form and location of its various entities together with the other necessary agreements, notwithstanding that much of the structure and form had already been agreed and that a timetable for agreeing the exact structure, form and location had been agreed. The Claimant and the Defendant agreed that each would do his part to agree or 'define' the exact structure form and location of the entities forming the fund but such an agreement is no different from an agreement to agree; see *Little v Courage*.[250] I accept that the object to be achieved was not wholly or completely indefinite and indeed that much of the structure and characteristics of the fund had been agreed. But sufficient remained to be agreed that the agreement evidenced by the letter and term sheet was in reality an agreement to agree with no indication of any objective criteria by reference to which agreement was to be reached on those matters which had not been agreed. Such an agreement is not recognised by the law as giving rise to enforceable obligations; see *Walford v Miles*[251] and *Multiplex Constructions v Cleveland Bridge*."[252]

---

[247] [2009] 2 P. & C.R. 14.
[248] [2007] EWCA Civ 285.
[249] [2011] EWHC 926 (Comm); *Barbudev v Eurocom Cable Management Bulgaria EOOD* [2011] EWHC 1560 (Comm).
[250] (1994) 70 P. & C.R. 469.
[251] [1992] 2 A.C. 128.
[252] [2006] EWHC 1341 (TCC) at [634]–[637], per Jackson J.

8.120   In *Morris v Swanton Care & Community Ltd*,[253] an agreement provided for one party to be entitled to provide services for four years and thereafter for "such further period as shall reasonably be agreed" by the parties. The Court of Appeal held that that part of the clause was no more than an agreement to agree, and therefore unenforceable. Dame Elizabeth Gloster said:

> "As a matter of grammar, the word 'reasonably' is an adverb that modifies the verb 'shall be agreed'. It is not the adjective 'reasonable' nor does it qualify the phrase the 'further period'. Although the verb 'agreed' is used in the passive form, it is clear that it is the parties who have to do the agreeing. On the proper construction of the relevant provisions, therefore, there was no existing agreement in place that the Consultancy Services would be extended by a reasonable period. To the contrary, the option is expressed to continue for 'such further period as shall reasonably be agreed'. Thus, any period of extension could be agreed, with the words 'shall reasonably' applying to the agreeing, and not to the further period itself. The claimant's argument seeks to transfer the 'reasonable' requirement to the period itself, on the basis that if the clause is read to provide for a reasonable period, the court can then determine what a reasonable period is. But that is wrong for two reasons: first, it is not what paragraph 1.1 of Schedule 5 says, and the exercise would require transposing reasonableness from agreeing to the further period. Secondly, the proposition is that, on the assumption that there was such a thing as an objectively reasonable period, that is what the parties acting reasonably should have agreed. The difficulty with this, apart from the actual terms of the clause, is that it presupposes that there is such a thing as a reasonable period which everyone could equally recognise as being reasonable, rather than the different commercial interests and different perspectives involved in any extension of the Earn-Out Consideration. Moreover, the court would have to identify some objective benchmark for determining the reasonable period without reaching an alternative subjective view or descending into the commercial fray; but that is not possible."

8.121   In some cases the court may be able to imply a term that the price to be agreed should be a fair price[254]; and if this is done the agreement will be capable of enforcement. Alternatively, the agreement may itself specify the consequences of a failure to agree, in which case there will be no need for any implication.[255] As Lord Kitchin put it in *Wells v Devani*[256]:

> "where it is apparent the parties intended to be bound and to create legal relations, it may be permissible to imply a term to give the contract such business efficacy as the parties must have intended. For example, an agreement may be enforceable despite calling for some further agreement between the parties, say as to price, for it may be appropriate to imply a term that, in default of agreement, a reasonable price must be paid."

8.122   The New Zealand Court of Appeal has drawn a distinction between a "process

---

[253] [2018] EWCA Civ 2763.
[254] *Corson v Rhuddlan Borough Council* [1990] 1 E.G.L.R. 255 CA; *Money v Ven-Lu-Ree Ltd* [1989] 3 N.Z.L.R. 129 PC.
[255] *Miller v Lakefield Estates Ltd* [1989] 1 E.G.L.R. 212 CA.
[256] [2019] UKSC 4; [2019] 2 W.L.R. 617.

contract" (i.e. an agreement to negotiate or to follow an agreed procedure) and the substantive contract agreement of which is the aim of the process. A contract to try to agree may be enforceable, depending on the specificity of its terms. However, a simple contract to negotiate in good faith cannot be enforced, because in this concept good faith is essentially a subjective concept and there are no objective criteria for the court to apply.[257] The distinction between a "process contract" and an agreement to agree was also made in Australia in *King Network Group Pty Ltd v Club of the Clubs Pty Ltd*[258] in which Young CJ in Eq. said:

"Thus, the prevailing view is that, whilst it may be a breach of a collateral contract, sometimes referred to as a 'process contract', to withdraw from negotiations without cause, there is no obligation to conclude the deal, let alone conclude the deal at the price suggested. A person who has agreed to negotiate in good faith is not prevented from taking the position that as the market is rising so should the price."

This distinction has not yet been drawn in England.

Where a contract depends on action by a third party there may be sufficient certainty. In *Anthracite Rated Investments (Jersey) Ltd v Lehman Brothers Finance SA*,[259] Briggs J said: **8.123**

"It is well settled that where the working out of a formula regulating the parties' rights under an agreement depends upon something to be done by a third party, the formula, and the rights dependent upon its implementation, do not fall to the ground merely because that party declines or is unable to act. In extremis, the court will step in and perform the relevant function."

Similarly, where a contract contains an obligation to use best endeavours to agree terms with a third party, that is a factor which may lead to the conclusion that the obligation has sufficient content to be enforceable.[260] In *Lambert v HTV Cymru (Wales) Ltd*,[261] Morritt LJ said: **8.124**

"I would draw distinction between the case of a contract itself and a contract to use all reasonable endeavours to procure such a contract. It seems to me that there is a material difference between a contract to do X and a contract to use all reasonable endeavours to procure that some third party does X. If one takes an example derived from the facts of *Scammell v Ouston* itself, it is plain from the contract in that case and the decision of the House of Lords that a contract to sell the van, the balance of the purchase price being paid on normal hire-purchase terms, was not sufficiently certain, because there was no sufficient definition of what normal hire-purchase terms were. However, if one contrasts that with a contract between A and B, where B is to use all reasonable endeavours to procure that C shall sell to A the named van on normal hire-purchase terms, for my part I do not see why the concept of what B is to achieve or to aim at is not suf-

---

[257] *Wellington City Council v Body Corporate 51702 (Wellington)* [2002] 3 N.Z.L.R. 486.
[258] [2008] NSWCA 344 [306].
[259] [2011] EWHC 1822 (Ch); [2011] 2 Lloyd's Rep. 538.
[260] *R&D Construction Group Ltd v Hallam Land Management Ltd* [2010] CSIH 96.
[261] [1998] F.S.R. 874.

ficiently certain to enable legal force and effect to be given to the contract between A and B.

In this case, where the obligation is to use all reasonable endeavours, it is clear and sufficiently certain what it is that the contracting party is to do. The aim at which the contracting party is to direct those efforts is likewise sufficiently certain, and nonetheless so because there is a range of possible goals at which those efforts are to be directed. As in the example of the sale of the van on hire-purchase terms, there may have been a hundred alternative forms of contract upon which A and C might subsequently agree, but that is no reason to excuse B from using all reasonable endeavours to procure a contract between A and C on any of them."

In *Dany Lions Ltd v Bristol Cars Ltd*,[262] Andrews J said that:

"... in determining whether a contractual obligation to use best or reasonable endeavours is or is not enforceable the initial focus should be on the object of the endeavours and whether it is sufficiently certain. If it is sufficiently certain, then the court will know precisely what it is that the party concerned must use his reasonable endeavours to achieve. However even in a case where there is certainty as to the object, there is still potentially the problem of whether there are sufficient objective criteria by which to evaluate the reasonableness of the endeavours."

She held on the facts that an obligation to use reasonable endeavours to enter into an agreement with a third party was too uncertain to be enforced.[263] But in *Astor Management AG v Atalaya Mining Plc*,[264] Leggatt J, approving the previous edition of this text, refused to follow *Dany Lions Ltd v Bristol Cars Ltd* which had held that an obligation to use best endeavours to reach agreement with a third party was unenforceable. He said:

"Far from being 'exceptional', I would say that it should almost always be possible to give sensible content to an undertaking to use reasonable endeavours (or 'all reasonable endeavours' or 'best endeavours') to enter into an agreement with a third party. There is no problem of uncertainty of object, as there is no inherent difficulty in telling whether an agreement with a third party has been made. Whether the party who gave the undertaking has endeavoured to make such an agreement (or used its best endeavours to do so) is a question of fact which a court can perfectly well decide. It may sometimes be hard to prove an absence of endeavours, or of best endeavours, but difficulty of proving a breach of a contractual obligation is an everyday occurrence and not a reason to hold that there is no obligation. Any complaint about lack of objective criteria could only be directed to the task of judging whether the endeavours used were 'reasonable', or whether there were other steps which it was reasonable to take so that it cannot be said that 'all reasonable endeavours' have been used. Where the parties have adopted a test of 'reasonableness', however, it seems to me that they

---

[262] [2014] EWHC 817 (QB).

[263] She does not appear to have been referred to the decision of the Court of Appeal *in Lambert v HTV Cymru (Wales) Ltd* which suggests the contrary. So too does the decision of the New Zealand Court of Appeal in *Mana v Fleming* [2007] NZCA 324.

[264] [2017] EWHC 425 (Comm); [2017] 1 Lloyd's Rep. 476.

are deliberately inviting the court to make a value judgment which sets a limit to their freedom of action."

It is considered that this is the better view.

Where a contract required the parties to attempt to resolve disputes through an alternative dispute resolution procedure as recommended to them by the Centre for Dispute Resolution, it was held that there was sufficient certainty in the procedure for the obligation to be legally binding.[265] In *Associated British Ports v Tata Steel UK Ltd*,[266] a licence agreement contained a clause which entitled either party in the event of any major physical or financial change in circumstances affecting the operation of a steelworks or the port serving it to serve notice on the other requiring the terms of the licence to be renegotiated, with provision for arbitration in default of agreement. Rose J held that this was more than a mere agreement to agree, but was a legally binding obligation. She held that the arbitrator would have the terms of the existing licence as a starting point and that the changes to the terms would reflect the major physical or financial change that gave rise to the arbitration. In addition, the parameters of the arbitrator's decision would be limited by the parties' submissions. **8.125**

The distinction between an unenforceable agreement to agree and an enforceable agreement is sometimes a narrow one. In *Management (Isle of Man) Ltd v Cable and Wireless Plc*,[267] parties were negotiating for a contribution to a legal liability for which both were potentially liable. What they actually agreed was that one party would contribute a fair share on principles to be agreed and discussed. Rix LJ said that the parties might have been bound if they had simply agreed that the one party would contribute "a fair share" or possibly a "fair share to be agreed" but not if they had agreed upon "a fair share on principles to be agreed". He explained: **8.126**

"In either event, there is a substantial and important distinction between [a fair share to be agreed and a fair share on principles to be agreed] and a simple agreement for a fair share. In the latter case, the court has itself been provided straightaway with the measure for its determination and can proceed to quantify the figure: *The Didymi*. In the former case the parties have agreed that they will themselves provide either the principles for finding the measure and/or the quantification of the share itself. It is like the distinction between agreeing, whether expressly or by implication, that the price of goods to be sold is to be a fair or reasonable price and on the other hand agreeing that the price is to be a price 'to be agreed'. In the first case the price will be set by the court (if none is previously agreed by the parties), but in the second case the parties have said that they, and not the court, will agree the price: see *May and Butcher Ltd v R*.[268] It is true that where a binding contract already exists, a provision that prices for future years are to be agreed is likely to remain a binding part of that contract: see *Mamidoil-Jetoil Greek Petroleum Co SA v Okta Crude Oil Refinery*,[269] an authority relied on by the judge below. However, *Mamidoil* distinguished

---

[265] *Cable & Wireless Plc v IBM United Kingdom Ltd* [2003] B.L.R. 89.
[266] [2017] EWHC 694 (Ch); [2017] 2 Lloyd's Rep. 11.
[267] [2005] 2 Lloyd's Rep. 597.
[268] [1934] 2 K.B. 17, at 21, 22.
[269] [2001] 2 Lloyd's Rep. 76, especially at 91.

between a long-term contract which undoubtedly binds the parties initially and an agreement like the present where there is an issue from the very beginning as to whether it ever amounted to a contract at all."

The distinction appears to be that the court can interpret "a fair share" as meaning that the share is to be ascertained by objective criteria, whereas "a fair share on principles to be agreed" leaves too much at large because the principles themselves are uncertain and cannot be made certain in the absence of further agreement.

8.127   In addition, where the issue is whether a contract has come into existence at all, the lack of certainty of the alleged contractual obligations may confirm the absence of any intention to create legal relations.[270]

8.128   In *Mamidoil-Jetoil Greek Petroleum Co SA v Okta Crude Oil Refinery AD*,[271] Rix LJ summarised the principles as follows:

"In my judgment the following principles relevant to the present case can be deduced from these authorities, but this is intended to be in no way an exhaustive list:

(i)   Each case must be decided on its own facts and on the construction of its own agreement. Subject to that,

(ii)   Where no contract exists, the use of an expression such as 'to be agreed' in relation to an essential term is likely to prevent any contract coming into existence, on the ground of uncertainty. This may be summed up by the principle that 'you cannot agree to agree'.

(iii)   Similarly, where no contract exists, the absence of agreement on essential terms of the agreement may prevent any contract coming into existence, again on the ground of uncertainty.

(iv)   However, particularly in commercial dealings between parties who are familiar with the trade in question, and particularly where the parties have acted in the belief that they had a binding contract, the courts are willing to imply terms, where that is possible, to enable the contract to be carried out.

(v)   Where a contract has once come into existence, even the expression 'to be agreed' in relation to future executory obligations is not necessarily fatal to its continued existence.

(vi)   Particularly in the case of contracts for future performance over a period, where the parties may desire or need to leave matters to be adjusted in the working out of their contract, the courts will assist the parties to do so, so as to preserve rather than destroy bargains, on the basis that what can be made certain is itself certain. *Certum est quod certum reddi potest.*

(vii)   This is particularly the case where one party has either already had the advantage of some performance which reflects the parties' agreement on a long term relationship, or has had to make an investment premised on that agreement.

(viii)   For these purposes, an express stipulation for a reasonable or fair measure or price will be a sufficient criterion for the courts to act on.

---

[270]   *Baird Textile Holdings v Marks & Spencer* [2001] C.L.C. 999 CA.
[271]   [2001] 2 Lloyd's Rep. 76.

But even in the absence of express language, the courts are prepared to imply an obligation in terms of what is reasonable.

(ix) Such implications are reflected but not exhausted by the statutory provision for the implication of a reasonable price now to be found in section 8(2) of the Sale of Goods Act 1979 (and, in the case of services, in section 15(1) of the Supply of Goods and Services Act 1982).

(x) The presence of an arbitration clause may assist the courts to hold a contract to be sufficiently certain or to be capable of being rendered so, presumably as indicating a commercial and contractual mechanism, which can be operated with the assistance of experts in the field, by which the parties, in the absence of agreement, may resolve their dispute." [272]

Similarly, in *BJ Aviation Ltd v Pool Aviation Ltd*,[273] Chadwick LJ said: **8.129**

"First, each case must be decided on its own facts and on the construction of the words used in the particular agreement. Decisions on other words, in other agreements, construed against the background of other facts, are not determinative and may not be of any real assistance.

"[21] Second, if on the true construction of the words which they have used in the circumstances in which they have used them, the parties must be taken to have intended to leave some essential matter, such as price or rent, to be agreed between them in the future—on the basis that either will remain free to agree or disagree about that matter—there is no bargain which the courts can enforce.

[22] Third, in such a case, there is no obligation on the parties to negotiate in good faith about the matter which remains to be agreed between them ...

[23] Fourth, where the court is satisfied that the parties intended that their bargain should be enforceable, it will strive to give effect to that intention by construing the words which they have used in a way which does not leave the matter to be agreed in the future incapable of being determined in the absence of future agreement. In order to achieve that result the court may feel able to imply a term in the original bargain that the price or rent, or other matter to be agreed, shall be a 'fair' price, or a 'market' price, or a 'reasonable' price; or by quantifying whatever matter it is that has to be agreed by some equivalent epithet. In a contract for sale of goods such a term may be implied by s 8 of the Sale of Goods Act 1979. But the court cannot imply a term which is inconsistent with what the parties have actually agreed. So if, on the true construction of the words which they have used, the court is driven to the conclusion that they must be taken to have intended that the matter should be left to their future agreement on the basis that either is to remain free to agree or disagree about that matter as his own perceived interest dictates there is no place for an implied term that, in the absence of agreement, the matter shall be determined by some objective criteria of fairness or reasonableness.

---

[272] A clause providing for expert determination in the event of failure to agree may have the same effect: *Tramtrack Croydon Ltd v London Bus Services Ltd* [2007] EWHC 107 (Comm).
[273] [2002] 2 P. & C.R. 25.

[24]   Fifth, if the court concludes that the true intention of the parties was that the matter to be agreed in the future is capable of being determined, in the absence of future agreement, by some objective criteria of fairness or reasonableness, then the bargain does not fail because the parties have provided no machinery for such determination, or because the machinery which they have provided breaks down. In those circumstances the court will provide its own machinery for determining what needs to be determined—where appropriate by ordering an inquiry ...".

8.130   In *MRI Trading AG v Erdenet Mining Corp LLC*,[274] the Court of Appeal, upholding Eder J,[275] followed and applied the principles in *Mamidoil-Jetoil Greek Petroleum Co SA v Okta Crude Oil Refinery AD* and *BJ Aviation Ltd v Pool Aviation Ltd*. They held on the facts that a requirement to agree certain charges and a shipping schedule under a contract for the sale of goods did not render the contract unenforceable.

Illustrations

1.   A contract for the sale of maize provided that the discharging port was to be agreed between sellers and buyers on the ship passing the Straits of Gibraltar. It was held that that provision was void for uncertainty.
   Mallozzi v Carapelli SpA[276]

2.   A business tenant withdrew an application to the court for the grant of a new tenancy as part of an overall agreement. Under the terms of the agreement the tenant was granted an option to take a new lease of a new building to be constructed by the landlord. The form of the lease was to be in the landlord's standard form with such amendments as might be mutually agreed. The rent was to be the greater of £33,000 per annum or such rent as might be agreed. The lease was to be for 25 years. It was held that the agreement was not void for uncertainty. There was sufficient material in the agreement to enable the court to discern a commencement date for the term; to imply a term that in default of agreement the rent was to be a fair rent; and that the other terms of the lease were to be such as the landlord reasonably required.
   Trustees of National Deposit Friendly Society v Beatties of London Ltd[277]

3.   A charterparty contained representations about the speed and fuel consumption of the vessel. A clause in the charterparty provided that if it failed to satisfy the representations "the hire shall be equitably decreased by an amount to be mutually agreed between owners and charterers". Conversely, if it performed better than the representations the hire was to be increased in the same manner. It was held that the obligation was legally binding and that the word "equitably" was not uncertain.
   Didymi Corp v Atlantic Lines and Navigation Co Inc[278]

4.   A lease contained an option to renew for a term of 21 years at a rent to be

---

[274] [2013] EWCA Civ 156; [2013] 1 Lloyd's Rep. 638.
[275] [2012] EWHC 1988 (Comm); [2013] 1 All E.R. (Comm) 1.
[276] [1976] 1 Lloyd's Rep. 407.
[277] [1985] 2 E.G.L.R. 59.
[278] [1988] 2 Lloyd's Rep. 108.

agreed (but not to exceed the rent reserved by the lease). It was held that it was an implied term that the rent should be a fair rent and that the option was not void for uncertainty.

Corson v Rhuddlan Borough Council[279]

5.   A developer and an airport operator entered into a written agreement which contained a clause by which they agreed to use reasonable endeavours to agree the terms of a joint venture regarding two airports, having regard to certain agreed principles. It was held that this was no more than an agreement to agree; and was therefore unenforceable.

London and Regional Investments Ltd v TBI Plc[280]

6.   An agreement for the operation of an airport contained an option to renew subject to the re-negotiation of the rent payable. It was held that this was an agreement to agree, and was therefore unenforceable.

BJ Aviation Ltd v Pool Aviation Ltd[281]

7.   A licence agreement provided that the parties should in good faith agree a variation order to the Underlying Contracts (which were defined) whereby one party should agree the provision of free issue materials to the other at cost price plus 5 per cent handling fee. It was held that the only thing to be agreed by the parties was a variation order, in circumstances where all the material obligations to be set out in the variation order were identified. The agreement was thus sufficiently certain to be enforceable.

Redd Factors Ltd v Bombardier Transportation UK Ltd[282]

8.   An option for the purchase of vessels provide for delivery dates for the vessels "to be mutually agreed upon". Although the parties intended the option to be legally binding, it was no more than an agreement to agree. There was no warrant for implying a term that the delivery dates should be within a reasonable time; and there was no other implication that could be made. The option was therefore void for uncertainty.

Teekay Tankers Ltd v STX Offshore & Shipbuilding Co Ltd[283]

18.   EFFECT OF UNCERTAINTY

The effect of uncertainty may be that no contract comes into existence; or it may be that one provision in an otherwise binding contract is unenforceable. Which of these two possibilities is likelier depends on the importance of the term which is uncertain. The more important the term, the more likely it is that the contract as a whole is unenforceable.

---

[279] [1990] 1 E.G.L.R. 255 CA. The correctness of *King's Motors (Oxford) Ltd v Lax* [1970] 1 W.L.R. 426 was doubted.
[280] [2002] EWCA Civ 355.
[281] [2002] 2 P. & C.R. 25.
[282] [2014] EWHC 3138 (QB).
[283] [2017] EWHC 253 (Comm); [2017] 1 Lloyd's Rep. 387.

8.131   Uncertainty may in principle have one of two results. The uncertainty may be such as to prevent any binding agreement from coming into existence; alternatively, there may be a binding agreement, but with the omission of the uncertain term.[284]

8.132   It is difficult to predict which of these two possibilities the court will adopt in any given case. In some cases the uncertain term is clearly severable from the remainder of the contract. Thus in *King's Motors (Oxford) Ltd v Lax*,[285] a lease contained an option to renew at a rent to be agreed. Clearly, the rent to be paid under any new lease is of fundamental importance. Accordingly, since the court was unable to discern any method for quantifying the rent, the option as a whole was declared void. Equally clearly, however, the lease in which the option was contained was a perfectly valid lease without the option; and therefore the avoidance of the option did not affect the validity of the lease.

8.133   Where the reason for the uncertainty is that the clause in question is unintelligible, or meaningless, the court must consider the remainder of the contract without the unintelligible or meaningless term. If the remainder of the contract is itself capable of taking effect as a complete contract, it seems that the court will give effect to it.[286]

8.134   Where, however, the problem arises from an almost infinite variety of possible meanings which may be placed on the term, with no criteria for selecting among them, and the term is one of importance to the parties, the court is more likely to hold that there is no binding agreement.[287]

8.135   Where the contract has been partly executed, it is, of course, more likely that the court will enforce the remainder of the agreement with the omission of the uncertain term. Thus where, for example, there is a conveyance of land containing some stipulation which is void for uncertainty, the uncertainty will not normally prevent the conveyance from vesting the land in the purchaser. In *Pearce v Watts*,[288] specific performance of an agreement for the sale of land was refused, because the agreement contained a reservation which was void for uncertainty. Jessel MR said:

> "If the conveyance were executed in this form, it is obvious, according to the present law, the whole land would pass to the purchaser, the reservation being void for uncertainty."

In that species of case the court does not hold that the uncertainty vitiates the entire instrument; it severs the uncertain term and gives effect to the remainder of the instrument as if the uncertain term had not been included in it.

Illustrations

1.   A landowner demised a stratum of coal to a miner. The lease reserved to the landlord the right of working coal not included in the demise provided that in

---

[284] See *Vitol BV v Compagnie Europeenne de Petroles* [1988] 1 Lloyd's Rep. 574 at 576, per Saville J.
[285] [1970] 1 W.L.R. 426.
[286] See, e.g. *Nicolene Ltd v Simmonds* [1953] 1 Q.B. 543 (see para.8.68) and *Richards (Michael) Properties Ltd v Corp of Wardens of St Saviour's Parish, Southwark* [1975] 3 All E.R. 416 (above); *United Group Rail Services Ltd v Rail Corp NSW* [2008] NSWSC 1364 (referring to this section).
[287] See, e.g. *Scammell and Nephew Ltd v Ouston* [1941] A.C. 251; *Bishop & Baxter Ltd v Anglo Eastern Trading and Industrial Co Ltd* [1944] K.B. 12 (see para.8.103, Illustration 2).
[288] (1875) L.R. 20 Eq. 492 (see para.8.37).

exercising the right the working of the coal demised should not be prevented or unduly interfered with. It was held that the reservation was unintelligible, and accordingly the lease took effect as if the reservation had not been included in it.

Mundy v Duke of Rutland[289]

2.   A franchise agreement contained a clause providing for renewal of the agreement with "uplifted minimum performance requirements", but did not specify what they were and did not provide for machinery to determine them. It was held that there was no binding agreement for renewal and that the original franchise agreement expired according to its terms.

Grow with US Ltd v Green Thumb (UK) Ltd[290]

---

[289]   (1882) 23 Ch. D. 81.
[290]   [2006] EWCA Civ 1201.

CHAPTER 9

MISTAKES AND INCONSISTENCIES

Our use of words is generally inaccurate and seldom completely correct, but our meaning is recognised none the less

St Augustine: *Confessions XI*, section 20

1.   CORRECTION OF MISTAKES BY INTERPRETATION

As part of the process of interpretation the court has power to correct obvious mistakes in the written expression of the intention of the parties. Once corrected, the contract is interpreted in its corrected form.

In *Wilson v Wilson*,[1] Lord St Leonards said: **9.01**

"Now it is a great mistake if it be supposed that even a Court of Law cannot correct a mistake, or error on the face of an instrument; there is no magic in words. If you find a clear mistake and it admits of no other construction, a Court of Law, as well as a Court of Equity, without impugning any doctrine about correcting those things which can only be shown by parol evidence to be mistakes— without, I say, going into those cases at all, both Courts of Law and of Equity may correct an obvious mistake on the face of an instrument without the slightest difficulty."

The reference to "courts of law" in distinction to "courts of equity" shows that his Lordship was considering the correction of errors as matters of interpretation rather than by way of the equitable remedy of rectification.[2] Although the principle is well-established its precise scope remains controversial.[3]

In *LSREF III Wight Ltd v Millvalley Ltd*,[4] Cooke J said: **9.02**

"… in order to construe a contract in a manner which is contrary to the language used, where there is no ambiguity in that language, the authorities make it plain that the court must be satisfied that something has gone wrong in the drafting, that there is a clear mistake and what correction ought to be made in the light of it to give effect to the parties' intention."

---

[1]   (1854) 5 H.L. Cas. 40 at 66.
[2]   In *Homburg Houtimport BV v Agrosin Ltd (The Starsin)* [2004] 1 A.C. 715, Lord Millett made a similar point by reference to the ability of courts of equity to correct errors in wills, at a time when there was no power to rectify a will.
[3]   *Marley v Rawlings* [2014] UKSC 2; [2015] A.C. 129.
[4]   [2016] EWHC 466 (Comm); 165 Con. L.R. 58; *Hayfin Opal Luxco 3 SARL v Windermere VII Cmbs Plc* [2016] EWHC 782 (Ch); [2018] 1 B.C.L.C. 118.

In *East v Pantiles (Plant Hire) Ltd*,[5] Brightman LJ described the circumstances in which a mistake in a written instrument could be corrected as a matter of interpretation:

> "Two conditions must be satisfied: first there must be a clear mistake on the face of the instrument; secondly it must be clear what correction ought to be made in order to cure the mistake.[6] If those conditions are satisfied, then the correction is made as a matter of construction. If they are not satisfied then either the claimant must pursue an action for rectification or he must leave it to a court of construction to reach what answer it can on the basis that the uncorrected wording represents the manner in which the parties decided to express their intention."

9.03   If it is no more than possible that a mistake has been made, the principle does not apply.[7] Equally, if it is not clear what correction should be made, the court cannot intervene.[8] In *G&S Brough Ltd v Salvage Wharf Ltd*,[9] Jackson LJ expressed the principle as follows:

> "Where a written agreement as drafted is a nonsense and it is clear what the parties were trying to say the court will, as a matter of construction, give effect to the obvious intention of the parties."

As Lord Hodge explained in *Arnold v Britton*[10]:

> "Even if, contrary to my view, one concluded that there was a clear mistake in the parties' use of language, it is not clear what correction ought to be made. The court must be satisfied as to both the mistake and the nature of the correction."

So, where there were three possible ways of correcting the alleged error, it could not be said that any one of them was clear.[11]

9.04   Before concluding that correction is required the court should first attempt to interpret the contract as it stands.[12] In *Multi-Link Leisure Developments Ltd v North Lanarkshire Council*,[13] Lord Hope said:

> "The court's task is to ascertain the intention of the parties by examining the words they used and giving them their ordinary meaning in their contractual context. It must start with what it is given by the parties themselves when it is conducting this exercise. Effect is to be given to every word, so far as possible,

---

5   [1982] 2 E.G.L.R. 111, applied in *Dalkia Utilities Services Plc v Celtech International Ltd* [2006] 1 Lloyd's Rep. 599; *Clydesdale Bank Plc v Weston Property Co Ltd* [2011] EWHC 1251 (Ch).
6   It is sufficient if the gist of the correction is clear: *KPMG LLP v Network Rail Infrastructure Ltd* [2007] EWCA Civ 363.
7   *Altera Voyageur Production Ltd v Premier Oil E&P UK Ltd* [2020] EWHC 1891 (Comm).
8   *Arnold v Britton* [2015] UKSC 36; [2016] A.C. 1619, per Lord Hodge.
9   [2009] EWCA Civ 21.
10   [2015] UKSC 36; [2015] A.C. 1619.
11   *Trillium (Prime) Property GP Ltd v Elmfield Road Ltd* [2018] EWCA Civ 1556; [2018] 1 P. & C.R. DG21; *Parker v Roberts* [2019] EWCA Civ 121; [2019] 1 P. & C.R. DG20; *Altera Voyageur Production Ltd v Premier Oil E&P UK Ltd* [2020] EWHC 1891 (Comm).
12   If the contract, as interpreted, is not absurd, it is unlikely that the court will interfere with its wording: *Bashir v Ali* [2011] EWCA Civ 707.
13   [2011] 1 All E.R. 175 (a Scottish appeal). There is no difference between the law of Scotland and the law of England and Wales in this respect: *Credential Bath Street Ltd v Venture Investment Placement Ltd* [2007] CSOH 208; 2008 Hous. L.R. 2.

in the order in which they appear in the clause in question. Words should not be added which are not there, and words which are there should not be changed, taken out or moved from the place in the clause where they have been put by the parties. It may be necessary to do some of these things at a later stage to make sense of the language. But this should not be done until it has become clear that the language the parties actually used creates an ambiguity which cannot be solved otherwise."

Both Lord St Leonards and Brightman LJ spoke of an error "on the face of the instrument". However, in order to decide whether there is such a mistake, the court may take into account such evidence of background facts as is admissible in order to interpret the contract.[14] In *Chartbrook Ltd v Persimmon Homes Ltd*,[15] Lord Hoffmann approved the judgment of Carnwath LJ in *KPMG LLP v Network Rail Infrastructure Ltd*,[16] and in particular that: **9.05**

"in deciding whether there is a clear mistake, the court is not confined to reading the document without regard to its background or context. As the exercise is part of the single task of interpretation, the background and context must always be taken into consideration."

All that is required is:

"that it should be clear that something has gone wrong with the language and that it should be clear what a reasonable person would have understood the parties to have meant. In my opinion, both of these requirements are satisfied."[17]

By the same token, in *Generali Italia SpA v Pelagic Fisheries Corporation*,[18] Foxton J said:

"Just as the court is entitled to have regard to the background and context of a document to determine whether there is a clear mistake, so too it must be entitled to have regard to the background and context in determining whether it is clear what correction ought to be made to correct that mistake. Indeed these will very often involve the same enquiry—reading the document with regard to its background and context may make it clear that there has been a mistake because it may make it clear what the parties intended to say, which is not what they have in fact said."

In order to invoke the principle it is necessary that something should have gone wrong with the language of the contract rather than with the bargain. The mistake must be one of language or syntax.[19] the court has said on numerous occasions that the process of contractual interpretation cannot be used to rectify a failure to think **9.06**

---

[14] *Holding & Barnes Plc v Hill House Hammond Ltd* [2002] L. & T.R. 7 CA. This passage in the previous edition of this book was approved by the CA in *KPMG LLP v Network Rail Infrastructure Ltd* [2007] EWCA Civ 363.
[15] [2009] 1 A.C. 1101.
[16] [2007] Bus. L.R. 1336.
[17] Applied in *Pink Floyd Music Ltd v EMI Records Ltd* [2010] EWCA Civ 1429; *State Street Bank and Trust Co v Sompo Japan Insurance Inc* [2010] EWHC 1461 (Ch).
[18] [2020] EWHC 1228 (Comm).
[19] *Scottish Widows Fund and Life Assurance Society v BGC International* [2012] EWCA Civ 607, per Arden LJ at [22].

through the financial consequences of the operation of a clause.[20] Thus in *Honda Motor Europe Ltd v Powell*,[21] Lewison LJ said:

"In my judgment it is still necessary in order to invoke this principle that something should have gone wrong with the language, as opposed to the implementation of the bargain, or the relevant decision to exercise powers ... .[22] The typical case in which the principle applies is where the clause in question is "an obvious nonsense" ... .[23] In addition even where the principle is invoked the question remains: what is the meaning that the instrument would convey to the reasonable reader?"

In *Trillium (Prime) Property GP Ltd v Elmfield Road Ltd*,[24] he said:

"Mr Dutton also argued that even if the language of the clause was apparently unambiguous, the commercial background and the commercial consequences of the literal interpretation showed that something had gone wrong with the language of the clause. The decision of the House of Lords in *Chartbrook Ltd v Persimmons Homes Ltd*[25] showed that in those circumstances the court could correct the mistake as a matter of interpretation. What is necessary to bring this principle into play is (a) that it should be clear that something has gone with the language and (b) that it is clear what a reasonable person would have understood the parties to have meant: *Chartbrook* at [22] and [25]. The first problem with this argument is that if anything has gone wrong with the rent review provisions, as Mr Dutton suggests, it is a failure to think through the consequences of what the parties agreed, rather than any deficiencies in drafting. A failure of that kind cannot be solved by the process of interpretation: *ING Bank NV v Ros Roca SA*[26]; *Scottish Widows Fund and Life Assurance Society v BGC International*[27]; *Honda Motor Europe Ltd v Powell*... ."[28]

Although the typical case is one where the clause in question is an obvious nonsense, the principle also extends to a case in which "the provision in question is inconsistent with some other provision which it is clear must have precedence".[29]

9.07   In *Homburg Houtimport BV v Agrosin Ltd (The Starsin)*,[30] Lord Bingham of Cornhill said:

"I take it to be clear in principle that the court should not interpolate words into a written instrument, of whatever nature, unless it is clear both that words have been omitted and what those omitted words were."

---

[20]   *Cathay Pacific Airways Ltd v Lufthansa Technik AG* [2020] EWHC 1789 (Ch); *Altera Voyageur Production Ltd v Premier Oil E&P UK Ltd* [2020] EWHC 1891 (Comm).
[21]   [2014] EWCA Civ 437.
[22]   *Scottish Widows Fund and Life Assurance Society v BGC International* [2012] EWCA Civ 607 at [21] (iii); *Cherry Tree Investments Ltd v Landmain Ltd* [2012] EWCA Civ 736; [2013] Ch. 305 at [131] and [144].
[23]   *JIS (1974) Ltd v MCP Investment Nominees I Ltd* [2003] EWCA Civ 721, per Carnwath LJ at [17], [18], [19] and [23].
[24]   [2018] EWCA Civ 1556; [2018] 1 P. & C.R. DG21.
[25]   [2009] UKHL 38; [2009] 1 A.C. 1101.
[26]   [2011] EWCA Civ 353; [2012] 1 W.L.R. 472, per Carnwath LJ at [24]; per Rix LJ at [80].
[27]   [2012] EWCA Civ 607; 142 Con. L.R. 27, per Arden LJ at [21].
[28]   [2014] EWCA Civ 437; [2014] Pens. L.R. 255, per Lewison LJ at [37].
[29]   *Scottish Widows Fund and Life Assurance Society v BGC International* [2012] EWCA Civ 607, per Arden LJ at [21].
[30]   [2004] 1 A.C. 715.

Lord Steyn said:

"As Lord Bingham has pointed out ... some words have been left out of clause 5. The deletion was plainly a mistake. In these circumstances the court should, in order to give effect to the reasonable expectations of the parties, fill the gap by inserting what had been omitted. What falls to be construed is the clause so reconstructed."

Lord Millett said:

"The clause does not make grammatical sense as it stands, and it is obvious that words have been omitted. The court must, therefore, supply the omission by implying at least the minimum necessary for the clause to make grammatical sense. This is what all the judges below did. But the authorities show that in a proper case the court will go further. Where it can see, not only that words have been omitted, but what those words are, then it is its duty to supply them. It is not necessary that the court should be certain precisely what words have been omitted; it is sufficient that it knows their gist.[31] The process is one of construction, not rectification; this is evident from the fact that the Court of Chancery not infrequently supplied omissions in wills at a time when it had no jurisdiction to rectify them."

In that case the words of a clause in a bill of lading had been modelled on a form in common use, but some of the words in that form had been omitted.[32] The House of Lords held that the words in the precedent should be interpolated into the bill of lading. Thus the extrinsic evidence of the precedent was critical to the process of identifying the omitted words.

It does not matter in principle that a draft agreement was tailor-made, rather than "off-the-peg", as in *The Starsin*. What matters is the help it can give in practice, as a matter of common sense rather than law, as to the nature of the mistake and how it should be corrected. Second, it does not matter that details have been changed in other parts of the draft. Third, it is sufficient that the court is satisfied about the gist of the correction that should be made.[33] In *KPMG LLP v Network Rail Infrastructure Ltd*,[34] Carnwath LJ said: **9.08**

"Once the court has identified an obvious omission, and has found in admissible background materials an obvious precedent for filling it, it should not be fatal that there may be more than one possible version of the replacement, or more than one explanation of the change."

In *The Prudential Assurance Co Ltd v Ayres*,[35] the Court of Appeal was satisfied that "something had gone wrong with the language" of a deed of guarantee and interpreted it in a way that did violence to its language but reflected what the par- **9.09**

---

[31] Applied in *Clydesdale Bank Plc v Weston Property Co Ltd* [2011] EWHC 1251 (Ch).
[32] The copying error in that case is technically known as homeoteleuton. The reader, like the author, may need to consult a dictionary.
[33] *KPMG LLP v Network Rail Infrastructure Ltd* [2007] Bus. L.R. 1336; *Company Developments (Finance) Ltd v Coffee Club Restaurants Ltd* [2011] EWCA Civ 766.
[34] [2007] Bus. L.R. 1336.
[35] [2008] 1 E.G.L.R. 5.

ties must have intended. In *ICM Computer Group Ltd v Stribley*,[36] the court was satisfied that something had gone wrong with the language of an amendment to a pension scheme and in effect added a clause to the written document. In *R & S Pilling (t/a Phoenix Engineering) v UK Insurance Ltd*,[37] a motor insurance policy certified that it met the statutory requirements of the Road Traffic Act 1988. On a literal interpretation of the scope of the cover, it did not. The Supreme Court applied a corrective interpretation, inserting words into the description of the cover, so as to make it conform to the statutory requirements. In *Re BCA Pension Plan*,[38] Snowden J corrected an obvious mistake in the rules of a pension scheme where both the mistake and the corrective interpretation needed to remedy it were obvious. In *Exmek Pharmaceuticals SAC v Alkem Laboratories Ltd*,[39] Burton J interpreted an arbitration clause which referred to the "law of the UK" as meaning the law of England and Wales. Likewise, in *LBG Capital No.1 Plc v BNY Mellon Corporate Trustee Services Ltd*,[40] the Court of Appeal corrected an obvious mistake in a tradable financial instrument. The Supreme Court upheld this decision[41] although Lord Neuberger doubted whether it was really a departure from the express words of the instrument.

9.10   However, where there is no doubt about the natural meaning of the contract and that meaning does not produce an arbitrary or irrational result, the fact that the contract seems unduly favourable to one party is not enough.[42] Nor it is enough that the parties have mistakenly failed to provide for a particular circumstance.[43] As Lord Neuberger of Abbotsbury MR put it in *Pink Floyd Music Ltd v EMI Records Ltd*[44]:

> "One is normally looking for an outcome which is 'arbitrary' or 'irrational', before a mistake argument will run."

9.11   Where the parties' mistake was not a mistake in expression, but a falsification of the expected timetable for a transaction, there was no error capable of correction by construction. Nothing had gone wrong with "the language"; what had gone wrong was a failure to anticipate the consequences of the language. The contract would have worked perfectly well if it had gone ahead in accordance with the originally expected timetable.[45]

9.12   The distinction between the correction of errors by interpretation and the equitable remedy of rectification[46] was pointed out in *North Circular Properties Ltd*

---

36   [2013] EWHC 2995 (Ch).
37   [2019] UKSC 16; [2019] 2 W.L.R. 1015.
38   [2015] EWHC 3492 (Ch); [2016] 4 W.L.R. 5.
39   [2015] EWHC 3158 (Comm); [2016] 1 Lloyd's Rep. 239.
40   [2015] EWCA Civ 1257; [2016] 2 All E.R. (Comm) 851.
41   [2016] UKSC 29; [2016] 2 Lloyd's Rep. 119.
42   *Bishops Wholesale Newsagency Ltd v Surridge Dawson Ltd* [2010] 2 B.C.L.C. 546; *Bashir v Ali* [2011] EWCA Civ 707; *LB Re Financing No.3 Ltd v Excalibur Funding No.1 Plc* [2011] EWHC 2111 (Ch).
43   *Scottish Widows Fund and Life Assurance Society v BGC International* [2012] EWCA Civ 607, per Arden LJ at [22].
44   [2010] EWCA Civ 1429. The stringency of the test is illustrated by *Campbell v Daejan Properties Ltd* [2012] EWCA Civ 1503; [2013] 1 E.G.L.R. 34.
45   *ING Bank NV v Ros Roca SA* [2011] EWCA Civ 353.
46   Described by Lord Hoffmann as a safety valve in *Chartbrook Ltd v Persimmon Homes Ltd* [2009] 1 A.C. 1101.

v Internal Systems Organisation Ltd.[47] The deputy judge said:

"Of course the court will not lightly, as part of the construction process, tamper with the actual words used, particularly in a commercial document such as a lease. On the other hand the law is not such an ass as to compel the court to hold the parties to the actual words used when it is, as in my judgment it is in this case, clear from the document itself, without looking at extrinsic evidence, that such words were used only by virtue of a draftsman's blunder. Such a process of correction of obvious drafting errors in the process of construction is of course distinct from the equitable doctrine of rectification. The former can only be adopted where the fact that a mistake has been made and the nature of the mistake can be ascertained with certainty from a consideration of the relevant instrument in the context of objective circumstances surrounding its execution. Rectification, on the other hand, will be appropriate in many other cases where the existence and nature of a mistake are apparent only from extrinsic evidence of the actual intention of the parties."

In *WW Gear Construction Ltd v McGee Group Ltd*,[48] Akenhead J said:

"Whilst the court does not readily accept that contractual parties have made a mistake in their written contracts, once it is clear that something has gone wrong with the language, the court will seek as a matter of construction and interpretation to determine what the parties really meant; in doing so, as with all contractual construction exercises, the court can as necessary have regard to the background to and context of the contract in question. If it is simply not possible to determine what was mutually intended from the wording, the background and the context, it may well be the case that the court has to say that the parties have produced a meaningless term or contract as the case may be. The construction exercise however is to be distinguished from the circumstances which give rise to a claim for rectification."

One difference between the correction of errors by interpretation and the **9.13** equitable remedy of rectification is that in the latter case (but not in the former) the court may have regard and give appropriate weight to the parties' pre-contractual negotiations.[49] Nevertheless, the principles of interpretation to correct a mistake and the equitable remedy of rectification are closely related.[50]

The assertion by the court of a power to correct errors is a reflection of the canon **9.14**

---

[47] Unreported 26 October 1984 (Ch. D.). Donald Rattee QC (sitting as a deputy judge). Sir Richard Buxton argued for the conclusion that the difference between rectification and construction has reduced almost to vanishing point in the light of the decision of the House of Lords in *Chartbrook Ltd v Persimmon Homes Ltd* [2009] 1 A.C. 1101: see [2010] C.L.J. 253. That argument was, in the author's opinion, largely attributable to the decision that whether a contract can be rectified is to be judged on the basis of an objectively manifested consensus which differs from the ultimate contract. It had previously been thought that evidence of the parties' subjective intention (as well as their negotiations) was admissible in an action for rectification. This part of the decision was highly controversial; and was significantly qualified by the Court of Appeal in *FSHC Group Holdings Ltd v GLAS Trust Corporation Ltd* [2019] EWCA Civ 1361. In addition, the remedy of rectification remains the appropriate remedy where the parties assert that a whole clause has been mistakenly omitted from the final agreement: *Cherry Tree Investments Ltd v Landmain Ltd* [2012] EWCA Civ 736; [2013] Ch. 305.

[48] [2010] EWHC 1460 (TCC) (correction of wrong cross-reference in the contract).

[49] *Pink Floyd Music Ltd v EMI Records Ltd* [2010] EWCA Civ 1429.

[50] *Oceanbulk Shipping & Trading SA v TMT Asia Ltd* [2010] UKSC 44.

of construction by which the court seeks to save a document rather than allow the intention of the parties to miscarry. This appears from the speech of Lord Brougham LC in *Langston v Langston*.[51] So also in *The Tropwind*,[52] Lord Denning MR said:

"We have on a few occasions rejected a sentence as meaningless. ... But this is only when it is impossible to make sense of it. Rather than find it meaningless, we should strive to find out what was really intended—by amending the punctuation, or by supplying words and so forth."

9.15   Although it is common to speak of the court supplying or striking out words this may not be strictly accurate. In *Re Sassoon*,[53] Romer LJ said:

"Now our attention was drawn during the argument to several cases, and many others are to be found in the books, where the court has departed, and in some cases departed widely, from the literal meaning of words contained in wills and settlements. Such cases are sometimes referred to as cases in which the court has 'supplied' or 'struck out' words. This is, perhaps, a convenient way of referring to them, but it is in strictness an entirely inaccurate way. Except in actions for rectification the court has no power whatsoever of adding to or subtracting from the words of a written instrument. A testator or a settlor may, however, in the instrument itself indicate sufficiently plainly that he is using certain words or phrases in other than their literal and ordinary meaning. In such cases he is said to have provided his own dictionary, and the court will construe such words and phrases in the light of that dictionary."

While this is undoubtedly true of many if not most cases, there are nevertheless cases in which the court has supplied whole phrases. It would be difficult to categorise such cases as cases where the court was doing no more than interpreting words in the instrument by reference to an idiosyncratic dictionary. Equally there are cases in which the court has construed a contract by striking out words where it is satisfied that they were included by clerical error.[54] There is even one case where the court appears to have supplied a whole clause which had been mistakenly omitted.[55]

9.16   In *Mannai Investment Co Ltd v Eagle Star Life Assurance Co Ltd*,[56] Lord Hoffmann gave a different explanation. He said:

"It is a matter of constant experience that people can convey their meaning unambiguously although they have used the wrong words. We start with an assumption that people will use words and grammar in a conventional way but quite often it becomes obvious that, for one reason or another, they are not doing so and we adjust our interpretation of what they are saying accordingly. We do so in order to make sense of their utterance: so that the different parts of the sentence fit together in a coherent way and also to enable the sentence to fit the background of facts which plays an indispensable part of the way we interpret what anyone is saying."

[51]   (1834) 2 Cl. & Fin. 194 (a will case).
[52]   [1982] 1 Lloyd's Rep. 232.
[53]   [1933] Ch. 858.
[54]   *Holding & Barnes Plc v Hill House Hammond Ltd* [2002] L. & T.R. 7 CA.
[55]   *ICM Computer Group Ltd v Stribley* [2013] EWHC 2995 (Ch). If correct, this case must be at the very limits of the principle.
[56]   [1997] A.C. 749 HL.

It is, he said, important to:

"distinguish between the meaning of words and the question of what would be understood as the meaning of a person who uses words. The meaning of words, as they would appear in a dictionary, and the effect of their syntactical arrangement, as it would appear in a grammar, is part of the material which we use to understand a speaker's utterance. But it is only a part; another part is our knowledge of the background against which the utterance was made. It is that background which enables us, not only to choose the intended meaning when a word has more than one dictionary meaning, but also, in the way I have explained, to understand a speaker's meaning, often without ambiguity, when he has used the wrong words."

This principle enables the court to take background facts into account in deciding whether a mistake has been made and, if so, what it is.[57] The application of this principle, although it has been called "common law rectification", is simply part of the overall process of interpreting a contract.[58]

However, where the document in question is a contract that is to be registered **9.17** in a register capable of inspection by the public, the court's power to intervene by interpretation rather than by rectification is more limited.[59]

2.   THE NATURE OF THE MISTAKE

The mistake to be corrected must be a mistake in expression. It may be a mistake in spelling or grammar; a mistake in the naming of persons referred to; the omission of words or the inclusion of words; or the use of the wrong words.

Many of the early cases involving the correction of errors by construction arose **9.18** out of the misuse of Latin in which legal documents were frequently written. "It is a rule of law, *mala grammatica non vitiat chartam*, neither false Latin nor false English will make a deed void when the intent of the parties doth plainly appear. It is therefore held that two negatives do not make an affirmative when the apparent intent is contrary. And it is another rule of law *falsa orthographia non vitiat concessionem*."[60]

However, the power of the court to correct errors goes beyond the mere correction **9.19** of spelling or grammar. In *Chipsaway International Ltd v Kerr*,[61] the Court of Appeal held that where it is clear that something has gone wrong with the language, such that the clause must be rewritten, the rewriting that is required is that which involves the minimum changes necessary to achieve a sensible meaning and which gives effect to the commercial purpose of the clause. In the author's opinion, this is too restrictive a description of the court's power. In *Chartbrook Ltd v Persim-*

---

[57] *Holding & Barnes Plc v Hill House Hammond Ltd* [2002] L. & T.R. 7 CA; *Homburg Hountimport BV v Agrosin Ltd* [2004] 1 A.C. 715.

[58] *KPMG LLP v Network Rail Infrastructure Ltd* [2007] EWCA Civ 363.

[59] See para.3.175 and especially *Cherry Tree Investments Ltd v Landmain Ltd* [2012] EWCA Civ 736; [2013] Ch. 305.

[60] *Sheppard's Touchstone*, 8th edn (1826), p.87. Examples of such cases are collected in *Norton on Deeds*, 2nd edn (1928), pp.103–104.

[61] [2009] EWCA Civ 320.

mon Homes Ltd,[62] Lord Hoffmann said that:

"there is not, so to speak, a limit to the amount of red ink or verbal rearrangement or correction which the court is allowed. All that is required is that it should be clear that something has gone wrong with the language and that it should be clear what a reasonable person would have understood the parties to have meant."[63]

Thus in *LB Re Financing No.3 Ltd v Excalibur Funding No.1 Plc*,[64] Briggs J said:

"Where something has gone wrong with the language, it is not in my judgment necessarily an objection to dealing with it in a way that avoids commercial absurdity that provisions have, apparently, to be rewritten, blue pencilled, or amplified so as to work rationally in particular circumstances."

Upon this principle the court may correct a mistaken reference to a party or a misnomer.[65]

9.20   In *Wilson v Wilson*,[66] a deed of separation between John Wilson and Mary Wilson contained a provision which apparently obliged the trustees of Mary Wilson to indemnify John Wilson against "the present debts and liabilities of the said John". The House of Lords held that the deed should be construed as if "Mary" had been substituted for "John" in that clause.

Similarly, in *Nittan (UK) Ltd v Solent Steel Fabrications Ltd*,[67] a company traded under the name of "Sargrove Automation". The contract named one of the parties as "Sargrove Electronic Controls Ltd", which was a real, but dormant company. The Court of Appeal read the name stated in the contract as the trading name of the company, holding that it was a case of mere misnomer.

9.21   The court may supply words erroneously omitted, particularly where the omitted words are part of a common form of wording. Thus in *Re Daniel's Settlement Trusts*,[68] a post-nuptial settlement declared trusts for every child or children of the marriage who being a son shall attain the age of 21 years in equal shares, and if there should be only one such child the whole to be in trust for such child, his or her executors. Assisted by the reference to "her", the Court of Appeal held that the trusts applied to daughters who had attained the age of 21.

Similarly, in *Re Hargraves' Trusts*,[69] a deed of trust declared trusts for such of the settlor's grandchildren "as being male shall have attained the age of 21 years or being female shall have married under that age". Farwell J held that daughters who attained the age of 21 without having married were entitled to benefit from the trusts. He said:

"When one reads this settlement as a whole, it is absolutely impossible, in my judgment, to come to any conclusion other than that there has been left out of what is a perfectly well recognised and settled form the words 'shall have at-

[62] [2009] 1 A.C. 1101.
[63] Applied in *Scottish Widows Fund and Life Assurance Society v BGC International* [2011] EWHC 729 (Ch).
[64] [2011] EWHC 2111 (Ch).
[65] See para.10.22.
[66] (1854) 5 H.L. Cas. 40.
[67] [1981] 1 Lloyd's Rep. 633.
[68] (1875) 1 Ch. D. 375.
[69] [1937] 2 All E.R. 545.

tained that age'. These words have no doubt been left out by some person who had to copy the form. … When the meaning is plainly written, throughout the document, from beginning to end, and I find a mistake made in copying a common form, which may operate to defeat the object for which the settlement was made, I am justified in construing the settlement in the way it was intended to be read."

The court may also supply the name of a grantor where the identity of the grantor appears from other parts of the deed. In *Lord Say and Seal's Case*,[70] Lord Say and Seal was intended to be the grantor. But the granting part of the deed did not say who was the grantor. The court supplied the name. **9.22**

The power of correction also extends to substituting antonyms. In *Bache v Proctor*,[71] Buller J referred to a case in the Common Pleas in which a bond was conditioned to be void if the obligor did not pay. The word "not" was rejected. In *Slough Estates Ltd v Slough Borough Council (No.2)*,[72] an applicant for planning permission had submitted a plan showing the land on which he wished to develop coloured in various colours. The planning permission granted permission to develop the land shown uncoloured on the plan. The Court of Appeal, reversing the trial judge, read the word "uncoloured" as meaning "coloured". However, it has been doubted whether as a matter of construction the court can construe a grant directly contrary to its express terms.[73] But it seems likely that the court will continue to assert such a power. **9.23**

So, for example, in *Fitzgerald v Masters*,[74] cl.8 of a contract for the sale of land provided:

"The usual conditions of sale … shall so far as they are inconsistent herewith be deemed to be embodied herein."

The High Court of Australia construed "inconsistent" as "consistent".
Dixon CJ and Fullagar J said in their joint judgment:

"There is a superficial difficulty in Cl. 8 because it purports to incorporate a set of conditions so far as they are inconsistent with what has been specifically agreed upon. No real difficulty, however, is created. Words may generally be supplied omitted or corrected, in an instrument, where it is clearly necessary in order to avoid absurdity or inconsistency. Here it would be indeed absurd to suppose that the parties having expressed their agreement on a number of special and essential matters, should intend to incorporate by reference a set of general conditions except so far as they were inconsistent with what they had specially agreed upon, and Cl. 8 must be read as if it said 'consistent' or 'not inconsistent'."

The court may also strike out words where it is satisfied that they have been included as a result of clerical error. In *Holding & Barnes Plc v Hill House Hammond Ltd (No.1)*,[75] seven leases were granted as part of the terms of sale of a business. The parties to all seven leases were the same. One of the leases contained **9.24**

---

70 (1711) 10 Mod. Rep. 40.
71 (1780) Doug. K.B. 382.
72 [1969] 2 Ch. 305.
73 See *Mill v Hill* (1852) 3 H.L. Cas. 828 at 851.
74 (1956) 95 C.L.R. 420.
75 [2002] L. & T.R. 7.

an apparently self-contradictory repairing obligation. The Court of Appeal held that when that lease was compared with the other six, it was obvious that words had been included by mistake. The obligation was construed as if the erroneously included words had been struck out.

9.25   The court may also correct errors in contractual machinery. In *North Circular Properties Ltd v Internal Systems Organisation Ltd*,[76] a lease provided for the increases of rent to become payable at the end of the sixth, eleventh, sixteenth and twenty-first years of the term. However, the review dates were later defined as meaning the fifth, tenth, fifteenth and twentieth years of the term. It was held that this was an obvious mistake, and the definition of the review dates was corrected to bring it into harmony with the dates from which the increases were to be payable. In *Monsolar IQ Ltd v Woden Park Ltd*,[77] a lease contained a rent review clause which operated by reference to the retail price index. Read literally its effect was to compound inflation year by year, rather than reflecting what the index was intended to achieve. That produced illogical and arbitrary results, which conflicted with the stated purpose of the rent review clause; and would result in an unafford-able rent. The court corrected the formula as a matter of interpretation.

Illustrations

1.   The obligatory part of a bond provided that the obligor was to become bound for 7,700. No species of money was mentioned. The court supplied the word "pounds".

Coles v Hulme[78]

2.   An arbitration agreement required the arbitrator to publish his award "on or before the 30th day of December next, or such further or ulterior date as the said [arbitrator] by a memorandum in writing under his hand to be indorsed hereon, what (if anything) is due". The missing verb was supplied by the court. Alderson B said:

"No one can doubt that the words 'shall appoint' have been left out."

Kirk v Unwin[79]

3.   A father appointed £5,000 to his daughter. By a later deed reciting the appointment he appointed another fund to her "upon the trusts and subject to the same provisions as are hereinbefore declared of and concerning the said sum of £5,000 hereinbefore appointed unto and for the benefit of" the daughter. It was held that the words "hereinbefore declared" should be construed as "hereinbefore recited to have been declared".

Hanbury v Tyrell[80]

---

[76]   Unreported 26 October 1984 (Ch. D.).
[77]   [2020] EWHC 1407 (Ch).
[78]   (1828) 8 B. & C. 568.
[79]   (1851) 6 Exch. 908.
[80]   (1856) 21 Beav. 322.

4.   A bill of sale to secure a loan of £70 and interest stipulated that principal and interest should be repaid by monthly instalments of "seven". The word "pounds" was supplied.
Mourmand v Le Clair[81]

5.   A conveyance was expressed to convey land coloured blue on a plan attached to the conveyance. The plan showed some land coloured blue and some coloured red. The court treated the conveyance as conveying the land coloured blue and red, and not merely the land coloured blue.
St Edmundsbury and Ipswich Diocesan Board of Finance v Clark (No.2)[82]

6.   A rent review clause provided that the rent was to be "such sum as shall be agreed between the parties before the expiration of 3 months after the date of posting of such notice as aforesaid in substitution for the said sum". No sum had been previously mentioned. The court inserted the words "specified in such notice or" at the beginning of the clause.
Wolverhampton and Dudley Breweries Plc v Trusthouse Forte Catering Ltd[83]

7.   A lease referred to such rent as may be fixed by an arbitrator nominated in accordance with the provisions of cl.3.04(b). The clause dealing with the appointment of arbitrators was cl.3.05(b). The court corrected the reference to the wrong clause.
Booker Industries Pty Ltd v Wilson Parking (QLD) Pty Ltd[84]

8.   A lease contained a clause that stated that "at all times during the term or at the expiration of the said term the lessee may offer to purchase the demised land from the lessor at a consideration equivalent to one thousand dollars ($1,000) per acre". The Privy Council held that the clause should be interpreted as giving the lessee an option to purchase, since a mere right to offer to purchase would be worthless.
Watson v Phipps[85]

9.   A deed of variation of a will was executed in order to reduce the incidence of inheritance tax. It varied the will by increasing the part of the estate which passed to the testator's widow. Clause 7 then provided that income of and from assets the subject of the deed should devolve as if the deed had not been executed. It was held that there was an obvious mistake, and that the income referred to was restricted to income arising prior to the date of the deed.
Schneider v Mills[86]

10.   A lease contained a break clause in the following terms:

"Either party shall be entitled by giving not less than six months' notice in writing to the other to terminate this lease at the end of the third year of the Term ('Termination Date') and provided that up to the Termination Date in the case of

[81]   [1903] 2 K.B. 216.
[82]   [1973] 1 W.L.R. 1572.
[83]   [1984] 2 E.G.L.R. 141.
[84]   (1982) 149 C.L.R. 600.
[85]   (1986) 60 A.J.L.R. 1.
[86]   [1993] 3 All E.R. 377.

a notice *given by the Landlord* the Tenant shall have paid the rents hereby reserved and shall have duly observed and performed the covenants on the part of the Tenant and the conditions herein contained this lease shall absolutely cease and determine on the Termination Date but without prejudice to any right or remedy of either party in respect of any antecedent breach by the other of the provisions of this lease."

The word "Landlord" was read as "Tenant", even though the effect of correcting the error was that the tenant had accepted an onerous condition, namely precise compliance with covenants.
Littman v Aspen Oil (Broking) Ltd[87]

11.   A contract defined the Termination Date as "the termination of the Mandate Letter pursuant to the terms thereof and which of such termination is provided in writing by the Variable Funding Noteholder or the Interim Servicer, as the case may be, to the Variable Funding Noteholder or the Interim Servicer, as the case may be". The word "which" was read as "notice" in order to make sense of the clause.
Royal Bank of Scotland Plc v Highland Financial Partners LLP[88]

12.   In a non-invalidation clause in an insurance policy "validated" was read as "invalidated".
Seashell of Lisson Grove Ltd v Aviva Insurance Ltd[89]

13.   A charterparty contained a clause that stated that it was to be governed by English law and that disputes should be resolved by the English courts. A bill of lading stated that all the terms of the charterparty "including the Law and Arbitration clause" were incorporated. It was held that since the charterparty contained no arbitration clause, but did contain a law and jurisdiction clause, the words of incorporation were sufficient to incorporate that clause. It was a case in which the reasonable reader would have understood that something had gone wrong with the language.
Caresse Navigation Ltd v Office National De L'electricite[90]

3.   MISTAKES IN EFFECT

The court will not by the process of interpretation correct a mistake about the legal effect of a written contract. However, such a mistake may be corrected by rectification where the mistake consists of a failure to appreciate what the words mean.

9.26   Where the mistake is not a mistake in expression, but a mistake as to the legal effect of a document, the court cannot correct the mistake by the process of interpretation. This is so even where the parties have themselves acted on a

---

[87]   [2006] 2 P. & C.R. 2.
[88]   [2010] EWCA Civ 809.
[89]   [2011] EWHC 1761 (Comm); [2012] 1 All E.R. (Comm) 754.
[90]   [2014] EWCA Civ 1366; [2015] 2 W.L.R. 43.

misinterpretation of the instrument. Thus in *North Eastern Railway v Lord Hastings*,[91] Lord Halsbury LC said:

"The words of a written instrument must be construed according to their natural meaning and it appears to me that no amount of acting by the parties can alter or qualify words which are plain and unambiguous."

Likewise, in *ING Bank NV v Ros Roca SA*,[92] what had gone wrong was not the language of the contract, but the fact that it had not gone ahead in accordance with the expected timetable. The words of the contract would have worked if the original timetable had been met. Accordingly, it could not be said that anything had gone wrong with the language of the contract. As Rix LJ put it: **9.27**

"these are errors of negotiation or commercial intuition, not errors of language in the expression of an agreement."

In *Honda Motor Europe Ltd v Powell*,[93] what had gone wrong was that pension trustees had overlooked the need to exercise a power to amend the rules of the scheme. Lewison LJ said:

"In my judgment it is still necessary in order to invoke this principle that something should have gone wrong with the language, as opposed to the implementation of the bargain, or the relevant decision to exercise powers."

Such circumstances might, however, give rise to an estoppel by convention or some other equitable remedy.[94] Thus in *Re Ethel and Mitchells and Butlers' Contract*,[95] a reconveyance to a mortgagor on payment of the mortgage was expressed to be conveyed to the mortgagor to hold "in fee". The effect of using that expression (rather than "in fee simple") was to transfer a life interest only, and to leave the legal estate outstanding in the mortgagee. Joyce J reluctantly held that he could not supply the word "simple" as a matter of construction. He said: **9.28**

"There cannot be any doubt about the intention of the parties with respect to the effect of the reconveyance in question, but it does not appear to me that I can come to the conclusion that the word 'simple' was intended to have been inserted, but has been omitted in the copying or by some similar accident, even if that would suffice. I cannot find that the parties when they executed the reconveyance did not really know and intend the deed to be drawn and to stand in the precise terms in which it is now found to be, although there cannot be the slightest doubt as to what they intended to be its operation and effect."

The same principle applies where the mistake relates to the factual application **9.29**

---

91 [1900] A.C. 260.
92 [2011] EWCA Civ 353.
93 [2014] EWCA Civ 437.
94 *Amalgamated Investment & Property Co Ltd v Texas Commerce International Bank Ltd* [1982] Q.B. 84. In *ING Bank NV v Ros Roca SA* [2011] EWCA Civ 353, the parties' mistake was corrected by this means.
95 [1901] 1 Ch. 945. It seems unlikely that, in view of the judge's findings, this case would be decided in the same way today.

of the contract. Thus in *Bodfield Ltd v Caldew Colour Plates Ltd*,[96] a rent review clause provided that the gross rental value of the property should be "the aggregate amount of rents actually paid or received by the lessee" subject to a proviso that the open market value should be substituted for any parts of the property "vacant or unoccupied by the lessee". The effect of the clause was that while the tenant remained in occupation of the whole of the property, the rent could not be increased. Walton J rejected the landlord's argument that the word "unoccupied" was an obvious mistake for "occupied". Similarly, where the terms of a break clause in a lease were not "obvious nonsense" on their face, but made the clause difficult to operate, the court could not correct the alleged error as a matter of construction.[97]

9.30   Where it is proved by extrinsic evidence that even deliberately chosen words do not carry into effect the intention of the parties the court may rectify the instrument to give effect to the real intention of the parties.[98] In *Re Butlin's Settlement Trusts*,[99] Brightman J said:

> "Furthermore, rectification is available not only in a case where particular words have been added, omitted or wrongly written as a result of careless copying or the like. It is also available where the words of the document were purposely used but it was mistakenly considered that they bore a different meaning from their correct meaning as a matter of true construction."

4.   THE QUALITY OF THE MISTAKE

A mistake will not be corrected by the court unless the court is sure both that a mistake has been made, and also what is required in order to give effect to the intention of the parties.[100]

9.31   The modern approach of the court was summarised in *East v Pantiles (Plant Hire) Ltd*,[101] by Brightman LJ as follows:

> "In *Snell's Principles of Equity*[102] the principle of rectification by construction is said to apply only to obvious clerical blunders or grammatical mistakes. I agree with that approach. Perhaps it might be summarised by saying that the principle applies where a reader with sufficient experience of the sort of document in issue would inevitably say to himself 'Of course X is a mistake for Y'."

---

[96]   [1985] 1 E.T.L.R. 110.

[97]   *JIS (1974) Ltd v MCE Investment Nominees I Ltd* [2003] EWCA Civ 721.

[98]   However, Sir Richard Buxton has made a powerful case for the conclusion that the difference between rectification and construction has reduced almost to vanishing point in the light of the decision of the House of Lords in *Chartbrook Ltd v Persimmon Homes Ltd* [2009] 1 A.C. 1101: see [2010] C.L.J. 253. This is, in the author's opinion, largely attributable to the decision that whether a contract can be rectified is to be judged on the basis of an objectively manifested consensus which differs from the ultimate contract. It had previously been thought that evidence of the parties' subjective intention (as well as their negotiations) was admissible in an action for rectification. This part of the decision remains highly controversial.

[99]   [1976] Ch. 251. This statement was approved by the Court of Appeal in *Co-operative Insurance Society Ltd v Centremoor Ltd* [1983] 2 E.G.L.R. 52; and by the HL in *Chartbrook Ltd v Persimmon Homes Ltd* [2009] 1 A.C. 1101.

[100] This section was referred to with apparent approval by the New South Wales Court of Appeal in *Kimberley Securities Ltd v Esber* [2008] NSWCA 301.

[101] [1982] 2 E.G.L.R. 111 applied in *Holding & Barnes Plc v Hill House Hammond Ltd* [2002] L & T.R. 103, per Sir Martin Nourse.

[102] 27th edn (1973), p.611.

What is required is both that it should be clear that something has gone wrong **9.32** with the language and also that it should be clear what a reasonable person would have understood the parties to have meant.[103] Both conditions must be satisfied.[104] Thus in *PEC Ltd v Thai Maparn Trading Co Ltd*,[105] Hamblen J confirmed that:

"The authorities make it plain that it must be clear not only that something has gone wrong with the language but also that what the language should be."

In *Coles v Hulme*,[106] Lord Tenterden CJ said:

"In every deed there must be such a degree of moral certainty as to leave in the mind of a reasonable person no doubt of the intent of the parties."

Similarly, in *Re Whitrick, deed*,[107] Jenkins LJ said:

"The reading of words into a will as a matter of necessary implication is a measure which any court of construction should apply with the greatest caution. Many wills contain slips and omissions which fail to provide for contingencies which, to anyone reading the will, might appear contingencies for which any testator would obviously wish to provide. The court cannot rewrite the testamentary provisions in wills which come before it for construction. This type of treatment of an imperfect will is only legitimate where the court can collect from the four corners of the document that something has been omitted and, further, collect with sufficient precision the nature of the omission."

And in *North Circular Properties Ltd v Internal Systems Organisation Ltd*,[108] the **9.33** deputy judge said that the correction of an error by construction could only be done:

"Where the fact that a mistake has been made and the nature of the mistake can be ascertained with certainty from a consideration of the relevant instrument in the context of objective circumstances surrounding its execution."

In *Homburg Houtimport BV v Agrosin Ltd (The Starsin)*,[109] Lord Bingham of Cornhill said:

"I take it to be clear in principle that the court should not interpolate words into a written instrument, of whatever nature, unless it is clear both that words have been omitted and what those omitted words were."

The court will not usually assume that an error has been made unless the clause **9.34** taken literally is absurd or repugnant to the remainder of the contract read as a whole. In *Wilson v Wilson*,[110] Lord Cranworth LC said:

"... I think that that is the necessary inference, or, if not, the whole thing is

---

[103] *Chartbrook Ltd v Persimmon Homes Ltd* [2009] 1 A.C. 1101.
[104] *ING Bank NV v Ros Roca SA* [2011] EWCA Civ 353; *Deutsche Trustee Co Ltd v Fleet Street Finance Three Plc* [2011] EWHC 2117 (Ch).
[105] [2012] 1 Lloyd's Rep. 295.
[106] (1828) 8 B. & C. 569.
[107] [1957] 1 W.L.R. 884 (a will case).
[108] Unreported 26 October 1984 (ChD).
[109] [2004] 1 A.C. 715. See further para.9.07.
[110] (1854) 5 H.L. Cas. 40 (where "John" was read as "Mary": see para.9.20).

insensible and irrational, and, consequently the articles cannot be carried into effect at all."

So too in *Fitzgerald v Masters*,[111] the High Court of Australia held that words could be supplied, omitted or corrected:

"where it is clearly necessary to avoid absurdity or inconsistency."

9.35   In *JIS (1974) Ltd v MCE Investment Nominees I Ltd*,[112] the court declined to correct an alleged mistake in a break clause in a lease. One reason was that the clause was not "obvious nonsense" on its face, although it was difficult to operate. As Lord Neuberger of Abbotsbury MR put it in *Pink Floyd Music Ltd v EMI Records Ltd*[113]:

"One is normally looking for an outcome which is 'arbitrary' or 'irrational', before a mistake argument will run."[114]

9.36   Where the court concludes that the draftsman may have made a mistake but that it is not clear that a mistake has been made, this principle of interpretation does not permit the court to intervene.[115]

9.37   Equally, where it is clear that a mistake of some kind has been made, but the court cannot ascertain the real intention of the parties with certainty, it must give effect to the instrument as it stands, unless the remedy of rectification is available.[116]. Accordingly, if it is not clear what correction should be made, the court cannot intervene.[117] In *G&S Brough Ltd v Salvage Wharf Ltd*,[118] Jackson LJ expressed the principle as follows:

"Where a written agreement as drafted is a nonsense and it is clear what the parties were trying to say the court will, as a matter of construction, give effect to the obvious intention of the parties."

As Lord Hodge explained in *Arnold v Britton*[119]:

"Even if, contrary to my view, one concluded that there was a clear mistake in the parties' use of language, it is not clear what correction ought to be made. The court must be satisfied as to both the mistake and the nature of the correction."

So, where there were three possible ways of correcting the alleged error, it could not be said that any one of them was clear.[120]

In *Doe d. Spencer v Godwin*,[121] a lease contained a proviso for re-entry upon breach of the tenant's covenants "hereinafter contained". There were no covenants

---

[111]   (1956) 95 C.L.R. 420.

[112]   [2003] EWCA Civ 721.

[113]   [2010] EWCA Civ 1429.

[114]   If the contract, as interpreted, is not absurd, it is unlikely that the court will interfere with its wording: *Bashir v Ali* [2011] EWCA Civ 707.

[115]   *Deutsche Trustee Co Ltd v Fleet Street Finance Three Plc* [2011] EWHC 2117 (Ch).

[116]   *Energy World Corp Ltd v Maurice Hayes and Associates Pty Ltd* (2007) 239 A.L.R. 457.

[117]   *Arnold v Britton* [2015] UKSC 36; [2016] A.C. 1619, per Lord Hodge.

[118]   [2009] EWCA Civ 21.

[119]   [2015] UKSC 36; [2015] A.C. 1619.

[120]   *Trillium (Prime) Property GP Ltd v Elmfield Road Ltd* [2018] EWCA Civ 1556; [2018] 1 P. & C.R. DG21; *Parker v Roberts* [2019] EWCA Civ 121; [2019] 1 P. & C.R. DG20.

[121]   (1815) 4 M. & S. 265.

after the proviso. Bayley J said:

"If we could clearly see the intention of the parties we ought to adopt that construction which would best give effect to that intention."

Although he said it was "plain" that a mistake had been made somewhere, it was not clear whether the mistake was in the omission of covenants after the proviso, or a mistake in the drafting of the proviso itself. The proviso was therefore given literal effect. It is unlikely that a modern court would have come to this answer. In *McKillen v Misland (Cyprus) Investments Ltd*,[122] one reason why the Court of Appeal rejected an attempt to correct an alleged error was that even if there had been an error it was not clear what provision should be substituted.

Nevertheless, it is not necessary to establish the precise form of words that would correct the mistake. It is sufficient if the court can ascertain the gist of the missing or wrongly included words.[123] If the court can do so, then it may insert the wrongly omitted words, even if the insertion goes further than is necessary merely to make grammatical sense of the contract.[124]   **9.38**

In practice, the most common reason for the court's refusal to correct an error as a matter of construction is a failure to demonstrate with the requisite degree of certainty not only that an error has been made, but also what the error was. Thus in *ING Bank NV v Ros Roca SA*,[125] the denominator in a formula referred to "EBITDA 2006".[126] It had been expected that the transaction would complete in 2006 at which point EBITDA 2006 would have been current EBITDA. However, the transaction was delayed. The result of applying the formula was to produce a result which was hard on one party. One objection to the principle of corrective interpretation was that the error was capable of being dealt in a number of different ways.   **9.39**

5.   FALSA DEMONSTRATIO

Where the words of description in a contract apply in part correctly and in part incorrectly to some subject matter, the incorrect part will be rejected, and the correct part read as if it stood alone.

One of the long-established principles of construction is enshrined in the Latin maxim *falsa demonstratio non nocet cum de corpore constat*.[127] In *Gesner Investments Ltd v Bombardier Inc*,[128] Rix LJ translated the principle as: **9.40**

"a plain misdescription did no harm."

It has been described as "a rule of good sense" and "a rational and useful canon

---

122 [2012] EWCA Civ 179.
123 *Homburg Hountimport BV v Agrosin Ltd* [2004] 1 A.C. 715, per Lord Millett; *KPMG LLP v Network Rail Infrastructure Ltd* [2007] EWCA Civ 363.
124 *Homburg Hountimport BV v Agrosin Ltd* [2004] 1 A.C. 715, per Lord Millett; *KPMG LLP v Network Rail Infrastructure Ltd* [2007] EWCA Civ 363.
125 [2011] EWCA Civ 353.
126 A common acronym meaning "earnings before interest, tax, depreciation and amortisation".
127 A false description does not vitiate when there is no doubt which person is meant.
128 [2011] EWCA Civ 1118. See also *Dry Bulk Handy Holding Inc v Fayette International Holdings Ltd* [2012] EWHC 2107 (Comm).

of construction".[129] It is analogous to a case in which one might conclude, from various details and circumstantial evidence that a witness was describing a particular motor car, even though his reading of the number plate was inaccurate.[130]

9.41   The application of the maxim is most frequent in the construction of parcels clauses in conveyances, but it may be applied equally to other kinds of documents.[131] Thus in *Adamastos Shipping Ltd v Anglo Saxon Shipping Ltd*,[132] a charterparty included a clause which stated "This bill of lading shall have effect subject to the carriage of goods by Sea Act of the United States ... 1936." The House of Lords held that the words "this bill of lading" should be read as "this charterparty". This has been described as "an elementary textbook example" of the application of the maxim.[133]

9.42   In *Kason Kek-Gardner Ltd v Process Components Ltd*[134] an agreement referred to a "registered trademark 46553 KEK". However, 46553 was not a registered trademark. There was a registered trademark "KEK" but it was number 2506657. Lewison LJ said:

> "This is a case in which there is nothing which is completely and accurately described as a registered trademark 46553 KEK. There is a trademark 46553 KEK, but it is not registered. On the other hand, there is a registered trademark KEK, but it has a different number. In those circumstances the court is entitled to apply the ancient principle *falsa demonstratio non nocet* ('a plain misdescription does no harm'). Either the number of the trademark mentioned in the PCL agreement must be rejected or the description of the trademark as 'registered' must be rejected; for the two cannot stand together. The trademark relating to KEK is one of a number of trademarks all described as registered; and in those circumstances the judge was entitled to place weight on that part of the description and to reject the number."

9.43   So too in *Finbow v Air Ministry*,[135] the Minister purported to approve certain categories of lettings of agricultural land. The approval, if effective, would have prevented the tenants from having security of tenure. The document containing the approval expressed the approval as having been given under the Agriculture Act 1947, although that Act had been replaced in slightly different terms by the Agricultural Holdings Act 1948. McNair J held the approval to be valid. He said:

> "To hold that the misdescription of his powers rendered the document a nullity, would, in my judgment, defeat the plain intention of the Minister to be deduced from the circumstances and the date of its execution. It is in my judgment, a plain case for the application of the maxim *falsa demonstratio non nocet* and the principle embodied in the maxim *magis res valeat quam pereat*. There is a total inconsistency and repugnancy between the Minister's manifest intention and the literal effect of the document, and in my judgment the former should prevail."

---

[129]   *Cowen v Truefitt Ltd* [1899] 2 Ch. 309, per Lindley MR and Sir F.H. Jeune.
[130]   An example given by Lord Hoffmann in *Synthon BV v SmithKline Beecham Plc* [2006] 1 All E.R. 685.
[131]   See *Yambou Development Co Ltd v Kauser* (2000) 59 W.I.R. 141, per Lord Millett.
[132]   [1959] A.C. 133.
[133]   *Miramar Maritime Corp v Holborn Trading Ltd* [1984] A.C. 676, per Lord Diplock.
[134]   [2017] EWCA Civ 2132; [2018] 2 All E.R. (Comm) 381.
[135]   [1963] 1 W.L.R. 697.

In *Morrell v Fisher*,[136] Alderson B summarised the rule thus: **9.44**

"The … rule means that if there be an adequate and sufficient description, with convenient certainty of what was meant to pass, a subsequent erroneous addition will not vitiate it. The characteristic of cases within the rule is, that the description so far as it is false, applies to no subject at all; and so far as it is true applies to one only."

To similar effect are the observations of Parke B in *Llewellyn v Earl of Jersey*[137]:

"Then the other rule of law applies, that as soon as there is an adequate and sufficient definition, with convenient certainty, of what is intended to pass by a deed, any subsequent erroneous addition will not vitiate it; according to the maxim *'falsa demonstratio non nocet'*."[138]

In *Carr v Thales Pension Trustees Ltd*[139] Nugee J summarised it thus:

"It is well established that once it is concluded that an instrument is intended to refer to a particular person or thing, an inaccurate description of that person or thing will not invalidate the reference, this principle being traditionally expressed in the Latin maxim *'falsa demonstratio non nocet cum de corpore constat'*, which can be translated as 'a misdescription does no harm'."

These summaries of the principle might lead to the conclusion that the first **9.45**
description prevails over "subsequent" descriptions. However, this is not so. In *Hardwick v Hardwick*,[140] Lord Selborne LC said:

"It is perfectly certain that if all the terms of description fit some particular property, you cannot enlarge them by extrinsic evidence so as to exclude anything which any part of those terms do not accurately fit. On the other hand, I apprehend that if the words of description when examined do not fit with accuracy, and if there must be some modification of some part of them in order to place a sensible construction on the will, then the whole thing must be looked at fairly in order to see what are the leading words of description, and what is the subordinate matter, and for this purpose extrinsic facts may be regarded."

These two sentences have been treated as embodying two principles of interpretation.[141]

The suggestion that the false description must follow the true one was specifi- **9.46**
cally argued and rejected in *Cowen v Truefitt Ltd*.[142] Lindley MR said:

"I must, however, protest against the way in which the doctrine was stated by the appellants' counsel—that the maxim *falsa demonstratio non nocet* only applies when there is some incorrect statement at the end of the sentence. That is whittling away the doctrine and making it ridiculous; it is a misapprehension."

---

[136] (1849) 4 Exch. 591; *Republic Bank Ltd v Lochan* [2015] UKPC 26.
[137] (1843) 11 M. & W. 183.
[138] The words *cum de corpore constat* should be added to do the maxim full justice: *Eastwood v Ashton* [1915] A.C. 900 at 914, per Lord Sumner.
[139] [2020] EWHC 949 (Ch).
[140] (1873) L.R. 16 Eq. 168 (a will case).
[141] *Re Bright-Smith* (1886) 31 Ch. D. 314.
[142] [1899] 2 Ch. 309; *Republic Bank Ltd v Lochan* [2015] UKPC 26.

Sir F.H. Jeune said:

"I agree that the doctrine is not to be cut down, as was suggested by the appellants' counsel, by saying that it is to be limited to cases where the false part of the description follows the true."

And Rigby LJ said:

"... I altogether reject the argument ... that in applying the doctrine of *falsa demonstratio* it is material in what part of the sentence the *falsa demonstratio* is found."

9.47   In order for the maxim to be applied, there must be an adequate and sufficient description of the subject in the absence of the rejected words. If the words sought to be rejected are themselves part of the essential description of the subject, the court cannot apply the maxim. So also if the description, taken as a whole does fit some subject without inaccuracy, the court cannot reject part of the description by the application of this principle.[143] In *Magee v Lavell*,[144] the plaintiff agreed to assign a tenancy of "the house and premises he now occupies, known by the sign of the 'White Hart' with stabling and garden". The assignee sought to reject the words "he now occupies". Coleridge CJ said:

"Now, considering the agreement in the first instance it seems to me that the words 'he now occupies' are operative words which cannot be rejected. It therefore follows that extrinsic evidence was necessarily admissible so far as to show what was in fact the subject matter to which the words were applicable. On looking to such evidence, it is clear that there was a perfectly sufficient subject matter to which they applied as a description and would satisfy the language of the contract. The subject matter is not cut down or varied by the subsequent words 'known as the "White Hart" with stabling and garden.' These words, taken together with the preceding words, are satisfied by the subject matter he did occupy, viz. so much of the premises known as the 'White Hart' as he did occupy with the stabling and garden."

9.48   Where there are conflicting descriptions, the court must of course choose between them. The maxim does not assist in that choice. As Lord Parker of Waddington said in *Eastwood v Ashton*[145]:

"It was suggested that help might be derived from the maxim, *falsa demonstratio non nocet*. It is clear, however that this maxim is useless until the court has made up its mind as to which of two conflicting descriptions ought under the circumstances to be considered the true description. When this is done the false description may, of course, be discarded, and the maxim merely calls attention to this obvious result."[146]

---

[143] However, there are other techniques of interpretation, discussed by Lord Hoffmann in *Mannai Investment Co Ltd v Eagle Star Life Assurance Co Ltd* [1997] A.C. 749, which may enable the court to say that the parties have used the wrong language, even though there is something that fits the verbal description.

[144] (1874) L.R. 9 C.P. 107.

[145] [1915] A.C. 900 at 912; *Republic Bank Ltd v Lochan* [2015] UKPC 26.

[146] Applied in *Carr v Thales Pension Trustees Ltd* [2020] EWCH 949 (Ch).

Illustrations

1.   A conveyance described a parcel of land as "No. 153b"; "a small piece marked on the plan"; "in the occupation of EJ" and as "34 perches". The plan was drawn to scale, and when measured on the ground was only 27 perches. The reference to 34 perches was rejected as a false description of that which was accurately described by the plan.
   Llewellyn v Earl of Jersey[147]

2.   A testatrix devised her land, "known by the name of D, situate in the parish of K, now in the occupation of J.E.". The testatrix owned land known as D, occupied by J.E., but part of it was not in the parish of K. It was held that the whole land passed.
   Hardwick v Hardwick[148]

3.   A testator devised a farm by the description "my freehold farm and lands situate at Edgware and now in the occupation of" J.B. The testator had a farm at Edgware occupied by J.B. but part of it was copyhold rather than freehold. The word "freehold" was rejected as a false description, and the whole farm was held to pass.
   Re Bright-Smith[149]

6.   WHEN THE PRINCIPLE DOES NOT APPLY

The principle of falsa demonstratio cannot be applied where there is a subject which fits the whole of the description contained in the instrument, nor where there is no subject which fits any part of the description.

The application of the maxim *falsa demonstratio* appears to be confined to cases where the written description is like the curate's egg: good in parts.[150] Where a subject exists which is precisely described by the written description, the maxim can have no application.

9.49

In *National Society for the Prevention of Cruelty to Children v Scottish National Society for the Prevention of Cruelty to Children*,[151] a Scotsman who had lived all his life in Scotland, by a will in Scottish form, bequeathed a legacy to "the National Society for the Prevention of Cruelty to Children". All the interests of the testator were Scottish, the legacy was placed in a series of legacies to Scottish charities, and the Scottish society had recently been brought to the attention of the testator. By contrast the National Society had its head office in London, was not active in Scotland, and there was no evidence that it was known to the testator. The House of Lords held that the National Society and not the Scottish Society was entitled to the legacy. Lord Loreburn said:

"... the accurate use of a name in a will creates a strong presumption against any

---

[147]   (1843) 11 M. & W. 183.

[148]   (1873) L.R. 16 Eq. 168.

[149]   (1886) 31 Ch. D. 314.

[150]   However, there are other techniques of interpretation, discussed by Lord Hoffmann in *Mannai Investment Co Ltd v Eagle Star Life Assurance Co Ltd* [1997] A.C. 749, which may enable the court to say that the parties have used the wrong language, even though there is something that fits the verbal description.

[151]   [1915] A.C. 207.

rival who is not the possessor of the name mentioned in the will. It is a very strong presumption and one which cannot be overcome except in exceptional circumstances. I use as a convenient method of expressing one's thought the term 'presumption'. What I mean is that what a man has said ought to be acted upon unless it is clearly proved that he meant something different."[152]

9.50 So too in *Smith v Jeffries*,[153] a written contract was made for the sale of "Ware potatoes". There was more than one variety of Ware potatoes, of which Regent's Wares were the best. The buyer wanted Regent's Wares, but the seller offered to deliver an inferior variety; Kidney Wares. It was held that evidence was inadmissible to qualify the written description. Kidney Wares fell exactly within the contractual description.

9.51 In some cases it has been said that the maxim can have no application because the words sought to be rejected are part of the essential description of the subject. This is a different way of saying that there is a subject which precisely fits that part of the description. Thus in *Magee v Lavell*,[154] an agreement to assign a tenancy referred to "the house and premises he [sc the assignor] now occupies, known by the sign of the White Hart". There was a coach house which belonged to the White Hart but was not occupied by the assignor. It was held that the coach house was not included in the agreement, because there was a subject matter which satisfied the full description. Coleridge CJ said:

> "Thus if we look to the mere terms of the agreement themselves, there is a subject-matter to which, by a reasonable construction, all the terms of the agreement are applicable."

In *Mellor v Walmesley*,[155] Vaughan Williams LJ held that measurements in a parcels clause could not be rejected, because they were:

> "not an addition to something which has been certainly described, but are part and parcel of the description itself. The words are not an inaccurate statement of a quality of that which had already been certainly described or defined, but are part and parcel of that description or definition."

Thus the measurements were held to define the amount of land passing under the conveyance. It follows that there was a subject (namely the land as so measured) which exactly fitted the full description. In both the last-mentioned cases the phrase sought to be rejected was read as restricting the apparent width of the parcels conveyed.

9.52 This approach is summarised in the Latin maxim *non accipi debent verba in demonstrationem falsam, quae competunt in limitationem veram*. The maxim was explained by Alderson B in *Morrell v Fisher*[156] as follows:

> "The other rule means that if it stand doubtful upon the words whether they

---

[152] In *Mannai Investment Co Ltd v Eagle Star Life Assurance Co Ltd* [1997] A.C. 749 at 778, Lord Hoffmann agreed with the principle as expressed by Lord Loreburn, although the result of the case might not be the same if decided today.
[153] (1846) 15 M. & W. 561.
[154] (1874) L.R. 9 C.P. 107.
[155] [1905] Ch. 165.
[156] (1840) 4 Exch. 591.

import a false reference or demonstration, or whether they be words of restraint that limit the generality of the former words, the law will never intend error or falsehood."

In other words, the court will, if it can, give effect to all the words of description, and interpret words sought to be rejected as words of limitation.

Conversely, it seems that when the description is wholly inaccurate, or would be unclear once the false elements had been rejected, the maxim cannot apply. In *Cowen v Truefitt Ltd*,[157] a lease of rooms on the second floor of 13 and 14 Old Bond Street contained a grant of free ingress and egress through the staircase and passages of No.13. There was no staircase in No.13 but there were two in No.14. The Court of Appeal held that the doctrine of *falsa demonstratio* was inapplicable. Lindley MR said:

9.53

"I do not know that the doctrine is applicable where the court can see, as it can see in this case, what it is that the parties really did mean by the particular document in question."

This reasoning seems to lead to the conclusion that where the presumed intention of the parties is clear, the maxim has no application to reject the false description, but where the intention is unclear the maxim may be used. Sir F.H. Jeune based his judgment on different reasons. He said:

"The learned judge proposed to apply it [sc. the doctrine] by striking out the words 'No. 13' as being a mere *falsa demonstratio*, but I do not think that the principle applies. I doubt whether the words 'staircase and passages' are a sufficiently clear description of a back staircase, for there are two staircases in No. 14, a back and a front. I think, if the principle is to be applied at all, the words 'No. 13' would have to be struck out all through; but when one considers that … the real mistake was in supposing that there was a staircase in No. 13, it is not, in my opinion a case of *falsa demonstratio* at all, but the clear words of the lease apply to something which is non-existent, so that the principle cannot be invoked in aid of the construction of the lease."

Two reasons for rejecting the maxim are given. The first is that the description shorn of the false part lacks sufficient clarity. The second is that the description as it stands is not ambiguous but points to something which does not exist. It is submitted that only the first of the two reasons is really convincing. Taken literally the words of the description in a *falsa demonstratio* case always point to something which is non-existent, otherwise the maxim would not have to be invoked at all. On the other hand, if the application of the maxim is likely to result in a contract which is still ambiguous or unclear, that is a good reason for not interfering with the words of the contract as drawn. In the result the court was able to rectify the lease, so that the tenant did have a means of access to and from the demised property.

9.54

Nor will the maxim apply where all the words of description can be reconciled by a process of interpretation.[158] Thus in *Eastwood v Ashton*,[159] a conveyance contained a description by name; a description by admeasurement; a description by

9.55

---

[157] [1899] 2 Ch. 309.
[158] *Re Brocket, Dawes v Miller* [1908] 1 Ch. 185.

occupation and a description by reference to a plan. It was held that the plan prevailed. Lord Sumner said:

> "Neither is it a case where the false description applies to no subject and the true description to one only. The falsity, or rather the vagueness, of the first part, when supplemented by the last, is corrected and becomes a whole, which refers with adequate certainty to one subject and defines it fully."

7. FALSE LABELS

The nature of the relationship between the parties is to be determined by the substance of the obligations into which they have entered; and if their contract is described by a label inconsistent with that substance, or if the parties incorrectly state what they believe to be the effect in law of their contract, the label or the statement will be rejected.[160]

9.56   Although parties are free to enter into what contracts they please (subject to questions of illegality and public policy), they are not competent to determine the nature of the relationship created by the terms of the contract into which they have freely entered. The meaning of the contract (in the sense of determining what is the substance of the obligations into which the parties have entered) is a question of interpretation; that is of ascertaining the meaning that would be understood by a reasonable reader with the background knowledge of the parties. However, the legal effect of the contract is to be determined as a matter of law; not as a matter of interpretation. Once the substance of the parties' obligations has been decided as a question of interpretation, the legal effect of their agreement is often a question of classification or categorisation of the contract.[161]

9.57   In *Welsh Development Agency v Export Finance Co Ltd*,[162] Dillon LJ said:

> "What is said is that in determining the legal categorisation of an agreement and its legal consequences the court looks at the substance of the transaction and not at the labels which the parties have chosen to put on it.
>
> This is trite law, but it is law which has fallen to be applied in different types of cases where different factors are the relevant factors for consideration. It is therefore not surprising that the words used by eminent judges in different cases in applying the principle do not all fit very harmoniously together.
>
> Thus the task of looking for the substance of the parties' agreement and disregarding the labels they have used may arise in a case where their written agreement is a sham intended to mask their true agreement. The task of the courts there is to discover by extrinsic evidence what their true agreement was and to disregard, if inconsistent with the true agreement, the written words of the sham agreement. ...
>
> But the question can also arise where, without any question of sham, there is

---

[159] [1915] A.C. 900.

[160] Cited with approval in *The Management Corporation Strata v Liang Huat Aluminium Ltd* [2001] B.L.R. 351 (CA of Singapore); *Fearnley v Australian Fisheries Management Authority* [2006] FCAFC 3 (Federal Court of Australia Full Court); *Warne v GDK Financial Solutions Pty Ltd* [2006] NSWSC 259; *Sturt Football Club Inc v Commissioner of State Taxation* [2010] SASC 279.

[161] See para.4.16. Cited with approval in *Fearnley v Australian Fisheries Management Authority* [2006] FCAFC 3.

[162] [1992] B.C.L.C. 148.

some objective criterion in law by which the court can test whether the agreement the parties have made does or does not fall into the legal category in which the parties have sought to place their agreement."

In *Pawsey v Armstrong*,[163] the plaintiff and the defendant agreed that the plaintiff **9.58** should have a share in the profits and losses of a business. The plaintiff alleged that he was a partner in the business but the defendant denied that it had been agreed that he should become a partner. Kay J said:

"Now, I confess, in my opinion the agreement to share profit and loss is quite conclusive of the relation between two persons who do so agree, and it is not possible for one of them afterwards to say 'I was not a partner' any more than it would be possible for a man and a woman who had gone through a ceremony of marriage before a Registrar, and had satisfied all the conditions of the law for making a valid marriage, to say that they were not man and wife, because at the time one had said to the other, 'Now, mind, we are not man and wife'; or to put another illustration—Suppose a man allowed his friend to invest £10,000 consols in his name, and said, 'I will hold the consols and pay the dividends to A.B. during his life, and then to CD, and afterwards to anybody whom you by will shall appoint, but, mind, I am not to be considered a trustee'—the stipulation that he was not to be a trustee would not prevent his being a trustee. The truth is, that there are certain legal relations which are entered into by agreeing to certain conditions, and when those conditions are agreed to, it is quite idle for people to superadd, a stipulation that the necessary legal consequences shall not follow from the arrangement."

In *Weiner v Harris*,[164] Cozens-Hardy MR said: **9.59**

"It is quite plain that by the mere use of a well-known legal phrase you cannot constitute a transaction that which you attempt to describe by that phrase. Perhaps the commonest instance of all, which has come before the Courts in many phases, is this: Two parties enter into a transaction and say 'It is hereby declared there is no partnership between us.' The Court pays no regard to that.[165] The Court looks at the transaction and says 'Is this, in point of law, really a partnership? It is not in the least conclusive that the parties have used a term or language intended to indicate that the transaction is not that which in law it is.' So here the mere fact that goods are said to be taken on sale or return is not in any way conclusive of the real nature of the contract. You must look at the thing as a whole and see whether that is the real meaning and effect of it."

So too in *Addiscombe Garden Estates Ltd v Crabbe*,[166] an agreement described **9.60** as a licence was held to be a tenancy. Jenkins LJ said:

"... the relationship is determined by the law, and not by the label which the parties choose to put upon it, and ... it is not necessary to go so far as to find the document a sham."

---

[163] (1881) 18 Ch. D. 698.
[164] [1910] 1 K.B. 224 at 290.
[165] This sentence overstates the modern approach, as explained later in this section.
[166] [1958] 1 Q.B. 513.

Similarly, in *Street v Mountford*,[167] the parties entered into a written agreement described as a licence, and containing a statement by the occupier that:

"I understand and accept that a licence in the above form does not and is not intended to give me a tenancy protected under the Rent Acts."

The House of Lords held that it did. Lord Templeman said:

"Both parties enjoyed freedom to contract or not to contract and both parties exercised that freedom by contracting on the terms set forth in the written agreement and on no other terms. But the consequences in law of the agreement, once concluded, can only be determined by a consideration of the effect of the agreement. If the agreement satisfied all the requirements of a tenancy, then the agreement produced a tenancy and the parties cannot alter the effect of the agreement by insisting that they only created a licence. The manufacture of a five-pronged implement for manual digging results in a fork even if the manufacturer, unfamiliar with the English language, insists that he intended to make and has made a spade."

In *Protectacoat Firthglow Ltd v Szilagyi*,[168] Smith LJ said:

"*Street v Mountford* ... contains dicta to similar effect in the context of a dispute about whether a contractual document created a licence or a tenancy. It was said that the parties cannot turn a tenancy into a licence merely by calling it one. The same must be true of a partnership; one cannot create a partnership by signing a document which calls itself a partnership agreement. And the same must also be true of a contract for the performance of work in return for pay. The court must look at the substance not the label."

9.61   In *Ferguson v Dawson (John) & Partners (Contractors) Ltd*,[169] the question was whether a building labourer was an employee or an independent contractor. Megaw LJ (with whom Browne LJ agreed) said:

"My own view would have been that a declaration by the parties, even if it be incorporated in the contract, that the workman is to be or is to be deemed to be self-employed, an independent contractor, ought to be wholly disregarded—not merely treated as not being conclusive—if the remainder of the contractual terms, governing the reality of the relationship, show the relationship of employer and employee. The Roman soldier would not have been a self-employed labourer only sub-contractor because of any verbal exchange between him and the centurion when he enlisted. I find difficulty in accepting that the parties, by a mere expression of intention as to what the legal relationship should be, can in any way influence the conclusion of law as to what the relationship is. I think it would be contrary to the public interest if that were so; for it would mean that

---

[167] [1985] A.C. 809.

[168] [2009] I.C.R. 835.

[169] [1976] 1 W.L.R. 1213. Others have not gone so far: see *Law v Local Board of Redditch* [1892] 1 Q.B. 127, per Lord Esher MR ("I do not think much reliance ought to be placed on those words but I do not think that they ought to be left out of account altogether"); *Wall v Rederiaktiebolaget Luggude* [1915] 3 K.B. 66, per Bailhache J. ("There are additional reasons why the estimated amount of the freight in clause 15 should be regarded as a penalty. One excellent reason is that it is so called, a reason which I am aware is not conclusive, but is certainly weighty.")

the parties by their own whim, by the use of a verbal formula, unrelated to the reality of the relationship, could influence the decision on whom the responsibility for the safety of workmen, as imposed by statutory regulations, should rest."

This approach was approved by the Supreme Court in *Autoclenz Ltd v Belcher*.[170]   **9.62**
where the court adopted a broader approach in relation to contracts of employment, as opposed to "ordinary contracts and, in particular ... commercial contracts." In the field of employment, therefore, the courts have asserted a greater freedom to disregard the terms of a written contract where it does not correspond with the reality on the ground.[171] In *Bates v Post Office (No.3)*,[172] however, Fraser J took a wider view. Having referred to *Autoclenz Ltd v Belcher*[173] he said:

"I consider the dicta in *Autoclenz* to have application wider than the field of employment law, and its application is this. There is no magic in a label, and the court will consider all the relevant circumstances including the terms of any written agreement in arriving at the true agreement between the parties. It is similar, if not identical, to the court's approach when the word 'agent' is used, as has been seen above. The label used by the parties is not determinative. However, when one is considering 'all the circumstances of the case', as Lord Clarke states at [35], this must be done at the time of contracting. Hindsight cannot be used, as that contravenes the general principles of contractual construction."

In *HMRC v Secret Hotels2 Ltd*,[174] Lord Neuberger, approving observations in *A1*   **9.63**
Lofts Ltd v Revenue and Customs Commissioners[175] said:

"When deciding on the categorisation of a relationship governed by a written agreement, the label or labels which the parties have used to describe their relationship cannot be conclusive, and may often be of little weight."

Indeed it has been held that ultimately, the label used to characterise the nature   **9.64**
of the contractual relationship can be a distraction, and in extreme cases can lead to error.[176]

In *Associated British Ports v Ferryways NV*,[177] the question was whether a document called a "letter of comfort" gave rise to legally enforceable obligations. Maurice Kay LJ said:

"I regard a letter of comfort, properly so called, as one that does not give rise to contractual liability. The label used by the parties is not necessarily determinative. It is a matter of construction of the document as a whole."

In *Spliethoff's Bevrachtingskantoor BV v Bank of China Ltd*,[178] Carr J held that in deciding whether a contract was a "see to it" guarantee or a performance bond, the fact that the word "guarantee" was used in the document was not helpful to the

---

[170] [2011] UKSC 41.
[171] *Uber BV v Aslam* [2018] EWCA Civ 2748; [2019] I.C.R. 845.
[172] [2019] EWHC 606 (QB).
[173] [2011] UKSC 41; [2011] I.C.R. 1157.
[174] [2014] UKSC 16.
[175] [2010] S.T.C. 214
[176] *Mainteck Services Pty Ltd v Stein Heurtey SA* [2014] NSWCA 184.
[177] [2009] EWCA Civ 189.
[178] [2015] EWHC 999 (Comm); [2015] 1 C.L.C. 651.

process of construction, let alone determinative. She preferred to look to the substance and international and commercial context of the obligations. That said, it is wrong in principle to seek to pigeonhole a contractual obligation into a predefined legal category. In *AXA SA v Genworth Financial International Holdings Inc*,[179] one of the questions was whether an obligation was an indemnity or a performance bond. Bryan J said:

"Should the Court seek to pigeonhole or classify Clause 10.8 as a particular species of contractual obligation, for example as an indemnity or a performance bond, and then identify the consequences of such classification? Or should it construe the contractual language of Clause 10.8 against the factual matrix, and in the context of the SPA as a whole, to determine its true meaning and effect applying established principles as to contractual construction? There can be no doubt that the latter is the correct approach to contractual construction."

He added:

"It is perfectly possible that a clause is not a 'classic' example of any particular type of familiar contractual provision, but instead a 'bespoke' provision, agreed by the parties in response to particular factual circumstances and particular commercial imperatives. In the present case it is common ground that it is not a guarantee, or a performance bond akin to a letter of credit issued by a financial institution."[180]

9.65   Where the contract contains a written statement of some fact which will in turn have particular legal consequences, the court may place more weight on the label that the parties have given it. In *Buchmann v May*,[181] a tenancy agreement contained a statement to the effect that the letting was made for the purpose of the tenant's holiday. A letting for the purpose of a holiday would not have been protected by the Rent Act 1977. The Court of Appeal held that the statement in the tenancy agreement was at least prima facie evidence of the purpose of the tenancy.

9.66   Moreover, it is probable that the label which the parties give to the relationship into which they have entered is of some relevance in seeking objectively to ascertain their presumed intention. Thus where the question is the meaning of a defined term in a contract, the label that the contract gives to the definition is a permissible aid to interpretation.[182] The label may also be of considerable importance in borderline cases in deciding whether a contract answers some legal description. In *Massey v Crown Life Insurance Co*,[183] Lord Denning MR said:

"... if the true relationship of the parties is that of master and servant under a contract of service, the parties cannot alter the truth of that relationship by putting a different label upon it. ... On the other hand, if the parties' relationship is ambiguous and is capable of being one or the other, then the parties can remove that ambiguity, by the very agreement itself which they make with one another.

---

179   [2019] EWHC 3376 (Comm); [2020] 1 Lloyd's Rep. 229.

180   He concluded that the clause in question was bespoke.

181   [1978] 2 All E.R. 993.

182   *Chartbrook Ltd v Persimmon Homes Ltd* [2009] A.C. 1101; *Cattles Plc v Welcome Financial Services Ltd* [2010] 2 B.C.L.C. 712. See para.5.95.

183   [1978] 1 W.L.R. 676, approved by the Privy Council in *Australian Mutual Provident Society v Chaplin* (1978) 18 A.L.R. 385; *Narich Pty Ltd v Commissioner of Pay-Roll Tax* [1984] I.C.R. 286.

The agreement itself then becomes the best material from which to gather the true legal relationship between them."

In *Stringfellow Restaurants Ltd v Quashie*,[184] Elias LJ said:

"It is trite law that the parties cannot by agreement fix the status of their relationship: that is an objective matter to be determined by an assessment of all the relevant facts. But it is legitimate for a court to have regard to the way in which the parties have chosen to categorise the relationship, and in a case where the position is uncertain, it can be decisive, as Lord Denning recognised in *Massey v Crown Life Insurance*."

Thus where there is real difficulty in characterising a transaction, the label that parties attach to it can be of value in resolving the difficulty.[185]

In *Antoniades v Villiers*,[186] Bingham LJ, referring to the speech of Lord Templeman in *Street v Mountford*,[187] said: **9.67**

"The House of Lords has not, I think, held that assertions in a document that it is a licence should be ignored. It has been held that the true legal nature of a transaction is not to be altered by the description the parties choose to give it. A cat does not become a dog because the parties have agreed to call it a dog. But in deciding whether an animal is a cat or a dog the parties' agreement that it is a dog may not be entirely irrelevant."

In *Dragonfly Consultancy Ltd v Revenue and Customs Commissioners*,[188] Henderson J said that:

"statements by the parties disavowing any intention to create a relationship of employment cannot prevail over the true legal effect of the agreement between them. It is true that in a borderline case a statement of the parties' intention may be taken into account and may help to tip the balance one way or the other. ... In the majority of cases, however, such statements will be of little, if any, assistance in characterising the relationship between the parties."

He added, however:

"If the actual contractual arrangements between the parties do include statements of intention, they should in my view be taken into account, and in a suitable case there may be material which would justify the inclusion of such a statement in the hypothetical contract. Even then, however, the weight to be attached to such a hypothetical statement would in my view normally be minimal, although I do not rule out the possibility that there may be borderline cases where it could be of real assistance."

Similarly, in *George Hunt Cranes Ltd v Scottish Boiler and General Insurance*   **9.68**

---

[184] [2012] EWCA Civ 1735.
[185] *MJP Media Services Ltd v HM Revenue and Customs* [2012] EWCA Civ 1558; [2013] S.T.C. 2218.
[186] [1988] 2 All E.R. 309 at 315. The House of Lords reversed the Court of Appeal on the basis that the agreements in question were obvious shams. However, Lord Oliver of Aylmerton said that if the documents had been genuine, he would, as a matter of construction, have agreed with the Court of Appeal. See [1990] A.C. 417.
[187] [1985] A.C. 809.
[188] [2008] S.T.C. 3030.

Co Ltd,[189] the question was whether a term in an insurance policy which required claims to be made within a certain time limit was a condition precedent to the liability of insurers. Potter LJ said:

"However, where one clause is labelled 'condition precedent', and a question arises as to the status of a clause not so labelled, the latter is not, ipso facto, precluded from being regarded as such. If, as in this case, the wording of the clause is apt to make its intention unambiguously clear, then in my view the absence of the rubric need not be fatal. As with any other contract, the task of construction requires one to construe the policy as a whole. However, in this respect, as it seems to me, if there is a clear expression of intention on the wording of the clause that it shall be treated as a condition precedent, that label or apparent intention cannot simply be ignored. It should at least be regarded as a starting point."

So also in *Wire TV Ltd v CableTel (UK) Ltd*,[190] Lightman J said:

"… in construing an agreement (which is not a sham) for the purpose of analysing its legal character and the legal rights and obligations to which it gives rise, regard must be had to the substance of the transaction as disclosed by the language used, and this includes the form and shape of the transaction and the labels chosen by the parties. The parties to a transaction frequently have a choice as to the way it shall be structured, whether there should be one or more contracts and as to the rights and obligations to be created: an example is as to how consideration shall be appropriated to different components in any package or to different packages of goods or services being sold or provided by the same vendor to the same purchaser. For the purposes of legal analysis the court must respect the structure and appropriation adopted, and cannot treat the transaction as giving rise to different legal rights and obligations because those different legal rights and obligations would have been more natural and more in accordance with some objective view of the substance of the transaction."

9.69   On the same principle where a contract describes a payment as "liquidated damages" the court will take the label into account, but it is not decisive of the question whether the payment is in truth a penalty.[191] Likewise where a contract for the supply of bunkers to a vessel described the parties as buyer and seller, that description was taken into account, although ultimately overridden by other terms of the contract and the surrounding circumstances, with the result that the contract was not a contract for the sale of goods to which the Sale of Goods Act 1979 applied.[192]

9.70   Where the party who issued the document rejects the label attached to it, the court will be more cautious in rejecting the label. Lord Bingham of Cornhill explained

---

[189] [2001] EWCA Civ 1964; [2002] All E.R. (Comm) 366.
[190] [1998] C.L.C. 244 at 258; *Maple Leaf Macro Volatility Master Fund v Rouvroy* [2009] EWHC 257 (Comm). Observations of Lightman J to similar effect in *Spectros International Plc v Madden* [1997] S.T.C. 114 were applied in *HMRC v Collins* [2009] EWHC 284 (Ch). See also *National Car Parks Ltd v The Trinity Development Co (Banbury) Ltd* [2002] 2 P. & C.R. 18, per Arden LJ at [25]–[29] and per Buxton LJ at [39]–[42].
[191] *Dunlop Pneumatic Tyre Co Ltd v New Garage and Motor Co Ltd* [1915] A.C. 79. See para.16.30.
[192] *PST Energy 7 Shipping LLC v OW Bunker Malta Ltd* [2015] EWHC 2022 (Comm).

in *JI MacWilliam Co Inc v Mediterranean Shipping Co SA; The Rafaela S*[193]:

> "It is always the task of the court to determine the true nature and effect of a legal document, and in performing that task the court is not bound by the label which the parties have chosen to apply to it. Where, however, the court is considering a bona fide mercantile document, issued in the ordinary course of trade, it will ordinarily be slow to reject the description which the document bears, particularly where the document has been issued by the party seeking to reject the description."

Where there is an identity of interest between both sides to a commercial transaction both sides are likely to be in agreement as to its real purpose and its true nature and substance. In such a case the label may carry greater weight.[194]   **9.71**

Where there is more than merely a label, but also a statement of the legal consequences that the parties desire to result from that label, the court will also be wary of rejecting it. In *Clear Channel UK Ltd v Manchester City Council*,[195] Jonathan Parker LJ said: **9.72**

> "On the other hand the fact remains that this was a contract negotiated between two substantial parties of equal bargaining power and with the benefit of full legal advice. Where the contract so negotiated contains not merely a label but a clause that sets out in unequivocal terms the parties' intention as to its legal effect, I would in any event have taken some persuading that its true effect was directly contrary to that expressed intention."[196]

Illustration

The question arose whether a contract was a first demand guarantee (independent of the underlying contract between principals) or a true guarantee dependent on the liability of the principal debtor. Although the contract described itself as a "guarantee" it did not use the language of guarantee. The label "guarantee" was rejected.

Gold Coast Ltd v Caja de Ahorros del Mediterraneo[197]

8.   INTERNAL INCONSISTENCY

If a clause in a contract is followed by a later clause which destroys the effect of the first clause, the later clause is to be rejected as repugnant and the earlier clause prevails. If, however, the later clause can be read as qualifying rather than destroying the effect of the earlier clause, or if the contract itself indicates which is to have priority, then the two are to be read together, and effect given to both.

It sometimes happens that two clauses in a contract are found to be in some   **9.73**

---

[193] [2005] 2 A.C. 423.
[194] *Progress Property Co Ltd v Moorgarth Group Ltd* [2011] 2 All E.R. 432.
[195] [2006] 1 E.G.L.R. 27. In *Scottish Widows Plc v Stewart* [2006] EWCA Civ 999, Lloyd LJ said that there was much force in this observation.
[196] In *Street v Mountford* [1985] A.C. 809 the tenancy agreement contained such a clause, but it was rejected. However, that was not a case of a contract negotiated between two parties of equal bargaining power, and the tenant did not appear to have had legal advice.
[197] [2002] 1 Lloyd's Rep. 671 CA.

measure inconsistent. This is particularly the case where the contract is based upon a standard form which the parties have not negotiated to which special clauses or conditions have been added. Provisions are inconsistent if they cannot sensibly be read together.[198]

In *Walker v Giles*,[199] Wilde CJ said:

"And as the different parts of the deed are inconsistent with each other, the question is, to which part effect ought to be given. There is no doubt, that, applying the approved rules of construction to this instrument, effect ought to be given to that part which is calculated to carry into effect the real intention, and that part which would defeat it should be rejected."

As a statement of general principle that cannot be criticised.

9.74   A more specific principle was described in *Forbes v Git*,[200] in which Lord Wrenbury said:

"The principle of law to be applied may be stated in a few words. If in a deed an earlier clause is followed by a later clause which destroys altogether the obligation created by the earlier clause, the later clause is to be rejected as repugnant and the earlier clause prevails. In this case the two clauses cannot be reconciled and the earlier provision in the deed prevails over the later. Thus if A covenants to pay £100 and the deed subsequently provides that he shall not be liable under his covenant, that later provision is to be rejected as repugnant and void, for it altogether destroys the covenant. But if the later clause does not destroy but only qualifies the earlier, then the two are to be read together and effect is to be given to the intention of the parties as disclosed by the deed as a whole. Thus if A covenants to pay £100 and the deed subsequently provides that he shall be liable to pay only at a future named date or in a future defined event or if at the due date of payment he holds a defined office, then the absolute covenant to pay is controlled by the words qualifying the obligation in manner described."

9.75   This approach has been applied not only to inconsistent obligations contained in different parts of a contract, but also to inconsistent provisions of any kind. In *Slingsby's Case*,[201] a conveyance to joint owners contained a covenant which purported to make them severally liable. The Court of Exchequer Chamber held that the words purporting to create the several liability should be rejected. Similarly, in *Joyce v Barker Bros (Builders) Ltd*,[202] a conveyance was expressed to be made to the purchasers "as beneficial joint tenants in common equal shares". Vinelott J rejected the words "in common equal shares" as being inconsistent with the prior beneficial joint tenancy. In doing so he applied *Slingsby's Case*, but described the rule as "an absolutely last resort in construction".

---

[198] *Pagnan SpA v Tradax Ocean Transportation SA* [1987] 3 All E.R. 565, per Dillon LJ.

[199] (1848) 6 C.B. 662.

[200] [1922] 1 A.C. 256. Contrast *Furnivall v Coombes* (1843) 5 Man. & G. 736 and *Williams v Hathaway* (1877) 6 Ch. D. 544.

[201] (1586) 5 Co. Rep. 18. The principle is also stated in *Shepherd's Touchstone*, 88.

[202] (1980) 40 P. & C.R. 512. In *Reardon Smith Line Ltd v Central Softwood Buying Corp Ltd* (1932) 42 Ll. L. Rep. 284, Slesser LJ would have been prepared to apply the principle if all else failed. In *Missing Link Network Integration P/L v Olamte P/L* [2005] NSWSC 430, White J applied the principle, having tried all other means to resolve an inconsistency between clauses.

A contrary principle applies to the construction of wills. In the case of inconsist-   **9.76**
ency between two provisions in a will, the later provision prevails.[203] A possible
rationale behind the rule was explained by Millett J in *Martin v Martin*[204] as follows:

> "... where there are two inconsistent provisions in a deed which cannot be
> reconciled, they are to be treated as if they were contained in separate deeds
> executed by the same parties, one after the other, and in the same order in which
> the two inconsistent provisions are to be found in the deed. That, of course,
> explains the difference in treatment between a deed and a will; for in the case of
> two inconsistent wills made by the same testator, the later revokes the former and
> prevails, whereas in the case of two inconsistent deeds the result will depend on
> whether the grantor had put it out of his power by the first deed to bring about
> the consequences purported to be effected by the second."

If the principle survives in the modern law,[205] it is one to be applied only as a last   **9.77**
resort. In *Peabody Trust Governors v Reeve*,[206] cl.5(a) of a tenancy agreement stated
that with the exception of any changes in rent the agreement could only be altered
by the agreement in writing of both the tenant and the Trust. However, cl.5(b) said
that "The terms of this Agreement may be varied by the Trust by a notice of variation served on the Tenant and the provisions of section 103 of the Housing Act 1985
shall apply to this Agreement as if this tenancy were a secure tenancy". Mr Gabriel
Moss QC, sitting as a judge of the Chancery Division, said that the two clauses were
irreconcilable and that, if necessary, he would apply the approach in *Forbes v Git*.
However, he added that:

> "I have to add that this solution seems to me to be one of last resort only. It is
> not clear why the two sub-clauses in the present case come in the order in which
> they do. It may be that they could just as easily have appeared in the reverse
> order. That would have led to the opposite solution if this were the only ap-
> plicable test. It is hardly satisfactory for the true agreement of the parties to be
> ascertained on grounds which may be arbitrary and I suspect it is only in rare
> cases that this approach will be applied."

Likewise, in *RSPCA v Sharp*,[207] Lord Neuberger of Abbottsbury MR said in relation to a will:

> "... as a free-standing point, the mere fact that one clause precedes another seems
> to me to be of minor potential relevance on the issue of how they interrelate with
> each other."

The contract may itself indicate which of two inconsistent clauses is to prevail.   **9.78**

---

[203] See *Re Hammond* [1938] 3 All E.R. 308.
[204] (1987) 54 P. & C.R. 238.
[205] The principle appeared to have some traction in *Westcoast (Holdings) Ltd v Wharf Land Subsidiary (No.1) Ltd* [2012] EWCA Civ 1003 (although ultimately it was not relied on). It was
distinguished (but not disapproved) in *Panavia Air Cargo Ltd v Southend-on-Sea Borough Council*
[1988] 1 E.G.L.R. 124. But the application of a mechanistic principle seems inimical to the modern
approach to the interpretation of contract.
[206] [2009] L. & T.R. 9.
[207] [2011] 1 W.L.R. 980. See also *Dunnes Stores (Bangor) Ltd v New River Trustee 11 Ltd* [2015] NICh
7.

In *The World Symphony*,[208] cl.3 of a charterparty defined the charter period as six months fifteen days more or less in charterers' option. Clause 18 provided "Notwithstanding the provisions of clause 3" should the vessel be upon a voyage at the expiry of the charter period, charterers should have the use of the vessel on the same terms until completion of the voyage. Butler-Sloss LJ said:

> "In my view, the words in cl. 18 'notwithstanding the provisions of cl. 3 hereof' are crucial. In construing two clauses in the time charter which, read together, display not only a tension but also an inconsistency, it is clear to me that cl. 18 must override cl. 3 ...".

In *Commissioner for Railways v Avrom Investments Pty Ltd*,[209] a lease provided that the lessee should erect buildings "in accordance with such building design plan and specification as the ... lessor may in his absolute discretion approve ... and notwithstanding anything hereinbefore contained the building design plan and specification of the said building shall be subject to the reasonable requirements of the lessor". The Privy Council held that the latter part of the clause overrode the former part, with the consequence that the lessor's requirements had to be reasonable; and he could not unreasonably refuse consent to plans. Lord Somervell said that the words "notwithstanding anything hereinbefore contained":

> "clearly indicate the cutting down of a right hereinbefore contained."

9.79   Similarly, a contract may provide that one clause has effect "subject to" another. As Staughton LJ explained in *Scottish Power Plc v Britoil (Exploration) Ltd*[210]:

> "Correctly used, the words 'subject to' mean that two provisions in the contract are in conflict, and that the first-mentioned is to be subject to, yield to, the second when the conflict occurs."

In *Interserve Construction Ltd v Hitachi Zosen Inova AG*,[211] a building contract made provision for termination in certain cases. In some of those cases the right to terminate was "subject to" the provisions of another clause which provided:

> "In the case of a default by the Contractor under heads (h), (p) or (q) of Sub-Clause 43.1, the Purchaser may (at its absolute discretion) notify the Contractor of the default and if the Contractor fails to commence and diligently pursue the rectification of the default within a period of seven (7) Days after receipt of notification, the Purchaser may by notice terminate the employment of the Contractor under the Contract."

Jefford J held that compliance with that clause was a condition precedent to the right to terminate. The reference in the clause to discretion was limited to the question whether to invoke the termination process at all.

9.80   In *Scottish Widows Fund and Life Assurance Society v BGC International*,[212] cl.3.3 of a contract provided that it was to be "without prejudice" to cl.2 of a different agreement. Arden LJ said:

---

[208] [1992] 2 Lloyd's Rep. 115 CA.
[209] [1959] 1 W.L.R. 389.
[210] (1997) 141 S.J.L.B. 246; *NHS Commissioning Board v Vasant* [2019] EWCA Civ 1245.
[211] [2017] EWHC 2633 (TCC); 176 Con. L.R. 52.
[212] [2012] EWCA Civ 607.

"... the important point is that the statement of intention in clause 3.3 was itself qualified because that clause is prefaced by a statement that clause 3.3 is to be 'without prejudice to' clause 2 of the Relevant lease. Those words are not said to be in error. This means that clause 2 is to be accorded precedence over clause 3.3. So clause 3.3 must take effect subject to whatever clause 2 means. Clause 2 is the paramount provision. On this basis, clause 3.3 cannot adversely impact on the parties' obligations under clause 2 of the Relevant lease."

However, contract documents should as far as possible be read as complement-   **9.81**
ing each other and therefore as expressing the parties' intentions in a consistent and coherent manner. Only in the case of a clear and irreconcilable discrepancy is it necessary to resort to the contractual order of precedence to resolve it.[213]

Illustrations

1.   Certain persons entered into a covenant that they and their successors would pay certain moneys. The covenant was followed by a proviso which purported to exempt them from personal liability. The provision was rejected.
     Furnivall v Coombes[214]

2.   The vicar of a parish and the incumbent of an ecclesiastical district within the parish entered into a building contract. The building was to be paid for out of funds to be raised. The contract provided that neither the vicar nor the incumbent nor their estates were to be bound by the contract after they had ceased to be entitled to apply the fund (e.g. if the vicar had been translated). The qualification was held to be good.
     Williams v Hathaway[215]

3.   A deed made between trustees of two separate estates contained a covenant by one set of trustees to pay to the other a certain sum of money, and to indemnify them against liability under a mortgage. The covenant was expressed to be given "as trustees but not so as to create any personal liability". It was held that the parties had attempted to qualify the covenant by using words which, if given effect, would destroy the effect of the covenant and indemnity. The words were therefore rejected.
     Watling v Lewis[216]

4.   A debenture contained a covenant by the issuing company that it would pay the principal sum secured by the debenture "on or after" a certain day. It was held that after the named day had passed the company was liable to repay on demand. Parker J said:

"But if there be a covenant to pay, with a proviso that the covenant shall only be enforced at the suit of the covenantor, the proviso would, in my opinion be void

[213] *RWE Npower Renewables Ltd v JN Bentley Ltd* [2014] EWCA Civ 150; *Alexander v West Bromwich Mortgage Co Ltd* [2015] EWHC 135 (Comm).
[214] (1843) 5 Man. & G. 736.
[215] (1877) 6 Ch. D. 544.
[216] [1911] 1 Ch. 414.

for repugnancy on the principle stated in *Sheppard's Touchstone* at p.273, and illustrated by the recent case of *Watling v Lewis*."

Re Tewkesbury Gas Company[217]

5.   A charterparty provided that cargo was to be loaded at the rate of 125 fathoms daily and discharged at the rate of 125 fathoms daily, during the ordinary working hours of the respective ports but according to the custom of the respective ports. It was held that the reference to the custom of the ports was inconsistent with the stipulation of a fixed number of lay days, and the latter prevailed.
Love and Stewart Ltd v Rowtor Steamship Co Ltd[218]

6.   A lease contained a rent review schedule which provided for certain steps to be taken within specified time limits. Paragraph 13 provided that time was not of the essence. Paragraph 14 provided that if a rent review was not completed by a certain date, the rent would increase automatically by 25 per cent. It was held that time was not of the essence of para.14, and that para.13 should not be read as limited to the paragraphs which preceded it.
Panavia Air Cargo Ltd v Southend-on-Sea Borough Council[219]

9.   INCONSISTENCY WITH MAIN OBJECT

Words and even whole clauses may be rejected if they are inconsistent with the main object of the contract, as ascertained from a reading of it as a whole.

9.82   In *Glynn v Margetson & Co*[220] Lord Halsbury LC said:

"Looking at the whole of the document, and seeing what one must regard ... as its main purpose, one must reject words, indeed whole provisions, if they are inconsistent with what one assumes to be the main purpose of the contract."[221]

Thus in that case where the main purpose of the contract was the carriage of oranges from Malaga to Liverpool the court refused to give effect to a wide deviation clause. In the Court of Appeal,[222] Fry LJ expressed himself similarly:

"I think that principle of construction is not confined to this class of documents, but is applicable to all documents. This principle is applicable wherever specific words are used to express the main object and intent of the instrument, and in some other part general words are used which in their utmost generality would be inconsistent with and destructive of the main object of the contract. When the Court in dealing with a contract or document of any kind finds that difficulty, it always, so far as I know, follows this principle, that the general words must be limited so that they shall be consistent with and shall not defeat the main object of the contracting parties."

---

[217] [1911] 2 Ch. 279.
[218] [1916] 2 A.C. 527 HL.
[219] [1988] 1 E.G.L.R. 124 CA.
[220] [1893] A.C. 351.
[221] See also *Homburg Houtimport BV v Agrosin Ltd* [2004] 1 A.C. 715, per Lord Millett at [183]–[184].
[222] Sub nom *Margetson v Glynn* [1892] 1 Q.B. 337.

There is, however, an important distinction between the formulation in the speech **9.83** of Lord Halsbury LC and the judgment of Fry LJ. The former spoke of "what one assumes" to be the main purpose of the contract. The latter, however, spoke of "specific words used to express the main object and intent of the instrument". As long as it is remembered that an assumption as to the main purpose of the contract can be derived only from the words of the contract itself, and a consideration of such evidence as is properly admissible, no practical difference will result from the two formulations. It would, however, be mistaken, to conclude that the court is free to make its own assumptions as to the main object of a contract, which was not firmly rooted in the words of the contract itself.

The principle just described is similar to that enshrined in the ejusdem generis **9.84** rule, and is sometimes expressed in the Latin maxim *generalia non derogant specialibus.*[223]

A similar principle is applied where clauses in a contract are inconsistent with **9.85** the interest created by the contract. Thus it is fundamental to the concept of a periodic tenancy that each party to the tenancy should be entitled to determine it. In *Centaploy Ltd v Matlodge Ltd,*[224] a periodic weekly tenancy contained a term to the effect that the tenancy should continue until determined by the lessee. Whitford J said:

> "It nevertheless appears to me that it must be basic to a tenancy that at some stage the person granting the tenancy shall have the right to determine and a tenancy in which the landlord is never going to have the right to determine at all is, as I see it, a complete contradiction in terms. Unless, therefore, some greater estate than a weekly tenancy was created by the agreements, the determination provisions must, in my view, be regarded as repugnant ...".

Thus where a tenancy purported to restrict the landlord's power to give notice to quit to particular circumstances, it was held that the restriction was inconsistent with the essential nature of an annual tenancy, and consequently the restrictions did not apply. But had the restriction been limited to a defined period of time, it would have been upheld.[225]

Illustration

A lease contained a rent review clause which required the open market rental value of the property to be assessed on the basis of a hypothetical letting on the terms of the lease. The lease contained a clause which restricted use of the property to use as offices by a named individual. It was held that a hypothetical letting which included that restriction was inconsistent with the fundamental purpose of the clause which was to determine an open market rent. The restriction was therefore rejected.
Law Land Co Ltd v Consumers' Association[226]

---

[223] General words do not derogate from particular words. The maxim was applied in *Telewest Communications Plc v Customs and Excise Commissioners* [2005] S.T.C. 481. See para.7.46.

[224] [1974] Ch. 1. See also *Doe d. Warner v Browne* (1807) 8 East. 165; *Cheshire Lines Committee v Lewis & Co* (1880) 50 L.J.Q.B. 121.

[225] *Prudential Assurance Co Ltd v London Residuary Body* [1992] 2 A.C. 386 HL, overruling *Clay (Charles) & Sons Ltd v British Railways Board* [1971] Ch. 725, and followed in *Mexfield Housing Co-operative Ltd v Berrisford* [2011] 2 W.L.R. 423.

[226] [1980] 2 E.G.L.R. 109.

10.   INCONSISTENCY BETWEEN WRITTEN AND PRINTED CLAUSES

In case of inconsistency between written (or typed) clauses in a contract specially negotiated by the parties and printed clauses forming part of the standard form, the written clauses will prevail.[227]

9.86   For hundreds of years many types of commercial contract have been made on standard forms. The earliest bill of exchange dates from 1381.[228] Another early example is contracts of insurance. In the hurry of business parties frequently omit to alter the printed words so as to make them exactly conform to the contract which they intended to make.[229] The printed form is designed to cope with a number of different contracts being made in different circumstances, whereas the written or typed clauses are designed to cope only with the particular contract in the course of being made. In such circumstances the court will place greater weight on the written clauses, and if necessary allow them to prevail against the printed clauses. This is a different facet of the principle discussed in the last preceding paragraph. In *Homburg Houtimport BV v Agrosin Ltd*,[230] Lord Bingham of Cornhill said:

> "It is common sense that greater weight should attach to terms which the particular contracting parties have chosen to include in the contract than to pre-printed terms probably devised to cover very many situations to which the particular contracting parties have never addressed their minds."

9.87   The principle has no application where the parties have contracted on the basis of a selection of standard terms.[231] Where parties have contracted on the basis of both standard terms and special terms, the court should try to arrive at an interpretation which is consistent with both. In *Alchemy Estates Ltd v Astor*,[232] Sales J said:

> "It is true that special terms take precedence over standard conditions if there is a clear conflict between them: see *Homburg BV v Agrostin Private Ltd*. However, where the parties have adopted both standard conditions and special conditions, and have not indicated that the standard conditions they have adopted are to be displaced in some respect by a special condition and there is no necessary inconsistency between them, then it appears that the parties' intention is that the standard conditions and the special conditions should be interpreted together as parts of one coherent contractual scheme."

9.88   Two hundred years earlier, in *Robertson v French*,[233] Lord Ellenborough had said:

> "The only difference between policies of insurance and other instruments in this respect is that the greater part of the printed language of them being invariable and uniform has acquired from use and practice a known and definite meaning, and that the words superadded in writing (subject indeed always to being

---

[227] This section was referred to with approval in *Wentworth Partners Estate Agents Pty Ltd v Gordony* [2007] NSWSC 1135.

[228] See *Garrard v Lewis* (1882) 10 Q.B.D. 30 at 32.

[229] *Western Assurance Company of Toronto v Poole* [1903] 1 K.B. 376 at 389, per Bigham J.

[230] [2004] 1 A.C. 715.

[231] *Milton Furniture Ltd v Brit Insurance Ltd* [2015] EWCA Civ 671.

[232] [2009] 1 P. & C.R. 5.

[233] (1803) 4 East. 130; *Mountain v Whittle* [1921] A.C. 615; *Cubitt Building and Interiors Ltd v Richardson Roofing (Industrial) Ltd* (2008) 119 Con. L.R. 137.

governed in point of construction by the language and terms with which they are accompanied) are entitled nevertheless, if there should be any reasonable doubt upon the sense and meaning of the whole, to have a greater effect attributed to them than to the printed words, inasmuch as the written words are the immediate language and terms selected by the parties themselves for the expression of their meaning, and the printed words are a general formality adapted equally to their case and that of all other contracting parties upon similar occasions and subjects."

This approach permits the court to give greater weight to the written clauses, but the written clauses are still to be "governed in point of construction" by the printed terms accompanying them. The written terms cannot, therefore, override clear printed terms, unless the court can safely conclude that something has gone wrong with the language. A similar point was made by Blackburn J in *Joyce v Realm Marine Insurance Co.*[234] He said:

    9.89

"The ordinary and general rule in the case of a policy of insurance, of course, is that we must construe the policy as we find it; it is a printed form, with written parts introduced into it, and we are to take the whole together, both the written and the printed parts. Although it has sometimes been endeavoured to be argued that we ought to bestow no more attention on the written parts than on the printed parts which are uniform in most policies of insurance, there is no doubt that we do, and ought to, make a difference between them. The part that is specially put into a particular instrument is naturally more in harmony with what the parties are intending than the other, although it must not be used to reject the other, or to make it have no effect."

In *Western Assurance Company of Toronto v Poole*,[235] Bigham J said:

"Of course, if I am right in supposing as I do that 'salvage charges' is an equivalent for suing and labouring expenses ... then the printed clause and the written clause are inconsistent, and the latter must prevail."

In *Renton (O H) & Co Ltd v Palmyra Trading Corp of Palmyra*,[236] Jenkins LJ described:

    9.90

"a recognised principle, which is not confined to bills of lading, but in its relation to bills of lading may be stated as being that where a bill of lading is concluded by means of a printed form containing general conditions, into which the parties write, type or otherwise incorporate the terms agreed upon in respect of the particular transaction in view (for example the termini of the voyage contracted for), and any of the printed conditions is found to be inconsistent with or repugnant to the main object and intention of the bill of lading as disclosed by the terms specially agreed, the court will limit or modify the conflicting printed condition to the extent necessary to enable effect to be given to such main object and intention, or in a case of complete repugnancy wholly reject it."

---

[234] (1872) L.R. 7 Q.B. 580.
[235] [1903] 1 K.B. 376.
[236] [1956] 1 Q.B. 462.

So also in *The Brabant*,[237] McNair J held that a typed clause in a charterparty prevailed over an inconsistent printed clause in the same charterparty.

And in *The Athinoula*,[238] Mocatta J said:

"Clause 18 is, as I have indicated, a typed clause, whereas cl. 8 is a printed clause; and where there is a conflict between two such clauses it is well established that the typed clause should prevail."

9.91   Most of the reported cases have thus far dealt with mercantile contracts, but the same approach is applied to other forms of contract. In *Addis v Burrows*,[239] the parties entered into a tenancy agreement on the basis of a printed form. The term was expressed to be from 1 January 1944, to 30 June 1945, for the term of one year and so on from year to year. The specific dates had been typed in but the words "for the term of one year" were part of the printed form. The Court of Appeal held that the typed words prevailed. Lord Greene MR said:

"apart from striking any words out, the fact that the parties have deliberately typed into this document words creating a tenancy for eighteen months made it clear that it must be so construed, and that, if necessary, the subsequent words in print must yield to that construction."

Similarly, in *Neuchatel Asphalte Co Ltd v Barnett*,[240] the principle was applied to a purported receipt. Denning LJ said:

"It is a well settled rule of construction that, if one party puts forward a printed form of words for signature by the other and it is afterwards found that those words are inconsistent with the main object and intention of the transaction as disclosed by the terms specially agreed, then the court will limit or reject the printed words so as to ensure that the main object of the transaction is achieved."

In that case, however, the principle was extended by Denning LJ for he applied it to a typed indorsement on the back of a cheque which he held to be inconsistent with the covering letter accompanying the cheque. Hodson and Morris LJJ, though concurring in the result, based their judgments on somewhat different grounds.

9.92   This principle of interpretation seems to rely on the ability of the court to recognise which parts of a contract are general terms not chosen by the parties, and which have been specially negotiated. In most mercantile contracts, recognition is achieved visually by the obvious contrast between writing (or typing) and print. The differentiation between the two species of clause is plain to see. No doubt the court would have no difficulty in applying the same approach to a contract for the sale of land incorporating the Standard Conditions of Sale or a building contract made by reference to the JCT forms. The courts do not, however, recognise that many other forms of conveyancing documents are taken from standard precedents, and construe such documents as if all their clauses had been individually negotiated

---

[237] [1967] 1 Q.B. 588.
[238] [1980] 2 Lloyd's Rep. 481.
[239] [1948] 1 K.B. 444; *Riley v Coglan* [1967] 1 W.L.R. 1300 (footballer's contract of employment).
[240] [1957] 1 W.L.R. 356.

between the parties. Indeed, it is doubtful whether evidence of the provenance of a contract is admissible as an aid to interpretation, unless it follows a printed form.[241]

The parties may, of course, provide that special conditions should prevail over printed conditions,[242] or, conversely, provide that printed clauses should prevail over typed or written ones.

9.93

A difference between different sizes of type or print has no legal significance.[243]

9.94

Marginal notes stand upon a different footing. Marginal notes are not generally an essential part of the contract upon which they are marginalia and in case of conflict between the marginal note and the body of the contract the latter will prevail.[244]

9.95

11.   INCONSISTENCY BETWEEN WORDS AND FIGURES

Where there is an inconsistency between written words and figures in a contract, prima facie the words prevail.

In *Saunderson v Piper*,[245] a bill of exchange contained an inconsistency between the amounts in words and figures. It was held that the words prevailed. Tindal CJ said:

9.96

"we cannot shake the rule of commercial writers, that where a difference appears between the figures and the words of a bill, it is safer to attend to the words."

In relation to bills of exchange, the rule has statutory confirmation in s.9(2) of the Bills of Exchange Act 1882.

The principle was recognised but confined to commercial documents by Simonds J in *Re Hammond*,[246] in which he said:

9.97

"No doubt there is a prima facie rule that, where words and figures conflict, the words ought to prevail, but no case has been brought to my notice where the rule has been applied otherwise than in the case of commercial documents."

He therefore refused to apply the principle to the construction of a will, but instead applied the rule that in a will the later of two provisions prevails. Since the figure followed the words, the figure prevailed.

The rationale behind the rule is that it is easier to make a mistake in the copying or transcribing of figures than in the writing out of the words expressing those figures. This no doubt is true when what is being done is the simple expression of

9.98

---

[241] Evidence of the provenance of a document, and of the changes which were made to a precedent would be extremely difficult to disentangle from evidence of the negotiation of the finished contract through its preparatory stages; and it is clear that evidence of negotiations is ordinarily inadmissible: see section para.3.43. However, where the terms of a contract have been taken from a printed form, the form may be used in order to supply words that have been erroneously omitted from the contract: *Homburg Houtimport BV v Agrosin Ltd* [2004] 1 A.C. 715. Likewise, where the clause has been taken from a published precedent, the precedent is admissible as an aid to interpretation: see para.3.31.

[242] See, e.g. *Pagnan SpA v Tradax Ocean Transportation SA* [1987] 3 All E.R. 565 CA.

[243] *Yorkshire Insurance Co Ltd v Campbell* [1917] A.C. 218; see para.5.118.

[244] *Garrard v Lewis* (1882) 10 Q.B.D. 30.

[245] (1839) 5 Bing. N.C. 425.

[246] [1938] 3 All E.R. 308.

a number. However, there are cases where the draftsman of a contract is attempting to describe in words a rather more sophisticated mathematical concept. In such cases it has been suggested that the judicious use of algebra will elucidate the meaning better than words.[247]

Illustration

A lease required a notice to be served triggering a rent review. The notice was to specify a rent. The notice served required the rent to be increased to "£8,850 (Eight thousand seven hundred and fifty pounds)". It was held that the words prevailed over the figure.
Durham City Estates v Felicetti[248]

12. INCONSISTENCY BETWEEN WRITTEN TERMS AND INCORPORATED TERMS

Where a contract incorporates the terms of another document, and the terms of that other document conflict with the terms of the host contract, the terms of the host contract will prevail.[249]

9.99   In *Sabah Flour and Feed Mills Sdn Bhd v Comfez Ltd*,[250] Parker LJ referred to authority and said:

"Those passages lend support to the proposition that if an incorporated document contains provisions which conflict with the provisions of the written document, then the terms of the written document would, in the ordinary way, prevail. For my part I am prepared to accept that is one rule of construction which may be applied in circumstances such as these."

So also in *Modern Building Wales Ltd v Limmer and Trinidad Co Ltd*,[251] Buckley LJ said:

"Where parties by an agreement import the terms of some other document as part of their agreement those terms must be imported in their entirety, in my judgment, but subject to this: that if any of the imported terms in any way conflicts with the expressly agreed terms, the latter must prevail over what would otherwise be imported."

9.100   The general principle that where a contract incorporates the terms of another document, and the terms of that other document conflict with the terms of the host contract, the terms of the host contract will prevail is not determinative in a case in which the terms of a contract of employment have to be gathered from a patchwork of sources. In such a case the court must resolve the inconsistency in the way which it believes best reflects the intentions of the parties and for that purpose

---

[247] *London Regional Transport v Wimpey Group Services Ltd* (1987) 53 P. & C.R. 356.
[248] [1990] 1 E.G.L.R. 143 CA.
[249] See also para.3.66.
[250] [1988] 2 Lloyd's Rep. 18 CA.
[251] [1975] 1 W.L.R. 1281 CA.

may have regard to the way in which the contract had been operated in practice and the realities of the situation.[252]

13. APPROACH TO POTENTIAL INCONSISTENCY

The court is reluctant to hold that parts of a contract are inconsistent with each other, and will give effect to any reasonable construction which harmonises such clauses.[253]

The general approach was explained by Lord Goff of Chieveley in *Yien Yieh* **9.101** *Commercial Bank Ltd v Kwai Chung Cold Storage Co Ltd*[254]:

> "Their Lordships wish to stress that to reject one clause in a contract as inconsistent with another involves a rewriting of the contract which can only be justified in circumstances where the two clauses are in truth inconsistent. In point of fact, this is likely to occur only where there has been some defect of draftsmanship. The usual case is where a standard form is taken and then adapted for a special need, as is frequently done in, for example, the case of standard forms of charterparty adapted by brokers for particular contracts. From time to time, it is discovered that the typed additions cannot live with the printed form, in which event the typed additions will be held to prevail as more likely to represent the intentions of the parties. But where the document has been drafted as a coherent whole, repugnancy is extremely unlikely to occur. The contract has, after all, to be read as a whole; and the overwhelming probability is that, on examination, an apparent inconsistency will be resolved by the ordinary processes of construction."

In *Karachiwalla v Nanji*,[255] Lord Radcliffe described the rejection of a clause on **9.102** the ground of inconsistency as a "desperate expedient". Thus an effort should be made to give effect to every clause in the agreement and a clause should not be rejected unless it is manifestly inconsistent with or repugnant to the rest of the agreement.[256] If there is an arguable rationale for a clause which is said to be inconsistent with another clause, then both can be given effect.[257] Similarly, in *Goldmile Properties Ltd v Lechouritis*,[258] Sedley LJ said:

> "It is axiomatic that where the provisions of any contract, including a lease, come into conflict, they are to be interpreted and applied so as to give proper effect, if possible, to both of them."

---

[252] *Pimlico Plumbers Ltd v Smith* [2017] EWCA Civ 51; [2017] I.C.R. 657. The point did not arise on the appeal to the Supreme Court: [2018] I.C.R. 1511.
[253] This section was referred to with approval in *Tri-MG Intra Asia Airlines BV v Norse Air Charter Ltd* [2009] 1 Lloyd's Rep. 258; *C v D* [2011] EWCA Civ 646; *Arnold v Britton* [2013] EWCA Civ 902; [2013] L. & T.R. 371 and *Foster v Action Aviation Ltd* [2013] EWHC 2439.
[254] [1989] 2 H.K.L.R. 639 PC. See *Taylor v Rive Droite Music Ltd* [2006] E.M.L.R. 4, where the principle was applied but the court disagreed on whether two clauses were inconsistent with each other or could be reconciled.
[255] [1959] A.C. 581.
[256] *Axa Re v Ace Global Markets* [2006] Lloyd's Rep. I.R. 683.
[257] *Kangol Ltd v Hay & Robertson Plc* [2005] F.S.R. 13.
[258] [2003] 2 P. & C.R. 1.

9.103   In *Solly v Forbes*,[259] Forbes and Ellerman had been in partnership. Solly gave Ellerman a release from a certain debt which the partnership had incurred, but without prejudice to his claim against Forbes. Forbes argued that the proviso was repugnant to the release. The argument failed. Dallas CJ said:

> "It is assumed that, wherever the word release is made use of, it must operate absolutely and unconditionally, tho' immediately and in the same sentence followed by words, which shew it to be partial and particular only, and the general words being in no respect repugnant to the special words, but the latter a qualification merely of the former, leaving the release to operate to every purpose except to the exclusion of the particular purpose, which the parties have declared it to be their intention it shall not exclude."

9.104   So too in *Renton (OH) & Co Ltd v Palmyra Trading Corp of Palmyra*,[260] it was argued that a provision in a bill of lading was inconsistent with the main object of the contract. The House of Lords rejected the contention. Lord Morton of Henryton said:

> "The contract contained in the bill of lading must be read as a whole. So read, it provides, in effect, that the goods must be carried to London unless there occurs an event specified in one or other of the provisos already mentioned; but if such event happens, the goods may be discharged elsewhere, and such discharge is to be deemed to be due fulfilment of the contract. No conflict arises when an obligation in a contract, unqualified in its terms as it is first stated, is subsequently qualified by a proviso modifying or altering the obligation if certain events happen which are outside the control of either party. The original obligation and the qualification of it both form part of the intention of the parties and neither part is repugnant to the other."

To similar effect is the decision of the Court of Exchequer in *Jessel v Bath*.[261] Likewise in *Pagnan SA v Tradax Ocean Transportation SA*[262] Bingham LJ said:

> "It is not enough if one term qualifies or modifies the effect of another: to be inconsistent a term must contradict another term or be in conflict with it, such that effect cannot fairly be given to both clauses."

9.105   In *Société Générale, London Branch v Geys*,[263] the Supreme Court approved the approach to potential inconsistency in *Pagnan SpA v Tradax Ocean Transportation SA*. Lord Hope said:

> "In any event the court's duty, when confronted with two provisions in a contract that seem to be inconsistent with each other, is plain. It must do its best to reconcile them if that can conscientiously and fairly be done."

---

[259] (1820) 2 Brod. & Bing. 38.

[260] [1957] A.C. 149.

[261] (1867) L.R. 2 Exch. 267.

[262] [1987] 3 All E.R. 565; applied in *Price Waterhouse v University of Keele* [2004] EWCA Civ 583; *Cobelfret Bulk Carriers NV v Swissmarine Services SA* [2010] 1 Lloyd's Rep. 317; *Public Company Rise v Nibulon SA* [2015] EWHC 684 (Comm); and *Septo Trading Inc v Tintrade Ltd* [2020] EWHC 1795 (Comm).

[263] [2012] UKSC 63; [2013] 1 All E.R. 1061; *125 OBS (Nominees1) v Lend Lease Construction (Europe) Ltd* [2017] EWHC 25 (TCC); 174 Con. L.R. 105.

The tension between the two must be such that one clause would "almost entirely" deprive the other clause of any effect; or one clause would emasculate the other.[264]

There is no difference in principle between alleged inconsistency between clauses of a contract contained in a single document, and clauses contained in two or more separate documents which together make up one contract; although there may be different nuances.[265] Nevertheless, tension between different contractual obligations is often found where the contractual provisions are contained in a number of different documents. The problem is particularly acute in major building or engineering contracts. In *MT Hojgaard AS v E.ON Climate and Renewables UK Robin Rigg East Ltd*,[266] Lord Neuberger said:

9.106

"Where a contract contains terms which require an item (i) which is to be produced in accordance with a prescribed design, and (ii) which, when provided, will comply with prescribed criteria, and literal conformity with the prescribed design will inevitably result in the product falling short of one or more of the prescribed criteria, it by no means follows that the two terms are mutually inconsistent. That may be the right analysis in some cases ... However, in many contracts, the proper analysis may well be that the contractor has to improve on any aspects of the prescribed design which would otherwise lead to the product falling short of the prescribed criteria, and in other contracts, the correct view could be that the requirements of the prescribed criteria only apply to aspects of the design which are not prescribed. While each case must turn on its own facts, the message from decisions and observations of judges in the United Kingdom and Canada is that the courts are generally inclined to give full effect to the requirement that the item as produced complies with the prescribed criteria, on the basis that, even if the customer or employer has specified or approved the design, it is the contractor who can be expected to take the risk if he agreed to work to a design which would render the item incapable of meeting the criteria to which he has agreed."

Sometimes, however, the parties may recognise the possibility of inconsistency, for example, where they are contracting on the basis of a standard form with special additions, or where the contract incorporates the provisions of some other document. The contract may provide for an order of precedence of its various provisions. In such a case, the court should not approach the contract with a predisposition to find no inconsistency. Instead the court should approach the document "in a cool and objective spirit to see whether there is inconsistency or not".[267] This view was confirmed by the Court of Appeal in *Alexander v West Bromwich*

9.107

---

[264] *Cobelfret Bulk Carriers NV v Swissmarine Services SA* [2010] 1 Lloyd's Rep. 317; *Apache North Sea Ltd v Euroil Exploration Ltd, Edison SPA* [2019] EWHC 3241 (Comm).

[265] *Cobelfret Bulk Carriers NV v Swissmarine Services SA* [2010] 1 Lloyd's Rep. 317.

[266] [2017] UKSC 59; [2017] Bus. L.R. 1610.

[267] *Pagnan SpA v Tradax Ocean Transportation SA* [1987] 3 All E.R. 565 at 574, per Bingham LJ. The judge below (Steyn J) held that it was "the Court's duty ... to reconcile seemingly inconsistent provisions if that result can conscientiously and fairly be achieved" ([1987] 1 All E.R. 81 at 89). And in the Court of Appeal Dillon LJ said that if the two clauses "can be read together, they should be and there is no inconsistency". In the case of a contract which expressly recognises the possibility of inconsistency, it is submitted that the approach of Bingham LJ is to be preferred. In *Cobelfret Bulk Carriers NV v Swissmarine Services SA* [2010] 1 Lloyd's Rep. 317, Beatson J followed the approach of Bingham LJ, as did Walker J in *British-American Insurance (Kenya) Ltd v Matelec Sal* [2013] EWHC 3278 (Comm) and Teare J in *Alexander v West Bromwich Mortgage Co Ltd* [2015]

Mortgage Co Ltd,[268] in which Hamblen LJ said:

> "Where there is an inconsistency clause, one should therefore approach the question of inconsistency without any pre-conceived assumptions. One should not strive to avoid or to find inconsistency. Rather one should 'approach the documents in a cool and objective spirit to see whether there is inconsistency or not'
> …
> It follows that in such a case the general approach to potential inconsistency summarised in *Lewison on the Interpretation of Contracts* (5th edn) at para.9.13 that the 'court is reluctant to hold that parts of a contract are inconsistent with each other' does not apply, as Lewison observes at p.508 (fn.206)."

9.108   In *RWE Npower Renewables Ltd v JN Bentley Ltd*,[269] Akenhead J said:

> "In this case, the parties did make some provision in Clause 2 of the signed contract and provided for an 'order of precedence' in the various documents with Contract Data Part 1 being the first and the Works Information and Contract Data Part 2 being well down the order. But the order of precedence is effectively prefaced by the words that all the documents are 'deemed to form and be read and construed as part of this Agreement'. Accordingly, this is a contract which is to be construed in the usual way by reference to all the documents forming part of the Contract. It is only if there is an ambiguity or discrepancy between two or more contract documents that one then needs to have regard to the order of precedence. I did not understand from Counsel that there was any material disagreement with this conclusion. It is obviously right. One can take an example where the Contract Data Part 1 document required the powerhouse to be painted white but the Works Information required it to be painted black. That is on its face an irreconcilable ambiguity and the contract would be construed as requiring white paint. What one can not and should not do is to carry out an initial contractual construction exercise on each of the material contract documents on any given topic and then, so to speak, compare the results of that exercise to see if there is an ambiguity. If it is possible to identify a clear and sensible commercial interpretation from reviewing all the contract documents which does not produce an ambiguity, that interpretation is likely to be the right one; in those circumstances, one does not need the 'order of precedence' to resolve an ambiguity which does not actually on a proper construction arise at all."

Akenhead J's decision was upheld by the Court of Appeal.[270] Moore-Bick LJ said:

> "I start, as did the judge, from the position that the contract documents should as far as possible be read as complementing each other and therefore as expressing the parties' intentions in a consistent and coherent manner. I also note, as he did, that Option X5 is worded in more general terms than clause 6.2, which identifies in rather greater detail the work comprised in each section. That is reflected in clause 1 of Part 1 of the Contract Data, which expressly recognises

---

EWHC 135 (Comm).

[268] [2016] EWCA Civ 496; [2017] 1 All E.R. 942; applied in *Dynniq UK Ltd v Lancashire CC* [2017] EWHC 3173 (TCC); 176 Con. L.R. 40.

[269] [2013] EWHC 978 (TCC).

[270] *RWE Npower Renewables Ltd v JN Bentley Ltd* [2014] EWCA Civ 150.

that the works 'are more comprehensively set out in Part 2, Works Information.'
Despite differences in detail, however, one would expect the two provisions to
complement each other and that only in the case of a clear and irreconcilable
discrepancy would it be necessary to resort to the contractual order of precedence
to resolve it."

In *EE Ltd v Mundio Mobile Ltd*,[271] Carr J said: **9.109**

"Agreements should be read as a whole and construed so far as possible to avoid
inconsistencies between different parts on the assumption that the parties had
intended to express their intentions in a coherent and consistent way. One expects
provisions to complement each other. Only in the case of a clear and irreconcilable discrepancy would it be necessary to resort to the contractual order of
precedence to resolve it."

However, this appears to be too stark a view. In *Alexander v West Bromwich*   **9.110**
Mortgage Co Ltd,[272] the Court of Appeal discussed what amounted to inconsistency.
Hamblen LJ said:

"An example given by Akenhead J in *RWE Npower Renewables v Bentley* ... is
where one part of the contract required a building to be painted black and another
part stated it should be painted white. That is an example of a clear and literal
contradiction between clauses. In my judgment, inconsistency is not limited to
such cases. As *Pagnan v Tradax* makes clear, it extends to cases where clauses
cannot 'fairly' or 'sensibly' be read together; not merely cases where they cannot literally be read together. One should approach that question having due
regard to considerations of reasonableness and business common sense."

As it was put in *GB Building Solutions Ltd v SFS Fire Services Ltd*[273]:   **9.111**

"In summary, the task for the court is to ascertain whether or not there is an
inconsistency (meaning a contradiction or conflict, whether a case of literal
inconsistency or a case where two clauses cannot fairly or sensibly be read
together) without adopting any predisposition for or against inconsistency being present. If there is an inconsistency then the order of precedence clause
provides the answer."

---

[271] [2016] EWHC 531 (TCC).
[272] [2016] EWCA Civ 496; [2017] 1 All E.R. 942, applied in *Dynniq UK Ltd v Lancashire CC* [2017]
EWHC 3173 (TCC); 176 Con. L.R. 40.
[273] [2017] EWHC 1289 (TCC); 172 Con. L.R. 18.

CHAPTER 10

PRELIMINARY PARTS OF A CONTRACT

Now, pay particular attention to this first clause because it's most important. Says the party of the first part shall be known in this contract as the party of the first part. How do you like that? That's pretty neat, eh?

The Marx Brothers: *A Night at the Opera*

1. MEANING OF THE PREMISES

The premises are those parts of a deed which precede the habendum.

The preliminary parts of a deed are called, in technical language, "the premises". The word "premises" is: **10.01**

"a word of conveyancing jargon, meaning strictly (and pace Viscount Hailsham in *Whitley v Stumbles*[1]) everything in a deed which precedes the habendum."[2]

A fuller description was given by Blackstone[3]:

"The premises may be used to set forth the number and names of the parties, with their additions or titles. They also contain the recital, if any of such deeds, agreements or matters of fact, as are necessary to explain the reasons upon which the present transaction is founded: and herein also is set down the consideration upon which the deed is made. And then follows the certainty of the grantor, grantee and thing granted."

These matters form the subject of this chapter.

2. PRESUMPTION OF DUE DATE

Where a document bears a date, prima facie it is taken to have been executed on the date it bears.

Evidence is always admissible to prove the date upon which a document was executed. In a case where the document is not dated, it will often be necessary to lead evidence. However, where the document is itself dated, the date itself is prima facie evidence of the date upon which the document was executed. In *Hunt v Mas-* **10.02**

---

[1]   [1930] A.C. 544 at 546.

[2]   *Maunsell v Olins* [1975] A.C. 373, per Lord Wilberforce (a case of statutory construction). The habendum is that part of the deed (traditionally beginning with the words "TO HOLD") which specifies the nature and quality of the estate being conveyed. From that origin the word "premises" has evolved into its popular meaning of "buildings" since the parcels clause identifying the property conveyed traditionally comes immediately before the habendum.

[3]   2 Bl.Com. 298.

sey,[4] the issue was whether a letter (which was dated) was written at a time when the writer was a minor. Denman CJ said:

"The letter must be presumed prima facie to have been written on the day on which it bore date."

Similarly, in *Anderson v Weston*,[5] Bosanquet J said:

"Now when a deed is produced, and the execution of that deed is proved by the subscribing witness, or by accounting for the absence of the subscribing witness by death or otherwise, and proving the signature, and that deed bears a date, as far as my experience goes, that date has uniformly been taken to be prima facie evidence that the deed was executed at the time when it purports to bear date."

10.03   The presumption is only a prima facie presumption, and may be rebutted by evidence. Thus in *Hall v Cazenove*,[6] evidence was admitted to show that a charterparty was wrongly dated; in *Steele v Mart*,[7] evidence was admitted to show that a lease was wrongly dated; in *Jayne v Hughes*,[8] evidence was admitted to show that a deed was wrongly dated; and in *Reffell v Reffell*,[9] evidence was admitted to show that a will was wrongly dated. In *Classic Maritime Inc v Lion Diversified Holdings Berhad*,[10] a guarantee dated 28 August 2008 stated that it was made in order to induce a contract of affreightment dated 13 August 2008. Cooke J held that evidence was admissible to explain the anomaly.

3.   NO DATE OR IMPOSSIBLE DATE

Where a contract is not dated or refers to an impossible date it takes effect from the date upon which it was executed.

10.04   It was laid down in *Clayton's Case*[11] that a deed takes effect from the date of delivery.[12] Where, therefore, a deed bears no date the date of delivery or execution must be proved by evidence. It is not thought that any different principle applies to contracts not under seal. Thus in *Morrell v Studd and Millington*,[13] Astbury J said:

"When a written document contains no date, parol evidence is admissible to show when it was written and from what date it was intended to operate."

Coke also laid down[14] that:

---

4   (1834) 5 B. & Ald. 902.
5   (1840) 6 Bing. N.C. 296.
6   (1804) 4 East. 477.
7   (1825) 4 B. & C. 272.
8   (1854) 10 Exch. 430.
9   (1866) L.R. 1 P. & D. 139.
10   [2010] 1 Lloyd's Rep. 59.
11   (1585) 5 Co. Rep. 1a.
12   Although traditionally a deed was "signed sealed and delivered", nowadays it is "executed as a deed".
13   [1913] 2 Ch. 648.
14   *Co. Litt.* 46b.

"if an indenture of lease bear date which is void, as the 30th February, etc., if in this case the term be limited to begin from the date it shall begin from the delivery as if there had been no date at all."

And in *Styles v Wardle*,[15] Bayley J said:

"A deed has no operation until delivery, and there may be cases in which, *ut res valeat*, it is necessary to construe date, delivery. When there is no date, or an impossible date, that word must mean delivery. But where there is a sensible date, that word in other parts of the deed means the day of the date, and not of the delivery."

4. SEQUENCE OF DOCUMENTS

Where two or more documents are executed on the same day as part of a composite transaction, and the order of execution is relevant, it will be assumed that they were executed in the correct order.

Where parties to a transaction involving the execution of multiple documents intend them to be executed in a particular order which is necessary to give effect to the intended transaction, the court should be ready to presume that they were executed in the correct order to give effect to the transaction.[16]   **10.05**

In *Aikman v Conway*,[17] Alderson B said: **10.06**

"It is good rule, that when two things are done on the same day, that shall be presumed to have been done first which ought to be so."

In *Gartside v Silkstone and Dodworth Coal and Iron Co*,[18] Fry J said:

"I think the law stands in this way, that when two deeds are executed on the same day, the court must inquire which was in fact executed first, but that if there is anything in the deeds themselves to shew an intention, either that they shall take effect pari passu or even that the later deed shall take effect in priority to the earlier, in that case the court will presume that the deeds were executed in such order as to give effect to the manifest intention of the parties."

It is not clear whether the presumption is a prima facie presumption or a conclusive presumption. If it is the latter, then it is perhaps more correctly described as a rule of law. Since the object of the presumption is to give effect to the "manifest intention" of the parties, it is submitted that it would be more desirable for the presumption to be irrebuttable. Support for this conclusion may be found in the judgment of Templeman J in *Keith Bayley Rodgers & Co v Cubes Ltd*.[19] That case raised the question whether a notice under a lease and a notice under the Landlord and Tenant Act 1954 were served in a particular order. The judge said: **10.07**

---

[15] (1825) 4 B. & C. 908 at 911.
[16] *In re Kilnoore Ltd (in liquidation) Unidare Plc v Cohen* [2006] Ch. 489.
[17] (1837) 3 M. & W. 71.
[18] (1882) 21 Ch. D. 762. In *Aikman v Conway* (1837) 3 M. & W. 71, Alderson B said:

> "It is a good rule, that when two things are done on the same day, that shall be presumed to have been done first which ought to be so".

[19] (1975) 31 P. & C.R. 412.

"Alternatively, when a landlord has power to serve two notices in sequence, notice exercising the break clause followed by notice under section 25, and he launches both notices on the same day, it is to be assumed that the notices were delivered in the correct sequence and it is not necessary to pester the postman to see which notice was delivered first."

10.08 However, in *Eaglehill Ltd v J Needham Builders Ltd*,[20] the House of Lords approved the following formulation of the principle:

"If two acts have been done one of which ought to have been done after the other if it was to be valid and the evidence which could reasonably be expected to be available does not show which was done first, they will be presumed to have been done in the proper order."

This formulation suggests that the presumption is rebuttable by evidence.

Illustration

As part of a scheme for transferring control of a block of flats, parties entered into a share sale agreement and a property sale agreement. In order for the property sale not to infringe the tenant's rights, it was important that the property sale should become unconditional before the share sale. All the agreements were executed on the same day. Lloyd J applied the presumption and inferred that the agreements were executed in the intended order.
Michaels v Harley House (Marylebone) Ltd[21]

5. DESCRIPTION OF PARTIES

The parties to a contract may be described in any way sufficient to identify them.

10.09 It is not necessary to describe parties to a deed by their full names. In *Simmons v Woodward*,[22] Lord Halsbury LC said:

"... where you are dealing with a grantee, you may describe that grantee in any way which is capable of ascertainment afterwards: you are not bound to give him a particular name; you are not bound to give his christian name or his surname; you may describe him by any description by which the parties to the instrument think it right to describe him."

10.10 So too it is permissible to describe a party to a contract by a reputed name, for:

"there may be cases where names acquired by use and habit may be taken by repute as the true christian name and surname of the parties."[23]

---

20 [1973] A.C. 992 at 1011 HL.
21 [1997] 1 W.L.R. 967. The judge's reasoning was disapproved by the Court of Appeal (though not on this point), but his order was upheld on other grounds: [2000] Ch. 104.
22 [1892] A.C. 100.
23 *Frankland v Nicholson* (1805) 3 M. & S. 259n, per Sir William Scott.

So in *Re Croxon*,[24] it was said that a surname may be acquired by assumption and reputation only.

Similar principles apply to persons carrying on a trade. In *Maugham v Sharpe*,[25] **10.11**
Sharpe and Baker carried on business as the City Investment and Advance Company. A conveyance was made to that entity. Erle CJ said:

> "It is clear that individuals may carry on business under any name and style which they may choose to adopt: and I see no reason why the defendants may not do so under the name of the City Investment and Advance Company. If parties pretend to be a corporation, and presume to usurp the rights and powers of a corporate body as against the Crown, they may render themselves liable to be proceeded with against for so doing. But, as between those parties, the City Investment and Advance Company are Sharpe and Baker, and consequently the conveyance in question is a conveyance to those individuals."

Where a person signs a contract in his own name, without qualification, he is **10.12**
prima facie to be deemed to be a person contracting personally, and in order to prevent this liability from attaching, it must be apparent from the other portions of the document that he did not intend to bind himself as principal.[26] In *Internaut Shipping GmbH v Fercometal SARL*,[27] Rix LJ said:

> "It may be asked, indeed the question was raised in the course of argument, why the principle whereby particular attention is paid to the form of the signature, which is in effect a maxim of construction and not a rule of law, exists: from where does it take its force? I would answer that it reflects the commercial facts of life, the promptings of commercial common sense. The signature is, as it were, the party's seal upon the contract; and that remains the case even where, as here, the contract has already been made ... Prima facie a person does not sign a document without intending to be bound under it, or, to put that thought in the objective rather than subjective form, without properly being regarded as intending to be bound under it. If therefore he wishes to be regarded as not binding himself under it, then he should qualify his signature or otherwise make it plain that the contract does not bind him personally."

Moreover, a person cannot usually escape liability under a covenant or contract **10.13**
which he has signed, merely by signing in a name which is not his own. In *Fung Ping Shan v Tong Shun*,[28] Lord Parker of Waddington, delivering the advice of the Privy Council, said:

> "A person who signs, seals, and delivers a deed of covenant cannot avoid liability under the deed by signing a name which he represents as, but which is not in fact, his own, nor can he saddle such liability on the person whose name he uses, unless he is the duly constituted attorney of such person."

---

[24] [1904] 1 Ch. 252.
[25] (1864) 17 C.B.N.S. 443.
[26] *Universal Steam Navigation Co Ltd v James McKelvie & Co* [1923] A.C. 492.
[27] [2003] 2 All E.R. (Comm) 760.
[28] [1918] A.C. 403.

6. PARTIES REFERRED TO BY CLASS RATHER THAN NAME

The parties to a contract need not be named at all provided that the class to which they belong is named.

10.14   A series of cases involving deeds of composition with creditors has established that persons may be party to and bound by a deed even though not named in it.

In *Gresty v Gibson*,[29] a deed was made between the debtor and all his creditors. The deed was held to be valid. Pollock CB said in argument:

"Certainly, if one were to covenant with persons under the description of all the members of a corporation, or of a firm, at a particular time, it would be valid; the only question is whether the description of the covenantees as creditors is not too vague and general."

This case was approved and followed in *Reeves v Watts*,[30] in which Blackburn J said:

"My own opinion certainly was strongly in favour of the proposition that a person may be made a party to a deed inter partes by description as belonging to the defined class; on the principle that *id certum est quod certum reddi potest*."

Illustration

A deed of composition was made between a debtor and several creditors whose names were subscribed "on behalf of themselves and all and every other the creditors" of the debtor. It was held that the deed was valid.
M'Laren v Baxter[31]

7. EVIDENCE ADMISSIBLE TO IDENTIFY PARTIES

Extrinsic evidence is admissible for the purpose of identifying the parties to a contract.[32]

10.15   Extrinsic evidence is admissible to identify the parties to a contract, by way of exception to the parol evidence rule.[33] However, although evidence is admissible to identify parties to a contract, where the parties are specifically named in a written contract, evidence is not admissible for the purpose of showing that others (who were not named) were also parties to the contract.[34] Accordingly, where the terms of an agreement unequivocally and exhaustively identify the parties to it, it is

---

[29] (1866) L.R. 1 Ex. 112.
[30] (1866) L.R. 1 Q.B. 413.
[31] (1867) L.R. 2 C.P. 559; *Isaacs v Green* (1867) L.R. 2 Exch. 352.
[32] This section was referred to with apparent approval in *Navig8 Inc v South Vigour Shipping Inc* [2015] EWHC 32 (Comm); [2015] 1 Lloyd's Rep. 436.
[33] *Hamid (t/a Hamid Properties) v Francis Bradshaw Partnership* [2013] EWCA Civ 470; *Yuchai Dongte Special Purpose Automobile Co Ltd v Suisse Credit Capital (2009) Ltd* [2018] EWHC 2580 (Comm).
[34] *Barbudev v Eurocom Cable Management Bulgaria EOOD* [2011] EWHC 1560 (Comm); [2011] 2 All E.R. (Comm) 951.

impermissible to seek to contradict it.[35] Likewise, where a contract identifies the principal upon whose behalf an agent enters a contract, it is not open to a party to suggest that the agent entered the contract on behalf of someone other than the identified principal. If the principal is not identified, then (subject to the terms of the contract) evidence may be adduced to identify the principal.[36] The existence of an "entire agreement" clause is a strong pointer to the conclusion that the right of an undisclosed principal to sue on the contract has been excluded.[37] The strength of such a clause is lower where the principal is disclosed.[38]

In *Homburg Houtimport BV v Agrosin Ltd (The Starsin)*,[39] Lord Millett said: **10.16**

"The identity of the parties to a contract is fundamental. It is not simply a term or condition of the contract. It goes to the very existence of the contract itself. If it is uncertain, there is no contract. Like the nature and amount of the consideration and the intention to create legal relations it is a question of fact and may be established by evidence. Such evidence is admissible even where the contract is in writing, at least so long as it does not contradict its express terms, and possibly even where it does."[40]

Similarly, in *Shogun Finance Ltd v Hudson*,[41] Lord Phillips of Worth Matravers said:

"Words in a language have one or more ordinary meaning, which will be known to anyone who speaks that language. Names are not those kind of words. A name is a word, or a series of words, that is used to identify a specific individual. It can be described as a label. Whenever a name is used, extrinsic evidence, or additional information, will be required in order to identify the specific individual that the user of the name intends to identify by the name—the person to whom he intends to attach the label. Almost all individuals have two or more names which they use to identify themselves and where a name is mentioned in a particular context, or a particular milieu, those who hear it may have the additional information that they need to identify to whom the speaker is referring.

Where a name appears in a written document, the document itself may contain additional information which will enable the reader to identify the individual to whom the writer intended to refer when he wrote the name."

In *Fung Ping Shan v Tong Shun*,[42] the respondent, a Chinese resident of Chicago,   **10.17**
and his nephew who lived in Victoria, Hong Kong, had names which were each properly transliterated in English as "Tong Shun", but which differed when written in Chinese characters. The nephew executed a deed by which land was conveyed to "Tong Shun of Victoria in the Colony of Hong Kong, thereinafter

---

[35] *Foster v Action Aviation Ltd* [2013] EWHC 2439 (Comm).
[36] *Aspen Underwriting Ltd v Kairos Shipping Ltd* [2017] EWHC 1904 (Comm); [2017] 2 C.L.C. 364.
[37] *Kaefer Aislamientos SA de CV v AMS Drilling Mexico SA de CV* [2019] EWCA Civ 10; [2019] 1 W.L.R. 3514; *Ivy Technology Ltd v Martin* [2020] EWHC 94 (Comm).
[38] *Filatona Trading Ltd v Navigator Equities Ltd* [2020] EWCA Civ 109.
[39] [2004] 1 A.C. 715; *Estor Ltd v Multifit (UK) Ltd* [2009] EWHC 2565 (TCC).
[40] However, in *Shogun Finance Ltd v Hudson* [2004] 1 A.C. 919, Lord Hobhouse of Woodborough (with whom Lord Walker of Gestingthorpe agreed) said that extrinsic evidence to identify a party could not be allowed to contradict the written contract. This approach was followed in *Barbudev v Eurocom Cable Management Bulgaria EOOD* [2011] EWHC 1560 (Comm).
[41] [2004] 1 A.C. 919.
[42] [1918] A.C. 403.

called 'the purchaser'". The deed witnessed that "the purchaser" had paid the consideration. The deed also contained covenants given by "the purchaser". The nephew signed the deed with the respondent's name written in Chinese characters, and he paid the consideration with money supplied by the respondent. Lord Parker of Waddington, delivering the advice of the Privy Council said:

"There can be no doubt that parol evidence as to the identity of a party to a deed is always admissible, but in considering such evidence it is of paramount importance to bear in mind the indicia of identity afforded by the deed itself. In the present case these indicia are as follows: the person to be looked for is a person who (1) is named Tong Shun; (2) resides at Victoria in the Colony of Hong Kong; (3) is a trader; (4) has paid the vendor [25,600] dollars; and (5) enters into a covenant with the vendor by signing, sealing, and delivering the indenture itself. The uncle's Chinese name may properly be rendered into English as Tong Shun, and he may, no doubt, be properly described as a trader. He also seems to have provided the 26,500 dollars paid to the vendor. But he was not resident in Hong Kong when the indenture was executed. On the contrary he resided at Chicago, his only connection with Hong Kong being that he was or had been a partner in certain businesses carried on in the Colony. He certainly did not either personally or by a properly constituted attorney sign seal or deliver the indenture, or thereby enter into any covenant with the vendor. The nephew on the other hand, has a Chinese name which may properly be rendered into English as Tong Shun; he resides in Victoria in that Colony; he is a trader. He paid the 26,500 dollars, though out of money provided by the uncle; he personally signed sealed and delivered the indenture, and he is the only person who could possibly be sued by the vendor on the covenant on the part of the purchaser therein contained."

10.18   Even though evidence is admissible, the task of deciding who was a party to a contract is still an objective exercise. In *Estor Ltd v Multifit (UK) Ltd*,[43] Akenhead J said:

"Where, as here in this case, one can not ascertain from the offer and acceptance who the employing party was, it must be legitimate to consider what the parties said to each other and what they did in the period leading up to the acceptance in order to determine who that party was intended to be. It was accepted, properly, by both Counsel, that in determining a factual issue such as this, the court needs to adopt an objective approach and to consider the facts known to both parties and what was said orally or in writing between the relevant individuals. The fact that one individual went to or left a meeting, believing privately that the contract was to be with a particular party, would be of little or no weight or assistance in determining who the contract was with, unless there was reliable evidence that that belief was expressed to others at the meeting. Obviously, where there was an issue as to the identity of a party entering into a contract, if there was evidence that representatives of each party had met before the contract was signed and had said to each other that the contract was to be between X and Y, that would be admissible and relevant in determining who the parties to the contract were to be. If however the evidence about what was said and done was not as explicit and clear as that, one needs to construe or infer objectively what reasonable parties would have assumed would be the position

---

[43]   [2009] EWHC 2565 (TCC).

based on what was said or done. Thus, it might well be the case that, if one party said that payments would be made by X, that would be evidence which would point, objectively albeit not necessarily conclusively, to X being one of the parties. Similarly, if X and Y in their discussions and correspondence prior to the creation of the contract only talked about X and Y in the context of their discussions, that might well be a factor which objectively pointed to those two parties being parties to the contract."

In *Hamid v Francis Bradshaw Partnership*,[44] Jackson LJ summarised the principles as follows: **10.19**

"In my view the principles which emerge from this line of authorities are the following:

i)   Where an issue arises as to the identity of a party referred to in a deed or contract, extrinsic evidence is admissible to assist the resolution of that issue.

ii) In determining the identity of the contracting party, the court's approach is objective, not subjective. The question is what a reasonable person, furnished with the relevant information, would conclude. The private thoughts of the protagonists concerning who was contracting with whom are irrelevant and inadmissible.

iii) If the extrinsic evidence establishes that a party has been misdescribed in the document, the court may correct that error as a matter of construction without any need for formal rectification.

iv) Where the issue is whether a party signed a document as principal or as agent for someone else, there is no automatic relaxation of the parol evidence rule. The person who signed is the contracting party unless (a) the document makes clear that he signed as agent for a sufficiently identified principal or as the officer of a sufficiently identified company, or (b) extrinsic evidence establishes that both parties knew he was signing as agent or company officer.

The expression "sufficiently identified" is "intended to include cases where there is an inconsequential misdescription of the entity on behalf of whom the individual was signing".

The same approach is adopted where a contract is purportedly made with a non-existent company. In *Goldsmith (F) (Sicklesmere) Ltd v Baxter*,[45] Stamp J said: **10.20**

"Looking at the memorandum alone, and without regard to the surrounding circumstances, I find that the person—the *persona ficta* said to be the vendor has the following characteristics: (1) it is named Goldsmith Coaches (Sicklesmere) Ltd; (2) its registered office is said to be at Sicklesmere; (3) it has an agent called Brewer who claims to act for it; (4) it is the beneficial owner of 'Shelley'.

---

44 [2013] EWCA Civ 470; [2013] B.L.R. 447; *Americas Bulk Transport Ltd v Cosco Bulk Carrier Ltd* [2020] EWHC 147 (Comm). In *Taylor v Rhino Overseas Inc* [2020] EWCA Civ 35, Arnold LJ noted some tension between this formulation and the more restrictive formulation in *Barbudev v Eurocom Cable Management Bulgaria EOOD* [2011] EWHC 1560 (Comm); [2011] 2 All E.R. (Comm) 951, but was content to assume that Jackson LJ's formulation was correct.
45 [1970] Ch. 85; *Front Carriers Ltd v Atlantic & Orient Shipping Corp* [2007] 2 Lloyd's Rep. 131.

Applying the rule that a contract is to be construed by reference to the surrounding circumstances or in the light of the known facts, I find; (1) there is no limited company which in law has the name Goldsmith Coaches (Sicklesmere) Ltd, but the plaintiff company is often known as 'Goldsmith Coaches' and carries on business as a bus and coach contractor, and it does so at Sicklesmere; (2) the plaintiff company's registered office is at Sicklesmere, in the very place at which it carries on the bus and coach business; (3) the plaintiff company has an agent called Brewster; and (4) it is the beneficial owner of 'Shelley'. I find in addition that there is no other company having those characteristics. Applying this process, if it be permissible, I conclude beyond peradventure that Goldsmith Coaches (Sicklesmere) Ltd is no more or less than an inaccurate description of the plaintiff company F. Goldsmith (Sicklesmere) Ltd."

10.21   However, although extrinsic evidence may be adduced to explain or identify a person named in a contract, evidence will not be allowed to contradict the written contract.[46]

Illustrations

1.   The defendant's agent wrote in a book of the plaintiff "Mr Newell, 32 sacks culasses, at 39s 28d to await orders". The plaintiff afterwards wrote to the agent about the flour he "had bought" and the agent replied referring to the flour he "had sold". It was held that the surrounding circumstances could be taken into account to identify the buyer and the seller.
Newell v Radford[47]

2.   Eliza Wray, Henry Wray, William James Wray and Joseph Turnbull carried on business in partnership under the name "William Wray" without the addition of "& Co". A conveyance purported to convey land to "William Wray". It was held that the conveyance took effect as a conveyance to the partners. Warrington J said:

"I have to ascertain who was meant by the person described as William Wray in the deed; and I find that I may instead of William Wray read the deed as a conveyance to the four partners."

Wray v Wray[48]

3.   A tenancy agreement described one of the parties as "tenant". Oral evidence was admitted to show that he entered into the agreement as agent or nominee of another.
Danziger v Thompson[49]

---

[46]   *Shogun Finance Ltd v Hudson* [2004] 1 A.C. 919. See also *Young v Schuler* (1883) 11 Q.B.D. 651; *JH Rayner (Mincing Lane) Ltd v Department of Trade and Industry* [1990] 2 A.C. 418.
[47]   (1867) L.R. 3 C.P. 52.
[48]   [1905] 2 Ch. 349.
[49]   [1944] K.B. 654. See also *Young v Schuler* (1883) 11 Q.B.D. 651 (evidence of agency admissible). But evidence is not admissible to show that a person described as tenant was acting as agent for an undisclosed principal: *Hanstown Properties v Green* [1978] 1 E.G.L.R. 85, nor where the terms of the written contract are inconsistent with agency: *JH Rayner (Mincing Lane) Ltd v Department of Trade and Industry* [1990] 2 A.C. 418.

8. MISNOMER

The court may correct an obvious misnomer as a matter of interpretation[50]

In *Nittan (UK) Ltd v Solent Steel Fabrications Ltd*,[51] the defendant acquired the   **10.22**
assets of a company called Sargrove Electronics Controls Ltd. It did not, however,
acquire the company itself. It began to trade under the name Sargrove Automation.
The defendant insured against product liability and the insurers issued an endorsement to the policy to the effect that the insured should be deemed to include
Sargrove Electronic Controls Ltd. It was held that Sargrove Electronic Controls Ltd
was a misnomer which could be corrected by the court. Brightman LJ said:

"In my opinion, in construing a document, the Court is at liberty, as a matter of
construction, to correct a misnomer. A misnomer is not, in my view, necessarily
a mistake which requires the equitable remedy of rectification. The misnomer
may be a mere clerical error. A simple example would be the use in a conveyance of the expression 'the vendor' when clearly 'the purchaser' was intended.
It is not necessary to rectify the conveyance to enable it to be read as the parties
plainly intended. The words 'Sargrove Electronic Controls Limited' are used
three times in the endorsement of May 30. The words mean 'Solent Steel trading as Sargrove Automation'—that is to say, carrying on the business of
manufacturers of electronic apparatus as stated in the wording of the earlier
endorsement."

However, in *Durnford Trading AG v OAO Atlantrybflot*,[52] Rix LJ said: **10.23**

"It seems to me that the doctrine of misnomer is of uncertain width. It is clearly
a doctrine of construction, but it is not plain to what extent it permits the reference to extrinsic evidence. *Davies v Elsby Brothers Ltd*[53] would suggest that
where there are two possible entities, the rule is a strict one: unless one can say
from the four corners of the document that the parties must have intended to refer
to one rather than the other entity, then the doctrine does not apply. If, however,
there is only one possible entity, then it is possible to use extrinsic evidence to
identify a misdescribed party. It is arguable that *Nittan v Solent Steel*[54] falls into
this latter category. Moreover, the cases, as does common sense, suggest that a
case of mere misnomer is not easily (query if ever?) concluded to be such without
the mistake being explicable."

In *Derek Hodd Ltd v Climate Change Capital Ltd*,[55] Henderson J held that there   **10.24**
are no special rules of interpretation applicable to a case of alleged misnomer. In
so doing he disagreed with the tentative view expressed by Rix LJ in *Dumford Trading AG v OAO Atlantrybflot*. Similarly, in *Liberty Mercian v Cuddy Civil Engineer-*

---

[50]   This section was referred to with apparent approval in *Tecnicas Reunidas Saudia for Services and
Contracting Co Ltd v Korea Development Bank* [2020] EWHC 968 (TCC).
[51]   [1981] 1 Lloyd's Rep. 633, distinguished in *Yamaha-Kemble Music (UK) Ltd v ARC Properties Ltd*
[1990] 1 E.G.L.R. 261. See also paras 9.01–9.39.
[52]   [2005] 1 Lloyd's Rep. 289.
[53]   [1961] 1 W.L.R. 170.
[54]   [1981] 1 Lloyd's Rep. 633.
[55]   [2013] EWHC 1665 (Ch).

ing Ltd,[56] Ramsey J doubted whether the view expressed by Rix LJ could survive the re-statement of principle in *Chartbrook v Persimmon Homes Ltd.*[57] He held that in the case of an alleged misnomer the two relevant questions were: first, whether it was clear from the contract read against the admissible background that a mistake had been made; and second, whether it was clear what correction should be made. In the light of these cases, it is thought that the tentative view of Rix LJ is too narrow.

10.25   But even if that view is correct, the court would be able to take into account the same evidence of the background as would be admissible for the purpose of interpreting the contract,[58] including any relevant course of dealing between the parties.[59] In the end the question is one of interpretation of the contract in question,[60] and therefore the material available and the techniques used in contractual interpretation ought to apply even where the allegation is one of misnomer.[61] In *Front Carriers Ltd v Atlantic and Orient Shipping Corp*,[62] it was held that whether there has been a misnomer is a question of construction, viewed against the objective background facts; which supports this view.

9.   THIRD PARTY MAY TAKE THE BENEFIT OF A CONTRACT

In some cases an identified third party may take the benefit of a contract.

10.26   In some cases a person not a party to a deed may be able to rely on s.56(1) of the Law of Property Act 1925 which provides:

> "A person may take an immediate or other interest in land or other property, or the benefit of any condition, right of entry, covenant or agreement over or respecting land or other property, although he may not be named as a party to the conveyance or other instrument."

A discussion of the effect of s.56 is a matter of substantive law, and consequently outside the scope of this book. However, it may be mentioned that the section received the attention of the House of Lords in *Beswick v Beswick.*[63] Their Lordships unanimously held that s.56 had not abolished privity of contract, and that a person could not sue on a contract merely because he would benefit by its performance. However, their Lordships were not unanimous in deciding what the section did achieve. It seems clear that s.56 does not apply to personal property but applies only to real property.[64] It may also be the case that s.56 is confined to docu-

---

[56]   [2013] EWHC 2688 (TCC).

[57]   [2009] 1 A.C. 1101.

[58]   *Gastronome (UK) Ltd v Anglo Dutch Meats (UK) Ltd* [2006] 2 Lloyd's Rep. 587. Henderson J expressly approved this statement in *Derek Hodd Ltd v Climate Change Capital Ltd* [2013] EWHC 1665 (Ch).

[59]   *Connex South Eastern Ltd v MJ Building Services Group Plc* [2005] 2 All E.R. 871.

[60]   *Seb Trygg Holding AG v Manches* [2005] 2 Lloyd's Rep. 129; *Front Carriers Ltd v Atlantic and Orient Shipping Corp* [2007] 2 Lloyd's Rep. 131.

[61]   This proposition was approved in *Tecnicas Reunidas Saudia for Services and Contracting Co Ltd v Korea Development Bank* [2020] EWHC 968 (TCC).

[62]   [2007] 2 Lloyd's Rep. 131.

[63]   [1968] A.C. 58.

[64]   Per Lord Reid at 77; Lord Hodson at 81 and Lord Guest at 87.

ments under seal, made strictly inter partes in which one party expressly purports to covenant with someone not a party or to make a grant to such a person.[65]

10.27 The law has been considerably changed as regards third parties by the Contracts (Rights of Third Parties) Act 1999.[66] Section 1 of that Act provides:

"(1)   Subject to the provisions of this Act, a person who is not a party to a contract (a "third party") may in his own right enforce a term of the contract if—

(a)   the contract expressly provides that he may, or

(b)   subject to subsection (2), the term purports to confer a benefit on him.

(2)   Subsection (1)(b) does not apply if on a proper construction of the contract it appears that the parties did not intend the term to be enforceable by the third party.

(3)   The third party must be expressly identified in the contract by name, as a member of a class or as answering a particular description but need not be in existence when the contract is entered into.

(4)   This section does not confer a right on a third party to enforce a term of a contract otherwise than subject to and in accordance with any other relevant terms of the contract.

(5)   For the purpose of exercising his right to enforce a term of the contract, there shall be available to the third party any remedy that would have been available to him in an action for breach of contract if he had been a party to the contract (and the rules relating to damages, injunctions, specific performance and other relief shall apply accordingly).

(6)   Where a term of a contract excludes or limits liability in relation to any matter references in this Act to the third party enforcing the term shall be construed as references to his availing himself of the exclusion or limitation.

(7)   In this Act, in relation to a term of a contract which is enforceable by a third party—

"the promisor" means the party to the contract against whom the term is enforceable by the third party, and "the promisee" means the party to the contract by whom the term is enforceable against the promisor."

10.28 In considering whether a contract term purports to confer a benefit on a third party for the purposes of the Contracts (Rights of Third Parties) Act 1999, it is not enough that the contract confers a benefit on a third party in a general sense. The

---

[65]   Per Lord Upjohn at 106 ("obiter and tentative") and Lord Pearce at 94; *Amsprop Trading Ltd v Harris Distribution Ltd* [1997] 1 W.L.R. 1025.

[66]   The Act came into force on 11 November 1999 except in the case of a contract made before 11 May 2000. It does not apply to the following kinds of contract: a contract on a bill of exchange, promissory note or other negotiable instrument; a contract binding on a company and its members under the Companies Act 1985 s.14; any incorporation document of a limited liability partnership or any limited liability partnership agreement; a contract for the carriage of goods by sea, a contract for the carriage of goods by rail or road, or for the carriage of cargo by air, which is subject to the rules of the appropriate international transport convention (except that an exclusion clause in a contract of carriage may be relied on by a third party). Nor does the Act give a third party the right to enforce any term of a contract of employment against an employee, any term of a worker's contract against a worker (including a home worker), or any term of a relevant contract against an agency worker: s.6.

focus must be on whether a particular term purports to confer a benefit on the third party.[67]

10.29 In order to satisfy s.1(1)(b), the claimant must show that the term of the contract relied upon purports to confer a benefit upon him. If the claimant succeeds in showing that the term purports to confer a benefit upon him, he is entitled to enforce the term directly against the defendant unless the defendant persuades the court that the parties did not intend the term to be enforceable by him.[68] If the contract is neutral on this question, subs.(2) does not disapply subs.1(b). Whether the contract does express a mutual intention that the third party should not be entitled to enforce the benefit conferred on him or is merely neutral is a matter of construction having regard to all relevant circumstances.[69]

10.30 Section 1(1)(b) is satisfied if on a true construction of the term in question its sense has the effect of conferring a benefit on the third party in question. There is within s.1(1)(b) no requirement that the benefit on the third party shall be the predominant purpose or intent behind the term or that it denies the applicability of s.1(1)(b) if a benefit is conferred on someone other than the third party.[70] However, the reference in s.1(1) to the term purporting to "confer" a benefit connotes that the language used by the parties shows that one of the purposes of their bargain (rather than one of its incidental effects if performed) was to benefit the third party. Thus a provision for payment of a sum to an agent on his principal's behalf is to be contrasted with an agreement by A and B that A will pay C (C not being A's agent or trustee). In the latter case (but not in the former) s.1(1)(b) will be satisfied.[71]

10.31 Whether there is express identification of a class of which the claimants are members for the purposes of s.1(3), will depend upon the construction of the contract as a whole, viewed against the admissible factual matrix.[72] The same contract term may suffice both for the purposes of s.1(2)(b) and also for the purposes of s.1(3).[73] Section 1(3), by use of the word "express", does not allow a process of construction by implication.[74] A class described as "any previous tenant" was sufficient express identification.[75] So also was a description of a segregated client account and the purpose of the account.[76]

10. RECITALS

The function of recitals is to narrate the history leading up to the making of the agreement in question or to express in general terms the intention with which the agreement was made.

10.32 Recitals are less common than they once were. Recitals were rarely used in commercial contracts, but were frequent in conveyancing documents and deeds effect-

---

[67] *Royal Bank of Scotland Plc v McCarthy* [2015] EWHC 3626 (QB).

[68] *Laemthong International Lines Co Ltd v Artis* [2005] 2 All E.R. (Comm) 167.

[69] *Nisshin Shipping Co Ltd v Cleaves & Co Ltd* [2004] 1 All E.R. (Comm) 481.

[70] *Prudential Assurance Co Ltd v Ayres* [2007] 28 E.G. 122.

[71] *Dolphin Maritime & Aviation Services Ltd v Sveriges Angartygs Assurans Forening* [2009] EWHC 716 (Comm).

[72] *Chudley v Clydesdale Bank Plc* [2019] EWCA Civ 344; [2020] Q.B. 284.

[73] *Chudley v Clydesdale Bank Plc* [2019] EWCA Civ 344; [2020] Q.B. 284.

[74] *Avraamides v Colwill* [2007] B.L.R. 76, explained in *Chudley v Clydesdale Bank Plc* [2019] EWCA Civ 344; [2020] Q.B. 284.

[75] *Prudential Assurance Co Ltd v Ayres* [2007] 28 E.G. 122.

[76] *Chudley v Clydesdale Bank Plc* [2019] EWCA Civ 344; [2020] Q.B. 284.

ing dispositions of property. The spread of registered title has diminished the usefulness of recitals in conveyancing transactions. Nevertheless, they are still used in some transactions, especially where the parties desire to record formally the background to the transaction, or where the transaction is supplemental to an earlier transaction. They can also be used to describe the purpose of the contract.[77]

In *Square Mile Partnership Ltd v Fitzmaurice McCall Ltd*,[78] Arden LJ said: **10.33**

"Steps taken in preparation for an agreement are usually referred to in the recitals to an agreement if they are referred to at all. Recitals of this kind can be useful for interpreting the agreement."

As Hammond J observed in *Dysart Timbers Ltd v Nielsen*[79]:

"The recitals ('background') are very important, for these are 'agreed' facts."

Likewise, in *OneSteel Manufacturing Pty Ltd v BlueScope Steel (AIS) Pty Ltd*,[80] Allsop P pointed out that:

"There may be other background facts, but the recitals reveal the background *chosen by the parties* by way of the identification of relevant context. The recitals can assist in interpretation of operative provisions, though they do not control the latter's operation when clear and unambiguous."[81]

In *IRC v Raphael*,[82] Lord Wright said:

"The nature of recitals as statements of fact which are in the contemplation of the parties, is illustrated by the Scotch term 'narrative'."

In *Rust Consulting Ltd v PB Ltd*,[83] a recital was taken as encapsulating the "factual matrix" against which the contract was to be interpreted.
In other cases recitals perform the function of: **10.34**

"a preliminary statement of what the maker of the deed intended should be the effect and purpose of the whole deed when made."[84]

As Campbell JA pointed out in *Franklins Pty Ltd v Metcash Trading Ltd*[85]:

"Recitals can be of various kinds—including statements of the factual background to the transaction, statements of the intention or object of the parties in entering the transaction, or statements that the parties (or one or other of them) have agreed to do or will do certain acts."

Where the recitals purport to record the intention of the parties to the document **10.35**

---

[77] *Dorchester Project Management Ltd v BNP Paribas Real Estate Advisory & Property Management UK Ltd* [2013] EWCA Civ 176.
[78] [2007] 2 B.C.L.C. 23.
[79] [2007] NZCA 198.
[80] [2013] NSWCA 27.
[81] Emphasis in original.
[82] [1935] A.C. 96.
[83] [2010] EWHC 3243 (TCC).
[84] *Mackenzie v Duke of Devonshire* [1896] A.C. 400, per Lord Halsbury LC.
[85] [2009] NSWCA 407 at [379].

(or, more frequently, the settlor of a settlement), the court is wary of attributing much weight to such a statement. In *Mackenzie v Duke of Devonshire*,[86] Lord Watson said:

> "I think that it is a very dangerous canon of construction to admit what may be a very partial statement of intention, quite consistent with other objects, to control the whole of the other language of the deed with the effect of striking out beneficiaries whom the truster may have intended to benefit. The narrative words come to no more than this: 'My intention is to do' so and so, and you may add this, 'and I have accomplished that purpose by the provisions which follow.' In such a case the safer and only legitimate course is to look at the provisions which follow, and to read them according to their natural and just construction."

10.36   In describing a recital as an expression of the intention of the parties to the deed, it should not be overlooked that the word intention may have different connotations in different circumstances. This was pointed out in *IRC v Raphael*[87] by Lord Warrington of Clyffe who said:

> "The fact is that the narrative and operative parts of a deed perform quite different functions, and 'intention' in reference to the narrative and the same word in reference to the operative parts respectively bear quite different significations. As appearing in the narrative part it means 'purpose'. In considering the intention of operative part the word means significance or import? 'The way in which anything is to be understood' (*Oxford English Dictionary*) supported by the illustration: 'The intention of the passage was sufficiently clear'."

11.   RECITALS AS AN AID TO INTERPRETATION

Recitals may be taken into account by the court as an aid to interpretation.

10.37   The recitals to a document may perform a different function to the operative part of the document, but nevertheless they are part of the document itself, or at least part of the context in which the contract is made. Since the circumstances surrounding the making of a contract may be relied on as an aid to interpretation, it follows that recitals may be similarly relied on.[88] Accordingly, a recital may set out the background and purpose of an agreement.[89] In order for a recital to be an aid to interpretation it must be capable of being read consistently with the operative parts of the contract.[90]

10.38   As Arden LJ said in *Square Mile Partnership Ltd v Fitzmaurice McCall Ltd*[91]:

> "Steps taken in preparation for an agreement are usually referred to in the recitals to an agreement if they are referred to at all. Recitals of this kind can be useful for interpreting the agreement."

---

[86]   [1896] A.C. 400.

[87]   [1935] A.C. 96.

[88]   *Franklins Pty Ltd v Metcash Trading Ltd* [2009] NSWCA 407 at [380]; *GB Gas Holdings Ltd v Accenture (UK) Ltd* [2010] EWCA Civ 912 at [34]; *AMEC Foster Wheeler Group Ltd v Morgan Sindall Professional Services Ltd* [2015] EWHC 2012 (TCC).

[89]   *Mulville v Sandelson* [2019] EWHC 3287 (Ch).

[90]   *Attorney General v River Dorée Holdings Ltd* [2017] UKPC 39.

[91]   [2007] 2 B.C.L.C. 23.

In *Orr v Mitchell*,[92] Lord Herschell LC said:

"No authority has been cited which establishes that according to the law of Scotland, where a provision contained in a deed has to be construed, it is not legitimate to look at the whole deed in order to determine what is the true construction of the provision in question. In the absence of such authority, I am of opinion that light may properly be sought from every part of the deed, though I do not of course, say that every part of it is of equal weight."

The law of Scotland does not appear to differ from the law of England and Wales **10.39** in this respect. In the same case Lord Macnaghten said:

"When the words in the dispositive or operative part of a deed of conveyance are clear and unambiguous they cannot be corrected by reference to other parts of the instrument. When those words are susceptible of two constructions the context may properly be referred to for the purpose of determining which of the two constructions is the true meaning. In order to justify a reference to the context for this purpose, it is not necessary that the language of the dispositive or operative clause should be ambiguous in the sense that without some help you cannot tell which of two meanings should be taken. The rule applies though one of the two meanings is the more obvious one, and would necessarily be preferred if no light could be derived from the rest of the deed. For the purpose of construing the dispositive or operative clause, the whole of the instrument may be referred to though the introductory narrative or recitals leading up to that clause are, perhaps, more likely to furnish the key of its true construction than the subsidiary clauses of the deed."

This approach treats recitals as being part of the context in which the contract is made, and hence admissible aids to interpretation. In most cases this will be enough. It has been said that:

"there is a distinction between the operative terms of a contract and the recitals. Although the recitals can assist in the construction of a contract, they are not themselves operative terms."[93]

However, in practice one does encounter recitals coming before the operative part **10.40** of the document which contain elaborate definition clauses clearly intended to govern the meaning of expressions used in the operative part of the contract itself. In such a case it seems obvious that whatever may be the technical rules about allowing recitals to govern the operative part of a deed, the court would not interpret the document without adopting the recited definitions.[94]

---

92 [1893] A.C. 238.
93 *Franklins Pty Ltd v Metcash Trading Ltd* [2009] NSWCA 407 at [380].
94 See *The Karen Oltmann* [1976] 2 Lloyd's Rep. 708 (referred to in para.3.60) and para.5.91.

12.   RECITALS AND CONTRACTS WHOSE MEANING IS CLEAR

Where the words of the operative part of the contract are clear they will not be controlled, cut down or qualified by the recitals.

10.41   In *Walsh v Trevanion*,[95] Patteson J said:

"… when the words in the operative part of a deed of conveyance are clear and unambiguous, they cannot be controlled by the recitals or other parts of the deed. On the other hand, when those words are of doubtful meaning, the recitals and other parts of the deed may be used as a test to discover the intention of the parties, and to fix the true meaning of those words."

Similarly, in *Holliday v Overton*,[96] Sir John Romilly MR said:

"… it is impossible by a recital to cut down the plain effect of the operative part of a deed."

10.42   Lord Halsbury L.C. expressed himself with characteristic forcefulness in *Mackenzie v Duke of Devonshire*[97] in the following terms:

"If the trust purposes are set forth in the paragraph of the deed which is appropriate to such purposes, it seems to me to be absolutely unarguable that the true meaning of those words, and the purposes of the trust so set forth, can be in any way controlled, qualified, or modified by the initial statement of what the motive of the author of the deed was. It would to my mind be disastrous to introduce such a system of construing a deed. One has known the language of a will sometimes perverted to perform the function which it was assumed the testator intended to be performed, but I never in my life heard of the language of a deed which contained a perfectly unambiguous provision being twisted from the natural ordinary meaning of the words by a preliminary statement of what the maker of the deed intended should be the effect and purpose of the whole deed when made."

In the same case Lord Davey said:

"I take it to be a settled principle of law that the operative words of a deed which are expressed in clear and unambiguous language are not to be controlled, cut down, or qualified by a recital or narrative of intention."

10.43   In *Ex p. Dawes, Re Moon*,[98] Lord Esher MR said:

"Now there are three rules applicable to the construction of such an instrument. If the recitals are clear and the operative part is ambiguous, the recitals govern the construction. If the recitals are ambiguous, and the operative part is clear, the operative part must prevail. If both the recitals and the operative part are clear, but they are inconsistent with each other, the operative part is to be preferred."

---

[95]   (1850) 15 Q.B. 733, applied in *The Management Corp Strata v Liang Huat Aluminium Ltd* [2001] B.L.R. 351 (CA of Singapore).

[96]   (1852) 14 Beav. 467.

[97]   [1896] A.C. 440.

[98]   (1886) 17 Q.B.D. 275, followed in *T&N Ltd (in administration) v Royal & Sun Alliance Plc* [2003] 2 All E.R. (Comm) 939.

Lopes LJ said:

"There are several well-established rules applicable to the construction of deeds. One is this, that if the operative part of a deed is clear, and the recitals are not clear the operative part must prevail. Again, if the recitals are clear, but the operative part is ambiguous, the recitals control the operative part. If, again, the operative part and the recitals are both clear, but one is inconsistent with the other, the operative part must prevail."

This principle was applied in *Gallaher International Ltd v Tlais Enterprises Ltd.*[99] As Coulson J put it in *Brookfield Construction (UK) Ltd v Foster & Partners Ltd,*[100] "in the event of a clash" a contractual definition must take precedence over a recital. Likewise, in *Ondhia v Ondhia,*[101] the recital to a settlement agreement did not override the clear words of the operative part of the agreement. In *J Toomey Motors Ltd v Chevrolet UK Ltd*[102] the court refused to hold that a recital operated as an obligation covering matters that were dealt with elsewhere in the contract.   **10.44**

In *Russell v Stone (t/a PSP Consultants)*[103] parties entered into a standstill agreement. The agreement recited that they had agreed to enter into the standstill agreement "to extend the period in which proceedings can be issued and thereby extending the limitation period". However, cl.2 of the agreement provided that time would be "suspended" from the date of the agreement; and cl.2(c) reserved the parties' right to raise any limitation or similar defence arguments that they might have up to the date of the agreement whether known or unknown. Coulson J held that cl.2, which merely suspended time, took precedence over the recital which referred to extending time.   **10.45**

Likewise in *Attorney-General v Dorée Holdings Ltd*[104] a recital could not be used to insert an additional condition into an option. As Sir Bernard Rix put it, in case of inconsistency between a recital and a substantive obligation: **10.46**

"… high authority dictates that in such circumstances preference must be given to a substantive provision over a recital."

Modern methods of interpretation, in which background plays a far larger part than used to be the case, may have tempered the apparent rigidity of older statements of principle requiring ambiguity before recourse could be had to recitals.   **10.47**

"insofar as these earlier decisions require a finding of 'ambiguity', and proceed on the basis that it is possible to read the operative provisions without the aid of context, those decisions should not be followed. It would follow then that the recitals in a deed can be looked at as part of the surrounding circumstances of the contract without a need to find ambiguity in the operative provisions of the contract."[105]

---

[99] [2008] EWHC 804 (Comm) at [997].
[100] [2009] B.L.R. 246.
[101] [2012] EWCA Civ 1927.
[102] [2017] EWHC 276 (Comm).
[103] [2017] EWHC 1555 (TCC); [2017] P.N.L.R. 34.
[104] [2017] UKPC 39.
[105] *Franklins Pty Ltd v Metcash Trading Ltd* [2009] NSWCA 407 at [380]. This observation reflects the opinion stated in previous editions of this book. It appears to have been approved by Coulson J in *Russell v Stone (t/a PSP Consultants)* [2017] EWHC 1555 (TCC); [2017] P.N.L.R. 34.

Illustrations

1.   A bond recited an agreement that a certain person should serve as an engineer in the East Indies at a monthly salary to commence from the day of his embarkation at Southampton. The operative part of the bond mentioned no place of embarkation but merely the destination. The principal left for the East Indies but failed to arrive. He did not embark at Southampton. It was held that the surety of the bond was liable notwithstanding that the principal did not embark at Southampton.
   Evans v Earle[106]

2.   A marriage settlement recited that, after acquired, property of the wife should be settled on the trusts of the settlement. The operative part contained a covenant to settle after acquired property by the husband alone. It was held that the covenant could not be controlled by the recital.
   Young v Smith[107]

3.   A marriage settlement recited an agreement that all real and personal property, which during the coverture should devolve or vest in the wife or the husband in her right to the value of £200, should be settled on the trusts of the settlement. In the operative part of the settlement the husband covenanted that if at any time during the coverture any real or personal estate should devolve on or vest in the wife or the husband in her right to the amount in value of £200 at any one time, the husband would make or do all things necessary as would effectually vest such real or personal estate in the trustees of the settlement. It was held that the recitals could not control the operative part and that the husband was not liable in respect of property over which he had no power and in which he had no interest.
   Dawes v Tredwell[108]

4.   Bailey and others gave a joint and several guarantee to a bank, limited to £2,500 in respect of a customer's overdraft. The guarantee was invalid. Subsequently he and others gave a joint and several bond reciting a desire for advances to the same customer over and above £2,500. The operative part of the bond secured payment of all moneys whatsoever which the customer should borrow and all other moneys which the bank might advance for the accommodation of the customer or otherwise on his account. Bailey argued that his liability under the bond was limited to advances in excess of £2,500. The Privy Council held that the operative part was clear and could not be controlled by the recital. Bailey was therefore liable for all moneys advanced by the bank.
   Australian Joint Stock Bank v Bailey[109]

---

[106] (1854) 10 Exch. 1.
[107] (1865-66) L.R. 1 Eq. 180.
[108] (1881) 8 Ch. D. 354.
[109] [1899] A.C. 396.

13. RECITALS AND CONTRACTS WHOSE MEANING IS OTHERWISE UNCLEAR

Where the operative part of a contract is unclear, the recitals may be used to control, cut down or qualify the operative part.[110]

The first of the three principles formulated by Lord Esher MR in *Ex p. Dawes, Re Moon*[111] was that: **10.48**

"If the recitals are clear and the operative part is ambiguous, the recitals govern the construction."

To similar effect is the following statement of Jessell MR in *Re Michell's Trusts*[112]:

"Another thing which I think we may consider settled by authority is, that where the words of a covenant are ambiguous and difficult to deal with, we may resort to the recitals to see whether they throw any light on its meaning."

In *Mr H TV Ltd v ITV2 Ltd*,[113] Flaux J said that "where there is ambiguity within the operative parts of a contract and a recital is clear, the recital will govern the construction of the contract".

It may be noted, however, that before his ennoblement as Lord Esher, Brett LJ   **10.49**
had said in *Leggott v Barrett*[114]:

"If there is any doubt about the construction of the governing words of [the] document, the recital may be looked at in order to determine what is the true construction; but if there is no doubt about the construction, the rights of the parties are governed entirely by the operative part of the writing or deed."

This formulation does not require the demonstration of a true ambiguity before   **10.50**
resort may be had to the recitals. As Lord Macnaghten said in *Orr v Mitchell*[115]:

"In order to justify a reference to the context for this purpose, it is not necessary that the language of the dispositive or operative clause should be ambiguous in the sense that without some help you cannot determine which of two meanings should be taken. The rule applies though one of the two meanings is the more obvious one, and would necessarily be preferred if no light could be derived from the rest of the deed."

An even broader view was taken by Holt LCJ in *Bath & Montagu's Case*,[116] in which he said:

"The reciting part of a deed is not a necessary part either in law or in equity. It may be made use of to explain a doubt of the intention and meaning of the parties, but it hath no other effect or operation."

---

[110] This section was referred to with approval in *Four Marketing Ltd v Bradshaw* [2016] EWHC 3292 (QB); *Russell v Stone (t/a PSP Consultants)* [2017] EWHC 1555 (TCC); [2017] P.N.L.R. 34 and *The Owners—Strata Plan No.69567 v Baseline Constructions Pty Ltd* [2013] NSWSC 409.
[111] (1886) 17 Q.B.D. 275.
[112] (1878) 9 Ch. D. 5. See also *Pearsall v Summersett* (1812) 4 Taunt. 593.
[113] [2015] EWHC 2840 (Comm).
[114] (1880) 15 Ch. D. 306.
[115] [1893] A.C. 238.
[116] (1693) 3 Cas. in Ch. 55.

10.51   It appears, therefore, that recitals may be used to control the operative part of a contract in any case where the language of the operative part is not absolutely clear. Such a conclusion would be consistent with the general principle that any contract must be interpreted as a whole and in the light of the background knowledge available to both parties when the contract was made. Whether the recitals are regarded as being part of the contract itself or merely part of that background knowledge, the result is the same. It is submitted therefore that recitals may govern or qualify the operative part of a contract even where the contract is not ambiguous in the true sense, provided that there is some doubt about its true meaning, when read as a whole.[117]

10.52   Thus in *Crouch v Crouch*,[118] a separation agreement recited that the husband agreed to pay the wife 5s per week for her maintenance during her life so long as she should remain chaste. The operative part of the deed contained a covenant by the husband to pay the said sum of 5s to his wife on Saturday in each week. It was held that the covenant was limited by the recital and the husband was only liable to make the weekly payment for as long as the wife remained chaste. Lord Coleridge J said:

> "The recital is particular because it states that the payment to the wife is to be made so long as she is chaste, but the operative part of the deed is ambiguous because it does not show when the 5s begins to be payable or how long the weekly payment is to last—whether it is to be payable for the life of the wife, and whether it is to be paid by the husband's executors in case he predeceases her. Therefore it seems to me that the recital is clear and the operative part ambiguous, and that being so, the recital governs the construction of the deed."

In *Ross v Bank of Commerce (Saint Kitts Nevis) Trust and Savings Association Ltd*,[119] the Privy Council interpreted an unclear document by reference to its recitals, even though the recitals themselves were badly expressed. In *Frankland v Frankland*,[120] the words of the relevant clause were not clear. Birss J thus looked at the recitals to the agreement in order to solve the problem of interpretation. As he pointed out:

> "In any event the overall purpose of a clause and a contract as a whole is something to take into account in the exercise of interpretation ... and in this contract an indication of the overall purpose is set out in the recitals. The recitals do not merely reflect the subjective intentions of the parties since the recitals are part of the words of the document agreed to by both of them."

10.53   On similar principles, where a contract is ambiguous, the court may resolve the ambiguity by looking at the way in which the consideration is expressed.[121] In *Bank of India v Patel*,[122] the consideration clause of a guarantee referred to the provision of "banking facilities". It was argued for the guarantor that the wide words of

---

[117] Approved in *Longdale Pty Ltd v Vence Pty Ltd* [2009] VSC 471; and see *Franklins Pty Ltd v Metcash Trading Ltd* [2009] NSWCA 407 at [380].
[118] [1912] 1 K.B. 378.
[119] [2012] UKPC 3.
[120] [2017] EWHC 3063 (Ch).
[121] *National Bank of Nigeria Ltd v Oba M.S. Awolesi* [1964] 1 W.L.R. 1311; *Bank of India v Trans Continental Commodity Merchants Ltd* [1982] 1 Lloyd's Rep. 506.
[122] [1982] 1 Lloyd's Rep. 507.

the operative part of the document, which were apt to cover money due on foreign exchange transactions, should be restricted to "banking facilities". For the purpose of dealing with the argument Bingham J assumed that "banking facilities" did not include foreign exchange facilities. His Lordship said:

"It is also plain that the whole document must be construed, and if the meaning of the substantive provisions is unclear regard may be paid to the way in which the consideration is expressed ... I am, however, of opinion, that the language of this guarantee was deliberately drawn in the widest possible language so as to cover any liability of the company to the Bank arising out of their mutual relations as banker and customer, however that liability might arise and whether it arose out of what may be called a pure banking activity or not. I consider the language of the substantive clause so clear as to obviate the need for reference to the introductory recital, but even if regard is paid to that recital and 'banking facilities' were assumed not to include foreign exchange facilities I could not read the recital as cutting down in any way the deliberately wide language which follows."

His decision was upheld by the Court of Appeal.[123]

Illustrations

1.   A deed of composition recited that the debtor was entitled to certain property specified in a schedule to the deed, and had agreed to assign all such property to his trustee for the purpose of securing a composition with his creditors. The operative part of the deed in pursuance of the said agreement assigned to the trustee all the property set out in the schedule and all the estate right title interest claim and demand of the debtor to the said property "and all other and estate (if any)" of the debtor. It was held that the general words of assignment were controlled by the recital and applied only to the property listed in the schedule.
   Ex p. Dawes, Re Moon[124]

2.   Parties to an agreement relating to trademarks were in dispute about whether the description of goods was confined to goods within a particular class of the Nice classification of trademarked goods. It was held, by reference to the recital, that the concern of the agreement was with the use of trademarks, rather than with their registration. Since the Nice classification was concerned with registration rather than use, the goods described were not limited to those falling within the Nice classification.
   Omega Engineering Incorporated v Omega SA[125]

---

[123]   [1983] 2 Lloyd's Rep. 298.
[124]   (1886) 17 Q.B.D. 275.
[125]   [2010] F.S.R. 625.

14. INCONSISTENCY BETWEEN RECITALS AND OPERATIVE PART

In the case of an inconsistency between the recitals and the operative part of the contract, the operative part prevails.[126]

10.54   The third of the three principles propounded by Lord Esher MR in *Ex p. Dawes, Re Moon*[127] was that:

> "If both the recitals and the operative part are clear, but they are inconsistent with each other, the operative part is to be preferred."

Sir John Romilly MR said in *Young v Smith*[128]:

> "I have always held that where the recitals and the operative part of a deed are at variance, the operative part must be officious and the recitals inofficious."

10.55   As Coulson J put it in *Brookfield Construction (UK) Ltd v Foster & Partners Ltd*,[129] "in the event of a clash" a contractual definition must take precedence over a recital.
In *Franklins Pty Ltd v Metcash Trading Ltd*,[130] Campbell JA observed:

> "That a recital can be looked at as part of the surrounding circumstances of the contract still leaves room for the rule ... that where the recital is in conflict with the true interpretation of an operative provision (according to the modern standards of interpretation), the operative provision prevails. Strictly speaking, that is not so much a rule of construction as a reflection of the fact that recitals are not operative provisions in a contract."

Illustration

A mortgage recited that there was a limit of €5 million on a covenantor's liability "whether by way of principal and interest or otherwise as well as other moneys whatsoever now or at any time hereafter owed or to be owed to the Mortgagee". The operative covenant in the deed of covenant provided that there would be a limit on liability "to a principal amount of €5,000,000 together with interest, costs and expenses of collection". The covenant prevailed over the recital, with the effect that the limit applied only to the amount of principal due.
Qatar National Bank QPSC v The Owner of the Yacht Force India[131]

15. RECITAL AS OBLIGATION

In an appropriate case the court may interpret a recital as carrying with it an obligation to carry into effect that which is recited.[132]

10.56   Any words in a contract which show an agreement to do a thing amount to an

---

[126] This proposition was approved in *Qatar National Bank QPSC v The Owner of the Yacht Force India* [2020] EWHC 103 (Admlty).
[127] (1886) 17 Q.B.D. 275.
[128] (1865) L.R. 1 Eq. 180.
[129] [2009] B.L.R. 246.
[130] [2009] NSWCA 407 at [390].
[131] [2020] EWHC 103 (Admlty).
[132] This section was referred to with apparent approval in *Franklins Pty Ltd v Metcash Trading Ltd*

obligation.[133] No special language is necessary. Accordingly, the court may interpret a recital as carrying with it an obligation. In *Aspdin v Austin*,[134] Lord Denman said that:

"where words of recital or reference manifested a clear intention that the parties should do certain acts, the courts have from these inferred a covenant to do such acts, and sustained actions of covenant for the non performance, as if the instruments had contained express covenants to perform them."

In *Mr H TV Ltd v ITV2 Ltd*,[135] Flaux J said:

"... it is well established that, where the wording of a recital manifests a clear intention that the parties should do certain acts, the Court may infer from that wording a covenant to do such acts as if the instrument had contained an express agreement to that effect."

Thus in *Sampson v Easterby*,[136] a lease of an undivided third part of mines recited an agreement made between the lessee and the lessor under which the lessee was to pull down an old smelting mill and replace it with another of larger dimensions. The lease itself contained no such covenant, but contained a covenant to keep the new mill in repair. Lord Tenterden CJ said: **10.57**

"It appears evidently to have been the intention of the parties that the building should be erected; and as no precise form of words is necessary to make a covenant, we think the recital of the agreement that the building should be erected, followed by the express covenants to maintain and leave it, do amount to a covenant in law to erect the building."

On appeal the decision was affirmed.[137] Alexander CB said:

"We are all of opinion that in this demise there is a distinct covenant on the part of the defendant below to erect a smelting mill. Any words in a deed which show an agreement to do a thing amount to a covenant ... and it is here recited that the defendant and others had, with the permission of Sir C. Turner and two others, taken down a smelting mill, and did engage to erect at their own expense a smelting mill of larger dimensions."

The essential feature of the case was not the express covenant to keep the new mill in repair but the recital of the antecedent agreement.[138]

In *Isaacson v Harwood*,[139] Cairns LJ said: **10.58**

"Now it is well settled that there is no magic in the words of a covenant. Whatever words are used by a party to a deed, if he intends that they shall operate as a covenant, he will be held liable. In the simple case of a debtor

---

[2009] NSWCA 407 at [392] and *Grehan v Maynooth Business Campus Owners Management Co Ltd* [2019] IEHC 829.

[133] 57 Com. Dig. "Covenant".

[134] (1844) 1 Q.B. 671.

[135] [2015] EWHC 2840 (Comm).

[136] (1830) 9 B. & C. 505.

[137] Sub nom *Easterby v Sampson* (1830) 6 Bing. 644.

[138] See *Stephens v Junior Army and Navy Stores Ltd* [1914] 2 Ch. 516.

[139] (1868) L.R. 3 Ch. App. 225.

acknowledging a debt by deed under seal, without any other object declared by the deed, no doubt it must be assumed that, although no words of covenant are used, the debtor meant to be bound, or else why should he go through the form of executing the deed?"

In *Burford UK Properties Ltd v Forte Hotels (UK) Ltd*,[140] Auld LJ made a similar point (although not specifically relating to recitals). He said that:

"there is no particular magic in the use in the lease of the word 'covenant' as against that of 'condition', 'provision', 'agreement' or 'proviso', and that a proviso, whether in the body of a lease or in a schedule to it, may, depending on its form and the context, have the same force and effect as a covenant."

10.59   However, an acknowledgment of a debt in a deed will not give rise to an implied obligation to pay where the acknowledgment is merely collateral to the purpose for which the deed was executed.[141]

10.60   So also in *Mackenzie v Childers*,[142] a building estate was offered for sale in plots. For 20 years each contract of sale of a plot referred to a deed of mutual covenant between the vendors and all the purchasers. The deed itself recited that it was intended to be a part of all future contracts of sale of the plots that the several purchasers should execute the deed and be bound by the stipulations in it. However, the vendors gave no express covenant to that effect. It was held that a covenant was to be inferred. Kay J said:

"No formal words are necessary to make a covenant in such a deed. A statement of a binding intention on the part of the vendors who execute the deed, made, on the face of it, for the purpose of inducing the several purchasers to buy, is as good a covenant as could be made by the most formal words."

10.61   But the court will in any case be cautious in spelling a covenant out of a recital, because that is not the part of the deed in which covenants are usually expressed.[143] The court must be satisfied that the language does not merely show that the parties contemplated that the thing might be done, but it must amount to a binding agreement upon them that the thing shall be done.[144] One circumstance where the court is reluctant to imply a covenant from a recital is where the contract already contains obligations relating to the same subject. In *Dawes v Tredwell*,[145] Jessell MR said:

"There is another rule that the recital of an agreement does not create a covenant where there is an express covenant to be found in the witnessing part relating to the same subject matter."

This is simply an aspect of the principle *expressio unius est exclusio alterius*.[146]

---

[140] [2003] EWCA Civ 1800.
[141] *Jackson v North East Railway Co* (1877) 7 Ch. D. 573.
[142] (1889) 43 Ch. D. 265.
[143] *Farrall v Hilditch* (1859) 5 C.B.N.S. 840; *Fairstate Ltd v General Enterprise and Management Ltd* (2010) 133 Con. L.R. 112.
[144] *James v Cochrane* (1852) 7 Exch. 170.
[145] (1881) 18 Ch. D. 354.
[146] See para.7.53.

However, before this principle can be applied the court must first be satisfied that the part of the contract in question is a recital, rather than an operative provision.[147]

It is of course difficult as a matter of language to construe a recital ("whereas A has agreed") as meaning "A hereby agrees".[148] One explanation of the cases discussed in this section is that by reciting an agreement, the parties are estopped from denying that the agreement was made.[149]

10.62

Illustrations

1.   A deed recited that the plaintiff was indebted to the defendant in the sum of £100 for which the defendant had begun an action and that the plaintiff being desirous of staying the action and securing the debt agreed to convey certain property to the defendant upon certain trusts to secure payment of the debt. It then recited that it had been agreed that the defendant should be at liberty to enter judgment against the plaintiff in the action but that no execution should issue until the security should be released. It was held that the recital amounted to a covenant by the defendant not to issue execution until realisation of the security.
   Farrell v Hilditch[150]

2.   A deed of separation recited an agreement between the husband and the wife to live apart. By the operative part the husband assigned property to trustees to pay the income to the wife, and covenanted to make up the wife's income to £300 a year. The deed contained no covenant by the wife to live apart. The question arose in the husband's bankruptcy whether the wife gave valuable consideration for the husband's covenant. It was held that a covenant by the wife to live apart ought to be implied from the recital, and that accordingly the wife had given valuable consideration.
   Re Weston[151]

3.   An ante-nuptial settlement made between the intended spouses and trustees recited an agreement that property belonging to the wife and then in the hands of trustee should be settled. By the testatum the wife declared that in pursuance of the agreement the trustees should hold the property upon certain trusts. The husband gave no covenant. It was held that there was an implied covenant on the part of the husband to do such things as were necessary to give effect to the settlement.
   Buckland v Buckland[152]

4.   A contract contained a recital that one party to it owned a percentage interest in an aircraft. Clause 1.1 of the contract stated that the recitals were to be deemed

---

[147]   *Honeywell Control Systems Ltd v Multiplex Constructions (UK) Ltd* [2007] EWHC 390 (TCC).

[148]   A recital is cast in the form of a statement of fact (usually past fact) whereas a promise is a matter of present obligation. A promise unlike a statement of fact is a "performative utterance" (i.e. something of which it cannot be said that it is true or false; it creates the obligation merely by being uttered): see J.L. Austin, *How to Do Things with Words*. The concept of the performative utterance has been applied by judges in the construction of contracts (*Amoco Gas Exploration Co v Teeside Gas Transportation* [2001] 1 All E.R. (Comm) 865, per Lord Hoffmann; *Union Camp Chemicals Ltd v ACE Insurance SA-NY* [2001] C.L.C. 1609 (TCC)) and statutes (*Sun Life Assurance Plc v Thales Tracs Ltd* [2001] 1 W.L.R. 1562).

[149]   See para.3.63.

[150]   (1859) 5 C.B.N.S. 840.

[151]   [1900] 2 Ch. 164.

[152]   [1900] 2 Ch. 534.

integral and interpretative parts of the contract. It was held that that clause did not convert the recital into an operative obligation capable of breach by either party. *National Private Air Transport Co v Sheikh Abedlelah M. Kaki*[153]

16.   RECITAL AS ESTOPPEL

Where a recital of fact is intended to be a statement of all parties, all parties are estopped from denying the truth of the recital. But where the recital is the statement of one party only, only that party is so estopped.

10.63   In *Greer v Kettle*,[154] Lord Maugham said:

> "Estoppel by deed is a rule of evidence founded on the principle that a solemn and unambiguous statement or engagement in a deed must be taken as binding between parties and privies and therefore as not admitting any contradictory proof."

10.64   However, the mere fact that a deed recites a certain fact or state of affairs does not necessarily mean that all parties to the deed are estopped from denying its truth. In *Stroughill v Buck*,[155] Patteson J said:

> "When a recital is intended to be a statement which all parties to the deed have mutually agreed to admit as true, it is an estoppel upon all. But when it is intended to be the statement of one party only, the estoppel is confined to that party, and the intention is to be gathered from construing the instrument."

Indeed, in *Greer v Kettle* itself, a surety was held not to be estopped by a recital in the deed of guarantee that the loan guaranteed was comprised in a certain charge.

10.65   In addition, in order to found an estoppel the recited statement must be clear and definite. In *Onward Building Society v Smithson*,[156] Bowen LJ said:

> "It would be very dangerous to extract a proposition by inference from the statements in a deed, and hold the party estopped from denying it; estoppel can only arise from a clear, definite statement. For instance it is not enough to say that a vendor is well entitled in fee at law or in equity: he cannot be estopped from denying that he has the legal estate unless there is an express statement in the deed that he has it."

10.66   An estoppel will only arise where the recital recites a statement of present fact. It will not arise where the recital purports to state the legal effect of the document. In *CP Holdings Ltd v Dugdale*,[157] Park J said:

> "X and Y enter into an agreement: 'Whereas we believe that the effect of the new agreement will be MNO, we now agree as follows.' X later wants to argue that the effect of the new agreement on its true construction is not MNO, but is PQR instead. He is not estopped from doing so. He may have an uphill struggle in his

---

[153] [2017] EWHC 1496 (Comm).
[154] [1938] A.C. 156.
[155] (1850) 14 Q.B. 781.
[156] [1893] 1 Ch. 1 at 14, CA.
[157] [1998] N.P.C. 97; [1998] 5 WLUK 410, followed in *PW & Co v Milton Gate Investments Ltd* [2004] Ch. 142.

arguments on construction, but he is not estopped from putting them forward. In a case like that it is rectification or nothing."

This is a reflection of the principle that although the parties are free to contract in whatever terms they please, the legal effect of what they have agreed is a question of law for the court.

In *Brudenell-Bruce v Moore*,[158] Newey J said:

10.67

"... if a recital contains a statement which a party to the deed is to be taken to have agreed to admit as true, the statement is binding on him."

In *Prime Sight Ltd v Lavarello*,[159] the Privy Council held that a fact recited in a deed should be treated as a species of estoppel by convention. Lord Toulson said:

10.68

"However, there is no logical reason to treat declaratory statements in a deed which are intended to be contractually binding as less effective than any other express or implied contractual convention. The law as stated by Spencer Bower not only carries the considerable authority of Dixon J,[160] who was a master of the common law, and is supported by earlier authorities to which reference has been made, but more fundamentally it accords with the principle of party autonomy which underlies the common law of contract."

There was no general reason of public policy which prevented parties from contracting on the assumed basis of facts that they knew to be untrue. Where a recital contains an assumed basis of fact, the real facts (if different) must be ignored in interpreting the contract.[161] The Privy Council discussed the ambit of this principle in *Chen v Ng*.[162] Although they referred to academic criticism of *Prime Sight Ltd v Lavarello*, they made it clear that they did not question its correctness.

An estoppel by deed does not preclude contradictory oral evidence admissible in accordance with equitable principles.[163]

10.69

Illustrations

1.   A charge by way of legal mortgage contained a statement that the mortgaged property was vested in the borrower for the unexpired residue of a leasehold term. The mortgagee sought to argue that the borrower acquired no legal estate before the charge took effect. Evershed MR said:

"the mortgagees may well be said to be unable to complain of the truth of the recital which they no doubt caused to be inserted in their own mortgage ...".

Church of England Building Society v Piskor[164]

2.   A deed of variation made between the assignee of the reversion to a lease and two guarantors of the original tenant contained an acknowledgment by the

---

[158] [2012] EWHC 1024 (Ch).
[159] [2013] UKPC 22.
[160] In *Grundt v Great Boulder Proprietary Gold Mines Ltd* (1937) 59 C.L.R. 641.
[161] *Richards v Wood* [2014] EWCA Civ 327.
[162] [2017] UKPC 27; [2018] 1 P. & C.R. DG2.
[163] *Ali v Khan* (2002) 5 I.T.E.L.R. 232; *Close Asset Finance Ltd v Taylor* [2006] EWCA Civ 788.
[164] [1954] Ch. 553.

guarantors that their obligations under the guarantee extended to the varied obligations of the tenant. It was held that this was insufficient to estop the guarantors from contending that the benefit of their guarantee had not been assigned to the assignee. *Re Distributors & Warehousing Ltd*[165]

17.   RECITALS AS EVIDENCE

Recitals in certain old deeds are evidence of the truth of the matters recited.

10.70   The principles of estoppel bind parties to deeds and their privies. However, a recital may also have an effect on a person who was not a party to the deed, and who is not yet a privy of such a person.

10.71   Where parties contract for the sale of an interest in land s.45(6) of the Law of Property Act 1925 provides:

"Recitals, statements, and descriptions of facts and matters and parties contained in deeds, instruments, Acts of Parliament, or statutory declarations, twenty years old at the date of the contract, shall, unless and except so far as they may be proved to be inaccurate, be taken to be sufficient evidence of the truth of such facts, matters, and descriptions."

Moreover, by s.45(1) of the Act, a purchaser of any property:

"shall assume, unless the contrary appears, that the recitals, contained in the abstracted instruments, of any deed, will, or other document, forming part of that prior title, are correct, and gave all the material contents of the deed, will, or other document so recited, and that every document so recited was duly executed by all necessary parties, and perfected, if and as required, by fine, recovery, acknowledgment, enrolment, or otherwise."

This provision applies only to deeds executed prior to the "time prescribed by law".[166] The time prescribed by law is 15 years.[167]

18.   CONSIDERATION

Where the consideration is stated in a written contract, evidence will not be admitted to contradict the statement. However, evidence is admissible to prove consideration additional to that stated in the contract.

10.72   In early times it used to be doubted whether evidence was admissible to prove any consideration, where consideration was expressly stated on the face of the contract. Thus in *Peacock v Monk*,[168] Lord Hardwicke LC said:

"Where any consideration is mentioned, as of love and affection only, if it is not said also and for other considerations, you cannot enter into proof of any other: the reason is because it would be contrary to the deed: for when the deed says,

---

[165] [1986] 1 E.G.L.R. 90. The substantive decision in the case is no longer good law.
[166] Law of Property Act 1925 s.45(1)(a).
[167] Law of Property Act 1969 s.23.
[168] (1748) 1 Ves. Sen. 127.

it is in consideration of such a particular thing, that imports the whole consideration, and is negative to any other."

That was a particularly strict application of the parol evidence rule.

Although at least in theory the parol evidence rule probably continues in being, since Lord Hardwicke's day the courts have adopted a more relaxed approach to the admission of extrinsic evidence in order to establish the true consideration for the transaction.   **10.73**

It is still the case that evidence may not be given which would contradict the written statement of the consideration. Thus where a deed stated that certain land had been sold for $16,000 evidence that no consideration was given was held to be inadmissible.[169]   **10.74**

On the other hand, the court now adopts the attitude that proof of consideration additional to that stated in the contract is not contradictory of it. Thus in *Clifford v Turrell*,[170] Knight-Bruce VC said: **10.75**

> "The rule is that where there is one consideration stated in the deed, you may prove any other consideration, which existed, not in contradiction to the instrument, and it is not in contradiction to the instrument to prove a larger consideration than that which is stated."

Shadwell VC said:

> "Rules of law may exclude parol evidence where a written instrument stands in competition with it, but it has long been settled that it is not within any rule of this nature to adduce evidence of a consideration additional to what is stated in a written instrument."[171]

On appeal[172] Lord Lyndhurst LC said:

> "… the settled rule of law is, that you may prove a further consideration which is consistent with the consideration stated on the face of the deed. You cannot be allowed to prove a consideration inconsistent with it, but you may prove another which stands with it."

So too in *Turner v Forwood*,[173] Lord Goddard CJ referred to *Clifford v Turrell* and said that it: **10.76**

> "appears to lay down in the clearest possible terms that, at any rate, where there is a nominal consideration—and I am not satisfied that it is confined to cases of nominal consideration—evidence is always admissible to show that the true consideration was something more than the consideration stated in the written agreement, be it under hand or under seal."

---

[169] *Tsang Chuen v Li Po Kwai* [1932] A.C. 715.
[170] (1841) 1 Y. & C. Ch. Cas. 138.
[171] This passage was approved by the Privy Council in *Frith v Frith* [1906] A.C. 254. See also *Pao On v Lau Yiu Long* [1980] A.C. 614 at 631, per Lord Scarman.
[172] (1845) 14 L.J. Ch. 390.
[173] [1951] 1 All E.R. 746.

10.77   In *Classic Maritime Inc v Lion Diversified Holdings Berhad*,[174] a guarantee dated 28 August 2008 stated that it was made in order to induce a contract of affreightment dated 13 August 2008. Cooke J held that evidence was admissible to explain the anomaly, and to rebut the argument that the consideration was past consideration.

10.78   Further, evidence is admissible to show that the consideration for a transaction was given by a third party. In *Tsang Chuen v Li Po Kwai*,[175] Lord Blanesburgh referred to a statement by Farwell J that a person who had sealed receipt could not be heard to say that the purchase money had not in fact been received and said:

> "It is not, Sir George Farwell goes on to say, as if the purchase money had been paid out of money found by the vendor himself or by some third person, and that fact was being deposed to. The distinction between the two cases is obvious: 'There is no contradiction of the deed in saying 'True, the purchase money was paid by him, but out of some third person's money'; there is a direct contradiction in saying that it was never paid at all."

The evidence that is admissible for these purposes includes evidence of pre-contractual negotiations.[176]

Illustrations

1.   A guarantee contained an agreement to guarantee the debts of a person "in consideration of your having this day advanced" a certain sum of money to him. It was held that evidence was admissible to show that the consideration expressed in the guarantee was not a past consideration.
Goldshede v Swan[177]

2.   A company acquired a patent from the holders of the patent in return for shares to be credited as fully paid. The patent holders wished the shares to be held on their behalf by a trustee. The transfer to the trustees recited a nominal consideration. It was held that evidence was admissible to prove the full consideration, and that it had been agreed that the shares should be credited as fully paid.
Re British and Foreign Cork Co (Leifchild's case)[178]

3.   A railway company applied to another for a loan. It was agreed between them that the railway company should have the loan and the lender should have running powers over the borrower's lines. The written agreement giving the running powers did not mention the loan. It was held that evidence was admissible to prove the loan as consideration for the agreement.
Llanelly Railway and Dock Co v London and North Western Railway Co[179]

4.   By a written agreement it was agreed that Y should receive all the money which would become due to G on the winding up of a society, on payment by Y of £100. The consideration was stated to be "money paid". It was held that evidence

---

[174] [2010] 1 Lloyd's Rep. 59.
[175] [1932] A.C. 715.
[176] *Latimer Management Consultants v Ellingham Investments Ltd* [2005] EWHC 1732 (Ch).
[177] (1847) 1 Exch. 154.
[178] (1865) L.R. 1 Eq. 231.
[179] (1873) 8 Ch. App. 942 (affirmed, L.R. 7 H.L. 550).

was admissible to prove that in addition to the stated consideration it had also been agreed that Y would vote for the winding up of the society.
Re Barnstaple Annuitant Society[180]

19. RECEIPT

The presence of a receipt for consideration in a contract is not conclusive evidence that the consideration has been paid, but in favour of a subsequent purchaser a receipt in a deed is sufficient evidence provided that the subsequent purchaser has no notice of non-payment.

At common law a receipt in a deed estopped the person who gave the receipt from asserting that the consideration for which the receipt had been given had not in fact been paid. **10.79**

Thus in *Baker v Dewey*,[181] Bayley J said:

"There is no principle more clearly established than that when a party has executed a deed by which he declares that he has received a certain sum of money he is for ever estopped from saying the deed is false."

In *Prime Sight Ltd v Lavarello*,[182] the Privy Council held that an acknowledgment in a deed of payment of the purchase price operated as an estoppel between the parties such that the seller's trustee in bankruptcy could not assert that the price had not been paid. **10.80**

The stringency of the common law did not, however, apply to receipts given under hand.[183] This was because there was no estoppel in the absence of a seal.

Moreover, in equity a receipt even under seal was not conclusive.[184] In *Burchell v Thompson*,[185] Lush J said: **10.81**

"There was a time when courts of common law and courts of equity were distinct, and their practice differed. Formerly, it was thought that at common law, if the receipt clause was contained in a deed, there was an estoppel, and that if it was not in the deed there was no estoppel. It has long been clearly recognised, however, that there is no estoppel in the one case any more than the other. Even before the Supreme Court of Judicature Act 1873, a party to a deed was not in every case estopped at common law from setting up the truth. Moreover, before the passing of that Act, whether the deed contained the receipt clause or not, it was always open to the party who had misled to show in a court of equity as against the grantor that the money had not been paid and to claim relief."

This principle applies as between vendor and purchaser and as between mortgagor and mortgagee.[186] Even in equity, however, third parties were entitled to rely upon the receipt, because then it is a matter of title rather than of personal **10.82**

---

[180] (1884) 50 L.T. 424.
[181] (1823) 1 B. & C. 704.
[182] [2013] UKPC 22.
[183] *Lampon v Corke* (1822) B. & Ald. 606.
[184] *Winter v Lord Anson* (1827) 3 Russ. 488.
[185] [1920] 2 K.B. 80.
[186] *Creque v Penn* [2007] UKPC 44.

obligation.[187] In *Bickerton v Walker*,[188] Fry LJ said:

"The presence of a receipt indorsed upon a deed for the full amount of the consideration money has always been considered a highly important circumstance. The importance attached to this circumstance seems at first sight a little remarkable when it is remembered that the deed almost always contains a receipt and often a release under the hand and seal of the parties entitled to the money. But there are circumstances which seem to justify the view which has prevailed as to its importance. A deed may be delivered as an escrow, but there is no reason for giving a receipt till the money is actually received, unless it be to enable the person taking the receipt to produce faith by it. A deed is not always, perhaps rarely, understood by the parties to it, but a receipt is an instrument level with the ordinary intelligence of men and women who transact business in this country, and which he who runs may read and understand."

So too in *Rimmer v Webster*,[189] Farwell J said:

"If a man acknowledges that he has received the whole of the purchase money from the person to whom he transfers property he voluntarily arms the purchaser with the means of dealing with the estate as the absolute legal and equitable owner, free from every shadow of encumbrance or adverse equity, and he cannot be heard to say that he has not in fact received the purchase money."

Since the enactment of the Supreme Court of Judicature Act 1873, the equitable rules have prevailed.[190]

10.83   So far as third parties are concerned the position is emphasised by s.68 of the Law of Property Act 1925 which provides:

"A receipt for consideration money or other consideration in the body of a deed or indorsed thereon shall, in favour of a subsequent purchaser, not having notice that the money or other consideration thereby acknowledged to be received was not in fact paid or given, wholly or in part, be sufficient evidence of the payment or giving of the whole amount thereof."

The section applies to deeds executed after 31 December 1881. It does not, of course, apply to receipts under hand only.

10.84   A receipt may also have a substantive effect. Section 115 of the Law of Property Act 1925 provides that a receipt indorsed on or written at the foot of or annexed to a mortgage for all money thereby secured, which states the name of the person who pays the money and is executed by the chargee by way of legal mortgage or the person in whom the mortgaged property is vested and who is legally entitled to give a receipt for the mortgage money shall operate, without any reconveyance, surrender or release:

(a)   where a mortgage takes effect by demise or subdemise, as a surrender of the term, so as to determine the term or merge the same in the reversion immediately expectant thereon;

---

[187]   *Creque v Penn* [2007] UKPC 44.
[188]   (1885) 31 Ch. D. 151.
[189]   [1902] 2 Ch. 163.
[190]   Judicature Act 1873 s.25(11); Supreme Court of Judicature Act 1925 s.44; Senior Courts Act 1981 s.49(1).

(b) where the mortgage does not take effect by demise or subdemise, as a reconveyance thereof to the extent of the interest which is the subject matter of the mortgage, to the person who immediately before the execution of the receipt was entitled to the equity of redemption;

and in either case, as a discharge of the mortgaged property from all principal money and interest secured by, and from all claims under the mortgage, but without prejudice to any term or other interest which is paramount to the estate or interest of the mortgagee or other person in whom the mortgaged property was vested.

10.85

Where the receipt shows that the money was paid by someone not entitled to the immediate equity or redemption, the receipt operates to transfer the mortgage to the payer, unless it is otherwise expressly provided, or the money is paid out of money in the hands of a trustee, and it is not expressly provided that the receipt is to operate as a transfer.[191]

---

[191] Law of Property Act 1925 s.115(2).

CHAPTER 11

THE SUBJECT MATTER OF THE CONTRACT

Cursed … is he that removeth the landmark … But it is the unjust judge that is the capital remover of landmarks when he defineth amiss of land and property

Bacon: *Of Judicature*

1.   PARCELS—A MIXED QUESTION OF FACT AND LAW

Whether a particular parcel of land is or is not included in a conveyance is a mixed question of fact and law.

In *Lyle v Richards*,[1] Lord Cranworth LC said: **11.01**

"Parcel or no parcel is a question for the jury, and it was properly left to them."

A jury was, of course, only entitled to determine questions of fact. However, Lord Cranworth went on immediately to say:

"But the judge was bound to explain to the jurymen, for their guidance, what was the true construction of any documents necessary for the decision of the question 'parcel or no parcel'."

The interaction between the (legal) construction of the conveyance in question,   **11.02**
and the (factual) application of the conveyance so construed to the facts on the ground produces a mixed question of law and fact. Thus in *Jackson v Bishop*,[2] Buckley LJ said:

"The consideration of these matters [i.e. inconsistencies in a plan], although they may in some respects be said to be questions of law arising on the interpretation of the conveyance can, in my opinion, only be mixed questions of fact and law, because the interpretation of the plan depends not only upon questions of construction in the sense in which lawyers use that term, but on the application of the data that are contained in the plan to the locus in quo, and in my view the solution of the problem cannot be purely a question of law; it must be a question of mixed fact and law and in so far as it involves an attempt to resolve inconsistencies the court is driven to have regard to evidence of the surrounding circumstances and to reach a conclusion in the light of the evidence."

In *Pennock v Hodgson*,[3] Mummery LJ summarised the law as follows: **11.03**

"(1)   The construction process starts with the conveyance which contains the

---

[1]   (1866) L.R. 1 H.L. Cas. 222.
[2]   (1979) 48 P. & C.R. 57.
[3]   [2010] EWCA Civ 873; *Vance v Collerton* [2019] EWHC 2866 (Ch).

parcels clause describing the relevant land, in this case the conveyance to the Defendant being first in time.

(2) An attached plan stated to be "for the purposes of identification" does not define precise or exact boundaries. An attached plan based upon the Ordnance Survey, though usually very accurate, will not fix precise private boundaries nor will it always show every physical feature of the land.

(3) Precise boundaries must be established by other evidence. That includes inferences from evidence of relevant physical features of the land existing and known at the time of the conveyance.

(4) In principle there is no reason for preferring a line drawn on a plan based on the Ordnance Survey as evidence of the boundary to other relevant evidence that may lead the court to reject the plan as evidence of the boundary."

11.04   In so far as the question is one of law, no burden of proof lies on anyone. If, however, surrounding circumstances are relied on, they must be proved.[4]

2. DECISIVENESS OF RESULT

Although in some cases the court may decline to reach a conclusion as to the construction of a clause in a contract, this is not possible in the case of a parcels clause.[5]

11.05   There are rare occasions upon which the court declines to construe the language of a contract, but instead decides the case by reference to some presumption analogous to the burden of proof.[6] This is rarely, if ever, possible in construing a parcels clause. As Megarry J said in *Neilson v Poole*[7]:

"… in the construction of the parcels clause of a conveyance and the ascertainment of a boundary the court is under strong pressure to produce a decisive result. The prime function of a conveyance is to convey. As to any particular parcel of land, either the conveyance conveys it, or it does not; the boundary between what is conveyed and what is not conveyed must therefore be proclaimed. The court cannot simply say that the boundaries are uncertain, and leave the plot conveyed fuzzy at the edges, as it were."

3. EVIDENCE ADMISSIBLE TO IDENTIFY THE SUBJECT MATTER OF CONTRACT

As a general rule extrinsic evidence is admissible to identify the subject matter of the conveyance.[8]

11.06   Since a conveyance invariably deals with some estate or interest in a physical and unique plot of land, the parties must connect the words of the document with the reality on the ground. Consequently, extrinsic evidence is admissible to identify the

---

4 *Scott v Martin* [1987] 1 W.L.R. 841.
5 This paragraph was approved in *Akhtar v Brewster* [2012] EWHC 3521 (Ch).
6 See paras 8.64 and 11.52.
7 (1969) 20 P. & C.R. 909.
8 This paragraph was referred to with apparent approval in *Freeguard v Rogers* [1999] 1 W.L.R. 375 CA; and by the New South Wales Court of Appeal in *County Securities Pty Ltd v Challenger Group Holdings Pty Ltd* [2008] NSWCA 193.

plot of land of which the conveyance speaks. In *Taylor v Hamer*,[9] the question was whether a flagged dog garden[10] was included in a sale. Sedley LJ said:

"[T]he meaning to be ascribed to 'the property' in the conveyance is the meaning it would be given by a reasonable person who knows what the parties knew at the time they contracted. This, of course, begins with the geographic area comprised in the registered titles ... [I]t includes the facts that the claimant had been shown premises that included the flagged dog garden, and that he had not been told before contract that this was no longer part of the realty. In my judgment, such facts are not within the exclusion zone of prior negotiation and subjective intent described in Lord Hoffmann's third principle in *ICS*.[11] They are the normal means by which the subject matter of any offer and acceptance is identified."

In all cases identification of the land is necessary. As Lord Wrenbury pointed out in *Great Western Railway v Bristol Corp*[12]: **11.07**

"A contract for the sale of Blackacre is unmeaning until you know by evidence what the name Blackacre conveys."

Thus in *Ogilvie v Foljambe*,[13] the parties agreed upon the sale of "Mr. Ogilvie's house". Evidence was admitted to identify the house. Sir William Grant MR said:

"The subject matter of the agreement is left, indeed, to be ascertained by extrinsic evidence; and for that purpose, such evidence may be received. The defendant speaks of 'Mr. Ogilvie's house,' and agrees 'to give £14,000 for the premises'; and parol evidence has always been admitted, in such a case, to shew to what house, and what premises, the treaty related."

In *Freeguard v Rogers*,[14] Peter Gibson LJ said that:

"when a property, the subject matter of a conveyancing document, is described as 'the property known as...' it is permissible, indeed inevitable, that recourse will be had to extrinsic evidence to identify the property so known."

In *Partridge v Lawrence*,[15] Peter Gibson LJ said that extrinsic evidence of the **11.08** background known to both parties was always admissible to interpret a conveyance, in accordance with Lord Hoffmann's second principle.

This principle is a manifestation of the maxim, *Id certum est quod certum reddi potest*.[16]

The courts of Australia are much more cautious in admitting extrinsic evidence **11.09** in interpreting conveyancing documents (e.g. grants of easements) because the Tor-

---

9 [2003] 1 E.G.L.R. 103.
10 A pet cemetery.
11 See para.1.36.
12 (1918) 87 L.J. Ch. 414.
13 (1817) 3 Mer. 53.
14 [1999] 1 W.L.R. 375 CA.
15 [2004] 1 P. & C.R. 176.
16 *Shardlow v Cotterrell* (1881) 20 Ch. D. 90, per Lush LJ; *Plant v Bourne* [1897] 2 Ch. 281. See para.8.76.

rens system of land registration is dependent on a publicly accessible register.[17] It is not clear whether the approach of the High Court of Australia will be applied in New Zealand.[18] Whether the move in England and Wales under the Land Registration Act 2002 to a system of title by registration (rather than registration of title) will cause a shift in prevailing judicial attitudes remains to be seen. However, the indications of the last few years are that the courts in England and Wales have become more rather than less willing to have recourse to extrinsic topographical evidence in interpreting conveyancing documents.

11.10   The principle is not confined to contracts for the sale of land. In *Macdonald v Longbottom*,[19] the defendant made a written offer to buy from the plaintiff "your wool" at a certain price per stone. Evidence was admitted to identify the wool, and in particular to quantify the amount for sale. In the Court of Queen's Bench, Erle J said:

> "It is the universal practice to admit parol evidence to identify the subject-matter of a contract."

On appeal in the Court of Exchequer Chamber Williams J said:

> "We all think the evidence was admissible. That evidence does not vary the written contract; it only identifies the subject-matter to which it refers."

11.11   So also in *Savory (EW) Ltd v World of Golf Ltd*,[20] the vendor of copyright gave a receipt in the following terms: "Five original card designs inclusive of all copyrights. Subjects: four golfing subjects: one Teddy Bear painting". Evidence was held to be admissible to identify the designs. However, in *Smith v Jeffryes*,[21] parties agreed on the sale of "sixty tons of Ware potatoes". Evidence that Ware potatoes were of three kinds and that the parties had intended to contract for the sale of "Regent's Wares", one of those kinds, was held to be inadmissible. Accordingly, the sellers were entitled to supply potatoes of any of the three kinds, since each of the three corresponded with the contract description. The buyer's complaint that the sellers had offered to deliver Kidney Wares rather than Regent's Wares was rejected.

11.12   Where the words of the contract are clear, evidence will not be admitted so as to contradict them.[22] In *Lord Waterpark v Fennell*,[23] Lord Cranworth said:

> "Where, indeed, words have a clear and definite meaning, no evidence can be admitted to explain or control them. Thus a demise of my messuage at Dale could not by any parol evidence be shown to have been meant to describe, not a messuage, but a sheet of water."

Similarly, in *Grigsby v Melville*,[24] Stamp LJ said:

> "The action is not an action for rectification of the conveyance to accord with the

---

[17] *Westfield Management Ltd v Perpetual Trustee Co Ltd* [2007] HCA 45.
[18] *Big River Paradise Ltd v Congreve* [2008] NZCA 78; *Thompson v Trounson* [2008] NZCA 84.
[19] (1859) 1 E. & E. 977; (1860) 1 E. & E. 987; applied in *County Securities Pty Ltd v Challenger Group Holdings Pty Ltd* [2008] NSWCA 193.
[20] [1914] 2 Ch. 566.
[21] (1846) 15 M. & W. 561.
[22] *Pennock v Hodgson* [2010] EWCA Civ 873.
[23] (1859) 7 H.L. Cas. 650.
[24] [1974] 1 W.L.R. 80. This was a hard case in which a conveyance of a semi-detached dwelling house was held to include a cellar used by and only accessible from the other dwelling. It might nowadays

true intention of the parties to it; and given the most cogent evidence to be found in the circumstances surrounding the transaction that it did not give effect to that intention that evidence would not in, my judgment, be admissible to contradict the plain language of the conveyance. It is the unhappy fact that conveyances sometimes do convey that which was not intended to be, or exclude that which should have been, conveyed."

The evidence which is admissible is limited to objective evidence of physical **11.13** features and so on. Direct evidence of subjective intention to convey is not admissible for this purpose. In *Lord Waterpark v Fennell*,[25] Lord Chelmsford LC said:

"Parol evidence is generally admissible to apply the words used in a deed and to identify the property comprised within it. You cannot indeed show that the words were intended to include a particular piece of land, but you may prove facts from which you may collect the meaning of the words so as to include or exclude a portion of land where the words are capable of either construction."

Similarly, in *Hamble Parish Council v Haggard*,[26] Millett J said:

"Neither the conveyance itself nor the plan attached to it enables the churchyard to be identified. Extrinsic evidence is therefore admissible to identify it. Such evidence does not include evidence of the parties' intentions and accordingly evidence of what was shown on the sale plan is not admissible for this purpose. The admissible evidence is restricted to evidence of the layout of the land and the use to which it was put and other similar evidence of the surrounding circumstances at the date of the conveyance.[27] I have to put myself into the shoes of the notional judge visiting the site in 1984 with the conveyance in one hand and gazing about him in order to try to identify on the ground those features which would enable him to ascertain the extent of the churchyard and the whereabouts of the retained land lying between the churchyard and the green strip."

Illustrations

1. By a contract in writing parties agreed the sale of

"24 acres of land, freehold, and all appurtenances thereto at Totmonslow, in the parish of Draycott, in the county of Stafford, and all the mines and minerals thereto appertaining".

Evidence was admitted to identify the 24 acres in question.
Plant v Bourne[28]

---

be one of those rare cases in which the court might conclude that something had gone wrong with the language of the conveyance, although the result might be justifiable on the basis that the creation of a flying freehold is a very unusual transaction.

[25] (1859) 7 H.L. Cas. 650.
[26] [1992] 4 All E.R. 147.
[27] The sale plan, being an objective fact, would nowadays be admissible as part of the background known to both parties: *Adam v Shrewsbury* [2006] 1 P. & C.R. 474.
[28] [1897] 2 Ch. 281.

2.   Parties agreed to the sale of "the mill property". Evidence was admitted to identify the mill property.
Murray v Spicer[29]

3.   A contract of sale and the subsequent conveyance described the land as "the property known as plot 1". Evidence was admitted to assist in identifying the land.
Spall v Owen[30]

4.   EVIDENCE OF PHYSICAL FEATURES

Evidence of the physical features of the land is admissible to enable the court to interpret a conveyance so as to arrive at the most sensible result.[31]

11.14   The traditional view was that extrinsic evidence was only admissible where the words of the conveyance were unclear. In *Willson v Greene*,[32] Foster J said:

"It is trite law to say that extrinsic evidence cannot be given to contradict a written document. Equally, a contract is superceded by the conveyance, so that I am not entitled to look at the contract to construe the conveyance, or the contract plan, and I disregard it. It was, however, agreed that if the parcels are vague and the plan is for identification purposes only the court can take into account the surrounding circumstances. I heard a great deal of argument as to what surrounding circumstances consisted of, but whatever the ambit of that phrase I am more than satisfied that where the parcels are approximate and the plan is for identification only the court can look at, and accept, a boundary as marked and agreed by the parties."

Likewise, in *Scarfe v Adams*,[33] Griffiths LJ said:

"The principle may be stated thus: if the terms of the transfer clearly define the land or interest transferred extrinsic evidence is not admissible to contradict the transfer. In such a case, if the transfer does not truly express the bargain between vendor and purchaser, the only remedy is by way of rectification of the transfer. But if the terms of the transfer do not clearly define the land or interest transferred, then extrinsic evidence is admissible so that the court may ... do the best it can to arrive at the true meaning of the parties upon a fair consideration of the language used."

11.15   This approach no longer represents the modern law.[34] In accordance with Lord Hoffmann's second principle,[35] the background knowledge available to the parties is always admissible in interpreting their contract. A conveyance of land is no different in this respect. In *Partridge v Lawrence*, Peter Gibson LJ said that the principle as expressed in *Scarfe v Adams* might not do sufficient justice to Lord

---

[29] (1868) L.R. 5 Eq. 527.
[30] (1981) 44 P. & C.R. 36, approved in *Targett v Ferguson* (1996) 72 P. & C.R. 106 CA and *Freeguard v Rogers* [1999] 1 W.L.R. 375 CA.
[31] This section was approved in *Akhtar v Brewster* [2012] EWHC 3521 (Ch).
[32] [1971] 1 W.L.R. 635.
[33] [1981] 1 All E.R. 843.
[34] It was nevertheless applied by the Court of Appeal in *Horn v Phillips* [2003] EWCA Civ 1877 but the point does not appear to have been argued.
[35] In *Investors Compensation Scheme Ltd v West Bromwich Building Society* [1998] 1 W.L.R. 896.

Hoffmann's second principle. In the light of those doubts, more recent decisions of the Court of Appeal have held that extrinsic evidence of background is, in principle, admissible. Thus in *Adam v Shrewsbury*,[36] Neuberger LJ said:

"[I]t seems to me important to bear in mind that the principles relating to the construction and effect of such documents should not, at least as a matter of principle, differ from the principles applicable to the interpretation of bilateral contractual documentation generally. That point is supported by the fact that, in *Partridge's* case, Peter Gibson LJ specifically relied on guidance given by Lord Hoffmann in *ICS Ltd. -v- West Bromwich Building Society*[37] to support his conclusion that what might be called extrinsic evidence should not be excluded when interpreting a conveyance or deed of grant. However, I accept that that approach must not be adopted indiscriminately, because documents granting or transferring interest in land will often have been drafted on the basis of principles, or approaches, laid down by courts and referred to and relied on in textbooks, over the years."[38]

In *Pennock v Hodgson*,[39] Mummery LJ said:

"Looking at evidence of the actual and known physical condition of the relevant land at the date of the conveyance and having the attached plan in your hand on the spot when you do this are permitted as an exercise in construing the conveyance against the background of its surrounding circumstances. They include knowledge of the objective facts reasonably available to the parties at the relevant date. Although, in a sense, that approach takes the court outside the terms of the conveyance, it is part and parcel of the process of contextual construction."

As Briggs LJ observed in *Parmar v Upton*[40]:

11.16

"... conveyances of land are no exception to the principle set out in the *ICS* case, namely that the meaning of words and phrases may be illuminated by setting them against the relevant factual matrix. The meaning of a plan is no less susceptible to that process of illumination than the words or phrases of a parcels clause. In short, the plan must be interpreted by reference to the features on the ground visible at the time of the conveyance of which the plan forms part."

In *Jackson v Bishop*,[41] Bridge LJ observed:

"It seems to me that the decision is one which must depend on the application

---

[36] [2006] 1 P. & C.R. 474.
[37] [1998] 1 W.L.R. 896 at 912.
[38] The principle does not require modification once it is accepted that in the case of a document like a conveyance which will pass from hand to hand the reasonable reader would only place weight on background facts that are unlikely to change; such as the physical features of the land conveyed. See para.3.175. This footnote was approved in *Network Rail Infrastructure Ltd v Freemont Ltd* [2013] EWHC 1733 (Ch). In *Wood v Waddington* [2014] EWHC 1358 (Ch), Morgan J suggested that this principle may need modification in the light of *Cherry Tree Investments Ltd v Landmain Ltd* (see para.3.175). However, *Cherry Tree Investments Ltd v Landmain Ltd* was not concerned with objective facts verifiable on inspection of the property in question; and the two principles may yet be capable of reconciliation.
[39] [2010] EWCA Civ 873.
[40] [2015] EWCA Civ 795.
[41] (1979) 48 P. & C.R. 57.

of the plan to the physical features on the ground, to see which out of two possible conclusions seems to give the more sensible result."

Similarly, in *White v Richards*,[42] Nourse LJ said:

"The nature and extent of a private right of way created by express grant depend on the intention of the parties, which must be ascertained from the words of the grant read in the light of the surrounding circumstances. Amongst those circumstances, the physical features of the way are sometimes decisive."

In the result, a grant of a right of way with motor vehicles over a track was held to be limited by the nature of the track to vehicles with a wheelbase no greater than eight feet, no more than nine feet wide and weighing no more than 10 tons laden.

11.17   In *Taylor v Lambert*,[43] Lloyd LJ said:

"As with any other document, a conveyance must be read in the light of relevant surrounding circumstances. [Counsel] submitted that a stricter approach should apply to a conveyance than to other documents, because of the imperative need for certainty of title. What appears from the document should not be at risk of being subverted by reference to circumstances existing at the time of the transaction which may not endure and therefore may not be readily discoverable later by parties whose title depends on the conveyance. That is an understandable reason for caution, but it is inevitable that the document should be read and understood in the light of the situation as it is on the ground at the relevant time. The point of the conveyance, after all, is to transfer to the purchaser a legal estate or interest in relation to a given area of land. What the extent of that land is has to be determined by reference to the conveyance but it is at least difficult, and probably impossible, to imagine a conveyancing document which could define the physical extent of the relevant land without some cross-reference to at least one or more points to be identified by inspection of the site."

11.18   One cogent reason for this was pointed out by Lord Hoffmann in *Alan Wibberley Building Ltd v Insley*[44]:

"The parcels may refer to a plan attached to the conveyance, but this is usually said to be for the purposes of identification only. It cannot therefore be relied upon as delineating the precise boundaries and in any case the scale is often so small and the lines marking the boundaries so thick as to be useless for any purpose except general identification. It follows that if it becomes necessary to establish the exact boundary, the deeds will almost invariably have to be supplemented by such inferences as may be drawn from topographical features which existed, or may be supposed to have existed, when the conveyances were executed."

11.19   Physical features may be taken into account even where the conveyance states

---

[42] (1993) 68 P. & C.R. 105 CA.

[43] [2012] EWCA Civ 3. See also *Drake v Fripp* [2011] EWCA Civ 1279; *Dixon v Hodgson* [2011] EWCA Civ 1612; *Paton v Todd* [2012] EWHC 1248 (Ch); *Hudson Industrial Services Ltd v Wood* [2012] EWCA Civ 599.

[44] [1999] 1 W.L.R. 894; *Parmar v Upton* [2015] EWCA Civ 795.

that the land conveyed is "defined by" a plan.[45] However, that is not to say that the title documents can be ignored.[46] As Mummery LJ put it in *Cameron v Boggiano*[47]:

"A mismatch between a clear plan and the actual physical features on the ground is not in itself a reason that could possibly justify ditching the title documents and determining the position of the disputed boundary by reference to the topographical features alone."

He added:

"Where the lack of sufficient clarity is in a plan marked 'for identification only' it is, in my view, easier to justify regard to the topography to assist in construing the contract/transfer plan than in a case like this where the plan was not so designated and has been prepared as a defining document. Even so, if that document is insufficiently clear to the reasonable layman with the plan in his hand to determine the position of the boundary ..., the court is entitled to seek assistance on the construction of the plan and title documents by taking account of the topographical features at the relevant date."

Where physical features are relied on, the existence of those features must be **11.20** proved in the usual way by the party relying on them.[48]

In practice many boundary disputes turn on the precise location of physical **11.21** features and their correlation with symbols shown on a plan or mentioned in the parcels clause. This is not really a question of construing the conveyance but of applying it to the physical facts on the ground. Often it is necessary to examine a host of old conveyancing documents in order to compare descriptions and plans; a process not aided when the deeds are in a phrase attributed to Lord Westbury "difficult to read, disgusting to touch and impossible to understand".[49] In such a case, the precise location of boundaries must be proved by acts of ownership.

The conveyance and any accompanying plan must be interpreted objectively. The **11.22** ultimate question is: what would the reasonable layman think he was buying?[50]

5.   ADMISSIBILITY OF EVIDENCE: SPECIAL RULES

Evidence of subsequent conduct is admissible as an aid to the interpretation of parcels clauses if it is probative of the parties' intention at the date of the conveyance.[51]

In a frequently quoted dictum in *Att.-Gen. v Drummond*,[52] Lord Sugden said: **11.23**

"One of the most settled rules of law for the construction of ambiguities in ancient instruments is, that you may resort to contemporaneous usage to ascertain the meaning of the deed; tell me what you have done under such a deed, and I will tell you what that deed means."

---

[45] *Harsten Developments Ltd v Bleaken* [2012] EWHC 2704 (Ch).
[46] *Dixon v Hodgson* [2011] EWCA Civ 1612.
[47] [2012] EWCA Civ 157.
[48] *Scott v Martin* [1987] 1 W.L.R. 841.
[49] See *Wroth v Tyler* [1974] Ch. 30 at 56.
[50] *Toplis v Green* [1992] E.G.C.S. 20 CA; *Targett v Ferguson* (1996) 72 P. & C.R. 106 CA.
[51] This section was approved in *Akhtar v Brewster* [2012] EWHC 3521 (Ch).
[52] (1842) 1 Dr. & War. 162. See also para.3.197.

11.24   This approach was extended by the Privy Council in *Watcham v Att.-Gen. of the East Africa Protectorate.*[53] In that case the Privy Council held established:

> "the principle that even in the case of a modern instrument in which there is a latent ambiguity, evidence may be given of user under it to show the sense in which the parties to it used the language they have employed, and their intention in executing the instrument as revealed by their language interpreted in this sense."

Their Lordships held that similar evidence could also be given in cases of patent ambiguity.

11.25   *Watcham's Case* has aroused considerable judicial comment. In a number of cases it has been distinguished "with, perhaps, a certain amount of zest".[54] In *Gaisberg v Storr,*[55] Cohen LJ said that *Watcham's Case* needed to be applied with care. In *Sussex Caravans Ltd v Richardson,*[56] a "judicial slingshot"[57] was cast by Harman LJ who said that *Watcham's Case* had:

> "been long under suspicion of the gravest kind from real property lawyers."

11.26   However, in *GWH (Midlands) Ltd v Giblett,*[58] Dankwerts LJ said:

> "I think that *Watcham v East African Protectorate* is still good law. It certainly holds that the acts of parties, contemporaneous or even later in date, may be admissible in proper circumstances to construe a document, whether ancient or modern, the meaning of which, without assistance, is in doubt."

And in *Neilson v Poole,*[59] Megarry J held that such evidence was admissible. He gave two principal reasons. First, he drew attention to the modern tendency to relax exclusionary rules of evidence in civil cases whenever it seems safe to do so. Secondly, he drew attention to the need for certainty in the passage quoted in para.11.05.

11.27   *Watcham's Case* was discussed by the House of Lords in *Schuler (L) AG v Wickman Machine Tool Sales Ltd.*[60] Lord Wilberforce said that it was:

> "a precedent which I had thought had long been recognised to be nothing but the refuge of the desperate."

He added:

> "Whether in its own field, namely, that of interpretation of deeds relating to real property by reference to acts of possession, it retains any credibility in the face of powerful judicial criticism is not before us."

Lord Reid took a rather less hostile view. He said:

---

53 [1919] A.C. 533.
54 *Neilson v Poole* (1969) 20 P. & C.R. 909 at 914, per Megarry J.
55 [1949] W.N. 337.
56 [1961] 1 W.L.R. 561.
57 Per Dankwerts LJ in *GWH (Midlands) Ltd v Giblett* (1962) E.G. 287.
58 (1962) 182 E.G. 287.
59 (1969) 20 P. & C.R. 909.
60 [1974] A.C. 235.

"There may be special reasons for construing a title to land in light of subsequent possession but I find it unnecessary to consider that question."

Lord Simon of Glaisdale said that:

"It is possible that the actual decision can be justified, as can certainly many of the authorities on which it purports to found, by well recognised exceptions to the rule against adduction of extrinsic evidence."

Finally, Lord Kilbrandon took the most favourable view of all. He said:

"The decision in *Watcham v Attorney-General of East Africa Protectorate*, which was referred to by Lord Denning M.R., does not, I believe, command universal confidence, though I would not question it so far as it merely lays down that, where the extent of a grant is stated in an ambiguous manner in a conveyance, it is legitimate to interpret the deed by the extent of the possession which proceeded on it. And I am not sure that I see any reason to confine such a rule to ancient deeds."

These criticisms of *Watcham's Case* were again considered by Megarry J in *St Edmundsbury & Ipswich Board of Finance v Clark (No.2)*.[61] Having referred to *Schuler's* case he said: **11.28**

"However, I think it important to consider what is the proper ambit of the doctrine. One may accept to the full that it does not apply to commercial contracts or, for that matter, to any language of obligation, whatever the document. If the question is what one party is obliged to do under some document, the effect of measuring the obligation by what in fact that person has done under the document is to convert into a binding obligation what may have been done as of grace or to promote good relations or to avoid argument. If a contracting party wishes to avoid being liable to do more than he has agreed to do, he must therefore abstain from doing anything more than he can be required to do; he must be churlish and insistent on his rights. Life would become intolerable if everyone insisted to the ultimate on the strict letter of his rights; and the danger of applying the doctrine to cases of obligation is that it would encourage such an insistence.

In the *Watcham* case itself, and in *Neilson v Poole*, the matter in dispute was a matter of boundaries; and the application of the doctrine in this field involves very different considerations. Parcels clauses and plans in a conveyance not infrequently give rise to disputes on the application of what appears on the piece of paper to what lies physically on the ground. Even if there is no uncertainty as to the meaning of the words used or the ambit of what is coloured on the plan, there may still be serious problems of application. Furthermore, in these problems of application the passage of time often brings its own cure: the passage of 12 years may stifle an incipient boundary dispute, whereas it would do nothing to resolve the extent of a contractual obligation.[62] In such circumstances, it seems to me that the doctrine may still play a useful part."

---

[61] [1973] 1 W.L.R. 1572 (affirmed [1975] 1 W.L.R. 468).
[62] The passage of 12 years will no longer give rise to title by adverse possession in the case of registered land. This may be one reason why courts in Australia (where land is held under the Torrens system of registration) are more cautious about admitting extrinsic evidence: see para.11.06.

11.29   In *Beale v Harvey*,[63] the Court of Appeal held that it was not bound by *Watcham's Case* and declined to follow it, because it was not consistent with the general law of contract. But *Beale v Harvey* was subsequently distinguished by the Court of Appeal in *Ali v Lane*,[64] which breathed new life into the principle established in *Watcham's Case*. Carnwath LJ said:

> "The conclusion I would be inclined to draw from this review is that *Watcham* remains good law within the narrow limits of what it decided. In the context of a conveyance of land, where the information contained in the conveyance is unclear or ambiguous, it is permissible to have regard to extraneous evidence, including evidence of subsequent conduct, subject always to that evidence being of probative value in determining what the parties intended.[65]
> The qualification is crucial. When one speaks of 'probative value' it is important to be clear what needs to be proved ...
> I would add that in principle reference to the intentions of the parties means the parties to the original conveyance. Thus in *Watcham* the user relied on by the Privy Council was that of the Watcham family, who were the beneficiaries of the original certificate. In none of the cases reviewed above was account taken of the conduct of subsequent owners. Megarry J might possibly have been willing to go further. Where the evidence of the intentions of the original parties is unclear, long and unchallenged usage may, as he said, be '... good reason for tending to construe the (original) conveyance as having done what the parties appear to have treated it as having done ...' I do not read that as necessarily confined to long usage by the original parties. We need not decide whether that is a permissible extension of the *Watcham* principle. It would only apply if there were evidence of a long period of acceptance of a specific boundary by a succession of parties on *both* sides of the boundary."

11.30   In *Haycocks v Neville*,[66] the Court of Appeal held that the trial judge was right to have admitted evidence of acts of ownership which took place after the conveyance in question. In *Bradford v James*[67] and *Piper v Wakeford*,[68] the Court of Appeal reaffirmed that evidence of undisputed subsequent acts is admissible if it is of probative value in determining what the parties intended at the time of the conveyance.

The law may now be taken as settled at least up to the level of the Court of Appeal.[69] Moreover in *Armbrister v Lightbourn*,[70] the Privy Council cited *Watcham v Attorney General of the East African Protectorate*[71] without any disapproval in support of the proposition that:

> "where there is doubt or inconsistency as to the description of land in a conveyance, extrinsic evidence is admissible to resolve the difficulty."

---

[63] [2004] 2 P. & C.R. 18.
[64] [2007] 1 P. & C.R. 26.
[65] See also *Tower Hamlets LBC v Barrett* [2006] 1 P. & C.R. 9 recognising "a somewhat anomalous exception" to the general law of contract in this field.
[66] [2007] 12 E.G. 156.
[67] [2008] B.L.R. 538.
[68] [2008] EWCA Civ 1378.
[69] *Norman v Sparling* [2014] EWCA Civ 1152; [2015] 1 P. & C.R. 104.
[70] [2012] UKPC 40; [2013] 1 P. & C.R. 17.
[71] [1919] A.C. 533.

They added that the case shows that "the admissible extrinsic evidence may include later events."

In *Wood v Waddington*,[72] Morgan J suggested that this principle may need modification in the light of *Cherry Tree Investments Ltd v Landmain Ltd*.[73] However, *Cherry Tree Investments Ltd v Landmain Ltd* was not concerned with objective facts verifiable on inspection of the property in question; and the two principles may yet be capable of reconciliation.

11.31

In practice many boundary disputes are ultimately determined by a consideration of acts of ownership over the disputed land. If one party to a boundary dispute can prove a consistent course of conduct evincing ownership,[74] then unless the title deeds are clear (in which case the dispute is unlikely to have arisen anyway) it is probable that the acts of ownership will carry the day.

11.32

6. DIFFERENT KINDS OF DESCRIPTION

Land conveyed may be described by name; by metes and bounds; by admeasurement; by occupation or by plan. In registered conveyancing land is described by reference to the title number at HM Land Registry.

In *Eastwood v Ashton*,[75] Lord Sumner said:

11.33

"As long as only one species of description is resorted to in describing parcels no harm is done, and often only good, by copious enumeration of particulars all belonging to that species. If the description is by name, certainty is increased by naming every close which has a separate name; if by metes and bounds, by setting out every bound; if by admeasurement, by stating not only acres and roods, but also poles. To do this is always troublesome and often impracticable, but at least it is not a cause of uncertainty. If, however, several different species of description are adopted, risk of uncertainty at once arises, for if one is full, accurate and adequate, any others are otiose if right, and misleading if wrong."

Where two or more of the descriptions conflict, the court must make up its mind which of them is to prevail. Once that choice has been made, the court may then apply the doctrine of *falsa demonstratio* to the other descriptions.[76]

11.34

Where the land is registered, a transfer of the registered estate must be in the appropriate prescribed form.[77] If a document deals with part of the land comprised in a registered title, it must have attached to it a plan identifying clearly the land dealt with.[78] However, a plan is not necessary if the land can be clearly identified on the title plan of the registered title. In that case it may be identified by reference to the title plan.[79]

11.35

---

[72] [2014] EWHC 1358 (Ch), reversed [2015] EWCA Civ 538 (but without reference to this point).
[73] See para.3.175.
[74] For example, erecting fences, planting or felling trees, cultivating the land, fishing in a pond, preventing trespass, granting tenancies and so on.
[75] [1915] A.C. 900.
[76] See [1915] A.C. 900 at 912, per Lord Parker of Waddington, cited in para.9.48.
[77] Land Registration Rules 2003 r.58.
[78] Land Registration Rules 2003 r.213(1).
[79] Land Registration Rules 2003 r.213(4).

7. PLANS

Whether a plan controls a verbal description or a verbal description controls a plan is a question of construction of the particular conveyance. There is no presumption either way.[80]

11.36   Where a conveyance refers to a plan, it will usually introduce it with some phrase to indicate whether the plan is to control the verbal description or vice versa. Where there is no such order of precedents, the plan may be used as part of the conveyance; because it is from the conveyance as a whole that the intention must be ascertained.[81]

11.37   Where the introductory phrase is to the effect that the property is "more particularly described" in the plan, the plan will prevail over the verbal description. As Lord Wrenbury observed in *Eastwood v Ashton*[82]:

> "The words 'more particularly' exclude, I conceive, that they [sc. the parcels] have already been exhaustively described. These words seem to me to mean that the previous description may be insufficient for exact delimitation, and that the plan is to cover all deficiencies, if any."

This dictum was applied by Morton J in *Wallington v Townsend*[83] to the words "more particularly delineated".

11.38   In *Dixon v Hodgson*,[84] the transfer stated that the property was "defined on the attached plan and shown edged red". Black LJ said:

> "It is important to note that the plan is not merely for identification; it defines the property transferred. Being the dominant description, it has to be accorded full weight in the same way as the plan was in *Beale v Harvey*.[85] Finding that the plan did not enable him to determine the precise position of the boundary, and that the low wall had been put in a different place from that intended, the Recorder appears largely to have abandoned the plan. I am not persuaded that that was the proper approach. Even if the plan cannot give the whole answer, it must surely be right to look at it to see what information it does reveal about the boundary, notably its fixed points, its relationship to other features marked on the plan, and its direction of travel. Whilst it perhaps seems a little odd to look upon it as part of the surrounding circumstances when it was intended to be definitive, if it has failed in that primary aim I would see it as a very significant part of the objective facts available to the parties at the relevant date."

11.39   Physical features may be taken into account even where the conveyance states that the land conveyed is "defined by" a plan.[86]

11.40   Where, however, the introductory phrase is to the effect that the plan is "for the

---

[80]   The equivalent section in a previous edition was approved by the Court of Appeal in *Smith v Royce Properties Ltd* [2002] 2 P. & C.R. 5 and *Akhtar v Brewster* [2012] EWHC 3521 (Ch).
[81]   *Lovering v Atkinson* [2020] UKPC 14. Although this was an appeal from Guernsey, the Privy Council applied English authorities.
[82]   [1915] A.C. 900.
[83]   [1939] 2 All E.R. 225 (not reported on this point at [1939] Ch. 588).
[84]   [2011] EWCA Civ 1612.
[85]   [2003] EWCA Civ 1883; [2003] 2 P. & C.R. 18.
[86]   *Harsten Developments Ltd v Bleaken* [2012] EWHC 2704 (Ch).

purpose of identification only", the verbal description will prevail over the plan. In *Webb v Nightingale*,[87] Romer LJ said:

> "Now, it seems to me that the words 'for the purpose of identification only' are virtually meaningless in the context in which they are found in this particular document, and I have the greatest doubt whether the draftsman had the smallest idea of what he meant by putting them in. Words of that kind are, of course, frequently used in conveyances in which the parcels are described in the body of the deed. In such cases the plan is merely to assist identification, and in the event of any inconsistency arising, is subordinate to the verbal description."

In *Strachey v Ramage*,[88] Rimer LJ said:

> "[31]   The formula 'for the purpose of identification only' is one whose use is time-honoured. Its ordinary sense is that a plan so described is intended to do no more than identify the position and situation of the land: it is specifically not intended to identify its precise boundaries. The use of such a plan is therefore strictly only appropriate for a case in which the *verbal* description in the parcels identifies the limits of the land with adequate precision since it is a formula which indicates that the verbal description is intended to be decisive in that respect. Such a plan 'cannot control the parcels in the body of any of the deeds' (*Hopgood v Brown*[89]); it 'cannot therefore be relied upon as delineating the precise boundaries and in any case the scale is often so small and the lines marking the boundaries so thick as to be useless for any purpose except general identification' (*Wibberley*, above, per Lord Hoffmann).
>
> [32]   The use of this formula—'for the purpose of identification only'—is to be contrasted with the case in which the parcels clause gives a verbal description of the land but also refers to the land as being 'more particularly delineated' on the plan. In such a case, in the event of any uncertainty as between the words and the plan, the latter will ordinarily prevail over the words and *will* control the verbal description (see, for example, *Wallington v Townsend*[90])."

In such cases topographical evidence may also be used, as Lord Hoffmann   **11.41** explained in *Alan Wibberley Building Ltd v Insley*[91]:

> "The parcels may refer to a plan attached to the conveyance, but this is usually said to be for the purposes of identification only. It cannot therefore be relied upon as delineating the precise boundaries and in any case the scale is often so small and the lines marking the boundaries so thick as to be useless for any purpose except general identification. It follows that if it becomes necessary to establish the exact boundary, the deeds will almost invariably have to be supplemented by such inferences as may be drawn from topographical features which existed, or may be supposed to have existed, when the conveyances were executed."

---

[87]   (1957) 169 E.G. 330.
[88]   [2008] 2 P. & C.R. 8.
[89]   [1955] 1 W.L.R. 213 at 228, per Jenkins LJ.
[90]   [1939] 2 All E.R. 225 at 235D to 236H.
[91]   [1999] 1 W.L.R. 894; *Parmar v Upton* [2015] EWCA Civ 795.

11.42   In *Neilson v Poole*,[92] both phrases were used in the same conveyance. Megarry J said:

> "the collocation of the phrase 'for the purposes of identification only' with the words 'more particularly delineated on the plan drawn hereon' may be said to be unfortunate; and in that I think I speak temperately. The effect of a phrase such as 'for the purposes of identification only,' or 'only for the purpose of identification,' seems to be confined to the use of the plan to ascertaining where the land is situated, and to prevent the plan from controlling the parcels in the body of the conveyance ... On the other hand, phrases such as 'more particularly delineated' or 'more particularly described' or 'more precisely delineated,' used in reference to a plan, are words which tend to show that in case of conflict or uncertainty the plan is to prevail over any verbal description. Where both forms of expression are used together, as in the present case, they may indeed tend to be mutually stultifying. Certainly I do not think that they give the plan any predominance."

In *Druce v Druce*,[93] Arden LJ said that the use of both phrases was likely to mean that the verbal description prevailed. She said:

> "It is well established that if a plan is attached to a conveyance for the purpose of identification only, the verbal description in the conveyance will prevail over any other indication in the plan. On the other hand, if the property is described by reference to the plan, the plan prevails—*Eastwood v Ashton*[94] which concerned a conveyance where the property was 'more particularly described in the plan'. If both phrases are used, that is to say if the plan is for the purpose of identification only and in addition the property is described as more particularly described or delineated on the plan, as I said, it is a question of interpretation of the conveyance whether the plan prevails over the verbal description in the conveyance itself. Thus, it seems to me that in most cases the likely construction is that the verbal description is to prevail. It is because the combination that I have given is absolutely clear by the inclusion of the word "only" that the plan is for the sole purpose of enabling the parties or the court to identify the property."

11.43   The plan may be neither dominant nor subordinate, but simply be part of a composite description. In *Horne v Struben*,[95] the introductory phrase was "as will further appear by the diagram". Delivering the advice of the Privy Council Lord Robertson said:

> "Now, as matter of construction, this is merely an appeal to the diagram for further elucidation of the text, and not a subordination of the text to the diagram."

11.44   Where the plan was expressed to be "for the purpose of delineation only", it was

---

[92]   (1969) 20 P. & C.R. 909.
[93]   [2004] 1 P. & C.R. 26.
[94]   [1915] A.C. 900.
[95]   [1902] A.C. 454.

held that the plan must not be taken to be drawn to scale but that the lines were to be correct diagrammatically.[96]

Even where the plan is for the purpose of identification only it may be looked at for the purpose of determining the boundaries of the land conveyed, provided that it does not conflict with the verbal description. In *Wigginton & Milner Ltd v Winster Engineering Ltd*,[97] Buckley LJ said: **11.45**

> "To the extent that the conveyance stipulates that one part of it shall prevail over another part of it in the event of there being any contradiction between them in the ascertainment of the parties' intention the court must of course give effect to that stipulation. So if the conveyance stipulates that the plan shall not control the description of the parcels, the court must have due regard to that stipulation; but in so far as the plan does not conflict with the parcels, I can see no reason why, because it is described as being 'for identification only' it should not be looked at in understanding the description of the parcels. The process of identification is in fact the process of discovering what land was intended to pass under the conveyance, and that is the precise purpose which the plan is said to serve. Accordingly, so long as the plan does not come into conflict with anything which is explicit in the description of the parcels, the fact that it is said to be 'for the purposes of identification only' does not appear to me to exclude it from consideration in solving problems which are left undecided by what is explicit in the description of any parcel."

Where there is no other means of ascertaining the boundary, such a plan must be used.[98] However, it does not follow that where the plan is for identification only, physical features on the ground will govern the extent of the land conveyed.[99] The fact that a plan is described as being for identification only is no justification for ignoring it.[100] As Mummery LJ said in *Cameron v Boggiano*[101]: **11.46**

> "A mismatch between a clear plan and the actual physical features on the ground is not in itself a reason that could possibly justify ditching the title documents and determining the position of the disputed boundary by reference to the topographical features alone."

Even if the plan is not referred to in the conveyance, the court may take it into account if the parcels give rise to difficulty, and the plan is bound in or drawn on the conveyance.[102] The position may be different if the plan is merely attached to the conveyance,[103] but it is thought that an agreed plan, whether or not referred to in the body of the conveyance, is likely to be admissible as part of the background knowledge available to the parties to the conveyance.[104] Where a plan includes "T marks" against boundary features, but the "T marks" are not referred to in the body **11.47**

---

[96]   *Re Freeman and Taylor's Contract* (1907) 97 L.T. 39.
[97]   [1978] 1 W.L.R. 1462. This passage was followed and applied by the Court of Appeal in *Scott v Martin* [1987] 1 W.L.R. 841 and *Johnson v Shaw* [2004] 1 P. & C.R. 123.
[98]   *Wigginton & Milner Ltd v Winster Engineering Ltd* [1978] 1 W.L.R. 841, per Bridge LJ.
[99]   *Spall v Owen* (1982) 44 P. & C.R. 36.
[100] *Gilks v Hodgson* [2015] EWCA Civ 5.
[101] [2012] EWCA Civ 157.
[102] *Leachman v Richardson (L & K) Ltd* [1969] 1 W.L.R. 1129.
[103] *Wyse v Leahy* (1875) I.R. 9 C.L. 384.
[104] *Adam v Shrewsbury* [2006] 1 P. & C.R. 474; *Dixon v Hodgson* [2011] EWCA Civ 1612.

of the transfer, they are a factor to be taken into account in determining the boundary, but they raise no legal presumption of ownership.[105]

11.48 Where there are inconsistencies within the plan itself, there is no rule of law regulating the resolution of the conflict. In *Jackson v Bishop*,[106] the plan contained figured dimensions which were inconsistent with the scale of the plan itself. Bridge LJ said:

> "It is true that the judge, in preferring the figured dimensions to the scale dimensions, purported to be following a dictum of Romer L.J. in an unreported decision of this court,[107] but for myself I doubt whether there is any rule of law one way or the other as to whether when a conflict is apparent between dimensions stated in figures on a conveyance plan and dimensions arrived at by scaling off the plan if the plan is drawn to scale, the one is to prevail over the other. It seems to me that the decision is one which must depend on the application of the plan to the physical features on the ground, to see which out of two possible conclusions seems to give the more sensible result."

The plan in question was a plan of a whole estate being sold in lots, while the figured dimensions were, presumably, confined to the sale of the particular plot. The principle that written clauses prevail over printed clauses does not appear to have been considered. There seems to be no reason in principle why that should not apply to plans.

11.49 However, in *Cook v JD Wetherspoon Plc*,[108] Sir Martin Nourse said:

> "It is impossible to hold, as a general proposition, that a dimension is almost invariably more accurate than a line on a plan. It may or may not be. Where you find a plan, however out of date and however small the scale, which can be scaled off to a reasonable degree of accuracy, you cannot ignore the conflict which that exercise may produce in relation to a dimension marked on the plan ... [W]here there is a conflict between (1) dimensions in figures on a plan by which the property conveyed or transferred is described and (2) dimensions arrived at by scaling off the plan, the conflict is to be resolved by reference to such inferences as may be drawn from topographical features which existed when the conveyance or transfer was executed."

Illustrations

1. A Crown grant of land lying between high water mark and low water mark and covered with water at ordinary tides went on to state that the land was "more particularly delineated and described" in a plan. It was held that the grant was a grant of the particular piece of land which was the foreshore at the date of the grant, and not a piece of land which shifted as the foreshore shifted. The plan rebutted any presumption to the contrary.
Baxendale v Instow Parish Council[109]

2. A conveyance introduced a plan "for the purpose of facilitating identifica-

---

[105] *Lanfear v Chandler* [2013] EWCA Civ 1497.
[106] (1979) 48 P. & C.R. 57, applied in *Wesleyvale Ltd v Harding Homes (East Anglia) Ltd* [2003] EWHC 2291.
[107] Perhaps *Webb v Nightingale* (1957) 169 E.G. 330, often described as unreported.
[108] [2006] 2 P. & C.R. 18.
[109] [1982] Ch. 14.

tion only". It was held that the plan could not control the verbal description in the parcels clause.

Hopgood v Brown[110]

3. A conveyance introduced a plan "for the purpose of identification only". The plan showed a boundary as a straight line. It was proved in evidence that before the conveyance was completed the parties had marked out a boundary on site which had a kink in it. It was held that the marked-out boundary prevailed over the plan.

Willson v Greene[111]

4. A lease recited that the landlord was in the course of constructing a new hotel and then demised a parcel of land and the new building to be erected by the landlord all of which premises were more particularly delineated and described and shown coloured red and blue on a plan. In fact the building was erected partly on land outside the areas shown coloured on the plan. It was held that the extent of the demise was controlled by the plan, and hence the whole of the building was not included in the demise.

Kensington Pension Developments Ltd v Royal Garden Hotel (Oddenino's) Ltd[112]

8. PLANS AS WARRANTIES

A plan showing a layout of property not yet built will not usually amount to a warranty that the property will be built as shown on the plan.

In *Tucker v Vowles*,[113] a vendor prepared a plan of a building estate showing lots   **11.50** with houses on them, one building to a plot. It was held that the vendor did not warrant that the estate should be developed in accordance with the plan, and that no building scheme to that effect was to be implied. Romer J said:

> "No doubt the vendors contemplated the estate being a residential one, and that substantially the plan of the estate which I have referred to should be worked out; but I do not think I ought to gather, as against the vendors, from the facts before me, that they must be taken to have contemplated that they would never in any respect change this plan, but would adhere to it exactly as drawn; or that they were bound by a definite arrangement that each plot should have one house, and nothing but a house, except possibly a greenhouse or conservatory."

So also in *Whitehouse v Hugh*,[114] a plan showed a plot on an estate bounded by   **11.51** a vacant space, which had been roughly made up as a road. The conveyance was subject to a stipulation entitling the vendor to allow variations of the plan. It was held that the plan did not amount to a representation that the road would continue in being. However, the court laid particular emphasis on the provision entitling the vendor to alter the plans. Vaughan Williams LJ said:

> "[counsel] relied upon the plans as shewing that there was a road; and as mak-

---

[110] [1955] 1 W.L.R. 213.
[111] [1971] 1 W.L.R. 635.
[112] [1990] 2 E.G.L.R. 117. In fact since the tenant had been let into possession of the whole building, that part of the building which was not within the demise became part of the demise by encroachment.
[113] [1893] 1 Ch. 195.
[114] [1906] 2 Ch. 283.

ing such a representation to those who came to purchase that those who put forward the plans would not go back from them. The answer to that contention is that that might have been true if it had not been for the fact that the 9th condition, subject to which the appellant took his conveyance, gave the society an absolute power to alter the scheme by closing the road in question."

9. Legal Presumptions

In the absence of other evidence, boundaries may be determined by the application of legal presumptions. These presumptions are not conclusive, but rebuttable.

11.52   Over time the law has evolved a series of presumptions for regulating the fixing of boundaries. Some of these are presumptions of law, and some are presumptions of construction.[115] A presumption of this kind:

"is very often decisive where there is no evidence at all as to what the boundaries are, but like any other presumption it is rebuttable, and very often it can be easily rebutted by the production of title deeds."[116]

11.53   Such a presumption may also be rebutted by evidence of surrounding circumstances.[117]

10. Land Bordering a Road or River

It is generally to be presumed that the owner of land abutting a highway or non-tidal river is the owner of one-half of the soil of the roadway or river bed, and that a conveyance of the land will carry with it that half of the roadway or river bed.

11.54   In *Giles v County Building Constructors (Hertford) Ltd*,[118] Brightman J summarised the law as follows:

"As I understand the law, there are two presumptions relative to the ownership of the soil of a roadway. One presumption operates in certain circumstances where the conveyancing history of the land and the road is unknown. This presumption supplies a fact of which there is no direct evidence, namely the ownership of the road. The presumption is that the owner of the land abutting on the road is also the owner of the adjoining section of road up to the middle line. There is no room for this presumption when the conveyancing history of the land and the road is known from the time when they were in common ownership as in the case before me. In such a case, there is, in certain circumstances, a totally different presumption which is more in the nature of a canon of construction that a conveyance of the land includes half the adjacent roadway."

If the vendor owns more than half the highway, the second presumption applies

---

[115] See *Giles v County Building Constructors (Hertford) Ltd* (1971) 22 P. & C.R. 978 at 981, per Brightman J.

[116] *Fisher v Winch* [1939] 1 K.B. 666 at 674, per Goddard LJ.

[117] See *Mappin Brothers v Liberty & Co Ltd* [1903] 1 Ch. 118 at 127.

[118] (1971) 22 P. & C.R. 978.

to that part of the highway that he does own.[119] If he owns the whole of the highway, the presumption will apply to the whole.[120]

The presumption applies to private streets and roads as well as to highways.[121] **11.55** It also applies to bridleways.[122] Whether the presumption applies at all to footpaths is uncertain.[123] However, it is doubtful whether the presumption applies to land sold in building plots, even though the roads have actually been laid out, but if it does it readily yields in such a case to indications of a contrary intention.[124] Where a ditch abutted a public footpath, but was not a highway ditch in the sense of a ditch built to take surface water from the highway, the presumption did not apply.[125]

In *Pearson v Foster*,[126] Newey J held that the presumption applied to land border- **11.56** ing an artificial channel, but went on to hold that the presumption was rebutted by the detailed description of the parcels conveyed and the careful colouring on the conveyance plan.

No similar presumption applies to land bounded by a railway.[127] **11.57**

The origin of the first presumption is the probability that the owners of the land **11.58** fronting the road:

"devoted the surface of their soil to the public, in order to confer a common benefit on all those desirous of using the highway, without, however, parting with the ownership of the soil itself."[128]

Where the ownership of the soil is known, the first presumption is rebutted.[129] The **11.59** second presumption applies where there is a conveyance of land bounding a road or river. In *Central London Railway v City of London Land Tax Commissioners*,[130] Swinfen Eady J said:

"It is a well-settled rule of construction that, where there is a conveyance of land, even though it is described by reference to a plan, and by colour, and by quantity, if it is said to be bounded on one side by a public thoroughfare, then half the road passes unless there is enough in the expressions of the instrument or in the surrounding circumstances to show that this is not the intention of the parties."

The second presumption is not rebutted by the land being described as contain- **11.60** ing an area which can be satisfied without including half the road or river bed; or by the land being described as bounded by the road or river bed; or by the road or river bed being left uncoloured on a plan; or by the grantor owning the land on both sides of the road or river bed; or because subsequent events not contemplated at the

---

[119] *Re White's Charities* [1898] 1 Ch. 659.
[120] *Commission for New Towns v JJ Gallagher Ltd* [2003] 2 P. & C.R. 3.
[121] *Lang v House* (1961) 178 E.G. 801.
[122] *Pardoe v Pennington* (1996) 75 P. & C.R. 264.
[123] *Gilks v Hodgson* [2015] EWCA Civ 5.
[124] *Leigh v Jack* (1879) 5 Ex. D. 264 at 274, per Cotton LJ; *Giles v County Building Contractors (Hertford) Ltd* (1971) 22 P. & C.R. 978.
[125] *Gilks v Hodgson* [2015] EWCA Civ 5.
[126] [2017] EWHC 107 (Ch).
[127] *Thompson v Hickman* [1907] 1 Ch. 550.
[128] *Leigh v Jack* (1879) 5 Ex. D. 264 at 274, per Cockburn CJ.
[129] Above and see *Berridge v Ward* (1861) 10 CB (NS) 400; *Mappin Brothers v Liberty & Co Ltd* [1903] 1 Ch. 118; *Pardoe v Pennington* (1996) 75 P. & C.R. 264 CA.
[130] [1911] 1 Ch. 467, echoing language used by Cotton LJ in *Micklethwait v Newlay Bridge Co* (1886) 33 Ch. D. 133 at 145 (in which the presumption was applied to land abutting a river).

date of the conveyance show it to have been disadvantageous to the grantor to have parted with the soil.[131] However, where the acreage specified in a conveyance did not include the road, and the parcels were identified by reference to numbered parcels on the ordnance map and also timber on the road was left out of an agreed valuation, the presumption was rebutted.[132] In considering whether the presumption applies or is rebutted the court will take into account the objective facts surrounding the making of the conveyance.[133]

11.61   In *Paton v Todd*,[134] Morgan J considered the two presumptions.[135] He concluded that:

> "The presumption may be rebutted by internal evidence within the relevant conveyance itself or by reference to practical and common sense factors which would have been known to the parties at the time of the conveyance."

On the facts he concluded that neither presumption applied. Where, however, the land in question does not immediately about the highway there is no room for the presumption to operate, and therefore no need for any rebuttal.[136]

11.   Hedges and Ditches

Where land is bounded by an artificial hedge and ditch it is presumed that the boundary runs along the edge of the ditch further from the hedge.

11.62   In *Fisher v Winch*,[137] Sir Wilfred Greene MR expressed the "well known presumption" that:

> "where there is nothing else to identify the boundary and there is a ditch and a bank, the presumption is that the person who dug the ditch dug it at the extremity of his land and threw the soil on his own land to make a bank."

Accordingly, the presumption is that the boundary runs along the edge of the ditch further from the bank. A hedge is usually planted on such a bank. The practice of the Ordnance Survey, upon whose maps the vast majority of conveyances are based, is to show by means of a line the centre line of the hedge, rather than the edge of the ditch. The court will now take judicial notice of the practice of the Ordnance Survey in this respect.[138]

The basis of this presumption was explained by Lawrence J in *Vowles v Miller*[139]:

> "The rule about ditching is this. No man, making a ditch, can cut into his neighbour's soil, but usually he cuts it to the very extremity of his own land: he

---

[131] See Robert F. Norton, *Norton on Deeds*, 2nd edn (London: Sweet & Maxwell, 1928), p.252 and *Micklethwait v Newlay Bridge Co* (1886) 33 Ch. D. 133 at 145 and at 152; *Republic Bank Ltd v Lochan* [2015] UKPC 26.

[132] *Pryor v Petre* [1894] 2 Ch. 11.

[133] *Commission for New Towns v JJ Gallagher Ltd* [2003] 2 P. & C.R. 3, where Neuberger J considered the facts in detail.

[134] [2012] EWHC 1248 (Ch).

[135] Morgan J's summary was described as "reliable" in *Gilks v Hodgson* [2015] EWCA Civ 5; [2015] 2 P. & C.R. 4.

[136] *Gilks v Hodgson* [2015] EWCA Civ 5; [2015] 2 P. & C.R. 4.

[137] [1939] 1 K.B. 666.

[138] *Davey v Harrow Corp* [1958] 1 Q.B. 60.

[139] (1810) 3 Taunt. 137 at 138.

is of course bound to throw the soil which he digs out, upon his own land; and often, if he likes it, he plants a hedge on top of it …".

This rule also involves two successive presumptions. First, it is presumed that **11.63** the ditch was dug after the boundary was drawn. Second, it is then presumed that the ditch was dug and the hedge grown in the manner described by Lawrence J If the first presumption is displaced by evidence which shows that the ditch was in existence before the boundary was drawn, for example as an internal drainage ditch which was later used as a boundary when part of the land was sold, then there is no room for the reasoning of Lawrence J to operate.[140] However, the mere fact that a ditch is a drainage ditch does not rebut the presumption.[141]

The presumption does not apply where there is a hedge, but no ditch; and the **11.64** mere existence of a hedge does not mean that the owner of the hedge is entitled to a "ditch width" beyond it.[142]

In *Avon Estates Ltd v Evans*,[143] it was held that the prima facie position **11.65** established by the presumption was not affected by the presence of "T" marks on the plan, where the meaning of the "T" marks could not be ascertained by reference to the body of the conveyance or other admissible material.[144]

The presumption was held to have been rebutted in *Harsten Developments Ltd* **11.66** *v Bleaken*[145] where the hedge long pre-dated the creation of the boundary upon the sale of part of land which had been in common ownership up to the date of the conveyance. The boundary was created by reference to the Ordnance map and was consequently the centre line of the hedge. But in *Parmar v Upton*,[146] the conveyance of land by reference to the Ordnance map was held to be of no assistance in rebutting the presumption, where the conveyance relied on conveyed only land on one side of the disputed boundary after the common boundary had been created. As Briggs LJ pointed out:

"Where a disputed boundary is created by a conveyance or (now) Transfer, where the land was formerly in common ownership, then that conveyance is of primary and frequently decisive effect in resolving any dispute as to the position of the boundary thereby created. The same may be said of a boundary agreement between owners on either side of a disputed boundary. By contrast, where as here it is clear that the relevant ownership boundary was created prior to the earliest surviving conveyance, so that those which survive deal merely with the land on one or the other side of that boundary, then the conveyancing history is prima facie unlikely to be decisive, and frequently of little assistance. This is for two simple reasons. First, if the conveyance of land on one side purports to convey land beyond the pre-existing boundary, then it is to that extent a *brutum fulmen*. The seller cannot convey that to which he has no title. Conversely, if the conveyance appears at first sight to stop short of the pre-existing boundary then a common sense construction of it must ask the question whether the parties really

---

[140] *Alan Wibberley Building v Insley* [1999] 1 W.L.R. 894 HL.

[141] *Parmar v Upton* [2015] EWCA Civ 795.

[142] *Collis v Amphlett* [1918] Ch. 232.

[143] [2013] EWHC 1635 (Ch).

[144] Part of the debate was whether the "T" marks indicated ownership of the boundary feature or merely an obligation to maintain it. It might be thought, however, that it would be unusual for one landowner to be liable to maintain a boundary feature that he did not own.

[145] [2012] EWHC 2704 (Ch).

[146] [2015] EWCA Civ 795.

intended to reserve to the seller an apparently useless strip along the edge of the land being transferred."

12. HORIZONTAL DIVISIONS

A conveyance of land is presumed to carry with it the airspace above and the soil below. There are, however, no clear presumptions determining boundaries as between individual parts of a building.[147]

11.67   In the thirteenth century, Accursus, a lawyer in Bologna, coined the phrase *cuius est solum eius est usque ad coelum at ad inferos*.[148] This maxim has often been said to represent the law of England,[149] and even now "does have something to offer us".[150] However, there is no clear authority to the effect that land means the whole of the space from the centre of the earth to the heavens:

> "so sweeping, unscientific and unpractical a doctrine is unlikely to appeal to the common law mind."[151]

11.68   However, the ownership of land will normally carry with it the ownership of the airspace above it at least of sufficient extent to prevent the erection of advertisements[152] or oversailing by cranes[153] even if not overflying by aircraft.[154]

11.69   A fortiori, a conveyance of land upon which a building stands, will normally carry with it the whole of the building. Thus a conveyance of property carried with it a room which projected above ground level into the property conveyed[155] and a cellar below which was only accessible from next door.[156] It will also carry with it underground mines and minerals. In the case of a residential lease of a ground floor flat or maisonette, there is no presumption that the subsoil is also demised. In such a case the extent of the demise:

> "must be ascertained by reference to the terms of the grant, consisting only in the actual words used (and any other indicia of the actual intentions of the parties) taken with the context in which they were used, in relation to which the state and extent of the freehold available is of course one factor."[157]

11.70   In *Star Energy Weald Basin Ltd v Bocardo SA*,[158] the issue was whether the surface owner owed land at a depth of up to 2,800 feet below the surface into which oil wells had been sunk. Lord Hope of Craighead said:

---

[147] This section was referred to with apparent approval in *Lejonvarn v Cromwell Mansions Management Ltd* [2011] EWHC 3838 (Ch); [2012] L. & T.R. 31.

[148] He who owns the soil owns up to heaven and down to hell. See *Bernstein v Skyviews and General Ltd* [1978] Q.B. 479. Its origins in later glosses on Roman law are explained in *Star Energy Weald Basin Ltd v Bocardo SA* [2010] 3 W.L.R. 654.

[149] For example, *Saunders v Smith* (1838) 2 Jur. 491, per Shadwell VC.

[150] *Star Energy Weald Basin Ltd v Bocardo SA* [2011] 1 A.C. 380, per Lord Hope.

[151] *Commissioner for Railways v Valuer General* [1974] A.C. 328 at 352, per Lord Wilberforce.

[152] *Kelsen v Imperial Tobacco Co (of Great Britain & Ireland) Ltd* [1957] 2 Q.B. 334.

[153] *Anchor Brewhouse Developments Ltd v Berkley House (Docklands) Developments Ltd* [1987] 2 E.G.L.R. 173.

[154] *Bernstein v Skyviews and General Ltd* [1978] Q.B. 479.

[155] *Laybourn v Gridley* [1892] 2 Ch. 53.

[156] *Grigsby v Melville* [1974] 1 W.L.R. 80.

[157] *Gorst v Knight* [2018] EWHC 613 (Ch); [2018] 2 P. & C.R. 8.

[158] [2010] 3 W.L.R. 654.

"The better view, as the Court of Appeal recognised,[159] is to hold that the owner of the surface is the owner of the strata beneath it, including the minerals that are to be found there, unless there has been an alienation of them by a conveyance, at common law or by statute to someone else. That was the view which the Court of Appeal took in *Mitchell v Mosley*.[160] Much has happened since then, as the use of technology has penetrated deeper and deeper into the earth's surface. But I see no reason why its view should not still be regarded as good law. There must obviously be some stopping point, as one reaches the point at which physical features such as pressure and temperature render the concept of the strata belonging to anybody so absurd as to be not worth arguing about. But the wells that are at issue in this case, extending from about 800 feet to 2,800 feet below the surface, are far from being so deep as to reach the point of absurdity. Indeed the fact that the strata can be worked upon at those depths points to the opposite conclusion."[161]

There are no clear presumptions relating to divisions between individual parts of buildings.[162] The problem usually arises in the context of leases. Some guidance may, however, be given. The demise of one floor of a building extends at least as far as the joists of the underside of the floor above it,[163] this being the tenant's ordinary expectation in the absence of cogent reasons to the contrary.[164] However, a demise of a "suite of rooms" will not include a common roof.[165] A demise of a top floor flat, together with the roof and roof space will include the air space above the roof.[166] In *Lejonvarn v Cromwell Mansions Management Ltd*,[167] the judge held that the presumption should not be applied blindly. Its application will depend on the context of the property in question. Where, therefore, a building had been divided into three flats by means of carefully drafted leases, the presumption did not apply so as to confer on the lessee of the basement flat the right to excavate the sub-soil.   **11.71**

In *H Waites Ltd v Hambledon Court Ltd*,[168] Morgan J reviewed the case-law. He held that a long lease of a garage included the air-space above it. Those cases that held that there was no presumption about the inclusion or exclusion of air-space or sub-soil: **11.72**

"make good sense where one is dealing with a part of a building which has been horizontally divided, where there are often good reasons for the demise to be limited to a stratum and so as not to include airspace (or subsoil). Those reasons do not apply with the same force in the case of a building, whether single storey

---

[159] [2010] Ch. 100 at [59].
[160] [1914] 1 Ch. 438.
[161] Section 43 of the Infrastructure Act 2015 now gives a right to use deep-level land for the purpose of exploiting petroleum or deep geothermal energy. Deep-level land is land at a depth of at least 300 metres below surface level.
[162] This proposition was approved in *Rosebery Ltd v Rocklee Ltd* [2011] All E.R. (D) 139 (Jan).
[163] *Sturge v Hackett* [1962] 1 W.L.R. 1257.
[164] *Graystone Property Investments Ltd v Margulies* (1984) 47 P. & C.R. 472.
[165] *Cockburn v Smith* [1924] 2 K.B. 119. It is otherwise where the demised property is the whole of a "terraced" building. In such a case the roof over the demise will be included in the demise: *Tennant Radiant Heat Ltd v Warrington Development Corp* [1988] 1 E.G.L.R. 41. See also *Phelps v City of London Corp* [1916] 2 Ch. 255.
[166] *Davies v Yadegar* [1990] 1 E.G.L.R. 71 CA; *Haines v Florensa* [1990] 1 E.G.L.R. 73 CA.
[167] [2011] EWHC 3838 (Ch); [2012] L. & T.R. 31.
[168] [2014] EWHC 651 (Ch).

or not and whether in a terrace or freestanding, where all of the building is demised, i.e. there is no horizontal division."

13.   EXTERNAL WALLS AND PROJECTIONS

A grant of part of a building will be presumed to include both sides of any external wall bounding it, and also anything fixed to the wall.

11.73   In *Hope Brothers Ltd v Cowan*,[169] Joyce J said:

"speaking generally in the case of a demise of one floor of a building, or of a room on any floor which is bounded or enclosed on one or more sides by an outside wall, unless the outside wall be excepted or reserved or there be some context which leads to a contrary conclusion, prima facie the premises demised comprise the whole; that is to say both sides of the outside wall."

So in the absence of a reservation, a landlord may be restrained from maintaining an advertisement on the walls enclosing the demised property.[170]

11.74   Where there is an external feature (whether ornamental or not) fixed to an outside wall, prima facie it will pass with a grant of the property to which it is fixed.[171] So also where the footings or eaves of a building project beyond the edge of the external wall they will be included in the property, but the column of air between them will not.[172]

14.   EXCEPTIONS AND RESERVATIONS

An exception is the retention by the grantor of a thing already in existence, and in case of doubt is construed against the grantor. A reservation is the creation of a new right in favour of the grantor, and in case of doubt is construed against the grantee.

11.75   In *Earl Cardigan v Armitage*,[173] Bayley J said:

"An exception is ever of part of the thing granted and of a thing *in esse*. A reservation is always of a thing not *in esse*, but newly created and reserved out of the thing granted."[174]

11.76   In *Mason v Clarke*,[175] a tenancy "reserved" to the landlord all the game, rabbits, wild fowl and fish. Denning LJ said:

"Although the landlord purported to 'reserve' the game, rabbits etc., this was not in strictness a reservation. It was long settled at common law that an 'exception' is only properly allowed of things *in esse*, such as trees or minerals; a

---

[169] [1913] 2 Ch. 312. This approach has been consistently followed: see *Goldfoot v Welch* [1914] 1 Ch. 213; *Sturge v Hackett* [1962] 1 W.L.R. 1257.

[170] *Re Webb's Lease* [1951] Ch. 808.

[171] *Sturge v Hackett* [1962] 1 W.L.R. 1257.

[172] *Truckell v Stock* [1957] 1 W.L.R. 161.

[173] (1823) 2 B. & C. 197.

[174] [1906] 2 Ch. 283. Similar statements may be found in ancient textbooks, approved in *Doe d. Douglas v Lock* (1835) 2 Ad. & El. 705.

[175] [1954] 1 Q.B. 460.

'reservation' is only properly admitted of services to be rendered by the tenant, such as paying rent or providing a beast (heriot), whereas a right to come and kill and carry away wild animals is only a liberty or licence—a profit a prendre— which can take effect only by grant and not by exception or reservation. Words of reservation of sporting rights operate, therefore, not by way of reservation proper, but by way of regrant by the tenant: *Wickham v Hawker*."[176]

In *St Edmundsbury & Ipswich Diocesan Board of Finance v Clark (No.2)*,[177]   **11.77**
Megarry J distinguished between three categories:

"First, there was an exception, whereby the vendor excluded from the conveyance some existing part of what was conveyed, as where he conveyed an entire
estate except a specified house or field. Second, there was a reservation in the
strict sense, whereby the vendor created in his own favour some new interest
which issued out of the property conveyed, as where he reserved a rent payable
to himself. Third, there was the creation of some other new interest in favour of
the vendor, such as an easement; and as a reservation stricto sensu was confined
to the creation of an interest issuing out of the property conveyed, an easement
in favour of the vendor could not strictly be created by reservation, but had to
be created by words of regrant. Where mere words of reservation were used, the
easement was nevertheless construed as having been created by regrant if the
purchaser had executed the conveyance: see *Durham and Sunderland Railway
Co v Walker*."[178]

A valid exception operates immediately and the subject of it does not pass to the   **11.78**
grantee.[179] Because it takes effect immediately it must be distinguished from a
defeasance of an estate limited to take effect at some future time (e.g. a right to
resume possession of land).[180]

An exception is construed against the grantor in any case of doubt. In *Savill Bros*   **11.79**
Ltd v Bethell,[181] Stirling LJ said:

"It is a settled rule of construction that where there is a grant and an exception
out of it, the exception is to be taken as inserted in favour of the grantor and to
be construed in favour of the grantee."

In an extreme case, an exception may be held to be repugnant to the grant and   **11.80**
rejected completely. Thus in *Horneby v Clifton*,[182] there was a grant of "The Three
Conies" in Fleet Street with all the chambers, cellars and shops, etc, reserving to
one of the grantors the shops for his sole use and occupation. It was held that the
exception of all the shops was repugnant to the grant and was consequently void.

Where an exception does not precisely identify the parcel of land to be excepted,   **11.81**
the uncertainty may be curable by election. However, the tide of authority is, on the

---

[176] (1840) 7 M. & W. 63. The significance of the distinction between a reservation "proper" and a regrant
was that until the enactment of the Law of Property Act 1925 s.65(1) a regrant was of no effect until
the grantee had executed the conveyance. Since 1926 a reservation operates at law as a regrant
without any execution of the conveyance by the grantee.
[177] [1973] 1 W.L.R. 1592.
[178] (1842) 2 Q.B. 940.
[179] *Cooper v Stuart* (1889) 14 App. Cas. 286, per Lord Watson.
[180] *Cooper v Stuart* (1889) 14 App. Cas. 286.
[181] [1902] 2 Ch. 523.
[182] (1566) 3 Dyer. 264b.

whole, against the use of election as a means of curing uncertainty in conveyancing.[183]

11.82   A reservation is construed, in case of doubt, in favour of the grantor (i.e. the person in whose favour the reservation is made). This suggestion appears to have been made first in modern times by Upjohn J in *Bulstrode v Lambert*[184] and repeated by Denning LJ in *Mason v Clarke*.[185] It was challenged by Megarry J in *Cordell v Second Clanfield Properties Ltd*[186] and in *St Edmundsbury and Ipswich Diocesan Board of Finance v Clark (No.2)*.[187] His Lordship based his reasoning on s.65(1) of the Law of Property Act 1925 which provides:

> "A reservation of a legal estate shall operate at law without any execution of the conveyance by the grantee of the legal estate out of which the reservation is made, or any regrant by him, so as to create the legal estate reserved, and so as to vest the same in possession (whether being the grantor or not) for whose benefit the reservation is made."

He held that the words "without any regrant" had altered the position at common law and held that:

> "With the statutory abolition of the fictitious regrant, reservations of easements fall into line with the broad and sensible approach that it is for him who wishes to retain something for himself to see that there is an adequate statement of what it is that he seeks to retain; and if after considering all the circumstances of the case there remains any real doubt as to the ambit of the right reserved, then that doubt should be resolved against the vendor."

11.83   However, on appeal[188] the Court of Appeal held that the view of Megarry J was wrong. Sir John Pennycuick said:

> "Formerly the law was that on a conveyance with words merely reserving an easement, the easement was held to be created, provided that the purchaser executed the conveyance, without the necessity for words of regrant. The law treated the language of reservation as having the same effect as would the language of regrant although there was not in terms a regrant, and in those circumstances regarded the purchaser as the proferens for present purposes. This was a relaxation of the strict requirements for creating an easement ...
>
> Section 65 must be read in the light, therefore, of two aspects of the preceding law. First: that previously the law was sufficiently relaxed from its prima facie stringency to permit the language of a mere reservation to have the effect of a regrant though it was not in truth a regrant by its language. Second: that for this purpose the purchaser must execute the conveyance if an easement was to be created; that is to say, although a regrant was not required. Against that background, are the words in s.65 'without ... any regrant by' the purchaser to be regarded as altering the law so that the purchaser is no longer to be regarded as the relevant proferens? Or are they to be regarded as merely maintaining for the avoidance

---

[183] This topic is discussed in para.8.31.
[184] [1953] 1 W.L.R. 1064.
[185] [1954] 1 Q.B. 460.
[186] [1969] 2 Ch. 9.
[187] [1973] 1 W.L.R. 1572.
[188] [1975] 1 W.L.R. 468.

of doubt the situation that has been already reached by the development of the law, i.e. that mere words of reservation could be rendered as having the same effect as would the language of regrant though without there being in terms any purported regrant by the purchaser? We would, apart from authority, construe the words in the latter sense, so that the only relevant change in the law is the absence of the requirement that the purchaser should execute the conveyance."

The court therefore held that a reservation in a conveyance was to be construed in favour of the grantor and against the grantee in case of any doubt. The view expressed was clearly obiter. In the author's opinion there is much to be said for the view taken by Megarry J.

It is somewhat surprising that the legal classification of a right as an exception **11.84** rather than as a reservation should carry with it such significance. In the case of a landlord's right of entry on demised property during the term of a lease, it would mean that different principles of interpretation would apply, depending on whether the right arose as a result of a reservation or a tenant's covenant to permit entry. It is all the more surprising since conveyancers (no doubt incorrectly) in practice use the two expressions almost interchangeably.[189] This is recognised by the court, for where the wrong word is used the court will substitute the correct one. Thus where a Crown grant reserved a parcel of land Lord Lindley said:

"If the strip of land in question belonged to the Crown at the date of the grant, the strip was excepted from the grant. The word 'reserving' would operate as an exception."[190]

In *Windsor-Clive v Rees*,[191] HH Judge Keyser QC examined the authorities on **11.85** the interpretation of exceptions and reservations in a tenancy agreement. He pointed out that there was an inconsistency of approach in some of the cases; and that a reservation (as opposed to an exception) took effect as a regrant by the tenant to the landlord. That potentially led to incoherence in the law. However, he said:

"I think that conflict and incoherence can be avoided, though some tension does remain. In my judgment, the correct position is not that there is a rule of interpretation, as such, that a reservation is construed restrictively against the landlord. Rather, as part of the normal method of construing written instruments, the court will have regard to the entirety of the text and to the main subject matter of the agreement and, in the normal course of things, is likely to suppose that the intention of the parties is to advance the main purpose of the agreement as shown by its subject matter. Thus in the case of a lease, which necessarily grants exclusive possession and the right to quiet enjoyment, the court will naturally be inclined to suppose that qualifications on these rights will emerge clearly from the lease. This is not a matter of applying a special rule that a certain kind of provision must be construed against a particular party. It is simply a matter of applying the normal approach to construction. Accordingly, if, having regard to all relevant matters, the court finds that the normal approach to

---

[189] See *ARC Aggregates Ltd v Branston Properties Ltd* [2020] EWHC 1976 (Ch).
[190] (1859) 7 H.L. Cas. 650.
[191] [2019] EWHC 1008 (Ch); [2019] 4 W.L.R. 74.

construction results in ambiguity, there is nothing irrational in resorting to the *contra proferentem* rule."

11.86 This general approach was confirmed by the Court of Appeal in the same case.[192]

15. CONVEYANCES "SUBJECT TO" OTHER INTERESTS

A conveyance of a legal estate expressed to be made subject to another legal estate not in existence immediately before the date of the conveyance operates as a reservation unless the contrary intention appears.

11.87 Section 65(1) of the Law of Property Act 1925 provides:

"A conveyance of a legal estate expressed to be made subject to another legal estate not in existence immediately before the date of the conveyance, shall operate as a reservation unless a contrary intention appears."

The mere fact that a similar right is in existence immediately before the date of the conveyance will not prevent s.65(2) from having effect to convert a right expressly referred to in the conveyance into a legal estate.[193]

11.88 Even without reliance on s.65(2), if land is conveyed "subject to" rights of way hitherto enjoyed, mere accommodations may thereby be elevated to the status of easements.[194] Moreover a conveyance "subject to" a right may create a trust to give effect to that right as between transferor and transferee.[195] This will not be so in every case, but only where the conscience of the new estate owner is affected.[196]

11.89 However, a conveyance of a reservation "subject to and with the benefit of" a lease will not operate as a waiver of the right to forfeit the lease for breach of covenant committed before the date of the conveyance.[197]

---

[192] *Rees v Windsor-Clive* [2020] EWCA Civ 816; [2020] 4 W.L.R. 105.
[193] *Wiles v Banks* (1983) 50 P. & C.R. 80.
[194] See *Pitt v Buxton* (1969) 21 P. & C.R. 127; *Pallister v Clark* (1975) 30 P. & C.R. 84.
[195] *Binions v Evans* [1972] Ch. 359; *Lyus v Prowsa Developments Ltd* [1982] 1 W.L.R. 1044.
[196] *Ashburn Anstalt v Arnold* [1989] Ch. 1 CA.
[197] *London and County (A. & D.) Ltd v Wilfred Sportsman Ltd* [1971] Ch. 764.

CHAPTER 12

EXEMPTION CLAUSES

A prince never lacks legitimate reasons to break his promise.

Niccolò Machiavelli: *The Prince*

1.   NATURE OF EXEMPTION CLAUSES

For the purposes of the interpretation of contracts, an exemption clause is one in which words of exception remove or limit a remedy for breach, or where they seek to prevent a liability from arising by removing, through a subsidiary provision, part of the benefit which it appears to have been the purpose of the contract to provide.

Many commercial contracts are made on standard forms, the majority of which   **12.01**
contain provisions designed to eliminate or limit the liability of one contracting
party to another.[1] It may be thought hazardous to attempt to encapsulate the essence of an exclusion clause. The importance of defining or classifying what an
exclusion clause is lies in part in the traditional hostility of the courts to exclusion
clauses, and in the development of principles of construction which are applied to
exclusion clauses; and in part because exemption clauses are subject to statutory
controls. In his work on *Exception Clauses*,[2] Professor Coote divides exception
clauses into two classes:

"Type A: exception clauses whose effect, if any, is upon the accrual of particular
primary rights.
    Thus where words relating to quality have been employed by a vendor of
goods, an exclusion of conditions, warranties, or undertakings as to quality, helps
determine the extent to which those words are contractually binding as, by the
same token, would a stipulation by the vendor that he should not be required to
make compensation for poor quality.
    Type B: exception clauses which qualify primary or secondary rights without
preventing the accrual of any particular primary right. Examples would be limitations on the time within which claims might be made, and limitations as to the
amount which might be recovered on a claim. By contrast, a clause which
purported to take away a buyer's right to reject goods would belong to Type A."

Recent cases have emphasised the need to distinguish between clauses that define   **12.02**
the parties' primary obligations on the one hand, and those which seek to limit or
exclude a remedy for breach. This question was considered by the Supreme Court

---

[1]   See E. MacDonald, *Exemption Clauses, Penalty Clauses and Unfair Terms*, 2nd edn (London:
    Bloomsbury Professional, 2006) for comprehensive coverage if a little out of date.
[2]   (1964) London.

in *Impact Funding Solutions Ltd v Barrington Support Services Ltd*,[3] which concerned the extent of cover under an insurance policy. The court held that the extent of cover was to be ascertained by reading the statement of cover and any exclusions together; and that the exclusions could not be treated as "exclusion clauses" in the traditional sense. Lord Hodge said:

> "But the general doctrine ... that exemption clauses should be construed narrowly, has no application to the relevant exclusion in this policy. An exemption clause, to which that doctrine applies, excludes or limits a legal liability which arises by operation of law, such as liability for negligence or liability in contract arising by implication of law."

Lord Toulson said:

> "The fact that a provision in a contract is expressed as an exception does not necessarily mean that it should be approached with a pre-disposition to construe it narrowly. Like any other provision in a contract, words of exception or exemption must be read in the context of the contract as a whole and with due regard for its purpose. As a matter of general principle, it is well established that if one party, otherwise liable, wishes to exclude or limit his liability to the other party, he must do so in clear words.... This applies not only where the words of exception remove a remedy for breach, but where they seek to prevent a liability from arising by removing, through a subsidiary provision, part of the benefit which it appears to have been the purpose of the contract to provide. The vice of a clause of that kind is that it can have a propensity to mislead, unless its language is sufficiently plain. All that said, words of exception may be simply a way of delineating the scope of the primary obligation."

The example he gave was of a decorator who agreed to paint the outside of a house "except the garage doors".

12.03   In *JP Morgan Bank v Springwell Navigation Corpn*,[4] Gloster J put the point thus:

> "There is a clear distinction between clauses which exclude liability and clauses which define the terms upon which the parties are conducting their business; in other words, clauses which prevent an obligation from arising in the first place... ."

12.04   Similarly, in *First Tower Trustees Ltd v CDS (Superstores International) Ltd*,[5] Leggatt LJ said:

> "Where a party relies on a term of its contract to argue that it has no liability under the contract to the other party, an issue can arise as to whether the term excludes liability for breach of the contract or merely shows that no relevant contractual obligation has been undertaken. This is a question of construction of the contract in question."

---

3   [2016] UKSC 57; [2017] A.C. 73; *Manchikalapati v Zurich Insurance Plc* [2019] EWCA Civ 2163.
4   [2008] EWHC 1186 (Comm) at [601].
5   [2018] EWCA Civ 1396; [2019] 1 W.L.R. 637.

As Briggs LJ put it in *Nobahar-Cookson v Hut Group Ltd*[6]:

"The court must still use all its tools of linguistic, contextual, purposive and common-sense analysis to discern what the clause really means."

A similar approach was adopted by Kerr J in *The Angelia*.[7] In that case cl.2 of a charterparty provided that unavoidable hindrances in transporting, loading or receiving the cargo, restraints of established authorities and any other causes or hindrances happening without the fault of the charterers, shippers or suppliers of cargo, preventing or delaying the supplying, loading or receiving of the cargo were excepted. Kerr J said: **12.05**

"It is true that on the basis of its wording clause 2 is properly to be described as an exception clause. This has the consequence, for instance, that it must be strictly construed. But its effect in the context of the question whether or not it can be relied on as an answer to an allegation of fundamental breach cannot depend on the semantic question whether the charterparty says: 'I promise to supply a cargo but shall not be liable if I do not do so due to unavoidable hindrances,' or 'I promise to supply a cargo unless prevented by unavoidable hindrances.' The conclusive answer to any allegation of fundamental breach is in my view that the relevant provision (whether it be properly described as an exception clause or as a qualification of the obligation) excuses non-performance due to circumstances which are not the fault of the charterers."

The key distinction is one between clauses that exclude liability and clauses which define the terms upon which the parties are conducting their business; in other words, clauses which prevent an obligation from arising in the first place.[8] Courts are more receptive than hitherto about concluding that clauses define the scope of obligations rather than exclude liability for breach. **12.06**

2. CLASSIFICATION OF EXEMPTION CLAUSES

Exemption clauses are encountered in many different forms. Some clauses prevent one party from being liable to the other in the event of what would otherwise be a breach of their contract; some clauses limit the amount of compensation which would otherwise be payable upon a breach of contract; and other clauses require one party to indemnify the other against the consequences of that other's default. In addition clauses which limit the time in which one party may bring a claim against the other are treated in the same way as exemption clauses.

A tripartite classification was made in *Kenyon, Son & Craven Ltd v Baxter Hoare & Co Ltd*.[9] Donaldson J said: **12.07**

"Protective conditions are of three distinct types: first those which limit or reduce

---

6   [2016] EWCA Civ 128; [2016] 1 C.L.C. 573.
7   [1973] 1 W.L.R. 210.
8   *JP Morgan Chase Bank v Springwell Navigation* [2008] EWHC 1186 (Comm); *Lobster Group Ltd v Heidelberg Graphic Equipment Ltd* [2009] EWHC 1919 (TCC). See also *Gardiner v Agricultural and Rural Finance Pty Ltd* [2007] NSWCA 235 at [215].
9   [1971] 1 W.L.R. 519.

what would otherwise be the defendants' duty; second, those which exclude the defendants' liability for breach of specified aspects of that duty, and third, those which limit the extent to which the defendant is bound to indemnify the plaintiff in respect of the consequences of breaches of that duty."

In terms of a classification, there is a considerable overlap between the first and second "distinct types", for there is little theoretical difference between limiting the defendant's duty and excluding liability for breach of duty.[10] In substance, therefore, this follows Professor Coote's classification.

12.08   In *Photo Productions Ltd v Securicor Transport Ltd*,[11] Lord Diplock analysed the obligations upon contracting parties created by the contract. He divided them into primary obligations (that is, what each party promised to do), general secondary obligations (that is, to pay damages in the event of a breach of a primary obligation) and anticipatory secondary obligations (that is, to pay damages for future non-performance of primary obligations in a case where the breach of the primary obligation has amounted to a repudiation of the contract accepted by the other party). Lord Diplock continued:

"... an exclusion clause is one which excludes or modifies an obligation, whether primary, general secondary or anticipatory secondary, that would otherwise arise under the contract by implication of law. Parties are free to agree to whatever exclusion or modification of all three types of obligations they please within the limits that the agreement must retain the legal characteristics of a contract and must not offend against the equitable rule about penalties, that is to say it must not impose on the breaker of a primary obligation a general secondary obligation to pay to the other party a sum of money that is manifestly in excess of the amount which would fully compensate the other party for the loss sustained by him in consequence of the breach of the primary obligation."

12.09   This description assimilates all categories of exclusion clause. However, the strands of the description reveal a division of exclusion clauses into six categories:

(i)   clauses which exclude primary obligations;
(ii)   clauses which modify primary obligations;
(iii) clauses which exclude general secondary obligations;
(iv)   clauses which modify general secondary obligations;
(v)   clauses which exclude anticipatory secondary obligations;
(vi)   clauses which modify anticipatory secondary obligations.

12.10   In essence categories (i) and (ii) are the same as Professor Coote's Type A, and ought not to be considered as exclusion clauses, as opposed to clauses defining what obligations the contracting party has undertaken. Categories (iii) to (vi), which themselves overlap conceptually, are comprehended in Professor Coote's Type B.

12.11   Timebar clauses were included in the following description given by Lord Wilberforce in *Suisse Atlantique Societe D'Armement Maritime SA v NV Rot-*

---

[10]   There may be a practical difference in the application of the Consumer Rights Act 2015. See especially s.66(4)(a) (defining "negligence" by reference to obligations express or implied of a contract).

[11]   [1980] A.C. 827. Lord Diplock foreshadowed this analysis in *Ward (RV) Ltd v Bignall* [1967] 1 Q.B. 534 and *Moschi v Lep Air Services Ltd* [1973] A.C. 331.

terdamsche Kolen Centrale[12]:

"I treat the words 'exceptions clause' as covering broadly such clauses as profess to exclude or limit, either quantitatively or as to the time within which action must be taken, the right of the injured party to bring an action for damages."

The principles of interpretation that apply to exemption clauses apply to other clauses of the same nature, such as a claims control clause in a reinsurance policy, or a condition precedent to reinsurers' liability.[13]   **12.12**

In *Dorset County Council v Southern Felt Roofing Ltd*,[14] a building contract   **12.13** expressly provided that the employer should bear the risk of loss caused by certain specified perils. The Court of Appeal held that although the clause was not in terms expressed as an exemption clause, it potentially had the effect of absolving one party from tortious liability to the other, and hence construed it in accordance with the principles developed in relation to exclusion clauses.

However, in *BHP Petroleum Ltd v British Steel Plc*,[15] it was held that an orthodox defects liability clause in a building contract was not an exemption clause. It operated for the benefit of both parties. The employer is entitled to have the defects rectified without having to engage and pay another contractor to carry out the rectification: the contractor or supplier is entitled to carry out the rectification himself which may normally be expected to be less expensive for him than having to reimburse the cost to the employer of having it done by others.

3. INTERPRETATION OF CONTRACT AS A WHOLE

In interpreting an exemption clause, it must be interpreted in the context of the contract as a whole, rather than in isolation.

For many years there was a strong body of judicial opinion suggesting that the   **12.14** correct approach to the interpretation of an exemption clause was to consider the remainder of the contract apart from the exemption clause, and then to consider whether the exemption clause affords a defence to what would otherwise be the legal liability of the party seeking to rely on the exemption clause. The foundation of this approach is the celebrated judgment of Scrutton LJ in *Rutter v Palmer*,[16] in which he said:

"In construing an exemption clause certain general rules may be applied:
First the defendant is not exempted from liability for the negligence of his servants unless adequate words are used; secondly, the liability of the defendant apart from the exempting words must be ascertained; then the particular clause in question must be considered; and if the only liability of the party pleading the exemption is a liability for negligence, the clause will more readily operate to relieve him."

---

[12] [1967] 1 A.C. 361.
[13] *Beazley Underwriting Ltd v Al Ahleia Insurance Co* [2013] EWHC 677 (Comm).
[14] (1989) 48 B.L.R. 96 CA.
[15] [2000] 2 Lloyd's Rep. 277; *Lobster Group Ltd v Heidelberg Graphic Equipment Ltd* [2009] EWHC 1919 (TCC).
[16] [1922] 2 K.B. 87.

So too in *Beaumont-Thomas v Blue Star Line Ltd*,[17] Scott LJ said:

"In order to construe any exception of liability for events happening in the performance of a contract, where the words of the exception are not so clear as to leave no doubt as to their meaning, it is essential first to ascertain what the contractual duty would be if there were no exception."

A similar statement was made by Denning LJ in *Karsales (Harrow) Ltd v Wallis*[18]:

"It is necessary to look at the contract apart from the exempting clauses and see what are the terms, express or implied, which impose an obligation on the party. If he has been guilty of a breach of those obligations in a respect which goes to the very root of the contract, he cannot rely on the exempting clauses."

12.15   Such an approach would treat exemption clauses in a markedly different way from other clauses in a contract, for it is a basic principle of interpretation that any contract must be construed as a whole.[19] The divergent approaches appear in a single judgment of Scrutton LJ in *Calico Printers' Association v Barclays Bank Ltd*.[20] In that case he said:

"First of all, in my view, you do not take part of the document and consider it by itself; you are to construe the whole document. The parties have used a set of words to express their legal relations to each other and it is no good saying: 'Here I find in sentence A clear words, so I need not trouble about sentence B, because sentence B, if it contradicts sentence A, I will reject as repugnant, and I will ... assume that these parties used these words not meaning anything by them, and therefore I need not trouble about them because they do use clear language in sentence A'."

However, later in his judgment he said:

"First of all, you construe the whole words that are used and not a portion of them. Then you look to see what could be the suggested liability without the clause which purports to exempt from liability."

The second passage seems to be somewhat at variance with the first, and indeed the tenor of the judgment was to the effect that the clause in question limited the primary obligation of the party.

12.16   More recent cases have stressed the need to interpret exclusion clauses in the context of the contract as a whole. This point of view was convincingly advanced by Professor Coote,[21] and now seems to have gained judicial acceptance.[22]

---

[17] [1939] 3 All E.R. 127.
[18] [1956] 1 W.L.R. 936. In so far as Lord Denning MR suggested that a party in fundamental breach cannot rely on an exemption clause, he was in error: see *Photo Production Ltd v Securicor Ltd* [1980] A.C. 827.
[19] See para.7.07.
[20] (1931) 145 L.T. 51.
[21] B. Coote, "Exemption Clauses", in John Bell (ed.), *The Cambridge Law Journal* (London: Sweet & Maxwell, 1964), pp.7–14.
[22] *JP Morgan Chase Bank v Springwell Navigation* [2008] EWHC 1186 (Comm); *Lobster Group Ltd v Heidelberg Graphic Equipment Ltd* [2009] EWHC 1919 (TCC). See also *Gardiner v Agricultural*

Thus in *Swiss Bank Corp v Brink's Mat Ltd*,[23] Bingham J said of an exclusion clause (cl.13):

"My task, therefore, is to construe cl. 13 (i) and (iii) in the context of the contract as a whole and of the business relationship between these parties."

Likewise, in *National Westminster Bank v Utrecht-America Finance Co*,[24] Clarke LJ said of an exclusion clause (cl.8.2(d)):

"like any clause, clause 8.2 (d) must be construed in its context and in the context of the contract as a whole having regard to its factual matrix or surrounding circumstances."

In *HIH Casualty and General Insurance Ltd v Chase Manhattan Bank*,[25] Lord Hoffmann, discussing whether a clause excluded liability for negligence, said: **12.17**

"The question, as it seems to me, is whether the language used by the parties, construed in the context of the whole instrument and against the admissible background, leads to the conclusion that they must have thought it went without saying that the words, although literally wide enough to cover negligence, did not do so. This in turn depends upon the precise language they have used and how inherently improbable it is in all the circumstances that they would have intended to exclude such liability."

Similarly, in *Dairy Containers Ltd v Tasman Orient Line CV*,[26] Lord Bingham of Cornhill said of an exemption clause:

"This clause must be construed in the context of the contract as a whole."

In *Renton (GH) & Co Ltd v Palmyra Trading Corp of Panama*,[27] a bill of lading   **12.18**
provided for the transport of cargo from Canada to London and Hull "or so near thereunto as the vessel may safely get". A further clause stated that in the event of strikes preventing the vessel from entering the port of discharge the master might discharge the cargo at port of loading or any other safe and convenient port, and that such discharge was to be deemed due fulfilment of the contract. In consequence of a strike at the ports of discharge the cargo was discharged at Hamburg. The shipowners were held not to be liable for failure to discharge at the named ports. The latter clauses were treated as modifying the primary obligations created by the earlier clause. Lord Morton of Henryton said:

"The contract contained in the bill of lading must be read as a whole. So read, it provides, in effect, that the goods must be carried to London unless there oc-curs an event specified in one or other of the provisos already mentioned; but if such event happens, the goods may be discharged elsewhere, and such discharge is to be deemed to be due fulfilment of the contract. No conflict arises when an

---

and Rural Finance Pty Ltd [2007] NSWCA 235 at [215]. Contra see Adams (1978) 41 M.L.R. 703; Adams and Brownsword (1988) 104 L.Q.R. 94.
[23] [1986] 2 Lloyd's Rep. 79.
[24] [2001] 3 All E.R. 733 CA.
[25] [2003] 2 Lloyd's Rep. 61.
[26] [2005] 1 W.L.R. 215.
[27] [1957] A.C. 149.

obligation in a contract, unqualified in its terms as it is first stated, is subsequently qualified by a proviso modifying or altering the obligation if certain events happen which are outside the control of either party. The original obligation and the qualification of it both form part of the intention of the parties and neither part is repugnant to the other."

In *Farstad Supply A/S v Enviroco Ltd*,[28] the question was whether cl.33.5 of a charterparty excluded the charter's liability for negligence. Lord Clarke said:

"Like any other term in a contract, clause 33.5 must be construed in its context as part of clause 33 as a whole, which must in turn be set in its context as part of the charterparty, which in its own turn must be considered against the relevant surrounding circumstances or factual matrix."

12.19   In *Impact Funding Solutions Ltd v AIG Europe Insurance Ltd*,[29] Lord Hodge said of an exclusion in an insurance policy:

"An exclusion clause must be read in the context of the contract of insurance as a whole. It must be construed in a manner which is consistent with and not repugnant to the purpose of the insurance contract. There may be circumstances in which in order to achieve that end, the court may construe the exclusions in an insurance contract narrowly ... But the general doctrine, to which counsel also referred, that exemption clauses should be construed narrowly, has no application to the relevant exclusion in this policy. An exemption clause, to which that doctrine applies, excludes or limits a legal liability which arises by operation of law, such as liability for negligence or liability in contract arising by implication of law ... The relevant exclusion clause in this policy is not of that nature. The extent of the cover in the policy is therefore ascertained by construction of all its relevant terms without recourse to a doctrine relating to exemption clauses."

12.20   Similarly, in *Smith v South Wales Switchgear Ltd*,[30] Lord Fraser of Tullybelton said that the indemnity clause considered in that case could not be read in isolation from its context in the clause as a whole and in the context of the general conditions of the contract.

Thus in *E.E. Caledonia Ltd v Orbit Valve Co Europe*,[31] Steyn LJ said:

"It is sometimes right to take into account an obligation to insure in construing an indemnity or exemption clause. That is so because that context may reveal an allocation of risks which are insurable and expected to be insured."

As Basten JA pointed out in *Gardiner v Agricultural and Rural Finance Pty Ltd*[32]:

"If the contract is read as a whole, one is, perhaps, more likely to reach the conclusion that what might otherwise be seen as an exception which excuses li-

---

[28]   [2010] 2 Lloyd's Rep. 387.
[29]   [2016] UKSC 57; [2017] A.C. 33.
[30]   [1978] 1 W.L.R. 165.
[31]   [1994] 1 W.L.R. 1515 CA.
[32]   [2007] NSWCA 235 at [215], referring to this section in a previous edition.

ability for failure to perform, will rather be construed as a limitation on the scope of performance."[33]

Although the exemption clause is construed in its context in the whole of the contract, that context may itself give grounds for limiting the literal meaning of the exclusion. In *Morley v United Friendly Society Plc*,[34] an insurance policy against personal injury excluded liability for injury resulting from "wilful exposure to needless peril". Beldam LJ said: **12.21**

> "An exclusion clause in an insurance policy has to be construed in a manner consistent with and not repugnant to the purpose of the policy. To construe the words 'wilful exposure to needless peril' so as to deprive the insured of benefit under the policy whenever it could be shown that his intentional acts had exposed him to substantial risk would severely restrict the scope of the indemnity against accidental bodily injury. To avoid liability insurers must show that the exposure to needless peril was wilful, not merely that intentional acts done by the deceased resulted in his being exposed to such peril."

In *A Turtle Offshore SA v Superior Trading Inc*,[35] Teare J said: **12.22**

> "However, contracts are not construed literally but, as it has been put in the past, with regard to the main purpose of the contract or, as it is now frequently put, in the context of the contract as a whole. Thus, however wide the literal meaning of an exemption clause, consideration of the main purpose of the contract or of the context of the contract as a whole may result in the apparently wide words of an exemption clause being construed in a manner which does not defeat that main purpose or which reflects the contractual context."

The same approach applies to a clause in a contract which allocates risk as between the parties.[36]   **12.23**

4.   GENERAL APPROACH TO EXEMPTION CLAUSES

The courts' traditional hostility to exclusion clauses has diminished in modern times, and it may vary with the extent of protection which the clause in question seeks to afford.[37]

In *Tradigrain SA v Intertek Testing Services (ITS) Canada Ltd*,[38] Moore-Bick LJ said: **12.24**

> "It is certainly true that English law has traditionally taken a restrictive approach to the construction of exemption clauses and clauses limiting liability for

---

33   See also *JP Morgan Chase Bank v Springwell Navigation* [2008] EWHC 1186 (Comm); *Lobster Group Ltd v Heidelberg Graphic Equipment Ltd* [2009] EWHC 1919 (TCC).
34   [1993] 1 Lloyd's Rep. 490 CA.
35   [2009] 1 Lloyd's Rep. 177 at [109].
36   Above.
37   This section was referred to with apparent approval in *Air Transworld Ltd v Bombardier Inc* [2012] EWHC 243 (Comm); [2012] 1 Lloyd's Rep. 349. The modern approach to the interpretation of exclusion clauses is discussed in Stelios Tofaris, "Commercial Construction of Exemption Clauses" [2019] L.M.C.L.Q. 270.
38   [2007] 1 C.L.C. 188.

breaches of contract and other wrongful acts. However, in recent years it has been increasingly willing to recognise that parties to commercial contracts are entitled to apportion the risk of loss as they see fit and that provisions which limit or exclude liability must be construed in the same way as other terms."

Similarly, in *Frans Maas (UK) Ltd v Samsung Electronics (UK) Ltd*,[39] Gross J said that:

"words, even in exclusion clauses, mean what they say and the parties will be held to the bargain into which they have entered. Further, it is a matter of construction rather than law as to whether liability for deliberate acts will be excluded, though of course the wording must be clear."

12.25   In *Mitchell (George) (Chesterhall) Ltd v Finney Lock Seeds Ltd*,[40] Lord Denning MR traced the history of the court's approach to the interpretation of exclusion clauses.[41] He concluded that the court has only permitted reliance on exclusion clauses where to do so was fair and reasonable, and that in other cases judges have used a variety of devices to prevent reliance on the clause. In *Photo Production Ltd v Securicor Ltd*,[42] Lord Salmon said:

"Clauses which absolve a party to a contract from liability for breaking it are no doubt unpopular, particularly when they are unfair."

So too in *Ailsa Craig Fishing Co Ltd v Malvern Fishing Co Ltd*,[43] Lord Wilberforce, considering a clause which attempted to limit the liability of one party to a fixed financial amount, said:

"Clauses of limitation are not regarded by the courts with the same hostility as clauses of exclusion; this is because they must be related to other contractual terms, in particular to the risks to which the defendant party may be exposed, the remuneration which he receives and possibly also the opportunity of the other party to insure."

12.26   As Lord Denning MR demonstrated in the passage referred to above, the court's hostility to exclusion clauses manifested itself in the court's tendency to adopt a strained and artificial construction in order to strike down the clause. This practice has now been disapproved by the House of Lords. The catalyst which prompted this far-reaching change in judicial attitude was undoubtedly the enactment of the Unfair Contract Terms Act 1977. Since then, the Unfair Terms in Consumer Contracts Regulations 1999 and now the Consumer Rights Act 2015 have carried the process further. The effect of these Acts, and the Regulations, except in so far as they affect the interpretation of contracts, is outside the scope of this book.[44] At the same time, in the case of commercial contracts between parties of equal bargaining power the courts have increasingly recognised that the principle of party autonomy entitles the parties to allocate risks as they think fit.

---

[39]   [2004] 2 Lloyd's Rep. 251.
[40]   [1983] Q.B. 284.
[41]   The passage is quoted in para.2.101.
[42]   [1980] A.C. 827.
[43]   [1983] 1 W.L.R. 964.
[44]   See E. MacDonald, *Exemption Clauses, Penalty Clauses and Unfair Terms*, 2nd edn (London: Bloomsbury Professional, 2006) for comprehensive coverage.

In *Photo Production Ltd v Securicor Ltd*,[45] Lord Diplock said: **12.27**

"... The reports are full of cases in which what would appear to be very strained constructions have been placed upon exclusion clauses, mainly in what today would be called consumer contracts and contracts of adhesion. As Lord Wilberforce has pointed out, any need for this kind of judicial distortion of the English language has been banished by Parliament's having made these kinds of contracts subject to the Unfair Contract Terms Act 1977. In commercial contracts negotiated between businessmen capable of looking after their own interests and of deciding how risks inherent in the performance of various kinds of contract can be most economically borne (generally by insurance), it is, in my view, wrong to place a strained construction on words in an exclusion clause which are clear and fairly susceptible of one meaning only even after due allowance has been made for the presumption in favour of the implied primary and secondary obligation."[46]

The sentiment was repeated by Lord Wilberforce in *Ailsa Craig Fishing Co Ltd v Malvern Fishing Co Ltd*,[47] in which he said that "one must not strive to create ambiguities by strained construction", and in *Mitchell (George) (Chesterhall) Ltd v Finney Lock Seeds Ltd*[48] by Lords Diplock and Bridge of Harwich. It may safely be said that the court will no longer give a strained interpretation to an exclusion clause.[49]

In *Persimmon Homes Ltd v Ove Arup & Partners Ltd*,[50] Stuart-Smith J noted that: **12.28**

"... there has been a shift in the approach of the Courts to limitation and exclusion clauses. This shift has come about for two reasons, which are related. The first is the passing of the Unfair Contract Terms Act 1977 ... the second is an increasing recognition that parties to commercial contracts are and should be left free to apportion and allocate risks and obligations as they see fit, particularly where insurance may be available to one or other or both parties to cover the risks being so allocated."

When that case went to the Court of Appeal,[51] Jackson LJ repeated that approach. He said:

"In major construction contracts the parties commonly agree how they will allocate the risks between themselves and who will insure against what. Exemption clauses are part of the contractual apparatus for distributing risk. There is no need to approach such clauses with horror or with a mind-set determined to cut them down. Contractors and consultants who accept large risks will charge for doing so and will no doubt take out appropriate insurance. Contractors and

---

45 [1980] A.C. 827.
46 For the meaning of these terms see para.12.08.
47 [1983] 1 W.L.R. 964.
48 [1983] 2 A.C. 803.
49 The courts in Australia take the same approach: *Darlington Futures Ltd v Delco Australia Pty Ltd* (1986) 61 A.L.J.R. 76; *Nissho Iwai Australia Ltd v Malaysian National Shipping Corp Bhd* (1986) 61 A.L.J.R. 76; *Glebe Island Terminals Pty Ltd v Continental Seagram Pty Ltd* [1994] 1 Lloyd's Rep. 213 (Supreme Court of New South Wales).
50 [2015] EWHC 3573 (TCC); [2016] B.L.R. 112.
51 [2017] EWCA Civ 373; [2017] 2 C.L.C. 28.

consultants who accept lesser degrees of risk will presumably reflect that in the fees which they agree."

In *Taberna Europe CDO II Plc v Selskabet AF 1.September 2008 in Bankruptcy*,[52] Moore-Bick LJ said that:

"The authorities show that there has been an increasing willingness in recent years to recognise that parties to commercial contracts are entitled to determine for themselves the terms on which they will do business."

12.29   Thus in *Interactive E-Solutions JLT v O3b Africa Ltd*,[53] Lewison LJ said:

"The traditional approach of the courts towards exclusion clauses has been one of hostility. A strict and narrow approach to their interpretation held sway. This began to change with the passing of the Unfair Contract Terms Act 1977. Since then the courts have become more accepting of such clauses, recognising (at least in commercial contracts made between parties of equal bargaining power) that exclusion and limitation clauses are an integral part of pricing and risk allocation."

In *Bikam OOD v Adria Cable Sarl*,[54] Simon J rejected a submission that exclusion and limitation clauses are to be construed restrictively; and also held that no residual hostility applies to clauses which attempt to limit the liability of parties to a fixed financial amount. Likewise, in *Fujitsu Services Ltd v IBM United Kingdom Ltd*,[55] Carr J said:

"There is no reason to approach the exercise of construing an exemption or limitation of liability clause in any way different to any other term in a contract."

5.   STRICT CONSTRUCTION

Exemption clauses in contracts have traditionally been interpreted strictly, but the degree of strictness may vary with the extent of the exemption conferred by the clause.

12.30   Parties who enter into contracts tend to assume that contractual promises will be performed and to concern themselves less with what the consequences of non-performance will be. Moreover, commercial considerations militate against making explicit the refusal of one party to accept liability for non-performance. In *Mannai Investment Co Ltd v Eagle Star Life Assurance Co Ltd*,[56] Lord Hoffmann considered the meaning of a "strict construction". He regarded it as a requirement that the communication in question should be "clear, unambiguous, incapable of misleading". It is considered that this is the sense in which the expression is used in reference to exclusion clauses.

---

52   [2016] EWCA Civ 1262; [2017] Q.B. 633.
53   [2018] EWCA Civ 62; [2018] B.L.R. 167; *The Atlantic Tonjer* [2019] EWHC 1213 (Comm); [2020] 1 Lloyd's Rep. 171.
54   [2012] EWHC 621 (Comm); [2012] Bus. L.R. D109.
55   [2014] EWHC 752 (TCC).
56   [1997] A.C. 749

In *Hollier v Rambler Motors (AMC) Ltd*,[57] Salmon LJ said: **12.31**

"It is well settled that a clause excluding liability for negligence should make its meaning plain on its face to an ordinarily literate and sensible person. The easiest way of doing that, of course, is to state expressly that the garage, tradesman or merchant, as the case may be, will not be responsible for any damage caused by his own negligence. No doubt merchants, tradesmen, garage proprietors and the like are a little shy of writing in an exclusion clause quite so blunt as that. Clearly it would not attract customers, and might even put many off."

The same point was pithily made by Lord Halsbury in *Nelson Line (Liverpool)* **12.32** *Ltd v James Nelson & Sons Ltd*[58]:

"Lord Blackburn used to say that the contest between commercial men and lawyers was that the commercial men always wished to write it short and the lawyers always wished to write it long; but a mixture of the two renders the whole thing unintelligible."

The court has therefore insisted that a party who wishes to relieve himself from **12.33** a legal liability must do so in clear words.[59] Thus in *Szymonowski & Co v Beck & Co*,[60] Scrutton LJ said:

"Now I approach the consideration of that clause applying the principle repeatedly acted upon by the House of Lords and this Court—that if a party wishes to exclude the ordinary consequences that would flow in law from the contract he is making he must do so in clear words."

And in *White v Warwick (John) & Co Ltd*,[61] Denning LJ said:

"In this type of case, two principles are well settled. The first is that, if a person desires to exempt himself from a liability which the common law imposes on him, he can do so by a contract freely and deliberately entered into by the injured party in words that are clear beyond the possibility of misunderstanding."

These principles have survived the five principles of interpretation formulated in **12.34** *Investors Compensation Scheme v West Bromwich Building Society*,[62] although they are not to be applied as rigid rules. Lord Bingham of Cornhill reiterated[63]:

"This clause must be construed in the context of the contract as a whole. The general rule should be applied that if a party, otherwise liable, is to exclude or limit his liability or to rely on an exemption, he must do so in clear words; unclear words do not suffice; any ambiguity or lack of clarity must be resolved against that party."

---

[57] [1972] 2 Q.B. 71.
[58] [1908] A.C. 16.
[59] *Alison (J) Gordon & Co Ltd v Wallsend Shipway and Engineering Co Ltd* (1927) 44 T.L.R. 323, per Scrutton LJ.
[60] [1923] 1 K.B. 457.
[61] [1953] 1 W.L.R. 1285.
[62] [1998] 1 W.L.R. 896.
[63] *Dairy Containers Ltd v Tasman Orient Line CV* [2005] 1 W.L.R. 215.

In *McGee Group Ltd v Galliford Try Building Ltd*,[64] Coulson J held:

"... a clause which seeks to limit the liability of one party to a commercial contract, for some or all of the claims which may be made by the other party, should generally be treated as an element of the parties' wider allocation of benefit, risk and responsibility. No special rules apply to the construction or interpretation of such a clause although, in order to have the effect contended for by the party relying upon it, a clause limiting liability must be clear and unambiguous."

12.35   Thus the exemption clause must cover exactly the nature of the liability in question. So a clause which excludes liability for breach of warranty will not exclude liability for a breach of condition; and a clause which excludes liability for breach of implied terms will not exclude liability for breach of express terms. In *Air Transworld Ltd v Bombardier Inc*,[65] Cooke J held that the clause in that case successfully excluded liability for alleged breach of implied conditions arising under the Sale of Goods Act 1979 despite the fact that the exclusion clause did not use the word "condition". The clause made it clear that every promise implied by law was excluded, and those promises included conditions that would otherwise have arisen under the Act. However, if the words of the contract are not clear then the implied conditions are not excluded.[66]

12.36   The degree of clarity required may vary according to the extent of the exemption sought to be conferred by the clause.[67] In *Photo Production Ltd v Securicor Ltd*,[68] Lord Diplock said:

"Since the presumption is that the parties by entering into the contract intended to accept the implied obligations,[69] exclusion clauses are to be construed strictly and the degree of strictness appropriate to their construction may properly depend on the extent to which they involve departure from the implied obligations. Since the obligations implied by law in a commercial contract are those which, by judicial consensus over the years or by Parliament in passing a statute, have been regarded as obligations which a reasonable businessman would realise that he was accepting when he entered into a contract of a particular kind, the court's view of the reasonableness of any departure from the implied obligations which would be involved in construing the express words of an exclusion clause in one sense that they are capable of bearing rather than another is a relevant consideration in deciding what meaning the words were intended by the parties to bear. But this does not entitle the court to reject the exclusion clause, however unreasonable the court itself may think it is, if the words are clear and fairly susceptible of one meaning only."

Photo Production Ltd v Securicor Ltd was the first of the cases in the House of Lords to disapprove the adoption of strained interpretations of exclusion clauses.

[2017] EWHC 87 (TCC); [2017] 1 C.L.C. 440.
[65] [2012] EWHC 243 (Comm); [2012] 1 Lloyd's Rep. 349.
[66] *Dalmare SpA v Union Maritime Ltd* [2012] EWHC 3537 (Comm); [2013] 1 Lloyd's Rep. 509.
[67] *BHP Petroleum Ltd v British Steel Plc* [2000] 2 Lloyd's Rep. 277 per Evans LJ; *Stocznia Gdynia SA v Gearbulk Holdings Ltd* [2009] 1 Lloyd's Rep. 461, per Moore-Bick LJ.
[68] [1980] A.C. 827.
[69] For example, to pay damages in the event of non-performance of primary obligations; see para.12.08.

It may therefore be said that although the court will not adopt a strained interpretation, it will still adopt a strict one.

In *Whitecap Leisure Ltd v John H Rundle Ltd*,[70] Moore-Bick LJ said:　　　　　**12.37**

"The modern approach to construction, which applies as much to exclusion and limitation clauses as to other contractual terms, is to ascertain the objective intention of the parties from the words used and the context in which they are found, including the document as a whole and the background to it: see *Mannai Investment Co Ltd v Eagle Star Life Assurance Co Ltd*,[71] and *Investors Compensation Scheme v West Bromwich Building Society*. However, in cases where there is uncertainty about the parties' intention, and therefore about the meaning of the clause, such uncertainty will be resolved against the person relying on the clause and the more significant the departure is said to be from what are accepted to be the obligations ordinarily assumed under a contract of the kind in question, the more difficult it will be to persuade the court that the parties intended that result."

Similarly, in *Stocznia Gdynia SA v Gearbulk Holdings Ltd*[72] Moore-Bick LJ said:

"The court is unlikely to be satisfied that a party to a contract has abandoned valuable rights arising by operation of law unless the terms of the contract make it sufficiently clear that that was intended. The more valuable the right, the clearer the language will need to be."

The more improbable it is that the other party would agree to excluding the liability of the proferens, the more exacting the application of the principle will be.[73] So in *Kudos Catering (UK) Ltd v Manchester Central Convention Complex Ltd*,[74] a suggested interpretation of an exclusion clause was rejected because it would leave the contract effectively devoid of contractual content since there would have been no sanction for non-performance.

There is also a difference in approach in interpreting exemption clauses in　　　　　**12.38**
contracts on the one hand, and exemption clauses in settlements and wills on the other. There are two related principles in play: one, that the burden of proving that a case falls within the provisions of an exemption clause lies with the party relying on the clause, so that any ambiguity will be resolved against him; the other, that in a case of ambiguity, the words of the document will be construed against the party who made the document and seeks to rely on them. In *Bogg v Raper*,[75] Millett LJ commented:

"In the case of a contract these two principles march together, for it is assumed that the party responsible for the inclusion of the exemption clause is the party able to rely on it. In the case of a will or settlement, however, the two principles point in different directions. The document is the unilateral work of the testator or settlor through whom the beneficiaries claim. There is no inherent improbability that he should intend to absolve his executors or trustees from liability

---

[70]　[2008] 2 Lloyd's Rep. 216; applied in *University of Wales v London College of Business Ltd* [2015] EWHC 1280 (QB). The modern approach to the interpretation of exclusion clauses is discussed in Stelios Tofaris, "Commercial Construction of Exemption Clauses" [2019] L.M.C.L.Q. 270.

[71]　[1997] A.C. 749.

[72]　[2009] 1 Lloyd's Rep. 461.

[73]　*Geys v Société Générale* [2013] 1 A.C. 523; [2013] I.C.R. 117.

[74]　[2013] EWCA Civ 38; [2013] 2 Lloyd's Rep. 270.

[75]　(1998) 1 I.T.E.L.R. 267.

from the consequences of their negligence. They accept office on the terms of a document for which they are not responsible, and are entitled to have the document fairly construed according to the natural meaning of the words used."

Even so, trustees' liability can be excluded only by clear and unambiguous words; and the court should not be astute to construe an exemption clause beyond its natural meaning.[76]

12.39   Where trustees contract with third parties, they may limit their liability to the assets of the trust fund by suitable words. There must be words negativing the personal liability which is an ordinary incident of trusteeship. The mere fact that they contract "as trustees" in not sufficient, whereas if they contract "as trustees only", that is enough.[77]

Illustrations

1.   A contract for the sale of common English sainfoin contained a provision stating "sellers give no warranty express or implied as to the growth description or any other matters". The sellers delivered giant sainfoin. It was held that the failure to deliver common English sainfoin was a breach of a condition of the contract, and that a clause which excluded liability for breach of warranty was not appropriate to exclude liability for breach of condition.
Wallis Son & Wells v Pratt & Haynes[78]

2.   A contract note for the sale of "200 yards reels" of sewing cotton provided that:

"the goods delivered shall be deemed to be in all respects in accordance with the contract and the buyers shall be bound to accept and pay for the same accordingly unless the sellers shall within 14 days after the arrival of the goods at their destination receive from the buyers notice of any matter or thing by reason whereof they may allege that the goods are not in accordance with the contract."

It was held that a claim for short delivery was not barred because the reference to the "goods delivered" meant that the clause did not bar claims where the allegation was that the goods had not been delivered.
Beck & Co v Szymanowski (K) & Co[79]

3.   The buyer of a Bugatti motor car told the sellers that he wanted a car which would be comfortable and suitable as a tourer. The order form contained a term guaranteeing the car against damage due to faulty material and excluding "any other guarantee or warranty, statutory or otherwise". The car proved to be uncomfortable and unsuitable as a tourer. It was held that that requirement was a condition of the contract. Liability was not therefore excluded by that part of the clause

---

[76]   *Wight v Olswang* (1999) 1 I.T.E.L.R. 783.
[77]   See *Investec Trust (Guernsey) Ltd v Glenalla Properties Ltd* [2018] UKPC 7; [2019] A.C. 271; *First Tower Trustees Ltd v CDS (Superstores International) Ltd* [2018] EWCA Civ 1396; [2019] 1 W.L.R. 637.
[78]   [1910] 2 K.B. 1003, per Fletcher Moulton LJ dissenting; affirmed [1911] A.C. 394.
[79]   [1924] A.C. 43.

excluding warranties, and the reference to "other guarantees" could not be read as referring to "other conditions".
Baldry v Marshall[80]

4.   A contract provided for the sale of a "new Singer car". The contract contained a clause which provided that "all conditions, warranties and liabilities implied by statute common law or otherwise are excluded". The sellers delivered a car which was not a new car. It was held that the failure to deliver a new car was a breach of an express term of the contract, and that a clause which excluded liability for breach of implied terms was no protection.
Andrews Brothers (Bournemouth) Ltd v Singer and Co Ltd[81]

5.   A hire purchase agreement contained a clause which provided that:

"no warranty, condition, description or representation whether express or implied on the part of the owner as to the state or quality of the vehicle is given or implied any statutory or other warranty, condition, description or representation whether express or implied as to the state, quality fitness or roadworthiness being hereby excluded".

It was held that the exclusion clause covered warranties etc contained in the agreement itself, but was not appropriate to exclude liability for a warranty given in an agreement collateral to it.
Webster v Higgin[82]

6.   A contract for the sale of pheasant feed contained a clause excluding liability for "latent defects". It was held that the clause was ineffective to exclude liability for breach of the implied condition that the goods would be reasonably fit for their purpose.
Kendall (Henry) & Sons v Lillico (William) & Sons[83]

7.   A clause in a computer hardware and software contract limited liability for the supply functioning and use of the goods. It was held that this did not cover loss caused by a delay in supply, but that the clause applied only once the goods had been supplied.
Pegler Ltd v Wang (UK) Ltd[84]

8.   A contract for a package holiday contained a clause which stated:

"Where the passenger occupies a motorcoach seat fitted with a safety belt, neither the Operators nor their agents or co-operating organisations will be liable for any injury, illness or death or for any damages or claims whatsoever arising from any accident or incident, if the safety belt is not being worn at the time of such accident or incident".

While travelling in a coach a holidaymaker got out of her seat to get something

---

80   [1925] 1 K.B. 260.
81   [1934] 1 K.B. 17.
82   [1948] 2 All E.R. 127.
83   [1969] 2 A.C. 31.
84   [2000] B.L.R. 218.

from a bag she had stowed in the overhead luggage shelf. The coach braked suddenly. She fell backwards and suffered injury. It was held that since she was not occupying a seat at the time of the incident the exclusion clause did not apply.
Insight Vacations Pty Ltd v Young[85]

6. EXEMPTION CLAUSE MUST BE UNAMBIGUOUS

A real doubt or ambiguity in an exemption clause will be resolved against the party seeking to rely on the clause.

12.40 As has been seen, one of the principles of interpretation of written contracts is that any ambiguity is resolved *contra proferentem*.[86] One of the most common areas of application of this general principle is in the context of exemption clauses. in *Newman v Framewood Manor Management Co Ltd*,[87] Arden LJ said:

> "As the exoneration clause has to be interpreted contra proferentem, it is only right to give it its narrower meaning."

12.41 Thus in *Dairy Containers Ltd v Tasman Orient Line CV*,[88] Lord Bingham of Cornhill said:

> "The general rule should be applied that if a party, otherwise liable, is to exclude or limit his liability or to rely on an exemption, he must do so in clear words; unclear words do not suffice; any ambiguity or lack of clarity must be resolved against that party."

Similarly, in *Hollins v Davy (J) Ltd*,[89] Sachs J said:

> "I need, of course, hardly add that all exemption clauses are construed *contra proferentem* so that if there were here two reasonable constructions of a word or phrase, then the construction least favourable to the defendants will be adopted."

Likewise, in *Acme Transport Ltd v Betts*,[90] Cumming-Bruce LJ said:

> "But the principles are that the language of an exemption clause is prima facie to be construed against the person who drafted it or put it forward ... that the language of an exemption clause must be sufficiently explicit to disclose the common intention of the parties without straining the language."

12.42 So in *Lee (John) & Son (Grantham) Ltd v Railway Executive*,[91] a warehouse was let by the defendant on terms which excluded the liability of the defendant for loss or damage "which but for the tenancy hereby created or anything done pursuant to the provisions hereof would not have arisen". The tenant's goods were damaged by fire caused by sparks from a steam engine. The defendant contended that the clause

---

[85] [2011] HCA 11 (High Court of Australia).
[86] See para.7.66.
[87] [2012] EWCA Civ 159; [2012] 2 E.G.L.R. 45; *Financial Services Authority v Asset LI Inc* [2013] EWHC 178 (Ch); *Great Elephant Corp v Trafigura Beheer BV* [2013] EWCA Civ 905; [2014] 1 Lloyd's Rep. 1 (a force majeure clause).
[88] [2005] 1 W.L.R. 215.
[89] [1963] 1 Q.B. 844.
[90] [1981] R.T.R. 190.
[91] [1949] 2 All E.R. 581.

exempted it from liability even if negligence was proved. The court held that the exemption was confined to liabilities created by the relationship of landlord and tenant. Evershed MR said:

"We are presented with two alternative readings of this document and the reading which one should adopt is to be determined, among other things, by a consideration of the fact that the defendants put forward the document. They have put forward a clause which is by no means free from obscurity and have contended that, on the view for which they argued, it has a remarkably, if not an extravagantly, wide scope, and I think that the rule *contra proferentem* should be applied and that the result is that the present claim is not one which obliges the first plaintiffs to give to the defendants a release and an indemnity."[92]

The underlying principle is that a party to a contract is not to be taken to have given up rights without clear language to that effect. In *Nobahar-Cookson v Hut Group Ltd*,[93] Briggs LJ explained:

12.43

"In my judgment the underlying rationale for the principle that, if necessary to resolve ambiguity, exclusion clauses should be narrowly construed has nothing to do with the identification of the *proferens*, either of the document as a whole or of the clause in question. Nor is it a principle derived from an identification of the person seeking to rely upon it. Ambiguity in an exclusion clause may have to be resolved by a narrow construction because an exclusion clause cuts down or detracts from the ambit of some important obligation in a contract, or a remedy conferred by the general law such as (in the present case) an obligation to give effect to a contractual warranty by paying compensation for breach of it. The parties are not lightly to be taken to have intended to cut down the remedies which the law provides for breach of important contractual obligations without using clear words having that effect."

He went on to explain:

"I approach the issue as to the construction of clause 5.1 upon the basis that there remains a principle that an ambiguity in its meaning may have to be resolved by a preference for the narrower construction, if linguistic, contextual and purposive analysis do not disclose an answer to the question with sufficient clarity."

A difficulty of interpretation is not the same as an ambiguity; nor should a strained interpretation be placed upon a clause in order to create an ambiguity. Thus in *Ailsa Craig Fishing Co Ltd v Malvern Fishing Co Ltd*,[94] Lord Wilberforce said:

12.44

"It was contended that the initial words ... were ambiguous and that their ambiguity invalidates the whole subclause. But I accept on this the conclusion of Lord Dunpark that the words are 'open to construction' and I agree on the construction which he prefers. The possibility of construction of a clause does not amount to an ambiguity: that disappears after the court has pronounced the meaning."

---

[92] More recently, however, Hoffmann J has described the operation of the *contra proferentem* principle of construction, when applied to a lease, as being in most cases "entirely arbitrary": *Amax International Ltd v Custodian Holdings Ltd* [1986] 2 E.G.L.R. 111. Admittedly, however, the case did not concern an exemption clause.
[93] [2016] EWCA Civ 128; [2016] 1 C.L.C. 573.
[94] [1983] 1 W.L.R. 964.

12.45   If the clause is unintelligible, it is an a fortiori case. Thus in *Nelson Line (Liverpool) Ltd v Nelson (James) & Sons Ltd*,[95] Lord Halsbury said:

> "The known condition of the law is that unless protected by protective clauses the defendant is liable; he has only put together, or jumbled together, a number of phrases to which no legal interpretation can be given, and the result is that the state of liability under the law remains what it was and the defendant is liable."

12.46   Moreover when a party wishes to exclude his liability, it is dangerous to use neologisms. Thus in *London & North Western Railway v Neilson*,[96] a railway company conveyed goods on terms that they were not to be liable for "loss, damage, misconveyance, delay or detention" of the goods during transit. One question which arose was whether the fate of the goods was a misconveyance. In the Court of Appeal,[97] Scrutton LJ said that if a carrier wished to exempt himself from liability for negligence of his employees "he must use ordinary English and not inventive words of doubtful meaning". In the House of Lords, Lord Dunedin approved the approach of Scrutton LJ, describing the word "misconveyance" as "a coined word of no recognised significance". Lord Sumner said that if the word bore the wide meaning for which the railway company contended:

> "it is so wrapped up in deliberate obscurity as to be unavailable to the railway company, when read, as it should be, *contra proferentem*."

12.47   Sometimes, even a clause which is clear will not suffice, for it may be in conflict with other clauses in the contract. Thus in *Elderslie Steamship Co Ltd v Borthwick*,[98] Lord Macnaghten said:

> "The clause which has been called the large print clause seems to me to be perfectly clear. The small print clause is equally clear. For my part I am unable to reconcile the two clauses. In such a case an ambiguous document is no protection."

Illustrations

1.   A charterparty stipulated that the ship "should be provided with a deck cargo if required at full freight, but at merchant's risk". Part of the deck cargo was jettisoned, and the shippers brought an action against the shipowners to recover a general average contribution. It was held that the words of the exception clause were not clear enough to relieve the shipowners from liability. Bowen LJ said:

> "It is difficult at first sight to free oneself from the idea that those who drew this contract were thinking of the jettison of a deck load of timber. But still, what is the sound principle to apply? Why, it is that those who wish to make exceptions in their own favour, and by which they are to be relieved from the ordinary laws of the sea, ought to do so in clear words; and on that principle I think this case

---

[95]   [1908] A.C. 16.
[96]   [1922] A.C. 263.
[97]   [1922] 1 K.B. 192.
[98]   [1905] A.C. 93.

ought to be decided, and my judgment goes upon the basis that the terms used here are not clear enough to absolve the shipowners."

Burton v English[99]

2. A building contract contained a clause which required the contractor to build in a workmanlike manner and in accordance with a stipulated specification. The specification provided that the work was to be carried out in accordance with the bye-laws of the local authority and to their satisfaction. It was argued that the contractor's liability was excluded if the local authority expressed satisfaction with the work. It was held that the contract was ambiguous in that respect, and should be construed against the contractor. Accordingly, the building owner was entitled to sue the contractor for defective workmanship, despite the local authority having expressed satisfaction with the work.

Billyack v Leyland Construction Co Ltd[100]

7. LIABILITY FOR NEGLIGENCE

An exemption clause will not relieve a party from liability for negligence unless it does so expressly or by other clear words, or unless that party has no liability other than a liability in negligence.

The traditional approach of the court was summarised by Lord Morton of Henryton in *Canada Steamship Lines Ltd v R.*[101] as follows:

12.48

"(1)   If the clause contains language which expressly exempts the person in whose favour it is made (hereafter called 'the *proferens*') from the consequences of the negligence of his own servants, effect must be given to that provision.[102]

(2)   If there is no express reference to negligence, the court must consider whether the words are wide enough, in their ordinary meaning, to cover negligence on the part of the servants of the *proferens*. If a doubt arises at this point, it must be resolved against the *proferens* ...

(3)   If the words used are wide enough for the above purpose, the court must then consider whether 'the head of damage may be based on some ground other than negligence' ... The 'other ground' must not be so fanciful or remote that the proferens cannot be supposed to have desired protection against it; but subject to this qualification ... the existence of a possible head of damage other than that of negligence is fatal to the *proferens* even if the words used are prima facie wide enough to cover negligence on the part of his servants."

Although this was a Canadian appeal, the law is the same in England.[103]

---

[99]   (1883) 12 Q.B.D. 218.

[100]   [1968] 1 W.L.R. 471.

[101]   [1952] A.C. 192.

[102]   The fact that the propositions refer only to negligence of the party's servants and not to his own negligence is of no significance: *Gillespie Brothers & Co Ltd v Bowles (Roy) Transport Ltd* [1973] Q.B. 400, per Buckley LJ.

[103]   *Gillespie Brothers & Co Ltd v Bowles (Roy) Transport Ltd* [1973] Q.B. 400, per Buckley LJ.

12.49   In *Rutter v Palmer*,[104] Scrutton LJ put forward three principles for determining whether an exclusion clause excluded liability for negligence. The two relevant principles, for present purposes are that:

"… The defendant is not exempted from liability for the negligence of his servants unless adequate words are used",

and:

"if the only liability of the party pleading the exemption is a liability for negligence, the clause will more readily operate to exempt him."

12.50   The application of the *Canada Steamship* guidelines is not confined to cases of personal injury.[105] In the context of carriage of goods by sea they also apply to the question whether liability is excluded for breach of fundamental obligations such as the seaworthiness of the vessel.[106] Lord Morton's guidelines apply to indemnity clauses as well as exemption clauses.[107] Indeed, at any rate in commercial contracts, the *Canada Steamship* guidelines (in so far as they survive) are now more relevant to indemnity clauses than to exemption clauses.[108]

12.51   The "*Canada Steamship*" principles have never attained the force of law. Indeed, it is controversial whether they retain any authoritative status.[109] They are, nevertheless, often applied. But it would be "a fatal error" to regard these propositions as if they were a codifying statute.[110] The three-stage approach provides a guideline or helpful framework for the court's analysis, but is not a rule of law to be applied with the rigour of a taxing statute.[111] Whether Lord Morton's three formulations are called "principles" or "tests" or "rules" or "rulings" or "guidelines", they are not provisions in a statute but aids to interpretation, and the court's duty is always to construe the clause in question to see what it means, what it plainly means to any ordinarily literate and sensible person, even if that results in the clause having no effect.[112]

12.52   As Aikens J said in *HIH Casualty and General Insurance Ltd v Chase Manhattan Bank*[113]:

"The court's task is still to discern what the parties intended by the wording they have agreed in the context of the particular type of contract under consideration. But although 'rules' of construction are a guide to the intention of the parties, they are not the masters of the parties' intention."

---

[104] [1922] 2 K.B. 8.
[105] *Greenwich Millennium Village Ltd v Essex Services Group Plc* [2014] EWCA Civ 960; [2014] 1 W.L.R. 3517.
[106] *Onego Shipping and Chartering BV v JSC Arcadia Shipping* [2010] 2 Lloyd's Rep. 221.
[107] *Shell UK Ltd v Total UK Ltd* [2010] 3 All E.R. 793.
[108] *Persimmon Homes Ltd v Ove Arup & Partners Ltd* [2017] EWCA Civ 373; [2017] 2 C.L.C. 28.
[109] See Adam Shaw-Mellors, "Negligence construction: does anything remain of Canada Steamship?" [2017] J.B.L. 610; Stelios Tofaris, "Commercial Construction of Exemption Clauses" [2019] L.M.C.L.Q. 270.
[110] *Lamport & Holt Lines Ltd v Coubro & Scrutton (M&I) Ltd* [1982] 2 Lloyd's Rep. 42, per Donaldson MR; *The Golden Leader* [1980] 2 Lloyd's Rep. 573.
[111] *CNM Estates (Tolworth Tower) Ltd v VeCREF I SARL* [2020] EWHC 1605 (Comm).
[112] *Lamport & Holt Lines Ltd v Coubro & Scrutton (M & I) Ltd*, per Stephenson LJ. See also *Sonat Offshore SA v Amerada Hess Development Ltd* (1987) 39 Build. L.R. 1; *Aprile SpA v Elin Maritime Ltd* [2019] EWHC 1001 (Comm); [2020] 1 Lloyd's Rep. 111.
[113] [2001] C.L.C. 48 at [45], approved in *National Westminster Bank v Utrecht-America Finance Co* [2001] 3 All E.R. 733 at [47] CA.

This general approach was confirmed when the case reached the House of Lords.[114] Lord Bingham of Cornhill said:

"There can be no doubting the general authority of these principles,[115] which have been applied in many cases, and the approach indicated is sound. The courts should not ordinarily infer that a contracting party has given up rights which the law confers on him to an extent greater than the contract terms indicate he has chosen to do; and if the contract terms can take legal and practical effect without denying him the rights he would ordinarily enjoy if the other party is negligent, they will be read as not denying him those rights unless they are so expressed as to make clear that they do. But ... Lord Morton was giving helpful guidance on the proper approach to interpretation and not laying down a code. The passage does not provide a litmus test which, applied to the terms of the contract, yields a certain and predictable result. The court's task of ascertaining what the particular parties intended, in their particular commercial context, remains."[116]

In the same case, Lord Hoffmann said:

"The question, as it seems to me, is whether the language used by the parties, construed in the context of the whole instrument and against the admissible background, leads to the conclusion that they must have thought it went without saying that the words, although literally wide enough to cover negligence, did not do so. This in turn depends upon the precise language they have used and how inherently improbable it is in all the circumstances that they would have intended to exclude such liability."[117]

In *Macquarie Internationale Investments Ltd v Glencore (UK) Ltd*,[118] Walker J **12.53** considered the decision of the House of Lords in *HIH Casualty and General Insurance Ltd v Chase Manhattan Bank* and said that in the light of that decision his primary task was to identify the commercial purpose of the contract as a whole, and the exclusion clause in particular.

In *Mir Steel UK Ltd v Morris*,[119] Rimer LJ referred to the *Canada Steamship* **12.54** guidelines and subsequent authority, and concluded:

"Those various comments about the *Canada Steamship* principles show that they should not be applied mechanistically and ought to be regarded as no more than guidelines. They do not provide an automatic solution to any particular case. The court's function is always to interpret the particular contract in the context in which it was made. It would be surprising if it were otherwise."

The court concluded that, on the facts, "any claim" in the context of a purchaser's obligation to settle claims included claims based on intentional wrongdoing.

---

114 [2003] 1 All E.R. (Comm) 349. See also Lord Bingham of Cornhill in *Dairy Containers Ltd v Tasman Orient Line CV* [2005] 1 W.L.R. 215.
115 For example, the principles in *Canada Steamships v R.*
116 Lord Steyn agreed with Lord Bingham.
117 Although Lord Hoffmann had said that all the "intellectual baggage" of interpretation had been discarded, he did not repudiate the utility of the *Canada Steamship* guidelines, although he, like many judges before him, stressed that they are not to be mechanistically applied. They continue to be applied by the courts: see *Colour Quest Ltd v Total Downstream UK Plc* [2009] EWHC 540 (Comm); *Jose v MacSalvors Plant Hire Ltd* [2009] EWCA Civ 1329; *Onego Shipping and Chartering BV v JSC Arcadia Shipping* [2010] 2 Lloyd's Rep. 221.
118 [2008] 2 B.C.L.C. 565.
119 [2012] EWCA Civ 1397; [2013] 2 All E.R. (Comm) 54 (sub nom *Lictor Anstalt v Mir Steel UK Ltd*).

12.55   In *Societe Generale, London Branch v Geys* Société Générale, London Branch v Geys,[120] the Supreme Court applied the first two *Canada Steamship* guidelines without qualification or comment. Lord Hope said:

> "The approach that ought to be taken to the construction of clauses of this kind is well-established. In *Canada Steamship Lines Ltd v The King*[121] Lord Morton of Henryton quoted with approval the principles applicable to clauses which purport to exempt one party to a contract from liability for negligence which were stated by Lord Greene MR in *Alderslade v Hendon Laundry Ltd*.[122] In summary, these principles are (1) that if the clause expressly exempts the party in whose favour it is made (the proferens) from liability for negligence, effect must be given to it; (2) if there is no express reference to negligence, the court must consider whether the words used are wide enough to cover it; and (3) if a doubt arises on this point it must be resolved in favour of the other party and against the proferens."

He did not mention the third of those guidelines. Nevertheless, in *Capita (Banstead 2011) Ltd v RFIB Group Ltd*,[123] Longmore LJ referred to the third of the guidelines without any disapproval in recording that the judge had referred to the principle that "a clause is not to be construed as exempting a party to a contract from negligence if there is any other potential basis of liability which falls within its wording".

12.56   In *Taberna Europe CDO II Plc v Selskabet AF 1.September 2008 in Bankruptcy*,[124] Moore-Bick LJ said that the law had moved on since *Canada Steamship* and pointed out that:

> "The authorities show that there has been an increasing willingness in recent years to recognise that parties to commercial contracts are entitled to determine for themselves the terms on which they will do business."

The exclusion clause in that case did not mention negligence, but the Court of Appeal held that it was effective to exclude liability for negligent misrepresentation. If the *Canada Steamship* guidelines had been applied, it is difficult to see how the Court of Appeal could have decided the case as it did. In *Persimmon Homes Ltd v Ove Arup & Partners Ltd*,[125] Jackson LJ pointed out that in *Canada Steamship* the court was concerned both with an exclusion clause and also an indemnity clause. He commented:

> "Over the last 66 years there has been a long running debate about the effect of that passage and the extent to which it is still good law. In hindsight we can see that it is not satisfactory to deal with exemption clauses and indemnity clauses in one single compendious passage. It is one thing to agree that A is not liable to B for the consequences of A's negligence. It is quite another thing to agree that B must compensate A for the consequences of A's own negligence."

---

[120] [2012] UKSC 63; [2013] 1 A.C. 523.
[121] [1952] A.C. 192, 208.
[122] [1945] K.B. 189, 192.
[123] [2015] EWCA Civ 1310; [2016] Q.B. 835. See also *Federal Republic of Nigeria v JP Morgan Chase Bank, NA* [2019] EWHC 347 (Comm).
[124] [2016] EWCA Civ 1262; [2017] Q.B. 663.
[125] [2017] EWCA Civ 373; [2017] 2 C.L.C. 28.

It appears, therefore, that the *Canada Steamship* guidelines may no longer represent the law.

Even if the guidelines do survive, it may not be appropriate to apply each of them where the clause in question takes the form of "not liable unless" or "only liable if".[126] In *HIH Casualty and General Insurance Ltd v Chase Manhattan Bank*,[127] Aikens J said:

12.57

> "It seems to me that the second and third 'rules' of construction are intended to deal with cases where the exemption or indemnity clause wording has been deliberately drawn in a wide and general way. It is for that reason that its effect will appear equivocal and so the court naturally asks: what did the parties actually intend to cover by these general words? I think that the *Canada Steamship* case rules of construction were not intended to apply to a particular clause that is specifically directed at exempting liability for the breach of a particular type of absolute duty, where the breach can be established whether or not negligence (or fraud) is proved."

Thus Lord Morton's guidelines were not appropriate where the clause in question sought to exclude liability for a unitary obligation which is not dependent on innocence or negligence (such as a duty of disclosure).[128] Where a clause excluded liability except for "gross negligence ... fraud or wilful default" it was held that although "gross negligence" was not a concept generally recognised in English law, in the context of the contract it required more than mere negligence; and connoted not only conduct undertaken with actual appreciation of the risks involved, but also serious regard of or indifference to an obvious risk.[129] In this context "wilful neglect or default" means deliberate and conscious neglect or default, or reckless carelessness.[130] Nor do these guidelines apply to "anti-set-off" clauses.[131]

12.58

In *Capita (Banstead 2011) Ltd v RFIB Group Ltd*,[132] Popplewell J set out the following principles:

12.59

> "(1)   A clear intention must appear from the words used before the Court will reach the conclusion that one party has agreed to exempt the other from the consequences of his own negligence or indemnify him against losses so caused. The underlying rationale is that clear words are needed because it is inherently improbable that one party should agree to assume responsibility for the consequences of the other's negligence ...
>
> (2)   The *Canada Steamship* principles are not to be applied mechanistically and ought to be considered as no more than guidelines; the task is always to ascertain what the parties intended in their particular commercial

---

126 *Monarch Airlines Ltd v Luton Airport Ltd* [1998] 1 Lloyd's Rep. 403; *CNM Estates (Tolworth Tower) Ltd v VeCREF I SARL* [2020] EWHC 1605 (Comm).

127 [2001] C.L.C. 48, approved in *HIH Casualty and General Insurance Ltd v New Hampshire Insurance Co* [2001] C.L.C. 1480 CA.

128 *HIH Casualty and General Insurance Ltd v Chase Manhattan Bank* [2001] C.L.C. 1853 CA.

129 *Camarata Property Inc v Credit Suisse Securities (Europe) Ltd* [2011] EWHC 211 (Comm); *Winnetka Trading Corp v Julius Baer International Ltd* [2011] EWHC 2030 (Ch); *CNM Estates (Tolworth Tower) Ltd v VeCREF I SARL* [2020] EWHC 1605 (Comm).

130 *In re City Equitable Fire Insurance Ltd* [1925] Ch. 407; *Kenyon Son & Craven Ltd v Baxter Hoare & Co Ltd* [1971] 1 Lloyd's Rep. 232; *Swiss Bank Corp v Brink's Mat Ltd* [1986] 2 Lloyd's Rep. 79.

131 *Continental Illinois National Bank & Trust Co of Chicago v Papanicolau* [1986] 2 Lloyd's Rep. 441; *Skipskredittforeningen v Emperor Navigation* [1998] 1 Lloyd's Rep. 66.

132 [2014] EWHC 2197 (Comm).

context in accordance with the established principles of construction ...
They nevertheless form a useful guide to the approach where the commercial context makes it improbable that in the absence of clear words one
party would have agreed to assume responsibility for the relevant
negligence of the other.

(3)　These principles apply with even greater force to dishonest wrongdoing,
because of the inherent improbability of one party assuming responsibility for the consequences of dishonest wrongdoing by the other. The law,
on public policy grounds, does not permit a party to exclude liability for
the consequences of his own fraud; and if the consequences of fraudulent
or dishonest misrepresentation or deceit by his agent are to be excluded,
such intention must be expressed in clear and unmistakeable terms on the
face of the contract. General words will not serve. The language must be
such as will alert a commercial party to the extraordinary bargain he is
invited to make because in the absence of words which expressly refer to
dishonesty the common assumption is that the parties will act honestly ..."

This summary of principle was not in dispute on appeal.[133]

12.60　　In deciding whether the *Canada Steamship* guidelines apply, the court must pay
particular attention to the nature of the contract. Thus in a chain of construction
contracts each contractor or sub-contractor will generally expect to be responsible
for his own shortcomings, but otherwise to pass liability down the chain. So in
Greenwich Millennium Village Ltd v Essex Services Group Plc,[134] a contractor was
entitled to be indemnified by a sub-contractor, even though the sub-contractor's fail-
ings ought to have been discovered by the main contractor. Jackson LJ said:

"In my view the rule of construction stated in *Canada Steamship* and *Walters v
Whessoe* is of general application. Nevertheless it is based upon the presumed
intention of the parties. In applying that rule the court must have regard to the
commercial context of the contract under consideration. In the case of a construction contract a failure by the indemnitee to spot defects perpetrated by its contractor or sub-contractor should not ordinarily defeat the operation of an indemnity
clause, even if that clause fails expressly to encompass damage caused by the
negligence of the indemnitee."

8.　EXPRESS EXCLUSION OF LIABILITY FOR NEGLIGENCE

**In order to constitute an express exemption of liability for negligence the mean-
ing of the clause must be clear to an ordinarily literate sensible person, and it
is likely that it must contain the word "negligent" or "negligence" or some
synonym for those words.**

12.61　　Lord Morton's first guideline dealt with an express exclusion of liability for
negligence. Many cases have attempted to answer the question whether the words

---

[133]　[2015] EWCA Civ 1310; [2016] Q.B. 835.
[134]　[2014] EWCA Civ 960; [2014] 1 W.L.R. 3517.

of the exemption clause were "adequate" to exclude negligence. In considering this question the test is whether the clause makes:

"its meaning plain on its face to any ordinarily literate and sensible person."[135]

Where, however, the contract is made in a specialised business by two practitioners in that business the standard is different. The test in such a case is whether it makes its meaning plain to a reasonable informed practitioner in that field.[136]

In *Gillespie Brothers & Co Ltd v Bowles (Roy) Transport Ltd*,[137] a contract contained a clause requiring forwarding agents to keep a carrier indemnified against "all claims or demands whatsoever" in excess of a stipulated sum. It was held that the indemnity covered claims due to the negligence of the carrier. Both Buckley and Orr LJJ. held that the clause was an express agreement to indemnify the carrier against claims arising from his own negligence within the first proposition laid down by Lord Morton of Henryton. However, this reasoning was criticised by the House of Lords in *Smith v South Wales Switchgear Co Ltd*.[138] Although this case concerned an indemnity clause rather than an exemption clause, the House of Lords held that the approach to construction in this respect was the same. Viscount Dilhorne said that:

12.62

"there must be a clear and unmistakeable reference to ... negligence",

and Lord Fraser of Tullybelton said:

"I do not see how a clause can 'expressly' exempt or indemnify the proferens against his negligence unless it contains the word 'negligence' or some synonym for it."

Accordingly, in *Lamport & Holt Lines Ltd v Coubro & Scrutton (M&I) Ltd*,[139] May LJ said:

"Although there may be cases in the future, when a different view may be justified, I think that Lord Morton's first test can only be satisfied if the relevant condition does contain expressly the word 'negligent' or 'negligence'."

Where an exemption clause does expressly refer to negligence, it is not necessary for the clause to spell out that the negligence referred to is that of one of the parties to the contract, rather than that of a stranger.[140]

12.63

Illustration

A contract of carriage provided that the owners of the goods carried should indemnify the carrier against all claims and demands whatever by whoever made

---

135 *Hollier v Rambler Motors (AMC) Ltd* [1972] 2 Q.B. 71, per Salmon LJ: *Lamport & Holt Lines Ltd v Coubro & Scrutton (M&I) Ltd* [1982] 2 Lloyd's Rep. 42, per Stephenson LJ.
136 *Industrie Chimiche Italia Centrale SpA v NEA Ninemia Shipping Co SA* [1983] 1 All E.R. 686.
137 [1973] Q.B. 400.
138 [1978] 1 W.L.R. 165, distinguished in *Marubeni Corp v Sea Containers Ltd* (unreported 17 May 1995) where the words "without any deductions or withholdings whatsoever" excluded the right of set-off. This case was referred to without criticism in *BOC Group Plc v Cention LLC* [1999] 1 All E.R. (Comm) 970.
139 [1982] 2 Lloyd's Rep. 42.
140 *Spriggs v Sotheby Parke Bernet & Co* [1986] 1 Lloyd's Rep. 487.

in excess of or in addition to the liability of the carrier to the owners under the contract. It was held that there was no clear and unmistakeable reference to negligence and hence the clause did not protect the carriers against loss caused by their own negligence.

Shell Chemicals UK Ltd v P & O Roadtanks Ltd[141]

9. LIABILITY FOR NEGLIGENCE EXCLUDED BY THE ORDINARY MEANING OF THE CLAUSE

Liability for negligence may be excluded without an express reference to negligence if a fair reading of the clause shows that the parties intended to exclude such liability.

12.64   Lord Morton's second guideline considered whether the ordinary meaning of the words on the exemption clause were wide enough to exclude liability for negligence. In *Gillespie Brothers Ltd v Bowles (Roy) Transport Ltd*,[142] Buckley LJ said:

> "It is ... a fundamental consideration in the construction of contracts of this kind that it is inherently improbable that one party to the contract should intend to absolve the other party from the consequences of the latter's own negligence ... The intention to do so must therefore be made perfectly clear, for otherwise the court will conclude that the exempted party was only intended to be free from liability in respect of damage occasioned by causes other than negligence for which he is answerable."

12.65   In answering the question whether the ordinary meaning of the clause is to exclude liability for negligence, fine distinctions of language have emerged. If the clause enumerates losses without dealing with causes, it may not protect against liability for negligence; but if it enumerates causes, and suggests that the contracting party is free from all losses however caused, he will be protected.[143] If, therefore, the clause excludes liability for loss "however caused" that is likely to exclude liability for negligence.

So in *Joseph Travers & Sons Ltd v Cooper*,[144] a contract exempted a barge owner for "any damage to goods however caused which can be covered by insurance". Phillimore LJ said:

> "If you say 'any loss' you are directing attention to the kinds of losses and not to their cause or origin, and you have not sufficiently made it plain that you mean 'any and every loss' irrespective of the cause, and therefore you have not brought home to the person who is entrusting the goods to you that you are not going to be responsible for your servants on your behalf exercising due care for them, or possibly even for your own personal want of care. But if you direct attention to the causes of any loss, if you say 'any loss,' 'however caused' or 'under any circumstances,' you give sufficient warning, and it is not necessary to say in

---

[141] [1995] 1 Lloyd's Rep. 297 CA.

[142] [1973] Q.B. 400; cited with approval by Viscount Dilhorne in *Smith v South Wales Switchgear Ltd* [1978] 1 W.L.R. 165.

[143] *Gibaud v Great Eastern Railway* [1921] 2 K.B. 426, per Scrutton LJ. See also *Hinks v Fleet* [1986] 2 E.G.L.R. 243 (cited in para.12.66).

[144] [1915] 1 K.B. 73.

express terms 'whether caused by my servants' negligence,' or in the bill of lading phrase 'neglect or default or otherwise'."

In *White v Blackmore*,[145] Roskill LJ said:

"It will be observed that the exclusion is of 'all liabilities arising out of accidents causing damage or personal injury (whether fatal or otherwise) howsoever caused.' Wider words of exemption are difficult to conceive. Indeed the words 'howsoever caused' have become in the last half century and more the classic phrase whereby to exclude liability for negligence."

In *Hinks v Fleet*,[146] an exemption clause was in the following terms:　　　　**12.66**

"Vehicles and caravans are admitted on condition that the Park Owner Shall not be liable for loss or damage to (a) any vehicle or caravan (b) anything in, on or about any vehicle or caravan however such loss or damage may be caused ...".

The Court of Appeal[147] held that the clause was sufficient to exclude liability for negligence.

Likewise, in *Brown v Drake International Ltd*,[148] Pill LJ said:

"The expression 'however caused' gives the clearest indication that negligence and breach of statutory duty are included. The expression should be given its plain meaning."[149]

An express allocation of risk is also relevant in considering whether liability for　　**12.67** negligence is excluded. If the contract provides for performance "at the customers' sole risk"[150] or "at the owner's risk"[151] liability for negligence is likely to be excluded. But even in such cases the width of an exemption clause may be cut down by a consideration of the contract as a whole.[152]

The question whether the parties have excluded liability for a particular type of　　**12.68** loss may also depend in part on whether the contract requires one party or the other to insure against the risk of that loss. If a party is expressly required to insure against a particular loss it is likely that the parties intended the risk of that loss to be borne by him (or his insurers).

Thus in *Archdale (James) & Co Ltd v Comservices Ltd*,[153] a building contract required the contractor to indemnify the employer against damage to property arising out of the execution of the works, provided that it was due to the negligence of the contractor. The contract also provided that the existing structure and the works should be at the sole risk of the employer as regards damage by fire, and required

---

[145] [1972] 2 Q.B. 651.
[146] [1986] 2 E.G.L.R. 243.
[147] May and Lloyd LJJ and Hollings J. May LJ gave the leading judgment, in which *Lamport and Holt Lines Ltd v Coubro & Scrutton (M&I) Ltd* was not referred to.
[148] [2004] EWCA Civ 1629.
[149] *Aprile SpA v Elin Maritime Ltd* [2019] EWHC 1001 (Comm); [2020] 1 Lloyd's Rep. 111 ("howsoever arising"). But a clause even in these wide terms will not exempt a fraudulent or dishonest breach: see para.12.107.
[150] *Rutter v Palmer* [1922] 2 K.B. 89.
[151] *Levison v Patent Steam Carpet Cleaning Co Ltd* [1978] Q.B. 69.
[152] *Svenssons Travaruaktiebolag v Cliffe Steamship Co* [1932] 1 K.B. 490; *Levison v Patent Steam Carpet Cleaning Co Ltd* [1978] Q.B. 69.
[153] [1954] 1 W.L.R. 459.

the employer to insure against fire. It was held that the contractor was not liable for damage by fire, even one which was caused negligently.

In *Scottish Special Housing Association v Wimpey Construction UK Ltd*,[154] the owners of houses contracted with a contractor to modernise them. The contract contained similar wording to that in the *Archdale* case. When work was being carried out on one of the houses it was damaged by fire. The question was whether the contract excluded liability for fires caused negligently. Lord Keith of Kinkel said:

> "Clause 20(C) provides that the existing structures and contents owned by the employer are to be at his sole risk as regards damage by inter alia fire. No differentiation is made between fire due to the negligence of the contractor and that due to other causes. The remainder of the catalogue of perils includes some which could not possibly be caused by the negligence of the contractor, such as storm, tempest and earthquake, but others which might be, such as explosion, flood and the bursting or overflowing of water pipes. There is imposed upon the employer an obligation to insure against loss or damage by all these perils, in quite general terms. I have found it impossible to resist the conclusion that it is intended that the employer shall bear the whole risk of damage by fire, including fire caused by the negligence of the contractor or that of sub-contractors."

12.69   The opportunity to insure (without any express contractual requirement to do so) was also considered to be "possibly" relevant by Lord Wilberforce in *Ailsa Craig Fishing Co Ltd v Malvern Fishing Co Ltd*.[155] In *E.E. Caledonia Ltd v Orbit Valve Co Europe*,[156] contractual provisions relating to insurance were considered by the Court of Appeal to be relevant to the interpretation of an exclusion or indemnity clause, because they might reveal an agreed allocation of risk. It is thought that provisions relating to insurance are always relevant to the question whether the parties to a contract have allocated the risk of a particular loss or cause of loss. Indeed in *Co-operative Retail Services Ltd v Taylor Young Partnership Ltd*,[157] the House of Lords held that where two parties entered into a contract which stipulated that one party had to obtain an insurance in the joint names for both, then one joint insured could not sue the other joint insured for damages where the loss was covered by the insurance because there was an implied term in the contract preventing such action. However, there is no rule of law to this effect; it is a question of interpretation of the contract.[158] It may be the true interpretation that a provision for insurance is to be taken as satisfying or curtailing a contractual obligation, or it may be the true interpretation that a contractual obligation is to be backed by insurance with the result that the contractual obligation stands or is enforceable even if for some reason the insurance fails or proves inadequate.[159]

12.70   Where the same facts gave rise to a claim in negligence and to a claim for breach of statutory duty, and the exemption clause did not cover negligence, it was held that it did not cover breach of statutory duty either.[160] Conversely, where a clause

---

[154] [1986] 1 W.L.R. 995.

[155] [1983] 1 W.L.R. 964.

[156] [1994] 1 W.L.R. 1515.

[157] [2002] 1 W.L.R. 1419. See also *GD Construction (St Albans) Ltd v Scottish & Newcastle Plc* [2003] B.L.R. 131.

[158] *Tyco Fire & Integrated Solutions (UK) Ltd v Rolls-Royce Motor Cars Ltd* [2008] B.L.R. 285.

[159] *Surrey Heath Borough Council v Lovell Construction Ltd* (1990) 48 B.L.R. 108.

[160] *E.E. Caledonia Ltd v Orbit Valve Co Europe* [1994] 1 W.L.R. 1515.

was sufficient to exclude liability for negligence, it also excluded liability for breach of statutory duty.[161]

If there is any ambiguity at this stage in the process of interpretation then, in ac-   **12.71**
cordance with Lord Morton's second guideline, it is resolved against the *proferens*.
So in *Price & Co v Union Lighterage Co*,[162] Lord Alverstone CJ said:

> "... when a clause in such a contract as this is capable of two constructions, one
> of which will make it applicable where there is no negligence on the part of the
> carrier or his servants, and the other will make it applicable where there is such
> negligence, it requires special words to make the clause cover non-liability in
> case of negligence."

It seems that the *contra proferentem* principle applies irrespective of the identity of the contracting party. As has been seen, the *contra proferentem* principle does not usually apply in the case of a Crown grant.[163] Yet in *Canada Steamship Lines Ltd v R.*[164] the principle was applied to a lease granted by the Crown, and the Crown was held not to be protected by an ambiguous indemnity clause.

Subject to certain exceptions, if there is a doubt about the meaning of a written   **12.72**
term in a consumer contract, the interpretation which is most favourable to the
consumer prevails.[165]

Illustrations

1.   The owner of a car deposited it with a dealer for sale on commission. The terms on which it was accepted included a term that "customers' cars are driven by your staff at customers' sole risk". It was held that the clause was sufficient to exempt the dealer from liability due to the negligence of his staff.
Rutter v Palmer[166]

2.   The terms upon which a garage accepted cars for repair included a term that "the company is not responsible for damage caused by fire to customers' cars on the premises". It was held that since many fires start without negligence, the clause was not clear enough to protect the company from liability for a fire caused by its employees' negligence.
Hollier v Rambler Motors (AMC) Ltd[167]

3.   A building contract for the construction of a naval jetty contained a clause which provided that the contractor was to be responsible for any loss or damage to the works "from any cause whatsoever". It was held that that clause prevented the contractor from recovering from the employer in respect of damage to the works caused by the employer's own negligence.
Farr (AE) Ltd v The Admiralty[168]

4.   A notice stated that the owners of a quay took steps to keep them in order

---

[161] *Brown v Drake International Ltd* [2004] EWCA Civ 1629.
[162] [1904] 1 K.B. 412.
[163] See para.7.66.
[164] [1952] A.C. 192.
[165] See para.7.102.
[166] [1922] 2 K.B. 89.
[167] [1972] 2 Q.B. 71.
[168] [1953] 1 W.L.R. 965.

but did not ensure that the berths were always level. The notice further stated that vessels using the quays were at the risk of their owners and that the owners of the quay would not be responsible for any damage resulting from using the quays or taking the ground there. It was held that the notice was sufficient to exempt the quay owners from liability for negligence.

The Ballyaton[169]

5.   A derrick was stowed on a vessel upon terms which included a clause providing that the riggers should not be liable for loss or damage "which may arise from or be in any way connected with any act or omission of any person or corporation employed by us or by any sub-contractors or engaged in any capacity in connection herewith". It was held that although this was not an express exclusion of liability for negligence, the words were wide enough to comprehend negligence. No other head of liability existed, other than remote or fanciful possibilities, and accordingly the clause effectively excluded liability for negligence.

Lamport & Holt Lines Ltd v Coubro & Scrutton (M&I) Ltd[170]

6.   A charterparty exempted the owners for liability for errors of navigation. It was held that errors of navigation could be either negligent or non-negligent. The clause was ambiguous and the ambiguity would be resolved against the owners.

Seven Seas Transportation Ltd v Pacifico Union Marina Corp[171]

7.   An auctioneer accepted property for sale on terms that included a clause providing that it should not be responsible for damage of any kind whether caused by negligence or otherwise. It was held that it was not necessary for the clause to refer to the auctioneer's own negligence. The clause therefore exempted the auctioneer from liability for loss even if caused by its own negligence.

Spriggs v Sotheby Parke Bernet & Co[172]

8.   A charterparty provided that cargo was to be carried "at charterers' risk". It was held that this was insufficient to confer an exemption from liability for negligence.

The Fantasy[173]

9.   A building contract stated that:

"The Vendor and the Purchaser shall forthwith enter in to the National House-Building Council's standard form of Agreement No HB5 (1986) (or any other standard form in current use at the relevant time for the like purpose) which said standard form is hereinafter called 'the NHBC Agreement'. The Vendor shall not be liable to the Purchaser or any successor in title of the Purchaser under the Agreement or any document incorporated therein in respect of any defect error or omission in the execution or the completion of the work save to the extent and

---

[169] [1961] 1 All E.R. 459.
[170] [1982] 2 Lloyd's Rep. 42.
[171] [1983] 1 All E.R. 672; affirmed [1984] 2 All E.R. 140.
[172] [1986] 1 Lloyd's Rep. 487.
[173] [1991] 2 Lloyd's Rep. 391, following *Svenssons Travaruaktiebolag v Cliffe Steamship Co* [1932] 1 K.B. 490.

for the period that it is liable under the provisions of the NHBC Agreement on which alone his rights and remedies are founded."

It was held that this clause excluded liability for negligence.
Robinson and PE Jones (Contractors) Ltd[174]

10. POSSIBLE HEADS OF DAMAGE OTHER THAN NEGLIGENCE

Where the only possible head of damage is negligence an exemption clause will usually be interpreted as exempting from liability for negligence. But where liability may realistically arise otherwise than through negligence, the exemption clause should usually be interpreted as not exempting from liability for negligence.

Lord Morton's third guideline considered whether there were possible heads of liability other than negligence. Whether this guideline continues to have any force is controversial.　　**12.73**

In *Lamport & Holt Lines v Coubro & Scrutton (M&I) Ltd*,[175] Donaldson LJ observed:　　**12.74**

"When parties make an agreement governing their future relationship, human nature being on balance more inclined to optimism than pessimism, the parties are more likely to be thinking in terms of non-negligent rather than negligent performance of the contract. The law reflects this fact by assuming that if there are two potential grounds of liability, both of them real and foreseeable, prima facie any words of exemption will be directed at the non-negligent ground of liability."

In *PJ Casson v Ostley*,[176] a building contract said that works, including structures "shall be at the sole risk of the client as regards loss or damage by fire". The Court of Appeal held that this did not exempt the builder from liability for fire negligently caused. Sedley LJ said that:

"the process of reasoning has in the end to go something like this: the words on the page make perfectly good sense in the defendant builder's favour; but if you apply them to his own negligent—or for that matter deliberate—acts they seem less sensible; so you ask whether the parties meant to go that far; before answering, you remind yourself that A does not ordinarily agree to absolve B from the consequences of B's own neglect or malice; you therefore look for words which make such absolution plain; and, finding none, you conclude that the words on the page do not mean what they say."

A different rationale for the rule, based more upon linguistic than psychological grounds, was given by Lord Greene MR in *Alderslade v Hendon Laundry Ltd*[177]:　　**12.75**

"Where the head of damage in respect of which limitation of liability is sought

---

[174] [2011] EWCA Civ 9.
[175] [1982] 2 Lloyd's Rep. 42.
[176] [2003] B.L.R. 147. See also *HIH Casualty and General Insurance Co v Chase Manhattan Bank* [2003] 1 All E.R. (Comm) 349 at [63] HL, per Lord Hoffmann.
[177] [1945] K.B. 189.

to be imposed by such a clause is one which rests on negligence and nothing else, the clause must be construed as extending to that head of damage, because otherwise it would lack subject-matter. Where on the other hand, the head of damage may be based on some other ground than that of negligence, the general principle is that the clause must be confined in its application to loss occurring through that other cause, to the exclusion of loss arising through negligence. The reason is that if a contracting party wishes in such a case to limit his liability in respect of negligence, he must do so in clear terms in the absence of which the clause is construed as relating to a liability not based on negligence."

12.76 The first limb of this formulation asserts that if there is no other head of liability than negligence, the clause "must" be construed as extending to negligence. However, this formulation goes further than that of Scrutton LJ in *Rutter v Palmer*,[178] who said:

"if the only liability of the party leading the clause is a liability for negligence, the clause will more readily operate to exempt him."

In these circumstances, it has been said that the word "must" should not be taken "au pied de la lettre",[179] and should be read as "should usually".[180]

12.77 A further gloss on Lord Greene's formulation is found in the third principle enunciated by Lord Morton of Henryton in *Canada Steamship Lines Ltd v R.*[181] He said that:

"The other ground must not be so fanciful or remote that the *proferens* cannot be supposed to have desired protection against it; but subject to this qualification, which is no doubt to be implied from Lord Greene's words, the existence of a possible head of damage other than that of negligence is fatal to the *proferens* even if the words used are prima facie wide enough to cover negligence on the part of his servants."

However, even this formulation has been said to be:

"liable to mislead unless full force is given to his caveat that the 'other ground' must not be so fanciful or remote that the proferens cannot be supposed to have desired protection against it."[182]

Lord Morton's third test is:

"not a rigid or mechanical rule. It simply is an aid in the process of construction. And the ordinary meaning of words in their contractual setting is the dominant factor."[183]

12.78 Moreover, where an exemption clause excludes liability for breach of a contractual obligation, it will also exclude liability for breach of the self-same

---

[178] [1922] 2 K.B. 87.

[179] *Hollier v Rambler Motors (AMC) Ltd* [1972] 2 Q.B. 71, per Salmon LJ.

[180] *Lamport & Holt Lines v Coubro & Scrutton (M&I) Ltd* [1982] 2 Lloyd's Rep. 42, per May LJ.

[181] [1952] A.C. 192.

[182] *Lamport & Holt Lines Ltd v Coubro & Scrutton (M&I) Ltd* [1982] 2 Lloyd's Rep. 42, per Donaldson LJ.

[183] *E.E. Caledonia Ltd v Orbit Valve Co Europe* [1994] 1 W.L.R. 1515 at 1522, per Steyn LJ.

obligation in tort.[184] Only if the contractual duty and the tortious duty are different may the clause be effective to exclude liability for one but not the other.

Illustrations

1.   Goods were accepted for laundering on terms which provided "The maximum amount allowed for lost or damaged articles is 20 times the charge made for laundering". It was held that since the laundry would not be under any liability for lost or damaged articles in the absence of negligence, the clause effectively limited its liability in the event of negligence.
   Alderslade v Hendon Laundry Ltd[185]

2.   A contract of hire of a tricycle provided that "Nothing in this agreement shall render the owners liable for any personal injuries to the riders of the machine hired". It was held that in the absence of the clause the owners of the tricycle would be liable in contract to supply a tricycle reasonably fit for its purpose and would also be liable in negligence. The clause was effective only to exclude liability for the contractual liability, and was ineffective to exclude liability for negligence.
   White v Warwick (John) & Co Ltd[186]

3.   A building contract provided that the employer should bear the risk of loss or damage to the works by fire, lightning, explosion, aircraft and other aerial devices. It was held that since the clause referred to perils which occur without negligence, and since a fire can start without negligence, and that such a risk was neither fanciful nor remote, the clause was not sufficiently clear to absolve the contractor from liability for fire caused by his negligence.
   Dorset County Council v Southern Felt Roofing[187]

11.   INTERPRETATION OF CLAUSE AS A WARNING

In some cases the court has held that a clause purporting to exempt one party from liability may be given sufficient content by interpreting it as a warning.

In *Olley v Marlborough Court Ltd*,[188] a hotelier displayed a notice in the hotel bedroom disclaiming liability for articles lost or stolen. It was held that even if the notice formed part of the contract between the hotelier and a hotel guest, it was ineffective to exclude liability. Denning LJ said:

12.79

"Ample content can be given to the notice by construing it as a warning that the hotel company is not liable, in the absence of negligence. As such it serves a useful purpose. It is a warning to the guest that he must do his part to take care of his things himself, and if need be, insure them."

---

[184]   *Lamport & Holt Lines Ltd v Coubro & Scrutton (M&I) Ltd* [1982] 2 Lloyd's Rep. 42; *Brown v Drake International Ltd* [2004] EWCA Civ 1629.
[185]   [1945] K.B. 189.
[186]   [1953] 1 W.L.R. 1285. This is an example of a "strained" construction, and it is possible that, in any event, no liability in negligence would have arisen: see *Tai Hing Cotton Mill Ltd v Liu Chong Hing Bank Ltd* [1986] A.C. 80.
[187]   (1989) 48 B.L.R. 96 CA. See *GD Construction (St Albans) Ltd v Scottish & Newcastle Plc* [2003] B.L.R. 131.
[188]   [1949] 1 K.B. 532.

This approach was followed by the Court of Appeal in *Hollier v Rambler Motors (AMC) Ltd*[189] in which Stamp LJ said:

> "I would hold that, where the words relied upon by the defendant are susceptible to a construction under which they become a statement of fact in the nature of a warning or to a construction which will exempt the defendant from liability for negligence, the former construction is to be preferred."

12.80   However, in *Spriggs v Sotheby Parke Bernet & Co*,[190] the Court of Appeal declined to hold that the clause there in question could be given sufficient effect as a warning. It is thought that the practice of giving content to a clause by interpreting it as a warning is an example of strained construction which ought no longer to be adopted.

12.   Liability for Fundamental Breach

There is no rule of law which prevents parties from excluding or limiting liability for fundamental breach. Whether the contract does so is a question of interpretation.

12.81   In the 1950s and early 1960s the High Court, and more especially the Court of Appeal, developed the doctrine that where one party had committed a fundamental breach of the contract (that is, a repudiatory breach entitling the other party to treat the contract as at an end) he was not permitted to rely on provisions in the contract which excluded or limited his liability. The doctrine was seen as a rule of law, which was to be applied irrespective of the intention of the parties. A typical formulation of the rule is that of Denning LJ in *Karsales (Harrow) Ltd v Wallis*[191]:

> "Notwithstanding earlier cases which might suggest the contrary, it is now settled that exempting clauses of this kind, no matter how widely they are expressed, only avail the party when he is carrying out his contract in its essential respects. He is not allowed to use them as a cover for misconduct or indifference or to enable him to turn a blind eye to his obligations. They do not avail him when he is guilty of a breach which goes to the root of the contract."

12.82   However, in *UGS Finance Ltd v National Mortgage Bank of Greece and National Bank of Greece SA*,[192] Pearson LJ expressed a contrary view. He said:

> "As to the question of 'fundamental breach,' I think there is a rule of construction that normally an exception or exclusion clause or similar provision in a contract should be construed as not applying to a situation created by a fundamental breach of contract. This is not an independent rule of law imposed by the court on the parties willy-nilly in disregard of their contractual intention. On the contrary it is a rule of construction based on the presumed intention of the parties."

12.83   When the question arose for decision by the House of Lords in *Suisse Atlantique*

---

[189] [1972] 2 Q.B. 71.
[190] [1986] 1 Lloyd's Rep. 487.
[191] [1956] 1 W.L.R. 936; see also *Yeoman Credit Ltd v Apps* [1962] 2 Q.B. 508; *Astley Industrial Trust Ltd v Grimley* [1963] 1 W.L.R. 584; *Charterhouse Credit Co Ltd v Tolly* [1963] 2 Q.B. 683.
[192] [1964] 1 Lloyd's Rep. 446.

Societe D'Armement Maritime SA v NV Rotterdamsche Kolen Centrale,[193] the House preferred the view of Pearson LJ.

Viscount Dilhorne said:

"In my view it is not right to say that the law prohibits and nullifies a clause exempting or limiting liability for a fundamental breach or breach of a fundamental term. Such a rule of law would involve a restriction on freedom of contract and in the older cases I can find no trace of it."

Lord Reid also said that no such rule of law ought to be adopted.[194] Lord Hodson said that the better view was that:

"as a matter of construction normally an exception or exclusive clause or similar provision in a contract should be construed as not applying to a situation created by a fundamental breach of contract."

Lord Upjohn also preferred the view of Pearson LJ, but none the less held that once a contract had been discharged by repudiation and acceptance, the exemption clauses ceased to apply. This point has now been shown to be erroneous. Finally, Lord Wilberforce said that it must be:

"A question of contractual intention whether a particular breach is covered or not and the courts are entitled to insist, as they do, that the more radical the breach the clearer must the language be if it is to be covered."

In subsequent cases the Court of Appeal interpreted *Suisse Atlantique* as affirming the principle that when one party has been guilty of a fundamental breach of the contract and the other party accepts it so that the contract comes to an end (or if it comes to an end automatically by reason of the breach) then the guilty party cannot rely on an exception or limitation clause to escape liability for his breach.[195] This interpretation was even extended to cases in which the injured party elected to affirm the contract[196] in a process of reasoning subsequently described as an "impossible acrobatic".[197]

12.84

This interpretation of *Suisse Atlantique* was firmly disavowed by the House of Lords in *Photo Production Ltd v Securicor Ltd.*[198] The House of Lords unanimously stated (in rather clearer terms than in *Suisse Atlantique*) that there was no rule of law which prevented an exemption clause from applying in the case of a fundamental breach of contract. Lord Wilberforce, with whom the rest of their Lordships agreed, said:

12.85

"I have no second thoughts as to the main proposition that the question whether, and to what extent, an exclusion clause is to be applied to a fundamental breach, or a breach of a fundamental term, or indeed to any breach of contract, is a matter of construction of the contract."

Lord Salmon added that the "so-called 'rule of law'" was "non-existent".

---

[193] [1967] 1 A.C. 361.
[194] [1967] 1 A.C. 361 at 405.
[195] *Harbutt's "Plasticine" Ltd v Wayne Tank and Pump Co Ltd* [1970] 1 Q.B. 447, per Lord Denning MR; *Farnworth Finance Facilities Ltd v Attryde* [1970] 1 W.L.R. 1053.
[196] *Wathes (Western) Ltd v Austins (Menswear) Ltd* [1976] 1 Lloyd's Rep. 14.
[197] *Photo Production Ltd v Securicor Ltd* [1980] A.C. 827, per Lord Wilberforce.
[198] [1980] A.C. 827.

12.86   And in *Mitchell (George) (Chesterhall) Ltd v Finney Lock Seeds Ltd*,[199] Lord Bridge of Harwich described the *Photo Production* case as having given:

> "the final quietus to the doctrine that a 'fundamental breach' of contract deprived the party in breach of the benefit of clauses in the contract excluding or limiting his liability."

12.87   Despite this death blow, in *The Chanda*,[200] Hirst J held that an exemption clause did not protect a carrier who carried goods in breach of an express term about the manner in which they were to be stowed. But he held that this conclusion was not based on the discredited fundamental breach principle but on an independent rule of construction derived from previous authority. This line of authority has since been disavowed by the Court of Appeal. In *Daewoo Heavy Industries v Kipriver Shipping ("The Kapitan Petko Voivoda")*,[201] the Court of Appeal overruled *The Chanda*. Longmore LJ said that cases about the unauthorised carriage of deck cargo were not a special case: "The duty of the court is merely to construe the contract which the parties have made".

12.88   Likewise, whether a clause exempts a party from liability for a deliberate breach of contract is a question of construction of the clause.[202]

13.   PRESUMPTIONS OF INTERPRETATION

Although there once was a presumption of interpretation that an exclusion clause is not intended to apply to a fundamental breach of contract, the courts have moved away from any such presumption.

12.89   In *Gibaud v Great Eastern Railway Co*,[203] Scrutton LJ said:

> "The principle is well known ... that if you undertake to do a thing in a certain way, or to keep a thing in a certain place, with certain conditions protecting it and have broken the contract by not doing the thing contracted for in the way contracted for, or not keeping the article in the place in which you have contracted to keep it, you cannot rely on the conditions which were only intended to protect you if you had carried out the contract in the way in which you had contracted to do it."

12.90   Although this has the appearance of a statement of law it is submitted that it is best seen as a statement of a principle or presumption of interpretation.[204] Even so, it needs some refinement. First, the parties must have contemplated some failure to perform in the manner contracted, otherwise the need for protective clauses would rarely arise. Second, even when it was interpreted as laying down a rule of law, the rule only applied to fundamental breaches. However, it may be said that in the normal case an exemption clause will not be construed as being applicable to a repudiatory breach of contract. This approach may be described as a presumption of interpretation, which is rebuttable by clear and unambiguous language.

---

[199]   [1983] 2 A.C. 803.
[200]   [1989] 2 Lloyd's Rep. 494.
[201]   [2003] 2 Lloyd's Rep. 1.
[202]   *Frans Maas (UK) Ltd v Samsung Electronics (UK) Ltd* [2004] 2 Lloyd's Rep. 251.
[203]   [1921] 2 K.B. 426.
[204]   See *The Cap Palos* [1921] P. 458, per Lord Sterndale MR and Atkin LJ.

In his judgment in *UGS Finance Ltd v National Mortgage Bank of Greece and National Bank of Greece SA*,[205] Pearson LJ said:

12.91

"I think there is a rule of construction that normally an exception or exclusion clause or similar provision in a contract should be construed as not applying to a situation created by a fundamental breach of contract."

This view was echoed in the speeches in *Suisse Atlantique*.[206] Lord Reid said:

"As a matter of construction it may appear that the terms of the exclusion clause are not wide enough to cover the kind of breach which has been committed. Such clauses must be construed strictly and if ambiguous the narrower meaning will be taken. Or it may appear that the terms of the clause are so wide that they cannot be applied literally; that may be because this would lead to an absurdity or because it would defeat the main object of the contract or perhaps for other reasons. And where some limit must be read into a clause it is generally reasonable to draw the line at fundamental breaches. There is no reason why a contract should not make provision for events which the parties do not have in contemplation or even which are unforeseeable, if sufficiently clear words are used. But if some limitation has to be read in it seems reasonable to suppose that neither party had in contemplation a breach which goes to the root of the contract."

Lord Upjohn said:

"But where there is a breach of a fundamental term the law has taken an even firmer line for there is a strong, though rebuttable, presumption that in inserting a clause of exclusion or limitation in their contract the parties are not contemplating breaches of fundamental terms and the clauses do not apply to relieve a party from the consequences of such a breach even where the contract continues in force."

And Lord Wilberforce added, in relation to cases where a seller supplied wholly different goods to those contracted for:

"Since the contracting parties could hardly have been supposed to contemplate such a mis-performance, or to have provided against it without destroying the whole contractual substratum, there is no difficulty here in holding exception clauses to be inapplicable."

In *Photoshop Production Ltd v Securicor Ltd*,[207] the House of Lords returned to the theme. Lord Wilberforce said:

12.92

"I have no second thoughts ... that the question whether, and to what extent, an exclusion clause is to be applied to a fundamental breach or to a breach of a fundamental term, or indeed to any breach of contract, is a matter of construction of the contract. Many difficult questions arise and will continue to arise in the infinitely varied situations in which contracts come to be breached—by repudiatory breaches, accepted or not, anticipatory breaches, by breaches of

[205] [1964] 1 Lloyd's Rep. 446 (approved by the House of Lords in *Suisse Atlantique Societe D'Armement Maritime SA v NV Rotterdamsche Kalen Centrale* [1967] 1 A.C. 361).
[206] [1967] 1 A.C. 361.
[207] [1980] 1 A.C. 827.

conditions or of various terms and whether by negligent or deliberate action or otherwise. But there are ample resources in the normal rules of contract law for dealing with these without the superimposition of a judicially invented rule of law."

12.93   In *Motis Exports Ltd v Dampskibsselskabet AF 1912*,[208] Stuart-Smith LJ said neither of these decisions had affected the principle that:

"Where general words are used in a printed form which are obviously intended to apply, so far as they are applicable, to the circumstances of a particular contract, which particular contract is to be embodied in or introduced into that printed form, I think you are justified in looking at the main object and intent of the contract and in limiting the general words used, having in view that object and intent."[209]

12.94   If the presumption still exists, it seems to add little to the general principle that because it is improbable that the parties intended to exclude liability for fundamental breach, clear words are needed to overcome the improbability.[210]

12.95   In *Internet Broadcasting Corp v MAR LLC (t/a MARHedge)*,[211] Mr Gabriel Moss QC (sitting as a judge of the Chancery Division) summarised the principles as follows:

"The principles I deduce from the authorities which are relevant to the present type of case of deliberate, repudiatory breach involving personal wrongdoing are as follows:

(1)   There is no rule of law applicable and the question is one of construction.

(2)   There is a presumption, which appears to be a strong presumption, against the exemption clause being construed so as to cover deliberate, repudiatory breach.

(3)   The words needed to cover a deliberate, repudiatory breach need to be very 'clear' in the sense of using 'strong' language such as 'under no circumstances ...'.

(4)   There is a particular need to use 'clear', in the sense of 'strong', language where the exemption clause is intended to cover deliberate wrongdoing by a party in respect of a breach which cannot, or is unlikely to be, covered by insurance. Language such as 'including deliberate repudiatory acts by [the parties to the contract] themselves ...' would need to be used in such a case.

(5)   Words which, in a literal sense, cover a deliberate repudiatory breach will not be construed so as to do so if that would defeat the 'main object' of the contract.

(6)   The proper function between commercial parties at arm's length and with equal bargaining power of an exemption clause is to allocate insurable risk, so that an exemption clause should not normally be construed in such cases so as to cover an uninsurable risk or one very unlikely to be

---

[208] [2000] 1 Lloyd's Rep. 211. See also *Mediterranean Shipping Co SA v Trafigura Beheer BV* [2007] EWCA Civ 794.

[209] See *Glynn v Margetson and Co* [1893] A.C. 357 and paras 7.50 and 9.82.

[210] See *Mediterranean Shipping Co SA v Trafigura Beheer BV* [2007] EWCA Civ 794.

[211] [2009] 2 Lloyd's Rep. 295.

capable of being insured, in particular deliberate wrongdoing by a party to the contract itself (as opposed to vicarious liability for others).

(7) Words which in a literal sense cover a deliberate repudiatory breach cannot be relied upon if they are 'repugnant' ...".

However, in *Astrazeneca UK Ltd v Albemarle International Corp*,[212] Flaux J held **12.96** that proposition (2) of the above summary was wrong because it effectively sought to revive the discredited doctrine of fundamental breach. After a thorough review of the authorities he concluded:

"Thus, in my judgment, the judgment in *Marhedge* is heterodox and regressive and does not properly represent the current state of English law. If necessary, I would decline to follow it. Even if the breach by Albemarle of its obligation to deliver DIP had been a deliberate repudiatory breach as AZ contends, the question whether any liability of Albemarle for damages for that breach was limited by clause M would simply be one of construing the clause, albeit strictly, but without any presumption."

The author considers that Flaux J's conclusion is compelling at least in the case **12.97** of a deliberate breach; and is consonant with the general move away from presumptions of interpretation that has followed Lord Hoffmann's restatement of the law in *Investors Compensation Scheme v West Bromwich BS*. In the case of a repudiatory breach, however, the courts still recognise the improbability of parties agreeing that there should be no liability for such a breach. It may be that this is what Flaux J had in mind by saying that the clause should be interpreted strictly.

14.   THE LIMITS OF AN EXEMPTION CLAUSE

The court will not interpret an exemption clause so as to deprive the contractual undertakings of one party of all effect.[213] On grounds of public policy a contract may not exempt a party from liability for fraud. If a contract purports to exclude liability for the fraud of a party's agent, it must do so in clear and unmistakable terms.

During the development of the heretical rule that a party in fundamental breach **12.98** of contract could not rely upon exemption clauses in the contract, from time to time judicial observations suggested that an exemption clause would not be construed so as to deprive one party's contractual undertakings of all legal effect. So in *Firestone Tyre Co Ltd v Vokins & Co Ltd*,[214] it was argued that an exemption clause had the effect that lightermen would only be liable for non-delivery of goods where it could be shown that the goods had been stolen in transit. Devlin J said:

"One may test the point by considering the construction of the contract if the phrase about pilferage of the goods were not there. The position would then be that the lightermen were saying: 'We will deliver your goods; we promise to

---

[212] [2011] EWHC 1574 (Comm).
[213] This principle was referred to with approval in *CNM Estates (Tolworth Tower) Ltd v VeCREF I SARL* [2020] EWHC 1605 (Comm).
[214] [1951] 1 Lloyd's Rep. 32.

deliver your goods at such and such a place, and in the condition in which we receive them, but we are not liable if they are lost or damaged from any cause whatsoever.' That is not in law a contract at all. It is illusory to say: 'We promise to do a thing but we are not liable if we do not do it.'"

12.99   This conclusion was clearly reached as a matter of interpretation of the contract. However, in *Mendelssohn v Normand Ltd*,[215] Lord Denning MR deployed the dictum of Devlin J in a different way. He held, on the basis of the dictum, that an exemption clause could be rejected as being repugnant to a prior oral promise. This conclusion was not in reality arrived at by interpreting the contract. The dictum was again deployed by Roskill LJ in *Evans (J) & Son (Portsmouth) Ltd v Merzario (Andrea) Ltd*.[216] In that case forwarding agents had promised shippers that their goods would be stowed below deck. However the agents' conditions of business (which were incorporated into the contract) reserved to the agents complete freedom in respect of the means, route and procedure to be followed in the handling and transportation of the goods. The goods were shipped on deck and were lost overboard. Roskill LJ said:

> "I ventured to ask ... what the position would have been if when the defendants' first quotation had come along there had been stamped on the face of that quotation: 'No containers to be shipped on deck'; and the container had been shipped on deck. [Counsel] bravely said that the exemption clauses would still have applied. With great respect, that is an impossible argument. In the words which Devlin J. used ... the defendants' promise that the container would be shipped on deck would be wholly illusory."

Roskill LJ treated the question as one of interpretation.

12.100   Indications that it might be a rule of law are to be found in the speech of Lord Wilberforce in *Suisse Atlantique Societe D'Armement Maritime SA v NV Rotterdamsche Kolen Centrale*.[217] He said:

> "One may safely say that the parties cannot, in a contract, have contemplated that the clause should have so wide an ambit as in effect to deprive one party's stipulations of all contractual force: to do so would be to reduce the contract to a mere declaration of intent. To this extent it may be correct to say that there is a rule of law against the application of an exceptions clause to a particular type of breach."

This observation suggests that if a clause purported to deprive one party's promises of contractual force the court would not give effect to such a clause however clear the construction. There is, however, an alternative conclusion for resolving the conflict between the basic ingredients of a contract and the effect of such a clause. That is by concluding that the so-called contract is not a contract at all, and is morally but not legally binding. Parties may enter into arrangements which at first sight look like contracts, but may by particular stipulations in them prevent them from having binding force.[218]

---

[215] [1970] 1 Q.B. 177.
[216] [1976] 1 W.L.R. 1078.
[217] [1967] 1 A.C. 361.
[218] For example, *Rose & Frank Co v Crompton (JR) & Bros Ltd* [1925] A.C. 445 (where contractual liability was negatived by an express term).

It is not wholly clear whether the principle formulated by Lord Wilberforce **12.101** (whether it be one of law or of interpretation) has survived the more recent decisions of the House of Lords. Slender indications suggest that it has. Thus in *Photo Production Ltd v Securicor Ltd*,[219] Lord Diplock said that parties were free to exclude or modify their primary obligations:

"within the limits that the agreement must retain the legal characteristics of a contract and must not offend against the equitable rule against penalties."

This too is framed in terms of a rule of law, although it is not clear whether the application of the rule would produce the result that the clause was invalid or that there was no legally binding contract.

The principle can apply to a single clause in a contract, as well as to the relation- **12.102** ship between different clauses. It is not one which requires ambiguity on a fair reading before the principle comes into play.[220] In practice, the court is likely to interpret an exemption clause so as to prevent it from having such a wide ranging effect. As Flaux J put it in *AstraZeneca UK Ltd v Albemarle International Corp*[221]:

"In construing an exception clause against the party which relies upon it ... the court will strain against a construction which renders that party's obligation under the contract no more than a statement of intent and will not reach that conclusion unless no other conclusion is possible. Where another construction is available which does not have the effect of rendering the party's obligation no more than a statement of intent, the court should lean towards that alternative construction."

This process may be seen in the decision of the House of Lords in *Tor Line AIB* **12.103** *v Alltrans Group of Canada Ltd*.[222] In that case a charterparty contained a wide exemption clause. The owners contended that it exempted them from liability where the vessel did not physically conform with the description in the charterparty. Lord Roskill (with whom the other Law Lords agreed) said:

"If one construes the words 'in any other case' literally, the second part of the second sentence and indeed the whole of the third sentence ... become surplusage because on that view there would necessarily be no other 'case' liability for which is not already excluded. Moreover, such a literal construction would mean ... that the owners would be under no liability if they never delivered the vessel at all for service under the charter or delivered a vessel of a totally different description from that stipulated in the preamble. My Lords I cannot think that this can be right. Some limitation must be read into the first part of the second sentence."

Similarly, in *Kudos Catering (UK) Ltd v Manchester Central Convention Complex Ltd*,[223] a suggested interpretation of an exclusion clause was rejected

---

[219] [1980] A.C. 827.
[220] *CNM Estates (Tolworth Tower) Ltd v VeCREF I SARL* [2020] EWHC 1605 (Comm).
[221] [2011] EWHC 1574 (Comm); [2011] 2 C.L.C. 252.
[222] [1984] 1 W.L.R. 48.
[223] [2013] EWCA Civ 38; [2013] 2 Lloyd's Rep. 270.

because it would leave the contract effectively devoid of contractual content since there would have been no sanction for non-performance.

12.104   The principle that a clause will not be interpreted so as to deprive the contractual undertakings of one party of all effect was discussed in *Transocean Drilling UK Ltd v Providence Resources Plc*.[224] Moore-Bick LJ said:

> "However, it should be seen as one of last resort and there is authority that it applies only in cases where the effect of the clause is to relieve one party from all liability for breach of any of the obligations which he has purported to undertake.[225] Only in such a case could it be said that the contract amounted to nothing more than a mere declaration of intent."

Where, therefore, the clause is clear, the court will apply it.[226]

12.105   On grounds of public policy a party may not exempt himself for liability for his own fraud.[227] It is probable that there is no absolute rule of law that precludes a contract from excluding liability for the fraud of a party's agent. However, if a contract purports to do so "such intention must be expressed in clear and unmistakable terms on the face of the contract".[228] General words, however comprehensive the legal analyst might find them to be, will not serve: the language used must be such as will alert a commercial party to the extraordinary bargain he is invited to make.[229] Thus a clause purporting to exempt one party from loss or damage "howsoever caused", "or otherwise howsoever" and "arising or resulting from ... any other cause whatsoever" will not exempt that party from liability for his own dishonesty.[230]

12.106   In *Regus (UK) Ltd v Epcot Solutions Ltd*,[231] an exemption clause in a licence of offices stated:

> "We will not in any circumstances have any liability for loss of business, loss of profits, loss of anticipated savings, loss of or damage to data, third party claims or any consequential loss."

It was argued (as a prelude to a submission that the clause was invalid under the Unfair Contract Terms Act 1977) that the clause excluded liability for fraud. Rix LJ rejected that argument. He said:

> "Clause 23 as a whole does not purport to exclude liability (in the case of the losses identified in clause 23(3)) for fraud or wilful, reckless or malicious damage. Nor would any such clause naturally be construed as purporting to exclude liability for fraud or wilful damage."

---

[224] [2016] EWCA Civ 372. See also *Motortrak Ltd v FCA Australia Pty Ltd* [2018] EWHC 990 (Comm).

[225] *Great North Eastern Railway Ltd v Avon Insurance Plc* [2001] EWCA Civ 780; [2001] Lloyd's Rep. I.R. 793.

[226] *Motortrak Ltd v FCA Australia Pty Ltd* [2018] EWHC 990 (Comm).

[227] *HIH Casualty and General Insurance Ltd v Chase Manhattan Bank* [2003] 2 Lloyd's Rep. 61; *Frans Maas (UK) Ltd v Samsung Electronics (UK) Ltd* [2004] 2 Lloyd's Rep. 251.

[228] *HIH Casualty and General Insurance Ltd v Chase Manhattan Bank* [2003] 2 Lloyd's Rep. 61.

[229] Above.

[230] *Mitsubishi Corp v Eastwind Transport Ltd (The Irbenskiy Proliv)* [2005] 1 Lloyd's Rep. 383; *Goodlife Foods Ltd v Hall Fire Protection Ltd* [2017] EWHC 767 (TCC); 172 Con. L.R. 73 (the point did not arise on the appeal).

[231] [2009] 1 All E.R. (Comm) 586.

Likewise, in *Trident Turboprop (Dublin) Ltd v First Flight Couriers Ltd*,[232] a clause in an aircraft lease stated that the lessee gave up "any rights against the Lessor ... regarding any warranty or representation ...". Aikens J said:

"In my view this language, particularly the use of the words 'any rights against the Lessor', was deliberately chosen to give wide coverage to the types of right that FFCL was giving up. It agreed to give up all rights in respect of all types of representation, other than fraudulent ones."

Where an exemption (or exoneration) clause in a trust deed exempts trustees from   **12.107**
liability except in the case of "actual fraud" this means what it says and does not make them liable for "constructive fraud" or "equitable fraud".[233] Whether a clause exempts a party from liability for a deliberate (but not fraudulent) breach of contract is a question of interpretation of the clause.[234]

Clauses sometimes purport to confer exemption except in the case of "wilful"   **12.108**
breach or misconduct. In *Forder v Great Western Railway*,[235] Lord Alverstone CJ defined wilful misconduct as follows:

"Wilful misconduct in such a special condition means misconduct to which the will is party as contradistinguished from accident, and is far beyond any negligence, even gross or culpable negligence, and involves that a person wilfully misconducts himself who knows and appreciates that it is wrong conduct on his part in the existing circumstances to do, or to fail or omit to do (as the case may be), a particular thing, and yet intentionally does, or fails or omits to do it, or persists in the act, failure, or omission regardless of consequences ... or acts with reckless carelessness, not caring what the results of his carelessness may be."

In *National Semiconductors (UK) Ltd v UPS Ltd*,[236] Longmore J said:

"If I summarise the principle in my own words, it would be to say that for wilful misconduct to be proved there must be either (1) an intention to do something which the actor knows to be wrong or (2) a reckless act in the sense that the actor is aware that loss may result from his act and yet does not care whether loss will result or not or ... 'he took a risk which he knew he ought not to take'."

In order to forestall an argument that an exclusion clause purports to cover fraud,   **12.109**
contracts often contain what has come to be known as a "fraud carve-out".[237] The scope of such a carve-out clearly depends on its detailed working. In *Interactive E-Solutions JLT v O3B Africa Ltd*,[238] on the particular wording of the clause, it was held that it covered claims where fraud was an essential part of the cause of action. Lewison LJ said:

---

232 [2008] 2 Lloyd's Rep. 581.
233 *Armitage v Nurse* [1998] Ch. 241.
234 *Frans Maas (UK) Ltd v Samsung Electronics (UK) Ltd* [2004] 2 Lloyd's Rep. 251.
235 [1905] 2 K.B. 532. See also *Lewis v Great Western Ry Co* 3 Q.B.D. 195.
236 [1996] 2 Lloyd's Rep. 212; approved in *Denfleet International Ltd v TNT Global SpA* [2007] 2 Lloyd's Rep. 504.
237 See the survey by Flaux J in *Standard Chartered Bank (Hong Kong) Ltd v Independent Power Tanzania Ltd* [2016] EWHC 2908 (Comm).
238 [2018] EWCA Civ 62; [2018] B.L.R. 167.

"In the context of legal liability for claimed loss, it seems to me that the only workable criterion is whether an allegation of fraud is a necessary ingredient of the legal basis on which loss is claimed: in other words, whether an allegation of fraud is a necessary averment to support a cause of action."

15. EXEMPTION FROM LIABILITY FOR CONSEQUENTIAL LOSS

Where a contract exempts one party from liability for consequential loss, it will normally be interpreted as exempting him only from such loss as is recoverable under the second limb of the rule in Hadley v Baxendale.

12.110   An exemption clause will often exempt one contracting party from liability for "consequential loss". A series of cases have considered the scope of an exemption in these terms.

12.111   Damages for breach of contract are recoverable in accordance with the rule in *Hadley v Baxendale*,[239] which is as follows:

"Where two parties have made a contract which one of them has broken, the damages which the other party ought to receive in respect of such a breach of contract should be such as may fairly and reasonably be considered either arising naturally, i.e. according to the usual course of things, from such breach of contract itself, or such as may reasonably be supposed to have been in the contemplation of both parties, at the time they made the contract, as the probable result of the breach of it."

Damage occurring naturally or directly is said to be within the first limb of the rule, while damage which the parties might reasonably have contemplated because of special knowledge at the date of the contract is said to fall within the second limb. The cases lay down the principle of interpretation that a clause which excludes liability for consequential loss excludes liability only for damages falling within the second limb of the rule and does not exclude liability for damages falling within the first limb.

12.112   In *Millar's Machinery Co Ltd v David Way and Son*,[240] a clause excluding "responsibility for consequential damages" was held by the Court of Appeal not to exclude liability for damage occurring naturally or directly. Maugham LJ is recorded in indirect speech as having held that "the word 'consequential' had come to mean 'not direct'", and Roche LJ as having applied this reading to the contract.

In *Saint Line v Richardsons Westgarth & Co Ltd*,[241] a clause exempted liability for "indirect or consequential" damage. Atkinson J said:

"In my judgment the words 'indirect or consequential' do not exclude liability for damages which are the natural result of the breaches complained of ... If one takes loss of profit, it is quite clear that such a claim may very well arise directly and naturally from the breach based on delay."

In *Croudace Construction Ltd v Cawoods Concrete Products Ltd*,[242] the distinc-

[239] (1854) 9 Exch. 341.
[240] (1935) 40 Com. Cas. 204.
[241] [1940] 2 K.B. 49.
[242] (1978) 8 B.L.R. 20.

tion drawn at first instance by Parker J between consequential loss and natural or direct loss for the purposes of an exclusion clause was held to be correct. Megaw LJ considered the court to be bound by *Millar's Machinery* which in any event he considered rightly decided.

In *British Sugar Plc v Projects Ltd*,[243] Waller LJ[244] rejected the submission that "consequential" loss, to a reasonable businessman, would include loss of profits.

In *Deepak Fertilisers Ltd v ICI Chemicals and Polymers Ltd*,[245] the Court of Appeal said of a clause which expressly excluded liability for loss of profits as well as "indirect or consequential damage": **12.113**

> "The direct and natural result of the destruction of the plant was that Deepak was left without a methanol plant, the reconstruction of which would cost money and take time, losing for Deepak any methanol production in the meantime. Wasted overheads incurred during the reconstruction of the plant, as well as profits lost during that period, are no more remote as losses than the cost of reconstruction. Lost profits cannot be recovered because they are excluded in terms, not because they are too remote. We consider that this court is bound by the decision in *Croudace* where a similar loss was not excluded by a similar exclusion and considered to be direct loss."

The Court of Appeal followed this line of cases in *Hotel Services Ltd v Hilton International Hotels (UK) Ltd*.[246]

In *British Sugar Plc v Projects Ltd*,[247] Waller LJ had said that: **12.114**

> "… once a phrase has been authoritatively construed by a court in a very similar context to that which exists in the case in point, it seems to me that a reasonable businessman must more naturally be taken to be having the intention that the phrase should bear the same meaning as construed in the case in point."

It is likely that at least at the level of the Court of Appeal similar clauses will be interpreted in similar fashion.[248] Nevertheless, in *Transocean Drilling UK Ltd v Providence Resources Plc*,[249] Moore-Bick LJ said:

> "It is questionable whether some of those cases would be decided in the same way today, when courts are more willing to recognise that words take their meaning from their particular context and that the same word or phrase may mean different things in different documents."

The words of the clause may compel a different result. In *Star Polaris LLC v* **12.115**

---

[243] (1997) 87 B.L.R. 42.
[244] With whom Evans and Aldous LJJ agreed.
[245] [1999] 1 Lloyd's Rep. 387.
[246] [2000] B.L.R. 235.
[247] (1997) 87 B.L.R. 42.
[248] See also *BHP Petroleum Ltd v British Steel Plc* [1999] 2 Lloyd's Rep. 583, where this was common ground; *Watford Electronics Ltd v Sanderson CFL Ltd* [2001] B.L.R. 143 at 154; *Ferryways NV v Associated British Ports* [2008] 1 Lloyd's Rep. 639; *Natixis SA v Marex Financial, Access World Logistics (Singapore) Pte Ltd* [2019] EWHC 2549 (Comm) at [537] (approving the text). However, in *Caledonia North Sea Ltd v British Telecommunications Plc* [2002] B.L.R. 139 at 159, Lord Hoffmann reserved the question whether this interpretation is correct.
[249] [2016] EWCA Civ 372.

HHIC-Phil Inc,[250] a shipbuilding contract contained a complete code for the attribution of liability. Article IX.4 provided:

> "Except as expressly provided in this Paragraph, in no circumstances and on no ground whatsoever shall the BUILDER have any responsibility or liability whatsoever or howsoever arising in respect of or in connection with the VESSEL or this CONTRACT after the delivery of the VESSEL. Further, but without in any way limiting the generality of the foregoing, the BUILDER shall have no liability or responsibility whatsoever or howsoever arising for or in connection with any consequential or special losses, damages or expenses unless otherwise stated herein."

Sir Jeremy Cooke held that the remainder of that article set out what responsibility the builder had and that, read in context, the second of the quoted sentences set out "a further and particular limitation of liability above and beyond" what had been stated in the preceding sentences.

12.116   In some cases the clause expressly refers to loss of profits. Thus in *Fujitsu Services Ltd v IBM United Kingdom Ltd*,[251] the clause provided that neither party would be liable for "loss of profits, revenue, business, goodwill, indirect or consequential loss or damage". Carr J held that the clause should be interpreted according to the natural meaning of the words. On the other hand, in *2 Entertain Video Ltd v Sony DADC Europe Ltd*[252] the relevant clause provided that: "Neither party shall be … for any indirect or consequential loss or damage including (to the extent only that such are indirect or consequential loss or damage only) but not limited to loss of profits, loss of sales, loss of revenue, damage to reputation, loss or waste of management or staff time or interruption of business." The claim was one for loss of profits on goods in a warehouse destroyed by fire. O'Farrell J said:

> "The direct and natural result of the fire was the destruction of the goods and the warehouse, causing lost profits and business interruption losses to the claimants. Therefore, the claims in this case do not appear to fall within the scope of the exclusion."

As far as the words in parentheses were concerned, she said:

> "The effect of the words in parentheses is to negate the illustration intended by the words of inclusion. The only way in which these words can be given effect is to treat the reference to 'loss of profits …' and following categories of loss as losses that might or might not fall within the exclusion. As such, they are of no assistance in determining whether the losses claimed in this case fall within or without the exclusion."

The overall result was that a claim for loss of profits was not excluded by the clause.

Illustration

A claims handling agreement contained a clause that said:

---

[250] [2016] EWHC 2941 (Comm); [2017] 1 Lloyd's Rep. 203.
[251] [2014] EWHC 752 (TCC).
[252] [2020] EWHC 972 (TCC).

"Neither party shall be liable to the other for any indirect or consequential loss (including but not limited to loss of goodwill, loss of business, loss of anticipated profits or savings and all other pure economic loss) arising out of or in connection with this Agreement".

It was argued that the clause covered loss of goodwill or loss of business as free-standing items, whether or not they were consequential losses. That argument was rejected. The use of the phrase "including but not limited to" was a strong pointer that the specified heads of loss were but examples of the excluded indirect loss. The elevation of all "pure economic loss" as a freestanding category for which liability was excluded potentially cut across recovery of even direct loss: yet the clause furnished the "limit" to direct loss recovery. The purported exclusion of the specified categories of loss in both direct and indirect form was not expressed clearly.

Makerstudy Insurance Co Ltd v Endsleigh Insurance Services Ltd[253]

16.   INDEMNITY CLAUSES

A clause by which one party agrees to indemnify another party against the consequences of that other's liability to third parties, is subject to the same principles of interpretation as an exclusion clause.[254]

Indemnity clauses in contracts fall into two broad categories.   **12.117**

The first category consists of clauses where one party agrees to indemnify the **12.118** other against liability which that other may have towards him. In such a case the indemnity is "the obverse of an exempting clause".[255] In substance such a clause is an exemption clause.[256]

The second category consists of clauses in which one party to the contract agrees **12.119** to indemnify the other party against liability which that other party may incur towards third parties. There is no legal impediment to the inclusion in a contract of an indemnity clause of either category. However, in order to be effective, particularly in relation to loss caused by the negligence of the party indemnified, clear and unambiguous language must be used.

The lease which was considered by the Privy Council in *Canada Steamship Lines* **12.120** *Ltd v R.*[257] contained an indemnity clause as well as an exemption clause. Accordingly, the principles enunciated by Lord Morton of Henryton in that case apply also to indemnity clauses. The rationale behind the approach of the court in construing exemption clauses is the inherent improbability that one party to a contract would wish to absolve the other from liability for breach of contract, especially when such breach is attributable to that other's negligence.[258] This consideration applies with greater force to an indemnity clause. In *Smith v South Wales Switchgear Ltd*,[259]

---

[253] [2010] EWHC 281 (Comm).
[254] This section was cited with approval in *Antiparos ENE v SK Shipping Co Ltd* [2008] 2 Lloyd's Rep. 237.
[255] *Smith v South Wales Switchgear Ltd* [1978] 1 W.L.R. 165, per Viscount Dilhorne. Lord Fraser of Tullybelton also described an indemnity as being in many cases "merely the obverse of exemption".
[256] *Farstad Supply A/S v Enviroco Ltd* [2010] 2 Lloyd's Rep. 387.
[257] [1952] A.C. 192. See para.11.33.
[258] See, e.g. *Gillespie Bros & Co Ltd v Bowles (Roy) Transport Ltd* [1973] Q.B. 400, per Buckley LJ.
[259] [1978] 1 W.L.R. 165.

Viscount Dilhorne said:

"when considering the meaning of such a clause one must, I think, regard it as even more inherently improbable that one party should agree to discharge the liability of the other party for acts for which he is responsible."

In the same case, Lord Keith of Kinkel, having referred to the guidelines laid down in *Canada Steamship Lines Ltd v R.*,[260] said:

"While they apply to the construction both of a clause relied on as exempting from certain liabilities a party who has undertaken to carry out contractual work and of a clause whereby such a party has agreed to indemnify the other party against liabilities which would ordinarily fall on him, they apply a fortiori in the latter case, since it represents a less usual and more extreme situation."

12.121   Indeed, in the modern law they are more relevant to indemnity clauses than to exclusion clauses. In *Persimmon Homes Ltd v Ove Arup and Partners Ltd*,[261] Jackson LJ explained:

"Over the last 66 years there has been a long running debate about the effect of that passage and the extent to which it is still good law. In hindsight we can see that it is not satisfactory to deal with exemption clauses and indemnity clauses in one single compendious passage. It is one thing to agree that A is not liable to B for the consequences of A's negligence. It is quite another thing to agree that B must compensate A for the consequences of A's own negligence."

12.122   The guidelines do not, however, apply where the clause in question seeks to transfer vicarious liability from one party to the contract to another.[262] An indemnity clause must be interpreted in the context of the contract as a whole; and will not usually be interpreted as covering things for which the indemnified is being remunerated by the contractual consideration.[263]

Illustrations

1.   A building contract contained an indemnity by the contractor to the occupier of the site of the works against every claim against the occupiers under any statute or at common law for death, arising out of the contractor's work from "any cause other than the negligence" of the occupier. A workman was killed owing to a breach of the relevant electricity regulations. It was held that "negligence" in the particular context of the indemnity meant negligence at common law and did not include a breach of statutory duty. The occupiers were entitled to be indemnified.
Murfin v United Steel Company Ltd[264]

---

[260] [1952] A.C. 192.
[261] [2017] EWCA Civ 373; [2017] 2 C.L.C. 28.
[262] *White (Arthur) (Contractors) Ltd v Tarmac Civil Engineering Ltd* [1967] 1 W.L.R. 1508; *Phillips Products Ltd v Hyland* [1987] 1 W.L.R. 659; *Thompson v Lohan (T) (Plant Hire) and Hurdiss (JW)* [1987] 1 W.L.R. 649.
[263] *ENE Kos 1 Ltd v Petrolio Brasiliero SA (No.2)* [2012] UKSC 17; [2012] 2 A.C. 164.
[264] [1957] 1 W.L.R. 104.

2.   A contract for the erection of an oil storage tank contained a provision requiring the contractor to indemnify the employer against "all claims arising out of the operations being undertaken" by the contractor under the contract, including personal injury and death. One of the contractor's workmen was killed owing to the negligence of the employer. It was held that the indemnity did not cover claims due to the employer's negligence because, in the absence of an express indemnity against negligence, words which in their ordinary meaning are wide enough to cover negligence should not be construed to do so if there is some other head of damage against which protection might reasonably have been desired.
Walters v Whessoe & Shell Refining Co Ltd[265]

3.   A developer entered into an agreement with a highway authority to construct a bypass. The developer agreed to indemnify the authority in respect of all actions, claims, demands, expenses and proceedings arising out of or in connection with or incidental to the carrying out of the works other than those arising out of or in consequence of any act, neglect, default or liability of the authority. It was held that having regard to the well-established distinction in the law of compulsory purchase between compensation payable for loss suffered as a result of the execution of works on the one hand, and compensation payable for loss arising out of the subsequent use of the works when completed on the other, the indemnity should be construed narrowly, and limited to an indemnity against compensation of the first kind.
Wiltshire County Council v Crest Estates Ltd[266]

4.   A building contract required the contractor to indemnify the employer any expense, liability, loss, claim or proceedings in so far as such loss, injury or damage arose out of or in the course of or by reason of the carrying out of the works. It was held that the contract required the contractor to pay the employer's costs of an appeal on the indemnity basis.
Rabilizirov v A2 Dominion London Ltd[267]

17.   CLAUSES LIMITING LIABILITY

A clause limiting a party's liability for breach of contract is subject to the same principles of interpretation as a clause excluding liability, but those principles are not applied so rigorously.

At one time it had been thought that clauses limiting (rather than excluding) liability for breach of contract were subject to the full rigour of the rules relating to exemption clauses. However, this is not so. In *Ailsa Craig Fishing Co Ltd v Malvern Fishing Co Ltd*,[268] Lord Wilberforce said: **12.123**

"Clauses of limitation are not regarded by the courts with the same hostility as clauses of exclusion; this is because they must be related to other contractual terms, in particular to the risks to which the defending party may be exposed, the

---

[265]   (1960) 6 Build. L.R. 23.
[266]   [2005] 4 P.L.R. 86.
[267]   [2019] EWHC 863 (QB).
[268]   [1983] 1 W.L.R. 964 (a Scottish appeal).

remuneration which he receives and possibly also the opportunity of the other party to insure."

12.124 The more practical effects of the lesser hostility were summarised by Lord Fraser of Tullybelton as follows:

"In my opinion these principles [sc the strict rules of interpretation] are not applicable in their full rigour when considering the effect of conditions merely limiting liability. Such conditions will of course be read *contra proferentem* and must be clearly expressed, but there is no reason why they should be judged by the specially exacting standards which are applied to exclusion and indemnity clauses. The reason for imposing such standards on these conditions is the inherent improbability that the other party to a contract including such a condition intended to release the *proferens* from a liability that would otherwise fall on him. But there is no such high degree of improbability that he would agree to a limitation of the liability of the *proferens*, especially when ... the potential losses that might be caused by the negligence of the *proferens* or its servants are so great in proportion to the sums that can reasonably be charged for the services contracted for. It is enough in the present case that the condition must be clear and unambiguous."

In *Price Waterhouse v The University of Keele*,[269] Buxton LJ said:

"The principle set out by Lord Fraser is wider than the general rule of *contra proferentem*, which latter depends for its applicability on discernment of an ambiguity in the language. Rather, Lord Fraser's principle applies in a case such as the present directly, and without nice analysis in terms of ambiguity, when a clause that seeks to exclude liability that would otherwise attach under the contract cannot be construed with ease or confidence whichever party's argument is addressed."

Lord Fraser's "important distinction"[270] was applied by the House of Lords in an English appeal, namely *Mitchell (George) (Chesterhall) Ltd v Finney Lock Seeds Ltd*.[271]

12.125 However there is no rigid distinction between a clause excluding liability and a clause limiting liability; it is doubtful "whether Lord Fraser intended to introduce one mechanistic rule (a distinction between limiting and excluding liability) to mitigate the rigour of another".[272] The High Court of Australia has rejected a rigid distinction between clauses that exclude liability and clauses that limit liability,[273] and this may well come to represent English law as well.

12.126 One possible route to this conclusion was suggested by Evans LJ in *BHP Petroleum Ltd v British Steel Plc*[274]:

---

[269] [2004] EWCA Civ 583.
[270] *Mitchell (George) (Chesterhall) Ltd v Finney Lock Seeds Ltd* [1983] 2 A.C. 803, per Lord Bridge of Harwich.
[271] [1983] 2 A.C. 803.
[272] *HIH Casualty and General Insurance Ltd v Chase Manhattan Bank* [2003] 2 Lloyd's Rep. 61, per Lord Hoffmann.
[273] *Darlington Futures Ltd v Delco Australia Property* (1986) 68 A.L.R. 385.
[274] [2000] 2 Lloyd's Rep. 277.

"I think it is unfortunate if the present authorities cannot be reconciled on the basis that no categorization is necessary and of a general rule that the more extreme the consequences are, in terms of excluding or modifying the liability that would otherwise arise, then the more stringent the courts' approach should be in requiring that the exclusion or limit should be clearly and unambiguously expressed."

In the author's opinion this is a sound approach. The approach advocated by Evans LJ in *BHP Petroleum Ltd v British Steel Plc* may be gaining ground. In *Societe Generale, London Branch v Geys* Société Générale, London Branch v Geys,[275] Lord Hope said:

"As Lord Dunedin said in *W&S Pollock & Co v Macrae*,[276] in order to be effective such clauses must be 'most clearly and unambiguously expressed.' In *Ailsa Craig Fishing Co Ltd v Malvern Fishing Co Ltd*[277] Lord Fraser of Tullybelton said that it was an ordinary principle that such conditions must be construed strictly against the proferens. The principle is commonly applied in cases where the contract which the other party has entered into with the proferens is in a standard form or in terms set out by the proferens which were not negotiable. The more improbable it is that the other party would agree to excluding the liability of the proferens, the more exacting the application of the principle will be."

A clause limiting liability must be distinguished from a clause providing for agreed damages in the event of a breach. The essential difference was summarised by Lord Upjohn in *Suisse Atlantique Societe D'Armement Maritime SA v NV Rotterdamsche Kolen Centrale*[278] as follows: **12.127**

"An agreed damages clause is for the benefit of both; the party establishing breach by the other party need prove no damage in fact; the other must pay that, no less but no more. But where liability for damage is limited by a clause then the person seeking to claim damages must prove them at least up to the limit laid down by the clause; the other party, whatever may be the damage in fact can refuse to pay more if he can rely on the clause."

So in that case a demurrage clause was held not to be a limitation clause, and consequently not subject to the rules of construction applicable to such clauses. In *Bikam OOD v Adria Cable Sarl*,[279] Simon J held that no residual hostility applies to clauses which attempt to limit the liability of parties to a fixed financial amount.

---

[275] [2012] UKSC 63; [2013] 1 A.C. 523.
[276] 1922 S.C. (HL) 192 at 199.
[277] [1983] 1 W.L.R. 964 at 969H.
[278] [1967] 1 A.C. 361.
[279] [2012] EWHC 621 (Comm).

18. Time Bar Clauses

Time bar clauses are treated as limitation clauses and are interpreted strictly and, in cases of real doubt, contra proferentem.[280]

12.128   Contracts often contain provisions regulating the time within which claims must be made under the contract. They are in the nature of private contractual statutes of limitation. The purpose of such a clause is to enable the recipient of a claim to investigate and verify or dispute the claim, soon after the events giving rise to the claim, having regard to both the formulation of the claim and the factual material supporting it.[281] In *Atlantic Shipping and Trading Co Ltd v Louis Dreyfus and Co*,[282] the House of Lords held that a time bar clause was to be construed in the same way as a clause excluding or limiting liability. The reason for the decision was that the time bar clause purported to remove a cause of action after the lapse of a stipulated time. This approach was followed by the House of Lords in the strict construction applied to the time bar clause in *Beck & Co v Szymanowski & Co*.[283] Accordingly, a time bar clause must be clear and unambiguous if effect is to be given to it.[284] Thus, if there is any residual doubt about the matter, the ambiguity is to be resolved in such a way as not to prevent an otherwise legitimate claim from being pursued.[285]

In the *Atlantic Shipping* case, Lord Sumner (with whom three of the Law Lords agreed) said:

> "There is no difference in principle between words which save them from having to pay at all and words which save them from paying as much as they would otherwise have had to pay."

12.129   Time bar clauses were also included in the following description given by Lord Wilberforce in *Suisse Atlantique Societe D'Armement Maritime SA v NV Rotterdamsche Kolen Centrale*[286]:

> "I treat the words 'exceptions clause' as covering broadly such clauses as profess to exclude or limit, either quantitatively or as to the time within which action must be taken, the right of the injured party to bring an action for damages."

In *Videocon Global Ltd v Goldman Sachs International*,[287] the Court of Appeal confirmed that time bar clauses are strictly construed, and in *Nobahar-Cookson v*

---

[280] Applied in *Odfjfell Seachem A/S v Continentale des Petroles et d'Investissements* [2005] 1 All E.R. (Comm) 421.

[281] *Babanaft International Co SA v Avant Petroleum Inc (The Oltenia)* [1982] 1 Lloyd's Rep. 448; *"Amalie Essberger" Tankreederei GmbH & Co KG v Marubeni Corporation* [2019] EWHC 3402 (Comm).

[282] [1922] 2 A.C. 250.

[283] [1924] A.C. 43; see para.12.39, Illustration 2. See also *Finagra v OT Africa Line* [1998] 2 Lloyd's Rep.622; *Transgrain Shipping BV v Deiulemar Shipping SpA* [2014] EWHC 4202 (Comm).

[284] *Zurich Insurance Plc v Maccaferri Ltd* [2016] EWCA Civ 1302.

[285] *The Sabrewing* [2007] EWHC 2482 (Comm); [2008] 1 Lloyd's Rep. 286; *"Amalie Essberger" Tankreederei GmbH & Co KG v Marubeni Corporation* [2019] EWHC 3402 (Comm).

[286] [1967] 1 A.C. 361.

[287] [2016] EWCA Civ 130; [2016] 1 C.L.C. 528.

Hut Group Ltd,[288] Briggs LJ said that "it is well-settled that contractual limitation periods for the notification or bringing of claims are forms of exclusion clause".[289]

In *BHP Petroleum Ltd v British Steel Plc*,[290] it was held that an orthodox defects **12.130** liability clause in a building contract was not an exemption clause. It operated for the benefit of both parties. The employer is entitled to have the defects rectified without having to engage and pay another contractor to carry out the rectification: the contractor or supplier is entitled to carry out the rectification himself which may normally be expected to be less expensive for him than having to reimburse the cost to the employer of having it done by others.

A time bar clause, like an arbitration clause, will survive the termination of a **12.131** contract by repudiation and acceptance.[291]

The House of Lords has pointed out an important distinction between exclusion **12.132** clauses and limitation clauses.[292] Since a time bar clause does not wholly remove the right of an injured party to claim against the other, it is submitted that it is more analogous to a limitation clause than to an exemption clause. In other words it limits a claim temporally rather than quantitatively. Nevertheless, it is clear that the time limit within which a claim must be made must be strictly complied with.

A time bar clause will usually bar claims unless notice of them is given within a **12.133** stipulated period. It is on the content of the notice and any documents required in support of the claim that the dispute usually turns. Where a charterparty contained a time bar unless a claim was made with "all supporting documents" it was held that failure to supply bills of lading in time barred the claim.[293] Although it has often been said that each clause turns on its own specific wording, the requirements of a claim notification clause will usually require the identification of the legal basis for a claim (e.g. referring to particular warranties said to have been broken), as well as its factual basis.[294] Time bar provisions should be construed with the object of clarity and certainty to ensure that claimants are in a position to know what will be required to be done in accordance with the time requirements of the provision; this will also enable the recipient of a claim to understand what documentation might legitimately be expected to be provided in support of a claim.[295]

The required contents of a valid notice is a question of interpretation of the **12.134** clause. Every notification clause turns on its own individual wording.[296] Whether a valid notice has been given in time depends on the meaning of the notice, objectively interpreted, rather than on the subjective understanding of the parties.[297]

Although the usual principles applicable to the interpretation of notices will ap- **12.135** ply,[298] the clause will nevertheless be treated as a limitation clause for that

---

[288] [2016] EWCA Civ 128; [2016] 1 C.L.C 573.

[289] Applied in *Towergate Financial (Group) Ltd v Hopkinson* [2020] EWHC 984 (Comm).

[290] [2000] 2 Lloyd's Rep. 277.

[291] *Port Jackson Stevedoring Pty Ltd v Salmond & Spraggon (Australia) Pty Ltd* [1981] 1 W.L.R.138.

[292] See *Ailsa Craig Fishing Co Ltd v Malvern Fishing Co Ltd* [1983] 1 W.L.R. 964 and para.12.123.

[293] *Tricon Energy Ltd v MTM Trading LLC* [2020] EWHC 700 (Comm).

[294] *Teoco UK Ltd v Aircom Jersey 4 Ltd* [2018] EWCA Civ 23; [2018] BCC 339; *Triumph Controls UK Ltd v Primus International Holding Co* [2019] EWHC 565 (TCC).

[295] *"Amalie Essberger" Tankreederei GmbH & Co KG v Marubeni Corporation* [2019] EWHC 3402 (Comm).

[296] *Forrest v Glasser* [2006] 2 Lloyd's Rep. 392; *ROK Plc v S Harrison Group Ltd* [2011] EWHC 270 (Comm) (where the authorities on different forms of wording are reviewed); *MUR Shipping BV v Louis Dreyfus Company Suisse SA* [2019] EWHC 3240 (Comm).

[297] *Stobart Group Ltd v Stobart* [2019] EWCA Civ 1376.

[298] *ROK Plc v S Harrison Group Ltd* [2011] EWHC 270 (Comm).

purpose.[299] The clear commercial purpose of the clause includes that the person to whom the notification is given should know at the earliest practicable date in sufficiently formal written terms that a particularised claim for breach of contract is to be made so that he may take such steps as are available to him to deal with it.[300] Thus the touchstone is "clarity sufficient to achieve certainty rather than a requirement of strict compliance which, if applied inflexibly, can lead to uncommercial results".[301] A compliant notification will usually refer to the contractual provision that has been broken. But the level of detail required will depend on the wording of the clause. Where the contract provided that "the nature of the Claim" be specified "in reasonable detail", it required, as a minimum, that the notice should identify the contractual provision under which the claim was said to arise.[302] But where the contract merely required claims to be notified, no detail of the claim was required.[303]

12.136   The clause may specify the person on whom notice is to be served. In *Zayo Group International Ltd v Ainger*,[304] a share purchase agreement provided that the "Management Vendors" (who were seven individuals) were not to be liable for breach of warranty unless given notice within a specified time. It was held that a failure to serve one of them in time resulted in none of them being liable.

12.137   Some clauses also specify what documents must be provided in support of a claim. The purpose of so doing is that claims may be investigated while the facts are still fresh.[305] So where a clause required the provision of "all available supporting documents", it required the provision of documents relevant to both liability and quantum.[306] In some cases a distinction has been drawn between primary and secondary documents.[307] Nevertheless, a clause which requires the provision of "all supporting documents" indicates "a fairly expansive approach, though of course, that is qualified by the requirement for documents to be supporting."[308]

12.138   The effect of failing to give the requisite notice in time will also depend on the wording of the clause. In *Bloomberg LP v Sandberg*,[309] cl.6 of a contract provided that "no proceedings shall be commenced against the Contractor after the expiry of twelve years from the date of issue of the last written statement by the Client that practical completion of the Project has been achieved". Fraser J held that this operated as a procedural bar only, and did not extinguish the underlying liability. Consequently, in principle the contractor could be liable to make contribution under the Civil Liability (Contribution) Act 1978.

On the other hand, where a contract provided that sellers were not to be "liable for a claim" unless notified within a particular period, a failure to notify had the ef-

---

[299] *Laminates Acquisition Co v BTR Australia Ltd* [2004] 1 All E.R. (Comm) 737.

[300] *Senate Electrical Wholesalers Ltd v Alcatel Submarine Networks Ltd* [1999] 2 Lloyd's Rep. 423.

[301] *National Shipping Co of Saudi Arabia v BP Oil Supply Co* [2011] EWCA Civ 1127; [2012] 1 Lloyd's Rep. 18; *Kassiopi Maritime Co Ltd v Fal Shipping Co Ltd* [2015] EWHC 318 (Comm); [2015] 1 Lloyd's Rep. 473.

[302] *ROK Plc v S Harrison Group Ltd* [2011] EWHC 270 (Comm).

[303] *Forrest v Glasser* [2006] 2 Lloyd's Rep. 392. This conclusion depended on the particular wording and structure of the clause.

[304] [2017] EWHC 2542 (Comm).

[305] *Babanaft International Co SA v AvantiPetroleum Inc (The Oltenia)* [1982] 1 Lloyd's Rep. 448.

[306] *Babanaft International Co SA v AvantiPetroleum Inc (The Oltenia)* [1982] 1 Lloyd's Rep. 448.

[307] *Kassiopi Maritime Co Ltd v FAL Shipping Co Ltd (The Adventure)* [2015] EWHC 318 (Comm); [2016] 2 All E.R. (Comm) 243.

[308] *MUR Shipping BV v Louis Dreyfus Co Suisse SA* [2019] EWHC 3240 (Comm); [2020] Bus. L.R. 1013.

[309] [2015] EWHC 2858 (TCC); 162 Con. L.R. 260.

fect of extinguishing the claim with the consequence that it could not be advanced by way of equitable set-off.[310]

Illustrations

1.   A contract for the sale of a partially erected house contained a clause which provided that if the purchaser discovered any structural defect within six months from completion and notified the vendors, the vendors would make good the defect without expense to the purchasers. It was held that the clause applied only to defects discovered by the purchaser within six months, and not to those discovered afterwards; and only required the vendor to make them good, without removing the purchaser's right to sue for damages.
   Hancock v Brazier (BW) (Anerley) Ltd[311]

2.   A charterparty provided that demurrage should be payable against an owner's invoice supported by notices and statements of facts from loading and discharging ports duly signed by shippers. Any claim for demurrage to be accordingly presented within twelve months from completion of final discharge. It was held that the clause was not sufficiently clear to require the documents to be presented within twelve months in order to prevent the claim becoming time barred.
   The Pera[312]

3.   Terms of sale provided that disputes "shall be settled by arbitration" and that notice of a claim was to be given within twelve months. The contract went on to provide that if notice was not given within twelve months the claim would be time barred. It was held that the effect of the time bar was that the dispute could not be litigated in the courts after the expiry of the twelve-month time limit for the commencement of an arbitration.
   Wholecrop Marketing Ltd v Wolds Produce Ltd[313]

19.   DEVIATION

An exemption clause will not protect a carrier if he deviates from the route contracted for, or a bailee if he does not keep the goods bailed in the place contracted for. These are probably anomalous rules of substantive law which have grown up for historical reasons.

At common law a carrier was required to follow the contractual route, or if none **12.139** was specified, then the usual and reasonable route, as to which evidence could be given.[314] If the vessel deviated (except where necessary for the safety of the voyage or to save human life) a breach of the contract was committed. In *Hain Steamship Co Ltd v Tate and Lyle Ltd*,[315] the House of Lords held that where the shipowner deviated, he committed a breach of contract of such gravity that he was no longer entitled to rely on exemption clauses contained in it. There had, indeed,

---

[310]   *Philp v Cook* [2017] EWHC 3023 (QB).
[311]   [1966] 1 W.L.R. 1317.
[312]   [1985] 2 Lloyd's Rep. 103 CA.
[313]   [2013] EWHC 2079 (Ch).
[314]   *Reardon Smith Lines Ltd v Black Sea and Baltic General Insurance Co Ltd* [1939] A.C. 562.
[315]   [1936] 2 All E.R. 597.

been a long line of authority[316] to that effect. A similar view in relation to the bailment of goods was expressed by Scrutton LJ in *Gibaud v Great Eastern Railway Co.*[317] This rule has been called the "four corners" rule, for once the carrier or bailee has stepped outside the "four corners" of the contract he will no longer be entitled to rely on clauses in the contract inserted for his protection. The law was summarised by Lord Hodson in *Suisse Atlantique Societe D'Armement Maritime SA v NV Rotterdamsche Kolen Centrale*[318] as follows:

> "Thus, under a contract of carriage or bailment if the carrier or bailee uses a place other than that agreed on for storing the goods, or otherwise exposes the goods to risks quite different from those contemplated by the contract, he cannot rely on clauses designed to protect him against liability within the four corners of the contract, and has only such protection as is afforded by the common law."

12.140   However, Lord Hodson was at pains to stress that the cases which illustrated this principle were all cases which depended on "the construction of the contract". In the same case Lord Wilberforce explained these cases as being based on ordinary principles of contractual intention. However, in *Photo Production Ltd v Securicor Ltd,*[319] he suggested that:

> "It may be preferable that they should be considered as a body of authority sui generis with special rules derived from historical and commercial reasons."[320]

An alternative explanation was given by Lord Diplock who said:

> "The bringing to an end of all primary obligations under the contract may also leave the parties in a relationship, typically that of bailor and bailee, in which they owe to one another by operation of law fresh primary obligations of which the contract is not the source."

12.141   Thus once the contract is removed as the source of the obligations, the exemption clause is also removed. The liabilities of the bailee will therefore be governed simply by his status as a bailee. However, the contract cannot be brought to an end unless a repudiatory breach has already occurred, and ex hypothesi it would have occurred at a time when the contract (and the exemption clause) continued to govern the relationship between the parties. It is submitted, therefore, that Lord Diplock's explanation does not wholly incorporate the deviation cases into the view of the law established by the *Photo Production* case. One possibility is acceptance of the repudiatory breach which deviation constitutes is retrospective in operation, but this would be contrary to well-established authority[321] and indeed to the *ratio* of *Photo Production* itself.

---

[316] Beginning with *Davis v Garrett* (1830) 6 Bing. 716.
[317] [1921] 2 K.B. 426. (See the citation quoted in para.12.89.)
[318] [1967] 1 A.C. 361.
[319] [1980] A.C. 827.
[320] In *Kenya Railways v Antares Co Pte Ltd* [1987] 1 Lloyd's Rep. 424, Lloyd LJ said that he favoured assimilating the deviation cases into the ordinary law of contract, and declined to extend further any special category of case. However, in *The Chanda* [1989] 2 Lloyd's Rep. 494, Hirst J held that an exemption clause did not protect a carrier who carried goods in breach of an express term about the manner in which they were to be stowed.
[321] *Heyman v Darwins Ltd* [1942] A.C. 356.

Accordingly, unless the Supreme Court were to overrule at least one previous **12.142** decision of the House of Lords[322] it is difficult to see how the deviation cases may be treated except as a body of substantive law with rules of its own.[323] In *Dera Commercial Estate v Derya Inc*,[324] Carr J, referring to this section, confirmed that *Hain Steamship Co Ltd v Tate and Lyle Ltd* remains binding on the lower courts, and has not been impliedly overruled by subsequent decisions of the House of Lords.

Professor Coote suggests[325] that deviation is an anomalous type of breach which **12.143** to all intents and purposes ipso facto determines the contract unless an aggrieved party elects to waive the breach.[326] Since the principles applicable to deviation cases are a matter of the substantive law of contracts of carriage and bailment, it is not proposed to deal with the subject further in this work.

20. EXCLUSION OF PARTICULAR RIGHTS OR REMEDIES

Clear words are necessary before the court will hold that a contract has taken away rights or remedies which one of the parties to it would have had at common law.[327]

Some contractual provisions seek to prevent parties from relying upon what **12.144** would otherwise be their legal rights at common law. In general, parties are permitted to do so.[328] However:

"in construing such a contract one starts with the presumption that neither party intends to abandon any remedies for its breach arising by operation of law, and clear express words must be used in order to rebut this presumption."[329]

This observation is "essentially one of common sense; parties do not normally

---

[322] For example, *Hain Steamship Co Ltd v Tate and Lyle Ltd* [1936] 2 All E.R. 597.

[323] For a contrary view see D. Yates, *Exclusion Clauses in Contracts*, 2nd edn (London: Sweet & Maxwell, 1982), pp.210–211 and D. Yates and A.J. Hawkins, *Standard Business Contracts* (London: Sweet & Maxwell, 1986), pp.205–206. In *Daewoo Heavy Industries Ltd v Klipriver Shipping Ltd* [2003] 1 All E.R. (Comm) 801, Longmore LJ said that it had not yet been conclusively decided whether the deviation cases and the warehouse cases must be regarded as dead and buried along with the doctrine of fundamental breach.

[324] [2018] EWHC 1673 (Comm); [2018] Bus. L.R. 2105.

[325] B. Coote, *"Exemption Clauses"*, in John Bell (ed.), *The Cambridge Law Journal* (London: Sweet & Maxwell, 1964), p.94,

[326] See also *Alexander v Railway Executive* [1951] 2 K.B. 82, although the observations on the effect of a fundamental breach on an exemption clause must be treated with caution in so far as they apply to cases other than contracts of carriage or bailment.

[327] This section was cited with approval in *Seadrill Management Services Ltd v OAO Gazprom* [2009] EWHC 1530 (Comm) (affirmed [2010] EWCA Civ 691); *Filatona Trading Ltd v Navigator Equities Ltd* [2020] EWCA Civ 109 and *CNM Estates (Tolworth Tower) Ltd v VeCREF I SARL* [2020] EWHC 1605 (Comm).

[328] Subject, of course, to rules of public policy (e.g. that the jurisdiction of the court as to matters of law cannot be ousted by agreement).

[329] *Gilbert-Ash (Northern) Ltd v Modern Engineering (Bristol) Ltd* [1974] A.C. 689, per Lord Diplock; *Stocznia Gdanska SA v Latvian Shipping Co* [1998] 1 W.L.R. 574 at 585, per Lord Goff of Chieveley. In *Nile Co for the Export of Agricultural Crops v Bennett (H & JM) (Commodities) Ltd* [1986] 1 Lloyd's Rep. 555, Evans J said that the words had to be "clear and unequivocal". This is a more stringent test than merely "clear" but was also used by Lord Diplock in the *Gilbert-Ash* case. See also *BICC Plc v Burndy Corp* [1985] Ch. 232; *Aston FFI (Suisse) SA v Louis Dreyfus Commodities Suisse SA* [2015] EWHC 80 (Comm), [2015] 1 Lloyd's Rep. 413.

give up valuable rights without making it clear that they intend to do so".[330] In *Bahamas Oil Refining Co International Ltd v Owners of the Cape Bari Tankschiffahrts GMBH & Co KG*,[331] Lord Clarke, giving the advice of the Privy Council said:

> "The Board accepts the submission that, for a party to be held to have abandoned or contracted out of valuable rights arising by operation of law, the provision relied upon must make it clear that that is what was intended."

12.145 Similarly, in *Trafalgar House Construction (Regions) Ltd v General Surety & Guarantee Co Ltd*,[332] Lord Jauncey of Tullichettle said:

> "There is no doubt that in a contract of guarantee parties may, if so minded, exclude any one or more of the normal incidents of suretyship. However, if they choose to do so clear and unambiguous language must be used to displace the normal legal consequences of the contract …".

In *HIH Casualty and General Insurance Ltd v Chase Manhattan Bank*,[333] Lord Bingham of Cornhill said:

> "The courts should not ordinarily infer that a contracting party has given up rights which the law confers on him to an extent greater than the contract terms indicate he has chosen to do; and if the contract terms can take legal and practical effect without denying him the rights he would ordinarily enjoy if the other party is negligent, they will be read as not denying him those rights unless they are so expressed as to make clear that they do."

12.146 It has been said that this principle provides a particularly clear demonstration of the ability of special principles of construction to serve the overall purpose of the general principles of contractual construction.[334] Recent cases in the Court of Appeal have, however, weakened the force of this principle. In *Scottish Power UK Plc v BP Exploration Operating Co Ltd*,[335] Christopher Clarke LJ said:

> "The fact that there are two possible meanings is the beginning of the inquiry, not its end. It is then necessary for the court to apply 'all its tools of linguistic, contextual, purposive and common-sense analysis to discern what the clause really means'. If as a result of so doing the answer becomes clear the court should give effect to it even though the interpretation may deprive a party of a right at law which he might otherwise have had. It is open to parties to make an agreement which has that effect."

Nevertheless, there is still a part for the principle (or presumption) to play, although as Christopher Clarke LJ explained, "the strength of the presumption is reduced in proportion to the degree of derogation from the common law position".

Thus, where, as in that case, a clause replaced a common law right to damages

---

[330] *Seadrill Management Services Ltd v OAO Gazprom* [2010] EWCA Civ 691; [2010] C.L.C. 934 per Moore-Bick LJ; *The Atlantic Tonjer* [2019] EWHC 1213 (Comm); [2020] 1 Lloyd's Rep. 171.
[331] [2016] UKPC 20; [2016] 2 Lloyd's Rep. 469.
[332] [1996] A.C. 199 at 208C.
[333] [2003] 1 All E.R. (Comm) 349.
[334] *CNM Estates (Tolworth Tower) Ltd v VeCREF I SARL* [2020] EWHC 1605 (Comm).
[335] [2016] EWCA Civ 1043.

with a different contractual remedy which might (in some circumstances) have been more valuable than the common law right, the principle had little, if any, part to play.

In *Harcap Ltd v FK Generators & Equipment Ltdi*,[336] Bryan J summarised the principles as follows: **12.147**

"(1) First, that, although the parties are not lightly to be taken to have intended to cut down the remedies which the law provides for breach of contract without using clear words, the Court must still use all its tools of linguistic, contextual, purposive and common-sense analysis to determine what the clause really means ...

(2) The strength of any presumption that parties do not intend to give up their rights or claims under the general law is reduced in proportion to the degree of derogation from the common law position. It is relevant that a clause is not a pure exclusion clause, but instead one which replaces common law rights with a different contractual remedy which may, in certain circumstances, be more valuable than a right to damages ... What is required to displace that presumption is set out in that case. In particular one looks to see if a contract only makes coherent sense if other remedies are excluded ...

(3) Parties are entitled expressly to stipulate not only the primary rights that they expect to receive under their contract, but also the secondary remedies to which one would have become entitled upon the other's breach of that contract. It accords with business common sense for contracting parties at the outset to agree a fair and easily ascertainable sum that will become payable as compensation for breach and the more difficult it is to prove loss the greater the advantage to both parties of contractually fixing an easily ascertainable sum to be paid in the event of such default ..."

In most cases, a right of set-off will only be excluded where the clause refers to   **12.148**
set-off expressly.[337] So a clause in a lease which required the rent to be paid "without deduction" did not exclude a right of equitable set-off.[338] A contractual provision which contained an irrevocable undertaking to pay each instalment in cash by way of electronic transfer of immediately available funds was likewise insufficient.[339] But a provision requiring payment "without any deduction or set off whatsoever" has been held sufficient to exclude any right of deduction or set-off.[340] The omission of the word "whatsoever" makes no difference.[341] The issue is ultimately a question of interpretation of the specific clause in the context of the contract in question. Whilst the failure to refer expressly to rights of set-off being excluded may

---

[336] [2017] EWHC 2765 (Comm).
[337] For example, *Hong Kong & Shanghai Banking Corp v Klockner & Co AG* [1990] 2 Q.B. 514; *The Fedora* [1986] 2 Lloyd's Rep. 441 CA; *Coca Cola Financial Corp v Finsat International Ltd* [1998] Q.B. 43 CA; *John Dee Group v WMH (21) Ltd* [1997] B.C.C. 518; *Society of Lloyds v Leighs* [1997] C.L.C. 1398 CA; *The Atlantic Tonjer* [2019] EWHC 1213 (Comm); [2020] 1 Lloyd's Rep 171.
[338] *Connaught Restaurants Ltd v Indoor Leisure Ltd* [1994] 1 W.L.R. 501 CA. However, in Australia there is a body of authority to the effect that a covenant to pay "without deduction" has the effect of excluding set-off. The authorities are collected in *Sandbanks Holdings Pty Ltd v Durkan* [2010] WASCA 122. See also *Lotus Cars Ltd v Marcassus Sport SARL* [2019] EWHC 3128 (Comm).
[339] *Albion Energy Ltd v Energy Investments Global BRL* [2020] EWHC 301 (Comm).
[340] *Star Rider Ltd v Inntrepreneur Pub Co* [1998] 1 E.G.L.R. 53.
[341] *Altonwood Ltd v Crystal Palace FC (2000) Ltd* [2005] EWHC 292 (Ch).

be highly pertinent, the intention of the parties to exclude such rights may be sufficiently clear from the use of other words. Accordingly, a clause requiring payment "in full without deduction withholding or qualification" was sufficient to exclude the right of set-off.[342] Where a contract provided that sellers were not to be "liable for a claim" unless notified within a particular period, a failure to notify had the effect of extinguishing the claim with the consequence that it could not be advanced by way of equitable set-off.[343] In interpreting an "anti set-off" clause the guidelines in *Canada Steamship Lines Ltd v R.*[344] do not apply.[345]

12.149 In *FG Wilson (Engineering) Ltd v John Holt & Co (Liverpool) Ltd*,[346] Popplewell J said:

"A right of set-off may be excluded by agreement of the parties. If set-off is to be excluded by contract, clear and unambiguous language is required[347] ... But no more than that is required. In particular such a term is not to be treated in the same way as an exclusion clause."[348]

He added that such a clause should not be approached in a mechanistic way:

"Whether the set-off would operate as a substantive defence or as a remedy, what matters in each case is whether there has been clearly expressed an intention that the payment is to be made without reference to the claim which would otherwise be set-off. Where the language used does not mention set-off, it may be difficult for a party to satisfy the requirement of clarity if the clause relied on does not in terms qualify the payment obligation. Conversely where the provision does expressly qualify the payment obligation, it may readily be construed as sufficiently clear to be effective (as in *Coca-Cola Financial Corp v Finsat Ltd* [1998] Q.B.43;*WRM v Wood and Rohlig (UK) Ltd v Rock Unique Ltd* [2011] EWCA Civ 18). But there is no principle of construction that a no set-off clause cannot be effective unless it is expressed in terms to qualify the payment obligation."

His decision was upheld on appeal[349] in which Longmore LJ said that it was "difficult to think of clearer words than that a party 'shall not apply any set-off'".

12.150 Where a clause in a contract extended rather than excluded a party's right to withhold payment it was not to be "read in a niggardly fashion"; and therefore extended to unliquidated claims.[350]

12.151 A similar approach applies where the contract seeks to restrict one party's right to adduce evidence in relation to a dispute which would be admissible were that

[342] *Lotus Cars Ltd v Marcassus Sport SARL* [2019] EWHC 3128 (Comm).
[343] *Philp v Cook* [2017] EWHC 3023 (QB).
[344] [1952] A.C. 192.
[345] *Continental Illinois National Bank & Trust Co of Chicago v Papanicolau* [1986] 2 Lloyd's Rep. 441; *Skipskredittforeningen v Emperor Navigation* [1998] 1 Lloyd's Rep. 66.
[346] [2012] EWHC 2477 (Comm); [2012] 2 Lloyd's Rep. 479.
[347] *Modern Engineering (Bristol) Ltd v Gilbert-Ash (Northern) Ltd* [1974] A.C. 689 at 717, 722–723; *Connaught Ltd v Indoor Leisure Ltd* [1994] 1 W.L.R. 501; *Esso Petroleum Co Ltd v Milton* [1997] 1 W.L.R. 938; *BOC Group Plc v Centeon LLC* [1999] 1 All E.R. (Comm) 970.
[348] *Continental Illinois National Bank & Trust Company of Chicago v Papanicolaou (The Fedora)* [1986] 2 Lloyd's Rep. 441; *WRM Group Ltd v Wood* [1998] C.L.C. 189.
[349] [2013] EWCA Civ 1232; [2014] 1 All E.R. 785.
[350] *Geldof Metaalconstructie NV v Simon Carves Ltd* [2010] B.L.R. 401.

dispute to be litigated in court[351] and where it seeks to prevent one party from relying on a non-contractual sample in support of a claim to reject goods[352]; or where it is alleged that the contract terms prevent a principal from suing on a contract made by his agent.[353] The same approach is also applied where it is alleged that a contract deprives an injured contracting party of damages to which he would otherwise be entitled,[354] and where it is alleged that an accrued obligation and corresponding right has been discharged by later events.[355] A similar approach applies in considering whether an exemption clause deprives one party of any remedy in the event of breach[356]; whether the right to sue for damages for breach of contract has been excluded by the terms of the contract[357] and whether the right to forfeit a deposit has been excluded by the terms of the contract.[358] The same approach applies to the question whether a clause excluded other valuable rights conferred by the contract.[359] A clause may be effective to exclude the right of set-off, yet not be clear enough to exclude the right to counterclaim for damages.[360]

In *Stocznia Gdynia SA v Gearbulk Holdings Ltd*,[361] it was common ground that **12.152** the test of construction for a court to apply in ascertaining whether the parties intended to oust any common law or extra-contractual remedies, such as to constitute the terms of the contract as a complete code, is by reference to a requirement for "clear words". Burton J held that the words of the clause in that case were not clear enough to disapply the common law relating to repudiation and acceptance. His decision on this point was upheld by the Court of Appeal[362] in which Moore-Bick LJ said:

"In paragraph 88 of his judgment in *Stocznia Gdanska S.A. v Latvian Shipping Co*[363] Rix L.J. expressed the view that where contractual and common law rights overlap it would be too harsh to regard the use of a contractual mechanism of termination as ousting the common law mechanism, at any rate against a background of an express reservation of rights. In this case I would go further. In my view it is wrong to treat the right to terminate in accordance with the terms of the contract as different in substance from the right to treat the contract as discharged by reason of repudiation at common law. In those cases where the contract gives a right of termination they are in effect one and the same."

He added:

"The court is unlikely to be satisfied that a party to a contract has abandoned

---

[351] *Lindsay (WN) & Co Ltd v European Grain and Shipping Agency Ltd* [1963] 1 Lloyd's Rep. 437; *European Grain & Shipping Ltd v R&H Hall Plc* [1990] 2 Lloyd's Rep. 139.
[352] *Verheijdens Veevoeder Commissiehandel BV v 1S Joseph Inc* [1981] 1 Lloyd's Rep. 102.
[353] *Filatona Trading Ltd v Navigator Equities Ltd* [2020] EWCA Civ 109.
[354] *The Selda* [1999] 1 Lloyd's Rep. 729 CA; *Pearce & High Ltd v Baxter* [1999] C.L.C. 749 CA.
[355] *Marine Trade SA v Pioneer Freight Futures Ltd* [2010] 1 Lloyd's Rep. 631.
[356] *Kudos Catering (UK) Ltd v Manchester Central Convention Complex Ltd* [2013] EWCA Civ 38; [2013] 2 Lloyd's Rep. 270.
[357] *RP Explorer Master Fund v Chilukuri* [2013] EWHC 103 (Ch); *IG Index Ltd v Ehrentreu* [2013] EWCA Civ 95.
[358] *Griffon Shipping LLC v Firodi Shipping Ltd* [2013] EWHC 593 (Comm); [2013] 2 Lloyd's Rep. 50 (affirmed [2013] EWCA Civ 1567; [2014] 1 Lloyd's Rep. 471).
[359] *Gard Marine & Energy Ltd v China National Chartering Co Ltd* [2013] EWHC 2199 (Comm); [2014] 1 Lloyd's Rep. 59.
[360] *IG Index Ltd v Ehrentreu* [2013] EWCA Civ 95.
[361] [2008] 2 Lloyd's Rep. 202.
[362] [2009] 1 Lloyd's Rep. 461.
[363] [2002] 2 Lloyd's Rep. 436.

valuable rights arising by operation of law unless the terms of the contract make it sufficiently clear that that was intended. The more valuable the right, the clearer the language will need to be."

12.153 Similarly, in *Dalkia Utilities Services Plc v Celtech International Ltd*,[364] cl.14 of a contract entitled one party to terminate it in a number of different circumstances, none of which would necessarily have amounted to a repudiatory breach of contract. Clause 15 contained provisions for payment in the event of termination. Christopher Clarke J held that cl.15 did not apply to a repudiatory breach that was accepted. He said:

> "Clause 14 contains nine separate categories of circumstances in which one party or the other may terminate the agreement. In all of these categories the right to terminate would or could arise in circumstances which did not give rise to a right of termination at common law. Clause 15 deals with the consequences that will follow according to which ground for termination has been invoked. The natural reading of clause 15.7, in that context, is that the only rights or remedies that will arise in respect of a termination on any of the bases provided for by clause 14 will be those specified in clause 15. Secondly, clause 15.7 does not seem to me sufficiently clear, as it would need to be, to exclude the parties' common law right to accept a repudiatory breach of contract (eg an outright refusal to perform) as discharging the innocent party from further liability and to claim damages for the loss of the contract. The presumption is that it does not unless there are clear express words to that effect."

12.154 Where an arbitration agreement states that the award will be "final and binding" or "final conclusive and binding" that is not clear enough to exclude the right of appeal under the Arbitration Act 1996.[365]

12.155 Where a clause in a contract does exclude a remedy, the clause will be narrowly construed. In *Acsim (Southern) Ltd v Danish Contracting and Development Co Ltd*,[366] a building contract provided that the rights of the parties as to set-off were fully set out in the contract and no other rights relating to set-off should be implied. The Court of Appeal held that the reference to "set-off" was to be construed as a reference to set-off as defined by judicial decisions, and did not prevent the employer from defending itself against a claim for payment on the ground that the value of the work for which the sum was claimed had been diminished by the contractor's breaches of contract.

12.156 In *Port of Tilbury (London) Ltd v Stora Enso Transport & Distribution Ltd*,[367] a contract contained a clause prohibiting set-off, deduction and counterclaim save as otherwise expressly permitted by the contract. Another clause in the contract permitted the withholding of a genuinely disputed sum. The question was whether the latter clause enabled one party to resist payment under a take or pay clause by reliance on an unliquidated claim where both liability and quantum were disputed. The Court of Appeal held that the clause was limited to challenges to the quantum of invoices, and did not permit the set-off of a disputed cross-claim.

---

[364] [2006] 1 Lloyd's Rep. 599.

[365] *Essex CC v Premier Recycling Ltd* [2007] B.L.R. 233; *Shell Egypt West Manzala GmbH v Dana Gas Egypt Ltd* [2010] 2 All E.R. (Comm) 442. Commonwealth authorities to the opposite effect are considered in both cases.

[366] (1989) 47 B.L.R. 55 CA.

[367] [2009] 1 Lloyd's Rep. 391.

A particular remedy may be excluded by implication, but only if the implica- **12.157**
tion is a necessary one.[368] Thus a requirement that payments under the contract be
made by direct debit may exclude the right of set-off by necessary implication.[369]

In *Tele2 International Card Co SA v Post Office Ltd*,[370] cl.16 of a contract **12.158**
provided:

"In no event shall any delay, neglect or forbearance on the part of any party in
enforcing (in whole or in part) any provision of this Agreement be or be deemed
to be a waiver thereof or a waiver of any other provision or shall in any way
prejudice any right of that party under this Agreement".

The question arose whether this clause prevented conduct amounting to an affirmation of the contract. Aikens LJ said:

"In short, clause 16 cannot prevent the fact of an election to abandon the right
to terminate from existing: either it does or it does not. This conclusion is
reinforced, I think, by the terms of clause 16 itself. Although it stipulates that 'in
no event shall any delay, neglect or forbearance' on the part of any party in
enforcing a provision of the Agreement '... be or be deemed to be a waiver' of
the provision or '... shall in any way prejudice any right of that party under this
Agreement', it does not deal at all with the issue of election of whether or not to
exercise a contractual right. The general law demands that a party which has a
contractual right to terminate a contract must elect whether or not to do so. This
clause does not attempt to say that the doctrine of election shall not apply—
even assuming that any contractual provision could exclude the operation of the
doctrine."

It is doubtful whether a clause in a contract could disapply the doctrine of **12.159**
election. There is a logical inconsistency in one party claiming that a contract is at
an end, while at the same time relying on a clause in the contract to support that
claim. In *Stocznia Gdynia SA v Gearbulk Holdings Ltd*,[371] Moore-Bick LJ said:

"One can now see that it is impossible for a party to terminate a contract, in the
sense of discharging both parties from further performance, whether by invoking a term which entitles him to do so or by exercising his rights under the
general law, and at the same time treat it as continuing, since the two are
inconsistent. Either the primary obligations remain for performance, or they do
not."

In the context of waiver of forfeiture of leases, similar clauses have been held
ineffective in *R. v Paulson*[372] and *Expert Clothing Service & Sales Ltd v Hillgate
House Ltd*.[373] However, clauses of this kind have been upheld in Australia[374] and
New Zealand.[375]

---

[368] *Liberty Mutual Insurance Co (UK) Ltd v HSBC Bank Plc* [2002] EWCA Civ 691.
[369] *Esso Petroleum Co Ltd v Milton* [1997] 1 W.L.R. 938 CA.
[370] [2009] EWCA Civ 9.
[371] [2009] 1 Lloyd's Rep. 461.
[372] [1921] 1 A.C. 271.
[373] [1986] Ch. 340.
[374] *Ovendale Pty Ltd v Anthony* (1966) 117 C.L.R. 539.
[375] *Inner City Businessmen's Club v James Kirkpatrick* [1975] 2 N.Z.L.R. 636.

12.160   In *Novasen SA v Alimenta SA*,[376] Popplewell J held that a similar approach applies to the question whether the contract enlarges the remedies that would be available at common law. He said:

> "The issue before me is the converse of that which was there being considered, which was whether a right to damages or other remedy conferred by law was excluded by contract; whereas in this case the question is whether the contract confers a right to damages where no such right would arise at law. Nevertheless in my view similar principles should apply. The parties should be taken to have contracted against the background that their remedies will, in the absence of specific contrary agreement, be regulated by the system of law chosen to govern their contractual relations. If no remedy, in the form of an entitlement to damages, is conferred by law, clear words will be required to confer a contractual entitlement to such remedy. That is especially so where (a) the contractual term is a standard clause drafted and adopted by a trade body and (b) the contractual term is to confer a right of recovery in circumstances where no loss has in fact been suffered. Such a remedy is contrary to the compensatory principle governing the quantum of damages for breach of contract."

12.161   Although the cases mainly concern remedies, the same principles apply to primary obligations. In *Seadrill Management Services Ltd v OAO Gazprom*,[377] the question was whether the owner of a drilling rig was in breach of an implied obligation to operate the rig with reasonable skill and care. The contract between the owner and a hirer contained a clause which provided that except for such obligations and liabilities specifically assumed by the rig operator, the hirer would be solely responsible and assumed liability for all consequences of operations by both parties. Moore-Bick LJ said:

> "When [the clause] refers to obligations and liabilities which the contractor has 'specifically assumed' it must naturally refer to the obligations which arise out of the express terms of the contract with all the incidents which the law ordinarily attaches to them, since those incidents are inherent in them. It may, of course, be possible for the parties to agree otherwise, but unless they have done so, they can only be presumed to have accepted that the ordinary incidents apply. To proceed on any other basis would make commercial life impossible. To say, therefore, that under this form of contract the contractor specifically assumes an obligation to operate the rig but does not specifically assume an obligation to do so carefully is to approach the question from the wrong end. Prima facie it assumes the obligation as expressed and all that the law attaches to it, unless there is agreement to the contrary."

Illustrations

1.   A contract for the sale of goods provided for particular machinery for resolving a dispute. The buyer was to advise the seller of any complaint. Inspections were then to be made, and a surveyor's report was consequently to be produced by the buyer. If no agreement was reached at that stage the parties were to "settle the

---

[376] [2013] EWHC 345 (Comm); [2013] 1 Lloyd's Rep. 648.
[377] [2010] EWCA Civ 691; [2010] 1 C.L.C. 934; followed in *JP Morgan Chase Bank, NA v Federal Republic of Nigeria* [2019] EWCA Civ 1641.

dispute". It was held that the machinery was effective with the exception of the last stage and accordingly prevented the buyers from rejecting the goods.
Nile Co for the Export of Agricultural Crops v Bennett (H & JM) Ltd[378]

2.   A building contract required the payment of monies by a contractor to a subcontractor pursuant to interim certificates. The contract provided that the contractor was to be at liberty to deduct from any certified payment the amount of any bona fide contra-account and/or other claims which the contractor had against the subcontractor. It was held that those words entitled the contractor to withhold payments under a right of set-off.
Gilbert Ash (Northern) Ltd v Modern Engineering (Bristol) Ltd[379]

3.   A lease required the tenant to pay the rent "without deduction". It was held that these words were not sufficiently clear to exclude the tenant's right to equitable set-off.
Connaught Restaurants Ltd v Indoor Leisure Ltd[380]

4.   A guarantee required payment "without set-off or counterclaim and without deductions or withholdings whatsoever". It was held that these words covered counterclaims based on negligence.
The Fedora[381]

5.   A building contract provided for payment in accordance with architect's certificates "less only (i) retention money as hereinafter described (ii) any sum previously paid". A third exception in the standard form permitting deduction by way of set-off for breach of contract by the contractor had been deleted. Having regard to the deletion it was held that the contract excluded the right of set-off.
Mottram Consultants Ltd v Bernard Sunley & Sons Ltd[382]

6.   A contract for the sale of goods said that in default of performance damages would be "based on the difference between the contract price and either the default price ... or the actual or estimated value of the goods". It was held that damages "based on" those criteria did not mean that damages were "limited to" those criteria and that a claim for wasted expenditure could be made.
The Selda[383]

21.   CONTRACTUAL ESTOPPEL AND NON-RELIANCE CLAUSES

In principle, parties to a contract are free to contract on the basis of an assumed state of facts, even if they know those facts to be untrue. Such an agreement will generally take effect as a contractual estoppel. But if a contract contains a clause acknowledging that a party has not relied on any representation in entering into it, the effect of the clause as a contractual estoppel will be subject to the effect, if any, of the Misrepresentation Act 1967 and the

---

[378]   [1986] 1 Lloyd's Rep. 555.
[379]   [1974] A.C. 689.
[380]   [1994] 1 W.L.R. 501 CA.
[381]   [1986] 2 Lloyd's Rep. 441 CA.
[382]   [1975] 2 Lloyd's Rep. 197 HL.
[383]   [1999] 1 Lloyd's Rep. 729 CA.

Consumer Rights Act 2015. However, such a clause cannot exclude liability for fraudulent misrepresentation by a party to the contract.

12.162   In *Peekay Intermark Ltd v Australia & New Zealand Banking Group Ltd*,[384] Moore-Bick LJ said:

> "56   There is no reason in principle why parties to a contract should not agree that a certain state of affairs should form the basis for the transaction, whether it be the case or not. For example, it may be desirable to settle a disagreement as to an existing state of affairs in order to establish a clear basis for the contract itself and its subsequent performance. Where parties express an agreement of that kind in a contractual document neither can subsequently deny the existence of the facts and matters upon which they have agreed, at least so far as concerns those aspects of their relationship to which the agreement was directed. The contract itself gives rise to an estoppel: see *Colchester Borough Council v Smith*.[385]
>
> 57   It is common to include in certain kinds of contracts an express acknowledgment by each of the parties that they have not been induced to enter the contract by any representations other than those contained in the contract itself. The effectiveness of a clause of that kind may be challenged on the grounds that the contract as a whole, including the clause in question, can be avoided if in fact one or other party was induced to enter into it by misrepresentation. However, I can see no reason in principle why it should not be possible for parties to an agreement to give up any right to assert that they were induced to enter into it by misrepresentation, provided that they make their intention clear, or why a clause of that kind, if properly drafted, should not give rise to a contractual estoppel of the kind recognised in *Colchester Borough Council v Smith*. However, that particular question does not arise in this case. A clause of that kind may (depending on its terms) also be capable of giving rise to an estoppel by representation if the necessary elements can be established."

In *Springwell Navigation Corp v JP Morgan Chase Bank*,[386] Aikens LJ said:

> "So, in principle and always depending on the precise construction of the contractual wording, I would say that A and B can agree that A has made no pre-contract representations to B about the quality or nature of a financial instrument that A is selling to B. Should it make any difference that both A and B know at and before making the contract, that A did, in fact, make representations, so that the statement that A had not is contrary to what each side knows is the case? Apart from the remarks of Diplock J in *Lowe v Lombank*, Mr Brindle did not show us any case that might support the proposition that parties cannot agree that X is the case even if both know that is not so. I am unaware of any legal principle to that effect.[387] The only possible exception might be if the particular agreement between A and B on the certain state of affairs concerned contradicts some other specific or more general rule of English public policy. Like Moore-Bick LJ

---

[384] [2006] 2 Lloyd's Rep. 511.

[385] [1991] Ch. 448, affirmed on appeal [1992] Ch. 421.

[386] [2010] EWCA Civ 1221.

[387] Accordingly, it is no answer to a contractual estoppel that both parties know the truth: *Wallis Trading Inc v Air Tanzania Co Ltd* [2020] EWHC 339 (Comm).

in *Peekay* I see commercial utility in such clauses being enforceable, so that parties know precisely the basis on which they are entering into their contractual relationship."

At one time it was suggested that such clauses would not be effective at all. Later cases suggested that they would only have effect as estoppels by representation where the necessary elements of such an estoppel could be established. These elements would require the representee to show that he had himself relied on the representation in entering into the contract.[388] This rather complicated analysis has now been replaced by a simpler one, based on estoppel by contract.[389] **12.163**

The analysis of such a clause as giving rise to a contractual estoppel has since been applied in many other cases.[390] One significant difference between the two kinds of estoppel is that in the case of a contractual estoppel reliance does not need to be established.[391] In *Chen v Ng*,[392] the Privy Council discussed the principles of contractual estoppel. They pointed out that: **12.164**

"Whether the context is a deed or some other contract, the description contractual or conventional estoppel may in reality be a confusing misnomer, in circumstances where the parties can (even if there is also reliance on the truth of the agreed proposition) simply be regarded as having committed themselves by contractual term to a particular proposition."

In *Bikam OOD v Adria Cable SARL*,[393] a compromise agreement stated the amount of net debt owed by one party to the other. Popplewell J held that the statement amounted to a contractual estoppel. He said: **12.165**

"Where parties settle in a contractual document a disagreement as to an existing state of affairs in order to establish a clear basis for the contract itself and for

---

[388] *Watford Electronics Ltd v Sanderson CFL Ltd* [2001] B.L.R. 143; *EA Grimstead & Son Ltd v McGarrigan* [1999] EWCA Civ 3029.

[389] Professor David McLauchlan discusses contractual estoppel in "The Entire Agreement Clause" (2012) 128 L.Q.R. 521. Professor McMeel describes the approach of the courts to contractual estoppel clauses as "documentary fundamentalism" and argues that the principle of contractual estoppel has pushed the desire for commercial certainty to unnecessary and potentially unjust extremes: "Documentary fundamentalism in the Senior Courts: the myth of contractual estoppel" [2011] L.M.C.L.Q. 185. In the author's opinion this development is the logical extension of the traditional approach to recitals. "Contractual estoppel" is no more than a convenient label. The true analysis is that the parties are simply bound by their contract: *Credit Suisse International v Stichting Vestia Groep* [2014] EWHC 3103 (Comm).

[390] *Bottin International Investments v Venson* [2006] EWHC 3112 (Ch); *Donegal International v Republic of Zambia* [2007] 1 Lloyd's Rep. 397; *Trident Turboprop (Dublin) Ltd v First Flight Couriers Ltd* [2008] 2 Lloyd's Rep. 581; *Raiffeisen Zentralbank Osterreich AG v Royal Bank of Scotland Plc* [2010] EWHC 1392 (Comm); *FoodCo LLP v Henry Boot Developments Ltd* [2010] EWHC 358 (Ch); *Cassa Di Risparmio Della Repubblica Di San Marino Spa v Barclays Bank Ltd* [2011] EWHC 484 (Comm); *Bank Leumi (UK) Plc v Wachner* [2011] EWHC 656 (Comm); *Standard Chartered Bank v Ceylon Petroleum Corp* [2011] EWHC 1785 (Comm); *Credit Suisse International v Stichting Vestia Groep* [2014] EWHC 3103 (Comm); *Wallis Trading Inc v Air Tanzania Co Ltd* [2020] EWHC 339 (Comm). Contractual estoppel is discussed by Jo Braithwaite, "The origins and implications of contractual estoppel" (2016) 132 L.Q.R. 120 and by Nelson Goh, "Non-reliance clauses and contractual estoppel: commercially sensible or anomalous?" [2015] J.B.L. 511.

[391] *Trident Turboprop (Dublin) Ltd v First Flight Couriers Ltd* [2008] 2 Lloyd's Rep. 581.

[392] [2017] UKPC 27; [2018] 1 P. & C.R. DG2.

[393] [2013] EWHC 1985 (Comm). See also *Barclays Bank Plc v Svizera Holdings BV* [2014] EWHC 1020 (Comm).

its subsequent performance, neither party can subsequently deny the existence of the facts and matters upon which they have agreed."

In *Wallis Trading Inc v Air Tanzania Co Ltd*,[394] an aircraft lease contained a representation and warranty by the lessee that the lease was a legal, valid and binding obligation on it, and that the entry into and performance of the lease did not conflict with any laws binding on it. Butcher J held that the representation and warranty estopped the lessee from contending that the lease was void for non-compliance with procurement legislation.

12.166 The agreement may relate to a future state of affairs as well as a present or past one.[395] However, in *Financial Services Authority v Asset LI Inc*,[396] Andrew Smith J held that a non-reliance clause could not affect what were promises about future conduct as opposed to representations of fact.

12.167 It is common to include in certain kinds of contracts an express acknowledgement by each of the parties that they have not been induced to enter the contract by any representations other than those contained in the contract itself.

In *Quest 4 Finance Ltd v Maxfield*,[397] Teare J said:

"The commercial purpose of the declaration of non-reliance, which is part of the relevant background, is to ensure, in the interests of certainty, that the rights of the parties are governed by the terms of the written contract. Thus the maker of the declaration is prevented from relying upon anything other than the true nature, meaning and effect of the document which he has signed; and the first part of the declaration confirms that he understands the nature, meaning and effect of the warranty."

12.168 The clause must make clear its effect.[398] As Jacob J put it in *Thomas Witter Ltd v TBP Industries Ltd*[399]:

"… if a clause is to have the effect of excluding or reducing remedies for damaging untrue statements then the party seeking that protection cannot be mealy-mouthed in his clause. He must bring it home that he is limiting his liability for falsehoods he may have told."

12.169 It is contrary to public policy for a party to a contract to exclude liability in the case of his own fraud. Moreover, it is not possible to exclude liability in the case of deceit unless the clause is very clearly worded and the deceit is not that of a party to the contract itself.[400] In *FoodCo LLP v Henry Boot Developments Ltd*,[401] Lewison J said:

"Precisely what statements are covered by a non-reliance clause is a question of construction of the clause. But this is subject to the important principles that, as a matter of public policy, a contracting party cannot exclude liability for his own

---

[394] [2020] EWHC 339 (Comm).
[395] *Credit Suisse International v Stichting Vestia Groep* [2014] EWHC 3103 (Comm).
[396] [2013] EWHC 178 (Ch).
[397] [2007] 2 C.L.C. 706.
[398] *Cassa Di Risparmio Della Repubblica Di San Marino Spa v Barclays Bank Ltd* [2011] EWHC 484 (Comm); *Standard Chartered Bank v Ceylon Petroleum Corp* [2011] EWHC 1785 (Comm).
[399] [1996] 2 All E.R. 573.
[400] *HIH Casualty and General Insurance Ltd v Chase Manhattan Bank* [2003] 2 Lloyd's Rep. 61.
[401] [2010] EWHC 358 (Ch).

fraud; and that if he wishes to exclude liability for the fraud of his agent he must do so in clear and unmistakable terms on the face of the contract."[402]

In *HIH Casualty and General Insurance Ltd v Chase Manhattan Bank*,[403] Lord Bingham said:

"... if a party to a written contract seeks to exclude the ordinary consequences of fraudulent or dishonest misrepresentation or deceit by his agent, acting as such, inducing the making of the contract, such intention must be expressed in clear and unmistakable terms on the face of the contract ... General words, however comprehensive the legal analyst might find them to be, will not serve: the language used must be such as will alert a commercial party to the extraordinary bargain he is invited to make."

There has been some debate about whether a non-reliance clause falls within the scope of the Misrepresentation Act 1967 (and now the Consumer Rights Act 2015). In *EA Grimstead & Son Ltd v McGarrigan*,[404] it was suggested that it did not because it did not purport to exclude liability for misrepresentations; rather it prevented representations from being made at all. However, in *Raiffeisen Zentralbank Osterreich AG v Royal Bank of Scotland Plc*,[405] Christopher Clarke J said:

12.170

"to tell the man in the street that the car you are selling him is perfect and then agree that the basis of your contract is that no representations have been made or relied on, may be nothing more than an attempt retrospectively to alter the character and effect of what has gone before and in substance be an attempt to exclude or restrict liability."

This statement was approved by the Court of Appeal in *Springwell Navigation Corp v JP Morgan Chase Bank*.[406]

In *First Tower Trustees Ltd v CDS (Superstores International) Ltd*,[407] the Court of Appeal distinguished between a true exclusion clause and one which did no more than define the parties' primary obligations. In so far as previous cases decided that a so-called "basis" clause was outside the scope of the Misrepresentation Act 1967 with the consequence that the test of reasonableness under the Unfair Contract Terms Act 1977 (and now the Consumer Rights Act 2015) did not apply, it was only terms of the latter type to which that approach applied. A non-reliance clause is a clause of the former type, with the consequence that the test of reasonableness applied.

12.171

In equity a party to a deed could not set up an estoppel in reliance on a deed in relation to which there is an equitable right to rescission or in reliance on an untrue statement in an untrue recital induced by his own representation, whether in-

12.172

---

[402] *HIH Casualty & General Insurance Ltd v Chase Manhattan Bank* [2003] 2 Lloyd's Rep. 61. If the clause does purport to exclude liability for fraudulent misrepresentations it is likely to be void.

[403] [2003] 2 Lloyd's Rep. 61.

[404] [1999] EWCA Civ 3029.

[405] [2010] EWHC 1392 (Comm).

[406] [2010] EWCA Civ 1221. See also *Cleaver v Schyde Investments Ltd* [2011] EWCA Civ 929 in which a clause in the Standard Conditions of Sale restricting the right to rescind for misrepresentation failed the test of reasonableness. The special conditions appear to have contained a "non-reliance" clause but this was not apparently relied on.

[407] [2018] EWCA Civ 1396; [2019] 1 W.L.R. 637.

nocent or otherwise, to the other party.[408] This exception also applies to a non-reliance clause or other form of contractual estoppel.[409] The principle may not apply where there has been a misrepresentation as to the effect of the contractual documents which give rise to the estoppel.[410]

---

[408] *Greer v Kettle* [1938] A.C. 156.
[409] *Slocom Trading Ltd v Tatik Inc* [2012] EWHC 3464 (Ch) at [297].
[410] *Standard Chartered Bank v Ceylon Petroleum Corp* [2011] EWHC 1785 (Comm) at [529].

CHAPTER 13

FORCE MAJEURE CLAUSES

She can't help it; the girl can't help it

Bobby Troup

1. FORCE MAJEURE CLAUSES

Although the expression "force majeure" has no clear meaning in English law, it is used as a description of a type of clause that excuses or suspends performance of contractual obligations on the occurrence of a specified event.

The expression "force majeure" comes from French law.[1] It has no clear meaning in English law. In *Thomas Borthwick (Glasgow) Ltd v Faure Fairclough Ltd*,[2] Donaldson J said that: **13.01**

"the precise meaning of this term, if it has one, has eluded lawyers for years."

From time to time judges have considered the meaning of the phrase with the assistance of expert evidence about foreign law. Although, strictly speaking, these are decisions on the facts, they can be taken as guides to what would fall within the compass of the phrase. In *Matsoukis v Priestman & Co*,[3] which concerned a contract for the building of a steamship, Bailhache J, having heard evidence from foreign lawyers, said that the phrase was wider than "Act of God", but could not define how much wider. He held that it covered a coal strike that interrupted the defendant's business, and accidents to machinery; but not a shipwrights' strike, bad weather, football matches or a funeral.   **13.02**

In *Lebeaupin v Richard Crispin and Co*,[4] Macardie J also considered the scope of the phrase. He quoted the following definition from a French legal textbook: **13.03**

"This term is used with reference to all circumstances independent of the will of man, and which it is not in his power to control, and such force majeure is sufficient to justify the non-execution of a contract. Thus, war, inundations, and epidemics, are cases of force majeure; it has even been decided that a strike of workmen constitutes a case of force majeure."

He added:

"This is a wide definition, but I think that it usefully though loosely suggests not

---

[1] Civil Code art.1148.
[2] [1968] 1 Lloyd's Rep. 714.
[3] [1915] 1 K.B. 681.
[4] [1920] 2 K.B. 714.

only the meaning of the phrase as used on the Continent, but also the meaning of the phrase as often employed in English contracts."

He held that it would cover war; any direct legislative or administrative interference (e.g. an embargo); strikes or accidental breakdown of machinery. It would not cover bad weather (except perhaps an abnormal tempest). He concluded:

"I take it that a 'force majeure' clause should be construed in each case with a close attention to the words which precede or follow it, and with a due regard to the nature and general terms of the contract. The effect of the clause may vary with each instrument."

13.04   In *British Electrical and Associated Industries (Cardiff) Ltd v Patley Pressings Ltd*,[5] McNair J held that the phrase was not "too vague to have contractual effect"; although he held that an agreement that was "subject to force majeure conditions" was too uncertain to give rise to a concluded contract. The reason was a narrow one: that force majeure clauses came in too many varieties, and that the court could not choose between them.

13.05   In practice either "force majeure" is used as a label or heading for a clause; or it is a term defined in the clause; or it is supplemented by a series of defined events which trigger the operation of the clause. A force majeure clause will usually define the event which brings the clause into operation and the effect of bringing the clause into operation. It may also deal with the process by which one party notifies the other that the specified event has occurred.[6]

13.06   It need hardly be said that the precise effect of a force majeure clause depends principally on its words.[7] Thus a "force majeure clause should be construed in each case with a close attention to the words that precede or follow it, and with a due regard to the nature and general terms of the contract".[8] As what matters is the language of the clause, the citation of cases dealing with very differently worded clauses is of limited if any assistance.[9]

2.   FORCE MAJEURE AS EXEMPTION CLAUSES

A force majeure clause may, depending on its terms, be viewed as equivalent to an exemption clause.

13.07   In *Fairclough, Dodd & Jones Ltd v JH Vantol Ltd*,[10] the contract contained a term extending the time of shipment in certain events. Lord Tucker said:

"It seems to me quite natural that merchants should for their convenience make provision for what is to happen in the event of difficulties arising in the performance of their contracts, even if such difficulties are not such as to render

---

5   [1953] 1 W.L.R. 280.
6   See Furmston, "Drafting of Force Majeure Clauses" and Berg, "Detailed Drafting of a Force Majeure Clause", in E. McKendrick, *Force Majeure and Frustration of Contract*, 2nd edn (Oxon: Informa Law from Routledge, 2013).
7   *Coastal (Bermuda) Petroleum Ltd v VTT Vulcan Petroleum SA (No.2)* [1996] 2 Lloyd's Rep. 383.
8   *Lebeaupin v Richard Crispin and Co* [1920] 2 K.B. 714.
9   *Classic Maritime Inc v Limbungan Makmur SDN BHD* [2019] EWCA Civ 1102; [2019] 4 All E.R. 1145.
10   [1957] 1 W.L.R. 136. See also *GH Renton & Co Ltd v Palmyra Trading Corp of Palmyra* [1957] A.C. 149 (force majeure clause not invalidated by Hague/Visby Rules).

performance impossible. Sellers, who for one of the specified causes are unable to make use of the vessel on which they intended to ship the goods, may have difficulty in making other arrangements and have to plan some way ahead. It seems to be altogether reasonable to provide in such circumstances for a fixed and definite period of extension which will facilitate commerce rather than to think only in terms of escape from breach or of impossibility of performance."

Having referred to the effect of an exemption clause he continued:

"Force majeure clauses are of different kinds. In the case of an exception clause it is generally true to say that it only operates on the happening of an event which would otherwise result in a breach, but there is nothing to prevent the parties providing for an extension of the time for performance or for a substituted mode of performance on the occurrence of a force majeure event whether or not such event would have prevented performance."

This case is often taken as establishing that a force majeure clause is not an **13.08** exemption clause. Thus in *J Lauritzen AS v Wijsmuller BV (The Super Servant Two)*,[11] a clause in a contract of carriage entitled the carrier to cancel its performance in the event of force majeure and certain specified events. Bingham LJ said that the clause was not "an exceptions clause". Dillon LJ said that the clause was "a cancellation clause and not an exceptions clause".

The rationale for this distinction is that, properly interpreted, a force majeure **13.09** clause qualifies what would otherwise be an absolute obligation, rather than providing for what is to happen in the event of a breach of that obligation. In *Crawford and Rowat v Wilson, Sons & Co*,[12] Lord Esher MR said:

"The charter is, therefore, not an absolute contract that the defendants shall take delivery of the cargo whatever may happen. It is a contract that they will do so unless prevented by 'unavoidable hindrances'".

Likewise, in *Reardon Smith Line Ltd v Ministry of Agriculture, Fisheries and Food*,[13] McNair J said:

"I have already observed earlier that the exception clause in these charterparties, ... quite clearly applies to delay in the supply or bringing down of the cargo, and that, properly construed, the clause qualifies the absolute obligation to supply cargo for loading on the vessel's arrival to the extent of the delay arising from the excepted causes."

The dividing line between a contract which says "I promise to perform but will **13.10** not be liable if I fail to do so for specified reasons" and one which says "I promise to perform unless prevented by specified reasons" is a difficult one to draw. Thus in *SHV Gas Supply & Trading SAS v Naftomar Shipping & Trading Co Inc*,[14] Christopher Clarke J said:

"A force majeure clause is an exceptions clause and must be construed strictly.

---

11 [1990] 1 Lloyd's Rep. 1.
12 (1896) 1 Com. Cas. 277.
13 [1960] 1 Q.B. 439 at 514.
14 [2006] 1 Lloyd's Rep. 163.

This clause, if operative, does not mean that the seller is not in breach in failing to ship within the agreed time. It affords relief from the consequences of breach by providing that the seller shall not be 'liable in damages or otherwise' for delay in the performance of that obligation. Such a provision clearly excludes any liability in damages."

13.11   In *The Angelia*,[15] Kerr J suggested that the relevant distinction was whether the specified reason was one within the control of the contracting party. He said:

"No case was cited on either side, nor have I been able to find one, in which it has ever been suggested that a party can commit a fundamental breach when the breach occurs due to circumstances beyond its control and the contract provides that non-performance due to such circumstances is to be excused. It seems to me that by its nature the doctrine cannot have any application in such a case. The authorities in which the doctrine has been applied by holding that a party cannot rely upon a protective provision in the contract have all been cases, so far as I can find, where the breach was due to a cause within the control of the defendant, so that, to put it colloquially, the breach was in some way the fault of the defendant; and where the nature of the fault, or the seriousness of its consequences, or both, were such that the relevant protective provision in the contract could on its true construction not be relied upon to excuse the breach."

13.12   It might have been thought that one other possible distinction might lie in the time at which the force majeure event takes place. If it takes place when the party relying on it is already in breach of contract (e.g. when a vessel is already on demurrage) then the clause is being invoked to excuse or eliminate the effect of an existing breach of contract, rather than preventing a breach from arising in the first place.[16] Thus in *The Forum Craftsman*,[17] Hobhouse J said:

"It is well established that contractual provisions can impinge upon this situation in a number of ways. They can affect the definition of the laytime; for example the expression 'weather working days' means that you only count that category of day when calculating the laytime allowed. Then there may be laytime exceptions which provide that time is not to count during some period even though the relevant period would otherwise be within the definition of the laydays. All these types of provision define the obligation and therefore answer the question whether or not there has been a breach, not whether there is any liability for a breach. They do not affect the liability to demurrage after the laytime has been exhausted.

Once the laytime has been exceeded, there has been a breach and a clause operating at this time may be of a type which excludes or limits the liability in demurrage or it may be one which suspends the continuing obligation to discharge and therefore, pro tanto, suspends the breach which would otherwise have given rise to the obligation to pay demurrage. These types of clauses, whether excusing breaches, relieving prima facie obligations, or simply excluding or reducing the liability in liquidated damages are all provisions of the character of exclusion or exceptions clauses and therefore must be clearly

---

[15]   [1973] 1 W.L.R. 210, disapproved in *The Nema* [1982] A.C. 724, but not on this point.
[16]   See, e.g. *Compania Naviera Aeolus SA v Union of India* [1964] A.C. 868.
[17]   [1991] 1 Lloyd's Rep. 81.

expressed if they are to have that effect. Unclear or ambiguous clauses will be ineffective for that purpose. This is an application of the ordinary rules of contractual construction governing such clauses. They must be clearly worded."

However, this distinction has subsequently been rejected. In *The Solon*,[18] Thomas J said: **13.13**

"When the question is whether a general exception clause applies to excuse performance of the relevant obligation during laytime or demurrage, the rule 'once on demurrage always on demurrage' is not relevant; it is the general principle that an ambiguous clause is no protection which applies. That is because the issue is whether the clause excuses the charterer from his obligations under the charter-party; during laytime there is the primary obligation to load the vessel within the laydays and after the expiry of the laydays, although the primary obligation to load continues, there is the secondary obligation to pay demurrage for breach of the obligation to load within the laydays. In both cases the question is whether the clause is sufficiently clear to excuse the charterer from performance of the relevant obligation."

He concluded that the relevant clause in the charterparty:

"... operated as an exceptions clause excusing what would otherwise be a breach and not as a clause that provided for an extension of time for performance."

One consequence of treating a force majeure clause as an exception clause is that any ambiguity will be resolved against the party seeking to rely on it.[19]   **13.14**

3. THE TRIGGERING EVENT

Where a force majeure clause is triggered by a specified event, an event falling within the literal words of the clause may be insufficient to trigger the clause, if it is an event that could not reasonably have been contemplated by the parties at the date of the contract. In such a case the contract may be held to have been frustrated.

In *Bailey v De Crespigny*,[20] Hannen J said: **13.15**

"There can be no doubt that a man may by an absolute contract bind himself to perform things which subsequently become impossible, or to pay damages for the non-performance, and this construction is to be put upon an unqualified undertaking, where the event which causes the impossibility was or might have been anticipated and guarded against in the contract, or where the impossibility arises from the act or default of the promissor.

But where the event is of such a character that it cannot reasonably be supposed to have been in the contemplation of the contracting parties when the contract was made, they will not be held bound by general words which, though large enough to include, were not used with reference to the possibility of the particular contingency which afterwards happens."

---

[18] [2000] 1 Lloyd's Rep. 292.
[19] *Great Elephant Corp v Trafigura Beheer BV* [2013] EWCA Civ 905.
[20] (1869) L.R. 4 Q.B. 180.

13.16   In *Metropolitan Water Board v Dick, Kerr & Co Ltd*,[21] building contractors agreed to construct a reservoir to be completed within six years, subject to a proviso that if by reason of (inter alia) any difficulties, impediments, or obstructions whatsoever and howsoever occasioned the contractors should, in the opinion of the engineer, have been unduly delayed or impeded in the completion of the contract it should be lawful for the engineer to grant an extension of the time for completion. The contract was made in July 1914. Two years later they were required to cease work by direction of the Ministry of Munitions under the Defence of the Realm Acts. It was argued that the Ministry's action fell within the scope of the clause and could be dealt with by an extension of time. The House of Lords held that the clause did not apply, with the consequence that the contract was frustrated. Lord Parmoor said:

> "This language is no doubt wide, and the general words may be large enough to include the contingency of legislative interference stopping the works or postponing their erection for an indefinite time. I think, however, that the language was used *alio intuitu*, and that it is not reasonable to hold that it had any reference to such a contingency, or that such a contingency was in the contemplation of the parties when framing the terms of the section. A mere extension of time at the discretion of the engineer is not in any sense an appropriate remedy for the contingency which has occurred. In my opinion neither party intended to leave the decision as to what should be done in such a contingency to the discretion of the engineer, under an ordinary extension of time clause in a works contract."

13.17   In *Fibrosa Spolka Akeyjna v Fairbairn Lawson Combe Barbour Ltd*,[22] parties entered into a contract in July 1939 for the supply of machinery to Poland. The contract stated that:

> "Should dispatch be hindered or delayed ... by any cause whatsoever beyond our reasonable control, including ... war ... a reasonable extension of time shall be granted."

War broke out in September 1939 and Poland was occupied by the Nazis. The House of Lords held that the clause did not cover that event. Viscount Simon said:

> "The appellants argued that there could be no frustration by reason of the war which broke out during the currency of the contract because this contingency was expressly provided for in clause 7, and, therefore, there was no room for an implied term such as has often been regarded as a suitable way in which to express and apply the doctrine of frustration. I entirely agree with the Court of Appeal that in the circumstances of the present case this is a bad point. The ambit of the express condition is limited to delay in respect of which 'a reasonable extension of time' might be granted. That might mean a minor delay as distinguished from a prolonged and indefinite interruption of prompt contractual performance which the present war manifestly and inevitably brings about."

13.18   In *Wong Lai Yin v Chinachem Investment Co Ltd*,[23] a contract for the building and subsequent sale of a building contained a force majeure clause specifying a number

---

[21]   [1918] A.C. 119; *Bank Line Ltd v Arthur Capel & Co* [1919] A.C. 435.
[22]   [1943] A.C. 32.
[23]   (1979) 13 Build L.R. 81.

of events which would give rise to an extension. Clause 22 of the contract provided that "should any unforeseen circumstances beyond the Vendor's control arise" then the vendor could terminate the contract. The building works were destroyed by a landslide part way through construction. The Privy Council held that cl.22 did not apply. Lord Scarman said:

"Clause 22 ... cannot be construed as making provision for the possibility of this particular unforeseen contingency. The clause, coming at the end of a contract, replete with specific provisions and time limits, was plainly intended to confer upon the vendor a remedy of rescission if a dispute arose or it became clear that he could not complete in accordance with the contract ... It does not follow from the provision of a summary remedy avoiding litigation in such circumstances that the parties must have agreed that their contract would continue after an unforeseen natural disaster having the consequences analysed and assessed by the judges below."

In *The Evia (No.2)*,[24] Robert Goff J said: **13.19**

"The Court has however to exercise care before concluding that a clause is intended to apply in circumstances which would, apart from the clause, have the effect of frustrating a contract. Obviously, there are contractual provisions which may be held to apply after frustration; but frustration presupposes the occurrence of an event which effects so radical a change in the contractual adventure that, on a true construction of the contract, it ceases to bind the parties. This being so, it is dangerous just to look at the clause and to consider whether on its literal meaning it applies in the event which has occurred."

In *The Playa Larga*,[25] the parties entered into a contract for the sale of Cuban   **13.20**
sugar. Before shipment began Cuba passed a law that made shipment illegal. The sellers argued that the contract had been frustrated; but the buyers countered by relying on a clause (r.120) in the contract which provided for an extension of time in the event of (among other things) "government intervention". Ackner LJ said:

"However, it is not enough to establish that the event relied upon as frustration comes within the clause, unless r. 120, properly construed, is intended to be a complete code. It is thus necessary not only to look at the event, but to look at the scope of the clause and the remedy which it purports to provide ... It contemplates a temporary interruption, which, after due notification to the buyer, is followed by extending the shipping period. Then, if the shipment is still prevented by the end of the extended period, it gives to the buyer the option of cancelling the contract. Rule 120 is not directed at events which strike at the contract as a whole and renders further performance by either party unthinkable."

Particular triggering events are not considered in this book.[26] A force majeure   **13.21**
clause often ends with a more general phrase such as "other events beyond the control" of the party. Whether such words are confined to events of the same kind

---

[24] [1981] 2 Lloyd's Rep. 613.
[25] [1983] 2 Lloyd's Rep. 171.
[26] Reference may be made to H. Beale, *Chitty on Contracts*, 33rd edn (London: Sweet & Maxwell, 2012), paras 15-159 and following.

as the specified triggering events depends on whether the *eiusdem generis* principle is applied. This principle is considered in para.7.130.

4.   EVENTS BEYOND CONTROL

A force majeure clause will usually be interpreted as applicable only where the specified triggering event is beyond the control of the party in question, and cannot be overcome. However, this principle may be excluded by the terms of the clause

13.22   In *Okta Crude Oil Refinery AD v Mamidoil-Jetoil Greek Petroleum Co SA*,[27] Aikens J said that:

> "... generally, force majeure clauses are concerned to excuse performance of contractual obligations in circumstances where the events giving rise to the failure to perform are outside the control of the contractual party wishing to rely on the clause and their effect could not have been avoided or mitigated by reasonable steps by the contracting party concerned. A particular clause could be broader than those general confines."

13.23   In *Bulman & Dickson v Fenwick & Co*,[28] a charterparty provided that a vessel, when loaded with coal, should proceed to one of certain named places on the Thames, as ordered, and there unload. Eighty-four running hours were allowed on each voyage for loading and discharging, and there was an exception of any delay caused by strikes. She was ordered to proceed to the Regent's Canal. She was prevented from unloading by a strike. Lord Esher MR said:

> "It is true that when the vessel arrived at the Regent's Canal there was a difficulty in taking delivery because of a strike of workmen; but a strike would in itself not be sufficient to exonerate the charterers from doing the best they could to accept delivery, and would not entitle them to fold their arms and do nothing. If, notwithstanding the strike, they could by reasonable exertion have taken delivery of the cargo within the proper time, the strike would not have afforded them any defence. But the jury have found that they could not, by any reasonable effort, have taken delivery. The delay, therefore, was caused entirely by the strike, and was within the exception in the charterparty."

13.24   This has been taken as a principle of interpretation of force majeure clauses, namely that the clause may only be relied on where the person relying on the clause has taken reasonable steps to avoid or overcome the contingency. Thus in *Hoecheong Products Co Ltd v Cargill Hong Kong Ltd*,[29] a contract for the sale of goods contained a force majeure clause entitling the seller to cancel the contract in certain events. Lord Mustill said:

> "The sellers would be required to show, first, that there had been an event of the kind stipulated by the clause operating at the relevant time; second, that this event had adversely affected the supply of the goods by the sellers; and third, that the sellers could not overcome this adverse effect by obtaining from a source other

---

[27]   [2003] 1 Lloyd's Rep. 1 at [53].
[28]   [1894] 1 Q.B. 179.
[29]   [1995] 1 W.L.R. 404.

than the one which they had planned goods which matched the requirements of the contract."

In *B & S Contracts and Design Ltd v Victor Green Publications Ltd*,[30] a contract **13.25** for the erection of stands at Olympia contained the following clause:

"Every effort will be made to carry out any contract based on an estimate, but the due performance of it is subject to variation or cancellation owing to an act of God, war, strikes, civil commotions, work to rule or go-slow or overtime bans, lock-out, fire, flood, drought or any other cause beyond our control, or owing to our inability to procure materials or articles except at increased prices due to any of the foregoing causes."

The contractor's workforce went on strike. The contractor could have settled the strike by paying the workforce what it had demanded. Griffiths LJ said:

"Clauses of this kind have to be construed upon the basis that those relying on them will have taken all reasonable efforts to avoid the effect of the various matters set out in the clause which entitle them to vary or cancel the contract: ... Quite apart from that general principle this particular clause starts with the following wording: 'Every effort will be made to carry out any contract based on an estimate,' which is saying in express terms that which the law will imply when construing such a clause."

Kerr LJ said:

"I think it convenient to begin by considering what the terms of the contract were, viz. whether or not the plaintiffs were entitled to rely on the force majeure clause and on the exception of strikes on the facts of this case. To rely upon a strike of one's own workforce is difficult for a party seeking to rely on an exception of strikes, but I entirely agree that it is perfectly possible if the circumstances justify such reliance. The cases cited in the books have generally been concerned with situations where a place of performance was strike-bound, particularly in the shipping cases referred to in Carver, Carriage by Sea, ... But in either case it is clear that where an exception of strikes is invoked, then like all other exceptions it is subject to the principle that the party seeking to rely on it must show that the strike and its consequences could not have been avoided by taking steps which were reasonable in the particular circumstances."

In *Sonat Offshore SA v Amerada Hess Development Ltd*,[31] a contract defined **13.26** "force majeure" by reference to a list of events followed by the phrase "other cause beyond the reasonable control of such party". Purchas LJ said:

"In the ordinary commercial sense I cannot accept the submission that the words 'other cause beyond the reasonable control of such party' can be construed disjunctively."

---

30   [1984] I.C.R. 419.
31   [1988] 1 Lloyd's Rep. 145.

In *Channel Island Ferries Ltd v Sealink UK Ltd*,[32] the parties entered into a joint venture agreement whereby Sealink were to provide to a new company two vessels on bareboat charter terms. They did not do so because the crews of the vessels took industrial action including sit-ins on the vessels. The contract contained a force majeure clause excusing performance in the event of:

"strikes … and any accident or incident of any nature beyond the control of the relevant party".

The Court of Appeal held that "a party must not only bring himself within the clause but must show that he has taken all reasonable steps to avoid its operation or mitigate its results".

13.27   Similarly, in *Okta Crude Oil Refinery AD v Mamidoil-Jetoil Greek Petroleum Co SA*,[33] a contract for the supply and handling of oil to and from a terminal in Macedonia contained a clause that said:

"Neither party shall be responsible for damage caused by delay or failure to perform in whole or in part the stipulations of the present Agreement, when such delay or failure is attributable to earthquakes, acts of God, strikes, riots, rebellion, hostilities, fire, flood, acts or compliance with requests of any governmental or EC authority, war conditions or other causes beyond the control of the party affected, whether or not similar to those enumerated."

Okta claimed the protection of the clause on the basis of a government request that they should not perform the contract. However, they had themselves asked the government to make that request. Longmore LJ said:

"The question is not whether the request of the governmental authority is *within* the control of Okta but, rather, whether it is *beyond* the control of Okta. For Okta to be able to rely on the clause they have to show that the failure to perform is attributable to a request, which was *beyond* Okta's control." (emphasis in original).

13.28   In *Frontier International Shipping Corp v Swissmarine Corp Inc*,[34] cl.9 of a charterparty said:

"In case of strikes, lockouts, civil commotions, or any other causes or accidents beyond the control of the consignee which prevent or delay the discharging, such time is not to count unless the vessel is already on demurrage."

Mr Nigel Teare QC (sitting as a judge of the Commercial Court) said:

"Clause 9 provides for both specified and unspecified events to interrupt the running of laytime. In my judgment, the natural construction of clause 9, which states that the 'consignee' is to pay demurrage, is that the words 'beyond the control of the consignee' apply not only to 'any other causes or accidents' but also to the specified events of strikes, lockouts and civil commotions. I have reached that conclusion essentially for two reasons. Firstly, by reason of the word 'other',

---

[32]   [1998] 1 Lloyd's Rep. 323.
[33]   [2003] 2 Lloyd's Rep. 635.
[34]   [2005] 1 Lloyd's Rep. 390.

the words 'beyond the control of the consignee' are capable of referring both to the specified events and to the unspecified causes. Secondly, it makes sense to exclude from the running of laytime events which are beyond the control of the consignee but does not make sense to exclude from laytime causes which are not beyond the control of the consignee. I accept that the words 'beyond the control of the consignee' are also capable, as a matter of language, of applying only to the unspecified causes but I do not consider that such a construction can have been the intention underlying clause 9. That is because there is sense in interrupting the running of laytime where a strike is beyond the control of the consignee but it is difficult to identify any reason for interrupting laytime where a strike is not beyond the control of the consignee."

This is not an invariable rule. It seems probable that the principle depends on an **13.29** interpretation of the clause that requires any triggering event to be beyond the control of the party relying on the clause. As the Singapore Court of Appeal put it in *Holcim (Singapore) Pte Ltd v Precise Development Pte Ltd*[35]:

"Whether the affected party must have taken all reasonable steps before he can rely on the force majeure clause depends, in the final analysis, on the precise language of the clause concerned. Nevertheless, it might well be the case that, at least where the clause in question relates to events that must be beyond the control of one or more of the parties, then the party or parties concerned ought to take reasonable steps to avoid the event or events stipulated in the clause. In such a situation (as is in fact the case in the present proceedings), there is, in our view, a persuasive case for requiring the affected party to take reasonable steps to avoid the effects of the event in question. The rationale for this approach is a simple and commonsensical one: to the extent that the party or parties concerned do not take reasonable steps to avoid the event or events in question, it cannot be said that the occurrence of the event or events was beyond the control of the party or parties concerned—in which case the clause would not apply."

In *Emeraldian Ltd Partnership v Wellmix Shipping Ltd*,[36] cl.5.10 of a charterparty **13.30** provided that:

"Time lost as a result of all or any of the causes hereunder shall not be computed as laytime, unless vessel is already on demurrage:

...

(iv)   Accident at the mines, railway or ports;

...

(viii) Partial or Total interruptions on railways or port;

...

(ix)   Any cause of whatsoever kind or nature, beyond the control of Seller, preventing cargo preparation, loading or berthing of the vessel."

Teare J said:

"Clause 5.10 lists a number of 'causes' in respect of which it is agreed that time

---

35 [2011] SGCA 1. See also *Goldlion Properties Ltd v Regent National Enterprises Ltd* [2009] HKCFA 58.
36 [2011] 1 Lloyd's Rep. 301.

lost as a result of them shall not be 'computed' as laytime. Sub-clauses (i)–(viii) specify several such causes or events. They do not contain within them a qualification that the listed causes must be 'beyond the control of Seller'. Sub-clause (ix) does contain that express qualification. There are no words which state expressly that that qualification is intended to apply to the causes listed in clauses (i)–(viii). It is therefore arguable that the phrase 'beyond the control of the Seller', having regard to its position within sub-clause (ix), is not capable of applying to the earlier sub-clauses … I consider that each of the sub-clauses should be given its ordinary meaning and that there is no good reason, in the absence of words manifesting an intention that the phrase 'beyond the control of the Sellers' in sub-clause (ix) should be extended to each of the other sub-clauses, to regard the phrase as extending to each of the other sub-clauses."

He held also that the clause in question was not strictly a force majeure clause, so that the principle of interpretation did not apply.

13.31   Where the triggering event arises because of one party's breach of contract that party is unlikely to be able to rely on a force majeure clause. In *Great Elephant Corp v Trafigura Beheer BV*,[37] a clause provided that:

"Neither the Seller nor the Buyer shall be held liable for failure or delay in performance of its obligations under this Contract, if such performance is delayed or hindered by the occurrence of an unforeseeable act or event which is beyond the reasonable control of either party ('force majeure')."

Longmore LJ said:

"… it would be absurd if Vitol could excuse themselves from the consequences of that breach by reference to the Force Majeure clause when it was their own breach of contract that caused the supposed force majeure in the first place. So to allow Vitol would be to allow them to take advantage of their own wrong."[38]

5.   EVENT CAUSED BY PARTY'S NEGLIGENCE

A force majeure clause will usually be interpreted as inapplicable if the triggering event has been caused by the contracting party's own negligence.

13.32   The courts interpret exemption clauses as not applying where a party seeks to rely on his own negligence, in the absence of clear words to the contrary.[39] Although a force majeure clause is not an exemption clause, similar principles of interpretation apply. In *The Super Servant Two*,[40] Bingham LJ said:

"The present clause is not, as the Judge accepted, an exceptions clause. It is not therefore directly covered by *Canada Steamship*. The clause is, however, one which confers on one party only a right exercisable in a very wide range of circumstances to nullify the contractual bargain made between the parties at no cost to itself and regardless of the loss which the other party may sustain. To such

---

[37] [2013] EWCA Civ 905; [2013] All E.R. (Comm) 992.
[38] This principle is considered in para.7.111.
[39] *Canada Steamship Lines Ltd v The King* [1952] A.C. 192.
[40] [1990] 1 Lloyd's Rep. 1.

a clause the broad approach indicated by *Canada Steamship* is in my judgment appropriate."

Although the clause in that case was wide enough to include events brought about by negligence, the general tenor of the clause was to the contrary; and it could be given a sensible application if it excluded events brought about by negligence.

6. PREVENTION OF PERFORMANCE

Where a clause excuses non-performance on the ground that performance has been prevented by a triggering event, it will usually apply only if performance has become legally or physically impossible, rather than uneconomic.

Many force majeure clauses excuse performance if it has been "prevented". In *Tennants (Lancashire) Ltd v CS Wilson & Co*,[41] Lord Finlay said that:

13.33

"'prevention' in such a clause must refer to physical or legal prevention and not an economical unprofitableness."

Lord Loreburn said:

"The argument that a man can be excused from performance of his contract when it becomes 'commercially' impossible ... seems to me a dangerous contention, which ought not to be admitted unless the parties have plainly contracted to that effect."

Likewise, in *Thames Valley Power Ltd v Total Gas & Power Ltd*,[42] Christopher Clarke J accepted the general proposition that:

13.34

"the fact that a contract has become expensive to perform, even dramatically more expensive, is not a ground to relieve a party on the grounds of force majeure or frustration."

Similarly, in *Tandrin Aviation Holdings Ltd v Aero Toy Store LLC*,[43] Hamblen J said:

"It is well established under English law that a change in economic/market circumstances, affecting the profitability of a contract or the ease with which the parties' obligations can be performed, is not regarded as being a force majeure event."

Where a clause applied in case of a prohibition "restricting export" it was held that the clause would only operate if "the prohibition does in fact restrict export of goods of the contractual description during the contractual shipment period. A causal connection has to be proven".[44] It is more natural to construe the clause as

13.35

---

[41] [1917] A.C. 495 (a dissenting speech).
[42] [2006] 1 Lloyd's Rep. 441.
[43] [2010] 2 Lloyd's Rep. 668.
[44] *Bunge SA v Nidera BV* [2013] EWHC 84 (Comm); [2013] 1 Lloyd's Rep. 621. It is not thought that this statement is affected by the subsequent appeal to the Supreme Court on a different point: *Bunge SA v Nidera BV* [2015] UKSC 43.

"describing the practical effect on the seller's ability to perform the contract".[45] If a party's own breach of contract has caused the event relied on as force majeure, he will not be entitled to rely on the clause as excusing performance.[46]

7.   HINDRANCE OR DELAY

A force majeure clause may refer to hindrance of or delay in performance; in which case it may apply even though performance is not impossible.

13.36   The contract in *Tennants (Lancashire) Ltd v CS Wilson & Co*[47] was one for the supply of chemicals over the year 1914. The contract said that "deliveries may be suspended pending any contingencies beyond the control of the sellers or buyers (such as ... war ...) causing a short supply of labour, fuel, raw material, or manufactured produce, or otherwise preventing or hindering the manufacture or delivery of the article". The outbreak of war put an end to any source of supply in Germany, and caused a substantial shortage, with a consequent rise in price. The sellers immediately gave notice suspending delivery to their buyers. Between August and the end of the year the sellers were able at an increased price to obtain enough magnesium chloride to satisfy the buyer's contract, if they disregarded their other contracts and the normal requirements of their business, but not enough to satisfy all their contracts. Lord Loreburn said:

"By 'hindering' delivery is meant interposing obstacles which it would be really difficult to overcome. I do not consider that even a great rise of price hinders delivery. If that had been intended different language would have been used, and I cannot regard shortage of cash or inability to buy at a remunerative price as a contingency beyond the sellers' control."

On the facts however, he concluded:

"To place a merchant in the position of being unable to deliver unless he dislocates his business and breaks his other contracts in order to fulfil one surely hinders delivery."

Lord Atkinson said:

"'Preventing delivery' means, in my view, rendering delivery impossible; and 'hindering' delivery means something less than this, namely, rendering delivery more or less difficult, but not impossible."

45 *Bunge SA v Nidera BV* [2013] EWCA Civ 1628; [2014] 1 Lloyd's Rep. 404 affirming [2013] EWHC 84 (Comm); [2013] 1 Lloyd's Rep. 621 It is not thought that this statement is affected by the subsequent appeal to the Supreme Court on a different point: *Bunge SA v Nidera BV* [2015] UKSC 43.
46 *Great Elephant Corp v Trafigura Beheer BV* [2013] EWCA Civ 905; [2013] All E.R. (Comm) 992.
47 [1917] A.C. 495.

8. CAUSATION

A force majeure clause will usually be interpreted to apply only where the triggering event is the cause of the failure to perform.

The need for a causal connection is common in cases of this kind.[48] In this respect **13.37** a force majeure clause differs from what has been called a contractual frustration clause which does no more than cancel future performance of the contract on the happening of a specified event.[49]

In *Bunten & Lancaster Ltd v Wilts Quality Products (London) Ltd*,[50] a contract **13.38** for the sale of nuts stated that the seller had the right to cancel the contract "in the event of their seller, failing to ship or deliver on account of ... failure of crops". Owing to a poor crop the price of nuts rose. McNair J held that the clause was not engaged. First he held that there was no "failure of crops" on the facts. Second he said that:

"I therefore am quite unable to infer that the sellers' reason for failing to deliver was failure of crop, or force majeure, or any matter of that kind. If I had to make a finding upon the matter, I would say the reasonable inference is that he failed to deliver because he was not prepared to pay the proper market price for the commodity at such time as would enable him to make proper delivery under this contract."

In *Avimex SA v Dewulf & Cie*,[51] Robert Goff J said:

"It follows that the sellers are unable to establish that the force majeure event on which they rely occasioned 'delay in shipment of the goods'; and for this reason they are unable to rely upon the force majeure notices to the buyers, quoted in pars 9 and 10 of the award."

In *Bremer Handelsgesellschaft mbH v Westzucker GmbH (No.2)*,[52] Donaldson LJ said:

"If shippers or other sellers wish to take the benefit of the clause, they must still prove that the embargo would have prevented fulfilment of the contract on the assumption that they would otherwise have been in a position to fulfil it."

In *The Radauti*,[53] Staughton J said:

"I would suggest it is more a question of causation, whether the incidence of a particular peril which could have been foreseen can really be said to have caused one party's failure of performance."

---

[48] *Bunge SA v Nidera BV* [2013] EWHC 84 (Comm); [2013] 1 Lloyd's Rep. 621; affirmed [2013] EWCA Civ 1628; [2014] 1 Lloyd's Rep. 404; *Public Co Rise v Nibulon SA* [2015] EWHC 684 (Comm).
[49] See the discussion in *Classic Maritime Inc v Limbungan Makmur SDN BHD* [2019] EWCA Civ 1102; [2019] 4 All E.R. 1145.
[50] [1951] 2 Lloyd's Rep. 30.
[51] [1979] 2 Lloyd's Rep. 57.
[52] [1981] 2 Lloyd's Rep. 130.
[53] [1987] 2 Lloyd's Rep. 276.

13.39   In *Pancommerce SA v Veechema BV*,[54] the Court of Appeal rejected the argument that "the new prohibition clause is designed to make it unnecessary to enquire whether the governmental restriction in fact had any effect upon the sellers' ability to deliver".

In *Agrokor AG v Tradigrain SA*,[55] cl.20 of the contract was a force majeure clause entitling the sellers to cancel the contract to the extent that government prohibition of export prevented fulfilment of the contract. Longmore J said:

> "(a) that it is for the sellers to prove that they are entitled to rely on cl. 20 or equivalent; and (b) that, in order to do so, the sellers must show not merely that there was a ban which restricted the export of wheat, but also that the ban had the effect of restricting the performance of the actual contracts with Tradigrain."

13.40   In *Seadrill Ghana Operations Ltd v Tullow Ghana Ltd*,[56] Teare J held that the triggering event must be the sole cause of the failure to perform. He said that the decision of the Court of Appeal in *Intertradex SA v Lesieur-Tourteaux SARL*[57]:

> "is regarded as one which establishes the proposition that a force majeure event must be sole cause of the failure to perform an obligation ... Ultimately, however, ... the question is one of construction of the contract before the court."

Accordingly, it must normally be shown that "but for" the force majeure event, the party in default would have performed its obligation.[58]

13.41   A contractual frustration clause is different. In *Bremer Handelgesellschaft v Vanden Avenne-Izegem PVBA*,[59] Lord Wilberforce said:

> "The clause applies 'in case of prohibition of export ... preventing fulfilment'—so that a question may arise of causation. Was it the prohibition that prevented fulfilment or something else? This question may be phrased more specifically by asking whether the seller must prove that he had the goods ready to ship within the contract period, and a ship to carry them. The answer to it, in my clear opinion, is in the negative. The occurrence of a 'frustrating' event—in this case the prohibition of export—immediately and automatically cancels the contract, or the portion of it affected by the prohibition."

13.42   In *Classic Maritime Inc v Limbungan Makmur SDN BHD*,[60] Males LJ explained the reason for the distinction:

> "It seems to me that where the effect of a clause is to discharge the parties from an obligation to perform in the future, as distinct from to relieve them from liability to pay damages for a past breach, that may well have at least a bearing on the nature of the causative effect on a party's performance which an event is required to have. In such a case, both parties need to know at once when the event

---

[54]   [1983] 2 Lloyd's Rep. 304.
[55]   [2000] 1 Lloyd's Rep. 497.
[56]   [2018] EWHC 1640 (Comm); [2019] 1 All E.R. (Comm) 34.
[57]   [1978] 2 Lloyd's Rep. 509.
[58]   *Classic Maritime Inc v Limbungan Makmur Sdn Bhd* [2018] EWHC 2389 (Comm); [2018] Bus. L.R. 2471. This decision was affirmed by the CA; [2019] EWCA Civ 1102; [2019] 4 All E.R. 1145.
[59]   [1978] 2 Lloyd's Rep. 109.
[60]   [2019] EWCA Civ 1102; [2019] 4 All E.R. 1145.

occurs whether they are under any continuing obligation. There is, therefore, much to be said for a simple and straightforward causation requirement (an embargo which makes it impossible for any goods to be shipped) without requiring investigation of matters known only to one party, such as whether it was able and willing to perform if the event had not occurred. Such a consideration has much less force after the event, when the time for performance is over and the only question is whether a party is liable to pay damages. Although none of this is spelled out in Lord Wilberforce's speech, it provides in my judgment a compelling justification for understanding his reasoning ... ."

9. ALTERNATIVE METHODS OF PERFORMANCE

A force majeure clause will usually be interpreted as being inapplicable where alternative methods of performance still exist.

In *Ross T Smyth & Co Ltd v WN Lindsay Ltd*,[61] a parcel of 500 tons of Sicilian horse beans was sold for shipment from a Sicilian port or ports as per bill or bills of lading to be dated October and/or November 1951. The contract provided that: **13.43**

"should the fulfilment of this contract be rendered impossible by prohibition of export ... any unfulfilled part thereof to be cancelled."

At the date of the contract the export of horse beans was permitted, but by a subsequent Italian regulation export was only allowed under specific licence from 1 November 1951. The sellers claimed to rely on the clause. Devlin J said:

"It appears to me that if a party is going to rely on a prohibition of export or frustration, whichever it is, he has to show that it covers the whole contract period. If the prohibition covers only a part of the period which the contract gives for shipment then performance of the contract is not rendered impossible for the seller, it is merely rendered more difficult for him. Instead of having the full rights which the contract apparently gives him—two months in which to select a date—he has to select a date within a more limited period, but that is not rendering performance impossible. The position is exactly the same under a contract of this sort, where there is liberty to ship on any date during a given period, as it would be in a contract which offers to one party an option of doing a thing in two or more ways, let us say, to pay in gold in New York or in sterling in London. If after the contract it becomes illegal for him to pay in gold in New York he is not thereby relieved altogether from his obligation, he is merely deprived of his option. He has to pay in sterling in London. He cannot elect to tender gold in New York and then say: 'That is the way I chose to perform the contract, and as I cannot perform it in that way I am excused from performance altogether.'"

Similarly, in *Warinco AG v Fritz Mauthner*,[62] Megaw LJ said: **13.44**

---

[61] [1953] 1 W.L.R. 1280.
[62] [1978] 1 Lloyd's Rep. 151; *Exportelisa SA v Rocco Guiseppe & Figli* [1978] 1 Lloyd's Rep. 433. The position may be different when the seller in a string has already made arrangements to ship the goods, by himself or by some shipper higher up in the string: *Tradax Export SA v Andre & Cie SA* [1976] 1 Lloyd's Rep. 416.

"It is, in general, no answer for the seller merely to say, and to prove, that he had intended, and had made arrangements, to perform the contract in a particular way or at a particular time, and that he could no longer, as a result of the event, carry it out in that way or at that time. In order to escape being in default, he has also, in general, to show, at least, that he could not have carried out the contract, in compliance with its terms, in some other way or at some other time within the contract period. The same applies where the contract gives him a number of ports from which the goods may be shipped, but he is obliged to supply goods shipped from one or the other of them."

10. NOTICE PROVISIONS

Where a force majeure clause requires the party relying on it to give notice to the other, it is a question of interpretation of the clause whether a failure to give notice in accordance with the clause precludes reliance on it.

13.45   Some force majeure clauses require the party who wishes to rely on the clause to give notice to the other party (often within a contractual time scale). The giving of such notice in time may be a condition precedent to that party's ability to rely on the clause. If so, then failure to comply with the condition precedent will preclude reliance on the clause. Whether such a contractual stipulation is a condition precedent which must be strictly fulfilled, or is no more than an intermediate term, is a question of interpretation in each case.

In *Tradax Export SA v Andre & Cie SA*,[63] Lord Denning MR said:

"These notices are conditions. The seller must satisfy them in order to get the benefit of the clauses. They are not merely exhortatory: nor is the remedy only in damages."

13.46   However, this has proved too dogmatic a view. In *Bremer Handelgesellschaft v Vanden Avenne-Izegem PVBA*,[64] the contract contained a prohibition of export clause which stated:

"In the event of shipment proving impossible during the contract period by reason of any of the causes enumerated herein, sellers shall advise buyers of the reasons therefor."

Lord Wilberforce said:

"Whether this clause is a condition precedent or a contractual term of some other character must depend on (i) the form of the clause itself, (ii) the relation of the clause to the contract as a whole, (iii) general considerations of law."

The clause in question was not a condition but was an intermediate term. One reason was that no definite time limits were prescribed. However, another clause in the same contract, which prescribed definite time limits for the giving of notice of triggering events, was said to be:

---

[63]   [1976] 1 Lloyd's Rep. 416.
[64]   [1978] 2 Lloyd's Rep. 109.

"a complete regulatory code in the matter of force majeure, and that accurate compliance with its stipulation is essential to avoid commercial confusion in view of the possibility of there being long strings of buyers and sellers."

The fact that a clause requiring notice to be given contains no fixed time limit does not necessarily preclude compliance with the clause from being a condition precedent. In *Mamidoil-Jetoil Greek Petroleum Co SA v Okta Crude Oil Refinery*,[65] the force majeure clause said that the party invoking the clause "shall give prompt notice" to the other party. Aikens J said: **13.47**

"The form of the notice provision is imperative: a party 'invoking force majeure shall give prompt notice to the other party'. The implication behind that imperative is that, if the party does not, then it cannot rely on force majeure. The reason for requiring notice to be given must be that the 'other party' can then investigate the alleged force majeure at the time. It can challenge whether it does prevent performance or delay in performance by the party invoking force majeure. Alternatively it can see if there are other means of enabling performance to be continued. Lastly, if the notice provision is only an innominate term, then I find it difficult to see when the innocent party could allege it had suffered additional damage as a result of not being told promptly of the force majeure event other than the very damages that it would wish to receive for the first party's failure to perform the contract at all. These factors would all lead me to conclude that the parties intended the notice provision to be a condition precedent."

It has been suggested that if notice provisions are conditions of the contract, the condition need not be complied with where it would be futile, useless and unnecessary to do so.[66] But there is no general principle that a condition precedent need not be complied with if it is futile to do so. Whether a contractual obligation has arisen in any given case in principle depends on what the particular contract says, interpreted in accordance with the ordinary principles of contract interpretation. There is no principle of law or even interpretive presumption which enables a contractual precondition to the accrual of a right or obligation to be disapplied just because complying with it is considered by the court to serve no useful purpose. However, there may be circumstances in which (depending on the terms of the contract) a condition precedent may, as a matter of construction and in the light of subsequent events, no longer apply or may cease to have effect.[67] **13.48**

In *Great Elephant Corp v Trafigura Beheer BV*,[68] the contract contained a force majeure clause. Clause 21 said: **13.49**

"immediately on the occurrence of force majeure ... promptly notify the other party in writing stating the details of the event or act constituting force majeure and stating also the measure being adopted by it to minimise or to remedy the consequences of the force majeure on the performance of this contract."

---

[65] [2003] 1 Lloyd's Rep. 1.
[66] *Barrett Bros (Taxis) Ltd v Davies* [1966] 1 W.L.R. 1334; *The Mozart* [1985] 1 Lloyd's Rep. 239; *Mansel Oil Ltd v Troon Storage Tankers SA* [2008] 2 Lloyd's Rep. 384 (affirmed on appeal: [2009] EWCA Civ 425).
[67] *Astor Management AG v Atalaya Mining Plc* [2018] EWCA Civ 2407; [2019] Bus. L.R. 106.
[68] [2012] EWHC 1745 (Comm); [2012] 2 Lloyd's Rep. 503 (unaffected by reversal of the decision by the Court of Appeal on different grounds: [2013] EWCA Civ 905; [2013] All E.R. (Comm) 992).

Teare J held that this was not a condition precedent to the right to rely on force majeure. He said:

"i)   The clause is not framed as a condition precedent.

ii)   The requirement is not for notice within a clear and specified number of days but notice which is immediate and prompt. What is immediate and prompt will depend upon factual context. Here, the notice requires not only the 'details' of the event but also the 'measures' being adopted to minimise the consequences of the event. Both of these requirements suggest that some delay in giving notice must be permitted. Thus identifying when a notice is not immediate or prompt may be difficult. This is not the context in which the parties are likely to have intended that failure to provide immediate or prompt notice would debar a party from relying upon a force majeure event.

iii)   Where a specific sanction is intended the parties tend to say so expressly."

11.   EXCLUSION OF FRUSTRATION

Where a force majeure clause deals fully and completely with an event that would otherwise frustrate the contract, the doctrine of frustration will generally be excluded.

13.50   The inter-relationship between a force majeure clause and the doctrine of frustration under the general law is difficult to summarise.

In *Select Commodities Ltd v Valdo SA*,[69] Tomlinson J said:

"These authorities demonstrate that where the parties have included in their contract a clause which is intended to and does deal fully and completely with the effects of an event which would otherwise, absent the clause, frustrate the contract, the doctrine of frustration is inapplicable to the effects of that event if it occurs. Put another way, an event for the effects of which full and complete provision is made in the contract cannot, by definition, effect so radical a change in the contractual adventure that, on a true construction of the contract, it ceases to bind the parties."

13.51   This formulation, while correct, does not answer the question when full and complete provision will be held to have been made. As has been seen, where an event falls within the literal words of a force majeure clause, the courts have held that the clause is inapplicable where the event in question could not have been contemplated by the parties. But even where it could have been foreseen (and sometimes when it has) the doctrine of frustration is not necessarily excluded. As Rix LJ explained in *Edwinton Commercial Corp v Tsavliris Russ (Worldwide Salvage & Towage) Ltd*[70]:

"In my judgment, the application of the doctrine of frustration requires a multifactorial approach. Among the factors which have to be considered are the terms of the contract itself, its matrix or context, the parties' knowledge, expectations, assumptions and contemplations, in particular as to risk, as at the time of contract, at any rate so far as these can be ascribed mutually and objectively, and

---

[69]   [2007] 1 Lloyd's Rep. 1.
[70]   [2007] 2 Lloyd's Rep. 517.

then the nature of the supervening event, and the parties' reasonable and objectively ascertainable calculations as to the possibilities of future performance in the new circumstances. Since the subject matter of the doctrine of frustration is contract, and contracts are about the allocation of risk, and since the allocation and assumption of risk is not simply a matter of express or implied provision but may also depend on less easily defined matters such as 'the contemplation of the parties', the application of the doctrine can often be a difficult one."

CHAPTER 14

CERTIFICATES, CONSENTS AND DEEMING CLAUSES

For now I am in holiday humour and like enough to consent

William Shakespeare: *As You Like It*

1.   CERTIFICATES

Where a contract provides for some matter to be determined by a certificate, the court will not treat the clause as an exemption clause, and will not, therefore, construe it strictly.

Contracts, particularly contracts for the sale of goods and building contracts, often provide for certain matters to be determined by a certificate. The word "certificate" has no standard meaning and that the question what constitutes a certificate is dependent on the commercial or legal context in which the certification clause appears.[1]   **14.01**

In *Fairfield Sentry Ltd v Migani*,[2] Lord Sumption said: **14.02**

"As a matter of language, a 'certificate' ordinarily means (i) a statement in writing, (ii) issued by an authoritative source, which (iii) is communicated by whatever method to a recipient or class of recipients intended to rely on it, and (iv) conveys information, (v) in a form or context which shows that it is intended to be definitive. There is no reason to think that a document must satisfy any further formal requirements, unless its purpose or legal context plainly requires them."

In *London and Regional (St George's Court) Ltd v Ministry of Defence*,[3] Coulson J said: **14.03**

"Under most standard forms of construction and engineering contracts, certification regimes are commonplace. The contract will spell out the particular issue that the certifier is required to decide; what information is to be provided to the certifier to allow him to reach that decision, and when it must be provided; and the circumstances in which the certifier will then decide, on the basis of the information provided by both sides, the answer to the issue before him. The certificate is the final step in a process designed to ensure fairness, with the mechanism spelled out carefully in the contract itself. Moreover, where the certificate is anything other than an interim or provisional statement of the position—if it is

---

[1]   *Fairfield Sentry Ltd v Migani* [2014] UKPC 9.
[2]   [2014] UKPC 9.
[3]   (2008) 121 Con. L.R. 26 at [59].

intended to be final, and oust the jurisdiction of the courts or an arbitrator to review it—then that must be made plain in the clearest possible terms."

His decision was upheld by the Court of Appeal.

In *Costain International Ltd v Attorney-General*,[4] Huggins VP said:

"As I understand it, a certificate is basically a document which speaks to the truth of some existing fact. Often the fact will be that a person other than the certifier has done something, but it may equally well be that the certifier himself has done something or has come to some opinion."

14.04 The general purpose of a clause which so provides is to avoid disputes. Accordingly, the certificate will frequently be held to be conclusive as to any matter of fact which it certifies. It therefore prevents one party from contesting that which is certified, even if the certificate is erroneous. It is this consideration which has on occasion led the court to treat a certification clause as if it were an exemption clause and to construe it strictly. Thus in *Kollerich & Cie SA v State Trading Corp of India*,[5] a contract for the sale of cement provided for its packing to be certified by a named organisation. Parker J said:

"The clause is one which is, as to the certificate, an exemptions clause and must therefore be narrowly construed."

14.05 However, such a clause differs from an exemption clause, as Cairns LJ pointed out in *Toepfer v Continental Grain Co*[6]:

"I see no grounds for saying that a provision of this kind should be construed with some special degree of strictness. It is not like an exception[7] clause which is designed to operate to give protection to one party. Either buyer or seller benefit from this clause if some error of judgment on the part of the inspector led him to certify a quality in the goods different from their actual quality."

14.06 It is considered that the view of Cairns LJ is the better view, and that certification clauses should not be treated with any special strictness. However, the court may adopt a stricter approach where the clause seeks to prevent one party to a dispute arising under the contract from adducing evidence which would otherwise be admissible.[8] The two different views were referred to (without discussion) by Lloyd J in *The Bow Cedar*.[9]

2. QUALITY OF PERFORMANCE

Where a contract provides for the quality of performance to be certified, it is a question of interpretation of the particular contract whether the issue of the certificate discharges the contractual obligation to perform or is an added protection for the other party.

14.07 Many contracts contain provisions which require the issue of a certificate in con-

---

[4]   (1983) 23 B.L.R. 54 HKCA.
[5]   [1979] 2 Lloyd's Rep. 442 (affirmed [1980] 2 Lloyd's Rep. 32).
[6]   [1974] 1 Lloyd's Rep. 11.
[7]   The report reads "exceptional" but this is presumably a mistake.
[8]   *Lindsay (WN) & Co Ltd v European Grain & Shipping Agency Ltd* [1963] 1 Lloyd's Rep. 487. See para.12.151.
[9]   [1980] 2 Lloyd's Rep. 601.

nection with the quality of performance. For example, a contract for the carriage of goods by sea may require the quality of the goods to be certified upon loading; or a building contract may require an architect to certify that the work has been carried out in a particular manner or to a certain value. Frequently such a contract will contain other provisions dealing with the quality of performance. For example, the goods may be sold by description, or the building works may be required to be carried out in accordance with a particular specification. In such cases the question arises whether those primary obligations remain in being and enforceable despite the issue of the certificate contemplated by the contract.

The distinction was drawn by Devlin J in *Minster Trust Ltd v Traps Tractors* **14.08**
Ltd[10]:

> "If work under a contract is to be completed to the satisfaction of a certifier, it may mean that his duty is merely to see that the requirements of the contract are met, or it may mean that he is entitled to impose a standard of his own. It may be that his standard is that to which the parties submit and that it constitutes the only provision in the contract about quality; or it may be that his standard is an added protection, so that performance under the contract must satisfy both the contract requirement and the certifier."

He drew a further distinction between different types of certificate:

> "… There is a distinction between a certificate that is given only for the purposes of a particular contract and one that, although it may be called for by a particular contract, is not related to that contract. The certifier may not then be an agent of either party. That is so in the case of a Lloyd's certificate or of a certificate by a public analyst, or others that may be obtainable on a fee. It has now become quite common to include among documents which have to be tendered against payment a certificate of inspection or of quality. Certificates of this sort are addressed to all the world or to all who may be concerned. If the phrase is not used as more than a label, they might be called certificates in rem, as compared with certificates in personam, which deal only with particular contracts as are addressed only to particular parties. The former carry the same meaning to all who read them. The latter may have to be interpreted in the light of particular contractual requirements or information known only to the addressees. A certificate in rem certifies a standard of quality extraneous to the contract. It may be the certifier's own standard or it may be taken from some public or independent source. A certificate in personam may be based on the certifier's own standards or on standards prescribed by the contract. It may be a certificate of quality or a certificate that the contract has been carried out."

In the case of a "certificate in rem" the court is more likely to hold that the issue **14.09**
of the certificate discharges the obligations as respects performance. As Diplock LJ observed in *Lindsay (WN) & Co Ltd v European Grain & Shipping Co Ltd*[11]:

> "Translated into the language of the Sale of Goods Act 1893 [such a contract is] a contract for the sale of goods by description, but the relevant description was 'goods which the specified person will certify as corresponding with the description stated in the contract'."

---

[10]   [1954] 1 W.L.R. 963.
[11]   [1963] 1 Lloyd's Rep. 437.

14.10   In other words, the contract is interpreted as one in which the parties have agreed that their obligations are to be whatever the certifier determines them to be.[12] In *VTC v PVS*,[13] a charterparty contained a warranty by the owner that the vessel would arrive at all ports with cargo tanks, pumps and lines "suitable to load the intended cargo as per Charters' representative and/or independent surveyor's satisfaction". Hamblen J held that whether there was a breach of warranty depended on whether the surveyor was or was not satisfied, rather than on whether the cargo tanks etc were in fact suitable to load the intended cargo.

14.11   In the case of the "certificate in personam" it is easier for the court to hold that the certificate is merely an added protection. So in *Newton Abbott Development Co Ltd v Stockman Bros*,[14] a builder agreed to build houses in accordance with plans and specifications and to carry out the work to the satisfaction of the surveyor and sanitary inspector of the local authority. The surveyor and sanitary inspector gave certificates of approval. It was held that the issue of the certificates did not absolve the builder from his primary obligations as respects the quality of the work, but merely gave the employer superadded protection. Although for some time it seemed that the court was more likely to hold that the mere issue of a certificate did not discharge the primary obligations to perform the contract, it seems that nowadays the court is more likely to hold[15] that where performance requires to be certified, the contract should be interpreted as meaning that the obligations are whatever the certifier decides them to be.[16]

Illustrations

1.   A contract for the supply of iron rails provided that the rails should be equal in quality to any made in Staffordshire, and also provided that the rails should be inspected and certified by the parties on delivery. It was held that, notwithstanding inspection and certification, the seller was still required to comply with the express term as to quality.
   Bird v Smith[17]

2.   A policy of marine insurance on cattle contained a provision that the fittings on the ship were to be approved by a Lloyd's surveyor. The fittings were so approved, but it turned out during the voyage that they were inadequate. The policy contained an implied warranty that the ship was seaworthy. It was held that the implied warranty was not excluded by the stipulation as to approval by a Lloyd's surveyor, and that the primary obligation remained enforceable.
   Sleigh v Tyser[18]

3.   A charterparty contained a clause which provided "Steamer to clean for the

---

[12]   *Beaufort Developments (NI) Ltd v Gilbert-Ash (NI) Ltd* [1999] A.C. 266.
[13]   [2012] EWHC 1100 (Comm); [2012] 2 Lloyd's Rep. 527.
[14]   (1931) 47 T.L.R. 616. See also *Billyack v Leyland Construction Co Ltd* [1968] 1 W.L.R. 471 (para.12.47, Illustration 2).
[15]   But not always: see *Universities Superannuation Scheme Ltd v Marks & Spencer Plc* [1999] 1 E.G.L.R. 13.
[16]   For example, *Beaufort Developments (NI) Ltd v Gilbert-Ash (NI) Ltd* [1999] A.C. 266; *Jones v Sherwood Computer Services* [1992] 1 W.L.R. 277 CA; *Norwich Union Life Assurance Society v P & O Property Holdings Ltd* [1993] 1 E.G.L.R. 164 CA; *Mercury Communications Ltd v Director General of Telecommunications* [1996] 1 W.L.R. 48 HL.
[17]   (1848) 12 Q.B. 786.
[18]   [1900] 2 Q.B. 333.

cargo in question to the satisfaction of the charterer's inspector". The charterparty also contained an express warranty of seaworthiness, and a stipulation requiring the captain to keep the tanks clean. It was held that the expression of satisfaction by the charterer's inspector did not absolve the owners from compliance with the express warranty of seaworthiness and the requirement to keep the tanks clean.

Petrofina SA of Brussels v Compagnia Italiana Trasporto alii Minerali of Genoa[19]

4.   A building contract required the manufacture of plant to be in accordance with an identified specification and to the reasonable satisfaction of the engineer. The engineer issued a certificate, but did not notice certain hidden defects. It was held that the fact that the engineer was satisfied did not discharge the contractor's primary obligation to build in accordance with the specification.

National Coal Board v Neil (William) & Son (St Helens) Ltd[20]

5.   A building contract provided that in the event of the progress of the works being in the opinion of the architect unsatisfactory, then upon the recommendation of the architect the employer might determine the contract. It was held that the criterion was for the opinion of the particular architect as to what was or was not satisfactory and not an objective criterion.

Loke Hong Kee (8) Pte Ltd v United Overseas Land Ltd[21]

6.   A building contract provided that where and to the extent that approval of the quality of materials or standards of workmanship was a matter for the opinion of the architect, such quality and standards should be to the reasonable satisfaction of the architect. It was held all questions of quality and workmanship were for the opinion of the architect, and that his final certificate prevented any complaint of defects being made.

Crown Estate Commissioners v John Mowlem & Co Ltd[22]

3.   OBLIGATIONS TO BE DETERMINED BY THIRD PARTY

A contract may provide that the parties' obligations are whatever a third party (often an expert) decides they are. In such a case the court's opinion on the true interpretation of the contract is irrelevant.

In *Beaufort Developments (NI) Ltd v Gilbert-Ash (NI) Ltd*,[23] Lord Hoffmann said: **14.12**

"The powers of the architect or arbitrator, whatever they may be, are conferred by the contract. It seems to me more accurate to say that the parties have agreed that their contractual obligations are to be whatever the architect or arbitrator interprets them to be. In such a case, the opinion of the court or anyone else as to what the contract requires is simply irrelevant. To enforce such an interpretation of the contract would be something different from what the parties had agreed. Provisions of this kind are common in contracts for the sale of property at a valuation or goods which comply with a specified description. The contract

---

19   (1937) 53 Lloyd's Rep. 650.
20   [1985] Q.B. 300.
21   (1982) 23 B.L.R. 35 PC.
22   (1994) 70 B.L.R. 1 CA.
23   [1999] 1 A.C. 266 at 273.

may say that the value of the property or the question of whether the goods comply with the description shall be determined by a named person as an expert. In such a case, the agreement is to sell at what the expert considers to be the value or to buy goods which the expert considers to be in accordance with the description. The court's view on these questions is irrelevant."

14.13   It is this principle which underpins the general rule that in the absence of fraud or collusion the parties are bound by an expert's determination, provided that he answers the right question.[24]

14.14   Thus, where a contract provided for the payment of 55 per cent of the open market value of certain shares "as determined by an independent chartered accountant", it was held that the determination of the value by the accountant was essential to the determination of the contractual entitlement. One of the factors which led the court to that conclusion was that there are many ways of valuing shares, and which method to adopt would be a matter of judgment for the independent accountant.[25] In other words the court's view of how the shares should be valued was irrelevant.

14.15   As a matter of interpretation of the contract, if it provides for payment only of an amount certified by a third party, then a determination by the third party is a condition precedent to the obligation to pay.[26] Where, however, ascertainment of a price or value by the contractually prescribed method is inessential to the substance of the contract and an objective criterion can be identified,[27] the court will provide its own machinery if the contractual machinery breaks down,[28] at least where the reason for the breakdown is not the default of the party seeking the alternative machinery.[29]

4.   OBLIGATIONS TO BE DECIDED BY ONE PARTY TO THE CONTRACT

A contract may provide for one party to the contract himself to decide some issue which arises under the contract, whether it is a question of interpretation or a matter of mixed fact and law. However, if the contract does not expressly provide for the possibility of intervention by the court if the decision-making party has acted unreasonably, perversely or in bad faith, a term to that effect is likely to be implied.

14.16   In *Re Brown v GIO Insurance Ltd*,[30] Chadwick LJ said:

"... I can see no objection in principle to a bargain in which one party is left to decide (i) what the facts are in relation to some matter which is to arise in the future and which is plainly intended to have some contractual consequence under a provision of the contract which they have made and (ii) whether or not that combination of facts does fall within that provision. The jurisdiction of the court is not ousted in those circumstances; provided that the agreement which the par-

---

[24]   See paras 14.47 and 18.34.
[25]   *Gillat v Sky Television Ltd* [2001] All E.R. (Comm) 461 CA.
[26]   *Sharpe v San Paulo Railway Co* (1873) L.R. 8 Ch. App. 597.
[27]   *BJ Aviation Ltd v Pool Aviation Ltd* [2002] 2 P. & C.R. 25.
[28]   *Sudbrooke Trading Estate Ltd v Eggleton* [1983] 1 A.C. 444.
[29]   *Infiniteland Ltd v Artisan Contracting Ltd* [2006] 1 B.C.L.C. 632.
[30]   [1998] C.L.C. 650. See also *The Glacier Bay* [1996] 1 Lloyd's Rep. 370; *Bradbury v British Broadcasting Corp* [2015] EWHC 1368 (Ch).

ties have reached on that matter allows the court to interfere if the decision-making party has acted unreasonably, perversely or in bad faith. It seems to me that the court will be ready (in the absence of express words to the contrary), to construe the contract, if necessary by implying an appropriate term, so as to impose on the decision-making party an obligation to act reasonably and in good faith."

So where a mortgage provided for the payment of interest at a rate determined by the lender, the Court of Appeal held that it was an implied term of the mortgage that the lender would not set the interest rate "dishonestly, for an improper purpose, capriciously or arbitrarily". It was also an implied term that the discretion to set an interest rate would not be exercised unreasonably in the sense that there was no material on which a reasonable person could have exercised the discretion in the way he did.[31] **14.17**

The mere fact that a choice is to be made by one party to the contract does not necessarily mean that he has a discretion. Thus in *Skidmore v Dartford & Gravesham NHS Trust*,[32] a contract of employment provided for three types of disciplinary offence. A different procedure applied to different types of offence. The contract provided that it was for the employer to decide into which type the particular case fell. Lord Steyn said: **14.18**

"The trust is entitled to decide what disciplinary route should be followed. That decision must, however, comply with the terms of the contract. If a non-conforming decision is taken and acted upon, there is a breach of contract resulting in the usual remedies. The only escape from this position would be if it could be shown that the parties agreed wording in their contract making it clear that the employer's decision would be final thereby excluding the role of the court except, of course, in cases of bad faith or possibly the absence of reasonable grounds for the decision. There is no such provision in the present contract. It does, of course provide that 'It is for the authority to decide under which category a case falls'. This provision merely states the obvious: the trust must take the initial decision to commence the appropriate disciplinary procedure. It is, however, quite insufficient to exclude the normal consequences of a failure to follow the agreed contractual procedures".

In *Sara & Hossein Asset Holdings Ltd v Blacks Outdoor Retail Ltd*,[33] a lease provided for the payment of a service charge. The landlord was to give the tenant a certificate of "the amount and total costs payable" by the tenant; and that certificate was to be conclusive in the absence of manifest error or fraud. It was held that there was a fundamental difference between the scope of a certificate given by and independent third party and one given by a party to the contract. The deputy judge said: **14.19**

"The natural and obvious construction of that provision is that the certificate is conclusive as to 'the amount of the total cost' of the services said to be comprised within the service charge. There is, however, a clear distinction between a

---

[31] *Paragon Finance Plc v Nash* [2002] 1 W.L.R. 685; *Malione v BPB Industries Ltd* [2002] I.R.L.R. 452 CA.
[32] [2003] I.C.R. 721 HL.
[33] [2020] EWHC 1263 (Ch).

certificate establishing 'the amount' of a cost, and the question of whether that cost should properly have been incurred in the first place, within the scope of the obligations in the lease. As to that latter question, Schedule 6 makes no provision for any conclusive determination by the landlord or indeed anyone else. It follows that, in the ordinary way, that must be a matter which the tenant can put in issue and which is capable of determination by the court in the event of a dispute between the parties."

5. WHETHER CERTIFICATE OR APPROVAL MAY BE UNREASONABLY WITHHELD

Where a contract is to be performed to the satisfaction of a third party, the third party is not usually required to act reasonably in deciding whether or not to express satisfaction or to issue a certificate. But where the contract is to be performed to the satisfaction of one of the parties to it, it will usually be implied that he should act reasonably.[34]

14.20   An important distinction must be drawn between contracts in which satisfaction is to be expressed by a third party and contracts in which satisfaction is to be expressed by one of the parties to it. In the former case, the parties will usually have entrusted the monitoring of performance to an independent outsider and may, consequently, be taken to have relied on his competence. There is therefore, no need to imply any term that the third party should act reasonably in deciding whether or not to approve performance. Indeed, the certificate will be binding on the parties, even if the certifier was negligent.[35] By contrast, in a case where one party to the contract is to give or withhold approval of performance by the other, the court will more readily imply a term that approval is not to be unreasonably withheld.

14.21   In *Caney v Leith*,[36] a contract for the sale of land was subject to the approval of the sellers' title by the buyers' solicitors. It was held that in the absence of bad faith or unreasonable conduct whether or not the solicitors approved title was conclusive. But Farwell J explained the meaning of "unreasonable conduct" in this context as follows:

"what do the judges mean when they talk about unreasonableness? In my judgment, when they are using the word 'unreasonable,' they are dealing with a position where the solicitors are not acting in good faith—that is to say, where, to assist their client, and get him out of the contract, or for some other reason, the solicitors refuse to approve the lease, without giving the matter any consideration at all, or where their reasons for disapproval are so patent and absurd that the court can say in a moment: 'This is ridiculous and the solicitors cannot possibly make such an objection as that'."

14.22   While it may not be necessary to go so far as to require the opinion to be so objectionable that it suggests bad faith on the part of the solicitor, Farwell J's approach of permitting a challenge only where the objection can quickly be seen to

---

[34]   The equivalent section in a previous edition was referred to with apparent approval in *Skidmore v Dartford & Gravesham NHS Trust* [2003] I.C.R. 721 HL. See also *Anders & Kern UK Ltd v CGU Insurance Plc* [2007] EWHC 377 (Comm).

[35]   See para.14.47. But the certifier may himself be liable in negligence to a dissatisfied party.

[36]   [1937] 2 All E.R. 532.

be absurd or ridiculous, is a test that has been widely adopted and is the appropriate approach to "unreasonableness" in this context.[37]

Thus in *Dallman v King*,[38] a lease provided that the tenant should spend £200 in **14.23** repairs to be inspected and approved by the landlord and to be done in a substantial manner; and the tenant was to be entitled to retain the money out of the first year's rent. It was held that the landlord's approval was not a condition precedent to the tenant's entitlement to retain the money. Tindal CJ said:

"It could never have been intended that he [the landlord] should be allowed to act capriciously to withhold his approval; that would have been a condition which would go to the destruction of the thing granted, and if so, according to the well known rule, the thing granted would pass discharged of the condition."

Similarly, in *Braunstein v Accidental Death Insurance Co*,[39] a policy of insur- **14.24** ance against death or injury in a railway accident provided that before payment of any sum insured:

"proof satisfactory to the directors of the Company should be furnished by the claimant of the death or accident, together with such further evidence or information, if any, as the directors should think necessary to establish the claim."

Crompton J said:

"Now I cannot conceive that any Company would put before a person desirous of effecting an insurance with them a stipulation that, in order to establish the occurrence of an accident insured against, their own directors might require any evidence, however chimerical, capricious, and unjust the asking for it might be. The putting of such a construction on a stipulation like this is opposed to the general rule, that when it is agreed that an act is to be done to the satisfaction of a party it must be understood to mean reasonably to his satisfaction. The cases where it is agreed between two parties that a disputed matter shall be determined by the certificate of a third person differ from the present, for there the act is to be done by a third person, whereas here it is to be done by one of the parties."

However, in *Price v Bouch*,[40] Millett J said: **14.25**

"There is no general principle of law that, whenever a contract requires the consent of one party to be obtained by the other, there is an implied term that such consent is not to be unreasonably refused. It all depends upon the circumstances of the particular contract."

Where, for example, it is difficult to lay down any objective standards, it may not **14.26** be possible to imply a term that the party giving or refusing consent must act reasonably. Thus in *Andrews v Bellfield*,[41] the defendant ordered a pony phaeton from the claimant, a coach-builder. The order was given "on the assumption that

37 *Regal Success Venture Ltd v Jonlin Ltd* [2000] 2 HKFCAR 364.
38 (1837) 4 Bing. N.C. 105.
39 (1861) 1 B. & S. 782.
40 (1987) 53 P. & C.R. 257. This statement was approved by the Court of Appeal in *Cryer v Scott Brothers (Sunbury) Ltd* (1988) 55 P. & C.R. 183.
41 (1857) 2 C.B.N.S. 779, distinguished in *Liverpool City Council v Walton Group Plc* [2002] 1 E.G.L.R. 149.

you undertake to execute it in a manner which shall meet my approval, not only on the score of workmanship, but also of convenience and taste". It was held that the defendant was entitled to reject the carriage provided only that he acted bona fide. One of the factors leading to that conclusion was that, as Willes J pointed out, *arguendo*, the jury could only judge according to the general conventional rules of taste. Since the contract required the carriage to satisfy the defendant's taste, no objective yardstick could be defined.

14.27   There are, in addition, further cases in which no implication has been made. In *Haegerstrand v Anne Thomas Steamship Co Ltd*,[42] a contract provided that if a steamer was not approved by the purchaser the deposit was to be returned immediately. It was held that the purchaser need not act reasonably in withholding approval. Vaughan Williams LJ said:

"I am of opinion that the true meaning of the contract is that there is a condition which makes the view of the purchaser final if honestly arrived at."

Indeed in *Docker v Hyams*,[43] Harman LJ went so far as to say (obiter):

"where the condition is that something is to be done to A's approval or to his satisfaction then he is the judge, and as long as he is honest he need not be reasonable."

His Lordship did not appear to have had in mind the distinction between third parties and parties to the contract itself. His observation was directed to the position of something being done to the satisfaction of one party to the contract, and it may be doubted whether, on that footing, the observation is correct.

14.28   In *Gan Insurance Co Ltd v Tai Ping Insurance Co Ltd*,[44] a reinsurance contract provided that no claim should be settled or admitted "without the prior approval of reinsurers". The Court of Appeal rejected a claim that approval could not be unreasonably withheld. However, Mance LJ held that:

"any withholding of approval by reinsurers should take place in good faith after consideration of and on the basis of facts giving rise to the particular claim and not with reference to considerations wholly extraneous to the subject-matter of the particular reinsurance."

14.29   In approaching the question of construction whether there are constraints on the withholding or approval, it may be that there is a presumption that the parties intended a discretion or approval to be exercised reasonably. In *Stadhard v Lee*,[45] Cockburn CJ said:

"We quite agree that stipulations and conditions of this kind should, where the language of the contract admits of it, receive a reasonable construction, as it is to be contended that the party in whose favour such a clause is inserted meant to secure only what is reasonable and just, and we therefore entirely accede to

[42]   (1904) 10 Com. Cas. 67.
[43]   [1969] 1 W.L.R. 1060.
[44]   [2001] 2 All E.R. (Comm) 299.
[45]   (1863) 3 B. & S. 364.

the propriety of the decision in *Dallman v King*.[46] But we are equally clear that, where from the whole tenor of the agreement it appears that, however unreasonable and oppressive a stipulation or condition may be, the one party intended to insist upon it and the other to submit to it, a court of justice cannot do otherwise than to give effect to the terms which have been agreed upon between the parties."

It is also possible that the approach of the court will differ according to whether **14.30** the contract under consideration is an executed contract or an executory contract. In the latter case, especially if the parties do not expect to change their positions until the contract is executed, there is less reason to construe the contract in such a way as to prevent one party from effectively bringing it to an end.

The question of the exercise of contractual discretion is considered further in para.14.69.

Illustrations

1. An employee was engaged subject to his performing his duties "to the satisfaction of the directors". The directors were genuinely dissatisfied with the employee, although a jury found that they had no reason to be. The employee failed in an action for wrongful dismissal. It was held that the discretion of the directors was not to be overridden by the differing view of the jury.
Diggle v Ogston Motor Co[47]

2. Shipbuilders were building a ship on commission. They entered into a subcontract with a company for the supply of propellers which were to be made in accordance with a certain specification and to the entire satisfaction of the commissioning owners. It was held that the owners who might know nothing of the contract between the shipbuilders and the suppliers of the propellers had the right to reject the propellers for any reason at all, and not merely on the ground of some failure to comply with the specification.
Cammell Laird and Co Ltd v Manganese Bronze and Brass Co Ltd[48]

3. An agreement between a prospective developer and a local authority provided for the developer to submit to the authority a consultative study for the proposed development. The agreement said that if the authority did not approve the consultative study, it could terminate the agreement. It was held that the authority's approval could not be unreasonably withheld.
Liverpool City Council v Walton Group Plc[49]

4. A deed of covenant between adjoining owners provided that one owner was not to make planning applications or carry out works without the consent of the other. It was held that consent could not be unreasonably withheld.
89 Holland Park Management Ltd v Hicks[50]

---

[46] (1837) 4 Bing. N.C. 105.
[47] (1915) 84 L.J.K.B. 2165.
[48] [1934] A.C. 402.
[49] [2002] 1 E.G.L.R. 149.
[50] [2013] EWHC 391 (Ch).

6. FORM OF CERTIFICATE AND INDENTITY OF CERTIFIER

A certificate need not be in any particular form, but it must be clear and readily understandable and must be given by the person named or described in the contract.

14.31   A certificate of quality is often one of the documents used in the sale of goods in transit. It must therefore be a document which is clear in its terms. In *Minster Trust Ltd v Traps Tractors Ltd*,[51] Devlin J said:

> "I think a certificate of this sort must, to satisfy the contract, be unambiguous and readily understandable. When a document is tendered under a contract, the recipient has often to make up his mind whether he is going to pay out money on it or to accept or to reject goods; he has no right and may not have time to cross-examine the certifier or to ask him to clear up doubts."

This formulation was approved by the Court of Appeal in *Token Construction Co Ltd v Charlton Estates Ltd*,[52] in which Roskill LJ said:

> "Though neither condition 2(e) nor condition 16 ... prescribes any form in which the architect is to grant any extension or to certify his opinion, it is, in my judgment, essential that, while the architect is left free to adopt what form of expression he likes for the grant or certificate, as the case may require, he must do so clearly so that the intent and substance of what he does is clear. The court should not be astute to criticise documents issued by an architect merely because he may not use the precise language which a lawyer might have selected in order to express a like determination, but whilst this amount of latitude is permissible, it cannot extend to the court's treating as due compliance with contractual requirements documents which, however liberally interpreted, do not plainly show that they were intended to comply with, and, fairly understood, do comply with those contractual requirements."

14.32   These cases are concerned with the information contained in the certificate. In such cases it seems likely that the court will adopt the same principles of interpretation as it adopts in the case of other unilateral utterances (e.g. notices). However, some contracts also prescribe formal conditions of validity for a certificate or determination, and in such cases the court may adopt a relatively strict approach to the question whether the form of the certificate satisfies the contractual requirements. Thus in order to be valid the certificate must be given by the person named or described in the contract. It is a question of interpretation of the contract whether this may be delegated.[53] Where the exercise requires special skill it is less easy to conclude that it may be delegated.[54]

14.33   Thus in *Kollerich & Cie SA v State Trading Corp of India*,[55] a contract for the sale of goods provided for the packing of the goods to be inspected and certified by one of two named agencies. The seller appointed one of the agencies, but it delegated the inspection to another firm. The appointed agency then issued a

---

[51] [1954] 1 W.L.R. 963.
[52] (1973) 1 B.L.R. 48 CA.
[53] *Carey Group Plc v AIB Group (UK) Ltd* [2011] EWHC 567.
[54] *Carey Group Plc v AIB Group (UK) Ltd*, above.
[55] [1979] 2 Lloyd's Rep. 442 (affirmed [1980] 2 Lloyd's Rep. 32).

certificate which wrongly stated that it had carried out the inspection. It was held that the certificate was ineffective. Parker J said:

> "It appears to make commercial nonsense of the clause to say that the intention of the parties was merely that the inspection should be carried out by not one of the two inspection agencies named but any person whom either of the inspection agencies chose to appoint. If that had been intended, it would seem that there is no purpose served by specifying two agencies and ensuring that both of them are agencies of international repute. The natural meaning of the words is that the inspection was to be carried out by one of those named agencies and by no one else. In my judgment a contractual certificate is a certificate following upon inspection by one of those named agencies and not a certificate following upon an inspection carried out by someone else and stating entirely falsely that they, the named agency, had attended and inspected."

In *Finchbourne Ltd v Rodrigues*,[56] a service charge payable under a lease was required to be certified by the landlord's managing agent, acting as an expert. It was held that a certificate issued by the person who owned the landlord company was not given by an expert and hence was not binding. So also in *Ess v Truscott*[57] and *Jones v Jones*,[58] a valuation was set aside on the ground that it was not made by the valuer named in the agreement. In some cases, however, the court is able to reach the conclusion that valuation by the valuer named in the agreement is inessential.[59] In *Re Malpass*,[60] a testamentary option was granted for the purchase of land "at the agricultural value thereof determined for probate purposes as agreed with the District Valuer". For various reasons the District Valuer would not value the land, and consequently no value could be agreed with him. Megarry VC held that the inclusion of the District Valuer in the process was not essential, and directed an inquiry to ascertain the agricultural value of the land. By contrast in *Gillatt v Sky Television Ltd*,[61] where a contract required the valuation of shares to be carried out by an independent chartered accountant, it was held that the fact that an independent chartered accountant was to carry out the valuation was fundamental because there were a number of different ways in which the shares could have been valued. The essential question is whether, apart from the contractual machinery, the court is able to find an objective criterion for assessing the value or amount. If it can, then the contractual machinery is less likely to be held to be essential. Where an agreement provided for the valuation of land by an "independent valuer", the independ-

14.34

---

[56]   [1976] 3 All E.R. 581.
[57]   (1837) 2 M. & W. 385.
[58]   [1971] 1 W.L.R. 840. In *George v Roach* (1942) 67 C.L.R. a newsagent agreed to sell his store and business at a valuation made by a named person, the circulation manager of a newspaper group, subject to a minimum price of £85 per £1 of weekly profit. The named individual refused to certify the value, and the contract was held to be void for uncertainty, even though the newsagent was prepared to accept the minimum figure. It is questionable whether this case was rightly decided. See also *Equitable Trust Co of New York v Dawson Partners Ltd* (1927) 27 Lloyd's Rep. 49.
[59]   However, if the breakdown in the contractual machinery is attributable to the default of one party, the court is unlikely to provide alternative machinery at his behest: *Infiniteland Ltd v Artisan Contracting Ltd* [2006] 1 B.C.L.C. 632.
[60]   [1985] Ch. 42.
[61]   [2000] 2 B.C.L.C. 103.

ence of the valuer was essential and if the valuer had not been independent, the valuation would have been set aside.[62]

14.35   In *Equitable Trust Co of New York v Dawson Partners Ltd*,[63] a contract required a certificate to be issued "by experts who are sworn brokers". A certificate by a single broker was held to be bad. Lord Sumner said:

> "There is no room for documents which are almost the same, or which will do just as well. Business could not proceed securely on any other lines."

14.36   A similar problem is encountered in restrictive covenants which prohibit building without the consent of an identified person (e.g. "the vendor"). Even though the benefit of the covenant may pass to a successor in title of the original vendor, this does not usually alter the requirement to obtain the consent of the identified person, rather than the consent of his successor.[64] However if the identified person dies, or, being a company, is dissolved, the entire prohibition may be discharged.[65]

Illustrations

1.   A lease provided for the payment of a service charge by the tenant. The amount of the charge was to be certified by the landlord's managing agents acting as expert. The landlord was a company wholly owned by the sole principal of the managing agents. It was held that they could not be described as experts, since that expression required an independent judgment. Accordingly, a certificate which they issued was bad.
Finchbourne Ltd v Rodrigues[66]

2.   A building contract provided that if the contractor should make default in one or more of certain specified respects, the architect might give a notice specifying the default. The architect gave notice that in his opinion the contractor was in default. It was held that the notice was not vitiated by the default being expressed as the architect's opinion.
Hounslow London Borough Council v Twickenham Garden Developments Ltd[67]

7.   FINALITY OF CERTIFICATE OR EXPERT DETERMINATION

A certificate given or expert determination made under a contract will usually be final as between the parties to the contract, even if the certifier is mistaken or negligent, unless the certifier or expert has materially departed from his instructions.

14.37   Since the purpose of a certification clause is generally to avoid disputes, the

---

62   *Hopkinson v Hickton* [2016] EWCA Civ 1057.
63   [1927] 27 Lloyd's Rep. 49.
64   See *Bell v Norman C Ashton Ltd* (1956) 7 P. & C.R. 359; *Re Beechwood Homes Ltd's Application* [1994] 2 E.G.L.R. 178 CA; *Briggs v McCusker* [1996] 2 E.G.L.R. 197.
65   *Crest Nicholson Residential (South) Ltd v McAllister* [2003] 1 All E.R. 46, not following *Re Beechwood Homes Ltd's Application* [1994] 2 E.G.L.R. 178 CA; *Churchill v Temple* [2011] 17 E.G. 72.
66   [1976] 3 All E.R. 581. See also *Concorde Graphics Ltd v Andromeda Investments SA* [1983] 1 E.G.L.R. 53.
67   [1971] Ch. 233 at 265.

certificate will usually be final as between the parties to the contract. Thus in *Fairfield Sentry Ltd v Migani*,[68] Lord Sumption said that one of the characteristics of a certificate was that it was intended to be definitive.

In most cases this will be expressly provided by the terms of the contract. If a **14.38** clause in a contract does provide that a certificate is to be conclusive evidence the clause will be strictly construed, with any ambiguity being resolved against the party relying on the certificate.[69] In *Olympic Airways SA v ACG Acquisition XX LLC*,[70] an aircraft lease contained obligations on the part of the lessor to deliver the aircraft in a prescribed condition. One of the clauses in the contract stated that delivery by the lessee to the lessor of a certificate of acceptance would be "conclusive proof" that the aircraft was satisfactory to the lessee. The Court of Appeal held that the effect of this clause was that the lessee could not subsequently complain of defects in the aircraft.

In *University of Brighton v Dovehouse Interiors Ltd*,[71] Carr J said: **14.39**

"'Conclusive evidence' clauses have a clear commercial purpose. They are intended to provide contractually agreed limits to the scope of disputes and to provide clarity as to the parties' obligations once a project is complete. They allow the parties to dictate if and to what extent a final certificate is and is not to be treated as conclusive as between them."

However, in *London and Regional (St George's Court) Ltd v Ministry of* **14.40** *Defence*,[72] Coulson J said that:

"it must be clear that, if the certificate relied on is said to be a final certificate, this is plain from the face of the certificate itself."

His decision was upheld by the Court of Appeal.

This result can, it is thought, be achieved by providing that the certifier is to act as an expert. The use of experts in dispute resolution is considered further in Ch.18.

Where the contract provides either expressly or by necessary implication that the **14.41** certificate is to be final, the certificate cannot be set aside on the ground that the certifier made a mistake.[73] But even if it is not so provided, it is considered that it will usually have been the intention of the parties that the certificate should be final.[74] However, whether a certificate is final is a question of interpretation of the contract. On the one hand, the court has repeatedly held that where the price of a commodity is to be fixed by a valuation, the valuation is final and binding on the parties even if the valuer made a mistake.[75] Thus in *Jones v Sherwood Computer Services Plc*,[76] a contract for the sale of shares provided for the value of the shares to be calculated by reference to the volume of sales determined by expert

---

68 [2014] UKPC 9.
69 *North Shore Ventures Ltd v Anstead Holdings, Inc* [2011] EWCA Civ 230.
70 [2013] EWCA Civ 369; [2013] 1 Lloyd's Rep. 658.
71 [2014] EWHC 940 (TCC); (2014) 153 Con. L.R. 147; *Trustees of the Marc Gilbard 2009 Settlement Trust v OD Developments and Projects Ltd* [2015] EWHC 70 (TCC).
72 (2008) 121 Con. L.R. 26 at [62].
73 *Arenson v Arenson* [1973] Ch. 346; *Toepfer v Continental Grain Co* [1974] 1 Lloyd's Rep. 11.
74 *Homepace Ltd v Sita South East Ltd* [2008] 1 P. & C.R. 24; *Clark v Clark* [2011] EWHC 2746 (Ch); [2011] 7 WLUK 734; *Fairfield Sentry Ltd v Migani* [2014] UKPC 9.
75 *Campbell v Edwards* [1976] 1 W.L.R. 403; *Baber v Kenwood Manufacturing Co Ltd* [1978] 1 Lloyd's Rep. 175.
76 [1992] 1 W.L.R. 277 CA, disapproving *Burgess v Purchase & Sons (Farms) Ltd* [1983] Ch. 216 in

accountants. It was held that provided that the expert had asked himself the right question, his determination could not be set aside on grounds of mistake.[77] It is difficult to see any difference in principle between the considerations which led the court to the conclusion that a valuation is usually intended by the parties to be binding upon them, and the considerations which led parties to include certification clauses in their contracts.[78] On the other hand, where a lease required the tenant to pay a service charge calculated in accordance with certain specified provisions, and the lease also required the landlord to certify its expenditure (but not the amount of the service charge payable by the tenant), it was held that the certificate was not conclusive, having regard to the purpose of the service charge, with the consequence that the landlord was entitled to recover a proportion of expenditure which had been omitted from previous certificates.[79] In *Aquila WSA Aviation Opportunities II Ltd v Onur Air Tasimacilik AS*,[80] it was a condition precedent to the commencement of the term of an aircraft lease that the lessee should sign an acceptance certificate. The certificate provided that it would be conclusive proof that the aircraft was in the condition required by the contract. It was held that the certificate took effect according to its terms, and that the lessee was precluded from raising allegations of defects.

14.42 The case of certificates in building contracts is, however, somewhat different. In such contracts the primary purpose of the certificate is to ensure a regular cash flow to the contractor during the progress of the work. In such cases the court is less likely to hold that a certificate, particularly an interim certificate, was intended to be conclusive.[81] In the case of a final certificate, the building contract will usually provide for disputes to be determined by arbitration and give the arbitrator power to open up and review certificates.

14.43 A mistake is made when an expert goes wrong in the course of carrying out his/her instructions. If an expert makes a mistake while carrying out his/her instructions, the parties are bound by it for the reason that they have agreed to be bound by it. Where the expert departs from instructions in a material respect, the parties

---

which it was held that a valuation which gave reasons which were demonstrably wrong was liable to be set aside. *Jones v Sherwood Computer Services Plc* was followed in *Nikko Hotels (UK) Ltd v MEPC Plc* [1991] 2 E.G.L.R. 103 and *P & O Property Holdings v Norwich Union Life Insurance Society Plc* [1993] 1 E.G.L.R. 164 CA. However, in *Mercury Communications Ltd v Director-General of Telecommunications* [1996] 1 W.L.R. 48 the House of Lords said that where parties entrust a decision under a contract to an expert, they do so on the basis that he will interpret the contract correctly. The House of Lords held that the contract had been incorrectly interpreted in that case and set aside the determination. This might be thought to herald a new approach. Nevertheless, in *British Shipbuilders Ltd v VSEL Consortium* [1997] 1 Lloyd's Rep. 106, Lightman J held that *Jones v Sherwood Computer Services Plc* remained good law. In *Amoco (UK) Exploration Co v Amerada Hess Ltd* [1994] 1 Lloyd's Rep. 330 the contract contained an express agreement that no legal proceedings should be begun in respect of matters remitted to the expert.

[77] In *Boat Park Ltd v Hutchinson* [1999] 2 N.Z.L.R. 74 the NZCA held that a contract to buy at a "valuation" required a valuation by a registered valuer in accordance with basic valuation principles and basic valuation methods; and that the court could inquire into the methods adopted in order to see whether the contract had been complied with.

[78] See *Homepace Ltd v Sita South East Ltd* [2007] EWHC 629, approving this section.

[79] *Universities Superannuation Scheme Ltd v Marks & Spencer Plc* [1999] 1 E.G.L.R. 13 (a decision which seems out of line with other authority).

[80] [2018] EWHC 519 (Comm). Although the judge analysed the case in terms of contractual estoppel, the same result would be achieved simply by holding that the contract provided for a conclusive certificate.

[81] See *Crestar Ltd v Carr* (1987) 37 Build. L.R. 113 in which the Court of Appeal held that interim certificates given under the JCT Minor Building Works Form were not conclusive.

have not agreed to be bound; and accordingly where the certifier has materially departed from his instructions, the certificate will not bind the parties.[82] Any departure from the contractual instruction is material unless it can truly be characterised as trivial or de minimis in the sense of it being obvious that it could make no possible difference to either party.[83] The cases draw a distinction between an expert giving the wrong answer to the right question (in which case the parties remain bound by his answer) and an expert asking himself the wrong question (in which case the parties are not bound by his answer).[84] The distinction between the two is often difficult to discern, particularly where the contract contains detailed criteria to be applied by the expert and the criteria are susceptible to different interpretations.

In *Cine-UK Ltd v Union Square Developments Ltd*[85] a rent review clause **14.44** provided for the decision of the independent surveyor to be final and binding "both on fact and law". It was held that the court had no power to intervene, because the interpretation of the lease was itself one of the matters remitted to the surveyor whose decision was to be final and binding. In the same case Lady Wolffe discussed the distinction between answering the wrong question, on the one hand, and answering the right question in the wrong way. As noted, the distinction between the two is often elusive. But the judge held that what had been entrusted to the surveyor was the determination of the market rent. The interpretation of the rent review clause was not a different question. It had been argued for the tenants that if the surveyor had misinterpreted part of the rent review clause she would have answered the wrong question. Rejecting that submission, Lady Wolffe said:

"On this approach, any error of law in the interpretation of a particular contractual provision (such as the scope of the disregard in clause 2.2.6 of part 4), even if done within the bounds of the relevant exercise (here, ascertaining the open market rent) is nonetheless to be characterised as asking the wrong question (eg because of departing from the 'contractual direction'). In my opinion, however, the effect of that approach is to conflate the two very questions the cases have articulated ('Did the Surveyor answer the wrong question?' with 'Did the Surveyor answer the right question, albeit in the wrong way?') to define the boundaries of the court's limited jurisdiction to review."

A contract will sometimes say that a certificate is to be binding save in the case **14.45** of "manifest error". The expression "manifest error" refers to "oversights and blunders so obvious and obviously capable of affecting the determination as to admit of no difference of opinion",[86] or "one that is obvious or easily demonstrable

---

[82] *Veba Oil Supply & Trading GmbH v Petrotrade Inc* [2002] 1 Lloyd's Rep 295; *Halifax Life Ltd v Equitable Life Assurance Society* [2007] 1 Lloyd's Rep. 528; *National Grid Co Plc v M25 Group Ltd* [1999] 1 E.G.L.R. 65.

[83] *Veba Oil Supply & Trading GmbH v Petrotrade Inc* [2002] 1 Lloyd's Rep. 295 CA, per Simon Brown and Tuckey LJJ; *AIC Ltd v ITS Testing Services (UK) Ltd; The Kriti Palm* [2007] 1 Lloyd's Rep. 555.

[84] See, e.g. *Nikko Hotels (UK) Ltd v MEPC Plc* [1991] 2 E.G.L.R. 103.

[85] [2019] CSOH 3; 2019 Hous. L.R. 8.

[86] *Veba Oil Supply & Trading GmbH v Petrotrade Inc* [2002] 1 Lloyd's Rep. 295 at 302; *Halifax Life Ltd v Equitable Life Assurance Society* [2007] 2 All E.R. (Comm) 672. This section was approved in *Septo Trading Inc v Tintrade Ltd* [2020] EWHC 1795 (Comm).

without extensive investigation".[87] If the mistake is obvious then it may be that it does not also need to be demonstrated immediately and conclusively.[88] In *Menolly Investments 3 Sarl v Cerep Sarl*,[89] Warren J considered a provision referring to "manifest error" in a certificate of practical completion given under a building contract. He said:

> "That is not to say that the only evidence admissible is the certificate itself. The certificate must, after all, be construed against the background of the contract under which it is given and its subject matter, as well as in the context of the factual matrix against which manifest error is to be judged. Mr McGhee gives the example of the complete absence of an extra storey which the contractor has promised to build. This of course is a fanciful example; if a certifier were actually to certify the building as practically complete in such a case, it is obvious that something serious has gone wrong and that the certificate cannot stand. But the point is that it is only possible to say that something has gone wrong if (a) reference is made to the contract (which includes provision of the extra storey) and (b) the position on the ground i.e. that the extra storey has not been built. It cannot be the case that the obvious error must be apparent on the face of the certificate itself."

14.46   Where a certificate is said not to be conclusive in the case of a "manifest error" that cannot entitle a party to a full-blown trial in order to investigate the accuracy of the certificate.[90] However, it has been held that where the allegation is that an expert has departed from the instructions given to him by the contract, that is a matter that can be investigated by a full-blown trial.[91] A certificate may be invalid for manifest error if it is given on the basis of a disputed interpretation of the contract which turns out to be wrong.[92]

14.47   However, if a decision is issued in a dispute where it is binding "save for manifest error" a party wishing to challenge the decision may face insuperable difficulties if the expert is not obliged to give reasons and fails to set out the reasons for his decision.[93]

Illustrations

1.   A building contract provided that upon a claim by the contractor for an extension of time the employer should finally determine and certify the overall extension to which he considered the contractor to be entitled. It also provided for the contractor to make claims for payment which were to be certified by the employer if the employer was satisfied that the works for which payment was claimed had

---

[87]   *IIG Capital LLC v Van Der Merwe* [2008] 2 Lloyd's Rep. 187; *North Shore Ventures Ltd v Anstead Holdings, Inc* [2011] EWCA Civ 230.

[88]   *North Shore Ventures Ltd v Anstead Holdings, Inc* [2011] EWCA Civ 230 per Smith LJ.

[89]   [2009] EWHC 516 (Ch).

[90]   *ABM Amro Commercial Finance Plc v McGinn* [2014] EWHC 1674 (Comm).

[91]   *Friends Life Management Services Ltd v A & A Express Building Ltd* [2014] EWHC 1463 (Ch). (This was common ground between the parties and thus not the subject of argument.)

[92]   *Amey Birmingham Highways Ltd v Birmingham City Council* [2018] EWCA Civ 264; [2018] B.L.R. 225. Likewise, an expert's determination on the basis of an incorrect interpretation of the contract is unlikely to be binding: *Great Dunmow Estates ltd v Crest Nicholson Operations Ltd* [2019] EWCA Civ 1683.

[93]   *Halifax Life Ltd v Equitable Life Assurance Society* [2007] 1 Lloyd's Rep. 528.

been properly executed. It was held that the employers' decisions were final and binding, although the decisions had to be reached honestly, fairly and reasonably.
Balfour Beatty Civil Engineering Ltd v Docklands Light Railway Ltd[94]

2. An agreement provided for the redetermination of the parties' shares in the proceeds of oil exploration. The redetermination was referred to an expert under the terms of a further agreement which, on its true construction, required the expert to use a particular computer programme for mapping the oil reservoir. The expert's determination was set aside on the ground that he had used a different computer programme from that specified in the agreement.
Shell UK Ltd v Enterprise Oil Plc[95]

8. SCOPE OF CERTIFICATE OR EXPERT DETERMINATION

A certificate or expert determination will only be final as to matters which clearly fall within the scope of the certificate or the remit of the expert.

A certificate cannot be final on any question of law, for a clause which so provided would be void as ousting the jurisdiction of the court.[96] However, where the question of law is the interpretation of the contract itself, a certificate or expert determination may be final if the contract, properly interpreted, means that the parties agreed that their obligations would be whatever the certifier or expert decided that they were.[97] Whether the terms of a contract exclude the jurisdiction of the court to interpret the contract turns on the interpretation of the provisions in the particular contract.[98] Where the contract contains detailed criteria to be adopted in reaching a decision, the court has jurisdiction to determine the meaning and legal effect of those criteria.[99] **14.48**

A certificate may be final on any matter of fact on which the contract provides that it should be. In contracts for the sale of goods the question is sometimes formulated by asking whether the issue of the certificate is part of the description of the goods to be sold. Thus in *Toepfer v Continental Grain Co*,[100] a contract provided for the sale of "No. 3 Hard Amber Durum Wheat of U.S. origin-quality/condition final at loading as per official certificate". A certificate was erroneously issued in respect of amber durum wheat which was not "hard". It was argued that the certificate was final only as to quality but not as to the description of the goods themselves. The Court of Appeal rejected the argument. Lord Denning MR said: **14.49**

"The 'description' of goods often includes a statement of their quality. Thus 'new-laid eggs' contains both quality and description all in one. 'Quality' is often part of the description. In this very case the word 'hard' is a word both of quality and of description. If a certificate is final as to the quality 'hard,' it is final as to that description also. The quality and the description cannot be separated. Finality as to the one means finality as to the other."

---

[94] (1996) 78 B.L.R. 42 CA.
[95] [1999] 2 Lloyd's Rep. 456.
[96] *Re Davstone Estates Ltd's Leases* [1969] 2 Ch. 378. In practice the courts tend not to construe clauses as purporting to have this effect.
[97] *Beaufort Developments (NI) Ltd v Gilbert-Ash (NI) Ltd* [1999] 1 A.C. 266.
[98] *National Grid Co Plc v M25 Group Ltd* [1999] 1 E.G.L.R. 65.
[99] *National Grid Co Plc v M25 Group Ltd* [1999] 1 E.G.L.R. 65; *Great Dunmow Estates Ltd v Crest Nicholson Operations Ltd* [2019] EWCA Civ 1683.
[100] [1974] 1 Lloyd's Rep. 11.

14.50   The decision was referred to with approval by the House of Lords in *Gill & Duffus SA v Berger & Co Inc*,[101] in which Lord Diplock said:

> "What *Toepfer v Continental Grain Co* decided was that where the description of the goods agreed to be sold included a statement as to their quality and provided that a certificate as to quality was to be final, the certificate was final as to the correspondence of the goods with that part of the description of them in the contract that referred to their quality ... notwithstanding that the certificate was proved to be inaccurate ... One must look to the contract as a whole to identify the kind of goods that the seller was agreeing to sell and the buyer to buy. In *Toepfer's* case it was not 'No.3 hard amber durum wheat' simpliciter but durum wheat of U.S. origin for which a certificate had been issued by a U.S. government official stating that its quality was that which is described in the trade as 'No.3 hard amber.'"

14.51   Where, however, the quality of the goods is not in question, but they are not the contract goods, a certificate as to quality will not be binding. In such a case the court is able to distinguish clearly between the quality of the goods and their description in the contract.[102]

14.52   The court may also adopt a restrictive approach as to the scope of the certificate or expression of satisfaction. In *Parson v Sexton*,[103] the defendant ordered an engine. Payment of the price was to be in two instalments and was expressed to be in consideration:

> "of your supplying us with a certain fourteen-horse engine ... and putting the same in thorough repair, and supplying a new sixteen-horse boiler ... and delivering and erecting the whole, and setting the whole to work."

The second instalment of the price was to be paid "on being satisfied with the work". It was held that the stipulation as to the defendant's satisfaction with the work referred only to the work of the plaintiff in erecting the engine and not to the engine itself.

14.53   So too in *Panamena Europe Navegacion v Leyland (Frederick) & Co Ltd*,[104] a contract for emergency ship repairs provided for payment of the repairers upon the issue of a certificate by the owners' surveyor that the work had been satisfactorily carried out and on receipt of a certificate from the ultimate charterer certifying the amount due. The House of Lords held that the owners' surveyor was confined to certifying the actual quality of the work done, and was not entitled to consider the manner in which the work had been carried out, and in particular whether there had been reasonable economy in time, labour and materials.

14.54   In *Neste Production Ltd v Shell UK Ltd*,[105] a contract relating to sharing the cost of oil exploration provided for the determination of a question to be referred to an expert. He was to determine the question in accordance with the terms of a clause in the contract. It was held that the question whether that clause had been varied by agreement did not fall within his remit, and hence could be determined by the

---

[101] [1984] 1 A.C. 382.
[102] *The Bow Cedar* [1980] 2 Lloyd's Rep. 601; *Daudruy van Cauwenberghe & Fils SA v Tropical Product Sales SA* [1986] 1 Lloyd's Rep. 535.
[103] (1847) 4 C.B. 899.
[104] [1947] A.C. 428.
[105] [1994] 1 Lloyd's Rep. 447.

court. Likewise in *North Shore Ventures Ltd v Anstead Holdings Inc*,[106] a certificate in a guarantee was to be conclusive as to "amount". It was held that the certificate could not determine whether the terms of the underlying agreement had been varied.[107]

Illustration

A contract for the manufacture of a glue-cutting machine provided that it was to be constructed with strong and sound workmanship to the approval of a specified person. It was held that approval was limited to the strength and workmanship of the machine and did not extend to its efficiency in cutting glue.
Ripley v Lordon[108]

9. CERTIFICATES AS CONDITIONS PRECEDENT

Where payment for goods or services is to be made upon the issue of a certificate, the issue of the certificate is a condition precedent to the right to sue for the price, unless the certifier has wrongfully refused to issue a certificate.

In *London and Regional (St George's Court) Ltd v Ministry of Defence*,[109] Coulson J said: **14.55**

"It is axiomatic that, if a certificate is intended to be a condition precedent to payment, the contract must demonstrate such an intention by express words, or upon reading the document as a whole."

His decision was upheld by the Court of Appeal.

In *Sharpe v San Paulo Railway Co*,[110] a building contract provided for payments to be made against certificates issued by an engineer. Mellish LJ said: **14.56**

"Wherever, according to the true construction of the contract, the party only agrees to pay what is certified by an engineer, or what is found to be due by an arbitrator, and there is no agreement to pay otherwise—that is to say, in every case where the certificate of the engineer or arbitrator is made a condition precedent to the right to recover, there the Court has no right to dispense with that which the parties have made a condition precedent, unless, of course there has been some conduct on the part of the engineer or the company which may make it inequitable that the condition precedent should be relied upon."

So also in *Babbage v Coulburn*,[111] a tenancy agreement provided that the tenant should yield up in repair and should pay for any breakages; the amount of the payment, if in dispute, to be settled by two valuers or their umpire. It was held that no action was maintainable by the landlord unless and until the amount of the payment for damage had been ascertained in the manner laid down in the agreement.   **14.57**

---

[106] [2011] EWCA Civ 230.
[107] This conclusion was tentatively expressed by the majority in view of the decision of the High Court of Australia in *Dobbs v National Bank of Australasia* (1935) 53 C.L.R. 643.
[108] (1860) 2 L.T. 154.
[109] (2008) 121 Con. L.R. 26 at [62].
[110] (1873) L.R. 8 Ch. App. 597.
[111] (1882) 9 Q.B.D. 235.

14.58   In *Henry Boot Construction Ltd v Alstom Combined Cycles Ltd*,[112] Dyson LJ held that as a matter of construction of a building contract the issue of a certificate was a condition precedent to the right to payment under the contract. He continued:

> "By 'condition precedent' I mean that the right to payment arises when a certificate is issued or ought to be issued, and not earlier. It does not, however, follow from the fact that a certificate is a condition precedent that the absence of a certificate is a bar to the right to payment. This is because the decision of the engineer in relation to certification is not conclusive of the rights of the parties, unless they have clearly so provided. If the engineer's decision is not binding, it can be reviewed by an arbitrator (if there is an arbitration clause which permits such a review) or by the court. If the arbitrator or the court decides that the engineer ought to have issued a certificate which he refused to issue, or to have included a larger sum in a certificate which he did issue, they can, and ordinarily will, hold that the contractor is entitled to payment as if such certificate had been issued and award or give judgment for the appropriate sum ... It is convenient to make such an award or to enter such a monetary judgment in order to avoid the risk of further proceedings in the event that the employer does not pay. For the reasons that follow, I consider that the right to payment arises when a certificate is issued or ought to be issued, and not when the work is done (although the doing of the work is itself a condition precedent to the right to a certificate)."

14.59   If, however, the certificate or determination is binding, then it will be a condition precedent to the right to payment. If no contractually binding certificate or determination is made then the obligation will not be enforceable unless the court orders substitute machinery.[113]

Illustrations

1.   A contract for the supply of coke provided that the coke was to be of a certain quality and to the satisfaction of the buyer's inspecting officer. If the inspecting officer was not satisfied, the buyer was free to buy elsewhere. It was held that the satisfaction of the inspecting officer was a condition precedent to the right to payment.
Grafton v Eastern Counties Railway[114]

2.   A building contract provided that the contractor would be paid "on the certificate of the architect". It was held that a certificate was a condition precedent to the right to payment.
Stevenson v Watson[115]

10.   CONSENTS IN CONVEYANCING TRANSACTIONS

Where a lease or conveyance prohibits some act without the consent of the landlord or some other person, the court will often imply a term that consent may not be arbitrarily withheld.

---

[112] [2005] 3 All E.R. 932.
[113] See para.14.12.
[114] (1853) 8 Ex. 699.
[115] (1879) 4 C.P.D. 148.

Most leases contain a wide variety of covenants on the part of the tenant, many **14.60**
of which prohibit the performance of some act without the consent of the landlord.
The most common example is a covenant against assigning, underletting or parting with possession without the landlord's consent. In the case of such covenants,
it is provided by s.19(1) of the Landlord and Tenant Act 1927 that the covenant is
deemed to be subject to a proviso that consent is not to be unreasonably withheld.
In *Bocardo SA v S&M Hotels Ltd*,[116] Megaw LJ suggested (obiter) that such a term
was to be implied at common law. He said:

> "Such a provision would, in strict law, be meaningless or ineffective, unless it
> were to have implied in it some such term as 'such consent not to be unreason-
> ably withheld.' For if the landlord was entitled to refuse consent at his own
> entirely unrestricted discretion, the provision for assignment with consent would
> add nothing to, and subtract nothing from, the effect in law of the contract as it
> would be without those words being included. For a contracting party is always
> entirely free to agree to a variation of the contract at the request of the other party.
> That applies equally where, as here, the variation of the contract would constitute
> a novation."

It may be doubted whether the words are quite as ineffective as Megaw LJ sug- **14.61**
gests, for the words contemplate that consent may be given without a variation of
the lease.[117] In any event, this approach was not followed by Mervyn Davies J in
Guardian Assurance Co Ltd v Gants Hill Holdings Ltd.[118] In that case a lease
contained a covenant which prohibited a tenant from using the demised property
for a particular purpose without the landlord's consent. The judge held that there
was no implied term that consent should not be unreasonably withheld. He said:

> "As I see it, if A and B choose in a lease to express what it is not necessary to
> express, one is not obliged to conclude that the expressed words bear not only
> the expressed meaning but also some additional implied meaning."

So also in *Pearl Assurance Plc v Shaw*,[119] a lease contained a covenant by the
tenant not to apply for planning permission without the landlord's consent. Vinelott
J refused to imply a term that consent would not be unreasonably withheld.

This approach is consistent with the strict approach of the House of Lords in **14.62**
Viscount Tredegar v Harwood,[120] in which the lease contained a clause which
required the tenant to keep the demised property insured in a named insurance office or some other responsible office to be approved by the landlord. It was held that
the landlord had the absolute right to withhold approval to any insurance company
other than that named in the lease, and he was not confined to reasonable grounds.

Similar conclusions have been reached in freehold transactions in the context of **14.63**

---

[116] [1980] 1 W.L.R. 17.
[117] *Pearl Assurance Plc v Shaw* [1985] 1 E.G.L.R. 92. And see *Forte & Co Ltd v General Accident Life
Assurance Co Ltd* (1987) 54 P. & C.R. 9 and the Landlord and Tenant Act 1927 s.19(3) (both in relation to use restrictions rather than restrictions on alienation to which Megaw LJ was referring).
[118] [1983] 2 E.G.L.R. 36.
[119] [1985] 1 E.G.L.R. 92.
[120] [1929] A.C. 72.

restrictive covenants. Thus in *Price v Bouch*,[121] a deed of mutual covenant provided that no buildings should be erected on certain land unless the plans were approved by a committee. Millett J held that there was no implied term to the effect that consent was not to be unreasonably withheld. He said:

"There is no general principle of law that, whenever a contract requires the consent of one party to be obtained by the other, there is an implied term that such consent is not to be unreasonably refused. It all depends upon the circumstances of the particular contract."

He concluded:

"Where the required consent is that of an individual who is free to consult his own interests exclusively, a provision that such consent must not be unreasonably refused is often included in order to prevent consent being withheld arbitrarily, or capriciously, or from improper motives. If that is the only effect of including such a provision, its implication in the present case is unnecessary; while if it goes beyond that, it produces consequences which are unlikely to have been intended by the parties and is an implication which in my judgment, ought not to be made."

14.64 In stating that there was no general principle of law, the judge did not have his attention drawn to the contrary observations of Crompton J in *Braunstein v Accidental Death Insurance Co*.[122] However, while it is no doubt correct to say that there is no such principle of law in the sense of a principle which overrides the intention of the parties, it is thought that the implication of such a term is a step which the court is readier to take than it used to be.

14.65 In *Cryer v Scott Brothers (Sunbury) Ltd*,[123] the Court of Appeal did take that step. A conveyance contained a restrictive covenant which provided that all building plans were to be submitted to the vendor's surveyor for approval. The court held that although Millett J was correct in stating that there was no general principle that consent should not be unreasonably withheld,[124] such a term should be implied. The parties had contemplated that the plot was to be developed by building, and a capricious refusal would have been liable to defeat the purpose of the grant. The term was therefore justified both to give business efficacy to the covenant and also on the officious bystander test.[125]

14.66 In *Lymington Marina Ltd v MacNamara*,[126] a berthing licence provided for the grant of sub-licences to a third party approved by the licensor. The Court of Appeal rejected the submission that a refusal of approval had to be objectively reasonable but held that there had to be implied "a term that the power to withhold ap-

[121] (1987) 53 P. & C.R. 257. In *Wrotham Park Estate Co v Parkside Homes Ltd* [1974] 1 W.L.R. 798 a restrictive covenant prohibited building except in strict accordance with a layout plan approved in writing by the covenantee or his surveyor. Counsel for the covenantee (G.H. Newsom QC) conceded that the covenantee had no right to refuse approval unreasonably, and in particular could not use the stipulation as a bargaining counter to demand money from a would-be developer. The concession was said to have been correct in *Cryer v Scott Brothers (Sunbury) Ltd* (1988) 55 P. & C.R. 183.
[122] (1861) 1 B. & S. 782 (see para.14.24).
[123] (1988) 55 P. & C.R. 183.
[124] *Braunstein v Accidental Death Insurance Co* (1861) 1 B. & S. 782 does not appear to have been cited.
[125] See paras 6.79–6.102.
[126] [2007] EWCA Civ 151; [2007] Bus. L.R. D 29.

proval should be exercised in good faith and that the approval will not be withheld arbitrarily". In so holding the court followed the more modern commercial cases[127] in preference to the more traditional conveyancing cases.[128]

14.67 In some cases, the court may find that there are other provisions in the instrument which, irrespective of any implied term, lead to the conclusion that consent cannot be unreasonably withheld. In *Commissioner for Railways v Avrom Investments Pty Ltd*,[129] a lease provided that the lessee should erect buildings "in accordance with such building design plan and specification as the ... lessor may in his absolute discretion approve ... and notwithstanding anything hereinbefore contained the building design plan and specification of the said building shall be subject to the reasonable requirements of the lessor". The Privy Council held that the latter part of the clause overrode the former part, with the consequence that the lessor's requirements had to be reasonable; and he could not unreasonably refuse consent to plans.

14.68 The trend of modern cases is to imply a term to the effect that any contractual discretion must be exercised honestly, rationally, and for the purpose for which it was conferred. Although this does not impose an objective standard of reasonableness, it must be doubtful whether the older cases which held that the decision maker was free to act as he chose remain good law. The exercise of contractual discretion is considered further in para.14.69.

Illustrations

1. Condition 6 of conditions of sale provided that no buildings should be erected on a lot except "detached or semi-detached residential premises of European type or such other buildings of European type as the Director of Public Works may approve of with garages and all proper outbuildings thereto" and a block of flats on one particular part of the lot. Condition 7 provided that: "The design of the exterior elevations plans height and disposition of any buildings to be erected on the lot shall be subject to the special approval of the Director of Public Works and no building shall be erected on the lot save in accordance with such approval". It was held that the Director was entitled to demand a premium for consent to build four blocks of flats, and that he was entitled to take into account matters extraneous to the purpose of conditions 6 and 7.
Hang Wah Chong Investment Co Ltd v Attorney-General of Hong Kong[130]

2. Clause 4(c) of a conveyance provided that the purchasers would not

"build erect or place on the property ... any building or other structure other than the cottage now erected thereon without first submitting detailed plans of the proposed building or structure to the vendors and obtaining the vendors written consent to the size nature materials and colour thereof."

It was held that consent could not be unreasonably withheld.
Rickman v Brudenell-Bruce[131]

---

127 In particular *Gan Insurance Co Ltd v Tai Ping Insurance Co Ltd* [2001] 2 All E.R. (Comm) 299 CA.
128 Such as *Viscount Tredegar v Harwood* [1929] A.C. 72.
129 [1959] 1 W.L.R. 389.
130 [1981] 1 W.L.R. 1141.
131 [2005] EWHC 3400 (Ch).

11. CONTRACTUAL DISCRETION

Where a contract confers a discretion on one party, and the exercise of that discretion may adversely affect the interests of the other party, it will usually be implicit that the discretion must be exercised honestly and rationally and for the purpose for which it was conferred. An exercise of contractual discretion may be challenged on the same grounds that apply to a challenge to an administrative decision in public law.[132]

14.69   Where a contract confers a discretion on one of the contracting parties, exercise of which may adversely affect the interests of the other, there is an obvious potential conflict of interest. For that reason, in recent years the courts have consistently held that there are implied limits on the permissible exercise of the discretion. The central question is whether, in any particular situation, the parties have agreed that one party should be a primary decision-maker in respect of a decision that affects both parties.[133] Accordingly, if a contract confers an apparently unfettered discretion, then that discretion must not be exercised capriciously or unreasonably. There is no breach of contract unless the exercise of discretion was outside the range of reasonable responses. If, by contrast, a contract confers a discretion which is only exercisable if conditions laid down by the contract are met, then the court will decide, as a matter of fact, whether those conditions were met.[134]

14.70   However as Mance LJ said in *Gan Insurance v Tai Ping Insurance*[135]:

"the authorities do not justify any automatic implication, whenever a contractual provision exists putting one party at the mercy of another's exercise of discretion. It all depends on the circumstances ... ."

14.71   The rationale of the principle is that:

"... the decision requires the contracting party to make some kind of assessment or to choose from a range of options. It is the exercise of that power which renders the implication of a term that it should not be exercised arbitrarily, capriciously or in an irrational manner, necessary."[136]

14.72   Accordingly, the principle applies:

"whenever the contract gives responsibility to one party to make an assessment or exercise a judgment on a matter which materially affects the other party's interests and about which there is room for reasonable differences of view."

14.73   In *Brogden v Investec Bank Plc*,[137] Leggatt J distinguished a number of different meanings of "discretion". He concluded:

---

[132] Judicial control over contractual discretion is discussed generally in "Controlling Contractual Discretion" [2013] C.L.J. 65; "A good faith goodbye? Good faith obligations and contractual termination rights" [2017] L.M.C. 360; "Implied obligations of good faith and proper purpose" (2019) 1 J.I.B.F.L. 9; "The exercise of contractual discretion" [2019] L.Q.R. 135. This section was referred to with approval in *Airport Industrial GP Ltd v Heathrow Airport Ltd* [2015] EWHC 3753 (Ch).

[133] *Kwik Lets Ltd v Khaira* [2020] EWHC 616 (QB).

[134] *Al-Mishlab v Milton Keynes Hospital NHS Foundation Trust* [2015] EWHC 191 (QB).

[135] [2001] 2 All E.R. (Comm) 299.

[136] *Property Alliance Group Ltd v Royal Bank of Scotland Plc* [2016] EWHC 3342 (Ch).

[137] [2014] EWHC 2785 (Comm). On appeal it was held that the clause in question did not confer a

"Both on the authorities and as a matter of principle, it seems to me that where a contract gives responsibility to one party for making an assessment or exercising a judgment on a matter which materially affects the other party's interests and about which there is ample scope for reasonable differences of view, the decision is properly regarded as a discretion which is subject to the implied constraints that it must be taken in good faith, for proper purposes and not in an arbitrary, capricious or irrational manner. Those limits apply in circumstances where the decision is final and binding on the other party in the sense that a court will not substitute its own judgment for that of the party who makes the decision. There is therefore also a discretion in the second sense distinguished earlier. The concern … is that the decision-maker's power should not be abused. The implication is justified as a matter of construction to give effect to the presumed intention of the parties."

Where a party to a contract has a right to terminate it, the principles applicable to the exercise of a contractual discretion do not apply.[138] Nor does the principle apply where one party to a contract is exercising an absolute contractual right.[139] But as Males LJ said in *Equitas Insurance Ltd v Municipal Mutual Insurance Ltd*[140]: **14.74**

"It is only possible to say whether a term conferring a contractual choice on one party represents an absolute contractual right after that process of construction has been undertaken. To say that a term provides for an absolute contractual right and therefore no term can be implied puts the matter the wrong way round."

Accordingly, the mere fact that the contracting party has a choice between two options does not without more displace the implied term.[141]

In *The Product Star (No.2)*,[142] a charterparty entitled charterers to divert the vessel if the master or the owners considered in their discretion that any port of loading or discharge was dangerous or impossible for the vessel to reach. The Court of Appeal held that the discretion must be exercised reasonably. Leggatt LJ said: **14.75**

"Where A and B contract with each other to confer a discretion on A, that does not render B subject to A's uninhibited whim. In my judgment the authorities show that not only must the discretion be exercised honestly and in good faith, but, having regard to the provisions of the contract by which it is conferred, it must not be exercised arbitrarily, capriciously or unreasonably."[143]

The trend of recent cases supports the view that such an implication will usu- **14.76**

---

discretion, so the court did not discuss the question further: [2016] EWCA Civ 1031.

[138] *Monde Petroleum SA v Westernzagros Ltd* [2016] EWHC 1472 (Comm); [2017] 1 All E.R. (Comm) 1009; *Taqa Bratani Ltd v Rockrose UKCS8 LLC* [2020] EWHC 58 (Comm); *Essex County Council v UBB Waste (Essex) Ltd* [2020] EWHC 1581 (TCC). See Foxton, "A good faith goodbye? Good faith obligations and contractual termination rights" [2017] L.M.C.L.Q. 360. Termination clauses are discussed in paras 17.95–17.124.

[139] *Cathay Pacific Airways Ltd v Lufthansa Technik AG* [2020] EWHC 1789 (Ch).

[140] [2019] EWCA Civ 718; [2020] Q.B. 418.

[141] *Super-Max Offshore Holdings v Malhotra* [2017] EWHC 3246 (Comm).

[142] [1993] 1 Lloyd's Rep. 397 CA. See also *The Glacier Bay* [1995] C.L.C. 242 (reversed on the construction of the particular clause [1996] C.L.C. 240 CA); *Balfour Beatty Civil Engineering Ltd v Docklands Light Railway Ltd* (1996) 78 B.L.R. 42 CA.

[143] "Unreasonably" is to be understood in a sense analogous to the *Wednesbury* sense: *Paragon Finance Plc v Nash* [2002] 1 W.L.R. 685 CA. Although it was said in *Lymington Marina Ltd v MacNamara* [2007] EWCA Civ 151; [2007] Bus. L.R. D 29 that general public law principles do not apply to the review by the court of the exercise of a contractual discretion, this appears to have been overtaken

ally be made. In *British Telecommunications Plc v Telefonica O2 UK Ltd*,[144] Lord Sumption said:

> "As a general rule, the scope of a contractual discretion will depend on the nature of the discretion and the construction of the language conferring it. But it is well established that in the absence of very clear language to the contrary, a contractual discretion must be exercised in good faith and not arbitrarily or capriciously ... This will normally mean that it must be exercised consistently with its contractual purpose."

It appears, therefore, that the default rule is that the implication will be made. In addition, in that case the exercise of discretion was also constrained by the regulatory framework within which the contract was made. The implied term is necessary to give effect to the reasonable expectations of the parties.[145] It is "likely to be implicit in any commercial contract under which one party is given the right to make a decision on a matter which affects both parties whose interests are not the same".[146]

14.77   Where a mortgage provided for the payment of interest at a rate determined by the lender, the Court of Appeal held that it was an implied term of the mortgage that the lender would not set the interest rate "dishonestly, for an improper purpose, capriciously or arbitrarily". It was also an implied term that the discretion to set an interest rate would not be exercised unreasonably in the sense that there was no material on which a reasonable person could have exercised the discretion in the way he did.[147] Commenting on that decision in *Horkulak v Cantor Fitzgerald International*,[148] Potter LJ, giving the judgment of the court, said:

> "It is pertinent to observe that, in cases of this kind, the implication of the term is not the application of a 'good faith' doctrine, which does not exist in English contract law; rather it is as a requirement necessary to give genuine value, rather than nominal force or mere lip-service, to the obligation of the party required or empowered to exercise the relevant discretion. While, in any such situation, the parties are likely to have conflicting interests and the provisions of the contract effectively place the resolution of that conflict in the hands of the party exercising the discretion, it is presumed to be the reasonable expectation and therefore the common intention of the parties that there should be a genuine and rational, as opposed to an empty or irrational, exercise of discretion. Thus the courts impose an implied term of the nature and to the extent described."

So also in *Khatri v Cooperatieve Centrale Raiffeisen-Boerenleenbank BA*,[149] Jacob LJ said:

> "The authorities establish that even where an employee's contract says that he

---

by the decision of the Supreme Court in *Braganza v BP Shipping Ltd* [2015] UKSC 17; [2015] 1 W.L.R. 1661.

[144] [2014] UKSC 42; [2014] Bus. L.R. 765.

[145] *Wetherill v Birmingham City Council* [2007] EWCA Civ 599 CA.

[146] *JML Direct Ltd v Freesat UK Ltd* [2010] EWCA Civ 34.

[147] *Paragon Finance Plc v Nash* [2002] 1 W.L.R. 685; *Gan Insurance Co Ltd v Tai Ping Insurance Co Ltd* [2001] 2 All E.R. (Comm) 299 CA.

[148] [2005] I.C.R. 402. See also *Lymington Marina Ltd v MacNamara* [2007] EWCA Civ 151; [2007] Bus. L.R. D 29; *JML Direct Ltd v Freesat UK Ltd* [2009] EWHC 616 (Ch); *Bradbury v British Broadcasting Corp* [2015] EWHC 1368 (Ch).

[149] [2010] EWCA Civ 397.

is entitled to a bonus on a purely discretionary basis that does not mean the employer is entirely free to decide whether to pay a bonus or not. On the contrary, in making his decision whether to pay a bonus, and if so how much, the employer must act in a rational and fair manner. The test is essentially one of *Wednesbury* unreasonableness."

In *Unique Pub Properties Ltd v Broad Green Tavern Ltd*,[150] Warren J referred to a number of these cases and said: **14.78**

"What I conclude from those authorities is this principle, namely that a contractual discretion must be exercised honestly and in good faith and must not be exercised arbitrarily, capriciously or unreasonably, unreasonableness being assessed in the sense that no reasonable person would exercise the discretion in the manner proposed. Sometimes the courts appear to approach these restrictions by way of implication. In others, they appear to approach the matter of one of construction. It does not matter which approach is more accurate, especially as the implication is, in any case, a facet of construction as explained by Lord Hoffmann."

In *Socimer International Bank Ltd v Standard Bank London Ltd*,[151] Rix LJ reviewed the authorities and said: **14.79**

"It is plain from these authorities that a decision-maker's discretion will be limited, as a matter of necessary implication, by concepts of honesty, good faith, and genuineness, and the need for the absence of arbitrariness, capriciousness, perversity and irrationality. The concern is that the discretion should not be abused. Reasonableness and unreasonableness are also concepts deployed in this context, but only in a sense analogous to *Wednesbury* unreasonableness, not in the sense in which that expression is used when speaking of the duty to take reasonable care, or when otherwise deploying entirely objective criteria: as for instance when there might be an implication of a term requiring the fixing of a reasonable price, or a reasonable time. In the latter class of case, the concept of reasonableness is intended to be entirely mutual and thus guided by objective criteria."

In *SNCB Holding v UBS AG*,[152] Cooke J said:

"A duty to exercise 'good faith' in doing something is one which is usually to be contrasted with a duty to exercise reasonable care. It connotes subjective honesty, genuineness and integrity, not an objective standard of any kind, whether reasonableness, care or objective fair dealing. It cannot be equated with 'utmost good faith' and although its exercise in practice may involve different actions or restraint, the concept is not one which goes beyond the notion of truthfulness, honesty and sincerity."

The use of "unreasonableness" (even "in the *Wednesbury* sense") as the descriptor of the test has now generally been replaced by the concept of rationality. In **14.80**

---

[150] [2012] EWHC 2154 (Ch); [2012] 2 P. & C.R. 344. See also *Braganza v BP Shipping Ltd* [2013] EWCA Civ 230.
[151] [2008] 1 Lloyd's Rep. 558.
[152] [2012] EWHC 2044 (Comm).

Hayes v Willoughby,[153] Lord Sumption pointed out that in recent years the concept of rationality had played an increasing part in controlling contractual discretion. He went on to say:

"Rationality is not the same as reasonableness. Reasonableness is an external, objective standard applied to the outcome of a person's thoughts or intentions. The question is whether a notional hypothetically reasonable person in his position would have engaged in the relevant conduct ... A test of rationality, by comparison, applies a minimum objective standard to the relevant person's mental processes. It imports a requirement of good faith, a requirement that there should be some logical connection between the evidence and the ostensible reasons for the decision, and (which will usually amount to the same thing) an absence of arbitrariness, of capriciousness or of reasoning so outrageous in its defiance of logic as to be perverse."[154]

14.81   In *Fondazione Enasarco v Lehman Brothers Finance SA*,[155] a case about the ISDA agreement, David Richards J said:

"... the relevant authorities now quite clearly establish that in considering whether the non-defaulting party has 'reasonably determined' its Loss, that party is not required to comply with some objective standard of care as in a claim for negligence, but, expressing it negatively, must not arrive at a determination which no reasonable non-defaulting party could come to. It is essentially a test of rationality, of the type developed in the quite different context of public law duties ... ."

In *Ludgate Insurance Co Ltd v Citibank NA*,[156] Brooke LJ referred to authority and said:

"These cases show that provided that the discretion is exercised honestly and in good faith for the purposes for which it was conferred, and provided also that it was a true exercise of discretion in the sense that it was not capricious or arbitrary or so outrageous in its defiance of reason that it can properly be categorised as perverse, the courts will not intervene."

14.82   Thus where a landlord had the right to choose between a number of different ways in which to perform his obligations, the choice had to be one that was rational.[157] So also where a management company had the power under the terms of a lease to consent to the keeping of a pet, it was an implied term that the decision would be reached in accordance with a reasonable process; and that the decision would be rational.[158] Likewise, the principle of rationality (rather than the external standard of reasonableness) applies to the exercise of a non-fiduciary power

---

[153] [2013] UKSC 17; [2013] 1 W.L.R. 935 (a case that concerned the Protection from Harassment Act 1997).

[154] In the same case Lord Reed was not sure that he understood the distinction. The author is inclined to agree with Lord Reed.

[155] [2015] EWHC 1307 (Ch).

[156] [1998] Lloyds Rep. 221. See also *Concord Trust v The Law Debenture Trust Corp Plc* [2004] EWHC 1216 (Ch); *Jani-King (GB) Ltd v Pula Enterprises Ltd* [2008] 1 All E.R. (Comm) 451.

[157] *Waaler v Hounslow LBC* [2017] EWCA Civ 45; [2017] 1 P. & C.R. 219.

[158] *Victory Place Management Co Ltd v Kuehn* [2018] EWHC 132 (Ch); [2018] H.L.R. 437.

conferred by the terms of a pension scheme.[159] An option for the purchase of shares provided that it could not be exercised without the consent of a majority of the board of directors of the company. It was held that the power to refuse consent had to be exercised in a way that was not arbitrary, capricious or irrational in the public law sense.[160] Similarly, where insurers had the right to avoid a policy of insurance for non-disclosure, that right was subject to an implied term that the right would not be exercised arbitrarily, capriciously or irrationally.[161]

Rationality, however, is not the only limitation on the exercise of contractual **14.83** discretion. The court may intervene on any other ground upon which it could review a decision in public law. In *Braganza v BP Shipping Ltd*,[162] a contract of employment provided that death in service benefit would not be payable if "in the opinion of the Company" the death occurred because of the employee's wilful act. The question was whether on the evidence the company was entitled to conclude that the employee had committed suicide. Lady Hale referred to the test applied to the review of a decision of an administrative body in *Associated Provincial Pictures Houses Ltd v Wednesbury Corp*,[163] namely:

"The court is entitled to investigate the action of the local authority with a view to seeing whether they have taken into account matters which they ought not to take into account, or conversely, have refused to take into account or neglected to take into account matters which they ought to take into account. Once that question is answered in favour of the local authority, it may still be possible to say that, although the local authority have kept within the four corners of the matters which they ought to consider, they have nevertheless come to a conclusion so unreasonable that no reasonable authority could ever have come to it."

Lady Hale pointed out that this test had two limbs:

"The first limb focusses on the decision-making process—whether the right matters have been taken into account in reaching the decision. The second focusses upon its outcome—whether even though the right things have been taken into account, the result is so outrageous that no reasonable decision-maker could have reached it."

She concluded that:

"... unless the court can imply a term that the outcome be objectively reasonable—for example, a reasonable price or a reasonable term—the court will only imply a term that the decision-making process be lawful and rational in the public law sense, that the decision is made rationally (as well as in good faith) and consistently with its contractual purpose."

This involved both limbs of the *Wednesbury* test. As a result of this decision the exercise of a contractual discretion will be easier to challenge.[164] So where a secured lending facility entitled the lender to commission a valuation at the borrower's

---

[159] *IBM United Kingdom Holdings Ltd v Dalgleish* [2017] EWCA Civ 1212.
[160] *Watson v watchfinder.co.uk Ltd* [2017] EWHC 1275 (Comm); [2017] Bus. L.R. 1309.
[161] *UK Acorn Finance Ltd v Markel (UK) Ltd* [2020] EWHC 922 (Comm).
[162] [2015] UKSC 17; [2015] 1 W.L.R. 1661.
[163] [1948] 1 K.B. 223.
[164] Lords Hodge and Kerr agreed with Lady Hale. Lords Neuberger and Wilson dissented; but their dis-

expense, it was had that the valuation had to be commissioned in pursuit of legitimate commercial aims rather than to vex the borrower.[165]

14.84   Public law concepts were applied in *Evangelou v McNicol*[166] (a case about the Labour party's constitution). Beatson LJ said that:

> "... a discretion conferred on a party under a contract is subject to control which limits the discretion as a matter of necessary implication by concepts of honesty, good faith and genuineness, and need for absence of arbitrariness, capriciousness, perversity and irrationality."

And that:

> "... the principles to be applied were the same as those applied in public law cases, i.e. not only that the decision is made rationally and in good faith, but also that it is made consistently with its contractual purpose and, we add, that all relevant matters have been taken into account and irrelevant matters not taken into account."[167]

14.85   Attempts to impose an objective test of reasonableness, rather than the *Wednesbury* test, have rarely been successful.[168] The mere fact that one of the parties to the contract is the decision-maker does not necessarily prevent the imposition of an objective test, particularly where the question is one of interpretation of express terms, rather than the implication of a term. In *Lehman Brothers Special Financing Inc v National Power Corporation*,[169] Robin Knowles J said:

> "... the choice to make a party to the contract the decision maker does not, in my judgment, compel a conclusion that 'reasonableness' is deployed to mean rationality. It will depend on the wording and the context. The question of the nature of the decision making required by the parties to a contract is not the same as the question of the parties' choice of decision maker. The fact that the role of decision maker may place a party in a position of conflict of interest does not mean that 'reasonableness' can only mean rationality; the contract parties will have chosen to accept the conflict of interest. And conflict of interest is no less an issue if rationality is required."

However, where the contracting party entrusted with the discretion is itself subject to public law duties and constraints on the exercise of powers, the court is less likely to find a contractual duty which overlaps with that party's public law duties and constraints.[170]

14.86   Because the implied term is not automatic, it is necessary to consider whether it meets the tests for an implied term. In *Anders & Kern UK Ltd v CGU Insurance Plc*,[171] Toulson LJ said that in deciding the scope of any duty which may be implied from words in a contract which say 'unless a party consents', or words to that ef-

---

sent was a dissent on the facts rather than the legal test: Lord Neuberger at [103].
[165] *Property Alliance Group Ltd v Royal Bank of Scotland Plc* [2018] EWCA Civ 355; [2018] 1 W.L.R. 3529.
[166] [2016] EWCA Civ 817.
[167] See also *Faieta v ICAP Management Services Ltd* [2017] EWHC 2995 (QB); [2018] I.R.L.R. 227.
[168] See *Mercuria Energy Trading Pte Ltd v Citibank NA* [2015] EWHC 1481 (Comm).
[169] [2018] EWHC 487 (Comm); [2019] 3 All E.R. 53.
[170] *Hampshire County Council v Beazer Homes Ltd* [2010] EWHC 3095 (QB).
[171] [2008] 2 All E.R. (Comm) 1185.

fect, the context is vital. Thus an insurer had no duty to give consent to a state of affairs that would have materially increased the risk against which the insurance was in place. Although he rejected the submission that consent could not be unreasonably withheld, it is thought that even if that term had been implied the result would have been the same; because it would not have been unreasonable for an insurer to refuse to consent to a state of affairs that would have increased his risk.

In *Lehman Brothers International (Europe) v Exxonmobil Financial Services*   **14.87**
BV,[172] Blair J considered the nature of a contractual discretion in the context of a financial instrument. He pointed out that where a commercial contract gives one party a discretion, two separate questions arise: (a) what are the bounds of the discretion? And, (b) what approach does the court adopt if the discretion is not exercised or improperly exercised? He rejected the submission that *Braganza v BP Shipping Ltd*[173] (which suggested that both limbs of the *Wednesbury* test should be applied to the exercise of a contractual discretion) should be applied to the exercise of discretion in a commercial context. As he put it:

"The contractual discretion in the present case is given to a commercial party to a contract with another commercial party on the wholesale financial markets where the decision is as to the valuation of securities in the case of default. The decision is one which can be (and may need to be) taken without delay, and in which the non-Defaulting Party is entitled to have regard to its own commercial interests. In this kind of situation, I do not agree with LBIE that *Braganza* requires the kind of analysis of the decision-making process that would be appropriate in the public law context."

In *Patural v DG Services (UK) Ltd*,[174] Singh J sounded a note of caution in rela-   **14.88**
tion to a contract of employment. He said:

"In particular, it is clear that the two limbs of Wednesbury to which Lady Hale referred have been imported into this area of law also. This is an interesting example of the continuing development of the common law and in particular of the potential for cross-fertilisation between concepts of public law and private law, including the law relating to contracts of employment. However, for my part, I would respectfully sound a note of caution. It is to be recalled that the fundamental basis of public law is that public authorities have only those powers which are conferred upon them by law and must act in the public interest. Private actors such as employers and business entities more generally do not necessarily have the same duties. They may do so depending on the context."[175]

Where there is an alternative and explicit control mechanism, the implication of   **14.89**
a term may well be unnecessary.[176] One such control mechanism will be a requirement that a test of objective reasonableness must be satisfied. Another is where the

---

[172] [2016] EWHC 2699 (Comm); [2016] 2 C.L.C. 578.
[173] [2015] UKSC 17; [2015] 1 W.L.R. 1661.
[174] [2015] EWHC 3659 (QB); [2016] I.R.L.R. 286.
[175] Lord Sales also sounded a note of caution in "Use of powers for proper purposes in private law" (2020) L.Q.R. 384.
[176] *Mid Essex Hospital Services NHS Trust v Compass Group UK and Ireland Ltd (t/a Medirest)* [2013] EWCA Civ 200.

contract contains provisions for a challenge to the exercise of a contractual power, leaving the court as the final arbiter whether its exercise was justified.[177]

14.90   It is necessary for the court to be satisfied that the party in question does have a real discretion to exercise. In *Mid Essex Hospital Services NHS Trust v Compass Group UK and Ireland Ltd (t/a Medirest)*,[178] Jackson LJ also referred to a number of the cases referred to in the text and continued:

> "An important feature of the above line of authorities is that in each case the discretion did not involve a simple decision whether or not to exercise an absolute contractual right. The discretion involved making an assessment or choosing from a range of options, taking into account the interests of both parties. In any contract under which one party is permitted to exercise such a discretion, there is an implied term.[179] The precise formulation of that term has been variously expressed in the authorities. In essence, however, it is that the relevant party will not exercise its discretion in an arbitrary, capricious or irrational manner. Such a term is extremely difficult to exclude, although I would not say it is utterly impossible to do so."

In the same case Lewison LJ said:

> "... where one party to a contract has a discretion to exercise which will potentially impact upon the contractual rights and entitlements of another party to the contract the courts are more willing than heretofore to interpret the provisions conferring that discretion as being subject to implicit limits. Thus where one party to a contract has a discretionary power to decide whether a port is safe (*The Product Star (No 2)*[180]); or discretion to decide whether an employee should be paid a bonus, and if so how much (*Horkulak v Cantor Fitzgerald International*[181]; *Khatri v Cooperative Centrale*[182]); or discretionary power to raise interest rates (*Paragon Finance plc v Nash*[183]) an arbitrary or capricious exercise of discretion will be invalid. Indeed in some cases a failure to exercise a discretion or an arbitrary or capricious exercise of discretion will amount to a freestanding breach of contract sounding in damages (*Horkulak v Cantor Fitzgerald International*). But the rationale for interpreting discretionary powers as subject to implicit limitations is that without such limitations the discretion would be unfettered; or, as Leggatt LJ put it in *The Product Star (No 2)*, the exercise of the power would be the decision maker's 'uninhibited whim'. It is, therefore, a necessary control mechanism."

14.91   The limited grounds upon which the court may review an exercise of contractual discretion has consequences for the interpretation of the contract. In *Daniels v Lloyds Bank Plc*,[184] Cockerill J explained:

> "That limited scope of review however means that one must look carefully first

---

[177] *Kwik Lets Ltd v Khaira* [2020] EWHC 616 (QB).
[178] [2013] EWCA Civ 200; *Myers v Kestrel Acquisitions Ltd* [2015] EWHC 916 (Ch).
[179] The author is not convinced that this is a critical point. Where, for example, one party is given a discretion to approve or reject a proposal, there does not seem to be any reason in principle why the term should not be implied.
[180] [1993] 1 Lloyd's Rep. 397.
[181] [2005] I.C.R. 402.
[182] [2010] EWCA Civ 397.
[183] [2002] 1 W.L.R. 685.
[184] [2018] EWHC 660 (Comm); [2018] I.R.L.R. 813.

at whether the discretion relied upon exists—just as one would look carefully at the purpose for which the discretion is said to be exercised. Further the question of purpose forms a part of the exercise of contractual construction when determining whether the discretion contended for exists."

If the contract expressly provides for an objective standard of reasonableness, **14.92** there is no discretion in the sense discussed. In *Yilport Konteyner Terminali v Buxcliff KG*,[185] Mr Edelman QC (sitting as a judge of the Commercial Court) held that the fixing of a price for the discharge of containers damaged as a result of a collision was not a question of discretion limited only by subjective reasonableness. It was a term of the contract that the charges applied had to be objectively reasonable.

In *Pacific Basin IHX Ltd v Bulkhandling Handymax A/S*,[186] a charterparty provided that the vessel should not be ordered to any place where "in the reasonable judgment" of the master or owners she was likely to be exposed to war risks. Teare J held that this was not a case of contractual discretion; or that if it was there was no need to imply any term about how it should be exercised because of the express term that the judgment had to be reasonable. He added:

> "The effect of that clause is that the Owners must make a judgment. It must be made in good faith; otherwise it would not be a judgment but a device to obtain a financial gain. Further, the judgment reached must be objectively reasonable. An owner who wishes to ensure that his judgment is objectively reasonable will make all necessary enquiries. If he makes no enquiries at all it may be concluded that he did not reach a judgment in good faith. But if he makes those enquiries which he considers sufficient but fails to make all necessary enquiries before reaching his judgment I do not consider that his judgment will on that account be judged unreasonable if in fact it was an objectively reasonable judgment and would have been shown to be so had all necessary enquiries been made."

Similarly, in *Barclays Bank Plc v UniCredit Bank AG*,[187] an agreement provided **14.93** for a discretion to be exercised "in a commercially reasonable manner". Popplewell J held that this required the reasonableness of the decision in question to be objectively judged. However, whether a decision was objectively reasonable was to be tested by asking whether a reasonable person in the position of the decision maker, having regard to his own interest, could have reached the decision in question. On appeal[188] Longmore LJ said:

> "It is not easy to express a test for commercial reasonableness for the purpose of this (let alone any other) contract but I would tentatively express it by saying that the party who has to make the relevant determination will not be acting in a commercially reasonable manner if he demands a price which is way above what he can reasonably anticipate would have been a reasonable return from the contract into which he has entered and which it is sought to terminate at an early date."

---

185 [2012] EWHC 3289 (Comm); [2013] 1 Lloyd's Rep. 378.
186 [2011] EWHC 2862 (Comm); [2012] 1 Lloyd's Rep. 151.
187 [2012] EWHC 3655 (Comm); [2013] 2 Lloyd's Rep. 1.
188 [2014] EWCA Civ 302; [2014] 2 Lloyd's Rep. 59.

14.94   In *Lehman Brothers Special Financing Inc v National Power Corporation*,[189] the ISDA agreement provided for a close-out sum to be calculated by one party to the contract who "will act in good faith and use commercially reasonable procedures in order to produce a commercially reasonable result". Robin Knowles J held that this required an objective standard to be applied; although even applying that standard a decision could be objectively reasonable within a range of outcomes.

14.95   In *The Federal Mogul Asbestos Personal Injury Trust v Federal-Mogul Ltd*,[190] a contract for the handling of claims provided that an attorney should have "absolute authority, discretion and control, which shall be exercised in a businesslike manner in the spirit of good faith and fair dealing" to deal with the claims. Eder J held that the mandatory requirement stating how the discretion should be exercised involved:

> "… to some extent at least, an objective test which, although somewhat open-textured, is certainly capable of review by a Court; and that, if the Court were to conclude that Reinsurers were acting in a manner which was not 'business-like' in the spirit of good faith and fair dealing having regard to the matters stipulated, then I see no reason why such unbusinesslike conduct would not constitute an ordinary breach of contract by Reinsurers."

However, asking whether a charge or a price is objectively reasonable is not the same as asking whether a reasonable person fixing the charge or price could have reached the decision in question. It appears, therefore, that in cases such as *Pacific Basin IHX Ltd v Bulkhandling Handymax A/S* and *Barclays Bank Plc v UniCredit Bank AG* the concept of objective reasonableness is being used in a different sense.

14.96   In other cases there may be other limitations on the exercise of a contractual discretion. Where, for example, a contract is made against the background of regulation by a Directive of the EU the discretion may be limited by reference to the purposes of the Directive.[191]

14.97   It is a question of interpretation of the contract whether the exercise of discretion may be delegated.[192] Where the exercise of discretion requires special skill it is less easy to conclude that the exercise of discretion may be delegated.[193]

12.   DEEMING CLAUSES

A deeming clause may operate in a number of different ways. It may expand the ordinary meaning to be given to a word or phrase in the contract. It may prescribe consequences of taking or failing to take some step; or the consequence of some external event. It may be used to put beyond doubt whether a given state of affairs falls within a contractual provision. It may be used to create a contractual estoppel. It may also qualify contractual obligations that would otherwise have arisen. Where a deeming clause is used, it will usually be conclusive as to the deemed meaning or consequence.

---

[189] [2018] EWHC 487 (Comm); [2019] 3 All E.R. 53.
[190] [2014] EWHC 2002 (Comm).
[191] *British Telecommunications Plc v Telefonica O2 UK Ltd* British Telecommunications Plc v Telefónica O2 UK Ltd [2014] UKSC 42.
[192] *Carey Group Plc v AIB Group (UK) Ltd* [2011] EWHC 567.
[193] *Carey Group Plc v AIB Group (UK) Ltd.*

A deeming clause is a familiar technique in drafting contracts. It can be used in **14.98**
a number of ways. The first is to expand the ordinary meaning of a word or phrase.
In *Dairy Containers Ltd v Tasman Orient Line CV*,[194] a contract for the carriage
of goods by sea contained a clause which said:

"for the purpose of this sub-paragraph the limitation of liability under the Hague
Rules shall be deemed to be £100 Sterling, lawful money of the United Kingdom
per package or unit and references in the Hague Rules, to carriage by sea, shall
be deemed to include references to carriage by inland waterways."

Lord Bingham of Cornhill said:

"In each instance, the need for the deeming provision arises because without it
the term in question does not have the meaning it is to be deemed to have. The
limitation of liability under the rules is not '£100 Sterling, lawful money of the
United Kingdom per package or unit': it is the limitation provided by art IV, r 5
as qualified by art IX. The references to carriage by sea in the rules do not include
carriage by inland waterways. Thus the purpose of the deeming provision is to
give the rules a meaning different from that which they would have in the
absence of a deeming provision."

In some contexts a provision that deems X to be Y has the effect of creating a **14.99**
fiction that X is Y, but not in a way that stops what would ordinarily be Y from also
being Y.[195] But in others it will have precisely that effect. Thus where a clause in a
lease provided that service of a notice on the landlord would "not be deemed to be
validly served" unless a copy of the notice was served on the landlord's managing
agents, service on the landlord alone was ineffective. In such a case "deemed"
means "treated".[196] Likewise, where a non-reliance clause in an aircraft lease
acknowledged that "the Lessor has not and shall not be deemed to have made any
warranties or representations" about the aircraft, the effect of the clause was that
if any representations had been made, it was deemed that they had not.[197]

The second way in which a deeming clause is used is to spell out the conse- **14.100**
quences of taking some step specified in the contract, or the consequences of some
external event. Thus if a contract provides that a notice sent by one party to the other
using a specified method of transmission (e.g. recorded delivery post) is deemed
to have been given, the party sending the notice is relieved from the burden of having to prove receipt.[198] In the case of provisions dealing with notices, one of the
purposes of these provisions is to establish a fair allocation of the risks of any failure
of communication. The other main purpose is to avoid disputes on issues of fact
(especially as to whether a letter went astray in the post or was accidentally lost,
destroyed or overlooked after delivery to the premises of the intended recipient)

---

[194] [2005] 1 W.L.R. 215.
[195] *Zaccardi v Caunt* [2008] NSWCA 202.
[196] *Hotgroup Plc v Royal Bank of Scotland Plc* [2010] EWHC 1241 (Ch).
[197] *Trident Turboprop (Dublin) Ltd v First Flight Couriers Ltd* [2008] 2 Lloyd's Rep. 581.
[198] *Moncure v Cahusac* [2006] UKPC 54.

where the true facts are likely to be unknown to the person giving the notice, and difficult for the court to ascertain.[199]

14.101   A deeming clause may also prescribe the consequences of failing to take some specified step. In *Burrough's Adding Machines Ltd v Aspinall*,[200] a contract between a manufacturer and a salesman provided for him to be paid commission. The contract said that all statements of account sent by the company to him "shall be deemed to be accepted by the salesman as correct" unless he gave written notice that they were not within 30 days of receiving the account. It was held that if he failed to give notice, he was bound by the account, even if it was wrong.

In *Starmark Enterprises Ltd v CPL Distribution Ltd*,[201] a rent review clause provided for the landlord to serve a notice specifying a new rent. It went on to provide that if the tenant did not serve a counter-notice within a prescribed period, he would be "deemed to have agreed to pay the increased rent specified in the rent notice". The deeming clause displaced the usual presumption that time is not of the essence of a rent review timetable. Arden LJ said:

> "That proviso may loosely be referred to as a 'deeming' provision. The word 'deem' as used in legal drafting denotes a device for introducing a fiction. The word 'deem' in this type of context signals that the draftsman is about to introduce a fiction as if proviso (2) had read 'if the lessees shall fail to serve a counter-notice within the period aforesaid they shall be deemed to have agreed that black is white'. The concept of agreement in this situation is an artificial one."

14.102   A third way in which a deeming clause may be used is to prescribe consequences of some external event. In *Pancommerce SA v Veechema BV*,[202] a force majeure clause stated that:

> "In case of prohibition of export … or in case of any executive or legislative act done by or on behalf of the government of the country of origin … restricting export, whether partially or otherwise, any such restriction shall be deemed by both parties to apply to this contract and to the extent of such total or partial restriction to prevent fulfilment … and to that extent this contract or any unfulfilled portion thereof shall be cancelled."

Bingham J said:

> "It also follows by virtue of the clause that the restriction is deemed to the extent of the restriction to prevent fulfilment. I accept without reservation that the purpose of this deeming provision is to outlaw any factual enquiry into whether, but for the restriction, the seller could have performed the contract and whether his position was short or long and whether he could or should have obtained goods of the contractual description elsewhere. But what, in my judgment, it does not do is forbid enquiry into the extent of the restriction. Quite the contrary. It is only to the extent of the restriction that the restriction is deemed to prevent fulfilment and only to that extent that the contract is cancelled."

14.103   Fourth, a deeming provision may be used to put beyond doubt whether a given

---

[199] *Blunden v Frogmore Investments Ltd* [2002] 2 E.G.L.R. 29 CA.
[200] (1925) 41 T.L.R. 276.
[201] [2002] Ch. 306.
[202] [1982] 1 Lloyd's Rep. 645 (on appeal [1983] 2 Lloyd's Rep. 304).

state of affairs falls within a contractual provision. In *Howells v IGI Insurance Co Ltd*,[203] cl.11 of an insurance policy taken out on a professional footballer said that if he played more than five games during a stated period:

"the Insured shall be deemed conclusively to have been fully rehabilitated and no claim shall be payable hereunder ... ."

Potter LJ said:

"It is plain that clause 11 is a deeming clause, designed to define and put beyond doubt the test or definition of permanent total disablement from employment as a professional footballer."

Thus in this kind of case a deeming clause may be no more than a definition clause. It can give a word or phrase "a lexicon meaning".[204]

Fifth, a deeming clause may be used to create a contractual estoppel. In *Trident Turboprop (Dublin) Ltd v First Flight Couriers Ltd*,[205] a clause in an aircraft lease provided: **14.104**

"The Lessee also agrees and acknowledges that save as expressly stated in this Agreement and the other Transaction Documents to which the Lessor is a party, the Lessor has not and shall not be deemed to have made any warranties or representations, express or implied, about the Aircraft, including but not limited to the matters referred to above."

Aikens J said:

"The parties who agree such a clause are thus agreeing that no representations were made by Trident (as lessor), or, if any representations were made, then it is 'deemed' that they were not. The legal effect of provisions such as this has been analysed by the courts in terms of an estoppel created by contract: ... As Moore-Bick LJ points out at para 56 in the *Peekay* case, it is commercially convenient and desirable for parties to a contract to agree that a certain state of affairs (i.e. that no pre-contractual representations were made) is the case, so as to provide a clear basis for the contract itself. If the parties do agree a certain factual basis on which the contract is made, the contractual agreement is that neither party can subsequently deny that basis. Hence the phrase 'estoppel by contract'."

Sixth, a deeming clause may qualify contractual obligations that would otherwise   **14.105**
arise. In *William Sindall Plc v Cambridgeshire County Council*,[206] a contract for the sale of land contained the following terms:

"14.   Without prejudice to the duty of the vendor to disclose all latent easements and latent liabilities known to the vendor to affect the property, the property is sold subject to any rights of way and water, rights of common and other rights, easements, quasi-easements, liabilities and public rights affecting the same.

---

203 [2003] Lloyd's Rep. I.R. 803.
204 *Bernhard Schulte Shipmanagement (Bermuda) Ltd Partnership v BP Shipping Ltd* [2010] 2 All E.R. (Comm) 795.
205 [2008] 2 Lloyd's Rep. 581.
206 [1994] 1 W.L.R. 1016.

17.   The purchaser shall be deemed to purchase with full notice of and subject to: ... (e) all easements, quasi-easements rights and privileges (whether of a public or private nature) now affecting the property but without any obligation on the part of the vendor to define the same."

Hoffmann LJ said of these clauses:

"They qualify the obligations to convey as beneficial owner and give vacant possession and therefore qualify any representation which could be implied from having undertaken those obligations."

14.106   In deciding whether a clause is a deeming clause, the court will apply the usual techniques of interpretation including, where appropriate, the *contra proferentem* principle[207] and, in the case of a time limit, any applicable presumption that time is not of the essence.[208] Clear and unambiguous language will usually be required.[209] Even if a clause is clearly a deeming provision, there may yet be difficulties in deciding what exactly is the deemed state of affairs.[210] In case of doubt, the deeming clause will be construed *contra proferentem* (i.e. against the person in whose favour it operates)[211]; all the more so if the deeming clause is in reality an exemption clause.[212]

14.107   It is thought that in most cases a deeming clause will be definitive, except where the deeming clause makes it explicit that the contrary may be proved. In *Abigroup Contractors Pty Ltd v ABB Services Pty Ltd*,[213] Giles JA pointed out that:

"The word 'deemed' may create a fictitious situation, or it may simply state an indisputable conclusion."

In *Starmark Enterprises Ltd v CPL Distribution Ltd*,[214] Arden LJ concluded:

"Proviso (2) is a deeming provision and the natural meaning of the word 'deem' in my judgment is to introduce a conclusive state of affairs. There has to be some indication that the deemed state of affairs is not to survive in particular circumstances to exclude that normal meaning."

In *Mears Ltd v Costplan Services (South East) Ltd*,[215] a building lease provided that the landlord would not make changes to the works that would "materially affect the size (and a reduction of more than 3% of the size of any distinct area shown upon the Building Documents shall be deemed material)" of the property. Coulson LJ said that the purpose of the clause was to provide "a mechanism by which a breach of contract can be indisputably identified".

---

[207] See para.7.66.
[208] *Bickenhall Engineering Co Ltd v Grandmet Restaurants Ltd* [1995] 1 E.G.L.R. 110; *Wilderbrook Ltd v Oluwu* [2006] 2 P. & C.R. 54.
[209] *Tai Hing Cotton Mill Ltd v Liu Chong Hing Bank Ltd* [1986] A.C. 80, 110; *Financial Institutions Services Ltd v Negril Negril Holdings Ltd* [2004] UKPC 40.
[210] *Barbados Trust Co v Bank of Zambia* [2007] 1 Lloyd's Rep. 495.
[211] *WJB Chiltern Plc v Olympia Securities Commercial Plc* [2003] EWHC 3464 (Ch).
[212] *Demco Investments & Commercial SA v SE Banken Forsakring Holding AB* [2005] 2 Lloyd's Rep. 650.
[213] [2004] NSWCA 181.
[214] [2002] Ch. 306.
[215] [2019] EWCA Civ 502; [2019] 4 W.L.R. 55.

In *Lafarge (Aggregates) Ltd v Newham London Borough Council*,[216] Cooke J said that:

"The word 'deemed' can mean 'presumed until the contrary is proved', but it can also be used as a word of definition, stating how matters are to be regarded definitively for the purposes of the contract or document in question."

He concluded that the deeming provision in that case was definitive. In *Carne v Debono*,[217] condition 12(h) of a contract for the sale of land provided that any notice given by either party to the other should be deemed to have been served at the expiration 48 hours after it has been posted. Browne-Wilkinson V-C said that:

"Condition 12(h) is a deeming provision which does not exclude the possibility of proving an earlier receipt. It is not a statement that for all purposes the document shall only be treated as having been received at a particular time."

In *Re Thundercrest Ltd*,[218] the articles of association of a company contained **14.108** provisions relating to the deemed service of documents. Judge Paul Baker QC said:

"The purpose of deeming provisions in the case of management of companies is clear. In the case of uncertainty as to whether a document has been delivered, with large numbers of shareholders and so forth, there has to be some rule under which those in charge of the management can carry on the business without having to investigate every case where some shareholder comes along and says he has not got the document. The directors have to proceed and transact the company's business on the basis of the deeming provisions. But, in my judgment, all that falls away when you find it is established without any possibility of challenge that the document has not been delivered."

If a contract deems a particular state of affairs to exist, the inevitable **14.109** consequences of that state of affairs must also be assumed to exist. As Lord Asquith put it in *East End Dwellings Co Ltd v Finsbury Borough Council*,[219] a case of statutory construction:

"If you are bidden to treat an imaginary state of affairs as real, you must surely, unless prohibited from doing so, also imagine as real the consequences and incidents which, if the putative state of affairs had in fact existed, must inevitably have flowed from or accompanied it."

However, the key adverb is "inevitably". A deeming provision (or a contractual assumption) does not carry with it consequences that are no more than arguable consequences of the counter-factual assumption.[220] By the same token a deeming provision should be taken further than is required to effect the express deeming. So where a building contract provided machinery for requiring the making good of defects, a deeming provision which deemed defects to have been made good under that procedure did not deprive the building owner of other remedies in relation to

---

[216] [2005] 2 Lloyd's Rep. 577.
[217] [1988] 1 W.L.R. 1107.
[218] [1995] 1 B.C.L.C. 117.
[219] [1952] A.C. 109.
[220] *Cornwall Coast Country Club v Cardgrange Ltd* [1987] 1 E.G.L.R. 146.

defects that were subsequently discovered.[221] Similarly, a provision in a building contract that a variation in dimensions of more than 3 per cent would be deemed to be material did not of itself mean that the resulting breach of contract was material, such as to enable one party to the contract to terminate it.[222]

14.110 A deeming clause which operates between the contracting parties may have no consequences as against third parties. In *Re Cosslett (Contractors) Ltd*,[223] a clause in a building contract stated that when on site plant and materials were deemed to be the property of the employer. It was held that the clause did not actually pass property in the plant and materials, but that the employer had a charge over them. Millett LJ said:

> "Where, however, as in the present case the contract provides only that the plant and materials 'shall be deemed' or 'shall be considered' to be the property of the employer, the words are regarded as ambiguous. In such a case other provisions of the contract may be taken into account in order to decide whether the contract has the effect of passing the legal property in the plant and materials to the employer or whether, as the prima facie meaning of the words suggests, it does not have this effect but merely entitles the employer to act as if the property in the plant and materials had passed to him."

14.111 A deeming clause may also not protect a contracting party against equitable duties. In *Rignall Developments Ltd v Halil*,[224] a contract for the sale of land contained a clause that deemed the purchaser to have made local searches and enquiries and to have knowledge of all matters that searches would have revealed. It was held that despite the deeming clause the vendor was bound in equity to disclose a defect in title of which he was aware.

Illustrations

1. A facility agreement allowed the lenders to assign their rights to other banks with "the prior written consent" of the borrower. The agreement provided that "such consent" would be deemed to be given if no reply had been received from the borrower within 15 days after the making of a request for consent. The Court of Appeal was divided over the effect of the deeming provision. Waller LJ held that what was deemed to be given was a prior written consent. Rix LJ held that what was deemed to be given was a written consent, but only at the expiry of the 15-day period. Hooper LJ held that what was deemed to be given was simply consent.
Barbados Trust Co v Bank of Zambia[225]

2. A partnership was carried on from freehold premises. The partnership deed said that for the purposes of ascertaining any partner's interest in the property "the figure appearing in the Partnership accounts shall be deemed to be the value of the whole". That figure was the historic cost of the property. An outgoing partner was entitled to a "just valuation" of his share. It was held that the historic cost, rather than the market value of the property, was the value to be taken into account. The

---

[221] *Swansea Stadium Management Co Ltd v City & County of Swansea* [2019] EWHC 989 (TCC).
[222] *Mears Ltd v Costplan Services (South East) Ltd* [2019] EWCA Civ 502; [2019] 4 W.L.R. 55.
[223] [1998] Ch. 495.
[224] [1988] Ch. 190.
[225] [2007] 1 Lloyd's Rep. 495.

purpose of the deeming provision was to require there to be taken as the value of the property an amount which, but for the provision, might not be taken as its value.
In re White (Dennis), decd White v Minnis[226]

3.   Tax advisers were engaged on the basis of a success fee as a percentage of tax saved. Condition 3 of their terms of engagement stated that if an invoice was not disputed within a specified time limit "you will be deemed to have agreed to its terms". It was held that although the deeming provision might preclude challenge to the number of hours worked, it did not preclude challenge to the question whether the event amounting to success had actually occurred.
WJB Chiltern Plc v Olympia Securities Commercial Plc[227]

4.   A provision in a share sale agreement contained a clause regulating the service of documents. Notice given in accordance with the clause was deemed to be served. Notice could be given to the vendors at a certain address, with a copy to their solicitors marked for the attention of a named individual. The contract also provided for any change of solicitor to be notified to the counterparty. It was held that sending a copy of the notice to a different firm of solicitors, was not good service for the purposes of the contract.
Vaughan v Von Essen Hotels 5 Ltd[228]

5.   A building sub-contract provided that when on site all the sub-contractor's equipment should be deemed to be the property of the Contractor. It was held that the deeming clause was ambiguous on the question whether property in the equipment actually passed to the contractor. The ambiguity was resolved by reference to other contract terms. Title to the equipment did not pass to the contractor.
Alstom Power Ltd v SOMI Impianti SRL[229]

---

[226] [2001] Ch. 393.
[227] [2003] EWHC 3464 (Ch).
[228] [2007] EWCA Civ 1349.
[229] [2012] EWHC 2644 (TCC).

CHAPTER 15

STIPULATIONS AS TO TIME

Hours, days, months which are the rags of Time

John Donne: *The Sunne*

This bloody tyrant, Time

William Shakespeare: *Sonnet 16*

DIVISIONS OF TIME AND ITS COMPUTATION

1. YEAR

The word "year" in a contract may mean a calendar year or a period of 12 months reckoned from a date other than 1 January; or it may mean a period of less than 12 months.

The calendar year begins on 1 January. It consists of 365 days in a common year and 366 days in a leap year. A period of a year is measured from one date in the year to the corresponding date in the following year. Thus an employee's service which began on 13 October in a year preceding a leap year and ending on 11 October in the leap year was held not to be service for a year, even though it had lasted for 365 days.[1]   **15.01**

Where the word "year" is used in a contract, it may mean the calendar year or a period of 12 months reckoned from some date other than 1 January, according to the context. In some cases it may mean both these things in different parts of the same document. Thus in *IRC v Hobhouse*,[2] the taxpayer entered into a covenant on 5 May to pay a certain sum of money on 1 May "in each year". The word "year" was held to mean calendar year. Later in the document it was provided that the covenant was to last for eight years from the date of the deed. In that context the word "year" was held to mean a period of 12 months from the date of the deed, rather than a calendar year.   **15.02**

Moreover, it may be proved that the word "year" bears a special meaning by custom. Thus in *Grant v Maddox*,[3] a contract under which an actress was engaged for three years at a weekly salary was held to entitle her to be paid only during the theatrical season, for the word "year" had that special meaning in theatrical circles.

Likewise the context of a particular contract may lead to the conclusion that a "year" is a period of less than 12 months. In *Boufoy-Bastick v The University of the*   **15.03**

---

[1] *R. v Worminghall (Inhabitants)* (1817) 6 M. & S. 350. This is a manifestation of the "corresponding date rule" as to which see para.15.10.
[2] [1956] 1 W.L.R. 1393.
[3] (1846) 15 M. & W. 737.

West Indies,[4] a university academic was entitled to a supplementary pension if on retirement he had completed "ten years" of continuous service. The Privy Council held that, in context, a "year" meant an academic year. Lord Wilson said:

> "Take a student at the university who arrived on campus on 1 September and left on the first day of the long vacation, which appears to be 11 June. Would he not contend, and would the reasonable onlooker not agree, that he had completed a year of his studies? Or take a prisoner sentenced to ten years. A variety of rules means that the sentence need not mean, and often does not mean, that the prisoner must serve a full ten years. These two preliminary examples indicate only that in particular contexts there can be some flexibility in the concept of a year."

2. QUARTERS

For some purposes the year may be divided into quarters. Depending on the context the quarters may be of three calendar months each, or may be a period between two quarter days.

15.04   Notably in the law of landlord and tenant the year is divided into quarters. The four usual quarter days are 25 March (Lady Day); 24 June (Midsummer); 29 September (Michaelmas) and 25 December (Christmas). In some agricultural tenancies the "old" quarter days are still used. These are 11 days later than the usual quarter days.[5] Evidence may be admissible to show that a reference in a contract not under seal to the quarter days was intended to be a reference to the old quarter days.[6]

15.05   Where a contract refers to quarters of a year, it is a question of construction whether the contract means a period of three calendar months or a period between two of the usual quarter days. In *East v Pantiles (Plant Hire) Ltd*,[7] the expression "two quarters of a year" was construed as meaning six calendar months.

15.06   In *Durham Tees Valley Airport Ltd v BMI Baby Ltd*,[8] Davis J considered the meaning of the word "summer" in the context of an agreement regulating flights from a regional airport. He said:

> "The word 'summer' can have varying meanings depending on context, as I see it. Sometimes it can be used to connote a 3 month season (June, July, August) to be contrasted with the other 3 month seasons of autumn, winter and spring. According to the Shorter Oxford English Dictionary, sometimes in popular usage it connotes the period from mid-May to mid-August. Sometimes again it may be used in contrast simply to winter, in denoting one half of the year. I was told, in evidence, that for the scheduling purposes of the International Air Transport Association, 'summer' is defined as meaning from the last Sunday in March (corresponding presumably to the start of British Summer Time) until the last Saturday in October, with 'winter' being for the remainder of the year: although there was no evidence that this particular definition was widely accepted for

---

[4]   [2015] UKPC 27.
[5]   The old quarter days are those which derive from the unreformed Gregorian calendar. The tax year begins on old Lady Day (6 April).
[6]   *Doe d. Hall v Benson* (1821) 4 B. & Ald. 588; *Doe d. Spicer v Lea* (1809) East. 312.
[7]   [1982] 2 E.G.L.R. 111. See also *Samuel Properties (Developments) Ltd v Hayek* [1972] 1 W.L.R. 1296.
[8]   [2009] EWHC 852 (Ch).

airport/airline contracts (which, as I have said, are individually negotiated). All the same, I think, on the whole, that it is this last sense it has here."

3. MONTH

At common law a month means a lunar month, but in contracts made after 1 January 1926, month means a calendar month unless the context otherwise requires.

For reasons which are obscure, at common law a month means a lunar month. **15.07** One reason is given by Blackstone,[9] namely that a lunar month is a uniform period and capable of quarterly division into weeks. However, this reason was described by Atkin LJ as "inadequate".[10] He continued:

"The result is to adopt a meaning which is nearly always contrary to the intention of the parties. The rule is fortunately almost destroyed by exceptions. It does not apply to mercantile documents, or to statutes, or to mortgages, or to cases where the context requires the meaning of calendar months. It never did apply in ecclesiastical law. In the residue of cases, however, it clearly does apply, as is established by a series of authorities which we cannot overrule."

It is doubtful whether the first exception to the rule is quite as wide as stated, for it seems that it only covered mercantile transactions in the City of London.[11] The other exceptions are, however, well supported by authority. The authorities are collected in *Simpson v Margitson*[12] and *Bruner v Moore*.[13] In *Phipps (P) & Co (Northampton and Towcester Breweries) Ltd v Rogers*,[14] the rule was held to apply to a lease of a public house. Similarly, in *Bruner v Moore*,[15] it was held to apply to an option to purchase a patent.

However, the common law rule was altered by s.61 of the Law of Property Act **15.08** 1925 which provides:

"In all deeds, contracts ... and other instruments executed, made or coming into operation after [1 January 1926], unless the context otherwise requires—

(a) "Month" means calendar month ...".

The position at common law is thus of historical interest only.

A month is made up of consecutive days. Thus in *Stewart (CA) & Co v Phs Van* **15.09** *Ommeren (London) Ltd*,[16] a charterparty provided for hire to be paid at a rate "per calendar month". The ship went off hire for part of the month. The owners argued that they were entitled to retain the whole of the hire on the ground that the payment of hire was a payment for the next 30 or 31 days on which the ship was on hire, not a payment for the ensuing calendar month. The argument failed, and the

---

9   2 Bl. Com. 141.
10 In *Phipps (P) & Co (Northampton and Towcester Breweries) Ltd v Rogers* [1925] 1 K.B. 14.
11 *Turner v Barlow* (1863) 3 F. & F. 946, explained in *Bruner v Moore* [1904] 1 Ch. 305.
12 (1847) 11 Q.B. 23.
13 [1904] 1 Ch. 305.
14 [1925] 1 K.B. 14.
15 [1904] 1 Ch. 305.
16 [1918] 2 K.B. 560.

charterers were held to be entitled to recover a proportionate part of the hire as money paid for a consideration which had failed.

4. THE CORRESPONDING DATE RULE

Where a contract provides for the performance of an act within a certain number of months, the period expires on the day of the month bearing the same number as the date on which the period begins or, if there is no such day, on the last day of the month.

15.10   In *Dodds v Walker*,[17] Templeman LJ formulated the corresponding date rule as follows:

> "When time is limited by reference to calendar months no account can be taken of the fact that some months are longer or shorter than others. February equals March. In my judgment if an act is authorised to be performed on any arbitrary day in any month of the year, then one month elapses on the corresponding day of the next month, provided that the day of the act itself is excluded from computation."

Stephenson LJ added one qualification:

> "If the relevant calendar month in which the period expires is too short to provide a corresponding date, the period expires on the last day of that month, but if that period expires in a calendar month which is long enough to provide a corresponding date, that date appears to me to be the date on which the period expires."

The decision of the Court of Appeal was affirmed by the House of Lords[18] in which Lord Diplock said:

> "The corresponding date rule is simple. It is easy of application. Except in a small minority of cases ... all that the calculator has to do is to mark in his diary the corresponding date in the appropriate subsequent month. Because the number of days in five months of the year is less than in the seven others the inevitable consequence of the corresponding date rule is that one month's notice given in a 30 day month is one day shorter than one month's notice given in a 31 day month and is three days shorter if it is given in February. Corresponding variations in the length of notice reckoned in days occurs where the required notice is a plurality of months."

Dodds v Walker was concerned with the construction of a statute, but there is no difference in principle between a statute and a contract in this respect.[19]

---

[17]   [1980] 1 W.L.R. 1061.
[18]   [1981] 1 W.L.R. 1027.
[19]   *Wang v University of Keele* [2011] UKEAT/0223/10/CEA; [2011] I.C.R. 1251; *Webber v NHS Direct* UKEAT/0627/11/DM.

5.   DAY

The word "day" may mean either a calendar day or a period of 24 consecutive hours, according to the context.

There are many different ways of reckoning a day. As a period of time a day is **15.11** the time occupied by the earth in one revolution on its axis, in which the same terrestrial meridian returns to the sun; a period of 24 hours reckoned from a definite or given point. A solar or astronomical day is reckoned from noon to noon, while the civil day in most civilised countries is reckoned from midnight to midnight.[20] A calendar day is reckoned from midnight to midnight.In its ordinary sense, the word "day" in a contract refers to a calendar day. Thus where a contract specifies a day for performance of an obligation, the obliged party has until the end of that day to perform it (midnight).[21]

However, the context of a particular contract may show that the word "day" **15.12** means a period of 24 hours reckoned from some other time of day. Thus in *Cornioot v Royal Exchange Assurance Corp*,[22] a policy of marine insurance was for a voyage to a port and "for 30 days in port after arrival". It was held that the period of 30 days began to run at the precise time of day at which the ship arrived, and not at midnight following its arrival. Mathew LJ said:

"It appears to me that in order to give effect to the intention of the parties, the expression '30 days' in the policy must be construed as meaning, not thirty calendar days as contended by the plaintiff, but thirty consecutive periods of twenty four hours after the arrival of the ship."

This is, however, by no means a rule of general application, even in insurance cases. It was distinguished by the Court of Appeal in *Cartwright v MacCormack*[23] in which it was held that a period of 15 days covered by a policy meant 15 calendar days and consequently began to run at midnight on the date of issue of the policy.

A "working day" normally means a calendar day which is a day of work as **15.13** distinguished from a holiday. Thus a working day consists of 24 hours, and not merely of that part of the day during which work is carried on. "Working":

"does not define a part of a day but describes the character of the day as a whole."[24]

In *Lafarge (Aggregates) Ltd v Newham London Borough Council*,[25] Cooke J said

---

[20]   *Oxford English Dictionary* "day" II 6. This dictionary definition may not be scientifically correct. Although Greenwich Mean Time assumes that the earth makes one complete revolution every 24 hours precisely, it is only a mean. In fact, the "equation of time" (i.e. the difference between the assumption made by GMT and reality) varies by up to a few microseconds each day.

[21]   *Latimore Pty Ltd v Lloyd* [2020] QSC 136.

[22]   [1904] 2 K.B. 40.

[23]   [1963] 1 W.L.R. 18.

[24]   *Reardon Smith Line Ltd v Ministry of Agriculture Fisheries and Food* [1963] A.C. 691 HL, disapproving *Alvion Steamship Corp Panama v Galban Lobo Trading Co SA of Havana* [1955] 1 Q.B. 430. See also *The Mathraki* [1990] 2 Lloyd's Rep. 84.

[25]   [2005] 2 Lloyd's Rep. 577. The judge did not find it necessary on the facts to decide whether a "working day" was confined to particular hours when offices were open; but it is submitted that once a working day has been identified, the whole of the day counts as a working day.

that:

> "In ordinary parlance in the UK, 'working days' are Mondays to Fridays, excluding Christmas, Easter and Bank Holidays."

Saturday was not therefore a working day, even though one of the parties to the contract habitually worked on Saturdays.

15.14　A "weather working day" is a working day on which weather permits work to be carried on.[26]

15.15　In some cases a reference in a contract to days has been held to mean working days.[27] Moreover, it has been suggested that where a contract requires the giving of a stipulated number of days' notice the notice may only be given during normal working hours, and if given later would not be effectively given until working hours next recommenced.[28] So in *Momm v Barclays Bank International Ltd*,[29] the question arose when a payment had been made between banks. Kerr J said:

> "A day is a day. For banking purposes it ends at the close of working hours, and otherwise at midnight. Commerce requires that it should be clearly ascertainable by the end of the day whether a payment due to be made on that day has been made or not."

However, in *Afovos Shipping Co SA v Pagnan*,[30] the House of Lords declined to accept this view which was dependent on "the modalities of the recipient bank". Accordingly it was held that where hire under a charterparty has to be paid to a bank on a particular day, the payer has until midnight on that day in which to make the payment. This is consistent with the principle that once a working day has been identified the whole of the day counts as a working day.

15.16　In some cases, however, a day may be a "conventional day"[31]; that is to say a

> "horizontal strip of 24 hours ... across the vertical strips represented by the calendar days of 24 hours ...".[32]

A "conventional day" begins at a time of day determined by the contract, and ends 24 hours later.

Illustrations

1.　A policy of insurance insured a ship during a voyage and for 30 days' stay in her last port of discharge. It was held that the period of 30 days began to run 24 hours after the arrival of the ship, as it was the practice of insurers and insured to treat the 24 hours after the arrival of the ship as part of the voyage.
Mercantile Marine Insurance Co v Titherington[33]

---

[26] *Reardon Smith Line Ltd v Ministry of Agriculture Fisheries and Food* [1963] A.C. 691 HL.
[27] *Commercial Steamship Co v Boulton* (1875) 10 Q.B.D. 346.
[28] *Rightside Properties Ltd v Gray* [1975] Ch. 72.
[29] [1977] Q.B. 790.
[30] [1983] 1 W.L.R. 195.
[31] *The Mathraki* [1990] 2 Lloyd's Rep. 84.
[32] *Reardon Smith Line Ltd v Ministry of Agriculture Fisheries and Food* [1963] A.C. 691.
[33] (1864) 5 B. & S. 765.

2.   An advice note stated that demurrage would be charged at a specified rate if certain goods were not unloaded and removed within 48 hours after the despatch of the notice, and that the defendant was to send for the goods not later than 18.00 and not later than 13.00 on Saturdays. The notice was received on a Saturday, and unloading began on that day and was completed on the following Tuesday. It was held that in calculating the period of 48 hours the whole of each day (except Sunday) was to be included, not merely that part of the day on which unloading could take place.

Lancashire and Yorkshire Railway Co v Swann[34]

6.   TIME OF DAY

Where an expression of time occurs in a contract the time referred to is taken to be Greenwich Mean Time (or British Summer time during the period of summer time) unless the contrary is specifically stated.

Section 9 of the Interpretation Act 1978 provides: **15.17**

"Subject to section 3 of the Summer Time Act 1972 (construction of references to points of time during the period of summer time), whenever an expression of time occurs in an Act, the time referred to shall, unless it is otherwise specifically stated, be held to be Greenwich mean time."

By s.23(3) of the Act, s.9 is applied to deeds and other instruments or documents. During the period of summer time[35] the time may be fixed by order either one or two hours ahead of Greenwich Mean Time. In practice, it is usually one hour ahead. Section 3(1) of the Summer Time Act 1972[36] provides that:

"wherever any reference to a point of time occurs in any ... deed notice or other document whatsoever, the time referred to shall, during the period of summer time, be taken to be fixed for general purposes by this Act."

However, the Act does not affect the use of Greenwich Mean Time for purposes of astronomy, meteorology or navigation, or affect the construction of any document mentioning or referring to a point of time in connection with any of those purposes.[37]

But it appears that if something is to be done on a particular day, the day begins at midnight local time and not Greenwich Mean Time.[38]

---

[34] [1916] 1 K.B. 263.

[35] See Summer Time Order 2002 (SI 2002/262). Summer time begins at one o'clock, Greenwich Mean Time, in the morning of the last Sunday in March and ends at one o'clock, Greenwich Mean Time, in the morning of the last Sunday in October. At the beginning of summer time clocks are put forward one hour, and at the end of summer time they are put back one hour.

[36] As amended by the Summer Time Order 2002 (SI 2002/262).

[37] Summer Time Act 1972 s.3(2).

[38] See *R. v Logan* [1957] 2 Q.B. 589 (a criminal case concerning the commencement of an English Act of Parliament as applied to the armed forces overseas).

7. FRACTIONS OF A DAY

In general, fractions of a day are ignored in construing contracts, although the particular context may indicate that regard is to be had to fractions of a day, particularly where questions of priority may depend upon the precise time at which an event occurs.

15.18   In *Pugh v Duke of Leeds*,[39] Lord Mansfield said:

"'Date' does not mean the hour or the minute, but the day of delivery; and in law there is no fraction of a day."

The general rule was stated at greater length by Sir William Grant MR in *Lester v Garland*[40] as follows:

"Our law rejects fractions of a day more generally than the civil law does. The effect is to render the day a sort of indivisible point; so that any act, done in the compass of it, is no more referable to anyone, than to any other, portion of it; but the act and the day are co-extensive; and therefore the act cannot properly be said to be passed, until the day is passed."

15.19   Thus in *Cartwright v MacCormack*,[41] a policy of insurance commenced at 11.45 on the date of the policy and stated that the cover was valid "for fifteen days from the commencement date of risk". It was held that the period of 15 days should be measured from midnight on the commencing day. Harman LJ said:

"… generally speaking, when a day is mentioned from which the time is to start running, fractions of a day ought to be disregarded and time should run from midnight."

15.20   However, fractions of a day may be taken into account where the circumstances warrant it. In *Re North Ex p. Hasluck*,[42] Lord Esher MR said:

"No general rule exists for the computation of time, either under the Bankruptcy Act or any other statute, or, indeed, where time is mentioned in a contract, and the rational mode of computation is to have regard in each case to the purpose for which the computation is to be made."

Rigby LJ added:

"It is said that the law takes no account of fractions of a day; but that is not a correct statement, if it means that the law will never inquire at what time a particular event took place; for instance a difference of five minutes in the registration of two deeds in the Middlesex Registry would be sufficient to determine a question of priorities, and the time of their respective registrations would, as a matter of course be looked at. If the doctrine is cut down to the proposition that in

---

[39]   (1777) 2 Cowp. 714.
[40]   (1808) 15 Ves. 248. Parties are, however, free to exclude the rule in *Lester v Garland*: *Trafford MBC v Total Fitness (UK) Ltd* [2003] 2 P. & C.R. 2 CA.
[41]   [1963] 1 W.L.R. 18.
[42]   [1895] 2 Q.B. 264.

the computation of time the law takes no account of fractions of a day, then it means one of two things: either that the fraction of a day is to be taken as one whole day, or that it is to be excluded altogether from the calculation; it does not help us to determine in any particular case whether the part is to be left out or kept in."

The nature of the contract may also bear on the question whether fractions of a **15.21** day are to be regarded. Thus in *Yeoman v R.*,[43] a charterparty provided for cargo to be discharged at a particular rate per working day, with demurrage to be paid at a certain rate per day and pro rata. Loading ought to have been completed by 09.00 on a particular day. The charterers argued that they were entitled to the whole of that day on the ground that the law took no account of fractions of a day. However, it was held that the demurrage became payable at 09.00 and not at the following midnight. Romer LJ said that:

"there is no reason upon the terms of the charterparty why, in calculating the time allowed for discharging the cargo, fractions of a day should not be taken into consideration."

By contrast, in *Commercial Steamship Co v Boulton*,[44] it was held that a portion of a day counted as a whole day for the purpose of demurrage payable at a rate per day.

In addition, where a composite bargain is to be effected by multiple contracts **15.22** entered into on the same day, it may be presumed that the documents were executed in the correct order.[45]

8. Inclusion or Exclusion of Days in Computing Time

Where, under a contract, a period of time is expressed to run from a certain day, the day named is generally excluded in computing the period. But where a period of time is expressed to begin on a certain day, the day named is gener- ally included in computing the period. However, the context may displace the general rule.

In *Ex p. Toohey's Ltd: Re Butler*,[46] Toohey CJ said: **15.23**

"The general rule is that in computing a period of time from the date, or the day of the date, of a deed, or any fixed day—that day is prima facie to be excluded, but the context or other admissible evidence may show that it is to be included; whereas in computing a period of time which commences on a fixed day, that day is included …".[47]

In *Lester v Garland*,[48] Sir William Grant MR stated that there was no general rule, **15.24** but held that in the circumstances of that case the date which started time running

---

43   [1904] 2 K.B. 429.
44   (1875) 10 Q.B.D. 346.
45   See para.10.05.
46   (1934) 34 S.R. (NSW) 277.
47   See also [2004] NSWSC 628, rightly criticising a previous edition of this work.
48   (1808) 15 Ves. 248.

should be excluded from the computation of time. He said:

> "It is not necessary to lay down any general rule upon this subject: but upon technical reasoning I rather think, it would be more easy to maintain, that the day of an act done, or an event happening, ought in all cases to be excluded, than that it should in all cases be included."

The proposition that there is no general rule was confirmed by Lord Esher MR in *Re North Ex p. Hasluck*,[49] in which he described Grant MR as having:

> "laid down what I conceive to be the wholesome view that no general rule exists."

15.25   However, it seems that willy-nilly general rules have developed. In *Webb v Fairmainer*,[50] Parke B said:

> "Whatever doubt there might have been upon the point before the decision in *Lester v Garland*, since that case the rule appears to be that the time is to be calculated exclusively of the day on which the contract was made."

And in *Dodds v Walker*,[51] Lord Diplock said:

> "It is also clear under a rule that has been consistently applied by the courts since *Lester v Garland* that, in calculating the period that has elapsed after the occurrence of the specified event ... the day on which the event occurs is excluded from the reckoning."

15.26   So where an interest (e.g. under a lease) is expressed to run from a particular date, prima facie the interest begins at midnight at the end of the named day. Thus in *Ackland v Lutley*,[52] Lord Denman said:

> "The general understanding is, that terms for years last during the whole anniversary of the day from which they are granted."

Since the anniversary of the day named is included, it follows that the named day itself must be excluded. So in *Meggeson v Groves*,[53] a tenancy was granted for a term from 25 March. It was held that the term began at midnight on that day.

15.27   The rule is not a rule of law and may be displaced in appropriate circumstances.[54] Thus in *Ladyman v Wirral Estates Ltd*,[55] Fisher J said:

> "It seems to me that a general rule can be derived from the authorities, namely, that, prima facie, a lease in those terms[56] commences from the first moment of the day following that named, but it seems to me equally to be well-established by the cases that this is only a prima facie indication, and that it can be displaced

---

[49]   [1895] 2 Q.B. 264.
[50]   (1838) 3 M. & W. 473.
[51]   [1981] 1 W.L.R. 1027.
[52]   (1839) 9 Ad. & El. 879.
[53]   [1917] 1 Ch. 158.
[54]   *Trafford MBC v Total Fitness (UK) Ltd* [2003] 2 P. & C.R. 2.
[55]   [1968] 2 All E.R. 197; *Whelton Sinclair v Hyland* [1992] 2 E.G.L.R. 158 CA.
[56]   For example, commencing from a named day.

if, on the construction of the lease or agreement for lease, a contrary intention can be derived."

In that case the lease reserved rent in advance payable on four specified days in the year, and the lease was expressed to run from one of those days. It was held that the named day was included in the term.

Where a period of time is required to be calculated as "beginning on" or "with" **15.28** a certain date, that date must be included in the calculation.[57] In the context of legislation Chadwick LJ summarised the position in *Zoan v Rouamba*[58] as follows:

"Where, under some legislative provision, an act is required to be done within a fixed period of time 'beginning with' or 'from' a specified day, it is a question of construction whether the specified day itself is to be included in, or excluded from, that period. Where the period within which the act is to be done is expressed to be a number of days, months or years from or after a specified day, the courts have held, consistently ... that the specified day is excluded from the period; that is to say, that the period commences on the day after the specified day ...

Where, however, the period within which the act is to be done is expressed to be a period beginning with a specified day, then it has been held, with equal consistency over the past forty years or thereabouts, that the legislature (or the relevant rule-making body, as the case may be) has shown a clear intention that the specified day must be included in the period."

It is considered that the same principles would apply to a contract.

Illustrations

1.   Letters patent dated 25 February 1825, were granted for a term of 14 years. It was held that they expired at midnight on 25 February 1839, the day of the letters patent having been included in the term.
Russell v Ledsam[59]

2.   A settlement dated 13 May 1892, required trustees to hold property on trust for 21 years and at the expiry of the term to sell the property. It was held that the term began at midnight on 12 May 1892.
English v Cliff[60]

9.   ACTION WITHIN A CERTAIN PERIOD

Where a person is required to perform an act within a certain period the day of the date or event from which the period runs will not be included in the period; and the act may be performed at any time up to the last moment of the last day of the period.

---

[57]   *Trow v lnd Coope (West Midlands) Ltd* [1967] 2 Q.B. 899, per Salmon LJ.
[58]   [2000] 1 W.L.R. 1509 at 1516–1517.
[59]   (1845) 14 M. & W. 574.
[60]   [1914] 2 Ch. 376.

15.29   In *Lester v Garland*,[61] a will required the testator's sister to give security, within six months after the testator's death, not to marry a certain person. Sir William Grant MR approved the submission of counsel that there was a distinction to be drawn between a case where the triggering event was an act to which the person against whom time runs was privy, and a case in which the triggering event was foreign to that person. In the former case there might be ground for including the day of the triggering event in reckoning the period, whereas in the latter case it would not be reasonable to do so. Since the testator's sister was not privy to the testator's death, the day of his death was not to be included in the period of six months.

The approach of Sir William Grant MR has evolved into a rule of construction, even where the person against whom time is to run is privy to the triggering event. So in *Webb v Fairmainer*,[62] goods were sold on 5 October to be paid for in two months. It was held that 5 October was to be excluded in reckoning the period of two months. However, like other "rules" of construction, the principle in *Lester v Garland* may be displaced by the language of the particular instrument. Thus where a notice was served on 8 October 2001 stating that it was giving 17 days' notice to terminate a lease, and also saying that "for the avoidance of all doubt" that the lease would terminate on 24 October, the Court of Appeal held that the notice was unambiguous in terminating the lease on 24 October and that the rule in *Lester v Garland* should not be used so as to create an ambiguity.[63]

15.30   Where a person is required to perform an act "within" a certain period the act may be performed up to the last moment of the last day of that period.[64] So in *Manorlike Ltd v Le Vitas Travel Agency and Consultancy Services Ltd*,[65] a lease contained a clause entitling the landlord to terminate it by not less than three months' notice. The landlord served notice on the tenant requiring the tenant to vacate the property "within a period of three months" from service of the notice. The notice was held to be good. Kerr LJ said:

> "To my mind the word 'within,' used in the context of a period of time, is capable of meaning 'before or at the expiry of' that period ... it is not necessarily shorter than the period itself."

Nourse LJ said:

> "The precise meaning of a preposition such as 'within' depends on the context in which it is used. Here it is used in a legal document and it is applied to a period of three months' notice. In such a context I see no difference between the meanings of 'within' and 'during,' in my view if someone is required to vacate premises within or during a specified period, he will comply with the requirement by walking out of the door either before, or on, the stroke of midnight on the last day of the period."

15.31   Similarly, if something is required to be done "by" a date, it may be done on the

---

[61]   (1808) 15 Ves. 248.
[62]   (1838) 3 M. & W. 473.
[63]   *Trafford MBC v Total Fitness (UK) Ltd* [2003] 2 P. & C.R. 2.
[64]   *Page v More* (1850) 15 Q.B. 684.
[65]   [1986] 1 All E.R. 573.

specified date itself. In *Eastaugh v Macpherson*,[66] Evershed MR said:

> "As a matter of definition ... I should be inclined to think that 'by the date' ought to mean 'on or before the date'."

By contrast if something is to be done "on the expiry of" a period, it is not done "within" that period.[67] Likewise where an appointment had to be made "before" a specified date, it could not validly be made on the specified date itself.[68]

Illustration

A hire agreement required the hire and other charges to be repaid by the hirer by a "single payment ... on the expiry of 12 months starting with the date of this agreement". It was held that it could not have been expected that the hire would be paid on the stroke of midnight; and that consequently the words were to be flexibly interpreted to permit payment a reasonable time after the expiry of 12 months.
Ketley v Gilbert[69]

10. ACTION FORTHWITH OR AS SOON AS POSSIBLE

Where something is to be done "forthwith" or "as soon as possible" it is to be done in the shortest practicable time having regard to the circumstances surrounding the making of the contract.[70]

An obligation to do something forthwith will not usually be construed as requiring instantaneous performance. Thus in *Staunton v Wood*,[71] a contract for the sale of cable bars provided for the bars to be delivered "forthwith" and for payment to be made 14 days after the date of the contract. It was held that the obligation to deliver "forthwith" required delivery at some time in the 14 days before payment became due. So too in *Hydraulic Engineering Co Ltd v McHaffie Goslett & Co*,[72] a contract required the manufacture of part of a machine called a gun "as soon as possible". The manufacturer did not have a foreman competent to cut the required pattern and consequently delayed in making the gun. It was held that a breach of the obligation had been committed. Bramwell LJ said:

15.32

> "... to do a thing 'as soon as possible' means to do it within a reasonable time, with an undertaking to do it in the shortest practicable time ... I quite agree that a manufacturer or tradesman is not bound to discard all other work for the occasion, in order to take in hand a thing which he promises to do 'as soon as possible': for instance a tailor, who accepts an order to make a coat 'as soon as possible' need not put down a half made vest in order to begin the coat; every customer knows at the time of giving the order that the manufacturer or tradesman may have other orders on hand."

[1954] 1 W.L.R. 1307.
[67] *Ketley v Gilbert* [2001] 1 W.L.R. 986.
[68] *Breadner v Granville-Grossman* [2000] 4 All E.R. 705.
[69] [2001] 1 W.L.R. 986.
[70] Cited with approval in *Trafigura Maritime Logistics PTE Ltd v Clearlake Shipping PTE Ltd* [2020] EWHC 995 (Comm).
[71] (1851) 16 Q.B. 638.
[72] (1878) 4 Q.B.D. 670.

15.33   However, the particular difficulties of the manufacturer were not to be taken into account in determining how soon was as soon as possible. Cotton LJ said that the manufacturers:

> "must be taken to have meant that they would make the 'gun' as quickly as it could be made in the largest establishment with the best appliances."

15.34   A rather less objective approach was adopted by Roche J in *Verelst's Administratrix v Motor Union Insurance Co Ltd*.[73] In that case the personal representatives of a deceased person were required to give notice of the deceased's death to an insurance company "as soon as possible". The administratrix did not know of the existence of the policy for a year after the death, but gave notice as soon as she discovered the policy. It was held that the words "as soon as possible" meant as soon as possible in the circumstances actually affecting the administratrix. Accordingly, the insurers were liable on the policy.

15.35   In *Re Coleman's Depositories*,[74] a policy of insurance covering the liability of an employer to compensate his workmen for injuries by accident in the course of their employment was made subject to a condition that the employer should give immediate notice of any accident causing injury to a workman. Fletcher Moulton LJ said that:

> "although the word 'immediate' is no doubt a strong epithet, I think that it might be fairly construed as meaning with all reasonable speed considering the circumstances of the case."

15.36   The inclusion of the words "as soon as possible" to describe the time of performance of a contractual obligation may have the effect of indicating that the obligation is a condition of the contract.[75] Likewise, in *Tarkin AG v Thames Steel UK Ltd*,[76] a contract for the sale of scrap metal provided that "Material is to be delivered in the port immediately upon the Buyer's request". Blair J held that "by the use of the word 'immediately', the parties made time of the essence in that respect".

Illustration

A contract for the laying of a submarine cable provided for a vessel to be brought "forthwith" alongside a wharf. It was held that "forthwith" did not mean immediately, but meant "without delay or loss of time."
Roberts v Brett[77]

---

[73]   [1925] 2 K.B. 137.
[74]   [1907] 2 K.B. 798. This dictum was followed and applied in *Aspen Insurance UK Ltd v Pectel Ltd* [2008] EWHC 2804 (Comm).
[75]   *The Post Chaser* [1981] 2 Lloyd's Rep. 695 (obligation to declare a ship to buyers under a c.i.f. contract "as soon as possible").
[76]   [2010] EWHC 207 (Comm).
[77]   (1865) 11 H.L. Cas. 337.

11. Period on Expiry of which Act is to be Done

Where something is to be done at the expiry of a certain period it may not be done before midnight on the last day of the period, but may be done as soon as possible thereafter.

In *English v Cliff*,[78] a settlement required trustees to hold property on trust for 21 years and at the expiry of the period of 21 years to sell the trust property and hold the proceeds on different trusts. The question arose whether the trust was void for perpetuity on the ground that the interest would not vest for more than 21 years. Warrington J held that the trust was valid. He said:

15.37

> "The trust in the present case is to arise at the expiration of the term of twenty one years, and if looked at from one point of view that trust arises coincidentally with the last moment of the term, although, if looked at from another point of view, it may be said to arise at some infinitesimally small fraction of time after the last moment of the term. In my opinion, however, the only sensible view to be taken of such a limitation is that the term determines and the trust arises at the very same moment of time, and if looked at in that way it is impossible to say that the trust arises at a later period than that allowed by law. It seems to me therefore that the term determines and the trust arises at mathematically and identically the same moment, and so far as that objection goes I am of opinion that the trust is a good one."

It follows that if something is to done "on the expiry of" a period, it is not done "within" that period.[79]

The Importance of Being Punctual

12. Time of the Essence as a Matter of Interpretation

It is a question of interpretation of the contract whether stipulations as to time are of the essence of the contract, although the meaning of the time stipulation itself is unaffected by the answer to that question.

In general, parties are free to stipulate whether or not stipulations as to time in a contract must be strictly complied with. They are also by and large free to prescribe the consequences of a failure to take some step within a timetable expressed in the contract. Thus a failure to comply with a time limit may itself entitle the other party to treat the contract as at an end, or it may deprive the party in default of some right or advantage which would otherwise have accrued to him.

15.38

In some cases (notably in the Sale of Goods Act 1979) statute has intervened. Otherwise, it is a question of interpretation whether time is of the essence of a particular contractual stipulation. In *Bunge Corp v Tradax Export SA*,[80] Lord Wilberforce said:

15.39

---

[78]   [1914] 2 Ch. 376.
[79]   *Ketley v Gilbert* [2001] 1 W.L.R. 986.
[80]   [1981] 1 W.L.R. 711.

"As to such a clause there is only one kind of breach possible, namely to be late, and the questions to be asked are: first what importance have the parties expressly ascribed to this consequence? And, second, in the absence of expressed agreement, what consequence ought to be attached to it having regard to the contract as a whole?"

Similarly, Lord Lowry said:

"It is by construing a contract (which can be done as soon as the contract is made) that one decides whether a term is, either expressly or by necessary implication, a condition, and not by considering the gravity of the breach of that term (which cannot be done until the breach is imminent or has occurred)."

15.40   However, in strict theory, the question whether time is or is not of the essence of a stipulation as to time does not affect the meaning of that stipulation itself. In *Tilley v Thomas*,[81] Rolt LJ said:

"Now as a matter of construction merely, I apprehend the words must have the same meaning in equity as in law. The rights and remedies consequent on that construction may be different in the two jurisdictions, but the grammatical meaning of the expression is the same in each. And if this be so, time is part of the contract, and if there is a failure to perform within the time the contract is broken in equity no less than at law. But in equity there may be circumstances which will induce the Court to give relief against the breach, and sometimes even though occasioned by the neglect of the suitor asking for relief. Not so at law. The legal consequences of the breach must there be allowed strictly to follow."

15.41   As Lord Wilberforce recognised, failure to comply with a time stipulation is a breach of the contract: it is a separate question whether parties have expressly or by necessary implication provided for particular consequences to flow from delay. Accordingly, where a party to a contract for the sale of land fails to complete on the contractual completion date, damages for breach of contract may be recovered against him, even though time is not of the essence of the completion date.[82]

13.   Whether Time is of the Essence

Time stipulations are not of the essence in a non-mercantile contract unless the contract expressly so provides; or the nature of the contract or the surrounding circumstances show that time should be taken to be of the essence. In mercantile contracts, however, time will usually be of the essence of time stipulations.

15.42   The common law traditionally regarded stipulations as to time in a contract as conditions of a contract which had to be strictly complied with. However, historically courts of equity took a different view. A court of equity would often relieve against a failure to comply strictly with a time limit (e.g. in the case of a mortgage which could always be redeemed after the contractual date for repayment had

---

[81] (1867) L.R. 3 Ch. App. 61.
[82] *Phillips v Lamdin* [1949] 2 K.B. 33; *Raineri v Miles* [1981] A.C. 1050.

passed) unless the time limit was "of the essence of the contract". The view of equity has prevailed. Section 41 of the Law of Property Act 1925 provides:

"Stipulations in a contract, as to time or otherwise, which according to rules of equity are not deemed to be or to have become of the essence of the contract, are also construed and have effect at law in accordance with the same rules."

This section received the close attention of the House of Lords in *United Scientific Holdings Ltd v Burnley Borough Council*,[83] in which it was held that time was not of the essence of a timetable in a rent review clause in the absence of contra-indications in the lease or in the inter-relation of the rent review clause with other clauses in the lease or with the surrounding circumstances. Lord Simon of Glaisdale said of s.41:

"I cannot read section 41 of the Law of Property Act 1925 as meaning other than that, whenever contractual stipulations as to time fall for consideration in any court, they shall not be construed as essential, except where equity would before 1875 have so construed them, i.e. only when the strict observance of the stipulated time for performance was a matter of express agreement or necessary implication."

However, this passage (and similar expressions of opinion in the speeches of Lords Diplock and Fraser of Tullybelton) cannot be extended into the sphere of mercantile contracts. This was made clear by the House of Lords in *Bunge Corp v Tradax Export SA*,[84] in which an attempt to extend the reasoning of the House of Lords into the realm of mercantile contracts was firmly rejected as being inconsistent with a long line of authority which had not been referred to their Lordships in the *United Scientific* case. **15.43**

In *Urban 1 (Blonk Street) Ltd v Ayres*,[85] Etherton C said: **15.44**

"It is necessary to distinguish between three types of contractual time provision. They are those which are conditions in the technical sense that any breach of them, however slight, is a repudiatory breach of contract which entitles the other party to terminate the contract immediately; those which are warranties in the technical sense that any breach of them, however serious, will only ever entitle the other party to damages and not to terminate the contract; and those which are so-called innominate terms, breach of which will only be a repudiation of the contract entitling the other party to terminate the contract if the breach deprives him or her of substantially the whole benefit which it was intended they should obtain from the contract or, in simpler language, which goes to the root of the contract: *Hong Kong Fir Shipping Co Ltd* at 69 to 70. It is a matter to be determined on ordinary principles of contractual interpretation into which of those categories the term falls."[86]

He went on to discuss the consequences of classifying a time stipulation.

---

[83] [1978] A.C. 904.
[84] [1981] 1 W.L.R. 711.
[85] [2013] EWCA Civ 816.
[86] See also *Petrocapital Resources Plc v Morrison & Foerster (UK) LLP* [2013] EWHC 2682 (Ch) at [163].

15.45   In *Reuter v Sala*,[87] a contract provided for the sellers to declare shipments of pepper by a particular date. Cotton LJ said:

"It was argued that the rules of courts of equity are now to be regarded in all courts, and that equity enforced contracts though the time fixed therein for completion had passed. This was in cases of contracts such as purchases and sales of land, where, unless a contrary intention could be collected from the contract, the Court presumed that time was not an essential condition. To apply this to mercantile contracts would be dangerous and unreasonable. We must therefore hold that the time within which the pepper was to be declared was an essential condition of the contract, and in such a case the decisions in equity, on which reliance is placed, do not apply."

So also in a mercantile contract the time for shipment[88]; the time for presentation of documents[89]; the time for delivery of goods[90]; and the time at which a ship is expected ready to load[91] have all been held to be of the essence of the contract (or, which comes to the same thing, to be conditions of the contract) while the time for payment is not. So also, the time during which cargo must be loaded under a charterparty will not usually be held to be of the essence of the contract, for delay is adequately catered for by demurrage.[92]

15.46   In addition, time limits in a unilateral contract, such as an option, are also of the essence, even in the case of a non-mercantile contract.[93]

15.47   However, as Browne-Wilkinson VC pointed out in *British and Commonwealth Holdings Ltd v Quadrex Holdings Ltd*,[94] the phrase time being of the essence "of the contract" can be misleading. He said:

"The basic question is whether the failure to comply with a contractual provision within the time limited by the contract constitutes a repudiation of the contract i.e. is time of the essence of that contractual provision.[95] The phrase 'time is of the essence of the contract' is capable of causing confusion since the question in each case is whether time is of the essence of the particular contractual term which has been breached."

He added:

"There is therefore no general concept that time is of the essence of a contract as a whole: the question is whether time is of the essence of a particular provision."

---

[87] (1879) 4 C.P.D. 239.

[88] *Bowes v Shand* (1887) 2 App. Cas. 455.

[89] *Toepfer v Lenersan-Poortman NV* [1980] 1 Lloyd's Rep. 143.

[90] *Hartley v Hymans* [1920] 3 K.B. 475.

[91] *The Mihalis Angelos* [1971] 1 Q.B. 164.

[92] *Universal Cargo Carriers Corp v Citati* [1957] 2 Q.B. 401.

[93] See para.15.60.

[94] [1989] Q.B. 842 at 856 CA.

[95] This statement assumes that the time limit is linked to an obligation. It may, however, be linked to a term of the contract which is framed as an option (e.g. the right to serve a notice of rent review). Except in the case of a unilateral contract, or true option, the same principle applies.

Where a contract contains clauses contemplating extensions of time for **15.48**
performance, that is a pointer to the conclusion that time is not of the essence.[96]

14.   TIME EXPRESSLY OF THE ESSENCE

**Time is of the essence of a time stipulation if, on the true construction of the
contract, the contract expressly so provides.**

The question whether time is of the essence of a contract may also be expressed, **15.49**
in more traditional common law language, as the question whether compliance with
a time stipulation is a condition of the contract. A court of equity and a court of law
might have answered this question differently where the words of the contract gave
no guidance. However, both a court of equity and a court of law gave effect to an
express contractual stipulation that time was to be of the essence of a time
stipulation.

> "Parties may say by express words that notwithstanding any rule of law or equity
> to the contrary, time shall be of the essence of the contract; or they may use words
> which in substance mean the same thing."[97]

Thus in *Steedman v Drinkle*,[98] a contract for the sale of land expressly provided
that time was to be of the essence of the contract. The Privy Council dismissed an
action for specific performance by the party in default.

Where a time limit is expressed to be a "condition precedent" or a "condition" **15.50**
it is considered that it will generally be of the essence of the contract,[99] because a
"condition" is the equivalent expression at common law for the phrase "time of the
essence" which is used in equity. Likewise, where time is said to be of the essence
of a contract, delay will amount to a breach of condition, and thus a repudiatory
breach.[100]

It is not always so easy to reach a conclusion as to whether time is of the es- **15.51**
sence of a contract as a matter of interpretation. In *Harold Wood Brick Co Ltd v Ferris*,[101] a contract for the sale of land had a contractual completion date of 31 August
1935. Another clause in the contract provided that if completion of the contract was
delayed beyond that date the purchase money should be placed on deposit "but the
purchase shall in any event be completed not later than" 15 September 1935. The
Court of Appeal held that those words made completion by 15 September of the essence of the contract. However, in *Touche Ross & Co v Secretary of State*,[102] the
Court of Appeal came to a contrary conclusion on similar words. A rent review
clause in a lease entitled the landlord to serve notice on the tenant calling for a rent
review. The clause provided that in default of agreement, the question what rent

---

96 *Fitzpatrick v Sarcon (No.177) Ltd* [2012] NICA 58 (Court of Appeal of Northern Ireland).
97 *Harold Wood Brick Co Ltd v Ferris* [1935] 2 K.B. 198, per Greer LJ.
98 [1916] 1 A.C. 275.
99 *United Scientific Holdings Ltd v Burnley Borough Council* [1978] A.C 904 at 925 HL; *Chelsea Building Society Ltd v R. & A. Millett (Shops) Ltd* [1994] 1 E.G.L.R. 148 (not following *North
Hertfordshire District Council v Hitchin Industrial Estates Ltd* [1992] 2 E.G.L.R. 121); *Kuwait Rocks
Co v AMN Bulkcarriers Inc* [2013] EWHC 865 (Comm).
100 *Parbulk II A/S v Heritage Maritime Ltd SA* [2011] EWHC 2917; [2012] 1 Lloyd's Rep. 87.
101 [1935] 2 K.B. 198.
102 (1983) 46 P. & C.R. 187.

should be paid "shall as soon as practicable and in any event not later than three months after the service of the said notice" be referred to a surveyor. Dillon LJ said:

"If the clause had simply said that 'the question shall as soon as possible be referred for decision to a surveyor' there would be no doubt that time was not of the essence. Equally, in the light of the *United Scientific Holdings*[103] case, if the clause had simply said that 'the question shall within three months after the service of the landlord's notice be referred' time would not have been of the essence. Prima facie, therefore, it seems to me somewhat hard to deduce, from the running together of those two alternatives into the composite phrase 'shall as soon as practicable and in any event not later than three months after service of the notice be referred,' that time is to be of the essence and that the parties are concerned to show that this is not just ordinary use of language to indicate a desire that the matter should not be unduly protracted: they are concerned to show that the time-limit is obligatory and really means what it says, unlike any mere time-limit in a rent review clause."

The court therefore held that time was not of the essence.[104]

15.52   In *HHR Pascal BV v W2005 Puppet II BV*,[105] the parties entered into a share purchase agreement relating to a company with a hotel portfolio, two of which were under construction. Completion was conditional on, inter alia, substantial completion of the reconstruction work. The agreement contained a detailed code for the giving of notice of projected completion of the works, and for the possibility of revision. One of the issues was whether the time limit for service of a notice was mandatory. Simon J said:

"The timing provisions were very clearly of the type which had to be strictly complied with in order, to use the words of Lord Wilberforce in *Bremer Handelsgesellschaft mbH v Vanden Avenne-Izegem PVBA*,[106] 'to avoid commercial confusion'. The language is emphatic: 'such notice *shall* be sent at least 10 Business Days in advance', and the terms are part of a scheme which provides for the exercise of rights by each party. On the face of it the validity of the notice depends on the precise observance of the specified conditions as to time; and there is nothing among the wider considerations, and no contrary indications, to displace that assumption."

15.53   In cases relating to the sale of goods a different approach is adopted. In such cases the court frequently asks itself whether stipulations dealing with the date of delivery or shipment are part of the description of the goods agreed to be sold. Correspondence with description is an implied condition of a contract for the sale of goods.[107]

---

[103] *United Scientific Holdings v Burnley Borough Council* [1978] A.C. 904.

[104] It might, however, have been thought that the very fact that two cumulative time limits were expressed indicated the importance that the parties attached to the long stop date. In *The Post Chaser* [1981] 2 Lloyd's Rep. 695, an obligation to declare a ship to buyers under a c.i.f. contract "as soon as possible" was held on its own to be a condition of the contract. The author finds the reasoning in *Touche Ross* unconvincing. This criticism appears to have been accepted in *Petrocapital Resources Plc v Morrison & Foerster (UK) LLP* [2013] EWHC 2682 (Ch).

[105] [2010] 1 All E.R. (Comm) 399.

[106] [1978] 2 Lloyd's Rep. 109 at 116.

[107] Sale of Goods Act 1979 s.13. Lord Wilberforce has said that many of the cases on s.13 and its predecessor are excessively technical and due for reconsideration by the House of Lords: see

Consequently, if a stipulation as to time of delivery is part of the description of the goods, late delivery will be a breach of a condition of the contract, and will entitle the buyer to reject the goods. Thus in *Bowes v Shand*,[108] Lord Cairns said that time of shipment was "part of the description of the subject matter of what is sold". Similarly, in *Wilson v Wright*,[109] the seller offered to sell potatoes "for Saturday's steamer". The buyer accepted by telegram, adding the words "next steamer", which was in fact Saturday's steamer. The Court of Appeal held that part of the description of the goods was that they must be shipped by that particular steamer. A similar conclusion was reached in *Macpherson Train & Co Ltd v Ross (Howard) & Co Ltd*,[110] where tinned peaches were sold "afloat per S.S. Morton Bay due London approximately June 8". The time of arrival of the ship was held to be part of the description of the goods. However, in *Aron (J.) and Co v Comptoir Wegimont*,[111] McCardie J said:

> "I hold that a contract requirement that goods are to be shipped at a given time is far more than a mere description of the goods. I hold that it is a condition precedent."

In other cases, the contract expressly provides for a date of delivery. It is then a question of interpretation whether the date of delivery is a condition or a warranty. In general, the courts have held that time of delivery is a condition (or, as it is put in the older cases, a condition precedent).

15.54

Illustrations

1.   A contract for the sale of cable bars provided for delivery to take place forthwith and to be paid for within 14 days of the contract. It was held that delivery of the goods before payment was a condition precedent.
Staunton v Wood[112]

2.   A contract for the sale of hemp provided for shipment between 1 May and 31 July 1898. The agreement contained a clause that if the goods did not arrive from loss of vessel or other unavoidable cause the contract was to be void. It was held that the stipulations to delivery were conditions precedent.
Ashmore & Son v Cox (CS) & Co[113]

3.   A contract for the manufacture of a pleasure yacht contained a clause whereby the builders were to use their best endeavours to complete by 1 May 1957, but that that delivery date could not be guaranteed. It was held that the builders had

---

Reardon Smith Lines Ltd v Ynguar Hansen Tangen [1976] 1 W.L.R. 989. Caution is therefore needed in relying upon such cases.

[108] (1887) 2 App. Cas. 455.
[109] [1937] 4 All E.R. 371.
[110] [1955] 1 W.L.R. 640.
[111] [1921] 3 K.B. 435.
[112] (1851) 16 Q.B. 638.
[113] [1899] 1 Q.B. 436.

an implied obligation to deliver within a reasonable time of the specified date, and that that obligation was a condition of the contract.

McDougall v Aeromarine of Emsworth Ltd[114]

4.   A rent review clause entitled the landlord to serve notice on the tenant calling for a rent review. The rent was to be referred to arbitration if the landlord so required by a further notice given within three months after the first notice "but not otherwise". It was held that the words "but not otherwise" made time of the essence of the service of the second notice.

Drebbond Ltd v Horsham District Council[115]

5.   A contract for the sale of sugar f.o.b. provided the buyers to specify a load port "at latest Monday 14.11.83". Time was held to be of the essence. Leggatt J said:

"there are no words in the English language by which a deadline can be appointed more concisely, more precisely and with more finality than the words 'at latest'; and I hold that they mean what they say."

Gill & Duffus SA v Societe pour l'Exportation des Sucres SA[116]

6.   A contract for the sale of goods contained a clause which required the sellers to declare a ship "as soon as possible" after vessel's sailing. It was held that although the time for compliance was not fixed, it was nevertheless an essential step in respect of which time was of the essence.

The Post Chaser[117]

7.   A rent review clause provided that it should be a condition precedent to the determination of the rent that the landlord should give the tenant a notice during the first six months of a specified year. It was held that time was of the essence of the giving of the notice.

Chelsea Building Society v R&A Millett (Shops) Ltd[118]

8.   A contract for the sale of scrap metal provided that "Material is to be delivered in the port immediately upon the Buyer's request". Blair J held that "by the use of the word 'immediately', the parties made time of the essence in that respect".

Tarkin AG v Thames Steel UK Ltd[119]

---

[114] [1958] 1 W.L.R. 1126.

[115] (1978) 37 P. & C.R. 237.

[116] [1985] 1 Lloyd's Rep. 621; affirmed [1986] 1 Lloyd's Rep. 322.

[117] [1982] 1 All E.R. 19. See, however, *British and Commonwealth Holdings Ltd v Quadrex Holdings Ltd* [1989] Q.B. 842 CA where it was held that the fact that time for compliance was not specified prevented time from being of the essence. Nevertheless, The Post Chaser was referred to with approval.

[118] [1994] 1 E.G.L.R. 148, not following *North Hertfordshire District Council v Hitchin Industrial Estates Ltd* [1992] 2 E.G.L.R. 121.

[119] [2010] EWHC 207 (Comm).

15. Time of the Essence because of Nature of the Contract

Where the subject matter of the contract is of a wasting nature or liable to great fluctuations in value, time will be of the essence of the contract.

Although the general attitude of equity was that time was not of the essence of the contract, there were exceptions to that approach. As Lord Parker put it in *Stickney v Keeble*,[120] the maxim that time is not of the essence of a contract: **15.55**

"never had any application to cases in which the stipulation as to time could not be disregarded without injustice to the parties, when, for example, the parties for reasons best known to themselves, had stipulated that the time fixed should be essential, or where there was something in the nature of the property or in the sur-rounding circumstances which would render it inequitable to treat it as a non-essential term of the contract."

Thus, where the nature of the property is precarious, time may be of the essence. In *Withy v Cottle*,[121] there was a contract to purchase a life annuity. The precarious-ness of human life indicated that time would be of the essence. No definitive answer was given, however, since the point arose on an interlocutory procedural application.

So also where the property is a wasting asset, time may be of the essence.

In *Hudson v Temple*,[122] Sir John Romily MR held that time stipulations in a contract for the sale of a lease with an unexpired residue of 24½ years were of the essence of the contract. A similar conclusion in relation to a lease was reached in *Tilley v Thomas*[123] and *Pips (Leisure Productions) Ltd v Walton*.[124]   **15.56**

Where the subject matter of the contract is not merely property, but also a busi-ness being sold as a going concern, time will be of the essence of the contract. Thus in *Cowles v Gate*,[125] time was held to be of the essence in a contract for the sale of a public house as a going concern. The same conclusion was reached in *Lock v Bell*,[126] in which the contract provided for completion to take place "on or about" a certain date.   **15.57**

Further, where the subject matter of the contract is liable to fluctuate in value, time will be regarded as being of the essence. Thus in *Re Schwabacher*,[127] Parker J said: **15.58**

"With regard to contracts for the sale of shares, I think that time is of the es-sence both at law and in equity. Shares continually vary in price from day to day, and that is precisely why courts of equity have considered such a contract to be one in which time is of the essence of the contract, and not like a contract for the sale and purchase of real estate, in which time is not of the essence of the contract."

---

[120] [1915] A.C. 386.
[121] (1823) Turn. & R. 78.
[122] (1860) 29 Beav. 536.
[123] (1867) L.R. 3 Ch. App. 61 (residential lease with 19 years unexpired).
[124] (1982) 45 P. & C.R. 415 (commercial lease with 15½ years unexpired).
[125] (1871) L.R. 7 Ch. App. 12.
[126] [1930] Ch. 35.
[127] (1908) 98 L.T. 127.

This principle was approved and applied by the Court of Appeal in *Hare v Nicoll*.[128] However, where the contract did not lay down a fixed completion date or a formula enabling a fixed completion date to be ascertained, time was not of the essence of the requirement to complete.[129]

15.59 Where a contract for the sale of land provides for the payment of a deposit on or shortly after exchange of contracts, the time for payment is of the essence of the contract.[130]

16. OPTIONS AND UNILATERAL CONTRACTS

A time stipulation in an option or unilateral contract is of the essence of the contract.

15.60 Both in the Court of Chancery and in the courts of common law the rules that were developed about particular stipulations not being of the essence of the contract (or not being conditions of the contract) applied only to synallagmatic contracts (that is, contracts of reciprocal obligations). They did not apply to unilateral or "if contracts".[131] Under contracts which are only unilateral one party (the promisor) undertakes to do or refrain from doing something on his part if another party (the promisee) does or refrains from doing something, but the promisee does not himself undertake to do or to refrain from doing that thing. The commonest contracts of this kind are options granted for good consideration to buy or to sell land or other property or to grant or to take a lease, competitions for prizes and the like.[132] In such cases time is of the essence of any time limits with which the promisee is to comply.

15.61 Two possible theoretical reasons may be advanced for this rule. First, the grant of an option constitutes the making of an irrevocable offer, and an offer must be accepted in exact compliance with its terms.[133] Secondly, the question whether an option has been complied with simply involves asking what have the parties agreed to do, rather than what are the consequences of their having failed to do what they have agreed to do.[134] However, as Lord Diplock explained in *United Scientific Holdings Ltd v Burnley Borough Council*[135]:

> "A more practical business explanation why a stipulation as to the time by which an option to acquire an interest in property should be exercised by the grantee must be punctually observed is that the grantor, so long as the option remains open, thereby submits to being disabled from disposing of his proprietary interest to anyone other than the grantee, and this without any guarantee that it will be disposed of to the grantee. In accepting such a fetter on his powers of disposition of his property, the grantor needs to know with certainty the moment when it has come to an end."

---

128 [1966] 2 Q.B. 130 (although the case concerned an option).
129 *British and Commonwealth Holdings Ltd v Quadrex Holdings Ltd* [1989] Q.B. 842 CA.
130 *Samarenko v Dawn Hill House Ltd* [2011] EWCA Civ 1445; [2013] Ch. 36.
131 See *United Scientific Holdings Ltd v Burnley Borough Council* [1978] A.C. 904, per Lord Diplock.
132 See *United Dominions Trust (Commercial) Ltd v Eagle Aircraft Services Ltd* [1968] 1 W.L.R. 74.
133 See *United Dominions Trust (Commercial) Ltd v Eagle Aircraft Services Ltd* [1968] 1 W.L.R. 74, per Lord Denning MR.
134 Above, per Diplock LJ.
135 [1978] A.C. 904.

However, although time is of the essence for the exercise of an option, it does **15.62** not follow that any further time stipulations relating to the consequences of that exercise are also of the essence.[136]

Illustrations

1.   An agreement for the sale of shares contained an option to repurchase. It was held that time was of the essence for the exercise of the option.
Hare v Nicoll[137]

2.   A clause in a shareholders' agreement gave a shareholder the right on 31 March 2004 to effect a buy-out of shares and property in exchange for payment of a sum calculated by reference to a formula. Another clause provided that if no notice intimating a desire to effect the buy-out had been served prior to 31 March the agreement would terminate automatically. The House of Lords held that although time was of the essence of the giving of the notice, time was not of the essence for completion of the purchase.
Simmers v Innes[138]

17.   CONDITIONAL CONTRACTS

A stipulated time by which a condition precedent in a conditional contract must be fulfilled will be of the essence of the contract.

In *Valentines Properties Ltd v Huntco Corp Ltd*,[139] Lord Nicholls of Birkenhead **15.63** said:

"Inherent in a time limit is the notion that the parties are drawing a line. Once the line is crossed, a miss is as good as a mile. The rigour of this principle is softened when the parties are taken to have intended otherwise. Then, in the legal jargon, time is not regarded as 'of the essence'. Failing a contrary indication, the law assumes that stipulations as to time are not of the essence in certain common form situations, such as the date for completion of a contract for the sale of land. But that is not this case. The law makes no such assumption regarding a date fixed by a conditional contract as the date by which the condition is to be fulfilled. In the absence of contrary indication, the date so fixed must be strictly adhered to, and the time allowed is not to be extended by reference to equitable principles."

Similarly, in *Aberfoyle Plantations Ltd v Cheng*,[140] Lord Jenkins said:

"[W]here a conditional contract of sale fixes (whether specifically or by reference to the date fixed for completion) the date by which the condition is to be fulfilled, then the date so fixed must be strictly adhered to, and the time allowed is not to be extended by reference to equitable principles."

---

[136] *Simmers v Innes* [2008] S.C. (HL) 137.
[137] [1966] 2 Q.B. 130.
[138] [2008] S.C. (HL) 137.
[139] [2001] 3 N.Z.L.R. 305; *HHR Pascal BV v W2005 Puppet II BV* [2010] 1 All E.R. (Comm) 399.
[140] [1960] A.C. 115.

15.64   However, before this principle comes into play the court must be satisfied that there is a time limit attached to fulfilment of the condition.[141]

18.   RENT REVIEW CLAUSES

Time is not of the essence of a time limit in a rent review clause unless: (1) the clause expressly so provides; or (2) there are contra-indications either in the rent review clause itself or in the relationship between the rent review clause itself and other clauses in the lease.

15.65   In *United Scientific Holdings Ltd v Burnley Borough Council*,[142] the House of Lords held as a matter of principle that time was to be assumed not to be of the essence of time limits in a rent review clause. Lord Diplock said:

> "So on the question of principle which these two appeals were brought to settle, I would hold that in the absence of any contra-indication in the express words of the lease or in the interrelation of the rent review clause itself and other clauses or surrounding circumstances, the presumption is that the timetable specified in a rent review clause for completion of the various steps for determining the rent payable in respect of the period following the review date is not of the essence of the contract."

15.66   This ruling was expressed as a presumption. It is of course a presumption of interpretation, not a rule of law. Since it is only a presumption of interpretation, the parties are free to modify it by their bargain. The first way of making time of the essence is by expressly saying so in the rent review clause itself. As Lord Diplock himself said:

> "... the best way of eliminating all uncertainty in future rent review clauses is to state expressly whether or not stipulations as to the time by which any step provided by the clause is to be taken, shall be treated as being of the essence."

15.67   In some cases Lord Diplock's suggestion has been adopted, and the question does not therefore arise. Accordingly, the express words which the court has usually considered are words which do not state expressly whether time is or is not of the essence. The cases fall into two groups.

15.68   The first group consists of cases concerning the degree of emphasis given by the clause to the time limit. Thus where a clause required the landlord to give a notice within a stipulated time "but not otherwise," time was held to be of the essence.[143] However, a clause which required the rent to be referred to a surveyor "as soon as practicable and in any event not later than three months" after a certain date, time was held not to be of the essence.[144] A provision that the rent shall not in any event

---

[141] See, e.g. *McGahon v Crest Nicholson Regeneration Ltd* [2010] 2 E.G.L.R. 84.

[142] [1978] A.C. 904.

[143] *Drebbond Ltd v Horsham District Council* (1978) 37 P. & C.R. 237 (see para.15.54, Illustration 4).

[144] *Touche Ross & Co v Secretary of State* (1983) 46 P. & C.R. 187 (see para.15.51). It might, however, have been thought that the very fact that two time limits were expressed indicated the importance that the parties attached to the long stop date. In *The Post Chaser* [1981] 2 Lloyd's Rep. 695, an obligation to declare a ship to buyers under a c.i.f. contract "as soon as possible" was held on its own to be a condition of the contract. The author finds the reasoning in *Touche Ross* unconvincing. This criticism appears to have been accepted in *Petrocapital Resources Plc v Morrison & Foerster*

be less than a fixed figure does not amount to a contra-indication making time of the essence.[145]

It is difficult to extract any coherent principles of construction from this group of cases, as so often most of them seem to have been decided largely as a matter "of impression".[146]

The second group of cases concern clauses in which the clause prescribes the **15.69** consequence of failing to take the particular step within the stipulated time. Such clauses are commonly referred to as deeming clauses or default clauses. In *Lewis v Barnett*,[147] a rent review clause provided for the landlord to initiate the review by a particular date by a trigger notice. It then provided that if the landlord had not applied for the appointment of a surveyor by a particular date then any trigger notice already served would become void. The Court of Appeal held that the clause meant what it said, and that consequently having failed to comply with the time limit, the landlord had lost the right to a rent review. The same approach was adopted by the Court of Appeal in *Trustees of Smith's (Henry) Charity v AWADA Trading and Promotion Services Ltd*.[148] In that case, the rent review clause contained an elaborate procedure requiring the service of notices and counter-notices by specified dates. An application for the appointment of a surveyor was also to be made by a specified date. At each stage the clause prescribed the consequences of untimely service. In particular it was stipulated that, in the event of non-service of the requisite counter-notice, the party on whom the notice was served was deemed to agree its contents. It was held that time was of the essence. Slade LJ said:

"Any form of expression which clearly evinces the concept of finality attached to the end of the period or periods prescribed will suffice to rebut the presumption."

This decision seemed to lay down as a general principle that where the parties provided precisely what should happen in the event of a failure to take the contemplated step in time, that consequence would follow if the step was not timeously taken.

However, a differently constituted Court of Appeal reached (by a majority) a dif- **15.70** ferent conclusion in *Mecca Leisure Ltd v Renown Investments (Holdings) Ltd*.[149] In that case the landlord was to serve a trigger notice of proposing a rent. The tenant was entitled to serve a counter-notice disputing the landlord's figure, but if he did not do so within a stipulated time he was "deemed to have accepted and agreed the same". It was held that time was not of the essence of the requirement to serve a counter-notice. Although the majority accepted that the presence of a "deeming" clause was a contra-indication, it was not a conclusive one. In *Starmark Enterprises v CPL Distribution Ltd*,[150] the Court of Appeal considered these two cases. It held

---

(UK) LLP [2013] EWHC 2682 (Ch).

[145] *Metrolands Investments Ltd v Dewhurst (JR) Ltd* [1986] 3 All E.R. 659.
[146] For "matters of impression" see para.2.103.
[147] [1982] 2 E.G.L.R. 127; followed in *Fordgate Bingley Ltd v Argyll Stores Plc* [1994] 2 E.G.L.R. 84.
[148] (1983) 46 P. & C.R. 74.
[149] (1985) 49 P. & C.R. 12. Courts in Scotland (*Visionhire Ltd v Britel Fund Trustees Ltd* [1982] 1 E.G.L.R. 128), Australia (*CR Mailman and Associates Pty Ltd v Wormald (Aust) Pty Ltd* (1991) 24 N.S.W.L.R. 80) and New Zealand (*Mobil Oil New Zealand Ltd v Mandeno* [1995] N.Z.L.R. 114) all rightly declined to follow this decision.
[150] [2002] Ch. 306.

that where a deeming provision specified the consequences of failing to take a particular step within a contractual time limit the court cannot override that provision. Consequently, the presence of a deeming provision will make time of the essence of the timetable.[151] The *Mecca Leisure* case was disapproved.[152]

15.71 The second way of displacing the presumption that time is not of the essence of a rent review timetable is by the interrelationship between the review clause and the other clauses in the lease. In practice this means the interrelationship between the rent review clause and a tenant's right to determine the lease. In *United Scientific Holdings Ltd v Burnley Borough Council*,[153] Lord Simon of Glaisdale said:

> "… where a rent review clause is associated with a true option (a 'break' clause, for example), it is a strong indication that time is intended to be of the essence of the rent review clause-if not absolutely, at least to the extent that the tenant will reasonably expect to know what new rent he will have to pay before the time comes for him to elect whether to terminate or renew the tenancy."

Whether the right to review the rent and the right to determine are contained in the same sub-clause of the lease[154] or in different sub-clauses[155] makes no difference. Nor does it matter whether the tenant may give notice to determine the lease after the last date for service of a landlord's review notice[156] or by the last date.[157] If, however, the landlord may serve a notice after the last date for service of a tenant's notice to determine, time will not be of the essence of the service of the landlord's notice, because the essential interrelationship will be absent.[158] So too where the step which must be taken within the stipulated time is not one which is in the landlord's control (e.g. the obtaining of a decision of an arbitrator) time is unlikely to be of the essence, even where that step is associated with a tenant's break clause.[159]

15.72 There is no reported case yet in which time was held to be of the essence of a rent review timetable merely because of surrounding circumstances.

Illustrations

1. A rent review clause entitled the landlord to serve a notice specifying a rent and provided that if the tenant did not serve a counter-notice within a stipulated period, the rent was to be "conclusively fixed" at the figure stated in the landlord's

---

[151] For deeming clauses see para.14.98.

[152] The following cases are now of doubtful authority: *Davstone (Holdings) Ltd v Al-Rifai* (1976) 32 P. & C.R. 18; *Taylor Woodrow Property Co Ltd v Lonrho Textiles Ltd* (1986) 52 P. & C.R. 28; *Power Securities (Manchester) v Prudential Assurance Co* [1987] 1 E.G.L.R. 121; and *Phipps-Faire Ltd v Malbern Construction* [1987] 1 E.G.L.R. 1129.

[153] [1978] A.C. 904.

[154] *Al Saloom v James (Shirley) Travel Service Ltd* (1981) 42 P. & C.R. 181.

[155] *Legal and General Assurance (Pension Management) Ltd v Cheshire County Council* (1983) 46 P. & C.R. 160.

[156] *Coventry City Council v Hepworth & Son Ltd* (1983) 46 P. & C.R. 170.

[157] *Legal and General Assurance (Pension Management) Ltd v Cheshire County Council* (1983) 46 P. & C.R. 160.

[158] *Woodhouse (Edwin) Trustee Co Ltd v Sheffield Brick Co Ltd* [1984] 1 E.G.L.R. 130.

[159] *Metrolands Investments Ltd v Dewhurst (J.R.) Ltd* [1986] 3 All E.R. 659, criticised in *Stephenson & Sons v Orca Properties Ltd* [1989] 2 E.G.L.R. 129.

notice. It was held that time was of the essence for the service of the counter-notice.
Mammoth Greeting Cards Ltd v Agra Ltd[160]

2.   A rent review clause provided for the tenant to serve a written counter-notice specifying the rent which the tenant considered should be the market rent within five weeks of the service of the landlord's notice. It went on to provide that if the tenant did not serve "such counter-notice" the landlord's figure should stand as the rent. It was held that this was insufficient to make time of the essence of the service of a counter-notice.
Bickenhall Engineering Co Ltd v Grandmet Restaurants Ltd[161]

3.   A rent review clause stated that the rent was to be agreed between the parties not later than two months before the review date, or determined by an independent surveyor at the request of the landlord. It went on to say that "if no such agreement or written request is made by the review date applicable the yearly rent payable for the year ending on such review date shall continue to be the rent reserved by this Lease for the next seven years of the said term". It was held that time was of the essence of the making of the request.
Secretary of State for Communities & Local Government v Standard Securities Ltd[162]

19.   MERCANTILE CONTRACTS

As a general rule time is of the essence of stipulations as to time in mercantile contracts.

In *Reuter v Sala*,[163] Cotton LJ asserted that to apply to mercantile contracts the view of equity that time is not an essential condition of the contract would be "dangerous and unreasonable". That the equitable approach does not generally apply to mercantile contracts was recognised by the House of Lords in *United Scientific Holdings Ltd v Burnley Borough Council*.[164] Lord Salmon said:

15.73

> "In commercial transactions, provisions as to time are usually but not always regarded as being of the essence of the contract. They are certainly so regarded where the subject matter of the contract is the acquisition of a wasting asset or of a perishable commodity or is something likely to change rapidly in value. In such cases if, e.g. the seller fails to deliver within the time specified in the contract, the buyer may well be seriously prejudiced."

Despite the decision in that case, the general rule that punctual performance is a condition of mercantile contracts is still good law. In *Bunge Corp v Tradax Export SA*,[165] the House of Lords reaffirmed the principle. Lord Roskill said:

---

[160] [1990] 2 E.G.L.R. 124; *Barrett Estate Services Ltd v Davis Greig (Retail) Ltd* [1991] 2 E.G.L.R. 123.
[161] [1995] 1 E.G.L.R. 110 CA.
[162] [2008] 1 P. & C.R. 429.
[163] (1879) 4 C.P.D. 239.
[164] [1978] A.C. 904.
[165] [1981] 1 W.L.R. 711.

"I agree with counsel that in a mercantile contract when a term has to be performed by one party as a condition precedent to the ability of the other party to perform another term, especially an essential term such as the nomination of a single loading port, the term as to time for the performance of the former obligation will in general fall to be treated as a condition."

15.74   In a contract for the sale of goods, unless a different intention appears from the contract, stipulations as to time of payment are not of the essence of the contract.[166] Whether any other stipulation as to time is of the essence of the contract or not depends on the terms of the contract.[167] In conformity with the approach to construction embedded in the common law, the court has consistently held that punctual performance is a condition of the contract. Thus compliance with a time stipulation has been held to be a condition of the contract in the case of an obligation to ship goods at a certain time[168]; to give notice of appropriation[169]; to tender documents against which payment under a commodities contract is to be made.[170] Even a term as to payment of a deposit under a contract for the sale of a ship has been held to be a condition of the contract.[171] So too in a charterparty payment of hire punctually is a condition of the contract, breach of which entitles the owner to withdraw the ship, even if the hire is eventually paid late.[172] It was, however, recognised by Lord Lowry in *Bunge Corp v Tradax Export SA*[173] that:

"The treatment of time limits in mercantile contracts does not appear ... to be justifiable by any presumption of fact or rule of law, but rather to be a practical expedient founded on and dictated by the experience of businessmen."

15.75   Yet even as a practical expedient it has serious limitations, not least in the identification of contracts which fall within the scope of the principle. As Lord Diplock observed in *United Scientific Holdings Ltd v Burnley Borough Council*[174]:

"I do not think that the question of principle ... can be solved by classifying the contract of tenancy as being of a commercial character. In some stipulations in commercial contracts as to the time when something must be done by one of the parties or some event must occur, time is of the essence; in others it is not."

15.76   Indeed in many non-commercial contracts the requirement of certainty would seem to be just as important as in commercial contracts. One feature of commercial contracts to which attention is often drawn is that the particular contract may be only one of a string of contracts, so that failure in prompt performance of one contract may have repercussions along the string. However, it is not easy to see

---

[166] Sale of Goods Act 1979 s.10 (1).
[167] Sale of Goods Act 1979 s.10(2).
[168] *Bowes v Shand* (1887) 2 App. Cas. 455.
[169] *Reuter v Sala* (1879) 4 C.P.D. 239; *Bunge GmbH v CCV Landbouwberland G.A.* [1978] 1 Lloyd's Rep. 217.
[170] *Toepfer v Lenersan-Poortman NV* [1980] 1 Lloyd's Rep. 143.
[171] *The Selene G.* [1981] 2 Lloyd's Rep. 180.
[172] *The Laconia* [1977] A.C. 850.
[173] [1981] 1 W.L.R. 711.
[174] [1978] A.C. 904. See also *National Carriers Ltd v Panalpina (Northern) Ltd* [1981] A.C. 675 where the House of Lords rejected the notion that a lease of land was subject to different contractual principles as compared with a contract relating to chattels.

how this differs in practical effect from a contract for the sale of a house which is frequently one of a chain, and in respect of which a failure in prompt performance may also have effects down the chain. A better starting point in respect of all contracts would be to attempt to examine the potential harm which might flow from delayed performance.[175]

Illustration

A charterparty provided that at the date of delivery the vessel should be classed in every way fit to carry fuel oil and vacuum gasoil and/or its products; that the vessel was not to be delivered before 1 November 1997 and, if not delivered by 30 November, that the charterers had the right to cancel. It also contained a "majors approval" clause, which provided:

> "Vessel is presently MOBIL ..., CONOCO ..., BP ... and SHELL ... acceptable. Owners guarantee to obtain within 60 days EXXON approval in addition to present approvals ... If for any reason, during the time charter period, owners would lose even one of such acceptances they must advise charterers at once and they must reinstate same within 30 days from such occurrence failing which charterers will be at liberty to cancel charterparty ...".

It was held that because of the combination of the word "guarantee" and the short time limit, compliance with the time limit for approval by EXXON was a condition of the contract.

BS & N Ltd (BVI) v Micado Shipping Ltd (Malta)[176]

---

[175] See Treitel, *The Law of Contract*, 9th edn (London: Sweet & Maxwell, 1995), p.742.
[176] [2001] 1 Lloyd's Rep. 341.

CHAPTER 16

CONDITIONS AND CONDITIONAL OBLIGATIONS

"Unimportant, of course, I mean" the King hastily said and went on to himself in an undertone "important-unimportant-unimportant-important" as if he were trying which word sounded best

Lewis Carroll: *Alice in Wonderland*

1. THE MEANING OF "CONDITION"

In English law the word "condition" may mean (i) a requirement which must be satisfied before any contract comes into existence; (ii) a requirement which must be satisfied before a party can be liable to perform his obligations under a contract; (iii) a term of the contract; (iv) an important term of the contract, breach of which will amount to a repudiation of the contract; (v) a requirement which if satisfied will automatically bring the contract to an end; or (vi) a requirement which if satisfied will entitle one party to bring the contract to an end.[1]

The word "condition" both historically and today is used in a wide variety of **16.01** senses.[2] Some of those senses were explained by the Court of Appeal in *Wickman Machine Tool Sales Ltd v Schuler (L) AG*.[3] In that case Lord Denning MR identified three meanings of the word "condition". The first was its "proper meaning"; that is:

"a prerequisite to the *very existence* of the agreement."

The second was the "common meaning;" that is a term, provision or stipulation. He said:

"When an agreement is made for the sale of land, it is always subject to 'conditions of sale'. The Law Society's 'Conditions of Sale' are in everyday use. When a building contract is made, it is usually subject to the R.I.B.A. conditions. Whenever a quotation is given or invoice sent, the printed form invariably says it is subject to the 'conditions' on the back. In all these cases the word 'conditions' simply means *terms* of the contract."

The third is its meaning "as a term of art".

---

[1] Cited with approval in *Total Gas Marketing Ltd v Arco British Ltd* [1998] 2 Lloyd's Rep. 209 at 220, per Lord Steyn.
[2] In "The Contractual Concept of Condition" (1953) 69 L.Q.R. 485, S.J. Stoljar identifies no less than 12 meanings of the word.
[3] [1972] 1 W.L.R. 840.

"A 'condition' in this sense is a stipulation in a contract which carries with it this consequence: if the promisor breaks a 'condition' in any respect, however slight, it gives the other party a right to be quit of his future obligations and to sue for damages unless he, by his conduct, waives the condition, in which case he is bound to perform his future obligations, but can sue for the damages he has suffered. A 'condition' in this sense is used in contrast to a 'warranty'. If a promisor breaks a warranty in any respect, however serious, the other party is not quit of his future obligations. He has to perform them. His only remedy is to sue for damages."

16.02   In the House of Lords,[4] Lords Reid and Simon of Glaisdale both indicated that where the word "condition" is used in a legal document, there is a presumption that it is used in its sense as a term of art.

In his dissenting judgment in the Court of Appeal, Stephenson LJ said:

"To my mind the natural and ordinary meaning of making something a condition of an agreement is that it is made something on which the agreement depends. If the condition is not performed the agreement goes. If the condition is one to be fulfilled before the agreement comes into force, it is what lawyers have called a condition precedent (or a contingent or causal condition), that is a condition of the agreement's coming into force, and if it is not performed there is no agreement. If the condition is to be performed after the agreement has come into force, it is what lawyers have called a condition subsequent, or a condition inherent (or a promissory condition), that is a condition of the agreement's continuing; and if it is not performed the agreement comes to an end. In a sense all conditions are conditions precedent, some to an agreement beginning, others to its continuing. One thing is a condition of another when its existence is essential to that other thing, when the existence of each depends on the existence of the other, and that is so whether one of the two things is to be done once (the simplest case) or is to be repeated or continued or is an agreement to do one or more things."

This two-fold classification has the great attraction of simplicity, but unfortunately, it does not adequately reflect the wide (and often inconsistent) variety of judicial usage of the word "condition".

16.03   In *Yule v Smith*,[5] Sackar J gave the following useful summary:

"23.   In order to identify and apply the legal principles relevant to the case before me, it is necessary to be clear about this terminology. A contingency is merely an event on the occurrence (or non-occurrence) of which an obligation to perform, or the existence of a contract, may depend. The word 'condition' or 'condition precedent' is sometimes used to describe a contractual term that states or provides for a contingency. However, the word 'condition' is of course distinguishable when it is used to describe a type of contractual term under the tripartite classification.

24.   Sometimes a party to the contract will be made responsible under the contract to procure the fulfilment of a contingency (or condition), but sometimes the contingency (or condition) is something which is out of the

---

[4]   [1974] A.C. 235.
[5]   [2013] NSWSC 209.

control of the parties to the contract (e.g. the actions of a third party or an event beyond their control). Conditions of the former type are described as promissory conditions because a party has promised to bring about the fulfilment of the condition, whereas conditions of the latter type are described as non-promissory.

25. As mentioned, where a contract contains a condition precedent, the non-fulfilment of the condition precedent results in either there being no contract (i.e. a condition precedent to contract), or alternatively no obligation to perform (i.e. condition precedent to performance). Which of the two actually occurs in a given case depends on the intention of the parties ...

26. The expression 'condition subsequent' refers to an event the occurrence of which terminates either an existing contractual relationship, or the obligation of one or more parties to perform. However, as noted by various text writers, the distinction implied by the words 'precedent' and 'subsequent' is largely semantic, as most conditions precedent can be expressed as conditions subsequent (and vice versa)."

In *Wood Preservation Ltd v Prior*,[6] Goff J identified the following four different types of conditional arrangements: **16.04**

(1) where the arrangement between the parties, which would otherwise be a contract, is subject to a condition precedent to the making of an agreement at all;

(2) where there is a contract under which one party assumes a unilateral obligation in a certain event, and there is no obligation on the other party to bring about that certain event;

(3) where there is a bilateral contract subject to a condition precedent with an immediate obligation on one of the parties to perform the condition or to use his best endeavours to perform it;

(4) where there is an immediate contract but on the basis that one of the parties will obtain some particular information or assurance or perform some particular term which goes to the root of the contract.

And in *Bashir v Commissioner of Crown Lands*,[7] the Privy Council held that a   **16.05**
stipulation in a contract could be both a condition and a covenant.[8] Similarly, in *Burford UK Properties Ltd v Forte Hotels (UK) Ltd*,[9] Auld LJ said that:

"there is no particular magic in the use in the lease of the word 'covenant' as against that of 'condition', 'provision', 'agreement' or 'proviso', and that a proviso, whether in the body of a lease or in a schedule to it, may, depending on its form and the context, have the same force and effect as a covenant."

In *Total Gas Marketing Ltd v Arco British Ltd*,[10] Lord Steyn said that conditions   **16.06**
could be divided into promissory conditions and contingent conditions. A promissory condition is one which is within the power of the promisor to bring about, whereas a contingent condition is one which is not within his power to bring about,

---

[6]   [1969] 1 W.L.R. 1077.
[7]   [1960] A.C. 44.
[8]   See also *Hyundai Merchant Marine Co Ltd v Karander Maritime Co Inc* [1996] C.L.C. 749.
[9]   [2003] EWCA Civ 1800.
[10]   [1998] 2 Lloyd's Rep. 209 at 220.

although he may undertake obligations to try to do so.[11] Contingent conditions can themselves be divided into conditions precedent and conditions subsequent. A condition precedent is a condition that must be fulfilled to bring about the creation of a contract or the enforceablity of an obligation; and a condition subsequent is a condition which, if fulfilled, extinguishes a contract or obligation to which it is subsequent.

2.   CONDITIONS PRECEDENT

A condition precedent is a condition which must be fulfilled before any binding contract is concluded at all. The expression is also used to describe a condition which does not prevent the existence of a binding contract, but which suspends performance of it or an obligation under it until fulfilment of the condition; or to describe a contractual obligation that must be performed by one party before another contractual obligation of the counterparty arises.

16.07   A condition precedent[12] is the "proper" meaning of condition, referred to in the last section. In *Bremer Handelsgesellschaft Schaft v Vanden Avenne Izegem*,[13] Lord Wilberforce said:

> "Whether this clause is a condition precedent or a contractual term of some other character must depend on (i) the form of the clause itself, (ii) the relation of the clause to the contract as a whole, (iii) general considerations of law."

16.08   In *Trans Trust SPRL v Danubian Trading Co Ltd*,[14] a contract for the sale of goods provided that payment was to be by cash against shipping documents from a confirmed credit. The question arose what was the nature of the buyer's obligation to procure the provision of a confirmed credit. Denning LJ said:

> "Sometimes it is a condition precedent to the formation of a contract, that is, it is a condition which must be fulfilled before any contract is concluded at all. In those cases the stipulation 'subject to the opening of a credit' is rather like a stipulation 'subject to contract'. If no credit is provided there is no contract between the parties. In other cases the contract is concluded and the stipulation for a credit is a condition which is an essential term of the contract. In those cases the provision of the credit is a condition precedent, not to the formation of a contract, but to the obligation of the seller to deliver the goods. If the buyer fails to provide the credit, the seller can treat himself as discharged from any further performance of the contract and can sue the buyer for damages for not providing the credit."

In the result it was held that the obligation to open a credit was not a condition precedent, but an essential obligation of the contract, breach of which entitled the seller to refuse to deliver and to sue for damages.

16.09   The formulation by Denning LJ divides conditions precedent into two groups; one where non-fulfilment of the condition prevents the existence of any binding

---

[11] *Michaels v Harley House (Marylebone) Ltd* [2000] Ch. 104 at 116.

[12] Sometimes called a "suspensive condition": see *Bentworth Finance Ltd v Lubert* [1968] 1 Q.B. 680.

[13] [1978] 2 Lloyd's Rep. 109; *WW Gear Construction Ltd v McGee Group Ltd* [2010] EWHC 1460 (TCC).

[14] [1952] 2 Q.B. 297.

agreement, and the other where non-fulfilment of the condition has the same effect as a breach of contract which goes to the root of the contract. However, there is an intermediate position. A condition may be such as not to prevent a binding contract from coming into existence, but to suspend immediate performance of the obligations it creates until fulfilment of the condition. Thus in *Bank of Nova Scotia v Hellenic Mutual Ltd (The Good Luck)*,[15] Lord Goff of Chieveley described the "classical sense" in English law of a condition precedent as being a provision:

"under which the coming into existence of (for example) an obligation, or the duty or further duty to perform an obligation, is dependent upon the fulfilment of the specified condition."[16]

In *Aspen Insurance UK Ltd v Pectel Ltd*,[17] Teare J said:

"It is well established that a general clause in an insurance policy purporting to make compliance with obligations in the policy a condition precedent to the underwriters being liable in respect of a claim can indeed have that effect ... The effect of such a general clause is that which the clause would have if it had been set out at the commencement of each particular clause which imposes an obligation upon the assured. This is the 'modern drafting technique' ... Whilst the words 'condition precedent' are often used in such clauses, other words can have the same effect so long as the clause is apt to make that effect the clear intention of the parties ... What has to be found is a 'conditional link' between the assured's obligation to give notice and the underwriters' obligation to pay the claim ...".

In *Marten v Whale*,[18] A agreed to sell to B a plot of land "subject to purchaser's   **16.10** solicitors' approval of title and restrictions", and at the same time and in consideration of the sale of the land B agreed to sell A a motor car. B allowed A to have the car on loan, and A sold it to C. Subsequently B's solicitors refused to approve the title. The question was whether A had "agreed to buy" the car, for if he had he was empowered to pass a good title to C. The Court of Appeal held that the arrangement amounted to a conditional contract and consequently title passed to C. Similarly, in *Smallman v Smallman*,[19] parties reached an agreement for a settlement of a divorce. The agreement was "subject to the approval of the court". Lord Denning MR said:

"In my opinion, if the parties have reached an agreement on all essential matters, then the clause 'subject to the approval of the court' does not mean there is no agreement at all. There is an agreement, but the operation of it is suspended until the court approves it. It is the duty of one party or the other to bring the agreement before the court for approval. If the court approves it, it is binding on the parties. If the court does not approve, it is not binding. But, pending the ap-

---

[15]   [1992] 1 A.C. 233.
[16]   In *Nautica Marine Ltd v Trafigura Trading LLC* [2020] EWHC 1986 (Comm) labelled the first sense as a "pre-condition" and the second sense as a "performance condition".
[17]   [2009] Lloyd's Rep. I.R. 440.
[18]   [1917] 2 K.B. 480.
[19]   [1972] Fam. 25.

plication to the court, it remains a binding agreement which neither party can disavow."[20]

16.11   The expression "condition precedent" is also used to describe a contingency which must be fulfilled in order to bring a particular contractual obligation into operation. That contingency may be the performance by one party of a contractual obligation of his own, or may be some other event (such as the giving of a notice). In *Persimmon Homes (South Coast) Ltd v Hall Aggregates (South Coast) Ltd*,[21] Coulson J said:

"It is trite law that, if one party's obligation to do something under a contract is contingent upon the happening of a particular event, the circumstances of that event must be identified unambiguously in the contract. It must be clear beyond doubt how and in what circumstances the relevant obligation has been triggered."

16.12   An option (or unilateral contract) is sometimes described as an "if" contract, because it only comes into operation as a bilateral contract "if" the option is exercised. Where a provision in a bilateral contract is an "if" provision, fulfilment of the contingency introduced by the word "if" is likely to be a condition precedent.[22] Likewise, where a contractual clause contains the phrase "provided always that":

"This type of wording is often the strongest sign that the parties intend there to be a condition precedent. What follows such a proviso is usually a qualification and explanation of what is required to enable the preceding requirements or entitlements to materialise."[23]

In *Burford UK Properties Ltd v Forte Hotels (UK) Ltd*,[24] Arden LJ said:

"One of the normal meanings of the words 'provided that' is 'on condition that' or 'on the assumption or footing that.'"

16.13   The question whether a contractual mechanism creates a condition precedent is a question of construction of the relevant provision in its contractual context, according to the normal principles.[25] In *Astrazeneca UK Ltd v Albemarle International Corp*,[26] Flaux J said:

"Whilst it is clear that, for performance of a provision in a contract to be a condition precedent to the performance of another provision, it is not necessary for the relevant provision to use the express words 'condition precedent' or something similar, nonetheless the court has to consider whether on the proper construction of the contract that is the effect of the provisions."

---

[20] Whether this is correct as a matter of matrimonial law is beyond the scope of this book: see *Xydhias v Xydhias* [1999] 2 All E.R. 386; *Soulsbury v Soulsbury* [2008] Fam. 1.
[21] [2008] EWHC 2379 (TCC) at [298].
[22] *Merton London Borough v Stanley Hugh Leach Ltd* (1985) 32 B.L.R. 51; *WW Gear Construction Ltd v McGee Group Ltd* [2010] EWHC 1460 (TCC).
[23] *WW Gear Construction Ltd v McGee Group Ltd* [2010] EWHC 1460 (TCC), per Akenhead J.
[24] [2003] EWCA Civ 1800.
[25] *Teesside Gas Transportation Ltd v CATS North Sea Ltd* [2019] EWHC 1220 (Comm).
[26] [2011] EWHC 1574 (Comm); *Gwynt Y Mor Ofto Plc v Gwynt Y Mor Offshore Wind Farm Ltd* [2020] EWHC 850 (Comm).

He added that:

"... in the absence of an express term, performance of one obligation will only be a condition precedent to another obligation where either the first obligation must for practical reasons clearly be performed before the second obligation can arise or the second obligation is the direct quid pro quo of the first, in the sense that only performance of the first earns entitlement to the second."[27]

Because the classification of a term as a condition precedent may have the effect of depriving a party to a contract of a right because of a trivial breach which has little or no prejudicial effect on the other and causes that other little or no loss, the court will usually require clear words to be used before coming to that conclusion.[28] In *Denso Manufacturing UK Ltd v Great Lakes Reinsurance (UK) Plc*,[29] Ms Sara Cockerill QC said: **16.14**

"The starting point for any argument that a party is discharged from liability because a condition was a condition precedent is that the courts are careful to scrutinise arguments that a particular term is a condition precedent. One critical issue is whether the relevant terms are capable of being conditions precedent."

Although the phrase "condition precedent" is often used expressly, any other form of clear words will have the same effect.[30] In *Dreams Ltd v Pavilion Property Trustees Ltd*,[31] an agreement for the surrender of a lease stated that the surrender "is with vacant possession". Miles J held that unless vacant possession was delivered, the landlord could not be compelled to accept the surrender. Although the argument centred on the question whether the obligation to deliver vacant possession was a condition precedent, it is considered that the real question was whether the obligation to deliver vacant possession on the one hand, and the obligation to accept the surrender on the other were concurrent conditions or dependent obligations.

Normally a condition precedent must be precisely fulfilled. However, it has been suggested that a condition precedent need not be fulfilled where it would be futile, useless and unnecessary to do so.[32] This will rarely be the case where compliance with the condition is necessary in order to bring into effect a contractual obligation in a particular manner.[33] In *Glencore Grain Ltd v Goldbeam Shipping Inc*,[34] Moore-Bick J said: **16.15**

"If the parties have stipulated that a notice must be given in order to bring some other provision of the contract into operation, I doubt whether it could ever be dispensed with on the grounds that to give such a notice would be futile."

---

[27] See also *DRC Distribution Ltd v Ulva Ltd* [2007] EWHC 1716 (QB); *Yukos Hydrocarbons Investments Ltd v Georgiades* [2020] EWHC 173 (Comm).

[28] *Heritage Oil and Gas Ltd v Tullow Uganda Ltd* [2014] EWCA Civ 1048; *Mishcon De Reya LLP v RJI (Middle East) Ltd* [2020] EWHC 1670 (QB).

[29] [2017] EWHC 391 (Comm); [2018] 4 W.L.R. 93.

[30] *Heritage Oil and Gas Ltd v Tullow Uganda Ltd* [2014] EWCA Civ 1048.

[31] [2020] EWHC 1169 (Ch).

[32] *Barrett Bros (Taxis) Ltd v Davies* [1966] 1 W.L.R. 1334; *The Mozart* [1985] 1 Lloyd's Rep. 239; *Mansel Oil Ltd v Troon Storage Tankers SA* [2008] 2 Lloyd's Rep. 384 (affirmed on appeal [2009] EWCA Civ 425).

[33] *Glencore Grain Ltd v Flacker Shipping Ltd (The Happy Day)* [2002] 2 Lloyd's Rep. 487.

[34] [2002] 2 Lloyd's Rep. 400.

Despite suggestions in earlier cases, there is no general principle that a condition precedent need not be complied with if it is futile to do so. Whether a contractual obligation has arisen in any given case in principle depends on what the particular contract says, interpreted in accordance with the ordinary principles of contract interpretation. There is no principle of law or even interpretive presumption which enables a contractual precondition to the accrual of a right or obligation to be disapplied just because complying with it is considered by the court to serve no useful purpose. However, there may be circumstances in which (depending on the terms of the contract) a condition precedent may, as a matter of construction and in the light of subsequent events, no longer apply or may cease to have effect.[35]

16.16   It has been said that a condition precedent "enables a party to know where it stands contemporaneously", and consequently cannot be retrospectively satisfied.[36] However, where a condition precedent merely suspends performance of other obligations, then it appears that it can be satisfied at a date later than the time for fulfilment of the condition. In that sense the satisfaction of the condition is retrospective, because the obligation whose performance is suspended then comes into operation.[37] In other cases a similar result has been reached by interpreting the condition precedent as not being tied to a particular date.[38]

16.17   It should perhaps be mentioned that in older cases[39] the expression "condition precedent" is more generally used in the sense of a term of the contract, breach of which entitled the other party to the contract to treat it as at an end. This usage was bound up with the old rules of pleading which required the plaintiff to aver performance or willingness or ability to perform all stipulations on his part in the precise words in which they were expressed in the contract. This rule treated all promises by each party to a contract as "conditions precedent" to all promises of the other; with the result that any departure from the promised manner of performance, however slight that departure may have been, discharged the other party from the obligation to continue to perform any of his own promises.[40] In modern law, however, the expression "condition precedent" (as opposed simply to "condition") should be restricted to cases where non-fulfilment of the condition prevents the formation of a binding agreement, or suspends the operation of the contract or particular obligations under it.

Illustrations

1.   A finance company claimed arrears of instalments under a hire purchase agreement relating to a car. The buyer of the car proved that the company's agents had agreed that the hire would not become payable until the company had provided a log-book for the car. Lord Denning MR said:

"The provision of the log-book was a condition on which the very existence of

---

[35]   *Astor Management AG v Atalaya Mining Plc* [2018] EWCA Civ 2407; [2019] Bus. L.R. 106.

[36]   *Sempra Oil Trading Sarl v Kronos Worldwide Ltd* [2004] 1 Lloyd's Rep. 260.

[37]   *Lomas v JFB Firth Rixson Inc* [2010] EWHC 3372 (Ch) following dictum of Austin J in *Enron Australia v TXU Electricity* [2003] NSWSC 1169.

[38]   *McGahon v Crest Nicholson Regeneration Ltd* [2011] 1 P. & C.R. 225.

[39]   For example, cases decided before the changes in pleading made by the Common Law Procedure Act 1852.

[40]   See *Hong Kong Fir Shipping Co Ltd v Kawasaki Kisen Kaisha Ltd* [1962] 2 Q.B. 26; *United Scientific Holdings Ltd v Burnley Borough Council* [1978] A.C. 904, per Diplock LJ and Lord Diplock respectively.

the contract depended. It was, in technical language, a suspensive condition. Until the log-book was provided there was no contract at all."

Bentworth Finance Ltd v Lubert[41]

2.   A written agreement provided for the sale to the defendant of a share in an invention of the plaintiff. The defendant was allowed to give evidence to the effect that the agreement was not to become binding until the invention had been approved by an engineer. He had not approved it. It was held that no agreement came into existence.

Pym v Campbell[42]

3.   A compromise agreement between a company and its former chief executive provided that "Subject to and conditional upon the terms set out below" the company would pay a lump sum. One of the terms was a warranty by the chief executive "as a strict condition of this agreement" that there were no circumstances of which he was aware that would amount to a repudiatory breach of his contract of employment. It was held that the truth of the warranty was a condition precedent to the company's liability to pay.

Collidge v Freeport Plc[43]

4.   A guarantee of a sub-tenant's obligations under a sub-lease contained a covenant by the tenant to give notice to the guarantor whenever the rent under the sub-lease was two months in arrears. It was held that the giving of such notice was not a condition precedent to the guarantor's liability under the guarantee.

Greene King Plc v Quisine Restaurants Ltd[44]

5.   An agreement for the sale of land provided that: "As a pre-condition to completion the Seller shall obtain (and supply true copies to the Buyer) all of the Emergency Lighting Certificates as soon as practicable and in any event prior to the date of Actual Completion." It was held that this was a condition precedent to the buyer's obligation to complete, but not to the seller's.

British Overseas Nominees Ltd v Analytical Properties Ltd[45]

6.   A settlement agreement provided for the release of claims "Subject to the satisfactory completion of all terms of this Agreement by" two named parties. It was held that the quoted phrase was not a condition precedent. The release therefore took effect even though not all the terms of the agreement had been fully performed.

Yukos Hydrocarbons Investments Ltd v Georgiades[46]

7.   An option agreement provided that it was to be exercised by the buyer giving written notice. It also provided that "on the exercise of the option" the buyer

---

[41] [1968] 1 Q.B. 680.
[42] (1856) 1 E. & B. 370.
[43] [2008] I.R.L.R. 697.
[44] [2012] EWCA Civ 698.
[45] [2014] EWHC 802 (Ch).
[46] [2020] EWHC 173 (Comm).

was to pay a deposit. Payment of the deposit was not a condition precedent to the valid exercise of the option.

Peacock v Imagine Property Developments Ltd[47]

3. SUBJECT TO CONTRACT

Save in exceptional circumstances, an arrangement made subject to contract means that execution or exchange of a formal written contract is a condition precedent to any legal liability.

16.18   Informal agreements for the sale of land are commonly made "subject to contract". The making of such agreements is not confined to land transactions.[48] In the case of negotiations for the grant of a lease there is a presumption that any informal agreement is "subject to lease".[49]

16.19   Where such an expression is used, it is generally interpreted to mean that the parties do not intend to be bound unless and until a formal written contract is executed or exchanged between them. So in *Rossdale v Denny*,[50] Russell J said:

> "... after considering all the authorities which have been brought to my attention it would appear that in every case with two exceptions, where the words 'subject to' appear, the documents in those cases have been held to amount only to a conditional offer or a conditional acceptance, as the case may be, but not such as to constitute a binding contract apart from the execution of a formal document."

Of the two exceptions, one[51] was decided upon special facts and the other[52] has been frequently doubted, not least by the Court of Appeal affirming the decision of Russell J.

16.20   In *Generator Developments Ltd v Lidl UK GmbH*,[53] Lewison LJ said of the phrase "subject to contract":

> "The meaning of that phrase is well-known. What it means is that (a) neither party intends to be bound either in law or in equity unless and until a formal contract is made; and (b) each party reserves the right to withdraw until such time as a binding contract is made. It follows, therefore, that in negotiating on that basis [both parties] took the commercial risk that one or other of them might back out of the proposed transaction ... In short a 'subject to contract' agreement is no agreement at all."

16.21   The phrase "subject to contract" has the same effect in the case of a proposed grant of a lease.[54] So in *Derby & Co Ltd v ITC Pension Trust Ltd*,[55] Oliver J said:

> "Where negotiations are carried out 'subject to contract' that means, and I think

---

[47]   [2018] EWHC 1113 (TCC).
[48]   *Confetti Records v Warner Music (UK) Ltd* [2003] E.M.L.R. 35.
[49]   *Leveson v Parfum Marcel Rochas (England) Ltd* (1966) 200 E.G. 407.
[50]   [1921] 1 Ch. 57.
[51]   *Filby v Hounsell* [1896] 2 Ch. 737.
[52]   *North v Percival* [1898] 2 Ch. 128.
[53]   [2018] EWCA Civ 396; [2018] 2 P. & C.R. 7; *Goodwood Investments Holdings Inc v Thyssenkrupp Industrial Solutions AG* [2018] EWHC 1056 (Comm); *Astra Asset Management UK Ltd v The Co-Operative Bank Plc* [2019] EWHC 897 (Comm),
[54]   *Longman v Viscount Chelsea* (1989) 58 P. & C.R. 189 CA; *Akiens v Salomon* (1992) 65 P. & C.R.

this is clear from the authorities, that they are conditional on the final engross-ment, execution and exchange of the formal lease, where the case is one of negotiations for the grant of a lease or tenancy."

The mere fact that the parties contemplate the preparation of a formal contract **16.22** will not necessarily prevent a binding agreement from coming into effect before the formal contract is executed. In *Rossiter v Miller*,[56] Lord Blackburn said:

"I think the decisions settle that it is a question of construction whether the par-ties finally agreed to be bound by the terms, though they were subsequently to have a formal agreement drawn up."

So also in *Von Hatzfeld-Wildenburg v Alexander*,[57] Parker J said:

"It appears to be well settled by the authorities that if the documents or letters relied on as constituting a contract contemplate the execution of a further contract between the parties, it is a question of construction whether the execution of the further contract is a condition or term of the bargain or whether it is a mere expression of the desire of the parties as to the manner in which the transaction already agreed to will in fact go through."

In *Branca v Cobarro*,[58] the parties entered into an agreement which contained a clause stating:

"This is a provisional agreement until a fully legalised agreement, drawn up by a solicitor and embodying all the conditions herewith stated is signed."

The Court of Appeal held that a binding agreement came into effect.

In exceptional cases, even a document headed "subject to contract" may not **16.23** negative the formation of a binding agreement. In *Richards (Michael) Properties Ltd v Corp of Wardens of St Saviour's Parish, Southwark*,[59] property was offered for sale by tender. As is usual, the tender documents contained detailed terms. The successful tender was accepted by letter, but by mistake the secretary who typed it typed the words "subject to contract" at the bottom. Goff J rejected those words as meaningless, and held that a binding contract came into existence.

Alpenstow Ltd v Regalian Properties Plc,[60] is a somewhat different case. The par-ties entered into a written agreement containing a right of pre-emption. In the event of the owner wishing to sell it was to offer to sell a share in the property by notice. Within 28 days of the notice, the grantee was to accept the notice "subject to contract". Within seven days thereafter a draft contract was to be submitted; the draft was to be approved within 28 days, subject to any amendment reasonably required, and contracts were to be exchanged within seven days thereafter. Nourse J held that the agreement was binding, and in particular pointed to the incompat-ibility between the freedom to withdraw from the transaction which the words "subject to contract" suggested, and the duty to submit a contract and to exchange it within a particular timetable.

---

363 CA.
[55] [1977] 2 All E.R. 890; *Longman v Chelsea (Viscount)* (1989) 58 P. & C.R. 189 CA.
[56] (1878) 3 App. Cas. 1124.
[57] [1912] 1 Ch. 284.
[58] [1947] K.B. 854.
[59] [1975] 3 All E.R. 416.
[60] [1985] 1 W.L.R. 721.

In both these cases, the court was careful to stress that no doubt was being cast on the meaning and effect of the "subject to contract" formula in an ordinary case.

16.24   In the maritime world the phrase "subject to details" is equivalent to "subject to contract".[61] In *The Junior K*,[62] Steyn J said:

> "The expression 'subject to details' enables owners and charterers to know where they are in negotiations and to regulate their business accordingly. It is a device which tends to avoid disputes and the assumption of those in the shipping trade that it is effective to make clear that there is no binding agreement at that stage ought to be respected."

In *Thoresen & Co (Bankok) Ltd v Fathom Marine Co Ltd*,[63] Langley J said:

> "Thus, in my judgment, it has been established for many years that the words 'subject details' have a recognized meaning when used in the context of the sale of ships: there is no binding agreement until all the details of the proposed formal agreement have been agreed."

16.25   In *The Botnica*,[64] proposed terms for the charter of a ship stated: "Offer for the MSV Botnica is subject to the signing of mutually agreeable contract terms and conditions". All the relevant terms were subsequently agreed, but one party did not sign. Aikens J held that there was no binding contract. He said that:

> "the clear and obvious meaning of the words, in particular the words 'is subject to ....', whose meaning and effect is well known to commercial men, is that there will not be a binding agreement until that 'subject' has been fulfilled. In this case that is done by each side signing the mutually agreeable contract terms and conditions."[65]

16.26   However, the Court of Appeal has held that it is not legitimate to extend the principle illustrated by the "subject to contract" cases from the field of bilateral negotiations to that of a unilateral act, such as the giving of consent to alterations, where the landlord's consent to alterations was required under the terms of a lease.[66]

Illustrations

1.   Property was offered for sale in lots upon detailed conditions of sale, one of which provided that the purchaser would be required to sign a contract embody-

---

[61]   *The Soholt* [1981] 2 Lloyd's Rep. 574; *The Junior K* [1988] 2 Lloyd's Rep. 583; *The CPC Gallia* [1994] 1 Lloyd's Rep. 68; *Nautica Marine Ltd v Trafigura Trading LLC* [2020] EWHC 1986 (Comm).

[62]   [1988] 2 Lloyd's Rep. 583.

[63]   [2004] 1 Lloyd's Rep. 622.

[64]   [2007] 1 Lloyd's Rep. 37.

[65]   It is thought that, as formulated, the proposition is too wide; because a binding agreement can be made, even though it is "subject to" the fulfilment of some condition, although its performance or performance of some of its obligations may be suspended in the interim. However, since the condition in that case was the signing of the agreement itself, the decision is correct. See paras 16.27-16.39.

[66]   *Prudential Assurance Co Ltd v Mount Eden Land Ltd* [1997] 1 E.G.L.R. 37.

ing those conditions. A written offer for part of the property was accepted in writing. It was held that a binding contract had come into existence.
Rossiter v Miller[67]

2.   An agreement for the sale of a house stated that it was "subject to the preparation by [the vendor's] solicitor and completion of a formal contract". It was held that no binding contract was created.
Lloyd v Nowell[68]

3.   An agreement was stated to be "subject to preparation and approval of formal contract". It was held that no binding contract was created.
Winn v Bull[69]

4.   An agreement for a lease of a number of houses in Shanghai, to be taken in stages, stipulated that "a proper contract" was to be made by a named solicitor. It was held by the Privy Council that that stipulation did not prevent a binding contract from coming into existence as it was isolated from the other stipulations in point of sequence and could have been performed at many different times.
Oxford v Provand[70]

4.   Subject to Survey

A contract made subject to satisfactory survey is a binding contract, but is not enforceable unless the purchaser receives a survey which, acting bona fide, he considers satisfactory.[71]

Until recently it has been widely thought that the phrase "subject to survey" is equivalent to "subject to contract" with the result that no binding contract comes into existence. So in *Graham and Scott (Southgate) Ltd v Oxlade*,[72] Cohen LJ said: **16.27**

> "Mr Stanley Rees ... submitted that the distinction between 'subject to contract' and 'subject to survey' is a distinction without a difference, since under a provision 'subject to survey' an intending purchaser could refuse to sign a contract if he were dissatisfied with a survey. With this view I agree."

However, as Cohen LJ recognised, in the case of a sale "subject to survey" the intending purchaser is only free to withdraw on one ground, namely an unsatisfactory survey. By contrast, under an agreement "subject to contract" either party can withdraw for any reason at all. Nevertheless, the view that there was no difference between the two phrases held sway. So in *Marks v Board*,[73] a house was agreed to be sold "subject to surveyor's report". Rowlatt J held that there was no binding   **16.28**

---

[67]   (1878) 3 App. Cas. 1124.
[68]   [1895] 2 Ch. 744.
[69]   (1877) 7 Ch. D. 29.
[70]   (1868) L.R. 2 P.C. 135.
[71]   This section was referred to with apparent approval in *Hyundai Merchant Marine Co Ltd v Americas Bulk Transport Ltd (The Pacific Champ)* [2013] EWHC 470 (Comm); [2013] 2 Lloyd's Rep. 320.
[72]   [1950] 2 K.B. 257 (a case concerning the entitlement of estate agents to commission).
[73]   (1930) 46 T.L.R. 424.

contract. That was followed by Megaw J in *Astra Trust Ltd v Adams and Williams*,[74] a case of a ship sold subject to satisfactory survey.

However, the latter case was doubted in *The Merak*,[75] where a contract for the sale of a ship "subject to inspection by the buyers at a port and date to be agreed" was held by the Court of Appeal to be binding.

16.29   The principles were reviewed by Walton J in *Ee v Kakar*,[76] in which he held that an agreement for the sale of a house "subject to survey" created a binding contract. He held that the expression "subject to survey" was a condition which suspended the enforcement of the purchaser's obligations, although if the purchaser had not obtained a survey within a reasonable time he would be taken to have waived the condition.

It is submitted that this approach is correct. To hold otherwise would invalidate many arrangements into which parties entered in the belief that they were binding.

5.   SUBJECT TO OTHER MATTERS

Where an agreement is made subject to other matters it is a question of interpretation: (a) whether the parties intended to be bound at all; and (b) whether the matter subject to which the agreement is made is sufficiently certain.

16.30   Agreements may be made subject to all sorts of matters. It is then a question of interpretation in each case whether the parties intended to enter into an immediately binding contract, performance of which was suspended pending fulfilment of the condition or whether they intended no contract to arise at all. If the former is the correct conclusion it is also necessary to consider whether the condition is sufficiently certain to be legally enforceable. If it is not, the whole contract will be void for uncertainty. An important factor in determining whether a "subject" is a precondition[77] or a performance condition[78] is whether the satisfaction of the "subject" depends upon the decision of a contracting party, or on that of a third party. A "subject" is more likely to be classified as a precondition rather than a performance condition if the fulfilment of the subject involves the exercise of a personal or commercial judgment by one of the putative contracting parties (e.g. as to whether that party is satisfied with the outcome of a survey or as to the terms on which it wishes to contract with any third party).[79]

16.31   As a matter of principle, it is submitted that there is a great difference between an agreement "subject to contract" and an agreement subject to something else. In the former case, the fact that the parties indicate that they expect their rights and obligations to be governed by a formal contract is itself an indication that they do not intend to be bound unless and until such a contract is made. They are therefore free to withdraw on any ground at all.[80] But where the suspensory condition is something else, it would seem to indicate that the parties did intend to be bound, subject to the right of one (or both) of them to withdraw if the stipulated condition

---

[74]   [1969] 1 Lloyd's Rep. 81.
[75]   [1976] 2 Lloyd's Rep. 250.
[76]   (1979) 40 P. & C.R. 223.
[77]   i.e. one that prevents the formation of a contact.
[78]   i.e. one that suspends performance of an obligation under a concluded contract.
[79]   *Nautica Marine Ltd v Trafigura Trading LLC* [2020] EWHC 1986 (Comm).
[80]   This is why *The Botnica* [2007] 1 Lloyd's Rep. 37 is correctly decided.

was not fulfilled. This seems to be inconsistent with the conclusion that one or other of them may withdraw for any reason at all (that is, that there is no contract).

Thus in *Windschuegl (Charles H) Ltd v Pickering (Alexander) & Co Ltd*,[81] Devlin J said:

> "The phrase 'subject to contract' has, of course, been construed as meaning that no contract is made, but I think that that is purely because of the word 'contract' in 'subject to contract'. The phrase means 'subject to the making of a contract hereafter' and, partly because it is becoming so usual now, has to be regarded as a term which signifies to anyone who uses it that the matter has not progressed beyond the stage of negotiations. But I do not think the same is true as applied to anything else, nor do I see why it should be."

In *Hudson v Buck*,[82] a lease was agreed to be sold subject to the approval of the title by the purchaser's solicitor. The purchaser's solicitor refused to approve the title. Fry J held that the contract was unenforceable. It was not, however, necessary to consider whether a contract had ever come into existence at all or whether it was merely a case of enforcement of the purchaser's obligations being suspended. In *Caney v Leith*,[83] an agreement for the sale of a lease was "subject to the purchaser's solicitor approving the lease". Farwell J treated the contract as a conditional contract which could not be enforced against the purchaser unless the condition was fulfilled. It is submitted that this is the correct analysis.   **16.32**

In *Batten v White (No.2)*,[84] land was agreed to be sold "subject to planning permission to develop and satisfactory drainage". Russell J held that a binding contract was created.   **16.33**

In *Goodwood Investments Holdings Inc v Thyssenkrupp Industrial Solutions AG*,[85] a contract was made subject to board approval. Males J said: **16.34**

> "When a person concludes an agreement on behalf of a company which is stated to be subject to its board approval, he makes clear that he does not have authority, or at any rate is not prepared, to commit the company unless and until the approval is given ... Since the directors are required to exercise an independent judgment whether the transaction is in the best interests of the company, it is very hard to see how there could in such circumstances be any implied promise binding the company to the effect that approval will be forthcoming or that it is a mere formality or a 'rubber stamping' exercise. Even an express promise would be problematical. If the negotiator makes clear that he is not authorised to commit the company, he can hardly be authorised to commit the board of directors to commit the company. Accordingly, when an agreement is concluded which is subject to board approval, neither party is bound until the approval is given."

More difficult problems have been created where property is sold subject to finance. In *Lee-Parker v Izzet (No.2)*,[86] a formal written contract for the sale of a house contained a special condition which provided that the sale was "subject to   **16.35**

---

[81] (1950) 84 Lloyd's Rep. 89 at 92 (an agreement for the sale of goods subject to import licence held to be binding).
[82] (1877) 7 Ch. D. 683.
[83] [1937] 2 All E.R. 532.
[84] (1960) 12 P. & C.R. 66.
[85] [2018] EWHC 1056 (Comm).
[86] [1972] 1 W.L.R. 775.

the purchaser obtaining a satisfactory mortgage". Goulding J held that until the condition was fulfilled there was no binding contract for sale, and that the condition was void for uncertainty. It is submitted that the decision is wrong on both points. Since the parties had entered into a formal written contract, it would seem to follow that they intended each to be bound subject to the purchaser's right to withdraw if he could not obtain a satisfactory mortgage. On the second point, it is submitted that the court ought to have been readier to imply a term that the purchaser should act in good faith (and perhaps reasonably) in deciding whether a mortgage offer was satisfactory to him.[87]

Lee-Parker v Izzet was distinguished in *Janmohamed v Hassam*,[88] in which Slade J upheld as binding a contract for the sale of a house which was subject to the purchaser obtaining an offer of mortgage on terms satisfactory to himself within one month.

16.36   In addition, agreements "subject to finance" are commonly upheld in Australia and New Zealand.[89] So in *Meehan v Jones*,[90] a contract was subject to the purchaser's nominees arranging "finance on satisfactory terms and conditions to enable them to complete the purchase". The High Court of Australia held that the contract was binding. It is considered that this approach should be followed in England and Wales.[91]

16.37   In *Novus Aviation Ltd v Alubaf Arab International Bank BSC*,[92] a contract to provide equity funding for the acquisition and leasing of commercial aircraft was said to be "conditional upon satisfactory review and completion of documentation for the purchase, lease, and financing". Leggatt J said:

"63. I agree that whether or not the documentation was 'satisfactory' would potentially depend upon the attitudes and aims of the particular investor. Terms of some of the key transaction documents, such as the aircraft leases, which one investor might consider essential or objectionable might be differently perceived by another. There is no general or universal standard by which documentation could be declared 'satisfactory' in some absolute sense. The implication of this, however, is not that the language cannot be given a definite or practical meaning. It is that the word 'satisfactory' would reasonably be understood to mean 'considered satisfactory by Alubaf'. There is no conceptual difficulty or uncertainty in applying that test. Whether Alubaf considered the documentation to be satisfactory is a question of fact.

64. At the same time, I do not think that the ability of Alubaf to reject documentation as unsatisfactory should be seen as completely unqualified. It is in the nature of a contractual discretion. It is now well established that, in the absence of very clear language to the contrary, a contractual discretion must be exercised in good faith for the purpose for which it was conferred, and must not

---

[87] See, e.g. *Hudson v Buck* (1877) 7 Ch. D. 683 where Fry J indicated that the purchaser's solicitors were not entitled to refuse to approve the title on arbitrary grounds; and see para.14.20.

[88] [1977] 1 E.G.L.R. 142.

[89] See Coote, "Agreements subject to finance" (1976) 40 Conv. (N.S.) 37.

[90] (1982) 149 C.L.R. 571.

[91] However, an alleged contract to obtain "third party finance" to pay off a bankrupt's debts as a preliminary to obtaining an annulment of the bankruptcy was too uncertain to have legal effect (*Schweppe v Harper* [2008] B.P.I.R. 1090); as was an alleged obligation on the part of a seller to cooperate with the buyer to enable appropriate financing arrangements to be put in place (*Wittmann (UK) Ltd v Willdav Engineering SA* [2007] EWCA Civ 824).

[92] [2016] EWHC 1575 (Comm); [2017] 1 B.C.L.C. 414.

be exercised arbitrarily, capriciously or unreasonably (in the sense of irrationally) ... ."

A narrower approach was taken in *Howard (John) and Co (Northern) Ltd v*   **16.38**
Knight (JP) Ltd,[93] in which a ship was agreed to be sold "subject to satisfactory running trials". Megaw J held that that stipulation prevented the formation of a binding contract. This case was considered by Walton J in *Ee v Kakar*[94] who refused to follow it. It is submitted that Walton J was right. The same narrow approach was followed by Mocatta J in *The John S. Darbyshire*,[95] where a time charter was "subject to satisfactory completion of two trial voyages". In fact, in that case, the vessel did not satisfactorily complete the first trial voyage, so the judge's decision could be upheld on that ground.

So also many international sales are made subject to the obtaining of an import   **16.39**
or export licence. This does not prevent a binding contract from arising; indeed one or other party may be in breach of contract if the licence is not obtained.

6. IMPLIED DUTIES TO FULFIL CONDITIONS

The parties are under an implied obligation not to prevent the fulfilment of a condition upon which a contract depends. In addition, one or both of them may be under an implied obligation to take steps to procure that the condition is fulfilled.

There is imposed on parties to a contract a general duty to cooperate in the   **16.40**
performance of the contract. This duty includes a duty not to prevent the fulfilment of conditions. Thus in *Mackay v Dick*,[96] a digging machine was sold if it fulfilled certain conditions, one of which was that it should be capable of excavating at a certain rate in the buyer's railway cutting. The buyer refused to give it a proper trial. The House of Lords held that he was in breach of the contract and liable for the price of the machine. So also in *Bournemouth & Boscombe Athletic FC v Manchester United FC*,[97] a professional footballer signed for a new club at a fee part of which was to be paid to his former club after he had scored 20 goals. He was dropped from the team before he had had a reasonable opportunity to score 20 goals. The new club was held to be in breach of contract.

Sometimes, however, the parties' duties with respect to the fulfilment of condi-   **16.41**
tions go further than merely not preventing their fulfilment. There may be imposed on one or both parties positive duties to procure the fulfilment of the condition; and those duties may be duties to use their best (or reasonable) endeavours to procure fulfilment or they may be absolute duties to do so. There is no clear pattern to be observed in the cases, each one of which turns on its own facts.

Where the condition to be fulfilled is one which is dependent on the discretion   **16.42**
of one party to the contract, or even of a third party, it will be an implied term that that person must act in good faith, and in some cases reasonably.[98] In *Hudson v*

---

93 [1969] 1 Lloyd's Rep. 364.
94 (1979) 40 P. & C.R. 223.
95 [1977] 2 Lloyd's Rep. 457.
96 (1881) 6 App. Cas. 251.
97 [1980] 1 WLUK 29; *The Times,* 22 May 1980.
98 See para.14.69.

Buck,[99] a lease was sold subject to the approval of the title by the purchaser's solicitor. Fry J indicated (obiter) that if the purchaser had acted unreasonably, as by not appointing a solicitor, or if the solicitor appointed had taken utterly unreasonable objections to the title, the purchaser might not have been able to take advantage of the condition. In *Caney v Leith*,[100] Farwell J observed of a similar stipulation:

"In my judgment when they [i.e. judges] are using the word 'unreasonable' they are dealing with a position where the solicitors are not acting in good faith—that is to say, where, to assist their client, and get him out of the contract, or for some other reason, the solicitors refuse to approve the lease, without giving the matter any consideration at all, or where their reasons for disapproval are so patent and absurd that the court can say in a moment: 'This is ridiculous and the solicitors cannot possibly make such an objection as that.'"

Where, however, it is not immediately apparent that the objection is bad, the condition will not have been fulfilled.

16.43   Where a contracting party is under a contingent conditional obligation, he may be in breach of contract if he puts it out of his power to perform the obligation in the event that the contingency were to arise. As Lord Kitchin put it in *Duval v 11–13 Randolph Crescent Ltd*[101]:

"It is well established that a party who undertakes a contingent or conditional obligation may, depending upon the circumstances, be under a further obligation not to prevent the contingency from occurring; or from putting it out of his power to discharge the obligation if and when the contingency arises."

Where, therefore, a lease of a flat contained an absolute covenant against alterations, and a landlord's covenant to enforce obligations at the request of lessees of other flats, the landlord would be in breach of covenant in licensing an alteration that would have been prohibited by the absolute covenant.[102]

Illustrations

1.   A contract for the sale of land was conditional on the purchaser's solicitor approving title and other restrictions. It was held that the buyer was bound to appoint a solicitor, to submit the title to him and to consult him in good faith. Moreover, it was held that the solicitor was bound to give an honest opinion.
Marten v Whale[103]

2.   Parties agreed a divorce settlement "subject to the approval of the court". It was held that it was the duty of one party or the other to bring the settlement before the court for approval.
Smallman v Smallman[104]

3.   Land was agreed to be sold subject to a condition that the buyer should

---

[99]   (1877) 7 Ch. D. 683.
[100]   [1937] 2 All E.R. 532.
[101]   [2020] UKSC 18.
[102]   *Duval v 11–13 Randolph Crescent Ltd* [2020] UKSC 18.
[103]   [1917] 2 K.B. 480.
[104]   [1972] Fam. 25.

receive planning permission to use the property as a transport depot. It was held that the buyer was under a duty to take all reasonable steps to obtain the permission (although those steps did not include appealing to the Minister).
Hargreaves Transport Ltd v Lynch[105]

4.   A house was sold subject to survey. It was held that the purchaser was bound to obtain a survey, consider it and act bona fide in evaluating it.
Ee v Kakar[106]

5.   Sellers agreed to sell goods f.o.b. a Brazilian port "subject to any Brazilian export licence". It was held that the sellers were under a duty to take all reasonable steps to obtain the licence.
Brauer & Co (Great Britain) Ltd v Clark (James) (Brush Materials) Ltd[107]

6.   A provider of aircraft maintenance services agreed to licence a hangar to an airline, subject to the consent of the airport authority. It was held that the service provider had an implied obligation to use best endeavours to procure the consent.
Ryanair Ltd v SR Technics Ireland Ltd[108]

7.   EXPRESS DUTIES TO FULFIL CONDITIONS: BEST ENDEAVOURS AND SIMILAR CLAUSES

Express duties relating to the fulfilment of conditions are often expressed as obligations to use "best endeavours", "all reasonable endeavours" or "reasonable endeavours". Although the content of such an obligation is a question of interpretation of the contract in question, it is probable that an obligation to use best endeavours is more onerous than an obligation to use reasonable endeavours.

It has been said that there is no real difference between an obligation to use "best endeavours" and an obligation to use "reasonable endeavours". Thus in *Overseas Buyers v Granadex*,[109] Mustill J said: **16.44**

"it was argued that the arbitrators can be seen to have misdirected themselves as to the law to be applied, for they have found that EIC did 'all that could reasonably be expected of them', rather than finding whether EIC used their 'best endeavours' to obtain permission to export, which is the test laid down by the decided cases. I can frankly see no substance at all in this argument. Perhaps the words 'best endeavours' in a statute or contract mean something different from doing all that can reasonably be expected—although I cannot think what the difference might be."

---

105   [1969] 1 W.L.R. 215. However, an express obligation to use best endeavours to obtain planning permission was held to require the promisor to appeal to the Secretary of State if the appeal had a reasonable chance of success: *IBM United Kingdom Ltd v Rockware Glass Ltd* [1980] F.S.R. 335.
106   (1979) 40 P. & C.R. 223.
107   [1952] 2 All E.R. 497.
108   [2007] EWHC 3089 (QB).
109   [1980] 2 Lloyd's Rep. 608 at 613.

16.45   In *Pips (Leisure Productions) Ltd v Walton*,[110] Megarry VC said, somewhat more tentatively that:

> "Best endeavours' are something less than efforts which go beyond the bounds of reason, but are considerably more than casual and intermittent activities. There must at least be the doing of all that reasonable persons reasonably could do in the circumstances."

16.46   In *IBM United Kingdom Ltd v Rockware Glass Ltd*,[111] a contract required the buyer to use its best endeavours to obtain planning permission. Buckley LJ said:

> "I can feel no doubt that, in the absence of any context indicating the contrary, this should be understood to mean that the purchaser is to do all he reasonably can to ensure that the planning permission is granted."

Geoffrey Lane LJ said:

> "Those words, as I see it, oblige the purchaser to take all those reasonable steps which a prudent and determined man, acting in his own interests and anxious to obtain planning permission, would have taken."

16.47   However, as has been subsequently pointed out, as "a matter of language and business common sense" one would surely conclude that the two obligations did not mean the same thing.[112] It is considered, therefore, that an obligation to use reasonable endeavours is less stringent than one to use best endeavours.[113] Thus in *Stepping Stones Child Care Centre (ACT) Pty Ltd v Early Learning Services Ltd*,[114] it was held In Australia that "an obligation to use 'reasonable endeavours' is not as onerous as one to use 'best endeavours' or 'all reasonable endeavours'." Lord Hodge took the same view in *Mactaggart & Mickel Homes Ltd v Hunter*.[115]

16.48   In *Electricity Generation Corp v Woodside Energy Ltd*,[116] the High Court of Australia appeared to accept that an obligation to use reasonable endeavours and an obligation to use best endeavours created substantially similar obligations. The court also said that three general points could be made about such clauses. First, an obligation expressed thus is not an absolute or unconditional obligation. Second, the nature and extent of an obligation imposed in such terms is necessarily conditioned by what is reasonable in the circumstances, which can include circumstances that may affect an obligee's business. An obligee's freedom to act in its own business interests, in matters to which the agreement relates, is not neces-sarily foreclosed, or to be sacrificed, by an obligation to use reasonable endeavours to achieve a contractual object. Third, some contracts containing an obligation to use or make reasonable endeavours to achieve a contractual object contain their own

---

[110] [1981] 2 E.G.L.R. 172. See also *Terrell v Mabie Todd & Co Ltd* [1952] 2 T.L.R. 574; and *Sheffield District Railway Co v Great Central Railway Co* (1911) 27 T.L.R. 451, where it was pointed out that the words mean what they say: they do not mean "second best endeavours".

[111] [1980] F.S.R. 335; *Sainsbury's Supermarkets Ltd v Bristol Rovers* (1883) Ltd [2015] EWHC 2002 (Ch).

[112] *Rhodia International Holdings Ltd v Huntsman International LLC* [2007] 1 C.L.C. 59. See also *Jolley v Carmel Ltd* [2000] 2 E.G.L.R. 154.

[113] *Rhodia International Holdings Ltd v Huntsman International LLC* [2007] 1 C.L.C. 59.

[114] [2013] ACTSC 173.

[115] [2010] CSOH 130.

[116] [2014] HCA 7.

internal standard of what is reasonable, by some express reference relevant to the business interests of an obligee.

In *Mana v Fleming*,[117] a contract for the sale of land was conditional on the purchasers entering into a contract for the sale of their own property on terms acceptable to them by a certain date. The contract also contained an obligation on the purchasers "to do all things reasonably necessary" to enable the condition to be fulfilled by the due date. The New Zealand Court of Appeal said:

> "It places a burden on purchasers to 'do all things', which is commensurate with the benefit they acquire through inclusion of a special condition. As a consequence, the purchasers will be in breach if there is something which was reasonably necessary but which was not done even though other necessary things were done. A thing is 'necessary' in this context if it is required to bring about the stipulated result within the agreed period."

They added:

> "The word 'reasonably' introduces a qualitative or relative measure of what is necessary; its effect is to modify the obligation by reference to what is reasonable in the circumstances.[118] The necessary things must be rational or in accord with reason, eliminating things which it would be unreasonable to require to be done in the circumstances. The purchaser is not required to go beyond the bounds of reason. He or she is required to do all that can be reasonably done to achieve the contractual object but no more.
>
> The word 'reasonably' must import an objective standard, and performance is to be measured by applying that standard to the relevant facts and circumstances. Adoption of an objective standard is consistent with principle. The Court is the arbiter of what is reasonably necessary in any case, viewed from the purchaser's perspective. Anything less than an objective standard would allow a subjective assessment according to the values of the party whose conduct is at issue. That would deprive the word 'reasonably' of any meaning and convert the contract into an option to purchase."

An obligation to use reasonable endeavours to achieve the aim probably only requires a party to take one reasonable course, not all of them; whereas an obligation to use best endeavours probably requires a party to take all the reasonable courses he can. In that context, it may well be that an obligation to use all reasonable endeavours (or to do all things reasonably necessary) equates with using best endeavours.[119] Any attempt to distinguish between the two has been described as a "pointless hair-splitting exercise". However, both forms of obligation are more onerous than a simple obligation to use "reasonable endeavours".[120]

In *Ampurius NU Homes Holdings Ltd v Telford Homes (Creekside) Ltd*,[121] an agreement for lease required the landlord to "use its reasonable endeavours to

16.49

16.50

16.51

---

[117] [2007] NZCA 324.

[118] See *Hospital Products Ltd v United States Surgical Corp* (1984) 156 C.L.R. 41 at 92, per Mason J (discussing a "best endeavours" provision).

[119] *Rhodia International Holdings Ltd v Huntsman International LLC* [2007] 1 C.L.C. 59.

[120] *KS Energy Services Ltd v BR Energy (M) Sdn Bhd* [2014] SGCA 16 (Singapore Court of Appeal), disagreeing with the author in *Jolley v Carmel Ltd* [2000] 2 E.G.L.R. 153. See Man Yip and Yihan Goh, "Default Standards for Non Absolute Obligation Clauses" [2014] L.M.C.Q. 320.

[121] [2012] EWHC 1820 (Ch) unaffected by the reversal of this decision on different grounds at [2013]

procure completion of the Landlord's Works by the Target Date or as soon as reasonably possible thereafter". Funding difficulties caused delay in carrying out the work, and it was argued that there was no breach provided that the landlord was using reasonable endeavours to obtain finance. Roth J rejected that argument. He said:

"However, I do not think that a 'reasonable endeavours' clause as regards the time of completion in what is, in this respect, a construction contract can extend to endeavours to have sufficient money to perform the contract. Although the language could literally bear that meaning, in my judgment, on an objective reading the qualification of 'reasonable endeavours', as opposed to an absolute obligation to complete, is designed to cover matters that directly relate to the physical conduct of the works, thereby providing an excuse for delay in such circumstances as inclement weather or a shortage of materials for which the Defendant was not responsible. The clause does not, in my view, extend to matters antecedent or extraneous to the carrying out of the work, such as having the financial resources to do the work at all."

In *Astor Management AG v Atalaya Mining Plc*,[122] a contract provided for one party to use all reasonable endeavours to procure a senior debt facility by a specified date. Leggatt J held that the obligation to use all reasonable endeavours did not cease to apply when the specified date arrived without the objective having been attained. He said that the clause meant that the party in question was obliged to use all reasonable endeavours to attain the objective by the specified date, "provided that is practicable and, if not, as soon as practicable thereafter". He added:

"Whether the party who gave the undertaking has endeavoured to make such an agreement (or used its best endeavours to do so) is a question of fact which a court can perfectly well decide. It may sometimes be hard to prove an absence of endeavours, or of best endeavours, but difficulty of proving a breach of a contractual obligation is an everyday occurrence and not a reason to hold that there is no obligation. Any complaint about lack of objective criteria could only be directed to the task of judging whether the endeavours used were 'reasonable', or whether there were other steps which it was reasonable to take so that it cannot be said that 'all reasonable endeavours' have been used. Where the parties have adopted a test of 'reasonableness', however, it seems to me that they are deliberately inviting the court to make a value judgment which sets a limit to their freedom of action."

16.52 In considering whether there has been a breach of obligation, an important consideration is whether the failure to take the steps in question would have achieved their objective.[123]

16.53 Whether an obligation to use reasonable endeavours to achieve an objective requires financial considerations or profitability to be left out of account in evaluating those endeavours is a question of interpretation of the particular clause.[124]

16.54 Where the contract provides for a party to use best endeavours to obtain a

EWCA Civ 577; [2013] 4 All E.R. 377.
[122] [2017] EWHC 425 (Comm); [2017] 1 Lloyd's Rep. 476. The point did not arise on appeal.
[123] *Mactaggart & Mickel Homes Ltd v Hunter* [2010] CSOH 130; *Minerva (Wandsworth) Ltd v Greenland Ram (London) Ltd* [2017] EWHC 1457 (Ch) at [255].
[124] *Gaia Ventures Ltd v Abbeygate Helical (Leisure Plaza) Ltd* [2019] EWCA Civ 823.

particular result it is considered that he must, if necessary, to some extent subordinate his own financial interests under the contract to the obtaining of that result.[125]

In *Jet2.com Ltd v Blackpool Airport Ltd*,[126] the operator of an airport entered into an agreement with an airline. The agreement required the parties to "co-operate together and use their best endeavours to promote Jet2.com's low cost services from" the airport. The Court of Appeal held by a majority that the obligation was enforceable. One issue that arose was the extent to which the party under the obligation could have regard to his own financial interest. Moore-Bick LJ said:

"It was a central plank of BAL's argument before the judge that the obligation to use best endeavours did not require it to act contrary to its own commercial interests, which, in the context of this case, amounts to saying that BAL was not obliged to accept aircraft movements outside normal hours if that would cause it financial loss. Some support for that conclusion can be found in the cases, notably *Terrell v Mabie Todd and Co Ltd* and *Yewbelle Ltd v London Green Developments Ltd*, but I think the judge was right in saying that whether, and if so to what extent, a person who has undertaken to use his best endeavours can have regard to his own financial interests will depend very much on the nature and terms of the contract in question. In *Terrell v Mabie Todd and Co Ltd* the context in which the undertaking was given was sufficient in my view to make it clear that the company was not expected to do more than could reasonably be expected of a prudent board of directors acting in the interests of the shareholders. In neither *Yewbelle Ltd v London Green Developments Ltd* nor *EDI Central Ltd v National Car Parks Ltd* was there any extended discussion of what sacrificing its own interests might involve, either in the context of the case under consideration or more generally. I approach with some caution the submission that BAL was entitled to refuse to accept aircraft movements outside normal opening hours if that caused it to incur a loss, because on the judge's findings the ability to schedule aircraft movements outside those hours was essential to Jet2's business and was therefore fundamental to the agreement. In those circumstances one would not expect the parties to have contemplated that BAL should be able to restrict Jet2's aircraft movements to normal opening hours simply because it incurred a loss each time it was required to accept a movement outside those hours, or because keeping the airport open outside normal hours proved to be more expensive than it had expected. On the other hand, I can see force in the argument that if, for example, it were to become clear that Jet2 could never expect to operate low cost services from Blackpool profitably, BAL would not be obliged to incur further losses in seeking to promote a failing business."

Longmore LJ said:

"The fact that he has agreed to use his best endeavours pre-supposes that he may well be put to some financial cost, so financial cost cannot be a trump card to enable him to extricate himself from what would otherwise be his obligation. As

---

[125] However, Beatson J appears to have taken a different view in *Jet2.Com Ltd v Blackpool Airport Ltd* [2010] EWHC 3166 (Comm). In *A Turtle Offshore SA v Superior Trading Inc* [2009] 1 Lloyd's Rep. 177, Teare J held that a party under an express best endeavours obligation was entitled to take into account his own financial interests, but in the context of considering whether there were other courses of action open to him. If there were not then he was obliged to take an expensive course of action.
[126] [2012] EWCA Civ 417.

AT Lawrence J said in the *Sheffield District Railway Co* case, best endeavours does not mean second best endeavours. But I would agree with Moore-Bick LJ ... that, if it became clear that Jet2 could never expect to operate low cost services profitably from Blackpool, BAL could not be expected themselves to incur losses after that time in seeking to promote (or effectively propping up) a failing business."

16.55   In some older cases, however, the courts have been more sympathetic to the financial position of the party under the obligation. In *Croft v Lumley*,[127] Lumley had an obligation to use his best endeavours to improve the Opera House. He closed it at the end of the season in 1852 and did not open it at all in the following year. The House of Lords held that this was not a breach of obligation. Lord Cranworth said:

"With regard to the first alleged breach of covenant that Lumley would use his best endeavours to improve the Opera House for the purpose for which it was demised to him, of which it was alleged there was a breach by his not having kept it open in the seasons of 1853 and 1854, your Lordships at the time of the argument intimated a very strong and decided opinion that the facts warranted no such conclusion; that there was no pretence for saying that there had been any breach of the covenant upon that ground; that the meaning of the covenant was, that he should, by having proper scenes, and by having the house properly painted and kept in order, improve the house, but not if he found that there would be no benefit in opening the house at all; if it would not pay the expenses of having theatrical representation at all, that he should at his own loss, with no benefit to the landlord, keep it open without any corresponding advantage. Your Lordships expressed so clear an opinion upon that point at the time of the argument, that your Lordships did not desire even to hear what might be the opinions of the learned Judges upon it. I happen to know, by communicating with them at the time, that they never had the slightest doubt upon the subject; but your Lordships did not put any question to them upon that point."

16.56   Where, by contrast, the obligation is an obligation to use reasonable endeavours, he need not subordinate his own financial interests to the agreed goal.[128] In *Phillips Petroleum Company United Kingdom Ltd v Enron Europe Ltd*,[129] an agreement for the supply of North Sea gas contained a number of obligations requiring the parties to use "reasonable endeavours". One was an obligation to use reasonable endeavours to coordinate the construction of their respective facilities. Another was an obligation to use reasonable endeavours to agree the date on which deliveries were to begin ("the Commissioning Date") and the date of a three-day test of the parties' respective capacities to receive and deliver gas ("the Run-In Test"). The same clause went on to say that in the absence of agreement, the Commissioning Date would be 25 September 1996, and the Run-In Test would take place on 25–28 September 1996. Because of a fall in the price of gas Phillips refused to agree dates earlier than the fall-back dates. Enron argued that each party was under an obligation to use reasonable endeavours to reach agreement on the Commissioning Date

---

[127] (1858) 6 H.L.C. 672.
[128] *EDI Central Ltd v National Car Parks* [2010] CSOH 141; *Electricity Generation Corp v Woodside Energy Ltd* [2014] HCA 7.
[129] [1997] C.L.C. 329.

and the Run-In Test having regard only to criteria of technical and operational practicability and without regard to selfish or commercial motives. The Court of Appeal rejected that argument. Kennedy LJ said:

> "I find it impossible to say that they [i.e. the contract terms] impose on the buyer a contractual obligation to disregard the financial effect on him, and indeed everything else other than technical or operational practicality, when deciding how to discharge his obligation to use reasonable endeavours to agree to a commissioning date prior to 25 September 1996. If the obligation were to be strait-jacketed in that way, that is something which to my mind would have been expressly stated, and, as Mr Pollock's argument really conceded, this is not a situation in which it would be appropriate for the court to imply a term, not least because it is unnecessary to do so for purposes of business efficiency. The fall-back provision expressly states what is to happen if no early commissioning date is agreed."

The same approach applies to an obligation to use "all reasonable" endeavours[130] **16.57** and to an obligation to use "all reasonable but commercially prudent" endeavours.[131] However, this is subject to the qualification that where the contract actually specifies certain steps have to be taken as part of the exercise of reasonable endeavours, those steps will have to be taken, even if that could on one view be said to involve the sacrificing of a party's commercial interests.[132] In most cases, the question whether the taking of a particular course of action would have constituted a reasonable endeavour is essentially one for the judgment of the court, to be arrived at upon an evaluation of all the evidence, which may where appropriate include expert evidence.[133] The question is whether the particular course of action would have had a "significant" or "substantial" chance of achieving the desired result; although in some contexts there is no difference between these adjectives and others such as "real" or "worthwhile".[134]

In some cases, however, it is not possible to apply an objective test. In *P&O* **16.58** *Property Holdings Ltd v Norwich Union Life Insurance Society*,[135] P&O were the developers of a shopping centre funded by Norwich Union. Under the terms of the development agreement P&O and Norwich Union were obliged to "use their reasonable endeavours to secure a letting of each lettable part of the Development". Norwich Union had advanced the maximum amount that it was required to advance under the terms of the development agreement. Because of weakness in the market, it was not possible to obtain good tenants at good rents without paying reverse premiums. The question before the House of Lords was whether Norwich Union could insist that in using its reasonable endeavours to obtain lettings P&O was bound to pay reverse premiums "if a hypothetical reasonable landlord (ignoring who is to bear the cost of such premium) would agree to the payment of such a reverse premium". The House held that it was not entitled to insist. The argument

---

[130] *Yewbelle Ltd v London Green Developments Ltd* [2008] 1 P. & C.R. 279; *Geys v Societe Generale, London Branch* [2010] EWHC 648 (Ch).
[131] *CPC Group Ltd v Qatari Diar Real Estate* [2010] EWHC 1535 (Ch); *Cypjane Pty Ltd v Babcock & Brown International Pty Ltd* [2011] NSWCA 173.
[132] *Rhodia International Holdings Ltd v Huntsman International LLC* [2007] 1 C.L.C. 59.
[133] *The Talisman* [1989] 1 Lloyd's Rep. 535.
[134] *Yewbelle Ltd v London Green Developments Ltd* [2008] 1 P. & C.R. 279. Compare *Sharneyford Supplies Ltd v Edge* [1987] Ch. 305, where the CA took a more stringent view.
[135] (1994) 68 P. & C.R. 261.

for Norwich Union was that an objective standard had to be applied in order to give content to the obligation. The House rejected the argument because the willingness of a landlord to pay a reverse premium would depend on his financial circumstances at the time. A landlord with a healthy cash flow, taking a long-term view, would be willing to make such payments. A landlord who had cash-flow difficulties would be looking for quick lets at the best rent available. The agreement did not enable one to say what kind of landlord was under consideration.

16.59 Where a party is under an obligation to use reasonable endeavours to obtain a desired result, he must continue to use those endeavours until the point is reached when all reasonable endeavours have been exhausted. In *Yewbelle Ltd v London Green Developments Ltd*,[136] Lewison J said:

> "I come back to the question: for how long must the seller continue to use reasonable endeavours to achieve the desired result? In his opening address, Mr Morgan said that the obligation to use reasonable endeavours requires you to go on using endeavours until the point is reached when all reasonable endeavours have been exhausted. You would simply be repeating yourself to go through the same matters again. I am prepared to accept this formulation, subject to the qualification that account must be taken of events as they unfold, including extraordinary events."[137]

16.60 However, if there is an insuperable difficulty in obtaining the desired result, his obligation ceases (or is discharged) even though other difficulties are capable of being surmounted.[138]

16.61 In *KS Energy Services Ltd v BR Energy (M) Sdn Bhd*,[139] the Singapore Court of Appeal conducted a thorough review of authorities from many jurisdictions. They concluded (omitting references to authority):

> "[W]e also endorse the guidelines below vis-à-vis the operation and extent of both 'all reasonable endeavours' and 'best endeavours' clauses:
>
> (a) Such clauses require the obligor 'to go on using endeavours until the point is reached when all reasonable endeavours have been exhausted' ..., or 'to do all that it reasonably could' ...
>
> (b) The obligor need only do that which has a significant ... or real prospect of success ... in procuring the contractually-stipulated outcome.
>
> (c) If there is an insuperable obstacle to procuring the contractually-stipulated outcome, the obligor is not required to do anything more to overcome other problems which also stood in the way of procuring that outcome but which might have been resolved ...

---

[136] [2006] EWHC 3166 (Ch).

[137] This part of the judgment was not affected by the appeal and was approved in *Centennial Coal Co Ltd v Xstrata Coal Pty Ltd* [2009] NSWCA 341.

[138] *Yewbelle Ltd v London Green Developments Ltd* [2008] 1 P. & C.R. 279. In *Mana v Fleming* [2007] NZCA 324, the NZCA took a different approach to causation, saying that:

> "It is sufficient for the vendor to prove that the purchasers failed to do all things which may be reasonably necessary to satisfy the condition in order to establish a material breach of the agreement. The vendor does not have to go further and establish that the proper performance of cl.8.7(2) would have enabled the purchasers to enter into an acceptable agreement as provided by the special condition, cl.15. Proof of a causal connection is unnecessary in order to prove an actionable breach."

[139] [2014] SGCA 16.

(d) The obligor is not always required to sacrifice its own commercial interests in satisfaction of its obligations ... but it may be required to do so where the nature and terms of the contract indicate that it is in the parties' contemplation that the obligor should make such sacrifice ...

(e) An obligor cannot just sit back and say that it could not reasonably have done more to procure the contractually-stipulated outcome in cases where, if it had asked the obligee, it might have discovered that there were other steps which could reasonably have been taken ...

(f) Once the obligee points to certain steps which the obligor could have taken to procure the contractually-stipulated outcome, the burden ordinarily shifts to the obligor to show that it took those steps, or that those steps were not reasonably required, or that those steps would have been bound to fail ...".

8. Time for Fulfilment of Conditions

As a general rule: (a) where a conditional contract fixes a date for completion the condition must be fulfilled by that date; (b) where a conditional contract fixes no date for completion, then the condition must be fulfilled within a reasonable time; and (c) where a conditional contract fixes a date by which the condition must be fulfilled, then the date so fixed must be strictly adhered to. Where the condition must be fulfilled within a reasonable time, it is a question of interpretation of the contract whether the reasonable time must be measured from the date of the contract, or whether it may take account of events as they unfold.

The period of time within which conditions in a contract must be satisfied depends upon the true interpretation of the contract, that is, upon the meaning that the contract would convey to a reasonable reader.[140] Nevertheless, a reasonably clear pattern emerges from the cases. **16.62**

In *Smith v Butler*,[141] parties agreed the sale of a lease of a public house. The lease was mortgaged, and the sale was subject to a condition that the consent of the mortgagee be obtained to the same amount of money remaining on mortgage after the sale. Romer LJ said: **16.63**

> "To my mind it is reasonably clear that the vendor has until the time fixed for completion, or, if no time for completion is fixed, then a reasonable time, in which to procure the assent of the mortgagee to the acceptance of the purchaser as mortgagor."

In *Re Sandwell Park Colliery Co*,[142] Maugham J treated a reasonable time as being co-extensive with the period before the contractual completion date.

The authorities were reviewed by the Privy Council in *Aberfoyle Plantations Ltd v Cheng*,[143] in which Lord Jenkins summarised the position thus: **16.64**

---

[140] *Aberfoyle Plantations Ltd v Cheng* [1960] A.C. 115.
[141] [1900] 1 Q.B. 694.
[142] [1929] 1 Ch. 277.
[143] [1960] A.C. 115.

"... their Lordships would adopt, as warranted by authority and manifestly reasonable in themselves, the following general principles: (i) where a conditional contract of sale fixes a date for the completion of the sale, then the condition must be fulfilled by that date; (ii) where a conditional contract of sale fixes no date for completion of the sale, then the condition must be fulfilled within a reasonable time; (iii) where a conditional contract of sale fixes (whether specifically or by reference to the date fixed for completion) the date by which the condition is to be fulfilled, then the date so fixed must be strictly adhered to, and the time allowed is not to be extended by reference to equitable principles."

16.65   Picking up the third of Lord Jenkins' principles, in *Valentines Properties Ltd v Huntco Corp Ltd*,[144] Lord Nicholls of Birkenhead said:

"Inherent in a time limit is the notion that the parties are drawing a line. Once the line is crossed, a miss is as good as a mile. The rigour of this principle is softened when the parties are taken to have intended otherwise. Then, in the legal jargon, time is not regarded as 'of the essence'. Failing a contrary indication, the law assumes that stipulations as to time are not of the essence in certain common form situations, such as the date for completion of a contract for the sale of land. But that is not this case. The law makes no such assumption regarding a date fixed by a conditional contract as the date by which the condition is to be fulfilled. In the absence of contrary indication, the date so fixed must be strictly adhered to, and the time allowed is not to be extended by reference to equitable principles."

16.66   Of course the language of a particular contract may lead to a different conclusion. In *29 Equities Ltd v Bank Leumi (UK) Ltd*,[145] parties agreed to the assignment of a lease. The contract incorporated the *National Conditions of Sale* (20th edn). The lease required the consent of the landlord to be obtained to the assignment and the contract was subject to the reversioner's licence being obtained. The contract gave the vendor a right to rescind "if the licence cannot be obtained". The judge at first instance held that the licence had to be obtained by the contractual completion date. The Court of Appeal disagreed and held that the correct approach was to ask, at the date when the vendor sought to exercise his right to rescind, whether, as a matter of fact, it could fairly be said that the landlord's licence cannot be obtained.

This type of case may be distinguishable from the type of case considered by Lord Jenkins in the third of the propositions set out above. In reaching his conclusions Lord Jenkins seems to have had in mind conditions precedent.[146] However, it is clear that a stipulation in a contract for the sale of a lease that the sale is subject to the landlord's consent is not usually treated as a condition precedent, but is a condition subsequent.[147] In other words, a binding contract comes into existence, but a failure to obtain the necessary licence will result in the discharge of the contract.

16.67   If it is the case that there is a binding contract between the parties, the need for

---

[144] [2001] 3 N.Z.L.R. 305.
[145] [1986] 1 W.L.R. 1490.
[146] See especially his citation from the judgment of Maugham J in *Re Sandwell Park Colliery Co* [1929] 1 Ch. 277.
[147] *Property and Bloodstock Ltd v Emerton* [1968] Ch. 94; *Shires v Brock* [1978] 2 E.G.L.R. 153 CA.

strict time limits is not so strong.[148] This is particularly so in the case of a contract for the sale of land, since the contract will almost always entitle either party, once the contractual completion date has passed, to serve notice on the other "making time of the essence" of the contract.

Thus in *McGahon v Crest Nicholson Regeneration Ltd*,[149] a contract provided:

> "This contract is conditional upon the grant to the Seller or to the Seller's nominee of a headlease of the block of which the Property forms or is to form part. If the said headlease has not been granted to the Seller by 1st June 2008 then either party shall have the right to rescind this Contract by serving written notice of rescission upon the other."

The Court of Appeal held that the second sentence of the clause did not import a time limit into the first. Thus the right to rescind the contract was not exercisable after the grant of the head lease even though it had not been granted by 1 June 2008.

In some cases, what is a reasonable time must be judged objectively as at the date   **16.68** of the contract.[150] Whether this is so is a question of interpretation of the contract in question. Thus where contracts for the sale of gas to be extracted from the North Sea were conditional on entry into an allocation agreement, the House of Lords held that accession to the allocation agreements had to take place before the first delivery of gas.[151] However, where a contract for the sale of land was conditional on the obtaining of planning permission, and the buyer had an obligation to take reasonable steps to obtain it, time for fulfilment of the condition continued to run so long as the buyer continued to perform his obligation without default or negligence on his part.[152] Similarly, in *Pantland Hick v Raymond & Reid*,[153] the House of Lords held that in determining the length of a reasonable time in which to unload cargo it was necessary to take into account not only the ordinary course of events, but also the extraordinary events (in that case a dockers' strike) which actually took place.

In *Peregrine Systems Ltd v Steria Ltd*,[154] Maurice Kay LJ approved the formula-   **16.69** tion[155] that the question whether a reasonable time has been exceeded is:

> "a broad consideration, with the benefit of hindsight, and viewed from the time at which one party contends that a reasonable time for performance has been exceeded, of what would, in all the circumstances which are by then known to have happened, have been a reasonable time for performance. That broad consideration is likely to include taking into account any estimate given by the performing party of how long it would take him to perform; whether that estimate has been exceeded and, if so, in what circumstances; whether the party for whose benefit the relevant obligation was to be performed needed to participate in the performance, actively, in the sense of collaborating in what was needed to be done, or passively, in the sense of being in a position to receive performance, or not at all; whether it was necessary for third parties to collaborate with the

---

[148] Compare the attitude of the courts towards options and unilateral contracts (see para.15.60).
[149] [2010] EWCA Civ 842; [2011] 1 P. & C.R. 225.
[150] *Re Longlands Farm* [1968] 3 All E.R. 552.
[151] *Total Gas Marketing Ltd v Arco British Ltd* [1998] 2 Lloyd's Rep. 209.
[152] *Jolley v Carmel Ltd* [2000] 3 E.G.L.R. 68, affirming [2000] 2 E.G.L.R. 153.
[153] [1893] A.C. 22.
[154] [2005] EWCA Civ 239; [2005] Info. T.L.R. 294.
[155] In *Astea (UK) Ltd v Time Group Ltd* [2003] EWHC 725.

performing party in order to enable it to perform; and what exactly was the cause, or were the causes of the delay to performance. The list is not intended to be exhaustive."

In *Automotive Latch Systems Ltd v Honeywell International Inc*,[156] Flaux J said that:

"it is clear that the court can and should look at all the material available, including looking at the question with hindsight. On that basis, although none of the cases specifically touches on this, I do not see why in principle, the reasonableness of the party's conduct should not also be assessed, where appropriate, by reference to matters which ante-date the entering of the contract."

16.70   Another factor which may be considered in assessing reasonableness of actions and delay is the extent to which a particular course of action has been dictated or encouraged or agreed or acquiesced in by the other party.[157]

9.   CONTINGENT AND PROMISSORY CONDITIONS

A condition may be contingent, in the sense that liability is contingent on its fulfilment, or promissory in which case fulfilment of the condition is part of the consideration moving from the promisor.

16.71   Conditions precedent are normally contingent conditions. In other words unless and until the condition is satisfied, no contract comes into existence, or liability under a contract is suspended. There may be obligations imposed in relation to the fulfilment of the condition, but such obligations are collateral to the substance of the agreement which is to come into operation once the condition has been fulfilled. For example, a sale of land may be conditional on planning permission being obtained. The purchaser may be under an obligation to use his best endeavours to obtain such permission, but that is collateral to the main substance of the agreement.

16.72   On the other hand, a condition may be promissory, in the sense that it represents the consideration moving from the promisor.[158] Thus in *Eastham v Leigh London and Provincial Properties Ltd*,[159] a company entered into an agreement for lease. The company was given licence to enter a site and to build a six-storey office block on it. The agreement provided that if the building were completed to the satisfaction of the owner's surveyor and the company had performed all its obligations under the contract, then the owners would grant the company a lease for 125 years. The Court of Appeal held that the contract was not a conditional contract.[160] Buckley LJ said:

"Although cl. 4 is couched in conditional language, in my view it amounts to no more than this: it provides that if the taxpayer company perform their part of the

---

[156] [2008] EWHC 2171 (Comm) at [142].

[157] *Automotive Latch Systems Ltd v Honeywell International Inc* [2008] EWHC 2171 (Comm).

[158] Lord Steyn drew this distinction in *Total Gas Marketing Ltd v Arco British Ltd* [1998] 2 Lloyd's Rep. 209.

[159] [1971] Ch. 871.

[160] For the purpose of the Finance Act 1972. Contrast, however, *Cornish v Brook Green Laundry Ltd* [1959] 1 Q.B. 394.

contract, then the landlords will perform their part of the contract; in other words it is a recognition of the fact that the obligations of the parties are mutual and that the granting of the lease will, in fact, follow the completion of performance of the obligations of the taxpayer company. That is not, in my judgment, a condition precedent to the contract at all; it is part of the terms of the contract. One may call it a condition if one pleases, but it does not make it a condition precedent to the existence of a contract; it merely indicates that it is part of the terms of the bargain, just as in all contracts for sale the terms of the bargain are customarily described as conditions of sale."

This usage is what Lord Denning MR described as the "common meaning".[161] **16.73** However, promises may be of greater or lesser importance, and it is necessary to isolate those (important) terms of a contract which may properly be called "conditions".

One important difference between the two types of condition is whether fulfil- **16.74** ment of the condition is within the power of one of the contracting parties. If it is, the condition is more likely to be promissory than contingent. In *Michaels v Harley House (Marylebone) Ltd*,[162] Robert Walker LJ said:

"He[163] recognised the important difference (mentioned by Goff J. in *Eastham v Leigh London and Provincial Properties Ltd*)[164] between a true condition precedent which it is not within a contracting party's power to bring about, even though he may undertake to use his best endeavours to bring it about, and a promissory condition which the party does have power to fulfil or to cause to be fulfilled."

In *UR Power GmbH v Kuok Oils and Grains Pte Ltd*,[165] Gross J said:

"In the case, therefore of a contingent condition precedent, a contract will not be binding until the specified event occurs. But in the case of a promissory condition precedent, the contract will be binding, albeit that the performance of an obligation by one party will be a condition precedent to the *liability* of the other. It is perhaps imprudent to be unduly dogmatic but the distinction between contingent and promissory conditions precedent may well turn on whether the agreement purports to impose on A … an obligation to bring about the stipulated event; if it does, the condition is or likely to be promissory; if not, the condition is or is likely to be contingent."

In *Total Gas Marketing Ltd v Arco British Ltd*,[166] Lord Slynn said that there was **16.75** a "common factor" linking both contingent and promissory conditions which he described thus:

"If the provision in an agreement is of fundamental importance then the result either of a failure to perform it (if it is promissory) or of the event not happen-

---

161 See para.16.01.
162 [2000] Ch. 104 at 116.
163 Lloyd J.
164 [1971] Ch. 871 at 880–881.
165 [2009] 2 Lloyd's Rep. 495.
166 [1998] 2 Lloyd's Rep. 209 at 220.

ing or the act not being done (if it is a contingent condition or a condition precedent or a condition subsequent) *may* be that the contract either never comes into being or terminates. That may be so, whether the parties expressly say so or not."

The effect of the non-fulfilment of a condition may be either to suspend a party's obligations or to bring them to an end.

10. CLASSIFICATION OF CONTRACTUAL OBLIGATIONS

Contractual obligations may be divided into conditions, warranties and intermediate terms (which lie between the other two). It is a question of interpretation into which category a particular obligation falls.

16.76   The question whether or not a contractual obligation was a condition tradition-ally arose in the context of one party to a contract alleging that the failure of the other party to perform his part of the bargain had discharged the contract. In former times, obligations were classified into conditions precedent (performance of which by one party was a condition precedent to performance by the other party) and war-ranties (non-performance of which by one party did not prevent the enforcement of the other party's obligations). Under the ancient system of pleading it would be alleged that performance by the defendant was a condition precedent to liability of the plaintiff and that since the defendant had not performed his side of the bargain the plaintiff was no longer bound. Where, however, the obligation was not a condi-tion precedent, the plaintiff could maintain his action even though he might be in breach. In the modern law a condition in this sense is a term the breach of which gives the injured party the right to bring the contract to an end.

16.77   In *Kingston v Preston*,[167] Lord Mansfield is reported as having said that there were three kinds of covenant:

(1)   such as are called mutual and independent, where either party may recover damages from the other, for the injury he may have received by a breach of the covenants in his favour, and where it is no excuse for the defendant, to allege a breach of the covenants on the part of the plaintiff;

(2)   covenants which are conditions and dependent, in which the performance of one depends on the prior performance of another, and, therefore until this prior condition is performed, the other party is not liable to an action on his covenant;

(3)   mutual conditions to be performed at the same time; and in these, if one party was ready, and offered to perform his part, and the other neglected or refused to perform his, he who was ready and has offered has fulfilled his engagement, and may maintain an action for the default of the other, though it is not certain that either is obliged to do the first act.

16.78   In more modern terminology the first category of covenants would be called war-ranties, and the second and third conditions. The traditional distinction between conditions and warranties was explained by Fletcher Moulton LJ in a dissenting judgment in *Wallis Son & Wells v Pratt and Haynes*[168]:

---

[167] *Anon* (1773) Lofft 194; 98 E.R. 606; sub nom *Kingston v Preston, cited in* 2 Doug. K.B. at 689.
[168] [1910] 2 K.B. 1003 (approved by HL [1911] A.C. 394).

"A party to a contract who has performed, or is ready and willing to perform his obligations under that contract is entitled to the performance by the other contracting party of all the obligations which rest upon him. But from a very early period of our law it has been recognised that such obligations are not of equal importance. There are some which go so directly to the substance of the contract, or in other words are so essential to its very nature that non-performance may fairly be considered by the other part as a substantial failure to perform the contract at all. On the other hand, there are obligations which, though they must be performed, are not so vital that failure to perform them goes to the substance of the contract. Both classes are equally obligations under the contract, and the breach of anyone of them entitles the other party to damages. But in the case of the former class he has the alternative of treating the contract as being completely broken by the non-performance and (if he takes the proper steps) he can refuse to perform any of the obligations resting upon himself and sue the other party for a total failure to perform the contract. Although the decisions are fairly consistent in recognising the distinction between the two classes of obligation under a contract there has not been a similar consistency in the nomenclature applied to them. I do not, however, propose to discuss this matter, because later usage has consecrated the term 'condition' to describe an obligation of the former class and 'warranty' to describe an obligation of the latter class."

This passage suggests the classification of contractual terms into two classes only. **16.79** The Sale of Goods Act 1893 (and the Sale of Goods Act 1979) assumed this to be so. However, it is now clear that there is a third category, namely the "intermediate term" or "innominate term". Breach of such a term may vary in its gravity, so that it cannot be predicated at the outset whether a breach will be sufficiently serious as to justify terminating the contract. In such circumstances the approach of the court is to look at the breach alleged to have given rise to the right to bring the contract to an end and to decide whether the occurrence of that breach deprived the innocent party of "substantially the whole benefit" which it was the intention of the parties that he should obtain from the further performance of the other party's contractual undertakings.[169] Accordingly, contractual terms may be divided into three broad classes:

(1)   terms breach of which will always give rise to a right to bring the contract to an end ("conditions");
(2)   terms breach of which may or may not give rise to such a right depending on the gravity of the breach ("intermediate terms" or "innominate terms");
(3)   terms breach of which will never give rise to a right to bring the contract to an end, but give rise only to a claim for compensation ("warranties").

The general approach was described by Kerr LJ in *State Trading Corp of India* **16.80** *v Golodetz*[170]:

"Unless the term in question has the effect of a condition precedent to some other aspect of the contract or has already been classified authoritatively as a condition in other contexts "the courts should not be too ready to interpret contractual clauses as conditions" per Lord Wilberforce in *Bunge Corp v Tradax Export AS*.

---

[169] See *Hongkong Fir Shipping Co Ltd v Kawasaki Kisen Kaisha Ltd* [1962] 2 Q.B. 26, per Diplock LJ.
[170] [1989] 2 Lloyds Rep. 277.

At the end of the day if there is no other more specific guide to the correct solution to a particular dispute the Court may have no alternative but to follow the general statement of Bowen LJ in *Bentsen v Taylor* ... by making what is in effect a value judgment about the commercial significance of the terms in question...".

Compliance with time limits is considered in Ch.15.

Illustration

Under the terms of a waste management contract the contractor was required to provide a performance bond. It was held that a failure to provide the bond was not a breach of a condition of the contract.
South Oxfordshire District Council v Sita UK Ltd[171]

11. INTERPRETATION AND FACT

It is a question of interpretation of the contract into which category an obligation falls. But if it falls into the second category (i.e. an innominate or intermediate term), it is a question of fact (rather than of interpretation) whether in particular circumstances one party is entitled to treat the contract as having been repudiated by the other.

16.81   In *Glaholm v Hays*,[172] Tindal CJ said:

"Whether a particular clause in a charter-party shall be held to be a condition, upon the non-performance of which by the one party, the other is at liberty to abandon the contract, and consider it at an end; or whether it amounts to an agreement only, the breach whereof is to be recompensed by an action for damages, must depend upon the intention of the parties to be collected, in each particular case, from the terms of the agreement itself and from the subject matter to which it relates."

16.82   So also in *Bettini v Gye*,[173] the question arose whether a stipulation that an opera singer should be in London "without fail" six days before the first night for the purpose of rehearsals was a condition or not. Blackburn J, delivering the judgment of the court, said:

"We think the answer to this question depends upon the true construction of the contract taken as a whole. Parties may think some matter, apparently of very little importance, essential; and if they sufficiently express an intention to make the literal fulfilment of such a thing a condition precedent, it will be one; or they may think that the performance of some matter, apparently of essential importance and prima facie a condition precedent, is not really vital, and may be compensated for in damages, and if they sufficiently expressed such an intention, it will not be a condition precedent."

---

[171] [2007] Env. L.R. 13.
[172] (1841) 2 M. & G. 257.
[173] (1876) 1 Q.B.D. 183.

More recently in *Bunge Corp v Tradax Export SA*,[174] Lord Lowry said: **16.83**

> "It is by construing a contract (which can be done as soon as the contract is made) that one decides whether a term is, either expressly or by necessary implication, a condition, and not by considering the gravity of the breach of that term (which cannot be done until the breach is imminent or has occurred). The latter process is not an aid to construing the contract, but indicates whether rescission or merely damages is the proper remedy for a breach for which the innocent party might be recompensed in one way or the other according to its gravity."

Where it is not possible to say that as a matter of interpretation a particular term **16.84** of a contract is a condition or that any breach of a particular term will give rise to a right to terminate, the court must then examine the facts at the date of the exercise of the right to terminate, in order to see whether those facts deprived the party exercising the right to terminate of substantially the whole benefit of the contract so as to give rise to that right.

Illustration

A clause in a contract for the maintenance of a council's leisure facilities stated that the council was entitled to terminate the contract if the contractor committed any breach of its obligations under the contract. It was held that the clause could not be literally applied because the notion that this term would entitle the council to terminate a contract such as this at any time for any breach of any term flew in the face of commercial common sense.

Rice (t/a Garden Guardian) v Great Yarmouth Borough Council[175]

12. WHEN A TERM IS A CONDITION

A term will be treated as a condition of a contract where the parties have provided for it to be so treated either expressly or by necessary implication.

As Blackburn J indicated in *Bettini v Gye*,[176] parties to a contract may provide **16.85** expressly that a particular obligation is to be a condition of the contract. So in *London Guarantee Co v Fearnley*,[177] a policy of insurance against losses caused by embezzlement stated that it was subject "to the conditions herein contained which shall be conditions precedent". One of the terms was a proviso that the insured should, if required by the insurers, prosecute the embezzler. The House of Lords (by a majority) held that the proviso did constitute a condition precedent to liability. Lord Watson said:

> "It cannot with any propriety be said that the stipulation in question goes to the root of the contract between these parties. Nevertheless, it may be a condition precedent, provided that it appears that the parties intended it should have that effect."

---

[174] [1981] 1 W.L.R. 711.
[175] [2000] All E.R. (D) 902.
[176] (1876) 1 Q.B.D. 183 (see para.15.37).
[177] (1880) 5 App. Cas. 911.

16.86 In *Personal Touch Financial Services Ltd v Simplysure Ltd*[178] a contract appointed Simplysure as representative to solicit renewals of medical insurance policies. Clause 7 of the contract provided that it was "a condition of the Agreement that the Appointed Representative be aware of and abides by the rules of the regulator". Sir Stanley Burnton said:

> "... the fact that a contractual provision is described as a condition of the agreement is not conclusive. Agreements often refer to all their terms as conditions, as in 'conditions of sale'. However, this was not such a case. The word 'condition' appears only once in the Agreement, in cl.7, and its use was emphasised by the introductory words 'it is a condition of the agreement'. While its use is not conclusive, it must be given due weight when the agreement is construed."

16.87 However, it is not necessary for the contract to use the word "condition" before a term will be held to be a condition of the contract. In *Dawsons Ltd v Bonnin*,[179] an insurance policy stated that the proposal was to be "the basis" of the contract. The House of Lords held (by a majority) that complete accuracy in the proposal was thereby made a condition of the policy.

In *BS & N Ltd v Micado Shipping Ltd*,[180] a charter of an oil tanker stated that it was approved by a number of oil majors for the carriage of fuel. The charterparty contained a clause which said: "Owners guarantee to obtain within 60 days EXXON approval in addition to present approvals". The combination of the word "guarantee" and the short time limit for obtaining approval were enough to make the obligation a condition of the contract.

16.88 In *Astrazeneca UK Ltd v Albemarle International Corp*,[181] Flaux J said:

> "Whilst it is clear that, for performance of a provision in a contract to be a condition precedent to the performance of another provision, it is not necessary for the relevant provision to use the express words "condition precedent" or something similar, nonetheless the court has to consider whether on the proper construction of the contract that is the effect of the provisions."

He added that:

> "... in the absence of an express term, performance of one obligation will only be a condition precedent to another obligation where either the first obligation must for practical reasons clearly be performed before the second obligation can arise or the second obligation is the direct quid pro quo of the first, in the sense that only performance of the first earns entitlement to the second."[182]

16.89 Conversely, the mere fact that a contract uses the word "condition" is not conclusive. In *Schuler (L) AG v Wickman Machine Tool Sales Ltd*,[183] a sales agency agreement required the agent to visit potential customers at least once a week to solicit orders. That term was part of a clause which began "It shall be condition of this agreement". The House of Lords held that the term was not a condition of the

[178] [2016] EWCA Civ 461; [2016] Bus. L.R. 1049.
[179] [1922] 2 A.C. 413.
[180] [2001] 1 All E.R. (Comm) 240; [2001] 1 Lloyd's Rep. 341
[181] [2011] EWHC 1574 (Comm).
[182] See also *DRC Distribution Ltd v Ulva Ltd* [2007] EWHC 1716 (QB).
[183] [1974] A.C. 235.

agreement, and that consequently the agreement could not be terminated merely on account of one missed visit. Lord Reid said:

"Schuler maintain that the use of the word 'condition' is in itself enough to establish this intention. No doubt some words used by lawyers do have a rigid inflexible meaning. But we must remember that we are seeking to discover intention as disclosed by the contract as a whole. Use of the word 'condition' is an indication—even a strong indication—of such an intention but it is by no means conclusive."

The majority held that meaning could be given to the use of the word "condition" by treating the term as specially important, but not so important as to give rise to an automatic right to terminate on breach.

The same approach was taken by the Privy Council in *Australia and New Zealand Banking Group Ltd v Beneficial Finance Corp Ltd.*[184] In that case liability under a guarantee was expressed to be "conditional" upon payments being made at quarterly intervals. The Privy Council held that liability was not terminated merely by reason of a short delay in one quarterly payment.   **16.90**

There is indeed, in the modern cases, a tendency against construing contractual terms as conditions. In *Cehave NV v Bremer Handelgesellschaft mbH,*[185] Roskill LJ said: **16.91**

"In my view a court should not be over ready, unless required by statute or authority so to do, to construe a term in a contract as a 'condition' any breach of which gives rise to a right to reject rather than as a term any breach of which sounds in damages … In principle, contracts are made to be performed and not to be avoided according to the whims of market fluctuation and where there is a free choice between two possible constructions I think the court should tend to prefer that construction which will ensure performance, and not encourage avoidance of contractual obligations."

Accordingly, the court rejected an argument that in the case of a contract for the sale of goods because the Sale of Goods Act 1893 did not cater for intermediate terms all contractual stipulations must either be conditions or warranties.

In *Tradax International SA v Goldschmidt SA,*[186] Slynn J said: **16.92**

"… in the absence of any clear agreement or prior decision that this was to be a condition, the court should lean in favour of construing this provision as to impurities as an intermediate term, only a serious and substantial breach of which entitled rejection."

Lord Roskill returned to the theme in *Bunge Corp v Tradax Export SA,*[187] in which he said:

"In short, while recognising the modern approach and not being over ready to construe terms as conditions unless the contract clearly requires the court so to do, none the less the basic principles of construction for determining whether or

---

[184] (1982) 44 A.L.R. 241.
[185] [1976] Q.B. 44.
[186] [1977] 2 Lloyd's Rep. 604.
[187] [1981] 1 W.L.R. 711.

not a particular term is a condition remains as before, always bearing in mind on the one hand the need for certainty and on the other the desirability of not, when legitimate, allowing rescission where the breach complained of is highly technical and where damages would clearly be an adequate remedy."

In the result, the House of Lords held that a term in a contract requiring the buyers to give at least 15 consecutive days' notice of probable readiness of a vessel was a condition of the contract. Lord Wilberforce laid particular emphasis on the fact that there was only one possible type of breach, that is, to be late. Others of their Lordships relied on a long line of authority to the effect that stipulations as to time in a mercantile contract are of the essence of the contract.

16.93 Although, as Lord Roskill explained, certainty is an important consideration, it is not entitled to undue weight in determining whether a term is a condition or innominate. As Hamblen LJ put it in *Grand China Logistics Holding (Group) Co Ltd v Spar Shipping AS*[188]:

"Whilst certainty is an important consideration in the construction of commercial contracts, I consider that undue weight should not be given to it in evaluating whether a term is a condition or an innominate term. That is because the operation of a condition is always more certain than that of an innominate term and so over-reliance on certainty would lead to a presumption that terms are conditions. There is no such presumption. On the contrary the modern approach is that a term is innominate unless a contrary intention is made clear."

In that case the Court of Appeal, upholding Popplewell J, held that punctual payment of hire under a charterparty was not a condition of the contract.

16.94 In *ARK Shipping Co LLC v Silverburn Shipping (IoM) Ltd*,[189] the Court of Appeal held that an obligation in a bareboat charterparty to keep the vessel with unexpired classification of a specified class was not a condition of the contract. Gross LJ said:

"(i) it is a matter of the intention of the parties on the true construction of the contract; (ii) where, upon the true construction of the contract, the parties have not made the term a condition, it will be innominate if a breach may result in trivial, minor or very grave consequences; (iii) unless it is clear that a term is intended to be a condition or (only) a warranty, it will be innominate."

16.95 It is also highly relevant to consider pre-existing authority on the type of term under consideration. Once a particular kind of term has been classified by the court as a condition, later cases are likely to follow the same classification. This is because the courts have repeatedly stressed the need for certainty in the law, particularly in relation to commercial contracts. For example, in *The Mihalis Angelos*,[190] in which an "expected readiness" clause in a charterparty was held to be a condition, Megaw LJ said:

"One of the essential elements of law is some measure of uniformity. One of the important elements of the law is predictability. At any rate in commercial law, there are obvious and substantial advantages in having, where possible, a firm

---

[188] [2016] EWCA Civ 982; [2016] 2 Lloyd's Rep. 447.
[189] [2019] EWCA Civ 1161, reversing [2019] EWHC 376 (Comm); [2019] 1 Lloyd's Rep. 554.
[190] [1971] 1 Q.B. 164.

and definite rule for a particular class of legal relationship: for example, as here the legal categorisation of a particular, definable type of contractual clause in common use."

And one of the grounds upon which Edmund Davies LJ based his decision in that case was that the clause had been "generally regarded as a condition".

When a term has to be performed by one party as a condition precedent to the ability of the other party to perform another term the term as to time for the performance of the obligation will in general fall to be treated as a condition.[191]   **16.96**

Where the contract spells out the consequences of a failure to comply with a particular term, and those consequences are those which would follow from a breach of a condition, then the term in question is likely to be held to be a condition of the contract. In *BNP Paribas v Wockhardt EU Operations (Swiss) AG*,[192] Christopher Clarke J said: **16.97**

> "Commercial parties to a contract for the sale and delivery of currency who specify that non-payment or non-delivery shall have the consequences which would follow from a breach of condition, both as to entitlement to terminate and measure of recovery, must be taken to have agreed that the term in question shall have that status. The expressions 'condition' and 'repudiatory breach' are legal shorthand for a term breach of which entitles the innocent party to terminate the contract and to claim damages for loss of bargain or a breach which has those consequences. When the parties have expressed those consequences for themselves they have no need of the shorthand."

A provision in a time charter requiring payment of hire, accompanied by an anti-technicality clause allowing two days' grace, was held to be a condition of the contract.[193] One of the reasons given by the judge was that an express right to terminate the contract on breach of the term in question is a strong indication that that term is a condition. However, in *Spar Shipping AS v Grand China Logistics Holding (Group) Co Ltd*,[194] Popplewell J disagreed. He pointed out that an express right to terminate may be no more than an option to cancel which does not, of itself, mean that the antecedent breach giving rise to the right is a condition of the contract. As he put it: **16.98**

> "A clause which merely provides a contractual remedy for default is not naturally to be interpreted as determining what remedies are available if the contractual remedy is not relied on."

After a comprehensive review of the authorities he concluded that payment of hire was not a condition of a charter party. His decision was upheld by the Court of Appeal.[195]

In addition, of course, many terms are classified by statute (e.g. the Sale of Goods Act 1979) as being either conditions or not.

---

[191] *Bunge Corp v Tradax SA* [1981] 1 W.L.R. 711.
[192] [2009] EWHC 3116 (Comm).
[193] *Kuwait Rocks Co v AMN Bulkcarriers Inc* [2013] EWHC 865 (Comm).
[194] [2015] EWHC 718 (Comm).
[195] [2016] EWCA Civ 982; [2016] 2 Lloyd's Rep. 447.

Illustrations

1.   A charterparty stipulated that the vessel was to proceed to Trieste, there load a cargo and sail to a port in the UK. It was provided that the vessel was to sail from England on or before 4 February next. It was held that the stipulation as to the time of sailing was a condition of the charterparty.
Glaholm v Hays[196]

2.   A charterparty stated that the vessel was "now at Amsterdam". It was held that that statement was a condition of the charterparty.
Behn v Burness[197]

3.   A charterparty described the vessel as "now sailed or about to sail from a pitch pine port" to the UK. She did not sail until three weeks later. It was held that the statement was a condition of the charterparty. Bowen LJ said:

> "There is no way of deciding that question [i.e. whether a term is a condition or a warranty] except by looking at the contract in the light of the surrounding circumstances, and then making up one's mind whether the intention of the parties, as gathered from the instrument itself, will best be carried out by treating the promise as a warranty sounding only in damages, or as a condition precedent by the failure to perform which the other party is relieved of his liability."

Bentsen v Taylor Sons & Co (No.2)[198]

4.   In a contract for the hire of a vehicle there is an implied stipulation that the vehicle will correspond with the description of the vehicle contracted to be hired. This term is a condition of the contract, but an implied stipulation that the vehicle will be fit for the purpose for which it is hired is not.
Astley Industrial Trust Ltd v Grimley[199]

5.   An agreement for the termination of a joint building construction venture contained financial provisions for ascertaining the balance of account. One of the ingredients was the amount owed to a subsidiary of one of the parties under a building contract with a third party. The amount owing was in dispute. The agreement provided that no settlement of the dispute was to be made without the approval of both parties to the agreement. It was held that that term was a condition of the agreement.
Cia Barca de Panama SA v Wimpey (George) & Co Ltd[200]

6.   Payment of a deposit under a contract of sale is not a condition precedent to the formation of a binding contract, but is a condition of the contract. Accordingly, non-payment of the deposit entitles the vendor to terminate the contract.
Millichamp v Jones[201]; *Damon Compania Naviera SA v Hapag-Lloyd International SA*[202]

---

[196]   (1841) 2 M. & G. 257.
[197]   (1863) 2 B. & S. 751.
[198]   [1893] 2 Q.B. 274.
[199]   [1963] 1 W.L.R. 584.
[200]   [1979] 1 Lloyd's Rep. 598.
[201]   [1982] 1 W.L.R. 1422 (sale of land); *Samarenko v Dawn Hill House Ltd* [2011] EWCA Civ 1445; [2013] Ch.36.
[202]   [1985] 1 W.L.R. 435 (sale of ships); *Samarenko v Dawn Hill House Ltd* [2011] EWCA Civ 1445;

7.   A contract for the sale of a ship provided for a deposit of 10 per cent to be lodged at a bank in Singapore; but also provided for the whole of the purchase price to be payable in full in Piraeus on closing. The place of payment of the purchase price was a condition of the contract.
The Aktor[203]

13.   CONDITIONS SUBSEQUENT

A condition subsequent is a condition which brings a subsisting liability to an end on the fulfilment of the condition.

In his dissenting judgment in the Court of Appeal in *Wickman Machine Tool Sales Ltd v Schuler (L) AG*,[204] Stephenson LJ said: **16.99**

"If the condition is to be performed after the agreement has come into force, it is what lawyers have called a condition subsequent, or a condition inherent (or a promissory condition), that is a condition of the agreement's continuing; and if it is not performed the agreement comes to an end."

However, it is submitted that this statement is incomplete in two respects.

First, a condition subsequent need not be a promissory condition at all; it may   **16.100**
be a contingent condition fulfilment of which is entirely outside the control of the parties. Secondly, non-fulfilment of a contingent condition will almost always bring the contract to an end automatically,[205] whereas breach of a promissory condition puts the injured party to his election whether to affirm the contract or accept the non-performance as a repudiation.

Thus in *Bashir v Commissioner of Crown Lands*,[206] the Privy Council approved   **16.101**
the following statement of O'Connor P in the court below:

"At common law, a condition is a qualification annexed to an estate, whereby the latter shall be either created (condition precedent) enlarged, or defeated (condition subsequent), upon its performance or breach. The main distinction between a condition subsequent for the cesser of the term of a lease upon the happening of a certain event and a lessee's covenant is that (subject to any right of relief from forfeiture given to the lessee) upon breach of condition the lessor may re-enter, because the estate of the lessee is determined; whereas a breach of covenant only gives him the right to recover damages (or to obtain an injunction) unless the right to re-enter is expressly reserved by the lease."

However, the Privy Council also held that it is possible for a stipulation in a lease

---

[2013] Ch.36.
[203] [2008] 2 Lloyd's Rep. 246.
[204] [1972] 1 W.L.R. 840.
[205] In some cases, it may be necessary for one party to notify the other of the occurrence of the condition in order to give him an opportunity to waive the condition: see *Yewbelle Ltd v London Green Developments Ltd* [2008] 1 P. & C.R. 279 (although the case itself concerned a condition precedent).
[206] [1960] A.C. 44.

to be both a covenant and a condition, and indicated that this situation is brought about by the common form proviso for re-entry (or forfeiture clause). But breach of a covenant giving rise to a right of re-entry under an express proviso does not automatically bring the term to an end. It puts the landlord to his election whether or not to exercise his right, and he may elect not to do so, in which case the lease continues.[207]

16.102   In *The Hollandia*,[208] Lord Diplock described a condition subsequent as one which "comes into operation only upon the occurrence of a future event that may or may not occur".

16.103   In *Head v Tattersall*,[209] the plaintiff bought a horse on a Monday. The horse was warranted to have been hunted with the Bicester hounds. The contract provided that "horses not answering the description must be returned before 5 o'clock on Wednesday evening next; otherwise the purchaser shall be obliged to keep the lot with all faults". After the sale, but before the plaintiff removed the horse, he was informed that it had never been hunted with the Bicester hounds, but he took it away anyway. It later met with an accident, and the plaintiff returned the horse by the contractual deadline. It was held that he was entitled to have his money back, notwithstanding that the horse was no longer in the physical condition in which it was sold.

16.104   In *Felixstowe Dock and Railway Co and European Ferries Ltd v British Transport Docks Board*,[210] the parties entered into an agreement relating to the purchase of shares. The agreement was expressly made "conditional upon" the passing of an Act of Parliament then in the course of promotion. It was held that the agreement was an immediately binding agreement. Lord Denning MR said:

> "So here, then, was a binding agreement and it was subject to a condition subsequent or defeasant. The condition was that if Parliament did not pass the Bill on or before Nov. 15, 1976, it would cease to be binding."

Similarly, under the National Conditions of Sale, a contract for the sale of a lease is "conditional" on the reversioner's licence being obtained. This provision is not a condition precedent which prevents the formation of a binding contract.[211] However, failure to obtain the licence without fault of either party is a condition subsequent which brings the contract to an end.[212]

Illustrations

1.   A contract for the sale of ships was "contingent on onward sale or charter to the United States government". Failing onward sale or charter "the purchase

---

[207] This is so even where the lease apparently provides that upon breach of covenant by the tenant the lease shall become void. This approach is based upon the principle that the lessee should not be entitled to take advantage of his own wrong. See *Quesnel Forks Gold Mining Co Ltd v Ward* [1920] A.C. 222, and para.7.108.

[208] [1983] 1 A.C. 565.

[209] (1871) L.R. 7 Exch. 7.

[210] [1976] 2 C.M.L.R. 655.

[211] *Property and Bloodstock Ltd v Emerton* [1966] Ch. 94.

[212] *Shires v Brock* [1978] 2 E.G.L.R. 153 CA.

memorandum shall be terminated, null and void". It was held that it was a conditional agreement liable to be defeated by a condition subsequent.
Global Container Lines Ltd v State Black Sea Shipping Co[213]

2. A contract for the sale of ships was subject to two conditions. The first was approval by the board of directors of a particular company; and the second was the obtaining by the seller of an export licence within 30 days of signing the contract. It was held that the first of these conditions was a true suspensory condition, but that the second was a condition subsequent.
Ignazio Messina & Co v Polskie Linie Oceaniczne[214]

14.   OPTIONS AND UNILATERAL CONTRACTS

In the case of unilateral contracts, such as options, all conditions must be strictly performed, otherwise no binding contract comes into existence at all.

Compliance with time stipulations in an option or unilateral contract has already   **16.105**
been considered.[215] Precisely the same principles apply to compliance with other conditions. As Lord Hoffmann graphically put it in *Mannai Investment Co Ltd v Eagle Star Life Assurance Co Ltd*[216]:

"If the clause had said that the notice had to be on blue paper, it would be no good serving a notice on pink paper, however clear it might have been that the tenant wanted to terminate the lease."

So in *Finch v Underwood*,[217] a tenant was entitled to renew his lease on condi-   **16.106**
tion that the tenant's covenants had been performed. At the end of the lease the property required repairs which the trial judge described as "trifling". The Court of Appeal held that the tenant was not entitled to renew. Mellish LJ said:

"The tenant must take the covenant to renew as he finds it; if it contains conditions precedent he must comply with them before he can claim the benefit of it, and if he has not done so a Court of Equity cannot relieve him."

The same approach was followed by the Court of Appeal in *West Country Cleaners (Falmouth) Ltd v Saly*,[218] where the tenant failed to comply with a covenant to decorate the property in the last year of the term. Dankwerts LJ said that the same principles which govern compliance with time stipulations in options apply to any other conditions to which the option is subject.[219]

One reason why this should be so was given by Diplock LJ in *United Dominions*   **16.107**

---

[213] [1999] 1 Lloyd's Rep. 127.
[214] [1995] 2 Lloyd's Rep. 566 (the alleged contract failed for other reasons).
[215] See para.15.55.
[216] [1997] A.C. 749. See also *Burman v Mount Cook Land Ltd* [2002] Ch. 256 CA.
[217] (1876) 2 Ch. D. 310.
[218] [1966] 1 W.L.R. 1485.
[219] It has been held in Australia that it may also be possible to interpret a condition precedent as requiring only substantial compliance, with the result that trivial or de minimis breaches may be disregarded: *Newtown Management Pty Ltd v Owners of Strata Plan* 67219 [2009] NSWSC 150. See also *Diab v Regent Insurance Co Ltd* [2006] Lloyd's Rep. I.R. 779, where Lord Scott of Foscote expressed the same view, although the point did not arise for decision. However, this is not yet the law of England and Wales.

Trust (Commercial) Ltd v Eagle Aircraft Services Ltd[220] in the following terms:

"… as respects the promisor, the initial inquiry is whether the event, which under the unilateral contract gives rise to obligations on the part of the promisor, has occurred. To that inquiry the answer can only be a simple 'Yes' or 'No'. The event must be identified by its description in the unilateral contract; but if what has occurred does not comply with that description, there is an end of the matter. It is not for the court to ascribe any different consequences to non-compliance with one part of the description of the event than to any other part if the parties by their contract have not done so. See the cases about options.[221] For the inquiry here is: 'What have the parties agreed to do?'—not 'What are the consequences of their having failed to do what they have agreed to do?' as it was in the *Hongkong Fir* case. Such an inquiry cannot arise under a unilateral contract unless and until the event giving rise to the promisor's obligations has occurred."

16.108   Nevertheless, some breaches have been made in this principle. In the first place, part of a bilateral[222] contract which is drafted using the language of options will not necessarily be treated as an option, with the strict consequences which flow from that. Whether it does amount to an option depends on the proper interpretation of the contract as a whole.[223]

16.109   Second, where a particular method of exercising the option is prescribed, it will not necessarily be mandatory. So in *Yates Building Co Ltd v Pullen (RJ) & Sons (York) Ltd*,[224] an option was stated to be exercisable by written notice sent by registered post or by the recorded delivery service. Written notice was received in due time, but it had been sent by ordinary post. It was held by the Court of Appeal that the notice had been validly given. A similar view in the context of a tender was reached by Buckley J in *Manchester Diocesan Council of Education v Commercial and General Investments Ltd*,[225] in which he said:

"It may be that an offeror, who by the terms of his offer insists on acceptance in a particular manner, is entitled to insist that he is not bound unless acceptance is effected or communicated in that precise way, although it seems probable that, even so, if the other party communicates his acceptance in some other way, the offeror may be conduct or otherwise waive his right to insist on the prescribed method of acceptance. Where, however, the offeror has prescribed a particular method of acceptance, but not in terms insisting that only acceptance in that mode shall be binding, I am of opinion that acceptance communicated to the offeror by any other mode which is no less advantageous to him will conclude the contract."

16.110   Third, where an option is conditional upon the performance of covenants, the grantee will not be disabled from exercising the option because of past breaches of

---

[220] [1968] 1 W.L.R. 74; applied in *Siemens Hearing Instruments Ltd v Friends Life Ltd* [2014] EWCA Civ 382; [2014] 2 P. & C.R. 95.
[221] *Weston v Collins* (1865) 12 L.T. 4; *Hare v Nicoll* [1966] 2 Q.B. 130.
[222] Or synallagmatic.
[223] See *United Scientific Holdings Ltd v Burnley Borough Council* [1978] A.C. 904 (concerning a rent review clause).
[224] (1975) 237 E.G. 183.
[225] [1970] 1 W.L.R. 241. This seems doubtful in the light of *Siemens Hearing Instruments Ltd v Friends Life Ltd* [2014] EWCA Civ 382; [2014] 2 P. & C.R. 95, if the method of acceptance is, as a matter of construction, a condition of the option.

covenant if the breaches are "spent" in the sense of not giving rise to a subsisting cause of action.[226]

Fourth, it may be possible to interpret the option as requiring the condition to be fulfilled only if the grantor of the option requires it to be fulfilled. In *Little v Courage Ltd*,[227] a lease contained an option to renew subject to the condition (among others) that the landlord and the tenant should have agreed a business plan. The Court of Appeal held that the condition should be construed as meaning that a business plan was to be agreed only if the landlord required it to be agreed. **16.111**

Fifth, where the question is not whether substantive conditions have been performed, but what a notice exercising an option means, the ordinary techniques of interpretation of the notice apply. Having interpreted the notice, it must then be matched against the contractual requirements to see whether it meets them.[228] However, where the case is one where it is an indispensable condition that a notice exercising an option should contain "specific information", the omission of that information invalidates the notice. Whether it is the case is a question of interpretation. In *Rennie v Westbury Homes (Holdings) Ltd*,[229] Dyson LJ said: **16.112**

> "A typical case of an 'indispensable condition' is where the contract states that the relevant notice shall be in writing and shall contain particular information. Some clauses may expressly say that 'the notice shall only be valid if …'. Where express language of this kind does not appear in the clause, it will be a question of construction whether it is an indispensable condition[230] for validity that the notice satisfies the requirements of the clause."

Illustrations

1.   A lease contained an option to renew conditional on performance by the tenant of his covenants. The tenant covenanted to decorate in the last year of the term. The tenant decorated the premises four months before the beginning of the last year of the term but not during that year itself. It was held that the tenant had failed to comply with the condition precedent and so the exercise of the option failed.
Bairstow Eves (Securities) Ltd v Ripley[231]

2.   A lease contained a break clause which stated that the notice exercising the break had to be "expressed to be given under section 24(2) of the Landlord and Tenant Act 1954". The notice that the tenant gave did not contain those words, although it complied with the clause in all other respects. The notice was held to be invalid.
Friends Life Ltd v Siemens Hearing Instruments Ltd[232]

15.   DEPENDENT AND INDEPENDENT OBLIGATIONS

A contractual obligation may give rise to a liability which may only be enforced by a party to the contract if he has performed or offered to perform his own

---

[226]   *Grey v Friar* (1854) 4 H.L. Cas. 565; *Bass Holdings Ltd v Morton Music Ltd* [1988] Ch. 493 CA.
[227]   (1993) 70 P. & C.R. 469 CA.
[228]   *Trafford MBC v Total Fitness (UK) Ltd* [2002] 2 P. & C.R. 2 CA.
[229]   [2007] EWCA Civ 1401.
[230]   The concept of an "indispensable" condition is puzzling, because if a requirement of an option is a condition, it is by definition indispensable.
[231]   [1992] 2 E.G.L.R. 47 CA.
[232]   [2014] EWCA Civ 382.

obligations under it ("a dependent obligation"); or it may be capable of enforcement whether or not the party seeking to perform has performed or offered to perform his own obligations ("an independent obligation"). Which species of obligation has been created is a question of interpretation, but if the obligation constitutes the whole or a substantial part of the consideration for the contract, the court is likely to interpret it as a dependent obligation.[233]

16.113   It has already been pointed out that under the old system of pleading a plaintiff had to be able to aver his willingness to perform his own obligations under the contract in order to be able to enforce the obligations of the other party.[234] This approach has led to two strands in the law: first, the classification of terms as conditions, warranties and intermediate terms[235] and, secondly, the question whether obligations are mutually dependent or are independent. The two strands are, in practice, frequently intertwined. Moreover, this latter question is often linked to the order in which contractual obligations are to be performed.[236]

16.114   In *Tito v Waddell (No.2)*[237] Megarry VC said:

"If an instrument grants rights and also imposes obligations, the court must ascertain whether on the true construction of the instrument it has granted merely qualified or conditional rights, the qualification or condition being the due observance of the obligations, or whether it has granted unqualified rights and imposed independent obligations. In construing the instrument, the more closely the obligations are linked to the rights, the easier it will be to construe the instrument as granting merely qualified rights. The question always must be one of the intention of the parties as gathered from the instrument as a whole."

16.115   So, for example, in a contract for the sale of land, the vendor's obligation to convey and the purchaser's obligation to pay the purchase price are dependent obligations. In *Heard v Wadham*,[238] Lord Kenyon CJ said:

"It is clear that these are dependent covenants, and can it be contended for an instant that though the one has not conveyed he may call on the other to pay the money?"

The same position applies to a contract for the sale of goods (although, in the language of the Sale of Goods Act 1979, delivery of the goods and payment are "concurrent conditions").[239]

16.116   In *Doherty v Fannigan Holdings Ltd*,[240] a share sale agreement provided for the payment of the price on a specified day. It further provided that the shares would be transferred on receipt of the price. The Court of Appeal, referring with approval to the equivalent section of a previous edition of this book, held that the obligation to pay and the reciprocal obligation to transfer the shares were depend-

---

[233] The equivalent section in a previous edition of this book was referred to with approval in *Aalders v PA Putney Finance Australia Pty Ltd* [2011] NSWSC 756 and *Sydney Attractions Group Pty Ltd v Schulman* [2013] NSWSC 858.
[234] See paras 16.07 and 16.76.
[235] See para.16.76.
[236] See the notes to *Pordage v Cole* (1670) 1 Wms. Saund. 320.
[237] [1977] Ch. 106.
[238] (1801) 1 East. 619.
[239] Sale of Goods Act 1979 s.28.
[240] [2018] EWCA Civ 1615; [2018] 2 B.C.L.C. 623.

ent obligations. Sir Colin Rimer said:

"I regard as irresistible the inference that the intention of clause 5.1 is that there is to be an immediate delivery of such documents upon receipt of the price and that the parties' objective was to achieve what would in practice be a simultaneous exchange. To attribute to the parties the intention that either should perform his or its completion obligation except against the performance of the other's is to fix them with unlikely, and uncommercial, intentions. No purchaser of the shares is going to part with £2m to the vendor except against the receipt of the share transfer documents, any more than the vendor is going to part with the documents except against the receipt of the £2m."

In *Dreams Ltd v Pavilion Property Trustees Ltd*,[241] an agreement for the surrender of a lease stated that the surrender "is with vacant possession". Miles J held that unless vacant possession was delivered, the landlord could not be compelled to accept the surrender. This case is best analysed as a case of dependent obligations, or concurrent conditions.

However, in the case of a contract which is not wholly executory, it is submit-   **16.117**
ted that the court is less willing to hold that obligations are dependent. Thus in *Carter v Scargill*,[242] the plaintiff sold his business to the defendant. The contract provided that the purchaser would make additional payments to the vendor in the event that the business was proved by the vendor's books to realise a certain weekly profit. Four years after the sale the plaintiff sued for the instalments. The court held that it was no defence that the business had not been proved by the books to realise the stipulated weekly profit. Field J said:

"Now, whatever might have been the question if it had been raised while the agreement was executory, we are clearly of opinion that, the defendant having received a substantial portion of the consideration, it is no longer competent to him to rely upon the non-performance of that which might have been originally a condition precedent."

Similarly, in the case of a lease, the court has repeatedly held that obligations   **16.118**
imposed upon landlord or tenant are independent obligations. Thus in *Edge v Boileau*,[243] Parke B said:

"Then it was contended that the covenant for quiet enjoyment and the covenants to be performed by the plaintiff were not to be read independently, but as dependent covenants, and that the payment of the rent and repairing were therefore conditions precedent. I should have thought that point very clear even without authority. But there appears to be a case directly in point, viz. *Dawson v Dyer*.[244] In that case the same argument was put before the court as in the present case, and the court held the argument untenable."[245]

---

[241] [2020] EWHC 1169 (Ch).
[242] (1873) L.R. 10 Q.B. 564.
[243] (1885) 16 Q.B.D. 117.
[244] (1833) 5 B. & Ad. 584.
[245] This case was followed by du Parcq J in *Taylor v Webb* [1937] 2 K.B. 283; reversed on other grounds by the Court of Appeal. The decision of the Court of Appeal was itself later overruled by the House of Lords in *Regis Property Co Ltd v Dudley* [1959] A.C. 370.

In *Yorkbrook Investments Ltd v Batten*,[246] a tenant of a flat covenanted to pay a maintenance charge. The landlord's maintenance and other obligations were prefaced with the words:

"subject to the Lessee paying the Maintenance Contribution pursuant to the obligations of clause 4 hereof."

The Court of Appeal held that the covenants were independent, and the tenant could enforce the landlord's obligations, even though he might be in arrear with the contribution.[247]

16.119   In *Motortrak Ltd v FCA Australia Pty Ltd*,[248] Moulder J said that:

"the principle is that the obligation will only be independent where the contract can be performed without any cooperation on the part of the other party."

16.120   One factor which may be material in deciding whether obligations were intended to be dependent or not is whether they appear in the same document. In *The Odenfeld*,[249] a charterparty fixed a certain rate of hire. A "side letter" entered into on the same day contained a funding arrangement indemnifying the charterers against excessive payments of hire. The question arose whether a repudiatory breach of the side letter involved a repudiation of the entire charterparty. Kerr J held that it did not, for a number of reasons. In the course of his judgment he said:

"the very fact that they were put into separate documents, with the charter appearing to be complete in itself, points to the conclusion that the respective obligations under them were intended to be independent and not interdependent."

16.121   The same effect may be achieved by drafting. In *Wilkinson v Clements*,[250] a building agreement contemplated the grant of separate leases of particular parcels of the land. It was held that an action would lie to enforce the grant of some of those leases notwithstanding that the lessee did not propose to build on the remaining plots. Mellish LJ said:

"... I do not find it laid down anywhere that it is impossible for the parties so to frame an agreement that there may be a specific performance of part. For instance, if they had said in terms, 'This agreement is to be construed as if it were three separate agreements for the several portions,' nobody, I suppose, would doubt that the court would treat it as if there were separate agreements, and would not say, 'If you meant them to be separate agreements you ought not to have put them on the same piece of paper, but on three separate pieces.' That being so, it is really a question of construction whether practically that is not what the parties have done, and the Court ought to carry out the agreement according to what it sees is really the intention and object of the parties in making it."

---

[246] (1986) 52 P. & C.R. 51.
[247] The breadth of the reasoning was questioned (obiter) by the CA in *Bluestorm Ltd v Portvale Holdings Ltd* [2004] 2 E.G.L.R. 38.
[248] [2018] EWHC 990 (Comm) at [107].
[249] [1978] 2 Lloyd's Rep. 357.
[250] (1872) L.R. 8 Ch. App. 96.

Illustrations

1.   By articles of marriage the wife's father covenanted to settle certain property on the husband and wife during their lives and after their death on their issue. The husband covenanted to insure his life and to settle the policy in like manner. The marriage took place, but the wife died before her father had settled the property. The husband had not insured his life. It was held that the husband had partly performed the contract by the fact of the marriage, and consequently was entitled to enforce the wife's father's obligation.
Jeston v Key[251]

2.   A settlement agreement provided for one party to pay the other a sum of money by a specified date without set-off or deduction. The payee agreed to release any claims or demands which she might have against the payer; assign any benefits or sums which she was entitled to receive under loan agreements entered into in connection with the joint venture; resign as director of the companies set up in connection with the joint venture; and transfer her shares in the relevant companies. It was held that the obligation to make the payment was an independent obligation, non-fulfilment of which entitled the payee to present a bankruptcy petition.
Mulville v Sandelson[252]

16.   PARTICIPIAL PHRASES

It is a question of interpretation whether a participial phrase (that is, a phrase beginning with a participle) qualifies an obligation in a contract, or creates its own obligation.

Some contractual obligations contain within them participial phrases. One such obligation is the familiar form of covenant for quiet enjoyment in a lease, which usually begins "the tenant paying the rent and performing and observing his covenants". A similar kind of obligation is a covenant against doing something without consent "such consent not to be unreasonably withheld". In such cases the question arises whether the participial phrase creates a new obligation, or merely qualifies an earlier one. In *Westacott v Hahn*,[253] Pickford LJ said:

16.122

"I think the only principle ... which is useful to the question before us is that covenant is a matter of intention, and that any words will make a covenant, whether participial or not, if it can clearly be seen that such was the intention of the parties. A participial clause, therefore, such as that in this case, may be only a qualification of the previous covenants of the lessee, or it may be a covenant by the lessor to perform what is mentioned in the clause. If it be such a covenant, it may be also a qualification in the sense that the lessor's performance may be a condition precedent to the lessee's obligation to perform his. In former days it seems to have been considered that a clause could not be both a covenant and a qualification, but I think that is not the law now."

---

[251]   (1871) L.R. 6 Ch. App. 610.
[252]   [2019] EWHC 3287 (Ch).
[253]   [1918] 1 K.B. 495.

16.123   Similarly, in *Burford UK Properties Ltd v Forte Hotels (UK) Ltd*,[254] Auld LJ said that:

> "there is no particular magic in the use in the lease of the word 'covenant' as against that of 'condition', 'provision', 'agreement' or 'proviso', and that a proviso, whether in the body of a lease or in a schedule to it, may, depending on its form and the context, have the same force and effect as a covenant."

16.124   In the case of a tenant's covenant against assignment without the landlord's consent, "such consent not to be unreasonably withheld", it is now settled as a rule of construction that the landlord incurs no liability in damages if consent is unreasonably withheld. The effect of the participial phrase is to qualify the tenant's covenant, so that if consent is unreasonably withheld, the tenant is released from the covenant as regards the particular assignment.[255]

Illustration

Landlord trustees offered to let a house at a rent of £100 per annum "the trustees putting the premises in reasonable tenantable repair inside and out". A lease was subsequently entered into, containing a tenant's repairing covenant and a covenant to pay outgoings. It was held that the tenant was not liable to pay the cost of rectifying a defect in the drains which predated the lease. The judgment does not, however, clearly indicate whether the landlords would themselves have been liable in damages for failing to put the house into tenantable repair before the date of the lease.
Henman v Berliner[256]

---

[254] [2003] EWCA Civ 1800.
[255] *Treloar v Bigge* (1874) L.R. 9 Ex. 151; *Ideal Film Renting Co Ltd v Nielsen* [1921] 1 Ch. 575; *Rose v Gossman* (1967) 201 E.G. 767. This rule of construction has been reversed by the Landlord and Tenant Act 1988 in relation to covenants against alienation; but it remains in relation to covenants against changing the use of property or against making alterations.
[256] [1918] 2 K.B. 236.

CHAPTER 17

PENALTIES, TERMINATION AND FORFEITURE CLAUSES

The severity of penalties is only a vain resource invented of little minds in order to substitute terror for that respect which they have no means of obtaining

J. J. Rousseau: *Discourse on Political Economy*

1. NATURE OF A PENALTY CLAUSE

A penalty clause is a clause which, on breach of a primary obligation of the contract, imposes upon a contract-breaker a detriment out of all proportion to the injured party's legitimate interest in performance of that primary obligation.

The rule against penalties is an exception to the general principle of English law that a contract should be enforced in accordance with its terms.[1] If a clause is a penalty clause it is unenforceable and the court has no discretion in the matter.[2] The traditional characterisation of a penalty was that it is a sum of money held over one or both parties "in terrorem", as opposed to being a genuine pre-estimate of damages.[3] However, Lord Radcliffe said that he did not find that:

17.01

> "that description adds anything of substance to the idea conveyed by the word 'penalty' itself, and it obscures that fact that penalties may quite readily be undertaken by parties who are not in the least terrorised by the prospect of having to pay them and yet are, as I understand it, entitled to claim the protection of the court when they are called upon to make good their promises."[4]

Thus where a hire purchase agreement provided for the hirer to make payments to the finance company on premature determination of the agreement, Lord Radcliffe said that the real purpose of the clause was to afford the finance company "a substantial guarantee against the loss of their hiring contract".[5] The use of the traditional phrase "in terrorem" has been dropped. Nevertheless, the real contrast

---

[1] *Euro London Appointments Ltd v Claessens International Ltd* [2006] 2 Lloyd's Rep. 436, per Chadwick LJ.
[2] *Else (1982) Ltd v Parkland Holdings Ltd* [1994] 1 B.C.L.C. 130.
[3] *Lord Elphinstone v The Monkland Iron and Coal Co Ltd* (1886) 11 App. Cas. 332, "that which was to be enforced in terrorem", per Lord Halsbury; *Clydebank Engineering and Shipbuilding Co Ltd v Yzquierdo y Castaneda* [1905] A.C. 6, "merely stipulated in terrorem", per Lord Robertson; *Dunlop Pneumatic Tyre Co Ltd v New Garage and Motor Co Ltd* [1915] A.C. 79, "a payment of money stipulated as in terrorem of the offending party", per Lord Dunedin.
[4] *Bridge v Campbell Discount Co Ltd* [1962] A.C. 600 at 622.
[5] *Bridge v Campbell Discount Co Ltd* [1962] A.C. 600 at 622.

was thought to be between a provision that is a deterrent and a provision that is compensatory.[6]

17.02   More recent cases have adopted a broader approach to the question whether a contractual provision is a penalty. The modern test has become more nuanced; and the ultimate question is whether the clause under attack goes beyond the legitimate interests of the injured party in performance of the contract. In *United International Pictures v Cine Bes Filmcilik ve Yapimcilik AS*,[7] Mance LJ said:

> "I have also have found valuable Colman J's further observation in *Lordsvale*[8] ... which indicate that a dichotomy between a genuine pre-estimate of damages and a penalty does not necessarily cover all the possibilities. There are clauses which may operate on breach, but which fall into neither category, and they may be commercially perfectly justifiable."

17.03   In *M&J Polymers Ltd v Imerys Minerals Ltd*,[9] Burton J held that a "take or pay" clause did not offend the rule against penalties where:

> "the take or pay clause was commercially justifiable, did not amount to oppression, was negotiated and freely entered into between parties of comparable bargaining power, and did not have the predominant purpose of deterring a breach of contract nor amount to a provision 'in terrorem'."

17.04   The Supreme Court considered the nature of penalties in *Cavendish Square Holdings BV v Makdessi* and *ParkingEye Ltd v Beavis*.[10] In their joint judgment, Lords Neuberger and Sumption[11] pointed to the distinction between a primary contractual obligation and a secondary obligation which arises only on breach of a primary obligation. They continued at [32]:

> "The true test is whether the impugned provision is a secondary obligation which

---

[6]   *ECGD v Universal Oil Products Co* [1983] 2 All E.R. 205, per Slade LJ, based upon an observation to similar effect by Diplock LJ in *Bernstein (Philip) (Successors) Ltd v Lydiate Textiles Ltd* [1962] C.A.T. 238; *Lordsvale Finance Plc v Bank of Zambia* [1996] Q.B. 752.

[7]   [2004] 1 C.L.C. 401. See also *Lansat Shipping Co Ltd v Glencore Grain BV* [2009] 2 Lloyd's Rep. 688; *Murray v Leisureplay Plc* [2005] EWCA Civ 963; *Lancore Services Ltd v Barclays Bank Plc* [2008] 1 C.L.C. 1039; *Steria Ltd v Sigma Wireless Communications Ltd* [2008] B.L.R. 79; *Edgeworth Capital (Luxembourg) SARL v Ramblas Investments BV* [2015] EWHC 150 (Comm); *MSC Mediterranean Shipping Co SA v Cottonex Anstalt* [2015] EWHC 283 (Comm). In *Imam-Sadeque v Bluebay Asset Management (Services) Ltd* [2012] EWHC 3511 (QB) and *Novasen SA v Alimenta SA* [2013] EWHC 345 (Comm); [2013] 1 Lloyd's Rep. 648. Popplewell J adopted as correct the formulation of principle in earlier editions of this book. That formulation was:

> "A penalty clause is a clause which without commercial justification provides for payment or forfeiture of a sum of money or a transfer of property by one party to another in the event of a breach of contract, the clause being designed to secure performance of the contract rather than to compensate the payee for loss occasioned by the breach."

However, that formulation has been reconsidered in the light to the decision of the Supreme Court in *Cavendish Square Holdings BV v Makdessi* [2015] UKSC 67; [2016] A.C. 1172.

[8]   *Lordsvale Finance Plc v Bank of Zambia* [1996] Q.B. 752.

[9]   (2008) 117 Con. L.R. 88.

[10]   [2015] UKSC 67; [2016] A.C. 1172. The case is discussed in Day, "A Pyrrhic victory for the doctrine against penalties" [2016] J.B.L. 115; [2016] J.B.L. 251; Fisher, "Rearticulating the rule against penalty clauses" [2016] L.M.C.L.Q. 169; Summers, "Unresolved issues in the law on penalties" [2017] L.M.C.L.Q. 95; Eldridge "The new law of penalties: mapping the terrain" [2018] J.B.L. 636; Rowan, "The 'legitimate interest in performance' in the law on penalties" [2019] C.L.J. 148.

[11]   With whom Lords Carnwath and Clarke agreed.

imposes a detriment on the contract-breaker out of all proportion to any legitimate interest of the innocent party in the enforcement of the primary obligation. The innocent party can have no proper interest in simply punishing the defaulter. His interest is in performance or in some appropriate alternative to performance. In the case of a straightforward damages clause, that interest will rarely extend beyond compensation for the breach. ... But compensation is not necessarily the only legitimate interest that the innocent party may have in the performance of the defaulter's primary obligations."

Lord Mance said:

"... the dichotomy between the compensatory and the penal is not exclusive. There may be interests beyond the compensatory which justify the imposition on a party in breach of an additional financial burden. ... What is necessary in each case is to consider, first, whether any (and if so what) legitimate business interest is served and protected by the clause, and, second, whether, assuming such an interest to exist, the provision made for the interest is nevertheless in the circumstances extravagant, exorbitant or unconscionable. In judging what is extravagant, exorbitant or unconscionable, I consider (despite contrary expressions of view) that the extent to which the parties were negotiating at arm's length on the basis of legal advice and had every opportunity to appreciate what they were agreeing must at least be a relevant factor."

Lord Hodge said:

"When the court makes a value judgment on whether a provision is exorbitant or unconscionable, it has regard to the legitimate interests, commercial or otherwise, which the innocent party has sought to protect."

The link between payment of the stipulated sum and the breach of contract is **17.05** crucial, for if the sum is payable without breach, it cannot be a penalty.[12] However, a clause may amount to a penalty even though it requires no payment, if it requires a transfer of property (e.g. shares) on breach of obligation.[13] Likewise a clause may be a penalty clause if it requires the retransfer of property which had previously been transferred to the contract breaker; and to a clause which requires a contract breaker to forfeit a deposit[14] or sum of money due or to become due to the other party in the event of breach. A clause entitling the innocent party to a breach of contract by the other party to withhold a payment otherwise due is also subject to the penalty rule.[15]

---

[12] See para.17.15.

[13] *Jobson v Johnson* [1989] 1 W.L.R. 1026, disapproved on other grounds in *Cavendish Square Holdings BV v Makdessi* [2015] UKSC 67 but agreeing on this point. See also *General Trading Co (Holdings) Ltd v Richmond Corp Ltd* [2008] 2 Lloyd's Rep. 475.

[14] However, deposits are subject to special rules: see para.17.83.

[15] *Cavendish Square Holdings BV v Makdessi* [2015] UKSC 67; [2016] A.C. 1172 at [156] (Lord Mance) and [226] (Lord Hodge). Lords Neuberger and Sumption were more doubtful, although they were prepared to assume that such a clause could be a penalty: [72] and [73]. Lord Clarke agreed with all four of them, and Lord Toulson agreed with Lords Mance and Hodge. It seems, therefore, that a majority of the Supreme Court considers that a clause entitling the injured party to withhold money may fall within the rule against penalties.

Illustrations

1.   A lease contained a clause which entitled the landlord to enter the property and to carry out repairs which the tenant ought to have carried out in conformity with his covenants and then to recover the cost of the repairs from the tenant. It was held that the nature of the sum recoverable by the landlord was a debt, and hence it was not a penalty.
   Jervis v Harris[16]

2.   A contract for the introduction of staff to clients provided for the introduction fee to be paid within seven days of the date of invoice. It also contained provision for a refund of the fee if the staff member left prematurely. It was a condition precedent to the refund that the introduction fee had been paid within seven days of the date of invoice. It was held that the two clauses were not independent; but that the condition precedent to the entitlement to a refund was not a penalty.
   Euro London Appointments Ltd v Claessens International Ltd[17]

3.   A contract for the building of a bespoke luxury yacht entitled the builder to terminate it if the buyer did not pay sums due under the contract within 45 days. A clause in the contract stated that in the event of termination the builder was entitled to retain or recover 20 per cent of the contract price "by way of liquidated damages", but otherwise should return the balance of all sums received from the buyer. It was held that the clause struck a balance between the interests of the parties. It was commercially justified and was therefore not a penalty.
   Azimut-Benetti SpA v Healey[18]

4.   A contract for gym membership for a fixed period provided that if the contract was terminated before the expiry of that period the member would have to pay the subscriptions that would have fallen due for the remainder of the period. It was held that such a provision without discount for accelerated payment was a penalty, but where a discount for accelerated payment was allowed, it was not a penalty.
   Office of Fair Trading v Ashbourne Management Services Ltd[19]

5.   A contractor provided a bespoke modular building to a school for use as a sixth form college to be hired by the school under a finance lease. The lease provided that in the event of termination by repudiation, the school would pay the contractor the full amount of all hire charges under the lease, discounted at 3 per cent per annum for accelerated payment. Because the building was a bespoke building there was little prospect of realising residual value from it if the school no longer wanted it. It was held that the clause was not a penalty.
   School Facility Management Ltd v Governing Body of Christ the King College[20]

---

[16]   [1996] Ch. 195 CA.
[17]   [2006] 2 Lloyd's Rep. 436.
[18]   [2011] 1 Lloyd's Rep. 473.
[19]   [2011] EWHC 1237 (Ch).
[20]   [2020] EWHC 1118 (Comm).

2. PENALTY A QUESTION OF CONSTRUCTION

Whether a clause is a penalty clause is a question of construction of the contract, to be determined at the date of the contract, and not at the date of the breach.

In *Dunlop Pneumatic Tyre Co Ltd v New Garage and Motor Co Ltd*,[21] Lord Dunedin said:

17.06

"The question whether a sum stipulated is penalty or liquidated damage is a question of construction to be decided upon the terms and inherent circumstances of each particular contract, judged of as at the time of the making of the contract, not as at the time of the breach."

In *Lordsvale Finance Plc v Bank of Zambia*,[22] Colman J said that:

"whether a provision is to be treated as a penalty is a matter of construction to be resolved by asking whether at the time the contract was entered into the predominant contractual function of the provision was to deter a party from breaking the contract or to compensate the innocent party for breach. That the contractual function is deterrent rather than compensatory can be deduced by comparing the amount that would be payable on breach with the loss that might be sustained if breach occurred."

And in *Law v Local Board of Redditch*,[23] Lopes LJ said:

"The distinction between penalties and liquidated damages depends on the intention of the parties to be gathered from the whole of the contract."

In *Cavendish Square Holdings BV v Makdessi*,[24] Lords Neuberger and Sumption said:

17.07

"The question whether a damages clause is a penalty falls to be decided as a matter of construction, therefore as at the time that it is agreed. ... This is because it depends on the character of the provision, not on the circumstances in which it falls to be enforced."

There has, however, been some dissent from this view. In *Bridge v Campbell Discount Co Ltd*, Lord Radcliffe said[25]:

17.08

"The court's jurisdiction to relieve against penalties depends on 'a question not of words or of forms of speech, but of substance and of things.'[26] It cannot really depend on a point of construction, though it is often spoken of as so depending."

This is undoubtedly correct, in the sense that there is rarely any dispute about

---

[21] [1915] A.C. 79 at 86.
[22] [1996] Q.B. 752, approved in *Cine Bes Filmcilik ve Yapimcilik v United International Pictures* [2004] 1 C.L.C. 401; *Murray v Leisureplay Plc* [2005] I.R.L.R. 946.
[23] [1892] 1 Q.B. 127 and *Lansat Shipping Co Ltd v Glencore Grain BV* [2009] 2 Lloyd's Rep. 688.
[24] [2015] UKSC 67; [2016] A.C. 1172.
[25] [1962] A.C. 600 at 624.
[26] *Clydebank Engineering and Shipbuilding Co Ltd v Yzquierdo y Castaneda* [1905] A.C. 6 at 15, per Lord Davey.

what the words of the impugned clause mean. In this sense it is probably better to treat the question whether a clause is or is not a penalty as a question of classification or characterisation rather than of construction.[27]

17.09   In *Paciocco v Australia and New Zealand Banking Group Ltd*,[28] Kiefel J pointed out that:

> "The question whether a sum to be paid on default is a penalty, as distinct from liquidated damages, was said by Lord Dunedin to be a question of construction, but his Lordship is not to be taken to suggest that it will be answered by the language of the contract alone. This is evident from the reference to the 'inherent circumstances' of the contract, which includes the position of the party whose interests are to be protected by the stipulation for the payment of the sum on default."

In the same case Gegeler J said:

> "Lord Dunedin evidently used the word 'construction' to refer to something beyond the attribution of legal meaning. He used it to encompass legal characterisation. His added reference to the 'inherent circumstances of each particular contract', although not then the subject of further elaboration, was not, in light of *Clydebank*, confined to circumstances which bore only on the attribution of legal meaning but extended to all of the circumstances which bore on the objective resolution of the ultimate question of characterisation."

17.10   It is clear that any evidence that is admissible in interpreting a contract is equally admissible in deciding whether a clause is a penalty. Thus in *Lombank Ltd v Excell*,[29] it was argued that since the question was one of interpretation, evidence of the surrounding circumstances was inadmissible on that question. Not surprisingly, that argument was rejected by the Court of Appeal, and Lord Radcliffe's observation was relied on in support of the court's conclusion. However, the fallacy that evidence is inadmissible on questions of interpretation has now been repeatedly and authoritatively exposed.[30] This approach entitles (and indeed requires) the court to examine "the facts and circumstances of each particular case"[31] even on a question of interpretation. In those circumstances, it is submitted that it is correct to describe the question whether a sum is a penalty or liquidated damages as one of construction.[32]

17.11   It may be that in this particular class of case there is a difference between interpretation and construction. Thus it has been held that the range of evidence available to decide this question is wider than the range available where the question is to decide what the contract means. Accordingly, evidence of the parties' pre-contractual negotiations has been admitted on the question whether a clause was or was not a penalty. The purpose of adducing that evidence is not so that the parties can demonstrate that they agreed to opt out of the remedies regime provided by the common law but rather that the reasons that they had for doing so constitute adequate justification for the discrepancy between the contractual measure of dam-

---

[27]   See para.9.56.
[28]   [2016] HCA 28.
[29]   [1964] 1 Q.B. 415.
[30]   See para.3.143.
[31]   *Lombank Ltd v Excell* [1964] 1 Q.B. 415 at 427, per Upjohn LJ.
[32]   See *Lansat Shipping Co Ltd v Glencore Grain BV* [2009] 2 Lloyd's Rep. 688.

ages and that provided by the common law.[33] Whether it is correct that evidence of the parties' negotiations is admissible on this question of interpretation is debatable.[34]

But since the test for deciding whether a clause is a penalty depends on whether **17.12** the injured party has a legitimate interest to protect, it is thought that a greater range of evidence is admissible on that question. It also seems probable that the evidence may include evidence of facts that existed at the date of the contract, but were not known to the contract-breaker at the date when the contract was made. Thus in *ParkingEye Ltd v Beavis*,[35] ParkingEye operated but did not own a car park. It paid a fee to the land owners for the right to manage the car park. A clause imposing a fee of £85 on a motorist who overstayed the permitted period of free parking was justified, not merely by reference to ParkingEye's legitimate interests but also by reference to the legitimate interests of the land owners. It seems doubtful whether the relationship between ParkingEye and the land owners could have been known to the motorist when he drove into the car park.

Where a contract has been amended, the question whether a sum payable on **17.13** breach is a penalty is to be judged as at the date of the amendment.[36]

In general, evidence of events subsequent to the making of the contract is ir- **17.14** relevant in deciding what it means. But in *Philips Hong Kong Ltd v The Attorney General of Hong Kong*,[37] Lord Woolf said that:

> "the fact that the issue has to be determined objectively, judged at the date the contract was made, does not mean that what actually happened subsequently is irrelevant. On the contrary it can provide valuable evidence as to what could reasonably be expected to be the loss at the time the contract was made."

3.   Sum must be Payable on Breach

A sum of money which is payable otherwise than on breach of contract cannot be a penalty, unless the same clause governs events some of which are, and some of which are not, breaches.

It is of the essence of a penalty that it is payable upon breach of contract.[38] Many **17.15** clauses give one party to the contract an option of terminating, or in some cases prolonging, the contract on payment of an additional sum. Such a sum is not a penalty but the price of the option. So in *Associated Distributors Ltd v Hall*,[39] a contract for the hire of a tandem gave the hirer the option to terminate the hiring by returning the goods. The agreement also entitled the owner to terminate the hiring in the event of default by the hirer. A clause provided that in the event of the termination of the agreement the hirer was to pay "by way of compensation for

---

[33] *Azimut-Benetti SpA v Healey* [2010] EWHC 2234 (Comm); [2011] 1 Lloyd's Rep. 473, following dicta in *Murray v Leisureplay Plc* [2005] EWCA Civ 963; [2005] I.R.L.R. 946.

[34] See *Cavendish Square Holdings BV v Makdessi* [2015] UKSC 67; [2016] A.C. 1172 at [28].

[35] [2015] UKSC 67; [2016] A.C. 1172 at [99].

[36] *Unaoil Ltd v Leighton Offshore Pte Ltd* [2014] EWHC 2965 (Comm).

[37] [1993] 61 B.L.R. 41.

[38] *Cavendish Square Holdings BV v Makdessi* [2015] UKSC 67; [2016] A.C. 1172. Using a footballing metaphor, judges have described the "penalty area" as a "narrow field": see *Bernstein (Philip) (Successors) Ltd v Lydiate Textiles Ltd* [1962] C.A.T. 238; *Edgeworth Capital (Luxembourg) SARL v Ramblas Investments BV* [2015] EWHC 150 (Comm).

[39] [1938] 2 K.B. 83.

depreciation" a sum which, together with previous payments, would equal half of the total amount payable under the agreement. The hirer terminated the agreement by returning the tandem. It was held that the owners were entitled to the "compensation". Slesser LJ, reversing the county court judge, said:

> "he evidently did not regard the fact that the particular case we have here to consider was a case of payment with the exercise of an option. It follows in this case that no question of penalty or liquidated damage arises at all, and therefore the money for which the hirer has made himself liable must be paid and the claim cannot be impeached on any principle of law."

17.16   In *Office of Fair Trading v Abbey National Plc*,[40] Andrew Smith J said:

> "Undoubtedly the law about penalties does not apply if the obligation is to pay for a service or upon an event other than a breach, even if the service supplied or the event takes place against the background of or accompanied by a contractual breach, and even if the service would not have been provided or the event would not have occurred but for the breach. A customer could not necessarily invoke the law about penalties to challenge charges payable for his bank lending him money simply because his account would not be overdrawn but for his own breach. If an obligation to pay is penal, it must require payment upon the breach itself."

Thus a clause in a contract which provided for a guaranteed minimum revenue stream was a primary obligation and hence could not be within the rules relating to penalties.[41]

17.17   The same approach is taken where the sum is payable, not on the exercise of an option, but merely on the occurrence of a specified event which does not involve breach of contract by the payer. Thus in *ECGD v Universal Oil Products Co*,[42] A agreed to build a refinery. Finance was provided by B and guaranteed by C. A and C entered into an agreement under which A undertook to reimburse C for any payments made by C to B. A defaulted under the finance agreement with B, and consequently C's guarantee was called on. C sought reimbursement from A, who alleged that the agreement was a penalty. The allegation failed. Slade LJ posed the question in the following way:

> "whether the doctrine of penalties is capable of applying in a case where the terms of a contract between A and B provide that A is to pay a stated sum in the event of non-performance by A of one or more of the contractual obligations owed by A not to B himself but to a third party, C."

The question was answered in the negative. This approach was approved in the House of Lords where Lord Roskill said that:

> "The clause was not a penalty clause because it provided for payment of money on the happening of a specified event other than a breach of a contractual duty by the contemplated payer to the contemplated payee."

---

[40]   [2008] EWHC 2325 (Comm).
[41]   *Associated British Ports v Ferryways NV* [2008] 2 Lloyd's Rep. 353 (not challenged on appeal: [2009] EWCA Civ 189).
[42]   [1983] 2 All E.R. 205. See also *Edgeworth Capital (Luxembourg) SARL v Ramblas Investments BV* [2015] EWHC 150 (Comm).

Thus, in *Lehman Brothers Special Financing Inc v Carlton Communications Ltd*,[43] a clause in an agreement relating to interest swaps suspended obligations to pay in the event of the payee becoming insolvent. It was held that the clause was not a penalty. Briggs J said: **17.18**

> "I acknowledge that, in an appropriate case, a contractual provision for the withholding of monies otherwise due may be analysed as a penalty[44] ... In the present case however, not only is the withholding of payment triggered by an event not constituting a breach of contract, it is also a provision operating even-handedly as between the parties, so that either may rely upon it when there is a continuing Event of Default affecting the other party. The circumstances are as far removed from oppression as could be imagined."

However, in *Braes of Doune Windfarm (Scotland) Ltd v Alfred McAlpine Business Services Ltd*,[45] Akenhead J held that a clause was a penalty because it had the effect of subjecting one party to a liability to pay damages for loss or damage caused by someone else.

In *Jervis v Harris*,[46] a lease contained a clause which entitled the landlord to enter   **17.19**
the property and to carry out repairs which the tenant ought to have carried out in conformity with his covenants and then to recover the cost of the repairs from the tenant. Although the tenant's breach of his own repairing obligations was the occasion that gave rise to the landlord's right to enter to repair, the sum of money was not payable on the tenant's breach, but in consequence of the landlord having first expended the money on repairs. This was one reason why it was held that the nature of the sum recoverable by the landlord was a debt, and hence it was not a penalty.

The effect of this principle is that the penalty rule may be avoided by careful   **17.20**
drafting.[47] Thus if, for example, the contract provides for a discount on early payment the penalty rule cannot apply. In *Cavendish Square Holdings BV v Makdessi*,[48] Lords Neuberger and Sumption said:

> "This means that in some cases the application of the penalty rule may depend on how the relevant obligation is framed in the instrument, ie whether as a conditional primary obligation or a secondary obligation providing a contractual alternative to damages at law. Thus, where a contract contains an obligation on one party to perform an act, and also provides that, if he does not perform it, he will pay the other party a specified sum of money, the obligation to pay the specified sum is a secondary obligation which is capable of being a penalty; but if the contract does not impose (expressly or impliedly) an obligation to perform the act, but simply provides that, if one party does not perform, he will pay the other party a specified sum, the obligation to pay the specified sum is a conditional primary obligation and cannot be a penalty."

"We would accept that the application of the penalty rule can still turn on ques-

---

43 [2011] EWHC 718 (Ch).
44 *Gilbert-Ash (Northern) Ltd v Modern Engineering (Bristol) Ltd* [1974] A.C. 689 at 723.
45 [2008] EWHC 426 (TCC).
46 [1996] Ch. 195 CA.
47 *Cavendish Square Holdings BV v Makdessi* [2015] UKSC 67 at [130] (Lord Mance) and [258] (Lord Hodge), although Lord Hodge considered that the concept of a disguised penalty might yet save the day.
48 [2015] UKSC 67; [2016] A.C. 1172 at [14] and [43].

tions of drafting, even where a realistic approach is taken to the substance of the transaction and not just its form."

Herbert v Salisbury and Yeovil Railway Co[49] is a striking example. Lord Romilly MR said:

"For instance it is quite clear that if a mortgagor agrees to pay 5 or 6 per cent interest, and the mortgagee agrees to take less, say 4 per cent if it is paid punctually, that is a perfectly good agreement; but if the mortgage interest is at 4 per cent, and there is an agreement that if it is not paid punctually, 5 or 6 per cent interest shall be paid, that is in the nature of a penalty which this court will relieve against."[50]

It may be thought that this is a triumph of form over substance.

17.21 The High Court of Australia has taken a different view on the need for a breach of contract. In *Andrews v Australia and New Zealand Banking Group Ltd*[51] they rejected the argument that a sum of money payable otherwise than on breach of contract cannot be a penalty. They considered the old law relating to conditions in bonds, and concluded that equity relieved against penalties for non-performance of conditions, even where there was no contractual obligation to satisfy the condition.[52] However the Supreme Court has expressly rejected this approach and has reaffirmed the view that the question of penalty is only engaged where the detriment arises as a result of a breach of a primary obligation of the contract. Relief against forfeiture in equity is a quite different exercise despite the fact that the rule against penalties and relief against forfeiture have common historical origins. Whereas the rule against penalties regulates the remedies available for breach of contract, leaving the parties' primary obligations untouched, equitable relief against forfeiture enables the court to impose substantive terms as a condition of relief.[53]

17.22 In *Paciocco v Australia and New Zealand Banking Group Ltd*,[54] the High Court of Australia adhered to its view that it was not necessary to attract the penalty doctrine that the sum had to be payable on breach of a primary obligation of the contract. Gageler J said that the Supreme Court in *Cavendish Square Holding BV v Makdessi*[55] were wrong (or at least had misunderstood the effect of the common law of Australia) in saying that the High Court had made a radical departure from the previous understanding of the law. On the question before the court however, which was the enforceability of late payment fees in a banking contract, the law was the same in both jurisdictions. Their Honours held that the essence of a penalty clause was to punish breach rather than to protect the injured party's legitimate interests, and to that extent disagreed with Lord Radcliffe that to describe a penalty clause as held over one party in terrorem added nothing to the analysis. Their

---

[49] (1866) L.R. 2 Eq. 221.
[50] It is not entirely clear whether Lord Romilly was invoking the penalty rule or the equitable jurisdiction to relieve against forfeiture.
[51] [2012] HCA 30. See Davies and Turner, *"Relief against penalties without a breach of contract"* [2013] C.L.J. 20.
[52] The author unsuccessfully advanced this argument to the Court of Appeal in *Jervis v Harris* [1996] Ch. 195. It has now been conclusively rejected by the Supreme Court: *Cavendish Square Holdings BV v Makdessi* [2015] UKSC 67; [2016] A.C. 1172.
[53] *Cavendish Square Holdings BV v Makdessi* [2015] UKSC 67; [2016] A.C. 1172.
[54] [2016] HCA 28.
[55] [2015] UKSC 67; [2016] A.C. 1172.

Honours all discussed the tests propounded by Lord Dunedin in *Dunlop Pneumatic Tyre Co Ltd v New Garage and Motor Co Ltd*.[56] Kiefel J said:

"The distinction drawn by Lord Dunedin between liquidated damages and a penalty, whilst useful, should not be understood as a limiting rule. It does not mean that if no pre-estimate is made at the time a contract is entered into, as is the case here, a sum stipulated will be a penalty. Nor does it mean that a sum reflecting, or attempting to reflect, other kinds of loss or damage to a party's interests beyond those directly caused by the breach will be a penalty."

In *Edgeworth Capital (Luxembourg) SARL v Ramblas Investments BV*[57] the Court **17.23** of Appeal held, following *Cavendish Square Holding BV v Makdessi*,[58] as they were bound to do, that a sum payable on the happening of a specified event rather than on breach of contract was not a penalty. Thus in *Vivienne Westwood v Conduit Street*,[59] Fancourt J described the question whether the sum in question was payable on breach as the "threshold question".

Illustrations

1.   A contract for the sale of goods f.o.b. provided for all carrying charges at loading incurred due to late arrival and/or late nomination of the vessel to be for the buyers' account. The contract also entitled the buyers to claim an extension of the shipping period. In that event the buyers were to make payments to the seller on a graduated scale. It was held that since there was provision for an extension, the supply of a ship during the extended period would not constitute a breach of contract, and consequently the liability to make the payments could not be a penalty.
Gonzalez (Thomas P) Corp v Waring (FR) (International) Pty Ltd[60]

2.   A contract for the sale of goods f.o.b. provided that if the buyers did not tender a vessel within the contractual loading period they would be in default. The buyers had a right to extend the delivery period by notice. In either event the buyers would have to pay carrying charges at a stipulated rate. Notice was duly given. It was held that the payments were the price of an option, and no question of penalty arose.
Fratelli Moretti SpA v Nidera Handelscompagnie BV[61]

3.   Dealers had agreed with a finance company for commission to procure offers from hirers to enter into hire purchase agreements with the finance company. They also agreed that if the hirers defaulted under the agreements they would pay the finance company an amount equal to any unreceived payments of hire due under

56 [1915] A.C. 79.
57 [2016] EWCA Civ 412; [2017] 1 All E.R. (Comm) 577. See also *Hayfin Opal Luxco 3 SARL v Windermere VII Cmbs Plc* [2016] EWHC 782 (Ch); [2018] 1 B.C.L.C. 118.
58 [2015] UKSC 67; [2016] A.C. 1172.
59 [2017] EWHC 350 (Ch); [2017] L. & T.R. 23.
60 [1980] 2 Lloyd's Rep. 160.
61 [1981] 2 Lloyd's Rep. 47.

the agreements. It was held that the clause was not capable of being a penalty clause.

Bernstein (Philip) (Successors) Ltd v Lydiate Textiles Ltd[62]

4. A house owner sold his house on terms that the buyer leased it back to him. The purchase price was payable as to 70 per cent on completion of the sale and as to the remaining 30 per cent on the expiry of 10 years and his giving up possession. The tenancy agreement said that if the landlords terminated the tenancy under a contractual right to do so, the former owner would not receive the final payment. It was held that that term was not a penalty because there was no sum payable on breach.

UK Housing Alliance (North West) Ltd v Francis[63]

5. A liquidated damages clause in a construction contract provided for sectional completion of the project. It did not amount to a penalty, even though delay in completing one section had a knock-on effect on completion of the remaining sections of the project, with the result that liquidated damages would be payable for late completion of those sections even if there was no further delay. The builder's delay in completing the first section was the cause of the delay in completing the remaining sections, and it was fair that he should pay liquidated damages in respect of all sections.

Liberty Mercian Ltd v Dean & Dyball Construction Ltd[64]

4. SUM PAYABLE ON BREACH AND OTHER EVENTS

Where a sum is payable on the occurrence of a number of events, one or more of which is a breach of contract by the payer, the sum is capable of being a penalty in circumstances in which it in fact becomes payable by virtue of the breach.

17.24 Many contracts provide for a sum to be payable on termination of the contract, and also provide for the circumstances in which the contract is determinable. Usually it will be determinable upon breach of contract by one or both parties. It may also be determinable in circumstances which have nothing to do with breach of contract (e.g. at the option of a party or on the death or bankruptcy of a party). The stipulated sum will be contractually payable whichever of the events results in the termination of the contract. Does the fact that the sum is payable in the event of a breach make it potentially a penalty, and if so does that taint it for termination on other grounds?

17.25 A difficulty which has been felt by some judges is that of consistent treatment of the same sum. Thus the view has been expressed that:

"if [a sum] is not a penalty for all purposes and in all relations, as, for instance, when the hirer brings it upon himself by exercising his option to terminate, it can-

---

[62] [1962] C.A.T. 238, reported sub nom. *Sterling Industries Facilities Ltd v Lydiate Textiles Ltd* (1962) 106 S.J. 669.
[63] [2010] EWCA Civ 117.
[64] [2009] 06 E.G. 102.

not be a penalty in any one situation, as, for instance, when the owner is suing for damages for breach of the hiring obligations."[65]

So in *Elsey & Co Ltd v Hyde*,[66] a hire purchase agreement provided for the payment of a sum by the hirer in the event of termination of the agreement. The agreement could be terminated by the return of the goods by the hirer, or on breach of contract by the hirer. Slater J said:

"It appears to me to be a strange conclusion, if this money is to be regarded as a penalty, where it was payable in one event, and not regarded as a penalty where it was payable in another event. I think, therefore, as it is to my mind not a penalty where it is payable on the return of the article by the hirer, it ought not to be regarded as a penalty where it was payable on the retaking of the article by the owner."

This is logically attractive, but probably erroneous. The reasoning was disapproved by the majority of the Court of Appeal in *Cooden Engineering Co Ltd v Stanford*.[67] Thus in *Bridge v Campbell Discount Co Ltd*,[68] Lord Radcliffe said: **17.26**

"A sum of money sued for in one set of circumstances, as on a hirer's breach, when alone the 'in terrorem' idea can have any application, may be a penalty in the eyes of the law without it being necessarily anything but the price of an option in another set of circumstances or a mere guarantee in another."

On this approach the court treats such a clause as applying severally to the various circumstances in which it can be brought into play, and analyses each one separately. The Law Lords were, however, divided on the question whether this approach was correct. Viscount Simonds was prepared to treat the clause as being of several application,[69] as was Lord Morton of Henryton.[70] Lord Denning, however, held that the court had a wide jurisdiction to relieve against "minimum payment" clauses, irrespective of the circumstances which brought the clause into play.[71] Lord Devlin held that since the clause was a sham in the case of termination for breach, it could not be valid in the case of termination by option.[72] **17.27**

It is submitted that the approach which treats the clause as being of several application is correct, for not only does it give effect to the express terms of the bargain so far as possible, but it also displays a more pragmatic attitude to the contract. **17.28**

So in *Associated Distributors Ltd v Hall*,[73] the hire purchase agreement provided for the payment of a sum by the hirer in the event of termination of the agreement. The agreement was in fact terminated by the exercise of an option to terminate by

---

[65] *Bridge v Campbell Discount Co Ltd* [1962] A.C. 600, per Lord Radcliffe.
[66] (1926) unreported, but cited in *Cooden Engineering Co Ltd v Stanford* [1953] 1 Q.B. 86.
[67] [1953] 1 Q.B. 86, approved by the House of Lords in *Bridge v Campbell Discount Co Ltd* [1962] A.C. 600.
[68] [1962] A.C. 600.
[69] [1962] A.C. 600 at 613.
[70] [1962] A.C. 600 at 614.
[71] [1962] A.C. 600 at 631. Lord Denning's view has not found favour; see *ECGD v Universal Oil Products Co* [1983] 2 All E.R. 205, citing *Bernstein (Philip) (Successors) Ltd v Lydiate Textiles Ltd* [1962] C.A.T. 238.
[72] [1962] A.C. 600 at 634.
[73] [1938] 2 K.B. 83; see para.17.15.

the hirer. The Court of Appeal held that the contractual sum payable was not a penalty, but left open the question whether it would have been if the agreement had been terminated by the owner on the ground of the hirer's default.

17.29   Accordingly, the better view seems to be that where a sum is contractually payable on the happening of a number of events, including a breach of contract by the payer, the sum is capable of being a penalty when the circumstances giving rise to payment are the breach of contract, but not when the circumstances giving rise to payment are otherwise.[74]

5.   TERMINOLOGY NOT DECISIVE

The fact that a sum of money payable on breach of contract is described by the contract as "liquidated damages" or "penalty" is relevant to but not decisive of its proper categorisation.

17.30   In *Dunlop Pneumatic Tyre Co Ltd v New Garage and Motor Co Ltd*,[75] Lord Dunedin said:

> "Though the parties to a contract who use the words 'penalty' or 'liquidated damages' may prima facie be supposed to mean what they say, yet the expression used is not conclusive. The Court must find out whether the payment stipulated is in truth a penalty or liquidated damages."

In *Tullett Prebon Group Ltd v El-Hajjali*,[76] Nelson J said:

> "The fact that the parties state that the clause is not a penalty clause and the fact that they are of equal bargaining power are not decisive factors but they are certainly relevant to the consideration of the court."

In *Cavendish Square Holdings BV v Makdessi*,[77] Lords Neuberger and Sumption said:

> "The classification of terms for the purpose of the penalty rule depends on the substance of the term and not on its form or on the label which the parties have chosen to attach to it."

17.31   In *Law v Local Board of Redditch*,[78] a building contract provided that in the event of non-completion of the work by a certain date the contractor was to "forfeit and pay" a certain sum to be recoverable "as and for liquidated damages". Lord Esher MR said:

> "Then the contract goes on to say that the sums so forfeited may be recovered

---

[74]   The statement in the text that where a sum is contractually payable on the happening of a number of events, including a breach of contract by the payer, the sum is capable of being a penalty when the circumstances giving rise to payment are the breach of contract, but not when the circumstances giving rise to payment are otherwise approved in *Office of Fair Trading v Abbey National Plc* [2008] EWHC 2325 (Comm) and *Maple Leaf Macro Volatility Master Fund v Rouvroy* [2009] 1 Lloyd's Rep. 475 at 518. See also *Lehman Brothers Special Financing Inc v Carlton Communications Ltd* [2011] EWHC 718 (Ch) where Briggs J reached the same conclusion.

[75]   [1915] A.C. 79.

[76]   [2008] I.R.L.R. 760.

[77]   [2015] UKSC 67.

[78]   [1892] 1 Q.B. 127.

'as and for liquidated damages'. I do not think much reliance ought to be placed on those words, for, even if the sums were called penalties, the same considerations might be applicable; but I do not think that they ought to be left out of account altogether. It seems to me that they go somewhat to shew that the parties intended that these sums should be liquidated damages and not penalties."[79]

Equally, however, where the clause itself uses the word "penalty", the court must determine whether the stipulated sum really is a penalty or is a genuine pre-estimate of loss. So in *Clydebank Engineering and Shipbuilding Co Ltd v Yzquierdo y Castaneda*,[80] the Spanish government entered into a contract for the building of four torpedo boats. The contract provided that "the penalty for late delivery" was to be £500 per week per vessel. The House of Lords held that the sum was to be regarded as liquidated damages. Similarly, in *Webster v Bosanquet*,[81] Lord Mersey said: **17.32**

"... whatever be the expression used in the contract in describing the payment, the question must always be whether the construction contended for renders the agreement unconscionable and extravagant and one which no Court ought to allow to be enforced."

Since the terminology used by the parties prima facie characterises the payment, it must follow that some sort of onus rests upon the party who seeks to challenge the contractual terminology. Thus in *Robophone Facilities Ltd v Blank*,[82] Diplock LJ said: **17.33**

"The onus of showing that such a stipulation is a 'penalty clause' lies on the party who is sued on it."

In *GPP Big Field LLP v Solar EPC Solutions SL*,[83] a clause described both as a penalty and as delay, damages were held not to amount to a penalty.   **17.34**

In *Brown's Bay Resort Ltd v Pozzoni*,[84] a lease of a restaurant and bar in a tourist resort contained a clause which stated: **17.35**

"Failure to respect every aspect of this contract could result in an interruption of the contract by either the owner or the tenant. If an interruption occurs then the party responsible will pay to the other party a penalty fee of US$4,000.00."

The Privy Council held that this was not a liquidated damages clause, which had the effect of barring the tenant's claim for damages for breach of contract. They did not have to decide whether it was an unenforceable penalty.

Illustrations

1.   A hire purchase agreement provided that on termination the hirer was to pay such sum as, together with previous payments, would amount to two-thirds of the

---

[79] In *Commissioner of Public Works v Hills* [1906] A.C. 368, it was pointed out by the Privy Council that a clause which provided for "forfeited" sums to be recoverable as "liquidated damages" was self-contradictory, since the word "forfeited" was peculiarly appropriate to a penalty.
[80] [1905] A.C. 6.
[81] [1912] A.C. 394.
[82] [1966] 1 W.L.R. 1428.
[83] [2018] EWHC 2866 (Comm).
[84] [2016] UKPC 10.

hire purchase price. The payment was expressed to be "by way of agreed compensation for depreciation of the vehicle". It was held that since the amount of the payment was greater the earlier the determination, it could not have been genuinely for depreciation, and consequently, when the agreement was determined on account of the hirer's breach, the sum was a penalty and irrecoverable.
Bridge v Campbell Discount Co Ltd[85]

2. A charterparty contained a clause which provided "penalty for non-performance of this agreement proved damages, not exceeding estimated amount of freight". It was held that the clause was a penalty clause, one "excellent reason" being that it was so called.
Wall v Rederiaktiebolaget Luggude[86]

6. GENERAL APPROACH TO CATEGORISATION

Since liquidated damages clauses serve the useful purpose of avoiding litigation and promoting commercial certainty, the court should not be astute to categorise as penalties clauses described as liquidated damages clauses.

17.36   In a negotiated contract between properly advised parties of comparable bargaining power, there is a strong initial presumption that the parties themselves are the best judges of what is legitimate in a provision dealing with the consequences of breach.[87]

17.37   In *Robophone Facilities Ltd v Blank*,[88] Diplock LJ said:

"It is good business sense that parties to a contract should know what will be the financial consequences to them of a breach on their part, for circumstances may arise when further performance of the contract may involve them in loss. And the more difficult it is likely to prove and assess the loss which a party will suffer in the event of a breach, the greater the advantages to both parties of fixing by the terms of the contract itself an easily ascertainable sum to be paid in that event. Not only does it enable the parties to know in advance what their position will be if a breach occurs as to avoid litigation at all, but, if litigation cannot be avoided, it eliminates what may be the very heavy legal costs of proving the loss actually sustained which would have to be paid by the unsuccessful party. The court should not be astute to descry a 'penalty clause' in every provision of a contract which stipulates a sum to be payable by one party to the other in the event of a breach by the former."

17.38   Similarly, in *Elsey v JG Collins Insurance Agencies Ltd*,[89] Dickson J said:

"It is now evident that the power to strike down a penalty clause is a blatant

---

[85] [1962] A.C. 600.
[86] [1915] 3 K.B. 66, approved by the House of Lords in *Watts, Watts and Co Ltd v Mitsui and Co Ltd* [1917] A.C. 227.
[87] *Cavendish Square Holdings BV v Makdessi* [2015] UKSC 67; [2016] A.C. 1172 at [35]; *GPP Big Field LLP v Solar EPC Solutions SL* [2018] EWHC 2866 (Comm).
[88] [1966] 1 W.L.R. 1428, approved by the Supreme Court in *Cavendish Square Holdings BV v Makdessi* [2015] UKSC 67; [2016] A.C. 1172.
[89] (1978) 83 D.L.R. 15 (Supreme Court of Canada) approved in *Esanda Finance Corp Ltd v Plessnig* [1989] A.L.J. 238 (High Court of Australia) and *Phillips Hong Kong Ltd v Attorney-General of Hong Kong* (1993) 61 B.L.R. 41 PC.

interference with freedom of contract and is designed for the sole purpose of providing relief against oppression for the party having to pay the stipulated sum. It has no place where there is no oppression."

In *Phillips Hong Kong Ltd v Attorney-General of Hong Kong*,[90] Lord Woolf said:

"... the court has to be careful not to set too stringent a standard and bear in mind that what the parties have agreed should normally be upheld. Any other approach will lead to undesirable uncertainty especially in commercial contracts."

Likewise, in *Murray v Leisureplay Plc*,[91] Buxton LJ said that: **17.39**

"at least in connexion with commercial contracts, great caution should be exercised before striking down a clause as penal."

In *Meretz Investments NV v ACP Ltd*,[92] Lewison J said:

"To characterise a clause as a penalty, with the consequence that the court will refuse to enforce it, is a blatant interference with freedom of contract, and should normally be reserved for cases of oppression. There is, in my judgment, nothing inherently oppressive in a contractual term which has the effect of precluding one party to the contract from continuing to enjoy benefits under the contract at a time when he is not adhering to his own obligations."

This part of his judgment was upheld on appeal.[93]

Where the parties are of unequal bargaining power that fact may be taken into   **17.40**
account in deciding whether a clause is a penalty.

In *Makdessi v Cavendish Square Holdings BV*,[94] Christopher Clarke LJ said that:

"iii)   The court will not be astute to find that a clause contained in a commercial contract is unenforceable because it is penal, especially if the parties are of equal bargaining power and have had high level legal advice. The court recognises the utility of liquidated damages clauses and that to hold them to be penal is an interference with freedom of contract. It is, therefore, predisposed to uphold clauses which fix the damages for breach ...

iv)   To that end it will adopt a robust approach. If the likely loss is within a range, an average figure or a figure somewhere within the range is likely to be acceptable. If the loss is difficult to assess a figure which is not outrageous may well be acceptable. A pre-estimate does not have to be right to be reasonable ... The fact that it may result in overpayment is not fatal and the parties are allowed a generous margin. Further the fact that a breach may give rise to trifling or substantial damage may not be determinative if the parties can be regarded as having regarded the trifling as unlikely;

---

[90] (1993) 61 B.L.R. 41 PC; *Lansat Shipping Co Ltd v Glencore Grain BV* [2009] EWCA Civ 855.
[91] [2005] I.R.L.R. 946.
[92] [2007] Ch. 197.
[93] [2008] Ch. 244.
[94] [2013] EWCA Civ 1539, reversed on the facts [2015] UKSC 67; [2016] A.C. 1172. It is thought that this statement of principle remains correct where the injured party's legitimate interest does not extend beyond compensation for the breach. See also *Imam-Sadeque v Bluebay Asset Management (Services) Ltd* [2012] EWHC 3511 (QB).

v) But the fact that the clause has been agreed between parties of equal bargaining power who have competent advice cannot be determinative. The question whether a clause is penal habitually arises in commercial contracts, which enjoy no immunity from the doctrine."

17.41 Accordingly, a liquidated damages clause will not be construed with the same strictness as an exemption clause, or even a limitation of liability clause. The reason for the difference of approach is that a liquidated damages clause prescribes the amount recoverable, whether the true measure of loss is greater or smaller than the amount prescribed.[95] In *Diestal v Stevenson*,[96] a contract for the sale of coal prescribed payment of one shilling for every ton of coal not delivered. The buyer was held to this and not allowed to claim damages for the greater loss actually caused by the seller's non-delivery. Similarly, in *Talley v Wolsey-Neech*,[97] the vendor under a sale and purchase agreement sought to recover lost interest but failed as he was held entitled only to recover the liquidated damages as defined by the relevant clause. A liquidated damages clause therefore has benefits for both parties to the contract, rather than being one-sided in its protection.[98]

17.42 The court does sometimes employ other techniques in order to validate a clause. In *Wallis v Smith*,[99] parties entered into a contract for the sale of a development estate for £70,000. The buyer was to pay a deposit of £5,000, £500 of which was to be paid on execution of the contract, and the balance within seven months. The agreement provided that if the buyer committed a substantial breach of the contract the deposit of £5,000 should be forfeited; and if it had not been paid the buyer should pay £5,000 as liquidated damages. The court upheld the clause by construing it as being inapplicable to the obligation to pay the first instalment of the deposit and by emphasising the expression "serious breach".

17.43 A different technique was employed in *Alder v Moore*.[100] A professional footballer was insured against disablement. He was injured and received a payment from the insurers. Under the terms of the policy no claim was to be paid unless the claimant signed a declaration that he would not take part in playing professional football in the future and that in the event of infringement he would forfeit the amount of the paid claim. The claimant signed a document stating that "I hereby declare and agree that I will take no part as a playing member of any form of professional football in the future and that in the event of infringement of this condition I will be subject to a penalty of the amount stated above". The Court of Appeal, by a majority, held that no contractual obligation was created by the words "I agree", and that consequently the sum was simply a sum payable on the happening of an event not involving a breach of contract. Accordingly, it was not capable of being a penalty.

---

[95] *Cellulose Acetate Silk Co Ltd v Widnes Foundry (1925) Ltd* [1933] A.C. 20.
[96] [1906] 2 K.B. 345.
[97] (1978) 38 P. & C.R. 45.
[98] *Suisse Atlantique Societe D'Armement Maritime SA v Rotterdamsche Kolen Centrale* [1967] 1 A.C. 361, per Lord Upjohn, discussing a demurrage clause.
[99] (1882) 21 Ch. D. 243.
[100] [1961] 2 Q.B. 57.

7. Protection of Legitimate Interest

A clause which imposes a detriment on a contract-breaker which is not out of proportion to any legitimate interest of the injured party in securing performance of the contract will not be a penalty. The legitimate interests capable of protection in this way are not restricted to compensation for loss.

The traditional view, heavily influenced by Lord Dunedin's speech in *Dunlop Pneumatic Tyre Co Ltd v New Garage and Motor Co Ltd*,[101] was that there was a dichotomy between clauses which were genuine pre-estimates of damage and penalty clauses. He proposed four tests which acquired the status of a quasi-statutory code and were treated as being of almost immutable rules of general application.[102] These tests, which are discussed below, are adequate to deal with more or less standard clauses in consumer contracts, but a broader approach is required in the case of many other contracts. This rigid dichotomy has now been abandoned. **17.44**

In *Cavendish Square Holdings BV v Makdessi*,[103] Lords Neuberger and Sumption said: **17.45**

"The real question when a contractual provision is challenged as a penalty is whether it is penal, not whether it is a pre-estimate of loss. These are not natural opposites or mutually exclusive categories. A damages clause may be neither or both. The fact that the clause is not a pre-estimate of loss does not therefore, at any rate without more, mean that it is penal."[104]

As they pointed out[105]:

"A damages clause may properly be justified by some other consideration than the desire to recover compensation for a breach. This must depend on whether the innocent party has a legitimate interest in performance extending beyond the prospect of pecuniary compensation flowing directly from the breach in question."

In the same case, Lord Mance said[106]:

"There may be interests beyond the compensatory which justify the imposition on a party in breach of an additional financial burden. The maintenance of a system of trade, which only functions if all trading partners adhere to it ... may itself be viewed in this light; so can terms of settlement which provide on default for payment of costs which a party was prepared to forego if the settlement was honoured ...; likewise, also the revision of financial terms to match circumstances disclosed or brought about by a breach ... What is necessary in each case is to consider, first, whether any (and if so what) legitimate business interest is served and protected by the clause, and, second, whether, assuming such an inter-

---

[101] [1915] A.C. 79.
[102] *Cavendish Square Holdings BV v Makdessi* [2015] UKSC 67 at [22] and [31].
[103] [2015] UKSC 67.
[104] [2015] UKSC 67 at [31].
[105] [2015] UKSC 67 at [28].
[106] [2015] UKSC 67 at [152].

est to exist, the provision made for the interest is nevertheless in the circumstances extravagant, exorbitant or unconscionable."

Lord Hodge said[107]:

"I therefore conclude that the correct test for a penalty is whether the sum or remedy stipulated as a consequence of a breach of contract is exorbitant or unconscionable when regard is had to the innocent party's interest in the performance of the contract. Where the test is to be applied to a clause fixing the level of damages to be paid on breach, an extravagant disproportion between the stipulated sum and the highest level of damages that could possibly arise from the breach would amount to a penalty and thus be unenforceable. In other circumstances the contractual provision that applies on breach is measured against the interest of the innocent party which is protected by the contract and the court asks whether the remedy is exorbitant or unconscionable."

17.46   Accordingly the object and purpose of the rule against penalties is vindicated if one considers whether the agreed sum is commensurate with the interest protected by the bargain.[108] A detriment imposed upon the contract-breaker will be a penalty if it is extravagant, exorbitant or unconscionable in its nature and impact.[109] The imposition of a higher rate of interest following a default in payment protects a legitimate interest, because a defaulter is a greater credit risk and money is more expensive for a less good credit risk than for a good credit risk.[110] By contrast, where contractual arrangements required the tenant of commercial property to pay a higher rent following any non-trivial breach of covenant, the requirement went beyond the landlord's legitimate interest in having a tenant which performed its obligations and maintaining the investment value of the property.[111]

17.47   In *127 Hobson Street Ltd v Honey Bees Preschool Ltd*,[112] the Supreme Court of New Zealand, having considered both English and Australian cases said:

"The test to be applied is as follows. A clause stipulating a consequence for breach of a term of the contract will be an unenforceable penalty if the consequence is out of all proportion to the legitimate interests of the innocent party in performance of the primary obligation. When we refer in this judgment to legitimate interests in performance, that includes an interest in enforcing performance or some appropriate alternative to performance. A consequence will be out of all proportion if the consequence can fairly be described as exorbitant when compared with those legitimate interests."

17.48   Although it is clear that a legitimate interest in performance goes beyond monetary compensation for loss caused by the breach, the concept itself was not defined by the Supreme Court.[113] In *127 Hobson Street Ltd v Honey Bees Preschool*

---

107 [2015] UKSC 67 at [255], endorsed by Lord Toulson at [293].
108 *Paciocco v Australia and New Zealand Banking Group Ltd* [2015] FCAFC 50, approved in *Cavendish Square Holdings BV v Makdessi* [2015] UKSC 67 at [152].
109 *Cavendish Square Holdings BV v Makdessi* [2015] UKSC 67 at [181].
110 *Cargill International Trading Pte Ltd v Uttam Galva Steels Ltd [2019] EWHC 476 (Comm)* at [48].
111 *Vivienne Westwood Ltd v Conduit Street Development Ltd* [2017] EWHC 350 (Ch); [2017] L. & T.R. 23.
112 [2020] NZSC 53.
113 The question is discussed in Rowan, "The 'legitimate interest in performance' in the law on penal-

Ltd,[114] the Supreme Court of New Zealand discussed that question. They held that a legitimate interest can extend to the broader impact of non-performance on the commercial interests the parties seek to achieve through the contract; including a desire to deter breach; and the protection of way or system of conducting business of which the contract forms a part.

Where the injured party has no legitimate interest in performance of the contract **17.49** other than to be compensated for loss flowing from a breach of contract, Lord Dunedin's tests are still a valuable tool. As Lords Neuberger and Sumption said[115]:

> "In the case of a straightforward damages clause, that interest will rarely extend beyond compensation for the breach, and we therefore expect that Lord Dunedin's four tests would usually be perfectly adequate to determine its validity."

Where a clause is categorised as a liquidated damages clause, the scope of the **17.50** clause is a question of interpretation of the particular contract. Different approaches to the effect on termination of the contract on the recoverability of liquidated damages for delay were considered by Sir Rupert Jackson in *Triple Point Technology Inc v PTT Public Co Ltd*.[116] He said:

> "In cases where the contractor fails to complete and a second contractor steps in, three different approaches have emerged to clauses providing liquidated damages for delay:
>
> (i) The clause does not apply;[117]
> (ii) The clause only applies up to termination of the first contract;[118]
> (iii) The clause continues to apply until the second contractor achieves completion.[119]"

Ultimately the question turns on the wording of the particular clause. One question that will arise is whether the purpose of the clause is limited to liquidating damages for delay in completion, or whether it also liquidates damage for failure to complete at all.

---

ties" [2019] C.L.J. 148.

[114] [2020] NZSC 53.

[115] [2015] UKSC 67 at [32].

[116] [2019] EWCA Civ 230; [2019] 1 W.L.R. 3549 (permission to appeal to the Supreme Court has been granted). See also McKendrick, "Liquidated damages, delay and the termination of contracts" [2019] J.B.L. 577; Peel, "Liquidated damages and termination" [2019] L.Q.R. 530.

[117] *British Glanzstoff Manufacturing Co Ltd v General Accident, Fire and Life Assurance Corpn Ltd* [1913] A.C. 143; *Chanthall Investments Ltd v FG Minter Ltd* 1976 SC 73; *Gibbs v Tomlinson* (1992) 35 Con. L.R. 86.

[118] *Greenore Port Ltd v Technical & General Guarantee Co Ltd* [2006] EWHC 3119 (TCC); *Shaw v MFP Foundations and Pilings Ltd* [2010] EWHC 1839 (TCC); *LW Infrastructure Pte Ltd v Lim Chin San Contractors Pte Ltd* [2012] B.L.R. 13; *Bluewater Energy Services BV v Mercon Steel Structures BV* (2014) 155 Con. L.R. 85.

[119] *Hall v Van der Heiden* [2010] EWHC 586 (TCC); *GPP Big Field LLP v Solar EPC Solutions SL* [2018] EWHC 2866 (Comm).

Illustrations

1.　On the sale of shares in a business the seller entered into a number of restrictive covenants to protect the goodwill of the business. The contract provided that on breach the seller would not be entitled to receive further payments for his shareholding, and could be required to transfer his remaining shares at net asset value. Those clauses did not amount to a penalty because the buyer had a legitimate interest in protecting the goodwill of the business, and the loyalty of the seller.
Cavendish Square Holdings BV v Makdessi[120]

2.　A motorist had a contractual licence to park in a car park. The first two hours were free, but any overstayer was liable to a payment of £85. The payment was not a penalty because the payment protected legitimate interests of the car park operator which included providing sufficient monies out of which to provide the first two hours' free parking.
ParkingEye Ltd v Beavis[121]

3.　An obligation imposed on a contractor under an engineering and construction contract to pay delay damages set at a specified sum per day was not an unenforceable penalty clause. The sum was no greater than a genuine estimate of the loss which the employer would suffer from the breach, and the employer had a legitimate interest in ensuring timely performance.
GPP Big Field LLP v Solar EPC Solutions SL[122]

4.　A company's articles of association contained "bad leaver" provisions, which required a bad leaver to transfer his shares at either 75 per cent of the fair value of the shares, or par or subscription value, whichever was less. It was held that the company had a legitimate interest in in the faithful and diligent performance by the shareholders of their duties as employees and/or directors of group companies which might properly be protected by differential pricing of their shares in the event of their premature withdrawal as a consequence of fraud or gross misconduct.
Gray v Braid Group (Holdings) Ltd[123]

8.　SUM PAYABLE EXTRAVAGANT AND UNCONSCIONABLE

Where the injured party's legitimate interest does not extend beyond compensation for a breach, a sum payable on breach of contract will be held to be a penalty if it is extravagant and unconscionable in amount in comparison with the greatest loss which could possibly flow from the breach.

17.51　　In *Dunlop Pneumatic Tyre Co Ltd v New Garage and Motor Co Ltd*,[124] Lord Dunedin identified a number of tests to assist in determining the question of construction whether a clause was a penalty clause or not.[125] These tests are likely

---

[120]　[2015] UKSC 67.
[121]　[2015] UKSC 67; [2016] A.C. 1172.
[122]　[2018] EWHC 2866 (Comm).
[123]　[2016] CSIH 68; 2017 S.C. 409 (by majority); *Richards v IP Solutions Group Ltd* [2016] EWHC 1835 (QB).
[124]　[1915] A.C. 79.
[125]　In *Ringrow Pty Ltd v BP Australia Pty Ltd* (2005) 222 A.L.R. 306, the High Court of Australia as-

to be adequate to determine whether a clause is a penalty in cases where the injured party's legitimate interests do not go beyond compensation for the breach.[126] However, like all such judge-made tests, they should not be applied as if they were a statute. The first test is:

"It will be held to be a penalty if the sum stipulated for is extravagant and unconscionable in amount in comparison with the greatest loss that could conceivably be proved to have followed from the breach."

17.52 Thus if a builder agrees to build a house in a year, and agrees that if he does not build the house for £50, he will pay £1 million, "the extravagance of that would be at once apparent".[127] However, Lord Radcliffe pointed out in *Bridge v Campbell Discount Co Ltd*[128] that:

"'Unconscionable' must not be taken to be a panacea for adjusting any contract between competent persons when it shows a rough edge to one side or the other ..."

The word is:

"merely a synonym for something which is extravagant or exorbitant."[129]

In *Paciocco v Australia and New Zealand Banking Group Ltd*,[130] 130 Kiefel J pointed out that:

"... 'extravagant', 'exorbitant' and 'unconscionable' are 'strong words'; despite the different expressions used, they all describe the plainly excessive nature of the stipulation in comparison with the interest sought to be protected by that stipulation."

She went on to say that it was not enough that the sum in question was merely "disproportionate".
In the same case Keane J said:

"Only in cases where gross disproportion is such as to point to a predominant punitive purpose have agreed payments payable on breach of contract been struck down as penalties."

17.53 There must be a degree of disproportion sufficient to point to oppressiveness.[131] Thus, in *Phillips Hong Kong Ltd v Attorney-General of Hong Kong*,[132] Lord Woolf said:

---

sumed that Lord Dunedin's tests continued to represent Australian law.
[126] *Cavendish Square Holdings BV v Makdessi* [2015] UKSC 67.
[127] *Clydebank Engineering and Shipbuilding Co Ltd v Yzquierdo y Castaneda* [1905] A.C. 6 at 10, per Lord Halsbury LC.
[128] [1962] A.C. 600 at 626.
[129] *Imperial Tobacco Co (of Great Britain and Northern Ireland) Ltd v Parslay* [1936] 2 All E.R. 515 at 521, per Lord Wright MR.
[130] [2016] HCA 28.
[131] *Ringrow Pty Ltd v BP Australia Pty Ltd* (2005) 222 A.L.R. 306.
[132] (1993) 61 B.L.R. 41 PC.

"Except possibly in the case of a situation where one of the parties is able to dominate the other as to the choice of the terms of a contract, it will normally be insufficient to establish that a provision is objectively penal to identify situations where the application of the provision could result in a larger sum being recovered by the injured party than his actual loss. Even in such situations so long as the sum payable is not extravagant, having regard to the range of losses that it could reasonably be anticipated it would have to cover at the time the contract was made, it can still be a genuine pre-estimate of the loss that would be suffered and so a perfectly valid liquidated damages provision. The use in argument of unlikely illustrations should therefore not assist a party to defeat a provision as to liquidated damages."

In *Alfred McAlpine Capital Projects Ltd v Tilebox Ltd*,[133] Jackson J said:

"There seem to be two strands in the authorities. In some cases judges consider whether there is an unconscionable or extravagant disproportion between the damages stipulated in the contract and the true amount of damages likely to be suffered. In other cases the courts consider whether the level of damages stipulated was reasonable."

17.54   Whether a sum is extravagant or exorbitant in this sense must be decided objectively. In *Hayfin Opal Luxco 3 SARL v Windermere VII Cmbs Plc*,[134] Snowden J said:

"... the penalty doctrine does not depend upon whether it is subjectively intended to, or does, provide a deterrent to the particular contract-breaker, but must be founded upon objective reference to some norm. Accordingly, the penalty doctrine focuses on the lack of proportionality between the amount of the secondary liability imposed and the innocent party's legitimate interest in performance of the primary obligation. Whether a clause is a penalty cannot therefore depend upon the ability of the particular contract-breaker to pay the specified amount, or the source from which he is to pay. An innocent party cannot save a clause from being a penalty by claiming that even though it provides for payment of a wholly disproportionate amount to the interest which he (the innocent party) has in performance, the contract-breaker is so rich that he will not notice the difference. Nor can he do so by promising to limit his claim to specified funds in the hands of the contract-breaker, if the available amount of those funds would still be capable of paying a wholly disproportionate amount, and payment might deprive the contract-breaker of the ability to pay debts due to other creditors with lower priority."

In *Vivienne Westwood v Conduit Street*,[135] Fancourt J said:

"in considering whether a contractual stipulation is or is not a penalty, one must address first the threshold issue: is a stipulation in substance a secondary obligation engaged upon breach of a primary contractual obligation; then identify the

---

[133] [2005] B.L.R. 271.
[134] [2016] EWHC 782 (Ch).
[135] [2017] EWHC 350 (Ch); [2017] L. & T.R. 23. See also *Holyoake v Candy* [2017] EWHC 3397 (Ch); *Cargill International Trading Pte Ltd v Uttam Galva Steels Ltd* [2019] EWHC 476 (Comm).

extent and nature of the legitimate interest of the promisee in having the primary
obligation performed, and then determine whether or not, having regard to that
legitimate interest, the secondary obligation is exorbitant or unconscionable in
amount or in its effect."

Whether the contractual function is penal rather than compensatory can be   **17.55**
deduced in the first instance by comparing the amount that would be payable on
breach with the loss that might be sustained if the breach occurred.[136] In looking at
the greatest loss which could flow from the breach one is not confined to loss which
would be recoverable in an action for damages. Recoverable damages are limited
by the rules of remoteness of damage, and loss which may have been caused by a
breach may be irrecoverable as being too remote. This problem may be overcome
by a liquidated damages clause. In *Robophone Facilities Ltd v Blank*,[137] Diplock LJ
said:

"... if at the time of the contract the plaintiff informs the defendant that his loss
in the event of a particular breach is likely to be £X by describing this sum as
liquidated damages in the terms of his offer to contract, and the defendant
expressly undertakes to pay £X to the plaintiff in the event of such breach, the
clause which contains the stipulation is not a 'penalty clause' unless £X is not a
genuine and reasonable estimate by the plaintiff of the loss which he will in fact
be likely to sustain. Such a clause is, in my view, enforceable, whether or not the
defendant knows what are the special circumstances which make the loss likely
to be £X rather than some lesser sum which it would be in the ordinary course
of things."

Lord Dunedin's test refers to the greatest loss which could "conceivably" flow   **17.56**
from the breach. Likewise, in *Cavendish Square Holdings BV v Makdessi*,[138] Lord
Hodge said:

"Where the test is to be applied to a clause fixing the level of damages to be paid
on breach, an extravagant disproportion between the stipulated sum and the highest level of damages that could possibly arise from the breach would amount to
a penalty and thus be unenforceable."

Similarly, in *Tullett Prebon Group Ltd v El-Hajjali*,[139] Nelson J said:

"For my part I consider that in most cases it will only be where a clause can be
shown to be extravagant and unconscionable in relation to the greatest conceivable loss that a clause will properly be found to be a penalty clause though each
case will depend upon its own individual circumstances and will have to be
determined on its own facts."

It might be thought, however, that this is too generous a test since it first involves   **17.57**
considering not what loss is likely to flow from the breach but what loss could possibly or conceivably flow from it; and then allows a generous margin by asking

---

[136] *Lordsvale Finance Plc v Bank of Zambia* [1996] Q.B. 752.
[137] [1966] 1 W.L.R. 1428.
[138] [2015] UKSC 67; [2016] A.C. 1172 at [255].
[139] [2008] I.R.L.R. 760.

whether the stipulated sum is extravagant or unconscionable in relation to that greatest conceivable loss.

17.58   In *Imperial Tobacco Co (of Great Britain and Northern Ireland) Ltd v Parslay*,[140] Lord Wright MR said that the "relevant disproportion" was that:

"between the stipulated sum and the possible or probable amount of the damage."

In *Alfred MacAlpine Capital Projects Ltd v Tilebox*,[141] Jackson J said:

"There must be a substantial discrepancy between the level of damages stipulated in the contract and the level of damages which is likely to be suffered before it can be said that the agreed pre-estimate is unreasonable."

He also added that:

"Although many authorities use or echo the phrase 'genuine pre-estimate', the test does not turn upon the genuineness or honesty of the party or parties who made the pre-estimate. The test is primarily an objective one, even though the court has some regard to the thought processes of the parties at the time of contracting."

These observations were followed in *General Trading Co (Holdings) Ltd v Richmond Corp Ltd*.[142]

17.59   In *BNP Paribas v Wockhardt EU Operations (Swiss) AG*,[143] Christopher Clarke J held that a clause that required payment of sums accrued due under a contract together with a sum equivalent to loss of bargain was not a penalty.

In *Coden Engineering Co Ltd v Stanford*,[144] a hire purchase agreement relating to a car provided that if the owners repossessed the car, the hirer was to pay all the outstanding instalments of hire which would have been payable if the agreement had not been terminated. The clause was held to impose a penalty. Somervell LJ said:

"Although it cannot be said that the amount exceeds the greatest loss that could possibly follow on the breach ... it will exceed it in all except the exceptional case where the car has become of no value."

Jenkins LJ[145] said:

"It is, of course, possible to imagine a case in which before repossession by the owners the value of the car had been reduced to nothing ... but apart from that exceptional case, which I think can for the present purpose reasonably be ignored, it seems that the sum payable under clause 11 ... must always exceed ... any damage to the owners which could flow from any breach of contract by the hirer on which a determination by the owners under clause 11 might be founded. Therefore ignoring the exceptional and improbable case I have mentioned, I think

---

[140] [1936] 2 All E.R. 515 at 521.
[141] [2005] B.L.R. 271.
[142] [2008] 2 Lloyd's Rep. 475.
[143] [2009] EWHC 3116 (Comm).
[144] [1953] 1 Q.B. 86.
[145] In a dissenting judgment (though not on this point).

the sum payable on determination under clause 11 can, in point of amount, fairly be brought within the intention though not strictly within the letter of the first test of a penalty given by Lord Dunedin …".

It appears, therefore, that in considering what loss might flow from a breach, **17.60** exceptional cases must be ignored. However, it is submitted that other improbable losses ought not to be ignored, since probable losses would be recoverable as damages by action, and a liquidated damages clause may legitimately extend the recoverability of damages in the sense of extending damages to areas of genuine loss which the court would find too "remote". As Lord Sumption explained in *Bunge SA v Nidera BV*[146]:

"… damages clauses are commonly intended to avoid disputes about damages, either by prescribing a fixed measure of loss (as in the case of a liquidated damages clause) or by a providing a mechanical formula in place of the more nuanced and fact-sensitive approach of the common law (as in cl.20 of GAFTA 49). In either case, it is inherent in the clause that it may produce a different result from the common law. For that reason there can be no scope for a presumption that the parties intended the clause to produce the same measure of damages as the compensatory principle would produce at common law. The mere fact that in some cases its application will over-or under-estimate the injured party's loss is nothing to the point. Such clauses necessarily assume that the parties are willing to take the rough with the smooth. However, I would accept a more moderate version of [the] presumption. A damages clause may be assumed, in the absence of clear words, not to have been intended to operate arbitrarily, for example by producing a result unrelated to anything which the parties can reasonably have expected to approximate to the true loss."

He added:

"… such clauses are not necessarily to be regarded as complete codes for the assessment of damages. A damages clause, like any other contractual provision, is conclusive of the matters with which it deals. It may also implicitly exclude considerations which, although not directly within its scope, cannot be applied consistently with its terms. But it is a question of construction whether the mere fact that it deals with damages means that it must have been intended to do so exhaustively, thereby impliedly excluding any considerations which it has not expressly addressed. To treat a damages clause as a complete code in this all-embracing sense is to tax the foresight of the draftsman in a way which is rarely appropriate unless the alternative is to undermine the coherence or utility of the clause."

There are three other cases in which a liquidated damages clause may **17.61** legitimately provide for a measure of damages greater than the loss which might be expected to flow from a particular breach. First, in *Dunlop Pneumatic Tyre Co Ltd v New Garage and Motor Co Ltd*,[147] Lord Parker of Waddington said:

---

[146] [2015] UKSC 43; [2015] Bus. L.R. 987.
[147] [1915] A.C. 79 at 99.

"Supposing it were recited in the agreement that the parties had estimated the probable damage from breach of one stipulation at from £5 to £15, and the probable damage from a breach of another stipulation at £2 to £12 and had agreed on a sum of £8 as a reasonable sum to be paid on the breach of either stipulation, I cannot think that the Court would refuse to give effect to the bargain between the parties."

17.62 The second case is where the damages are impossible to estimate with any accuracy. Thus as Lord Halsbury LC observed in *Clydebank Engineering and Shipbuilding Co Ltd v Yzquierdo y Castaneda*[148]:

"The very reason why the parties do in fact agree to such a stipulation is that sometimes, although undoubtedly there is damage and undoubtedly damages ought to be recovered, the nature of the damage is such that proof of it is extremely complex, difficult and expensive."

And Lord Dunedin himself said[149]:

"It is no obstacle to the sum stipulated being a genuine pre-estimate of damage, that the consequences of the breach are such as to make precise pre-estimation almost an impossibility. On the contrary, that is just the situation when it is probable that pre-estimated damage was the true bargain between the parties."

As Lord Mance put it in *Cavendish Square Holdings BV v Makdessi*[150]:

"The impossibility of measuring loss from any particular breach is a reason for upholding, not for striking down, such a provision."

17.63 The third case, as already discussed, is where the clause protects a legitimate interest of the injured party in securing performance of the contract in addition to being compensated for the particular breach.[151] In *Cine Bes Filmcilik Ve Yapim Click v United International Pictures*,[152] Mance LJ said that:

"a dichotomy between a genuine pre-estimate of damages and a penalty does not necessarily cover all the possibilities.[153] There are clauses which may operate on breach, but which fall into neither category, and they may be commercially perfectly justifiable."

Whether a detriment imposed on a contract-breaker on breach of contract is commercially justifiable on the ground that the injured party has a legitimate interest in performance of the contract beyond mere compensation for the breach is now set to be the touchstone of validity of the clause.

17.64 The customary non-returnable deposit of 10 per cent of the purchase price paid

---

[148] [1904] A.C. 6 at 11.
[149] In *Dunlop Pneumatic Tyre Co Ltd v New Garage and Motor Co Ltd* [1915] A.C. 79 at 87.
[150] [2015] UKSC 67; [2016] A.C. 1172 at [143].
[151] *Cavendish Square Holdings BV v Makdessi* [2015] UKSC 67; [2016] A.C. 1172.
[152] [2004] 1 C.L.C. 401.
[153] In *Murray v Leisureplay Plc* [2005] I.R.L.R. 946, Buxton LJ thought that they did. It is thought that the view expressed by Mance LJ is the better one.

under a contract for the sale of land may fall into this category,[154] as may a reasonable increase in the rate of interest payable in case of default,[155] unless the rate of interest itself has no legitimate justification.[156]

It appears that the court will not intervene where the stipulated sum is clearly less than the damage likely to be suffered. In *Temloc Ltd v Erill Properties Ltd*,[157] developers entered into a contract with builders on the JCT form. The form included a clause requiring the contractors to pay liquidated damages for delay at a rate stated in the Appendix to the contract. The Appendix, as filled in, stated that the rate was to be "£ nil". The developers argued that this had the effect of excluding the liquidated damages clause from the contract leaving damages for delay at large. The Court of Appeal rejected this argument and held that the parties had quantified the damage as nil and that consequently no damages for delay were recoverable.   **17.65**

A liquidated damages clause (if valid) operates in substitution for a general assessment of the claimant's losses caused by delay. It does not enable the wronged party to recover compensation for the same losses twice over.[158]   **17.66**

Illustrations

1.   A contract for the engagement of an actor required the actor to conform to the regulations of the theatre. He was to be paid £3.6s.8d. for each night. The agreement provided that if either party failed to comply with the agreement or any part thereof he should pay to the other the sum of £1,000 as liquidated damages. It was held that the sum was a penalty.
   Kemble v Farren[159]

2.   An agreement provided for the sale of household furniture and stock in trade at a valuation. It further provided that if either party did not comply with the agreement "in every particular" he should forfeit and pay the sum of £50. A breach might have been the non-payment of the purchase money or the non-delivery of a very small portion of the goods. It was held that the sum was a penalty.
   Betts v Burch[160]

3.   An agreement entitled one of the parties to deposit mineral refuse on certain land, and obliged him to level and soil the land within a stipulated time. The agreement provided that if the work was not completed in accordance with the contract, a payment was to be made at the rate of £100 per acre for all ground unrestored. The sum was held to be liquidated damages.
   Lord Elphinstone v Monkland Iron and Coal Co Ltd[161]

4.   A hire purchase agreement relating to a juke box provided for payments to be made by the hirer in the event of termination, including a payment for

---

[154] See *Workers Trust & Merchant Bank Ltd v Dojap Investments Ltd* [1993] A.C. 573 PC.
[155] *Lordsvale Finance Plc v Bank of Zambia* [1996] Q.B. 752.
[156] *Cargill International Trading Pte Ltd v Uttam Galva Steels Ltd* [2019] EWHC 476 (Comm).
[157] (1987) 39 Build. L.R. 30.
[158] *Triple Point Technology Inc v PTT Public Co Ltd* [2019] EWCA Civ 230; [2019] 1 W.L.R. 3549 (permission to appeal to the Supreme Court has been granted).
[159] (1829) 6 Bing. 141.
[160] (1859) 4 H. & N. 506.
[161] (1886) 11 App. Cas. 332.

depreciation. Arithmetically the effect of the agreement was that the owners would receive more than the total amount of hire if the agreement was terminated in the first eight months, and thereafter the charge for depreciation was progressively reduced until it vanished in the eighteenth month. The sum was held not to be a penalty.

Phonographic Equipment (1958) Ltd v Muslu[162]

5.   A charterparty provided that in the event of late redelivery, if market rates had risen in the meantime, the charter would be liable to pay at the increased rate as from 30 days before the last day for redelivery. It was held that the clause amounted to a penalty, because the ordinary measure of damages for late redelivery would not have required the charter to pay the increased rate earlier than the last day for redelivery.

Lansat Shipping Co Ltd v Glencore Grain BV[163]

9.   SUM PAYABLE ON BREACH OF CONTRACT TO PAY MONEY

Where a sum is payable on a breach of contract to pay money, it will be a penalty if the sum payable on breach is greater than the sum which ought to have been paid under the contract. This does not, however, prohibit a requirement to pay interest at a reasonable rate.

17.67   Lord Dunedin's second test[164] is:

"It will be held to be a penalty if the breach consists only in not paying a sum of money, and the sum stipulated is a sum greater than the sum which ought to have been paid."

So also in *Kemble v Farren*,[165] Tindal CJ said:

"But that a very large sum should become immediately payable, in consequence of the non-payment of a very small sum, and that the former should not be considered as a penalty, appears to be a contradiction in terms …".

17.68   Although this proposition was accepted as representing the law in *Wallis v Smith*,[166] Jessel MR questioned its rationale. He said:

"It has always appeared to me that the doctrine of the English law as to non-payment of money—the general rule being that you cannot recover damages because it is not paid by a certain day, is not quite consistent with reason. A man may be utterly ruined by the non-payment of a sum of money on a given day, the damages may be enormous, and the other party may be wealthy. However that is our law. If, however, it were not our law the absurdity would be apparent. I see no reason apart from our law why a man may not stipulate 'You shall pay me £500 on a given day.' It maybe of almost vital importance to him. He may have

---

[162]   [1961] 1 W.L.R. 1379.

[163]   [2009] EWCA Civ 855.

[164]   *Dunlop Pneumatic Tyre Co Ltd v New Garage and Motor Co Ltd* [1915] A.C. 79 at 87. This test is a corollary to the first test.

[165]   (1829) 6 Bing. 141.

[166]   (1882) 21 Ch. D. 243 at 257.

to deposit it as security for the granting of concessions of enormous value, and the other party may know it. He may have to make a payment on a stamp for a most valuable patent, and the other party may know that he relies upon it. It is not unreasonable, as it appears to me, in those cases to say, 'If you do not pay the £500, or it may be £50, on that date you shall pay £5,000 for the damage I shall sustain.'"

The common law rule as to the recovery of damages for non-payment of money was also said by Lord Dunedin to be one possible foundation for his second test. However, in recent times the foundation has become weakened, since it is now possible to recover special damages for non-payment or late payment of money, and such damages are not limited to interest on the principal sum.[167] In addition, given the flexibility of the new test of "legitimate interest in performance", it may be that Lord Dunedin's second test should now be qualified, at least to the extent that in the circumstances he mentions, there is a rebuttable presumption that the stipulated sum is a penalty.   **17.69**

In *Nutting v Baldwin*,[168] names at Lloyd's formed an association to prosecute claims for negligence. The rules of the association required each name to pay subscriptions to finance the litigation. The rules also provided that if any name did not pay his subscription, the committee of the association could declare him to be a defaulting member, in which case he was excluded from the fruits of the litigation. Rattee J held that this did not amount to a penalty because it was an essential part of the arrangement that both claims and the costs of prosecuting the claims should be pooled. This appears to be a case in which Lord Dunedin's second test was not applied, but outflanked.   **17.70**

Illustrations

1. A contract between a football club and a supplier for the supply of replica kit provided that if the club were late in paying, they had to pay interest at 5 per cent per week. If the suppliers were late in delivering, they had to pay 20 pence per garment per day. The interest rate was equivalent to 260 per cent per annum. It was held that the requirement to pay interest was a penalty.
Jeancharm Ltd v Barnet Football Club Ltd[169]

2. A loan agreement was provided for an uplift of 1 per cent for late payment of a debt. That was held to be a genuine pre-estimate of loss on the basis that it indicated that the borrower was a risky borrower.
Lordvale Finance Plc v Bank of Zambia[170]

---

[167] *Wadsworth v Lydell* [1981] 1 W.L.R. 598, approved by the House of Lords in *President of India v La Pintada Cia Navegacion SA* [1985] A.C. 104. In an age of inflation some real loss will almost inevitably flow from the late payment of money for the payment of the same nominal sum at a date later than that contracted for will be worth less in real terms.

[168] [1995] 1 W.L.R. 201.

[169] [2003] EWCA Civ 58.

[170] [1996] Q.B. 752.

10.   ACCELERATED PAYMENT

A clause will not generally be construed as a penalty clause where it provides for the whole of a debt payable in instalments to become due on failure to pay one or more instalments on time.

17.71   Although it is a general principle of construction that payment of a sum of money is a penalty when it is payable on breach of an obligation to make a smaller payment, this is not so where the sum to be paid is part of a larger outstanding debt.[171]

17.72   The essence of a penalty is that it is a payment which is made upon a breach of contract. What distinguishes the cases of accelerated payment is that the whole debt is already outstanding and that payment of the whole amount of the debt must be made whether or not there is a breach of obligation. So in *Wallingford v Mutual Society*,[172] Lord Selborne LC said:

> "The real matter seems to stand thus. These mortgage bonds were given to secure the £6,000, which sum was treated as advanced, although money did not pass, and also the premiums, which would become due by instalments according to the rules of the society; and the payment of which under those rules was liable to be accelerated, if any of the instalments was not punctually paid. I cannot think that such an acceleration of payments has anything in common with a penalty. It was a contract for certain payments which were *debita in praesenti* although *solvendo in futuro* …".

Similarly, in *Protector Endowment Loan and Annuity Co v Grice*,[173] Cockburn CJ said:

> "The clauses in question in the present case were essential parts of the contract; it is an agreement for a discharge by quarterly instalments of the whole debt, but if there is a failure to perform the agreement, a condition is inserted that the whole amount shall become payable at once; it is not merely a mode of securing payment of the instalments. If the payment of an additional sum of money is mentioned only for the purpose of inducing persons to fulfil their contract, it is not to be literally enforced in a court of justice; but here it was contemplated that the terms of the contract should be fulfilled, and we do not doubt that it was intended that the whole amount should become due upon non-payment of an instalment."

17.73   However, in *Wadham Stringer Finance Ltd v Meaney*,[174] Woolf J held that where an accelerated payment clause comes into operation as the result of a breach of contract, it is capable of being a penalty. It is not clear by what process of reasoning he reached this conclusion.

In order to fall within this exception, the court must be satisfied that the debt is genuinely due before the acceleration of its payment. In *O'Dea v Allstates Leasing System (WA) Pty Ltd*,[175] a leasing agreement for a commercial vehicle provided

---

[171] This principle was applied in *Hunt v Kallinicos* [2009] NSWCA 5.
[172] (1880) 5 App. Cas. 685.
[173] (1880) 5 Q.B.D. 592.
[174] [1981] 1 W.L.R. 39.
[175] (1983) 152 C.L.R. 359.

that the entire rent was due to the lessor on signing the agreement, with the proviso that if the lessees observed all their obligations under the lease, the rent could be paid by monthly instalments. After a few months the lessors repossessed the vehicle and claimed the difference between the instalments paid by the lessees and the whole rent. The High Court of Australia held that the accelerated payment clause was a penalty.

Where a debt is replaced by a smaller debt, but the original debt revives if the smaller debt is not paid, that will not amount to a penalty. In *Thompson v Hudson*,[176] Lord Westbury said:

"A penalty is a punishment, an infliction, for not doing, or for doing something; but if a man submits to receive, at a future time and on the default of his debtor, that which he is now entitled to receive, it is impossible to understand how that can be regarded as a penalty."

So in *Lloyd's v Twinn*,[177] Scott VC said:

"A contractual provision the effect of which is that a debtor who owes, say, £1,000 may discharge his liability if he pays £500 by a specified date but if he does not do so must pay the £1,000 is not a penalty provision. If the substance of a contractual provision is as described it does not matter in the least that the contractual provision takes a form under which, first, the liability to pay £1,000 is replaced by a liability to pay £500, second, the £500 is to be paid by a specified date and, third, if the debtor fails to pay the £500 by that date his liability to pay the £1,000 revives. In considering whether a provision is a penalty, the law will look to the substance, not to the form."

11.   SUM PAYABLE FOR BREACH OF MORE THAN ONE OBLIGATION

Where the injured party's legitimate interest does not extend beyond compensation for a breach there is a presumption that a stipulated sum is a penalty where it is made payable on the occurrence of one or more of several breaches, some of which may cause serious damage and others insignificant damage.

Originally it appears to have been a relatively inflexible rule that where a single sum was payable on more than one breach of contract, it was a penalty. Thus in *Astley v Weldon*,[178] Heath J said: 17.74

"Where articles contain covenants for the performance of several things, and then one large sum is stated at the end to be paid upon breach of performance, that must be considered to be a penalty. But where it is agreed that if a party do a particular thing, such a sum shall be paid by him, there the sum may be treated as liquidated damages."

This inflexible approach no longer prevails. In *Lord Elphinstone v Monkland Iron*   17.75

---

[176]   (1869) 4 H.L. 1.
[177]   (2000) 97(15) L.S.G. 40.
[178]   (1801) 2 B. & P. 346, followed in *Kemble v Farren* (1829) 6 Bing. 141.

and Coal Co Ltd,[179] Lord Watson said:

"When a single slump [*sic*] sum is made payable by way of compensation, on the occurrence of one or more of all of several events, some of which may occasion serious and others but trifling damage, the presumption is that the parties intended the sum to be penal, and subject to modification."

Lord Herschell LC also drew attention to the fact that:

"The agreement does not provide for the payment of a lump sum upon the non-performance of anyone of many obligations differing in importance."

Lord Watson's formulation was adopted by Lord Dunedin as his third test[180]:

"There is a presumption (but no more) that it is a penalty when 'a single lump sum is made payable by way of compensation, on the occurrence of one or more of several events, some of which may occasion serious and others but trifling damage.'"

17.76   In *Willson v Love*,[181] Lord Esher MR said that Lord Watson's formulation meant the same thing as if it had read "some of which may occasion serious and others less serious damage". However, this reading was disapproved in *Dunlop Pneumatic Tyre Co Ltd v New Garage and Motor Co Ltd*,[182] in which Lord Atkinson pointed out that:

"this alteration would mean that the damage resulting from each event should be almost uniform in amount, a construction which would mean that the stipulated compensation must presumably be a penalty in almost every conceivable case."[183]

In the *Dunlop* case,[184] Lord Parker of Waddington drew a further distinction between:

"cases in which the damage likely to accrue from each stipulation is the same in kind and cases in which the damage likely to accrue varies in kind with each stipulation."

17.77   In the former case it seems that he would not have regarded any presumption as arising, whereas in the latter case there would be a rebuttable presumption that the sum was a penalty. The presumption may be rebutted where the damage caused by the various breaches is of such an uncertain nature that it cannot be accurately ascertained. As Lord Mance put it in *Cavendish Square Holdings BV v Makdessi*[185]:

---

[179] (1886) 11 App. Cas. 332.
[180] *Dunlop Pneumatic Tyre Co Ltd v New Garage and Motor Co Ltd* [1915] A.C. 79 at 87. Lord Dunedin abandoned Lord Watson's phrase "slump sum" in favour of the more familiar "lump sum".
[181] [1896] 1 Q.B. 626.
[182] [1915] A.C. 79 at 94.
[183] He added that Lord Watson's statement had been approved without the alteration in *Clydebank Engineering and Shipbuilding Co Ltd v Yzquierdo y Castaneda* [1905] A.C. 6 and *Webster v Bosanquet* [1912] A.C. 394.
[184] [1915] A.C. 79 at 98.
[185] [2015] UKSC 67; [2016] A.C. 1172 at [143].

"The impossibility of measuring loss from any particular breach is a reason for upholding, not for striking down, such a provision."

In such a case, however, the court must be satisfied that there is no question of extortion.[186] The presumption may also be rebutted where the stipulated amount varies according to the gravity of the breach:

17.78

"for instance, if you find that it is so much per acre for ground which has been spoilt by mining operations, or if you find, as in the present case, that it is so much per week during the whole time for which the non-delivery of vessels beyond the contract time is delayed—then you infer that prima facie the parties intended the amount to be liquidated damages and not penalty."[187]

In *Imam-Sadeque v Bluebay Asset Management (Services) Ltd*,[188] Popplewell J referred to the presumption that a clause is a penalty when a single lump sum is made payable by way of compensation, on the occurrence of one or more or all of several events, some of which may occasion serious and others but trifling damage. He continued:

17.79

"Nevertheless care must be taken not to elevate what is no more than a presumption into a rule, and so subvert the rationale behind the penalty doctrine. It is a presumption because in the circumstances described by Lord Dunedin in the passage quoted, the innocent party will often be able to recover his loss as damages for breach of contract, so that there is no injustice to him in rendering the clause unenforceable. The corollary is that where it is foreseeable that it may be impossible or difficult for the innocent party to recover his true loss as damages, the Court will more readily uphold the clause. ... Provided that the amount payable under the clause does not exceed the greatest loss which could realistically be suffered as a result of foreseeable breaches, this is in my view a powerful factor for upholding the clause, because in such cases depriving the innocent party of his bargain and confining him to his remedy in damages involves injustice to that party."

In *Cavendish Square Holdings BV v Makdessi*,[189] Christopher Clarke LJ said that:

17.80

"... the fact that the same sum is payable on different breaches of either the same stipulation, or different stipulations where the damage likely to arise from the breaches is of the same kind, may not save the clause. The fact that there is only one stipulation involved or that loss of the same kind may result from breaches of different stipulations may not tell you very much, because the breach and the loss resulting therefrom may vary very widely in character and extent. A similarity in kind may mask a myriad of differences. If the range of possible breaches and of likely losses from such breaches is large but, on a scale from 0 to 100, most cases would fall within the 30–70 range, a figure of 90 could be hard to

---

[186] [1915] A.C. 79 at 96, per Lord Atkinson and at 103, per Lord Parmoor.
[187] *Clydebank Engineering and Shipbuilding Co Ltd v Yzquierdo y Castaneda* [1905] A.C. 6 at 16, per Lord Davey. See also *Public Works Commissioner v Hills* [1906] A.C. 368 at 376, per Lord Dunedin.
[188] [2012] EWHC 3511 (QB).
[189] [2013] EWCA Civ 1539. Although this case was reversed by the Supreme Court at [2015] UKSC 67; [2016] A.C. 1172 it is thought that this statement of principle remains correct in cases where the injured party's legitimate interest does not extend beyond compensation for the breach of contract.

justify, particularly if one set of breaches could only fall in the 30–50 bracket. In the latter case a figure of 70 might be unjustifiable."

17.81   The presumption may be rebutted where the stipulated sum is payable only in the event of a serious breach.[190] Mindful of the consequences of striking down a clause as a penalty clause, the court will do its best to interpret a liquidated damages clause as applying only to serious breaches.[191]

Illustrations

1.   A manufacturer supplied products to dealers who undertook not to tamper with the marks on the goods, not to sell goods at less than the manufacturer's list prices, and not to supply persons whose supplies the manufacturer had decided to suspend, and to pay £5 as liquidated damages for every product sold in breach of the agreement. It was held that the payment was not a penalty.
Dunlop Pneumatic Tyre Co Ltd v New Garage and Motor Co Ltd[192]

2.   A manufacturer supplied motor cars to a dealer who undertook not to sell cars or parts below the manufacturer's list price, not to sell cars to other dealers and not to exhibit any car without the manufacturer's permission. He agreed to pay £250 for each breach of the agreement as "the agreed damage which the manufacturer will sustain". It was held that the sum was a penalty.
Ford Motor Co v Armstrong[193]

3.   An investor complained that his instructions had not been properly carried out by an online trading service. His complaint was settled by an agreement in which he was paid $40,000 and agreed not to make derogatory claims against the service. The agreement provided that he would be liable to refund the $40,000 if he committed any breach of the agreement. It was held that that provision was a penalty.
CMC Group Plc v Zhang[194]

12.   OBLIGATIONS TO TRANSFER PROPERTY

A clause which requires a contract-breaker to transfer property in the event of a breach of contract is subject to the penalty rule in the same way as an obligation to pay money in the event of a breach of contract.

17.82   In *Jobson v Johnson*[195] it was conceded that an obligation to transfer property at an undervalue fell within the ambit of the penalty rule. The correctness of this

---

[190]   *Wallis v Smith* (1882) 21 Ch. D. 243.
[191]   *Webster v Bosanquet* [1912] A.C. 394; *Cenargo Ltd v Izar Construcciones Navale SA* [2002] 2 C.L.C. 1151.
[192]   [1915] A.C. 79.
[193]   (1915) 31 T.L.R. 267. The difference between this case and *Dunlop's* case seems to lie only in the amount of the agreed payment.
[194]   [2006] EWCA Civ 408.
[195]   [1989] 1 W.L.R. 1026; *Else (1982) Ltd v Parkland Holdings Ltd* [1994] 1 B.C.L.C. 130.

concession has now been confirmed by the Supreme Court in *Cavendish Square Holdings BV v Makdessi*.[196] Lords Neuberger and Sumption said[197]:

"... it seems to us that there is no reason why an obligation to transfer assets (either for nothing or at an undervalue) should not be capable of constituting a penalty. While the penalty rule may be somewhat artificial, it would heighten its artificiality to no evident purpose if it were otherwise. Similarly, the fact that a sum is paid over by one party to the other party as a deposit, in the sense of some sort of surety for the first party's contractual performance, does not prevent the sum being a penalty, if the second party in due course forfeits the deposit in accordance with the contractual terms, following the first party's breach of contract."

Lord Hodge said[198]:

"... I see no reason in principle why the rule against penalties should not extend to clauses that require the contract-breaker to transfer property to the innocent party on breach."

Having considered previous cases he concluded[199]:

"I am satisfied therefore that the rule against penalties can be applied to a contractual term that provides for the transfer on breach of contract of property from the contract-breaker to the innocent party."

13. DEPOSITS

A clause providing for the forfeiture of a deposit will not be treated as a penalty provided that the deposit is a reasonable amount.

By custom there is an exception to the rule against penalties in the case of a deposit. A deposit is paid as an earnest of performance of a contract, and if the contract is completed the deposit is applied towards payment of the purchase price. If the contract is not completed the deposit is liable to forfeiture. The right to forfeit the deposit does not depend on the vendor showing that he has suffered any loss. **17.83**

In *Linggi Plantations Ltd v Jagatheesan*,[200] Lord Hailsham of St Marylebone said: **17.84**

"The truth is that a reasonable deposit has always been regarded as a guarantee of performance as well as a payment on account, and its forfeiture has never been regarded as a penalty in English law or common English usage."

In *Griffon Shipping LLC v Firodi Shipping Ltd*,[201] Teare J said of deposits:

[196] [2015] UKSC 67; [2016] A.C. 1172.
[197] [2015] UKSC 67; [2016] A.C. 1172 at [16]. Lord Mance appears to have reached the same conclusion.
[198] [2015] UKSC 67; [2016] A.C. 1172 at [230].
[199] [2015] UKSC 67 at [233].
[200] [1972] 1 M.L.J. 89 PC.
[201] [2013] EWHC 593 (Comm); [2013] 2 Lloyd's Rep. 50.

"I have noted the submission of counsel for the Buyers that the construction of the MOA favoured by the arbitration tribunal is consistent with commercial sense but am unable to accept it. The first part of the submission is that since deposits are an anomaly because they enable the innocent party to retain a sum in excess of its actual loss the court should not expand the scope and operation of a deposit. It is true that deposits enable a party to retain a sum in excess of its actual loss but that is in the nature of a deposit. The requirement to pay a deposit encourages the buyer to perform. 'It is a guarantee that the purchaser means business'.[202] The encouragement flows from the fact that the deposit may indeed exceed the seller's damages. The prevalent use of deposits in the sale of property, whether the property be real estate or ships, indicates that they have a real and accepted purpose. I do not regard that purpose as uncommercial or anomalous. The second part of the submission is that there is good commercial reason for the buyer paying loss of bargain damages where he fails to pay the deposit because the seller can immediately 'walk away and put the vessel back on the market' and will 'have probably lost relatively few opportunities' so that loss of bargain damages would be appropriate. However, as with the first part of the submission, this ignores the commercial purpose of deposits. Moreover, it has long been recognised that a deposit which has been paid will be forfeited if the buyer fails to perform even though the deposit exceeds the loss of bargain damages. In those circumstances there is, in my judgment, no commercial or business sense in permitting a buyer to improve his position by the simple expedient of not paying the deposit."

Teare J's decision was upheld on appeal.[203]

17.85 However, it is critical that the deposit is a reasonable amount. In *Workers Trust & Merchant Bank Ltd v Dojap Investments Ltd*,[204] Lord Browne-Wilkinson said:

"It is not possible for the parties to attach the incidents of a deposit to the payment of a sum of money unless such sum is reasonable as earnest money."

17.86 Whether a deposit is a reasonable sum is a question of fact. This question is to be decided objectively, and is not determined by the practice of a particular class of vendor. By long usage the customary deposit under a contract for the sale of land in the UK has been 10 per cent of the purchase price, and if a vendor alleges that a greater sum is reasonable, he must show special circumstances which justify that.[205]

However, it has been held in Australia that a contractual provision requiring a deposit of 5 per cent to be topped up to 10 per cent on the purchaser's default was void as being a penalty.[206]

17.87 Where it is sought to justify a deposit larger than the customary 10 per cent the justification must relate to the function of a deposit as an earnest of performance and as compensation for the vendor's withdrawal of his asset from the property market pending completion; and must provide an objective justification. The question is not whether the deposit represents a genuine pre-estimate of the vendor's

---

[202] See *Soper v Arnold* (1889) 14 App. Cas. 429 at 435, per Lord Macnaghten.

[203] [2013] EWCA Civ 1567; [2014] 1 Lloyd's Rep. 461.

[204] [1993] A.C. 573 PC.

[205] [1993] A.C. 573 PC. 10 per cent is also the conventional amount of a deposit in Hong Kong: *Polyset Ltd v Panhandat Ltd* (2002) 5 H.K.C.F.A.R. 234 (which contains a full review of the authorities).

[206] *Luu v Sovereign Developments Pty Ltd* [2006] NSWCA 40; *Iannello v Sharpe* [2007] NSWCA 61.

potential loss.[207] In *Cadogan Petroleum Holdings Ltd v Global Process Systems LLC*,[208] a contract for the sale of gas plants provided for payment in stages. However, property in the plants was to remain in the seller until payment in full. Eder J held that these instalments of the purchase price did not fall within the rules relating to deposits. He said that since the payments were not triggered by any breach of contract they could not fall within the principles applicable to penalties, and therefore the limitation on those principles laid down by the deposit cases could not apply.[209]

Surprisingly, it has also been held in Australia that where a deposit of 10 per cent **17.88** was payable in two instalments, the second to be paid on completion of the contract, the requirement to pay the second instalment was void as being a penalty.[210]

14.   RATES OF INTEREST

Where the rate of interest payable on a loan is liable to increase in the event of default by the borrower, the increased rate may be penal if it operates with retrospective effect or if the increase is exceptionally large. But where the increase is modest and operates prospectively, it will not be struck down as a penalty.

In the case of mortgages, it has been repeatedly held that a provision by which **17.89** the rate of interest payable increases in the event of a default by the borrower will be unenforceable as a penalty.[211] This was treated as settled law by the House of Lords in *Wallingford v Mutual Society*.[212] A distinction arose between a case in which a rate of interest was payable, but liable to be reduced in the event of punctual payment, and a case in which a rate of interest was payable but liable to increase in the event of default. The former case involved no penalty; the latter case did. In *Herbert v Salisbury and Yeovil Railway Co*,[213] Lord Romilly MR said:

> "For instance it is quite clear that if a mortgagor agrees to pay 5 or 6 per cent interest, and the mortgagee agrees to take less, say 4 per cent if it is paid punctually, that is a perfectly good agreement; but if the mortgage interest is at 4 per cent, and there is an agreement that if it is not paid punctually, 5 or 6 per cent interest shall be paid, that is in the nature of a penalty which this court will relieve against."[214]

It may be thought that this is a triumph of form over substance.

However, where the rate of interest was only liable to increase with prospective **17.90** effect, the increased rate was enforceable. In *Burton v Slattery*,[215] interest was pay-

---

[207] *Polyset Ltd v Panhandat Ltd* [2002] 5 H.K.C.F.A.R. 234.
[208] [2013] EWHC 214 (Comm); [2013] 2 Lloyd's Rep. 26.
[209] The judge also considered whether to grant relief against forfeiture and decided that he would not. The distinction between the penalty rule and relief against forfeiture was discussed by the Supreme Court in *Cavendish Square Holdings BV v Makdessi* [2015] UKSC 67.
[210] *Boyarsky v Taylor* [2008] NSWSC 1415.
[211] *Lady Holies v Wyse* (1693) 2 Vern. 289; *Strode v Parker* (1694) 2 Vern. 316.
[212] (1880) 5 App. Cas. 685.
[213] (1866) L.R. 2 Eq. 221.
[214] It is not entirely clear whether Lord Romilly was invoking the penalty rule or the equitable jurisdiction to relieve against forfeiture.
[215] (1725) 5 Bro. P.C. 233.

PENALTIES, TERMINATION AND FORFEITURE CLAUSES

able on a mortgage debt at the rate of 5 per cent, but if any instalment was not repaid, the rate was to increase to 8 per cent with effect from three months after the date of payment. The House of Lords held that the higher rate of interest was recoverable.

In *Herbert v Salisbury and Yeovil Railway Co*,[216] a purchaser was let into possession of land under a contract for sale. The contract provided for interest to be paid on the purchase price at the rate of 4 per cent up to the due date for payment and at the rate of 5 per cent thereafter, but if the price had not been paid within six months, the rate was to increase again to 8 per cent. Lord Romilly MR upheld the claim to interest at 8 per cent.

17.91   The authorities were reviewed by Colman J in *Lordsvale Finance Plc v Bank of Zambia*.[217] In that case a bank loan provided for the rate of interest to be increased by 1 per cent in the event of default by the borrower. He distinguished between cases where the rate of interest operated retrospectively (in which case the increase would be penal) and cases where it would operate prospectively. In the latter case, the increase is commercially justifiable as referable to the increased credit risk of the defaulting borrower, and will be upheld, provided that the increase is itself modest. It seems, however, that the modesty of the increase is not an essential factor, provided that it can be justified. In *Cargill International Trading Pte Ltd v Uttam Galva Steels Ltd*,[218] Bryan J upheld a default interest rate of LIBOR plus 12 per cent which, in the evidence, was the commercial norm for Indian companies in the steel industries comparable to Uttam.

17.92   Since many contracts differentiate between a rate of interest payable on default, and a rate of interest payable in other circumstances, the distinction is consonant with commercial practice. The justification for an increase in interest rates on default is that the credit risk is increased, and the costs of administering the loan may also increase.[219]

17.93   Where interest changes from simple interest to compound interest in the event of a default in payment, that may be an indication of a penalty.[220] If there is no legitimate justification for the rate of interest, that too may be an indication of a penalty.[221]

17.94   However, where a rate of interest is agreed between two commercial parties in the economic circumstances of the time, it should not lightly be set aside as amounting to a penalty.[222]

Illustrations

1.   A contract between a football club and a supplier for the supply of replica kit provided that if the club were late in paying, they had to pay interest at 5 per cent per week. If the suppliers were late in delivering, they had to pay 20 pence per

---

[216] (1866) L.R. 2 Eq. 221.
[217] [1996] Q.B. 752.
[218] [2019] EWHC 476 (Comm).
[219] *Cavendish Square Holdings BV v Makdessi* [2015] UKSC 67 at [148] (Lord Mance) and [222] (Lord Hodge); *Lombard North Central Plc v European Skyjets Ltd* [2020] EWHC 679 (QB) (5% default interest rate unlikely to be penal).
[220] *Donegal International Ltd v Republic of Zambia* [2007] 1 Lloyd's Rep. 397.
[221] *Cargill International Trading Pte Ltd v Uttam Galva Steels Ltd* [2019] EWHC 476 (Comm) (LIBOR plus 12% upheld).
[222] *Taiwan Scot Co Ltd v Masters Golf Co Ltd* [2009] EWCA Civ 685.

garment per day. The interest rate was equivalent to 260 per cent per annum. It was held that the requirement to pay interest was a penalty.

Jeancharm Ltd v Barnet Football Club Ltd[223]

2. A settlement agreement for the repayment of debt required repayment with interest at the rate of 6 per cent. However, it provided that upon default in repayment the interest would increase from 6 per cent to 8 per cent, and instead of being simple interest, would be compounded quarterly. It was held that the default interest provision was a penalty.

Donegal International Ltd v Republic of Zambia[224]

15. OPTIONS TO TERMINATE

An option to terminate is construed in the same manner as any other option, and accordingly any condition must be strictly complied with. But where the right of termination is unqualified, it will generally be exercisable in accordance with its terms.

Many contracts contain express provisions entitling one or both parties to bring the contract to an end. Common examples are break clauses in leases, withdrawal clauses in charterparties, a clause entitling a finance company to repossess goods and a vendor's right to terminate a contract for the sale of land.   **17.95**

The clause itself will not be strictly interpreted but any condition precedent to its exercise must be precisely fulfilled.[225] In *Mardorf Peach & Co Ltd v Attica Sea Carriers Corp of Liberia*,[226] Lord Wilberforce, contrasting a withdrawal clause in a charterparty and a forfeiture clause on a lease, nevertheless accepted that in the case of a charterparty: **17.96**

"the owner has to show that the conditions necessary to entitle him to withdraw have been strictly complied with."

So in *Afovos Shipping Co SA v Pagnan (R) and Lli (F)*,[227] a charterparty gave the owner the option of withdrawing the ship failing punctual and regular payment of the hire. However, before exercising the option, the owner was required to give 48 hours' notice. The House of Lords held that the notice could not be validly given before midnight on the day appointed for payment, even though it was in practice virtually impossible for the hire to have been paid after banking hours.   **17.97**

Similar principles apply to the interpretation of options to determine in leases. Almost all such options contain time limits within which the option must be exercised, and such time limits must be strictly complied with.[228] So also must any conditions relating to the performance of the tenant's covenants[229] or the forma-   **17.98**

---

[223] [2003] EWCA Civ 58.
[224] [2007] 1 Lloyd's Rep. 397.
[225] See paras 15.63and 16.105.
[226] [1977] A.C. 850 at 870. See also *Afovos Shipping Co SA v Pagnan (R) and Lli (F)* [1982] 1 W.L.R. 848, per Kerr LJ.
[227] [1983] 1 W.L.R. 195.
[228] *United Scientific Holdings Ltd v Burnley Borough Council* [1978] A.C. 904.
[229] *Grey v Friar* (1854) 4 H.L. Cas. 565; *Simons v Associated Furnishers Ltd* [1931] 1 Ch. 379.

tion by the landlord of a particular intention (e.g. to redevelop).[230] If the option requires notice to be given in a particular form, that too must be strictly complied with.[231]

17.99 In addition, the clause must be exercised strictly in accordance with its terms. So where a clause in a charterparty entitled the owners to withdraw the vessel failing punctual payment of hire, it was held that they could not withdraw the vessel temporarily. Either the vessel was withdrawn or it was not.[232]

17.100 Nevertheless, in interpreting an option to terminate the court will give effect to the business purpose of the clause, and will not uphold an interpretation which would have the effect of making the option illusory.[233] So where an option is conditional on the performance of covenants, a spent breach of covenant in respect of which there is no subsisting cause of action will not prevent the exercise of the option.[234] In *Parkinson v Barclays Bank Ltd*,[235] a lease for 21 years contained a clause entitling the landlord to terminate it at the expiry of the fourteenth year of the term if it required the premises for the purpose of the business carried on by it. The Court of Appeal held that it was sufficient if the landlord required some part of the premises at some time during the last seven years of the term, and that it was not necessary for the landlord to have an immediate requirement. The court's conclusion might have been different if the option had been exercisable at any time rather than at one fixed date. Cohen LJ said:

> "One principle of construction is that if of two constructions one gives business efficacy to a document, while the other leads to an improbable conclusion, the court must prefer the former. I think that this is essentially a case where that principle applies ...".

17.101 Applying this approach it has been held that an option to terminate a service contract was validly exercised even though the letter on which the validity of the exercise turned had been sent earlier than contemplated by the clause.[236]

17.102 It is important to distinguish between two types of condition that must be fulfilled. There may be substantive conditions, such as the giving of a notice by a certain date, or the occurrence of some event (e.g. breach of an obligation), or the existence of a state of affairs (e.g. compliance with obligations). These conditions must be fulfilled precisely. As Lord Hoffmann graphically put it in *Mannai Investment Co Ltd v Eagle Star Life Assurance Co Ltd*[237]:

> "If the clause had said that the notice had to be on blue paper, it would be no good serving a notice on pink paper, however clear it might have been that the tenant wanted to terminate the lease."[238]

---

[230] *IRC v Southend-on-Sea Estates Co Ltd* [1915] A.C 428.
[231] *Siemens Hearing Instruments Ltd v Friends Life Ltd* [2014] EWCA Civ 382; [2014] 2 P. & C.R. 95.
[232] *The Agios Giorgis* [1976] 2 Lloyd's Rep. 192; *The Mihalios Xilas* [1978] 1 W.L.R. 1257.
[233] It may be thought that in *Fitzhugh v Fitzhugh* [2012] EWCA Civ 694; [2012] 2 P. & C.R. 14 insufficient weight was given to this principle.
[234] *Bass Holdings Ltd v Morton Music Ltd* [1988] Ch. 493.
[235] [1951] 1 K.B. 368.
[236] *Ellis Tylin Ltd v Co-Operative Retail Services Ltd* [1999] B.L.R. 205. It is not entirely clear whether the court distinguished between the satisfaction of substantive conditions and the mere communication of information.
[237] [1997] A.C. 749. See also *Burman v Mount Cook Land Ltd* [2002] Ch. 256 CA.
[238] *Siemens Hearing Instruments Ltd v Friends Life Ltd* [2014] EWCA Civ 382; [2014] 2 P. & C.R. 95.

On the other hand, there are conditions that relate to the communication of **17.103** information. Whether these conditions have been fulfilled is determined by applying the ordinary principles of interpretation to the communication in question. Where the question is not whether substantive conditions have been performed, but what a notice exercising an option means, the ordinary techniques of interpretation of the notice apply. Having interpreted the notice, it must then be matched against the contractual requirements to see whether it meets them.[239]

In many cases a right to terminate a contract is unqualified. The question has **17.104** arisen in such cases whether there is any implied qualification of such a right (such as a requirement of good faith, or a requirement to give reasons). The cases suggest that no such qualification will be implied.

Chapman v Honig[240] concerned the validity of a notice to quit terminating a **17.105** tenancy. Pearson LJ said:

"Common experience is that, when the validity of an act done in purported exercise of a right under a contract or other instrument is disputed, the inquiry is limited to ascertaining whether the act has been done in accordance with the provisions of the contract or other instrument. I cannot think of any case in which such an act might be invalidated by proof that it was prompted by some vindictive or other wrong motive. Motive is disregarded as irrelevant. A person who has a right under a contract or other instrument is entitled to exercise it and can effectively exercise it for a good reason or a bad reason or no reason at all."

In *Reda v Flag Ltd*,[241] an employment contract provided for termination without **17.106** cause. The Privy Council held that no qualification to that right could be implied. Lord Millett said:

"Flag had an express contractual right, which it exercised, to bring the appellants' contracts of employment to an end at any time during the contract period without cause. Their Lordships agree with Flag that that is an end of the matter. As the Court of Appeal observed, 'the very nature of such a power is that its exercise does not have to be justified.'"

In *Lomas v IFB Firth Rixon Inc*,[242] Longmore LJ said: **17.107**

"The right to terminate is no more an exercise of discretion, which is not to be exercised in an arbitrary or capricious (or perhaps unreasonable) manner, than the right to accept repudiatory conduct as a repudiation of a contract. ... But no one would suggest that there could be any impediment to accepting repudiatory conduct as a termination of the contract based on the fact that the innocent party can elect between termination and leaving the contract on foot. The same applies to elective termination."

---

[239] *Trafford MBC v Total Fitness (UK) Ltd* [2002] 2 P. & C.R. 2 CA. The proposition in the text was approved in *The Party Bus Co Ltd v Attorney-General* [2012] NZCA 194 and *Batchelar Centre Ltd v Westpac New Zealand Ltd* [2015] NZHC 272.
[240] [1963] 2 Q.B. 502.
[241] [2002] UKPC 38; [2002] I.R.L.R. 747.
[242] [2012] EWCA Civ 419; [2013] B.C.L.C. 27; *Monk v Largo Foods Ltd* [2016] EWHC 1837 (Comm); *Kwik Lets Ltd v Khaira* [2020] EWHC 616 (QB).

17.108   In *TSG Building Services Plc v South Anglia Housing Ltd*,[243] cl.1.1 of a contract for gas servicing provided that the parties would work together and individually in the spirit of trust, fairness and mutual cooperation for the benefit of the programme. Another clause provided for a right of termination on notice. Akenhead J decided that on its true interpretation the right to terminate was not expressly circumscribed. He continued:

> "The parties had gone as far as they wanted in expressing terms in Clause 1.1 about how they were to work together in a spirit of 'trust fairness and mutual cooperation' and to act reasonably. Even if there was some implied term of good faith, it would not and could not circumscribe or restrict what the parties had expressly agreed in Clause 13.3, which was in effect that either of them for no, good or bad reason could terminate at any time before the term of four years was completed. That is the risk that each voluntarily undertook when it entered into the Contract, even though, doubtless, initially each may have thought, hoped and assumed that the Contract would run its full term."

17.109   In *Monde Petroleum SA v Westernzagros Ltd*,[244] Mr Richard Salter QC said:

> "In my judgment a contractual right to terminate is a right which may be exercised irrespective of the exercising party's reasons for doing so. Provided that the contractual conditions (if any) for the exercise of such a right (for example, the occurrence of an event of default) have been satisfied, the party exercising such a right does not have to justify its actions."

17.110   In *Taqa Bratani Ltd v Rockrose UKCS8 LLC*,[245] HH Judge Pelling QC reviewed the cases and concluded:

> "In my judgment these authorities speak with a single voice—where the parties choose to include within their agreement a provision that entitles one or more of the parties to terminate the agreement between them, that clause takes effect in accordance with its terms."

17.111   In *Cathay Pacific Airways Ltd v Lufthansa Technik AG*,[246] the same principle was applied to an option to remove engines from a long-term contract for aircraft engine maintenance, even though the exercise of the option did not terminate the whole agreement.

16.   TERMINATION CLAUSES

A contract may provide that a right of termination can be exercised in the event of a non-repudiatory breach. But a clause in a contract that purports to enable one party to terminate it if the other party commits any breach of contract is likely to be interpreted as being limited to repudiatory breaches. Where a contract contains termination provisions they will not usually preclude termination at common law by repudiation and acceptance.[247]

---

[243] [2013] EWHC 1151; [2013] B.L.R. 484; *Monk v Largo Foods Ltd* [2016] EWHC 1837 (Comm).
[244] [2016] EWHC 1472 (Comm); [2017] 1 All E.R. (Comm) 1009 (this point did not arise on appeal).
[245] [2020] EWHC 58 (Comm); *Essex County Council v UBB Waste (Essex) Ltd* [2020] EWHC 1581 (TCC).
[246] [2020] EWHC 1789 (Ch).
[247] This section was approved in *Bates v Post Office (No.3)* [2019] EWHC 606 (QB) at [898].

It is open to the parties to agree that, as regards a particular obligation, any breach **17.112** shall entitle the party not in default to treat the contract as repudiated.[248] Thus it is open to the parties to provide that a non-repudiatory breach will entitle the injured party to terminate. It is a question of interpretation whether they have done so.[249]

So, where a bond issue defined events of default as including a failure to perform or comply with its obligations it was held that no further requirement of materiality was required before the bond trustee was entitled to accelerate repayment.[250]

It is also, of course, open to the parties to provide that a contract may be **17.113** terminated without breach simply by the giving of notice. But any such provision must be interpreted in the context of the contract as a whole. Thus what appears to be a free-standing right to terminate a contract at any time may on examination be construed as a more limited right, especially where the contract purports to be for a fixed term.[251] Although it may not be appropriate to interpret a termination clause contra proferentem, a court should be cautious about concluding that one party is entitled to terminate a relatively long-term contract, unless the contract is clear as to the circumstances in which the party seeking to terminate is entitled to do so.[252]

Many contracts contain provisions entitling one party to terminate it if the other **17.114** commits "any" breach of contract. The courts have evolved a principle of interpretation that limits the right to terminate to cases in which the breach in question is repudiatory.

In *Antaios Compania SA v Salen AB*,[253] a charterparty contained a clause entitling the owners to withdraw the vessel "on any breach of this charter party." The House of Lords held that the right of termination was limited to repudiatory breaches. Lord Diplock upheld the reasoning of the arbitrators who had decided that:

> "'any other breach of this charter party' in the withdrawal clause means a repudiatory breach—that is to say: a fundamental breach of an innominate term or breach of a term expressly stated to be a condition, such as would entitle the shipowners to elect to treat the contract as wrongfully repudiated by the charterers."

In *Rice (t/a The Garden Guardian) v Great Yarmouth Borough Council*,[254] a contract for the provision of leisure management and grounds maintenance services contained a clause entitling the council to terminate it if the contractor committed "a breach" of contract. The Court of Appeal held that the right of termination was limited to repudiatory breaches. Hale LJ said that:

---

[248] *Bunge Corp v Tradax Export SA* [1981] 1 W.L.R. 711.
[249] *BNP Paribas v Wockhardt EU Operations (Swiss) AG* (2009) 132 Con. L.R. 177.
[250] *Bank of New York Mellon v GV Films Ltd* [2010] 2 All E.R. (Comm) 285.
[251] *Digital Integration Ltd v Software 2000* [1998] E.C.C. 289.
[252] *Sutton Housing Partnership Ltd v Rydon Maintenance Ltd* [2016] EWHC 1122 (TCC).
[253] [1988] 1 A.C. 191.
[254] [2003] T.C.L.R. 1.

"the notion that this term would entitle the council to terminate a contract such as this at any time for any breach of any term flies in the face of commercial common sense."[255]

Likewise, in *Dominion Corporate Services Ltd v Debenhams Properties Ltd*,[256] an agreement for lease entitled a party to terminate it if "either party shall in any respect fail or neglect to observe or perform any of the provisions of this Agreement". Kitchin J held that this right was limited to termination in the event of failure to perform in a way that amounted to a repudiatory breach.

17.115 In other cases the contract provides that the right to terminate only arises if there has been a "substantial" or "material" breach. Whether a breach is "substantial" or "material" must be judged objectively.[257]

In *Crane Co v Wittenborg AS*,[258] a contract entitled the parties to terminate it in the event of "substantial" breach. Mance LJ doubted whether there was any difference between this description and repudiatory breach. The fact that the contract provided for the possibility of remedying the breach made no difference. Mance LJ said:

"The requirement, in the case of a remediable breach, that a notice to remedy should have been given and a 90 day period should have elapsed before any termination does not persuade me that the parties must have had in mind breaches which were less than repudiatory. I therefore consider that substantial should be read as equivalent to repudiatory."

17.116 However, in *Leofelis SA v Lonsdale Sports Ltd*,[259] a trade mark licence entitled the licensor to terminate it if "the Licensee commits a breach of this Agreement; PROVIDED THAT if the breach is capable of remedy termination shall only occur if the breach shall not have been remedied within 30 days of the Licensee having been given notice in writing specifying the breach and requiring it to be remedied." It was argued that the right only applied to repudiatory breaches. The Court of Appeal rejected the argument. Lloyd LJ said:

"I would reject this argument. In the absence of the proviso in cl.11.2.1, there might be something to be said for it. However, the proviso makes it clear that the clause applies to breaches which can be remedied, and also requires TMLC to give Leofelis the opportunity to remedy the breach. I cannot see that the clause can properly be construed as limited to repudiatory breaches. If it were, the clause would add nothing to the position under the general law."

17.117 This view appears to be gaining ground. In *ENE Kos 1 Ltd v Petrolio Brasiliero SA (No.2)*,[260] Lord Sumption said:

---

[255] One objection to this conclusion is that the clause adds nothing to the parties' rights at common law. If that is right, then inclusion of the clause in the contract serves no useful purpose. Later cases have made this point. See also Whittaker, "Termination Clauses" in Burrows and Peel (eds), *Contract Terms* (Oxford: Oxford University Press, 2007); J.W. Carter and W. Courtney, "Breach of condition and express termination right: a distinction with a difference" (2017) 133 L.Q.R. 395.

[256] [2010] EWHC 1193 (Ch). See also *Peregrine Systems Ltd v Steria Ltd* [2004] EWHC 275 (TCC).

[257] *Fitzroy House Epworth Street (No.1) Ltd v Financial Times Ltd* [2006] 1 W.L.R. 2207.

[258] [1999] 12 WLUK 675.

[259] [2008] E.T.M.R. 63.

[260] [2012] UKSC 17; [2012] 4 All E.R. 1.

"There is no legal policy specific to termination rights restricting their availability or the consequences of their exercise more narrowly than the language of
the contract or the general law."

Likewise, in *Firodi Shipping Ltd v Griffon Shipping LLC*,[261] Tomlinson LJ said:

"Whatever the position now, a contractual remedy of termination which has no
need to characterise the defaulting Buyers' conduct as repudiatory is a valuable
addition to Sellers' armoury. The circumstances out of which Buyers' repudiation must be spelled are not always clear cut. A contractual right of termination
exercisable upon the happening or non-happening of an event usually brooks of
less argument."

Similarly, in *Newland Shipping and Forwarding Ltd v Toba Trading FZC*,[262] Leggatt J said:

"In principle, a contractual right to cancel or terminate a contract (these terms
generally being interchangeable) arises when the contract says it arises."

In *Dalkia Utilities Services Plc v Celtech International Ltd*,[263] the right to **17.118**
terminate arose on "material" breach. It was common ground that the word "material" meant that the breach in question did not have to be repudiatory, otherwise the
contract would have added nothing to the remedies available at common law.[264] In
the author's opinion this is the better view.

In *Glolite Ltd v Jasper Conran Ltd*,[265] Neuberger J said that:

"Whether a breach of an agreement is 'material' must depend upon all the facts
of the particular case, including the terms and duration of the agreement in question, the nature of the breach, and the consequences of the breach."

In *Gallagher International Ltd v Tias Enterprises Ltd*,[266] Christopher Clarke J
said:

"Materiality had to be assessed in the context in which the question arises which,
here, is the possible termination of a five-year agreement. In order for a breach
to be material it does not have to be repudiatory ... In *Phoenix Media Ltd v
Cobweb Information*,[267] Neuberger J, as he then was, said:

'Materiality involves considering the following: the actual breaches, the
consequence of the breaches to [the innocent party]; [the guilty party's]
explanation for the breaches; the breaches in the context of TEL Agreement;

---

261 [2013] EWCA Civ 1567; [2014] 1 Lloyd's Rep. 471.
262 [2014] EWHC 661 (Comm).
263 [2006] 1 Lloyd's Rep. 599.
264 However, in considering whether a tenant exercising a break clause had "materially" complied with
its covenants, Morritt C said that: "The words 'substantial' and 'material', depending on the context,
are interchangeable": *Fitzroy House Epworth Street (No.1) Ltd v Financial Times Ltd* [2006] 1
W.L.R. 2207. See also *DB Rare Books Ltd v Antiqbooks* [1995] 2 B.C.L.C. 306.
265 [1998] 1 WLUK 280; *The Times*, 28 January 1998. See also *National Power Plc v United Gas Co
Ltd* [1998] 7 WLUK 694; *Fortman Holdings Ltd v Modem Holdings* [2001] EWCA Civ 1235.
266 [2008] EWHC 804 (Comm).
267 [2000] 5 WLUK 424.

the consequences of holding TEL Agreement determined and the consequences of holding TEL Agreement continues.'

I respectfully regard that as a helpful checklist."[268]

17.119 The contract may provide for a party in breach to be given the opportunity to remedy the breach before a right of termination can be exercised. Such was the case in *FL Schuler AG v Wickman Machine Tool Sales Ltd*.[269] Lord Reid said:

> "The question then is what is meant by the word 'remedy'. It could mean obviate or nullify the effect of a breach so that any damage already done is in some way made good. Or it could mean cure so that matters are put right for the future. I think that the latter is the more natural meaning. The word is commonly used in connection with diseases or ailments and they would normally be said to be remedied if they were cured although no cure can remove the past effect or result of the disease before the cure took place. And in general it can only be in a rare case that any remedy of something that has gone wrong in the performance of a continuing positive obligation will, in addition to putting it right for the future, remove or nullify damage already incurred before the remedy was applied. To restrict the meaning or remedy to cases where all damage past and future can be put right would leave hardly any scope at all for this clause. On the other hand, there are cases where it would seem a misuse of language to say that a breach can be remedied. For example, a breach of clause 14 by disclosure of confidential information could not be said to be remedied by a promise not to do it again."

17.120 If a contract does contain a provision requiring a warning notice to be given to the defaulting party, so that the latter may remedy the breach, the existence of the opportunity to remedy the breach may lead to the conclusion that a failure to remedy entitles the giver of the notice to terminate the contract, even if the breach in question is not repudiatory.[270]

17.121 Where a contract contains a termination clause that will not usually preclude termination at common law. In *Stocznia Gdynia SA v Gearbulk Holdings Ltd*,[271] Moore-Bick LJ said:

> "In paragraph 88 of his judgment in *Stocznia Gdanska S.A. v Latvian Shipping Co*[272] Rix L.J. expressed the view that where contractual and common law rights overlap it would be too harsh to regard the use of a contractual mechanism of termination as ousting the common law mechanism, at any rate against a background of an express reservation of rights. In this case I would go further. In my view it is wrong to treat the right to terminate in accordance with the terms of the contract as different in substance from the right to treat the contract as discharged by reason of repudiation at common law. In those cases where the contract gives a right of termination they are in effect one and the same."

---

[268] See also *Crosstown Music Co 1 LLC v Rive Droite Music Ltd* [2009] EWHC 600 (Ch) (not appealed on this point).

[269] [1974] A.C. 235; *Force India Formula One Team Ltd v Etihad Airways PJSC* [2011] E.T.M.R. 10.

[270] *Obrascon Huarte Lain SA v Her Majesty's Attorney General for Gibraltar* [2014] EWHC 1028 (TCC), affirmed [2015] EWCA Civ 712.

[271] [2009] 1 Lloyd's Rep. 461.

[272] [2002] 2 Lloyd's Rep. 436.

Similarly, in *Dalkia Utilities Services Plc v Celtech International Ltd*,[273] cl.14 of **17.122** a contract entitled one party to terminate it in a number of different circumstances, none of which would necessarily have amounted to a repudiatory breach of contract. Clause 15 contained provisions for payment in the event of termination. Christopher Clarke J held that cl.15 did not apply to a repudiatory breach that was accepted. He said:

"Clause 14 contains nine separate categories of circumstances in which one party or the other may terminate the agreement. In all of these categories the right to terminate would or could arise in circumstances which did not give rise to a right of termination at common law. Clause 15 deals with the consequences that will follow according to which ground for termination has been invoked. The natural reading of clause 15.7, in that context, is that the only rights or remedies that will arise in respect of a termination on any of the bases provided for by clause 14 will be those specified in clause 15. Secondly, clause 15.7 does not seem to me sufficiently clear, as it would need to be, to exclude the parties' common law right to accept a repudiatory breach of contract (e.g. an outright refusal to perform) as discharging the innocent party from further liability and to claim damages for the loss of the contract. The presumption is that it does not unless there are clear express words to that effect."

Where a contract contains a termination clause, no particular formality is neces- **17.123** sary (unless the contract so provides) to exercise the right.[274] Any communication which clearly conveys that the right is being exercised will suffice.[275] Neverthe-less, in interpreting a termination clause the court must still adopt a commercially sensible interpretation. In determining whether a termination clause has been validly exercised, there must be substantive compliance with the contractual provisions, and any notice exercising the right to terminate must be in sufficiently clear terms to communicate to the recipient clearly the decision to exercise the contractual right to terminate. It is, however, a question of interpretation of the contract whether each and every specific requirement is an indispensable condition which renders termina-tion ineffective in the absence of full compliance. But any interpretation needs to be tempered by reference to commercial common sense.[276]

Where a party to a contract has a right to terminate it, the principles applicable **17.124** to the exercise of a contractual discretion have been held not to apply.[277]

17. FORFEITURE CLAUSES

A forfeiture clause is a clause which brings an interest to a premature end by reason of a breach of covenant or condition, and the court will penetrate the

---

[273] [2006] 1 Lloyd's Rep. 599.
[274] This section was approved in *Lehman Brothers International (Europe) v Exxonmobil Financial Services BV* [2016] EWHC 2699 (Comm).
[275] *Newland Shipping and Forwarding Ltd v Toba Trading FZC* [2014] EWHC 661 (Comm).
[276] *Obrascon Huarte Lain SA v Her Majesty's Attorney General for Gibraltar* [2014] EWHC 1028 (TCC), affirmed [2015] EWCA Civ 712. In the case of a true unilateral contract (which includes an option to terminate), if as a matter of interpretation the right to terminate depends on a condition, that condition will in practice be indispensable: *Siemens Hearing Instruments Ltd v Friends Life Ltd* (see para.16.112).
[277] *Monde Petroleum SA v Westernzagros Ltd* [2016] EWHC 1472 (Comm); 167 Con. L.R. 15; *Monk v Largo Foods Ltd* [2016] EWHC 1837 (Comm).

disguise of a forfeiture clause dressed up to look like something else. A forfeiture clause is not to be construed strictly, but is to receive a fair construction.

17.125 Almost invariably a formal lease of land contains a forfeiture clause which entitles the landlord to re-enter for breach of covenant or condition. In *Clays Lane Housing Co-operative Ltd v Patrick*,[278] the Court of Appeal accepted the submission that:

> "a right to determine a lease by a landlord is a right of forfeiture if (a) when exercised, it operates to bring the lease to an end earlier than it would 'naturally' terminate; and (b) it is exercisable in the event of some default by the tenant."[279]

17.126 The court will treat as a forfeiture clause any arrangement which possesses these characteristics. So in *Plymouth Corp v Harvey*,[280] a lease contained a proviso for re-entry on breach of covenant. The tenant was in breach of covenant. The landlord gave the tenant time to remedy the breach and to provide an effective sanction, the tenant executed a deed of surrender in escrow and handed it to a third party to deliver to the landlord if he were satisfied that the tenant had failed to remedy the breach within the stipulated time. Plowman J held that this was merely an attempt to "change the mechanics" of forfeiture, and that the arrangement took effect as a forfeiture clause. A similar result followed in *Clarke (Richard) and Co Ltd v Widnall*.[281] In that case a tenancy was terminable by 12 months' notice. It contained a clause which entitled the landlord to terminate the tenancy on three months' notice in the event of a breach of covenant by the tenant. The Court of Appeal held that it took effect as a forfeiture clause. Where, however, the length of notice is no shorter than the notice which would be required in the absence of any breach, the clause is not a forfeiture clause.[282] The primary significance of the distinction is that if the clause is not a forfeiture clause, the tenant cannot obtain relief against forfeiture.

17.127 In *Celestial Aviation Trading 71 Ltd v Paramount Airways PVT Ltd*,[283] cl.13.2 of an aircraft lease provided that on the occurrence of an event of default the lessor could terminate the lease and take possession of the aircraft. The events of default included a failure to pay sums due. Hamblen J said:

> "The loss of the right to continued possession of the aircraft for the substantial remaining term of the leases on a single default in payment can be regarded as involving forfeiture. This is borne out by the authorities which recognise that loss of a right of possession may be sufficient to engage the forfeiture jurisdiction."

---

278 (1984) 49 P. & C.R. 72.

279 The reference to "natural" termination in this definition means in the case of a lease for a fixed term, the contractual expiry date, and in the case of a periodic tenancy, the date on which the tenancy could be terminated by notice to quit. Although this is an acceptable working definition, many forfeiture clauses entitle the landlord to forfeit for breach of conditions which do not involve default by the tenant (e.g. the insolvency of a surety for the tenant as in *Halliard Property Co Ltd v Segal (Jack) Ltd* [1978] 1 W.L.R. 377).

280 [1971] 1 W.L.R. 549.

281 [1976] 1 W.L.R. 845.

282 *Clays Lane Housing Co-operative Ltd v Patrick* (1984) 49 P. & C.R. 72.

283 [2011] 1 Lloyd's Rep. 9.

A cancellation clause in a charterparty has also been described as a forfeiture **17.128** clause, which "should not be lightly applied".[284]

However, where an insurance policy contained a term that required the insured **17.129** to make a claim for loss to the insurers within fifteen days after the occurrence of the loss, it was held that the term was not a forfeiture clause, against which equity could grant relief,[285] but was a condition precedent to the insurers' liability to indemnify which had to be complied with.[286]

As with other rights to terminate contracts, any condition precedent must be **17.130** strictly complied with. Thus the breach of covenant giving rise to the forfeiture must be proved. In *Croft v Lumley*,[287] Channell B said:

> "I think that the condition ought to be construed with this amount of strictness, that it ought clearly to appear the condition was meant to include and did incorporate the covenant on the breach whereof the right to re-enter is claimed; but that the question whether the covenant itself is broken (having once ascertained that the condition for re-entry applies to and includes it) is to be determined by reference to the rules which prevail in construing ordinary contracts between party and party."

So also in *Doe d. Davis v Elsam*,[288] Lord Tenterden said:

> "I do not think provisoes of this sort are to be construed with the strictness of conditions at common law. These are matters of contract between the parties, and should, in my opinion be construed as other contracts."

The court will not be astute to correct the language of a forfeiture clause. So **17.131** where a proviso for re-entry was incomprehensible the court declined to construe it.[289] In *Doe d. Spencer v Goodwin*,[290] a proviso entitled the landlord to re-enter for breach of covenant "hereinafter" contained. The court refused to read "hereinafter" as "hereinbefore" even though there were no tenant's covenants after the proviso. Bayley J said:

> "Now here it is plain there is a mistake somewhere, but where it lies I am at a loss to discover … whether the error lies in the insertion of those words, or in the omission of other covenants. I am at a loss to conceive with any sufficient certainty to be able to determine that those words ought to be struck out."

Once it has been determined that the condition of re-entry applies to the particular **17.132** covenant, the question whether the covenant has been broken is to be determined on ordinary principles of interpretation. In *Goodtitle d Luxmoore v Saville*,[291] Lord Ellenborough CJ said:

---

[284] *Noemijulia Steamship Co Ltd v Minister of Food* [1951] 1 K.B. 223; *The North Sea* [1997] 2 Lloyd's Rep. 324; *The Qatar Star* [2011] 1 Lloyd's Rep. 350. The main debate in this context has been whether relief against forfeiture (or an analogous injunction) is available.
[285] The possibility that equity might be able to extend time for compliance was left open.
[286] *Diab v Regent Insurance Co Ltd* [2007] 1 W.L.R. 797 PC.
[287] (1858) 6 H.L. Cas. 672.
[288] (1828) Moo. & M. 189.
[289] *Doe d. Wyndham v Carew* (1841) 2 Q.B. 317.
[290] (1815) 4 M. & S. 265.
[291] (1812) 16 East. 87.

"In the construction of covenants of this sort, they are neither entitled to favour or disfavour, whether they are to create a forfeiture or continue an estate; but we are to put a fair construction upon them, according to the apparent intention of the contracting parties."

Similarly, in *Bristol Corp v Westcott*,[292] Cotton LJ said:

"I agree that, although it is a question of forfeiture, we must construe the covenant fairly, ascertain its meaning without regard to forfeiture, and then see whether upon that ascertained meaning, a forfeiture has been incurred."

17.133 This view is not always applied. For example, in *Creery v Summersell and Flowerdew & Co Ltd*,[293] Harman J said of a use covenant in a lease:

"Covenants of this sort which may work a forfeiture have always been strictly construed against the lessor, and that rule I propose to follow."

Similar statements may be found in other cases.[294] That approach may well be a little less powerful than it was many years ago, on the basis that such canons of construction are now given rather less weight.[295] However, even though less weight is given to it the logic of this approach is not entirely clear, for as Jessel MR pointed out in *Bristol Corp v Westcott*,[296] the construction of a covenant:

"must be the same in an action for damages for breach of the covenant as in an action for the recovery of the land on the ground that the proviso for re-entry has come into operation by reason of such breach."

17.134 It is thought that this is the better view. Thus, in *Mansel Oil Ltd v Troon Storage Tankers SA*,[297] Christopher Clarke J said:

"Nor do I ignore the fact that the cancellation clause is a form of forfeiture clause … That cannot, however, mean that the charterparty should be interpreted in an uncommercial manner."

---

[292] (1879) 12 Ch. D. 461 at 467.
[293] [1949] Ch. 751.
[294] e.g. *Crusoe d. Blencowe v Bugby* (1771) 2 Wm. Bl. 766; *Chaplin v Smith* [1926] 1 K.G. 198; *Lam Kee Sdn Bhd v Lam Shes Tong* [1975] A.C. 247.
[295] *Akici v LR Butlin Ltd* [2006] W.L.R. 201, per Neuberger LJ.
[296] (1879) 12 Ch. D. 461.
[297] [2008] 2 Lloyd's Rep. 384.

CHAPTER 18

DISPUTE RESOLUTION

Sensible lawyers in every age would say that judges should be the last resort in any case because no one can predict what they will do.

Richard Marius: *Thomas More: A Biography*

1.   INCORPORATION OF ARBITRATION CLAUSES

Whether a contract incorporates an arbitration clause is a question of construction of the contract. Where the arbitration clause is contained in a party's standard terms or in the terms of a previous contract between the same parties, general words of incorporation will generally suffice. But where the arbitration clause is contained in a contract made between different parties, or between one of them and a third party, clearer words are necessary.

Part 1 of the Arbitration Act 1996 applies where the arbitration agreement is in writing.[1] Section 6(2) of the Arbitration Act 1996 provides that the reference in an agreement to a written form of arbitration clause or to a document containing an arbitration clause constitutes an arbitration agreement if the reference is such as to make that clause part of the agreement. The authorities recognise a distinction in approach between cases in which the parties incorporate the terms of a contract between two other parties or between one of them and a third party and those in which they incorporate standard terms.[2] In *The Federal Bulker*[3] the issue was whether a clause in a charterparty requiring bills of lading to provide for arbitration of "all disputes arising out of this contract" was incorporated in bills which provided "all terms ... as per charterparty ... to be considered as fully incorporated as if fully written". The Court of Appeal held that the arbitration clause was not incorporated. Bingham LJ said:

> "64   Generally speaking, the English law of contract has taken a benevolent view of the use of general words to incorporate by reference standard terms to be found elsewhere. But in the present field a different, and stricter, rule has developed, especially where the incorporation of arbitration clauses is concerned. The reason no doubt is that a bill of lading is a negotiable commercial instrument and may come into the hands of a foreign party with no knowledge and no ready means of knowledge of the terms of the charterparty. The cases show that a strict test of incorporation having, for

18.01

---

[1]   Section 5(1). There is an agreement in writing if: (a) the agreement is made in writing (whether or not it is signed by the parties); (b) the agreement is made by the exchange of communications in writing; or (c) the agreement is evidenced in writing: s.5(2).

[2]   *Habas Sinai Ve Tibbi Gazlar Istihsal Endustrisi AS v Sometal Sal* [2010] EWHC 29 (Comm), containing a full review of the authorities, on which the text of this section is largely based.

[3]   [1981] 1 Lloyd's Rep. 103.

better or worse, been laid down, the Courts have in general defended this rule with some tenacity in the interests of commercial certainty. If commercial parties do not like the English rule, they can meet the difficulty by spelling out the arbitration provision in the bill of lading and not relying on general words to achieve incorporation.

65   The importance of certainty in this field was emphasised by Lord Denning, M.R. in *The Annefield* ... by Sir John Donaldson, M.R. in *The Varenna* ... and by Lord Justice Oliver in the same case ... This is indeed a field in which it is perhaps preferable that the law should be clear, certain and well understood than that it should be perfect. Like others, I doubt whether the line drawn by the authorities is drawn where a modern commercial lawyer would be inclined to draw it. But it would, I think, be a source of mischief if we were to do anything other than try to give effect to settled authority as best we can."

18.02   In *International Research Corp Plc v Lufthansa Asia Pacific Pte Ltd*,[4] it was held by the High Court of Singapore that:

"... the approach towards incorporating an arbitration clause in one contract into another is extremely strict."

After a lengthy analysis and review of authority, the judge concluded that an arbitration clause did apply to obligations arising out of a supplemental agreement made between different parties to those who entered into the original agreement.

18.03   In *The Nerano*,[5] a bill of lading said on its face that the "conditions as per charterparty" were incorporated, and on its reverse that all "terms and conditions liberties exceptions and arbitration clause" of the charterparty were incorporated. The express reference to the arbitration clause was sufficient to incorporate it. Saville LJ said:

"In the present case the parties have not merely used general words of incorporation. They have expressly identified and specified the charterparty arbitration clause as something to be incorporated into their contract. Such a clause does not impose unusual burdens on the parties: it is a common agreement in contracts of all kinds for the carriage of goods by sea."

18.04   The incorporation of terms is to be distinguished from mere notice of terms; the fact that the holder of a bill of lading has notice of terms in a charterparty does not mean that those terms are incorporated in the bill of lading.[6] In *Caresse Navigation Ltd v Office National De L'electricite*[7] a charterparty contained a clause that stated that it was to be governed by English law and that disputes should be resolved by the English courts. A bill of lading stated that all the terms of the charterparty "including the Law and Arbitration clause" were incorporated. The Court of Appeal held that since the charterparty contained no arbitration clause, but did contain a law and jurisdiction clause, the words of incorporation were sufficient to

---

4   [2012] SGHC 226; [2013] 1 Lloyd's Rep. 24. See also *British-American Insurance (Kenya) Ltd v Matelec Sal* [2013] EWHC 3278 (Comm).

5   [1996] 1 Lloyd's Rep. 1.

6   *The Varenna* [1984] Q.B. 599; *Siboti K/S v BP France SA* [2003] 2 Lloyd's Rep. 364.

7   [2014] EWCA Civ 1366; [2015] 2 W.L.R. 43, affirming [2013] EWHC 3081 (Comm); [2014] 1 Lloyd's Rep. 337.

incorporate that clause. It was a case in which the reasonable reader would have understood that something had gone wrong with the language.

In *The Athena (No.2)*,[8] Langley J described the cases in which the strict test of incorporation of an arbitration agreement was applied as being "two-contract" cases; whereas in "single contract" cases, general words of incorporation sufficed. He said:

18.05

"In principle, English law accepts incorporation of standard terms by the use of general words and, I would add, particularly so when the terms are readily available and the question arises in the context of dealings between established players in a well-known market. The principle ... does not distinguish between a term which is an arbitration clause and one which addresses other issues. In contrast, and for the very reason that it concerns other parties, a 'stricter rule' is applied in charterparty/bills of lading cases. The reason given is that the other party may have no knowledge nor ready means of knowledge of the relevant terms. Further, as the authorities illustrate, the terms of an arbitration clause may require adjustment if they are to be made to apply to the parties to a different contract."

He said, however, that an extension of the stricter rule should not be encouraged. He concluded:

"General words of incorporation may serve to incorporate an arbitration clause save in the exceptional two-contract cases ... in which some express reference to arbitration or perhaps provision of the relevant clause is also required."

In *Habas Sinai Ve Tibbi Gazlar Istihsal Endustrisi AS v Sometal Sal*,[9] Christopher Clarke J said:

18.06

"48.   I accept that, if the terms of an earlier contract or contracts between the parties are said to have been incorporated it is necessary for it to be clear which terms those were. But, like Langley J, I do not regard this to be the position only if the terms said to be incorporated include an arbitration or jurisdiction clause. Whenever some terms other than those set out in the incorporating document are said to be incorporated it is necessary to be clear what those terms are. Since arbitration clauses are not terms which regulate the parties' substantive rights and obligations under the contract but are terms dealing with the resolution of disputes relating to those rights and obligations it is also necessary to be clear that the parties did intend to incorporate such a clause. But, if a contract between A and B incorporates all the terms of a previous contract between them other than the terms newly agreed in the later contract, there should be no lack of clarity in respect of what is to be incorporated.

49.   There is a particular need to be clear that the parties intended to incorporate the arbitration clause when the incorporation relied on is the incorporation of the terms of a contract made between different parties, even if one of them is a party to the contract in suit. In such a case it may not be evident that the parties intended not only to incorporate the substantive provisions of the other contract but also provisions as to the resolution of disputes between different parties, particularly if a degree of verbal

---

8   [2007] 1 Lloyd's Rep. 280.
9   [2010] EWHC 29 (Comm).

manipulation is needed for the incorporated arbitration clause to work. These considerations do not, however, apply to a single contract case."

18.07   The more restrictive approach requires express reference to the arbitration or jurisdiction clause before it will be taken to be incorporated into the contract. This more restrictive approach will apply to cases in which A and B make a contract incorporating terms agreed between A (or B) and C.

Common examples are a bill of lading incorporating the terms of a charter to which A is a party[10]; reinsurance contracts incorporating the terms of an underlying insurance; excess insurance contracts incorporating the terms of the primary layer of insurance; and building or engineering sub-contracts incorporating the terms of a main contract or sub-sub-contracts incorporating the terms of a sub-contract.

18.08   It will also apply where A and B make a contract incorporating terms agreed between C and D.

Bills of lading, reinsurance[11] and insurance contracts and building contracts 'may fall into this category.

18.09   However, it will not apply where A and B make a contract in which they incorporate standard terms.

These may be the standard terms of one party set out on the back of an offer letter or an order, or contained in another document to which reference is made; or terms embodied in the rules of an organisation of which A or B or both are members; or they may be terms standard in a particular trade or industry.

18.10   Nor will it apply where A and B make a contract incorporating terms previously agreed between A and B in another contract or contracts to which they were both parties.[12]

18.11   Even when the wording of one contract is prima facie of sufficient width to incorporate the arbitration clause in another, such incorporation may be defeated if undue manipulation is required.[13] In the absence of clear language one relevant consideration is the extent to which the clause in question is apt and workable if transplanted from one contract to another.[14] As Hamblen J explained in *Onego Shipping BV v JS Arcadia Shipping*[15]:

---

[10]   See, e.g. *OK Petroleum AB v Vitol Energy SA* [1995] 2 Lloyd's Rep. 160, per Colman J. ("In particular, in approaching the question whether a charterparty arbitration clause is incorporated by general words of incorporation into a bill of lading contract, the courts have repeatedly held that great weight is to be attached to the consideration that an arbitration clause between shipowner and charterer is not 'germane' or relevant to those contractual rights and obligations which arise under the bill of lading contract. There is in the authorities a well-developed approach to construction of general words of incorporation that only such provisions will be incorporated as are in substance relevant or germane to, and, if incorporated, capable of being operated in conjunction with the subject-matter of the bill of lading.")

[11]   See, e.g. *Assicurazioni Generali SPA v Ege Sigorta AS* [2002] Lloyd's Rep. I.R. 480, per Colman J. ("... general words of incorporation in a reinsurance contract will not generally incorporate jurisdiction clauses from the primary policy. The reason for this is that such clauses are not germane to the primary risk reinsured, but are merely ancillary provisions which the parties to the reinsurance would not normally intend to incorporate.")

[12]   *Habas Sinai Ve Tibbi Gazlar Istihsal Endustrisi AS v Sometal Sal* [2010] EWHC 29 (Comm).

[13]   *Siboti K/S v BP France SA* [2003] 2 Lloyd's Rep. 364.

[14]   *Giffen (Electrical Contractors) Ltd v Drake & Scull Engineering Ltd* (1993) 37 Con. L.R. 84.

[15]   [2010] 2 Lloyd's Rep. 221.

"Verbal manipulation is a process which should be carried out intelligently rather than mechanically and only in so far as it is necessary to avoid insensible results."

2. WHETHER PARTIES BOUND TO ARBITRATE

If the contract gives a reasonably clear indication that arbitration is envisaged by both parties as a means of dispute resolution, it will be interpreted as binding them to refer disputes to arbitration even though the clause is not expressed in mandatory terms.

In *Mangistaumunaigaz Oil Production Association v United World Trade Inc*,[16] **18.12** an oil purchase contract provided for "Arbitration, if any, by ICC rules in London". It was argued that these words were ambiguous and left in doubt whether the parties did intend to create a mandatory reference to arbitration. Potter J said:

"In my opinion the clause as a whole, read in the context of an international contract for the sale of oil, demonstrates that the parties intended to settle any dispute which might arise between them by arbitration according to ICC rules in London with English law to apply. The alternative is that, by providing for arbitration 'if any', the parties were merely binding themselves in advance to the arbitral rules and venue which would govern any ad hoc agreement for arbitration which they might subsequently make if a dispute arose. The terms of the written contract suggest no need or reason to take so unusual a course. I consider that the commercial sense of an agreement of this kind, and the presumed contractual intention of the parties in importing the words used, can best be effected either by treating the words 'if any' as surplusage, or as being an abbreviation for the words 'if any dispute arises'. Any other construction appears to me to strain common sense and to breach the overall rule of construction which is to give effect to the presumed intention of the parties having regard to the context in which the words appear."

In *Lobb Partnership Ltd v Aintree Racecourse Co Ltd*,[17] Colman J said:

"The English courts have consistently taken the view that, provided that the contract gives a reasonably clear indication that arbitration is envisaged by both parties as a means of dispute resolution, they will treat both parties as *bound* to refer disputes to arbitration even though the clause is not expressed in mandatory terms."

Thus where the clause provided that disputes "shall" be referred to arbitration, **18.13** the parties were bound to arbitrate.[18] A clause will be an arbitration agreement if the binding agreement to arbitrate needs to be triggered by an election to arbitrate.[19] The fact that only one party to the contract has the ability to refer disputes to an arbitrator does not prevent the clause from being an arbitration agreement.[20] If there

---

[16] [1995] 1 Lloyd's Rep. 617.
[17] [2000] B.L.R. 65.
[18] *William McIlroy Swindon Ltd v Quinn Insurance Ltd* [2010] EWHC 2448 (TCC).
[19] *Westfal-Larsen & Co A/S v Ikerigi Compania Naviera SA; The Messiniaki Bergen* [1983] 1 All E.R. 382.
[20] *Woolf v Collis Removal Service* [1948] 1 K.B. 11; *Pittalis v Sherefettin* [1986] Q.B. 868; *Lobb*

is an ambiguity in the clause, it will be resolved using the same constructional techniques as apply to any other contractual provision.[21]

18.14 In *Hermes One Ltd v Everbread Holdings Ltd*,[22] a shareholders' agreement provided that if a dispute could not be resolved within a stipulated time "any party may submit the dispute to binding arbitration". The Privy Council held that arbitration was not compulsory but that a party had the option to require arbitration, even after another party had begun litigation. Their Lordships observed, however:

> "But clauses depriving a party of the right to litigate should be expected to be clearly worded—even though the commercial community's evident preference for arbitration in many spheres makes any such presumption a less persuasive factor nowadays than it was once."

They added:

> "The fact remains that there is an obvious linguistic difference between a promise that disputes shall be submitted to arbitration and a provision, agreed by both parties, that 'any party may submit the dispute to binding arbitration'."

3. PRESUMPTION OF ONE-STOP ARBITRATION

Where a contract incorporates an arbitration clause there is a presumption that the parties intended all their substantive disputes to be determined by arbitration.[23]

18.15 As Lord Macmillan pointed out in *Heyman v Darwins Ltd*[24]:

> "Arbitration clauses in contracts vary widely in their language for there is no limitation on the liberty of contracting parties to define as they please the matters which they desire to submit to arbitration."[25]

18.16 At one time the courts paid close attention to the precise words of an arbitration clause in order to decide whether particular disputes fell within its scope.[26] Distinctions were drawn between such forms of words as disputes "arising under" and "arising out of" the agreement. However, these linguistic nuances no longer play any real part in interpreting an arbitration agreement. The question was settled by the decision of the House of Lords in *Fiona Trust and Holding Corp v Privalov*,[27] in which Lord Hoffmann said:

> "In my opinion the construction of an arbitration clause should start from the as-

---

Partnership Ltd v Aintree Racecourse Co Ltd [2000] B.L.R. 65.

21 *Lobb Partnership Ltd v Aintree Racecourse Co Ltd* [2000] B.L.R. 65.

22 [2016] UKPC 1; [2016] 1 W.L.R. 4098.

23 This section was cited with apparent approval in *Amtrust Europe Ltd v Trust Risk Group SpA* [2014] EWHC 4169 (Comm). There is no similar presumption in Australia. The authorities are discussed in *Inghams Enterprises Pty Ltd v Hannigan* [2020] NSWCA 82.

24 [1942] A.C. 356.

25 The Singapore High Court conducted a review of a number of different types of arbitration clause in *Dyna-Jet Pte Ltd v Wilson Taylor Asia Pacific Pte Ltd* [2016] SGHC 238; [2017] 1 Lloyd's Rep. 59.

26 Earlier authorities are collected in H. Beale, *Chitty on Contracts*, 33rd edn (London: Sweet & Maxwell, 2018), para.32-030.

27 [2007] Bus. L.R. 1719. See also *Bilta (UK) Ltd v Nazir* [2010] 2 Lloyd's Rep. 29; *Deutsche Bank AG v Tongkah Harbour Public Co Ltd* [2011] EWHC 2251 (QB).

sumption that the parties, as rational businessmen, are likely to have intended any dispute arising out of the relationship into which they have entered or purported to enter to be decided by the same tribunal. The clause should be construed in accordance with this presumption unless the language makes it clear that certain questions were intended to be excluded from the arbitrator's jurisdiction. As Longmore LJ remarked … : 'if any businessman did want to exclude disputes about the validity of a contract, it would be comparatively easy to say so'."

In the same case Lord Hope said:

"It is the kind of clause to which ordinary businessmen readily give their agreement so long as its general meaning is clear. They are unlikely to trouble themselves too much about its precise language or to wish to explore the way it has been interpreted in the numerous authorities, not all of which speak with one voice. Of course, the court must do what it can to provide charterers and shipowners with legal certainty at the negotiation stage as to what they are agreeing to. But there is no conflict between that proposition and the guidance which Longmore LJ gave in paras 17–19 of the Court of Appeal's judgment about the interpretation of jurisdiction and arbitration clauses in international commercial contracts. The proposition that any jurisdiction or arbitration clause in an international commercial contract should be liberally construed promotes legal certainty. It serves to underline the golden rule that if the parties wish to have issues as to the validity of their contract decided by one tribunal and issues as to its meaning or performance decided by another, they must say so expressly. Otherwise they will be taken to have agreed on a single tribunal for the resolution of all such disputes."

O'Farrell J applied the presumption of one-stop arbitration in *Emmott v Michael Wilson & Partners*.[28]

In *Deutsche Bank AG v Tongkah Harbour Public Co Ltd*,[29] Blair J said: **18.17**

"In construing an arbitration clause, the assumption is that the parties, as rational business people, are likely to have intended any dispute arising out of the relationship into which they entered to be decided by the same tribunal.[30] Similarly, where the question arises (as here) in the context of dispute resolution provisions in multiple related agreements, the assumption is that the parties do not generally intend a dispute to be litigated in two different tribunals. Where the provisions in one agreement give jurisdiction to the court, and in another refer disputes to arbitration, the allocation of jurisdiction is fundamentally one of construction."[31]

In *Monde Petroleum SA v Westernzagros Ltd*,[32] Popplewell J said: **18.18**

"The presumption in favour of one-stop adjudication may have particular potency

---

28 [2016] EWHC 3010 (Comm); [2017] 1 Lloyd's Rep. 21.
29 [2011] EWHC 2251 (QB).
30 *Fiona Trust & Holding Corp v Privalov* [2007] UKHL 40; *Norscot Rig Management PVT Ltd v Essar Oilfields Services Ltd* [2010] EWHC 195 (Comm); [2010] 2 Lloyd's Rep. 209 at [16(iv)].
31 *UBS AG v HSH NordBank AG* [2009] 2 Lloyd's Rep. 272 at [83], per Lord Collins; *Sebastian Holdings Inc v Deutsche Bank AG* [2011] 1 Lloyd's Rep. 106 at [41]–[42] and [49], per Thomas LJ.
32 [2015] EWHC 67 (Comm); [2015] 1 Lloyd's Rep. 330; *Sodzawiczny v Ruhan* [2018] EWHC 1908 (Comm); [2018] Bus. L.R. 2419; *C v D1* [2015] EWHC 2126 (Comm), applied in *Petroleum Company of Trinidad and Tobago Ltd v Samsung Engineering Trinidad Co Ltd* [2017] EWHC 3055

where there is an agreement which is entered into for the purpose of terminating an earlier agreement between the same parties or settling disputes which have arisen under such an agreement. Where parties to a contractual dispute enter into a settlement agreement, the disputes which it can be envisaged may subsequently arise will often give rise to issues which relate both to the settlement agreement itself and to the previous contract which gave rise to the dispute. It is not uncommon for one party to wish to impeach the settlement agreement and to advance a claim based on his rights under the previous contract. In such circumstances rational businessmen would intend that all aspects of such a dispute should be resolved in a single forum. Where the settlement/termination agreement contains a dispute resolution provision which is different from, and incompatible with, a dispute resolution clause in the earlier agreement, the parties are likely to have intended that it is the settlement/termination agreement clause which is to govern all aspects of outstanding disputes, and to supersede the clause in the earlier agreement … ."

18.19   The presumption will generally apply only to disputes arising out of the relationships created or purported to have been created by the contract.[33] It will not apply to other disputes even if they arise between the same parties. But in the case of disputes arising out of other relationships an arbitration clause that is widely enough drawn may capture them.

18.20   In *Yegiazaryan v Smagin*,[34] the Court of Appeal reiterated that the presumption "is particularly strong where, as in this case, the dispute-resolution clause is in a contract entered into to resolve disputes under an earlier contract."

18.21   The mere fact that the allegations sought to be raised include allegations of criminality does not displace the presumption.[35] An arbitration clause will enable the arbitral tribunal to decide whether the contract is vitiated by fraud or misrepresentation; or was procured by duress.[36] It is only if the dispute concerns the validity of the arbitration agreement itself that the dispute will fall outside its scope. The scope of an arbitration agreement may extend to a claim in insolvency proceedings to avoid a transaction as being a transaction at an undervalue[37]; or conduct in the affairs of a company alleged to amount to unfair prejudice.[38] However the presumption applies only to substantive disputes. It does not apply to ancillary applications for security so long as there is no attempt to have the merits of the dispute heard other than by the agreed arbitral tribunal.[39] But the parties are free to exclude the court's power to grant ancillary relief (such as a freezing order); and a widely worded *Scott v Avery* clause has been held to have this effect.[40]

(TCC); [2018] 1 Lloyd's Rep. 242.

[33] *Microsoft Mobile OY v Sony Europe* [2018] 1 All ER (Comm) 419; *Terre Neuve SARL v Yewdale Ltd* [2020] EWHC 772 (Comm).

[34] [2016] EWCA Civ 1290; [2017] 1 Lloyd's Rep. 102.

[35] *Interprods Ltd v De La Rue International Ltd* [2014] EWHC 68 (Comm).

[36] *El Nasharty v J Sainsbury Plc* [2008] 1 Lloyd's Rep. 360.

[37] *Nori Holding Ltd v Public Joint Stock Company "Bank Otkritie Financial Corpn"* [2018] EWHC 1343 (Comm); [2019] Bus. L.R. 146, not following the decision of the Singapore Court of Appeal in *Larsen Oil & Gas Pte Ltd v Petroprod Ltd* [2011] 3 S.L.R. 414.

[38] *Fulham Football Club (1987) Ltd v Richards* [2011] EWCA Civ 855; [2012] Ch. 333.

[39] *The Rena K* [1978] 1 Lloyd's Rep. 545; *Petromin SA v Secnav Marine Ltd* [1995] 1 Lloyd's Rep. 603; *In re Q's Estate* [1999] 1 Lloyd's Rep. 931; *Ispat Industries Ltd v Western Bulk Pte Ltd* [2011] EWHC 93 (Comm).

[40] *B v S* [2011] 2 Lloyd's Rep. 18.

The presence of a service of suit clause in the contract permitting service in the US does not displace the presumption.[41] **18.22**

The same approach will apply where the parties enter into a tri-partite relationship embodied in a single document (e.g. owners, charterers and guarantor).[42] Similarly, where the question arises in the context of dispute resolution provisions in multiple related agreements, the assumption is that the parties do not generally intend a dispute to be litigated in two different tribunals.[43] **18.23**

Although this approach is now well settled in England and Wales, the New South Wales Court of Appeal has declined to adopt it.[44]

4. FACTORS THAT MAY DISPLACE THE PRESUMPTION

The presumption of one-stop arbitration may be displaced where the contract expressly contemplates that some disputes may be litigated; where parties enter into a series of contracts containing different dispute resolution procedures; or where they have chosen resolution by an expert rather than an arbitrator.

Where a contract contained both a choice of jurisdiction clause and an arbitration clause (thus contemplating that some disputes would be litigated and others arbitrated) the presumption in favour of one-stop arbitration did not apply.[45] Likewise where the overall contractual arrangements contain two or more differently expressed choices of jurisdiction and/or law in respect of different agreements, the presumption does not apply. In such a case the question is resolved by a careful and commercially-minded construction of the agreements providing for the resolution of disputes. This may include enquiring under which of a number of inter-related contractual agreements a dispute actually arises, and seeking to do so by locating its centre of gravity and thus which jurisdiction clause is "closer to the claim". It may also be relevant that one or more of the agreements is a standard form.[46] **18.24**

In *BNP Paribas SA v Trattamento Rifiuti Metropolitani SPA*,[47] Hamblen LJ summarised the correct approach to such cases: **18.25**

"(1)   Where the parties' overall contractual arrangements contain two competing jurisdiction clauses, the starting point is that a jurisdiction clause in one contract was probably not intended to capture disputes more naturally seen as arising under a related contract ...

(2)   A broad, purposive and commercially-minded approach is to be followed ...

(3)   Where the jurisdiction clauses are part of a series of agreements they should be interpreted in the light of the transaction as a whole, taking into

---

41 *Ace Capital Ltd v CMS Energy Corp* [2009] Lloyd's Rep. I.R. 414.
42 *Stellar Shipping Co LLC v Hudson Shipping Lines* [2010] EWHC 2985 (Comm).
43 *Deutsche Bank AG v Tongkah Harbour Public Co Ltd* [2011] EWHC 2251 (QB).
44 *Rinehart v Welker* [2012] NSWCA 95.
45 *Secretary of State for Transport v Stagecoach South Western Trains Ltd* [2010] 1 Lloyd's Rep. 175.
46 *Trust Risk Group Spa v Amtrust Europe Ltd* [2015] EWCA Civ 437; *Costain Ltd v Tarmac Holdings Ltd* [2017] EWHC 319 (TCC); [2017] 1 Lloyd's Rep. 331.
47 [2019] EWCA Civ 768; [2019] 2 Lloyd's Rep. 1 (authorities omitted); *Airbus SAS v Generali Italia SpA* [2019] EWCA Civ 805; [2020] 1 All E.R. (Comm) 191; *Albion Energy Ltd v Energy Investments Global BRL* [2020] EWHC 301 (Comm).

account the overall scheme of the agreements and reading sentences and phrases in the context of that overall scheme ...

(4)   It is recognised that sensible business people are unlikely to intend that similar claims should be the subject of inconsistent jurisdiction clauses ...

(5)   The starting presumption will therefore be that competing jurisdiction clauses are to be interpreted on the basis that each deals exclusively with its own subject matter and they are not overlapping, provided the language and surrounding circumstances so allow ...

(6)   The language and surrounding circumstances may, however, make it clear that a dispute falls within the ambit of both clauses. In that event the result may be that either clause can apply rather than one clause to the exclusion of the other ... ."

18.26   Equally the presumption does not apply where the parties have chosen determination by an expert rather than an arbitrator.[48] The question in such a case is one of interpretation of the clause.[49]

18.27   In *Guidance Investments Ltd v Guidance Hotel Investment Co BSC*,[50] it was common ground that the presumption did not apply because the arbitration clause was limited to one kind of dispute. Even where the presumption applies the clause will not catch a claim which is purely tortious.[51]

5.   CAPACITY IN WHICH THIRD PARTY IS TO ACT

Whether a clause providing for dispute resolution is an arbitration agreement or some other form of dispute resolution is a question of interpretation of the agreement. The indicia of arbitration are: (a) there is a dispute or a difference between the parties which has been formulated in some way or another; (b) the dispute or difference has been remitted by the parties to the person to resolve in such a manner that he is called upon to exercise a judicial function; (c) where appropriate, the parties must have been provided with an opportunity to present evidence and/or submissions in support of their respective claims in the dispute; and (d) the parties have agreed to accept his decision.

18.28   Many contracts include provisions for the resolution of disputes or potential disputes. A person who decides them may be an arbitrator or an expert; or may have some other role.

18.29   In *Re Carus-Wilson and Green*,[52] a contract for the sale of land provided that the timber was to be paid for at a valuation made by two valuers appointed by the parties, who were to appoint an umpire to decide if the valuers did not agree. The valuers did not agree, so the umpire decided. The question was whether the umpire was an arbitrator. Lord Esher MR said:

"The question here is, whether the umpire was merely a valuer substituted for

---

[48] *Barclays Bank Plc v Nylon Capital LLP* [2011] EWCA Civ 826; *Empyreal Energy Ltd v Daylighting Power Ltd* [2020] EWHC 1971 (TCC).

[49] *UBS AG v HSH NordBank AG* [2009] 2 Lloyd's Rep. 272; *Sebastian Holdings Inc v Deutsche Bank AG* [2011] 1 Lloyd's Rep. 106; *Deutsche Bank AG v Tongkah Harbour Public Company Ltd* [2011] EWHC 2251 (QB).

[50] [2013] EWHC 3413 (Comm).

[51] *Ryanair Ltd v Esso Italiana Srl* [2013] EWCA Civ 1450.

[52] (1887) 18 Q.B.D 7.

the valuers originally appointed by the parties in a certain event, or arbitrator. If it appears from the terms of the agreement by which a matter is submitted to a person's decision, that the intention of the parties was that he should hold an inquiry in the nature of a judicial inquiry, and hear the respective cases of the parties, and decide upon evidence laid before him, then the case is one of an arbitration. The intention in such cases is that there shall be a judicial inquiry worked out in a judicial manner. On the other hand, there are cases in which a person is appointed to ascertain some matter for the purpose of preventing differences from arising, not of settling them when they have arisen, and where the case is not one of arbitration but of a mere valuation. There may be cases of an intermediate kind, where, though a person is appointed to settle disputes that have arisen, still it is not intended that he shall be bound to hear evidence or arguments. In such cases it may be often difficult to say whether he is intended to be an arbitrator or to exercise some function other than that of an arbitrator. Such cases must be determined each according to its particular circumstances."

In *Arenson v Casson Beckman Rutley & Co*,[53] Lord Wheatley summarised the indicia of an arbitration agreement as follows: **18.30**

"The indicia are as follows: (a) there is a dispute or a difference between the parties which has been formulated in some way or another; (b) the dispute or difference has been remitted by the parties to the person to resolve in such a manner that he is called upon to exercise a judicial function; (c) where appropriate, the parties must have been provided with an opportunity to present evidence and/or submissions in support of their respective claims in the dispute; and (d) the parties have agreed to accept his decision."

Even where these indicia are present the decision maker may be an expert rather that the arbitrator if the clause expressly states the capacity in which he is to act,[54] or if other indications in the clause point towards that conclusion.[55] The mere fact that a clause refers to an "umpire" is neutral on the question of whether the clause as a whole is an arbitration agreement.[56] **18.31**

Illustrations

1. A clause in an insurance contract stated that:

"This contract is governed by the laws of England and any dispute or difference arising hereunder between the Assured and the Insurers shall be referred to a Queen's Counsel of the English Bar to be mutually agreed between the Insurers and the Assured or in the event of disagreement by the Chairman of the Bar Council."

It was held that this was an arbitration agreement.
David Wilson Homes Ltd v Survey Services Ltd[57]

2. A rent review clause provided that the rent was to be

---

53 [1977] A.C. 405.
54 *Palacath Ltd v Flanagan* [1985] 2 All E.R. 161.
55 *North Eastern Co-operative Society Ltd v Newcastle upon Tyne City Council* [1987] 1 E.G.L.R. 142.
56 *Safeway Food Stores Ltd v Banderway Ltd* [1983] 2 E.G.L.R. 116.
57 [2001] 1 All E.R. (Comm) 449.

"determined by an independent surveyor agreed between the lessors and the lessee or (in default of agreement) by an arbitrator to be nominated by the President of the Royal Institution of Chartered Surveyors on the application of either party and this lease shall be deemed for this purpose to be a submission to arbitration within the Arbitration Act 1950 or any statutory modification or re-enactment thereof for the time being in force".

It went on to say that:

"The fees payable to the independent surveyor or arbitrator hereinbefore mentioned for such assessment as aforesaid shall be borne by the parties hereto equally".

It was held that an independent surveyor appointed by agreement (rather than by the President of the RICS) was to act as an expert rather than an arbitrator.
North Eastern Co-operative Society Ltd v Newcastle upon Tyne City Council[58]

3.   A contract contained a clause that stated "Disputes may be dealt with as provided in para.1.8 of the RIBA Conditions but shall otherwise be referred to the English Courts". The relevant RIBA Condition was an arbitration agreement. It was held that the contract contained a binding arbitration agreement and that the jurisdiction clause only came into effect if neither party referred a dispute to arbitration.
Lobb Partnership Ltd v Aintree Racecourse Co Ltd[59]

6.   DETERMINATION BY EXPERT

A contract may provide for resolution of disputes by an expert. Whether a person is to act as expert or arbitrator is a question of interpretation of the contract.

18.32   There is no objection to a clause providing that an expert is to be the final judge of fact relating to a contract. It was at one time thought that a clause which enabled an expert to determine questions of interpretation of the contract was void as ousting the jurisdiction of the court. However, the better view is that in such a case the true analysis is that the parties have agreed that their rights and obligations are whatever the expert says they are.[60]

18.33   A clause may combine both an element of expert determination and also a reference to arbitration if the expert determination does not produce a concluded result. In *Turville Heath Inc v Chartis Insurance UK Ltd*,[61] an insurance policy contained a clause in the following terms:

"If you and we fail to agree on the amount of loss, either party may make a written demand that each selects an independent appraiser ... The independent appraiser will select an arbitrator within fifteen (15) days ... The independent appraisers will then appraise the loss and submit any differences to the arbitrator. A decision in writing agreed to by the two appraisers or either appraiser and the arbitrator will be binding."

---

58   [1987] 1 E.G.L.R. 142.
59   [2000] B.L.R. 65.
60   See para.14.12.
61   [2012] EWHC 3019 (TCC).

Edwards-Stuart J said that:

"the clause does not cease to be an arbitration clause simply because it provides that a decision in writing agreed by the two appraisers will be binding on the parties. That ... means no more than that if the appraisers are agreed as to the amount of the loss, there is no dispute to put before an arbitrator. Or, putting it another way, he submitted that there is nothing objectionable in the parties being able to withdraw their dispute from the arbitral process at any time. In almost any dispute resolution process it is open to parties to resolve their dispute by agreement and terminate the process."

However, the difficulty was that in the event of submission to the arbitrator, his decision was only binding if one of the appraisers agreed with it. For that reason, the clause could not be considered to be a valid arbitration clause.

7. VALIDITY OF EXPERT'S DETERMINATION

A determination by an expert acting within his remit will be valid unless (a) his determination is tainted by fraud or collusion; (b) he has answered the wrong question; (c) he has departed materially from the instructions contained in the contract; or (d) the interpretation of the contract was not within his remit and he has misinterpreted it.

In *Homepace Ltd v Sita South East Ltd*,[62] Lloyd LJ said: **18.34**

"Each case depends on the terms of the contract under which the determination is made, both as to what it is that the expert has to decide, and as to how far his decision is binding on the parties. In each case it is necessary to examine the determination, in order to see whether it lies within the scope of the expert's authority. If it does not, then it has no effect as between the parties. If on the other hand it does, then the contract also governs the question whether the determination is binding or whether, and if so to what extent or on what grounds, the determination can be questioned."

In *Great Dunmow Estates Ltd v Crest Nicholson Operations Ltd*,[63] Patten LJ said:

"... the scope and nature of an expert's jurisdiction is determined by the contract between the parties. They determine what the expert is to decide and have it within their power to agree that his decision on those matters should be final without recourse to the courts. The expert has no other source of authority and is unregulated in terms of his powers by statute. The scope of his remit and the finality of his decisions on matters within his authority are therefore dependent on the proper construction and terms of the contract which the parties have made. This includes the question whether that very issue of jurisdiction is itself a matter for the expert or one for the court to adjudicate upon."

The starting point is that where a contract provides for some matter to be   **18.35**
determined by an expert, his determination will bind the parties. In *Campbell v*

---

[62] [2008] 1 P. & C.R. 24; *Empyreal Energy Ltd v Daylighting Power Ltd* [2020] EWHC 1971 (TCC).
[63] [2019] EWCA Civ 1683. For an Irish perspective, see *Dunnes Stores v McCann* [2020] IESC 1.

Edwards,[64] Lord Denning MR said:

"It is simply the law of contract. If two persons agree that the price of property should be fixed by a valuer on whom they agree, and he gives that valuation honestly and in good faith, they are bound by it. Even if he has made a mistake they are still bound by it. The reason is because they have agreed to be bound by it. If there were fraud or collusion, of course, it would be different. Fraud or collusion unravels everything."

18.36 If the expert has answered the wrong question then his determination will not be binding. In *Jones v Sherwood Computer Services*,[65] Dillon LJ said:

"On principle, the first step must be to see what the parties have agreed to remit to the expert, this being, as Lord Denning MR said in *Campbell v Edwards*, a matter of contract. The next step must be to see what the nature of the mistake was, if there is evidence to show that. If the mistake made was that the expert departed from his instructions in a material respect, e.g. if he valued the wrong number of shares, or valued shares in the wrong company, or if, as in *Jones (M) v Jones (RR)*,[66] the expert had valued machinery himself whereas his instructions were to employ an expert valuer of his choice to do that, either party would be able to say that the certificate was not binding because the expert had not done what he was appointed to do."

18.37 The cases have drawn a distinction between answering the right question (but wrongly) and answering the wrong question.[67] In *Veba Oil Supply & Trading Gmbh v Petrotrade Inc*,[68] Simon Brown LJ said:

"A mistake is one thing; a departure from instructions quite another. A mistake is made when an expert goes wrong in the course of carrying out his instructions. The difference between that and an expert not carrying out his instructions is obvious ...".

18.38 Where a valuer of shares was alleged to have valued on the basis of erroneous hypotheses it was held that:

---

[64] [1976] 1 W.L.R. 403.

[65] [1992] 1 W.L.R. 277 disapproving *Burgess v Purchase & Sons (Farms) Ltd* [1983] Ch. 216 in which it was held that a valuation which gave reasons which were demonstrably wrong was liable to be set aside. *Jones v Sherwood Computer Services Plc* was followed in *Nikko Hotels (UK) Ltd v MEPC Plc* [1991] 2 E.G.L.R. 103 and *P&O Property Holdings v Norwich Union Life Insurance Society Plc* [1993] 1 E.G.L.R. 164 CA. However, in *Mercury Communications Ltd v Director-General of Telecommunications* [1996] 1 W.L.R. 48 the House of Lords said that where parties entrust a decision under a contract to an expert, they do so on the basis that he will interpret the contract correctly. The House of Lords held that the contract had been incorrectly interpreted in that case and set aside the determination. This might be thought to herald a new approach. Nevertheless, in *British Shipbuilders Ltd v VSEL Consortium* [1997] 1 Lloyd's Rep. 106, Lightman J held that *Jones v Sherwood Computer Services Plc* remained good law. In *Amoco (UK) Exploration Co v Amerada Hess Ltd* [1994] 1 Lloyd's Rep. 330 the contract contained an express agreement that no legal proceedings should be begun in respect of matters remitted to the expert.

[66] [1971] 1 W.L.R. 840.

[67] *Nikko Hotels (UK) Ltd v MEPC Plc* [1991] 2 E.G.L.R. 103.

[68] [2002] 1 All E.R. 703.

"if he adopts a hypothesis that would not be adopted by other valuers, then he may have made an error in his valuation, but it does not mean that he has valued something different. It means he has made a mistake."[69]

The distinction is not always an easy one to grasp especially where the ground of complaint is that the expert has misinterpreted the contract; and the misinterpretation has led him to the wrong answer.[70]   **18.39**

In *British Shipbuilders v VSEL Consortium Plc*,[71] Lightman J summarised the principles as follows:

"(1)   Questions as to the role of the expert, the ambit of his remit (or jurisdiction) and the character of his remit (whether exclusive or concurrent with the jurisdiction vested in the court) are to be determined as a matter of construction of the agreement).

(2)   If the agreement confers upon the expert the exclusive remit to determine a question, (subject to (3) and (4) below) the jurisdiction of the court is excluded because (as a matter of substantive law) for the purposes of ascertaining the rights and duties of the parties under the agreement the determination of the expert alone is relevant and any determination of the court is irrelevant. It is irrelevant whether the court would have reached a different conclusion or whether the court considers that the expert's decision is wrong, for the parties have in either event agreed to abide by the decision of the expert.

(3)   If the expert in making his determination goes outside his remit e.g. by determining a different question from that remitted to him or in his determination fails to comply with any conditions which the agreement requires him to comply with in making his determination, the court may intervene and set his decision aside. Such a determination by the expert as a matter of construction of the agreement is not a determination which the parties agreed should affect the rights and duties of the parties, and the court will say so.

(4)   Likewise, the court may set aside a decision of the expert where ... the agreement so provides if his determination discloses a manifest error.

(5)   The court has jurisdiction ahead of the determination by the expert to determine a question as to the limits of his remit or the conditions which the expert must comply with in making his determination, but (as a rule of procedural convenience) will (save in exceptional circumstances[72]) decline to do so. This is because the question is ordinarily merely hypothetical, only proving live if, after seeing the decision of the expert, one party considers that the expert got it wrong. To apply to the court in anticipation of his decision (and before it is clear that he has got it wrong) is likely to prove wasteful of time and costs—the saving of which may be presumed to have been the, or at least one of the, objectives of the parties in agreeing to the determination by the expert."

As stated in the first of these principles, whether the court has concurrent jurisdic-   **18.40**

---

[69]   *Doughty Hanson & Co Ltd v Roe* [2008] 1 B.C.L.C. 404.
[70]   See *Barclays Bank Plc v Nylon Capital LLP* [2011] EWCA Civ 826 where Lord Neuberger MR pointed out some of the conceptual difficulties.
[71]   [1997] 1 Lloyd's Rep. 106.
[72]   The word "exceptional" should now be omitted: *Barclays Bank Plc v Nylon Capital LLP* [2011] EWCA Civ 826.

tion with the expert to decide questions of interpretation of the contract is itself a question of interpretation. In *Norwich Union Life Insurance Society v P&O Property Holdings Ltd*,[73] a building contract required disputes about "practical completion" to be referred to an expert. The question arose whether the court could rule on the meaning of that expression. Nicholls VC said:

> "Parties to a contract such as this enter into a clause such as clause 6(9) with the object of obtaining a speedy and conclusive determination on the matter in dispute by the tribunal they have chosen. They are not readily to be taken to have intended that any necessary prerequisite to that determination, which raises a question of law, is to be outside the matter so remitted. On the contrary, they are unlikely to have intended that fine and nice distinctions were to be drawn between factual matters which fall within the expert's remit and questions of law or questions of mixed law and fact which do not."

He held that questions of construction of the agreement fell within the remit of the expert and that it would require clear words to give the court concurrent jurisdiction.

18.41   Some doubt was cast on this approach in *Mercury Communications Ltd v Director General of Telecommunications*.[74] The Director General was to determine the terms of a licence. Those terms were to secure that the operator paid "the cost of anything done pursuant to or in connection with the agreement including fully allocated costs attributable to the services to be provided and taking into account relevant overheads". The Director made a determination but it was argued that he had misinterpreted the clause. Lord Slynn said:

> "What has to be done in the present case under condition 13, as incorporated in clause 29 of the agreement, depends upon the proper interpretation of the words 'fully allocated costs' which the defendants agree raises a question of construction and therefore of law, and 'relevant overheads' which may raise analogous questions. If the Director misinterprets these phrases and makes a determination on the basis of an incorrect interpretation, he does not do what he was asked to do. If he interprets the words correctly then the application of those words to the facts may in the absence of fraud be beyond challenge. In my view when the parties agreed in clause 29.5 that the Director's determination should be limited to such matters as the Director would have power to determine under condition 13 of the BT licence and that the principles to be applied by him should be 'those set out in those conditions' they intended him to deal with such matters and such principles as correctly interpreted. They did not intend him simply to apply such meaning as he himself thought they should bear. His interpretation could therefore be reviewed by the court. There is no provision expressly or impliedly that these matters were remitted exclusively to the Director, even though in order to carry out his task he must be obliged to interpret them in the first place for himself. Nor is there any provision excluding altogether the intervention of the court. On the contrary clause 29.5 contemplates that the determination shall be implemented 'not being the subject of any appeal or proceedings'. In my opinion, subject to the other points raised, the issues of construction are ones which are not removed from the court's jurisdiction by the agreement of the parties."

---

[73]   [1993] 1 E.G.L.R. 164.
[74]   [1996] 1 W.L.R. 48.

In his dissenting judgment in the Court of Appeal[75] (upheld in the House of   **18.42**
Lords), Hoffmann LJ had said:

> "So in questions in which the parties have entrusted the power of decision to a
> valuer or other decision-maker, the courts will not interfere either before or after
> the decision. This is because the courts' views about the right answer to the ques-
> tion are irrelevant. On the other hand, the court will intervene if the decision-
> maker has gone outside the limits of his decision-making authority.
>   One must be careful about what is meant by 'the decision-making authority'.
> By 'decision-making authority' I mean the power to make the wrong decision,
> in the sense of a decision different to that which the court would have made.
> Where the decision-maker is asked to decide in accordance with certain
> principles, he must obviously inform himself of those principles and this may
> mean having, in a trivial sense, to 'decide' what they mean. It does not follow
> that the question of what the principles mean is a matter within his decision-
> making authority in the sense that the parties have agreed to be bound by his
> views. Even if the language used by the parties is ambiguous, it must (unless void
> for uncertainty) have a meaning."

The approach of Hoffmann LJ is the correct approach. In *Barclays Bank Plc v*   **18.43**
Nylon Capital LLP,[76] the Court of Appeal held that the court will not generally
intervene in a matter which is within the jurisdiction of the expert save in the narrow circumstances circumscribed as a matter of contractual interpretation of such
clauses. Thomas LJ described the circumstances in which the court could decide
the question of the expert's jurisdiction in advance of his decision:

> "The court has to determine first whether it is faced with a dispute which is real
> and not hypothetical and then if it is real, whether it is in the interests of justice
> and convenience to determine the matter in issue itself rather than allowing the
> expert to determine it first."

Where the contract contains detailed instructions to the decision maker the   **18.44**
tendency of the courts is to hold that it has jurisdiction to interpret those instructions.
Thus in *National Grid Co Plc v M25 Group Ltd*,[77] a rent review clause contained
instructions to the valuer about what he was to take into account and what he was
to disregard. The Court of Appeal held that it had jurisdiction to rule on the meaning of disputed instructions. Mummery LJ said:

> "In this lease, however, the parties agreed that, in determining the question
> referred to him, the valuer should observe certain agreed contractual directions
> ... The valuer must ascertain the rent in accordance with these contractual
> criteria. He can only lawfully do what he was appointed to do under the lease.
> If he does something that he was not appointed to do, he is acting outside his
> terms of reference. He does not have a completely free hand in deciding the ques-
> tion of what increase ought to be made in the rent payable. Whether he is acting
> within the perimeter of his contractual power depends on ascertaining the cor-
> rect limits of the power conferred on him by the lease. Those limits are
> ascertained by a process of construction of the lease. The terms of the lease do

---

[75]   [1994] C.L.C. 1125; approved in *Barclays Bank Plc v Nylon Capital LLP* [2011] EWCA Civ 826.
[76]   [2011] EWCA Civ 826.
[77]   [1999] 1 E.G.L.R. 65.

not confer on the valuer, either expressly or by implication, the sole and exclusive power to construe the lease."

The balance of authority now favours preservation of the court's ability to rule on matters of contractual interpretation.[78] It appears, therefore, that the court's jurisdiction will only be excluded by express words or necessary implication.

18.45 Where the contract contains instructions to the expert about his methodology, the parties will not be bound if he fails to follow that methodology in a material respect. In such circumstances the court is not concerned with the effect of the failure on the result. A material departure vitiates the decision.[79] Any departure is material unless it can truly be characterised as trivial or de minimis, in the sense of it being obvious that it could make no possible difference to either party.[80] In one case the contract relating to oil exploration required the expert to use a particular computer program for mapping the contours of the sea bed. He used a different program, with the result that his determination was not binding.[81]

18.46 Where the contract provides for the expert to have particular attributes, a determination by one without those attributes will not be binding. So where an agreement provided for the valuation of land by an "independent valuer", it would have been a material departure from the contract if the valuer had not been independent, and the valuation would have been set aside.[82]

Illustrations

1.   A mining lease entitled the tenant to terminate it if "Minerals" as defined by lease were exhausted. Whether they were exhausted was to be certified by a surveyor. It was held that the court had jurisdiction to interpret the definition; and that where the surveyor had misinterpreted the definition of Minerals, his certificate was not binding.
Homepace Ltd v Sita South East Ltd[83]

2.   Completion of a share sale agreement depended on whether a certificate of practical completion had been issued under a related building contract. The building contract allowed for sectional completion. It was held that where the certifier had misinterpreted the contract, the certificate was invalid.
Menolly Investments 3 Sarl v Cerep Sarl[84]

3.   A settlement agreement required a valuer to value a shareholding in a company. A clause in the agreement stated that the books and records of the company included its handwritten takings, which were warranted to be materially

---

[78]   *Great Dunmow Estates Ltd v Crest Nicholson Operations Ltd* [2019] EWCA Civ 1683.
[79]   *Shell UK v Enterprise Oil* [1999] 2 Lloyd's Rep. 456; *Veba Oil Supply & Trading Gmbh v Petrotrade Inc* [2002] 1 All E.R. 703.
[80]   *Veba Oil Supply & Trading Gmbh v Petrotrade Inc* [2002] 1 All E.R. 703.
[81]   *Shell UK v Enterprise Oil* [1999] 2 Lloyd's Rep. 456.
[82]   *Hopkinson v Hickton* [2016] EWCA Civ 1057.
[83]   [2008] 1 P. & C.R. 24.
[84]   [2009] 125 Con. L.R. 75.

accurate. A valuation that did not refer to the handwritten takings at all was held not to be contractually binding.

Begum v Hossain[85]

8.   EXPERT'S DETERMINATION BINDING

A valid expert determination binds the parties, even if the words "final and binding" are not used. Some clauses expressly permit challenge on the ground of "manifest error". A manifest error is one that is obvious or easily demonstrable without extensive investigation.[86]

In *Premier Telecom Communications Group Ltd v Webb*,[87] Moore-Bick LJ said   **18.47**
that:

"… it all comes down to the construction of the contract under which the expert was appointed to act. Only by construing the contract can one identify the matters that were referred for his decision, the meaning and effect of any special instructions and the extent to which his decisions on questions of law or mixed fact and law were intended to bind the parties."

In *Homepace Ltd v Sita South East Ltd*,[88] a mining lease entitled the tenant to   **18.48**
terminate it if "Minerals" as defined by lease were exhausted. Whether they were exhausted was to be certified by a surveyor. Lloyd LJ said:

"The structure of these provisions seems to me to be such that, despite the absence of any words such as 'final and binding', the surveyor is given exclusive power to determine the questions to which his certificate is directed, whether it be as to the exhaustion of all Minerals, or as to their not being economically recoverable, and with no prospect of being so within ten years. If his certificate does no more (and no less) than determine one or other of those matters, it seems to me that it is not open to either party (it would in practice be the landlord) to contend that this is not the correct view of the facts. There would be no point to the certificate if the question to which it relates were to remain in contention between the parties after a valid certificate has been issued."

Some clauses permit a challenge on the ground of "manifest error". In *Conoco*   **18.49**
(UK) Ltd v Phillips Petroleum Co (UK) Ltd,[89] Morison J said that a "manifest error" referred to "oversights and blunders so obvious as to admit of no difference of opinion". In *IIG Capital LLC v Van Der Merwe*,[90] Lewison J said that:

---

85 [2015] EWCA Civ 717.
86 This section was referred to with approval in *Walton Homes Ltd v Staffordshire County Council* [2013] EWHC 2554 (Ch).
87 [2014] EWCA Civ 994.
88 [2008] 1 P. & C.R. 24.
89 *Unreported, 19 August 1996*, cited with apparent approval in *Veba Oil Supply & Trading Gmbh v Petrotrade Inc* [2002] 1 All E.R. 703; *Franbar Holdings Ltd v Casualty Plus Ltd* [2011] EWHC 1161 (Ch). See also *Galaxy Energy International Ltd (BVI) v Eurobunker SPA* [2001] C.L.C. 1725 (a manifest error is one that is "plain and obvious").
90 [2008] 1 All E.R. (Comm) 435. This formulation was approved on appeal: [2008] 2 All E.R. (Comm) 1173.

"A 'manifest error' is one that is obvious or easily demonstrable without extensive investigation."

18.50 In *Axa Sunlife Services Plc v Campbell Martin Ltd*,[91] the Court of Appeal held that a "manifest error" was one that was obvious; and that in determining whether an error was obvious, regard could be had to extrinsic evidence. Thus in an appropriate context it is not only legitimate but necessary in deciding whether there has been a manifest error to look beyond the document or instrument said to contain it.[92]

18.51 If the mistake is obvious then it may be that it does not also need to be demonstrated immediately and conclusively.[93] In *Menolly Investments 3 Sarl v Cerep Sarl*,[94] Warren J considered a provision referring to "manifest error" in a certificate of practical completion given under a building contract. He said:

"That is not to say that the only evidence admissible is the certificate itself. The certificate must, after all, be construed against the background of the contract under which it is given and its subject matter, as well as in the context of the factual matrix against which manifest error is to be judged. Mr McGhee gives the example of the complete absence of an extra storey which the contractor has promised to build. This of course is a fanciful example; if a certifier were actually to certify the building as practically complete in such a case, it is obvious that something serious has gone wrong and that the certificate cannot stand. But the point is that it is only possible to say that something has gone wrong if (a) reference is made to the contract (which includes provision of the extra storey) and (b) the position on the ground i.e. that the extra storey has not been built. It cannot be the case that the obvious error must be apparent on the face of the certificate itself."

18.52 In *Natoli v Walker*,[95] Kirby P said:

"Obviously, there is difficulty in the word 'manifest'. What may be 'manifest' to one judicial officer may fail to persuade another. The criterion cannot be the swiftness of mind of the sharpest intellect. Nor can it be the perception of one whose whole career has been devoted to examining and reflecting upon building contracts. An objective, not a subjective, test for what is 'manifest' is contemplated. But the word will not go away. Against the background of its history in this context it requires swift and easy persuasion and rapid recognition of the suggested error."

9. ALTERNATIVE DISPUTE RESOLUTION CLAUSES

Machinery providing for alternative dispute resolution will be upheld where: (a) the process is sufficiently certain in that there should not be the need for an agreement at any stage before matters can proceed; (b) the administrative processes for selecting a party to resolve the dispute and to pay that person are

---

91 [2011] EWCA Civ 133.
92 *IG Index Plc v Colley* [2013] EWHC 478 (QB) §814 (the expression "manifest error" was in fact a defined term in that case).
93 *North Shore Ventures Ltd v Anstead Holdings, Inc* [2011] EWCA Civ 230, per Smith LJ.
94 [2009] EWHC 516 (Ch).
95 (1994) 217 A.L.R. 201 at 215.

defined; and (c) the process or at least a model of the process is set out. Where a contract contains valid machinery for resolving potential disputes between the parties, it will usually be necessary for the parties to follow that machinery, and the court will not permit an action to be brought in breach of the agreement.

The courts in England and Wales have consistently held that an agreement to   **18.53**
negotiate or to conciliate disputes is not enforceable. The courts in Singapore, on the other hand, are prepared to uphold agreements to negotiate with a view to settling disputes.[96]

However, where the contract contains provisions requiring disputes to be submit-   **18.54**
ted to mediation, the court will strive to uphold them. As Colman J put it in *Cable & Wireless Plc v IBM UK Ltd*[97]:

"However, the English courts should nowadays not be astute to accentuate uncertainty (and therefore unenforceability) in the field of dispute resolution references. There is now available a clearly recognised and well-developed process of dispute resolution involving sophisticated mediation techniques provided by trained mediators in accordance with procedures designed to achieve settlement by the means most suitable for the dispute in question."

He added:

"Before leaving this point of construction I would wish to add that contractual references to ADR which did not include provision for an identifiable procedure would not necessarily fail to be enforceable by reason of uncertainty. An important consideration would be whether the obligation to mediate was expressed in unqualified and mandatory terms or whether, as is the case with the standard form of ADR orders in this court, the duty to mediate was expressed in qualified terms: 'shall take such serious steps as they may be advised'. The wording of each reference will have to be examined with these considerations in mind. In principle, however, where there is an unqualified reference to ADR, a sufficiently certain and definable minimum duty of participation should not be hard to find."

In *Holloway v Chancery Mead Ltd*,[98] Ramsay J identified the requirements of a   **18.55**
valid ADR clause as follows:

"It seems to me that considering the above authorities the principles to be derived are that the ADR clause must meet at least the following three requirements: First, that the process must be sufficiently certain in that there should not be the need for an agreement at any stage before matters can proceed. Secondly, the administrative processes for selecting a party to resolve the dispute and to pay

---

[96]   The authorities are reviewed in *International Research Corporation Plc v Lufthansa Asia Pacific Pte Ltd* [2012] SGHC 226; [2013] 1 Lloyd's Rep. 24.
[97]   [2003] B.L.R. 89. See also *G4S Cash Centres (UK) Ltd v Clydesdale Bank Plc* [2011] CSIH 48.
[98]   [2008] 1 All E.R. (Comm) 653.

that person should also be defined. Thirdly, the process or at least a model of the process should be set out so that the detail of the process is sufficiently certain."

18.56   Similarly, in *Aiton Australia Pty Ltd v Transfield Pty Ltd*,[99] Einstein J said that a valid dispute resolution clause must satisfy the following minimum requirements:

> "It must be in the form described in *Scott v Avery*.[100] That is, it should operate to make completion of the mediation a condition precedent to commencement of court proceedings.
>
> The process established by the clause must be certain. There cannot be stages in the process where agreement is needed on some course of action before the process can proceed because if the parties cannot agree, the clause will amount to an agreement to agree and will not be enforceable due to this inherent uncertainty.
>
> The administrative processes for selecting a mediator and in determining the mediator's remuneration should be included in the clause and, in the event that the parties do not reach agreement, a mechanism for a third party to make the selection will be necessary.
>
> The clause should also set out in detail the process of mediation to be followed—or incorporate these rules by reference. These rules will also need to state with particularity the mediation model that will be used."[101]

18.57   In *Sulamerica CIA Nacional de Seguros SA v Enesa Engenhara SA*,[102] Cooke J accepted the statements of principle in *Holloway v Chancery Mead Ltd*, but held that the mediation clause in his case was unenforceable. He said:

> "First, there is no unequivocal commitment to engage in mediation let alone a particular procedure, albeit that various provisions are made about a mediation. The parties agree that 'they will seek to have the Dispute resolved amicably by mediation' but do not bind themselves to do so in clear terms. They only agree in general terms to attempt to resolve differences in mediation. Second, there is no agreement to enter into any clear mediation process, whether based on a model put in place by an ADR organisation or otherwise. Third, there is no provision in Condition 11 for selection of the mediator. There are therefore stages in the process where agreement is needed on a course of action before a mediation can proceed. The parties would need to agree upon the identity of the mediator, the location of the mediation and the process in which the parties had to engage.
>
> In this connection it is noteworthy that, when insurers suggested mediation on 7th October, they enclosed a draft mediation agreement and a document setting out an explanation as to how the process might work in Brazil. Implicit within that suggestion was the recognition that Condition 11 was not enough to establish what the parties had to do and that there was a need for a further agreement."

---

99   (1999) 153 F.L.R. 236 at [69].
100   (1856) 5 H.L. Cas. 811.
101   But His Honour added: "This is not to suggest that the process need be overly structured. Certainly, if specificity beyond essential certainty were required, the dispute resolution procedure may be counter-productive as it may begin to look much like litigation itself".
102   [2012] EWHC 42 (Comm); [2012] 1 Lloyd's Rep. 275.

The Court of Appeal agreed with Cooke J.[103] On the question of principle Moore-Bick LJ said:

"I have little doubt that the parties intended condition 11 to be enforceable and thought they had achieved that objective. In those circumstances the court should be slow to hold they have failed to do so. However, in order for any agreement to be effective in law it must define the parties' rights and obligations with sufficient certainty to enable it to be enforced. The task of the court when questions of this kind arise, therefore, is to determine whether the clause under consideration fulfils that requirement. Although clauses providing for mediation and other forms of dispute resolution procedure are becoming increasingly common, I do not think it helpful to go beyond that in attempting to define the minimum ingredients necessary to enable such provisions to be given legal effect. Each case must be considered on its own terms."

In considering the particular clause he said:

"… condition 11 does not set out any defined mediation process, nor does it refer to the procedure of a specific mediation provider. The first paragraph contains merely an undertaking to seek to have the dispute resolved amicably by mediation. No provision is made for the process by which that is to be undertaken and none of the succeeding paragraphs touches on that question. I agree with the judge, therefore, that condition 11 is not apt to create an obligation to commence or participate in a mediation process. The most that might be said is that it imposes on any party who is contemplating referring a dispute to arbitration an obligation to invite the other to join in an ad hoc mediation, but the content of even such a limited obligation is so uncertain as to render it impossible of enforcement in the absence of some defined mediation process. I think that the judge was right, therefore, to hold that condition 11 is incapable of giving rise to a binding obligation of any kind."

In *Flight Training International Inc v International Fire Training Equipment Ltd*,[104] a contract provided for disputes to be: **18.58**

"submitted to the Advisory, Conciliation and Arbitration Services (ACAS) London. Legal fees and costs shall be paid by either party which does not prevail at mediation."

Cresswell J said:

"Where a dispute resolution clause refers disputes to a body that provides conciliation, mediation and arbitration services and the only reference in the clause is to mediation, this provides a strong indication of an intention to select mediation as opposed to conciliation or arbitration services."

Hildyard J considered *Sulamerica CIA Nacional* and other cases in *Wah v Grant*   **18.59**

---

[103] *Sul America CIA Nacional de Seguros SA v Enesa Engenhara SA* [2012] EWCA Civ 638; [2012] 1 Lloyd's Rep. 671.
[104] [2004] 2 All E.R. (Comm) 568.

Thornton International Ltd[105] in which he distilled the following principle:

"In the context of a positive obligation to attempt to resolve a dispute or difference amicably before referring a matter to arbitration or bringing proceedings the test is whether the provision prescribes, without the need for further agreement, (a) a sufficiently certain and unequivocal commitment to commence a process (b) from which may be discerned what steps each party is required to take to put the process in place and which is (c) sufficiently clearly defined to enable the Court to determine objectively (i) what under that process is the minimum required of the parties to the dispute in terms of their participation in it and (ii) when or how the process will be exhausted or properly terminable without breach."

He went on to say:

"However, especially when the relevant provision is but one part of a concluded and otherwise legally enforceable contract, the court will strain to find a construction which gives it effect. For that purpose it may imply criteria or supply machinery sufficient to enable the court to determine both what process is to be followed and when and how, without the necessity for further agreement, the process is to be treated as successful, exhausted or properly terminated. The court will especially readily imply criteria or machinery in the context of a stipulation for agreement of a fair and reasonable price."

18.60   In *Peterborough City Council v Enterprise Managed Services Ltd*,[106] Edwards-Stuart J applied those observations to a dispute resolution clause which required disputes to be resolved by adjudication. He said that if necessary the court could fix the level of the adjudicator's fee, which was all that was left to the parties' agreement.

18.61   In *Emirates Trading Agency LLC v Prime Mineral Exports Private Ltd*,[107] clause 11 of the contract provided that:

"In case of any dispute or claim arising out of or in connection with or under this LTC … the Parties shall first seek to resolve the dispute or claim by friendly discussion. Any party may notify the other Party of its desire to enter into consultation to resolve a dispute or claim. If no solution can be arrived at in between the Parties for a continuous period of 4 (four) weeks then the non-defaulting party can invoke the arbitration clause and refer the disputes to arbitration."

Teare J conducted a thorough review of the authorities, including authorities from Australia[108] and Singapore and concluded that the clause created enforceable obligations. He held that where commercial parties have agreed a dispute resolution clause which purports to prevent them from launching into an expensive arbitration without first seeking to resolve their dispute by friendly discussions the

---

[105] [2012] EWHC 3198 (Ch); [2013] 1 Lloyd's Rep. 11; also reported as *Tang v Grant Thornton* [2013] 1 All E.R. (Comm) 1226.
[106] [2014] EWHC 3193 (TCC).
[107] [2014] EWHC 2104 (Comm); [2015] 1 W.L.R. 1145.
[108] Including *United Group Rail Services v Rail Corp New South Wales* (2009) 127 Con. L.R. 202 referred to below.

courts should seek to give effect to the parties' bargain. Moreover, there was a public interest in giving effect to dispute resolution clauses which require the parties to seek to resolve disputes before engaging in arbitration or litigation. He held further that there was an implied obligation to seek to do so in good faith. The presence of a time limit was an important feature of the clause.[109] He concluded thus:

"The agreement is not incomplete; no term is missing. Nor is it uncertain; an obligation to seek to resolve a dispute by friendly discussions in good faith has an identifiable standard, namely, fair, honest and genuine discussions aimed at resolving a dispute. Difficulty of proving a breach in some cases should not be confused with a suggestion that the clause lacks certainty. In the context of a dispute resolution clause pursuant to which the parties have voluntarily accepted a restriction upon their freedom not to negotiate it is not appropriate to suggest that the obligation is inconsistent with the position of a negotiating party. Enforcement of such an agreement when found as part of a dispute resolution clause is in the public interest, first, because commercial men expect the court to enforce obligations which they have freely undertaken and, second, because the object of the agreement is to avoid what might otherwise be an expensive and time consuming arbitration."

18.62   In *Ohpen Operations UK Ltd v Invesco Fund Managers Ltd*,[110] O'Farrell J reviewed the authorities and stated:

"The following principles can be derived from the above authorities as applicable where a party seeks to enforce an alternative dispute resolution provision by means of an order staying proceedings:

i)   The agreement must create an enforceable obligation requiring the parties to engage in alternative dispute resolution.

ii)   The obligation must be expressed clearly as a condition precedent to court proceedings or arbitration.

iii) The dispute resolution process to be followed does not have to be formal but must be sufficiently clear and certain by reference to objective criteria, including machinery to appoint a mediator or determine any other necessary step in the procedure without the requirement for any further agreement by the parties.

iv)   The court has a discretion to stay proceedings commenced in breach of an enforceable dispute resolution agreement. In exercising its discretion, the Court will have regard to the public policy interest in upholding the parties' commercial agreement and furthering the overriding objective in assisting the parties to resolve their disputes."

18.63   Where the contract contains provision for the process of appointment of a person to resolve a dispute, that process must be complied with. In *Cream Holdings Ltd v*

---

[109] It might also have been held that whether or not the obligation to seek to resolve the dispute was enforceable, the stand-still period before either party could invoke arbitration was independently enforceable in the same principle as a lock-out agreement. *Pitt v PHH Asset Management Ltd* [1994] 1 W.L.R. 327, which makes this distinction, was cited to the judge, but not mentioned in his judgment.

[110] [2019] EWHC 2246 (TCC), followed in *Plekhanov v Yanchenko* [2020] EWHC 1076 (Comm).

Davenport,[111] Mummery LJ said:

> "Agreed formal requirements are aimed at eliminating, or at least reducing, the risk of avoidable, time wasting and cost consuming disputes about whether or not a person has been appointed to a position and on what terms. There is, in general, more to the appointment of a person to perform any duties than simply selecting a name to fill the position. Appointment is a process which should be formal and precise."

18.64   Where a contract contains valid machinery for resolving potential disputes between the parties, it will usually be necessary for the parties to follow that machinery; and the court will not permit an action to be brought in breach of the agreement.[112] In *Racecourse Betting Control Board v Secretary for Air*,[113] MacKinnon LJ said that:

> "the court makes people abide by their contracts, and, therefore, will restrain a plaintiff from bringing an action which he is doing in breach of his agreement with the defendant that any dispute between them shall be otherwise determined."

18.65   In *Channel Tunnel Group Ltd v Balfour Beatty Construction Ltd*,[114] cl.67 of a contract required any dispute to be submitted to a panel of experts, with the possibility of a subsequent arbitration. Lord Mustill said:

> "This is not the case of a jurisdiction clause, purporting to exclude an ordinary citizen from his access to a court and featuring inconspicuously in a standard printed form of contract. The parties here were large commercial enterprises, negotiating at arms length in the light of a long experience of construction contracts, of the types of disputes which typically arise under them, and of the various means which can be adopted to resolve such disputes. It is plain that clause 67 was carefully drafted, and equally plain that all concerned must have recognised the potential weaknesses of the two-stage procedure and concluded that despite them there was a balance of practical advantage over the alternative of proceedings before the national courts of England and France. Having made this choice I believe that it is in accordance, not only with the presumption exemplified in the English cases cited above that those who make agreements for the resolution of disputes must show good reasons for departing from them, but also with the interests of the orderly regulation of international commerce, that having promised to take their complaints to the experts and if necessary to the arbitrators, that is where the appellants should go. The fact that the appellants now find their chosen method too slow to suit their purpose, is to my way of thinking quite beside the point."

18.66   In *Gillatt v Sky Television Ltd*,[115] Mr Gillatt was entitled under a contract (the TAS Agreement) to a payment of 55 per cent of the open market value of certain shares as determined by an independent chartered accountant. He did not take the neces-

---

[111]   [2009] B.C.C. 183.
[112]   *O'Brien v TTT Moneycorp Ltd* [2019] EWHC 1491 (Comm).
[113]   [1944] Ch. 114.
[114]   [1993] A.C. 334.
[115]   [2000] 2 B.C.L.C. 103.

sary steps to secure the appointment of the accountant. A claim for payment was dismissed. Mummery LJ said:

"There is no question in this case of the 'breakdown' of machinery for the determination of value, either as a result of the parties failing to perform their legal obligations or as a result of the nominated valuer being unable or unwilling to fulfil his role. There was no legal obligation on the parties in the TAS Agreement to agree on the value of the shares or to agree on the accountant to be appointed or to agree on invoking the assistance of the President of the Institute. It was open to Mr Gillatt before this action was started to seek the appointment and the determination of the independent accountant without the co-operation of Sky. But for reasons of his own, which are not disclosed in the evidence, he did not attempt to do so. It is not a case of a breakdown of contractual machinery; it is a case of a failure by the party claiming payment to take the necessary contractual steps to ascertain entitlement to payment. There is, in my view, no question of the court becoming entitled in these circumstances to substitute something different (i.e. its own opinion on open market value) in place of what was contractually agreed between the parties (i.e. the opinion of the accountant) for the determination of Mr Gillatt's entitlement, but which Mr. Gillatt has simply disregarded."

In *Infiniteland Ltd v Artisan Contracting Ltd*,[116] Chadwick LJ said: **18.67**

"I can see no reason, in principle, why a party, say 'A', who chooses not to allow the contractual machinery to operate should be able to ask the court, nevertheless, to enforce the contract against the other party, say 'B'. It is no answer, in such a case, to say that the machinery is non-essential. It is the machinery upon which the parties agreed when they made their bargain. A cannot be heard to insist on the agreed machinery—as a defence to a claim made against him—if it is he who has not allowed it to operate. But, equally, as it seems to me, in such a case A cannot insist on imposing on B other machinery to which B has never agreed. B is not to be denied the benefit of the machinery to which he has agreed—in resisting a claim made against him—by A's unilateral refusal to allow that machinery to operate."

In *Harper v Interchange Group Ltd*,[117] Aikens J referred to these two cases and   **18.68**
said:

"The clauses in question in these two cases were dealing with two different situations and both are different in terms from the present case. But in each case the contract clauses provide a mechanism for determination of the value of a payment to be made by one party to the other. As Mummery LJ pointed out ... the cases emphasise the importance of upholding, if possible, the validity of contracts and the intention of the parties to them. They also illustrate the approach of the court in seeking to prevent contracts from becoming ineffective as a result of one party taking advantage of its failure to perform a contractual obligation. In another context the court's willingness in principle to enforce a dispute—

---

[116] [2006] 1 B.C.L.C. 632.
[117] [2007] EWHC 1834 (Comm).

resolution agreement between parties was emphasised by Lord Mustill in *Channel Tunnel Group Ltd v Balfour Beatty Construction Ltd.*"

He held that the contractual steps amounted to "a comprehensive agreement between the parties of a contractual mechanism for resolving disputes" with the consequence that a failure to operate the contractual machinery precluded the bringing of an action in court. By the same token where a contract incorporated a particular procedure for the appointment of an arbitrator, and the procedure was not followed, the resulting appointment was invalid and the appointee's award was likewise invalid.[118] But if the contractual procedure is optional rather than mandatory, then it is open to the parties to by-pass it.[119]

18.69   Likewise if the clause is no more than an agreement to agree (as where the clause provided for mediation with the consent of the parties) the parties will not be bound to follow the procedure.[120] Thus in *Elizabeth Bay Developments Pty Ltd v Boral Building Services Pty Ltd*,[121] a clause provided simply that mediation was to be administered by the Australian Commercial Dispute Centre. The Guidelines of that Centre (which it was conceded were incorporated into the contract) required that prior to mediation the parties must sign an agreement "consistent with these guidelines". Giles J held that the clause was void for uncertainty. He said:

> "... by the incorporation of the guidelines the parties had agreed (inter alia) to sign mediation agreements the terms of which were not settled beyond the necessity that they be consistent with the guidelines. The agreements to mediate were open ended, indeed unworkable because the process to which the parties had committed themselves would come to an early stop when, prior to the mediation, it was asked what the parties had to sign and the question could not be answered.
>
> No doubt it would be possible to prepare an agreement consistent with the guidelines, but there would be an infinite combination of provisions which would not be inconsistent with the guidelines, and for this reason alone the agreement of the parties fell down for lack of certainty and the process which they should follow in their mediation. The deficiency was not overcome by regard to other provisions in the guidelines because the guidelines themselves called for signature of a mediation agreement as to what was clearly an important step in the process."

18.70   Judge Peter Coulson QC summarised the law in *DGT Steel & Cladding Ltd v Cubitt Building & Interiors Ltd*[122] as follows:

> "I derive from the authorities noted above the following three principles which seem to me to be relevant and applicable to contracts containing a binding adjudication agreement. (a) The court will not grant an injunction to prevent one party from commencing and pursuing adjudication proceedings, even if there is already court or arbitration proceedings in respect of the same dispute: see

---

[118] *Sumukan Ltd v Commonwealth Secretariat (No.2)* [2008] Bus. L.R. 858.
[119] *Halifax Financial Services Ltd v Intuitive Systems Ltd* [1999] 1 All E.R. (Comm) 303.
[120] *Balfour Beatty Construction Northern Ltd v Modus Corovest (Blackpool) Ltd* [2008] EWHC 3029 (TCC).
[121] (1995) 36 N.S.W.L.R. 709 at 715.
[122] [2008] Bus. L.R. 132.

Herschel Engineering Ltd v Breen Property Ltd 70 Con LR 1. (b) The court has an inherent jurisdiction to stay court proceedings issued in breach of an agreement to adjudicate (see *Cape Durasteel Ltd v Rosser & Russell Building Services Ltd* 46 Con LR 75) just as it has with any other enforceable agreement for ADR: see *Channel Tunnel Group Ltd v Balfour Beatty Construction Ltd* [1993] AC 334, *Cott UK Ltd v FE Barber Ltd* [1997] 3 All ER 540 and *Cable & Wireless plc v IBM United Kingdom Ltd* [2002] 2 All ER (Comm) 1041. (c) The court's discretion as to whether or not to grant a stay should be exercised in accordance with the principles noted above. If a binding adjudication agreement has been identified then the persuasive burden is on the party seeking to resist the stay to justify that stance: see *Cott UK Ltd v FE Barber Ltd* and *Cable & Wireless plc v IBM United Kingdom Ltd*."

Where a dispute resolution clause contained a "carve-out" entitling either party to apply to court for an interim injunction without going through the agreed mechanism, it was held that the court could only deal with the application for an interim injunction; and the carve-out did not enable the substantive dispute to bypass the agreed contractual mechanism.[123]   **18.71**

The courts in Australia have recognised the enforceability of clauses that require the parties to negotiate a dispute resolution procedure in good faith.[124] It is doubtful whether this represents the current state of English law.[125]   **18.72**

10.   CONTRACTUAL DISPUTE RESOLUTION CLAUSE AS CONDITION PRECEDENT

A contractual dispute resolution clause may be a condition precedent to a party's right to bring an action. Depending on the wording of the clause, it may bar all proceedings or only proceedings relating to the substance of the dispute.

The validity of a condition precedent to the right to bring an action for breach of contract was established by the decision of the House of Lords in *Scott v Avery*,[126] where the condition precedent was expressly stated. Where it is not expressly stated it is a question of construction whether compliance with the contractual dispute resolution machinery is a condition precedent to the right to litigate. As the Privy Council said in *Collins v Locke*[127]:   **18.73**

"The questions to be considered in the case of such clauses are, whether an arbitration or award is necessary before a complete cause of action arises, or is made a condition precedent to an action, or whether the agreement to refer disputes is a collateral and independent one. That question must be determined in each case by the construction of the particular contract, and the intention of the parties to be collected from its language."

---

[123] *Ardentia Ltd v British Telecommunications Plc* (2008) 119 Con. L.R. 50.
[124] *Computershare Ltd v Perpetual Registrars Ltd (No.2)* [2000] VSC 233; *United Group Rail Services Ltd v Rail Corp New South Wales* (2009) 74 N.S.W.L.R. 618.
[125] See *DS-Rendite-Fonds NR.106 VLCC Titan Glory GMBH & Co Tankschiff KG v Titan Maritime SA* [2015] EWHC 2488 (Comm).
[126] (1856) 5 H.L. Cas. 811.
[127] (1878–79) L.R. 4 App. Cas. 674.

18.74   It is not essential in order to exclude a right of action at law that the contract should in terms prescribe that the award of the specially constituted tribunal shall be a condition precedent of any legal proceedings.[128] In *Babbage v Coulborn*[129] a lease required the tenant to deliver up the property in repair at the end of the tenancy and "in the event of any loss, damage, or breakage ... the same to be made good or paid for by the tenant, the amount of such payment, if in dispute, to be referred to and settled by two valuers, one to be appointed by the landlord and the other by the tenant or their umpire in the usual way". After the end of the tenancy the landlord had the dilapidations assessed by a surveyor and sued the tenant for damages. Field J said:

> "I think that the county court judge was right in holding that the action was not maintainable until the amount of the payment for damage had been ascertained by two valuers or their umpires."

18.75   By contrast in *Cubitt Building and Interiors Ltd v Richardson Roofing (Industrial) Ltd*,[130] a clause in the contract stated that: "If any dispute or difference arises under the sub-contract either party may refer it to adjudication in accordance with Clause 38A". Akenhead J held that "one cannot construe the adjudication provisions in a way that makes adjudication a pre-condition to the institution of the final dispute resolution process agreed by the parties which is arbitration ...".

18.76   One question that has arisen is whether a *Scott v Avery* clause bars only proceedings dealing with a substantive dispute, or whether it also bars ancillary court proceedings (such as an application for an anti-suit injunction, a freezing order or security for costs).

In *Mantovani v Carapelli*,[131] the question was whether the clause barred proceedings in Italy for security. Donaldson J said:

> "The clause prohibits all legal proceedings in respect of the dispute before a final award has been obtained and the Italian proceedings to obtain security for the claim are proceedings in respect of the dispute even if they are not designed to determine it."

Donaldson J was upheld on appeal. Lawton LJ said:

> "The prohibition is against bringing 'any action or other legal proceedings'. The words 'other legal proceedings' are wide enough to cover proceedings in Italy for the form of order which in England would be called a Mareva injunction."

18.77   In *Toepfer International v Societe Cargill France*,[132] the question was whether one party was entitled to an anti-suit injunction restraining the other from proceedings with an action begun in breach of the clause. Phillips LJ said:

> "We have not found very satisfactory an approach which, as a matter of implication, applies a *Scott v. Avery* clause to ancillary proceedings outside England but not to ancillary proceedings within the English court. Be that as it may, we are

---

[128] *Cipriani v Burnett* [1933] A.C. 83.
[129] (1892) 9 Q.B.D. 235.
[130] [2008] EWHC 1020 (TCC).
[131] [1978] 2 Lloyd's Rep. 63 (Donaldson J); [1980] 1 Lloyd's Rep. 375 CA.
[132] [1980] 1 Lloyd's Rep. 375.

satisfied that, as a matter of construction, a *Scott v. Avery* clause cannot apply to injunctive proceedings brought for the purpose of enforcing the clause itself."[133]

In *B v S*,[134] a contract for the sale of goods contained a clause that stated:　**18.78**

"Neither party hereto ... shall bring any action or other legal proceedings against the other of them in respect of any such dispute until such dispute shall first have been heard and determined by the arbitrators, ... and it is hereby expressly agreed and declared that the obtaining of an Award from the arbitrators ... shall be a condition precedent to the right of either party hereto ... to bring any action or other legal proceedings against the other of them in respect of any such dispute."

The issue was whether this clause precluded the grant of a freezing order, or applied only to proceedings dealing with the substantive dispute under the contract. Flaux J held that as a matter of construction of the clause it barred all proceedings, including an application for a freezing order. He distinguished earlier authorities on the basis that orders in aid of arbitration had been granted under mandatory provisions of the Arbitration Act 1950, whereas the equivalent provisions of the Arbitration Act were no longer mandatory and had been excluded by agreement.

It seems probable, however, that the court would still hold that it has power to grant an anti-suit injunction if one party, in breach of the clause, were to start proceedings in court.

Illustrations

1.　A tenant had a right to renew a lease on terms to be agreed; but if they could not be agreed then the landlord agreed to "purchase by valuation" buildings erected by the tenant. The Privy Council held that a valuation was a condition precedent to a right of action.
Hallen v Spaeth[135]

2.　Tickets sold for a sweepstake in connection with a race meeting stated:

"This ticket is sold subject to the condition that in the event of any dispute arising with respect to any matters connected with the drawing of the sweepstake, or the awarding of the prizes, the decision of the stewards of the Trinidad Turf Club thereon shall be accepted as final."

The Privy Council held that the terms of the ticket made a decision by the stewards a condition precedent to any action to recover the stakes.
Cipriani v Burnett[136]

---

[133] However, the court would, if permitted, have construed the clause as limited to barring substantive rather than ancillary proceedings.
[134] [2011] EWHC 691 (Comm).
[135] [1923] A.C. 634.
[136] [1933] A.C. 83.

11. INCORPORATION OF CHOICE OF JURISDICTION CLAUSE

Where the Judgments Regulation[137] applies, a choice of jurisdiction clause will only be incorporated into the contract where the parties clearly consent to it. Whether they have done so is to be decided as a question of EU law rather than domestic law. In other respects, the question whether a jurisdiction clause forms part of the contract is decided in the same way as the question whether an arbitration clause has been incorporated.

18.79 Article 25 of the Judgments Regulation provides that:

"If the parties, regardless of their domicile, have agreed that a court or the courts of a Member State are to have jurisdiction to settle any disputes which have arisen or which may arise in connection with a particular legal relationship, that court or those courts shall have jurisdiction, unless the agreement is null and void as to its substantive validity under the law of that Member State. Such jurisdiction shall be exclusive unless the parties have agreed otherwise. The agreement conferring jurisdiction shall be either:

(a) in writing or evidenced in writing;

(b) in a form which accords with practices which the parties have established between themselves;

(c) in international trade or commerce, in a form which accords with a usage of which the parties are or ought to have been aware and which in such trade or commerce is widely known to, and regularly observed by, parties to contracts of this type involved in the particular trade or commerce concerned."

Article 17 of the Lugano Convention is in similar terms.

18.80 In *Powell Duffryn Plc v Petereit*,[138] the ECJ said in relation to the equivalent provision in the Brussels Convention:

"The concept of 'agreement conferring jurisdiction' is decisive for the assignment, in derogation from the general rules on jurisdiction, of exclusive jurisdiction to the court of the Contracting State designated by the parties. Having regard to the objectives and general scheme of the Brussels Convention, and in order to ensure as far as possible the equality and uniformity of the rights and obligations arising out of the Convention for the Contracting States and persons concerned, therefore, it is important that the concept of 'agreement conferring jurisdiction' should not be interpreted simply as referring to the national law of one or other of the States concerned."

18.81 In *Benincasa v Dentalkit Srl*,[139] the ECJ said that a clear distinction must be

---

[137] Council Regulation EC No.1215/2012 replacing EC No.44/2001 as from 10 January 2015. The new text does not differ from the old art.24. The Judgments Regulation will continue to apply to proceedings begun before 31 December 2020: Withdrawal Agreement art.67(1); The European Union (Withdrawal Agreement) Act 2020. For proceedings after that date the UK has applied to accede to the Lugano Convention which differs in some respects from the Judgments Regulation.

[138] (C-214/89) [1992] E.C.R. I-1745.

[139] (C-269/95) [1997] E.C.R. I-5451; [1997] E.T.M.R. 447.

drawn between a jurisdiction clause and the substantive provisions of the contract in which it is incorporated. It added:

"A jurisdiction clause, which serves a procedural purpose, is governed by the provisions of the Convention, whose aim is to establish uniform rules of international jurisdiction. In contrast, the substantive provisions of the main contract in which that clause is incorporated, and likewise any dispute as to the validity of that contract, are governed by the *lex causae* determined by the private international law of the State of the court having jurisdiction."

In *Knorr-Bremse Systems v Haldex Brake Products*,[140] it was held that: **18.82**

(i)   The concept of an agreement is an autonomous concept of Community law.

(ii)   If under Community law a valid agreed jurisdiction clause is found to exist as between the original contracting parties, it will bind a successor to the rights and obligations of one of those parties.

(iii)   The principle that a successor is bound is part of Community law; but whether there has been such a succession in any particular case is a question for the national law governing the substantive contract.

(iv)   If there has been no succession, the court seised must ascertain whether the person against whom the jurisdiction clause is invoked actually accepted the jurisdiction clause relied on against him.

(v)   The court must decide this question by reference to the requirements laid down in the first paragraph of art.23 of the Judgments Regulation, which is also a matter of Community law, rather than the national law applicable to the substantive provisions of the contract.

(vi)   The formal requirements of that paragraph are strict.

(vii)   It is for the party relying on the jurisdiction clause to demonstrate clearly and precisely that the formal requirements are met.

(viii)   The scope of a valid jurisdiction clause, in the sense of delimiting the disputes that fall within it, is a question of the national law governing the contract.[141]

EU law requires "real consent" to, or "actual acceptance" of, a jurisdiction clause,   **18.83**
which must be "clearly and precisely demonstrated".[142] Where the contract refers expressly to one party's standard terms it is not necessary for there to have been a specific reference to the jurisdiction clause for the purposes of establishing the real

---

[140] [2008] F.S.R. 30; partially approved in *Deutsche Bank AG v Asia Pacific Broadband Wireless Communications Inc* [2008] 2 C.L.C. 520.

[141] *Benincasa v Dentalkit Srl* (C-269/95) [1997] E.C.R. I-5451; [1997] E.T.M.R. 447.

[142] *Estasis Salotti v RUWA* [1977] 1 C.M.L.R. 345; *MSG v Les Gravieres* [1997] Q.B. 731; *Coreck Maritime GmbH v Handelsveen* [2001] C.L.C. 550; *Knorr-Bremse Systems v Haldex Brake Products* [2008] F.S.R. 30; *Africa Express Line Ltd ("AEL") v Socofi SA* [2010] I.L.Pr. 15; *Coys of Kensington Automobiles Ltd v Pugliese* [2011] EWHC 655 (QB). However, since the question whether the court has jurisdiction always arises on an interlocutory basis before trial, it is recognised that it is possible that a trial may falsify the basis on which jurisdiction has been assumed. For that reason it has been held in England that any fact and matter on which the assumption of jurisdiction by the court depends has to be shown to exist by reference to the test of a "good arguable case": *Canada Trust v Stolzenberg* [1998] 1 W.L.R. 547; *Bols Distilleries BV v Superior Yacht Services Ltd* [2007] 1 W.L.R. 12; *Deutsche Bank AG v Asia Pacific Broadband Wireless Communications Inc* [2008] 2 C.L.C. 520; *Four Seasons Holdings Inc v Brownlie* [2017] UKSC 80; [2018] 1 W.L.R. 192.

consent required by art.23.[143] In *Salotti v RÜWA Polstereimaschinen GmbH*,[144] the ECJ held, in relation to the equivalent provision in the Brussels Convention, that the requirement of writing is fulfilled:

    (a) where a clause conferring jurisdiction is included among the general conditions of one of the parties printed on the back of a contract, but *only* if the contract signed by both parties contains an express reference to those general conditions; or

    (b) where the contract refers to a prior written offer which refers to general conditions including a jurisdiction clause, only if the express reference can be checked by a party exercising reasonable care and the general conditions (including the jurisdiction clause) have been communicated to the other party with the prior offer.

18.84 The parties' agreement may be contained in more than one document, e.g. by an exchange of correspondence,[145] or where there is an express reference in the written contract itself by way of incorporation of other written terms which include a clause conferring jurisdiction.[146] Where there is an express reference in the written contract by way of incorporation of other written terms which include a clause conferring jurisdiction, art.23 is fulfilled even if the party signing did not have a copy of those conditions in their possession or readily available or did not understand what was incorporated.[147] Identification of the parties is a question of national law rather than community law; and it is not necessary for there to be a written record of the parties to the agreement.[148]

18.85 Where the terms of a wholly separate contract are incorporated, different considerations apply. Only those terms directly germane to the parties' agreement are carried over. The presumption is that these usually exclude a jurisdiction clause.[149] However, in the end it is a question of construction of the contract. As Moore-Bick J put it in *AIG Europe SA v QBE International Insurance Ltd*[150]:

> "In each case the Court must construe the language of the contract in the context of its commercial background and ask itself whether a consensus on the subject matter of the jurisdiction clauses is clearly and precisely demonstrated."

18.86 If under EU law a valid agreed jurisdiction clause is found to exist as between the original contracting parties, it will bind a successor to the rights and obligations of one of those parties. In such a case there is no need to show that the successor specifically consented to the jurisdiction clause.[151] Thus if a jurisdiction clause included in a carrier's printed conditions of carriage is effective as between the carrier and the shipper, then it is also effective between the carrier and any

---

[143] *Credit Suisse Financial Products v Société Générale d'Entreprises* [1997] C.L.C. 168; *7E Communications Ltd v Vertex Antennentechnik GmbH* [2007] 1 W.L.R. 2175.

[144] [1976] E.C.R. 1831; [1977] 1 C.M.L.R. 345.

[145] *7E Communications Ltd v Vertex Antennentechnik GmbH* [2007] 1 W.L.R. 2175; *Africa Express Line Ltd ("AEL") v Socofi SA* [2010] I.L.Pr. 15.

[146] *Credit Suisse Financial Products v Société Générale d'Enterprises* [1997] C.L.C. 168.

[147] *Polskie Ratownictwo Okretowe v Rallo Vito & C SNC* [2010] 1 Lloyd's Rep. 384; *Coys of Kensington Automobiles Ltd v Pugliese* [2011] EWHC 655 (QB).

[148] *Antonio Gramsci Shipping Corp v Stepanovs* [2011] 1 Lloyd's Rep. 647, not following *Knorr-Bremse Systems v Haldex Brake Products* [2008] F.S.R. 30.

[149] *Africa Express Line Ltd ("AEL") v Socofi SA* [2010] 2 Lloyd's Rep. 181.

[150] [2001] 2 Lloyd's Rep. 268; *Siboti v BP France* [2003] 2 Lloyd's Rep. 364.

[151] *Coreck Maritime v Handelsveem* [2000] E.C.R. I-9337.

subsequent holders, provided that under the relevant national law, the holder of the bill of lading succeeded to the shipper's rights and obligations under it.[152] On the same principle a shareholder who acquired shares in a company was bound by a jurisdiction clause contained in the company's constitutional documents.[153]

Although the agreement may be in writing, it may in the alternative be evidenced in writing. There is no need for the agreement to be signed.[154] The writing relied on need not emanate from the party against whom the jurisdiction clause is being enforced.[155] Further, a failure to raise an objection within a reasonable time to the terms of a written confirmation following an oral agreement may establish the formalities required by art.23.[156] **18.87**

If neither the Judgements Regulation nor any international convention applies, then the same principles as determine whether an arbitration clause has been incorporated into a contract determine whether a choice of jurisdiction clause has been incorporated.[157] Thus in *Assicurazioni Generali SpA v Ege Sigorta AS*,[158] Colman J said: **18.88**

"... general words of incorporation in a reinsurance contract will not generally incorporate jurisdiction clauses from the primary policy. The reason for this is that such clauses are not germane to the primary risk reinsured, but are merely ancillary provisions which the parties to the reinsurance would not normally intend to incorporate."

Illustrations

1.   A contract of insurance contained a clause by which the parties agreed to submit all disputes to the jurisdiction of the Courts of Athens. A reinsurance contract stated "CONDITIONS: Wording as original". It was held that this general reference to incorporation was insufficient to incorporate the jurisdiction clause.
    AIG Europe (UK) Ltd v Ethniki[159]

2.   "Conditions: All terms, Clauses and conditions as original and to follow the original in all respects including settlements". It was held that this general reference to incorporation was insufficient to incorporate the jurisdiction clause.
    AIG Europe SA v QBE International Insurance Ltd[160]

---

[152] *The Tilly Russ* [1985] Q.B. 931; *Coreck Maritime v Handelsveem* [2000] E.C.R. I-9337.
[153] *Powell Duffryn Plc v Petereit* (C-214/89) [1992] E.C.R. I-1745.
[154] *Powell Duffryn Plc v Petereit* (C-214/89) [1992] E.C.R. I-1745.
[155] *F Berghoefer GmbH & Co KG v ASA SA* (C-221/84) [1985] E.C.R. 2699.
[156] *Iveco Fiat SpA v Van Hool NV* [1986] E.C.R. 3337.
[157] *AIG Europe (UK) Ltd v Anonymous Greek Co of General Insurance (The Ethniki)* [1998] 4 All E.R. 301 and [2000] 2 All E.R. 566; *AIG Europe SA v QBE International Insurance Ltd* [2001] 2 Lloyd's Rep. 268; *Siboti K/S v BP France SA* [2003] 2 Lloyd's Rep. 364.
[158] [2002] Lloyd's Rep. I.R. 480.
[159] [2000] 2 All E.R. 566. The court applied English law to determine the question, although they said that had they applied European law the result would have been the same.
[160] [2001] 2 Lloyd's Rep. 268.

3. "All the terms whatsoever of the said charter apply to and govern the rights of the parties concerned in this shipment." It was held that this general reference to incorporation was insufficient to incorporate the jurisdiction clause.
Siboti v BP France[161]

4. Parties entered into a contract for the supply of gasoil in July 2008 on the seller's standard terms which included a jurisdiction clause. A second contract was made between them at a meeting in August 2008; but the written terms, which were the same terms as those of the first contract, were not sent until the following day. It was held that the jurisdiction clause was incorporated into the second contract.
Vitol SA v Arcturus Merchant Trust Ltd[162]

12. EXCLUSIVE AND NON-EXCLUSIVE JURISDICTION CLAUSES

Whether a clause is an exclusive jurisdiction clause or a non-exclusive jurisdiction clause is a question of interpretation of the contract. If the clause is framed as a positive obligation to submit disputes to the chosen jurisdiction it is likely to be an exclusive jurisdiction clause. In cases to which the Judgments Regulation[163] applies, there is a presumption that a jurisdiction clause is an exclusive jurisdiction clause.

18.89   A clause conferring jurisdiction on the courts of a particular legal system may be exclusive (in which case the parties have agreed that disputes may only be referred to the courts of the chosen jurisdiction) or non-exclusive, in which case the parties have conferred additional jurisdiction on those courts.

18.90   The cases draw a distinction between a positive (or transitive) obligation to submit disputes to the courts of the chosen jurisdiction and a mere submission to that jurisdiction. In the former case the clause is regarded as an exclusive jurisdiction clause. In the latter case it is regarded as a non-exclusive jurisdiction clause.

In *Austrian Lloyd Steamship Co v Gresham Life Assurance Society Ltd*,[164] the clause stated:

> "For all disputes which may arise out of the contract of insurance, all the parties interested expressly agree to submit to the jurisdiction of the Courts of Budapest having jurisdiction in such matters".

Romer LJ said:

> "The question is this: Does the condition merely mean that, if one of the parties to the contract is sued by the other in the Court of Budapest, he will not take any objection to its jurisdiction; or, does it mean that the parties mutually agree that, if any dispute arises under the contract, it shall be determined by the Court in Budapest? Having regard to the nature of the contract and its language, I am of the opinion that the latter construction is the correct one. It is not as if the insurance company only had agreed that they would submit to the jurisdiction of the Court of Budapest: both parties mutually agree to submit to that jurisdiction in

---

[161] [2003] 2 Lloyd's Rep. 364.
[162] [2009] EWHC 800 (Comm).
[163] Council Regulation EC No.1215/2012 replacing EC No.44/2001 as from 10 January 2015.
[164] [1903] 1 K.B. 249.

respect of any dispute which may arise under the contract. If there had been an agreement by the parties in similar terms to submit to the decision of a particular individual, I think there could have been no doubt that it would have amounted to an agreement to submit any dispute under the contract to the arbitration of that person. In this case, instead of nominating a particular individual as arbitrator, the parties agree to submit any dispute arising under the contract to the Courts at Budapest."

In *Cannon Screen Entertainment Ltd v Handmade Films (Distributors) Ltd*,[165]   **18.91**
Hobhouse J considered the effect of this decision. He said:

"The phrase in the *Austrian Lloyd* case was 'agree to submit' but in that case it was construed in a transitive sense as an agreement to submit disputes to a particular court in the same way as one can agree to submit disputes to the decision of the arbitrator. The clauses which I have to construe do not lend themselves to a transitive construction; the sense is that the parties submit themselves to the jurisdiction of the court not that the parties submit disputes. In the *Austrian Lloyd* case it was open to the court to construe the words as if they read 'agree to submit all such disputes'. I do not consider that it would be appropriate to make such an inferential insertion in these clauses. Words are an accurate tool and relatively small differences in wording will produce different contractual effects. In these clauses the parties have used neither the word exclusive nor a sentence construction which is transitive."

He held, therefore, that the clause was a non-exclusive clause.

The distinction between "transitive" and "intransitive" clauses has since been   **18.92**
made on many occasions.[166] In other cases the question has been resolved in favour of an exclusive jurisdiction clause on the ground that the instruction about jurisdiction is mandatory. Thus in *Hin-Pro International Logistics Ltd v Compania Sud Americana De Vapores SA*,[167] the clause provided that disputes "shall be subject to ... the jurisdiction of the English High Court in London". Christopher Clarke LJ said:

"... the words 'shall be subject to' are imperative and directory. They are not words which are apt simply to provide an option. That is certainly the case in relation to the applicable law and, prima facie, the same should be so in relation to jurisdiction."

In *Sinochem International Oil (London) Co Ltd v Mobil Sales and Supply Corp*,[168] Rix J said:

"The test which has been developed for distinguishing an exclusive from a non-exclusive jurisdiction clause is whether on its proper construction the clause obliges the parties to resort to the relevant jurisdiction, irrespective of whether the word 'exclusive' is used: *Dicey and Morris* 13th. ed 2000 at para.12-078. Or

---

[165] Unreported, 11 July 1989, QBD cited in *British Aerospace v Dee Howard* [1993] 1 Lloyd's Rep. 368.
[166] However, as Langley J observed in *The Athena (No.2)* [2007] 1 Lloyd's Rep. 280 "The language of 'transitive' and 'intransitive' does not leap to every mind".
[167] [2015] EWCA Civ 40; [2015] 2 Lloyd's Rep. 1.
[168] [2000] 1 Lloyd's Rep. 670, applied in *Standard Bank Plc v Agrinvest International Inc* [2008] 1 Lloyd's Rep. 532.

to put the issue in another way: is the obligation contained in the clause the intransitive one to submit to a jurisdiction if it is chosen by the other contracting party, or is it the transitive one to submit all disputes to the chosen jurisdiction?"

Similarly, in *Sabah Shipyard (Pakistan) Ltd v Pakistan*,[169] Waller LJ said:

"In my view clause 1.9.1 does not lend itself to a transitive construction, and when taken with clause 2.6, it seems to me that it is not an exclusive clause in the sense of making it a breach of contract for either party to commence proceedings in a jurisdiction other than England."

In *Axa Re v Ace Global Markets Ltd*,[170] Gloster J said:

"In my judgment, the jurisdiction clause, even taken on its own, is not necessarily an exclusive jurisdiction agreement, because it does not transitively require all disputes to be submitted to an English court."

18.93   However, the fact that the clause is framed in an intransitive sense is not conclusive. In *Continental Bank NA v Aeakos Compania Naviera SA*,[171] an agreement between borrowers and a lender contained a clause which stated:

"Each of the borrowers ... hereby irrevocably submits to the jurisdiction of the English courts ... but the bank reserves the right to proceed under this agreement in the courts of any other country claiming or having jurisdiction in respect thereof."

The Court of Appeal held that the clause was exclusive as regards the borrowers, but non-exclusive as regards the bank. Steyn LJ said:

"We regard the concluding words as significant: 'but the bank reserves the right to proceed under this agreement in the courts of any other country claiming or having jurisdiction in respect thereof.' The juxtaposition of a submission by the defendants to the jurisdiction of the English courts and the option reserved in favour of the bank to sue elsewhere brings into play the *expressio unius exclusio alterius* canon of construction.[172] It suggests that a similar option in favour of the defendants was deliberately omitted. In our judgment the language of clause 21.02 evinces a clear intention that the defendants, but not the bank, would be obliged to submit disputes in connection with the loan facility to the English courts."

18.94   So also in *Middle Eastern Oil v National Bank of Abu Dhabi*,[173] a banking contract contained a term that stated:

"The Bank and the Customer submit to the jurisdiction of the Civil Courts of the United Arab Emirates but without prejudice to the Bank's general right to take proceedings, where necessary, in any court wheresoever".

---

[169] [2003] 2 Lloyd's Rep. 571.
[170] [2006] Lloyd's Rep. I.R. 683.
[171] [1994] 1 W.L.R. 588; *Bank of New York Mellon v GV Films* [2010] 1 Lloyd's Rep. 365.
[172] See para.7.53.
[173] [2009] 1 Lloyd's Rep. 251.

Teare J said:

"The words used in the phrase 'The Bank and the Customer submit to the jurisdiction of the Civil Courts of the United Arab Emirates' are capable of meaning that the bank and the customer agree that they will submit disputes concerning their banking relationship to the jurisdiction of the Civil Courts of the UAE. But they are also capable of meaning that the bank and the customer agree that if one commences proceedings against the other concerning their banking relationship in the civil courts of the UAE the other will submit to the jurisdiction of those courts, leaving untouched the parties' right to commence proceedings elsewhere is they are able to do so. However, the clause must be construed as a whole. The clause ends by saying: 'but without prejudice to the Bank's general right to take proceedings, where necessary, in any court wheresoever.' This indicates that the draftsman has addressed the question of proceedings concerning the banking relationship being brought in other jurisdictions and has expressly provided that the bank may do so. No mention is made of the customer being able to do so. In my judgment the obvious inference to be drawn from that omission is that, properly construed, the jurisdiction clause was intended to oblige the customer to commence proceedings concerning its banking relationship in the courts of the UAE but not to oblige the Bank to do so. The customer's general right to do so was prejudiced. The bank's general right to do so was not prejudiced. That is the meaning which, in my judgment, the clause would convey to a reasonable person in the situation of the parties at the time they entered into their banking relationship."

In some cases the presence in the contract of an English choice of law clause has been seen as decisive. The strength of this factor is increased in a case where none of the contracting parties is English or Welsh. In *Sohio Supply Co v Gatoil (USA) Inc*,[174] a contract for the sale of oil was made between two Delaware corporations. The contract stated that: "This agreement shall be governed by the laws of England under the jurisdiction of the English court without recourse to arbitration". The jurisdiction clause was held to be an exclusive clause. Staughton LJ said: **18.95**

"To my mind, it is manifest that these business men intended that clause to apply to all disputes that should arise between them. I think of no reason at all why they should choose to go to the trouble of saying that the English courts should have non-exclusive jurisdiction. I can think of every reason why they should choose that some court, in this case the English court, should have exclusive jurisdiction. Then, both sides would know where all cases were to be tried."

In *Svendborg v Wansa*,[175] the court reached the same conclusion. Staughton LJ said:

"I conclude that the clause does confer exclusive jurisdiction on the English courts. My reasons are in substance, first those which I stated in *Sohio Supply Co v Gatoil (USA) Inc*[176] and in particular that I could think of no reason why businessmen should choose to go to the trouble of saying that the English courts should have non-exclusive jurisdiction. My second reason is that the parties in

---

174 [1989] 1 Lloyd's Rep. 588.
175 [1997] 2 Lloyd's Rep. 183; *Maersk Sealand v Akar* [2003] EWHC 797 (Comm).
176 [1989] 1 Lloyd's Rep. 588.

the second part of the clause were plainly saying that English law was to be mandatory if the American Carriage of Goods by Sea Act did not apply, it seems to me that they must have intended English *jurisdiction* likewise to be mandatory in that event."

18.96 Waller J espoused a similar rationale in *British Aerospace Plc v Dee Howard Co.*[177] He said that "there is no real purpose as I see it in submitting disputes to the jurisdiction of the English court as well as choosing English law unless the intention is to make England exclusive". However, as Langley J said in *The Athena (No.2)*[178]: "even a non-exclusive jurisdiction clause does have a purpose. It makes it difficult, if not impossible, to argue that the chosen forum is not an appropriate one for the resolution of the dispute".[179] Likewise in *Hin-Pro International Logistics Ltd v Compania Sud Americana De Vapores SA*[180] Christopher Clarke LJ also saw benefit in a non-exclusive English jurisdiction clause, especially when coupled by an English choice of law clause.

18.97 Article 17 of the Lugano Convention provides:

"If the parties, one or more of whom is domiciled in a Contracting State, have agreed that a court or the courts of a Contracting State are to have jurisdiction to settle any disputes which have arisen or which may arise in connection with a particular legal relationship, that court or those courts shall have exclusive jurisdiction."

By contrast, art.25 of the Judgments Regulation provides:

"If the parties, regardless of their domicile, have agreed that a court or the courts of a Member State are to have jurisdiction to settle any disputes which have arisen or which may arise in connection with a particular legal relationship, that court or those courts shall have jurisdiction. Such jurisdiction shall be exclusive unless the parties have agreed otherwise."[181]

In *Starlight Shipping Co v Allianz Marine & Aviation Versicherungs AG,*[182] Burton J applied the presumption in the Judgment Regulation, which he described as a principle of interpretation, that a jurisdiction clause was an exclusive jurisdiction clause. His decision was upheld on appeal.[183]

18.98 However, even in a case to which the Lugano Convention applies, the parties may validly contract that the courts of a contracting state are to have non-exclusive jurisdiction. Whether they have done so is a question of construction of the contract.[184]

---

[177] [1993] 1 Lloyd's Rep. 368. Rix J made the same point in *Sinochem International Oil (London) Co Ltd v Mobil Sales and Supply Corp* [2000] 1 Lloyd's Rep. 670.
[178] [2007] 1 Lloyd's Rep. 280.
[179] If the contract is one which expressly provides that it is to be governed by English law, it would seem to be very difficult to argue that England is not an appropriate forum even without a choice of jurisdiction clause.
[180] [2015] EWCA Civ 40; [2015] 2 Lloyd's Rep. 1.
[181] In the former Judgments Regulation the equivalent article (art.23) applied only in cases where one or more of the parties was domiciled in a Member State.
[182] [2011] EWHC 3381 (Comm); [2012] 1 Lloyd's Rep. 162.
[183] [2014] EWCA Civ 1010.
[184] *Kurz v Stella Musical Veranstaltungs GmbH* [1992] Ch.196; *Insured Financial Structures Ltd v*

13. SCOPE OF JURISDICTION CLAUSES

Where a contract incorporates a choice of jurisdiction clause there is a presumption that the parties intended all their disputes to be determined by the courts of their chosen jurisdiction.

Fiona Trust & Holdings Corp v Privalov[185] concerned an arbitration clause rather than a choice of jurisdiction clause. In the Court of Appeal Longmore LJ said: **18.99**

"Ordinary businessmen would be surprised at the nice distinctions drawn in the cases and the time taken up by argument in debating whether a particular case falls within one set of words or another very similar set of words. If businessmen go to the trouble of agreeing that their disputes be heard in the courts of a particular country or by a tribunal of their choice they do not expect (at any rate when they are making the contract in the first place) that time and expense will be taken in lengthy argument about the nature of particular causes of action and whether any particular cause of action comes within the meaning of the particular phrase they have chosen in their arbitration clause."

He added:

"As it seems to us any jurisdiction or arbitration clause in an international commercial contract should be liberally construed.[186] The words 'arising out of' should cover 'every dispute except a dispute as to whether there was ever a contract at all' ...".

The House of Lords approved the approach of Longmore LJ.[187]

Accordingly, the same approach also applies to jurisdiction clauses; whether they   **18.100** are exclusive jurisdiction clauses[188] or non-exclusive jurisdiction clauses.[189] Accordingly, in construing a jurisdiction clause, a broad and purposive construction must be followed.[190] In *UBS AG v HSH Nordbank AG*,[191] Lawrence Collins LJ said:

"Whether a jurisdiction clause applies to a dispute is a question of construction. Where there are numerous jurisdiction agreements which may overlap, the parties must be presumed to be acting commercially, and not to intend that similar claims should be the subject of inconsistent jurisdiction clauses."

A jurisdiction clause, like an arbitration clause, is a separable agreement from the   **18.101** agreement as a whole. This is true both as a matter of domestic law[192] and as a mat-

---

Elektrocieplownia Tychy SA [2003] Q.B. 1260.
[185] [2007] 2 Lloyd's Rep. 267.
[186] *UBS AG v HSH Nordbank AG* [2010] 1 All E.R. (Comm) 727 at [82]–[83].
[187] *Fili Shipping Co Ltd v Premium Nafta Products Ltd* [2007] Bus. L.R. 1719 sub nom.
[188] *Skype Technologies SA v Joltid Ltd* [2009] EWHC 2783 (Ch); *Cavell USA Inc v Seaton Insurance Co* [2008] 2 C.L.C. 898, reversed in part [2009] 2 C.L.C. 991.
[189] *Cinnamon European Structured Credit Master Fund v Banco Commercial Portugues SA* [2010] I.L.Pr. 11. See also *Celltech R & D Ltd v MedImmune Inc* [2005] F.S.R. 491.
[190] *Sebastian Holdings Inc v Deutsche Bank AG* [2011] 1 Lloyd's Rep. 106.
[191] [2009] 2 Lloyd's Rep. 272.
[192] *Mackender v Feldia* [1967] 2 Q.B. 590; *Fiona Trust v Privalov* [2007] 2 C.L.C. 553.

ter of European law.[193] It follows that disputes about the validity of the contract must, on the face of it, be resolved pursuant to the terms of the clause. It is only if the jurisdiction clause is itself under some specific attack that a question can arise whether it is right to invoke the jurisdiction clause. Examples of this might be fraud or duress alleged in relation specifically to the jurisdiction clause.[194]

18.102   The scope of a jurisdiction clause (in the sense of what disputes fall within it) is a question of domestic law, even in a case to which the Judgments Regulation[195] applies.[196]

18.103   It is generally to be assumed on these principles that just as parties to a single agreement do not intend as rational businessmen that disputes under the same agreement be determined by different tribunals, parties to an arrangement between them set out in multiple related agreements do not generally intend a dispute to be litigated in two different tribunals.[197] However, where there are multiple related agreements, the task of the court in determining whether a dispute falls within the jurisdiction clauses of one or more related agreements, depends upon the intention of the parties as revealed by the agreements against these general principles.[198] The presumption may be rebutted in a case in which the parties have entered into different agreements relating to different aspects of an overall transaction where the agreements contain clauses conferring jurisdiction on the courts of different countries.[199] As Rix J put it in *Credit Suisse First Boston (Europe) Ltd v MLC Bermuda Ltd*[200]:

> "where different agreements are entered into for different aspects of an overall relationship, and those different agreements contain different terms as to jurisdiction, it would seem to be applying too broad and indiscriminate a brush simply to ignore the parties' careful selection of palette."

Thus where different but related agreements contain overlapping and inconsistent dispute resolution clauses, the nature of the claim and the particular agreement out of which the claim arose ought to be considered. Where a claim arose out of or was more closely connected with one agreement than the other, the claim ought to be subject to the dispute resolution regime contained in the former agreement, even if the latter was, on a literal reading, wide enough to cover the claim.[201]

---

[193]   *Benincasa v Dentalkit Srl* [1997] E.C.R. I-3767.

[194]   *Deutsche Bank AG v Asia Pacific Broadband Wireless Communications Inc* [2008] 2 C.L.C. 520.

[195]   Council Regulation EC 1215/2012 (replacing EC No.44/2001 as from 10 January 2015).

[196]   *Knorr-Bremse Systems v Haldex Brake Products* [2008] F.S.R. 30; *Deutsche Bank AG v Asia Pacific Broadband Wireless Communications Inc* [2008] 2 C.L.C. 520; *Cinnamon European Structured Credit Master Fund v Banco Commercial Portugues SA* [2010] I.L.Pr. 11.

[197]   *Sebastian Holdings Inc v Deutsche Bank AG* [2011] 1 Lloyd's Rep. 106. But in the same case the CA approved the statement in *Dicey Morris & Collins on Conflicts of Laws* (2010 supplement, para.12-094) that: "There is no presumption that a jurisdiction (or arbitration) agreement in contract A, even if expressed in wide language, was intended to capture disputes under contract B; the question is entirely one of construction". There is a tension between these two propositions.

[198]   *Sebastian Holdings Inc v Deutsche Bank AG* [2011] 1 Lloyd's Rep. 106; *PT Thiess Contractors Indonesia v PT Kaltim Prima Coal* [2011] EWHC 1842 (Comm).

[199]   *Satyam Computer Services Ltd v Upaid Systems Ltd* [2008] 2 All E.R. (Comm) 465; *UBS AG v HSN Nordbank AG* [2008] I.L.Pr. 46.

[200]   [1999] 1 Lloyd's Rep. 767.

[201]   *Transocean Offshore International Ventures Ltd v Burgundy Global Exploration Corp* [2010] 2 S.L.R. 821; *PT Thiess Contractors Indonesia v PT Kaltim Prima Coal* [2011] EWHC 1842 (Comm).

In *Costain Ltd v Tarmac Holdings Ltd*,[202] Coulson J followed the approach of Rix **18.104**
J in *Credit Suisse First Boston (Europe) Ltd v MLC (Bermuda) Ltd*[203] holding that,
where parties enter into different contracts covering different aspects of their
relationships, or where there are linked contracts with different dispute resolution
clauses, the presumption of one-stop arbitration may not apply. In such a case, what
is required is a careful and commercially-minded construction of the agreements
providing for the resolution of disputes. This may include enquiring under which
of a number of inter-related contractual agreements a dispute actually arises, and
seeking to do so by locating its centre of gravity and thus which dispute resolution
clause is "closer to the claim". In determining the intention of the parties and
construing the agreement, some weight may also be given to the fact that the terms
are standard forms plainly drafted by one of the parties.

Chugai Pharmaceutical Co Ltd v UCB Pharma SA[204] concerned a worldwide pat- **18.105**
ent licence, one of which was a US patent. The licence contained a clause conferring exclusive jurisdiction on the English courts. The question arose whether an
English court could rule on whether a particular product infringed the claims of a
US patent. Henry Carr J said:

"(i)   Parties are taken to consider what, in all the circumstances, are the
         judicial arrangements which meet their commercial needs and, if the par-
         ties have done so, the court needs strong grounds before it will impose
         its will over and against the express intention of the parties.

(ii)   That has particular importance in patent licence cases. Patent licences
         commonly provide that patents may only be declared invalid in the
         countries in which they are registered, but infringement is to be
         determined by the court of a single state.

(iii)   Most patentees and licensees recognise that issues of construction arise
         both in relation to infringement and validity, hence 'squeeze' argu-
         ments are common. However, attacks on validity have to be conducted
         in the country where the patent is registered. It is only the courts of the
         country of registration which have jurisdiction to revoke. Therefore, the
         very nature of a patent licence agreement covering a number of countries
         involves the potentiality for proceedings to be generated in more than
         one jurisdiction.

(iv)   Therefore, one option for the parties is to agree that validity has to be
         dealt with on a country-by-country basis, thereby acknowledging the
         reality that only national courts can revoke, but that all issues of infringe-
         ment should be determined by one court.

(v)   From a commercial point of view, the latter course makes good sense.
         To have all issues of infringement determined by one court gives rise to
         a greater chance of consistency. It will in many cases reduce the amount
         of litigation involved and it will mean that only one court, and perhaps
         in some cases only one judge, need be educated so as to understand the
         patented technology involved."

A jurisdiction clause in one contract (contract A) may have the effect of captur- **18.106**
ing disputes arising under another contract (contract B). The principle is based on

---

[202] [2017] EWHC 319 (TCC); [2017] 1 Lloyd's Rep. 331.
[203] [1999] CLC 579; [1999] 1 Lloyd's Rep. 767.
[204] [2017] EWHC 1216 (Pat); [2017] Bus. L.R. 1455.

the interpretation of the jurisdiction clause in contract A, rather than on incorporation of the clause in contract B. It will normally apply where the parties to contract A and contract B are the same; and where contract A and contract B are interdependent, or have been concluded at the same time as part of a single package or transaction, or (if concluded at different times) dealt with the same subject-matter.[205]

18.107   The presumption in favour of a "one-stop shop" does not have the effect that a choice of jurisdiction clause will be abrogated by a later contract made with a different party.[206] A jurisdiction clause in an agreement providing security for release of a ship may not extend to underlying claims between owners and charterers.[207] Similarly, a jurisdiction clause may not capture claims against non-parties, even if the claims arise out of or are related to the contract containing the clause.[208]

18.108   Where there are two jurisdiction clauses in different agreements between the same parties, then, for the purpose of ascertaining which governs the dispute in question, the court should strive not to construe them as overlapping but rather mutually exclusive in scope. This is so even if it may cause the jurisdictional fragmentation of a particular claim.[209] While fragmentation of dispute resolution may have to be accepted if that is what the parties must be taken to have agreed, that is not a conclusion which should be lightly reached.[210]

18.109   Although the presumption of "one-stop" adjudication applies to contractual jurisdiction clauses,[211] such a clause will not usually catch a claim which is purely tortious.[212] But a claim framed in tort (or delict) may be sufficiently closely connected with the contract as to fall within the scope of a jurisdiction clause.[213] In addition, the clause may expressly provide for such claims to be within its scope.[214] In some cases, a jurisdiction clause may be enforced by one contracting party (A) to prevent another contracting party (B) from suing a third party (C) in tort in a different jurisdiction. A jurisdiction clause is more likely to have that effect where A and C are alleged to be joint tortfeasors.[215]

14.   CHOICE OF LAW CLAUSES

At common law and under the Rome Convention a choice of law clause will only be valid if the chosen law applicable to the contract is the law of a state. However, a supra-national body of law may be relevant to questions of interpretation of such a contract. The same probably applies to a contract made after 1 December 2009.

18.110   At common law the question whether a contract provided for a choice of law is

---

[205] *Terre Neuve SARL v Yewdale Ltd* [2020] EWHC 772 (Comm).

[206] *ACP Capital Ltd v IFR Capital Plc* [2008] I.L.Pr. 47.

[207] *Angara Maritime Ltd v Oceanconnect UK Ltd* [2011] 1 All E.R. (Comm) 193.

[208] *Morgan Stanley & Co International Plc v China Haisheng Juice Holdings Co Ltd* [2010] 2 All E.R. (Comm) 514.

[209] *Monde Petroleum SA v Western Zagroz Ltd* [2015] EWHC 67 (Comm); [2015] 1 Lloyd's Rep. 330; *Deutsche Bank AG v Comune Di Savona* [2017] EWHC 1013 (Comm); [2018] 1 B.C.L.C. 358.

[210] *Airbus SAS v Generali Italia SpA* [2019] EWCA Civ 805; [2019] Bus. L.R. 2997.

[211] *Starlight Shipping Co v Allianz Marine & Aviation Versicherungs AG* [2014] EWCA Civ 1010.

[212] *Ryanair Ltd v Esso Italiana Srl* [2013] EWCA Civ 1450.

[213] *Airbus SAS v Generali Italia SpA* [2019] EWCA Civ 805; [2019] Bus. L.R. 2997.

[214] See *Etihad Airways PJSC v Flöther* [2019] EWHC 3107 (Comm).

[215] *Clearlake Shipping Pte Ltd v Xiang Da Marine Pte Ltd* [2019] EWHC 2284 (Comm); [2020] 1 All E.R. (Comm) 61.

a question of construction of the contract. In *Compagnie D'Armement Maritime SA v Compagnie Tunisienne de Navigation SA*,[216] Lord Diplock said:

"... when any question arises between parties to a contract as to the proper law applicable to it, is to determine whether the parties intended by their contract to exercise any choice at all and, if they did, to determine what was the system of law which they selected. In determining this the English court applies the ordinary rules of English law relating to the construction of contracts."[217]

Where there was no express choice of jurisdiction clause a choice of jurisdiction could nevertheless sometimes be inferred from other provisions of the contract. For instance an arbitration clause providing for arbitration in England is a strong indication that the parties intended the contract to be governed by English law, since that is the system of law which an arbitrator can be assumed to be most familiar. But that inference can be rebutted by other factors.[218] For the same reason, a choice of jurisdiction clause is taken as a strong indication that the law of the chosen jurisdiction is the proper law of the contract.[219] But a tacit choice may only be found where it is reasonably clear that it is a genuine choice by the parties.[220] A choice of law clause may be a "floating" choice, in the sense that it gives one of the parties an option to require that a particular system of law applied. So where a contract provided "Subject to Venezuelan Law and/or Venezuelan Jurisdiction if required", it was held that the clause gave the Venezuelan principal the option to demand Venezuelan law and/or jurisdiction.[221] **18.111**

Article 1 of the Rome Convention[222] provides that the Convention applies to contractual obligations in any situation involving a choice between the laws of different countries. Article 3(1) provides that: **18.112**

"A contract shall be governed by the law chosen by the parties. The choice must be express or demonstrated with reasonable certainty by the terms of the contract or the circumstances of the case. By their choice the parties can select the law applicable to the whole or a part only of the contract."

---

216 [1971] A.C. 572.
217 Where the contract contains a choice of law clause applicable to its substantive provisions, and also an arbitration clause, the contract must be read as a whole (including the arbitration clause): *Kabab-Ji SAL (Lebanon) v Kout Food Group (Kuwait)* [2020] EWCA Civ 6.
218 *Compagnie D'Armement Maritime SA v Compagnie Tunisienne de Navigation SA* [1971] A.C. 572.
219 *Hamlyn & Co v Talisker Distillery* [1894] A.C. 202; *Mackender v Feldia AG* [1967] 2 Q.B. 590; *Hellenic Steel Co v Svolamar Shipping Co Ltd* [1991] 1 Lloyd's Rep. 370.
220 *Egon Olendorff v Liberia Corp* [1996] C.L.C. 482; *Samcrete Egypt Engineers and Contractors SAE v Land Rover Exports Ltd* [2002] C.L.C. 533; *British Arab Commercial Bank Plc v Bank of Communications* [2011] 1 Lloyd's Rep. 664.
221 *Heath Lambert Ltd v Sociedad de Corretaje de Seguros* [2004] 1 Lloyd's Rep. 495.
222 Incorporated into English Law by the Contracts (Applicable Law) Act 1990. However, in relation to contracts made on or after 17 December 2009 the Rome Convention is superseded by the Rome 1 Regulation (Regulation (EC) 593/2008): Contracts (Applicable Law) Act 1990 s.4A. It is intended that the substantive rules of the Rome Conventions (Rome I and Rome II) will continue to form a part of the law of England and Wales after the UK's departure from the EU: Law Applicable to Contractual Obligations and Non-Contractual Obligations (Amendment etc) (EU Exit) Regulations 2019 (SI 2019/834).

The Convention precludes two systems of law from governing the same contract.[223]

The fact that art.3 requires that a choice of law be demonstrated with reasonable certainty is significant. It means that if it is argued that a choice of law is implicit rather than express, then the contract taken as a whole must point ineluctably to the conclusion that the parties intended their contract to be governed by the law in question. Whether there has been an implied choice of law is to be objectively decided.[224]

18.113   Although the contract may incorporate specific rules of foreign law into a contract otherwise governed by English law, as Potter LJ explained in *Shamil Bank of Bahrain EC v Beximco Pharmaceuticals Ltd*[225]:

> "The doctrine of incorporation can only sensibly operate where the parties have by the terms of their contract sufficiently identified specific 'black letter' provisions of a foreign law or an international code or set of rules apt to be incorporated as terms of the relevant contract such as a particular article or articles of the French Civil Code or the Hague Rules. By that method, English law is applied as the governing law to a contract into which the foreign rules have been incorporated."[226]

18.114   Thus a contract cannot be governed by a supra-national body of law, such as *lex mercatoria*,[227] Sharia'a,[228] or halacha.[229] This is also the position at common law.[230] So where a contract provided that "Subject to the principles of Glorious Sharia'a, this agreement shall be governed by and construed in accordance with the laws of England", it was held that the contract was entirely governed by English law.[231] Potter LJ said:

> "The general reference to principles of Sharia'a in this case affords no reference to, or identification of, those aspects of Sharia'a law which are intended to be incorporated into the contract, let alone the terms in which they are framed. It is plainly insufficient for the defendants to contend that the basic rules of the Sharia'a applicable in this case are not controversial. Such 'basic rules' are neither referred to nor identified. Thus the reference to the 'principles of ... Sharia'a' stand unqualified as a reference to the body of Sharia'a law generally. As such, they are inevitably repugnant to the choice of English law as the law of the contract and render the clause self-contradictory and therefore meaningless."

18.115   However, a body of supra-national law may be relevant to the interpretation of

---

[223] *Shamil Bank of Bahrain EC v Beximco Pharmaceuticals Ltd* [2004] 2 All E.R. (Comm) 312.

[224] *Lawlor v Sandvik Mining & Construction Mobile Crushers and Screens Ltd* [2013] EWCA Civ 365.

[225] [2004] 2 All E.R. (Comm) 312.

[226] It has been suggested that this is really a question of certainty in identifying the foreign law relied on: see *Halpern v Halpern* [2008] Q.B. 195.

[227] See *Halpern v Halpern* [2008] Q.B. 195.

[228] Islamic law: see *Shamil Bank of Bahrain EC v Beximco Pharmaceuticals Ltd* [2004] 2 All E.R. (Comm) 312.

[229] Jewish law: see *Halpern v Halpern* [2008] Q.B. 195.

[230] *Amin Rasheed Shipping Corp v Kuwait Insurance Co* [1984] A.C. 50; *Musawi v RE International (UK) Ltd* [2008] 1 Lloyd's Rep. 326.

[231] *Shamil Bank of Bahrain EC v Beximco Pharmaceuticals Ltd* [2004] 2 All E.R. (Comm) 312.

the contract.[232] Where a contract provides that it is to be governed by English law, it is to be interpreted in accordance with English principles of interpretation, even if the origins of the form of the contract can be traced to a different jurisdiction.[233]

The objection to a supra-national body of law does not apply to an arbitration agreement.[234]

In relation to contracts made on or after 17 December 2009 the Rome Convention is superseded by the Rome 1 Regulation.[235] The text of the Regulation differs from that of the Rome Convention. Article 1 says that it applies "in situations involving a conflict of laws, to contractual obligations in civil and commercial matters", rather than in a situation requiring a choice between the laws "of different countries". Recital (13) says: **18.116**

"This Regulation does not preclude parties from incorporating by reference into their contract a non-State body of law or an international convention."

It seems probable that this recital is intended to permit parties to incorporate by reference non-state bodies of law as contractual terms (as envisaged in *Shamil Bank of Bahrain EC v Beximco Pharmaceuticals Ltd*[236]) rather than as the law applicable to the contract.[237]

By art.3(1): **18.117**

"A contract shall be governed by the law chosen by the parties. The choice shall be made expressly or clearly demonstrated by the terms of the contract or the circumstances of the case. By their choice the parties can select the law applicable to the whole or to part only of the contract."

Recital (12) states that an agreement between the parties to confer on one or more courts or tribunals of a Member State exclusive jurisdiction to determine disputes under the contract should be one of the factors to be taken into account in determining whether a choice of law has been clearly demonstrated. In interpreting the Rome 1 Regulation the Giuliano-Lagarde report may be taken into account.[238] This states:

"The choice of law by the parties will often be express but the Convention recognises the possibility that the Court may, in the light of all the facts, find that the parties have made a real choice of law although this is not expressly stated in the contract. For example, the contract may be in a standard form which is known to be governed by a particular system of law even though there is no express statement to this effect, such as a Lloyd's policy of marine insurance. In other cases a previous course of dealing between the parties under contracts

---

[232] See *Halpern v Halpern* [2008] Q.B. 195, despite the fact that art.10 of the Rome Convention states that the applicable law will govern interpretation of the contract.
[233] *Astrazeneca Insurance Co Ltd v XL Insurance (Bermuda) Ltd* [2013] EWHC 349 (Comm).
[234] *Halpern v Halpern* [2008] Q.B. 195.
[235] Regulation (EC) 593/2008; Contracts (Applicable Law) Act 1990 s.4A. It is intended that the substantive rules of the Rome Conventions (Rome I and Rome II) will continue to form a part of the law of England and Wales after the UK's departure from the EU: Law Applicable to Contractual Obligations and Non-Contractual Obligations (Amendment etc) (EU Exit) Regulations 2019 (SI 2019/834).
[236] [2004] 2 All E.R. (Comm) 312.
[237] But it should be noted that recital (13) looks forward to the possibility of the adoption by the EU of rules of substantive contract law and standard terms and conditions which the parties might be able to adopt.
[238] Contracts (Applicable Law) Act 1990 s.3(3)(a).

containing an express choice of law may leave the court in no doubt that the contract in question is to be governed by the law previously chosen where the choice of law clause has been omitted in circumstances which do not indicate a deliberate change of policy by the parties. In some cases the choice of a particular forum may show in no uncertain manner that the parties intend the contract to be governed by the law of that forum, but this must always be subject to the other terms of the contract and all the circumstances of the case. Similarly references in a contract to specific Articles of the French Civil Code may leave the court in no doubt that the parties have deliberately chosen French law, although there is no expressly stated choice of law. Other matters that may impel the court to the conclusion that a real choice of law has been made might include an express choice of law in related transactions between the same parties, or the choice of a place where disputes are to be settled by arbitration in circumstances indicating that the arbitrator should apply the law of that place.

This Article does not permit the court to infer a choice of law that the parties might have made where they had no clear intention of making a choice."

18.118　　In *FR Lürssen Werft GMBH & Co KG v Halle*,[239] Aikens LJ explained:

"It is clear from the cases that to show there has been an implied choice of law within article 3 of the Rome Convention it has to be demonstrated that there was a real choice of the applicable law. This has to be demonstrated with reasonable certainty and sufficient clarity either from the terms of the contract itself or the surrounding circumstances or both. Those phrases are not alternatives. One can examine both the terms of the contract and the surrounding circumstances to see if the choice had been demonstrated with reasonable clarity."

18.119　　In some cases the parties may impliedly choose a system of law. But the bar is a high one. In *Lawlor v Sandvik Mining and Construction Mobile Crushers and Screens Ltd*,[240] Lord Toulson said:

"The objective nature of the test means that the party asserting an implied choice of law has to satisfy the court to the required standard that, on an objective view, the parties must have taken it without saying that their contract should be governed by that law—or, in Lord Diplock's formulation, that the contract taken as a whole points ineluctably to the conclusion that the parties intended it to be governed by that law. He does not have to prove that there was in fact a subjective conscious choice (for, as I have said, evidence of subjective intention would be inadmissible), but he does have to satisfy the court that the only reasonable conclusion to be drawn from the circumstances is that the parties should be taken to have intended the putative law to apply."

A jurisdiction clause may have this effect. The inference that it does is stronger where the jurisdiction clause is an exclusive one. An assumption that a particular system of law would apply is insufficient to amount to a real choice.[241]

18.120　　Arbitration agreements are outside the scope of Rome 1.[242] They are, therefore, governed by the common law. Where the contract contains an arbitration clause, the

---

[239] [2011] 1 Lloyd's Rep. 265.
[240] [2013] EWCA Civ 365; [2013] 2 Lloyd's Rep. 98.
[241] *GDE LLC v Anglia Autoflow Ltd* [2020] EWHC 105 (Comm).
[242] Regulation 1(2)(e).

law applicable to the arbitration is likely to be that which applies to the substantive contract. But this is not always the case. Even if the arbitration agreement forms part of a substantive contract, its proper law may not be the same as that of the substantive contract. The proper law of the arbitration agreement is to be determined by undertaking a three-stage inquiry into (i) express choice, (ii) implied choice, and (iii) closest and most real connection. As a matter of principle, those three stages ought to be embarked on separately and in that order, since any choice made by the parties ought to be respected, but it has been said on many occasions that, in practice, stage (ii) often merges into stage (iii), because identification of the system of law with which the agreement has its closest and most real connection is likely to be an important factor in deciding whether the parties have made an implied choice of proper law.[243] Where there is an express choice of law in the main contract it might amount to an express choice of the arbitration agreement law. Whether it does is a matter of construction of the whole contract, including the arbitration agreement, applying the principles of construction of the main contract law if different from English law. In all other cases there is a strong presumption that the parties have impliedly chosen the curial law as the arbitration agreement law unless there are powerful countervailing factors in the relationship between the parties or the circumstances of the case.[244] The topic is discussed in detail in Joseph: *Jurisdiction and Arbitration Agreements and their Enforcement*.[245]

---

[243] *Sulamérica Cia Nacional de Seguros SA v Enesa Engelharia SA* [2012] EWCA Civ 638; [2013] 1 W.L.R. 102.

[244] *Enka Insaat ve Sanayi AS v OOO Insurance Company Chubb* [2020] EWCA Civ 574, reversing [2019] EWHC 3568 (Comm); [2020] 1 Lloyd's Rep. 71. The Supreme Court affirmed the decision of the Court of Appeal but for different reasons: [2020] UKSC 38; [2020] 1 W.L.R. 4117.

[245] 3rd edition.

INDEX

LEGAL TAXONOMY
FROM SWEET & MAXWELL

This index has been prepared using Sweet & Maxwell's Legal Taxonomy. Main index entries conform to keywords provided by the Legal Taxonomy except where references to specific documents or non-standard terms (denoted by quotation marks) have been included. These keywords provide a means of identifying similar concepts in other Sweet & Maxwell publications and online services to which keywords from the Legal Taxonomy have been applied. Readers may find some minor differences between terms used in the text and those which appear in the index. Suggestions to *sweetandmaxwell.taxonomy@tr.com*.

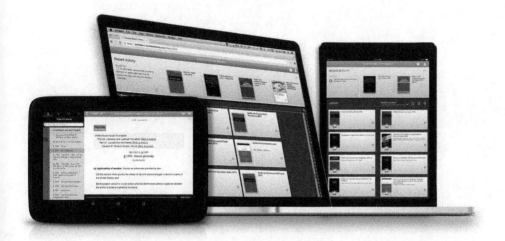

Also available:

Contractual Duties: Performance, Breach, Termination and Remedies, 3rd edn

Professor Neil Andrews; Professor Graham Virgo; Professor Andrew Tettenborn

ISBN: 9780414078574
Publication date: July 2020
Formats: Hardback/ProView eBook/Westlaw UK

This work provides guidance from three leading contract academics on the duties at play in contract disputes. Of great practical importance, the law discussed in this book determines when, how and with what consequences a party may exit their bargain.

There are substantial case law updates, including numerous Supreme Court decisions, across all four key areas of the book since the last edition appeared in 2017, notably, on force majeure, recoverable loss, whether a party can complain of breach when himself in default.

Also available as a Standing order

Illegality and Public Policy, 5th edn

Professor Richard E Buckley

ISBN: 9780414078482
Publication date: August 2020
Formats: Hardback/ProView eBook/Westlaw UK

This text sets out fully and clearly the law relating to illegality, public policy and restraint of trade in the context of contracts. Offering practical examples of situations in which illegality issues may arise and outlining possible solutions, the book also explores possible reforms of the law in the UK and Commonwealth jurisdictions aimed at overcoming its perceived uncertainly and rigidity.

Also available as a Standing order

Misrepresentation, Mistake and Non-Disclosure, 5th edn

John Cartwright

ISBN: 9780414071186

Publication date: November 2019

Formats: Hardback/ProView eBook/Westlaw UK

Professor Cartwright explains in detail the doctrines of misrepresentation, mistake and non-disclosure as they affect the validity of contracts. He analyses the consequences of each, focusing in particular on the remedies available to parties in each case. Taking account of major developments in case law and legislation in these areas, the potential impact of the UK leaving the European Union is also considered.

Also available as a Standing order

Contact us on :   Tel: +44 (0)345 600 9355   Order online:

sweetandmaxwell.co.uk